Computer Graphics
Using OpenGL

Computer Graphics

Using OpenGL

Second Edition

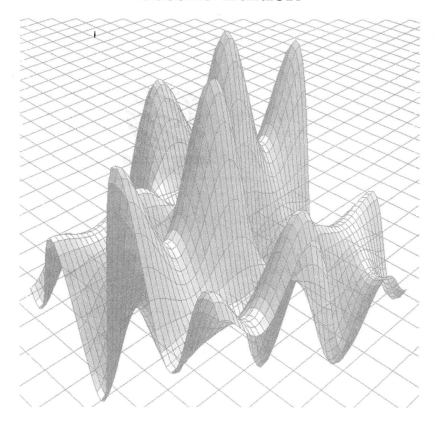

F. S. Hill, Jr.

Department of Electrical and Computer Engineering
University of Massachusetts

Prentice
Hall

Prentice Hall International, Inc.

Publisher: **Alan Apt**
Vice president and editorial director of ECS: **Marcia Horton**
Executive managing editor: **Vince O'Brien**
Managing editor: **David A. George**
Production editor: **Irwin Zucher**
Manufacturing buyer: **Pat Brown**
Vice president and director of production and manufacturing, ESM: **David W. Riccardi**
Cover director: **Heather Scott**
Assistant to art director: **John Christiana**
Cover art: *Labyrinth* © **Stephen Baker**
Editorial assistant: **Toni Holm**
Composition: **Prepare, Inc.**

© 2001 by Prentice Hall
Prentice-Hall, Inc.
Upper Saddle River, New Jersey 07458

© 1990 Macmillan Publishing Company

Printed in the United States of America

10 9 8 7 6 5

ISBN 0-13-320326-3

Prentice-Hall International (UK) Limited, *London*
Prentice-Hall of Australia Pty. Limited, *Sydney*
Prentice-Hall Canada Inc., *Toronto*
Prentice-Hall Hispanoamericana, S.A., *Mexico*
Prentice-Hall of India Private Limited, *New Delhi*
Prentice-Hall of Japan, Inc., *Tokyo*
Pearson Education Asia Pte. Ltd
Editora Prentice-Hall do Brasil, Ltda., *Rio de Janeiro*
Prentice-Hall, Upper Saddle River, *New Jersey*

To Merilee
and to Greta, Jessie, and Rosy

Preface

This book provides an introduction to computer graphics for students who wish to learn the basic principles and techniques of the field and who, in addition, want to write substantial graphics applications themselves. The field of computer graphics continues to enjoy tremendous vitality and growth. The ever-increasing number of feature-length animated movies has generated heady excitement about what graphics can do, and the ready access to graphics everyone now has through computer games and the Internet is stimulating people to learn how to do it themselves.

Graphics systems are getting better, faster, and cheaper at a bewildering rate, and many new techniques are emerging each year from researchers and practitioners around the world, but the underlying principles and approaches constitute a stable and coherent body of knowledge. Much of this knowledge can be acquired through a single course in graphics, and this book attempts to organize the ideas and methods to bring the reader from the beginning, with modest programming skills, to being able to design and produce significant graphics programs.

INTENDED AUDIENCE

The book is designed as a text for either a one- or two-semester course at the senior undergraduate or first-year graduate level. It can also be used for self-study. It is aimed principally at students majoring in computer science or engineering, but will also suit students in other fields, such as physics and mathematics.

Mathematical Background Required

The reader should have the equivalent of one year of college mathematics; knowledge of elementary algebra, geometry, trigonometry, and elementary calculus also is assumed. Some exposure to vectors and matrices is useful, but not essential, as vector and matrix techniques are introduced in the context of graphics as they are needed, and an appendix also summarizes the key ideas.

Computer graphics tends to use a lot of mathematics to express the geometric relationships between lines, surfaces, and the viewing eye. Although no single mathematical notion is difficult in itself, the sheer number of tools required can be daunting. The book places particular emphasis on revealing the reasons for using this or that technique and on showing how the objects of interest in a graphics program are properly described by the mathematical objects we use.

Computer Programming Background Required

In general, the reader should have at least one semester of experience writing computer programs in C, C++, or Java. A lot of the programming in graphics involves the direct translation of geometric relationships into code and so uses straightforward variables, functions, arrays, looping, and testing, which is similar from language to language. C++ is used throughout the book, but much of the material will be familiar to someone whose computer language background is only C.

It is helpful for the reader to have experience as well in manipulating `struct`'s in C or classes in C++.

These are used to capture the rather complicated structure of some graphical objects that reside in a scene, where the object (say, a castle or an airplane) consists of many parts and these parts themselves consist of complex subparts. Some experience with elementary linked data structures such as linked lists or trees is also desirable, but not essential.

A reader with knowledge of C but not C++ will need to pick up the basics of object-oriented programming. We define a number of useful classes (such as the

`Window`, `Mesh`, `Scene`, `Camera`, and `Texture` classes) and show why they are so convenient and usable. Some of the hallmarks of object-oriented programming, such as inheritance and polymorphism, are used in a few contexts to make the programmer's job easier, but we do not place inordinate emphasis on a pure object-oriented approach.

PHILOSOPHY

The book has been completely reorganized and rewritten from the first edition, but the basic philosophy remains: Computer graphics is learned by doing it: One must write and test real programs to comprehend fully what is going on. A principal goal of the book is to show readers how to translate a particular design "task" first into its underlying geometric components, to find a suitable mathematical representation for the objects involved, and finally to translate this representation into suitable algorithms and program code. Readers start by learning how to develop simple routines to produce pictures. Then methods for rendering drawings of ever more complex objects are presented in a step-by-step fashion.

Exercises and Problems

More than 440 drill exercises appear throughout the book. Most of these are of the "stop-and-think" variety that require no programming and that allow readers to test their grasp of the material themselves. Some urge the student to implement some of the new ideas in program code.

In addition, "case studies" appear at the end of each chapter, amounting to 100 in all. These exercises are normally programming projects suitable for homework assignments and range from the simple to the challenging. They expand on the material within their chapter and often extend ideas in new directions. Whether or not the case studies are actually carried out by students, they should be studied as an integral part of the chapter.

A suggested "level of effort" is associated with each case study, to indicate the approximate investment in time a student may need to accomplish the task. Programming is an unpredictable business and students' abilities vary, but the rough guide is as follows:

Level of Effort

I: A simple project that can be implemented in an evening, suitable to be made due at the next class meeting.
II: A more extensive project that might be assigned to be due in a week, so that a student has time to think about designing the program and has adequate time for the iterative (and sometimes frustrating) testing and debugging cycle that projects always seem to require.
III: A major project that might require three weeks to design and implement. Such a project requires substantial design effort and careful program layout, but would (correctly) be viewed as a major accomplishment by the student.

Use of OpenGL

A frequent stumbling block that appears as one first brushes up against computer graphics is getting started making pictures. It is easy enough to write a program, but there must be an underlying tool that ultimately draws the lines and curves on the screen. Fortunately, such a tool exists and is readily available. OpenGL emerged from Silicon Graphics, Inc., in 1992 and has become a widely adopted graphics application programming interface (API). It provides the actual drawing tools through a collection of functions that are called within an application. As described in Appendix 1, it is available (usually through free downloads over the Internet) for all types of computer systems encountered in colleges, universities, and industry. OpenGL is easy to install and learn, and its longevity as a standard API is being nurtured by the OpenGL Architecture Review Board (ARB), an industry consortium responsible for guiding the evolution of the software.

One aspect of OpenGL that makes it so well suited for use in a computer graphics course is its "device independence," or portability. Many university computer laboratories contain a variety of different computers. A student can develop and run a program on any available computer. The program can then be run on a different computer, for testing or grading purposes perhaps, and the graphics will be the same on the two machines.

OpenGL offers a rich and highly usable API for 2D graphics and image manipulation, but its real power emerges with 3D graphics. Using OpenGL, students can progress rapidly and produce stunning animations in only a single-semester course.

Use of C++ as the Programming Language

C++ is now familiar enough to most students in engineering and computer science through a first programming course, that it is the natural choice of language to use. It offers several advantages over C, such as passing parameters to functions by reference, which reduces the need for explicit pointers and simplifies reading the code. File I/O also is greatly simplified through streams, and in general, the syntax for all kinds of I/O is clearer in C++ than in C. To keep things simple, in C++ no emphasis is placed on implementing operators.

Furthermore, it is easy to develop handy utility classes in C++, such as those for a 2D or 3D point, a line, a window, or a color, which make code simpler and more robust. Students see the benefit of hiding the details of a geometric object within the object itself and of imbuing the object with the ability to do things like draw itself or test whether it intersects another object. The `Canvas` class developed in Chapter 3 offers a good example, as it maintains its own notion of a window, a viewport, and a current position, and it can draw basic figures with very little programming effort.

Emphasis on 3D Computer Graphics

Because playing games on personal computers has become so popular, and so many dazzling animations are appearing in movies, students are particularly interested in developing 3D graphics applications. Accordingly, several chapters from the first edition have been rewritten and rearranged in order to get to topics in 3D graphics as quickly as possible. In a number of situations, concepts are presented for the 2D case and the 3D case together, which helps to clarify the distinctions between the two.

Describing 3D Scenes with the use of Scene Design Language

It can be very awkward and time consuming to design a scene of many 3D objects using "raw" OpenGL commands. So a simple Scene Design language (SDL) is introduced in Chapter 5 (and fully defined in an appendix). Using this language, students can describe scenes with familiar terms like "cube," "sphere," and "rotate" and can build files of such instructions that can be read into their program at run time. An appendix (and the book's Web Site) provides code for an interpreter that can read an SDL file and build a list of objects described in the file. It is then a simple matter to use OpenGL to draw the scene from the object list.

This same language and interpreter is put to fine use in Chapter 14, in which the student develops code for ray tracing a scene described using SDL. Students can therewith design and ray trace much more elaborate and interesting scenes than would be possible otherwise.

Optional Use of POSTSCRIPT®

In recent years, POSTSCRIPT has become a de facto standard page-layout language, offering a rich set of operators for drawing text and graphics in a device-independent manner. POSTSCRIPT usually works invisibly within a laser printer, receiving commands from a word-processing or page-layout program and converting them to lines, dots, and characters. But it is possible for a student to prepare a "script" of POST-SCRIPT commands and direct it to a printer, whereupon the onboard POSTSCRIPT interpreter creates the intended graphics. Beautiful graphics can be created in this way. Therefore, POSTSCRIPT provides an excellent example of a concise and powerful 2D graphics language, with many of the same capabilities as OpenGL to carry out transformations and perform rendering.

The POSTSCRIPT language is introduced in an appendix, and students interested in approaching graphics this way are shown how to create interesting scripts that produce pleasing pictures. The appendix also shows how to download and work with GhostScript, which provides an on-screen POSTSCRIPT interpreter, so that pictures can be easily previewed and debugged during their development.

ORGANIZATION OF THE BOOK AND COURSE PLANS

There is much more in this book than can be covered in a one-semester course or even in a two-semester course. The book has been arranged so that the instructor can select different groups of chapters for close study, depending on the length of the course and the interests and backgrounds of the students in the class. Several such paths through the book are suggested here, after the principal topics in each chapter are described.

Brief Overview of Each Chapter

Chapter 1. This chapter gives an overview of the computer graphics field, with examples of how various of its subfields are using graphics. The different kinds of graphics display systems available are described, along with the types of "primitives" (polygons, text, images, etc.) that a graphic system displays. The chapter also describes some of the many kinds of input devices (mouse, tablet, data glove, etc.) that are in common use.

Chapter 2. This chapter gets students started with writing graphics applications. Programming using OpenGL is described, and several complete line-drawing applications (including the popular Sierpinski gasket) are developed. Techniques are discussed for using OpenGL to draw various primitives such as polylines and polygons and for using the mouse and keyboard in an interactive graphics application. Case studies at the end of the chapter provide interesting programming projects to help students get a clear initial sense of how a graphics application is implemented.

Chapter 3. Chapter 3 develops the central notion of the window-to-viewport mapping, for sizing and positioning pictures on the display. Do-it-yourself management of windows and viewports is discussed, as is using OpenGL to handle the details. A first clipping algorithm is developed. Zooming, panning, and tilting to achieve interesting visual effects are described, as is the simple animation of figures. A `Canvas` class is developed that encapsulates all of the tools. The drawing of complex polygon-based figures, circles, and arcs is discussed, as is the parametric form for representing both 2D and 3D curves.

Chapter 4. This chapter reviews vectors and their basic operations and shows the great benefits to be gained by using vector tools in graphics. Students who are familiar with vectors can read the chapter quickly, focusing on how vectors describe relations between the geometric objects they manipulate in their programs. Where possible, vector operations are treated without regard for the dimensionality of the space in question, but the use of the cross product in 3D is given special emphasis.

The notion of a coordinate frame is introduced, and it is shown how such frames make it natural to work with homogeneous coordinates. Affine combinations of points are discussed to clarify the difference between vectors and points (to help avoid a common pitfall that arises when one writes graphics applications). Several applications involving interpolation, elementary Bezier curves, and line intersections are developed. The fundamental algorithm to clip a line against a convex polygon is developed in detail, and more advanced clipping algorithms are addressed in the case studies. (An interesting project for "2D ray tracing" is suggested in one case study.)

Chapter 5. Transformations are of central importance in computer graphics, and students sometimes have difficulty developing intuitions about them—particularly about 3D transformations. This chapter develops the underlying theory of transforming figures and coordinate systems using affine transformations in both the 2D and 3D cases. Homogeneous coordinates are employed from the start for describing transformations. Special care is given to rotations in 3D, which are notoriously difficult to visualize.

Tools are added to the `Canvas` class set forth in Chapter 3 to shift, scale, and rotate figures through the "current transformation," and OpenGL's matrix operations are enlisted to facilitate this feature. An overview of the OpenGL viewing pipeline is then developed, and the roles of the modelview, projection, and viewport transformations are described. The drawing of 3D objects using OpenGL's tools is developed. The use of Scene Description Language (SDL) is introduced, and it is shown how to use the SDL interpreter to read in a description of a 3D scene from a file and to draw the objects represented in the file.

Chapter 6. In this chapter, tools are developed for modeling and drawing complicated mesh objects. Sample meshes are developed, including polyhedra such as the dodecahedron and buckyball and more complex shapes such as arches, domes, "tubes" that undulate through space, and surfaces of revolution. Techniques are developed for rendering these objects either with flat or smooth shading.

Chapter 7. This chapter develops tools for the flexible viewing of 3D scenes. The "synthetic camera" that forms perspectival views is defined, and its relationship to the low-level viewing tools OpenGL provides is discussed. A convenient `Camera` class is built that encapsulates the details of manipulating the camera and makes it easy to "fly" the camera through a scene in an animation.

The mathematics of perspective projections is then developed in detail, along with a discussion of how OpenGL produces perspective views through matrix manipulations. The clipping algorithm that operates in homogeneous coordinate space (which OpenGL also uses) is developed in detail. Methods for producing stereo views are introduced. The chapter closes with a taxonomy of the many kinds of projections used in art, architecture, and engineering and shows how to produce each kind of projection in a program.

Chapter 8. Chapter 8 tackles ways to make pictures of 3D scenes more realistic. Shading models are developed that compute the various light components that reflect off of objects that are bathed in light. Methods for using OpenGL to set up light sources and alter the surface material properties of objects are described. OpenGL's depth-buffer method of removing hidden surfaces is described in detail. Techniques for "painting" texture onto the surface of an object to make it more realistic are developed, for both procedural and "image" textures. Finally, methods for adding simple shadows to pictures are presented.

Chapter 9. This chapter delves into the fascinating area of fractals and ways to generate images of them. Methods are presented for refining a curve's shape to maintain "self-similarity," which, in the limit, produces a fractal. Methods are also presented for drawing very complex curves based on a small set of "string-replacement" rules. Tiling the plane with a small set of shapes, including "reptiles," is described.

Methods are described for drawing complex images known as "strange attractors." These methods use the repeated application of a few affine transformations. The inverse problem of how to find a set of affine transformations whose attractor is a given image is presented and leads to a discussion of fractal image compression that exploits the technique. The celebrated Mandelbrot set and Julia sets are introduced, and tools to draw them are developed.

Chapter 10. Chapter 10 discusses powerful graphics methods for manipulating images formed on a raster display.

The basic pix map is revisited as a fundamental object for storing and manipulating images, and a number of operations for manipulating pix maps are developed. The classical Bresenham's algorithm for drawing lines is described in detail. Ways to describe "regions" in a pix map and to fill them with a color or pattern are developed. Particular attention is given to filling a polygonal region. The phenomenon of aliasing that plagues graphics programmers is discussed, and some techniques for reducing aliasing are developed. The techniques of dithering and error diffusion that produce the effect of more colors than a device can display also are described.

Chapter 11. This chapter is devoted to the design and drawing of "smooth" curves and surfaces. The theory of Bezier and B-spline curves is described, along with that for rational B-splines, which leads to a discussion of NURBS curves. Interactive curve design is presented, wherein a designer specifies a set of "control points" with a mouse and uses a curve-generation algorithm to preview the curve associated with those points. The curve may either interpolate the points or merely be attracted to them.

Complex surface design using Bezier, B-spline, and NURBS patches is also developed, and the issue of joining two patches together seamlessly is addressed.

Chapter 12. This chapter examines some intricacies of the human color vision system and addresses the problem of representing colors numerically. The CIE standard chromaticity diagram is described, along with various ways to use it in color calculations. The color gamuts of various devices also are discussed, as are different color spaces and conversions of colors between them. The problem of efficient color quantization, which attempts to reduce the number of different colors in an image without destroying its visual quality, is developed.

Chapter 13. In this chapter, several methods are developed for performing proper hidden surface removal (HSR) in pictures of 3D scenes. The difference between "image-precision" and "object-precision" algorithms is discussed, along with ways to preprocess the polygonal faces in a scene for rapid HSR. The depth-buffer method first seen in Chapter 8 is examined more deeply.

Several HSR methods based on sorting the list of faces to allow rapid rendering, including the binary space partition approach, are discussed. A scan-line HSR method also is developed, and its advantages over the depth-buffer method are described. Further HSR methods based on a "divide-and-conquer" approach are also discussed.

Chapter 14. Chapter 14 introduces the powerful ray-tracing approach to rendering scenes with high realism. Working through this chapter, the student can first develop a primitive, but simple, ray tracer and then add on capabilities to ultimately produce a full ray tracer that can generate dazzling images. Methods to intersect rays with various shapes are described, followed by ways to render the objects using different shading models. The physically based Cook–Torrance reflection model, which OpenGL cannot provide, is developed for use in ray tracing. Techniques for painting texture onto ray-traced surfaces—both 3D textures such as marble and image-based textures—are described in detail. Methods to speed up ray tracing using bounding boxes are also developed.

A great advantage of ray tracing is that it automatically performs HSR and makes it easy to create exact shadows of objects. In addition, it allows one to simulate the reflection of light from shiny surfaces, as well as the refraction of light through transparent objects. Methods to accomplish each of these aims are described. The chapter ends with a thorough discussion of ray tracing complex objects formed by using "constructive solid geometry."

Suggested Paths through the Book

All suggested paths through the book include Chapters 1 through 5 as fundamental, although Chapter 4 can be perused independently by students who are familiar with vectors. Chapter 9 can be tackled after Chapter 5 with no loss in continuity, as can Chapter 10. The 2D parts of Chapter 11 also may be studied after Chapter 5.

Possible Course Plans

- For a *one-semester undergraduate course* in which interest is highest in **3D graphics**: Chapters 1 through 5, with parts of Chapter 6 and Chapter 7 and parts of Chapter 9.
- If *extending the material to a two-semester course*, add the rest of Chapter 7 and parts of Chapters 8, 10, and 11.
- For a *one-semester undergraduate course* in which interest is highest in **2D and raster graphics**: Chapters 1 through 3, along with the POSTSCRIPT appendix and parts of Chapters 4 and 5. Also include Chapter 9.
- If extending the material to a *two-semester course*, add parts of Chapters 7 and 8, and include Chapters 10 and 11 and parts of Chapter 12.
- For a *one-semester graduate course* in which interest is highest in **3D graphics**: Chapters 1 through 7, with parts of Chapters 8 and 9.
- If *extending the material to a two-semester course*, add the rest of Chapter 8, and include parts of Chapters 10 and all of Chapters 11 through 14.
- For a *one-semester graduate course* in which interest is highest in **2D and raster graphics**: Chapters 1 through 3, along with the POSTSCRIPT appendix and parts of Chapters 4 through 8. Include Chapter 9 and 10 as well.
- If *extending the material to a two-semester course*, add Chapters 11 and 12 and parts of Chapters 13 and 14.

SUPPLEMENTS

An accompanying instructor's manual provides solutions to most of the exercises and suggests additional projects. Complete demonstration programs of techniques developed in the text are explained and listed.

Materials are also available through the book's site on the Internet: http://www.prenhall.com/hill.

Many samples of code and utility libraries are available here as well, as are images and textures. All may be used freely.

ACKNOWLEDGMENTS

This book and the first edition have grown out of notes used in courses I have been teaching at the University of Massachusetts for the last 19 years. During this time, a large number of students have helped to develop demonstrations and make suggestions for improving the courses. They have also produced many exquisite graphical samples, some of which appear here. Some students who have been particularly helpful in the first and second editions are Tarik Abou-Raya, Earl Billingsley, Dennis Chen, Daniel Dee, Brett Diamond, Jay Greco, Tom Kopec, Adam Lavine, Russell

Turner, Bill Verts, Shel Walker, Noel Llopis, Russell Swan, A. Chandrashekhara, Emmanuel Agu, Tom Laramee, Chang Su, Xiongzi Li, Jung-Yao Huang, Anjul Srivastava, Steve Morin, and Elwood Anderson. I apologize for any inadvertent omissions.

Several colleagues have provided inspiration and guidance during the germination of the book. I am particularly grateful to Charles Hutchinson for his support in starting the graphics effort at the university, to Michael Wozny for his enthusiasm and encouragement in the development of that effort, and to Charle Rupp for the many creative ideas in graphics he passed on to me. I would especially like to thank Daniel Bergeron, who made substantial contributions to the coherence and readability of the first edition.

I would also like to thank the following individuals, and many others who are not mentioned by name, for their advice and help: Edward Hammerand, Arkansas State University; Deborah Walters, SUNY at Buffalo; Suzanne M. Lea, University of North Carolina at Greensboro; John Neitzke, Northeast Missouri State University; Norman Hosay, University of New Haven; David F. McAllister, North Carolina State University; John DeCatrel, Florida State University; Steve Cunningham, California State University, Stanislaus; Paul Heckbert, Carnegie Mellon University; Angelo Yfantis, University of Nevada; Lee H. Tichenor, Western Illinois University; Norman Wittels, Worcester Polytechnic Institute; Edward Angel, University of New Mexico; Matthew Ward, Worcester Polytechnic Institute; Richard E. Neapolitan, Northeastern Illinois University; Jack E. Bresenham, Winthrop University; Michael Goss, Colorado State University; Bikash Sabata, Wayne State University; and Paul T. Barham, North Carolina State University.

Portions of the book were written while I was on sabbatical working with Dr. Hermann Maurer at the Institute for Information Processing and Computer Supported Media, Technical University Graz, in Graz, Austria, and portions were written while I was on a Fulbright grant at the Indian Institute of Science in Bangalore. I am grateful for the stimulation and support I received during these visits.

Special thanks to my project manager Ana Arias Terry, for her guidance and encouragement during the preparation of the book, and to Irwin Zucker, the production editor, whose expertise and care during production have markedly improved it. Finally, thanks to my parents, to my wife Merilee, and to Greta, Jessie, and Rosy, for all their patience and support while this book slowly took shape.

NOTE TO THE READER: HOW TO VIEW THE STEREO PICTURES

Several stereoscopic figures appear in the book to clarify discussions of 3D situations. They appear as a pair of nearly identical figures placed side by side. To gain the full value of these pictures, coerce your left eye to look at the left-hand picture alone and your right eye to look at the right-hand one alone. This may take practice: Some people catch on quickly, others only after many bleary-eyed attempts, and some people never. Of course, the figures still help to clarify the discussion even without the stereo effect.

One way to practice viewing these figures is to hold the index fingers of each hand upright in front of you, about 2 inches apart, and to stare "through them" at a blank wall in the distance. Each eye, naturally, sees two fingers, but they seem to overlap in the middle. This overlap is precisely what is desired when looking at stereo figures: Each eye sees two figures, but the "middle ones" are brought into perfect overlap. When the "middle fingers" fuse together like this, the brain constructs a single 3D image out of them. Some people find it helpful to place a piece of white cardboard between the two figures and to rest their nose on it. The cardboard barrier prevents each eye from seeing the image intended for the other eye.

Brief Contents

APPENDIXES

Contents

5 *Transformations of Objects*   209

6 *Modeling Shapes with Polygonal Meshes*   287

8 *Rendering Faces for Visual Realism*   408

11   *Curve and Surface Design*   597

About the Author

F. S. Hill, Jr., is Professor of Electrical and Computer Engineering at the University of Massachusetts—A,herst. He received a Ph. D. degree from Yale University in 1968, worked for three years in digital data transmission at Bell Telephone Laboratories, and joined the University in 1970. He is the author of numerous articles in the field of signal processing, communications, and computer graphics. He has been editor and associate editor of the IEEE Communications Society Magazine. He is also a Fellow of the IEEE. He is coauthor of *Introduction to Engineering* and has won several awards for outstanding teaching.

1 Introduction to Computer Graphics

"Begin at the beginning," the King said gravely, "and go on till you come to the end; then stop."

Lewis Carroll, Alice in Wonderland

The machine does not isolate the man from the great problems of nature but plunges him more deeply into them

Antoine de Saint-Exupéry

Goals of the Chapter

▲ To provide an overview of the computer graphics field.

▲ To describe the important input and output graphics devices.

PREVIEW

Section 1.1 introduces the area of computer graphics, and Section 1.2 gives a number of examples of how computer-generated graphics are used today. Section 1.3 looks at the primitive ingredients that make a computer-generated picture; in particular, Section 1.3.4 introduces the notion of a raster image, which is used throughout the book. In Section 1.4, we describe a number of graphics display devices that are in common use today, and Section 1.5 surveys various input devices that are employed in "interactive graphics" applications.

"Any sufficiently advanced technology is indistinguishable from magic."

Arthur C. Clarke

1.1 WHAT IS COMPUTER GRAPHICS?

Good question! People use the term "computer graphics" to mean different things in different contexts. Most simply, computer graphics are **pictures** that are generated by a computer. Everywhere you look today, there are examples to be found, especially in magazines and on television. This book was typeset using a computer: Every character (even this one: **G**) was "drawn" from a library of character shapes stored in computer memory. Books and magazines abound with pictures created on a computer. Some look so natural, you can't distinguish them from photographs of a "real" scene. Others have an artificial or surreal feeling, intentionally fashioned to achieve some visual effect. And movies today often show scenes that never existed, but were carefully crafted by computer, mixing the real and the imagined.

1

"Computer graphics" also refers to the **tools** used to make such pictures. The purpose of this book is to show what the tools are and how to apply them. There are both hardware and software tools. Hardware tools include video monitors and printers that display graphics, as well as input devices, like a mouse or trackball, that let a user point to items and draw figures. The computer itself, of course, is a hardware tool, along with its special circuitry to facilitate graphical display and capture images.

As for software tools, you are already familiar with the usual ones: the computer's operating system, editor, compiler, and debugger, found in any programming environment. For graphics, there must also be a collection of "graphics routines" that produce the pictures themselves. For example, all graphics libraries have functions to draw a simple line or circle (or characters such as **G**). Some go well beyond this, containing functions to draw and manage windows with pull-down menus and dialog boxes or to set up a "camera" in a three-dimensional coordinate system and to make "snapshots" of objects stored in some data base.

In this book, we show how to write programs that utilize graphics libraries and how to add functionality to those programs. Not too long ago, programmers were compelled to use highly "device-dependent" libraries, designed for use on one specific computer system with one specific type of display device. This made it very difficult to "port" a program to another system or to use the program with another device: Usually the programmer had to make substantial changes to the program to get it to work, and the process was time consuming and highly prone to errors. Happily, the situation is far better today: Device-independent graphics libraries are now available that allow the programmer to use a common set of functions within an application and to run the same application on a variety of systems and displays. OpenGL is such a library and serves as the main tool we use in this book. The OpenGL way of creating graphics is used widely in both universities and industry. We begin a detailed discussion of Open GL in Chapter 2.

Finally, "computer graphics" often means the whole **field of study** that involves these tools and the pictures they produce. (So the term is also used in the singular form: "Computer graphics is. ...") The field is acknowledged by many to have started in the early 1960s, with Ivan Sutherland's pioneering doctoral thesis at MIT on "Sketchpad". Interest in graphics grew quickly, in both academia and industry, and there were rapid advances in display technology and in the algorithms used to manage pictorial information. SIGGRAPH[1], a special-interest group in graphics, was formed in 1969 and is very active today around the world. (The must-not-miss annual SIGGRAPH meeting now attracts 30,000 participants.) More can be found at *http://www.siggraph.org*. Today, there are hundreds of companies around the world having some aspect of computer graphics as their main source of revenue, and the subject of computer graphics is taught in most computer science or electrical engineering departments in colleges and universities.

Computer graphics is a very appealing field of study. You learn to write programs that create pictures, rather than streams of text or numbers. Humans respond readily to pictorial information and are able to absorb much more information from pictures than from a collection of numbers. Our eye–brain system is highly attuned to recognizing visual patterns. Reading text is, of course, one form of pattern recognition: We instantly recognize characters, form them into words, and interpret their meaning. But we are even more acute when glancing at a picture. What might be an inscrutable blather of numbers when presented as text becomes an instantly recognizable shape or pattern when presented graphically. The amount of information in a picture can be enormous. We not only recognize what's "in it," but also glean a world of information from its subtle details and texture.

---

[1]   SIGGRAPH is a special-interest group in the Association for Computing Machinery ACM.

People study computer graphics for many reasons. Some just want a better set of tools for plotting curves and presenting the data they encounter in their other studies or work. Some want to write computer-animated games, while others are looking for a new medium for artistic expression. Everyone wants to be more productive and to communicate ideas better, and computer graphics can be a great help.

There is also the "input" side. A program generates output—pictures or otherwise—from a combination of the algorithms executed in the program and the data the user inputs into the program. Some programs accept input crudely, through characters and numbers typed at the keyboard. Graphics programs, on the other hand, emphasize more familiar types of input: the movement of a mouse on a desktop, the strokes of a pen on a drawing tablet, or the motion of the user's head and hands in a virtual-reality setting. We examine many techniques of "interactive computer graphics" in this book; that is, we combine the techniques of natural user input with those that produce pictorial output.

1.2 WHERE COMPUTER-GENERATED PICTURES ARE USED

Computer graphics can draw pictures of actual objects with dazzling realism. But it can also draw things that never existed or could never exist. The programmer describes an object of interest through some algorithm in a program, and the program generates a picture from this model.

In this section, we look briefly at some applications that use computer graphics, to demonstrate the range of situations that can benefit from graphics. Later we shall describe several of these applications in detail as case studies.

1.2.1 Art, Entertainment, and Publishing

Computer graphics is widely used in the production of movies, television programs, books, and magazines. The cost of graphics systems has decreased markedly in recent years, and powerful software tools have been developed to utilize such systems. Talented designers can now routinely use computers to create special effects, animation, and high-quality publications.

Movie Production, Animation, and Special Effects

Computer-animated commercials are seen regularly on television, and some very impressive animations are being integrated into feature movies. Plates 1 and 2 show dazzling examples of individual frames taken from some animations.

Animations are created by writing a sequence of images onto film or videotape, each image being only slightly different from the one before. When the film or videotape is played back at 20 to 30 frames a second, the human eye blends the images and sees smooth motion.

Computer Games

Plate 3 shows an image from a computer game. The player moves joysticks and pulls triggers, and the computer-generated image responds instantly. Special hardware is often used to speed up the generation of successive images. Arcade games provide some of the greatest challenges to graphics programmers, as the action must be realistic and at the same time very fast.

Browsing on the World Wide Web

We live in a networked world, and many people regularly "surf" the World Wide Web. Plate 4 shows a sample image from a browser. The user moves the mouse to a spot on the screen and clicks to choose the next Web site to visit, whereupon a page of information is sent over the Internet. The browser must rapidly interpret the data on the page and draw it on the screen as high-quality text and graphics.

Slide, Book, and Magazine Design

Plate 5 shows a sample screen from a **page layout** program, used to design the final "look" of each page of a book or magazine. The user can interactively move text and graphics around to find the most pleasing arrangement.

Another form of publishing is sometimes called "presentation graphics." In a business setting, high-quality slides are designed to be shown to a group of customers or management. Plate 6 shows a sample slide. Often, slides contain bar charts or pie charts that summarize complex information in a readily understandable form. These graphics must be of high quality and have visual appeal in order to make a particular point.

A **paint system** is another tool for generating images by computer. The user fashions the image by sketching—often using a tablet or light pen—and by selecting colors and patterns to create the desired effects. Figure 1.1 shows a paint system being used, and Plate 7 shows a picture created with such a system. The system provides an assortment of tools: Previously rendered images can be retrieved from mass storage and merged with new images, "palettes" of different colors can be accessed and displayed, and many different textures can be created by means of simple commands. These systems are often used to create pages you encounter on the World Wide Web.

FIGURE 1.1 A user creating an image on a paint system. (ZBrush interface. Courtesy of Ofer Alon.www.pixologic.com.)

Mapmaking is another form of publishing. Plate 8 shows a detailed map. Mapmaking is an exacting activity because a huge amount of information and detail must be integrated together with great accuracy.

1.2.2 Computer Graphics and Image Processing

The fields of computer graphics and image processing are blending together more each year, so that it is becoming harder (and less important) to know where the boundary between them lies. In this book we focus on computer graphics, but also describe a number of techniques that historically would have been confined to the image-processing field.

The main task in computer graphics is to create pictures and images—to synthesize them on the basis of some description, or model, in a computer. The main task in image processing, on the other hand, is to improve or alter images that were created elsewhere, perhaps digitized from photographs or captured by a video recorder. Processing can remove "specks" of noise from an image, enhance the contrast of the image, sharpen its edges, and fix its colors. Software routines can be used to search for certain features in an image and highlight them to make them more noticeable or understandable.

Figure 1.2a shows an image obtained by digitally scanning a photograph. Part b shows the image after its contrast has been enhanced, specks of noise have been removed, and its edges have been sharpened.

a)   b)

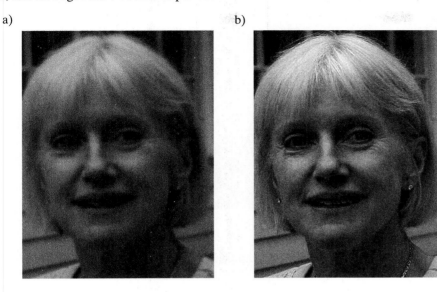

FIGURE 1.2 Enhancing an image. (a) Original. (b) Enhanced.

Plate 9 shows a whimsical blending of graphics and image processing.

The movie industry has capitalized in dramatic ways on the marriage of computer graphics and image processing.

1.2.3 Monitoring a Process

Highly complex systems like factories, power plants, and air traffic control systems must be carefully monitored; often, there must be a "human in the loop" to watch out for impending trouble. The operator must be given information, on a **status display**, that is current and that can be interpreted instantly. Measurements are made of the system every second or so, and the data are transmitted to the monitoring station, to be converted to graphical information and presented to the operator.

For example, Figure 1.3 shows a display from a manufacturing process. The user sees a schematic representation of the process, giving the whole picture at a glance. Various icons can flash or change color to alert the user to changes that need attention.

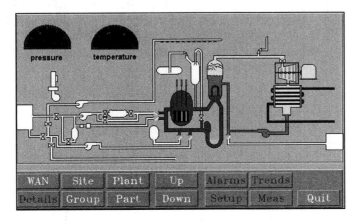

FIGURE 1.3 Monitoring a manufacturing process. (Courtesy of Dataviews Corporation.)

FIGURE 1.4 A woman wears a head-mounted display and data gloves to interact with a virtual world. (Courtesy of NASA.)

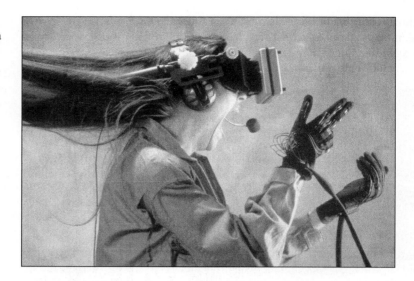

1.2.4 Displaying Simulations

Some systems, that are displayed graphically actually exist and can be measured in real time. Others have never been built, perhaps could never be built, and exist only as equations and algorithms in a computer. But they can still be tested and "run through their paces" as if they existed, and valuable information can be obtained. Computer graphics has the ability to display objects as if they already physically exist, when in actuality they are only models inside a computer.

A variety of systems can be profitably simulated: the movement of a robot as it shuffles down the slope of an active volcano, the response of the human body to the introduction of a foreign substance, and the effect of global warming due to an increase in hydrocarbons. The classic example is a flight simulator, as shown in Plate 10. The system is an airplane with a certain shape and flying characteristics, along with a "world" consisting of a landing field, mountains, other planes, and, of course, "air," all modeled appropriately. In a flight simulator, the dynamics of the airplane's motion are modeled on a computer. During a simulated flight, as the pilot moves the controls, the program calculates new positions and speeds for the simulated plane. The pilot sees a simulated view outside the cockpit. Flight simulator programs are among the most demanding and difficult graphics applications to write, because they must respond so rapidly.

Another form of simulation has recently become popular: the simulation of "virtual worlds". Figure 1.4 shows a woman interacting with a virtual world using a head-mounted display and data gloves. As she turns her head the graphical display shows different views of a computer-generated world, and she can move her "virtual hands" to touch different objects in the world. She sees a picture of her "hands" in the world, and when she "grasps" an object she sees it being clutched and responding to her hand movements.

Plate 11 shows another example where you sit at a terminal viewing and interacting with a world stored on remote computers in the World Wide Web. You use the mouse to propel yourself through this world, and "chat" with people you meet by typing messages. These people are graphical representations of other users representation of you, and chatting back at you.

1.2.5 Computer-aided Design

A number of disciplines make heavy use of interactive computer graphics to facilitate the design of some system or product. For example, Plate 12 shows the process of designing the casing of an electric soldering iron. The computer holds a model of the device in memory, and a picture based on the model is displayed for the user to examine. The designer can rotate the object and zoom in for a closer look, perhaps using a trackball or "data glove" to carry out the manipulation. To speed up the rendering, a **wire-frame** drawing (Plate 12a) is used, whereby the shape of the object is suggested by a grid of connected lines.

Presumably, the designer would scrutinize the current model and then indicate certain changes in its shape, whereupon the model would be updated and rendered again. When the shape seems about right, the user requests a more realistic view, as in Plate 12b. This view might take longer to produce, because the algorithms that produce full-color renderings with shadows, glossy highlights, and fine detail can be very complex.

Analysis and simulation can be used here, too. The shape of the soldering iron might have the right visual appeal, but the casing might be too weak or too heavy or might be uncomfortable to grip. Algorithms can be applied to the model to analyze its weight and heft, and to test whether the inner workings of the soldering iron will fit properly inside the casing. Further algorithms can test whether the particular shape is too expensive to produce in steel or aluminum and even whether the internal parts can be assembled conveniently in the final manufacturing process! The computer can be a powerful ally throughout design and manufacturing. Our principal interest in this book is in producing images of an object that provide the designer with the right information.

Computer-aided Architectural Design

Computer graphics can also help architects design buildings. Here the model might be a floor plan of a house. An architect can make adjustments to the floor plan, moving a wall here or adjusting a window there (with the mouse, of course), and then see a fully rendered version showing how the house would appear, as in Plate 13. Different textures, such as brick or stucco, can be tried out. Using interactive controls, the architect can even "walk through" the house and show a client how he or she will experience the house when it finally is built.

Electrical Circuit Design

Figure 1.5 is another example in which computer-aided design offers enormous benefits. Here the model is a symbolic description of an electronic circuit that might form part of a new computer. The designer can add new circuit elements (called "gates") by selecting from a menu of icons (small pictures that represent the elements) and "dragging" the icon to the desired position in the circuit. By means of simple pointing actions, the designer can add, delete, and connect gates. Then, simulation software can test how a real version of the circuit would perform. On the basis of the results of the simulation, the designer adjusts the circuit and tests it again.

1.2.6 Scientific Analysis and Visualization

Scientific data are often complex, and relationships among the variables of an experiment can be difficult to visualize. Graphics provides a superb tool for presenting scientific information in a way that can be easily grasped. When data are displayed in the right way, you often have new insights into the underlying process you are investigating. By displaying data properly, you can also communicate ideas better to colleagues.

FIGURE 1.5 Digital logic design application. (Courtesy of Chris Vadnais and Capilano Computing Systems, Ltd.)

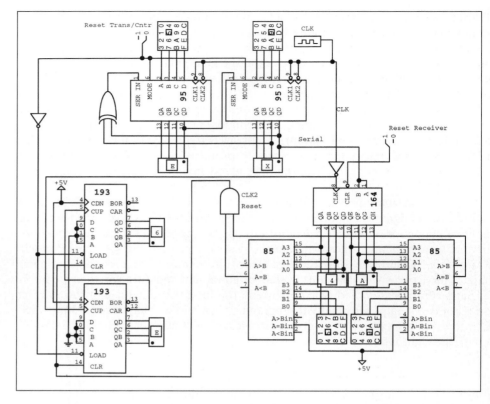

Figure 1.6 is an example of the graphical display of complex scientific data. In the figure, a surface is seen to undulate in a fashion the eye can grasp immediately. The height of the surface represents one quantity (such as temperature or viscosity) that is displayed against two other quantities to produce a three-dimensional plot. By con-

FIGURE 1.6 Display of complex scientific data.

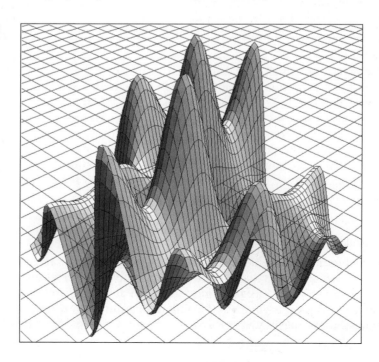

trast, if these data were presented as just a table of numbers, one would have to study the table laboriously in order to obtain the same information.

Plate 14 shows the structure of a complex molecule of "fullerine", named after Buckminster Fuller. It consists of 60 carbon atoms arranged in a particular geometric pattern and provides a third stable form of carbon (along with graphite and diamond). (We examine its shape further in chapter 6.) The geometric arrangement is made immediately apparent using computer graphics. This particular rendition of the molecule was created to be not only clear and revealing but also beautfiul.

Plate 15 shows a complex image built up by scanning a human head. Areas of different colors immediately inform a physician about the state of health of each part of the brain.

In Plate 16, graphics are used to present a huge amount of weather data in a form that can be readily recognized and analyzed, to assist in predicting future weather.

In addition to assisting humans in understanding measured data, computer graphics is well suited for providing insight into complex mathematical ideas. Several powerful programs (*Mathematica*, MatLab, MathCad, etc.) have been developed recently that allow a user to enter equations and "rules" pertaining to various quantities and then to see the resulting objects displayed in some fashion. For instance, Figure 1.7a shows a surface generated by a mathematical formula. The surface is displayed using *Mathematica* by typing the single instruction

a)

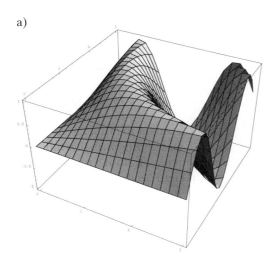

b)

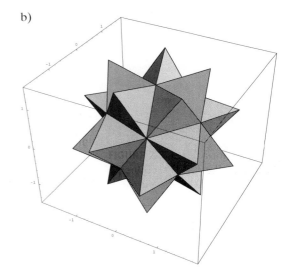

```
ParametricPlot3D[{t,u,Sin[t u]},{t,0,3},{u,0,3}]
```

FIGURE 1.7 *Mathematica* displays of (a) a complex mathematical surface and (b) a mathematically defined solid object.

In graphical form, the intricacies of the formula are nicely revealed at a glance, and the user can adjust some parameters in order to examine the surface from different viewpoints. Figure 1.7b also uses *Mathematica* to draw a complex three-dimensional object (a stellated icosahedron) to assist the user in studying its structure.

Minimal surfaces are a class of mathematically defined surfaces with special properties. Soap are sometimes observed to organize themselves as minimal surfaces. Plate 17 shows a computer-generated picture of a new minimal surface, discovered recently by Professor David Hoffman and his colleagues. The researchers' intuitions about the existence of this special surface were guided using computer graphics.

Plate 18 shows a portion of the beguiling Mandelbrot set (examined in Chapter 9) which has been called "the most complex object in mathematics."

1.3 ELEMENTS OF PICTURES CREATED IN COMPUTER GRAPHICS

What makes up a computer-drawn picture? The basic objects out of which such pictures are composed are called **output primitives**. One useful categorization of these is the following:

- polylines
- text
- filled regions
- raster images

We will see that these types overlap somewhat, but this terminology provides a good starting point. We describe each type of primitive in turn and hint at typical software routines that are used to draw it. More details on these tools are given in later chapters, of course. We also discuss the various attributes of each output primitive. The **attributes** of a graphic primitive are the characteristics that affect how it appears, such as color and thickness.

1.3.1 Polylines

FIGURE 1.8 (a) A polyline drawing of a dinosaur. (Courtesy of Susan Verbeck.) (b) A plot of a mathematical function. (c) A wire-frame rendering of a three-dimensional object.

A *polyline* is a connected sequence of straight lines. Each of the examples in Figure 1.8 contains several polylines: In (a), one polyline extends from the nose of the dinosaur to its tail; in (b); the plot of the mathematical function is a single polyline and in (c) the "wireframe" picture of a chess pawn contains many polylines that outline its shape.

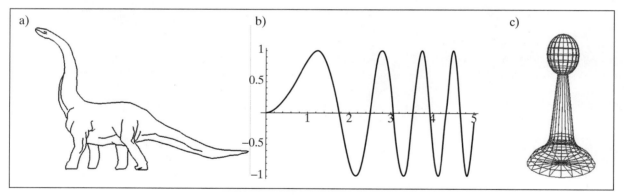

Note that a polyline can appear as a smooth curve. Figure 1.9 shows a blowup of a curve, revealing its underlying short line segments. The eye blends them into an apparently smooth curve.

FIGURE 1.9 A curved line made up of straight-line segments.

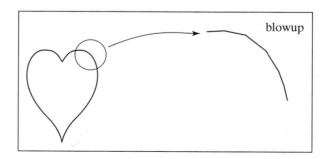

Pictures made up of polylines are sometimes called **line drawings.** Some devices, like a pen plotter, are specifically designed to produce line drawings.

The simplest polyline is a single straight-line segment. A line segment is specified by its two endpoints, say (x_1, y_1) and (x_2, y_2). A drawing routine for a line might look like

```
drawLine(x1, y1, x2, y2);
```

This routine draws a line between the two endpoints. We develop such a tool later and show many examples of its use. At that point, we get specific about how coordinates such as x_1 are represented (by integers or by real numbers) and how colors can be represented in a program.

A special case arises when a line segment shrinks to a single point and is drawn as a "dot." Even the lowly dot has important uses in computer graphics, as we shall see later. A dot might be programmed using the routine

```
drawDot(x1, y1);
```

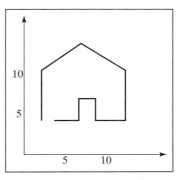

When there are several lines in a polyline, each one is called an **edge**, and two adjacent lines meet at a **vertex**. The edges of a polyline can cross one another, as seen in Figure 1.8. Polylines are specified as a list of vertices, each given by a coordinate pair:

$$(x_0, y_0), (x_1, y_1), (x_2, y_2), \ldots, (x_n, y_n). \tag{1.1}$$

FIGURE 1.10 A sample polyline.

For instance, the polyline shown in Figure 1.10 is given by the sequence $(2, 4)$, $(2, 11), (6, 14), (12, 11), (12, 4), \ldots$ (What are the remaining vertices in this polyline?) To draw polylines, we will need a tool such as the routine

```
drawPolyline(poly);
```

where the variable `poly` is a list containing all the endpoints (x_i, y_i) in some fashion. There are various ways to capture a list in a program, each having its advantages and disadvantages.

A polyline need not form a closed figure, but if the first and last points are connected by an edge, the polyline is a **polygon**. If, in addition, no two edges cross, the polygon is called **simple.** Figure 1.11 shows some interesting polygons; only *A* and *D* are simple. Polygons are fundamental in computer graphics, partly because they are so easy to define, and many drawing (rendering) algorithms have been finely tuned to operate optimally with polygons. Chapter 3 describes polygons in depth.

FIGURE 1.11 Examples of polygons.

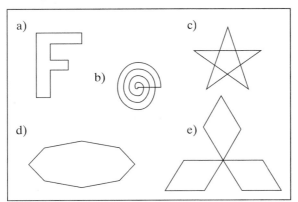

Attributes of Lines and Polylines

Important attributes of a polyline are the color and thickness of its edges, the manner in which the edges are dashed, and the manner in which thick edges blend together at their endpoints. Typically, all of the edges of a polyline are given the same attributes.

The first two polylines in Figure 1.12 are distinguished by the line-thickness attribute. The third polyline is drawn using dashed segments.

FIGURE 1.12 Polylines with different attributes.

When a line is thick, its ends have shapes, and a user must decide how two adjacent edges "join." Figure 1.13 shows various possibilities. Case (a) shows "butt-end" lines that leave an unseemly groove at the joint. Case (b) shows rounded ends on the lines, so they join smoothly. Case (c) shows a mitered joint, and Case (d) shows a trimmed mitered joint. Software tools are available in some packages to allow the user to choose the type of joining. Some methods are quite expensive computationally.

FIGURE 1.13 Some ways of joining two thick lines in a polyline.

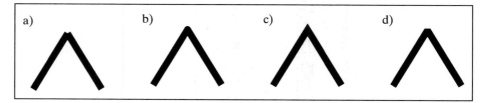

The attributes of a polyline are sometimes set by calling routines such as

`setDash(dash7)` or `setLineThickness(thickness)`.

1.3.2 Text

Some graphics devices have two distinct display modes: a **text mode** and a **graphics mode**. The text mode is used for the simple input and output of characters to control the operating system or edit the code in a program. Text displayed in this mode uses a built-in character generator that is capable of drawing alphabetic, numeric, and punctuation characters, as well as a selection of special symbols such as ♥, ∞, and ⊕. Usually, these characters cannot be placed arbitrarily on the display, but rather, can be put only in some row and column of a built-in grid.

The graphics mode offers a richer set of character shapes than the text mode does, and characters can be placed arbitrarily. Figure 1.14 shows some examples of text drawn graphically.

FIGURE 1.14 Some text drawn graphically.

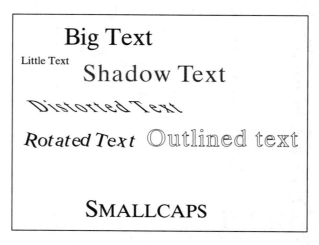

A routine to draw a character string might look like

```
drawString(x, y, string);
```

This routine places the starting point of the string at position (x, y) and draws the sequence of characters stored in the variable `string`.

Text Attributes

There are many text attributes, the most important of which are the text's font (type-face), color, size, spacing, and orientation.

Font A **font**, or **typeface**, is a specific set of character shapes in a particular style and size. Figure 1.15 shows various fonts.

FIGURE 1.15 Some examples of fonts.

The shape of each character can be defined by a polyline (or more complicated curves, such as Bezier curves; see Chapter 11), as shown in Figure 1.16a, or by an arrangement of dots, as shown in Figure 1.16(b). Graphics packages come with a set of predefined fonts, and additional fonts can be purchased from companies that specialize in designing them.

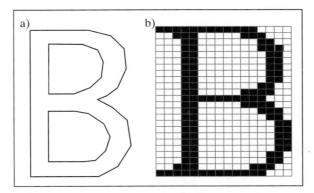

FIGURE 1.16 A character shape defined by (a) a polyline and (b) a pattern of dots.

Characters may also be drawn tilted along some direction. Tilted strings are often used to annotate parts of a graph.

The graphic presentation of high-quality text is a complex subject. Barely perceptible differences in detail can change pleasing text into ugly text. Indeed, we see so much printed material in our daily lives, that we subliminally expect characters to be displayed with certain shapes, spacings, and subtle balances.

1.3.3 Filled-Regions

The **filled-region** (sometimes called "fill area") primitive is a shape filled with some color or pattern. The boundary of a filled region is often a polygon (although more complex regions are considered in Chapter 10). Figure 1.17 shows several filled

FIGURE 1.17 Examples of filled polygons.

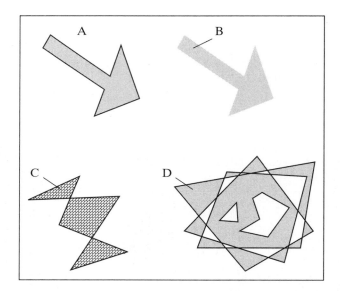

polygons. Polygon *A* is filled with its edges visible, whereas *B* is filled with its border left undrawn. Polygons *C* and *D* are non-simple. Polygon *D* even contains polygonal holes. Such shapes can still be filled, but one must specify exactly what is meant by a polygon's "interior," since filling algorithms differ depending on the definition. Algorithms for performing the filling action are discussed in Chapter 10.

To draw a filled polygon, one would use a routine like

```
fillPolygon(poly, pattern);
```

where the variable `poly` holds the data for the polygon—the same kind of list as for a polyline—and the variable `pattern` contains some description of the pattern to be used for filling.

Figure 1.18 shows the use of filled regions to shade the different faces of a three-dimensional object. Each polygonal face of the object is filled with a certain shade of gray that corresponds to the amount of light that would reflect off that face. This combination of shading makes the object appear to be bathed in light from a certain direction. The shading of three-dimensional objects is discussed in Chapter 8.

The attributes of a filled region include the attributes of the enclosing border that encloses the region, as well as the pattern and color of the filling.

FIGURE 1.18 Filling polygonal faces of three-dimensional objects to suggest proper shading.

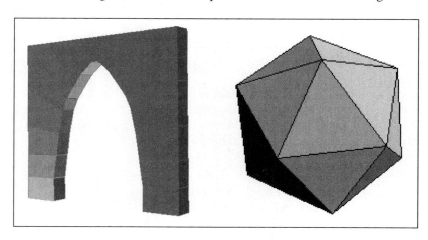

1.3.4 Raster Image

Figure 1.19(a) shows a **raster image** of a chess piece. The image is made up of many small "cells," in different shades of gray, as revealed in the blowup shown in Figure 1.19(b). The individual cells are often called "**pixels**" (short for "picture elements"). Normally, your eye is unable to see the individual cells; instead, it blends them together and synthesizes an overall picture.

a) b)

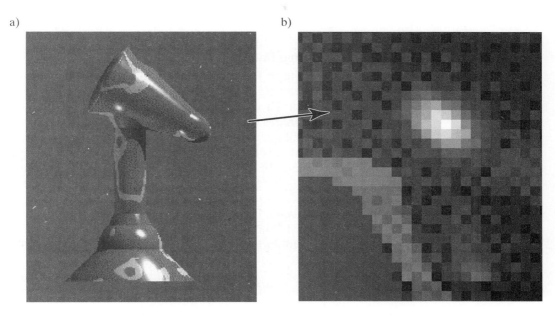

A raster image is stored in a computer as an array of numerical values. The array is thought of as being rectangular, with a certain number of rows and a certain number of columns. Each numerical value represents the value of the pixel stored there. The array as a whole is often called a "**pixel map**." The term "**bitmap**" is also used (although some people think this term should be reserved for those pixel maps wherein each pixel is represented by a single bit having the value 0 or 1.)

Figure 1.20(a) shows a simple example of a figure that is represented by a 18-by-19 array (18 rows by 19 columns) of cells in three shades of gray. Suppose the three

FIGURE 1.19 (a) A raster image of a chess piece. (b) A blowup of the image. (Ray tracing courtesy of Andrew Slater.)

FIGURE 1.20 A simple figure represented as a bit map.

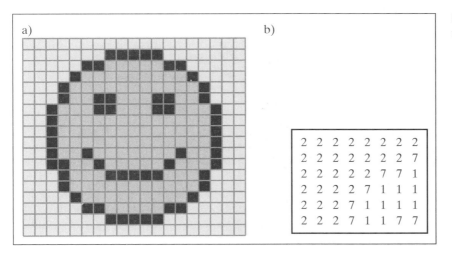

a) b)

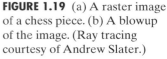

2	2	2	2	2	2	2	2
2	2	2	2	2	2	2	7
2	2	2	2	2	7	7	1
2	2	2	2	7	1	1	1
2	2	2	7	1	1	1	1
2	2	2	7	1	1	7	7

gray levels are encoded as the values 1, 2, and 7. Figure 1.20(b) shows the numerical values of the pixel map for the upper left 6-by-8 portion of the image.

How are raster images created? The three principal sources are as follows:

1. **Hand-designed Images.**

   With this technique, a designer figures out what values are needed for each cell and types them into memory. Sometimes a paint program can be used to help automate the process: The designer can draw and manipulate various graphical shapes, viewing what has been made so far. When satisfied, the designer stores the result in a file. The icon in Figure 1.20 was created this way.

2. **Computed Images.**

   According to this methodology, an algorithm is used to render a scene, which might be modeled abstractly in computer memory. As a simple example, a scene might consist of a single yellow, smooth sphere illuminated by a light source that emanates orange light. The model contains descriptions of the size and position of the sphere, the placement of the light source, and the hypothetical camera that is to take the picture. The raster image plays the role of the film in the camera. In order to create the raster image, an algorithm must calculate the color of light that falls on each pixel of the image in the camera. This is the way in which ray-traced images, such as the chess piece in Figure 1.19 are created. (See Chapter 14.)

   Raster images also frequently contain images of straight lines. A line is created in an image by setting the proper pixels to the line's color. But quite a bit of computation may be required to determine the sequence of pixels that "best fit" the ideal line between two given endpoints. Bresenham's algorithm (see Chapter 10) provides a very efficient approach to determining these pixels.

   Figure 1.21(a) shows a raster image featuring several straight lines, a circular arc, and some text characters. Figure 1.21(b) shows a close-up of the raster image in order to expose the individual pixels that are "on" the lines. For a horizontal or vertical line, the black square pixels line up nicely, forming a sharp line. But for the other lines and for an arc, the "best" collection of pixels produces only an approximation to the "true" line desired. In addition, the result shows the dread "**jaggies**" that have a relentless presence in raster images.

FIGURE 1.21 (a) A collection of lines and text. (b) Blowup of part (a), having "jaggies."

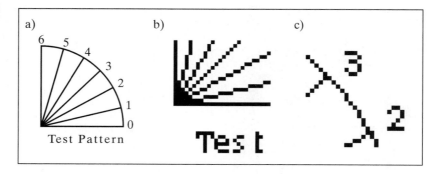

3. **Scanned Images.**

   A photograph or television image can be digitized. In effect, a grid is placed over the original image, and at each grid point, the digitizer reads into memory the "closest" color in its repertoire. The bitmap thereby created is then stored in a file for later use. The image of the kitten in Figure 1.22 was formed in this way.

FIGURE 1.22 A scanned image.

Because raster images are simply arrays of numbers, they can be subsequently processed to good effect by a computer. For instance, Figure 1.23 shows three successive enlargements of the kitten image of Figure 1.22. The enlargements are formed by "pixel replication" (discussed in detail in Chapter 10). Each pixel has been replicated 3 times in each direction in part (a), 6 times in part (b), and 12 times in part (c).

FIGURE 1.23 Three successive blowups of the kitten image of Figure 1.22. (a) Three-times enlargement. (b) Six-times enlargement. (c) Twelve-times enlargement.

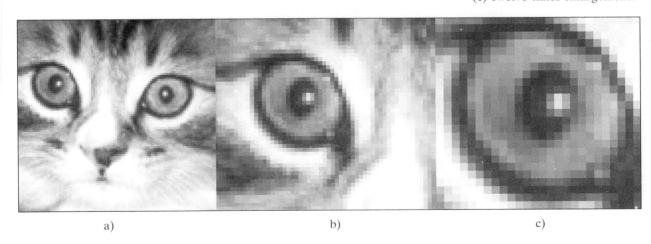

a)   b)   c)

As another example, one often needs to "clean up" a scanned image—for instance, to remove specks of noise or to reveal important details. Figure 1.24(a) shows the kitten image of Figure 1.22 with gray levels altered to increase the contrast and make details more evident, and Figure 1.24(b) shows the effect of "edge enhancement," achieved by a form of filtering the image.

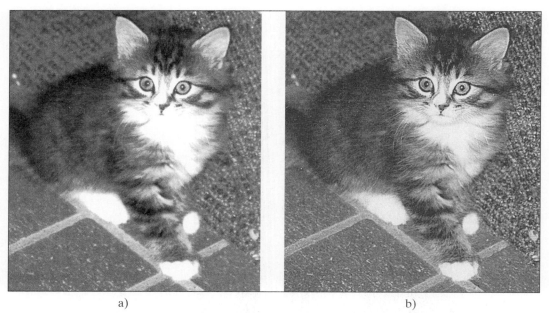

a)   b)

FIGURE 1.24 Examples of image enhancement.

Figure 1.25 shows two examples of editing an image to accomplish some visual effect. Part (a) shows the kitten image "embossed," and in part (b) the image is distorted geometrically.

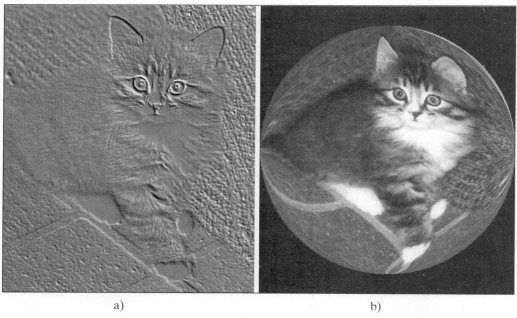

a)   b)

FIGURE 1.25 Examples of altering an image for visual effect.

1.3.5 Representation of Shades of Gray and Color in Raster Images

An important aspect of a raster image is the manner in which the various shades of gray or colors are represented in the bitmap. We briefly survey the most common methods.

1.3.5.1 Gray-scale Raster Images

If there are only two pixel values in a raster image, it is called **bi-level.** Figure 1.26(a) shows a simple bi-level image, representing a familiar arrow-shaped cursor frequently

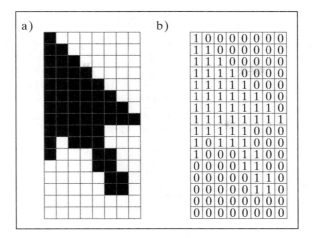

a)   b)

1	0	0	0	0	0	0	0
1	1	0	0	0	0	0	0
1	1	1	0	0	0	0	0
1	1	1	1	0	0	0	0
1	1	1	1	1	0	0	0
1	1	1	1	1	1	0	0
1	1	1	1	1	1	1	0
1	1	1	1	1	1	1	1
1	1	1	1	1	0	0	0
1	0	1	1	1	0	0	0
1	0	0	0	1	1	0	0
0	0	0	0	1	1	0	0
0	0	0	0	0	1	1	0
0	0	0	0	0	1	1	0
0	0	0	0	0	0	0	0
0	0	0	0	0	0	0	0

FIGURE 1.26 (a) A bilevel image of a cursor. (b) A bit map of the image.

seen on a computer screen. The raster of this image consists of 16 rows of 8 pixels each. Figure 1.26(b) shows a bitmap of this image as an array of 1's and 0's. The image at the left associates black with a 1 and white with a 0, but this association might just as easily be reversed. Since one bit of information is sufficient to distinguish two values, a bi-level image is often referred to as a "**one-bit-per-pixel**" image.

When the pixels in a gray-scale image take on more than two values, each pixel requires more than a single bit to represent it in memory. Gray-scale images are often classified in terms of their **pixel depth,** the number of bits needed to represent their gray levels. Since an n-bit quantity has 2^n possible values, there can be 2^n gray levels in an image with pixel depth n. The most common values are as follows:

- Two bits per pixel produce 4 gray levels.
- Four bits per pixel produce 16 gray levels.
- Eight bits per pixel produce 256 gray levels.

Figure 1.27 shows 16 gray levels ranging from black to white. Each of the 16 possible pixel values is associated with a binary-valued **quadruple**, such as 0110 or 1110. Here, 0000 represents black, 1111 denotes white, and the other 14 values represent gray levels in between.

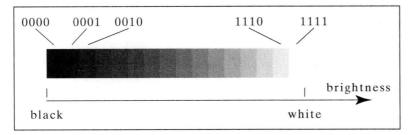

FIGURE 1.27 Sixteen levels of gray.

Many gray-scale images[2] employ 256 gray levels, since that number usually gives a scanned image of acceptable quality. Each pixel is represented by some eight-bit value, such as 01101110. The pixel value usually represents "brightness," with black represented by 00000000, white by 11111111, and a medium gray by 10000000. Figure 1.22 uses 256 gray levels.

---

[2] Thousands are available on the Internet, frequently as gif, jpg, or tif images.

Effect of Pixel Depth: Gray-scale Quantization

Sometimes an image that initially uses eight bits per pixel is altered so that fewer bits per pixel are utilized. This might occur if a particular display device is incapable of displaying 256 levels, or if the full image takes up too much memory. Figures 1.28 through 1.30 show the effect on the image of the kitten of Figure 1.22 if pixel values are simply truncated to fewer bits. The loss in fidelity is hardly noticeable for the images in Figure 1.28, which use six and five bits per pixel (providing 64 and 32 different shades of gray, respectively).

FIGURE 1.28 The image of Figure 1.22 reduced to (left) six bits per pixel and (right) five bits per pixel.

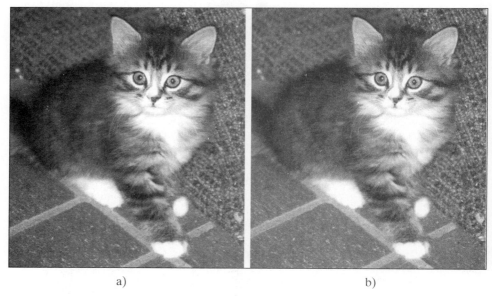

a)   b)

But there is a significant loss in quality in the images of Figure 1.29. Part (a) shows the effect of truncating each pixel value to four bits, so that there are only 16 possible shades of gray. For example, pixel value 01110100 is replaced with 0111. In part (b), the 8 possible levels of gray are clearly visible. Note that some areas of the figure that show gradations of gray in the original now show a "lake" of uniform gray.

FIGURE 1.29 The image of Figure 1.22 reduced to (left) four bits per pixel and (right) three bits per pixel.

a)   b)

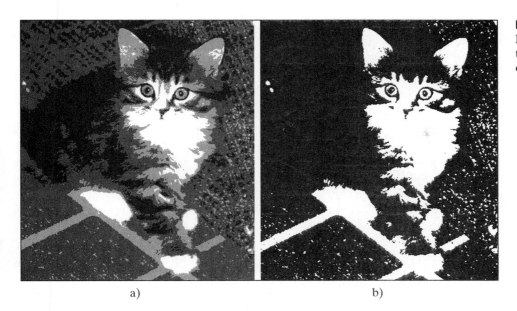

a)   b)

FIGURE 1.30 The image of Figure 1.22 reduced to (left) two bits per pixel and (right) one bit per pixel.

This effect is often called **banding**, since areas that should show a gradual shift in the gray level instead show a sequence of uniform gray "bands."

Figure 1.30 shows the cases of two bits and one bit per pixel. In part (a), the four levels are clearly visible and there is a great deal of banding. In part (b) there is only black and white, and much of the original information about the image has been lost. In Chapter 10, we show techniques, such as dithering, for improving the quality of an image when too few bits are used for each pixel.

1.3.5.2 Color Raster Images

Color images are desirable because they match our daily experience more closely than do gray-scale images. Color raster images have become more common in recent years as the cost of high-quality color displays has come down. The cost of scanners that digitize color photos has also become reasonable.

Each pixel in a color image has a "color value," a numerical value that somehow represents a color. There are a number of ways to associate numbers with colors (see Chapter 12 for a detailed discussion), but one of the most common is to describe a color as a combination of amounts of red, green, and blue light. Each pixel value is an **ordered triple**, such as (23, 14, 51), that prescribes the intensities of the red, green, and blue components in that order.

The number of bits used to represent the color of each pixel is often called the **color depth** of the pixel. Each value in the (red, green, blue) triple has a certain number of bits, and the color depth is the sum of these values. A color depth of three allows one bit for each component. For instance, the pixel value (0, 1, 1) means that the red component is "off," but both green and blue are "on." In most displays, the contributions from each component are added together (see Chapter 12 for exceptions, such as in printing), so (0,1,1) would represent the addition of green and blue light, which is perceived as cyan. Since each component can be on or off, there are eight possible colors, as tabulated in Figure 1.31. As expected, equal amounts of red, green, and blue, (1, 1, 1), produce white.

A color depth of three rarely offers enough precision for specifying the value of each component, so larger color depths are used. Because a byte is such a natural quantity to manipulate on a computer, many images have a color depth of eight. Each pixel then has one of 256 possible colors. A simple approach allows three bits for

color value	displayed
0,0,0	black
0,0,1	blue
0,1,0	green
0,1,1	cyan
1,0,0	red
1,0,1	magenta
1,1,0	yellow
1,1,1	white

FIGURE 1.31 A common correspondence between color value and perceived color.

each of the red and the green components, and two bits for the blue component. But more commonly, the association of each byte to a particular color is more complicated and uses a "color lookup" table, as discussed in the next section.

The highest quality images, known as **true-color** images, have a color depth of 24 and so use a byte for each component. This seems to achieve as good color reproduction as the eye can perceive: More bits do not improve an image. But such images require a great deal of memory: three bytes for every pixel. A high-quality image of 1,080 by 1,024 pixels requires over 3 million bytes!

Plates 19 through 21 show some color raster images having different color depths. Plate 19 shows a full-color image with a color depth of 24 bits. Plate 20 shows the degradation this image suffers when the color depth is reduced to 8 by simply truncating the red and green components to 3 bits each and the blue component to 2 bits. Plate 21 also has a color depth of 8, so its pixels contain only 256 colors, but the particular colors that are used have been carefully chosen for best reproduction. Methods for doing this are discussed in Chapter 12.

1.4 GRAPHICS DISPLAY DEVICES

In this section, we present an overview of some hardware devices that are used to display computer graphics. The devices include video monitors, plotters, and printers. A rich variety of graphics displays has been developed over the last 30 years, and new ones are appearing all the time. The quest is to display pictures of ever higher quality that recreate more faithfully what is in the artist's or engineer's mind. In what follows, we look over the types of pictures that are being produced today, how they are being used, and the kinds of devices used to display them. In the process, we look at ways to measure the "quality" of an image and see how different kinds of display devices measure up.

1.4.1 Line-Drawing Displays

Some devices are line drawers. Because of the technology of the time, most early computer graphics were generated by line-drawing devices. The classic example is the **pen plotter**, which moves a pen invisibly over a piece of paper to some spot that is specified by the computer, puts the pen down, and then sweeps the pen across to another spot, leaving a trail of ink of some color. Some plotters have a carousel that holds several pens that the program can exchange automatically in order to draw in different colors. Usually, the choice of available colors is very limited: A separate pen is used for each color. The "quality" of a line drawing is related to the precision with which the pen is positioned and the sharpness of the lines that are drawn.

There are various kinds of pen plotters. **Flatbed plotters** move the pen in two dimensions over a stationary sheet of paper. **Drum plotters** move the paper back and forth on a drum to provide one direction of motion, while the pen moves back and forth at the top of the drum to provide the other direction.

Figure 1.32 shows an example of a drum plotter. There are also video displays called "vector," "random-scan," or "calligraphic" displays that produce line drawings. These devices have internal circuitry specially designed to sweep an electronic beam from point to point across the face of a cathode-ray tube, leaving a glowing trail. Since each line segment to be displayed takes very few data values (for two endpoints and perhaps a color), vector displays can draw a picture very rapidly (hundreds of thousands of vectors per second).

FIGURE 1.32 Example of a drum plotter. (Courtesy of Hewlett Packard Company. Reprinted with permission.)

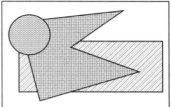

Vector displays, however, cannot show smoothly-shaded regions or scanned images. Region filling is usually simulated by **cross-hatching** with different line patterns, as suggested in Figure 1.33. Today raster displays have largely replaced vector displays, except in very specialized applications.

FIGURE 1.33 Cross-hatching to simulate filling a region.

1.4.2 Raster Displays

Most displays used for computer graphics nowadays are raster displays. The most familiar raster displays are the **video monitor** connected to personal computers and workstations [see Figure 1.34(a)], and the **flat-panel** display common to portable personal computers [see Figure 1.34(b)]. Other common displays produce **hard** copy of an image: the **laser printer, dot matrix printer, ink-jet plotter**, and **film recorder**.

FIGURE 1.34 (a) Video monitors on PC. (b) Flat-panel display.

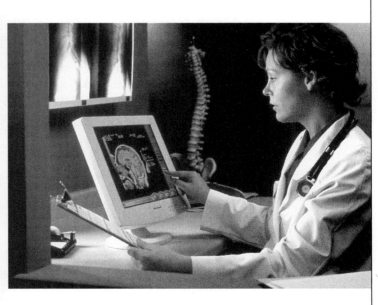

a)   b)

Raster devices have a **display surface** on which the image is presented. This surface has a certain number of pixels that it can show, such as 480 rows, each containing 640 pixels. So such a display surface can show $480 \times 640 \approx 307,000$ pixels simultaneously. All raster displays have a built-in coordinate system that associates a given pixel in an image with a given physical position on the display surface. Figure 1.35 shows an example. The horizontal coordinate sx increases from left to right, and the vertical coordinate sy increases from top to bottom. This "upside-down" coordinate system is typical of raster devices.

FIGURE 1.35 The built-in coordinate system for the surface of a raster display.

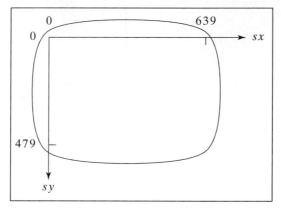

Raster displays are always connected one way or another to a **frame buffer**, a region of memory sufficiently large to hold all of the pixel values for the display (i.e., to hold the bit map of the image). The frame buffer may be physical memory on board the display, or it may reside in the host computer. For example, a graphics card that is installed in a personal computer actually houses the memory required for the frame buffer.

Figure 1.36 suggests how an image is created and displayed. The graphics program is stored in system memory and is executed instruction by instruction by the central processing unit (CPU). The program computes appropriate values for each pixel in the desired image and loads the values into the frame buffer. (This is the part we focus on later when it comes to programming: building tools that write the "correct" pixel values into the frame buffer.) A "scan controller" takes care of the actual display process, running autonomously (rather than under program control) and doing the same thing pixel after pixel. The scan controller causes the frame buffer to "send" each pixel through a converter to the appropriate physical spot on the display surface. The converter takes a pixel value such as 01001011 and converts it to the corresponding quantity that produces a spot of color on the display.

FIGURE 1.36 Block diagram of a computer with raster display.

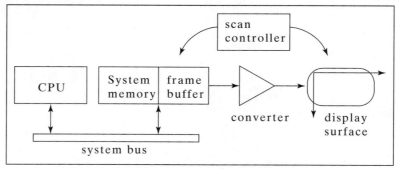

The Scanning Process

Figure 1.37 provides more detail regarding the scanning process. The main issue is how each pixel value in the frame buffer is "sent" to the right place on the display surface. Think of each of the pixels in the frame buffer as having a two-dimensional address

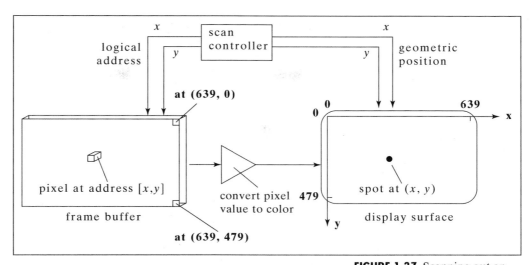

FIGURE 1.37 Scanning out an image from the frame buffer to the display surface.

(x, y). For address $(136, 252)$, for instance, there is a specific memory location that holds the value of the pixel. Call this location mem[136][252].

The scan controller sends logical address $(136, 252)$ to the frame buffer, which emits the value mem[136][252]. The controller also simultaneously "addresses" a physical (geometric) position $(136, 252)$ on the display surface. Position $(136, 252)$ corresponds to a certain physical distance of 136 units horizontally and 252 units vertically from the upper left-hand corner of the display surface. Different raster displays use different units.

The value mem[136][252] is converted to a corresponding intensity or color in the conversion circuit, and that intensity or color is sent to the proper physical position, $(136, 252)$, on the display surface. To scan out the image in the entire frame buffer, every pixel value is visited once, and its corresponding spot on the display surface is "excited" with the proper intensity or color. In some devices, this scanning must be repeated many times per second, in order to "refresh" the picture. The video monitor to be described next is such a device.

Video Monitors

Video monitors are based on a cathode-ray tube, or **CRT**, similar to the display in a television set. Figure 1.38 adds some details to the general description set forth previuosly for a system using a video monitor as its display device. In particular, the conversion process from pixel value to "spot of light" is illustrated. The system shown has a color depth of six bits; the frame buffer is shown as having six bit "planes." Each pixel uses one bit from each of the planes.

FIGURE 1.38 Operation of a color video monitor display system.

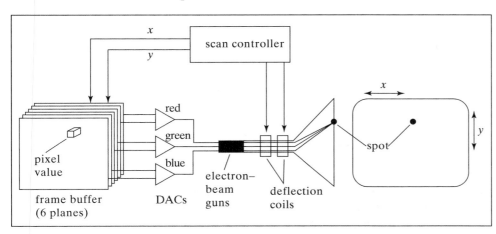

FIGURE 1.39 Input–output characteristic of a two-bit DAC.

Input	Voltage/brightness
00	0 * Max
01	0.333 * Max
10	0.666 * Max
11	1 * Max

The red, green, and blue components of a pixel each use a pair of bits. The pairs are fed to three **digital-to-analog converters** (DACs), which convert logical values like 01 into actual voltages. The correspondence between digital input values and output voltages is shown in Figure 1.39, where Max is the largest voltage level the DAC can produce.

The three voltage levels drive three "guns" inside the CRT, which in turn excite three electron beams with intensities proportional to the voltages. The deflection coils divert the three beams so that they stimulate three tiny phosphor dots at the proper place, (x, y), on the inside of the cathode-ray tube. Because of the phosphor materials used, one dot glows red when stimulated, another glows green, and the third glows blue. The dots are so close together that your eye sees one composite dot and perceives a color that is the sum of the three component colors. Thus, the composite dot can be made to glow in a total of $4 \times 4 \times 4 = 64$ different colors.

As described earlier, the scan controller addresses one pixel value, mem[x][y], in the frame buffer at the same time it "addresses" one position, (x, y), on the face of the CRT by sending the proper signal to the deflection coils. Because the glow of a phosphor dot quickly fades when the stimulus is removed, a CRT image must be **refreshed** rapidly (typically, 60 times a second) to prevent disturbing **flicker**. During each "refresh interval," the scan controller scans quickly through the entire memory of the frame buffer, sending each pixel value to its proper spot on the screen's surface.

Scanning proceeds row by row through the frame buffer, each row providing pixel values for one **scan line** across the face of the CRT. The order of scanning is usually from left to right along a **scan line** and from top to bottom by scan line. (Historians say that this convention has given rise to terms like "scan line," as well as to the habit of numbering scan lines downward with zero at the top, resulting in upside-down coordinate systems.)

Some of the more expensive systems have a frame buffer that supports 24 planes of memory. Each of the DACs has eight input bits, so there are 256 levels of red, 256 of green, and 256 of blue, for a total of $2^{24} = 16$ million colors.

At the other extreme are **monochrome** video displays, which display a single color in different intensities. A single DAC converts pixel values in the frame buffer to voltage levels, which drive a single electron-beam gun. The CRT has only one type of phosphor, so it can produce various intensities of only one color. Note that six planes of memory in the frame buffer gives $2^6 = 64$ levels of gray.

The color display of Figure 1.38 has a *fixed* association with a displayed color. For instance, the pixel value 001101 sends 00 to the "red DAC," 11 to the "green DAC," and 01 to the "blue DAC," producing a mix of bright green and dark blue—bluish green. Similarly, 110011 is displayed as a bright magenta and 000010 as a medium bright blue.

1.4.3 Indexed Color and the Lookup Table

Some systems use an alternative method of associating pixel values with colors—a **color lookup table** (or **LUT**), which offers a *programmable* association between a pixel value and the final displayed color. Figure 1.40 shows a simple example. The color depth is

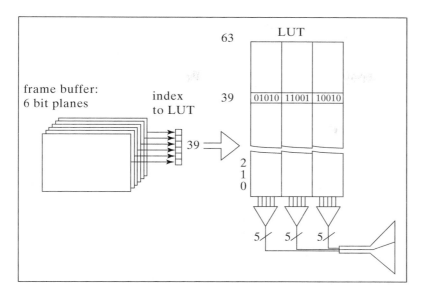

FIGURE 1.40 A color display system that incorporates an LUT.

again six, but the 6 bits stored in each pixel go through an intermediate step before they drive the CRT. These bits are used as an *index* into a table of 64 values, say, `LUT[0] ... LUT[63]`. (Why are there exactly 64 entries in this LUT?) For instance, if a pixel value is 39, the values stored in `LUT[39]` are used to drive the DACs, as opposed to having the bits in the value 39 itself drive them. As shown in the figure, `LUT[39]` contains the 15-bit value 01010 11001 10010. Five of these bits (01010) are routed to drive the "red DAC," 5 others drive the "green DAC," and the last 5 drive the "blue DAC."

Each of the `LUT[ ]` entries can be set under program control, using some system routine such as `setPalette()`. For example, the instruction

```
setPalette(39, 17, 25, 4);
```

would set the value in LUT[39] to the 15-bit quantity 10001 11001 00100 (since 17 is 10001 in binary, 25 is 11001, and 4 is 00100).

To make a particular pixel—say, the one at location $(x, y) = (479, 532)$—glow in the designated color, the value 39 is stored in the frame buffer, using `drawDot()` defined earlier:

```
drawDot(479, 532, 39);        // set pixel at (479, 532) to value 39
```

Each time the frame buffer is "scanned out" to the display, this pixel is read as the value 39, which causes the value stored in LUT[39] to be sent to the DACs. This programmability offers a great deal of flexibility in choosing colors, but of course, it comes at a price: The program (or programmer) has to figure out which colors to use! We consider this dilemma further in Chapter 10.

What is the potential of this system for displaying colors? In the system of Figure 1.40, each entry of the LUT consists of 15 bits, so each color can be set to one of $2^{15} = 32K = 32,768$ possible colors. The set of 2^{15} possible colors that the system is capable of displaying is called its **palette**, so we say that this display "has a palette of 32K colors."

The problem is that each pixel value lies in the range 0...63, and only 64 different colors can be stored in the LUT at one time. Therefore, this system can display a maximum of 64 different colors *at one time*—that is, during one scan-out of the entire frame buffer, something like 1/60 of a second. The contents of the LUT are not changed in the middle of a scan-out of the image, so one whole scan-out uses a fixed set of 64 palette colors. Usually, the contents of the LUT remain fixed for many scan-outs, although a program can change the contents of a small LUT during the brief dormant period between two successive scan-outs.

In more general terms, suppose that a raster display system has a color depth of b bits (so that there are b bit planes in its frame buffer) and that each LUT entry is w bits wide. Then

The system can display 2^w colors, any 2^b at one time.

■ EXAMPLE

1. A system with $b = 8$ bit planes and an LUT width $w = 12$ can display 4,096 colors, any 256 of them at a time.
2. A system with $b = 8$ bit planes and an LUT width $w = 24$ can display $2^{24} = 16,777,216$ colors, any 256 at a time.
3. If $b = 12$ and $w = 18$, the system can display 256K = 262,144 colors, 4,096 at a time.

No relationship is enforced between the number of bit planes, b, and the width of the LUT, w. Normally, w is a multiple of three, so the same number of bits ($w/3$) drives each of the three DACs. Also, b never exceeds w, so the palette is at least as large as the number of colors that can be displayed at one time. (Why would you never design a system with $w < b$?)

Note that the LUT itself requires very little memory—only 2^b words of w bits each. For example, if $b = 12$ and $w = 18$, there are only 9,216 bytes of storage in the LUT. So what is the motivation for having an LUT in a raster display system? Usually, it is a need to reduce the cost of memory. Increasing b increases significantly the amount of memory needed for the frame buffer, mainly because there are so many pixels. The tremendous amount of memory that is required can add significantly to the cost of the overall system.

To compare the costs of two systems, one with an LUT and one without, Figure 1.41 shows an example of two 1,024-by-1,280-pixel displays (so that each of them supports about 1.3 million pixels). Both systems allow colors to be defined with a precision of 24 bits, often called "true color."

FIGURE 1.41 Comparison of two raster display systems.

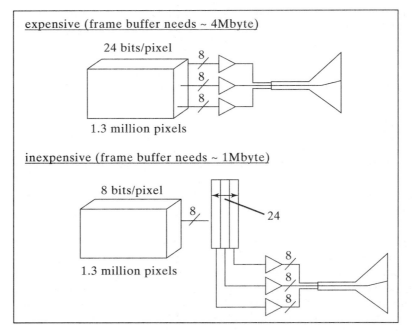

expensive (frame buffer needs ~ 4Mbyte)

24 bits/pixel

8

8

8

1.3 million pixels

inexpensive (frame buffer needs ~ 1Mbyte)

8 bits/pixel

8

24

1.3 million pixels

8

8

8

System #1 (expensive) The first system has a 24-bit-per-pixel frame buffer and no LUT, so each of its 1.3 million pixels can be set to any one of 2^{24} colors. Eight bits drive each of the DACs. (The number "8" and the slash through the line into each DAC indicate the presence of eight bit lines feeding into the DAC.) The amount of memory required for the frame buffer in this system is $1,024 \times 1,280 \times 24$ bits, which is almost 4 megabytes.

System #2 (inexpensive) The second has an 8-bit-per-pixel frame buffer along with an LUT, and the LUT is 24 bits wide. The system can display 2^{24} different colors, but only 256 at a time. The amount of memory required for the frame buffer is $1,024 \times 1,280 \times 8$ which is about 1 megabyte. (The LUT requires a trivial 768 bytes of memory.) If memory costs a significant amount per megabyte, this system is much less expensive than the first.

Putting an LUT in an inexpensive system attempts to compensate for the small number of different pixel values possible. The LUT allows the programmer to create a full set of colors, even though a given image can contain only a restricted set of them.

Displays with LUTs are still quite common today because memory costs remain high. The situation is changing rapidly, however, as the price of memory plummets. Many reasonably priced personal computers today have 24-bit frame buffers.

PRACTICE EXERCISES

1.4.1 Why not always have an LUT?

Since an LUT is inexpensive and offers the advantage of flexibility, why not have an LUT even in a system with 24 bits per pixel?

1.4.2 Configure your own system

For each of the systems that follow:

a. Draw the circuit diagram, similar to Figure 1.41.
b. Label the number of bits associated with the frame buffer, the DACs, and the LUT (if present);
c. Calculate (in bytes) the amount of storage required for the frame buffer and the LUT (if present):
   i. $b = 15$, no LUT;
   ii. $b = 15$, $w = 24$;
   iii. $b = 8$, $w = 18$;
   iv. $b = 12$, no LUT. ■

1.4.4 Other Raster Display Devices

Video monitors are not the only raster display devices: various other kinds have recently been developed. Portable "laptop" computers often have **flat-panel** displays, as suggested in Figure 1.42. Each pixel is addressed by a horizontal grid wire and a vertical grid wire. To turn a pixel "on," the corresponding horizontal and vertical grid wires are excited, producing an electric field at the location of the pixel, causing that spot to change its brightness.

The exact mechanism of converting the electric field to a visible dot depends on the technology used. In the case of a **liquid crystal display** (LCD), the electric field alters the polarization of long crystalline molecules in the LCD material. This modification either allows light to pass through the panel or prevents it from passing through. **Active matrix panels** are LCD panels that have a tiny transistor at each pixel location. The transistor responds to the electric field and adjusts the liquid crystals by

FIGURE 1.42 Flat-panel displays.

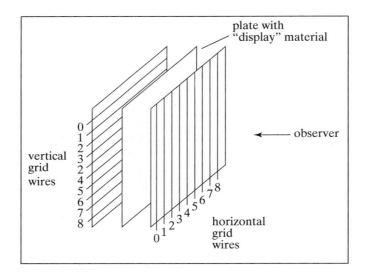

an amount proportional to the field, thus allowing the display of different levels of brightness. In addition, the transistors provide some "memory" that holds the crystals in their adjusted state, so that the display need not be refreshed. This arrangement produces a much brighter display. Color LCD panels are available that have resolutions of 800 by 1,000 pixels.

The **plasma panel** display has a geometry similar to that shown in Figure 1.42, but the material in the plate effectively places a tiny neon bulb at each pixel location. This bulb is turned on or off by the electric field. Like the active matrix display, the plasma panel need not be refreshed.

Several other kinds of raster displays are discussed in the references [e.g., Foley90].

1.4.5 Hard-Copy Raster Devices

One frequently wants a permanent version of an image, usually on paper or film. A number of raster devices produce hard copy of a raster image. Each draws pictures by transferring information from the frame buffer, dot by dot, to the display medium.

- *Film recorders*. In a **film recorder**, the "screen" is a strip of photographic film, and the electron beam exposes the film as it sweeps over it (once) in a raster pattern. Sometimes film recorders are separate devices with their own frame buffers, and sometimes they are simply cameras mounted directly on a CRT display. Film recorders are frequently used to make movies or high-quality 35-mm slides. Also, videotape recorders are available that make an electronic hard copy of any image stored in their frame buffer, to be played back on a television set.
- *Laser printer*. **Laser printers** also scan out raster patterns from an internal frame buffer, rapidly sweeping a laser beam over an internal drawing surface. At certain spots over which the beam is swept, the surface becomes electrically charged, causing a powder "toner" to adhere to the spots. The toner is then transferred to the paper to create the picture. Laser printers offer much higher resolution than do dot matrix printers, capitalizing on the great precision with which a laser beam can be positioned.
- *Inkjet plotter*. **Inkjet plotters** produce hard-copy raster images in color. A tiny nozzle sweeps over the paper and squirts the proper color of ink at each "pixel position."

Figure 1.43a shows text and graphics produced on the kind of dot matrix printer that is frequently used with personal computers, and Figure 1.43b shows output from a laser printer. Dot matrix printers place dots at a density of only 70 or so dots per inch

a)

b)

```
displayed.        esident campus
at we needn      e programs to t
to exclude       ne course to ea
version tak      ard a degree la
implificati      ates. This flexib
```

FIGURE 1.43 Blowups of dot matrix and laser printer images.

(dpi). Laser printers, on the other hand, can produce densities of 600 or more dpi and so can produce very high-quality graphics.

Even higher densities can be achieved by printers used in the publishing industry, such as the Linotronic typesetter, which prints at 2,540 dots per inch. This book was printed on such a device.

Many printers today are equipped with an internal microprocessor that is programmed to interpret PostScript,[3] a **page description language** that can generate high-quality text and graphics on a printed page. Figure 1.44 shows a brief "script" written in PostScript. When the file containing this script is printed, the onboard PostScript interpreter creates the picture shown in Figure 1.44b.

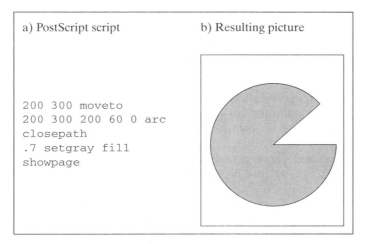

a) PostScript script   b) Resulting picture

```
200 300 moveto
200 300 200 60 0 arc
closepath
.7 setgray fill
showpage
```

FIGURE 1.44 A PostScript script and the resulting image.

PostScript is a **device-independent** language, so the same commands can be sent to different printers, and except for variations in quality, the same basic page is printed. (On printers having higher dot densities, there is a noticeable increase in the sharpness of lines, text, and patterns.) PostScript is widely used for laser printers, and we discuss it in several places in the book.

PostScript can be used as a powerful programming language to create graphics. Appendix 4 introduces the PostScript language and shows how to write small program "scripts" in PostScript that, when sent to a printer, print the resulting graphics.

---

[3] PostScript is a trademark of Adobe Systems, Inc.

1.5 GRAPHICS INPUT PRIMITIVES AND DEVICES

Many input devices let the user control the computer. You can look at an input device in two ways: what it *is*, and what it *does*. Physically, each device is some piece of machinery, such as a mouse, a keyboard, or a trackball. The device fits in the hand in a certain way and is natural for the user to manipulate. The device measures the user's manipulations and sends corresponding numerical information back to the graphics program.

We first look at what input devices do, by examining the kinds of data each sends to the program. We then look at a number of input devices in common use today.

1.5.1 Types of Input Graphics Primitives

Each device transmits a particular kind of data (e.g., a number, a string of characters, or a position) to the program. The different types of data are called **input primitives**. Two different physical devices may transmit the same type of data, so, logically, they generate the same graphics primitives.

The important input primitives are as follows.

String The **string** is the most familiar input primitive, producing a **string of characters** and thus modeling the action of a keyboard. When an application requests a string, the program pauses while the user types in the string, followed by a termination character. The program then resumes with the string stored in memory.

Choice A **choice** reports a **selection** from a fixed number of items. The programmer's model is a bank of buttons, or a set of buttons on a mouse.

Valuator A **valuator** produces a real value between 0.0 and 1.0, which can be used to fix the length of a line, the speed of an action, or perhaps the size of a picture. The model in the programmer's mind is a knob that can be turned from 0 to 1 in smooth gradations.

Locator A basic requirement in interactive graphics is to allow the user to point to a position on the display. The **locator** input primitive performs this function, because it produces a **coordinate pair** (x, y). The user manipulates an input device (usually a mouse) in order to position a visible cursor to some spot and then triggers the choice. This action returns the values of x and y, along with the value of the trigger, to the application.

Pick The **pick** input primitive is used to identify a portion of a picture for further processing. Some graphics packages allow a picture to be defined in terms of **segments**, which are groups of related graphics. These packages provide tools to define segments and to give them identifying names. When using `pick()`, the user "points" to a part of a picture with some physical input device, and the package figures out which segment is being pointed to. The primiteve `pick()` then returns the name of the segment to the application, enabling the user to erase, move, or otherwise manipulate the segment.

The graphics workstation is initialized when an application starts running: Among other things, each logical input primitive is associated with one of the installed physical devices.

1.5.2 Types of Physical Input Devices

We now look at the other side of input devices: the physical machine that is connected to the personal computer or workstation.

Plate 1.
A selected frame from Mulan.
(Disney Enterprises, Inc.)

Plate 2.
A selected image from Toy Story.
(Disney Enterprises, Inc.)

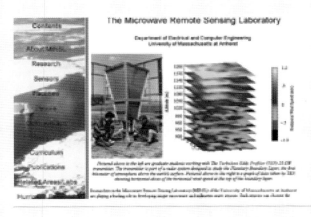

Plate 3.
A sample image from the computer-based game Rogue Spear:Urban Operations. *(Courtesy of Red Storm Entertainment)*

Plate 4.
Browsing on the Web. *(Courtesy of The Microwave Remote Sensing Laboratory, University of Massachusetts)*

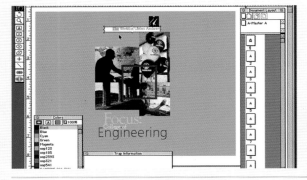

Plate 5.
An image from a page layout program.
(*Courtesy of Thomas F. Sweeney, Jr.*)

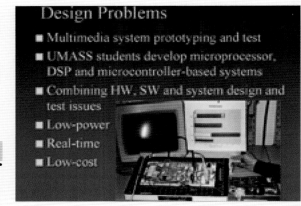

Plate 6.
An example slide for a presentation.
(*Courtesy of Wayne Burleson*)

Plate 7.
An image created with a paint system.
(*Courtesy of Ofer Alon www.pixologic.com*)

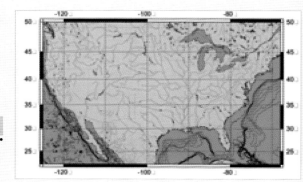

Plate 8.
Producing a complex map. (*Courtesy of Paul Wessel and Walter H. F. Smith*)

Plate 9.
Mixing graphics and images.

Plate 10.
Simulated view out of a cockpit window.
(Courtesy of Evans & Sutherland, Inc.)

Plate 11.
Interacting with a Virtual World.
(Courtesy of ActiveWorld.com, Inc.)

a.

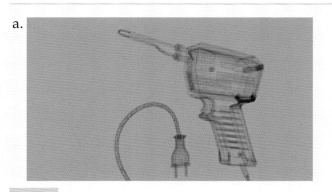

b.

Plate 12.
Designing mechanical structures. *(Courtesy of Renzo and Adriano Del Fabbro)*

Plate 13.
Designing a house. *(Courtesy of Renzo and Adriano Del Fabbro)*

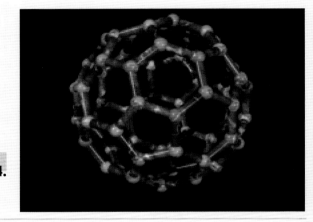

Plate 14.
A simulation of a Fullerine molecule. *(Courtesy of Sascha Rogmann www.rogmann.com)*

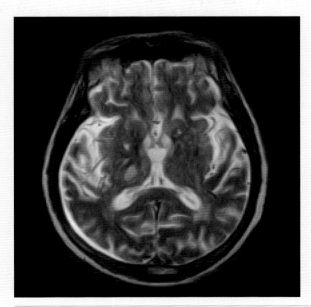

Plate 15.
Image of brain formed using an MRI scan. *(Courtesy of the Computer Vision Laboratory, Computer Science Department, University of Massachusetts, and the Departments of Neurology and Radiology, Baystate Medical Center, Springfield, Massachusetts)*

Keyboard All workstations are equipped with a keyboard, which sends strings of characters to the application upon request. Hence, a keyboard is usually used to obtain a `string` input primitive. Some keyboards have cursor keys or function keys, which are often used to produce `choice` input primitives.

Buttons Sometimes a separate bank of buttons is installed on a workstation. The user presses one of the buttons to perform a `choice` input function.

Mouse The **mouse** is perhaps the most familiar input device of all, because it is easy and comfortable to operate. As the user slides the mouse over the desktop, the mouse sends information about the changes in its position to the workstation. Software within the workstation keeps track of the mouse's position and moves a **graphics cursor**—a small dot or cross—on the screen accordingly. The mouse is most often used to perform a `locate` or a `pick` function. Usually, there are some buttons on the mouse that the user can press to trigger the desired action.

Tablet Like a mouse, a **tablet** is used to generate `locate` or `pick` input primitives. As shown in Figure 1.45, the tablet provides an area on which the user can slide a stylus. The tip of the stylus contains a microswitch. By pressing down on the stylus, the user can trigger the logical function that is desired.

FIGURE 1.45 A graphics tablet.

The tablet is particularly handy for digitizing drawings: The user can tape a picture onto the surface of the tablet and then move the stylus over it, pressing down to send information about each new point that is selected to the workstation. A menu is sometimes printed on the tablet and the user *picks* an item by pressing down the stylus on the inside of one of the boxes associated with a particular item. Suitable software maps each such box into the desired function on the application that is running.

Joystick and Trackball

Figure 1.46 shows two similar input devices that control the position of a cursor on the display. The arcade-style **joystick** in part (a) has a lever that can be pivoted in any direction to indicate position. The **trackball** in part (b) has a large ball that can be rotated

FIGURE 1.46 Joystick and trackball.

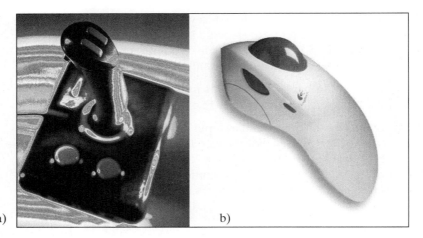

a)   b)

in any direction with the thumb to alter the position of the cursor. For each of these devices, internal circuitry converts physical motion into electrical signals, just as in the mouse. The devices are used primarily for `locator` and `valuator` functions.

Knobs Figure 1.47 shows a bank of knobs that the user can turn to "dial in" a value. Each knob performs a logical *valuator* function. Banks of knobs such as these are often part of a workstation that is used for the interactive design of three-dimensional objects. The user can rotate a displayed object in three dimensions by adjusting the position of three separate knobs. Also, two knobs can be used to control the *x* and *y* positions of a cursor on a display, so that, together, the knobs can perform the *locator, stroke*, and *pick* functions.

FIGURE 1.47 A bank of knobs. (Courtesy of Tektronix, Inc.)

Space Ball and Data Glove The space ball and the data glove pictured in Figure 1.48 are relatively new input devices. Both are designed to give a user explicit control over several variables at once, by performing hand and finger motions. Sensors inside each device pick up subtle hand motions and translate them into *valuator* values that get passed back to the application. These devices are particularly suited to situations in which the hand movements themselves make sense in the context of the program (such as when the user is controlling a virtual robot hand) and the effects of such motions are simulated on the screen for the user to observe.

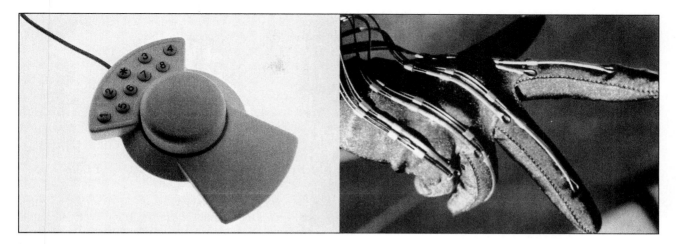

Digitizing Three-dimensional Objects and Capturing Motion

Figure 1.49 shows a device that can measure the locations of points in space, allowing three-dimensional shapes to be captured. As the laser beam scans the solid object in an x, y raster pattern, information on distance is stored. Figure 1.50 shows a similar device that can track the position of several points on a moving body, allowing, for example, the detailed motions of a dancer to be captured.

FIGURE 1.48 The space ball (Courtesy of Logicad 3D, a Logitech Company) and data glove (Courtesy of NASA Headquarters).

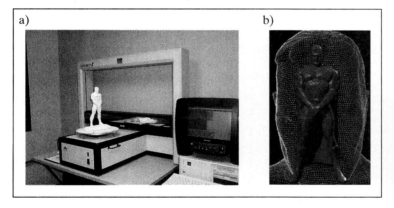
a)   b)

FIGURE 1.49 Digitizing a three-dimensional shape (Courtesy of Digiboties, Inc.)

FIGURE 1.50 Capturing a dancer's motion (Courtesy of Motion Analysis, Inc.).

Other devices have been used in the past, such as the light pen, thumbwheel, paddle, etc. (Complete descriptions of these devices can be found in books such as [Foley93] and [Rogers98].)

1.6 SUMMARY

In this chapter, we introduced the field of computer graphics and discussed the variety of places computer graphics is used today in the creation of pictures. We described many kinds of drawing devices, the most widely used of which are the raster video display and the laser printer. We also defined the major **output primitives**—polylines, text, filled regions, and raster images—and described the attributes that are normally associated with each. Because of its importance both as a vehicle for pictures and as a mechanism within display devices, the raster image was emphasized. The key property of a raster image is that it consists of a collection of numbers, and each number can take on only a fixed set of values, making the image discrete in two spatial dimensions, as well as in the color–brightness dimension. Of equal importance is the natural association of pixel values with memory locations in a computer, which we shall exploit many times throughout this text.

We described various kinds of graphical input devices used for interactive computer graphics and discussed the **input primitives** that they normally produce.

1.7 FURTHER READING

A number of books provide a good introduction to the field of computer graphics. Hearn and Baker [Hearn94] give a leisurely and interesting overview of the field with lots of examples. Foley and Van Dam [Foley93] and David Rogers[Rogers98] give additional technical details on the many kinds of graphics input and output devices. An excellent series of five books known as "Graphics Gems" [Gems], first published in 1990, brought together many new ideas from graphics researchers and practitioners around the world.

There are also a number of journals and magazines that give good insight into new techniques in computer graphics. The most accessible is the Institute of Electrical and Electronic Engineers' (IEEE's) *Computer Graphics and Applications*, which often features survey articles on new areas in graphics. The classic repositories of new results in graphics are the annual Proceedings of SIGGRAPH [SIGGRAPH], and the Association for Computing Machinery's [ACM's] Transactions on Graphics [TOGS]. Another, more recent, arrival is the *Journal of Graphics Tools* [jgt].

2

Getting Started: Drawing Figures

Machines exist; let us then exploit them to create beauty, a modern beauty, while we are about it. For we live in the twentieth century.

Aldous Huxley

Goals of the Chapter

▲ To get started writing programs that produce pictures.

▲ To learn the basic ingredients found in every OpenGL program.

▲ To develop some elementary graphics tools for drawing lines, polylines, and polygons.

▲ To develop tools that allow the user to control a program with the mouse and keyboard.

PREVIEW

Section 2.1 discusses the basics of writing a program that makes simple drawings. The importance of device-independent programming is discussed, and the characteristics of windows-based and event-driven programs are described. Section 2.2 introduces the use of OpenGL as the device-independent application programmer interface (API) that is emphasized throughout the book and shows how to draw various graphics primitives. Sample drawings, such as a picture of the Big Dipper, a drawing of the Sierpinski gasket, and a plot of a mathematical function illustrate the use of OpenGL. Section 2.3 discusses how to make pictures based on polylines and polygons, and begins the building of a personal library of graphics utilities. Section 2.4 describes interactive graphics programming, whereby the user can indicate positions on the screen with the mouse or press keys on the keyboard to control the action of a program. The chapter ends with a number of case studies that embellish ideas discussed earlier and that delve deeper into the main ideas of the chapter.

2.1 GETTING STARTED MAKING PICTURES

Like many disciplines, computer graphics is mastered most quickly by doing it: by writing and testing programs that produce a variety of pictures. It is best to start with simple tasks. Once these are mastered, you can try variations, see what happens, and move towards drawing more complex scenes.

To get started, you need an environment that lets you write and execute programs. With respect to graphics, this environment must also include both hardware to display pictures (usually a CRT display, which we shall call the "screen") and a library of software tools that your programs can use to perform the actual drawing of graphics primitives.

Every graphics program begins with some initializations that establish the desired display mode and set up a coordinate system for specifying points, lines, etc. Figure 2.1 shows some of the variations one might encounter. In part (a), the entire screen is used for drawing: The display is initialized by switching it into "graphics mode," and the coordinate system is established as shown. Coordinates x and y are measured in pixels, with x increasing to the right and y increasing downward.

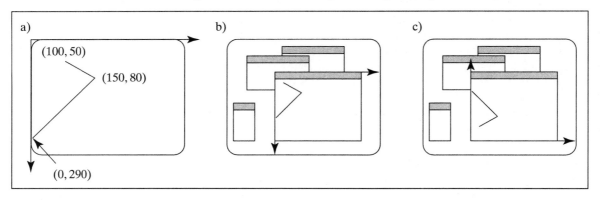

FIGURE 2.1 Some common varieties of display layouts.

In part (b), a more modern, "window-based," system is shown. This system can support a number of different rectangular *windows* on the display screen at one time. Initialization involves creating and "opening" a new window (which we shall call the **screen window**)[1] for graphics. Graphics commands use a coordinate system that is attached to the window: Usually, x increases to the right and y increases downward.[2] Part (c) shows a variation in which the initial coordinate system is "right side up," with y increasing upward.[3]

Normally, each system has some elementary drawing tools that help the user to get started. The most basic tool has a name like `setPixel(x, y, color)`, which sets the individual pixel at location (x, y) to the color specified by `color`. Sometimes this tool goes by a different name, such as `putPixel()`, `SetPixel()`, or `drawPoint()`. Along with `setPixel()`, there is almost always a tool for drawing a straight line— for example, `line(x1, y1, x2, y2)`, which draws a line between $(x1, y1)$ and $(x2, y2)$. In other systems, this tool might be called `drawLine()` or `Line()`. The commands

```
line(100, 50, 150, 80);
line(150, 80, 0, 290);
```

would draw the pictures shown in each system in Figure 2.1. Other systems have no `line()` command, but rather, use `moveto(x, y)` and `lineto(x, y)`. These instructions stem from the analogy to a pen plotter, wherein the pen has some **current position.** The notion is that `moveto(x, y)` moves the pen invisibly to location (x, y), thereby setting the current position to (x, y); `lineto(x, y)` draws a line from the current position to (x, y) and then updates the current position to this

---

[1]   The word "window" is overused in graphics; we shall take care to distinguish the various usages of the term.

[2]   Some sample systems are Unix workstations using X Windows, an IBM PC running Windows 95 under the Windows Application Programming Interface, and an Apple Macintosh using the built-in QuickDraw library.

[3]   An example is any window-based system using OpenGL.

particular (x, y). Each command moves the pen from its current position to a new position. The new position then becomes the current position. The pictures in Figure 2.1 would be drawn using the commands

```
moveto(100, 50);
lineto(150, 80);
lineto(0, 290);
```

With a given system, the energetic programmer can develop a whole tool kit of sophisticated functions that utilize these elementary tools, thereby building up a powerful library of graphics routines. The final graphics applications are then written by making use of this personal library.

An obvious problem is that each graphics display uses different basic commands to drive it, and every environment has a different collection of tools for producing the graphics primitives. This variation makes it difficult to *port* a program from one environment to another (and sooner or later, everyone is faced with reconstructing a program in a new environment), so the programmer must build the necessary tools on top of the new environment's library. This reconstruction task may require major alterations in the overall structure of a library or application, as well as a significant effort on the part of the programmer.

2.1.1 Device-independent Programming and OpenGL

It is a boon when a uniform approach to writing graphics applications is made available, such that the *same* program can be compiled and run on a variety of graphics environments, with the guarantee that it will produce nearly identical graphical output on each display. This is known as **device-independent** graphics programming. OpenGL offers such a tool: Porting a graphics program requires only that you install the appropriate OpenGL libraries on the new machine; the application itself requires no change, calling the same functions in this library with the same parameters. In the end, the same graphical results are produced. The OpenGL way of creating graphics has been adopted by a large number of companies, and OpenGL libraries exist for all of the important graphics environments.[4]

OpenGL is often called an "application programming interface" (API): a collection of routines that the programmer can call, along with a model of how the routines work together to produce graphics. The programmer "sees" only the interface and is therefore shielded from having to cope with the specific hardware or software idiosyncrasies on the resident graphics system.

OpenGL is at its most powerful when drawing images of complex three-dimensional (3D) scenes. It might be viewed as overkill for simple drawings of two-dimensional (2D) objects. But it works well for 2D drawing, too, and affords a *unified* approach to producing pictures. We start by using the simpler constructs in OpenGL, capitalizing for simplicity on the many default states it provides. Later, when we write programs to produce elaborate 3D graphics, we tap into OpenGL's more powerful features.

Although we will develop most of our graphics tools using the power of OpenGL, we will also "look under the hood" and examine how the classical graphics algorithms work. It is important to see how such tools might be implemented, even if you use the ready-made OpenGL versions for most applications. In special circumstances, you may wish to use an alternative algorithm for some task, or you may encounter a new problem that OpenGL does not solve. You also may need to develop a graphics application that does not use OpenGL at all.

---

[4] Appendix 1 discusses how to obtain and get started with OpenGL in different environments.

2.1.2 Windows-based Programming

As mentioned earlier, many modern graphics systems are *windows based* and manage the display of multiple overlapping *windows*. The user can move windows around the screen by means of the mouse and can resize the windows. Using OpenGL, we will do our drawing in one of these windows, as we saw in Figure 2.1(c).

Event-driven Programming

Another property of most windows-based programs is that they are *event driven*. This means that the program responds to various events, such as the click of a mouse, the press of a key on a keyboard, or the resizing of a window on a screen. The system automatically manages an *event queue*, which receives messages stating that certain events have occurred and deals with them on a first-come, first-served, basis. The programmer organizes a program as a collection of *callback functions* that are executed when events occur. A callback function is created for each type of event that might take place. When the system removes an event from the queue, it simply executes the callback function associated with the type of that event. For programmers used to building programs with a "do this, then do this ..." structure, some rethinking is required. The new structure is more like "do nothing until an event occurs, and then do the specified thing."

The method of associating a callback function with a particular type of event is often quite system dependent. But OpenGL comes with a *Utility Toolkit* (see Appendix 1), which provides tools to assist with event management. For instance,

```
glutMouseFunc(myMouse);      // register the mouse action function
```

registers the function `myMouse()` as the function to be executed when a mouse event occurs. The prefix "glut" indicates that this function is part of the Open*GL* *U*tility *T*oolkit. The programmer puts code in `myMouse()` to handle all of the possible mouse actions that are of interest.

Figure 2.2 shows a skeleton of an example `main()` function for an event-driven program. We will base most of our programs in this book on this skeleton. There are four principal types of events we will work with, and a "glut" function is available for each:

- `glutDisplayFunc(myDisplay);` Whenever the system determines that a window should be redrawn on the screen, it issues a "redraw" event. This happens when the window is first opened and when the window is exposed by moving another window off of it. Here, the function `myDisplay()` is registered as the callback function for a redraw event.
- `glutReshapeFunc(myReshape);` Screen windows can be reshaped by the user, usually by dragging a corner of the window to a new position with the mouse.

FIGURE 2.2 A skeleton of an event-driven program using OpenGL.

```
void main()
{
        initialize things⁵
        create a screen window
        glutDisplayFunc(myDisplay);    // register the redraw function
        glutReshapeFunc(myReshape);    // register the reshape function
        glutMouseFunc(myMouse);        // register the mouse action function
        glutKeyboardFunc(myKeyboard);  // register the keyboard action function
        perhaps initialize other things
        glutMainLoop();                // enter the unending main loop
}
        all of the callback functions are defined here
```

---

⁵ Notes shown in italics in fragments of code are pseudocode rather than actual program code. They suggest the actions that real code substituted there should accomplish.

(Simply moving the window does not produce a reshape event.) Here, the function myReshape() is registered with the reshape event. As we shall see, myReshape() is automatically passed arguments that report the new width and height of the reshaped window.

- glutMouseFunc(myMouse); When one of the mouse buttons is pressed or released, a mouse event is issued. Here, myMouse() is registered as the function to be called when a mouse event occurs. The function myMouse() is automatically passed arguments that describe the location of the mouse and the nature of the action initiated by pressing the button.

- glutKeyboardFunc(myKeyboard); This command registers the function myKeyboard() with the event of pressing or releasing some key on the keyboard. The function myKeyboard() is automatically passed arguments that tell which key was pressed. Conveniently, it is also passed data indicating the location of the mouse at the time the key was pressed.

If a particular program does not make use of a mouse, the corresponding callback function need not be registered or written. Then mouse clicks have no effect in the program. The same is true for programs that do not use a keyboard.

The final function shown in Figure 2.2 is glutMainLoop(). When this instruction is executed, the program draws the initial picture and enters an unending loop, in which it simply waits for events to occur. (A program is normally terminated by clicking in the "go away" box that is attached to each window.)

2.1.3 Opening a Window for Drawing

The first task in making pictures is to open a screen window for drawing. This effort can be quite involved and is system dependent. Because OpenGL functions are device independent, they provide no support for controlling windows on specific systems. But the OpenGL Utility Toolkit *does* include functions to open a window on whatever system you are using.

Figure 2.3 fleshes out the skeleton of Figure 2.2 above to show the entire main() function for a program that will draw graphics in a screen window. The first five function calls use the OpenGL Utility Toolkit to open a window for drawing. In your first graphics programs, you can just copy these functions as is; later, we will see what the various arguments mean and how to substitute others for them to achieve certain

FIGURE 2.3 Code using the OpenGL Utility Toolkit to open the initial window for drawing.

```
// appropriate #includes go here - see Appendix 1

void main(int argc, char** argv)
{
        glutInit(&argc, argv); // initialize the toolkit
        glutInitDisplayMode(GLUT_SINGLE | GLUT_RGB); // set the display mode
        glutInitWindowSize(640,480); // set window size
        glutInitWindowPosition(100, 150); // set the window position on screen
        glutCreateWindow("my first attempt"); // open the screen window

        // register the callback functions
        glutDisplayFunc(myDisplay);
        glutReshapeFunc(myReshape);
        glutMouseFunc(myMouse);
        glutKeyboardFunc(myKeyboard);

        myInit();               // additional initializations as necessary
        glutMainLoop();         // go into a perpetual loop

}
```

effects. The first five functions initialize and display the screen window in which our program will produce graphics. We give a brief description of what each one does:

- `glutInit(&argc, argv);` This function initializes the OpenGL Utility Toolkit. Its arguments are the standard ones for passing information about the command line; we will make no use of them here.
- `glutInitDisplayMode(GLUT_SINGLE | GLUT_RGB);` This function specifies how the display should be initialized. The built-in constants `GLUT_SINGLE` and `GLUT_RGB`, which are ORed together, indicate that a single display buffer should be allocated and that colors are specified using desired amounts of red, green, and blue. (Later we will alter these arguments: For example, we will use double buffering for smooth animation.)
- `glutInitWindowSize(640,480);` This function specifies that the screen window should initially be 640 pixels wide by 480 pixels high. When the program is running, the user can resize the window as desired.
- `glutInitWindowPosition(100, 150);` This function specifies that the window's upper left corner should be positioned on the screen 100 pixels over from the left edge and 150 pixels down from the top. When the program is running, the user can move this window wherever desired.
- `glutCreateWindow("my first attempt");` This function actually opens and displays the screen window, putting the title "my first attempt" in the title bar.

The remaining functions in `main()` register the callback functions as described earlier, perform any initializations specific to the program at hand, and start the main event loop processing. The programmer (you) must implement each of the callback functions as well as `myInit()`.

2.2 DRAWING BASIC GRAPHICS PRIMITIVES

We want to develop programming techniques for drawing a large number of geometric shapes that make up interesting pictures. The drawing commands will be placed in the callback function associated with a redraw event, such as the `myDisplay()` function.

We first must establish the coordinate system in which we will describe graphical objects and prescribe where they will appear in the screen window. Computer graphics programming, it seems, involves an ongoing struggle with defining and managing different coordinate systems. So we start simply and work up to more complex approaches.

We begin with an intuitive coordinate system that is tied directly to the coordinate system of the screen window [see Figure 2.1(c)], and that measures distances in pixels. Our first sample screen window, shown in Figure 2.4, is 640 pixels wide by 480

FIGURE 2.4 The initial coordinate system for drawing.

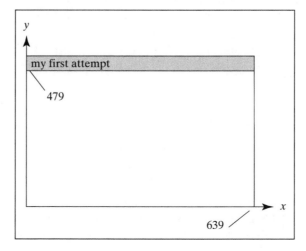

pixels high. The x-coordinate increases from 0 at the left edge to 639 at the right edge. The y-coordinate increases from 0 at the bottom edge to 479 at the top edge. We establish this coordinate system later, after examining some basic primitives.

OpenGL provides tools for drawing all of the output primitives described in Chapter 1. Most of them, such as points, lines, polylines, and polygons, are defined by one or more *vertices*. To draw such objects in OpenGL, you pass it a list of vertices. The list occurs between the two OpenGL function calls `glBegin()` and `glEnd()`. The argument of `glBegin()` determines which object is drawn. For instance, Figure 2.5 shows three points drawn in a window 640 pixels wide and 480 pixels high. These dots are drawn using the command sequence:

```
glBegin(GL_POINTS);
  glVertex2i(100, 50);
  glVertex2i(100, 130);
  glVertex2i(150, 130);
glEnd();
```

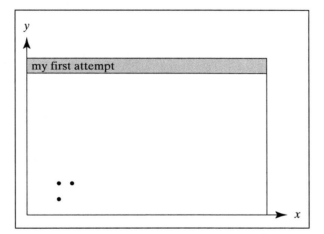

FIGURE 2.5 Drawing three dots.

The constant `GL_POINTS` is built-into OpenGL. To draw other primitives, you replace `GL_POINTS` with `GL_LINES`, `GL_POLYGON`, etc. Each of these will be introduced in turn.

As we shall see later, these commands send the information about a vertex down a "graphics pipeline," in which it goes through several processing steps. For present purposes, just think of the information as being sent more or less directly to the coordinate system in the screen window.

Many functions in OpenGL, such as `glVertex2i()`, have several variations, that distinguish the number and type of arguments passed to the function. Figure 2.6 shows how such function calls are formatted.

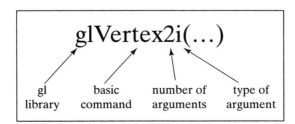

FIGURE 2.6 Format of OpenGL commands.

The prefix "gl" indicates a function from the OpenGL library (as opposed to "glut" for the GL Utility Toolkit). Then comes the basic command root, followed by the number of arguments being sent to the function (often, 3 and 4), and, finally, the type of argument (i for an integer, f or d for a floating-point value, etc., as we describe shortly). When we wish to refer to the basic command without regard to the specifics of its arguments, we will use an asterisk, as in glVertex*().

To generate the same three-dot picture as in Figure 2.5, you could, for example, pass the function floating-point values instead of integers, using the following commands:

```
glBegin(GL_POINTS);
  glVertex2d(100.0, 50.0);
  glVertex2d(100.0, 130.0);
  glVertex2d(150.0, 130.0);
glEnd();
```

OpenGL Data Types

OpenGL works internally with specific data types. For instance, functions such as glVertex2i() expect integers of a certain size (32 bits). It is well known that some systems treat the C or C++ data type int as a 16-bit quantity, whereas others treat it as a 32-bit quantity. There is no standard size for float or double either. To ensure that OpenGL functions receive the proper data types, it is wise to use the built-in names, such as GLint or GLfloat, for OpenGL types. The OpenGL types are listed in Figure 2.7. Some of these types will not be encountered until later in the book.

FIGURE 2.7 Command suffixes and argument data types.

Suffix	Data type	Typical C or C++ type	OpenGL type name
b	8-bit integer	signed char	GLbyte
s	16-bit integer	short	GLshort
i	32-bit integer	int or long	GLint, GLsizei
f	32-bit floating point	float	GLfloat, GLclampf
d	64-bit floating point	double	GLdouble, GLclampd
ub	8-bit unsigned number	unsigned char	GLubyte, GLboolean
us	16-bit unsigned number	unsigned short	GLushort
ui	32-bit unsigned number	unsigned int or unsigned long	GLuint, GLenum, GLbitfield

As an example, a function using the suffix i "expects" a 32-bit integer, but your system might translate int as a 16-bit integer. Therefore, if you wished to encapsulate the OpenGL commands for drawing a dot in a generic function such as drawDot(), you might be tempted to use the following code:

```
void drawDot(int x, int y)              ← danger: passes ints
{       // draw dot at integer point (x, y)
  glBegin(GL_POINTS);
    glVertex2i(x, y);
  glEnd();
}
```

This code passes `ints` to `glVertex2i()`. This will work on systems that use 32-bit `ints`, but might cause trouble on those that use 16-bit `ints`. It is safer to write `drawDot()` as in Figure 2.8 and to use `GLints` in your programs. When you recompile your programs on a new system, `GLint` `GLfloat`, etc. will be associated with the appropriate C++ types (in the OpenGL header `GL.h`; see Appendix 1) for that system, and these types will be used consistently throughout the program.

```
void drawDot(GLint x, GLint y)
{      // draw dot at integer point (x, y)
  glBegin(GL_POINTS);
    glVertex2i(x, y);
  glEnd();
}
```

FIGURE 2.8 Encapsulating OpenGL details in the generic function `drawDot()`.[6]

The OpenGL "State"

OpenGL keeps track of many *state variables*, such as the current size of a point, the current color of a drawing, the current background color, etc. The value of a state variable remains active until a new value is given. The size of a point can be set with `glPointSize()`, which takes one floating-point argument. If the argument is 3.0, the point is usually drawn as a square, three pixels on a side. (For additional details on this and other OpenGL functions, consult the appropriate OpenGL documentation, some of which is on-line; see Appendix 1.) The color of a drawing can be specified using

```
glColor3f(red, green, blue);
```

where the values of red, green, and blue vary between 0.0 and 1.0. For example, some of the colors listed in Figure 1.31 could be set using the following string of commands:

```
glColor3f(1.0, 0.0, 0.0);    // set drawing color to red
glColor3f(0.0, 0.0, 0.0);    // set drawing color to black
glColor3f(1.0, 1.0, 1.0);    // set drawing color to white
glColor3f(1.0, 1.0, 0.0);    // set drawing color to yellow
```

The background color is set with `glClearColor(red, green, blue, alpha)`, where `alpha` specifies a degree of transparency and is discussed later. (Use 0.0 for now.) To clear the entire window to the background color, use `glClear(GL_COLOR_BUFFER_BIT)`. The argument `GL_COLOR_BUFFER_BIT` is another constant built into OpenGL.

Establishing the Coordinate System

Our method for establishing an initial choice of coordinate system will seem obscure here, but will become clearer in the next chapter, when we discuss windows, viewports, and clipping. Here, we just take the few required commands on faith. The `myInit()` function in Figure 2.9 is a good place to set up the coordinate system. As we shall see later, OpenGL routinely performs a large number of transformations. It uses matrices to do this, and the commands in `myInit()` manipulate certain matrices to accomplish the desired goal. The `gluOrtho2D()` routine sets the transformation we need for a screen window that is 640 pixels wide by 480 pixels high.

---

[6] Using this function instead of the specific OpenGL commands makes a program more readable. It is not unusual to build up a personal collection of such utilities.

FIGURE 2.9 Establishing a simple coordinate system.

```
void myInit(void)
{
  glMatrixMode(GL_PROJECTION);
  glLoadIdentity();
  gluOrtho2D(0, 640.0, 0, 480.0);
}
```

Putting It All Together: A Complete OpenGL program

Figure 2.10 shows a complete program that draws the lowly three dots of Figure 2.5. It is easily extended to draw more interesting objects, as we shall see. The initialization in `myInit()` sets up the coordinate system, the point size, the background color, and the drawing color. The drawing is encapsulated in the callback function `myDisplay()`. Because this program is not interactive, no other callback functions are used. `glFlush()` is called after the dots are drawn, to ensure that all data are completely processed and sent to the display. This is important in some systems that

FIGURE 2.10 A complete OpenGL program to draw three dots.

```
#include<windows.h>    // use as needed for your system
#include<gl/Gl.h>
#include<gl/glut.h>
//<<<<<<<<<<<<<<<<<<<<<<<<< myInit >>>>>>>>>>>>>>>>>>>>
 void myInit(void)
 {
    glClearColor(1.0,1.0,1.0,0.0);        // set white background color
    glColor3f(0.0f, 0.0f, 0.0f);           // set the drawing color
    glPointSize(4.0);                    // a 'dot' is 4 by 4 pixels
    glMatrixMode(GL_PROJECTION);
    glLoadIdentity();
    gluOrtho2D(0.0, 640.0, 0.0, 480.0);
}
//<<<<<<<<<<<<<<<<<<<<<<<<< myDisplay >>>>>>>>>>>>>>>>>>
void myDisplay(void)
{
    glClear(GL_COLOR_BUFFER_BIT);        // clear the screen
    glBegin(GL_POINTS);
        glVertex2i(100, 50);             // draw three points
        glVertex2i(100, 130);
        glVertex2i(150, 130);
    glEnd();
    glFlush();                           // send all output to display
}
//<<<<<<<<<<<<<<<<<<<<<<<<< main >>>>>>>>>>>>>>>>>>>>>>>
void main(int argc, char** argv)
{
    glutInit(&argc, argv);               // initialize the toolkit
    glutInitDisplayMode(GLUT_SINGLE | GLUT_RGB); // set display mode
    glutInitWindowSize(640,480);         // set window size
    glutInitWindowPosition(100, 150);    // set window position on screen
    glutCreateWindow("my first attempt"); // open the screen window
    glutDisplayFunc(myDisplay);          // register redraw function
    myInit();
    glutMainLoop();                      // go into a perpetual loop
}
```

operate over a network: Data are buffered on the host machine and sent to the remote display only when the buffer becomes full or a `glFlush()` is executed.

2.2.1 Drawing Dot Constellations

A dot constellation is some pattern of dots or points. We describe several examples of interesting dot constellations that are easily produced using the basic program in Figure 2.10. In each case, the appropriate function is named in `glutDisplayFunc()` as the callback function for the redraw event. You are strongly encouraged to implement and test each example, in order to build up your experience with graphics.

■ **EXAMPLE 2.2.1 The Big Dipper**

Figure 2.11 shows a pattern of eight dots representing the Big Dipper, a familiar sight in the night sky.

The names and positions of the eight stars in the Big Dipper (in one particular view of the night sky), are given by the following ordered triplets: {Dubhe, 289, 190}, {Merak, 320, 128}, {Phecda, 239, 67}, {Megrez, 194, 101}, {Alioth, 129, 83}, {Mizar, 75, 73}, {Alcor, 74, 74}, {Alkaid, 20, 10}. Since so few data points are involved, it is easy to list them explicitly, or "**hardwire**" them into the code. (When many dots are to be drawn, it is more convenient to store them in a file and then have the program read them from the file and draw them. We do this in a later chapter.) These points can replace the three points specified in Figure 2.10. It is useful to experiment with this constellation, trying different point sizes, as well as different background and drawing colors.

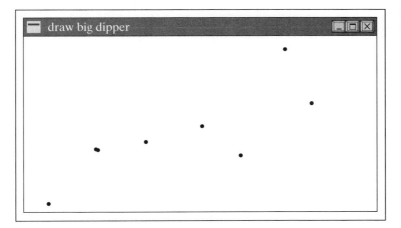

FIGURE 2.11 Two simple dot constellations.

■ **EXAMPLE 2.2.2 Drawing the Sierpinski gasket**

Figure 2.12 shows the Sierpinski gasket. Its dot constellation is generated *procedurally*, which means that each successive dot is determined by a procedural rule. Although the rule here is very simple, the final pattern is a fractal (See Chapter 9.) We first approach the rule for generating the Sierpinski gasket in an intuitive fashion. In Case Study 2.2, we see that it is one example of an *iterated function system*.

The Sierpinski gasket is produced by calling `drawDot()` many times with dot positions $(x_0, y_0), (x_1, y_1), (x_2, y_2),\ldots$, determined by a simple algorithm. Denote the kth point $p_k = (x_k, y_k)$. Each point is based on the previous point p_{k-1}. The procedure is as follows:

FIGURE 2.12 The Sierpinski Gasket.

1. Choose three fixed points T_0, T_1, and T_2 to form some triangle, as shown in Figure 2.13(a).

FIGURE 2.13 Building the Sierpinski gasket.

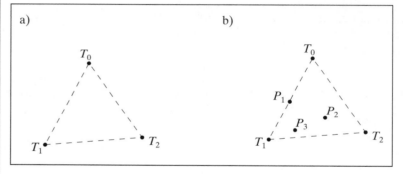

2. Choose the initial point p_0 to be drawn by selecting one of the points T_0, T_1, and T_2 at random.

Now iterate the following steps until the pattern is satisfyingly filled in:

3. Choose one of the three points T_0, T_1, and T_2 at random; call it T.
4. Construct the next point p_k as the **midpoint**[7] between T and the previously found point p_{k-1}. That is,

   $$p_k = \text{midpoint of } p_{k-1} \text{ and } T.$$

5. Draw p_k using `drawDot()`.

Figure 2.13(b) shows a few iterations of the foregoing procedure. Suppose the initial point p_0 happens to be T_0, and let T_1 be chosen next. Then p_1 is formed so that it lies halfway between T_0 and T_1. Suppose T_2 is chosen next, so that p_2 lies halfway between p_1 and T_2. Next, suppose T_1 is chosen again, so that p_3 is formed as shown, etc. This process goes on generating and drawing points (conceptually, forever), and the pattern of the Sierpinski gasket quickly emerges.

---

[7] To find the midpoint between two points, say, (3, 12) and (5, 37), simply *average* their x and y components individually by adding them and dividing by two. So the midpoint of (3, 12) and (5, 37) is $\big((3 + 5)/2,$ $(12 + 37)/2\big) = (4, 24)$.

It is convenient to define a simple class, GLintPoint, that describes a point whose coordinates are integers:[8]

```
class GLintPoint{
public:
    GLint x, y;
};
```

We then build and initialize an array of three such points, T[0], T[1], and T[2], to hold the three corners of the triangle using GLintPoint T[3]= {{10,10},{300,30},{200, 300}}. There is no need to store each point p_k in the sequence as it is generated, since we simply want to draw it and then move on. So we set up a variable point to hold this changing point. At each iteration, point is updated to hold the new value.

We use i=random(3) to choose one of the points T[i] at random. random(3) returns one of the values 0, 1, and 2 with equal likelihood. It is defined as[9]

```
int random(int m)
{
    return rand()%m;
}
```

Figure 2.14 shows the remaining details of the algorithm, which generates 1,000 points of the Sierpinski gasket.

```
void Sierpinski(void)
{
  GLintPoint T[3]= {{10,10},{300,30},{200, 300}};

  int index = random(3);        // 0, 1, or 2 equally likely
  GLintPoint point = T[index];  // initial point
  drawDot(point.x, point.y);    // draw initial point
  for(int i = 0; i < 1000; i++) // draw 1000 dots
  {
    index = random(3);
    point.x = (point.x + T[index].x) / 2;
    point.y = (point.y + T[index].y) / 2;
    drawDot(point.x,point.y);
  }
  glFlush();
}
```

FIGURE 2.14 Generating the Sierpinski gasket.

■ EXAMPLE 2.2.3 Simple "Dot Plots"

Suppose you wish to learn the behavior of some mathematical function $f(x)$ as x varies. For example, how does

$$f(x) = e^{-x} \cos(2\pi x)$$

vary for values of x between 0 and 4? A quick plot of $f(x)$ versus x, such as that shown in Figure 2.15, can reveal a lot.

---

[8] If C rather than C++ is being used, a simple `typedef struct{GLint x, y;}GLintPoint;` is useful here.

[9] Recall that the standard function rand() returns a pseudorandom value in the range 0 to 32767. The modulo function reduces it to a value in the range 0 to 2.

FIGURE 2.15 A "dot plot" of $e^{-x}\cos(2\pi x)$ versus x.

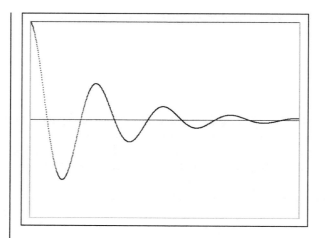

To plot this function, simply "sample" it at a collection of equispaced x-values, and plot a dot at each coordinate pair $(x_i, f(x_i))$. Choosing some suitable increment, say, 0.005, between consecutive x-values, we see that the process runs basically as follows:

```
glBegin(GL_POINTS);
   for(GLdouble x = 0; x < 4.0 ; x += 0.005)
        glVertex2d(x, f(x));
glEnd();
glFlush();
```

But there is a problem here: The picture that it produced will be impossibly tiny because values of x between 0 and 4 map to the first four pixels at the bottom left of the screen window. Further, the negative values of $f(.)$ will lie below the window and will not be seen at all. We therefore need to scale and position the values to be plotted so that they cover the screen window area appropriately. Here we do it by brute force, in essence picking some values to make the picture show up adequately on the screen. Later we develop a general procedure that copes with these adjustments, the so-called procedure of mapping from world coordinates to window coordinates.

Scaling x Suppose we want the range from 0 to 4 to be scaled so that it covers the entire width of the screen window, given in pixels by `screenWidth`. Then we need only scale all x-values by `screenWidth`/4, using

```
sx = x * screenWidth /4.0;
```

which yields 0 when x is 0 and `screenWidth` when x is 4.0, as desired.

Scaling and shifting y The values of $f(x)$ lie between −1.0 and 1.0, so we must scale and shift them as well. Suppose we set the screen window to have a height of `screen-Height` pixels. Then, to place the plot in the center of the window, we scale by `screenHeight`/2 and shift up by `screenHeight`/2:

```
sy = (y + 1.0) * screenHeight / 2.0;
```

As desired, this yields 0 when y is −1.0, and `screenHeight` when y is 1.0.

Note that the conversions from x to sx and from y to sy are of the form

$$sx = Ax + B$$

and

$$sy = Cy + D \tag{2.1}$$

for properly chosen values of the constants $A, B, C,$ and D. A and C perform scaling; B and D perform shifting. The operation of scaling and shifting is basically a form of "affine transformation." We study affine transformations in depth in Chapter 5; they provide a more consistent approach that maps any specified range in x and y to the screen window.

We need only set the values of $A, B, C,$ and D appropriately, and draw the dot plot using the following code:

```
GLdouble A, B, C, D, x;
A = screenWidth / 4.0;
B = 0.0;
C = screenHeight / 2.0;
D = C;
glBegin(GL_POINTS);
   for(x = 0; x < 4.0 ; x += 0.005)
      glVertex2d(A * x + B, C * f(x) + D);
glEnd();
glFlush();
```

Figure 2.16 shows the entire program for drawing the dot plot, to illustrate how the various ingredients fit together. The initializations are similar to those for the program that draws three dots in Figure 2.10. Notice that the width and height of the screen window are defined as constants and used where needed in the code.

PRACTICE EXERCISES

2.2.1 Dot plots for any function f( )

Consider drawing a dot plot of the function $f(.)$ like the one in Example 2.2.3, where it is known that as x varies from x_{low} to x_{high}, $f(x)$ takes on values between y_{low} and y_{high}. Find the appropriate scaling and translation factors of Equation 2.1 so that the dots will lie properly in a screen window with width W pixels and height H pixels. ■

2.3 MAKING LINE DRAWINGS

Hamlet: Do you see yonder cloud that's almost in shape of a camel? Polonius: By the mass, and 'tis like a camel, indeed. Hamlet: Methinks it is like a weasel. - William Shakespeare, Hamlet

As discussed in Chapter 1, line drawings are fundamental in computer graphics, and almost every graphics system comes with "driver" routines to draw straight lines. OpenGL makes it easy to draw a line: Use GL_LINES as the argument to glBegin(), and pass it the two endpoints as vertices. Thus, to draw a line between (40, 100) and (202, 96), use the following code:

```
glBegin(GL_LINES);       // use constant GL_LINES here
    glVertex2i(40, 100);
    glVertex2i(202, 96);
glEnd();
```

```
#include<windows.h> // use proper includes for your system
#include<math.h>
#include<gl/Gl.h>
#include<gl/glut.h>
const int screenWidth = 640;    // width of screen window in pixels
const int screenHeight = 480;   // height of screen window in pixels
GLdouble A, B, C, D;  // values used for scaling and shifting
//<<<<<<<<<<<<<<<<<<<<<<<<< myInit >>>>>>>>>>>>>>>>>>>>>
 void myInit(void)
 {
    glClearColor(1.0,1.0,1.0,0.0);      // background color is white
    glColor3f(0.0f, 0.0f, 0.0f);        // drawing color is black
    glPointSize(2.0);           // a 'dot' is 2 by 2 pixels
    glMatrixMode(GL_PROJECTION);    // set "camera shape"
    glLoadIdentity();
    gluOrtho2D(0.0, (GLdouble)screenWidth, 0.0, (GLdouble)screenHeight);
    A = screenWidth / 4.0; // set values used for scaling and shifting
    B = 0.0;
    C = D = screenHeight / 2.0;
}
//<<<<<<<<<<<<<<<<<<<<<<<<< myDisplay >>>>>>>>>>>>>>>>>>
void myDisplay(void)
{
  glClear(GL_COLOR_BUFFER_BIT);     // clear the screen
  glBegin(GL_POINTS);
  for(GLdouble x = 0; x < 4.0 ; x += 0.005)
  {
    Gldouble func = exp(-x) * cos(2 * 3.14159265 * x);
    glVertex2d(A * x + B, C * func + D);
   }
  glEnd();
  glFlush();      // send all output to display
}
//<<<<<<<<<<<<<<<<<<<<<<<<< main >>>>>>>>>>>>>>>>>>>>>>>>
void main(int argc, char** argv)
{
  glutInit(&argc, argv);            // initialize the toolkit
  glutInitDisplayMode(GLUT_SINGLE | GLUT_RGB); // set display mode
  glutInitWindowSize(screenWidth, screenHeight); // set window size
  glutInitWindowPosition(100, 150); // set window position on screen
  glutCreateWindow("Dot Plot of a Function"); // open the screen window
  glutDisplayFunc(myDisplay);       // register redraw function
  myInit();
  glutMainLoop();         // go into a perpetual loop
}
```

FIGURE 2.16 A complete program for drawing the "dot plot" of a function.

This code might be encapsulated for convenience in the routine `drawLineInt()`:

```
void drawLineInt(GLint x1, GLint y1, GLint x2, GLint y2)
  {
    glBegin(GL_LINES);
      glVertex2i(x1, y1);
      glVertex2i(x2, y2);
    glEnd();
  }
```

An alternative routine, `drawLineFloat()`, could be implemented similarly. (How?)

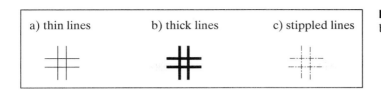

FIGURE 2.17 Simple picture
built from four lines.

If more than two vertices are specified between glBegin(GL_LINES) and glEnd(),
they are taken in pairs, and a separate line is drawn between each pair. The tic-tac-toe
board shown in Figure 2.17(a) would be drawn using the following commands:

```
glBegin(GL_LINES);
    glVertex2i(10, 20);  // first horizontal line
    glVertex2i(40, 20)
    glVertex2i(20, 10);  // first vertical line
    glVertex2i(20, 40);
    four more calls to glVertex2i() here for the other two lines
glEnd();
glFlush();
```

OpenGL provides tools for setting the attributes of lines. A line's color is set in the
same way as that for points, using glColor3f(). Figure 2.17(b) shows the use of
thicker lines, as set by glLineWidth(4.0). The default thickness is 1.0. Figure
2.17(c) shows stippled (dotted or dashed) lines. The details of stippling are addressed
in Case Study 2.5 at the end of the chapter.

2.3.1 Drawing Polylines and Polygons

Recall from Chapter 1 that a **polyline** is a collection of line segments joined end to
end. It is described by an ordered list of points, as in the equation

$$p_0 = (x_0, y_0), p_1 = (x_1, y_1), \ldots, p_n = (x_n, y_n). \tag{2.2}$$

In OpenGL, a polyline is called a "line strip" and is drawn by specifying the vertices,
in turn, between glBegin(GL_LINE_STRIP) and glEnd(). For example, the code

```
glBegin(GL_LINE_STRIP);  // draw an open polyline
    glVertex2i(20,10);
    glVertex2i(50,10);
    glVertex2i(20,80);
    glVertex2i(50,80);
glEnd();
glFlush();
```

produces the polyline shown in Figure 2.18(a). Attributes such as color, thickness,
and stippling may be applied to polylines in the same way they are applied to single
lines. If it is desired to connect the last point with the first point to make the polyline

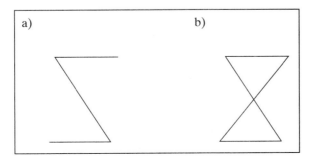

FIGURE 2.18 A polyline and a
polygon.

into a polygon, simply replace GL_LINE_STRIP with GL_LINE_LOOP. The resulting polygon is shown in Figure 2.18(b).

Polygons drawn using GL_LINE_LOOP cannot be filled with a color or pattern. To draw filled polygons, you must use glBegin(GL_POLYGON), as described later.

■ EXAMPLE 2.3.1 Drawing line graphs

In Example 2.2.3, we looked at plotting a function $f(x)$ versus x with a sequence of dots at positions $(x_i, f(x_i))$. A line graph is a straightforward extension of that concept: The dots are simply joined by line segments to form a polyline. Figure 2.19 shows an example, based on the function

FIGURE 2.19 A plot of a mathematical formula.

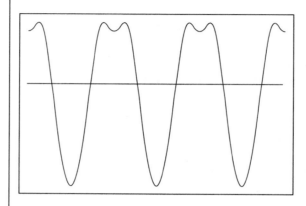

$$f(x) = 300 - 100 \cos(2\pi \ x/100) + 30 \cos(4\pi \ x/100) + 6 \cos(6\pi \ x/100)$$

as x varies in steps of 3 for 100 steps. A blowup of this figure would show a sequence of connected line segments; in a normal-sized picture, they blend together and appear as a smoothly varying curve.

The process of plotting a function with line segments is almost identical to that for producing a dot plot, so the program of Figure 2.16 can be used with only slight adjustments. We must scale and shift the lines being drawn here, to properly place them in the window. This requires the computation of the constants A, B, C, and D in the same manner as we did before. (See Equation 2.1.) Figure 2.20 shows the changes necessary for the inner drawing loop in the myDisplay() function.

FIGURE 2.20 Plotting a function using a line graph.

```
glBegin(GL_LINE_STRIP);
for(Gldouble x = 0; x < 4.0; x += 0.005)
{
    define func
    glVertex2d(A * x + B, C * func + D);
}
glEnd();
glFlush;
```

■ EXAMPLE 2.3.2 Drawing polylines stored in a file

Most interesting pictures made up of polylines contain a rather large number of line segments. It is convenient to store a description of the polylines in a file, so that the picture can be redrawn at will. (Several interesting examples may be found on the Internet; see the preface to the text.)

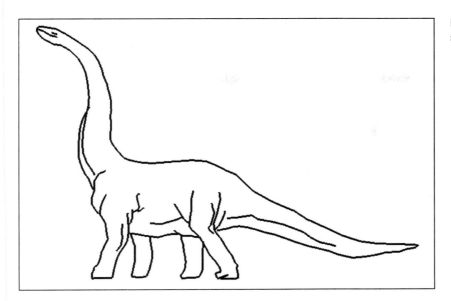

FIGURE 2.21 Drawing polylines stored in a file.

It is not hard to write a routine that draws the polylines stored in a file. Figure 2.21 shows an example of what might be drawn.

Suppose the file `dino.dat` contains a collection of polylines, in the following format (the comments are not part of the file):

```
21                      number of polylines in the file
4                       number of points in the first polyline
169  118                first point of first polyline
174  120                second point of first polyline
179  124
178  126
5                       number of points in the second polyline
298  86                 first point of second polyline
304  92
310  104
314  114
314  119
29
32  435
10  439
 . . .                  etc.
```

(The entire file is available on the web site for this book. See the preface.) Figure 2.22 shows a routine in C++ that will open such a file and then draw each of the polylines it contains. The file having the name contained in the string `fileName` is read and each polyline is drawn. The routine could be used in place of `myDisplay()` in Figure 2.16 as the callback function for the redraw event. The values of A, B, C, and D would have to be chosen judiciously to scale the polylines properly. We develop a general approach to do this in Chapter 3.

This version of `drawPolyLineFile()` in Figure 2.22 does very little error checking. If the file cannot be opened—perhaps because the wrong name is passed to the function—the routine simply returns control to the main program. If the file contains bad data, such as real values where integers are expected, the results are unpredictable. As presented, the routine should be considered only as a starting point for developing a more robust version.

```
#include <fstream.h>
void drawPolyLineFile(char * fileName)
{
    fstream inStream;
    inStream.open(fileName, ios ::in); // open the file
    if(inStream.fail())
        return;
    glClear(GL_COLOR_BUFFER_BIT);      // clear the screen
    GLint numpolys, numLines, x ,y;
    inStream >> numpolys;              // read the number of polylines
    for(int j = 0; j < numpolys; j++) // read each polyline
    {
        inStream >> numLines;
        glBegin(GL_LINE_STRIP);        // draw the next polyline
        for (int i = 0; i < numLines; i++)
        {
            inStream >> x >> y;        // read the next x, y pair
            glVertex2i(x, y);
        }
        glEnd();
    }
    glFlush();
    inStream.close();
}
```

FIGURE 2.22 Drawing polylines stored in a file.

■ **EXAMPLE 2.3.3 Parameterizing figures**

Figure 2.23 shows a simple house consisting of a few polylines. It can be drawn using code shown partially in Figure 2.24. (What code would be suitable for drawing the door and window?)

This is not a very flexible approach. The position of each endpoint is hardwired into the code, so hardwirededHouse() can draw only one house in one size and one location. More flexibility is achieved if we **parameterize** the figure and pass the parameter values to the routine. In that way, we can draw **families** of objects, distin-

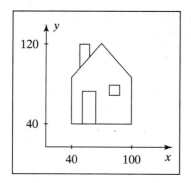

FIGURE 2.23 A House.

```
void hardwiredHouse(void)
{
    glBegin(GL_LINE_LOOP);
    glVertex2i(40, 40); // draw the shell of house
    glVertex2i(40, 90);
    glVertex2i(70, 120);
    glVertex2i(100, 90);
    glVertex2i(100, 40);
    glEnd();
    glBegin(GL_LINE_STRIP);
    glVertex2i(50, 100); // draw the chimney
    glVertex2i(50, 120);
    glVertex2i(60, 120);
    glVertex2i(60, 110);
    glEnd();
    . . . // draw the door
    . . . // draw the window
}
```

FIGURE 2.24 Drawing a house with "hardwired" dimensions.

```
void parameterizedHouse(GLintPoint peak, GLint width, GLint height)
  // the top of house is at the peak; the size of house is given
  //  by the height and width
{
  glBegin(GL_LINE_LOOP);
    glVertex2i(peak.x,                peak.y);  // draw shell of house
    glVertex2i(peak.x + width / 2, peak.y - 3 * height /8);
    glVertex2i(peak.x + width / 2  peak.y -      height);
    glVertex2i(peak.x - width / 2, peak.y -      height);
    glVertex2i(peak.x - width / 2, peak.y - 3 * height /8);
  glEnd();
  draw the chimney in the same fashion
  draw the door
  draw the window
}
```

FIGURE 2.25 Drawing a parameterized house.

guished by different parameter values. Figure 2.25 shows this approach. The parameters specify the location of the peak of the roof and the width and height of the house. The details of drawing the chimney, door, and window are left as an exercise.

This routine may be used to draw a "village," as shown in Figure 2.26, by making successive calls to parameterizedHouse() with different parameter values. (How is a house "flipped" upside down? Can *all* of the houses in the figure be drawn using the routine given?)

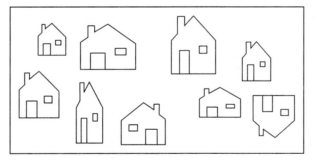

FIGURE 2.26 A "village" of houses drawn using parameterizedHouse().

■ EXAMPLE 2.3.4 Building a polyline drawer

As we shall see, some applications compute and store the vertices of a polyline in a list. It is natural, therefore, to add to our growing toolbox of routines a function that accepts the list as a parameter and draws the corresponding polyline. The list might be in the form of an array or a linked list. Here we use the array form and define the class to hold it in Figure 2.27.

```
class GLintPointArray{
    const int MAX_NUM = 100;
    public:
        int num;
        GLintPoint pt[MAX_NUM];
};
```

FIGURE 2.27 Data type for a linked list of vertices.

Figure 2.28 shows a possible implementation of the polyline-drawing routine. The routine also takes a parameter closed: If closed is nonzero, the last vertex in the polyline is connected to the first vertex. The value of closed sets the argument of glBegin(). The routine simply sends each vertex of the polyline to OpenGL.

FIGURE 2.28 A linked list data
type, and drawing a polyline or
polygon.

```
void drawPolyLine(GLintPointArray poly, int closed)
{
        glBegin(closed ? GL_LINE_LOOP : GL_LINE_STRIP);
          for(int i = 0; i < poly.num; i++)
          glVertex2i(poly.pt[i].x, poly.pt[i].y);
        glEnd();
        glFlush();
}
```

2.3.2 Line Drawing using `moveto()` and `lineto()`

As we have noted earlier, a number of graphics systems provide line-drawing tools
based on the functions `moveto()` and `lineto()`. These functions are so common
that it is important to be familiar with their use. We shall fashion our own `moveto()`
and `lineto()` functions that operate by calling OpenGL tools. In Chapter 3, we shall
also dive "under the hood" to see how you would build `moveto()` and `lineto()`
functions based on first principles if a powerful library like OpenGL were not available.

Recall that `moveto()` and `lineto()` manipulate a hypothetical pen whose position is called the **current position**, or CP. We can summarize the effects of the two
functions as follows:

    moveto(x, y):   set CP to (x, y)
    lineto(x, y):   draw a line from CP to (x, y), and then update CP to (x, y)

A line from (x_1, y_1) to (x_2, y_2) is therefore drawn using the two calls `moveto(x1,
y1)` and `lineto(x2, y2)`. A polyline based on the list of points $(x_0, y_0), (x_1, y_1), \ldots,$
(x_{n-1}, y_{n-1}) is easily drawn using the following code:

```
moveto(x[0], y[0]);
for(int i = 1; i < n; i++)
   lineto(x[i], y[i]);
```

It is straightforward to build `moveto()` and `lineto()` on top of OpenGL. To do this,
we must define and maintain our own CP. For the case of integer coordinates, the implementation shown in Figure 2.29 would do the trick.

FIGURE 2.29 Defining
`moveto()` and `lineto()` in
OpenGL.

```
GLintPoint CP;          // global current position

//<<<<<<<<<<<<< moveto >>>>>>>>>>>>>
void moveto(GLint x, GLint y)
{
   CP.x = x; CP.y = y; // update the CP
}
//<<<<<<<<<<<<< lineTo >>>>>>>>>>>>>>>>
void lineto(GLint x, GLint y)
{
   glBegin(GL_LINES);  // draw the line
      glVertex2i(CP.x, CP.y);
      glVertex2i(x, y);
   glEnd();
   glFlush();
   CP.x = x; CP.y = y; // update the CP
}
```

2.3.3 Drawing Aligned Rectangles

A special case of a polygon is the **aligned rectangle**, so called because its sides are aligned with the coordinate axes. We could create our own function to draw an aligned rectangle (how?), but OpenGL provides the ready-made function

```
glRecti(GLint x1, GLint  y1, GLint x2, GLint y2);
// draw a rectangle with opposite corners (x1, y1) and (x2, y2);
// fill the rectangle with the current color;
```

This command draws the aligned rectangle on the basis of two given points. In addition, the rectangle is filled with the current color. Figure 2.30 shows what is drawn by the following code:

```
glClearColor(1.0,1.0,1.0,0.0); // white background
glClear(GL_COLOR_BUFFER_BIT);  // clear the window
glColor3f(0.6,0.6,0.6);               // bright gray
glRecti(20,20,100,70);
glColor3f(0.2,0.2,0.2);               // dark gray
glRecti(70, 50, 150, 130);
glFlush();
```

Notice that the second rectangle is "painted over" the first one. We examine other "drawing modes" in Chapter 10.

Figure 2.31 shows two further examples. Part (a) is a "flurry" of randomly chosen aligned rectangles that might be generated by code such as the following[10]:

FIGURE 2.30 Two aligned rectangles filled with colors.

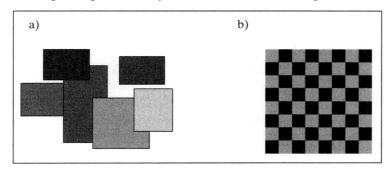

FIGURE 2.31 (a) Random flurry of rectangles. (b) A checkerboard.

```
void drawFlurry(int num, int numColors, int Width, int Height)
// draw num random rectangles in a Width by Height rectangle
{
  for (int i = 0; i < num; i++)
  {
    GLint x1 = random(Width);      // place corner randomly
    GLint y1 = random(Height);
    GLint x2 = random(Width);      // pick the size so it fits
    GLint y2 = random(Height);
    GLfloat lev = random(10)/10.0;// random value, in range 0 to 1
    glColor3f(lev,lev,lev);        // set the gray level
    glRecti(x1, y1, x2, y2);       // draw the rectangle
  }
  glFlush();
}
```

Part (b) is the familiar checkerboard, with alternating gray levels. Practice Exercise 2.3.1 asks you to generate this drawing.

---

[10] Recall from Example 2.2.2 random(N) returns a randomly chosen value between 0 and $N - 1$.

2.3.4 Aspect Ratio of an Aligned Rectangle

The principal properties of an aligned rectangle are its size, position, color, and shape. Its shape is embodied in its **aspect ratio**, and we shall be referring to the aspect ratios of rectangles throughout the book. The **aspect ratio** of a rectangle is simply the ratio of its width to its height:[11]

$$\text{aspect ratio} = \frac{\text{width}}{\text{height}}. \tag{2.3}$$

Rectangles with various aspect ratios are shown in Figure 2.32.

FIGURE 2.32 Examples of aspect ratios of aligned rectangles.

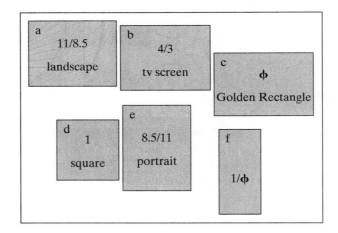

Rectangle *A* has the shape of a piece of 8.5-by-11-inch paper laid on its side in the so-called **landscape** orientation (i.e., with the rectangle's width larger than its height). The aspect ratio of Rectangle *A* is 1.294. Rectangle *B* has the aspect ratio of a television screen, 4/3, and *C* is the famous **golden rectangle** described in Case Study 2.3. Its aspect ratio is close to $\phi = 1.618034$. Rectangle *D* is a square with aspect ratio equal to 1, and *E* has the shape of a piece of standard paper in **portrait** orientation, with an aspect ratio of .7727. Finally, *F* is tall and skinny, with an aspect ratio of $1/\phi$.

PRACTICE EXERCISES

2.3.1 Drawing the checkerboard

(Try your hand at this exercise before looking at the answers.) Write the routine `checkerboard(int size)` that draws the checkerboard shown in Figure 2.31(b). Place the checkerboard with its lower left corner at $(0, 0)$. Each of the 64 squares has a length of `size` pixels. Choose two nice colors for the squares. **Solution:** The ijth square has lower left corner at (`i*size`, `j*size`) for $i = 0, \ldots, 7$ and $j = 0, \ldots, 7$. The color can be made to alternate between (r_1, g_1, b_1) and (r_2, g_2, b_2) by using the following code:

```
if((i + j)%2 ==0) // if i + j is even
   glColor3f( r1, g1, b1);
else

   glColor3f(r2, g2, b2);
```

---

[11] Be careful, however: Some authors define it as the ratio of height to width.

2.3.2 Alternative ways to specify a rectangle

An aligned rectangle can be described in other ways than by specifying two opposite corners. Two of these other possibilities are to specify

- its center point, height, and width; or
- its upper left corner, width, and aspect ratio.

Write functions `drawRectangleCenter()` and `drawRectangleCornerSize()` that pass these alternative parameters, and use glRecti() to draw the rectangle.

2.3.3 Different aspect ratios

Write a routine that draws a filled rectangle of aspect ratio R. Suppose the display has a drawing space of 400 by 400. Arrange the size of the rectangle so that it is as large as possible. That is, if $R > 1$, the rectangle spans across the drawing space, from left to right, and if $R < 1$, it spans from top to bottom.

2.3.4 Drawing the parametrized house

Fill in the details of `parametrizedHouse()` in Figure 2.25 so that the door, window, and chimney are drawn in their proper proportions for given values of `height` and `width`. Choose pleasing sizes and positions for various shapes.

2.3.5 Scaling and positioning a figure by using parameters

Write the function `void drawDiamond(GLintPoint center, int d)` that draws the simple diamond shown in Figure 2.33, centered at `center` and having size `d`. Use this function to draw a "flurry" of diamonds, as suggested in Figure 2.34. ■

2.3.5 Filling Polygons

So far we can draw unfilled polygons in OpenGL, as well as aligned rectangles filled with a single solid color. OpenGL also supports filling more general polygons with a pattern or color. The restriction is that the polygons must be *convex*.

> **DEFINITION: Convex polygon:** A polygon is convex if a line connecting any two points of the polygon lies entirely within it.

Several polygons are shown in Figure 2.35. Of these, only D, E, and F are convex. (Check to make sure that each of these polygons satisfies the definition of convexity.) D is certainly convex: All triangles are. A is not even simple (recall Chapter 1),

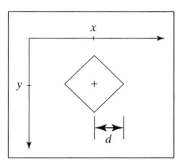

FIGURE 2.33 A simple diamond.

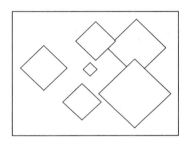

FIGURE 2.34 A "flurry" of diamonds.

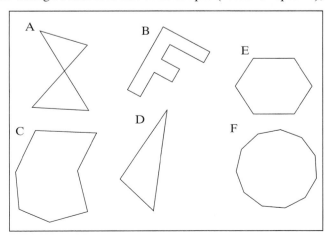

FIGURE 2.35 Convex and nonconvex polygons.

so it cannot be convex. Both B and C "bend inward" at some point. (Find two points on B such that the line joining them does not lie entirely inside B.)

To draw a convex polygon based on vertices $(x_0, y_0), (x_1, y_1), \ldots, (x_n, y_n)$ use the usual list of vertices, but place them between a `glBegin(GL_POLYGON)` and a `glEnd()`:

```
glBegin(GL_POLYGON);
    glVertex2f(x0, y0);

    glVertex2f(x1, y1);
    . . .
    glVertex2f(xn, yn);
glEnd();
```

The polygon will be filled in the current color. It can also be filled with a stipple pattern (see Case Study 2.5), and later we will paint images into polygons as part of applying a texture.

Figure 2.36 shows a number of filled convex polygons. In Chapter 10, we will examine an algorithm for filling any polygon, convex or not.

FIGURE 2.36 Several filled convex polygons.

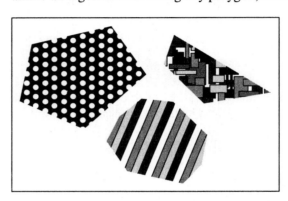

2.3.6 Other Graphics Primitives in OpenGL

OpenGL supports the drawing of five other objects as well. Figure 2.37 shows examples of each of them. To draw a particular one, the constant shown with it is used in `glBegin()`. The following list explains the function of each of the five constants:

FIGURE 2.37 Other geometric primitive types.

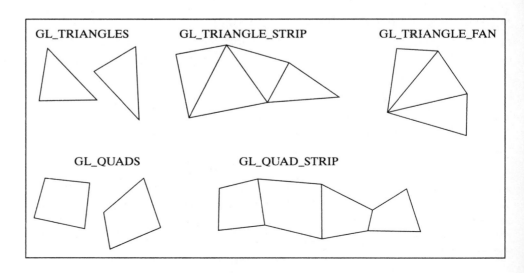

- GL_TRIANGLES: takes the listed vertices three at a time and draws a separate triangle for each.
- GL_QUADS: takes the vertices four at a time and draws a separate quadrilateral for each.
- GL_TRIANGLE_STRIP: draws a series of triangles based on triplets of vertices: v_0, v_1, v_2, then v_2, v_1, v_3, then v_2, v_3, v_4, etc. (in an order such that all triangles are "traversed" in the same way, e.g., counterclockwise).
- GL_TRIANGLE_FAN: draws a series of connected triangles based on triplets of vertices: v_0, v_1, v_2, then v_0, v_2, v_3, then v_0, v_3, v_4, etc.
- GL_QUAD_STRIP: draws a series of quadrilaterals based on foursomes of vertices: first v_0, v_1, v_3, v_2, then v_2, v_3, v_5, v_4, then v_4, v_5, v_7, v_6, etc. (in an order such that all quadrilaterals are "traversed" in the same way, e.g., counterclockwise).

2.4 SIMPLE INTERACTION WITH THE MOUSE AND KEYBOARD

Interactive graphics applications let the user control the flow of a program by natural human motions: pointing and clicking the mouse and pressing various keys on the keyboard. The position of the mouse at the time of the click or the identity of the key that is pressed is made available to the application program and is processed as appropriate.

Recall that when the user presses or releases a mouse button, moves the mouse, or presses a keyboard key, an event occurs. Using the OpenGL Utility Toolkit (GLUT) the programmer can register a callback function with each of these events by using the following commands:

- `glutMouseFunc(myMouse)`, which registers `myMouse()` with the event that occurs when the mouse button is pressed or released;
- `glutMotionFunc(myMovedMouse)`, which registers `myMovedMouse()` with the event that occurs when the mouse is moved while one of the buttons is pressed;
- `glutKeyboardFunc(myKeyboard)` which registers `myKeyBoard()` with the event that occurs when a keyboard key is pressed.

We next see how to use each of these functions.

2.4.1 Mouse Interaction

How are data pertaining to the mouse sent to the application? You must design the callback function `myMouse()` to take four parameters, so that it has the prototype

```
void myMouse(int button, int state, int x, int y);
```

Then, when a mouse event occurs, the system calls the registered function, supplying it with values for these parameters. The value of `button` will be one of

```
GLUT_LEFT_BUTTON, GLUT_MIDDLE_BUTTON, and GLUT_RIGHT_BUTTON,
```

with the obvious interpretation, and the value of `state` will be one of `GLUT_UP` and `GLUT_DOWN`. The values `x` and `y` report the position of the mouse at the time of the event. (Be alert, however: The `x` value is the number of pixels from the left of the window, as expected, but the `y` value is the number of pixels *down* from the top of the window!)

■ **EXAMPLE 2.4.1 Placing dots with the mouse**

We start with an elementary, but important, example. Each time the user presses down the left mouse button, a dot is drawn in the screen window at the mouse position. If the user presses the right button, the program terminates. The following version of myMouse() does the job. (Note that, because the *y*-value of the mouse position is the number of pixels from the top of the screen window, we draw the dot, not at (x, y), but at (x, screenHeight−y), where screenHeight is assumed here to be the height of the window, in pixels):

```
void myMouse(int button, int state, int x, int y)
{
        if(button == GLUT_LEFT_BUTTON && state == GLUT_DOWN)
            drawDot(x, screenHeight -y);
        else if(button == GLUT_RIGHT_BUTTON && state == GLUT_DOWN)
        exit(-1);
}
```

The argument of −1 in the standard function exit() simply returns −1 back to the operating system; this value is usually ignored.

■ **EXAMPLE 2.4.2 Specifying a rectangle with the mouse**

Here, we want the user to be able to draw rectangles whose dimensions are entered with the mouse. The user clicks the mouse at two points that specify opposite corners of an aligned rectangle, and the rectangle is drawn. The data for each rectangle need not be retained: each new rectangle replaces the previous one. The user can clear the screen by pressing the right mouse button.

The routine shown in Figure 2.38 stores the corner points in the static array corner[], which is made static so that values are retained in the array between successive calls to the routine. The variable numCorners keeps track of how many corners have been entered so far; when this number reaches two, the rectangle is drawn, and numCorners is reset to zero.

FIGURE 2.38 A callback routine to draw rectangles entered with the mouse.

An alternative method for designating a rectangle uses a **rubber rectangle** that grows and shrinks as the user moves the mouse. This is discussed in detail in Section 10.3.3.

```
void myMouse(int button, int state, int x, int y)
{
    static GLintPoint corner[2];
    static int numCorners = 0;            // initial value is 0
    if(button == GLUT_LEFT_BUTTON && state == GLUT_DOWN)
    {
        corner[numCorners].x = x;
        corner[numCorners].y = screenHeight - y;    // flip y coordinate
        numCorners++;                               // have another point
        if(numCorners == 2)
        {
            glRecti(corner[0].x, corner[0].y, corner[1].x, corner[1].y);
            numCorners = 0;        // back to 0 corners
        }
    }
    else if(button == GLUT_RIGHT_BUTTON && state == GLUT_DOWN)
            glClear(GL_COLOR_BUFFER_BIT);           // clear the window
    glFlush();
}
```

■ **EXAMPLE 2.4.3 Controlling the Sierpinski gasket with the mouse**

It is simple to extend the Sierpinski gasket routine described earlier so that the user can specify the three vertices of the initial triangle with the mouse. We use the same process as in the previous example: Gather the three points in an array corners [], and when three points are available, draw the Sierpinski gasket. The meat of the myMouse() routine is therefore as follows:

```
static GLintPoint corners[3];
static int numCorners = 0;
if(button == GLUT_LEFT_BUTTON && state == GLUT_DOWN)
{
   corner[numCorners].x = x;
   corner[numCorners].y = screenHeight - y; // flip y coordinate
   if(++numCorners == 3)
   {
     Sierpinski(corners);              // draw the gasket
     numCorners = 0;                   // back to 0 corners
   }
}
```

Here, Sierpinski() is the same as in Figure 2.14, except that the three vertices of the triangle are passed as parameters.

■ **EXAMPLE 2.4.4 Create a polyline using the mouse**

Figure 2.39 shows a polyline being created with mouse clicks. Here, instead of having each new point replace the previous one, we choose to retain all the points clicked, for later use. The user enters a succession of points with the mouse, and each point is stored in the next available position of the array. If the array becomes full, no further points are accepted. After each click of the mouse, the window is cleared and the entire current polyline is redrawn. The polyline is reset to empty if the right mouse button is pressed.

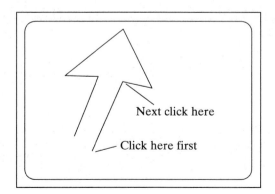

FIGURE 2.39 Interactive creation of a polyline.

Next click here

Click here first

Figure 2.40 shows one possible implementation of this procedure. Note that last keeps track of the last index used so far in the array List []; it is incremented as each new point is clicked and is set to −1 to make the lists empty. If it were desirable to make use of the points in List outside of myMouse(), the variable List could be made global.

```
void myMouse(int button, int state, int x, int y)
{
    #define NUM 20
    static GLintPoint List[NUM];
    static int last = -1;              // last index used so far

  // test for mouse button as well as for a full array
    if(button == GLUT_LEFT_BUTTON && state == GLUT_DOWN && last < (NUM -1))
    {
        List[++last].x = x;         // add new point to list
        List[ last].y = screenHeight - y;
        glClear(GL_COLOR_BUFFER_BIT);     // clear the screen
        glBegin(GL_LINE_STRIP);        // redraw the polyline
          for(int i = 0; i <= last; i++)
            glVertex2i(List[i].x, List[i].y);
        glEnd();
        glFlush();
    }
    else if(button == GLUT_RIGHT_BUTTON && state == GLUT_DOWN)
      last = -1;              // reset the list to empty
}
```

FIGURE 2.40 A polyline drawer based on mouse clicks.

Mouse Motion

An event of a different type is generated when the mouse is moved (more than some minimal distance) while some button is held down. The callback function—say, `myMovedMouse()`—is registered with this event by using

```
glutMotionFunc(myMovedMouse);
```

The callback function must take two parameters and have the prototype `void my-MovedMouse(int x, int y);` The values of x and y are, of course, the position of the mouse when the event occurred.

■ **EXAMPLE 2.4.5 "Freehand" drawing with a fat brush**

Suppose we want to create a curve by sweeping the mouse along some trajectory with a button held down. In addition, we want it to seem that the drawing "brush" has a square shape. This can be accomplished by designing `myMovedMouse()` to draw a square at the current mouse position:

```
void myMovedMouse(int mouseX, int mouseY)
{
    GLint x = mouseX;                     //grab the mouse position
    GLint y = screenHeight - mouseY;        // flip it as usual
    GLint brushSize = 20;
    glRecti(x,y, x + brushSize, y + brushSize);
    glFlush();
}
```

2.4.2 Keyboard Interaction

As mentioned earlier, pressing a key on the keyboard queues a keyboard event. The callback function `myKeyboard()` is registered with that type of event through `glutKeyboardFunc(myKeyboard)`. The function must have the prototype

```
void myKeyboard(unsigned int key, int x, int y);
```

The value of key is the ASCII value[12] of the key pressed. The values x and y report the position of the mouse at the time that the event occurred. (As before, y measures the number of pixels down from the top of the window.)

The programmer can capitalize on the many keys on the keyboard to offer the user a large number of choices to invoke at any point in a program. Most implementations of myKeyboard() consist of a long switch statement, with a case for each key of interest. Figure 2.41 shows one possibility. Pressing p draws a dot at the mouse position; pressing the left arrow key adds a point to some (global) list, but does no drawing;[13] pressing E causes an exit from the program. Note that if the user holds down the p key and moves the mouse around, a rapid sequence of points is generated to make a "freehand" drawing.

```
void myKeyboard(unsigned char theKey, int mouseX, int mouseY)
{
  GLint x = mouseX;
  GLint y = screenHeight - mouseY; // flip the y value as always
  switch(theKey)
  {
    case 'p':
        drawDot(x, y);    // draw a dot at the mouse position
        break;
    case GLUT_KEY_LEFT: List[++last].x = x; // add a point
                        List[  last].y = y;
        break;
    case 'E':
        exit(-1);         //terminate the program
    default:
     break;               // do nothing
  }
}
```

FIGURE 2.41 An example of the keyboard callback function.

2.5 SUMMARY

The hard part in writing graphics applications is getting started: pulling together the hardware and software ingredients in a program to make the first few pictures. The OpenGL application programmer interface (API) helps enormously here, providing a powerful, yet simple, set of routines to make drawings. One of the API's great virtues is device independence, which makes it possible to write programs for one graphics environment and use the same program without changes in another environment.

Most graphics applications are written today for a windows-based environment. The program opens a window on the screen that can be moved and resized by the user and responds to mouse clicks and keystrokes. We saw how to use OpenGL functions that make it easy to create such a program.

Primitive drawing routines were applied to making pictures composed of dots, lines, polylines, and polygons, and were combined into more powerful routines that form the basis of one's personal graphics toolbox. Several examples illustrated the use of the tools therein and described methods for interacting with a program by using the keyboard and mouse. The case studies presented next offer additional programming examples that explore in more depth the topics discussed so far or that branch out to interesting related topics.

---

[12] "ASCII" stands for "American Standard Code for Information Interchange." Tables of ASCII values are readily available on the Internet. See also ascii.html at the Web site for this book.

[13] Names for the various "special" keyboard keys, such as the function keys, arrow keys, and "home," may be found in the include file glut.h.

2.6 CASE STUDIES

While using this text, it is best to try out new ideas as they are introduced, to solidify the ideas presented. This is particularly true in the first few chapters, since getting started with one's first graphics programs often presents a hurdle that one must surmount. To focus this effort, each chapter ends with some **case studies** which describe programming projects that both are interesting in themselves and concentrate on the ideas developed in the chapter.

Some of the case studies are simple exercises that only require fleshing out some pseudocode given in the text and then running the program through its paces. Others are much more challenging and could be the basis of a major programming project within a course. It is always difficult to judge how much time someone else will need to accomplish any project. The "**level of effort**" that accompanies each case study is a rough guess at best.

Level of Effort

There are three levels of effort:

I: A simple exercise. It could be assigned for the next class.

II: An intermediate exercise. It probably will take several days to complete.[14]

III: An advanced exercise. It would probably be assigned two weeks or so ahead of time.

CASE STUDY 2.1 PSEUDORANDOM CLOUDS OF DOTS

Level of Effort: II. The random-number generator (RNG) `random(N)` (see Example 2.2.2) produces a value between 0 and $N - 1$ each time it is called. It uses the standard C++ function `rand()` to generate values. Each value appears to be randomly selected and to have no relation to its predecessors.

In fact, the successive numbers that `rand()` produces are not generated randomly at all, but rather through a very regular mechanism whereby each number n_i is determined from its predecessor n_{i-1} by a specific formula. A typical formula is

$$n_i = \left[n_{i-1}A + B \right] \bmod N, \tag{2.4}$$

where A, B, and N are suitably chosen constants. One set of numbers that works fairly well is $A = 1{,}103{,}515{,}245$, $B = 12{,}345$, *and* $N = 32{,}767$. Multiplying n_{i-1} by A and adding B forms a large value, and the modulo operation brings the value into the range from 0 to $N - 1$. The process begins with some "seed" value chosen for n_0.

Because the numbers only give an appearance of randomness, they are called **pseudorandom** numbers. The choices of the values for A, B, and N are very important, and slightly different values give rise to very different characteristics in the sequence of numbers. More details can be found in [Knuth98].

Scatter Plots

Some experiments yield data consisting of many pairs of numbers (A_i, B_i), and the goal is to infer visually how the *a*-values and *b*-values are related. For instance, a large number of people are measured, and one wonders if there is a strong correlation between a person's height and weight.

A scatter plot can be used to give visual insight into the data. For each person, data are plotted as a dot at position (*height*, *weight*) so only the `drawDot()` tool is needed. Figure 2.42 gives an example. It suggests that a person's height and weight are roughly linearly related, although some people (such as A) are idiosyncratic, being light weight, yet quite tall.

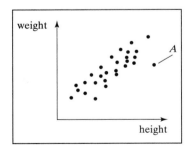

FIGURE 2.42 A scatter plot of people's height versus weight.

---

[14] A "day of programming" means several two-hour "sessions," with plenty of thinking (and resting) time between sessions. It also assumes a reasonably skilled programmer (with at least two semesters of programming in hand) who is familiar with the idiosyncrasies of the language and the platform being used. It does *not* allow for those dreadful hours we all know too well of being stuck with some obscure bug that presents a brick wall of frustration until it is ferreted out and squashed.

Here we use scatter plots to visually test the quality of a random-number generator. Each time the function `random(N)` is called, it returns a value in the range $0..N - 1$ that is apparently chosen at random, unrelated to values previously returned. But are successive values truly unrelated?

One simple test builds a scatter plot based on pairs of successive values returned by `random(N)`. The routine calls `random(N)` twice in succession and plots the first value against the second:

```
for(int i = 0; i < num; i++)
    drawDot(random(N), random(N));
```

Or, in "raw" OpenGL, we may place the `for` loop between `glBegin()` and `glEnd()`:

```
glBegin(GL_POINTS);
    for(int i = 0; i < num; i++)          // do it num times
        glVertex2i(random(N), random(N));
glEnd();
```

The second way is more efficient, avoiding the overhead associated with making many calls to `glBegin()` and `glEnd()`.

Figure 2.43 shows a typical plot that might result. There should be a "uniform" density of dots throughout the square, to reassure you that the values $0..N - 1$ occur with about equal likelihood and that there is no discernible relationship between one value and its successor.

Figure 2.44 shows what can happen with an inferior RNG. In (a), there is too high a density of certain values, so the distribution is not uniform in $0..N - 1$. In (b), there is high correlation between a number and its successor: When one number is large, the other tends to be small. And c) shows perhaps the worst situation of all: After a few dozen values have been generated, the pattern *repeats*, and no new dots are generated!

FIGURE 2.43 A constellation of 500 random dots.

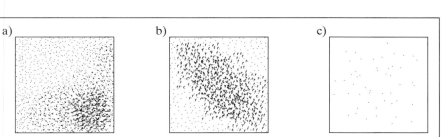

FIGURE 2.44 Scatter plots produced by inferior random-number generators.

Plotting dot constellations such as these can provide a rough first check on the uniformity of the numbers that are generated. The test is far from thorough test, however [Knuth98].

Write a program that produces random dot plots, using some different RNGs to produce the (x, y) pairs. Try different constants A, B, and N in the basic RNG, and see the effect this has on the dot constellations. (*Warning*: If the dot constellation suddenly "freezes" such that no new dots appear, it may be that the pattern of numbers is simply repeating.)

CASE STUDY 2.2 INTRODUCTION TO ITERATED FUNCTION SYSTEMS

From his paradise no one shall ever evict us - David Hilbert, defending Cantor's set theory

Level of Effort: II. The repetitive operation of drawing the Sierpinski gasket is an example of an **iterated function system (IFS)**, which we shall encounter a surprising number of times throughout this book. Many interesting computer-generated figures (fractals, the Mandelbrot set, etc.) are based on variations of this IFS.

A hand calculator provides a tool for experimenting with a simple IFS: Enter some (positive) number *num* and press the square-root key. This produces a new number, $\sqrt{num}$. Press the square-root key again to take the new number's square root, yielding $\sqrt{\sqrt{num}}$. Keep doing this until you tire of it. With this operation, you are *iterating* with the square-root function, and each result is used as the input for the next square root. An initial value of *num* = 64 yields the sequence: 64, 8, 2.8284, 1.68179, ... (Is there a value to which this sequence converges?)

Figure 2.45 presents the system schematically, showing that each output value is *fed back* to have its square root formed, again and again.

FIGURE 2.45 Taking the square root repetitively.

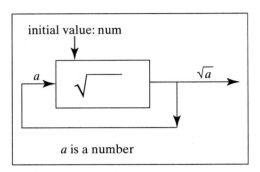

initial value: num

a $\sqrt{a}$

a is a number

In this example, the function being iterated is $f(x) = \sqrt{x}$, or symbolically, $f(.) = \sqrt{.}$, the "square rooter." Other functions $f(.)$ can be used instead, such as the following:

- $f(.) = 2(.)$;   the "doubler"; doubles its argument.
- $f(.) = \cos(.)$;   the "cosiner."
- $f(.) = 4(.)(1 - (.))$ the "logistic" function, used in chaos theory. (See Chapter 3.)
- $f(.) = (.)^2 + c$ for a constant c used to define the Mandelbrot set. (See Chapter 9.)

It is sometimes helpful to give a name to each number that emerges from the IFS. We call the kth such number d_k and say that the process begins at $k = 0$ by "injecting" the initial value d_0 into the system. Then the sequence of values generated by the IFS is

$$d_0,$$
$$d_1 = f(d_0),$$
$$d_2 = f(f(d_0)),$$
$$d_3 = f(f(f(d_0))),$$
$$\vdots$$

so d_3 is formed by applying function $f(.)$ three times. This is called **the third iterate** of $f()$ applied to the initial value d_0. More succinctly, we can denote the **kth iterate** of $f()$ by

$$d_k = f^{[k]}(d_0), \qquad (2.5)$$

meaning the value produced after $f(.)$ has been applied k times to d_0. (*Note:* This does *not* mean that the value $f(d_0)$ is raised to the kth power.) We can also use the recursive form and say that

$$d_k = f(d_{k-1}) \text{ for } k = 1, 2, 3, \dots, \text{ for a given value of } d_0.$$

The sequence of values $d_0, d_1, d_2, d_3, d_4, \dots$ is called "the **orbit** of d_0" for the system.

Example: The orbit of 64 for the function $f(.) = \sqrt{.}$ is 64, 8, 2.8284, 1.68179, ..., and the orbit of 10,000 is 100, 10, 3.162278, 1.77828, ... (What is the orbit of 0? What is the orbit of 0.1?)

Example: The orbit of 7 for the "doubler" $f(.) = 2 \cdot (.)$ is 7, 14, 28, 56, 112, ... The k-th iterate is $7 * 2^k$.

Example: The orbit of 1 for $f(.) = \sin(.)$ can be found using a hand calculator; the result is 1, .8414, .7456, .6784, ..., which *very* slowly approaches the value 0. (What is the orbit of 1 for $\cos(.)$? In particular, to what value does the orbit converge?)

Project 1: Plotting the Hailstone Sequence

Consider iterating the intriguing function

$$f(x) = \begin{cases} x/2 & \text{if } x \text{ is even} \\ 3x + 1, & \text{if } x \text{ is odd} \end{cases} . \tag{2.6}$$

Even-valued arguments are cut in half, whereas odd ones are enlarged. For example, the orbit of 17 is the sequence 17, 52, 26, 13, 40, 20, 10, 5, 16, 8, 4, 2, 1 .... Once a power of two is reached, the sequence falls "like a hailstone" to 1 and becomes trapped in a short repetitive cycle (which one?). The following is an unanswered question in mathematics:

Unanswered Question: Does *every* orbit fall to 1?

That is, does a positive integer exist, which, when used as a starting point and iterated with this "hailstone function," does *not* ultimately crash down to 1? No one knows, but the intricacies of the sequence have been widely studied (See [Hayes84] or numerous sources on the internet, such as www.cecm.sfu.ca/organics/papers/lagarias/.)

Write a program that plots the course of the sequence $y_k = f^{[k]}(y_0)$ versus k. The user gives a starting value y_0 between 1 and 4,000,000,000 (unsigned longs will hold values of this size). Each value y_k is plotted as the point (k, y_k). Each plot continues until y_k reaches a value of 1 (if it ever does at all).

Because the hailstone sequence can be very long, and the values of y_k can grow very large, it is essential to scale the values before they are displayed. Recall from Section 2.2 that appropriate values of $A, B, C,$ and D are determined so that when the value (k, y_k) is plotted at screen coordinates

```
sx = (A * k + B)
```

and

```
sy = (C * yk + D)
```

the entire sequence fits on the screen.

Note that you do not know how long the sequence will be or how large y_k will get, until after the sequence has been generated. A simple solution is to run the sequence invisibly first, keeping track of the largest value, yBiggest, attained by y_k, as well as the number of iterations, kBiggest, required for the sequence to reach unity. These values are then used to determine $A, B, C,$ and D. The sequence is then rerun and plotted.

To improve the final plot, we do the following:

a. Draw horizontal and vertical axes.
b. Plot the logarithm of y_k rather than y_k itself.

A Curious Question: What is the largest yBiggest and what is the largest kBiggest encountered for any hailstone sequence with starting value between 1 and 1,000,000?

Iterating with functions that produce points

Iterating numbers through some function $f(.)$ is interesting enough, but iterating *points* through a function is even more so, since we can use drawDot() to build patterns out of the different points that emerge. So we consider a function $f(p)$ that takes one point $p = (x, y)$ as input and produces another point as output. Each newly formed point is fed back into the same function again to generate yet another new point, as suggested in Figure 2.46. Here, p_{k-1} is used to create the kth iterate, $p_k = f^{[k]}(p_0)$, which is then fed back to produce p_{k+1}, etc.

Once again, we call the sequence of points $p_0, p_1, p_2, \ldots$ the **orbit of p_0**.

FIGURE 2.46 Iterated function sequence generator for points.

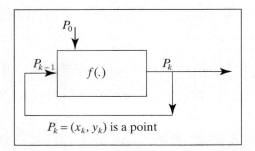

$P_k = (x_k, y_k)$ is a point

■ **Aside: The Sierpinski gasket seen as an IFS**

In terms of an IFS, the kth dot, p_k, of the Sierpinski gasket is formed from p_{k-1} using

$$p_k = ((p_{k-1} + T[\text{random}(3)])/2,$$

where it is understood that the x and y components must be formed separately. Thus, the function that is iterated is

$$f(.) = ((.) + T[\text{random}(3)])/2.$$

Project 2: The Gingerbread Man

The "gingerbread man" shown in Figure 2.47 is based on another IFS, and it can be drawn as a dot constellation. This figure has become a familiar creature in chaos theory [Peitgen88, Gleick87, Schroeder91] because it is a form of "strange attractor": the successive dots are "attracted" into a region resembling a gingerbread man with curious hexagonal holes.

FIGURE 2.47 A typical gingerbread man.

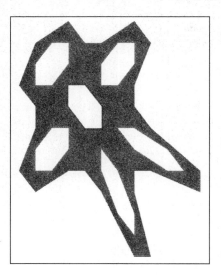

There is no randomness in the process that generates the gingerbread man: Each new point q is formed from the previous point p according to the following two rules:

$$q.x = M(1 + 2L) - p.y + |p.x - LM|; \tag{2.7}$$
$$q.y = p.x.$$

Observe that the constants M and L are carefully chosen to scale and position the gingerbread man on the display. (The values $M = 40$ and $L = 3$ might be good choices for a 640-by-480-pixel display.)

Write a program that allows the user to choose the starting point for the iterations with the mouse and then draws the dots for the gingerbread man. (If a mouse is unavailable, one good starting point is $(115, 121)$.) Fix suitable values of M and L in the routine, but experiment with other values as well.

You will notice that, for a given starting point, only a certain number of dots appear before the pattern repeats (i.e., it stops changing). Different starting points give rise to different patterns. Arrange your program so that you can add to the picture by inputting additional starting points with the mouse.

PRACTICE EXERCISES

2.6.1 A fixed point on the gingerbread man

Show that the process given in Equations (2.7) has the "fixed point" $((1 + L)M, (1 + L)M)$. That is, the result of subjecting this point to the process of that equation is the same point. (This would be a very uninteresting starting point for generating the gingerbread man!) ■

CASE STUDY 2.3 THE GOLDEN RATIO AND OTHER JEWELS

Level of Effort: I. The aspect ratio of a rectangle is an important attribute. Over the centuries, one aspect ratio has been particularly celebrated for its pleasing qualities in works of art: that of the golden rectangle. Considered the most pleasing of all rectangles, the golden rectangle is neither too narrow nor too squat. It figures in the Greek Parthenon (see Figure 2.48), Leonardo da Vinci's *Mona Lisa*, Salvador Dali's *Sacrament of the Last Supper*, and much of M. C. Escher's works.

FIGURE 2.48 The Greek Parthenon fitting within a golden rectangle.

The golden rectangle is based on a fascinating quantity: the golden ratio $\phi = 1.618033989\ldots$. The value ϕ appears in a surprising number of places in computer graphics.

Figure 2.49 shows a golden rectangle with sides of length ϕ and 1. This shape has the unique property that if a square is removed from the rectangle, the piece that remains will again be a golden rectangle! What value must ϕ have to make this work? Note in the figure that the smaller rectangle has height 1, so to be golden, it must have width $1/\phi$. Thus,

$$\phi = 1 + \frac{1}{\phi}, \tag{2.8}$$

which is easily solved to yield

$$\phi = \frac{1 + \sqrt{5}}{2} = 1.618033989\ldots. \tag{2.9}$$

This is approximately the aspect ratio of a standard 3-by-5 index card. From Equation 2.8, we see also that $\phi - 1 = 1/\phi = .618033989\ldots$. This is the aspect ratio of a golden rectangle lying on its short end.

FIGURE 2.49 The golden rectangle.

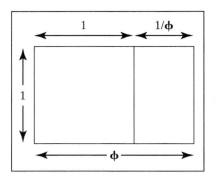

The number ϕ is remarkable mathematically in many ways, two favorites being

$$\phi = \sqrt{1 + \sqrt{1 + \sqrt{1 + \sqrt{1 + \ldots}}}} \qquad (2.10)$$

and

$$\phi = 1 + \cfrac{1}{1 + \cfrac{1}{1 + \cfrac{1}{1 + \ldots}}} \qquad (2.11)$$

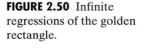

FIGURE 2.50 Infinite regressions of the golden rectangle.

Both of these formulas are easy to prove (how?) and display a pleasing simplicity in the use of the single digit 1.

The idea that the golden rectangle contains a smaller version of itself suggests a form of "infinite regression" of figures within figures within figures, *ad infinitum*. Figure 2.50 demonstrates this regression. We simply keep removing squares from each remaining golden rectangle.

Write an application that draws the regression of golden rectangles centered in a screen window 600 pixels wide by 400 pixels high. (First determine where and how big the largest golden rectangle is that will fit in this window. Your picture should regress down until the smallest rectangle is about one pixel in size.)

There is much more to be said about the golden ratio, and many delights can be found in [Gardner61], [Hill78], [Huntley70], and [Ogilvy69]. For instance, in the next chapter we see golden pentagrams, and in Chapter 6 we see that two of the Platonic solids, the dodecahedron and the icosahedron, contain three mutually perpendicular golden rectangles!

PRACTICE EXERCISES

2.6.2 Other golden things

Equation 2.10 shows ϕ as a repeated square root involving the number 1. What is the value of

$$W = \sqrt{k + \sqrt{k + \sqrt{k + \sqrt{k + \cdots}}}}.$$

2.6.3 On ϕ and golden rectangles

a. Show that Equations 2.10 and 2.11 are valid.
b. Find the point at which the two dotted diagonals shown in Figure 2.50 lie, and show that this is the point to which the sequence of golden rectangles converges.
c. Use Equation 2.8 to derive the relationship

$$\phi^2 + \frac{1}{\phi^2} = 3. \qquad (2.12)$$

2.6.4 Golden orbits

An examination of Equations 2.10 and 2.11 reveals that the golden ratio ϕ is <u>the limiting</u> value of applying certain functions again and again. The first function is $f(.) = \sqrt{1 + (.)}$. What is the second function? Viewing these expressions in terms of iterated functions, we see that ϕ is the value to which orbits converge for some starting values. (The starting value is hidden in the "…" of the expressions.) Explore with a hand calculator what starting values one can use and still have the process converge to ϕ. ■

CASE STUDY 2.4 BUILDING AND USING POLYLINE FILES

Level of Effort: II. Complex pictures such as Figure 2.21 are based on a large collection of polylines. The data for the polylines are typically stored in a file, so the picture can be reconstructed at a later time by reading the polylines into a program and redrawing each line. A reasonable format for such a file was described in Section 2.3.1, as was the routine `draw-PolyLineFile()`, which does the drawing.

The file "dino.dat," which stores the dinosaur in Figure 2.21, is available as `dino.dat` on the Web site for this book. (See the preface.) Other polyline files are also available there.

a. Write a program that reads polyline data from a file and draws each polyline in turn. Generate at least one interesting polyline file of your own on a text processor, and use your program to draw a picture based on data from the file.
b. Extend the program in Part (a) to accept some other file formats. For instance, have the program accept **differentially coded** x- and y-coordinates. In this format the first point (x_1, y_1) of each polyline is encoded as before, but each remaining point (x_i, y_i) is encoded after subtracting the previous point from it. Thus, the file contains $(x_i - x_{i-1}, y_i - y_{i-1})$. In many cases, there are fewer significant digits in the difference than in the original point values, allowing more compact files. Experiment with this format, and create several data files that use it.
c. Adapt the preceding file format so that a "color value" is associated with each polyline in the file. This color value appears in the file on the same line as the number of points in the associated polyline. Experiment with this format, and create several polyline files that use it.
d. Adjust the polyline drawing routine so that it draws a closed polygon whenever a minus sign precedes the number of points in a polyline. Thus, in the file

−3		← negative, so this is a polygon
0	0	first point in this polygon
35	3	second point in this polygon
57	8	also connect this to the first point of the polygon
5		← positive, so leave it open as usual
0	1	
12	21	
23	34	
⋮		

the first polyline is drawn as a triangle, with its last point connected to its first. Experiment with this format, and create several files that use it.

CASE STUDY 2.5 STIPPLING OF LINES AND POLYGONS

Level of Effort: II. Often, one wants a line to be drawn with a dot–dash pattern or a polygon to be filled with a pattern representing some image. OpenGL provides convenient tools to do this.

Line Stippling

It is straightforward to define a stipple pattern for use with line drawing. Once the pattern is specified, it is applied to subsequent line drawing as soon as it is enabled with the command

```
glEnable(GL_LINE_STIPPLE);
```

and until it is disabled with the command

```
glDisable(GL_LINE_STIPPLE).
```

The function

```
glLineStipple(GLint factor, GLushort pattern);
```

defines the stipple pattern. The value of `pattern` (which is of type `GLushort`, an unsigned 16-bit quantity) is a sequence of 0's and 1's that define which dots along the line are drawn: A 1 stipulates that a dot is drawn; a 0 stipulates that it is not. The pattern in scanned from the low-order bit up to the high-order bit. The pattern is repeated as many times as necessary to draw the desired line. Figure 2.51 shows several examples. The pattern is given compactly in hexadecimal notation. For example, 0xEECC specifies the bit pattern 1110111011001100. The variable `factor` specifies how much to "enlarge" `pattern`: Each bit in the pattern is repeated `factor` times. For instance, the pattern 0xEECC with factor 2 yields 11111100111111001111000011110000. In drawing a stippled polyline, for example, with `glBegin(GL_LINE_STRIP); glVertex*(); glVertex*(); glVertex*(); . . . glEnd();`, the pattern continues from the end of one line segment to the beginning of the next, until `glEnd()`.

FIGURE 2.51 Sample stipple patterns.

pattern	factor	resulting stipple
0xFF00	1	....
0xFF00	2	....
0x5555	1	....
0x3333	2	.. ..
0x7733	1	... ...

Write a program that allows the user to type in a `pattern` (in hexadecimal notation) and a value for `factor`, and then draws stippled lines laid down with the mouse.

Polygon Stippling

It is also not difficult to define a stipple pattern for filling a polygon, but there are more details to cope with. After the pattern is specified, it is applied to subsequent polygon filling once it is enabled with the command `glEnable(GL_POLYGON_STIPPLE)`, until it is disabled with the command `glDisable(GL_POLYGON_STIPPLE)`.

The function

```
glPolygonStipple(const GLubyte * mask);
```

attaches the stipple pattern to subsequently drawn polygons, based on a 128-byte array `mask[]`. These 128 bytes provide the bits for a mask that is 32 bits wide and 32 bits high. The pattern is "tiled" throughout the polygon (which is invoked with the usual `glBegin(GL_POLYGON); glVertex*();. . . .; glEnd();` commands). The pattern is specified by an array definition, such as

```
GLubyte mask[]={0xff, 0xfe, 0x34, ... };
```

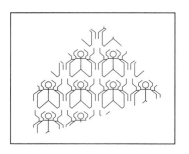

FIGURE 2.52 A sample stippled polygon.

The first four bytes prescribe the 32 bits across the bottom row, from left to right; the next four bytes give the next row up, etc. Figure 2.52 shows the result of filling a specific polygon with a "fly" pattern specified in the OpenGL "red book" [woo97].

Write a program that defines an interesting stipple pattern for a polygon and then allows the user to lay down a sequence of convex polygons with the mouse, each filled with the pattern defined.

CASE STUDY 2.6 POLYLINE EDITOR

Level of Effort: III. Drawing programs often allow one to enter polylines using a mouse and then to *edit* the polylines until they present the desired picture. Figure 2.53(a) shows a house in the process of being drawn; the user has just clicked at the position shown, and a line has been drawn from the previous point to the one designated by the mouse.

Figure 2.53(b) shows the effect of moving a point. The user positions the cursor near the vertex of some polyline, presses down the mouse button, and "drags" the chosen point to some other location before releasing the button. Upon release of the button, the previous lines connected to this point are erased, and new lines are drawn to it.

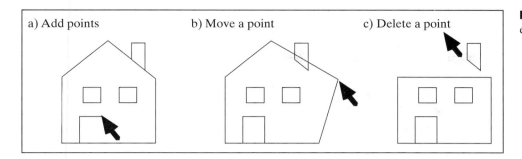

FIGURE 2.53 Creating and editing polylines.

Figure 2.53(c) shows how a point is deleted from a polyline. The user clicks near the vertex of some polyline, and the two line segments connected to that vertex are erased. Then the two other endpoints of the segments just erased are connected with a line segment.

Write a program that allows the user to enter and edit pictures made up of as many as 60 polylines. The user interacts with the screen by pressing keyboard keys and pointing and clicking with the mouse. The functionality of the program should include the following "actions":

- `begin   ('b')`:   (create a new polyline)
- `delete ('d')`:   (delete the next point pointed to)
- `move    ('m')`:   (drag the point pointed to to a new location)
- `refresh ('r')`:   (erase the screen and redraw all the polylines)
- `quit    ('q')`:   (exit from the program)

A list of polylines can be maintained in an array such as: `GLintPointArray polys[60]`. The verb `begin`, activated by pressing the key `'b'`, permits the user to create a new polyline, which is stored in the first available "slot" in array `polys`. The verb `delete` requires that the program identify which point of which polyline lies closest to the point currently designated by the mouse. Once that point is identified, the "previous" and "next" vertices in the chosen polyline are found. The two line segments connected to the chosen vertex are erased, and the previous and next vertices are joined with a line segment. The verb `move` finds the vertex closest to the currently designated point and waits for the user to click the mouse a second time, at which point the vertex is moved to this new point.

What other functions might you want in a polyline editor? Discuss how you might save the array of polylines in a file and read it in later. Also, discuss what a reasonable mechanism might be for inserting a new point inside a polyline.

CASE STUDY 2.7 BUILDING AND RUNNING MAZES

Level of Effort: III. The task of finding a path through a maze seems forever fascinating. (See [Ball74].) You can generate an elaborate maze on a computer and use graphics to watch it be traversed. Figure 2.54 shows a rectangular maze with 100 rows and 150 columns. The goal is to find a path from the opening at the left edge to the opening at the right edge. Although you can traverse the maze manually by trial and error, it is more interesting to develop an algorithm to do it automatically.

Write and execute a program that (a) generates and displays a rectangular maze of R rows and C columns and (b) finds (and displays) the path through the maze from start to end. The program generates mazes randomly, but they must be **proper**; that is, every one of the R-by-C cells is connected by a unique, albeit tortuous, path to every other cell. Think of a maze as a graph, as suggested by Figure 2.55. A node of the graph corresponds to each cell in which either a path terminates or two paths meet, and each path is represented by a branch. So a node occurs at every cell for which there is a choice of which way to go next. For instance, when Q is reached there are three choices, whereas at M there are only two.

FIGURE 2.54 A maze.

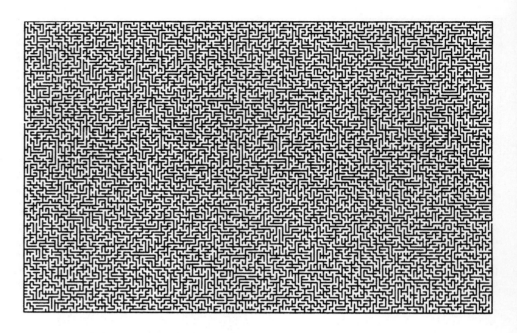

How should a maze be represented? One way is to state, for each cell, whether its north wall is intact and its east wall is intact, suggesting the following data structure:

```
char northWall[R][C], eastWall[R][C];
```

If `northwall[i][j]` is 1, the *ij*th cell has a solid upper wall; otherwise the wall is missing. The zeroth row is a phantom row of cells below the maze whose north walls make up the bottom edge of the maze. Similarly, `eastwall[i][0]` specifies where any gaps appear in the left edge of the maze.

FIGURE 2.55 A simple maze and its graph.

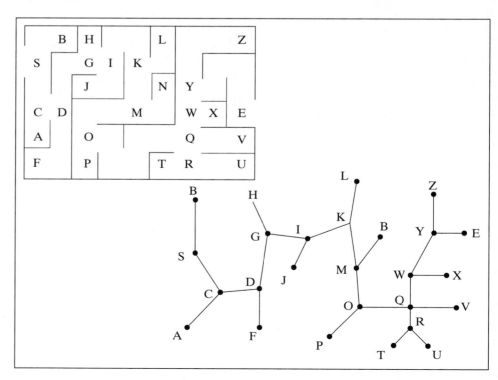

Generating a Maze Start with all walls intact, so that the maze is a simple grid of horizontal and vertical lines. The program draws this grid. An invisible "mouse" whose job is to "eat" through walls to connect adjacent cells is initially placed in some arbitrarily chosen cell. The mouse checks the four neighbor cells (above, below, left, and right) and, for each neighbor, asks whether it has all four walls intact. If not, the cell has previously been visited and so is already on some path. The mouse may detect several candidate cells that haven't been visited: It chooses one randomly and eats through the connecting wall, saving the locations of the other candidates on a stack. The wall that is eaten is erased, and the mouse repeats the process. When it becomes trapped in a dead end—surrounded by visited cells—it pops an unvisited cell and continues. When the stack is empty, all cells in the maze have been visited. A "start" and "end" cell is then chosen randomly, most likely along some edge of the maze. It is delightful to watch the maze being formed dynamically as the mouse eats through walls. (*Question:* Might a queue be better than a stack for storing candidates? How would it affect the order in which later paths are created?)

Running the Maze To run the maze, we use a "backtracking" algorithm. At each step, the mouse tries to move in a random direction. If there is no wall, it places its position on a stack and moves to the next cell. The cell that the mouse is in can be drawn with a red dot. When the mouse runs into a dead end, it can change the color of the cell to blue and backtrack by popping the stack. The mouse can even put a wall up to avoid ever trying the dead-end cell again.

Addendum Proper mazes aren't too challenging, because you can always traverse them using the "shoulder-to-the-wall" rule, wherein you trace the maze by rubbing your shoulder along the left-hand wall. At a dead end, you sweep around and retrace the path, always maintaining contact with the wall. Because the maze is a "tree," you will ultimately reach your destination. In fact, there can even be cycles in the graph and you will still always find the end, as long as both the starting and ending cells are on outer boundaries of the maze. (Why?) To make things more interesting, place the starting and ending cells in the interior of the maze, and also let the mouse eat some extra walls (maybe randomly 1 in 20 times). In this way, some cycles may be formed that encircle the ending cell and defeat the "shoulder-to-the-wall" method.

2.7 FURTHER READING

Several books provide an introduction to using OpenGL. The *OpenGL Programming Guide* by Woo, Neider, and Davis [Woo97] is an excellent source. There is also a wealth of information available on the Internet. (See, for instance, the OpenGL repository at http://www.opengl.org/ and the complete manual for openGL at http://www.sgi.com/software/opengl/manual.html.)

3

More Drawing Tools

Computers are useless. They can only give you answers.

Pablo Picasso

Even if you are on the right track, you'll get run over if you just sit there.

Will Rogers

Goals of the Chapter

▲ To introduce viewports and clipping.

▲ To develop the window-to-viewport transformation.

▲ To develop a classical clipping algorithm.

▲ To create tools to draw in world coordinates.

▲ To develop a C++ class to encapsulate the drawing routines.

▲ To develop ways to select windows and viewports for optimum viewing.

▲ To draw complex pictures using relative drawing and turtle graphics.

▲ To build figures based on regular polygons and their offspring.

▲ To draw arcs and circles.

▲ To describe parametrically defined curves and to see how to draw them.

PREVIEW

Section 3.1 introduces world coordinates and the world window. Section 3.2 describes the window-to-viewport transformation. This transformation simplifies graphics applications by letting the programmer work in a reasonable coordinate system, yet have all pictures mapped as desired to the display surface. The section also discusses how the programmer (or user) chooses the window and viewport to achieve the desired drawings. A key property is that the aspect ratios of the window and viewport must agree, or distortion results. Some of the choices can be automated. Section 3.3 develops a classical clipping algorithm that removes any parts of the picture that lie outside the world window.

Section 3.4 builds a useful C++ class called *Canvas* that encapsulates the many details of initialization and handling of variables that are required for a drawing program. Its implementation in an OpenGL environment is developed. A programmer can use the tools in *Canvas* to make complex pictures and remain confident that the underlying data are protected from inadvertent mishandling.

Section 3.5 develops routines for relative drawing and "turtle graphics" that add handy methods to the programmer's tool kit. Section 3.6 examines how to draw interesting figures based on regular polygons, and Section 3.7 discusses the drawing of arcs and circles. The chapter ends with several case studies, including the development of the *Canvas* class for a non-OpenGL environment, in which all the details of clipping and the window-to-viewport transformation must be explicitly developed.

Section 3.8 describes different representations for curves and develops the very useful parametric form that permits straightforward drawing of complex curves. Both two-dimensional and three-dimensional curves are considered.

3.1 INTRODUCTION

It is as interesting and as difficult to say a thing well as to paint it.

Vincent van Gogh

In Chapter 2, our drawings used the basic coordinate system of the screen window: coordinates that are essentially in pixels, extending from zero to some value `screen-Width` $-$ 1 in *x*, and from zero to some value `screenHeight` $-$ 1 in *y*. This means that we can use only positive values of *x* and *y*, and the values must extend over a large range (several hundred pixels) if we hope to get a drawing of some reasonable size.

In a given problem, however, we may not want to think in terms of pixels: It may be much more natural to think in terms of *x* varying from, say, -1 to 1, and *y* varying from -100.0 to 20.0. (Recall how awkward it was to scale and shift values in the program for producing a dot plot in Figure 2.16.) Clearly, we want to make a separation between the values we use in a program to *describe* geometrical objects and the size and position of the *pictures* of those objects on the display.

In this chapter, we develop methods that let the programmer or user describe objects in whatever coordinate system best fits the problem at hand and that automatically scale and shift the picture of an object so that it "comes out right" in the screen window. The space in which objects are described is called **world coordinates**, which are the usual Cartesian *xy*-coordinates used in mathematics, based on whatever units are convenient.

We define a rectangular **world window**[1] in world coordinates. The world window specifies which part of the "world" should be drawn. The understanding is that whatever lies inside the window should be drawn and whatever lies outside should be clipped away and not drawn.

In addition, we define a rectangular **viewport** in the screen window. A mapping (consisting of scalings and shiftings) between the world window and the viewport is established so that when all the objects in the world are drawn, the parts that lie inside the world window are automatically mapped to the inside of the viewport. Accordingly, the programmer thinks in terms of "looking through a window" at the objects being drawn and placing a "snapshot" of whatever is seen in that window into the viewport on the display. This window–viewport approach makes it much easier to do natural things like "zooming in" on a detail in a scene or "panning around" the scene.

We first develop the mapping part that provides the automatic change of coordinates. Then we see how clipping is done.

---

[1] As mentioned, the term "window" has a bewildering set of meanings in graphics, which often leads to confusion. We shall try to keep the different meanings clear by saying "world window," "screen window," etc., when necessary.

3.2 WORLD WINDOWS AND VIEWPORTS

We use an example to motivate the use of world windows and viewports. Suppose you want to examine the nature of a certain mathematical function, say, the sinc function famous in the signal-processing field. This function is defined by

$$\text{sinc}(x) = \frac{\sin(\pi x)}{\pi x}. \tag{3.1}$$

You want to know how the function bends and wiggles as x varies. Suppose you know that as x varies from $-\infty$ to ∞, the value of $\text{sinc}(x)$ varies over much of the range -1 to 1, and that $\text{sinc}(x)$ is particularly interesting for values of x near zero. So you want a plot that is centered at $(0, 0)$, and that shows $\text{sinc}(x)$ for closely spaced x-values between, say, -4.0 and 4.0. Figure 3.1 shows a plot of $\text{sinc}(x)$, generated by using a simple OpenGL display function (after a suitable world window and viewport were specified, of course). The code is as follows:

FIGURE 3.1 A plot of the "sinc" function.

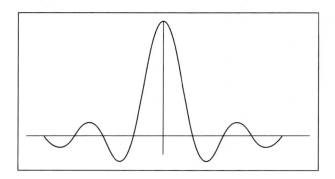

```
void myDisplay(void)
{
    glBegin(GL_LINE_STRIP);
    for(GLfloat x = -4.0; x < 4.0; x += 0.1)
    {
        GLfloat y = sin(3.14159 * x) / (3.14159 * x);
        glVertex2f(x, y);
    }
    glEnd();
    glFlush();
}
```

Note that the code operates in a *natural* coordinate system for the problem at hand: x is made to vary in small increments from -4.0 to 4.0. The key issue here is how the various (x, y) values become scaled and shifted so that the picture appears properly in the screen window.

We accomplish the proper scaling and shifting by setting up a world window and a viewport and then establishing a suitable mapping between them. The window and viewport are both aligned rectangles specified by the programmer. The window is expressed in world coordinates. The viewport is a portion of the screen window. Figure 3.2 is an example of a world window and a viewport. The notion is that whatever lies in the world window is scaled and shifted so that it appears in the viewport; everything else is clipped off and not displayed.

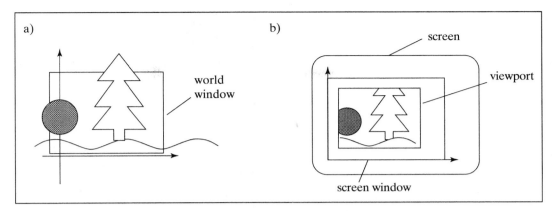

FIGURE 3.2 A world window and a viewport.

We want to describe not only how to do scaling and shifting in *OpenGL*, which is very easy, but also *how* scaling and shifting are done, in order to give insight into the low-level algorithms used. We work with only a 2D version here, but later we shall see how these ideas extend naturally to 3D "worlds" viewed with a "camera."

3.2.1 The Mapping from the Window to the Viewport

Figure 3.3 shows a world window and a viewport in more detail. The world window is described by its *left*, *top*, *right*, and *bottom* borders as $W.l$, $W.t$, $W.r$, and $W.b$, respectively[2]. The viewport is described likewise in the coordinate system of the screen window (opened at some place on the screen) by $V.l$, $V.t$, $V.r$, and $V.b$, which are measured in pixels.

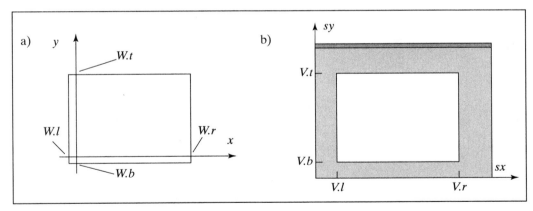

FIGURE 3.3 Specifying the window and viewport.

The world window can be of any size and shape and in any position, as long as it is an aligned rectangle. Similarly, the viewport can be any aligned rectangle, although it is, of course, usually chosen to lie entirely within the screen window. Further, the world window and viewport do not have to have the same aspect ratio, although distortion results if their aspect ratios differ. As suggested in Figure 3.4, distortion occurs because the figure in the window must be stretched to fit into the viewport. We shall see later how to set up a viewport with an aspect ratio that always matches that of the screen window, even when the user resizes the window.

---

[2]   For the sake of brevity, we use *l* for *left*, *t* for *top*, etc. in mathematical formulas.

FIGURE 3.4 A picture mapped from a window to a viewport. Here some distortion is produced.

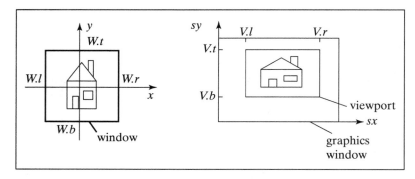

Given a description of the window and viewport, we derive a **mapping** or **transformation**, called the **window-to-viewport mapping.** This mapping is based on a formula that produces a point (sx, sy) in the screen window coordinates for any given point (x, y) in the world. We want the mapping to be "proportional," in the sense that if x is, say, 40% of the way over from the left edge of the window, then sx is 40% of the way over from the left edge of the viewport. Similarly, if y is some fraction f of the height of the window from the bottom, sy must be the *same* fraction f up from the bottom of the viewport.

Proportionality forces the mappings to have the *linear* form

$$sx = Ax + C,$$
$$sx = By + D,$$

(3.2)

for some constants $A, B, C,$ and D. The constants A and B scale the x and y coordinates, and C and D shift (or *translate*) them.

How can $A, B, C,$ and D be determined? Consider first the mapping for x. As shown in Figure 3.5, proportionality dictates that $sx - V.l$ be the same fraction of the total $(V.r - V.l)$ as $x - W.l$ is of the total $(W.r - W.l)$, so that

FIGURE 3.5 Proportionality in mapping x to sx.

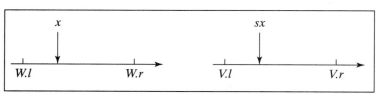

$$\frac{sx - V.l}{V.r - V.l} = \frac{x - W.l}{W.r - W.l},$$

or

$$sx = \frac{V.r - V.l}{W.r - W.l}x + \left(V.l - \frac{V.r - V.l}{W.r - W.l}W.l\right).$$

Now, identifying A as the part that multiplies x and C as the constant part, we obtain:

$$A = \frac{V.r - V.l}{W.r - W.l}$$

and

$$C = V.l - AW.l$$

Similarly, proportionality in y dictates that

$$\frac{sy - V.b}{V.t - V.b} = \frac{y - W.b}{W.t - W.b},$$

and writing sy as $By + D$ yields

$$B = \frac{V.t - V.b}{W.t - W.b}, D = V.b - BW.b.$$

Summarizing, we have, for the **window-to-viewport transformation**,

$$sx = Ax + C$$

and

$$sy = By + D, \tag{3.3}$$

with

$$A = \frac{V.r - V.l}{W.r - W.l}, C = V.l - AW.l$$

and

$$B = \frac{V.t - V.b}{W.t - W.b}, D = V.b - BW.b.$$

The mapping can be used with *any* point (x, y) inside or outside the window. Points inside the window map to points inside the viewport, and points outside the window map to points outside the viewport.

One should carefully check the following properties of this mapping using Equation 3.3:

a. if x is at the window's left edge $(x = W.l)$, then sx is at the viewport's left edge $(sx = V.l)$.
b. if x is at the window's right edge, then sx is at the viewport's right edge.
c. if x is a fraction f of the way across the window, then sx is a fraction f of the way across the viewport.
d. if x is outside the window to the left $(x < w.l)$, then sx is outside the viewport to the left $(sx < V.l)$, and analogously if x is outside to the right.

Also, one should check similar properties for the mapping from y to sy.

■ **EXAMPLE 3.2.1**

Consider the window and viewport of Figure 3.6. The window has $(W.l, W.r, W.b, W.t) = (0, 2.0, 0, 1.0)$, and the viewport has $(V.l, V.r, V.b, V.t) = (40, 400, 60, 300)$.

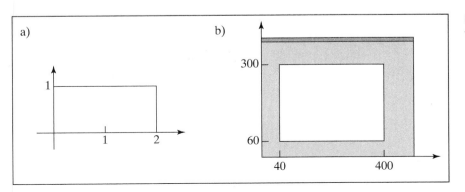

FIGURE 3.6 An example of a window and a viewport.

Using the formulas in Equation 3.3, we obtain

$$A = 180, C = 40, B = 240, \text{ and } D = 60.$$

Thus, for this example, the window-to-viewport mapping is

$$sx = 180x + 40;$$
$$sy = 240y + 60.$$

We check that this mapping properly maps various points of interest, such as the following:

• Each corner of the window is indeed mapped to the corresponding corner of the viewport. For example, $(2.0, 1.0)$ maps to $(400, 300)$.
• The center of the window, $(1.0, 0.5)$, maps to the center of the viewport, $(220, 180)$.

PRACTICE EXERCISE

3.2.1 Building the mapping

Find values of $A, B, C,$ and D for the case of a world window of $(-10.0, 10.0, -6.0, 6.0)$ and a viewport of $(0, 600, 0, 400)$.   ■

Doing It in OpenGL

OpenGL makes it very easy to use the window-to-viewport mapping, automatically passing each vertex it is given (via a `glVertex2*()` command) through a sequence of transformations that carry out the desired mapping. OpenGL also automatically clips off parts of objects lying outside the world window. All we need do is to set up the transformations properly, and OpenGL does the rest.

For 2D drawing, the world window is set by the function `gluOrtho2D()`, and the viewport is set by the function `glViewport()`. These functions have the prototypes

```
void gluOrtho2D(GLdouble left, GLdouble right, GLdouble bottom,
GLdouble top);
```

which sets the window to have a lower left corner of (`left`, `bottom`) and an upper right corner of (`right`, `top`), and

```
void glViewport(GLint x, GLint y, GLint width, GLint height);
```

which sets the viewport to have a lower left corner of (x, y) and an upper right corner of (x + `width`, y + `height`).

By default, the viewport is the entire screen window: If W and H are the width and height of the screen window, respectively, the default viewport has lower left corner at $(0, 0)$ and upper right corner at (`W`, `H`).

Because OpenGL uses matrices to set up all its transformations, `gluOrtho2D()`[3] must be preceded by two "setup" functions: `glMatrixMode(GL_PROJECTION)` and `glLoadIdentity()`. (We discuss what is going on behind the scenes here more fully in Chapter 5.)

Thus, to establish the window and viewport used in Example 3.2.1, we would use the following code:

```
glMatrixMode(GL_PROJECTION);
glLoadIdentity();
gluOrtho2D(0.0, 2.0, 0.0, 1.0);        // sets the window
glViewport(40, 60, 360, 240);          // sets the viewport
```

---

[3]   The root "ortho" appears because setting the window this way is actually setting up a so-called orthographic projection in 3D, as we shall see in Chapter 7.

Hereafter, every point (x, y) sent to OpenGL by using `glVertex2*(x, y)` undergoes the mapping of Equation 3.3, and edges are automatically clipped at the window boundary. (In Chapter 7, we see the details of how this is done in 3D; in that discussion, it also becomes clear how the 2D version is simply a special case of the 3D version.)

We will make programs more readable if we encapsulate the commands that set the window into a function `setWindow()` as shown in Figure 3.7. We also show `setViewport()`, which hides the OpenGL details of `glViewport(..)`. To make setViewport easier to use, its parameters are slightly rearranged to match those of `setWindow()`, so they are both in the order `left, right, bottom, top`.

```
//--------------- setWindow ---------------------
void setWindow(float left, float right, float bottom, float top)
{
      glMatrixMode(GL_PROJECTION);
      glLoadIdentity();
      gluOrtho2D(left, right, bottom, top);
}
//--------------- setViewport ------------------
void setViewport(int left, int right, int bottom, int top)
{
      glViewport(left, bottom, right - left, top - bottom);
}
```

FIGURE 3.7 Handy functions to set the window and viewport.

Note that for convenience we use simply the type `float` for the parameters to `setWindow()`. The parameters `left`, `right`, etc. are automatically cast to type GLdouble when they are passed to `gluOrtho2D()`, as specified by this function's prototype. Similarly we use the type `int` for the parameters to `setViewport()`, knowing the arguments to `glViewport()` will be properly cast.

It is worthwhile to look back and see what we used for a window and viewport in the early OpenGL programs given in Chapter 2. In Figures 2.10 and 2.17, the programs used the following instructions:

1. in `main()`:
```
glutInitWindowSize(640,480);    // set screen window size
```
This instruction sets the size of the screen window to 640 by 480. The default viewport was used, since no `glViewport()` command was issued; the default viewport is the entire screen window.

2. in `myInit()`:
```
glMatrixMode(GL_PROJECTION);
glLoadIdentity();
gluOrtho2D(0.0, 640.0, 0.0, 480.0);
```
This set of instructions set the world window to the aligned rectangle with corners $(0, 0)$ and $(640.0, 480.0)$, just matching the size of the viewport, so the underlying window-to-viewport mapping did not alter anything. This was a reasonable first choice for getting started.

■ **EXAMPLE 3.2.2 Plotting the sinc function, revisited**

Putting the foregoing ingredients together, we can see what it takes to plot the sinc() function shape of Figure 3.1. With OpenGL, it is just a matter of defining the window and viewport. Figure 3.8 shows the required code, assuming that we want to plot the function from closely spaced x-values between −4.0 and 4.0 into a viewport of width 640 and height 480. (The window is set to be a little wider than the range of the plot, to leave some cosmetic space around the plot.)

```
void myDisplay(void) // plot the sinc function, using world coordinates
{
   setWindow(-5.0, 5.0, -0.3, 1.0);   // set the window
   setViewport(0, 640, 0, 480);    // set the viewport
   glBegin(GL_LINE_STRIP);
   for(GLfloat x = -4.0; x < 4.0; x += 0.1)      // draw the plot
      glVertex2f(x, sin(3.14159 * x) / (3.14159 * x));
   glEnd();
   glFlush();
}
```

FIGURE 3.8 Plotting the sinc function.

FIGURE 3.9 The dinosaur inside its world window.

FIGURE 3.10 Tiling the display with copies of the dinosaur.

∎ EXAMPLE 3.2.3 Drawing polylines from a file

In Chapter 2, we drew the dinosaur shown in Figure 3.9 using the routine `draw-PolylineFile("dino.dat")` of Figure 2.22. The polyline data for the figure was stored in a file called `"dino.dat"`." The world window and viewport had not yet been introduced, so we just took certain things on faith or by default and, luckily, still got a picture of the dinosaur.

Now we can see why that worked: The world window we used happened to enclose the data for the dinosaur. (See Case Study 2.4.) All of the polylines in `dino.dat` lay inside a rectangle with corners $(0, 0)$ and $(640, 480)$, so none were clipped with that choice of a window.

Armed with tools for setting the window and viewport, we can take more control of the situation. The next two examples are illustrative.

∎ EXAMPLE 3.2.4 Tiling the screen window with the dinosaur motif

To add some interest to the way the screen looks, we can draw a number of copies of the dinosaur in some pattern. Laying lots of copies of the same thing side by side to cover the entire screen window is called **tiling** the window. The picture that is copied at different positions is often called a **motif**. Tiling a screen window is easily achieved by using a different viewport for each instance of the motif. Figure 3.10a shows a tiling involving 25 copies of the motif. This tiling was generated with the following code:

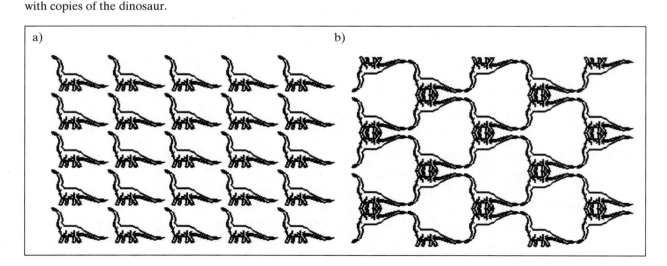

```
setWindow(0, 640.0, 0, 440.0);           // set a fixed window
for(int i=0; i < 5; i++)                 // for each column
   for(int j=0; j < 5; j++)              // for each row
   {
     glViewport(i * 64, j * 44, 64, 44); // set the next viewport
     drawPolylineFile("dino.dat");       // draw it again
   }
```

(It is easier to use glViewport() here than setViewport(). What would the arguments to setViewport() be if we chose to use it instead?) Note that each copy is drawn in a viewport of size 64 by 44 pixels whose aspect ratio (64/44) matches that of the world window. Thus, each dinosaur is drawn without distortion.

Figure 3.10(b) shows another tiling, but here alternate motifs are flipped upside down to produce an intriguing effect. This was done by flipping the window upside down every other iteration: interchanging the top and bottom values in setWindow().[4] (Check to make sure that this flip of the window properly affects B and D in the window-to-viewport transformation of Equation 3.3, which is our means of flipping the picture in the viewport.) Then the code for the double loop was changed to the following:

```
for(int i = 0; i < 5; i++)
   for(int j = 0; j < 5; j++)
   {
     if((i+j) % 2 == 0)                         // if (i+j) is even
       setWindow(0.0, 640.0, 0.0, 440.0); // right-side-up window
     else
       setWindow(0.0, 640.0, 440.0, 0.0); // upside-down window
     glViewport(i * 64, j * 44, 64, 44);  // set the next viewport
     drawPolylineFile("dino.dat");        // draw it again
   }
```

■ **EXAMPLE 3.2.5 Clipping parts of a figure**

A picture can also be *clipped*, by proper setting of the window. OpenGL automatically clips off parts of objects that lie outside the world window. The leftmost picture of Figure 3.11 consists of a collection of hexagons of different sizes, each rotated slightly relative to its neighbor. Suppose the hexagons are drawn by exe-

FIGURE 3.11 Using the window to clip parts of a figure.

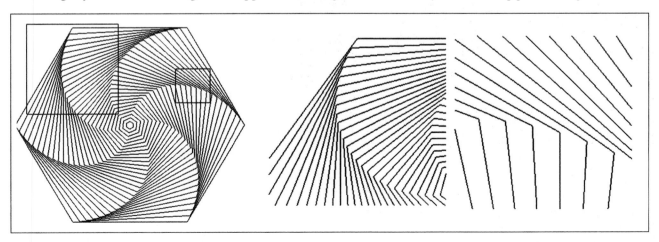

---

[4] It might seem easier to invert the viewport, but OpenGL does not permit a viewport to have a negative height.

cuting some function `hexSwirl()`. (We shall see how to write `hexSwirl()` in Section 3.6.) Shown overlapping the hexagons are two boxes that indicate different choices of a window. The middle and rightmost pictures of Figure 3.11 show what is drawn if these boxes are used for the world windows. It is important to keep in mind that the *same* entire object is drawn in each case, using the following code:

```
setWindow(...); // the window is changed for each picture
setViewport(...); // use the same viewport for each picture
hexSwirl(); // the same function is called
```

What is *displayed*, on the other hand, depends on the setting of the window.

Zooming and Roaming

The example in Figure 3.11 points out how changing the window can produce useful effects. Making the window smaller is much like **zooming in** on the object with a camera. Whatever is in the window must be stretched to fit into the fixed viewport, so when the window is made smaller, the portion inside becomes more enlarged. Similarly making the window larger is equivalent to **zooming out** from the object. (Visualize how the dinosaur would appear if the window were enlarged to twice the size it has in Figure 3.9.) A camera can also **roam** (sometimes called "pan") around a scene, taking in different parts of it at different times. This is easily accomplished by shifting the window to a new position.

■ **EXAMPLE 3.2.6　Zooming in on a figure in an animation**

Consider putting together an animated sequence in which the camera zooms in on some portion of the hexagons in Figure 3.11. To accomplish this task, we make a series of pictures, often called **frames**, using a slightly smaller window for each one. When the frames are displayed in rapid succession, the visual effect is of the camera zooming in on the object.

Figure 3.12 shows a few of the windows used; they are concentric and have a fixed aspect ratio, but their size diminishes for each successive frame. Visualize what is drawn in the viewport for each of these windows.

FIGURE 3.12 Zooming in on the swirl of hexagons.

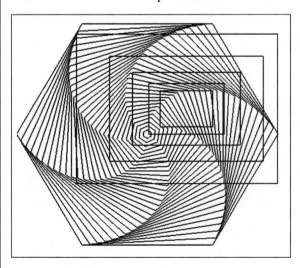

A skeleton of the code to achieve this zooming effect is shown in Figure 3.13. For each new frame, the screen is cleared, the window is made smaller (about a fixed center and with a fixed aspect ratio), and the figure within the window is drawn in a fixed viewport.

```
float cx = 0.3, cy = 0.2; //center of the window
float H, W = 1.2, aspect = 0.7; // window properties
set the viewport
for(int frame = 0; frame < NumFrames; frame++) // for each frame
{
        clear the screen        // erase the previous figure
        W *= 0.7;               // reduce the window width
        H = W * aspect;         // maintain the same aspect ratio
        setWindow(cx - W, cx + W, cy - H, cy + H); //set the next window
        hexSwirl();             // draw the object
}
```

FIGURE 3.13 Making an animation.

Achieving a Smooth Animation

The previous approach is not completely satisfying, because of the time it takes to draw each new figure. What the user sees is a repetitive cycle of the following two actions:

A. Instantaneous erasure of the current figure.
B. A (possibly) slow redrawing of the new figure.

The problem is that the user sees the line-by-line creation of the new frame, which can be distracting. What the user would like to see is the following repetitive cycle:

A. A steady display of the current figure.
B. Instantaneous replacement of the current figure by the *finished* new figure.

The trick is to draw the new figure "somewhere else" while the user stares at the current figure and then to move the completed new figure instantaneously onto the user's display. OpenGL offers **double buffering** to accomplish this task. Memory is set aside for an extra screen window that is not visible on the actual display, and all drawing is done to that window, or buffer. (The use of such "off-screen memory" is discussed fully in Chapter 10.) The command glutSwapBuffers() then causes the image in the buffer to be transferred onto the screen window and become visible to the user.

To make OpenGL reserve a separate buffer for this use, we employ the command GLUT_DOUBLE rather than GLUT_SINGLE in the routine used in main() to initialize the display mode:

```
glutInitDisplayMode(GLUT_DOUBLE | GLUT_RGB);
```

The command glutSwapBuffers() would be placed directly after hexSwirl() in the code of Figure 3.13. Then, even if it takes a substantial period for the polyline to be drawn, at least the image will change abruptly from one figure to the next in the animation, producing a much smoother and visually comfortable effect.

PRACTICE EXERCISE

3.2.2 Whirling swirls

As another example of clipping and tiling, Figure 3.14(a) shows the swirl of hexagons of Figure 3.12 with a particular window defined. The window is kept fixed in this example, but the viewport varies with each drawing. Figure 3.14(b) shows a number of copies of this figure, laid side by side to tile the display. Try to pick out the individual swirls. (Some of the swirls have been flipped. Which ones?) The result is dazzling to the eye, in part due to the eye's tendency to synthesize many small elements into an overall pattern.

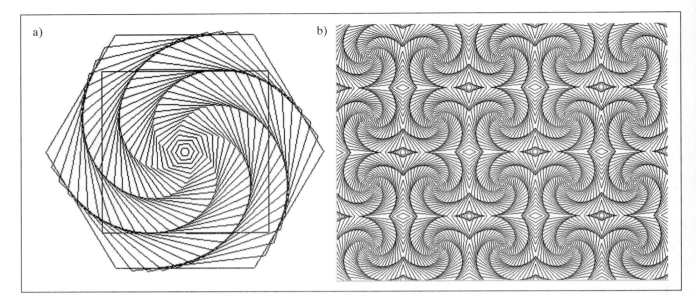

a)   b)

FIGURE 3.14 (a) Whirling hexagons in a fixed window. (b) A tiling formed using many viewports.

Except for the flipping, the code shown next creates the pattern of Figure 3.14(b). The function `myDisplay()` sets the window once and then draws the clipped swirl again and again in different viewports. The code is as follow:

```
void myDisplay(void)
{
    clear the screen
    setWindow(-0.6, 0.6, -0.6, 0.6); // the portion of the
                                          swirl to draw
    for(int i = 0; i < 5; i++)      // make a pattern of 5-by-4
                                          copies
        for(int j = 0; j < 4; j++)
        {
            int L = 80; // the amount to shift each viewport
            geViewport(i * L, L + i * L, L, L);
            hexSwirl();
        }
}
```

Type this code into an OpenGL environment, and experiment with the figures it draws. Taking a cue from a previous example, determine how to flip alternating figures upside down.   ■

3.2.2 Setting the Window and Viewport Automatically

Let us see how to choose the window and viewport in order to produce appropriate pictures of a scene. In some cases, the programmer (or possibly the user at run time) can input the window and viewport specifications to achieve a certain effect; in other cases, one or both of these specifications are set up automatically, according to some requirement for the picture. In this section, we discuss a few alternative selections.

Setting of the Window

Often, the programmer does not know where the object of interest lies, or how big it is, in world coordinates. Like the dinosaur earlier, the object might be stored in a file, or it might be generated procedurally by some algorithm whose details are not known. In either case, it is convenient to let the application determine a good window to use.

The usual approach is to find a window that includes the entire object. To achieve this, the object's extent must be found. The **extent** (or **bounding box**) of an object is the aligned rectangle that just covers the object. Figure 3.15 shows a picture made up of several line segments. The extent of the figure, shown as a dashed line, is (*left*, *right*, *bottom*, *top*) = (0.36, 3.44, −0.51, 1.75).

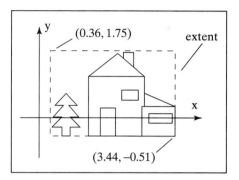

FIGURE 3.15 Using the extent as the window.

How can the extent be computed for a given object? If all the endpoints of the object's lines are stored in an array pt[i], for $i = 0, 2, \ldots, n - 1$, the extent can be computed by finding the extreme values of the x- and y-coordinates in this array. For instance, the left side of the extent is the smallest of the values pt[i].x. Once the extent is known, the window can be made identical to it.

If, on the other hand, an object is procedurally defined, there may be no way to determine its extent ahead of time. In such a case, for finding the routine the extend may have to be run twice, a different way each time:

Pass 1. Execute the drawing routine, but do no actual drawing; just compute the extent. Then set the window.
Pass 2. Execute the drawing routine again. Do the actual drawing.

Automatic Setting of the Viewport to Preserve the Aspect Ratio

Suppose you want to draw the largest undistorted version of a figure that will fit in the screen window. To do that, you need to specify a viewport that has the same aspect ratio as the world window. A common wish is to find the *largest* such viewport that will fit inside the screen window on the display.

Suppose the aspect ratio of the world window is known to be R and the screen window has width W and height H. There are two distinct situations: The world window may have a larger aspect ratio than the screen window ($R > W/H$), or it may have a smaller aspect ratio ($R < W/H$). The two situations are shown in Figure 3.16. We consider each in turn.

FIGURE 3.16 Possible aspect ratios for the world and screen windows.

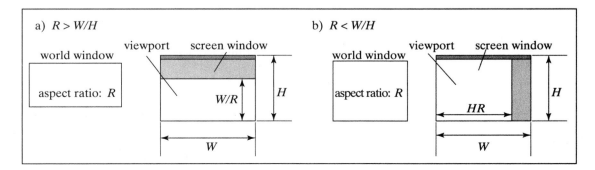

Case (a): $R > W/H$. Here the world window is short and stout relative to the screen window, so the viewport with a matching aspect ratio R will extend fully across the screen window, but will leave some unused space above or below. At its largest, therefore, the viewport will have width W and height W/R, so it is set with the following command (check that this viewport does indeed have aspect ratio R):

```
setViewport(0, W, 0, W/R);
```

Case (b): $R < W/H$. Here the world window is tall and narrow relative to the screen window, so the viewport of matching aspect ratio R will reach from the top to the bottom of the screen window, but will leave some unused space to the left or right. At its largest, the viewport will have height H, but width HR, so it is set with the command

```
setViewport(0, H * R, 0, H);
```

■ EXAMPLE 3.2.7 A tall window

Suppose the window has aspect ratio $R = 1.6$ and the screen window has $H = 200$ and $W = 360$, and hence, $W/H = 1.8$. Therefore, Case (b) applies, and the viewport is set to have a height of 200 pixels and a width of 320 pixels.

■ EXAMPLE 3.2.8 A short window

Suppose $R = 2$ and the screen window is the same as in the previous example. Then Case (a) applies, and the viewport is set to have a height of 180 pixels and a width of 360 pixels.

Resizing the Screen Window; the Resize Event

In a windows-based system the user can resize the screen window at run time, typically by dragging one of its corners with the mouse. This action generates a **resize** event that the system can respond to. A function in the OpenGL utility toolkit, `glutReshapeFunc()`, specifies a function to be called whenever this event occurs:

```
glutReshapeFunc(myReshape); // specifies the function called on a
                            // resize event
```

(This statement appears in `main()`, along with the other calls that specify callback functions.) The registered function is also called when the window is first opened and must have the prototype

```
void myReshape(GLsizei W, GLsizei H);
```

When this function is executed, the system automatically passes it the new width and height of the screen window, which the function can then use in its calculations. (`GLsizei` is a 32-bit integer; see Figure 2.7.)

What should `myReshape()` do? If the user makes the screen window bigger, the previous viewport could still be used (why?), but the user might instead desire to increase the viewport to take advantage of the larger window size. If the user makes the screen window smaller, crossing any of the boundaries of the viewport, he or she will almost certainly want to compute a new viewport.

Making a Matched Viewport

One common approach is to find a new viewport that both fits into the new screen window and has the same aspect ratio as the world window. Matching the aspect ratios of the viewport and world window in this way will prevent distortion in the new picture. Figure 3.17 shows a version of `myReshape()` that does the desired matching: It finds the largest matching viewport (i.e., one that matches the aspect ratio R

```
void myReshape(GLsizei W, GLsizei H)
{
        if(R > W/H) // use (global) window aspect ratio
              setViewport(0, W, 0, W/R);
        else
              setViewport(0, H * R, 0, H);
}
```

FIGURE 3.17 Using a reshape function to set the largest matching viewport upon a resize event.

of the window) that will fit into the new screen window. The routine obtains the width and height of the new screen window through its arguments. The code is a simple embodiment of the result in Figure 3.16.

PRACTICE EXERCISES

3.2.3 Find the bounding box for a polyline

Write a routine that computes the extent of the polyline stored in the array of points pt[i], for $i = 0, 2, \ldots, n - 1$.

3.2.4 Matching the viewport

Find the matching viewport for a window with aspect ratio 0.75 when the screen window has width 640 and height 480.

3.2.5 Centering the viewport (Don't skip this one!)

Adjust the myReshape() routine of Figure 3.17 so that the viewport, rather than lying in the lower left corner of the display, is centered both vertically and horizontally in the screen window.

3.2.6 How to squash a house

Choose a window and a viewport so that a square is squashed to half its proper height. What are the coefficients A, B, C, and D in this case?

3.2.7 Calculation of the mapping

Find the coefficients A, B, C, and D of the window-to-viewport mapping for a window given by $(-600, 235, -500, 125)$ and a viewport given by $(20, 140, 30, 260)$. Does distortion occur for figures drawn in the world? Change the right border of the viewport so that distortion will not occur. ■

3.3 CLIPPING LINES

Clipping is a fundamental task in graphics, needed to keep those parts of an object that lie outside a given region from being drawn. A large number of clipping algorithms have been developed. In an OpenGL environment, each object is automatically clipped to the world window with the use of a particular algorithm (which we examine in detail in Chapter 7 for both 2D and 3D objects).

Because OpenGL does the clipping for you, you may be tempted to skip a study of the clipping process. But the ideas that are used to develop a clipper are basic and arise in diverse situations; we shall examine a variety of approaches to clipping in later chapters. (Also, it is useful to know how to pull together a clipper as needed when a tool like OpenGL is not being used.)

In this section, we develop an algorithm that clips off outlying parts of each line segment presented to it. This algorithm can be incorporated into a line-drawing routine if we do not have the benefit of clipping performed by OpenGL. In Case Study 3.3, we develop an implementation of a class of algorithms that draw clipped lines.

3.3.1 Clipping a Line

In this section, we describe a classic line-clipping algorithm, the Cohen–Sutherland clipper, that computes which part (if any) of a line segment with endpoints `p1` and `p2` lies inside the world window and then reports back the endpoints of that part.

We shall develop a routine `clipSegment(p1, p2, window)` that takes two 2D points and an aligned rectangle and clips the line segment defined by the endpoints `p1` and `p2` to the window boundaries. If any portion of the line remains within the window, the new endpoints are placed in `p1` and `p2`, and a value of 1 is returned (indicating that some part of the segment is visible). If the line is completely clipped out, a value of 0 is returned. (No part is visible.)

Figure 3.18 shows a typical situation covering some of the many possible actions of a clipper. The function `clipSegment( )` does one of four things to each line segment:

FIGURE 3.18 Clipping lines at window boundaries.

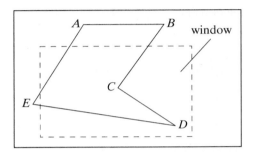

- If the entire line lies within the window (e.g., like segment CD), the function returns a value of 1.
- If the entire line lies outside the window (e.g., like segment AB), the function returns a value of 0.
- If one endpoint is inside the window and one is outside (e.g., like segment ED), the function clips the portion of the segment that lies outside the window and returns a value of 1.
- If both endpoints are outside the window, but a portion of the segment passes through it (e.g., like segment AE), the function clips both ends and returns a value of 1.

There are many possible arrangements of a segment with respect to the window. The segment can lie to the left, to the right, above, or below the window; it can cut through any one (or two) window edges, and so on. We therefore need an organized and efficient approach that identifies the prevailing situation and computes new endpoints for the clipped segment. Efficiency is important because a typical picture contains thousands of line segments, each of which must be clipped against the window. The Cohen–Sutherland algorithm applies a rapid divide-and-conquer approach to the problem. Other clipping methods are discussed beginning in Chapter 4.

3.3.2 The Cohen–Sutherland Clipping Algorithm

The Cohen–Sutherland algorithm quickly detects and dispenses with two common cases, called "trivial accept" and "trivial reject." As shown in Figure 3.19, both endpoints of the segment AB lie within window W, and so the whole segment AB must lie inside W. Therefore, AB can be *trivially accepted*: It needs no clipping. This situ-

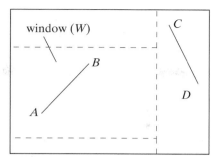

FIGURE 3.19 Trivial acceptance or rejection of a line segment.

ation occurs frequently when a large window is used that encompasses most of the line segments. On the other hand, both endpoints *C* and *D* lie entirely *to one side* of *W*, and so segment *CD* must lie entirely outside *W*. Accordingly, *CD* is *trivially rejected*, and nothing is drawn. This situation arises frequently when a small window is used with a dense picture that has many segments outside the window.

Testing for a Trivial Accept or Trivial Reject

We want a fast way to detect whether a line segment can be trivially accepted or rejected. To facilitate this task, an "inside-outside code word" is computed for each endpoint of the segment. Figure 3.20 shows how this computation is done. Point *P* is to the left and above the window *W*. These two facts are recorded in a code word for *P*: A T (for TRUE) is seen in the field for "is to the left of" and "is above." An F (for FALSE) is seen in the other two fields, "is to the right of" and " is below."

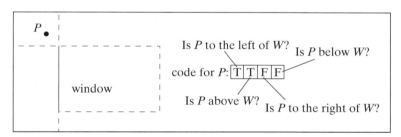

FIGURE 3.20 Encoding how point *P* is disposed with respect to the window.

For example, if *P* is inside the window, its code is FFFF; if *P* is below, but neither to the left nor right of the window, its code is FFFT. Figure 3.21 shows the nine different regions that are possible, each with its code.

TTFF	FTFF	FTTF
TFFF	FFFF	FFTF
	window	
TFFT	FFFT	FFTT

FIGURE 3.21 Inside–outside codes for a point.

We form a code word for each of the endpoints of the line segment being tested. The conditions of trivial accept and reject are easily related to these code words:

- *Trivial accept:* Both code words are FFFF;
- *Trivial reject:* The code words have a T in the *same* position; both points are to the left of the window, or both are above, etc.

The actual formation of the code words and tests can be implemented efficiently using the bit manipulation capabilities of C or C++, as we describe in Case Study 3.3.

Chopping When There Is Neither Trivial Accept nor Trivial Reject

The Cohen–Sutherland algorithm uses a divide-and-conquer strategy. If the segment can be neither trivially accepted nor rejected, it is broken into two parts at one of the window boundaries. One part lies outside the window and is discarded. The other part is potentially visible, so the entire process is repeated for this segment against another of the four window boundaries. The entire procedure gives rise to the following strategy:

```
do{
        form the code words for p1 and p2
        if (trivial accept) return 1;
        if (trivial reject) return 0;
        chop the line at the "next" window border; discard the "outside" part;
    } while(1);
```

The algorithm terminates after at most four passes through the loop, since, at each iteration, we retain only the portion of the segment that has "survived" testing against previous window boundaries, and there are only four such boundaries. Thus, after at most four iterations, trivial acceptance or rejection is assured.

How is the chopping at each boundary done? Figure 3.22 shows an example involving the right edge of the window.

FIGURE 3.22 Clipping a segment against an edge.

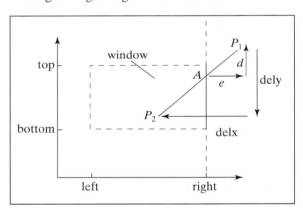

The location of point A must be computed. Its x-coordinate is clearly `W.right`, the position of the right edge of the window. Its y-coordinate requires adjusting `p1.y` by the amount d shown in the figure. But, by similar triangles,

$$\frac{d}{dely} = \frac{e}{delx},$$

where e is `p1.x - W.right` and the statements

```
delx = p2.x - p1.x;                                              (3.4)
dely = p2.y - p1.y;
```

give the differences between the coordinates of the two endpoints. Thus, d is easily determined, and the new value of `p1.y` is found by adding an increment to the old one:

```
p1.y += (W.right - p1.x) * dely / delx                           (3.5)
```

Similar reasoning is used for clipping against the other three edges of the window.

In some of the calculations the term `dely/delx` occurs, and in others it is `delx/dely`. One must always be concerned about dividing by zero, and in fact, `delx` is zero for a vertical line and `dely` is zero for a horizontal line. But as discussed in the exercises, the perilous lines of code are never executed when a denominator is zero, so division by zero will not occur.

The foregoing ideas are collected in the routine `clipSegment( )` shown in Figure 3.23. The endpoints of the segment are passed by reference, since changes made to the endpoints by `clipSegment()` must be visible in the calling routine. (The type `Point2` holds a 2D point, and the type `RealRect` holds an aligned rectangle. Both types are described fully in Section 3.4.)

```
int clipSegment(Point2& p1, Point2& p2, RealRect W)
{
     do{
          if(trivial accept) return 1; // some portion survives
          if(trivial reject) return 0; // no portion survives

          if(p1 is outside)
          {
               if(p1 is to the left)   chop against the left edge
               else if(p1 is to the right) chop against the right edge
               else if(p1 is below)  chop against the bottom edge
               else if(p1 is above)  chop against the top edge
          }
          else      // p2 is outside
          {
               if(p2 is to the left) chop against the left edge
                    else if(p2 is to the right) chop against the right edge
               else if(p2 is below)  chop against the bottom edge
               else if(p2 is above) chop against the top edge
          }
     }while(1);
}
```

FIGURE 3.23 The Cohen–Sutherland line clipper (pseudocode).

Each time the `do` loop is executed, the code for each endpoint is recomputed and tested. When trivial acceptance and trivial rejection fail, the algorithm tests whether `p1` is outside the window, and if it is, that end of the segment is clipped to a window boundary. If `p1` is inside the window, then `p2` must be outside (why?), so `p2` is clipped to a window boundary.

This version of the algorithm clips in the order left, then right, then bottom, and then top. The choice of order is immaterial if segments are equally likely to lie anywhere in the world. A situation that requires all four clips is shown in Figure 3.24. The

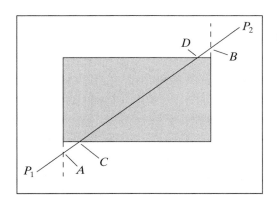

FIGURE 3.24 A segment that requires four clips.

first clip changes p1 to *A* ; the second alters p2 to *B*; the third finds p1 still outside and below and so changes *A* to *C* ; and the last changes p2 to *D*. For any choice of ordering for the chopping tests, there will always be a situation in which all four clips are necessary.

Clipping is a fundamental operation that has received a lot of attention over the years. Accordingly, several other approaches have been developed. We examine some of them in the case studies at the end of the chapter and in Chapter 4.

PRACTICE EXERCISE

3.3.1 Hand simulation of clipSegment()

Go through the clipping routine by hand for the case of a window given by (*left*, *right*, *bottom*, *top*) = (30, 220, 50, 240) and the following line segments:

1. *p*1 = (40, 140), *p*2 = (100, 200);   2. *p*1 = (10, 270), *p*2 = (300, 0);
3. *p*1 = (20, 10), *p*2 = (20, 200);   4. *p*1 = (0, 0), *p*2 = (250, 250);

In each case, determine the endpoints of the clipped segment, and for a visual check, sketch the situation on graph paper.   ■

3.4 DEVELOPING THE CANVAS CLASS

One must not always think that feeling is everything. Art is nothing without form.
Gustave Flaubert

There is significant freedom in working in world coordinates and in having primitives be clipped and properly mapped from the window to the viewport. But this freedom must be managed properly. There are so many interacting ingredients (points, rectangles, mappings, etc.) in the "soup," that we should encapsulate them and restrict how the application programmer accesses them, to avoid subtle bugs. We should also ensure that the various ingredients are properly initialized.

It is natural to use classes and take advantage of the opportunity they offer for hiding data. So we develop a class called *Canvas* that provides a handy drawing canvas on which to draw the lines, polygons, etc. of interest. This class provides simple methods for creating the desired screen window and establishing a world window and viewport, and it ensures that the window-to-viewport mapping is well defined. It also offers the routines moveTo() and lineTo() that many programmers find congenial, as well as the useful "turtle graphics" routines we develop later in the chapter.

There are many ways to define the *Canvas* class; the choice presented here should be considered only as a starting point for your own version. We implement the class in this section using OpenGL, exploiting all of the operations OpenGL does automatically (such as clipping). But in Case Study 3.4, we describe an entirely different implementation (based on Turbo C++ in a DOS environment), for which we have to supply all of the tools. In particular, an implementation of the Cohen–Sutherland clipper is used.

3.4.1 Some Useful Supporting Classes

It will be convenient to have some common data types available for use with *Canvas* and other classes. We define them here as classes[5] and show simple constructors and other functions for handling objects of each type. Some of the classes also have a

---

[5]   Students preferring to write in C can define similar types using the struct construction.

draw function to make it easy to draw instances of the class. Other functions (methods) will be added later as the need arises. Some of the methods are implemented directly in the class definitions; the implementation of others is requested in the exercises, and only the declaration of the method is given.

class Point2: A Point Having Real Coordinates

The first supporting class embodies a single point expressed with floating-point coordinates. It is shown with two constructors, a function set() to set the coordinate values and two functions to retrieve the individual coordinate values. The code is as follows:

```
class Point2
{
  public:
    Point2() {x = y = 0.0f;}      // constructor1
    Point2(float xx, float yy) {x = xx; y = yy;} // constructor2
    void set(float xx, float yy) {x = xx; y = yy;}
    float getX() {return x;}
    float getY() {return y;}
    void draw(void) { glBegin(GL_POINTS); // draw this point
                      glVertex2f((GLfloat)x, (GLfloat)y);
                      glEnd();}
  private:
    float x, y;
};
```

Note that values of x and y are cast to the type GLfloat when glVertex2f() is called. This is most likely unnecessary since the type GLfloat is defined on most systems as float anyway.

class IntRect: An Aligned Rectangle with Integer Coordinates

To describe a viewport, we need an aligned rectangle having integer coordinates. The class IntRect provides this functionality in the following code:

```
class IntRect
{
  public:
    IntRect() {l = 0; r = 100; b = 0; t = 100;}// constructors
    IntRect(int left, int right, int bottom, int top)
        {l = left; r = right; b = bottom; t = top;}
    void set(int left, int right, int bottom, int top)
        {l = left; r = right; b = bottom; t = top;}
    void draw(void); // draw this rectangle using OpenGL
  private:
    int l, r, b, t;
};
```

class RealRect: An Aligned Rectangle with Real Coordinates

A world window requires the use of an aligned rectangle having real values for its boundary position. (This class is so similar to IntRect that some programmers would use templates to define a class that could hold either integer or real coordinates.) The code is

```
class RealRect
{
  same as intRect except use float instead of int
};
```

102   **Chapter 3** ■ More Drawing Tools

PRACTICE EXERCISE

3.4.1 Implementing the classes

Flesh out the preceding classes by adding other functions you think would be useful
and by implementing the functions, such as `draw()` for `intRect`, that have previously been declared.   ■

3.4.2 Declaration of Class `Canvas`

We declare the interface for *Canvas* in `Canvas.h` as shown in Figure 3.25. The data
members of `Canvas.h` include the current position, a window, a viewport, and the
window-to-viewport mapping.

FIGURE 3.25 The header file
`Canvas.h`.

```
class Canvas {
 public:
   Canvas(int width, int height, char* windowTitle); // constructor
   void setWindow(float l, float r, float b, float t);
   void setViewport(int l, int r, int b, int t);
   IntRect getViewport(void);  // divulge the viewport data
   RealRect getWindow(void); // divulge the window data
   float getWindowAspectRatio(void);
   void clearScreen();
   void setBackgroundColor(float r, float g, float b);
   void setColor(float r, float g, float b);
   void lineTo(float x, float y);
   void lineTo(Point2 p);
   void moveTo(float x, float y);
   void moveTo(Point2 p);
   others later
 private:
   Point2 CP;          // current position in the world
   IntRect viewport; // the current window
   RealRect window;   // the current viewport
   others later
};
```

The *Canvas* constructor takes the width and height of the screen window, along
with the title string for the window, as arguments and creates the window desired,
performing all of the appropriate initializations. *Canvas* also includes functions to set
and return the dimensions of the window and the viewport, and to control the drawing and background color. (There is no explicit mention of data for the window-to-
viewport mapping in this version, as this mapping is managed "silently" by OpenGL.
In Case Study 3.4, we add members to hold the mapping for an environment that requires it.) Other functions shown are versions of `lineTo()` and `moveTo()` that do
the actual drawing (in world coordinates, of course). We add "relative drawing tools"
in the next section.

Figure 3.26 shows how the *Canvas* class might typically be used in an application.
A single global object `cvs` is created, which initializes and opens the desired screen
window. The object is made global so that callback functions such as `display()`
can "see" it. (We cannot pass `cvs` as a parameter to such functions, as their prototypes
are fixed by the rules of the OpenGL Utility Toolkit.) The `display()` function here
sets the window and viewport and then draws a line, using *Canvas* member functions.
Then a rectangle is created and drawn using its own member function.

```
Canvas cvs(640, 480, "try out Canvas");    // global canvas object

//<<<<<<<<<<<<<<<<<<<<<<<<<<< display >>>>>>>>>>>>>>>>>>>>>>
void display(void)
{
  cvs.clearScreen();  // clear screen
  cvs.setWindow(-10.0, 10.0, -10.0, 10.0);
  cvs.setViewport(10, 460, 10, 460);
  cvs.moveTo(0, -10.0);  // draw a line
  cvs.lineTo(0, 10.0);
  RealRect box( -2.0, 2.0, -1.0, 1.0); // construct a box
  box.draw(); // draw the box
  . . .
}
//<<<<<<<<<<<<<<<<<<<<< main >>>>>>>>>>>>>>>>>>>>>>>>>>>>>>>>>
void main(void)
{
  // the window is opened in the Canvas constructor
  cvs.setBackgroundColor(1.0, 1.0, 1.0); // background is white
  cvs.setColor(0.0, 0.0, 0.0);  // set drawing color
  glutDisplayFunc(display);
  glutMainLoop();
}
```

FIGURE 3.26 Typical usage of the *Canvas* class.

The main() routine does no initialization: This has all been done in the *Canvas* constructor. The routine main() simply sets the drawing and background colors, registers the function display(), and enters the main event loop. (Could these OpenGL-specific functions also be "buried" in *Canvas* member functions?)

3.4.3 Implementation of Class Canvas

We next show some details of an implementation of the class Canvas when OpenGL is available. (Case Study 3.4 discusses an alternative implementation.) The constructor, shown in Figure 3.27, passes the desired width and height (in pixels) to glut-InitWindowSize() and the desired title string to glutCreateWindow(). Some fussing must be done to pass glutInit() the arguments it needs, even though no use is made of them here. (Normally, main() passes glutInit() the command-line

FIGURE 3.27 The constructor for the OpenGL version of *Canvas*.

```
//<<<<<<<<<<<<<<<<<<<<< Canvas constructor >>>>>>>>>>>>>>>>
Canvas:: Canvas(int width, int height, char* windowTitle)
{
  char* argv[1];    // dummy argument list for glutInit()
  char dummyString[8];
  argv[0] = dummyString; // hook up the pointer
  int argc = 1;    // to satisfy glutInit()

  glutInit(&argc, argv);
  glutInitDisplayMode(GLUT_SINGLE | GLUT_RGB);
  glutInitWindowSize(width, height);
  glutInitWindowPosition(20, 20);
  glutCreateWindow(windowTitle); // open the screen window
  setWindow(0, (float)width, 0, (float)height); //default world window
  setViewport(0, width, 0, height); // default viewport
  CP.set(0.0f, 0.0f);   // initialize the CP to (0, 0)
}
```

arguments, as we saw earlier. This cannot be done here, since we use a global Canvas object, `cvs`, which is constructed before `main()` is called.)

Figure 3.28 shows the implementation of some of the remaining *Canvas* member functions. (Others are requested in the exercises.) The function `moveTo()` simply updates the current position; `lineTo()` sends the CP as the first vertex and the new point (x, y) as the second vertex. Note that we do not need to use the window-to-viewport mapping explicitly here, since OpenGL automatically applies it. The function `setWindow()` passes its arguments to `gluOrtho2D()`—after properly casting their types—and loads them into *Canvas* `window`.

FIGURE 3.28 Implementation of some *Canvas* member functions.

```
//<<<<<<<<<<<<<<<<<<<<<<< moveTo >>>>>>>>>>>>>>>>>>>>>>>>
void Canvas:: moveTo(float x, float y)
{
  CP.set(x, y);
}
//<<<<<<<<<<<<<<<<<<<<<<< lineTo >>>>>>>>>>>>>>>>>>>>>>>>
void Canvas:: lineTo (float x, float y)
{
  glBegin (GL_LINES);
    glVertex2f ((GLfloat) CP.x, (GLfloat) CP.y);
    glVertex2f ((GLfloat) x, (GLfloat) y);      // draw the line
  glEnd();
  CP.set (x, y);      // update the CP
  glFlush();
}
//<<<<<<<<<<<<<<<<<<<<<<< set Window >>>>>>>>>>>>>>>>>>>>>>>>
void Canvas:: setWindow (float l, float r, float b, float t)
{
  glMatrixMode (GL_PROJECTION);
  glLoadIdentity();
  gluOrtho2D ((GLdouble)l, (GLdouble)r, (GLdouble)b, (GLdouble)t);
  window.set (l, r, b, t);
}
```

PRACTICE EXERCISES

3.4.2 Flesh out each of the following member functions

```
a. void setViewport(int l, int r, int b, int t);
b. IntRect getViewport(void);
c. RealRect getWindow(void);
d. void clearScreen(void);
e. void setBackgroundColor(float r, float g, float b);
f. void setColor(float r, float g, float b);
g. void lineTo(Point2 p);
h. void moveTo(Point2 p);
i. float getWindowAspectRatio(void);
```

3.4.3 Using *Canvas* for a simulation: Fibonacci numbers

The growth in the size of a rabbit population is said to be modeled by the equation

$$y_k = y_{k-1} + y_{k-2},$$

where y_k is the number of bunnies at the kth generation. This model says that the number in the current generation is the sum of the numbers in the previous two generations. The initial populations are $y_0 = 1$ and $y_1 = 1$. Successive values of y_k are formed by substituting earlier values, and the resulting sequence is the well-known **Fibonacci sequence**; $1, 1, 2, 3, 5, 8, 13 \ldots$. A plot of the sequence y_k versus k reveals the nature of this growth pattern. Use the *Canvas* class to write a program that draws such a plot for a sequence of length N. Adjust the size of the plot appropriately for different N. (The sequence grows very rapidly, so you may instead wish to plot the logarithm of y_k versus k.) Also, plot the sequence of ratios $p_k = y_k/y_{k-1}$, and watch how quickly p_k converges to the golden ratio.

3.4.4 Another simulation: sinusoidal sequences

The following difference equation generates a sinusoidal sequence:

$$y_k = ay_{k-1} - y_{k-2} \qquad \text{for} \qquad k = 1, 2, \ldots.$$

Here, a is a constant between 0 and 2, y_k is 0 for $k < 0$, and $y_0 = 1$. In general, one cycle consists of S points if we set $a = 2\cos(2\pi/S)$. A good picture results with $S = 40$. Write a routine that draws sequences generated in this fashion, and test it for various values of S. ■

3.5 RELATIVE DRAWING

If we add just a few more drawing tools to our tool kit (which is the emerging class *Canvas*), certain drawing tasks become much simpler. It is often convenient to have drawing take place at the current position (CP) and to describe positions relative to the CP. We develop functions, therefore, whose parameters denote *changes* in position: The programmer specifies how far to go along each coordinate to the next desired point.

3.5.1 Developing moveRel() and lineRel()

Two new routines are `moveRel()` and `lineRel()`. The function `moveRel()` is simple: It just "moves" the CP through the displacement (`dx`, `dy`). The function `lineRel(float dx, float dy)` does this, too, but it first draws a line from the old CP to the new one. Both functions are shown in Figure 3.29.

```
void Canvas :: moveRel(float dx, float dy)
{
        CP.set(CP.x + dx, CP.y + dy);
}

void Canvas :: lineRel(float dx, float dy)
{
        float x = CP.x + dx, y = CP.y + dy;
        lineTo(x, y);
        CP.set(x, y);
}
```

FIGURE 3.29 The functions `moveRel()` and `lineRel()`.

■ **EXAMPLE 3.5.1 An arrow marker**

Markers of different shapes can be placed at various points in a drawing to add emphasis to the display. Figure 3.30 shows pentagram markers used to highlight the data points in a line graph.

FIGURE 3.30 Placing markers
for emphasis.

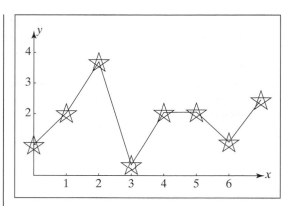

Because the same figure is drawn at several different points, it is convenient to be able to say simply `drawMarker()` and have the figure be drawn at the CP. Then the line graph of Figure 3.30 can be drawn, along with the markers, using code suggested by the following pseudocode:

```
moveTo(first data point);
drawMarker();                    // draw a marker there
for(each remaining data point)
{
    lineTo(the next point);   // draw the next line segment
    drawMarker();              // draws it at the CP
}
```

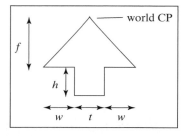

FIGURE 3.31 Model of an
arrow.

FIGURE 3.32 Drawing an arrow
using relative moves and draws.

Figure 3.31 shows an arrow-shaped marker, drawn using the routine in Figure 3.32. The arrow is positioned with its uppermost point at the CP. For flexibility, the arrow shape is parameterized through the four size parameters f, h, t, and w as shown. The function `arrow()` uses only `lineRel()`, and no reference is made to absolute positions. Note that, although the CP is altered while drawing is going on, at the end the CP has been set back to its initial position. Hence, the routine produces no "side effects" (beyond the drawing itself).

```
void arrow(float f, float h, float t, float w)
{ // assumes global Canvas object: cvs
    cvs.lineRel(-w - t / 2, -f);   // down the left side
    cvs.lineRel(w, 0);
    cvs.lineRel(0, -h);
    cvs.lineRel(t, 0);        // across
    cvs.lineRel(0, h);        // back up
    cvs.lineRel(w, 0);
    cvs.lineRel(-w - t / 2, f);
}
```

3.5.2 Turtle Graphics

The last tool we add for now is surprisingly convenient. It keeps track not only of "where we are" with the CP, but also "the direction in which we are headed." This is a form of **turtle graphics**, which has been found to be a natural way to do graphics programming.[6] The notion is that a "turtle", which is conceptually similar to the pen in

---

6   Turtle graphics was introduced by Seymour Papert at MIT as part of the LOGO language for teaching children how to program. (See, e.g., [Abelson81].)

a pen plotter, migrates over the page, leaving a trail behind itself that appears as a line segment. The turtle is positioned at the CP, headed in a certain direction called the **current direction**, CD, the number of degrees measured counterclockwise (CCW) from the positive *x*-axis.

It is easy to add functionality to the *Canvas* class that will "control the turtle." First, CD is added as a private data member. Then we add three functions:

1. turnTo(float angle). This function turns the turtle to the given angle and is implemented as

   ```
   void Canvas:: turnTo(float angle) {CD=angle;}
   ```

2. turn(float angle). This routine turns the turtle through angle degrees counterclockwise; it is implemented as

   ```
   void Canvas:: turn(angle){CD += angle;}
   ```

   We use a negative argument to make a right turn. Note that a turn is a relative change in direction; we do not specify a direction, only a *change* in direction. This simple distinction provides enormous power in drawing complex figures with the turtle.

3. forward(float dist, int isVisible). This instruction moves the turtle forward in a straight line from the CP through a distance dist in the current direction CD and updates the CP. If isVisible is nonzero, a visible line is drawn; otherwise nothing is drawn.

Figure 3.33 shows that, in going forward in the direction CD, the turtle just moves in the *x* direction a distance $dist \times \cos(\pi \times CD/180)$ and in the *y* direction a distance $dist \times \sin(\pi \times CD/180)$, so the implementation of forward() is immediate:

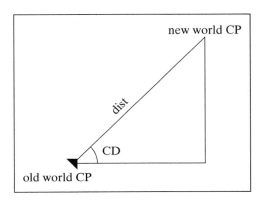

FIGURE 3.33 Effect of the forward() routine.

```
void Canvas:: forward(float dist, int isVisible)
{
        const float RadPerDeg=0.017453393;    //radians per degree
        float x = CP.x + dist * cos(RadPerDeg * CD);
        float y = CP.y + dist * sin(RadPerDeg * CD);
        if(isVisible)
               lineTo(x, y);
        else
               moveTo(x, y);
}
```

Turtle graphics makes it easy to build complex figures out of simpler ones, as we see in the next two examples.

■ EXAMPLE 3.5.2 Building a figure upon a hook motif

The three-segment "hook" motif shown in Figure 3.34(a) can be drawn using the commands

```
forward(3 * L, 1);   // L is the length of the short sides
turn(90);
forward(L, 1);
turn(90);
forward(L, 1);
turn(90);
```

for some choice of L. Suppose that procedure hook() encapsulates these instructions. Then the shape in Figure 3.34(b) is drawn using four repetitions of hook(). The figure can be positioned and oriented as desired by choices of the initial CP and CD.

FIGURE 3.34 Building a figure out of several turtle motions.

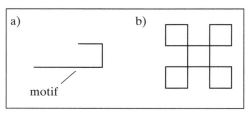

■ EXAMPLE 3.5.3 Polyspirals

A large family of pleasing figures called *polyspirals* can be generated easily with turtle graphics. A polyspiral is a polyline wherein each successive segment is larger (or smaller) than its predecessor by a fixed amount and is oriented at some fixed angle to the predecessor. A polyspiral is rendered by the following pseudocode:

```
for(some number of iterations)
{
    forward(length,1);   // draw a line in the current direction
    turn(angle);         // turn through angle degrees
    length += increment; // increment the line length
}
```

Each time a line is drawn, both its length and direction are incremented. If increment is 0, the figure neither grows nor shrinks. Figure 3.35 shows several polyspirals. The implementation of the preceding routine is requested in the exercises.

FIGURE 3.35 Examples of polyspirals. Angles are (a) 60°, (b) 89.5°, (c) −144°, and (d) 170°.

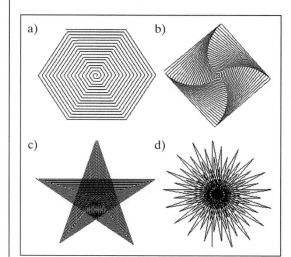

PRACTICE EXERCISES

3.5.1 Drawing turtle figures

Write routines that use turtle motions to draw the three figures shown in Figure 3.36. Can the turtle draw the shape in Part (c) without "lifting the pen" and without drawing any line twice?

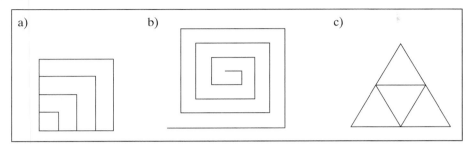

FIGURE 3.36 Other simple turtle figures.

3.5.2 Drawing a well-known logo

Write a routine that makes a turtle draw the outline of the logo shown in Figure 3.37. (Your routine need not fill the polygons.)

3.5.3 Driving the turtle with strings

We can use a shorthand notation to describe a figure. Suppose that

F means `forward(d, 1);`   (for some distance d),
L means `turn(60);`   (a left turn),

and

R means `turn(-60).`   (a right turn).

FIGURE 3.37 A famous logo.

What does the following sequence of commands produce?
    FLFLFLFRFLFLFLFRFLFLFLFR. (See Chapter 9 for a generalization of this sequence that produces fractals!)

3.5.4 Drawing meanders

A **meander**[7] is a pattern like that in Figure 3.38(a), often made up of a continuous line meandering along some path. One frequently sees meanders on Greek vases, Chinese plates, or floor tilings from various countries. The motif for the meander of Figure 3.38(a) is shown in Figure 3.38(b). After each motif is drawn, the turtle is turned (how much?) to prepare it for drawing the next motif.

FIGURE 3.38 Example of a meander.

Write a routine that draws the preceding motif and a routine that draws the meander. (Meanders are most attractive if the graphics package at hand supports the control of line thickness—as OpenGL does—so that `forward()` draws thick lines.) A dazzling variety of more complex meanders can be designed, as suggested in later exercises.

---

[7]   Based on the name Maeander (in modern form, Menderes), a winding river in Turkey.

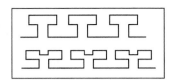

FIGURE 3.39 Additional figures for meanders.

FIGURE 3.40 Hierarchy of meander motifs.

3.5.5 Other classes of meanders

Figure 3.39 shows two additional types of meanders. Write routines that employ turtle graphics to draw them.

3.5.6 Drawing elaborate meanders

Figure 3.40 shows a sequence of increasingly complex motifs for meanders. Write routines that draw a meander for each of these motifs. What does the next most complicated motif in this sequence look like, and what is the general principle behind constructing these motifs?

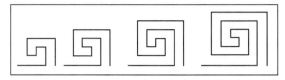

3.5.7 Implementing polyspiral

Write the routine `polyspiral(float length, float angle, float incr, int num)`, which draws a polyspiral consisting of `num` segments, the first having length `length`. After each segment is drawn, `length` is incremented by `incr`, and the turtle turns through angle `angle`.

3.5.8 Is a polyspiral an IFS?

Can a polyspiral be described in terms of an IFS, as defined in Chapter 2? Specify the function that is iterated by the turtle at each iteration.

3.5.9 Recursive form for `Polyspiral()`

Rewrite `polyspiral()` in a recursive form, so that `polyspiral()` with argument `dist` calls `polyspiral()` with argument `dist+inc`. Put a suitable stopping criterion in the routine.   ■

3.6 FIGURES BASED ON REGULAR POLYGONS

To generalize is to be an idiot.

William Blake

Bees … by virtue of certain geometrical forethought … know that the hexagon is greater than the square and triangle, and will hold more honey for the same expenditure of material.

Pappus of Alexandria

The regular polygons form a large and important family of shapes that are often encountered in computer graphics. We need efficient ways to draw them. In this section, we examine how to do this and how to create a number of figures that are variations of the regular polygon.

3.6.1 The Regular Polygons

First we define of a regular polygon:

> **DEFINITION:** A polygon is **regular** if it is simple, if all its sides have equal lengths, and if adjacent sides meet at equal interior angles.

As discussed in Chapter 1, a polygon is **simple** if no two of its edges cross each other (more precisely, only adjacent edges can touch and only at their shared endpoint). We give the name **n-gon** to a regular polygon having n sides. Familiar examples are the 4-gon (a square), 5-gon (a regular pentagon), 8-gon (a regular octagon), and so on. A 3-gon is an equilateral triangle. Figure 3.41 shows various examples. If the number of sides of an n-gon is large the polygon approximates a circle in appearance. In fact this is used later as one way to implement the drawing of a circle.

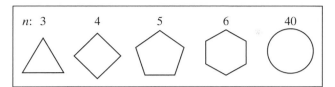

FIGURE 3.41 Examples of n-gons.

The vertices of an n-gon lie on a circle, the so-called parent circle of the n-gon, and their locations are easily calculated. The case of the hexagon is shown in Figure 3.42; the vertices lie equispaced every 60° around the circle. The parent circle of radius R (not shown) is centered at the origin, and the first vertex P_0 has been placed on the positive x-axis. The other vertices follow accordingly, as $P_i = (R\cos(ia), R\sin(ia))$, for $i = 1, \ldots, 5$, where a is $\pi/3$ radians. Similarly, the vertices of the general n-gon lie at

$$P_i = (R\cos(2\pi i/n), R\sin(2\pi i/n)), \quad \text{for } i = 0, \ldots, n - 1. \tag{3.6}$$

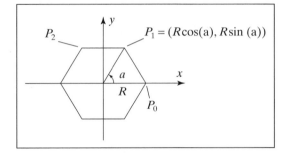

FIGURE 3.42 Finding the vertices of a 6-gon.

It is easy to modify this n-gon. To center it at position (cx, cy), we need only add cx and cy to the x- and y-coordinates, respectively. To scale the n-gon by factor S, we need only multiply R by S. To rotate through angle A, we need only add A to the arguments of $\cos()$ and $\sin()$. More general methods for performing geometrical transformations are discussed in Chapter 5.

It is simple to implement a routine that draws an n-gon, as shown in Figure 3.43. The n-gon is drawn centered at (cx, cy), with radius `radius`, and is rotated through `rotAngle` degrees.

FIGURE 3.43 Building an n-gon in memory.

```
void ngon(int n, float cx, float cy, float radius, float rotAngle)
{         // assumes global Canvas object, cvs
    if(n < 3) return;       // bad number of sides
    double angle = rotAngle * 3.14159265 / 180;  // initial angle
    double angleInc = 2 * 3.14159265 /n;          //angle increment
    cvs. moveTo(radius * cos(angle) + cx, radius * sin(angle) + cy);
    for(int k = 0; k < n; k++)  // repeat n times
    {
        angle += angleInc;
        cvs.lineTo(radius * cos(angle) + cx, radius * sin(angle) + cy);
    }
}
```

■ **EXAMPLE 3.6.1 Turtle-driven *n*-gon**

It is also simple to draw an *n*-gon using turtle graphics. Figure 3.44 shows how to draw a regular hexagon. The initial position and direction of the turtle are indicated by the small triangle. The turtle simply goes forward six times, making a CCW turn of 60 degrees between each move. The code is as follows:

FIGURE 3.44 Drawing a hexagon.

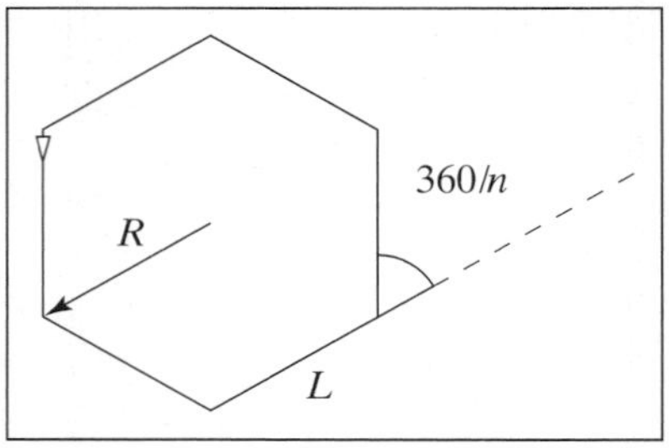

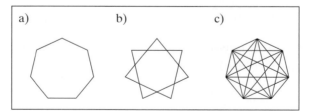

```
for (i = 0; i < 6; i++)
{
        cvs.forward(L, 1);
        cvs.turn(60);
}
```

One vertex is situated at the initial CP, and both the CP and the CD are left unchanged by the process. Drawing the general *n*-gon, as well as some variations of it, is discussed in the exercises.

3.6.2 Variations on *n*-Gons

Interesting variations based on the vertices of an *n*-gon can also be drawn. The vertices may be connected in a number of ways to produce a variety of figures, as suggested in Figure 3.45. The standard *n*-gon is drawn in Figure 3.45(a) by connecting adjacent vertices, but Figure 3.45(b) shows a **stellation** (or starlike figure) formed by connecting every other vertex. And Figure 3.45(c) shows the interesting **rosette**, formed by connecting each vertex to every other vertex. We discuss the rosette next; other figures are described in the exercises.

FIGURE 3.45 A 7-gon and its offspring. (a) The 7-gon. (b) A stellation. (c) A "7-rosette."

a)   b)   c)

■ **EXAMPLE 3.6.2 The rosette and the golden 5-rosette**

The **rosette** is an *n*-gon with each vertex joined to every other vertex. Figure 3.46 shows 5-, 11-, and 17-rosettes. A rosette is sometimes used as a test pattern for computer graphics devices. Its orderly shape readily reveals any distortions, and the resolution of the device can be determined by noting the amount of "crowding" and blurring exhibited by the bundle of lines that meet at each vertex.

Rosettes are easy to draw: Simply connect every vertex to every other. Pseudocode for drawing a rosette is as follows:

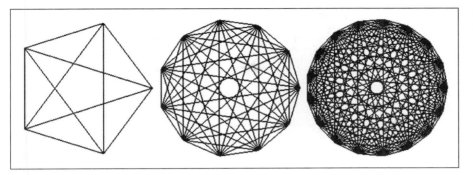

FIGURE 3.46 The 5-, 11-, and 17-rosettes.

```
void Rosette(int N, float radius)
{
    Point2 pt[big enough value for largest rosette];
    generate the vertices pt[0],....,pt[N-1], as in Figure 3.43
    for(int i = 0; i < N - 1; i++)
        for(int j = i + 1; j < N ; j++)
        {
            cvs.moveTo(pt[i]); // connect all the vertices
            cvs.lineTo(pt[j]);
        }
}
```

The 5-rosette is particularly interesting because it embodies many instances of the golden ratio ϕ. (See Chapter 2.) Figure 3.47(a) shows a 5-rosette, which is made up of an outer pentagon and an inner pentagram. The Greeks saw a mystical significance in this figure. Its segments have an interesting relationship: Each segment is ϕ times longer than the next smaller one. (See the exercises.) Also, because the edges of the pentagram form an inner pentagon, an infinite regression of pentagrams is possible, as is shown in Figure 3.47(b).

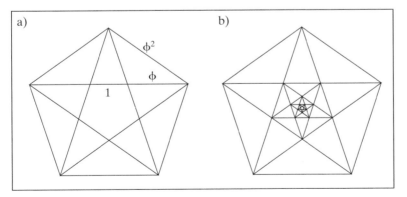

FIGURE 3.47 5-Rosette and infinite regressions of pentagons and pentagrams.

■ **EXAMPLE 3.6.3 Figures based on two concentric *n*-gons**

Figure 3.48 shows some shapes built upon two concentric parent circles, the outer of radius R and the inner of radius fR for some fraction f. Each figure uses a variation of an *n*-gon whose radius alternates between the inner and outer radii. Parts (a) and (b) show familiar company logos based on 6-gons and 10-gons. Part (c) is based on the 14-gon, and part (d) shows the inner circle explicitly.

FIGURE 3.48 A family of famous logos.

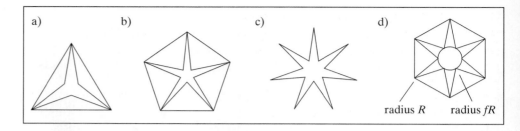

PRACTICE EXERCISES

3.6.1 Stellations and rosettes

The pentagram is drawn by connecting every other point as one traverses around a 5-gon. Extend this scheme to an arbitrary odd-valued n-gon, and develop a routine that draws this so-called stellated polygon. Can the procedure be done with a single initial `moveTo()`, followed only by `lineTo()`s (that is, without "lifting the pen")? What happens if n is even?

3.6.2 How many edges in an N-rosette?

Show that a rosette based on an N—gon—an N-rosette—has $N(N - 1)/2$ edges. This number is the same as the number of "clinks" one hears when N people are seated around a table and everybody clinks glasses with everybody else.

3.6.3 Prime rosettes

If a rosette has a prime number N of sides, it can be drawn without "lifting the pen"— that is, by using only `lineTo()`. Start at vertex v_0 and draw to each of the others in turn: $v_1, v_2, v_3, \dots$, until v_0 is again reached and the polygon is drawn. Then go around again drawing lines, but skip a vertex each time—that is, increment the index by two— thereby drawing to $v_2, v_4, \dots, v_0$. This will require going around twice to arrive back at v_0. (A *modulo* operation is performed on the indices, so that their values remain between 0 and $N - 1$.) Then repeat the procedure, incrementing by 3: $v_3, v_6, v_0, \dots,$ v_0. Each repetition draws exactly N lines. Because there are $N(N - 1)/2$ lines in all, the process repeats $(N - 1)/2$ times. Also, because the number of vertices is a prime, no pattern is ever repeated until the drawing is complete. Develop and test a routine that draws prime rosettes in this way.

3.6.4 Rosettes with an odd number of sides

If n is prime, we know that the n-rosette can be drawn as a single polyline without "lifting the pen". It can also be drawn as a single polyline for any *odd* value of n. Devise a method that does this.

3.6.5 The geometry of the star pentagram

Show that the length of each segment in the 5-rosette stands in the golden ratio to that of the next smaller segment. One way to tackle this problem is to demonstrate that the triangles of the star pentagram are "golden triangles" with an inner angle of $\pi/5$ radians. Show that $2\cos(\pi/5) = \phi$ and $2\cos(2\pi/5) = 1/\phi$. Another approach uses only two families of similar triangles in the pentagram and the relation $\phi^3 = 2\phi + 1$ satisfied by ϕ.

3.6.6 Erecting triangles on n-gon legs

Write a routine that draws figures like the logo in Part (a) of Figure 3.48 for any value of f, positive or negative. What is a reasonable geometric interpretation of negative f?

3.6.7 Drawing the star with relative moves and draws

Write a routine to draw a pentagram that uses only relative moves and draws, centering the star at the CP.

3.6.8 Draw a pattern of stars

Write a routine to draw the pattern of 21 stars shown in Figure 3.49. The small stars are positioned at the vertices of an *n*-gon.

3.6.9 New points on the "7-gram"

Figure 3.50 shows a figure formed from the seven points of a 7-gon centered at the origin. The first point lies at $(R, 0)$. Instead of connecting consecutive points around the 7-gon, two intermediary points are skipped. (This is a form of "stellation" of an *n*-gon.) Find the coordinates of point P, where two of the edges intersect.

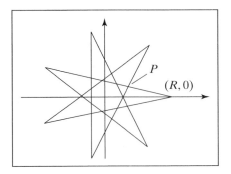

FIGURE 3.49 A star pattern.

FIGURE 3.50 A "7-gram."

3.6.10 Turtle drawings of the *n*-gon

Write a function `turtleNgon(int numSides, float length)` that uses turtle graphics to draw an *n*-gon with `numSides` sides of length `length`.

3.6.11 Polygons sharing an edge

Write a routine that draws *n*-gons, for $n = 3, \ldots, 12$, on a common edge, as in Figure 3.51.

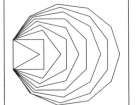

FIGURE 3.51 *n*-Gons sharing a common edge.

3.6.12 A more elaborate figure

Write a routine that renders the shape in Figure 3.52 by drawing repeated hexagons rotated relative to one another.

3.6.13 Drawing a famous logo

The esteemed logo shown in Figure 3.53 consists of three instances of a motif, rotated a certain amount with respect to each other. Write a routine that draws this shape using turtle graphics.

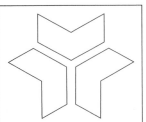

FIGURE 3.53 Logo of the University of Massachusetts.

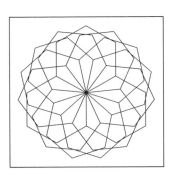

FIGURE 3.52 Repeated use of turtle commands.

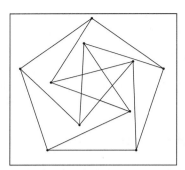

FIGURE 3.54 Rotating "pentathings."

3.6.14 Rotating pentagons: animation

Figure 3.54 shows a pentagram oriented with some angle of rotation within a pentagon, with corresponding vertices joined together. Write a program that animates this figure. The configuration is drawn using some initial angle A of rotation for the pentagram. After a short pause, this pentagram is erased, but then is redrawn at a slightly larger angle A. The process repeats until a key is pressed.   ▪

3.7 DRAWING CIRCLES AND ARCS

Drawing a circle is equivalent to drawing an n-gon that has a large number of vertices. The n-gon resembles a circle (unless it is scrutinized too closely). The routine `drawCircle()` shown in Figure 3.55 draws a 50-sided n-gon, by simply passing its parameters on to `ngon()`. It would be more efficient to write `drawCircle()` from scratch, basing it on the code of Figure 3.43.

FIGURE 3.55 Drawing a circle based on a 50-gon.

```
void drawCircle(Point2 center, float radius)
{
     const int numVerts = 50;
       ngon(numVerts, center.getX(), center.getY(), radius, 0);
}
```

3.7.1 Drawing Arcs

Many figures in art, architecture, and science involve arcs of circles placed in pleasing or significant arrangements. An arc is conveniently described by the position of the center c and radius R of its "parent" circle, along with its beginning angle a and the angle b through which it sweeps. Figure 3.56 shows such an arc. We assume that if b is positive, the arc sweeps in a CCW direction from a: if b is negative, the arc sweeps in a CW fashion. A circle is a special case of an arc, with a sweep of 360°.

FIGURE 3.56 Defining an arc.

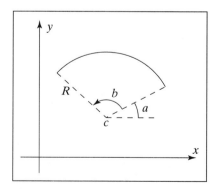

We want a routine, `drawArc( )`, that draws an arc of a circle. The function shown in Figure 3.57 approximates the arc by part of an n-gon, using `moveTo( )` and `lineTo( )`. Successive points along the arc are found by computing a $\cos()$ and $\sin()$ term each time through the main loop. If `sweep` is negative, the angle automatically decreases each time through.

```
void drawArc(Point2 center, float radius, float startAngle, float sweep)
{    // startAngle and sweep are in degrees
    const int n = 30; // number of intermediate segments in arc
    float angle = startAngle * 3.14159265 / 180; // initial angle in radians
    float angleInc = sweep * 3.14159265 /(180 * n); // angle increment
    float cx = center.getX(), cy = center.getY();
    cvs.moveTo(cx + radius * cos(angle), cy + radius * sin(angle));
    for(int k = 1; k < n; k++, angle += angleInc)
        cvs.lineTo(cx + radius * cos(angle), cy + radius * sin(angle));
}
```

FIGURE 3.57 Drawing an arc of a circle.

The CP is left at the last point on the arc. (In some cases, one may wish to omit the initial moveTo() to the first point on the arc, so that the arc is connected to whatever shape was being drawn when drawArc() is called.)

A much faster arc-drawing routine is developed in Chapter 5 that avoids the repetitive calculation of so many sin() and cos() functions. That routine may be used freely in place of the procedure presented here.

With drawArc( ) in hand, it is a simple matter to build the routine drawCircle(Point2 center, float radius) that draws an entire circle. (How?)

The routine drawCircle( ) is called by specifying a center and radius, but there are other ways to describe a circle, that have important applications in interactive graphics and computer-aided design. Two familiar ones are the following:

1. **The center is given, along with a point on the circle.** Here, drawCircle( ) can be used as soon as the radius is known. If c is the center and p is the given point on the circle, the radius is simply the distance from c to p, found using the usual Pythagorean theorem.
2. **Three points are given through which the circle must pass.** It is known that a unique circle passes through any three points that do not lie in a straight line. Finding the center and radius of this circle is discussed in Chapter 4.

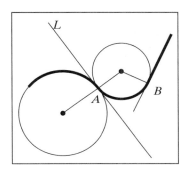

FIGURE 3.58 Blending arcs using tangent circles.

■ **EXAMPLE 3.7.1 Blending arcs together**

More complex shapes can be obtained by using parts of two circles that are tangent to one another. Figure 3.58 illustrates the underlying principle. The two circles are tangent at point A, where they share tangent line L. Because of this, the two arcs shown by the thick curve blend together seamlessly at A with no visible break or corner. Similarly, the arc of a circle blends smoothly with any tangent line, as at point B.

FIGURE 3.59 The yin–yang symbol.

PRACTICE EXERCISES

3.7.1 Circle figures in philosophy

In Chinese philosophy and religion, the two principles of yin and yang interact to influence all creatures' destinies. Figure 3.59 shows the exquisite yin–yang symbol. The dark portion, yin, represents the feminine aspect, and the light portion, yang, represents the masculine. Describe in detail the geometry of this symbol, assuming that it is centered in some coordinate system.

3.7.2 The seven pennies

Describe the configuration shown in Figure 3.60 in which six pennies fit snugly around a center penny. Use symmetry arguments to explain why the fit is exact—that is, why each of the outer pennies *exactly* touches its three neighbors.

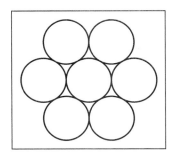

FIGURE 3.60 The seven circles.

FIGURE 3.61 A famous logo.

3.7.3 A famous logo

Figure 3.61 shows a well-known automobile logo formed by erecting triangles inside an equilateral triangle, with the outer triangle replaced by two concentric circles. After determining the "proper" positions for the three inner points, write a routine to draw this logo.

3.7.4 Drawing clocks and such

Circles and lines may be made tangent in a variety of ways to create pleasing, smooth curves, as in Figure 3.62(a). Figure 3.62(b) shows the underlying lines and circles. Write a routine that draws this basic clock shape

FIGURE 3.62 Blending arcs to form smooth curves.

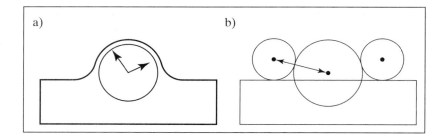

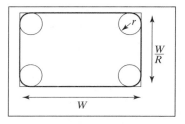

FIGURE 3.63 A rounded rectangle.

3.7.5 Drawing rounded rectangles

Figure 3.63 shows an aligned rectangle with rounded corners. The rectangle has width W and aspect ratio R, and each corner is described by a quarter circle of radius $r = gW$, for some fraction g. Write a routine `drawRoundRect(float W, float R, float g)` that draws this rectangle centered at the CP, which should be left at the center upon exit from the routine.

3.7.6 Shapes involving arcs

Figure 3.64 shows two interesting shapes that involve circles or arcs. One is similar to the Atomic Energy Commission symbol. (How does it differ from that symbol?) Write and test two routines that draw these figures.

FIGURE 3.64 Shapes based on arcs.

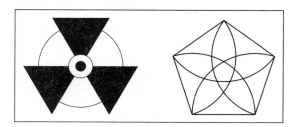

3.7.7 A teardrop

A teardrop shape that is used in many ornamental figures is shown in Figure 3.65(a). As shown in part (b), it consists of a circle of a given radius R, snuggled down into an angle ϕ. What are the coordinates of the circle's center C for a given R and ϕ? What are the initial angle of the arc and its sweep? Develop a routine to draw a teardrop at any position and in any orientation.

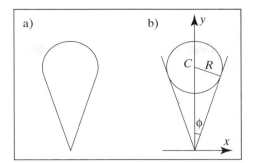

FIGURE 3.65 The teardrop and its construction.

3.7.8 Drawing patterns of teardrops

Figure 3.66 shows some uses of the teardrop. Write a routine that draws each drawing.

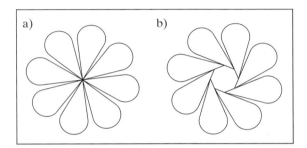

FIGURE 3.66 Some figures based on the teardrop.

3.7.9 Pie charts

A sector is formed by connecting each end of an arc to the center of a circle. The familiar pie chart is formed by drawing a number of sectors. A typical example is shown in Figure 3.67. Pie charts are used to illustrate how a whole is divided into parts, as when a pie is split up and distributed. The eye quickly grasps how big each "slice" is relative to the others. Often, one or more of the slices is "exploded" away from the pack as well, as shown in the figure. Sectors that are exploded are simply shifted slightly away from the center of the pie chart in the proper direction.

To draw a pie chart, we must know the relative sizes of the slices. Write and test a routine that accepts data from the user and draws the corresponding pie chart. The user enters the fraction of the pie each slice represents, along with an *e* if the slice is to be drawn exploded or an *n* otherwise. ■

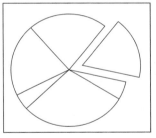

FIGURE 3.67 A pie chart.

3.8 USING THE PARAMETRIC FORM FOR A CURVE

There are two principal ways to describe the shape of a curved line: implicitly and parametrically. The **implicit form** describes a curve by a function $F(x, y)$ that provides a relationship between the x and y coordinates: The point (x, y) lies on the curve if and only if it satisfies the equation

$$F(x, y) = 0. \tag{3.7}$$

For example, the straight line through the points A and B has the implicit form

$$F(x, y) = (y - A_y)(B_x - A_x) - (x - A_x)(B_y - A_y), \tag{3.8}$$

and the circle with radius R centered at the origin has the implicit form

$$F(x, y) = x^2 + y^2 - R^2. \tag{3.9}$$

A benefit of using the implicit form is that you can easily test whether a given point lies on the curve: Simply evaluate $F(x, y)$ at the point in question. For certain classes of curves, it is meaningful to speak of an inside and an outside of the curve, in which case $F(x, y)$ is also called the **inside–outside function**, with the understanding that

$$F(x, y) = 0 \quad \text{for all } (x, y) \text{ on the curve,}$$
$$F(x, y) > 0 \quad \text{for all } (x, y) \text{ outside the curve,} \tag{3.10}$$

and

$$F(x, y) < 0 \quad \text{for all } (x, y) \text{ inside the curve.}$$

(Is $F(x, y)$ of Equation (3.9) a valid inside–outside function for the circle?)

Some curves are **single valued** in x, in which case there is a function $g(.)$ such that all points on the curve satisfy $y = g(x)$. For such curves, the implicit form may be written $F(x, y) = y - g(x)$. (What is $g(.)$ for the line of Equation (3.8)?) Other curves are single valued in y, (so there is a function $h(.)$ such that points on the curve satisfy $x = h(y)$). And some curves are not single valued at all: $F(x, y) = 0$ cannot be rearranged into either the form $y = g(x)$ or the form $x = h(y)$. The circle, for instance, can be expressed as

$$y = \pm\sqrt{R^2 - x^2} \tag{3.11}$$

but here there are two functions, not one.

3.8.1 Parametric Forms for Curves

A parametric form for a curve produces different points on the curve, based on the value of a parameter. Parametric forms can be developed for a wide variety of curves, and they have much to recommend them, particularly when one wants to draw or analyze the curve. A parametric form suggests the movement of a point through time, which we can translate into the motion of a pen as it sweeps out the curve. The path of a particle traveling along the curve is fixed by two functions, $x(\ )$ and $y(\ )$, and we speak of $(x(t), y(t))$ as the **position** of the particle at time t. The curve itself is the totality of points "visited" by the particle as t varies over some interval. For any curve, therefore, if we can dream up suitable functions $x(\ )$ and $y(\ )$, they will represent the curve concisely and precisely.

The familiar Etch-a-Sketch[8] shown in Figure 3.68 provides a vivid analogy. As knobs are turned, a stylus hidden in the box scrapes a thin visible line across the screen. One knob controls the horizontal position of the stylus, and the other directs its vertical position. If the knobs are turned in accordance with $x(t)$ and $y(t)$, the parametric curve is swept out. (Complex curves require substantial manual dexterity.)

FIGURE 3.68 Etch-a-Sketch drawings of parametric curves. (Drawing by Suzanne Casiello.)

---

[8]   Etch-a-Sketch is a trademark of Ohio Art.

Examples: The Line and the Ellipse

The straight line of Equation (3.8) passes through points A and B. We choose a parametric form that visits A at $t = 0$ and B at $t = 1$, obtaining

$$x(t) = A_x + (B_x - A_x)t \qquad\qquad (3.12)$$

and

$$y(t) = A_y + (B_y - A_y)t.$$

Thus, the point $P(t) = (x(t), y(t))$ sweeps through all of the points on the line between A and B as t varies from 0 to 1. (Check this out!)

Another classic example is the **ellipse**, a slight generalization of the circle. The ellipse is described parametrically by

$$x(t) = W \cos(t) \qquad\qquad (3.13)$$

and

$$y(t) = H \sin(t), \qquad \text{for } 0 \le t \le 2\pi,$$

where W is the "half width" and H the "half height" of the ellipse. (Some of the geometric properties of the ellipse are explored in the exercises.) When W and H are equal, the ellipse is a circle of radius W. Figure 3.69 shows an ellipse, along with the component functions $x(.)$ and $y(.)$.

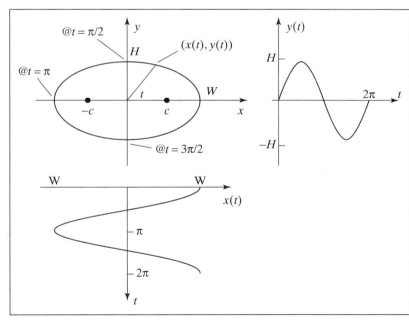

FIGURE 3.69 An ellipse described parametrically.

As t varies from 0 to 2π, the point $P(t) = (x(t), y(t))$ moves once around the ellipse, starting (and finishing) at $(W, 0)$. The figure shows where the point is located at various times t. It is useful to visualize drawing the ellipse on an Etch-a-Sketch. The knobs are turned back and forth in an undulating pattern, one mimicking $W \cos(t)$ and the other $H \sin(t)$. (This action is surprisingly difficult to perform manually.)

Finding an Implicit Form from a Parametric Form

Suppose we want to check that the parametric form in Equation (3.13) truly represents an ellipse. How do we find the implicit form from the parametric form? The basic step is to combine the two equations for $x(t)$ and $y(t)$ to somehow eliminate the variable t. The result is a relationship that must hold for *all t*. It is not always easy to see how to do this, because there are no simple guidelines that apply to all parametric forms. For the ellipse, however, we can square both x/W and y/H and use the well-known relationship $\cos{(t)}^2 + \sin{(t)}^2 = 1$ to obtain the familiar equation for an ellipse:

$$\left(\frac{x}{W}\right)^2 + \left(\frac{y}{H}\right)^2 = 1. \tag{3.14}$$

The exercises that follow explore properties of the ellipse and other "classical curves." They develop useful facts about the **conic sections**—facts which will be used later. Read the exercises over, even if you do not stop to solve each one.

PRACTICE EXERCISES

3.8.1 On the geometry of the ellipse

An ellipse is the set of all points such that the sum of the distances to two foci is constant. The point $(c, 0)$ shown in Figure 3.69 forms one focus, and $(-c, 0)$ forms the other. Show that H, W, and c are related by: $W^2 = H^2 + c^2$.

3.8.2 How eccentric!

The **eccentricity**, $e = c/W$ of an ellipse is a measure of the ellipse's deviation from circularity, with an eccentricity of 0 for a true circle. As interesting examples, the planets in our solar system have very nearly circular orbits, with e ranging from $1/143$ (Venus) to $1/4$ (Pluto). Earth's orbit exhibits $e = 1/60$. As the eccentricity of an ellipse approaches unity, the ellipse flattens into a straight line. But e has to get very close to unity before this happens. What is the ratio H/W of height to width for an ellipse that has $e = 0.99$?

3.8.3 The other conic sections

The ellipse is one of the three conic sections, which are curves formed by cutting ("sectioning") a circular cone with a plane, as shown in Figure 3.70. The conic sections are as follows:

- Ellipse: The plane cuts one nappe of the cone.
- Hyperbola: The plane cuts both nappes of the cone.
- Parabola: The plane is parallel to the side of the cone.

The parabola and hyperbola have interesting and useful geometric properties. Both of them have simple implicit and parametric representations.

FIGURE 3.70 The classical conic sections.

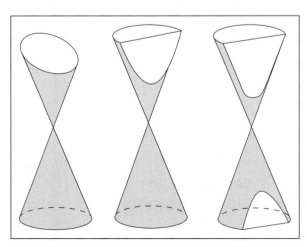

Show that the following parametric representations are consistent with the implicit forms given:

- **Parabola:**   Implicit form: $y^2 - 4ax = 0$.

$$x(t) = at^2 \qquad\qquad\qquad\qquad\qquad\qquad\qquad (3.15)$$
$$y(t) = 2at.$$

- **Hyperbola:**   Implicit form: $(x/a)^2 - (y/b)^2 = 1$.

$$x(t) = a \sec(t); \qquad\qquad\qquad\qquad\qquad\qquad (3.16)$$
$$y(t) = b \tan(t).$$

What range for the parameter t is used to sweep out the hyperbola? (*Note:* A hyperbola is defined as the locus of all points for which the *difference* in its distances from two fixed foci is a constant. If the foci here are at $(-c, 0)$ and $(+c, 0)$, show that a and b must be related by $c^2 = a^2 + b^2$.   ▦

3.8.2 Drawing Curves Represented Parametrically

It is straightforward to draw a curve when its parametric representation is available. This is a major advantage of the parametric form over the implicit form. Suppose a curve C has the parametric representation $P(t) = (x(t), y(t))$ as t varies from 0 to T. [See Figure 3.71(a).] Suppose further that we want to draw a good approximation to the curve, using only straight lines. Then we just take **samples** of $P(t)$ at closely spaced instants. A sequence $\{t_i\}$ of times is chosen, and for each t_i, the position $P_i = P(t_i) = (x(t_i), y(t_i))$ of the curve is found. The curve $P(t)$ is then approximated by the polyline based on this sequence of points P_i, as shown in Figure 3.71(b).

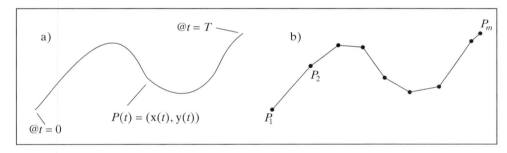

FIGURE 3.71 Approximating a curve by a polyline.

Figure 3.72 shows a fragment of code that draws the curve $(x(t), y(t))$ when the desired array of sample times $t[i]$ is available.

FIGURE 3.72 Drawing an ellipse using points equispaced in t.

```
// draw the curve (x(t), y(t)) using
// the array t[0],...,t[n-1] of "sample-times"

glBegin(GL_LINES);
    for(int i = 0; i < n; i++)
        glVertex2f(x(t[i]), y(t[i]));
glEnd();
```

If the samples are spaced sufficiently close together, the eye will naturally blend the line segments together and will see a smooth curve. Samples must be closely spaced in t-intervals in which the curve is "wiggling" rapidly, but may be placed less densely in those intervals in which the curve is undulating slowly. The required "closeness" or "quality" of the approximation depends on the situation.

Code can often be simplified if it is needed only for a specific curve. The ellipse in Equation 3.13 can be drawn using n equispaced values of t with the following code:

```
#define TWOPI 2 * 3.14159265
glBegin(GL_LINES);
    for(double t = 0; t <= TWOPI; t += TWOPI/n)
        glVertex2f(W * cos(t), H * sin(t));
glEnd();
```

For drawing purposes, parametric forms circumvent all of the difficulties of implicit and explicit forms. Curves can be multivalued, and they can intersect with themselves any number of times. Verticality presents no special problem: $x(t)$ simply becomes constant over some interval in t. Later, we shall see that drawing curves which lie in 3D space is just as straightforward: Three functions of t are used, and the point at t on the curve is $(x(t), y(t), z(t))$.

PRACTICE EXERCISES

3.8.4 A sample curve

Compute and plot by hand the points that would be drawn by the preceding fragment of code for $W = 2$ and $H = 1$, at the five values of $t = 2\pi i/9$, for $i = 0, 1, \ldots, 4$.

3.8.5 Drawing a Logo

FIGURE 3.73 A familiar "eye" made of circles and ellipses.

A well-known logo consists of concentric circles and ellipses, as shown in Figure 3.73. Suppose you have a drawing tool `drawEllipse(W, H, color)` that draws the ellipse of Equation 3.13 filled with color `color`. (Assume that as each color is drawn, it completely obscures any previously drawn color.) Choose suitable dimensions for the ellipses, and give the sequence of commands required to draw the logo.   ■

Some specific examples of curves used in computer graphics will help to cement the ideas presented in this section.

3.8.3 Superellipses

An excellent variation of the ellipse is the **superellipse**, a family of ellipselike shapes that can produce good effects in many drawing situations. The implicit formula for the superellipse is

$$\left(\frac{x}{W}\right)^n + \left(\frac{y}{H}\right)^n = 1, \tag{3.17}$$

where n is a parameter called the *bulge*. Looking at the corresponding formula for the ellipse in Equation 3.14, we see that the superellipse becomes an ellipse when $n = 2$. The superellipse has the parametric representation

$$\begin{aligned} x(t) &= W \cos(t)|\cos(t)^{2/n-1}|, \\ y(t) &= H \sin(t)|\sin(t)^{2/n-1}|, \end{aligned} \tag{3.18}$$

for $0 \le t \le 2\pi$. The exponent on the $\sin()$ and $\cos()$ functions is really $2/n$, but the peculiar form shown is used to avoid trying to raise a negative number to a fractional power. Check that the form presented reduces nicely to the equation for the ellipse when $n = 2$. Also, check that the parametric form for the superellipse is consistent with the implicit equation.

Figure 3.74(a) shows a family of **supercircles**, special cases of superellipses for which $W = H$. Figure 3.74(b) shows a scene composed entirely of superellipses, suggesting the range of shapes possible.

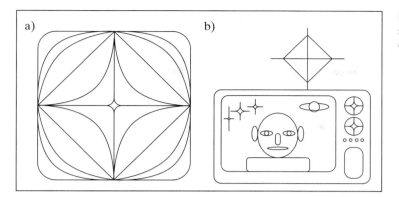

FIGURE 3.74 (a) Family of supercircles. (b) Scene composed of superellipses.

For $n > 1$ the bulge is outward, whereas for $n < 1$ it is inward. When $n = 1$, the supercircle becomes a square. (In Chapter 6 we shall look at three-dimensional "superquadrics," surfaces that are sometimes used in CAD systems to model solid objects.)

Superellipses were first studied in 1818 by the French physicist Gabriel Lamé. More recently, in 1959, the extraordinary inventor Piet Hein (best known as the originator of the Soma cube and the game Hex) was approached with the problem of designing a traffic circle in Stockholm. The circle had to fit inside a rectangle (with $W/H = 6/5$) determined by other roads and had to permit a smooth flow of traffic, as well as be pleasing to the eye. An ellipse proved to be too pointed at the ends for the best traffic patterns, so Hein sought a fatter curve with straighter sides and dreamed up the superellipse. He chose $n = 2.5$ as the most pleasing bulge. Stockholm quickly accepted the superellipse motif for its new center. The curves were "strangely satisfying, neither too rounded nor too orthogonal, a happy blend of elliptical and rectangular beauty" [Gardner75, p. 243]. Since that time, superellipse shapes have appeared in furniture, textile patterns, and even silverware. More can be found out about them in the [Gardner75] and [Hill79b].

The **superhyperbola** can also be defined [Barr81]. Just replace $\cos(t)$ by $\sec(t)$ and $\sin(t)$ by $\tan(t)$ in Equation 3.18. When $n = 2$, the familiar hyperbola is obtained. Figure 3.75 shows some sample superhyperbolas. As the bulge n increases beyond 2, the curve bulges out more and more, and as the bulge decreases below 2, the curve bulges out less and less, becoming straight for $n = 1$ and pinching inward for $n < 1$.

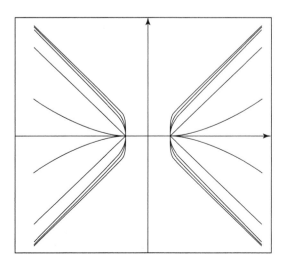

FIGURE 3.75 The superhyperbola family.

3.8.4 Polar Coordinate Shapes

Polar coordinates may be used to represent many interesting curves. As shown in Figure 3.76, each point on the curve is represented by an angle θ and a radial distance r. If r and θ are each made a function of t, then as t varies the curve $\big(r(t), \theta(t)\big)$ is swept out. Of course, this curve also has the Cartesian representation $\big(x(t), y(t)\big)$, where

FIGURE 3.76 Polar coordinates.

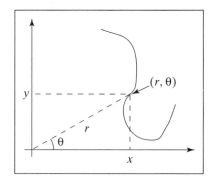

$$x(t) = r(t)\cos\big(\theta(t)\big) \tag{3.19}$$

and

$$y(t) = r(t)\sin\big(\theta(t)\big).$$

But a simplification is possible for a large number of appealing curves. In those instances, the radius r is expressed directly as a function of θ and the parameter that sweeps out the curve is θ itself. For each point (r, θ), the corresponding Cartesian point (x, y) is given by

$$x = f(\theta)\cos(\theta) \tag{3.20}$$

and

$$y = f(\theta)\sin(\theta).$$

Curves given in polar coordinates can be generated and drawn as easily as any others: The parameter is θ, which is made to vary over an interval appropriate to the shape. The simplest example is a circle with radius K (i.e., $f(\theta) = K$). The form $f(\theta) = 2K\cos(\theta)$ is another simple curve (which one?). Figure 3.77 shows some shapes that have simple expressions in polar coordinates. Among these shapes are the following:

FIGURE 3.77 Examples of curves with simple polar forms.

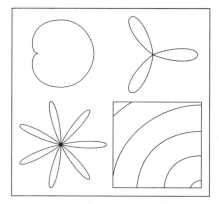

- *Cardioid:* $f(\theta) = K\big(1 + \cos(\theta)\big)$.
- *Rose curves:* $f(\theta) = K\cos(n\theta)$, where n specifies the number of petals in the rose. Two cases are shown.
- *Archimedean spiral:* $f(\theta) = K\theta$.

In each case, the constant K gives the overall size of the curve. Because the cardioid is periodic, it can be drawn by varying θ from 0 to 2π. The rose curves are periodic when n is an integer, and the Archimedean spiral keeps growing forever as θ increases from 0. The shape of this spiral has found wide use as a cam for converting rotary motion to linear motion. (see [Yates46] and [Seggern90].

The **conic sections** (the ellipse, parabola, and hyperbola) all share the polar form

$$f(\theta) = \frac{1}{1 \pm e \cos(\theta)}, \tag{3.21}$$

where e is the eccentricity of the section. For $e = 1$, the shape is a parabola; for $0 \le e < 1$, it is an ellipse; and for $e > 1$, it is a hyperbola.

The Logarithmic Spiral

The **logarithmic spiral** (or "equiangular spiral") $f(\theta) = Ke^{a\theta}$, shown in Figure 3.78(a), is also of particular interest [Coxeter61]. This curve cuts all radial lines at a constant angle α, where $a = \cot(\alpha)$. The logarithmic spiral is the only spiral that has the same shape for any change of scale: Enlarge a photo of such a spiral any amount, and the enlarged spiral will fit (after a rotation) exactly on top of the original curve. Similarly, rotate a picture of an equiangular spiral, and it will seem to grow larger or smaller [Steinhaus69].[9] This preservation of shape seems to be used by some animals, such as the mollusk known as a chambered nautilus. [See Figure 3.78(b).] As the animal grows, its shell also grows along a logarithmic spiral in order to provide a home of constant shape [Gardner61].

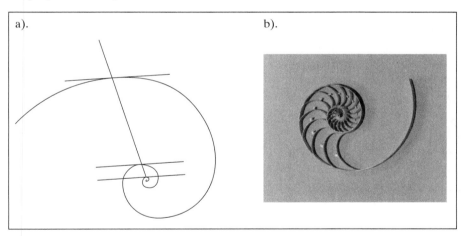

a).   b).

FIGURE 3.78 (a) The logarithmic spiral and (b) the chambered nautilus.

Other families of curves are discussed in the exercises and case studies, and an exhaustive listing and characterization of interesting curves is given in [Yates46, Seggern90, Shikin95].

3.8.5 3D Curves

Curves that meander through 3D space may also be represented parametrically and will be discussed fully in later chapters. To create a parametric form for a 3D curve, we invent three functions $x(.)$, $y(.)$, and $z(.)$, and say that the curve is "at" $P(t) = \big(x(t), y(t), z(t)\big)$ at time t. Following are some examples:

---

[9] This curve was first described by Descartes in 1638. Jacob Bernoulli (1654–1705) was so taken by it that his tombstone in Basel, Switzerland, was engraved with it, along with the inscription *Eadem mutata resurgo*: "Though changed, I shall arise the same."

The helix

The circular helix is given parametrically by

$$x(t) = \cos(t)$$
$$y(t) = \sin(t)$$ (3.22)
$$z(t) = bt,$$

for some constant b. The curve is illustrated in Figure 3.79 as a stereo pair. (See the preface for a discussion of viewing stereo pairs.) If you find this presentation unwieldy, just focus on one of the figures.

FIGURE 3.79 The helix, displayed as a stereo pair.

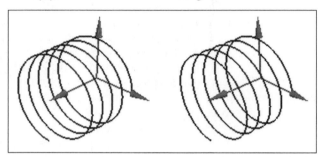

Many variations on the circular helix are possible, such as the elliptical helix, given by $P(t) = (W \cos(t), H \sin(t), bt)$, and the conical helix, with equation $P(t) = (t \cos(t), t \sin(t), bt)$. (Sketch these.) Any 2D curve $(x(t), y(t))$ can, of course, be converted to a helix by appending $z(t) = bt$, or some other form for $z(t)$.

The toroidal spiral

A toroidal spiral, given by

$$x(t) = (a \sin(ct) + b) \cos(t),$$
$$y(t) = (a \sin(ct) + b) \sin(t)$$ (3.23)
$$z(t) = a \cos(ct)$$

is formed by winding a string about a torus (a three-dimensional solid in the shape of a doughnut). Figure 3.80 shows the case $c = 10$, so the string makes 10 loops around the torus. We examine tubes based on this spiral in Chapter 6.

FIGURE 3.80 3.80. A toroidal spiral, displayed as a stereo pair.

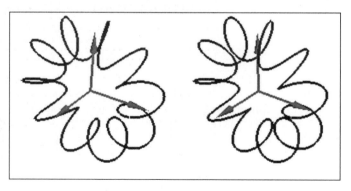

PRACTICE EXERCISES

3.8.6 Drawing superellipses

Write a routine drawSuperEllipse(...) that draws a superellipse. The routine takes as parameters c, the center of the superellipse; the size parameters W and H; the bulge n; and m, the number of "samples" of the curve to use in fashioning the polyline approximation.

3.8.7 Drawing polar forms

Write routines to draw an *n*-petaled rose and an equiangular spiral.

3.8.8 Golden cuts

Find the specific logarithmic spiral that makes "golden cuts" through the intersections of the infinite regression of golden rectangles, as shown in Figure 3.81. (Recall Chapter 2.) How would a picture like this be drawn algorithmically?

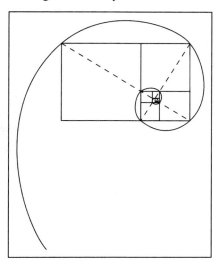

FIGURE 3.81 The spiral and the golden rectangle.

3.8.9 A useful implicit form of a function

Define a suitable implicit form for the rose curve defined earlier in polar coordinates by the equation $f(\theta) = K \cos(n\theta)$.

3.8.10 Inside–outside functions for polar curves

Discuss whether there is a single method that will yield a suitable inside–outside function for *any* curve given in polar coordinate form, as in Equation 3.20. Give examples or counterexamples. ■

3.9 SUMMARY

In this chapter, we developed several tools that make it possible for the applications programmer to think and work directly in the most convenient "world" coordinate system for the problem at hand. Objects are defined ("modeled") using high-precision real coordinates, without concern for where or how big the picture of the object will be on the screen. These concerns are deferred to the later selection of a window and a viewport—either manually or automatically—that define both how much of the object is to be drawn and how it is to appear on the display. This approach separates the modeling stage from the viewing stage, allowing the programmer or user to focus on the relevant issues at each phase, without being distracted by details of the display device.

The use of windows makes it very easy to "zoom" in or out on a scene, or "roam" around to different parts of a scene. Such actions are familiar from everyday life with cameras. The use of viewports allows the programmer to place pictures or collections of pictures at the desired spots on the display in order to compose the final picture we discussed. We discussed various methods for ensuring that the window and viewport have the same aspect ratio to prevent distortion.

Clipping is a fundamental technique in graphics, and we developed a classical algorithm for clipping line segments against the world window. The algorithm allows the programmer to designate which portion of the picture will actually be rendered: parts outside the window are clipped off. OpenGL automatically performs clipping, but in other environments a clipper must be incorporated explicitly.

We developed the *Canvas* class to encapsulate many underlying details and provide the programmer with a single, uniform tool for fashioning drawing programs. Canvas hides OpenGL details in convenient routines, such as `setWindow()`, `setViewport()`, `move-To()`, `lineTo()`, and `forward()`, and ensures that all proper initializations are carried out. In a case study, we shall implement *Canvas* in a more basic, non-OpenGL environment, where explicit clipping and window-to-viewport mapping routines are required. In such an environment, the value of hiding data within the *Canvas* class is even more apparent.

A number of additional tools were developed for performing relative drawing and turtle graphics, and for creating drawings that include regular polygons, arcs, and circles. The parametric form for a curve was introduced and shown to be a very natural description of any curve. The parametric form makes it simple to draw a curve, even those that are multivalued, that cross over themselves, or that have regions in which the curve moves vertically.

3.10 CASE STUDIES

One of the symptoms of an approaching nervous breakdown is the belief that one's work is terribly important.

Bertrand Russell

CASE STUDY 3.1 STUDYING THE LOGISTIC MAP AND SIMULATION OF CHAOS

Level of Effort: II. Iterated function systems (IFSs) were discussed at the end of Chapter 2. Another IFS provides a fascinating look into the world of **chaos** (see [Gleick87]), and requires the proper setting of a window and viewport. A sequence of values is generated by the repeated application of a function $f(.)$ called the **logistic map**. The function describes a parabola via the equation

$$f(x) = 4\lambda x(1 - x) \tag{3.24}$$

where λ is some chosen constant between 0 and 1. Beginning at a given point x_0 between 0 and 1, the function $f(.)$ is applied iteratively to generate the **orbit** (recall the definition of the term in Chapter 2):

$$x_k = f^{[k]}(x_0).$$

How does this sequence behave? A world of complexity lurks here. The action of the sequence can be made most vivid by displaying it graphically in a certain fashion. Figure 3.82 shows the parabola $y = 4\lambda x(1 - x)$ for $\lambda = 0.7$ as x varies from 0 to 1.

FIGURE 3.82 The logistic map for $\lambda = 0.7$.

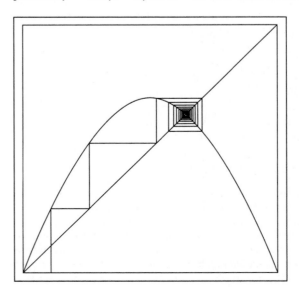

A starting point of $x_0 = 0.1$ is chosen, and at that point a vertical line is drawn up to the parabola, showing the value $f(x_0) = 0.252$. Next, we must apply the function to the new value $x_1 = 0.252$. This is shown visually by moving horizontally over to the line $y = x$, as illustrated in the figure. Then, to evaluate $f(\ )$ at this new point, a line is again drawn up vertically to the parabola. The process repeats forever, as with other IFSs. From the previous position (x_{k-1}, x_k), a horizontal line is drawn to (x_k, x_k) from which a vertical line is drawn to (x_k, x_{k+1}). The figure shows that, for $\lambda = 0.7$, the values quickly converge to a stable "attractor," a fixed point such that $f(x) = x$. (What is the value of this point for $\lambda = 0.7$?) Note that the attractor does not depend on the starting point: The sequence *always* converges quickly to a final value.

If λ is set to small values, the action will be even simpler: A single attractor will appear at $x = 0$. But when the "λ-knob" is increased, something strange begins to happen. Figure 3.83a shows what results when $\lambda = 0.85$. The "orbit" that represents the sequence falls into an endless repetitive cycle, never settling down to a final value. There are several attractors here, one at each vertical line in the limit cycle shown in the figure. And when λ is increased beyond the critical value $\lambda = 0.892486418\ldots$ the process becomes truly chaotic.

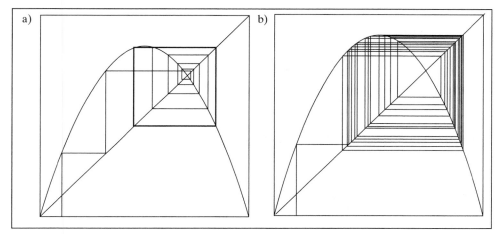

a)   b)

FIGURE 3.83 The logistic map for (a) $\lambda = 0.85$ and (b) $\lambda = 0.9$.

The case of $\lambda = 0.9$ is shown in Figure 3.83(b). For most starting points, the orbit is still periodic, but the number of orbits observed between the repetitions is now extremely large. Other starting points yield truly aperiodic motion, and very small changes in the starting point can lead to very different behavior. Before the truly remarkable character of this phenomenon was first recognized by Mitchell Feigenbaum in 1975, most researchers believed that very small adjustments to a system should produce correspondingly small changes in its behavior and that simple systems such as this one could not exhibit arbitrarily complicated behavior. Feigenbaum's work spawned a new field of inquiry into the nature of complex nonlinear systems, known as chaos theory [Gleick87]. It is intriguing to experiment with this logistic map.

Write and execute a program that permits the user to study the behavior of repeated iterations of the logistic map, as shown in Figure 3.83. Set up a suitable window and viewport so that the entire logistic map can be clearly seen. The user gives the values of x_0 and λ, and the program draws the limit cycles produced by the system.

CASE STUDY 3.2 IMPLEMENTATION OF THE COHEN–SUTHERLAND CLIPPER IN C OR C++

Level of Effort: II. The basic flow of the Cohen–Sutherland algorithm was described in Section 3.3.2. In this case study, we flesh out some details of its implementation in C or C++, exploiting for efficiency the low-level bit manipulations these languages provide.

We first need to form the "inside–outside" code words that report how a point P is positioned relative to the window. (See Figure 3.20.) A single eight-bit word `code` suffices: Four of its bits are used to capture the four pieces of information. Point P is tested against each window boundary in turn; if P lies outside that boundary, the proper bit of `code` is set to 1 to represent TRUE.

Figure 3.84 shows how this test can be carried out. First `code` is initialized to 0, and then its individual bits are set as appropriate using a bitwise OR operation. The values 8, 4, 2, and 1 are simple masks. For instance, since 8 is 00001000 in binary, bitwise OR-ing a value with 8 sets the fourth bit from the right end to 1.

FIGURE 3.84 Setting bits in the "inside–outside" code word for a point *P*.

```
unsigned char code = 0;          // initially all bits are 0
...
if(P.x < window.l) code |= 8;    // set bit 3
if(P.y > window.t) code |= 4;    // set bit 2
if(P.x > window.r) code |= 2;    // set bit 1
if(P.y < window.b) code |= 1;    // set bit 0
```

In the clipper, both endpoints P1 and P2 (see Figure 3.22) are tested against the window, and their code words `code1` and `code2` are formed. We then must test for "trivial accept" and "trivial reject":

- **Trivial accept.** Both endpoints are inside the window, so both `code1` and `code2` are identically 0. In C or C++, this is quickly determined using the bitwise OR operation: a trivial accept occurs if (`code1 | code2`) is 0.
- **Trivial reject.** A trivial reject occurs if both endpoints lie outside the window *on the same side*: both to the left of the window, both above, both below, or both to the right. This condition is equivalent to their codes having at least one 1 in the *same* bit position. For instance, if `code1` is 0110 and `code2` is 0100, then P1 lies above and to the right of the window, while P2 lies above, but neither to the left nor to the right, of the window. Since both points lie above the window, no part of the line can lie inside the window. So trivial rejection is easily tested using the bitwise AND of `code1` and `code2`; if each of them has some 1 in the same position, then `code1 & code2` does also, and (`code1 & code2`) will be nonzero.

Chopping When There is Neither Trivial Accept Nor Trivial Reject

Another implementation issue is efficient chopping of the portion of a line segment that lies outside the window, as in Figure 3.22. Suppose it is known that point P with code word `code` lies outside the window. Then the individual bits of `code` can be tested to see on which side of the window P lies, and the chopping can be accomplished as in Equation (3.5). Figure 3.85 shows a chopping routine that finds the new point (such as *A* in Figure 3.22) and replaces P with it. The routine uses the bitwise AND of `code` with a mask to determine where P lies relative to the window.

FIGURE 3.85 Chopping the segment that lies outside the window.

```
ChopLine(Point2 &P, unsigned char code)
{
        if(code & 8){        // to the Left
             P.y += (window.l - P.x) * dely / delx);
             P.x = window.l;
        }
        else if(code & 2){        // to the Right
             P.y += (window.r - P.x) * dely / delx;
             P.x = window.r;
        }
        else if(code & 1){        // below
             P.x += (window.b - P.y) * delx / dely;
             P.y = window.b;
        }
        else if(code & 4){        // above
             P.x += (window.t - P.y) * delx / dely;
             P.y = window.t;
        }
}
```

Write a complete implementation of the Cohen–Sutherland algorithm, putting together the pieces described here with those in Section 3.3.2. If you do this in the context of a *Canvas* class implementation, as discussed in the next case study, consider how the routine should best access the private data members of the window and the points involved, and develop the code accordingly.

Test the algorithm by drawing a window and a large assortment of randomly chosen lines, showing the parts that lie inside the window in red and those that lie outside in black.

PRACTICE EXERCISES

3.10.1 Why will a "divide by zero" never occur?

Consider a *vertical* line segment such that `delx` is zero. Why is the code `P.y += (window.1 - P.x) * dely / delx)` that would cause a divide by zero never reached? Similarly, explain why each of the four statements that compute `delx/dely` or `dely/delx` are never reached if the denominator happens to be zero.

3.10.2 Do two chops in the same iteration?

The performance of the Cohen–Sutherland algorithm would appear to be improved if we replaced lines such as "`else if(code & 2)`" with "`if(code & 2)`" and tried to do two line "chops" in succession. Show, however, that this approach can lead to erroneous endpoints being computed and, hence, to disaster. ■

CASE STUDY 3.3 IMPLEMENTING CANVAS IN TURBO C++

Level of Effort: III. It is interesting to develop a drawing class such as *Canvas* in which all the details are worked out, to see how the many ingredients go together. Sometimes it is even necessary to do this, as when a supporting library like OpenGL is not available. We design *Canvas* here for a popular graphics platform that uses Borland's Turbo C++.

We want an implementation of the *Canvas* class that has essentially the same interface as that in Figure 3.25. Figure 3.86 shows the version we develop here (omitting parts that are simple repetitions of Figure 3.25). The constructor takes a desired width and height, but no title, since Turbo C++ does not support titled screen windows. Several new private data members internally manage clipping and the window-to-viewport mapping.

FIGURE 3.86 Interface for the Canvas class in Turbo C++.

```
class Canvas {
  public:
     Canvas(int width, int height);  // constructor
     setWindow(),setViewport(), lineTo(), etc .. as before
  private:
     Point2 CP;        // current position in the world
     IntRect viewport; // the current window
     RealRect window;  // the current viewport
     float mapA, mapB, mapC, mapD;  // data for the window-to-viewport mapping
     void makeMap(void); // builds the map
     int screenWidth, screenHeight;
     float delx,dely;        // increments for clipper
     char code1, code2;      // outside codes for clipper
     void ChopLine(tPoint2 &p, char c);
     int clipSegment(tPoint2 &p1, tPoint2 &p2);
};
```

Implementation of the *Canvas* Class

We show some of the *Canvas* member functions here, to illustrate what must be done to manage the window-to-viewport mapping and clipping.

1. **The Canvas Constructor**

   First the constructor is passed the desired width and height of the screen. Then Turbo C++ is placed in graphics mode at the highest resolution supported by the graphics system used. The actual screen width and height available are tested, and if either one is less than was requested, the program terminates. Finally, a default window and viewport are established, and the window-to-viewport mapping is built (inside `setViewport()`.) The code is as follows:

   ```
   Canvas:: Canvas(int width, int height)
   {
           int gdriver = DETECT, gmode; //Turbo C++: use best
                                          resolution screen
           initgraph(&gdriver, &gmode, ""); // go to "graphics" mode
           screenWidth = getmaxx() + 1;  // size of available screen
           screenHeight = getmaxy() + 1;
           assert(screenWidth >= width); // as wide as asked for?
           assert(screenHeight >= height); // as high as asked for?
           CP.set(0.0, 0.0);
           window.set(-1.0,1.0,-1.0,1.0); // default window
           setViewport(0,screenWidth, 0, screenHeight); // sets
                                          // default map, too

   }
   ```

2. **Setting the Window, the Viewport, and the Mapping**

   Whenever either the window or viewport is set, the window-to-viewport mapping is updated to ensure that it is current. A degenerate window of zero height causes an error. The mapping uses window and viewport data to compute the four coefficients A, B, C, and D that are required. The following is the code for these operations:

   ```
   //<<<<<<<<<<<<<<<<<<<<<<<< set Window >>>>>>>>>>>>>>>>>>>>>>
   void Canvas:: setWindow(float l, float r, float b, float t)
   {
           window.set(l, r, b, t);
           assert(t != b); //degenerate !
           makeMap();    // update the mapping
   }
   //<<<<<<<<<<<<<<<<<<<<<< setViewport >>>>>>>>>>>>>>>>>>>>>>
   void Canvas:: setViewport(int l, int r, int b, int t)
   {
           viewport.set(l, r, b, t);
           makeMap();    // update the mapping
   }
   //<<<<<<<<<<<<<<<<<< makeMap >>>>>>>>>>>>>>>>>>>>>>>>>
   void Canvas:: makeMap(void)
   {           // set mapping from window to viewport
           intRect vp = getViewport(); // local copy of viewport
           RealRect win = getWindow(); // local copy of window
           float winWid = win.r - win.l;
           float winHt = win.t - win.b;
           assert(winWid != 0.0); assert(winHt != 0.0); // degenerate!
           mapA = (vp.r - vp.l)/winWid;  // fill in mapping values
           mapC =   vp.l - map.A * win.l;
           mapB = (vp.t - vp.b)/winHt;
           mapD =   vp.b - map.B * win.b;
   }
   ```

3. `moveTo()`, and `lineTo()` with clipping

The routine `moveTo()` converts a point from world coordinates to screen coordinates and calls the specific Turbo C++ `moveto()` routine to update the internal current position maintained by the software. `Moveto()` also updates *Canvas'* world coordinate CP. The routine `lineTo()` works similarly, but it must first determine which part, if any, of the segment lies within the window. To do this, it uses `clipSegment()`, described in Section 3.3 and in Case Study 3.2, which returns the `first` and `second` endpoints of the inside portion of the segment. If any portion of the segment lies in the window, `clipSegment()`, it moves to `first` and draws a line to `second`. `clipSegment()` finishes with a `moveTo()`, to ensure that both the *Canvas* CP and the internal Turbo C++ CP will be current.

In the following code, `ChopLine` and `clipSegment` are the same as in Case Study 3.2:

```
//<<<<<<<<<<<<<<<<<<<<<<<<<< moveTo >>>>>>>>>>>>>>>>>>
void Canvas:: moveTo(float x, float y)
{
        int sx = (int)(mapA * x + mapC);
        int sy = (int)(mapB * y + mapD);
        moveto(sx, sy);                  // a Turbo C++ routine
        CP.set(x, y);
}
//<<<<<<<<<<<<<<<<<<<<<< lineTo >>>>>>>>>>>
void Canvas:: lineTo(float x, float y)
{ // Draw a line from CP to (x,y), clipped to the window
        Point2 first = CP;  // initial value of first
        Point2 second(x, y);  // initial value of second
        if(clipSegment(first, second)) // any part inside?
        {
            moveTo(first.x, first.y); // to world CP
            int sx = (int)(mapA * second.x + mapC);
            int sy = (int)(mapB * second.y + mapD);
            lineto(sx,sy);  // a Turbo C++ routine
        }
        moveTo(x, y);       // update CP
}
```

Write a full implementation of the *Canvas* class in Turbo C++ (or a similar environment that requires you to implement clipping and mapping). Cope appropriately with setting the drawing and background colors. (This operation is usually quite system specific.) Test your class by using it in an application that draws polyspirals, as specified by the user.

CASE STUDY 3.4 DRAWING ARCHES

Level of Effort: II. Arches have been used throughout history in architectural compositions. Their structural strength and ornamental beauty make them very important elements in structural design, and a rich variety of shapes have been incorporated into cathedrals, bridges, doorways, etc.

Figure 3.87 shows two basic arch forms. The arch in Part (a) is centered at the origin and has a width of $2W$. The arch begins at height H above the baseline. Its principal element is a half circle with radius $R = W$. The ratio H/W can be adjusted according to taste. For instance, H/W might be related to the golden ratio.

Figure 3.87(b) shows an idealized version of the second most famous arch shape, the **pointed**, or "equilateral," arch, often seen in cathedrals.[10] Here, two arcs of radius $R = 2W$ meet directly above the center. (Through what angle does each arc sweep?)

---

[10] From J. Fleming, H. Honour, and N. Pevsner, *Dictionary of Architecture* (London: Penguin Books, 1980).

FIGURE 3.87 Two basic arch forms.

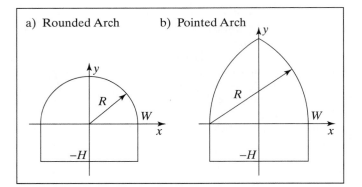

The **ogee**[11] (or "keel") arch is shown in Figure 3.88. This arch was introduced about 1300 A.D. and was popular in architectural structures throughout the late Middle Ages. Circles of radius fR rest on top of a rounded arch of radius R for some fraction f. This configuration fixes the position of the two circles. (What are the coordinates of point C?) On each side, two arcs blend together to form a smooth pointed top. It is interesting to work out the parameters of the various arcs in terms of W and f.

Develop routines that can draw each of the types of arch just described. Also, write an application that draws an interesting collection of such arches in a castle, mosque, or bridge of your design.

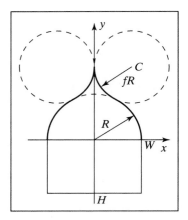

FIGURE 3.88 The ogee arch.

CASE STUDY 3.5 SOME FIGURES USED IN PHYSICS AND ENGINEERING

Level of Effort: II. This case study works with a collection of interesting pictures that arise in certain topics within physics and engineering. The first picture illustrates a physical principle of circles intersecting at right angles; the second creates a chart that can be used to study electromagnetic phenomena; the third develops symbols that are used in designing digital systems.

1. Electrostatic Fields

   The pattern of circles shown in Figure 3.89 is studied in physics and electrical engineering as the electrostatic field lines that surround electrically charged wires. This kind of pattern

FIGURE 3.89 Families of orthogonal circles.

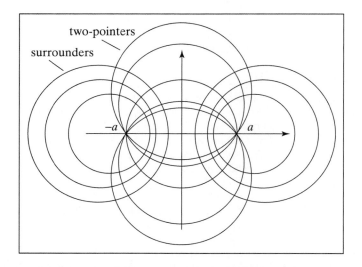

---

[11] From the Old French *ogive*, meaning an S-shaped curve.

also appears in mathematics in connection with the analytic functions of a complex variable. Here, we view the patterns simply as an elegant array of circles and consider how to draw them.

There are two families of circles, which we will call "two-pointers" and "surrounders." The two-pointers family consists of circles that pass through two given points. Suppose the two points are $(-a, 0)$ and $(a, 0)$. The two-pointers can be distinguished by some parameter m, and for each value of m, two different circles are generated. The circles have centers and radii respectively given by

$$\text{center} = \left(0, \pm a\sqrt{m^2 - 1}\right) \quad \text{and} \quad \text{radius} = am$$

as m varies from 1 to infinity.

Circles in the surrounders family surround one of the points $(-a, 0)$ and $(a, 0)$. The centers and radii of the surrounders are also distinguished by a parameter, n, and have the respective values

$$\text{center} = (\pm an, 0) \quad \text{and} \quad \text{radius} = a\sqrt{n^2 - 1}$$

as n varies from 1 to infinity. The surrounder circles are also known as "circles of Appolonius," and they arise in problems of pursuit [Ball74]. The distances from any point on a circle of Appolonius to the points $(-a, 0)$ and $(a, 0)$ have a constant ratio. (What is this ratio in terms of a and n?)

The surrounder family is intimately related to the two-pointer family: Every surrounder circle "cuts" through every two-pointer circle at a right angle. The families of circles are thus said to be **orthogonal** to one another.

Write and execute a program that draws the two families of orthogonal circles. Choose sets of values of m and n so that the picture is well balanced and pleasing.

2. **Smith Charts**

Another pattern of circles is found in Smith charts, familiar in electrical engineering in connection with electromagnetic transmission lines. Figure 3.90 shows the two orthogonal families found in Smith charts. Here, all members of the families pass through a common point $(1, 0)$. Circles in family A have centers at $(1 - m, 0)$ and radii m, and circles in family B have centers at $(1, \pm n)$ and radii n, where both m and n vary from 0 to π. Write and execute a program that draws these families of circles.

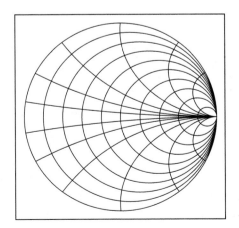

FIGURE 3.90 The Smith Chart.

3. **Logic Gates for Digital Circuits**

Logic gates are familiar to scientists and engineers who study basic electronic circuits found in computers. Each type of gate is symbolized in a circuit diagram by a characteristic shape, several of which are based on arcs of circles. Figure 3.91(a) shows the shape of the so-called NAND gate, according to a worldwide standard.[12] The NAND gate is basically a rounded arch placed on its side. The lone arc used has a radius of 13 units relative to the other elements, so the NAND gate must be 26 units in height.

FIGURE 3.91 Standard graphic symbols for the nand and nor gates.

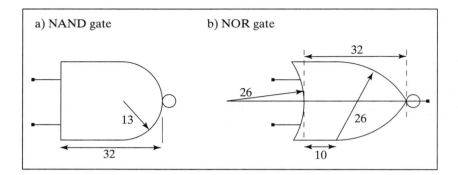

Figure 3.91(b) shows the standard symbol for a NOR gate. It is similar to a pointed arch turned on its side. Three arcs are used, each having a radius of 26 units. (The published standard shown has an error in it that makes it impossible for certain elements to fit together. What is the error?)

Write a program that can draw both types of circuit at any size and position in the world. [For the NOR gate, find and implement a reasonable correction to the error in Figure 3.91(b).] Also, arrange matters so that your program can draw these gates rotated by 90°, 180°, or 270°.

CASE STUDY 3.6 TILINGS

Level of Effort: II. Computer graphics offers a powerful tool for creating pleasing pictures based on geometric objects. One of the most intriguing types of pictures is that which apparently repeats forever in all directions. These pictures are variously called **tilings** and **repeat patterns**.

1. Basic Tilings

   Figure 3.92 shows a basic tiling. A **motif**, in this case four quarter circles in a simple arrangement, is designed in a square region of the world. To draw a tiling over the plane based on this motif, a collection of viewports is created side by side that covers the display surface, and the motif is drawn once inside each viewport.

FIGURE 3.92 A motif and the resulting tiling.

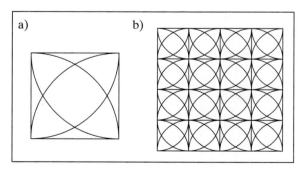

---

[12] The Institute of Electrical and Electronic Engineers (IEEE) publishes many things, including standard definitions of terminology and graphic shapes of circuit elements. These drawings are taken from the standard document IEEE Std. 91–1984.

Write a program that

a. chooses a square window in the world and draws some interesting motif in it (possibly clipping portions of it, as in Figure 3.14) and
b. successively draws the picture in a set of viewports that abut one another and together cover the display surface.

Execute your program with at least two motifs.

2. Truchet Tiles

A slight variation of the method of Part I selects successive motifs randomly from a "pool" of candidate motifs. Figure 3.93(a) shows the well-known Truchet tiles,[13] which are based on two quarter circles centered at opposite corners of a square. Tile 0 and tile 1 differ only by a 90° rotation.

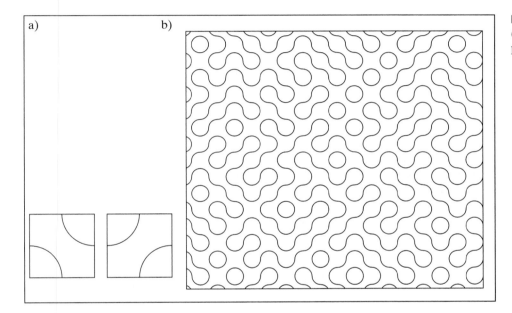

FIGURE 3.93 Truchet Tiles. (a) The two tiles. (b) A Truchet pattern.

Write an application that draws Truchet tiles over the entire viewport. Each successive tile uses tile 0 or tile 1, selected at random.

Curves other than arcs can be used as well, as suggested in Figure 3.94. What conditions should be placed on the angle with which each curve meets the edge of the tile in order to avoid sharp corners in the resulting curve? This notion can also be extended to include more than two tiles.

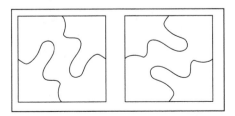

FIGURE 3.94 Extension of Truchet tiles.

Extend the preceding program so that it introduces random selections of two or more motifs, and execute the program on the motifs you have designed. Make sure that you have designed motifs that blend together properly.

[13] C. Smith, "The Tiling Patterns of Sebastian Truchet and the Topology of Structural Hierarchy," *Leonardo*, 20:4, pp. 373–385, 1987.

CASE STUDY 3.7 PLAYFUL VARIATIONS ON A THEME

Level of Effort: II. In Section 3.8, we discussed how to draw a curve represented parametrically by $P(t)$: Take a succession of instants $\{t_i\}$ and connect the successive "samples" $\big(x(t_i), y(t_i)\big)$ by straight lines. A wide range of pictures can be created by varying the way in which the samples are taken. We suggest several possibilities.

For each of the methods described next for obtaining t-samples, write a program that draws each of the following four shapes:

a. an ellipse
b. a hyperbola
c. a logarithmic spiral
d. a five-petaled rose curve

1. **Unevenly Spaced Values of t**

    Instead of using a constant increment between values of t in sampling the functions $x()$ and $y()$, use a varying increment. It is interesting to experiment with different choices to see what visual effects can be achieved. Some possibilities for a sequence of $n + 1$ t-values between 0 and T (suitably chosen for the shape of the curve at hand) are as follows:

    - $t_i = T\sqrt{i/n}$: The samples cluster closer and closer together as i increases.
    - $t_i = T(i/n)^2$: The samples spread out as i increases.
    - $t_i = T(i/n) + A\sin(ki/n)$ The samples cluster together cyclically or spread apart. The constants A and k are chosen to alter the amount and speed of the variation.

2. **Randomly Selected t-Values**

    The t-values can be chosen randomly by devising a function

    $$t_i = \text{randChoose}\,(0, T)$$

    that returns a value randomly selected from the range 0 to T each time it is called.

    Figure 3.95 shows the polyline generated in this fashion for points on an ellipse. It is interesting to watch such a picture develop on a display. A flurry of seemingly unrelated lines first appears, but soon the eye detects some order in the chaos and sees an elliptical "envelope" emerging around the cloud of lines.

FIGURE 3.95 A random ellipse polyline.

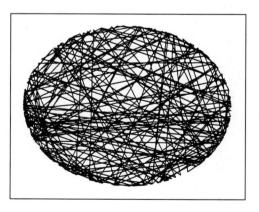

Alternatively, a sequence of increasing t-values can be used, generated by the function

$$t_i = t_{i-1} + \text{randChoose}\,(0, r),$$

where r is some small positive value.

3. **Connecting Vertices in Different Orders**

    In a popular children's game, pins are driven into a board in some pattern, and a piece of thread is woven around the pins in some order. The t-values here define the positions of the pins in the board, and `LineTo()` plays the role of the thread.

The samples of $P(t)$ are prestored in a suitable array P[i], i = 0,1,..,n. The polyline is drawn by passing in an interesting way through a sequence of values of i. That is, the sequence $i_0, i_1, \ldots$ is generated from values between 0 and n, and for each index i_k, a call to worldLineTo(P[i_k]) is made. Some possibilities are as follows:

- The "Random Deal": the sequence $i_0, i_1, \ldots$ is a random permutation of the values $0, 1, \ldots, n$, as in dealing a fixed number of cards from a shuffled deck.
- Every pair of points is connected by a straight line. So every pair of values in the range $0, 1, \ldots, n$ appears in adjacent spots somewhere in the sequence $i_0, i_1, \ldots$. The prime rosette gives one example in which lines are drawn connecting each point to every other point.
- One can also draw "webs," as suggested in Figure 3.96. Here, the index values cycle many times through the possible values, skipping by some M each time. This is easily done by forming the next index from the previous one using $i = (i + M) \bmod(n + 1)$.

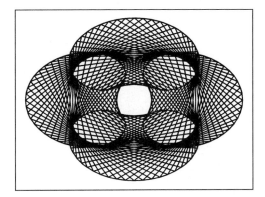

FIGURE 3.96 Adding "webs" to a curve.

CASE STUDY 3.8 CIRCLES ROLLING AROUND CIRCLES

Level of Effort: II. Another large family of interesting curves can be useful in graphics. Consider the path traced by a point rigidly attached to a circle as the circle rolls around another fixed circle. The curves produced by this path are called **trochoids**, and Figure 3.97 shows how they are generated. The point that will do the tracing is attached to the rolling circle (of radius b) at the end of a rod k units from the center of the circle. The fixed circle has radius a. There are two basic kinds of trochoids: When the circle rolls externally [Figure 3.97(a)], an **epitrochoid** is generated, and when it rolls internally [Figure 3.97(b)], a **hypotrochoid** is generated. The children's game Spirograph[14] is a familiar tool for drawing trochoids, which have the following parametric forms:

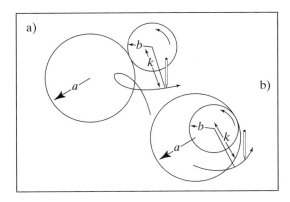

FIGURE 3.97 Circles rolling around circles.

---

[14] A trademark of Kenner Products.

The epitrochoid

$$x(t) = (a + b)\cos(2\pi t) - k\cos\left(2\pi\frac{(a+b)t}{b}\right);$$

$$y(t) = (a + b)\sin(2\pi t) - k\sin\left(2\pi\frac{(a+b)t}{b}\right). \tag{3.25}$$

The hypotrochoid

$$x(t) = (a - b)\cos(2\pi t) + k\cos\left(2\pi\frac{(a-b)t}{b}\right);$$

$$y(t) = (a - b)\sin(2\pi t) - k\sin\left(2\pi\frac{(a-b)t}{b}\right). \tag{3.26}$$

An ellipse results from the hypotrochoid when $a = 2b$ for any k.

When the point doing the tracing lies on the rolling circle ($k = b$), the shapes traced out are called **cycloids**. Some familiar special cases of cycloids are the following:

Epicycloids

　　Cardioid: $b = a$.
　　Nephroid: $2b = a$.

Hypocycloids

　　Line segment: $2b = a$.
　　Deltoid: $3b = a$.
　　Astroid:[15] $4b = a$.

Some of these curves are shown in Figure 3.98. Write a program that can draw both epitrochoids and hypotrochoids. The user can choose which family to draw and can enter the required parameters. Execute the program to draw each of the special cases listed.

FIGURE 3.98 Examples of cycloids. (a) Nephroid. (b) $a/b = 10$. (c) Deltoid. (d) Astroid.

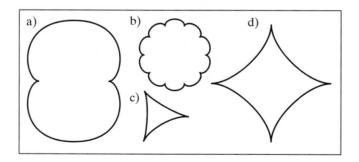

CASE STUDY 3.9 SUPERELLIPSES

Level of Effort: I. Write and execute a program to draw superellipses. To draw each superellipse, the user indicates opposite corners of its bounding rectangle, and types a value for the bulge, whereupon the specified superellipse is drawn.

(Optional). Extend the program so that it can draw rotated superellipses. The user types an angle after typing the bulge.

---

[15] Note that the astroid is also a superellipse! It has a bulge of 2/3.

3.11 FURTHER READING

In getting started with graphics, it is very satisfying to write applications that produce fascinating curves and patterns. These lead you to explore the deep connection between mathematics and the visual arts. Many books are available that offer guidance and provide myriad examples. McGregor and Watt's *The Art of Graphics for the IBM PC* [Mcgregor86] offers many algorithms for creating interesting patterns. Some particularly noteworthy books on curves and geometry are Jay Kappraff's *Connections* [Kappraff91], A. K. Dewdney's *The Armchair Universe* [Dewdney88], Stan Ogilvy's *Excursions in Geometry*[Ogilvy69], D. Pedoe's *Geometry and the Visual Arts* [Pedoe76], Roger Sheperd's *Mind Sights* [Sheperd90], and the series of books on mathematical excursions by Martin Gardner, such as *Time Travel* [Gardner88] and *Penrose Tiles to Trapdoor Ciphers* [Gardner89]). Coxeter has written elegant books on geometry, including *Introduction to Geometry* [Coxeter69] *Mathematical Recreations and Essays* [Ball74], and Hoggar's *Mathematics for Computer Graphics* [Hoggar92] discusses many features of IFSs.

4 *Vectors Tools for Graphics*

The knowledge at which geometry aims is knowledge of the eternal, and not of aught perishing and transient.

Plato

For us, whose shoulders sag under the weight of the heritage of Greek thought and who walk in the paths traced out by the heroes of the Renaissance, a civilization without mathematics is unthinkable.

Andre Weil

Let us grant that the pursuit of mathematics is a divine madness of the human spirit.
Alfred North Whitehead

All that transcends geometry, transcends our comprehension.

Blaise Pascal

Goals of the Chapter

▲ To review vector arithmetic and to relate vectors to objects of interest in graphics.

▲ To relate geometric concepts to their algebraic representations.

▲ To describe lines and planes parametrically.

▲ To distinguish points and vectors properly.

▲ To exploit the dot product in graphics.

▲ To develop tools for working with objects in 3D space, including the cross product of two vectors.

PREVIEW

This chapter develops a number of useful tools for dealing with geometric objects encountered in computer graphics. Section 4.1 motivates the use of vectors in graphics and describes the principal graphical coordinate systems. Section 4.2 reviews the basic ideas pertaining to vectors and describes the key operations performed on vectors. Although most of the results presented apply to any number of dimensions, vectors in 2D and 3D are stressed. Section 4.3 reviews the powerful dot product operation and applies it to a number of geometric tasks, such as performing orthogonal projections, finding the distance from a point to a line, and determining the direction of a ray "reflected" from a shiny surface. Section 4.4 reviews the cross product of two vectors and discusses its important applications in 3D graphics.

Section 4.5 introduces the notion of a coordinate frame and homogeneous coordinates; the emphasis is on the idea that points and vectors are significantly different types of geometric objects. The section also develops the two principal mathematical representations of a line and a plane, showing where each is useful. Affine combinations of points are introduced, and an interesting kind of animation known as "tweening" is described, of which Bezier curves are an application.

Section 4.6 examines the central problem of finding where two line segments intersect, which is vastly simplified by using vectors. The section also discusses the problem of finding the unique circle determined by three points. Section 4.7 examines the issue of finding where a "ray" hits a line or plane and applies the notions that are involved to the clipping problem. Section 4.8 focuses on clipping lines against convex polygons and polyhedra, developing the powerful Cyrus–Beck clipping algorithm along the way.

The chapter ends with case studies that extend the tools presented and that provide opportunities to enrich one's graphics programming skills. Tasks include processing polygons, performing experiments in 2D "ray tracing," drawing rounded corners on figures, rendering animation by tweening, and developing advanced clipping tools.

4.1 INTRODUCTION

In computer graphics, we work, with objects defined in a 3D world (with 2D objects and worlds being just special cases thereof). All objects to be drawn, as well as the "cameras" used to draw them, have shape, position, and orientation. We must write computer programs that somehow describe these objects and how light bounces around to illuminate them, so that the final pixel values on the display can be computed. Think of an animation in which a camera flies through a hilly scene containing various buildings, trees, roads, and cars. What does the camera "see"? Whatever it does "see" has to be converted ultimately to numbers. It's a tall order.

The two fundamental mathematical disciplines that come to our aid in graphics are *vector analysis* and *transformations*. By studying these disciplines in detail, we develop methods to describe the various geometric objects we will encounter, and we learn how to convert geometric ideas to numbers. The result is a collection of crucial algorithms that we can call upon in graphics programs.

In this chapter, we examine the fundamental operations of vector algebra and see how they are used in graphics; Transformations are addressed in Chapter 5. We start at the beginning and develop a number of important tools and methods of attack that will appear again and again throughout the book. If you have previously studied vectors, much of this chapter will be familiar, but the numerous applications of vector analysis to geometric situations should still be scrutinized. Although the chapter might strike you as appearing out of a mathematics text, having the information it presents collected in one place and related to the real problems we encounter in graphics will be useful.

Why Are Vectors So Important?

A preview of some situations in which vector analysis comes to the rescue might help to motivate the study of vectors. Figure 4.1 shows three geometric problems that arise in graphics. Many other examples could be given as well.

Part (a) presents a computer-aided design problem: The user has placed three points on the display with the mouse and wants the unique circle that passes through

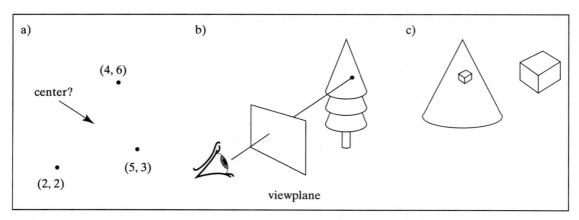

FIGURE 4.1 Three sample geometric problems that yield readily to vector analysis.

them to be drawn. (Can you visualize this circle?) For the coordinates given, where is the center of the circle located? We shall see in Section 4.6 that this problem is thorny without the use of vectors, but almost trivial when the right vector tools are used.

Part (b) shows a camera situated in a scene that contains a Christmas tree. The camera must form an image of the tree on its "viewplane" (similar to the film plane of a physical camera), and the image must be transferred to a screen window on the user's display. Where does the image of the tree appear on this plane, and what is its exact shape? To answer these questions, we need a detailed study of perspective projections, which will be greatly aided by the use of vector tools. (If this seems too easy, imagine that you are developing an animation involving a sphere and the camera is zooming in on the sphere along some trajectory, rotating as it does so. Write a routine that generates the whole sequence of images!)

Part (c) shows a shiny cone in which the reflection of a cube can be seen. Given the positions of the cone, cube, and viewing camera, where *exactly* does the reflected image appear, and what is its color and shape? In studying ray tracing in Chapter 14, we will make extensive use of vectors, and we will see that this problem is readily solved.

Some Basics

All points and vectors we work with are defined relative to some coordinate system. Figure 4.2 shows the coordinate systems that are normally used. Each system has an *origin* called ϑ and some axes emanating from ϑ. The axes are usually oriented at right angles to one another. Distances are marked along each axis, and a point is given coordinates according to how far along each axis it lies. Part (a) shows the usual two-dimensional system. Part (b) shows a *right-handed* 3D coordinate system, and part (c) shows a *left-handed* 3D coordinate system.

FIGURE 4.2 The familiar two- and three-dimensional coordinate systems.

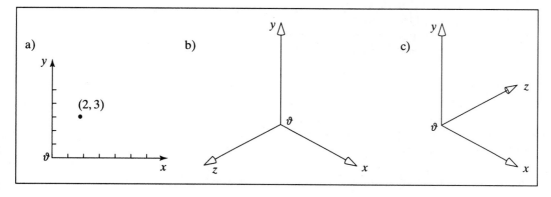

In a right-handed system, if you rotate your *right* hand around the *z*-axis by sweeping from the positive *x*-axis around to the positive *y*-axis, as shown in the figure, your thumb points along the positive *z*-axis. In a left-handed system, you must do this with your *left* hand to make your thumb point along the positive *z*-axis. Right-handed systems are more familiar and are conventionally used in mathematics, physics, and engineering. In this text, we use a right-handed system when setting up models for objects. But left-handed systems also have a natural place in graphics, when dealing with viewing systems and "cameras."

We first look at the basics of vectors, how one works with them, and how they are useful in graphics. In Section 4.5 we return to fundamentals and show an important distinction between points and vectors that, if ignored, can cause great difficulties in graphics programs.

4.2 REVIEW OF VECTORS

Not only Newton's laws, but also the other laws of physics, so far as we know today, have the two properties which we call invariance under translation of axes and rotation of axes. These properties are so important that a mathematical technique has been developed to take advantage of them in writing and using physical laws... called vector analysis. Richard Feynman

Vector arithmetic provides a unified way to express geometric ideas algebraically. In graphics, we work with vectors of two, three, and four dimensions, but many results need only be stated once, and they apply to vectors of any dimension. This broad applicability makes it possible to bring together the various cases that arise in graphics into a single expression, which can then be applied to a variety of tasks.

Viewed geometrically, vectors are objects having length and direction. They represent various physical entities, such as force, displacement, and velocity. A vector is often drawn as an arrow of a certain length pointing in a certain direction. It is valuable to think of a vector geometrically as a *displacement* from one point to another.

Figure 4.3 uses vectors to show how the stars in the Big Dipper are moving over time [Kerr79]. The current location of each star is shown by a point, and a vector shows the velocity of each star. The "tip" of each arrow shows the point where its star will be located in 50,000 years; producing a very different Big Dipper indeed!

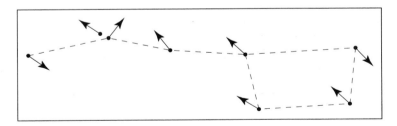

FIGURE 4.3 The Big Dipper now and in AD 50,000.

Figure 4.4a shows, in a 2D coordinate system, the two points $P = (1, 3)$ and $Q = (4, 1)$. The displacement from P to Q[1] is a vector **v** having components $(3, -2)$, calculated by subtracting the coordinates of the points individually. To "get from" P to Q, we shift down by 2 and to the right by 3. Because a vector is a displacement, it has a size and a direction, but no inherent location; the two arrows labeled **v** in the

---

[1]   Uppercase letters are conventionally used for points, boldface lowercase letters for vectors.

FIGURE 4.4 A vector as a displacement.

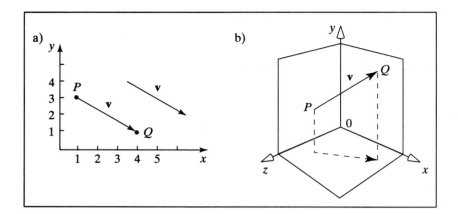

figure are in fact the same vector. Figure 4.4b shows the corresponding situation in three dimensions: **v** is the vector from point P to point Q. One often states that

The **difference** between two points is a vector: $\mathbf{v} = Q - P$.

Turning this around, we also say that a point Q is formed by displacing point P by vector **v**; we say that **v** "offsets" P to form Q. Algebraically, Q is then the **sum**: $Q = P + \mathbf{v}$. Also,

The **sum** of a point and a vector is a point: $P + \mathbf{v} = Q$.

At this point, we represent a vector through a list of its components; an n-dimensional vector is given by an *n-tuple*:

$$\mathbf{w} = (w_1, w_2, \ldots, w_n). \tag{4.1}$$

Mostly, we will be interested in 2D vectors such as $\mathbf{r} = (3.4, -7.78)$ and 3D vectors such as $\mathbf{t} = (33, 142.7, 89.1)$. Later, when it becomes important, we will explore the distinction between a vector and its *representation* and, in fact, will use a slightly expanded notation to represent vectors (and points). Writing a vector as a *row matrix* like $\mathbf{t} = (33, 142.7, 89.1)$ fits nicely on the page, but when it matters, we will instead write vectors as *column matrices*, such as

$$\mathbf{r} = \begin{pmatrix} 3.4 \\ -7.78 \end{pmatrix} \quad \text{and} \quad \mathbf{t} = \begin{pmatrix} 33 \\ 142.7 \\ 89.1 \end{pmatrix}.$$

It matters when we want to multiply a point or a vector by a matrix, as we shall see in Chapter 5.

4.2.1 Operations with Vectors

Vectors permit two fundamental operations: You can add them, and you can multiply them by **scalars** (real numbers).[2] So if **a** and **b** are two vectors, and s is a scalar, it is meaningful to form both $\mathbf{a} + \mathbf{b}$ and the product $s\mathbf{a}$. For example, if $\mathbf{a} = (2, 5, 6)$ and $\mathbf{b} = (-2, 7, 1)$, we can form the two vectors

$$\mathbf{a} + \mathbf{b} = (0, 12, 7)$$

and

$$6\mathbf{a} = (12, 30, 36),$$

---

[2] There are also systems in which scalars can be complex numbers; we do not work with them here.

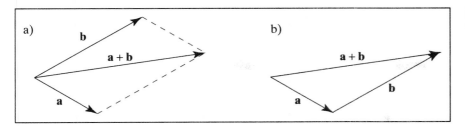

FIGURE 4.5 The sum of two vectors.

always performing the operations *componentwise*. Figure 4.5 shows a two-dimensional example, using $\mathbf{a} = (1, -1)$ and $\mathbf{b} = (2, 1)$. We can represent the addition of two vectors graphically in two different ways. In Figure 4.5(a), we show both vectors "starting" at the same point, thereby forming two sides of a parallelogram. The sum of the vectors is then a diagonal of this parallelogram—the diagonal that emanates from the starting point of the vectors. This view—the "parallelogram rule" for adding vectors—is the natural picture for forces acting at a point: The diagonal gives the resultant force.

Alternatively, in Figure 4.5(b), we show one vector (**b**) starting at the head of the other (**a**) and draw the sum as emanating from the tail of **a** to the head of **b**. The sum completes the triangle, which is the simple addition of one displacement to another. The components of the sum are clearly the sums of the components of its parts, as the algebra dictates.

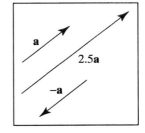

FIGURE 4.6 Scaling a vector.

Figure 4.6 shows the effect of scaling a vector. For $s = 2.5$, the vector $s\,\mathbf{a}$ has the same direction as **a**, but is 2.5 times as long. When s is negative, the direction of $s\mathbf{a}$ is opposite that of **a**: The case of $s = -1$ is shown in the figure.

Subtraction follows easily once adding and scaling have been established: $\mathbf{a} - \mathbf{c}$ is simply $\mathbf{a} + (-\mathbf{c})$. Figure 4.7 shows the geometric interpretation of this operation, forming the difference of **a** and **c** as the sum of **a** and $-\mathbf{c}$ [Figure 4.7(b)]. With the parallelogram rule, this sum is seen to be equal to the vector that emanates from the head of **c** and terminates at the head of **a** [Figure 4.7(c)]. This vector is recognized as one diagonal of the parallelogram constructed using **a** and **c**. Note that the other diagonal is the one that represents the sum $\mathbf{a} + \mathbf{c}$.

FIGURE 4.7 Subtracting vectors.

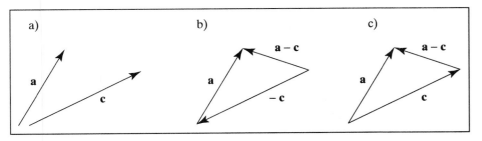

4.2.2 Linear Combinations of Vectors

With methods in hand for adding and scaling vectors, we can define a linear combination of vectors. To form a **linear combination** of two vectors, **v** and **w** (having the same dimension), we scale each of them by some scalars, say, a and b, and add the weighted versions to form the new vector, $a\mathbf{v} + b\mathbf{w}$. The more general definition for combining m such vectors is as follows:

> **DEFINITION:** A **linear combination** of the m vectors $\mathbf{v}_1, \mathbf{v}_2, \ldots, \mathbf{v}_m$ is a vector of the form
>
> $$\mathbf{w} = a_1\mathbf{v}_1 + a_2\mathbf{v}_2 + \ldots + a_m\mathbf{v}_m, \tag{4.2}$$
>
> where $a_1, a_2, \ldots, a_m$ are scalars.

For example, the linear combination $2(3, 4, -1) + 6(-1, 0, 2)$ forms the vector $(0, 8, 10)$. In later chapters we shall deal with rather elaborate linear combinations of vectors, especially when we seek to represent curves and surfaces using spline functions.

Two special types of linear combinations, "affine" and "convex" combinations, are particularly important in graphics.

Affine Combinations of Vectors

A linear combination of vectors is an **affine combination** if the coefficients $a_1, a_2, \ldots,$ a_m add up to unity. Thus, the linear combination in Equation (4.2) is affine if

$$a_1 + a_2 + \ldots + a_m = 1. \tag{4.3}$$

For example, $3\mathbf{a} + 2\mathbf{b} - 4\mathbf{c}$ is an affine combination of $\mathbf{a}$, $\mathbf{b}$, and $\mathbf{c}$, but $3\mathbf{a} + \mathbf{b} - 4\mathbf{c}$ is not. The coefficients of an affine combination of two vectors $\mathbf{a}$ and $\mathbf{b}$ are often forced to sum to unity by writing one vector as some scalar t and the other as $(1 - t)$, as in

$$(1 - t)\mathbf{a} + (t)\mathbf{b}. \tag{4.4}$$

Affine combinations of vectors appear in various contexts, as do affine combinations of points, as we shall see later.

Convex Combinations of Vectors

Convex combinations have an important place in mathematics and numerous applications in graphics. A **convex combination** arises as a further restriction on an affine combination: Not only must the coefficients of the linear combination sum to unity, but each coefficient must also be nonnegative. Thus, the linear combination of Equation (4.3) is **convex** if:

$$a_1 + a_2 + \ldots + a_m = 1 \tag{4.5}$$

and

$$a_i \geq 0, \text{for } i = 1, \ldots, m.$$

As a consequence, all a_i must lie between 0 and 1. (Why?)

Accordingly, $.3\mathbf{a} + .7\mathbf{b}$ is a convex combination of $\mathbf{a}$ and $\mathbf{b}$, but $1.8\mathbf{a} - .8\mathbf{b}$ is not. The set of coefficients $a_1, a_2, \ldots, a_m$ is sometimes said to form a **partition of unity**, suggesting that a unit amount of "material" is partitioned into pieces. Convex combinations frequently arise in applications in which one is making a unit amount of some brew and can combine only positive amounts of the various ingredients. Such combinations appear in unexpected contexts. For instance, we shall see in Chapter 11 that spline curves are in fact convex combinations of certain vectors, and in our discussion of color in Chapter 12, we shall find that colors can be considered as vectors and that any color of unit brightness may be considered to be a convex combination of three primary colors!

We will find it useful to talk about the "set of all convex combinations" of a collection of vectors. The set of all convex combinations of the two vectors $\mathbf{v}_1$ and $\mathbf{v}_2$ is the set of all vectors

$$\mathbf{v} = (1 - a)\mathbf{v}_1 + a\mathbf{v}_2 \tag{4.6}$$

as the parameter a is allowed to vary from 0 to 1. (Why?) What is this set? Rearranging the equation, we see that

$$\mathbf{v} = \mathbf{v}_1 + a(\mathbf{v}_2 - \mathbf{v}_1). \tag{4.7}$$

Figure 4.8(a) shows $\mathbf{v}$ to be the vector that is $\mathbf{v}_1$ plus some fraction of $\mathbf{v}_2 - \mathbf{v}_1$, so the tip of $\mathbf{v}$ lies on the line joining $\mathbf{v}_1$ and $\mathbf{v}_2$. As a varies from 0 to 1, $\mathbf{v}$ takes on all the positions on the line from $\mathbf{v}_1$ to $\mathbf{v}_2$, and only those positions.

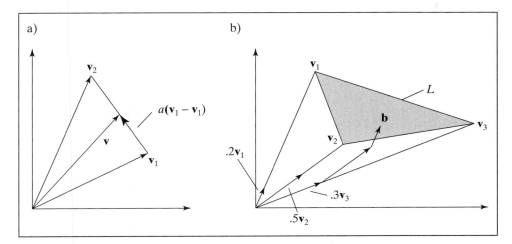

FIGURE 4.8 The set of vectors representable by convex combinations.

Figure 4.8(b) shows the set of all convex combinations of three vectors. We choose two parameters a_1 and a_2, both lying between 0 and 1, and form the linear combination

$$\mathbf{q} = a_1\mathbf{v}_1 + a_2\mathbf{v}_2 + (1 - a_1 - a_2)\mathbf{v}_3, \tag{4.8}$$

where we also insist that a_1 plus a_2 not exceed unity. The vector $\mathbf{v}$ is a convex combination, since none of its coefficients is ever negative and they sum to unity. Figure 4.8(b) shows the three position vectors $\mathbf{v}_1 = (2, 6)$, $\mathbf{v}_2 = (3, 3)$, and $\mathbf{v}_3 = (7, 4)$. By the proper choices of a_1 and a_2, any vector lying within the shaded triangle of vectors can be represented, and no vectors outside this triangle can be reached. The vector $\mathbf{b} = .2\mathbf{v}_1 + .5\mathbf{v}_2 + .3\mathbf{v}_3$, for instance, is shown explicitly as the vector sum of the three weighted ingredients. (Note how it is built up out of "portions" of the three constituent vectors.) So the set of all convex combinations of these three vectors "spans" the shaded triangle. (The proof of this statement is requested in a later exercise.)

If $a_2 = 0$, any vector in the line L that joins $\mathbf{v}_1$ and $\mathbf{v}_3$ can be "reached" by the proper choice of a_1. For example, the vector that is 20 percent of the way from $\mathbf{v}_1$ to $\mathbf{v}_3$ along L is given by $.8\mathbf{v}_1 + 0\mathbf{v}_2 + .2\mathbf{v}_3$.

4.2.3 The Magnitude of a Vector; Unit Vectors

If a vector $\mathbf{w}$ is represented by the n-tuple $(w_1, w_2, \ldots, w_n)$, how might its magnitude (equivalently, its *length* or *size*) be defined and computed? We denote the magnitude by $|\mathbf{w}|$ and define it as the distance from the tail to the head of the vector. On the basis of the Pythagorean theorem, we obtain

$$|\mathbf{w}| = \sqrt{w_1^2 + w_2^2 + \ldots + w_n^2}. \tag{4.9}$$

For example, the magnitude of $\mathbf{w} = (4, -2)$ is $\sqrt{20}$, and that of $\mathbf{w} = (1, -3, 2)$ is $\sqrt{14}$. A vector of zero length is denoted as $\mathbf{0}$. Note that if $\mathbf{w}$ is the vector from point A to point B, then $|\mathbf{w}|$ will be the distance from A to B. (Why?)

It is often useful to scale a vector so that the result has unity length. This type of scaling is called **normalizing** a vector, and the result is known as a **unit vector**. For example, we form the normalized version of $\mathbf{a}$, denoted $\hat{\mathbf{a}}$, by scaling $\mathbf{a}$ with the value $1/|\mathbf{a}|$:

$$\hat{\mathbf{a}} = \frac{\mathbf{a}}{|\mathbf{a}|}. \tag{4.10}$$

Clearly, $|\hat{\mathbf{a}}| = 1$ (why?), and $\hat{\mathbf{a}}$ is a unit vector having the same direction as $\mathbf{a}$. For example, if $\mathbf{a} = (3, -4)$, then $|\mathbf{a}| = 5$, and the normalized version is $\hat{\mathbf{a}} = \left(\frac{3}{5}, \frac{-4}{5}\right)$. At times, we refer to a unit vector as a **direction**. Note that any vector can be written as its magnitude times its direction: If $\hat{\mathbf{a}}$ is the normalized version of $\mathbf{a}$, vector $\mathbf{a}$ may always be written as $\mathbf{a} = |\mathbf{a}|\,\hat{\mathbf{a}}$.

PRACTICE EXERCISES

4.2.1 Representing vectors as linear combinations

With reference to Figure 4.8, what values or range of values for a_1 and a_2 create the following sets?

a. $\mathbf{v}_1$.
b. The line joining $\mathbf{v}_1$ and $\mathbf{v}_2$.
c. The vector midway between $\mathbf{v}_2$ and $\mathbf{v}_3$.
d. The centroid of the triangle.

4.2.2 The set of all convex combinations

Show that the set of all convex combinations of three vectors $\mathbf{v}_1$, $\mathbf{v}_2$, and $\mathbf{v}_3$ is the set of vectors whose tips lie in the "triangle" formed by the tips of the three vectors. *Hint*: Each point in the triangle is a combination of $\mathbf{v}_1$ and some point lying between $\mathbf{v}_2$ and $\mathbf{v}_3$.

4.2.3 Factoring out a scalar

Show how scaling a vector $\mathbf{v}$ by a scalar s changes the length of $\mathbf{v}$. That is, show that $|s\mathbf{v}| = |s||\mathbf{v}|$. Note the dual use of the magnitude symbol $|\ \ |$, once for a scalar and once for a vector.

4.2.4 Normalizing vectors

Normalize each of the following vectors:

a. $(1, -2, .5)$.
b. $(8, 6)$
c. $(4, 3)$.   ▪

4.3 THE DOT PRODUCT

Two other powerful tools that facilitate working with vectors are the dot (or inner) product and the cross product. The dot product produces a scalar; the cross product operates only on three-dimensional vectors and produces another vector. In this section we review the basic properties of the dot product, principally to develop the notion of perpendicularity. We then use the dot product to solve a number of important geometric problems in graphics. After that, the cross product is introduced and is employed to solve a number of 3D geometric problems.

The **dot product** of two vectors is simple to define and compute. For two-dimensional vectors, (a_1, a_2) and (b_1, b_2), it is simply the scalar whose value is $a_1 b_1 + a_2 b_2$. Thus, to calculate the dot product, we multiply corresponding components of the two vectors and add the results. For example, the dot product of $(3, 4)$ and $(1, 6)$ is 27, and that of $(2, 3)$ and $(9, -6)$ is 0.

The definition of the dot product generalizes easily to n dimensions:

DEFINITION: THE DOT PRODUCT The dot product d of two n-dimensional vectors $\mathbf{v} = (v_1, v_2, \ldots, v_n)$ and $\mathbf{w} = (w_1, w_2, \ldots, w_n)$ is denoted as $\mathbf{v} \cdot \mathbf{w}$ and has the value

$$d = \mathbf{v} \cdot \mathbf{w} = \sum_{i=1}^{n} v_i w_i \qquad (4.11)$$

▪ EXAMPLE 4.3.1

- The dot product of $(2, 3, 1)$ and $(0, 4, -1)$ is 11.
- $(2, 2, 2, 2) \cdot (4, 1, 2, 1.1) = 16.2$.
- $(1, 0, 1, 0, 1) \cdot (0, 1, 0, 1, 0) = 0$.
- $(169, 0, 43) \cdot (0, 375.3, 0) = 0$.

4.3.1 Properties of the Dot Product

The dot product exhibits four major properties that we frequently exploit and that follow easily from its basic definition:

1. Symmetry: $\mathbf{a} \cdot \mathbf{b} = \mathbf{b} \cdot \mathbf{a}$
2. Linearity: $(\mathbf{a} + \mathbf{c}) \cdot \mathbf{b} = \mathbf{a} \cdot \mathbf{b} + \mathbf{c} \cdot \mathbf{b}$
3. Homogeneity: $(s\mathbf{a}) \cdot \mathbf{b} = s(\mathbf{a} \cdot \mathbf{b})$
4. $|\mathbf{b}|^2 = \mathbf{b} \cdot \mathbf{b}$

The first property is that the order in which the two vectors are combined does not matter: The dot product is **commutative**. The next two properties have to do with the fact that the dot product is **linear**: The dot product of a sum of vectors can be expressed as the sum of the individual dot products, and scaling a vector scales the value of the dot product. The last property asserts that taking the dot product of a vector with itself yields the **square of the length** of the vector. This property appears frequently in the form $|\mathbf{b}| = \sqrt{\mathbf{b} \cdot \mathbf{b}}$.

The manipulations in Example 4.3.2 show how the foregoing properties can be used to simplify an expression involving dot products. The result itself will be used in the next section.

▪ EXAMPLE 4.3.2 Simplification of $|\mathbf{a} - \mathbf{b}|^2$

Simplify the expression for the square of the length of the difference of two vectors $\mathbf{a}$ and $\mathbf{b}$ to obtain the relation

$$|\mathbf{a} - \mathbf{b}|^2 = |\mathbf{a}|^2 - 2\mathbf{a} \cdot \mathbf{b} + |\mathbf{b}|^2. \qquad (4.12)$$

The derivation proceeds as follows: Give the name C to the expression $|\mathbf{a} - \mathbf{b}|^2$. Then by the fourth property, C is a dot product; that is,

$$C = |\mathbf{a} - \mathbf{b}|^2 = (\mathbf{a} - \mathbf{b}) \cdot (\mathbf{a} - \mathbf{b}).$$

Using linearity, we obtain $C = \mathbf{a} \cdot (\mathbf{a} - \mathbf{b}) - \mathbf{b} \cdot (\mathbf{a} - \mathbf{b})$. From the symmetry and linearity properties, we simplify this further to $C = \mathbf{a} \cdot \mathbf{a} - 2\mathbf{a} \cdot \mathbf{b} + \mathbf{b} \cdot \mathbf{b}$. Finally, the fourth property yields $C = |\mathbf{a}|^2 - 2\mathbf{a} \cdot \mathbf{b} + |\mathbf{b}|^2$, the desired result.

By replacing the minus sign with a plus sign in Eq. (4.12), the following similar and useful relation emerges:

$$|\mathbf{a} + \mathbf{b}|^2 = |\mathbf{a}|^2 + 2\mathbf{a} \cdot \mathbf{b} + |\mathbf{b}|^2. \qquad (4.13)$$

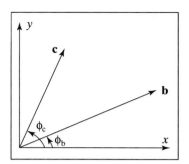

FIGURE 4.9 Finding the angle between two vectors.

4.3.2 The Angle between Two Vectors

The most important application of the dot product is in finding the angle between two vectors or between two intersecting lines. Figure 4.9 shows the 2D case, where the vectors **b** and **c** lie at angles ϕ_b and ϕ_c, respectively, relative to the x-axis. Now, from elementary trigonometry,

$$\mathbf{b} = \left(|\mathbf{b}| \cos \phi_b, |\mathbf{b}| \sin \phi_b\right)$$

and

$$\mathbf{c} = \left(|\mathbf{c}| \cos \phi_c, |\mathbf{c}| \sin \phi_c\right).$$

Thus, the dot product of **b** and **c** is

$$\mathbf{b} \cdot \mathbf{c} = |\mathbf{b}||\mathbf{c}| \cos \phi_c \cos \phi_b + |\mathbf{b}||\mathbf{c}| \sin \phi_b \sin \phi_c$$
$$= |\mathbf{b}||\mathbf{c}| \cos\left(\phi_c - \phi_b\right),$$

so we have, for any two vectors **b** and **c**,

$$\mathbf{b} \cdot \mathbf{c} = |\mathbf{b}||\mathbf{c}| \cos(\theta), \tag{4.14}$$

where θ is the angle from **b** to **c**. Hence, $\mathbf{b} \cdot \mathbf{c}$ varies as the cosine of the angle from **b** to **c**. The same result holds for vectors of three, four, or any number of dimensions.

To obtain a slightly more compact form, we divide through both sides by $|\mathbf{b}||\mathbf{c}|$ and use the unit vector notation $\hat{\mathbf{b}} = \mathbf{b}/|\mathbf{b}|$ to obtain

$$\cos(\theta) = \hat{\mathbf{b}} \cdot \hat{\mathbf{c}}. \tag{4.15}$$

This is the desired result: The cosine of the angle between two vectors **b** and **c** is the dot product of the normalized vectors.

■ **EXAMPLE 4.3.3**

Find the angle between $\mathbf{b} = (3, 4)$ and $\mathbf{c} = (5, 2)$.

SOLUTION:

Form $|\mathbf{b}| = 5$ and $|\mathbf{c}| = 5.385$ so that $\hat{\mathbf{b}} = (3/5, 4/5)$ and $\hat{\mathbf{c}} = (.9285, .3714)$. The dot product $\hat{\mathbf{b}} \cdot \hat{\mathbf{c}} = .85422 = \cos(\theta)$; hence, $\theta = 31.326°$. This result can be checked by plotting the two vectors on graph paper and measuring the angle between them.

4.3.3 The Sign of b · c, and Perpendicularity

Recall that $\cos(\theta)$ is **positive** if $|\theta|$ is less than 90°, **zero** if $|\theta|$ equals 90°, and **negative** if $|\theta|$ exceeds 90°. Because the dot product of two vectors is proportional to the cosine of the angle between them, we can observe immediately that two vectors (of any nonzero length) are

less than	90° apart	if $\mathbf{b} \cdot \mathbf{c} > 0$;
exactly	90° apart	if $\mathbf{b} \cdot \mathbf{c} = 0$;
more than	90° apart	if $\mathbf{b} \cdot \mathbf{c} < 0$.

$$(4.16)$$

These results are indicated in Figure 4.10. The sign of the dot product is used in many algorithmic tests.

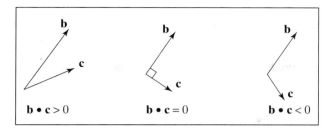

FIGURE 4.10 The sign of the dot product.

The case in which the vectors are 90° apart, or **perpendicular**, is of special importance.

DEFINITION: Vectors **b** and **c** are perpendicular if **b** · **c** = 0. (4.17)

Other names for "perpendicular" are **orthogonal** and **normal**, and we shall use all three interchangeably.

The most familiar examples of orthogonal vectors are those aimed along the axes of 2D and 3D coordinate systems, as shown in Figure 4.11. In part (a), the 2D vectors $(1, 0)$ and $(0, 1)$ are mutually perpendicular unit vectors. The 3D counterparts of these vectors are so commonly used that they are called the "standard unit vectors" and are given the names **i**, **j**, and **k**.

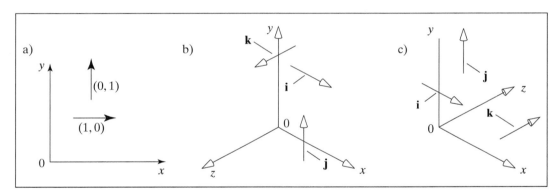

DEFINITION: The **standard unit vectors** in 3D have components

$\mathbf{i} = (1, 0, 0),$ $\mathbf{j} = (0, 1, 0),$ and $\mathbf{k} = (0, 0, 1).$ (4.18)

FIGURE 4.11 The standard unit vectors.

Part (b) of the figure shows these components in a right-handed system, and part (c) shows them in a left-handed system. Note that **k** always points in the positive z direction.

Using these definitions, we can write any 3D vector such as (a, b, c) in the alternative form

$(a, b, c) = a\mathbf{i} + b\mathbf{j} + c\mathbf{k}.$ (4.19)

■ **EXAMPLE 4.3.4**

Notice that $\mathbf{v} = (2, 5, -1)$ is clearly the same as $2(1, 0, 0) + 5(0, 1, 0) - 1(0, 0, 1)$, which is recognized as $2\mathbf{i} + 5\mathbf{j} - \mathbf{k}$.

The form shown in Equation (4.19) presents a vector as a sum of separate elementary component vectors, so it simplifies various pencil-and-paper calculations. This form is particularly convenient in dealing with the cross product, discussed in Section 4.4.

PRACTICE EXERCISES

4.3.1 Alternative proof of $b \cdot c = |b||c| \cos \theta$

Note that **b** and **c** form two sides of a triangle, and the third side is **b** − **c**. Use the law of cosines to obtain the square of the length of **b** − **c** in terms of the lengths of **b** and **c** and the cosine of θ. Compare your answer with Equation (4.12) to obtain the desired result.

4.3.2 Find the angle

Calculate the angle between the vectors $(2, 3)$ and $(-3, 1)$, and check the result visually, using graph paper. Then compute the angle between the 3D vectors $(1, 3, -2)$ and $(3, 3, 1)$.

4.3.3 Testing for perpendicularity

Which pairs of the following vectors are perpendicular to one another: $(3, 4, 1)$, $(2, 1, 1)$, $(-3, -4, 1)$, $(0, 0, 0)$, $(1, -2, 0)$, $(4, 4, 4)$, $(0, -1, 4)$, and $(2, 2, 1)$?

4.3.4 Pythagorean theorem

Refer to Equations (4.12) and (4.13). For the case in which **a** and **b** are perpendicular, these expressions have the same value, which seems to make no sense geometrically. Show that it all works out fine, and relate the result to the Pythagorean theorem.

4.3.4 The 2D "Perp" Vector

Suppose the 2D vector **a** has components (a_x, a_y). What vectors are perpendicular to **a**? One way to obtain such a vector is to interchange the x- and y-components and negate one of them.[3] Let $\mathbf{b} = (-a_y, a_x)$. Then the dot product $\mathbf{a} \cdot \mathbf{b} = 0$, so **a** and **b** are indeed perpendicular. For instance, if $\mathbf{a} = (4, 7)$, then $\mathbf{b} = (-7, 4)$ is a vector normal to **a**. There are infinitely many vectors normal to any **a**, since any scalar multiple of **b**, such as $(-21, 12)$ and $(7, -4)$, is also normal to **a**. (Sketch several of these vectors for a given **a**.)

It is convenient to have a symbol for one *particular* vector that is normal to a given 2D vector **a**. We use the symbol ⊥ (pronounced "perp") for this purpose.

> **DEFINITION:** Let $\mathbf{a} = (a_x, a_y)$. Then
> $$\mathbf{a}^{\perp} = (-a_y, a_x) \tag{4.20}$$
> is the **counterclockwise perpendicular** to **a**.

Note that **a** and $\mathbf{a}^{\perp}$ have the same length: $|\mathbf{a}| = |\mathbf{a}^{\perp}|$. Figure 4.12(a) shows an arbitrary vector **a** and the resulting $\mathbf{a}^{\perp}$. Note that moving from the direction **a** to the direction $\mathbf{a}^{\perp}$ requires a left turn. (Making a right turn is equivalent to turning in the direction $-\mathbf{a}^{\perp}$.)

FIGURE 4.12 The vector $\mathbf{a}^{\perp}$ perpendicular to **a**.

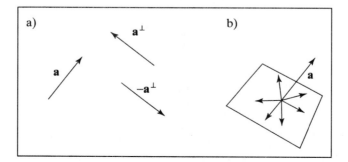

---

[3]　This is equivalent to the familiar fact that perpendicular lines have slopes that are negative reciprocals of one another. In Chapter 5, we see that the "interchange and negate" operation arises naturally in connection with a rotation of 90 degrees.

We show in the next section how this notation can be put to good use. Figure 4.12(b) shows that in three dimensions no single vector lies in "the" direction perpendicular to a given 3D vector **a**, since *any* of the vectors lying in the plane perpendicular to **a** will do. However, the cross product developed later will provide a simple tool for dealing with such vectors.

PRACTICE EXERCISES

4.3.5 Some pleasant properties of $a^\perp$

It is useful in some discussions to view the "perp" symbol $\perp$ as an operator that performs a "rotate 90° left" operation on its argument, so that $\mathbf{a}^\perp$ is the vector produced by applying the $\perp$ to vector **a**, much as $\sqrt{x}$ is the value produced by applying the square-root operator to x. Viewing $\perp$ in this way, show that it has the following properties:

a. Linearity: $(\mathbf{a} + \mathbf{b})^\perp = \mathbf{a}^\perp + \mathbf{b}^\perp$ and $(A\mathbf{a})^\perp = A\mathbf{a}^\perp$ for any scalar A
b. $\mathbf{a}^{\perp\perp} = (\mathbf{a}^\perp)^\perp = -\mathbf{a}$ (two perps make a reversal)

4.3.6 The "perp dot" product

Interesting things happen when we form the dot product of the perp of a vector with another vector, as in $\mathbf{a}^\perp \cdot \mathbf{b}$. We call this operation the "perp dot product" [Hill, 1995]. Use the basic definition of $\mathbf{a}^\perp$ to show that

$$\begin{aligned}
\mathbf{a}^\perp \cdot \mathbf{b} &= a_x b_y - a_y b_x &&\text{(value of the perp dot product)} \\
\mathbf{a}^\perp \cdot \mathbf{a} &= 0 &&\text{($\mathbf{a}^\perp$ is perpendicular to } \mathbf{a}\text{)} \\
|\mathbf{a}^\perp|^2 &= |\mathbf{a}|^2 &&\text{($\mathbf{a}^\perp$ and } \mathbf{a}\text{ have the same length)} \\
\mathbf{a}^\perp \cdot \mathbf{b} &= -\mathbf{b}^\perp \cdot \mathbf{a}, &&\text{($\mathbf{a}^\perp$ is antisymmetric)}
\end{aligned} \tag{4.21}$$

The fourth fact shows that the perp dot product is antisymmetric: Moving the $\perp$ from one vector to the other reverses the sign of the dot product. Other useful properties of the perp dot product will be discussed as they are needed.

4.3.7 Calculate a perp dot product

Compute $\mathbf{a} \cdot \mathbf{b}$ and $\mathbf{a}^\perp \cdot \mathbf{b}$ for $\mathbf{a} = (3, 4)$ and $\mathbf{b} = (2, 1)$.

4.3.8 It's a determinant

Show that $\mathbf{a}^\perp \cdot \mathbf{b}$ can be written as the determinant

$$\mathbf{a}^\perp \cdot \mathbf{b} = \begin{vmatrix} a_x & a_y \\ b_x & b_y \end{vmatrix}.$$

(For definitions of matrices and determinants, see Appendix 2.)

4.3.9 Other goodies

a. Show that $(\mathbf{a}^\perp \cdot \mathbf{b})^2 + (\mathbf{a} \cdot \mathbf{b})^2 = |\mathbf{a}|^2 |\mathbf{b}|^2$.
b. Show that if $\mathbf{a} + \mathbf{b} + \mathbf{c} = \mathbf{0}$, then $\mathbf{a}^\perp \cdot \mathbf{b} = \mathbf{b}^\perp \cdot \mathbf{c} = \mathbf{c}^\perp \cdot \mathbf{a}$.   ■

4.3.5 Orthogonal Projections and the Distance from a Point to a Line

Three geometric problems arise frequently in graphics applications: **projecting** a vector onto a given vector, **resolving** a vector into its components in one direction and another, and finding the distance between a point and a line. All three problems are simplified if we use the perp vector and the perp dot product.

Figure 4.13a shows the basic ingredients. We are given two points A and C and a vector **v**. The following questions arise:

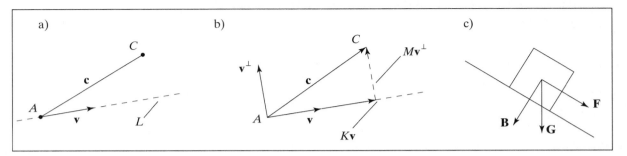

FIGURE 4.13 Resolving a vector into two orthogonal vectors.

a. How far is the point C from the line L that passes through A in the direction **v**?

b. If we drop a perpendicular from C onto L, where does it hit L?

c. How do we decompose the vector $\mathbf{c} = C - A$ into a part along the line L and a part perpendicular to L?

Figure 4.13(b) defines some additional quantities: $\mathbf{v}^{\perp}$ is the vector **v** rotated 90 degrees CCW. Dropping a perpendicular from C onto line L, we say that the vector **c** is **resolved** into the portion $K\mathbf{v}$ along **v** and the portion $M\mathbf{v}^{\perp}$ perpendicular to **v**, where K and M are some constants to be determined. Then we have

$$\mathbf{c} = K\mathbf{v} + M\mathbf{v}^{\perp}. \tag{4.22}$$

Given **c** and **v**, we want to solve for K and M. Once these are found, we say that the **orthogonal projection** of **c** onto **v** is $K\mathbf{v}$ and that the distance from C to the line is $|M\mathbf{v}^{\perp}|$.

Figure 4.13(c) shows a situation in which the questions a, b, and c might arise. We wish to analyze how the gravitational force vector **G** acts on the block shown to pull it down the incline. To do this, we must resolve **G** into the force **F** acting along the incline and the force **B** acting perpendicular to the incline. That is, we seek **F** and **B** such that $\mathbf{G} = \mathbf{F} + \mathbf{B}$. (Are the vectors **B** and **F** correct in the figure?)

Equation (4.22) is really two equations: The left- and right-hand sides must agree for the x-components, and they also must agree for the y-components. There are two unknowns: K and M. So we have two equations in two unknowns, and Cramer's rule can be applied. But who remembers Cramer's rule? We use a trick here that is easy to remember and immediately reveals the solution; it is equivalent to Cramer's rule, but simpler to apply.

The trick in solving two equations in two unknowns is to eliminate one of the variables. We do this by forming the dot product of both sides with the vector **v**:

$$\mathbf{c} \cdot \mathbf{v} = K\mathbf{v} \cdot \mathbf{v} + M\mathbf{v}^{\perp} \cdot \mathbf{v}. \tag{4.23}$$

Happily, the term $\mathbf{v}^{\perp} \cdot \mathbf{v}$ vanishes (why?), yielding

$$K = \frac{\mathbf{c} \cdot \mathbf{v}}{\mathbf{v} \cdot \mathbf{v}}.$$

Similarly, we "dot" both sides of Equation (4.22) with $\mathbf{v}^{\perp}$ to obtain

$$M = \frac{\mathbf{c} \cdot \mathbf{v}^{\perp}}{\mathbf{v} \cdot \mathbf{v}},$$

where we have used the third property in Equation (4.21). Putting all this together, we have

$$\mathbf{c} = \left(\frac{\mathbf{v} \cdot \mathbf{c}}{|\mathbf{v}|^2}\right)\mathbf{v} + \left(\frac{\mathbf{v}^{\perp} \cdot \mathbf{c}}{|\mathbf{v}|^2}\right)\mathbf{v}^{\perp} \qquad \text{(resolving } \mathbf{c} \text{ into } \mathbf{v} \text{ and } \mathbf{v}^{\perp}\text{)}. \tag{4.24}$$

This equality holds for any vectors **c** and **v**. The part along **v** is known as the **orthogonal projection** of **c** onto the vector **v**. The second term gives the "difference term" explicitly and compactly; its size is the distance from C to the line:

$$\text{distance} = \left| \frac{\mathbf{v}^{\perp} \cdot \mathbf{c}}{|\mathbf{v}|^2} \mathbf{v}^{\perp} \right| = \frac{|\mathbf{v}^{\perp} \cdot \mathbf{c}|}{|\mathbf{v}|}.$$

(Check that the second form really equals the first.) Referring to Figure 4.13(b), we can say that **the distance from a point** C **to the line through** A in the direction **v** is

$$\text{distance} = \frac{|\mathbf{v}^{\perp} \cdot (C - A)|}{|\mathbf{v}|}. \tag{4.25}$$

■ **EXAMPLE 4.3.5**

Find the orthogonal projection of the vector **c** $= (6, 4)$ onto **a** $= (1, 2)$. (Sketch the relevant vectors.)

SOLUTION:

Evaluate the first term in Equation 4.24, obtaining the vector $(14, 28)/5$.

■ **EXAMPLE 4.3.6** How far is the point $C = (6, 4)$ from the line that passes through $(1, 1)$ and $(4, 9)$?

SOLUTION:

Set $A = (1, 1)$, use $\mathbf{v} = (4, 9) - (1, 1) = (3, 8)$, and evaluate *distance* in Equation 4.25: The result is *distance* $= 31/\sqrt{73}$.

PRACTICE EXERCISES

4.3.10 Resolve it!

Express the vector **g** $= (4, 7)$ as a linear combination of **b** $= (3, 5)$ and **b**$^{\perp}$. How far is $(4, 2) + \mathbf{g}$ from the line through $(4, 2)$ that moves in the direction **b**?

4.3.11 A block pulled down an incline

A block rests on an incline tilted 30° from the horizontal. Gravity exerts a force of one newton on the block. What component of gravity moves the block along the incline?

4.3.12 How far is it?

How far from the line through $(2, 5)$ and $(4, -1)$ does the point $(6, 11)$ lie? Check your result on graph paper. ■

4.3.6 Applications of Projection: Reflections

To display the reflection of light from a mirror or the behavior of billiard balls bouncing off one another, we need to find the direction that an object takes upon being reflected at a given surface. In a case study at the end of this chapter, we describe an application that traces a ray of light as it bounces around inside a reflective chamber or a billiard ball as it bounces around a pool table. At each bounce, the ray of light or the billiard ball is reflected in a new direction, as derived in this section.

When light reflects from a mirror, we know that the angle of reflection must equal the angle of incidence. We next show how to use vectors and projections to compute the direction in which the light is reflected. We can think in terms of two-dimensional vectors for simplicity, but because the derivation does not explicitly state the dimensions of the vectors involved, the same result applies in three dimensions for reflection from a surface.

Figure 4.14(a) shows a ray having direction **a**, hitting line L, and reflecting in (an as yet unknown) direction **r**. The vector **n** is perpendicular to the line. Angle θ_1 must equal angle θ_2. How is **r** related to **a** and **n**? Figure 4.14(b) shows **a** resolved into a portion **m** along **n** and a portion **e** orthogonal to **n**. Because of symmetry, **r** has the same component **e** orthogonal to **n**, but the opposite component along **n**, so **r** = **e** − **m**. Because **e** = **a** − **m**, it follows that **r** = **a** − 2**m**. Now, **m** is the orthogonal projection of **a** onto **n**, so by Equation (4.24),

$$\mathbf{m} = \frac{\mathbf{a} \cdot \mathbf{n}}{|\mathbf{n}|^2} \mathbf{n} = (\mathbf{a} \cdot \hat{\mathbf{n}})\hat{\mathbf{n}}. \tag{4.26}$$

(Recall that $\hat{\mathbf{n}}$ is a unit vector in the direction of **n**.) Accordingly, we obtain the result

$$\mathbf{r} = \mathbf{a} - 2(\mathbf{a} \cdot \hat{\mathbf{n}})\hat{\mathbf{n}} \qquad \text{(direction of the reflected ray).} \tag{4.27}$$

In three dimensions, physics demands that the reflected direction **r** lie in the plane defined by **n** and **a**. Equation (4.27) indeed supports this requirement, as we subsequently show in Chapter 5.

FIGURE 4.14 Reflection of a ray from a surface.

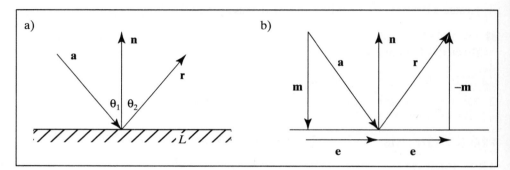

■ EXAMPLE 4.3.7

Let **a** = $(4, -2)$ and **n** = $(0, 3)$. Then Equation (4.27) yields **r** = $(4, 2)$, as expected. Both the angle of incidence and the angle of reflection are equal to $\tan^{-1}(2)$.

PRACTICE EXERCISES

4.3.13 Find the reflected direction

For **a** = $(2, 3)$ and **n** = $(-2, 1)$, find the direction of the reflection.

4.3.14 Lengths of the incident and reflected vectors

Using Equation (4.27) and properties of the dot product, show that $|\mathbf{r}| = |\mathbf{a}|$. ■

4.4 THE CROSS PRODUCT OF TWO VECTORS

The **cross product** (also called the **vector product**) of two vectors is another vector. It has many useful properties, but the one we use most often is that it is perpendicular to both of the given vectors. The cross product is defined only for three-dimensional vectors.

Given the 3D vectors **a** = (a_x, a_y, a_z) and **b** = (b_x, b_y, b_z), their cross product is denoted as **a** × **b**. It is defined in terms of the standard unit vectors **i**, **j**, and **k** [see Equation (4.18)] by

$$\mathbf{a} \times \mathbf{b} = (a_y b_z - a_z b_y)\mathbf{i} + (a_z b_x - a_x b_z)\mathbf{j} + (a_x b_y - a_y b_x)\mathbf{k}. \tag{4.28}$$

(The cross product can actually be derived from more fundamental principles; see the exercises.) As this form is rather difficult to remember, the cross product is often written as the easily remembered determinant

$$\mathbf{a} \times \mathbf{b} = \begin{vmatrix} \mathbf{i} & \mathbf{j} & \mathbf{k} \\ a_x & a_y & a_z \\ b_x & b_y & b_z \end{vmatrix}. \tag{4.29}$$

(See Appendix 2 for a review of determinants.) Thus, remembering how to form the cross product requires only remembering how to form a determinant.

■ EXAMPLE 4.4.1

For $\mathbf{a} = (3, 0, 2)$ and $\mathbf{b} = (4, 1, 8)$, direct calculation shows that $\mathbf{a} \times \mathbf{b} = -2\mathbf{i} - 16\mathbf{j} + 3\mathbf{k}$. What is $\mathbf{b} \times \mathbf{a}$?

From Equation (4.29), one can easily show that the cross product satisfies the following algebraic properties:

$$\mathbf{i} \times \mathbf{j} = \mathbf{k};$$
1. $\mathbf{j} \times \mathbf{k} = \mathbf{i};$
   $\mathbf{k} \times \mathbf{i} = \mathbf{j}.$
2. $\mathbf{a} \times \mathbf{b} = -\mathbf{b} \times \mathbf{a}$ (antisymmetry)
3. $\mathbf{a} \times (\mathbf{b} + \mathbf{c}) = \mathbf{a} \times \mathbf{b} + \mathbf{a} \times \mathbf{c}$ (linearity)   (4.30)
4. $(s\mathbf{a}) \times \mathbf{b} = s(\mathbf{a} \times \mathbf{b})$ (homogeneity)

These equations are true in both left-handed and right-handed coordinate systems. Note the logical (alphabetical) ordering of vectors in the equation $\mathbf{i} \times \mathbf{j} = \mathbf{k}$, which also provides a handy mnemonic device for remembering the direction of cross products.

PRACTICE EXERCISES

4.4.1 Demonstrate the four properties
Prove each of the preceding four properties of the cross product.

4.4.2 Derivation of the cross product
The form of the cross product given in Equation 4.28, presented as a definition, can actually be derived from more fundamental ideas. We need only assume that

a. The cross-product operation is linear.
b. The cross product of a vector with itself is zero.
c. $\mathbf{i} \times \mathbf{j} = \mathbf{k}$, $\mathbf{j} \times \mathbf{k} = \mathbf{i}$, and $\mathbf{k} \times \mathbf{i} = \mathbf{j}$.

By writing $\mathbf{a} = a_x\mathbf{i} + a_y\mathbf{j} + a_z\mathbf{k}$ and $\mathbf{b} = b_x\mathbf{i} + b_y\mathbf{j} + b_z\mathbf{k}$, apply these assumptions to derive the proper form for $\mathbf{a} \times \mathbf{b}$.

4.4.3 Is a × b perpendicular to a?
Show that the cross product of the vectors $\mathbf{a}$ and $\mathbf{b}$ is indeed perpendicular to $\mathbf{a}$.

4.4.4 Vector products
Find a vector $\mathbf{b} = (b_x, b_y, b_z)$ that satisfies the cross-product relation $\mathbf{a} \times \mathbf{b} = \mathbf{c}$, where $\mathbf{a} = (2, 1, 3)$ and $\mathbf{c} = (2, -4, 0)$. Is there only one such vector?

4.4.5 Nonassociativity of the cross product
Show that the cross product is not associative. That is, show that $\mathbf{a} \times (\mathbf{b} \times \mathbf{c})$ is not necessarily the same as $(\mathbf{a} \times \mathbf{b}) \times \mathbf{c}$.

4.4.6 Another useful fact

Show, by direct calculation on the components, that the length of the cross product has the form

$$|\mathbf{a} \times \mathbf{b}| = \sqrt{|\mathbf{a}|^2|\mathbf{b}|^2 - (\mathbf{a} \cdot \mathbf{b})^2}.$$ ■

4.4.1 Geometric Interpretation of the Cross Product

By definition the cross product $\mathbf{a} \times \mathbf{b}$ of two vectors is another vector, but how is it related geometrically to that vector, and why is it of interest? Figure 4.15 gives the answer. The cross product $\mathbf{a} \times \mathbf{b}$ has the following useful properties (whose proofs are requested in the exercises for this subsection):

FIGURE 4.15 Interpretation of the cross product.

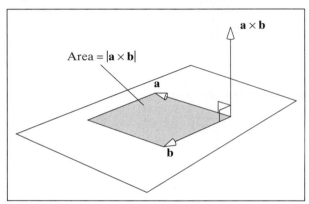

1. $\mathbf{a} \times \mathbf{b}$ is perpendicular (orthogonal) to both $\mathbf{a}$ and $\mathbf{b}$.
2. The length of $\mathbf{a} \times \mathbf{b}$ equals the area of the parallelogram determined by $\mathbf{a}$ and $\mathbf{b}$. This area is equal to

    $$|\mathbf{a} \times \mathbf{b}| = |\mathbf{a}||\mathbf{b}| \sin(\theta), \quad (4.31)$$

    where θ is the angle between $\mathbf{a}$ and $\mathbf{b}$, measured from $\mathbf{a}$ to $\mathbf{b}$ or $\mathbf{b}$ to $\mathbf{a}$, whichever produces an angle less than $180°$. As a special case, $\mathbf{a} \times \mathbf{b} = \mathbf{0}$ if, and only if, $\mathbf{a}$ and $\mathbf{b}$ have the same or opposite directions or if either has zero length. What is the magnitude of the cross product if $\mathbf{a}$ and $\mathbf{b}$ are perpendicular?
3. The sense of $\mathbf{a} \times \mathbf{b}$ is given by the right-hand rule when one is working in a right-handed system. For example, twist the fingers of your right hand from $\mathbf{a}$ to $\mathbf{b}$; then $\mathbf{a} \times \mathbf{b}$ will point in the direction of your thumb. (When working in a left-handed system, use your left hand instead.) Note that the fact that $\mathbf{i} \times \mathbf{j} = \mathbf{k}$ supports this property.

■ EXAMPLE 4.4.2

Let $\mathbf{a} = (1, 0, 1)$ and $\mathbf{b} = (1, 0, 0)$. These vectors are easy to visualize, as they both lie in the x, z-plane. (Sketch them.) The area of the parallelogram defined by $\mathbf{a}$ and $\mathbf{b}$ is easily seen to be unity. Because $\mathbf{a} \times \mathbf{b}$ is orthogonal to both $\mathbf{a}$ and $\mathbf{b}$, we expect it to be parallel to the y-axis and hence be proportional to $\pm\mathbf{j}$. In either a right-handed or a left-handed system, sweeping the fingers of the appropriate hand from $\mathbf{a}$ to $\mathbf{b}$ reveals a thumb pointed along the positive y-axis. Direct calculation based on Equation (4.28) confirms all of this: $\mathbf{a} \times \mathbf{b} = \mathbf{j}$.

PRACTICE EXERCISE

4.4.7 Proving the properties

Prove the preceding three properties given for the cross product. ■

4.4.2 Finding the Normal to a Plane

As we shall see in the next section, we sometimes must compute the components of the normal vector **n** to a plane. If the plane is known to pass through three specific points, the cross product provides the tool to accomplish this task. Any three points P_1, P_2, and P_3 determine a unique plane, as long as the points do not lie in a straight line. Figure 4.16 is illustrative.

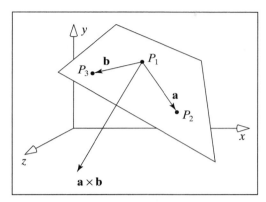

FIGURE 4.16 Finding the plane through three given points.

To find the normal vector to the plane shown, we build two vectors, $\mathbf{a} = P_2 - P_1$ and $\mathbf{b} = P_3 - P_1$. Their cross product $\mathbf{n} = \mathbf{a} \times \mathbf{b}$ must be normal to both **a** and **b**, so it is normal to every line in the plane. (Why?). It is therefore the desired normal vector. (What happens if the three points do lie in a straight line?) Any scalar multiple of this cross product is also a normal vector, including $\mathbf{b} \times \mathbf{a}$ which points in the direction opposite to $\mathbf{a} \times \mathbf{b}$.

■ **EXAMPLE 4.4.3**

Find the normal vector to the plane that passes through the points $(1, 0, 2), (2, 3, 0)$, and $(1, 2, 4)$.

SOLUTION:

By direct calculation, $\mathbf{a} = (2, 3, 0) - (1, 0, 2) = (1, 3, -2)$, and $\mathbf{b} = (1, 2, 4) - (1, 0, 2) = (0, 2, 2)$, so their cross product $\mathbf{n} = (10, -2, 2)$.

Since a cross product involves the subtraction of various quantities [see Equation (4.28)], this method for finding **n** is vulnerable to numerical inaccuracies, especially when the angle between **a** and **b** is small. Later, we develop a more robust method for finding normal vectors in practice.

PRACTICE EXERCISES

4.4.8 Does the choice of points matter?

Is the same plane obtained as in Example 4.4.3 if we use the points in a different order, say, $\mathbf{a} = (1, 0, 2) - (2, 3, 0)$ and $\mathbf{b} = (1, 2, 4) - (2, 3, 0)$? Show that the same plane does result.

4.4.9 Finding some planes

For each of the following triplets of points, find the normal vector to the plane (if it exists) that passes through the triplet:

a. $P_1 = (1, 1, 1), P_2 = (1, 2, 1), P_3 = (3, 0, 4)$.
b. $P_1 = (8, 9, 7), P_2 = (-8, -9, -7), P_3 = (1, 2, 1)$.
c. $P_1 = (6, 3, -4), P_2 = (0, 0, 0), P_3 = (2, 1, -1)$.
d. $P_1 = (0, 0, 0), P_2 = (1, 1, 1), P_3 = (2, 2, 2)$.

4.4.10 Finding the normal vectors

Calculate the normal vectors to each of the faces of the two objects shown in Figure 4.17. The cube has vertices $(\pm1, \pm1, \pm1)$, and the tetrahedron has vertices $(0, 0, 0)$, $(0, 0, 1)$, $(1, 0, 0)$, and $(0, 1, 0)$. ■

FIGURE 4.17 Finding the normal vectors to faces.

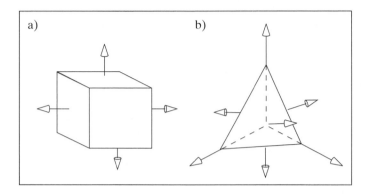

4.5 REPRESENTATIONS OF KEY GEOMETRIC OBJECTS

In the preceding sections, we have discussed some basic ideas of vectors and their application to important geometric problems that arise in graphics. Now we develop the fundamental ideas that facilitate working with lines and planes, which are central to graphics and whose "straightness" and "flatness" makes them easy to represent and manipulate.

What does it mean to "represent" a line or plane, and why is that important? The goal is to come up with a formula or equation that distinguishes points that lie on the line from those that do not. This might be an equation that is satisfied by all points on the line and only those points. Or it might be a function that returns different points on the line as some parameter is varied. The representation allows one to answer such questions as Is point *P* on the line? and Where does the line *intersect* another line or some other object. Importantly, a line lying in a plane divides the plane into two parts, and we often need to ask whether point *P* lies on one or the other side of the line.

To deal properly with lines and planes, we must, somewhat unexpectedly, go back to basics and review how points and vectors differ and how each is represented. The need for this review arises because, to represent a line or plane, we must "add points together" and "scale points," operations that are, in fact, nonsensical when applied to points. To see what is really going on, we introduce the notion of a coordinate frame, which makes clear the significant difference between a point and a vector and reveals in what sense it remains legitimate to "add points." The use of coordinate frames leads ultimately to the notion of "homogeneous coordinates," which are a central tool in computer graphics, and greatly simplify many algorithms. We will make explicit use of coordinate frames in only a few places in the book, most notably when changing coordinate systems and "flying" cameras around a scene.[4] (See Chapters 5, 6, and 7.) But even when not explicitly mentioned, an underlying coordinate frame will be present in every situation.

---

[4] This is an area where graphics programmers can easily go astray: Their programs produce pictures that look fine for simple situations, but that become mysteriously and glaringly wrong when things get more complex.

4.5.1 Coordinate Systems and Coordinate Frames

One doesn't discover new lands without consenting to lose
sight of the shore for a very long time. André Gide

In discussing vectors in previous sections, we have said, for instance, that a vector **v** $= (3, 2, 7)$, meaning that it is a certain ordered triple. We say the same for a point, as in point $P = (5, 3, 1)$. This makes it seem that points and vectors are the same thing. But points and vectors are, in fact, very different: Points have a location, but no size or direction, whereas vectors have a size and direction, but no location.

What we mean by **v** $= (3, 2, 7)$, of course, is that the vector **v** has the components $(3, 2, 7)$ in the underlying coordinate system. Similarly, $P = (5, 3, 1)$ means that point P has the coordinates $(5, 3, 1)$ in the underlying coordinate system. Normally, this confusion between the object and its representation presents no problem. A problem arises when there is more than one coordinate system (a very common occurrence in graphics) and when one transforms points or vectors from one system into another.

We usually think of a coordinate system as three axes emanating from an origin, as in Figure 4.2(b). But in fact, a coordinate system is "located" somewhere in "the world," and its axes are best described by three vectors that point in mutually perpendicular directions. In particular, it is important to make explicit the "location" of the coordinate system, so we extend the notion of a 3D coordinate system[5] to that of a 3D coordinate "frame." A **coordinate frame** consists of a specific point, ϑ, called the *origin*, and three mutually perpendicular unit vectors,[6] **a**, **b**, and **c**. Figure 4.18 shows a coordinate frame "residing" at some point ϑ within "the world," with its vectors **a**, **b**, and **c** drawn so that they appear to emanate from ϑ like axes.

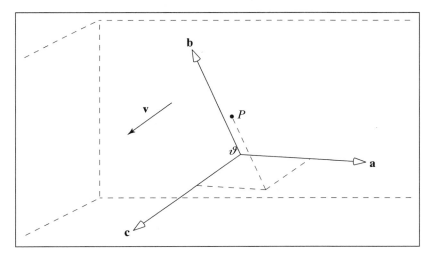

FIGURE 4.18 A coordinate frame positioned in "the world."

Now, to represent a vector **v**, we find three numbers (v_1, v_2, v_3) such that

$$\mathbf{v} = v_1\mathbf{a} + v_2\mathbf{b} + v_3\mathbf{c} \qquad (4.32)$$

and say that **v** "has the representation" (v_1, v_2, v_3) in this system.

---

[5] The ideas for a 2D system are essentially identical.

[6] In more general contexts, the vectors need not be mutually perpendicular, but rather only "linearly independent" (such that, roughly, none of them is a linear combination of the other two). The coordinate frames we work with will always have perpendicular axis vectors.

On the other hand, to represent a point, P, we view its location as an offset from the origin by a certain amount: We represent the vector $P - \vartheta$ by finding three numbers (p_1, p_2, p_3) such that

$$P - \vartheta = p_1\mathbf{a} + p_2\mathbf{b} + p_3\mathbf{c}$$

and then, equivalently, write P itself as

$$P = \vartheta + p_1\mathbf{a} + p_2\mathbf{b} + p_3\mathbf{c}. \tag{4.33}$$

The representation of P is not just a triple, but a triple along with an origin. P is "at" a location that is offset from the origin by $p_1\mathbf{a} + p_2\mathbf{b} + p_3\mathbf{c}$. The basic idea is to make the origin of the coordinate system *explicit*. This becomes important only when there is more than one coordinate frame and in transforming one frame into another.

Note that when we earlier defined the standard unit vectors $\mathbf{i}, \mathbf{j}$, and $\mathbf{k}$ as $(1, 0, 0)$, $(0, 1, 0)$, and $(0, 0, 1)$, respectively, we were actually defining their *representations* in an underlying coordinate frame. Since, by Equation (4.32), $\mathbf{i} = 1\mathbf{a} + 0\mathbf{b} + 0\mathbf{c}$, vector $\mathbf{i}$ is actually just $\mathbf{a}$ itself! It's a matter of naming: whether you are talking about the vector or about its representation in a coordinate frame. We usually do not bother to distinguish the two.

Note that one cannot explicitly say where ϑ is or cite the directions of $\mathbf{a}, \mathbf{b}$, and $\mathbf{c}$: To do so requires having some other coordinate frame in which to represent this one. In terms of its own coordinate frame, ϑ has the representation $(0, 0, 0)$, $\mathbf{a}$ has the representation $(1, 0, 0)$, etc.

The Homogeneous Representation of a Point and a Vector

It is useful to represent both points and vectors using the *same* set of basic underlying objects, $(\mathbf{a}, \mathbf{b}, \mathbf{c}, \vartheta)$. From Equations 4.32 and 4.33, the vector $\mathbf{v} = v_1\mathbf{a} + v_2\mathbf{b} + v_3\mathbf{c}$ needs the four coefficients $(v_1, v_2, v_3, 0)$, whereas the point $P = p_1\mathbf{a} + p_2\mathbf{b} + p_3\mathbf{c} + \vartheta$ needs the four coefficients $(p_1, p_2, p_3, 1)$. The fourth component designates whether the object does or does not include ϑ. We can formally write any $\mathbf{v}$ and P using matrix multiplication (multiplying a row vector by a column vector; see Appendix 2) as

$$\mathbf{v} = (\mathbf{a}, \mathbf{b}, \mathbf{c}, \vartheta)\begin{pmatrix} v_1 \\ v_2 \\ v_3 \\ 0 \end{pmatrix} \tag{4.34}$$

and

$$P = (\mathbf{a}, \mathbf{b}, \mathbf{c}, \vartheta)\begin{pmatrix} P_1 \\ P_2 \\ P_3 \\ 1 \end{pmatrix}. \tag{4.35}$$

Here, the row matrix captures the nature of the coordinate frame, and the column vector captures the representation of the specific object of interest. Thus, vectors and points have different representations: Vectors have 0 as a fourth component whereas points have 1 as a fourth component. Equations (4.34) and (4.35) are examples of the **homogeneous representation** of vectors and points.[7] The use of homogeneous coordinates is one of the hallmarks of computer graphics, as it both helps to keep straight the distinction between points and vectors and provides a compact notation

---

[7]   Actually, we are only going part of the way in this discussion. As we shall see in Chapter 7 when we study projections, homogeneous coordinates in that context permit an additional operation, which makes them truly homogeneous. Until we examine projections, however, this operation need not be introduced.

when one works with affine transformations. It pays off in a computer program to represent the points and vectors of interest in homogeneous coordinates as ordered quadruples, by appending a 1 or a 0 as a fourth component.[8] This is particularly helpful when we must convert between one coordinate frame and another in which points and vectors are represented.

It is simple to convert between the "ordinary" representation of a point or vector (as an ordered triple for 3D objects and an ordered pair for 2D objects) and the homogeneous form.

To go from ordinary to homogeneous coordinates,

If the object is a point, append a 1.
If the object is a vector, append a 0.

To go from homogeneous coordinates to ordinary coordinates,

If the object is a vector, its final coordinate is 0. So delete the 0.
If the object is a point, its final coordinate is 1. So delete the 1.

OpenGL uses 4D homogeneous coordinates for all its vertices. If you send it a triple in the form (x, y, z), it converts it immediately to $(x, y, z, 1)$. If you send it a 2D point (x, y), it first appends a 0 for the z-component and then a 1, to form $(x, y, 0, 1)$. All computations are done within OpenGL in 4D homogeneous coordinates.

Linear Combinations of Vectors

Some things work out quite nicely in homogeneous coordinates when we combine vectors coordinate-wise. All the definitions and manipulations are consistent:

- The difference of two points $(x, y, z, 1)$ and $(u, v, w, 1)$ is $(x - u, y - v, z - w, 0)$, which is, as expected, a vector.
- The sum of a point $(x, y, z, 1)$ and a vector $(d, e, f, 0)$ is $(x + d, y + e, z + f, 1)$, another point.
- Two vectors can be added: $(d, e, f, 0) + (m, n, r, 0) = (d + m, e + n, f + r, 0)$, which produces another vector.
- It is meaningful to scale a vector: $3(d, e, f, 0) = (3d, 3e, 3f, 0)$.
- It is meaningful to form *any* linear combination of vectors. Let the vectors be $\mathbf{v} = (v_1, v_2, v_3, 0)$ and $\mathbf{w} = (w_1, w_2, w_3, 0)$. Then, using arbitrary scalars a and b, we form $a\mathbf{v} + b\mathbf{w} = (av_1 + bw_1, av_2 + bw_2, av_3 + bw_3, 0)$, which is a valid vector.

Forming a linear combination of vectors is well defined, but does it make sense for points? The answer is no, except in one special case, which we explore next.

4.5.2 Affine Combinations of Points

Consider forming a linear combination of two points, $P = (P_1, P_2, P_3, 1)$ and $R = (R_1, R_2, R_3, 1)$, using the scalars f and g:

$$fP + gR = (fP_1 + gR_1, fP_2 + gR_2, fP_3 + gR_3, f + g).$$

We know that this is a valid vector if $f + g = 0$. (Why?) But we shall see that it is *not* a valid point, unless $f + g = 1$! Recall from Equation (4.3) that when the coefficients of a linear combination sum to unity, the equation is called an "affine" combination. So we see that the only linear combination of points that is valid is an affine combination. For example, the object $0.3P + 0.7R$ is a valid point, as are $2.7P - 1.7R$

---

8   In the 2D case, points are triples $(p_1, p_2, 1)$ and vectors are triples $(v_1, v_2, 0)$.

and the midpoint $0.5P + 0.5R$, but $P + R$ is not a point. For three points, P, R, and Q, we can form the valid point $0.3P + 0.9R - 0.2Q$, but not $P + Q - 0.9R$. Thus, **any affine combination of points is a legitimate point.**

But what is wrong geometrically with forming *any* linear combination of two points, say,

$$E = fP + gR,$$

when $f + g$ is different from unity? What is wrong is that a problem arises if we shift the origin of the coordinate system [Goldman85]. Suppose the origin is shifted by vector $\mathbf{u}$, so that P is shifted to $P + \mathbf{u}$ and R is shifted to $R + \mathbf{u}$. If E is a valid point, it, too, must be shifted to the new point $E' = E + \mathbf{u}$. But instead, we have

$$E' = fP + gR + (f + g)\mathbf{u},$$

which is *not* $E + \mathbf{u}$, unless $f + g = 1$.

The failure of a simple sum $P_1 + P_2$ of two points to be a true point is shown in Figure 4.19. Points P_1 and P_2 are shown in two coordinate systems, one offset from the other. Viewing each point as the head of a vector bound to its origin, we see that the sum $P_1 + P_2$ yields two different points in the two systems. Therefore, $P_1 + P_2$ depends on the choice of coordinate system. Note, by way of contrast, that the affine combination $0.5(P_1 + P_2)$ does *not* depend on this choice.

FIGURE 4.19 Adding points is not a valid operation.

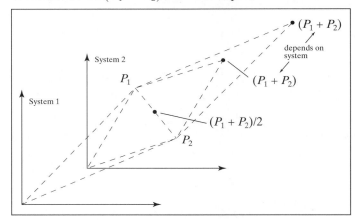

A Point Plus a Vector is an Affine Combination of Points

There is another way of examining affine sums of points that is interesting in its own right and that also leads to a useful tool in graphics. This way doesn't require the use of homogeneous coordinates.

Consider forming a point as a point A offset by a vector $\mathbf{v}$ that has been scaled by scalar t: $A + t\mathbf{v}$. This is the sum of a point and a vector, so it is a valid point. If we take as vector $\mathbf{v}$ the difference between some other point B and A (i.e., $\mathbf{v} = B - A$), then we have the point

$$P = A + t(B - A), \tag{4.36}$$

which is also a valid point. But now rewrite Equation (4.37) algebraically as

$$P = tB + (1 - t)A, \tag{4.37}$$

and it is seen to be an affine combination of points. (Why?) This further validates writing affine sums of points; in fact, any affine sum of points can be written as a point plus a vector. (See the exercises on p. 169.) If you are ever uncomfortable writing an affine sum of points as in Equation 4.37 (a form we will use often), simply understand that it *means* the point given by Equation 4.36.

■ **EXAMPLE 4.5.1 The Centroid of a triangle**

Consider the triangle T with vertices A, B, and C shown in Figure 4.20. We use the preceding ideas to show that the three **medians** of T meet at a point that lies two-thirds of the way along each median. This point is the centroid (center of gravity)[9] of T.

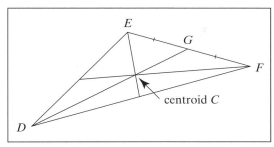

FIGURE 4.20 The centroid of a triangle as an affine combination.

By definition, the median from D is the line from D to the midpoint of the opposite side. Thus, $G = (E + F)/2$. We first ask where the point that is two-thirds of the way from D to G lies? Using the parametric form, we see that the desired point must be $D + (G - D)t$ with $t = 2/3$, which yields the affine combination

$$C = \frac{D + E + F}{3}.$$

(Try it!) Here's the cute part [Pedoe70]: Since this result is *symmetrical* in D, E, and F, it must also be two-thirds of the way along the median from E and two-thirds of the way along the median from F. Hence, the three medians meet there, and C is the centroid.

This result generalizes nicely for a regular polygon of N sides: The centroid is simply the average of the locations of the N vertices, another affine combination. For an arbitrary polygon, the formula is more complex.

PRACTICE EXERCISES

4.5.1 Any affine combination of points is valid

Consider three scalars a, b, and c that sum to unity and three points A, B, and C. The affine combination $aA + bB + cC$ is a valid point, because using $c = 1 - a - b$, we see that it is the same as $aA + bB + (1 - a - b)C = C + a(A - C) + b(B - C)$, the sum of a point and two vectors. (Check this out!) To generalize, given the affine combination of points $w_1 A_1 + w_2 A_2 + \ldots + w_n A_n$, where $w_1 + w_2 + \ldots + w_n = 1$, show that it can be written as a point plus a vector and is therefore a valid point.

4.5.2 Shifting the coordinate system [Goldman85]

Consider the general situation of forming a linear combination of m points:

$$E = \sum_{i=1}^{m} a_i P_i.$$

We ask whether E is a point, a vector, or nothing at all? By considering the effect of a shift in each P_i by $\mathbf{u}$, show that E is "shifted" to $E' = E + S\mathbf{u}$, where

$$S = \sum_{i=1}^{m} a_i$$

---

[9]   The reference to gravity arises because, if a thin plate is cut in the shape of T, the plate hangs level if suspended by a thread attached at the centroid. Gravity pulls equally on all sides of the centroid, so the plate is balanced.

is the sum of the coefficients. Also, show that

i. E is a point if $S = 1$.
ii. E is a vector if $S = 0$.
iii. E is meaningless for other values of S.   ■

4.5.3 Linear Interpolation of Two Points

The affine combination of points expressed in Equation (4.36), viz.,

$$P = A(1 - t) + Bt,$$

performs a **linear interpolation** between the points A and B. That is, the x-component $P_x(t)$ provides a value that is fraction t of the way between the values A_x and B_x, and similarly for the y-component (and in 3D, the z-component). This is a sufficiently important operation to warrant a name, and $lerp()$ (for linear interpolation) has become popular. In one dimension, $lerp(a, b, t)$ provides a number that is the fraction t of the way from a to b. Figure 4.21 gives a simple implementation of `lerp()`.

FIGURE 4.21 Linear interpolation effected by `lerp()`.

```
float lerp(float a, float b, float t)
{
        return a + (b - a) * t;   // return a float
}
```

In a similar manner, one often wants to compute the point $P(t)$ that is the fraction t of the way along the straight line from point A to point B. This point is often called the "tween" (for "in-between") at t of points A and B. Each component of the resulting point is formed as the `lerp()` of the corresponding components of A and B. A procedure

```
Point2 Canvas:: Tween(Point2 A, Point2 B, float t)  // tween A and B
```

is easily written (how?) to implement "tweening." A 3D version is almost the same.

■ **EXAMPLE 4.5.2**

Let $A = (4, 9)$ and $B = (3, 7)$. Then `Tween(A, B, t)` returns the point $(4 - t, 9 - 2t)$, so that `Tween`$(A, B, 0.4)$ returns $(3.6, 8.2)$. (Check this on graph paper.)

4.5.4 "Tweening" for Art and Animation

Interesting animations can be created that show one figure being "tweened" into another. The procedure is simplest if the two figures are polylines (or families of polylines) based on the same number of points. Suppose the first figure, A, is based on the polyline with points A_i and the second polyline, B, is based on points B_i, for $i = 0, \ldots, n - 1$. Then we can form the polyline $P(t)$, called the "tween at t," by forming the points

$$P_i(t) = (1 - t)A_i + tB_i.$$

If we look at a succession of values of t between 0 and 1, say, $t = 0, 0.1, 0.2, \ldots, 0.9, 1.0$, we see that this polyline begins with the shape of A and ends with the shape of B, but in between it is a blend of the two shapes. For small values of t, it looks like A, but as t increases, the polyline warps (smoothly) towards a shape close to B. For $t = 0.25$, for instance, point $P_i(0.25)$ of the tween is 25% of the way from A to B.

Figure 4.22 shows a simple example in which polyline A has the shape of a house and polyline B has the shape of the letter T. The point R on the house corresponds to the point S on the T. The various tweens of point R on the house and point S on the T lie on the line between R and S. The tween for $t = 1/2$ lies at the midpoint of RS. The in-between polylines show the shapes of the tweens for $t = 0, 0.25, 0.5, 0.75,$ and 1.0.

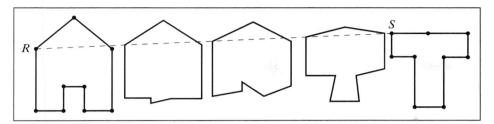

FIGURE 4.22 Tweening a T into a house.

```
void Canvas:: drawTween(Point2 A[], Point2 B[], int n, float t)
{   // draw the tween at time t between polylines A and B
  for(int i = 0; i < n; i++)
  {
      Point2 P;
      P = Tween(A[i], B[i],t);
      if(i == 0)  moveTo(P.x, P.y);
      else   lineTo(P.x, P.y);
  }
}
```

FIGURE 4.23 Tweening two polylines.

Figure 4.23 is the routine `drawTween()`, which draws a tween of two polylines A and B, each having n vertices, at the specified value of t.

The routine `drawTween()` could be used in an animation loop that tweens A and B back and forth, first as t increases from 0 to 1, then as t decreases back to 0, etc. Double buffering, as discussed in Chapter 3, is used to make the transition from one displayed tween to the next instantaneous one. The code is as follows:

```
for(t = 0.0, delT = 0.1; ; t += delT)   // tween back and forth forever
{
    clear the buffer
    drawTween(A, B, n, t);
    glutSwapBuffers();
    if( t >= 1.0 || t <= 0.0)  delT = - delT; // reverse the flow of t
}
```

Figure 4.24 shows an artistic use of this technique based on two sets of polylines. Three tweens are shown. (what values of t are used?) Because the two sets of polylines are drawn sufficiently far apart, there is room to draw the tweens between them with no overlap, so that all five pictures fit nicely in one frame.

FIGURE 4.24 From man to woman. (Courtesy of Marc Infield.)

Susan E. Brennan of Hewlett Packard Corporation in Palo Alto, California, has produced caricatures of famous figures with the use of this method. (See [Dewdney88].) Figure 4.25 is an example. The second and fourth faces are based on digitized points for Elizabeth Taylor and John F. Kennedy. The third face is a tween, and the other three are based on **extrapolation**. That is, values of t larger than 1 are used, so that the term $(1 - t)$ is negative. Extrapolation can produce caricaturelike distortions, in some sense "going to the other side" of polyline B from polyline A. Values of t less than 0 are also used here, with a similar effect.

FIGURE 4.25 Face caricature: Tweening and extrapolation. (Courtesy of Susan Brennan.)

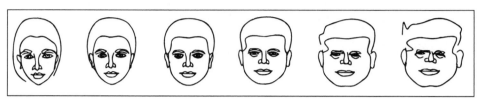

Tweening is used in the film industry to reduce the cost of producing animations such as cartoons. In earlier days an artist had to draw 24 pictures for each second of film, because movies display 24 frames per second. With the assistance of a computer, however, an artist need draw only the first and final pictures, called **key frames**, in certain sequences and let the others be generated automatically. For instance, if the characters are not moving too rapidly in a certain one-half-second portion of a cartoon, the artist can draw and digitize the first and final frames of this portion, and the computer can create 10 tweens using linear interpolation, thereby saving a great deal of the artist's time. (See the case study at the end of this chapter for a programming project that produces these effects.)

PRACTICE EXERCISES

4.5.3 A limiting case of tweening

What is the effect of tweening when all of the points A_i in a polyline A are the same? How is a polyline B distorted in appearance in each tween?

4.5.4 An extrapolation

Let polyline A be a square with vertices $(1, 1)$, $(-1, 1)$, $(-1, -1)$, and $(1, -1)$ and polyline B be a wedge with vertices $(5, -2)$, $(4, 3)$, $(4, 0)$, and $(3, -2)$. Sketch (by hand) the shape $P(t)$ for $t = -1, -0.5, 0.5$, and 1.5.

4.5.5 Extrapolation versus tweening

Suppose that five polyline pictures are displayed side by side. From careful measurement, you determine that the middle three are in-betweens of the first and the last, and you calculate the values of t used. But someone claims that the last is actually an extrapolation of the first and the fourth. Is there any way to tell whether this is true? If it is an extrapolation, can the value of t that was used be determined? If so, what is it? ■

4.5.5 Preview: Quadratic and cubic tweening and Bezier Curves

In Chapter 11, we address the problem of designing complex shapes called Bezier curves. The underlying idea is simply tweening between a collection of points. With linear interpolation, we "partition unity" into the pieces $(1 - t)$ and t, and we use these pieces to "weight" the points A and B. We can extend this idea to quadratic interpolation by partitioning unity into three pieces: We just write

$$1 = ((1 - t) + t)^2$$

and expand the formula to produce the three pieces $(1 - t)^2, 2(1 - t)t$, and t^2. These obviously sum to unity, so they can be used to form the affine combination of points A, B, and C:

$$P(t) = (1 - t)^2 A + 2t(1 - t)B + t^2 C. \tag{4.38}$$

This is the Bezier curve for the points A, B, and C. Figure 4.26(a) shows the shape of $P(t)$ as t varies from 0 to 1. The curve flows smoothly from A to C. (Notice that it misses the middle point.) Going further, one can expand $((1 - t) + t)^3$ into four pieces (which ones?) that can be used to do "cubic interpolation" between four points A, B, C and D, as shown in Figure 4.26(b).

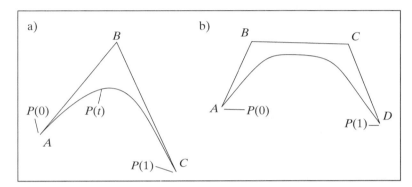

FIGURE 4.26 Bezier curves as tweening.

PRACTICE EXERCISE

4.5.6 Try it out

Draw three points A, B, and C on a piece of graph paper. For each of the values $t = 0$, $.1, .2, \ldots, .9, 1$, compute the position of $P(t)$ in Equation 4.38, and draw the polyline that passes through these points. Is it always a parabola? ■

4.5.6 Representing Lines and Planes

We now turn to developing the principal forms in which lines and planes are represented mathematically. It is quite common to find data structures within a graphics program that capture a line or plane using one of these forms.

Lines in 2D and 3D Space

A **line** is defined by two points, say, C and B. [See Figure 4.27(a)]. It is infinite in length, passing through the points and extending forever in both directions. A **line segment** (**segment** for short) is also defined by two points, its **endpoints,** but extends only from one endpoint to the other [Figure 4.27(b)]. Its **parent** line is the infinite line that passes through its endpoints. A **ray** is "semi-infinite": It is specified by a point and a direction, starting at that point and extending infinitely far in a given direction [Figure 4.27(c)].

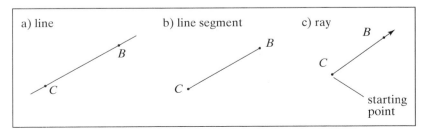

FIGURE 4.27 Lines, segments, and rays.

These objects are very familiar, yet it is useful to collect their important representations and properties in one spot. We also describe the most important representation of all for a line in computer graphics: the **parametric representation**.

Parametric representation of a line

The construction represented in Equations (4.36) and (4.37) is very useful, because as t varies, the point P traces out all of the points on the straight line defined by C and B. This construction therefore gives us a way to name and compute any point along the line. We do so by using a **parameter** t that distinguishes one point on the line from another. Call the line L, and give the name $L(t)$ to the position associated with t. Using $\mathbf{b} = B - C$, we have

$$L(t) = C + \mathbf{b}t. \tag{4.39}$$

As t varies, so does the position of $L(t)$ along the line. (One often thinks of t as time and uses language such as "at time $0 \dots$," "as time goes on $\dots$," or "later" to describe different parts of the line.) Figure 4.28 shows vector $\mathbf{b}$ and the line L passing through C and B. (A 2D version is illustrated, but the 3D version uses the same ideas.) Note where $L(t)$ is located for various values of t. If $t = 0$, $L(0)$ evaluates to C, so at $t = 0$, we are "at" point C. At $t = 1$, $L(1) = C + (B - C) = B$. As t varies, we add a longer or shorter version of $\mathbf{b}$ to the point C, resulting in a new point along the line. When t is larger than 1, the new point lies somewhere on the opposite side of B from C; when t is less than 0, the new point lies on the side of C opposite from B.

FIGURE 4.28 Parametric representation $L(t)$ of a line.

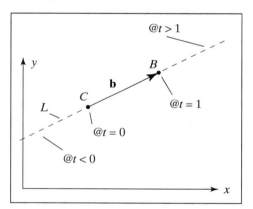

For a fixed value of t, say, $t = 0.6$, Equation (4.39) gives a formula for exactly one point along the line through C and B: the particular point $L(0.6)$. Thus, the equation describes a point. But since one can view it as a function of t that generates the coordinates of *every* point on L as t varies, the equation is called the **parametric representation of line L**.

The line, ray, and segment of Figure 4.27 are all represented by the same $L(t)$ of Equation (4.39). They differ parametrically only in the values of t that are relevant:

For the segment, $0 \le t \le 1$;
for the ray, $0 \le t < \infty$; $\qquad\qquad$ (4.40)
for the line, $-\infty < t < \infty$.

The ray "starts" at C when $t = 0$, passes through B at $t = 1$, and then continues forever as t increases. C is often called the "starting point" of the ray.

A very useful fact is that $L(t)$ lies a "fraction t of the way" between C and B when t lies between 0 and 1. For instance, when $t = 1/2$, the point $L(0.5)$ is the **midpoint** between C and B, and when $t = 0.3$, the point $L(0.3)$ is 30% of the way from C to B.

This is clear from Equation (4.39), since $|L(t) - C| = |\mathbf{b}||t|$ and $|B - C| = |\mathbf{b}|$, so the value of $|t|$ is the ratio of the distances $|L(t) - C|$ to $|B - C|$, as claimed.

One can also speak of the "speed" with which the point $L(t)$ "moves" along line L. Since it covers a distance $|\mathbf{b}|t$ in time t, the point moves at a constant speed $|\mathbf{b}|$.

■ EXAMPLE 4.5.2 A line in 2D

Find a parametric form for the line that passes through $C = (3, 5)$ and $B = (2, 7)$.

SOLUTION:

Build vector $\mathbf{b} = B - C = (-1, 2)$ to obtain the parametric form $L(t) = (3 - t, 5 + 2t)$.

■ EXAMPLE 4.5.3 A line in 3D

Find a parametric form for the line that passes through $C = (3, 5, 6)$ and $B = (2, 7, 3)$.

SOLUTION:

Build vector $\mathbf{b} = B - C = (-1, 2, -3)$ to obtain the parametric form $L(t) = (3 - t, 5 + 2t, 6 - 3t)$.

Other parametrizations for a straight line are possible, although they are rarely used. For instance, the point

$$W(t) = C + \mathbf{b}t^3$$

also "sweeps" over every point on L. It lies at C when $t = 0$ and reaches B when $t = 1$. Unlike $L(t)$, however, $W(t)$ "accelerates" along its path from C to B.

Point Normal Form for the Equation of a Line (the Implicit Form)

This form for the equation of a line is written in a way that better reveals the underlying geometry of the line. The familiar equation of a line in 2D has the form

$$f x + g y = 1, \tag{4.41}$$

where f and g are constants. The notion is that every point (x, y) that satisfies this equation lies on the line, so the equation provides a condition for a point to be on the line. (This is true only for a line in 2D; a line in 3D requires two equations. So, unlike the parametric form that works perfectly well in both 2D and 3D, the point normal form only applies to lines in 2D.)

Equation (4.41) can be written using the dot product: $(f, g) \cdot (x, y) = 1$. So, for every point on a line, a certain dot product must have the same value. We examine the geometric interpretation of the "vector" (f, g) and, in so doing, develop the point normal form of a line. This form is very useful in such tasks as clipping, eliminating hidden lines, and tracing rays. Formally, the point normal form makes no mention of dimensionality: A line in 2D has a point normal form, and a plane in 3D has one.

Suppose, then, that we know that line L passes through points C and B, as in Figure 4.29. What is the point normal form of L? If we can find a vector $\mathbf{n}$ that is

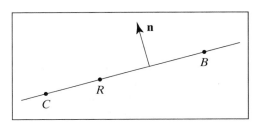

FIGURE 4.29 Finding the point normal form for a line.

perpendicular to L, then, for any point $R = (x, y)$ on L, the vector $R - C$ must be perpendicular to $\mathbf{n}$, so we have the following condition on R:

$$\mathbf{n} \cdot (R - C) = 0 \qquad \text{(point normal form).} \qquad (4.42)$$

This is the **point normal** equation for the line, expressing the fact that a certain dot product must turn out to be zero for *every* point R on the line. This point employs as data *any* point lying on the line and *any* vector normal to the line.

We still must find a suitable $\mathbf{n}$. Let $\mathbf{b} = B - C$ denote the vector from C to B. Then $\mathbf{b}^{\perp}$ will serve well as the desired $\mathbf{n}$. For purposes of building the point normal form, any scalar multiple of $\mathbf{b}^{\perp}$ works just as well for $\mathbf{n}$.

■ **EXAMPLE 4.5.4 Find the point normal form**

Suppose line L passes through points $C = (3, 4)$ and $B = (5, -2)$. Then $\mathbf{b} = B - C = (2, -6)$ and $\mathbf{b}^{\perp} = (6, 2)$. (Sketch $\mathbf{b}^{\perp}$) Choosing C as the point on the line, we have, for the point normal form, $(6, 2) \cdot ((x, y) - (3, 4)) = 0$, or $6x + 2y = 26$. Both sides of this equation can be divided by 26 (or any other nonzero number) if desired.

It is also easy to find the normal to a line, given the equation of the line, say, $fx + gy = 1$. Writing this equation once again as $(f, g) \cdot (x, y) = 1$, we find that the normal $\mathbf{n}$ is simply (f, g) (or any multiple thereof). For instance, the line given by $5x - 2y = 7$ has normal vector $(5, -2)$, or, more generally, $K(5, -2)$ for any nonzero K.

It is also straightforward to find the parametric form for a line if you are given its point normal form. Suppose it is known that line L has the point normal form $\mathbf{n} \cdot (P - C) = 0$, where $\mathbf{n}$ and C are given explicitly. The parametric form is then $L(t) = C + \mathbf{n}^{\perp}t$. (Why?) You can also obtain the parametric form if the equation of the line is given, by (1) finding the normal $\mathbf{n}$ as in the previous paragraph, (2) finding a point (C_x, C_y) on the line by choosing any value for C_x, and (3) using the equation to find the corresponding C_y.

Moving from One Representation to Another

We have described three different ways to characterize a line. Each representation uses certain data that distinguish one line from another. These are the data that would be stored in a suitable data structure within a program to capture the specifics of each line that is of interest. For instance, the data associated with the representation that specifies a line parametrically, as in $C + \mathbf{b}t$, would be information about the point C and the direction $\mathbf{b}$. We summarize this situation by saying that the relevant datum is $\{C, \mathbf{b}\}$.

The three representations and their data are as follows:

- The two-point form: say, C and B; datum = $\{C, B\}$.
- The parametric form: $C + \mathbf{b}t$; datum = $\{C, \mathbf{b}\}$.
- The point normal (implicit) form (in 2D only): $\mathbf{n} \cdot (P - C) = 0$; datum = $\{C, \mathbf{n}\}$.

Note that a point C on the line is common to all three forms. Figure 4.30 shows how the data in each representation can be obtained from the data in the other representations. For instance, given $\{C, \mathbf{b}\}$ of the parametric form, the normal $\mathbf{n}$ of the point normal form is obtained simply as $\mathbf{b}^{\perp}$.

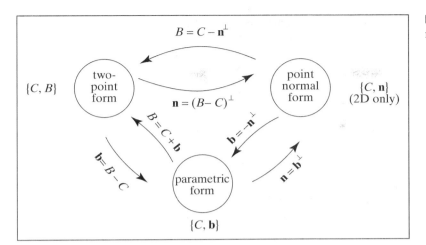

FIGURE 4.30 Moving between representations of a line.

PRACTICE EXERCISE

4.5.7 Find the point normal form

Find the point normal form for the line that passes through $(-3, 4)$ and $(6, -1)$. Sketch the line and its normal vector on graph paper. ■

Planes in 3D Space

Because there is such a heavy use of polygons in 3D graphics, planes seem to appear everywhere. A polygon (a "face" of an object) lies in its "parent" plane, and we often need to clip objects against planes or find the plane in which a certain face lies.

Like lines, planes have three fundamental forms: the three-point form, the parametric representation, and the point normal form. We examined the three-point form in Section 4.4.2.

The Parametric Representation of a Plane

The parametric form for a plane is built on three ingredients: one of its points, C, and two (nonparallel) vectors, **a** and **b**, that lie in the plane, as shown in Figure 4.31. If we are given the three (noncollinear) points A, B, and C in the plane, then we take **a** $= A - C$ and **b** $= B - C$.

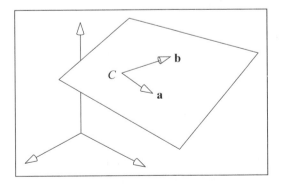

FIGURE 4.31 Defining a plane parametrically.

To construct a parametric form for this plane, note that any point in the plane can be represented by a vector sum: C, plus some multiple of **a**, plus some multiple of **b**. Using parameters s and t to specify the multiples, we have $C + s\mathbf{a} + t\mathbf{b}$. This provides the desired parametric form

$$P(s, t) = C + \mathbf{a}s + \mathbf{b}t \tag{4.43}$$

Given any values of s and t, we can identify the corresponding point on the plane. For example, the position at $s = t = 0$ is C itself, and that at $s = 1$ and $t = -2$ is $P(1, -2) = C + \mathbf{a} - 2\mathbf{b}$.

Note that two parameters are involved in the parametric expression for a surface, whereas only one parameter is needed for a curve. In fact, if one of the parameters is fixed (say, $s = 3$), then $P(3, t)$ is a function of one variable and represents a straight line: $P(3, t) = (C + 3\mathbf{a}) + \mathbf{b}t$.

It is sometimes handy to arrange the parametric form into a form in which its "components" are explicit. We do so by collecting terms, which yields

$$P(s, t) = (C_x + a_x s + b_x t, C_y + a_y s + b_y t, C_z + a_z s + b_z t). \tag{4.44}$$

We can rewrite the parametric form in Equation (4.43) explicitly in terms of the given points A, B, and C. We just use the definitions of $\mathbf{a}$ and $\mathbf{b}$ to obtain

$$P(s, t) = C + s(A - C) + t(B - C),$$

which can be rearranged into the *affine combination* of points

$$P(s, t) = sA + tB + (1 - s - t)C. \tag{4.45}$$

■ **EXAMPLE 4.5.5 Find a parametric form, given three points in a plane**

Consider the plane passing through $A = (3, 3, 3)$, $B = (5, 5, 7)$, and $C = (1, 2, 4)$. From Equation (4.43), it has the parametric form $P(s, t) = (1, 2, 4) + (2, 1, -1)s + (4, 3, 3)t$. This equation can be rearranged to the component form $P(s, t) = (1 + 2s + 4t)\mathbf{i} + (2 + s + 3t)\mathbf{j} + (4 - s + 3t)\mathbf{k}$ or to the affine combination form $P(s, t) = s(3, 3, 3) + t(5, 5, 7) + (1 - s - t)(1, 2, 4)$.

The point Normal Form for a Plane

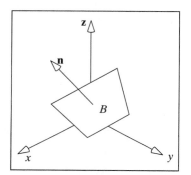

FIGURE 4.32 Determining the equation of a plane.

Planes can also be represented in point normal form, and the classic equation for a plane emerges at once.

Figure 4.32 shows a portion of plane P in three dimensions. A plane is completely specified by giving (1) a single point $B = (b_x, b_y, b_z)$ that lies within it and (2) the direction $\mathbf{n} = (n_x, n_y, n_z)$ normal to the plane. Just as the vector normal to a line in two dimensions orients the line, the normal to a plane orients the plane in space.

The normal $\mathbf{n}$ is understood to be perpendicular to any line lying in the plane. For an arbitrary point $R = (x, y, z)$ in the plane, the vector from R to B must be perpendicular to $\mathbf{n}$, giving

$$\mathbf{n} \cdot (R - B) = 0. \tag{4.46}$$

This is the point normal equation of the plane. It is identical in form to that for the line: a dot product set equal to 0. All points in a plane form vectors with B that have the same dot product with the normal vector. By spelling out the dot product and using $\mathbf{n} = (n_x, n_y, n_z)$, we see that the point normal form is the traditional equation for a plane, viz.,

$$n_x x + n_y y + n_z z = D, \tag{4.47}$$

where $D = \mathbf{n} \cdot (B - 0)$. For example, given the equation for a plane, such as $5x - 2y + 8z = 2$, you know immediately that the normal to that plane is $(5, -2, 8)$ or any multiple of this. (How do you find a point in the plane?)

■ **EXAMPLE 4.5.6 Find a point normal form**

Let plane P pass through $(1, 2, 3)$ with normal vector $(2, -1, -2)$. The point normal form of this plane is $(2, -1, -2) \cdot ((x, y, z) - (1, 2, 3)) = 0$. The equation for the plane may be written out as $2x - y - 2z = -6$.

■ EXAMPLE 4.5.7 Find a parametric form, given the equation of a plane

Find a parametric form for the plane $2x - y + 3z = 8$.

SOLUTION:

By inspection, the normal to the plane is $(2, -1, 3)$. There are many parametrizations; we need only find one. For C, choose any point that satisfies the equation; $C = (4, 0, 0)$ will do. Find two (noncollinear) vectors, each having a dot product of 0 with $(2, -1, 3)$; some hunting reveals that $\mathbf{a} = (1, 5, 1)$ and $\mathbf{b} = (0, 3, 1)$ will work. Thus, the plane has the parametric form $P(s, t) = (4, 0, 0) + (1, 5, 1)s + (0, 3, 1)t$.

■ EXAMPLE 4.5.8 Finding two noncollinear vectors

Given the normal $\mathbf{n}$ to a plane, what is an easy way to find two noncollinear vectors $\mathbf{a}$ and $\mathbf{b}$ that are both perpendicular to $\mathbf{n}$? In the previous exercise, we invented two that work; here we use the fact that the cross product of *any* vector with $\mathbf{n}$ is normal to $\mathbf{n}$. So we take a simple choice, such as $(0, 0, 1)$, and construct $\mathbf{a}$ as its cross product with $\mathbf{n}$:

$$\mathbf{a} = (0, 0, 1) \times \mathbf{n} = (-n_y, n_x, 0).$$

(Is this vector indeed normal to $\mathbf{n}$?) We can use the same idea to form a vector $\mathbf{b}$ that is normal to both $\mathbf{n}$ and $\mathbf{a}$:

$$\mathbf{b} = \mathbf{n} \times \mathbf{a} = (-n_x n_z, -n_y n_z, n_x^2 + n_y^2).$$

(Check to make sure that $\mathbf{b} \perp \mathbf{a}$ and $\mathbf{b} \perp \mathbf{n}$.) So $\mathbf{b}$ is certainly not collinear with $\mathbf{a}$.
  We apply this method to the plane $(3, 2, 5) \cdot (R - (2, 7, 0)) = 0$. We set $\mathbf{a} = (0, 0, 1) \times \mathbf{n} = (-2, 3, 0)$ and $\mathbf{b} = (-15, -10, 13)$. The plane therefore has the parametric form

$$P(s, t) = (2 - 2s - 15t, 7 + 3s - 10t, 13t).$$

Check: Is $P(s, t) - C = (-2s - 15t, -3s - 10t, 13t)$ indeed normal to $\mathbf{n}$ for *every* s and t?

PRACTICE EXERCISE

4.5.8 Find the plane

Find a parametric form for the plane coincident with the y, z-plane. ■

Moving from One Representation to Another

Just as with lines, it is useful to be able to move between the three representations of a plane, to manipulate the data that describe a plane into the form best suited to a problem.
  For a plane, the three representations and their data are as follows:

- The three-point form, say, C, B, and A; datum $= \{C, B, A\}$.
- The parametric form, $C + \mathbf{a}s + \mathbf{b}t$; datum $= \{C, \mathbf{a}, \mathbf{b}\}$.
- The point normal (implicit) form, $\mathbf{n} \cdot (P - C) = 0$; datum $= \{C, \mathbf{n}\}$.

A point C on the plane is common to all three forms. Figure 4.33 shows how the data in each representation can be obtained from the data in the other representations. Check each transformation carefully. Most of these cases were developed explicitly in Section 4.4.2 and in this section. Some are developed in the exercises. The trickiest is probably the calculation in Example 4.5.8. Another case that deserves some explanation is finding three points in a plane, given the point normal form. One point,

FIGURE 4.33 Moving between representations of a plane.

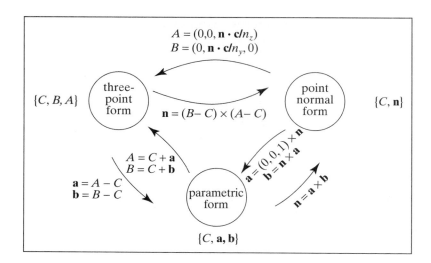

C, is already known. The other two are found using special values in the point normal form itself, which is the equation $n_x x + n_y y + n_z z = \mathbf{n} \cdot C$. We choose, for convenience, $A = (0, 0, a_z)$ and use the equation to find $a_z = \mathbf{n} \cdot C / n_z$. Similarly, we choose $B = (0, b_y, 0)$ and use the equation to find $b_y = \mathbf{n} \cdot C / n_y$.

Planar Patches

Just as we can restrict the parameter t in the representation of a line to obtain a ray or a segment, we can restrict the parameters s and t in the representation of a plane.

In the parametric form of Equation (4.43), the values for s and t can range from $-\infty$ to ∞, and thus, the plane can extend forever. In some situations we want to deal with only a "piece" of a plane, such as a parallelogram that lies in it. Such a piece is called a **planar patch**, a term that invites us to imagine the plane as a quilt of many patches joined together. Later, we examine curved surfaces made up of patches that are not necessarily planar. Much of the practice of modeling solids involves piecing together patches of various shapes to form the skin of an object.

A planar patch is formed by restricting the range of allowable parameter values for s and t. For instance, one often restricts s and t to lie only between 0 and 1. The patch is positioned and oriented in space by appropriate choices of $\mathbf{a}, \mathbf{b}$, and C. Figure 4.34(a) shows the available range of s and t as a square in **parameter space**, and Figure 4.34(b) shows the patch that results from this restriction in object space.

FIGURE 4.34 Mapping between two spaces to define a planar patch.

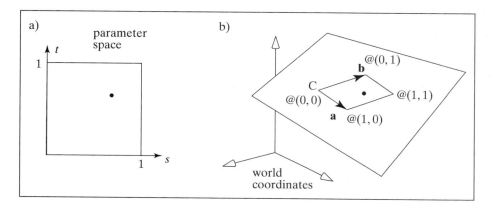

To each point (s, t) in parameter space, there corresponds one 3D point in the patch $P(s, t) = C + \mathbf{a}s + \mathbf{b}t$. The patch is a parallelogram whose corners correspond to the four corners of parameter space and are situated at

$$P(0, 0) = C,$$
$$P(1, 0) = C + \mathbf{a}, \qquad\qquad (4.48)$$
$$P(0, 1) = C + \mathbf{b},$$

and

$$P(1, 1) = C + \mathbf{a} + \mathbf{b}.$$

The vectors $\mathbf{a}$ and $\mathbf{b}$ determine both the size and the orientation of the patch. If $\mathbf{a}$ and $\mathbf{b}$ are perpendicular, the grid will become rectangular, and if, in addition, $\mathbf{a}$ and $\mathbf{b}$ have the same length, the grid will become square. Changing C just shifts the patch without altering its shape or orientation.

■ **EXAMPLE 4.5.9 Make a patch**

Let $C = (1, 3, 2)$, $\mathbf{a} = (1, 1, 0)$, and $\mathbf{b} = (1, 4, 2)$. Find the corners of the planar patch.

SOLUTION:

From the preceding table, we obtain the four corners $P(0, 0) = (1, 3, 2)$, $P(0, 1) = (2, 7, 4)$, $P(1, 0) = (2, 4, 2)$, and $P(1, 1) = (3, 8, 4)$.

■ **EXAMPLE 4.5.10 Characterize a patch**

Find the values of $\mathbf{a}, \mathbf{b}$, and C that create a square patch of length 4 on a side, centered at the origin and parallel to the x, z-plane.

SOLUTION:

The corners of the patch are $(2, 0, 2)$, $(2, 0, -2)$, $(-2, 0, 2)$, and $(-2, 0, -2)$. Choose any corner, say $(2, 0, -2)$, for C. Then $\mathbf{a}$ and $\mathbf{b}$ each have length 4 and are parallel to either the x- or the z-axis. Choose $\mathbf{a} = (-4, 0, 0)$ and $\mathbf{b} = (0, 0, 4)$.

PRACTICE EXERCISE

4.5.9 Find a Patch

Find point C and some vectors $\mathbf{a}$ and $\mathbf{b}$ that create a patch having the four corners $(-4, 2, 1)$, $(1, 7, 4)$, $(-2, -2, 2)$, and $(3, 3, 5)$. ▪

4.6 FINDING THE INTERSECTION OF TWO LINE SEGMENTS

We often need to compute the point at which two line segments in 2D space intersect. Sometimes the computation appears in related tasks, such as determining whether or not a polygon is simple. Finding the intersection of two line segments will illustrate the power of parametric forms and dot products.

The Problem: Given two line segments, determine whether they intersect, and if they do, find their point of intersection.

The Solution: Suppose one segment has endpoints A and B and the other segment has endpoints C and D. As shown in Figure 4.35, the two segments can be situated in many different ways: They can miss each other (a and b), overlap in one point (c and d), or even overlap over some region (e). They may or may not be parallel. We need an organized approach that handles all of these possibilities.

FIGURE 4.35 Many cases for two line segments.

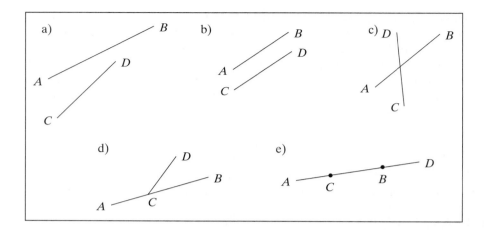

Every line segment has a **parent line**: the infinite line of which it is part. Unless two parent lines are parallel, they will intersect at some point. We first locate this point.

We set up parametric representations for each of the line segments in question. Call AB the segment from A to B. Then

$$AB(t) = A + \mathbf{b}t, \tag{4.49}$$

where, for convenience, we define $\mathbf{b} = B - A$. As t varies from 0 to 1, all points on the finite line segment are visited. If t is allowed to vary from $-\infty$ to ∞, the entire parent line is swept out.

Similarly, we call the segment from C to D by the name CD and give it the parametric representation (using a new parameter, say, u)

$$CD(u) = C + \mathbf{d}u, \tag{4.50}$$

where $\mathbf{d} = D - C$. We use different parameters for the two lines, t for one and u for the other, in order to describe different points on the lines independently. (If the same parameter were used, the points on the two lines would be locked together.)

For the parent lines to intersect, there must be specific values of t and u for which the Equations (4.49) and (4.50) are equal:

$$A + \mathbf{b}t = C + \mathbf{d}u.$$

Defining $\mathbf{c} = C - A$ for convenience, we can write this condition in terms of three known vectors and two (unknown) parameter values:

$$\mathbf{b}t = \mathbf{c} + \mathbf{d}u. \tag{4.51}$$

Like Equation (4.22), Equation (4.51) yields two equations in two unknowns. We solve it the same way: Dot both sides with $\mathbf{d}^\perp$ to eliminate the term in $\mathbf{d}$, giving $\mathbf{d}^\perp \cdot \mathbf{b}t = \mathbf{d}^\perp \cdot \mathbf{c}$. There are two main cases to consider: The term $\mathbf{d}^\perp \cdot \mathbf{b}$ is zero, and it is not zero.

Case 1: The Term $\mathrm{d}^\perp \cdot \mathrm{b}$ *Is Not Zero*

Here we can solve for t, obtaining

$$t = \frac{\mathbf{d}^\perp \cdot \mathbf{c}}{\mathbf{d}^\perp \cdot \mathbf{b}}. \tag{4.52}$$

Similarly, after using one additional property of perp dot products (which one?), we dot both sides of Equation (4.51) with $\mathbf{b}^\perp$ to obtain

$$u = \frac{\mathbf{b}^\perp \cdot \mathbf{c}}{\mathbf{d}^\perp \cdot \mathbf{b}}. \tag{4.53}$$

Now we know that the two parent lines intersect, and we know where. But this doesn't mean that the line segments themselves intersect. If t lies outside the interval $[0, 1]$, segment AB doesn't "reach" the other segment, and similarly if u lies outside of $[0, 1]$. If both t and u lie between 0 and 1, the line segments *do* intersect at some point I whose location is easily found by substituting the value of t into Equation (4.49):

$$I = A + \left(\frac{\mathbf{d}^{\perp} \cdot \mathbf{c}}{\mathbf{d}^{\perp} \cdot \mathbf{b}} \right) \mathbf{b} \qquad \text{(the intersection point).} \qquad (4.54)$$

■ **EXAMPLE 4.6.1**

Given the endpoints $A = (0, 6)$, $B = (6, 1)$, $C = (1, 3)$, and $D = (5, 5)$, find the intersection of the lines AB and CD, if such intersection exists.

SOLUTION:

$\mathbf{d}^{\perp} \cdot \mathbf{b} = -32$, so $t = 7/16$ and $u = 13/32$, which both lie between 0 and 1. Therefore, the segments do intersect. The intersection lies at $(x, y) = (21/8, 61/16)$. This result may be confirmed visually by drawing the segments on graph paper and measuring the observed intersection.

Case 2: The Term $\mathbf{d}^{\perp} \cdot \mathbf{b}$ *Is Zero*

In this case, we know that $\mathbf{d}$ and $\mathbf{b}$ are parallel. (Why?) The segments might still overlap, but that can happen only if the parallel parent lines are identical. A test for this condition is developed in the exercises that follow.

PRACTICE EXERCISES

These exercises discuss the development of a routine that performs the complete intersection test on two line segments.

4.6.1 When the parent lines overlap

We explore Case 2 of this section, in which the term $\mathbf{d}^{\perp} \cdot \mathbf{b} = 0$, so the parent lines are parallel. We must determine whether the parent lines are identical and, if so, whether the segments themselves overlap.

To test whether the parent lines are the same, we see whether C lies on the parent line through A and B.

a. First show that the equation for the parent line is $b_x(y - A_y) - b_y(x - A_x) = 0$. Then substitute C_x for x and C_y for y and see whether the left-hand side is sufficiently close to zero (i.e., whether it is less than some tolerance, such as 10^{-8}). If not, the parent lines do not coincide, and no intersection exists.

b. If the parents lines are the same, the final test is to see whether the segments themselves overlap. To do this, show how to find the two values t_c and t_d at which the line through A and B reaches C and D, respectively. Because the parent lines are identical, we can use just the x-component. Segment AB begins at 0 and ends at 1, and by examining the ordering of the four values $0, 1, t_c$, and t_d, we can readily determine the relative positions of the two lines.

c. Now show that there is an overlap, unless both t_c and t_d are less than zero or both are larger than unity. If there is an overlap, the endpoints of the overlap can easily be found from the values of t_c and t_d.

d. Finally, given the endpoints $A = (0, 6)$, $B = (6, 2)$, $C = (3, 4)$, and $D = (9, 0)$, determine the nature of any intersection.

4.6.2 The algorithm for determining the intersection

Write the routine `segIntersect()` that would be used in the context of `if(segIntersect(A, B, C, D, InterPt)) <do something>`. This routine takes four points representing the two segments and returns 0 if the segments do not intersect and 1 if they do. If the segments do intersect, the location of the intersection is placed in `interPt`. The routine returns -1 if the parent lines are identical.

4.6.3 Testing the simplicity of a polygon

Recall that a polygon P is simple if there are no edge intersections, except at the endpoints of adjacent edges. Fashion a routine `int isSimple(Polygon P)` that takes a brute-force approach and tests whether any pairs of edges of the list of vertices of the polygon intersect, returning 0 if so and 1 if not. (`Polygon` is some suitable class for describing a polygon.) This is a simple algorithm, but not the most efficient one. (See [Moret91] and [Preparata85] for more elaborate attacks that involve some sorting of edges in x and y.)

4.6.4 Line-segment intersections

For each of the following pairs of segments, determine whether the segments intersect and, if so, where:

1. $A = (1, 4)$, $B = (7, 1/2)$, $C = (7/2, 5/2)$, $D = (7, 5)$.
2. $A = (1, 4)$, $B = (7, 1/2)$, $C = (5, 0)$, $D = (0, 7)$.
3. $A = (0, 7)$, $B = (7, 0)$, $C = (8, -1)$, $D = (10, -3)$.   ■

4.6.1 Application of Line Intersections: The Circle through Three Points

Suppose a designer wants a tool that draws the unique circle that passes through three given points. The user specifies three points A, B, and C, on the display with the mouse as suggested in Figure 4.36(a), and the circle is drawn automatically, as shown in Figure 4.36(b). The unique circle that passes through three points is called the **excircle** or **circumscribed circle**, of the triangle defined by the points. Which circle is it? We need a routine that can calculate its center and radius.

FIGURE 4.36 Finding the excircle.

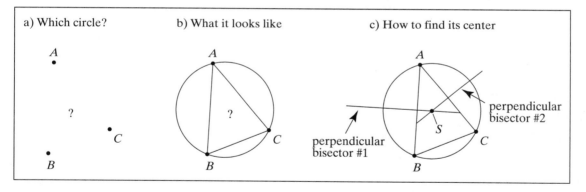

a) Which circle?

b) What it looks like

c) How to find its center

Figure 4.36(c) shows how to find the excircle. The center S of the desired circle must be equidistant from all three vertices, so it must lie on the **perpendicular bisector** of *each* side of triangle ABC. (The perpendicular bisector is the locus of all points that are equidistant from two given points.) Thus, we can determine S if we can compute where two of the perpendicular bisectors intersect.

We first show how to find a parametric representation of the perpendicular bisector of a line segment. Figure 4.37 shows a segment S with endpoints A and B. Its perpendicular bisector L is the infinite line that passes through the midpoint M of segment S and is oriented perpendicular to it. But we know that M is given by $(A + B)/2$ and that the direction of the normal is given by $(B - A)^{\perp}$, so the perpendicular bisector has the parametric form

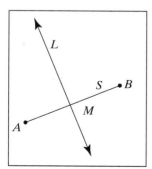

FIGURE 4.37 The perpendicular bisector of a segment.

$$L(t) = \frac{1}{2}(A + B) + (B - A)^{\perp}t \quad \text{(the perpendicular bisector of } AB\text{)}.\tag{4.55}$$

Now we are in a position to compute the excircle of three points. Returning to Figure 4.35(c), we seek the intersection S of the perpendicular bisectors of AB and AC. For convenience, we define the following vectors:

$$\mathbf{a} = B - A;$$
$$\mathbf{b} = C - B; \qquad\qquad (4.56)$$
$$\mathbf{c} = A - C.$$

To find the perpendicular bisector of AB, we need the midpoint of AB and a direction perpendicular to AB. The midpoint of AB is $A + \mathbf{a}/2$. (Why?) The direction perpendicular to AB is $\mathbf{a}^{\perp}$. So the parametric form for the perpendicular bisector is $A + \mathbf{a}/2 + \mathbf{a}^{\perp}t$. Similarly, the perpendicular bisector of AC is $A - \mathbf{c}/2 + \mathbf{c}^{\perp}u$, using the parameter u. Point S lies where these two perpendicular bisectors meet, at the solution of the equation

$$\mathbf{a}^{\perp}t = \mathbf{b}/2 + \mathbf{c}^{\perp}u$$

(where we have used $\mathbf{a} + \mathbf{b} + \mathbf{c} = \mathbf{0}$). To eliminate the term in u, we take the dot product of both sides of this equation with $\mathbf{c}$, obtaining $t = (1/2)(\mathbf{b} \cdot \mathbf{c})/(\mathbf{a}^{\perp} \cdot \mathbf{c})$. To find S, we use this value for t in the representation of the perpendicular bisector. We thus have $A + \mathbf{a}/2 + \mathbf{a}^{\perp}t$, which yields the simple *explicit* form[10]

$$S = A + \frac{1}{2}\left(\mathbf{a} + \frac{\mathbf{b} \cdot \mathbf{c}}{\mathbf{a}^{\perp} \cdot \mathbf{c}}\mathbf{a}^{\perp}\right) \qquad \text{(center of the excircle).} \qquad (4.57)$$

The radius of the excircle is the distance from S to any of the three vertices—that is, $|S - A|$. So we just form the magnitude of the last term in Equation (4.57). After some manipulation (check this out), we obtain

$$\text{radius} = \frac{|\mathbf{a}|}{2}\sqrt{\left(\frac{\mathbf{b} \cdot \mathbf{c}}{\mathbf{a}^{\perp} \cdot \mathbf{c}}\right)^2 + 1} \qquad \text{(radius of the excircle).} \qquad (4.58)$$

Once S and the radius are known, we can use `drawCircle()` from Chapter 3 to draw the desired circle.

■ **EXAMPLE 4.6.2**

Find the perpendicular bisector L of the segment S having endpoints $A = (3, 5)$ and $B = (9, 3)$.

SOLUTION:

By direct calculation, the midpoint $M = (6, 4)$, and $(B - A)^{\perp} = (2, 6)$, so L has the representation $L(t) = (6 + 2t, 4 + 6t)$. It is useful to plot both S and L to see this result.

Every triangle also has an **inscribed circle**, which is sometimes necessary to compute in a computer-aided design context. In a case study at the end of the chapter, we examine how to do this and also discuss the beguiling **nine-point circle**.

PRACTICE EXERCISE

4.6.5 A perpendicular bisector

Find a parametric expression for the perpendicular bisector of the segment with endpoints $A = (0, 6)$ and $B = (4, 0)$. Plot the segment and the line. ■

---

[10] Other closed-form expressions for S have appeared previously (e.g., in [Goldman90] and [Lopex92]).

4.7 INTERSECTIONS OF LINES WITH PLANES; CLIPPING

The task of finding the intersection of a line with another line or with a plane arises in a surprising variety of situations in graphics. We have already seen one approach in Section 4.6 that finds where two line segments intersect. That approach used parametric representations for both line segments and solved two simultaneous equations.

In this section, we develop an alternative method that works for both lines and planes. It represents the intersecting line by a parametric representation and the line or plane being intersected in a point normal form. The method is very direct and clearly reveals what is going on. We develop it once and then apply the results to the problem of clipping a line against a convex polygon in 2D or a convex polyhedron in 3D. In Chapter 7, we see that this intersection technique is an essential step in viewing 3D objects. In Chapter 14, we use the same intersection technique to get started tracing rays.

In 2D, we want to find where a line intersects another line; in 3D, we want to find where a line intersects a plane. Both of these problems can be solved at once, because the formulation is in terms of dot products and the same expressions arise whether the vectors that are involved are 2D or 3D. (We also address the problem of finding the intersection of two planes in the exercises at the end of the section; its solution, too, is based on dot products.)

Consider a line described parametrically by $R(t) = A + \mathbf{c}t$. We also refer to this line as a *ray*. We want to compute where it intersects the object characterized by the point normal form $\mathbf{n} \cdot (P - B) = 0$. In 2D, this object is a line; in 3D, it is a plane. Whichever it is, Point B lies on it, and vector $\mathbf{n}$ is normal to it. Figure 4.38(a) shows the ray hitting a line, and Figure 4.38(b) shows it hitting a plane. We want to find the location of the "hit point."

FIGURE 4.38 Where does a ray hit a line or a plane?

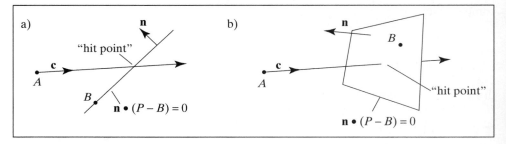

Suppose the points hits at $t = t_{\text{hit}}$, the "hit time." At this value of t, the line and ray must have the same coordinates, so $A + \mathbf{c}t_{\text{hit}}$ must satisfy the equation of the point normal form of the line or plane. Therefore, we substitute this unknown "hit point" into the point normal equation to obtain the following condition on t_{hit}:

$$\mathbf{n} \cdot (A + \mathbf{c}t_{\text{hit}} - B) = 0.$$

This equation may be rewritten as

$$\mathbf{n} \cdot (A - B) + \mathbf{n} \cdot \mathbf{c}t_{\text{hit}} = 0,$$

which is a linear equation in t_{hit}. Its solution is

$$t_{\text{hit}} = \frac{\mathbf{n} \cdot (B - A)}{\mathbf{n} \cdot \mathbf{c}} \qquad \text{(hit time, 2D and 3D cases).} \tag{4.59}$$

As always with a ratio of terms, we must examine the eventuality that the denominator of t_{hit} is zero. This occurs when $\mathbf{n} \cdot \mathbf{c} = 0$, or when the ray is aimed parallel to the plane, in which case there is no hit at all.[11]

---

[11] If the numerator is also zero, the ray lies entirely in the line (2D) or plane (3D). (Why?)

When the hit time has been computed, it is simple to find the location of the hit point: We merely substitute t_{hit} into the representation of the ray:

hit point $P_{hit} = A + ct_{hit}$ (hit point, 2D and 3D cases).   (4.60)

In the practice exercises at the end of the section, we will also need to know generally in which direction the ray strikes the line or plane: "along with" the normal $\mathbf{n}$ or "counter to" $\mathbf{n}$. (This orientation will be important because we will need to know whether the ray is exiting from an object or entering it.) Figure 4.39 shows the two possibilities for a ray hitting a line. In Part (a), the angle between the direction $\mathbf{c}$ of the ray and $\mathbf{n}$ is less than 90°, so we say that the ray is aimed "along with" $\mathbf{n}$. In Part (b), the angle is greater than 90°, so the ray is aimed "counter to" $\mathbf{n}$.

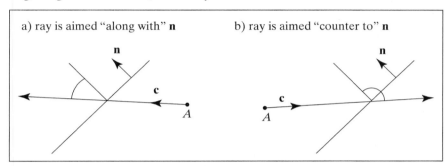

a) ray is aimed "along with" $\mathbf{n}$ b) ray is aimed "counter to" $\mathbf{n}$

FIGURE 4.39 The direction of the ray is "along" or "against" $\mathbf{n}$.

It is easy to test which of these possibilities exists, since the *sign* of $\mathbf{n} \cdot \mathbf{c}$ tells immediately whether the angle between $\mathbf{n}$ and $\mathbf{c}$ is less than or greater than 90°. Putting these ideas together, we have the following three possibilities:

If $\mathbf{n} \cdot \mathbf{c} > 0$,   the ray is aimed "along with" the normal.

If $\mathbf{n} \cdot \mathbf{c} = 0$,   the ray is parallel to the line.   (4.61)

If $\mathbf{n} \cdot \mathbf{c} < 0$,   the ray is aimed "counter to" the normal.

PRACTICE EXERCISES

4.7.1 Intersections of rays with lines and planes

Find when and where the ray $A + \mathbf{c}t$ hits the object $\mathbf{n} \cdot (P - B) = 0$ (a line in 2D, a plane in 3D):

a. $A = (2, 3)$, $\mathbf{c} = (4, -4)$, $\mathbf{n} = (6, 8)$, $B = (7, 7)$.
b. $A = (2, -4, 3)$, $\mathbf{c} = (4, 0, -4)$, $\mathbf{n} = (6, 9, 9)$, $B = (-7, 2, 7)$.
c. $A = (2, 0)$, $\mathbf{c} = (0, -4)$, $\mathbf{n} = (0, 8)$, $B = (7, 0)$.
d. $A = (2, 4, 3)$, $\mathbf{c} = (4, 4, -4)$, $\mathbf{n} = (6, 4, 8)$, $B = (7, 4, 7)$.

4.7.2 Rays hitting planes

Find the point where the ray $(1, 5, 2) + (5, -2, 6)t$ hits the plane $2x - 4y + z = 8$.

4.7.3 What is the intersection of two planes?

Geometrically, we know that two planes intersect in a straight line. But which line? Suppose the two planes are given by $\mathbf{n} \cdot (P - A) = 0$ and $\mathbf{m} \cdot (P - B) = 0$. Find the parametric form of the line in which they intersect. You may find the following procedure easiest:

a. First obtain a parametric form for one of the planes, say, $B + \mathbf{a}s + \mathbf{b}t$ for the second plane.
b. Then substitute this form into the point normal form for the first plane, thereby obtaining a linear equation that relates the parameters s and t.
c. Solve for s in terms of t, say, $s = E + Ft$. (Find expressions for E and F.)
d. Write the desired line as $B + \mathbf{a}(E + Ft) + \mathbf{b}t$.   ■

4.8 POLYGON INTERSECTION PROBLEMS

Polygons are the fundamental objects that are used in both 2D and 3D graphics. In 2D graphics, their straight edges make it easy to describe and draw polygons. In 3D graphics, an object is often modeled as a polygonal "mesh": a collection of polygons that fit together to make up the object's "skin." If the skin forms a closed surface that encloses some space, the mesh is called a *polyhedron*. We study meshes and polyhedra in depth in Chapter 6.

Figure 4.40 shows a 2D polygon and a 3D polyhedron that we might need to analyze or render in a graphics application. The following three important questions arise with such objects:

FIGURE 4.40 Intersection problems involving a line and a polygonal object.

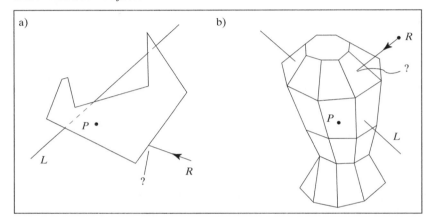

a. Is a given point P inside or outside the object?
b. Where does a given ray R first intersect the object?
c. Which part of a given line L lies inside the object, and which part lies outside?

As a simple example, which part(s) of the line $3y - 2x = 6$ lie inside the polygon whose vertices are $(0, 3), (-2, -2), (-5, 0), (0, -7), (1, 1)$?

4.8.1 Working with Convex Polygons and Polyhedra

The general case of intersecting a line with any polygon or polyhedron is quite complex; we address it in Section 4.8.4. Things are much simpler when the polygon or polyhedron is convex, because a convex polygon is completely described by a set of "bounding lines"; in 3D, a convex polyhedron is completely described by a set of "bounding planes". So we need only test the line against a set of unbounded lines or planes.

Figure 4.41 illustrates the 2D case. Part (a) shows a convex pentagon, and part (b) shows the bounding lines L_0, L_1, etc., of the pentagon. Each bounding line defines two

FIGURE 4.41 Convex polygons and polyhedra.

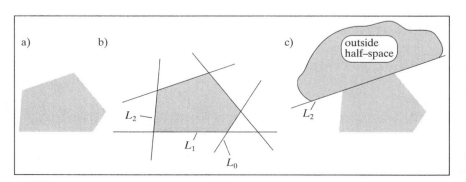

half-spaces: the inside half-space that contains the polygon and the outside half space that shares no points with the polygon. Part (c) of the figure shows a portion of the outside half-space associated with the bounding line L_2.

■ EXAMPLE 4.8.1 Finding the bounding lines

Figure 4.42(a) shows a unit square; its four bounding lines are given by $x = 1$, $x = -1$, $y = 1$, and $y = -1$. In addition, for each bounding line, we can identify the outward normal vector: the one that points into the outside half-space of the bounding line. The outward normal vector for the line $y = 1$ is, of course, $\mathbf{n} = (0, 1)$. (What are the other three outward normal vectors?)

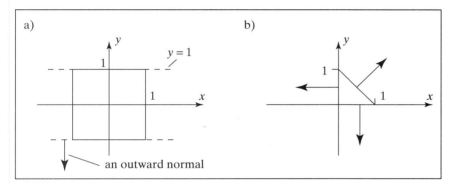

FIGURE 4.42 Examples of convex polygons.

The triangle in part (b) has three bounding lines. (What is the equation of each line?) The point normal forms for the three lines are as follows:

$$(-1, 0) \cdot \big(P - (0, 0)\big) = 0;$$
$$(0, -1) \cdot \big(P - (0, 0)\big) = 0;$$
$$(1, 1) \cdot \big(P - (1, 0)\big) = 0.$$

Note that in each case the outward normal is used.

The big advantage in dealing with convex polygons is that we perform intersection tests only on infinite lines, and we do not need to check whether an intersection lies "beyond" an endpoint. (Recall the complexity of the intersection tests in Section 4.7.) In addition, the point normal form can be used, which simplifies the calculations.

For a convex polyhedron in 3D, each plane has an inside and an outside half-space and an outward-pointing normal vector. The polyhedron is the intersection of all the inside half-spaces (the set of all points that are simultaneously in the inside half-space of every bounding plane).

4.8.2 Ray Intersections and Clipping for Convex Polygons

In Section 4.7, we developed a method that finds where a ray hits an individual line or plane. We can use this method to find where a ray hits a convex polygon or polyhedron.

The Intersection Problem

Figure 4.43 shows a ray $A + \mathbf{c}t$ intersecting a polygon P. We want to know all of the places where the ray hits P. Because P is convex, the ray hits P exactly twice: It enters once and exits once. Call the values of t at which the ray enters and exits t_{in} and t_{out}, respectively. The problem is then to compute the values of t_{in} and t_{out}. Once these hit times are known, we, of course, know the hit points themselves:

$$\text{Entering hit point} = A + \mathbf{c}t_{\text{in}};$$
$$\text{Exiting hit point} = A + \mathbf{c}t_{\text{out}}.$$

(4.62)

FIGURE 4.43 Ray $A + \mathbf{c}t$ intersecting a convex polygon.

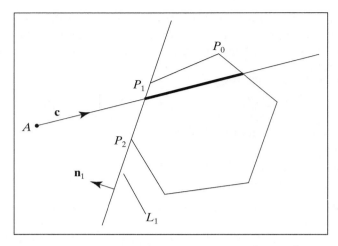

The ray is inside P for all t in the interval $[t_{in}, t_{out}]$.

Note that finding t_{in} and t_{out} solves not only the intersection problem, but also the clipping problem: If we know t_{in} and t_{out}, we know which part of the line $A + \mathbf{c}t$ lies inside P. Usually, the clipping problem is stated as follows: For the two points A and C, which part of segment AC lies inside P? We treat this problem next.

The Clipping Problem

Figure 4.44 shows several aspects of the clipping problem. Part (a) shows the case where A and C both lie outside P, but a portion of the segment AC lies inside P. If we consider segment AC as part of a ray given by $A + \mathbf{c}t$, where $\mathbf{c} = C - A$, then point A corresponds to the point on the ray at $t = 0$, and C corresponds to the point at $t = 1$. These "ray times" are labeled in the figure. To find the clipped segment, we compute t_{in} and t_{out} as just described. The segment that "survives" clipping has endpoints $A + \mathbf{c}t_{in}$ and $A + \mathbf{c}t_{out}$. In Figure 4.44(b), point C lies inside P, so t_{out} is larger than unity. The clipped segment has endpoints $A + \mathbf{c}t_{in}$ and C. In Part (c), both A and C lie inside P, so the clipped segment is AC.

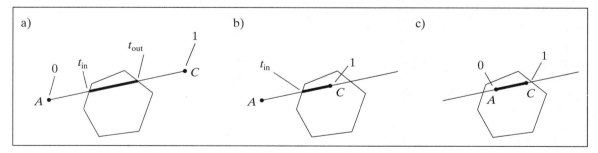

FIGURE 4.44 A segment clipped by a polygon.

In general, we compute t_{in} and compare it with zero. The larger of the values zero and t_{in} is used as the "time" for the first endpoint of the clipped segment. Similarly, the smaller of the values unity and t_{out} is used to find the second endpoint. So the endpoints of the clipped segment are

$$A' = A + \mathbf{c}\max(0, t_{in}) \tag{4.63}$$

and

$$C' = A + \mathbf{c}\min(t_{out}, 1).$$

Now, how are t_{in} and t_{out} computed? We must consider each of the bounding lines of P in turn and find where the ray $A + \mathbf{c}t$ intersects that line. We suppose that each bounding line is stored in point normal form as the pair $\{B, \mathbf{n}\}$, where B is some point on the line and $\mathbf{n}$ is the *outward-pointing normal* for the line; that is, $\mathbf{n}$ points to the outside of the polygon. Because it is outward pointing, the test of Equation 4.61 translates to the following conditions:

If $\mathbf{n} \cdot \mathbf{c} > 0$,   the ray is exiting from P.

If $\mathbf{n} \cdot \mathbf{c} = 0$,   the ray is parallel to the line.   (4.64)

If $\mathbf{n} \cdot \mathbf{c} < 0$ the ray is entering P.

For each bounding line, we find

  a. the hit time of the ray with the bounding line [use Equation (4.59)];
  b. Whether the ray is entering or exiting the polygon [use Equation (4.64)].

If the ray is entering, we know that the time at which the ray ultimately enters P (if it enters it at all) cannot be *earlier* than the newly found hit time. We keep track of the earliest possible entering time as t_{in}. For each entering hit time t_{hit}, we replace t_{in} by $\max(t_{in}, t_{hit})$. Similarly, we keep track of the *latest* possible exit time as t_{out}, and for each exiting hit we replace t_{out} by $\min(t_{out}, t_{hit})$.

It helps to think of the interval $[t_{in}, t_{out}]$ as the **candidate interval** of t—the interval of t inside of which the ray *might* lie inside the object. Figure 4.45 gives an example for the clipping problem. We know that the point $A + \mathbf{c}t$ *cannot* be inside P for any t outside of the candidate interval. As each bounding line is tested, the candidate interval gets reduced as t_{in} is increased or t_{out} is decreased: Pieces of it get "chopped" off. To get started, we initialize t_{in} to zero and t_{out} to unity for the line-clipping problem, so the candidate interval is $[0, 1]$. The algorithm is then as follows:

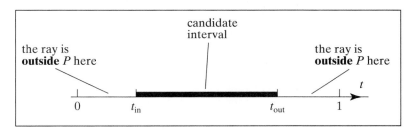

FIGURE 4.45 The candidate interval for a hit.

1. Initialize the candidate interval to $[0, 1]$.[12]
2. For each bounding line, use Equation (4.59) to find the hit time t_{hit} and determine whether it is an entering or exiting hit:
   - If t_{hit} is an entering hit, set $t_{in} = \max(t_{in}, t_{hit})$.
   - If t_{hit} is an exiting hit, set $t_{out} = \min(t_{out}, t_{hit})$.
   If at any point t_{in} becomes greater than t_{out}, the ray misses P entirely, and testing is terminated.
3. If the candidate interval is not empty, then, from Equation (4.63), the segment from $A + \mathbf{c}t_{in}$ to $A + \mathbf{c}t_{out}$ lies inside P. For the line-clipping problem, these are the endpoints of the clipped line. For the ray intersection problem, they are the entering and exiting points of the ray.

Note that we stop testing as soon the candidate interval vanishes. This is called an **early out**: If we determine early in the processing that the ray is outside of the polygon, we save time by immediately exiting from the test.

---

[12] For the ray intersection problem, where the ray extends infinitely far in both directions, we set $t_{in} = -\infty$ and $t_{out} = \infty$. In practice, t_{in} is set to a large negative value and t_{out} to a large positive value.

Figure 4.46 shows a specific example of clipping: We seek the portion of segment AC that lies in polygon P. We initialize t_{in} to zero and t_{out} to unity. The ray "starts" at A at $t = 0$ and proceeds to point C, reaching it at $t = 1$. We test the ray against each bounding line $L_0, L_1, \ldots$, in turn and update t_{in} and t_{out} as necessary.

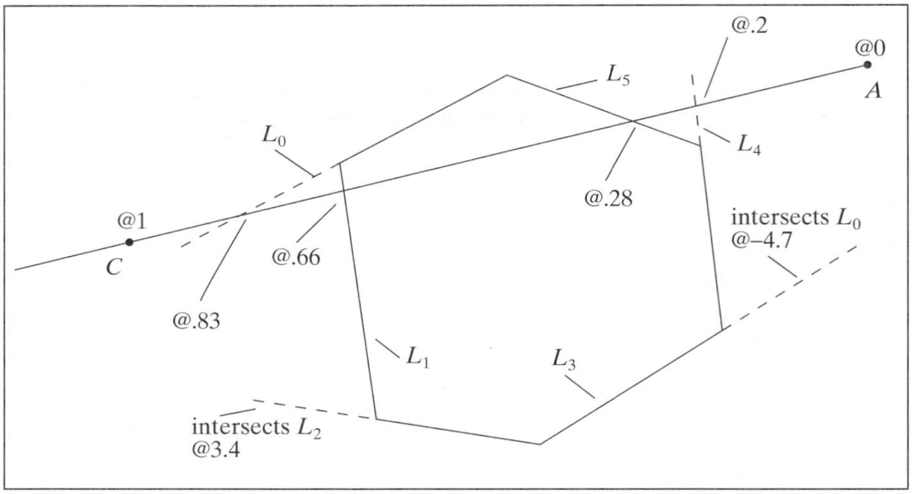

FIGURE 4.46 Testing when a ray lies inside a convex polygon.

Suppose that when we test the ray against line L_0 we find an exiting hit at $t = 0.83$. This sets t_{out} to 0.83, and the candidate interval is now $[0, 0.83]$. We then test the ray against L_1 and find an exiting hit at $t = 0.66$. This reduces the candidate interval to $[0, 0.66]$. The test against L_2 gives an exiting hit at $t = 3.4$. This tells us nothing new: We already know that the ray is outside for $t > 0.66$. The test against L_3 gives an entering hit at $t = -4.7$, which is earlier than the current t_{in}. The test with L_4 gives an entering hit at $t = 0.2$, so t_{in} is updated to 0.2. Finally, testing against L_5 gives an entering hit at $t = 0.28$, and we are done: The candidate interval is $[0.28, 0.66]$. In fact, the ray *is* inside P for all t between 0.28 and 0.66.

Line test	t_{in}	t_{out}
0	0	0.83
1	0	0.66
2	0	0.66
3	0	0.66
4	0.2	0.66
5	0.28	0.66

FIGURE 4.47 Updates on the values of t_{in} and t_{out}.

Figure 4.47 shows the sequence of updates to t_{in} and t_{out} that occur as each of the preceding lines is tested.

4.8.3 The Cyrus–Beck Clipping Algorithm

Let us now use the ideas we have just presented to build a routine that performs the clipping of a line segment against any convex polygon. The method was originally developed by Cyrus and Beck [Cyrus78]. Later, a highly efficient clipper for rectangular windows based on similar ideas was devised by Liang and Barsky [Liang84]. The latter is discussed in a case study at the end of the chapter.

The routine that implements the Cyrus–Beck clipper has the following interface:

```
int CyrusBeckClip(Line& seg, LineList& L) ;
```

The parameters are the line segment, `seg`, to be clipped (which contains the first and second endpoints, named `seg.first` and `seg.second`, respectively) and the list of bounding lines of the polygon. The routine clips `seg` against each line in `L` as described in Section 4.8.2 and places the clipped segment back into `seg`. (This is why `seg` must be passed by reference.) The routine returns the following values:

- 0 if no part of the segment lies in P (the candidate interval became empty);
- 1 if some part of the segment does lie in P.

Figure 4.48 shows pseudocode for the Cyrus–Beck algorithm. The types `LineSegment`, `LineList`, and `Vector2` are suitable data types to hold the quantities in

```
int CyrusBeckClip(LineSegment& seg, LineList L)
{
  double numer, denom; // used to find hit time for each line
  double tIn = 0.0, tOut = 1.0;
  Vector2 c, tmp;
  form vector: c = seg.second - seg.first
  for(int i = 0; i < L.num; i++) // chop at each bounding line
  {
      form vector tmp = L.line[i].pt - first
      numer = dot(L.line[i].norm, tmp);
      denom = dot(L.line[i].norm, c);
      if(!chopCI(tIn, tOut numer, denom,)) return 0; // early out
  }
  // adjust the endpoints of the segment; do second one 1st.
  if (tOut < 1.0 ) // second endpoint was altered
  {
      seg.second.x  = seg.first.x + c.x * tOut;
      seg.second.y  = seg.first.y + c.y * tOut;
  }
  if (tIn > 0.0)  // first endpoint was altered
  {
      seg.first.x  = seg.first.x + c.x * tIn;
      seg.first.y  = seg.first.y + c.y * tIn;
  }

      return 1; // some segment survives

}
```

FIGURE 4.48 Pseudocode for Cyrus–Beck clipper for a convex polygon, 2D case.

question. (See the exercises at the end of the section). Variables numer and denom hold the numerator and denominator, respectively, of t_{hit} of Equation (4.59):

$$numer = \mathbf{n} \cdot (B - A);$$
$$denom = \mathbf{n} \cdot \mathbf{c}. \tag{4.65}$$

Note that the value of seg.second is updated first, since we must use the old value of seg.first in updating for both seg.first and seg.second.

The routine chopCI() is shown in Figure 4.49. It uses numer and denom of Equation (4.65) to calculate the time at which the ray hits a bounding line, utilizes Equation (4.64) to determine whether the ray is entering or exiting the polygon, and "chops" off the piece of the candidate interval CI that is thereby found to be outside the polygon.

If the ray is parallel to the line, it could lie entirely in the inside half-space of the line or entirely out of it. It turns out that numer = $\mathbf{n} \cdot (B - A)$ is exactly the quantity needed to tell which of these cases obtains. See the exercises that follow.

The 3D Case: Clipping a Line against a Convex Polyhedron

The Cyrus–Beck clipping algorithm works in three dimensions in exactly the same way as it does in two. In 3D, the edges of the window become planes defining a convex region, and the line segment is a line suspended in space. ChopCI() needs no changes at all (since it uses only the values of dot products, through numer and denom). The data types in CyrusBeckClip() must, of course, be extended to 3D types, and when the endpoints of the line are adjusted, the z-component must be adjusted as well.

FIGURE 4.49 Clipping against a single bounding line.

```
int chopCI(double& tIn, double& tOut, double numer, double denom)
{
  double tHit;
  if(denom < 0)        // ray is entering
  {
     tHit = numer / denom;
     if(tHit > tOut) return 0;      // early out
     else if(tHit > tIn) tIn = tHit; // take larger t
  }
  else if(denom > 0)           // ray is exiting
  {
     tHit = numer / denom;
     if(tHit < tIn) return 0;      // early out
     if(tHit < tout) tOut = tHit; // take smaller t
  }
  else              // denom is 0: ray is parallel
  if(numer <= 0) return 0;   // missed the line

  return 1; // CI is still non-empty
}
```

PRACTICE EXERCISES

4.8.1 Data types for variables in the cyrus–beck clipper

Provide useful definitions for data types, either as structs or classes, for `LineSegment`, `LineList`, and `Vector2` used in the Cyrus–Beck clipping algorithm.

4.8.2 What does numer $<= 0$ do?

Sketch the vectors involved in the value of `numer` in `chopCI()`, and show that when the ray $A + \mathbf{c}t$ moves parallel to the bounding line $\mathbf{n} \cdot (P - B) = 0$, it lies wholly in the inside half-space of the line if and only if `numer` > 0.

4.8.3 Find the clipped line

Find the portion of the segment with endpoints $(2, 4)$ and $(20, 8)$ that lies within the quadrilateral window with corners at $(0, 7)$, $(9, 9)$, $(14, 4)$, and $(2, 2)$. ▪

4.8.4 Clipping against Arbitrary Polygons

In the previous section, we saw how to clip a line segment against a convex polygon. We generalize this procedure to a method for clipping a segment against *any* polygon.

The basic problem is to find where the ray $A + \mathbf{c}t$ lies inside polygon P given by the list of vertices $P_0, P_1, \dots, P_{N-1}$. Figure 4.50 shows an example.

FIGURE 4.50 Where is a ray inside an arbitrary polygon P?

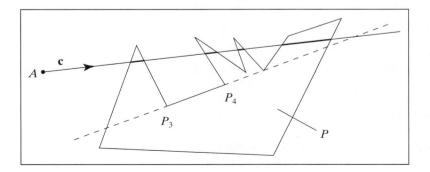

It is clear that, in general, the ray can enter and exit from P multiple times and that the result of clipping a segment against P may result in a *list* of segments rather than a single one. Also, of course, P is no longer described by a collection of infinite bounding lines in point normal form; we must work with the N finite segments such as $P_3 P_4$ that form its edges.

The problem is close to the one we dealt with in Section 4.7: finding the intersection of two line segments. Now we are intersecting one line segment with the sequence of line segments associated with P.

We represent each edge of P parametrically (rather than in point normal form). For instance, the edge $P_3 P_4$ is represented as $P_3 + \mathbf{e}_3 u$, where $\mathbf{e}_3 = P_4 - P_3$ is the **edge vector** associated with P_3. In general, the ith edge is given by $P_i + \mathbf{e}_i u$, for u in $[0, 1]$ and $i = 0, 1, \ldots, N - 1$ where $\mathbf{e}_i = P_{i+1} - P_i$, and, as always, we equate P_N with P_0.

Recall from Section 4.7 that the ray $A + \mathbf{c}t$ hits the ith edge when t and u have the proper values to make $A + \mathbf{c}t = P_i + \mathbf{e}_i u$. Letting vector $\mathbf{b}_i = P_i - A$, we seek the solution (values of t and u) of

$$\mathbf{c}t = \mathbf{b}_i + \mathbf{e}_i u.$$

Equations (4.52) and (4.53) hold the answers. Converted to the current notation, they read

$$t = \frac{\mathbf{e}_i^\perp \cdot \mathbf{b}_i}{\mathbf{e}_i^\perp \cdot \mathbf{c}}$$

and

$$u = \frac{\mathbf{c}^\perp \cdot \mathbf{b}_i}{\mathbf{e}_i^\perp \cdot \mathbf{c}}.$$

If $\mathbf{e}_i^\perp$ is zero, the ith edge is parallel to the direction $\mathbf{c}$ of the ray, and there is no intersection. A true intersection exists with the ith edge only if u falls in the interval $[0, 1]$.

We need to find all of the genuine hits of the ray with edges of P and place them in a list of the hit times. Call this list `hitList`. Then pseudocode for the process would look like the following:

```
initialize hitList to empty
for(int i = 0; i < N; i++)    // for each edge of P
{
      build bi, ei for the i-th edge
      solve for t, u
      if(u lies in [0,1])
            add t to the hitList
}
```

What we do now with this list depends on the problem at hand.

The Ray Intersection Problem

Where does the ray *first* hit P? This question is answered by finding the smallest value of t, in `hitList`. Call this value t_{min}. Then the hit spot is, as always, $A + \mathbf{c}t_{min}$.

The line-clipping problem

To solve this problem, we need the sequence of t-intervals in which the ray is inside P. We thus must sort `hitList` and then take the t-values in pairs. The ray enters P at the first time in each pair and exits from P at the second time of each pair.

■ **EXAMPLE 4.8.2 Clip** *AB* **to Polygon** *P*

Suppose the line to be clipped is *AB*, as shown in Figure 4.51, for which $A = (1, 1)$ and $B = (8, 2)$. *P* is given by the list of vertices $(3, 2), (2, 0), (6, -1), (6, 2), (4, 1)$. Taking each edge in turn, we get the following values of *t* and *u* at the intersections:

Edge	*u*	*t*
0	0.3846	0.2308
1	−0.727	−0.2727
2	0.9048	0.7142
3	0.4	0.6
4	0.375	0.375

The hit with edge 1 occurs at *t* outside of $[0, 1]$ so it is discarded. We sort the remaining *t*-values and arrive at the following sorted hit list: $\{0.2308, 0.375, 0.6, 0.7142\}$. Thus, the ray enters *P* at $t = 0.2308$, exits it at $t = 0.375$, reenters it at $t = 0.6$, and exits it for the last time at $t = 0.7142$.

FIGURE 4.51 Clipping a line against a polygon.

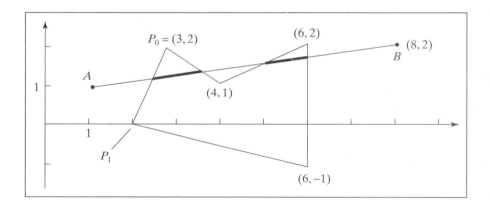

PRACTICE EXERCISE

4.8.4 Clip a line

Find the portions of the line from $A = (1, 3.5)$ to $B = (9, 3.5)$ that lie inside the polygon with list of vertices $(2, 4), (3, 1), (4, 4), (3, 3)$.   ■

4.8.5 More Advanced Clipping

Clipping algorithms are fundamental to computer graphics, and a number of efficient ones have been developed. We have examined two approaches to clipping so far: The **Cohen–Sutherland** clipping algorithm, studied in Chapter 2, clips a line against an aligned rectangle; the **Cyrus–Beck** clipper generalizes that algorithn to clipping a line against any convex polygon or polyhedron. But situations arise in which one needs more sophisticated clipping. We mention two such methods here, and develop the details of both in case studies at the end of the chapter.

The **Sutherland–Hodgman** clipper is similar to the Cyrus–Beck method, performing clipping against a convex polygon. But instead of clipping a single line segment, it clips an entire polygon (which need not be convex) against the convex polygon. Most importantly, its output is again a *polygon* (or possibly a set of polygons). Sometimes it is important to retain the polygonal structure during clipping, since the clipped polygons may need to be filled with a pattern or color. This is not possible if the edges of the polygon are clipped individually.

The **Weiler–Atherton** clipping algorithm clips any polygon P against *any* other polygon W, convex or not. It can output the part of P that lies inside W (**interior clipping**) or the part of P that lies outside W (**exterior clipping**). In addition, both P and W can have "holes" in them. As might be expected, this algorithm is somewhat more complex than the others we have examined, but its power makes it a welcome addition to one's toolkit in a variety of applications.

4.9 SUMMARY

Vectors offer a convenient way to express many geometric relations, and the operations supported by vectors provide a powerful means of manipulating geometric objects algebraically. Many computer graphics algorithms are simplified and made more efficient through the use of vectors. Because most vector operations are expressed the same way, independently of the dimensionality of the underlying space, it is possible to derive results that are equally true in 2D or 3D space.

The dot product of two vectors is a fundamental quantity that simplifies finding the length of a vector and the angle between two vectors. It can be used to find such things as the orthogonal projection of one vector onto another, the location of the center of the excircle of three points, and the direction of a reflected ray. The dot product is often used to test whether two vectors are orthogonal to one another and, more generally, to test when the angle between the vectors is less than, or more than, 90°. It is also used in working with a 2D vector $\mathbf{a}^\perp$ that lies 90° to the left of a given vector $\mathbf{a}$. In particular, the dot product $\mathbf{a}^\perp \cdot \mathbf{b}$ reports useful information about how $\mathbf{a}$ and $\mathbf{b}$ are disposed relative to each other.

The cross product also reveals information about the angle between two vectors in 3D and, in addition, evaluates to a vector that is perpendicular to them both. It is often used to find a vector that is normal to a plane.

In developing an algorithm, it is crucial to have a concise representation of the graphical objects involved. The two principal forms for doing this are the parametric representation and the implicit form. The parametric representation "visits" each of the points on the object as a parameter is made to vary, so the parameter "indexes into" different points on the object. The implicit form expresses an equation that all points on the object, and only those points, must satisfy. Often, it takes the form $f(x, y) = 0$ in 2D or $f(x, y, z) = 0$ in 3D, where $f()$ is some function. Not only does the value of $f()$ for a given point tell when the point is on the object, but when a point lies off of the object, the sign of $f()$ can reveal on *which* side of the object the point lies. In this chapter we addressed finding representations of the two fundamental "flat" objects in graphics: lines and planes. For such objects, both the parametric form and implicit form are linear in their arguments. The implicit form can be revealingly written as the dot product of a normal vector and a vector lying within the object.

It is possible to form arbitrary linear combinations of vectors, but not of points. For points, only affine combinations are allowed, or else chaos reigns if the underlying coordinate system is ever altered, as it frequently is in graphics. Affine combinations of points are useful in graphics, and we showed that they form the basis of "tweening" for animations and for Bezier curves.

The parametric form of a line or ray is particularly useful for such tasks as finding where two lines intersect or where a ray hits a polygon or polyhedron. These problems are important in themselves, and they also underlie clipping algorithms that are so prominent in graphics. The Cyrus–Beck clipper, which finds where a line that is expressed parametrically shares the same point in space as a line or plane that is expressed implicitly, addresses a larger class of problems than the Cohen–Sutherland clipper of Chapter 2. We will examine the Cyrus–Beck clipper in several other contexts later in the text.

In the case studies that are presented next, the vector tools developed so far are applied to some interesting graphics situations, and their power is seen even more clearly. Whether or not you intend to carry out the required programming to implement these miniprojects, it is valuable to read through them and imagine what course you would pursue to solve them.

4.10 CASE STUDIES

CASE STUDY 4.1 ANIMATION WITH TWEENING

Level of Effort: II. Devise two interesting polylines, such as A and B shown in Figure 4.52. Ensure that A and B have the same number of points, perhaps by adding an artificial extra point in the top segment of B.

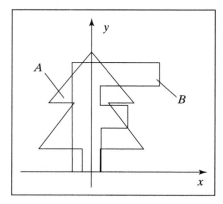

FIGURE 4.52 Tweening two polylines.

a. Develop a routine similar to `drawTween(A, B, n, t)` of Figure 4.23 that draws the tween at t of the polylines A and B.
b. Develop a routine that draws a sequence of tweens between A and B as t varies from 0 to 1, and experiment with the routine. Use the double buffering offered by OpenGL to make the animation smooth.
c. Extend the routine so that after t increases gradually from 0 to 1, it decreases gradually back to 0 and then repeats, so the animation repeatedly shows A mutating into B and then back into A. This alternation should continue until a key is pressed.
d. Develop a routine that allows the user to enter two polylines with the mouse, after which the polylines are tweened. The user presses key "A" and begins to lay down points to form polyline A; then the user presses key "B" and lays down the points for polyline B. Pressing "T" terminates the process and begins the tweening, which continues until the user types "Q". Allow for the case where the user inputs a different number of points for A than for B: Your program automatically creates the required number of extra points along line segments (perhaps at their midpoints) of the polyline having fewer points.

CASE STUDY 4.2 CIRCLES GALORE

Level of Effort: II. Write an application that allows the user to input the points of a triangle with a mouse. The program then draws the triangle along with its **inscribed circle**, **excircle**, and **nine-point circle**, each in a different color. Arrange matters so that the user can then move vertices of the triangle to new locations with the mouse, whereupon the new triangle with its three circles are redrawn.

We saw how to draw the excircle in Section 4.6.2. Here we show how to find the inscribed circle and the nine-point circle.

The Inscribed Circle

This is the circle that just "snuggles up" inside the given triangle and is tangent to all three sides.[13] Figure 4.53(a) shows a triangle ABC along with its inscribed circle. As was the case with the excircle, the hard part is finding the center of the inscribed circle. A straightforward method[14] recognizes that the inscribed circle of ABC is simply the excircle of a different set of three points, RST, as shown in the figure.

---

[13] Note that finding the incircle also solves the problem of finding the unique circle that is tangent to three non-collinear lines in the plane.

[14] Suggested by Russell Swan.

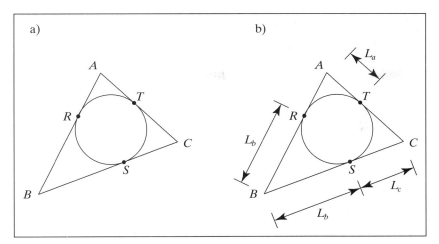

FIGURE 4.53 The inscribed circle of *ABC* is the excircle of *RST*.

We need only find the locations of R, S, and T and then use the excircle method of Section 4.6.2. Figure 4.53(b) shows the distances of R, S, and T from A, B, and C. By the symmetry of a circle, the distances $|B - R|$ and $|B - S|$ must be equal, and there are two other pairs of lines that have the same length. Using the definitions of Equation (4.56) for $\mathbf{a}, \mathbf{b}$, and $\mathbf{c}$, we therefore have

$$|\mathbf{a}| = L_b + L_a, \qquad |\mathbf{b}| = L_b + L_c, \qquad \text{and} \qquad |\mathbf{c}| = L_a + L_c,$$

which can be combined to solve for L_a and L_b:

$$2L_a = |\mathbf{a}| + |\mathbf{c}| - |\mathbf{b}|; \qquad 2L_b = |\mathbf{a}| + |\mathbf{b}| - |\mathbf{c}|.$$

With L_a and L_b known, we find that

$$R = A + L_a \frac{\mathbf{a}}{|\mathbf{a}|},$$

$$S = B + L_b \frac{\mathbf{b}}{|\mathbf{b}|},$$

and

$$T = A - L_a \frac{\mathbf{c}}{|\mathbf{c}|}. \qquad (4.66)$$

(Check these expressions!)

We can encapsulate the calculation of R, S, and T from A, B, and C in a simple routine `get-TangentPoints(A, B, C, R, S, T)`. The advantage is that if we have a routine `ex-circle()` that takes three points and computes the center and radius of the excircle defined by them, we can use the *same* routine to find the inscribed circle. Experiment with these tools.

The Nine-point Circle

A triangle has nine particularly interesting points:

- the midpoints of the three sides;
- the feet of the three altitudes;
- the midpoints of the lines joining the orthocenter (where the three altitudes meet) to the vertices.

Remarkably, a single circle passes through all nine points! Figure 4.54 shows **the nine-point circle**[15] for a sample triangle. The nine-point circle is perhaps most easily drawn as the excircle of the midpoints of the sides of the triangle.

---

[15] "This circle is the first really exciting one to appear in any course on elementary geometry," according to Daniel Pedoe, *Circles* (New York: Pergamon Press, 1957).

FIGURE 4.54 The nine-point circle.

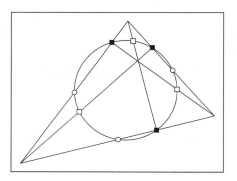

CASE STUDY 4.3 IS POINT **Q** INSIDE CONVEX POLYGON **P**?

Level of Effort: II. Suppose you are given the specification of a convex polygon P. Suppose further that you are asked to determine whether or not a particular point Q lies inside P. But from the discussion on convex polygons in Section 4.8.1, we know that this is equivalent to asking whether Q lies on the inside half-space of *every* bounding line of P. For each bounding line L_i, we need only test whether the vector $Q - P_i$ is more than 90° away from the outward-pointing normal. In other words,

$$Q \text{ lies in } P \text{ if } (Q - P_i) \cdot n_i < 0 \qquad \text{for } i = 0, 1, \dots, N - 1. \tag{4.67}$$

Figure 4.55 illustrates the test for the particular bounding line that passes through P_1 and P_2. For a point Q that lies inside P, the angle with $\mathbf{n}_1$ is greater than 90°. For a point Q' that lies outside P, the angle is less than 90°.

FIGURE 4.55 Is point Q inside polygon P?

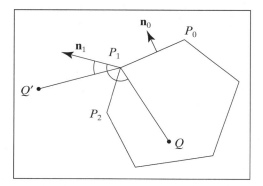

Write and test a program that allows the user to do each of the following:

a. Lay down the vertices of a convex polygon P with the mouse.
b. Successively lay down test points Q with the mouse.
c. Print "is inside" or "is not inside", depending on whether the point Q is or is not inside P.

CASE STUDY 4.4 REFLECTIONS IN A CHAMBER (2D RAY TRACING)

Level of Effort: II. This case study applies some of the tools and ideas introduced in this chapter to a fascinating, yet simple, simulation. The simulation performs a kind of ray tracing, based in a 2D world for easy visualization. Three-dimensional ray tracing is discussed in detail in Chapter 14.

The simulation traces the path of a single tiny ball as it bounces off various walls inside a "chamber." Figure 4.56(a) shows a cross section of a convex chamber W that has six walls and contains three convex "pillars." The ball begins at point S and moves in a straight line in direction **c** until it hits a barrier, whereupon it "reflects" off the barrier and moves in a new direction, again in a straight line. It continues to do this forever. Figure 4.56(b) shows an example of the polyline path that a ray representing the ball traverses.

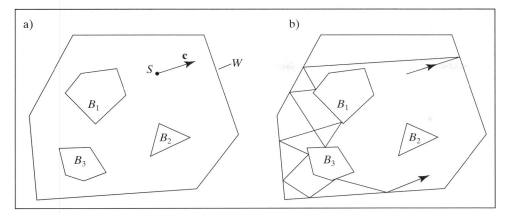

FIGURE 4.56 A 2D ray-tracing experiment.

For any given position S and direction $\mathbf{c}$ of the ray, tracing its path requires two operations:

- Finding the first wall of the chamber "hit" by the ray.
- Finding the new direction the ray will take as it reflects off this first wall.

Both of these operations have been discussed in the chapter. Note that as each new ray is created, its starting point is always on some wall, the "hit point" of the previously hit wall.

We represent the chamber by a list of convex polygons: $\text{pillar}_0, \text{pillar}_1, \dots$, and arrange that pillar_0 is the "chamber" inside which the action takes place. The pillars are stored in suitable arrays of points. For each ray beginning at S and moving in direction $\mathbf{c}$, the entire array of pillars is scanned, and the intersection of the ray with each pillar is determined. This test is done using the Cyrus–Beck algorithm of Section 4.8.3. If there is a hit with a pillar, the "hit time" is taken to be the time at which the ray "enters" the pillar. We encapsulate the test in the routine

```
int rayHit(Ray thisRay, int which, double& tHit);
```

which calculates the hit time `tHit` of the ray `thisRay` against $\text{pillar}_{\text{which}}$, returning 1 if the ray hits the pillar and 0 if it misses. A suitable type for `Ray` is `struct{Point2 startPt; Vector2 dir;}` or the corresponding class; it captures the starting point S and direction $\mathbf{c}$ of the ray.

We want to know which pillar the ray hits first. This question is answered by keeping track of the earliest hit time as we scan through the list of pillars. Only positive hit times need to be considered: Negative hit times correspond to hits at spots in the direction opposite that of the ray's travel. When the earliest hit point is found, the ray is drawn from S to it.

We must find the direction of the reflected ray as it moves away from the latest hit spot. The direction $\mathbf{c}'$ of the reflected ray is given in terms of the direction $\mathbf{c}$ of the incident ray by Equation (4.27) and is

$$\mathbf{c}' = \mathbf{c} - 2(\mathbf{c} \cdot \hat{\mathbf{n}})\hat{\mathbf{n}}, \tag{4.68}$$

where $\hat{\mathbf{n}}$ is the unit normal to the wall of the pillar that was hit. If a pillar inside the chamber was hit, we use the outward-pointing normal; if the chamber itself was hit, we use the inward-pointing normal.

Write and execute a program that draws the path of a ray as it reflects off the inner walls of the chamber W and the walls of the convex pillars inside the chamber. Arrange things so that the user can read in the list of pillars from an external file. Also, have the user specify the ray's starting position and direction. (See Chapter 11 for the "elliptipool" 2D ray-tracing simulation.)

CASE STUDY 4.5 CYRUS–BECK CLIPPING

Level of Effort: II. Write and execute a program that clips a collection of lines against a convex polygon. The user specifies the polygon by laying down a sequence of points with the mouse (after the pressing the key "C" to terminate the polygon and begin clipping). Then a sequence of lines is generated, each having randomly chosen endpoints.

For each such line, first the whole line is drawn in red, and then the portion that lies inside the polygon is drawn in blue.

CASE STUDY 4.6 CLIPPING A POLYGON AGAINST A CONVEX POLYGON: SUTHERLAND–HODGMAN CLIPPING

Level of Effort: III. The clipping algorithms we have studied so far clip individual line segments against polygons. When, instead, a *polygon* is clipped against a window, it can be fragmented into several polygons in the clipping process, as suggested in Figure 4.57(a). The polygon may need to be filled with a color or pattern, which means that each of the clipped fragments must be associated with that pattern, as suggested in Figure 4.57(b). Therefore, a clipping algorithm must keep track of edges *ab*, *cd*, and so on, and must fashion a new polygon (or several polygons) out of the original one. It is also important that an algorithm not retain extraneous edges, such as *bc*, as part of the new polygon, because such edges would be displayed when they should in fact be invisible.

FIGURE 4.57 Clipping a polygon against a polygon.

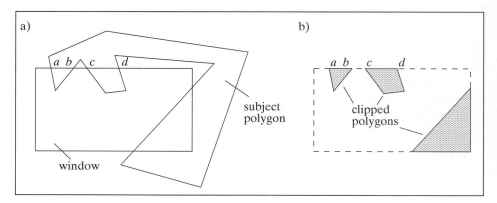

The polygon to be clipped will be called the *subject* polygon *S*. The polygon against which *S* is clipped will be called the *clip* polygon *C*. How do we clip polygon *S*, represented by a list of vertices, against polygon *C*, to generate a collection of lists of vertices that properly represents the set of clipped polygons?

We examine here the **Sutherland–Hodgman** clipping algorithm, which is quite simple and clips any subject polygon (convex or not) against a convex clip polygon. The algorithm can leave extraneous edges that must be removed later.

Because of the many different cases that can arise, we need an organized method for keeping track of the clipping process. The Sutherland–Hodgman algorithm takes a divide-and-conquer approach: It breaks a difficult problem into a set of simpler ones. It is built on the Cyrus–Beck approach, but must work with a *list* of vertices that represent a polygon, rather than a simple pair of vertices.

Like the Cyrus–Beck algorithm, the Sutherland–Hodgman algorithm clips polygon *S* against each bounding line of polygon *C* in turn, leaving only the part that is inside *C*. Once all of the edges of *C* have been used this way, *S* will have been clipped against *C* as desired. Figure 4.58 shows the algorithm as applied to a seven-sided subject polygon *S* and a rectangular clip polygon *C*. We will describe each step in the process for this example. *S* is characterized by the list of vertices *a*, *b*, *c*, *d*, *e*, *f*, *g*. *S* is clipped against the top, right, bottom, and left edges of *C* in turn, and at each stage a new list of vertices is generated from the old one. The list describes one or more polygons and is passed along as the subject polygon for clipping against the next edge of *C*.

The basic operation, then, is to clip the polygon(s) described by an input list of vertices against the current clip edge of *C* and produce an output list of vertices. To do this, we traverse the input list, forming successive edges with pairs of adjacent vertices. Each such edge *E* has a first and a second endpoint we call *s* and *p*, respectively. There are four possible situations for endpoints *s* and *p*: both can be inside the clip edge, both can be outside of it, one can be on one side of the clip edge and the other can be on the other side, and vice versa. In each case, certain

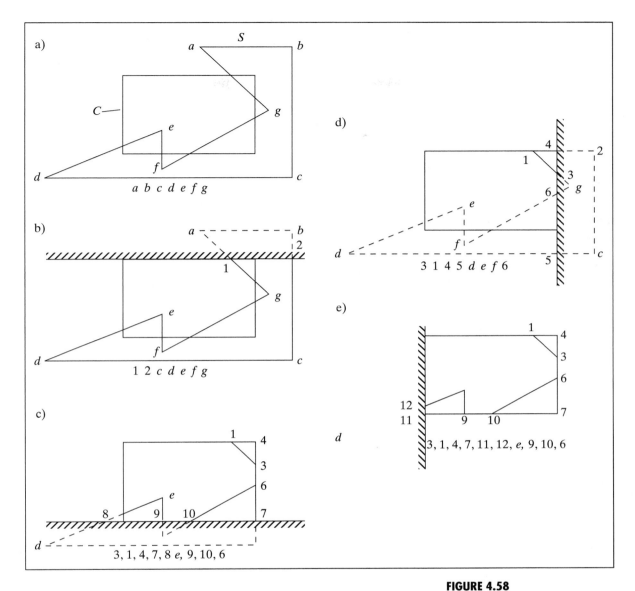

FIGURE 4.58
Sutherland–Hodgman polygon clipping.

points are output to (appended onto) the new list of vertices, as shown in Figure 4.59. The possibilities and actions are summarized as follows:

a. Both s and p are inside: p is output.
b. s is inside and p is outside: Find the intersection i and output it.
c. Both s and p are outside: Nothing is output.
d. s is outside and p is inside: Find intersection i, and output i and then p.

Now follow the progress of the Sutherland–Hodgman algorithm in Figure 4.58. Consider clipping S against the top edge of C. The input list of vertices for this phase is a, b, c, d, e, f, g. For convenience, the first edge from the list is taken as that from g to a, the edge that "wraps around" from the end of the list to its first element. Thus, point s is g and point p is a here. Edge g, a, meaning the edge from g to a, intersects the clip edge at a new point, "1," which is output to the new list. (The output list from each stage in the algorithm is shown below the subsequent drawing in Figure 4.58.) The next edge in the input list is a, b. Since both endpoints are above the clipping edge, nothing is output. The third edge, b, c, generates two output points, 2 and c,

FIGURE 4.59 Four cases for each edge of S.

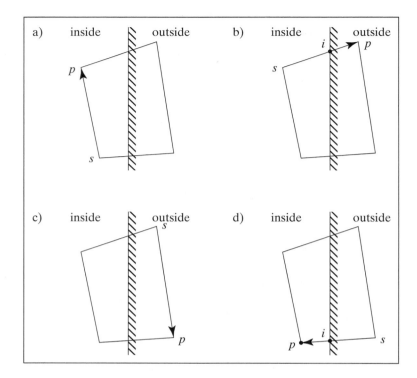

and the fourth edge, c, d, outputs point d. The process continues until the last edge, f, g, is tested, producing g. The new list of vertices for the next clipping stage is therefore $1, 2, c, d, e, f, g$. It is illuminating to follow the example in Figure 4.58 carefully in its entirety to see how the algorithm works.

Notice that extraneous edges (3, 6 and 9, 10) are formed that connect the three polygonal fragments produced by the clipping algorithm. Such edges can cause problems in some polygon-filling algorithms. It is possible, but not trivial, to remove these offending edges [Sutherland74].

Implement the Sutherland–Hodgman clipping algorithm, and test it on a variety of sample polygons. The user lays down the convex polygon C with the mouse and then does the same with the subject polygon S. Each is drawn in red as it is being laid down. Clipping is then performed, and all clipped polygons are drawn in blue.

CASE STUDY 4.7 CLIPPING ONE POLYGON AGAINST ANOTHER: WEILER–ATHERTON CLIPPING

Level of Effort: III. Weiler–Atherton clipping is the most general clipping mechanism of all we have studied. It clips any subject polygon against any (possibly nonconvex) clip polygon. The polygons may even contain holes.

The Sutherland–Hodgman algorithm examined in Case Study 4.6 exploits the convexity of the clipping polygon through the use of inside and outside half-spaces. In some applications, however, such as removing hidden surfaces and rendering shadows, one must clip one concave polygon against another. Clipping is more complex in such cases. The Weiler–Atherton approach clips any polygon against any other, even when they have holes. It also allows one to form the set-theoretic **union**, **intersection**, and **difference** of two polygons, as we discuss in Case Study 4.8.

We start with a simple example, shown in Figure 4.60. Here, two concave polygons, SUBJ and CLIP, are represented by the lists of vertices (a, b, c, d) and (A, B, C, D), respectively. We adopt the convention of listing vertices so that the interior of the polygon is to the right of each edge as we move cyclically from vertex to vertex through the list. For instance, the interior of SUBJ lies to the right of the edge from c to d and to the right of that from d to a. This is akin to listing vertices in "clockwise" order.

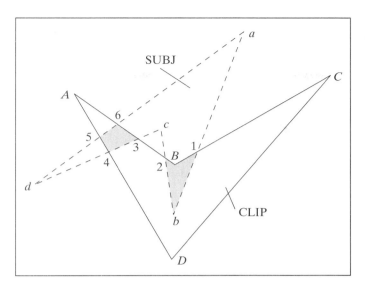

FIGURE 4.60 Weiler–Atherton clipping.

All of the intersections of the two polygons are identified and stored in a list. (See later.) In this example, there are six such intersections. To clip SUBJ against CLIP, traverse around SUBJ in the "forward direction" (i.e., so that its interior is to the right), until an "entering" intersection is found—one for which SUBJ is moving from the outside to the inside of CLIP. Here we first find 1, and it goes to an output list that records the clipped polygon(s).

The process is simple to state in geometric terms: Traverse along SUBJ, moving segment by segment, until an intersection is encountered (2 in the example). The idea now is to turn away from following SUBJ and to follow CLIP instead. There are two ways to turn. First, turn so that CLIP is traversed in its forward direction. This keeps the inside of both SUBJ and CLIP to the right. Then, upon finding an intersection, turn and follow along SUBJ in its forward direction, and so on. Each vertex or intersection encountered is put on the output list. Repeat the "turn and jump between polygons" process, traversing each polygon in its forward direction, until the first vertex is revisited. The output list at this point consists of $(1, b, 2, B)$.

Now check for any other entering intersections of SUBJ. Number 3 is found, and the process repeats, generating the output list $(3, 4, 5, 6)$. Further checks for entering intersections show that they have all been visited, so the clipping process terminates, yielding the two polygons $(1, b, 2, B)$ and $(3, 4, 5, 6)$. An organized way to implement this "follow in the forward direction and jump" process is to build the following two lists by traversing each polygon (so that its interior is to the right) and listing both vertices and intersections in the order they are encountered:

SUBJLIST: $a, 1, b, 2, c, 3, 4, d, 5, 6$

CLIPLIST: $A, 6, 3, 2, B, 1, C, D, 4, 5$

(What should be done if no intersections are detected between the two polygons?) Therefore, traversing a polygon amounts to traversing a list, and jumping between polygons is effected by jumping between lists.

Notice that once the lists are available, there is very little geometry in the process—just a "point outside polygon" test to properly identify an entering vertex. The proper direction in which to traverse each polygon is embedded in the ordering of its list. The progress of the algorithm as applied to the preceding example is traced in Figure 4.61.

A more complex example involving polygons with holes is shown in Figure 4.62. The vertices that describe holes also are listed in an order such that the interior of the polygon lies to the right of an edge. (For holes, this is sometimes called "counterclockwise order.") The same rule is used as earlier: Turn and follow the other polygon in its forward direction. Beginning with entering intersection 1, the polygon $(1, 2, 3, 4, 5, i, 6, H)$ is formed. Then, starting with entering intersection 7, the polygon $(7, 8, 9, c, 10, F)$ is created. What entering intersection should be used to generate the third polygon? This is a valuable exercise for building SUBJLIST and CLIPLIST and for tracing through the operation of the Weiler–Atherton clipping algorithm.

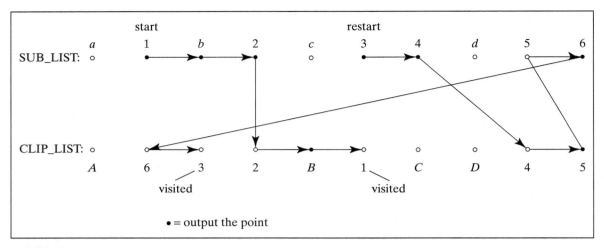

FIGURE 4.61 Applying the Weiler–Atherton method.

As with many algorithms that base decisions on intersections, we must examine how this one deals with cases where edges of CLIP and SUBJ are parallel and overlap over a finite segment. To do so, we generate SUBJ and CLIP polygons, either in files or by letting the user lay down polygons with the mouse. In this implementation, we carefully consider how the algorithm will operate in situations such as the following:

- Some edges of SUBJ and CLIP are parallel and overlap over a finite segment.
- SUBJ or CLIP or both are nonsimple polygons.
- Some edges of SUBJ and CLIP overlap only at their endpoints.
- CLIP and SUBJ are disjoint.
- SUBJ lies entirely within a hole of CLIP.

FIGURE 4.62 Weiler–Atherton clipping: polygons with holes.

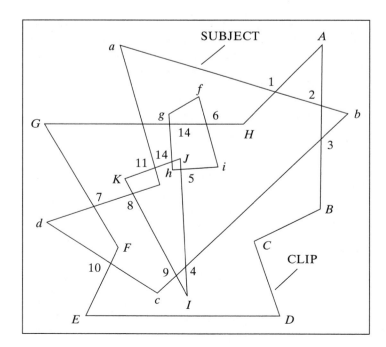

CASE STUDY 4.8 BOOLEAN OPERATIONS ON POLYGONS

Level of Effort: III. If we view a polygon as a set of points (the set of all points on the boundary or in the interior of the polygon), then the result of the Weiler–Atherton clipping operation is the **intersection** of the two polygons—the set of all points that are in both CLIP and SUBJ. The polygons output by the Weiler–Atherton algorithm consist of points that lie both within the original SUBJ and within the CLIP polygons. In this case study, we generalize from intersections to other set-theoretic operations on polygons, often called "Boolean" operations. Such operations arise frequently in modeling [Mortenson85] as well as in graphics. (See Chapter 14.) In general, for any two sets of points, A and B, we have the following three set-theoretic operations:

- Intersection: $A \cap B = \{$all points in both A and $B\}$.
- Union: $A \cup B = \{$*all points in A* or in B or both$\}$.
- Difference: $A - B = \{$all points in A, but not in $B\}$.

A similar definition holds for the difference $B - A$. Examples of these sets are shown in Figure 4.63.

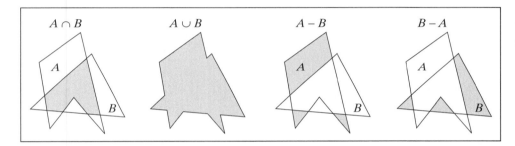

FIGURE 4.63 Polygons formed by Boolean operations on polygons.

It is not hard to adjust the Weiler–Atherton method, which already performs intersections, to perform the union and difference operations on polygons A and B.

1. *Computing the union of A and B.* To apply this operation, we traverse around A in the forward direction until an exiting intersection is found—one for which A is moving from the inside to the outside of B. We output the intersection and traverse along A until another intersection with B is found. We then turn to follow B in its forward direction. At each subsequent intersection, we output the vertex and turn to follow the other polygon in its forward direction. Upon returning to the initial vertex, we look for other exiting intersections that have not yet been visited.
2. *Computing the difference $A - B$ (outside clipping).* Whereas finding the intersection of two polygons results in clipping one against the other, the difference operation "shields" one polygon from another. That is, the difference SUBJ − CLIP consists of the parts of SUBJ that lie outside CLIP. No parts of SUBJ are drawn that lie within the border of CLIP, so the region defined by CLIP is effectively protected, or shielded.

To implement this algorithm, we traverse around A until an entering intersection into B is found. Then we turn to B, following it in the reverse direction (so that B's interior is to the left). Upon reaching another intersection, we jump to A again. At each intersection, we jump to the other polygon, always traversing A in the forward direction and B in the reverse direction. Some examples of forming the union and difference of two polygons are shown in Figure 4.64. Applying the union and difference operations generates the following polygons:

POLYA ∪ POLYB
4, 5, g, h (a hole)
8, B, C, D, 1, b, c, d
2, 3, i, j (a hole)
6, H, E, F, 7, f (a hole)

FIGURE 4.64 Forming the union and difference of two polygons.

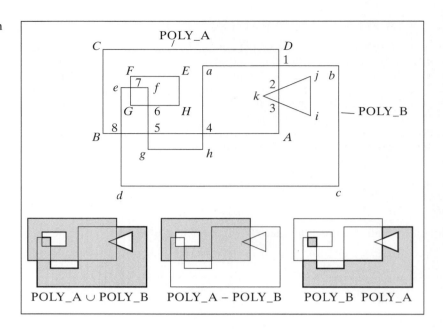

POLY_A ∪ POLY_B   POLY_A − POLY_B   POLY_B POLY_A

POLYA − POLYB

$4, 5, 6, H, E, F, 7, e, 8, B, C, D, 1, a$

$2, 3, k$

POLYB − POLYA

$1, b, c, d, 8, 5, g, h, 4, A, 3, i, j, 2$

$7, f, 6, G$

Notice how the holes (E, F, G, H) and (k, i, j) in the polygons are properly handled, and observe that the algorithm generates holes as needed. (Holes are polygons listed in counterclockwise fashion.)

Adapt the Weiler–Atherton method so that it can form the union and difference of two polygons, and execute your routines on a variety of polygons. Generate polygons A and B, either in files or algorithmically, to assist in the testing. Draw the polygons A and B in two different colors and the result of the operation in a third color.

4.11 FURTHER READING

Many books provide a good introduction to vectors. A favorite is Hoffmann's *About Vectors*. The Graphics Gems series [Gems] is an excellent source of new approaches and results in vector arithmetic and geometric algorithms by computer graphics practitioners. Three excellent articles are Alan Paeth's "A Half-Angle Identity for Digital Computation: The Joys of the Half Tangent" [Paeth91], Ron Goldman's "Triangles" [Goldman90], and Lopez–Lopez's "Triangles Revisited" [Lopez92]. Two books that delve more deeply into the nature of geometric algorithms are Moret and Shapiro's *Algorithms From P to NP* [Moret91] and Preparata and Shamos's *Computational Geometry, an Introduction* [Preparata85].

5

Transformations of Objects

Minus times minus is plus, the reason for this we need not discuss.

W. H. Auden

"If I eat one of these cakes," she thought, "it's sure to make some change in my size." So she swallowed one ... and was delighted to find that she began shrinking directly.

Lewis Carroll, Alice in Wonderland

Many of the brightly colored tile-covered walls and floors of the Alhambra in Spain show us that the Moors were masters in the art of filling a plane with similar interlocking figures, bordering each other without gaps. What a pity that their religion forbade them to make images!

M. C. Escher

Goals of the Chapter

▲ To develop tools for transforming one picture into another.

▲ To introduce the fundamental concepts of affine transformations, which perform combinations of rotations, scalings, and translations.

▲ To develop functions that apply affine transformations to objects in computer programs.

▲ To develop tools for transforming coordinate frames.

▲ To see how to set up a camera to render a 3D scene using OpenGL.

▲ To learn to design scenes in the Scene Design language SDL, and to write programs that read SDL files and draw the scenes they describe.

PREVIEW

The main goal in this chapter is to develop techniques for working with a particularly powerful family of transformations called affine transformations, both with pencil and paper and in a computer program, with and without OpenGL. Section 5.1 motivates the use of 2D and 3D transformations in computer graphics and sets up some basic definitions. Section 5.2 defines 2D affine transformations and establishes terminology for them in terms of a matrix. The notation of coordinate frames is used to keep clear what objects are being altered and how they are altered. The section shows how elementary affine transformations can perform scaling, rotation, translation, and shearing. Section 5.2.5 demonstrates that one can combine as many affine transformations as one wishes, and the result is another affine transformation, also characterized by a matrix. Section 5.2.7 discusses key properties of all affine transformations—most notably, that they preserve straight lines, planes, and parallelism—and shows why such transformations are so prevalent in computer graphics.

Section 5.3 extends the ideas of Section 5.2 to 3D affine transformations and shows that all of the basic 2D properties hold in 3D as well. 3D transformations—particularly 3D rotations—are more complex than 2D ones, however, and more difficult to visualize, so special attention is paid to describing and combining various rotations.

Section 5.4 discusses the relationship between transforming points and transforming coordinate systems. Section 5.5 shows how transformations are managed within a program when OpenGL is available and how transformations can greatly simplify many operations commonly needed in a graphics program. Modeling transformations and the use of the "current transformation" are motivated through a number of examples. Section 5.6 discusses modeling 3D scenes and drawing them using OpenGL. A "camera" is defined which is positioned and oriented so that it takes the desired snapshot of the scene. The section discusses how transformations are used to size and position objects as desired in a scene. Some sample 3D scenes are modeled and rendered, and the code required to do so is examined. This section also introduces the Scene Description Language (SDL) and shows how to write an application that can draw any scene described in the language. The presentation requires the development of a number of classes to support reading and parsing SDL files and creating lists of objects that can be rendered. These classes are available from the book's Web site.

The chapter ends with a number of case studies that elaborate on the main ideas and provide opportunities to work with affine transformations in graphics programs. One case study asks you to develop routines that perform transformations when OpenGL is not available. Also described are ways to decompose an affine transformation into its elementary operations and the development of a fast routine for drawing arcs of circles that capitalizes on the equivalence between a rotation and three successive shears.

5.1 INTRODUCTION

Affine transformations are a fundamental cornerstone of computer graphics and are central to OpenGL as well as most other graphics systems. They are also a problem for many programmers because it is often difficult to get them right. One particularly delicate area is the confusion of points and vectors. The two seem very similar and are frequently expressed in a program by using the same data type—perhaps a list of three numbers like $(3.0, 2.5, -1.145)$. But this practice can lead to disaster in the form of serious bugs that are very difficult to ferret out, principally because points and vectors do *not* transform the same way. We need a way to keep them straight, which is offered by using *coordinate frames* and appropriate homogeneous coordinates, as introduced in Chapter 4.

5.2 INTRODUCTION TO TRANSFORMATIONS

The universe is full of magical things, patiently waiting for our wits to grow sharper.

E. Phillpotts

We have already seen some examples of transformations, at least in 2D. In Chapter 3, for instance, the window-to-viewport transformation was used to scale and translate objects situated in the world window to their final size and position in the viewport.

We want to build on those ideas and gain more flexible control over the size, orientation, and position of objects of interest. In the following sections we develop the required tools, based on the powerful **affine transformation**, which is a staple in computer graphics. We operate in both two and three dimensions.

Figure 5.1(a) shows two versions of a simple house, drawn before and after each of its points has been transformed. In this case the house has been scaled down in size, rotated a small amount, and then moved up and to the right. The overall transformation is a combination of three elementary ones: scaling, rotation, and translation. Figure 5.1(b) shows a 3D house before and after it is similarly transformed: Each 3D point in the house is subjected to a scaling, a rotation, and a translation by the transformation.

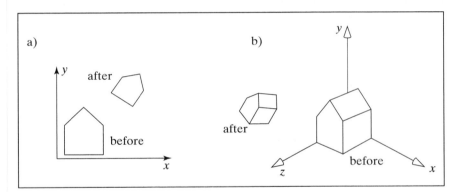

FIGURE 5.1 Drawings of objects before and after they are transformed.

Transformations are very useful in a number of situations:

a. We can compose a "scene" out of a number of objects, as in Figure 5.2. Each object, such as the arch, is most easily designed (once for all) in its own "master" coordinate system. The scene is then fashioned by placing a number of "instances" of the arch at different places and with different sizes, using the proper transfor-

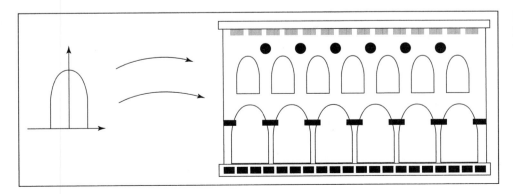

FIGURE 5.2 Composing a picture from many instances of a simple form.

FIGURE 5.3 Composing a 3D scene from primitives.

mation for each. Figure 5.3 shows a 3D example, in which the scene is composed of many instances of cubes that have been scaled and positioned in a "city."

b. Some objects, such as the snowflake shown in Figure 5.4, exhibit certain symmetries. We can design a single "motif" and then fashion the whole shape by appropriate reflections, rotations, and translations of the motif.

FIGURE 5.4 Using a "motif" to build up a figure.

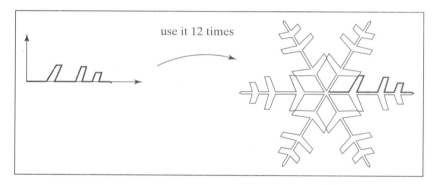

c. A designer may want to view an object from different vantage points and make a picture from each one. The scene can be rotated and viewed with the same camera, but, as suggested in Figure 5.5, it is more natural to leave the scene alone

FIGURE 5.5 Viewing a scene from different vantage points.

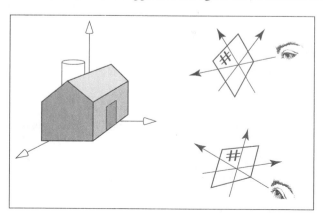

and move the camera to different orientations and positions for each snapshot. Positioning and reorienting a camera can be carried out through the use of 3D affine transformations.

   d. In a computer animation, several objects must move relative to one another from frame to frame. This effect can be achieved by shifting and rotating the separate local coordinate system of each object as the animation proceeds. Figure 5.6 shows an example.

FIGURE 5.6 Animating by transforming shapes.

Where Are We Headed? Using Transformations with OpenGL

The first few sections of this chapter present the basic concepts of affine transformations and show how they produce certain geometric effects, such as scaling, rotations, and translations, both in 2D and 3D space. Ultimately, of course, the goal is to produce graphical drawings of objects that have been transformed to the proper size, orientation, and position so that they produce the desired scene. A number of graphics platforms, including OpenGL, provide a "graphics pipeline," or a sequence of operations that are applied to all points that are "sent through." A drawing is produced by processing each point.

    Figure 5.7 shows a simplified view of the OpenGL graphics pipeline. An application sends the pipeline a sequence of points $P_1, P_2, P_3, \ldots$ using commands like the now familiar

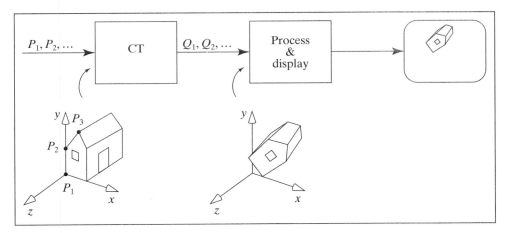

FIGURE 5.7 The OpenGL pipeline.

```
glBegin(GL_LINES);
   glVertex3f(...); // send P1 through the pipeline
   glVertex3f(...); // send P2 through the pipeline
   glVertex3f(...); // send P3 through the pipeline
                   ⋮
glEnd();
```

As shown in the figure, these points first encounter a transformation called the "current transformation" (CT), which alters their values into a different set of points, say, $Q_1, Q_2, Q_3, \ldots$. Just as the original points P_i describe some geometric object, the points Q_i describe the transformed version of the same object. These points are then sent through additional steps and ultimately are used to draw the final image on the display.

The CT therefore provides a crucial tool in the manipulation of graphical objects, and it is essential for the application programmer to know how to adjust the CT so that the desired transformations are produced. After developing the underlying theory of affine transformations, we turn in Section 5.5 to showing how this is done.

Object Transformations versus Coordinate Transformations

There are two ways to view a transformation: as an **object transformation** or as a **coordinate transformation**. An object transformation alters the coordinates of each point on the object according to some rule, leaving the underlying coordinate system fixed. A coordinate transformation defines a new coordinate system in terms of the old one and then represents all of the object's points in this new system. The two views are closely connected, and each has its advantages, but they are implemented somewhat differently. We shall first develop the central ideas in terms of object transformations and then relate them to coordinate transformations.

5.2.1 Transforming Points and Objects

We look first at the general idea of a transformation and then at the particular case of an affine transformation.

A transformation alters each point P in space (2D or 3D) into a new point Q by means of a specific formula or algorithm. Figure 5.8 shows 2D and 3D examples.

FIGURE 5.8 Mapping points into new points.

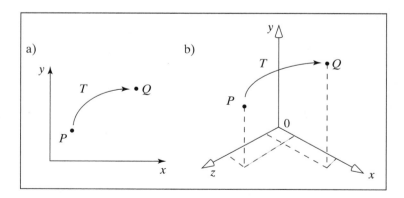

As the figure illustrates, an arbitrary point P in the plane is **mapped** to another point Q. We say that Q is the **image** of P under the mapping T. Part (a) shows a 2D point P being mapped to a new point Q; Part (b) shows a *3D* point P being mapped to a new Q. We transform an object by transforming each of its points, using, of course, the same function $T()$ for each point. We can map whole collections of points at once. The collection might be all the points on a line or all the points on a circle.

The **image** of line L under T, for instance, consists of the images of all the individual points of L.[1]

Most mappings of interest are continuous, so the image of a straight line is still a connected curve of some shape, although not necessarily a straight line. Affine transformations, however, do preserve lines, as we shall see: The image under T of a straight line is also a straight line. Most of this chapter will focus on affine transformations, but other kinds of transformations can be used to create special effects. Figure 5.9, for instance, shows a complex warping of a figure that cannot be achieved with an affine transformation. The transformation that is employed might be used for visual effect or to emphasize important features of an object.

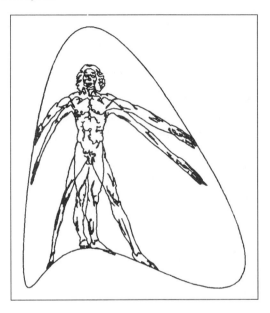

FIGURE 5.9 A complex warping of a figure.

To keep things straight, we use an explicit coordinate frame when performing transformations. Recall from Chapter 4 that a coordinate frame consists of a particular point ϑ called the origin and some mutually perpendicular vectors (called **i** and **j** in the 2D case and **i**, **j**, and **k** in the 3D case) that serve as the axes of the coordinate frame.

We take the 2D case first, as it is easier to visualize. In whichever coordinate frame we are using, points P and Q have the representations

$$P = \begin{pmatrix} P_x \\ P_y \\ 1 \end{pmatrix}$$

and

$$Q = \begin{pmatrix} Q_x \\ Q_y \\ 1 \end{pmatrix},$$

respectively. Recall that this means that the point P "is at" location $P = P_x\mathbf{i} + P_y\mathbf{j} + \vartheta$, and similarly for Q. P_x and P_y are familiarly called the "coordinates" of P. The

---

[1] More formally, if S is a set of points, its **image** $T(S)$ is the set of all points $T(P)$, where P is some point in S.

transformation operates on the representation P and produces the representation Q according to some function $T()$; that is,

$$\begin{pmatrix} Q_x \\ Q_y \\ 1 \end{pmatrix} = T\begin{pmatrix} P_x \\ P_y \\ 1 \end{pmatrix},$$ (5.1)

or, more succinctly,

$$Q = T(P).$$ (5.2)

The function $T()$ could be complicated, as in

$$\begin{pmatrix} Q_x \\ Q_y \\ 1 \end{pmatrix} = T\begin{pmatrix} \cos(P_x)e^{-P_y} \\ \dfrac{\ln(P_y)}{1 + P_x^2} \\ 1 \end{pmatrix},$$

and such transformations might have interesting geometric effects, but we restrict ourselves to much simpler families of functions: those that are *linear* in P_x and P_y. This property characterizes the affine transformations.

5.2.2 The Affine Transformations

What is algebra, exactly? Is it those three-cornered things?

J. M. Barrie

Affine transformations are the most common transformations used in computer graphics. Among other things, they make it easy to scale, rotate, and reposition figures. A succession of affine transformations can easily be combined into a simple overall affine transformation, and affine transformations permit a compact matrix representation.

Affine transformations have a simple form: The coordinates of Q are linear combinations of those of P. That is,

$$\begin{pmatrix} Q_x \\ Q_y \\ 1 \end{pmatrix} = \begin{pmatrix} m_{11}P_x + m_{12}P_y + m_{13} \\ m_{21}P_x + m_{22}P_y + m_{23} \\ 1 \end{pmatrix}$$ (5.3)

for some six given constants m_{11}, m_{12}, etc. Q_x consists of portions of both of P_x and P_y, and so does Q_y. This "cross-fertilization" between the x- and y-components gives rise to rotations and shears.

The affine transformation of Equation (5.3) has a useful matrix representation that helps to organize one's thinking:[2]

$$\begin{pmatrix} Q_x \\ Q_y \\ 1 \end{pmatrix} = \begin{pmatrix} m_{11} & m_{12} & m_{13} \\ m_{21} & m_{22} & m_{23} \\ 0 & 0 & 1 \end{pmatrix} \begin{pmatrix} P_x \\ P_y \\ 1 \end{pmatrix}$$ (5.4)

[Just multiply the right side out to see that the equation is the same as Equation (5.3). In particular, note how the third row of the matrix forces the third component

---

[2]   See Appendix 2 for a review of matrices.

of Q to be 1.] For an affine transformation, the third row of the matrix is always $(0, 0, 1)$.

Vectors can be transformed as well as points. Recall that if vector V has coordinates V_x and V_y, then its coordinate-frame representation is a column vector with a third component of zero. Transformed by the same affine transformation as Equation (5.4) for points—that is,

$$\begin{pmatrix} W_x \\ W_y \\ 0 \end{pmatrix} = \begin{pmatrix} m_{11} & m_{12} & m_{13} \\ m_{21} & m_{22} & m_{23} \\ 0 & 0 & 1 \end{pmatrix} \begin{pmatrix} V_x \\ V_y \\ 0 \end{pmatrix}, \tag{5.5}$$

the original vector clearly becomes another vector: Its third component is always zero.

PRACTICE EXERCISE

5.2.1 Apply the transformation

An affine transformation is specified by the matrix

$$\begin{pmatrix} 3 & 0 & 5 \\ -2 & 1 & 2 \\ 0 & 0 & 1 \end{pmatrix}.$$

Find the image Q of point $P = (1, 2)$.

Solution. $\begin{pmatrix} 8 \\ 2 \\ 1 \end{pmatrix} = \begin{pmatrix} 3 & 0 & 5 \\ -2 & 1 & 2 \\ 0 & 0 & 1 \end{pmatrix} \begin{pmatrix} 1 \\ 2 \\ 1 \end{pmatrix}.$ ◾

5.2.3 Geometric Effects of Elementary 2D Affine Transformations

Affine transformations produce combinations of four elementary transformations: translation, scaling, rotation, and shear.

Figure 5.10 shows an example of the effect of each kind of transformation, applied individually.

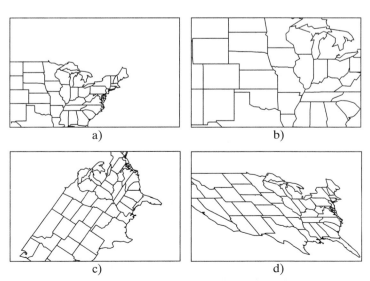

a)

b)

c)

d)

FIGURE 5.10 Transformations of a map: (a) translation; (b) scaling; (c) rotation; (d) shear.

Translation

Often, one wants to translate a picture into a different position on a graphics display. The translation part of the affine transformation arises from the third column of the matrix

$$\begin{pmatrix} Q_x \\ Q_y \\ 1 \end{pmatrix} = \begin{pmatrix} 1 & 0 & m_{13} \\ 0 & 1 & m_{23} \\ 0 & 0 & 1 \end{pmatrix} \begin{pmatrix} P_x \\ P_y \\ 1 \end{pmatrix}, \tag{5.6}$$

or simply

$$\begin{pmatrix} Q_x \\ Q_y \\ 1 \end{pmatrix} = \begin{pmatrix} P_x + m_{13} \\ P_y + m_{23} \\ 1 \end{pmatrix}.$$

So, in ordinary coordinates, $Q = P + \mathbf{d}$, where the "offset vector" $\mathbf{d}$ is (m_{13}, m_{23}).

For example, if the offset vector is $(2, 3)$, every point will be altered into a new point that is two units farther to the right and three units above the original point. The point $(1, -5)$, for instance, is transformed into $(3, -2)$, and the point $(0, 0)$ is transformed into $(2, 3)$.

Scaling

Scaling changes the size of a picture and involves two scale factors, S_x and S_y, for the x- and y-coordinates, respectively:

$$(Q_x, Q_y) = (S_x P_x, S_y P_y).$$

Thus, the matrix for a scaling by S_x and S_y is simply

$$\begin{pmatrix} S_x & 0 & 0 \\ 0 & S_y & 0 \\ 0 & 0 & 1 \end{pmatrix}. \tag{5.7}$$

Scaling in this fashion is more accurately called **scaling about the origin**, because each point P is moved S_x times farther from the origin in the x-direction and S_y times farther from the origin in the y-direction. If a scale factor is negative, then there is also a **reflection** about a coordinate axis. Figure 5.11 shows an example in which the scaling $(S_x, S_y) = (-1, 2)$ is applied to a collection of points. Each point is both reflected about the y-axis and scaled by 2 in the y-direction.

FIGURE 5.11 A scaling and a reflection.

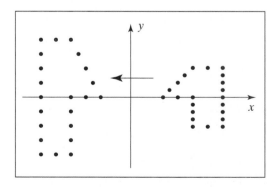

There are also "pure" reflections, for which each of the scale factors is +1 or −1. An example is

$$T(P_x, P_y) = (-P_x, P_y), \tag{5.8}$$

which produces a mirror image of a picture by "flipping" it horizontally about the y-axis, replacing each occurrence of x with $-x$. (What is the matrix of this transformation?)

If the two scale factors are the same $(S_x = S_y = S)$, the transformation is a **uniform scaling**, or a magnification about the origin, with magnification factor $|S|$. If S is negative, there are reflections about both axes. A point is moved outward from the origin to a position $|S|$ times farther away from the origin. If $|S| < 1$, the points will be moved closer to the origin, producing a reduction (or "demagnification"). If, on the other hand, the scale factors are not the same, the scaling is called a **differential scaling**.

PRACTICE EXERCISE

5.2.2 Sketch the effect

A pure-scaling affine transformation uses scale factors $S_x = 3$ and $S_y = -2$. Find and sketch the image of each of the three objects in Figure 5.12 under this transformation. (Make use of the facts—to be verified later—that an affine transformations maps straight lines to straight lines and ellipses to ellipses.) ■

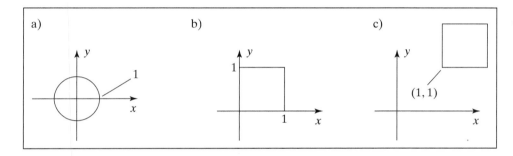

FIGURE 5.12 Objects to be scaled.

Rotation

A fundamental graphics operation is the rotation of a figure about a given point through some angle. Figure 5.13 shows a set of points rotated about the origin through an angle of $\theta = 60°$.

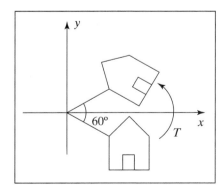

FIGURE 5.13 Rotation of points through an angle of 60°.

When $T(\ )$ is a rotation about the origin, the offset vector **d** is zero and $Q = T(P)$ has the form

$$Q_x = P_x \cos(\theta) - P_y \sin(\theta), \tag{5.9}$$

$$Q_y = P_x \sin(\theta) + P_y \cos(\theta).$$

As we show next, this form causes positive values of θ to perform a counterclockwise (CCW) rotation. In terms of its matrix form, a pure rotation about the origin is given by

$$\begin{pmatrix} \cos(\theta) & -\sin(\theta) & 0 \\ \sin(\theta) & \cos(\theta) & 0 \\ 0 & 0 & 1 \end{pmatrix}. \tag{5.10}$$

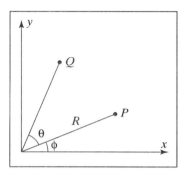

FIGURE 5.14 Derivation of the rotation mapping.

■ **EXAMPLE 5.2.1**

Find the transformed point Q caused by rotating $P = (3, 5)$ about the origin through an angle of $60°$.

SOLUTION:

For an angle of $60°$, $\cos(\theta) = .5$ and $\sin(\theta) = .866$, and Equation (5.9) yields $Q_x = (3)(0.5) - (5)(0.866) = -2.83$ and $Q_y = (3)(0.866) + (5)(0.5) = 5.098$. Check this result on graph paper by swinging an arc of $60°$ from $(3, 5)$ and reading off the position of the mapped point. Also, check numerically that Q and P are at the same distance from the origin. (What is this distance?)

Derivation of the Rotation Mapping We wish to demonstrate that Equation (5.9) is correct. Figure 5.14 shows how to find the coordinates of a point Q that results from rotating point P about the origin through an angle θ. If P is at a distance R from the origin, at some angle ϕ, then $P = (R\cos(\phi), R\sin(\phi))$. Now Q must be at the same distance as P and at angle $\theta + \phi$. Using trigonometry, we find that the coordinates of Q are

$$Q_x = R\cos(\theta + \phi),$$
$$Q_y = R\sin(\theta + \phi).$$

We substitute into this equation the two familiar trigonometric relations

$$\cos(\theta + \phi) = \cos(\theta)\cos(\phi) - \sin(\theta)\sin(\phi)$$

and

$$\sin(\theta + \phi) = \sin(\theta)\cos(\phi) + \cos(\theta)\sin(\phi)$$

and use $P_x = R\cos(\phi)$ and $P_y = R\sin(\phi)$ to obtain Equation (5.9).

PRACTICE EXERCISE

5.2.3 Rotate a point

Use Equation (5.9) to find the image of each of the following points after a rotation about the origin:

a. $(2, 3)$ through an angle of $-45°$
b. $(1, 1)$ through an angle of $-180°$.
c. $(60, 61)$ through an angle of $4°$.

In each case, check the result on graph paper, and numerically compare the distances of the original point and its image from the origin.

SOLUTION:

a. $(3.5355, .7071)$; b. $(-1, -1)$; c. $(55.5987, 65.0368)$.   ■

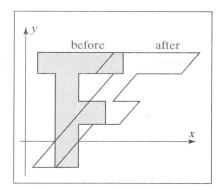

FIGURE 5.15 An example of shearing.

Shearing

Figure 5.15 shows an example of shearing "in the x-direction" (or "along x"). In this case, the y-coordinate of each point is unaffected, whereas each x-coordinate is translated by an amount that increases linearly with y. A shear in the x-direction is given by

$$Q_x = P_x + hP_y,$$
$$Q_y = P_y,$$

where the coefficient h specifies what fraction of the y-coordinate of P is to be added to the x-coordinate. The quantity h can be positive or negative. The matrix associated with this type of shear is

$$\begin{pmatrix} 1 & h & 0 \\ 0 & 1 & 0 \\ 0 & 0 & 1 \end{pmatrix}. \tag{5.11}$$

Shearing is sometimes used to make italic letters out of regular letters. One can also have a shear "along y," for which $Q_x = P_x$ and $Q_y = gP_x + P_y$ for some value g, so that the matrix is given by

$$\begin{pmatrix} 1 & 0 & 0 \\ g & 1 & 0 \\ 0 & 0 & 1 \end{pmatrix}. \tag{5.12}$$

■ **EXAMPLE 5.2.2**

Into which point does $(3, 4)$ shear when $h = .3$ in Equation (5.11)?

SOLUTION:

$Q = (3 + (.3)4, 4) = (4.2, 4)$.

■ **EXAMPLE 5.2.3**

Let $g = 0.2$ in Equation (5.12). To what point does $(6, -2)$ map?

SOLUTION:

$Q = (6, 0.2 \cdot 6 - 2) = (6, -0.8)$.

A more general shear "along" an arbitrary line is discussed in a case study at the end of the chapter. A notable feature of a shear is that its matrix has a determinant of unity. As we see later, this implies that the area of a figure is unchanged when it is sheared.

PRACTICE EXERCISE

5.2.4 Shearing lines

Consider the shear for which $g = .4$ and $h = 0$. Experiment with various sets of three collinear points to build some assurance that the sheared points are still collinear. Then, assuming that lines do shear into lines, determine into what objects the following line segments shear:

a. the horizontal segment between $(-3, 4)$ and $(2, 4)$.
b. the horizontal segment between $(-3, -4)$ and $(2, -4)$.
c. the vertical segment between $(-2, 5)$ and $(-2, -1)$.
d. the vertical segment between $(2, 5)$ and $(2, -1)$.
e. the segment between $(-1, -2)$ and $(3, 2)$;

5.2.4 The Inverse of an Affine Transformation

Most affine transformations of interest are **nonsingular**, which means that the determinant of m in Equation (5.4), which evaluates to[3]

$$\det M = m_{11}m_{22} - m_{12}m_{21} \tag{5.13}$$

is nonzero. Notice that the third column of M, which represents the amount of translation, does not affect the determinant. This is a direct consequence of the two zeroes appearing in the third row of M. We shall make special note on those rare occasions that we use singular transformations.

It is reassuring to be able to undo the effect of a transformation. This is particularly easy to do with nonsingular affine transformations. If point P is mapped into point Q according to $Q = MP$, we simply premultiply both sides by the **inverse** of M, denoted M^{-1}, and write

$$P = M^{-1}Q. \tag{5.14}$$

The inverse of M is given by[4]

$$M^{-1} = \frac{1}{\det M} \begin{pmatrix} m_{22} & -m_{12} \\ -m_{21} & m_{11} \end{pmatrix}. \tag{5.15}$$

We therefore obtain the following matrices for the elementary inverse transformations:

- *Scaling* [use M as found in Equation 5.7)]:

$$M^{-1} = \begin{pmatrix} \frac{1}{S_x} & 0 & 0 \\ 0 & \frac{1}{S_y} & 0 \\ 0 & 0 & 1 \end{pmatrix}.$$

- *Rotation* [use M as found in Equation (5.10)]:

$$M^{-1} = \begin{pmatrix} \cos(\theta) & \sin(\theta) & 0 \\ -\sin(\theta) & \cos(\theta) & 0 \\ 0 & 0 & 1 \end{pmatrix}.$$

---

[3] See Appendix 2 for a review of determinants.
[4] See Appendix 2 for a review of inverse matrices.

- *Shearing* [use the version of M in Equation (5.11)]:

$$M^{-1} = \begin{pmatrix} 1 & -h & 0 \\ 0 & 1 & 0 \\ 0 & 0 & 1 \end{pmatrix}.$$

- *Translations* (the inverse transformation simply subtracts the offset rather than adds it):

$$M^{-1} = \begin{pmatrix} 1 & 0 & -m_{13} \\ 0 & 1 & -m_{23} \\ 0 & 0 & 1 \end{pmatrix}.$$

PRACTICE EXERCISES

5.2.5 What is the inverse of a rotation?

Show that the inverse of a rotation through θ is a rotation through $-\theta$. Is this reasonable geometrically? Why?

5.2.6 Inverting a shear

Is the inverse of a shear also a shear? Show why or why not.

5.2.7 An Inverse matrix

Compute the inverse of the matrix

$$M = \begin{pmatrix} 3 & 2 & 1 \\ -1 & 1 & 0 \\ 0 & 0 & 1 \end{pmatrix}.$$

5.2.5 Composing Affine Transformations

Progress might have been all right once, but it has gone on too long.

Ogden Nash

It is rare that we want to perform just one elementary transformation; usually, an application requires that we build a compound transformation out of several elementary ones. For example, we may want to

- translate by $(3, -4)$,
- then rotate through $30°$,
- then scale by $(2, -1)$,
- then translate by $(0, 1.5)$,
- and, finally, rotate through $-30°$.

How do these individual transformations combine into one overall transformation? The process of applying several transformations in succession to form one overall transformation is called **composing** (or **concatenating**) the transformations. As we shall see, when two affine transformations are composed, the resulting transformation is (happily) also affine.

Consider what happens when two 2D transformations, $T_1(\ )$ and $T_2(\ )$, are composed. As suggested in Figure 5.16, $T_1(\ )$ maps P into Q, and $T_2(\ )$ maps Q into W. What is the transformation $T(\ )$ that maps P directly into W? That is, what is the nature of $W = T_2(Q) = T_2\big(T_1(P)\big)$?

Suppose the two transformations are represented by the matrices M_1 and M_2. Thus, P is first transformed to the point $M_1 P$, which is then transformed to $M_2(M_1 P)$. By associativity, the latter is just $\big(M_2 M_1\big)P$, and so we have

$$W = MP, \tag{5.16}$$

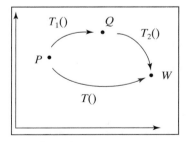

FIGURE 5.16 The composition of two transformations.

where the overall transformation is represented by the single matrix

$$M = M_2 M_1. \tag{5.17}$$

When homogeneous coordinates are used, affine transformations are composed by simple matrix multiplication. Notice that the matrices appear in *reverse* order to that in which the transformations are applied: If we first apply T_1 with matrix M_1 and then apply T_2 with matrix M_2 to the result, the overall transformation has the matrix $M_2 M_1$, with the second matrix appearing first in the product as you read from left to right. (Just the opposite order will be seen when we transform coordinate systems.)

By applying the same reasoning, any number of affine transformations can be composed simply by multiplying their associated matrices. In this way, transformations based on an arbitrary succession of rotations, scalings, shears, and translations can be formed and captured in a single matrix.

■ **EXAMPLE 5.2.4 Build one**

Build a transformation that

a. rotates through 45 degrees,
b. then scales in x by 1.5 and in y by -2,
c. and, finally, translates through $(3, 5)$.

Find the image under this transformation of the point $(1, 2)$.

SOLUTION:

Construct the three matrices and multiply them in the proper order (first one last, etc.) as follows:

$$\begin{pmatrix} 1 & 0 & 3 \\ 0 & 1 & 5 \\ 0 & 0 & 1 \end{pmatrix} \begin{pmatrix} 1.5 & 0 & 0 \\ 0 & -2 & 0 \\ 0 & 0 & 1 \end{pmatrix} \begin{pmatrix} .707 & -.707 & 0 \\ .707 & .707 & 0 \\ 0 & 0 & 1 \end{pmatrix} = \begin{pmatrix} 1.06 & -1.06 & 3 \\ -1.414 & -1.414 & 5 \\ 0 & 0 & 1 \end{pmatrix}.$$

Now, to transform the point $(1, 2)$, we enlarge it to the triple $(1, 2, 1)$, multiply that by the composite matrix to obtain $(1.94, 0.758, 1)$, and drop the 1 to form the image point $(1.94, 0.758)$. It is instructive to use graph paper and to perform each of these transformations in turn to see how $(1, 2)$ is mapped.

5.2.6 Examples of Composing 2D Transformations

Art is the imposing of a pattern on experience, and our aesthetic enjoyment is recognition of the pattern.

Alfred North Whitehead

In this section, we examine some important examples of composing 2D transformations and see how they behave.

■ **EXAMPLE 5.2.5 Rotating about an arbitrary point**

So far, all of the rotations we have considered have been about the origin. But suppose we wish instead to rotate points about some other point in the plane. As suggested in Figure 5.17, the desired "pivot" point is $V = (V_x, V_y)$, and we wish to rotate points such as P through an angle θ to position Q. To do this, we must relate the rotation about V to an elementary rotation about the origin.

The figure shows that if we first translate all points so that V coincides with the origin, then a rotation about the origin (which maps P' to Q') will be appropriate. Once this rotation is done, the whole plane is shifted back to restore V to its orig-

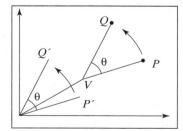

FIGURE 5.17 Rotation about a point.

inal location. The rotation therefore consists of the following three elementary transformations:

1. Translate point P through vector $\mathbf{v} = (-V_x, -V_y)$.
2. Rotate about the origin through angle θ.
3. Translate P back through $\mathbf{v}$.

Creating a matrix for each elementary transformation and multiplying the matrices out produces

$$\begin{pmatrix} 1 & 0 & V_x \\ 0 & 1 & V_y \\ 0 & 0 & 1 \end{pmatrix} \begin{pmatrix} \cos(\theta) & -\sin(\theta) & 0 \\ \sin(\theta) & \cos(\theta) & 0 \\ 0 & 0 & 1 \end{pmatrix} \begin{pmatrix} 1 & 0 & -V_x \\ 0 & 1 & -V_y \\ 0 & 0 & 1 \end{pmatrix} = \begin{pmatrix} \cos(\theta) & -\sin(\theta) & d_x \\ \sin(\theta) & \cos(\theta) & d_y \\ 0 & 0 & 1 \end{pmatrix},$$

where the overall translation components are

$$d_x = -\cos(\theta)V_x + \sin(\theta)V_y + V_x,$$
$$d_y = -\sin(\theta)V_x - \cos(\theta)V_y + V_y.$$

Because the same $\cos(\theta)$ and $\sin(\theta)$ terms appear in this result as in a rotation about the origin, we see that a rotation about an arbitrary point is equivalent to a rotation about the origin followed by a complicated translation through (d_x, d_y).

As a specific example, we find the transformation that rotates points through $30°$ about $(-2, 3)$ and determine into which point the point $(1, 2)$ maps. A $30°$ rotation uses $\cos(\theta) = 0.866$ and $\sin(\theta) = 0.5$. The offset vector is then $(1.232, 1.402)$, so the transformation applied to any point (P_x, P_y) is

$$Q_x = 0.866P_x - 0.5P_y + 1.232,$$
$$Q_y = 0.5P_x + 0.866P_y + 1.402.$$

Applying this transformation to $(1, 2)$ yields $(1.098, 3.634)$. This is the correct result, as can be checked by sketching it on graph paper. (Do it!)

■ **EXAMPLE 5.2.6 Scaling and shearing about arbitrary "pivot" points**

In a manner similar to that of Example 5.2.5, we often want to scale all points about some pivot point other than the origin. Because the elementary scaling operation of Equation (5.7) scales points about the origin, we do the same "shift–transform–unshift" sequence as for rotations. This scaling and generalizing the shearing operation are explored in the exercises at the end of the section.

■ **EXAMPLE 5.2.7 Reflections about a tilted line**

Consider the line through the origin that makes an angle of β with the x-axis, as shown in Figure 5.18. Point A reflects into point B, and each house shown reflects

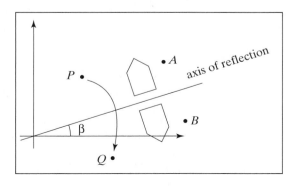

FIGURE 5.18 Reflecting a point about a tilted axis.

into the other. We want to develop the transformation that reflects any point P about the line, called the *axis of reflection*, to produce point Q. Is this an affine transformation?

To show that it is affine, we build the transformation out of three parts:

- a rotation through the angle β (so that the axis of reflection coincides with the x-axis);
- a reflection about the x-axis;
- A rotation back through β that "restores" the axis of reflection.

Each of these transformations is represented by a matrix, and the overall transformation is given by the product of the three matrices, so the overall transformation *is* affine. Check that each of the steps is properly represented in the following three matrices and that the product is also correct:

$$\begin{pmatrix} c & s & 0 \\ -s & c & 0 \\ 0 & 0 & 1 \end{pmatrix} \begin{pmatrix} 1 & 0 & 0 \\ 0 & -1 & 0 \\ 0 & 0 & 1 \end{pmatrix} \begin{pmatrix} c & -s & 0 \\ s & c & 0 \\ 0 & 0 & 1 \end{pmatrix} = \begin{pmatrix} c^2 - s^2 & -2cs & 0 \\ -2cs & s^2 - c^2 & 0 \\ 0 & 0 & 1 \end{pmatrix}.$$

Here, c stands for $\cos(-\beta)$ and s for $\sin(-\beta)$. Using trigonometric identities, we can write the final matrix (check this out!) as

$$\begin{pmatrix} \cos(2\beta) & \sin(2\beta) & 0 \\ \sin(2\beta) & -\cos(2\beta) & 0 \\ 0 & 0 & 1 \end{pmatrix} \quad \{\text{a reflection about the axis at angle } \beta\} \qquad (5.18)$$

This has the general look of a rotation matrix, except that the angle has been doubled and minus signs have crept into the second column. But in fact, it is the matrix for a reflection about the axis at angle β.

PRACTICE EXERCISES

5.2.8 The classic: The window-to-viewport transformation

We developed this transformation in Chapter 3. Rewriting Equation 3.2 in the current notation, we have

$$M = \begin{pmatrix} A & 0 & C \\ 0 & B & D \\ 0 & 0 & 1 \end{pmatrix},$$

where the components $A, B, C,$ and D depend on the window and viewport and are given in Equation (3.3). Show that this transformation is composed of

- a translation through $(-W.l, -W.b)$ to place the lower left corner of the window at the origin,
- a scaling by (A, B) to size things,
- and a translation through $(V.l, V.b)$ to move the viewport to the desired position.

5.2.9 Form for a rotation about a point

Show that the transformation of Figure 5.17 can be written out as

$$Q_x = \cos(\theta)(P_x - V_x) - \sin(\theta)(P_y - V_y) + V_x,$$
$$Q_y = \sin(\theta)(P_x - V_x) + \cos(\theta)(P_y - V_y) + V_y.$$

This form clearly reveals that the point is first translated by $(-V_x, -V_y)$, is then rotated, and is then translated by (V_x, V_y).

5.2.10 Where does it end up?

Where is the point $(8, 9)$ after it is rotated through $50°$ about the point $(3, 1)$? Find the M matrix.

5.2.11 Seeing it two ways

On graph paper, place the point $P = (4, 7)$ and the result Q of rotating P about $V = (5, 4)$ through $45°$. Now rotate P about the origin through $45°$ to produce Q', which is clearly different from Q. The difference of Q and Q' is $V - VM$. Show the point $V - VM$ on the graph, and check that $Q - Q'$ equals $V - VM$.

5.2.12 What if the axis doesn't go through the origin?

Find the affine transformation that produces a reflection about the line given parametrically by $L(t) = A + \mathbf{b}t$. Show that the transformation reduces to Equation (5.18) when $A + \mathbf{b}t$ does pass through the origin. How is $\mathbf{b}$ related to β?

5.2.13 Reflection in $x = y$

Show that a reflection about the line $x = y$ is equivalent to a reflection in x followed by a $90°$ rotation.

5.2.14 Scaling about an arbitrary point

Fashion the affine transformation that scales points about a pivot point (V_x, V_y). Test the overall transformation on some sample points, to confirm that the scaling operation is correct. Compare this transformation with the transformation for rotation about a pivot point.

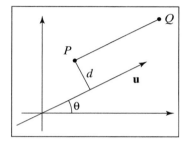

5.2.15 Shearing along a tilted axis

Fashion the transformation that shears a point along the axis described by a vector $\mathbf{u}$ tilted at an angle θ, as shown in Figure 5.19. Point P is shifted along $\mathbf{u}$ an amount that is a fraction f of the displacement d of P from the axis.

FIGURE 5.19 Shearing along a tilted axis.

5.2.16 Transforming three points

Any affine transformation is completely determined by specifying what it does to three points. To illustrate this relationship, find the affine transformation that converts triangle C with vertices $(-3, 3), (0, 3)$, and $(0, 5)$ into equilateral triangle D with vertices $(0, 0), (2, 0)$, and $(1, \sqrt{3})$, as shown in Figure 5.20. In solving this problem, use the following sequence of three elementary transformations:

1. Translate C down by 3 and right by 3 to place vertex c at c'.
2. Scale in x by $2/3$ and in y by $\sqrt{3}/2$ so that C matches D in width and height.
3. Shear by $-1/\sqrt{3}$ in the x-direction to align the top vertex of C with that of D.

Check that this transformation does in fact transform triangle C into triangle D. Also, find the inverse of the transformation, and show that it converts triangle D back into triangle C.

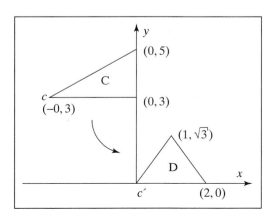

FIGURE 5.20 Converting one triangle into another.

5.2.17 Fixed points of an affine transformation

The point F is a *fixed point* of the affine transformation $T(p) = Mp$ if $T(F) = F$; that is, if F satisfies $MF = F$.

a. Show that when the third column of M is $(0, 0, 1)$, such that there is no translation, the origin is always a fixed point of T.
b. Show that if F is a fixed point of T, then, for *any* P, $T(P) = M(P - F) + F$.
c. What is a fixed point for a rotation about point V? Show that this point satisfies the relationship in Part (b).
d. What is the fixed point for a scaling with scale factors S_x and S_y about point V?
e. Consider the "fifth iterate" of $T()$ applied to P, given by $R = T(T(T(T(T(P)))))$. (Recall the iterated function systems described at the end of Chapter 2.) Use the result in Part (b) to show a simple form for the output R in terms of the fixed point F of $T()$, viz., $R = M^5(P - F) + F$.

5.2.18 Finding matrices

Give the explicit form of the three-by-three matrix representing each of the following transformations:

a. Scaling by a factor of 2 in the x-direction and then rotating about $(2, 1)$.
b. Scaling about $(2, 3)$ and following by translation through $(1, 1)$.
c. Shearing by 30% in x, scaling by 2 in x, and then rotating about $(1, 1)$ through 30°.

5.2.19 Normalizing a box

Find the affine transformation that maps the box with corners $(0, 0)$, $(2, 1)$, $(0, 5)$, and $(-2, 4)$ into the square with corners $(0, 0)$, $(1, 0)$, $(1, 1)$, and $(0, 1)$. Sketch the boxes.

5.2.20 Some transformations commute

Show that uniform scaling **commutes** with rotation, in that the resulting transformation does not depend on the order in which the individual transformations are applied. Show also that two translations commute, as do two scalings. Finally, show that differential scaling does *not* commute with rotation.

5.2.21 Reflection plus a rotation

Show that a reflection in x followed by a reflection in y is the same as a rotation by 180°.

5.2.22 Two successive rotations

Suppose that $R(\theta)$ denotes the transformation that produces a rotation through the angle θ. Show that applying $R(\theta_1)$ followed by $R(\theta_2)$ is equivalent to applying the single rotation $R(\theta_1 + \theta_2)$. Thus, successive rotations are additive.

5.2.23 A Succession of shears

Find the composition of a pure shear along the x-axis followed by a pure shear along the y-axis. Is this still a shear? Sketch by hand an example of what happens to a square centered at the origin and subjected to a simultaneous shear versus a succession of shears along the two axes.   ■

5.2.7 Some Useful Properties of Affine Transformations

We have seen how to represent 2D affine transformations with matrices, how to compose complex transformations from a sequence of elementary ones, and the geometric effect of different 2D affine transformations. Before moving on to 3D transformations, it is useful to summarize some general properties of affine transformations. These properties are easy to establish, and because no reference is made to the dimensionality of the objects being transformed, they apply equally well to 3D affine transformations. The only fact about 3D transformations that we need to know at this point is that, like their 2D counterparts, they can be represented in homogeneous coordinates by a matrix.

Affine Transformations Preserve Affine Combinations of Points

We know that an affine combination of two points P_1 and P_2 is the point

$$W = a_1 P_1 + a_2 P_2,$$

where $a_1 + a_2 = 1$. What happens when we apply an affine transformation $T()$ to the point W? We claim that $T(W)$ is the *same* affine combination of the transformed points; that is,

$$T(a_1 P_1 + a_2 P_2) = a_1 T(P_1) + a_2 T(P_2). \tag{5.19}$$

For instance, $T(0.7\,(2, 9) + 0.3\,(1, 6)) = 0.7T((2, 9)) + 0.3T((1, 6))$.

Proving the general statement is simply a matter of linearity. Using homogeneous coordinates, we see that the point $T(W)$ is MW, and, from the linearity of matrix multiplication, it follows that

$$MW = M(a_1 P_1 + a_2 P_2) = a_1 M P_1 + a_2 M P_2,$$

which, in ordinary coordinates, is just $a_1 T(P_1) + a_2 T(P_2)$, as claimed. The property that affine combinations of points are preserved under affine transformations seems fairly elementary and abstract, but it turns out to be pivotal to the power of affine transformations. It is sometimes taken as the *definition* of an affine transformation.

Affine Transformations Preserve Lines and Planes

Affine transformations preserve collinearity and "flatness," so the image of a straight line is another straight line. To see this, recall that the parametric representation $L(t)$ of a line through A and B is itself an affine combination of A and B:

$$L(t) = (1 - t)A + tB.$$

This equation represents an affine combination of points, so by the previous result, the image of $L(t)$ is the same affine combination of the images of A and B:

$$Q(t) = (1 - t)T(A) + tT(B). \tag{5.20}$$

This formula is the equation of another straight line passing through $T(A)$ and $T(B)$. Using it in computer graphics vastly simplifies drawing transformed line segments: We need only compute the two transformed endpoints $T(A)$ and $T(B)$ and then draw a straight line between them! This saves having to transform *each* of the points along the line, which is obviously impossible.

The argument is the same to show that a plane is transformed into another plane. Recall from Equation (4.45) that the parametric representation for a plane can be written as an affine combination of points:

$$P(s, t) = sA + tB + (1 - s - t)C.$$

When each point is transformed, this equation becomes

$$T(P(s, t)) = sT(A) + tT(B) + (1 - s - t)T(C),$$

which is clearly also the parametric representation of some plane.

The preservation of collinearity and "flatness" guarantees that polygons will transform into polygons and planar polygons (those whose vertices all lie in a plane) will transform into planar polygons. In particular, triangles will transform into triangles.

Parallelism of Lines and Planes is Preserved

If two lines or planes are parallel, their images under an affine transformation are also parallel. This is easy to show. We do it first for lines. Take an arbitrary line $A + \mathbf{b}t$ having direction $\mathbf{b}$. This line transforms to the line given in homogeneous coordinates by $M(A + \mathbf{b}t) = MA + (M\mathbf{b})t$, which has direction vector $M\mathbf{b}$. This new direction does *not* depend on point A. Thus, two different lines, $A_1 + \mathbf{b}t$ and $A_2 + \mathbf{b}t$ that have the same direction will transform into two lines, both having the direction $M\mathbf{b}$, so the lines are parallel. An important consequence of this property is that *parallelograms map into other parallelograms*.

The same argument applies to a plane: Its direction vectors [see Equation (4.43)] transform into new direction vectors whose values do not depend on the location of the plane. A consequence of this property is that parallelepipeds[5] map into other parallelepipeds.

■ EXAMPLE 5.2.8 How is a grid transformed?

Because affine transformations map parallelograms into parallelograms, they are rather limited in how much they can alter the shape of geometrical objects. To illustrate this limitation, apply any 2D affine transformation T to a unit square grid, as in Figure 5.21. Because a grid consists of two sets of parallel lines, T maps the square grid to another grid consisting of two sets of parallel lines. To get an idea of how objects are warped by the transformation, think of the grid as "carrying along" whatever objects are defined in it. That is all that an affine transformation can do: warp figures in the same way that one grid is mapped into another. The new lines can be tilted at any angle, they can be any (fixed) distance apart, and the two new axes need not be perpendicular. And, of course, the whole grid can be positioned anywhere in the plane. The same result applies in 3D: All that a 3D affine transformation can do is map a cubical grid into a grid of parallelepipeds.

FIGURE 5.21 A transformed grid.

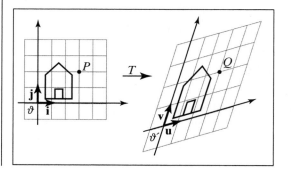

The Columns of the Matrix Reveal the Transformed Coordinate Frame

It is useful to examine the columns of the matrix M of an affine transformation, for they prescribe how the coordinate frame is transformed. Suppose, then, that the matrix M is given by

$$M = \begin{pmatrix} m_{11} & m_{12} & m_{13} \\ m_{21} & m_{22} & m_{23} \\ 0 & 0 & 1 \end{pmatrix} = (\mathbf{m}_1 \vdots \mathbf{m}_2 \vdots m_3), \tag{5.21}$$

---

[5] As we shall see later, a parallelepiped is the 3D analog of a parallelogram: It has six sides that occur in pairs of parallel faces.

so that the columns of the matrix are $\mathbf{m}_1, \mathbf{m}_2,$ and m_3. The first two columns are vectors (their third component is a 0), and the last column is a point (its third component is a 1). As always, the coordinate frame of interest is defined by the origin ϑ and the basis vectors $\mathbf{i}$ and $\mathbf{j}$, which have the representations

$$\vartheta = \begin{pmatrix} 0 \\ 0 \\ 1 \end{pmatrix}, \mathbf{i} = \begin{pmatrix} 1 \\ 0 \\ 0 \end{pmatrix}, \text{and } \mathbf{j} = \begin{pmatrix} 0 \\ 1 \\ 0 \end{pmatrix}.$$

Notice that the vector $\mathbf{i}$ transforms into the vector $\mathbf{m}_1$ (check this out) according to

$$\mathbf{m}_1 = M\mathbf{i},$$

and similarly, $\mathbf{j}$ maps into $\mathbf{m}_2$ and ϑ maps into the point m_3. These mappings are illustrated in Figure 5.22(a). The coordinate frame $(\mathbf{i}, \mathbf{j}, \vartheta)$ transforms into the coordinate frame $(\mathbf{m}_1, \mathbf{m}_2, m_3)$, and these new objects are precisely the columns of the matrix.

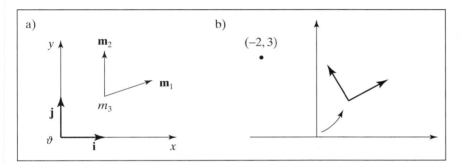

FIGURE 5.22 The transformation forms a new coordinate frame.

The axes of the new coordinate frame are not necessarily perpendicular, nor must they be of unit length. (They are still perpendicular if the transformation involves only rotations and uniform scalings.) Any point $P = P_x\mathbf{i} + P_y\mathbf{j} + \vartheta$ transforms into $Q = P_x\mathbf{m}_1 + P_y\mathbf{m}_2 + m_3$. It is sometimes very revealing to look at the matrix of an affine transformation in this way.

■ **EXAMPLE 5.2.9 Rotation about a point**

The transformation explored in Example 5.2.5, a rotation of $30°$ about the point $(-2, 3)$, yields the matrix

$$\begin{pmatrix} .866 & -.5 & 1.232 \\ .5 & .866 & 1.402 \\ 0 & 0 & 1 \end{pmatrix}.$$

As shown in Figure 5.22(b), the coordinate frame therefore maps into the new coordinate frame with origin at $(1.232, 1.402, 1)$ and coordinate axes given by the vectors $(0.866, 0.5, 0)$ and $(-0.5, 0.866, 0)$. Note that these axes are still perpendicular, since only a rotation is involved.

Relative Ratios Are Preserved

Affine transformations have yet another useful property. Consider a point P that lies a fraction t of the way between two given points, A and B, as shown in Figure 5.23. Apply the affine transformation $T(\ )$ to A, B, and P. We claim that the transformed point, $T(P)$, also lies the *same* fraction t of the way between the images $T(A)$ and $T(B)$. This is not hard to show. (See the exercises at the end of the section.)

FIGURE 5.23 Relative ratios are preserved.

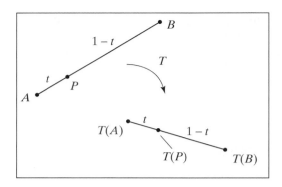

As a special case, midpoints of lines map into midpoints. This property leads to a nice geometric result: The diagonals of any parallelogram bisect each other. (*Proof*: Any parallelogram is an affine-transformed square (why?), and the diagonals of a square bisect each other, so the diagonals of a parallelogram also bisect each other.) The same applies in 3D space: The diagonals of any parallelepiped bisect each other.

As an interesting aside, note that, in addition to preserving lines, parallelism, and relative ratios, affine transformations preserve ellipses and ellipsoids, as we see in Chapter 6.

Effect of Transformations on the Areas of Figures

In computer-aided design (CAD) applications, it is often important to compute the area or volume of an object. For instance, how is the area of a polygon affected when all of its vertices are subjected to an affine transformation? It is clear geometrically that neither translations nor rotations have any effect on the area of a figure, but scalings certainly do, and shearing might.

The following result is simple and is developed in the exercises: When the 2D transformation with matrix M is applied to an object, its area is multiplied by the *magnitude of the determinant* of M:

$$\frac{\text{area after transformation}}{\text{area before transformation}} = |\det M|. \tag{5.22}$$

In 2D, the determinant of M in Equation (5.4) is $m_{11}m_{22} - m_{12}m_{21}$.[6] Thus, for a pure scaling, as in Equation (5.7), the new area is $S_x S_y$ times the original area, whereas for a shear along one axis, the new area is the same as the original area! Equation (5.10) also confirms that a rotation does not alter the area of a figure, since $\cos^2(\theta) + \sin^2(\theta) = 1$.

In 3D, similar arguments apply, and we can conclude that the volume of a 3D object is scaled by $|\det M|$ when the object is transformed by the 3D transformation based on the matrix M.

■ **EXAMPLE 5.3.0 The area of an ellipse**

What is the area of the ellipse that fits inside a rectangle with width $2W$ and height $2H$?

SOLUTION:

This ellipse can be formed by scaling the unit circle $x^2 + y^2 = 1$ by the scale factors $S_x = W$ and $S_y = H$, a transformation for which the matrix M has determinant WH. The unit circle is known to have area π, so the ellipse has area πWH.

---

[6] This quantity can be negative. Give an example where this happens.

Every Affine Transformation Is Composed of Elementary Operations

We can construct complex affine transformations by composing a number of elementary ones. It is interesting to turn the question around and ask, What elementary operations "reside in" a given affine transformation?

Basically, a matrix M may be factored into a product of elementary matrices in various ways. One particular way of factoring the matrix M associated with a 2D affine transformation (See Case Study 5.3) yields the result

$$\tilde{M} = (\text{translation})(\text{shear})(\text{scaling})(\text{rotation})$$

That is, any three-by-three matrix $\tilde{M}$ that represents a 2D affine transformation can be written as the product of (reading from right to left) a translation matrix, a rotation matrix, a scaling matrix, a shear matrix, and a translational matrix. The specific components of each matrix are given in the case study mentioned.

In 3D, things are somewhat more complicated. The four-by-four matrix M that represents a 3D affine transformation can be written as

$$M = (\text{translation})(\text{scaling})(\text{rotation})(\text{shear}_1)(\text{shear}_2),$$

the product of (reading from right to left), a shear matrix, another shear matrix, a rotation matrix, and a scaling matrix, and a translation matrix. This result is developed in Case Study 5.6.

PRACTICE EXERCISES

5.2.24 Generalizing the argument

Show that if W is an affine combination of the N points P_i, $i = 1, \ldots, N$, and $T()$ is an affine transformation, then $T(W)$ is the same affine combination of the N points $T(P_i), i = 1, \ldots, N$.

5.2.25 Show that relative ratios are preserved

Consider a point P given by $A + \mathbf{b}t$, where $\mathbf{b} = B - A$. Find the distances $|P - A|$ and $|P - B|$ from P to A and from P to B, respectively, showing that they lie in the ratio t to $1 - t$. Is this true if t lies outside of the range 0 to 1? Do the same for the distances $|T(P) - T(A)|$ and $|T(P) - T(B)|$.

5.2.26 Effect on area

Show that a 2D affine transformation causes the area of a figure to be multiplied by the factor given in Equation (5.22). (*Hint:* Consider a geometric figure to be made up of many very small squares, each of which is mapped into a parallelogram, and then find the area of this parallelogram.) ■

5.3 3D AFFINE TRANSFORMATIONS

The same ideas apply to 3D affine transformations as apply to 2D affine transformations, but, of course, the expressions are more complicated, and it is considerably harder to visualize the effect of a 3D transformation.

Again, we use coordinate frames and suppose that we have an origin ϑ and three mutually perpendicular axes in the directions $\mathbf{i}, \mathbf{j}$, and $\mathbf{k}$. (See Figure 4.18.) Point P in this frame is given by $P = \vartheta + P_x\mathbf{i} + P_y\mathbf{j} + P_z\mathbf{k}$ and so has the representation

$$P = \begin{pmatrix} P_x \\ P_y \\ P_z \\ 1 \end{pmatrix}.$$

Now, suppose $T()$ is an affine transformation that transforms point P to point Q. Then, just as in the 2D case, $T()$ is represented by a matrix $\tilde{M}$ that is now 4 by 4, viz.,

$$M = \begin{pmatrix} m_{11} & m_{12} & m_{13} & m_{14} \\ m_{21} & m_{22} & m_{23} & m_{24} \\ m_{31} & m_{32} & m_{33} & m_{34} \\ 0 & 0 & 0 & 1 \end{pmatrix}, \tag{5.23}$$

and we can say that the representation of point Q is found by multiplying P by $\tilde{M}$:

$$\begin{pmatrix} Q_x \\ Q_y \\ Q_z \\ 1 \end{pmatrix} = M \begin{pmatrix} P_x \\ P_y \\ P_z \\ 1 \end{pmatrix}. \tag{5.24}$$

Notice once again that for an affine transformation, the final row of the matrix is a string of zeroes followed by a lone 1. (This will cease to be the case when we examine projective matrices in Chapter 7.)

5.3.1 The Elementary 3D Transformations

In this section, we consider the nature of elementary 3D transformations individually and then compose them into general 3D affine transformations.

Translation

For a pure translation, the matrix M has the simple form

$$\begin{pmatrix} 1 & 0 & 0 & m_{14} \\ 0 & 1 & 0 & m_{24} \\ 0 & 0 & 1 & m_{34} \\ 0 & 0 & 0 & 1 \end{pmatrix}.$$

Check that $Q = MP$ is simply a shift in Q by the vector $\mathbf{m} = (m_{14}, m_{24}, m_{34})$.

Scaling

Scaling in 3D is a direct extension of the 2D case, with a matrix

$$\begin{pmatrix} S_x & 0 & 0 & 0 \\ 0 & S_y & 0 & 0 \\ 0 & 0 & S_z & 0 \\ 0 & 0 & 0 & 1 \end{pmatrix}, \tag{5.25}$$

where the three constants S_x, S_y, and S_z cause scaling of the corresponding coordinates. Scaling is about the origin, just as in the 2D case. Figure 5.24 shows the effect of scaling in the z-direction by 0.5 and in the x-direction by a factor of two. Notice that

FIGURE 5.24 Scaling the basic barn.

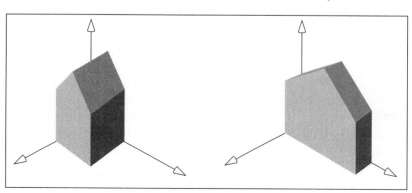

the figure shows various lines before and after being transformed; it capitalizes on the important fact that straight lines transform to straight lines.

Shearing

Three-dimensional shears appear in greater variety than do their two-dimensional counterparts. The matrix for the simplest elementary shear is the identity matrix with one zero term replaced by some value, as in

$$\begin{pmatrix} 1 & 0 & 0 & 0 \\ f & 1 & 0 & 0 \\ 0 & 0 & 1 & 0 \\ 0 & 0 & 0 & 1 \end{pmatrix}, \tag{5.26}$$

which produces $Q = (P_x, fP_x + P_y, P_z)$; that is, P_y is offset by some amount proportional to P_x, and the other components are unchanged. This causes an effect similar to that in 2D shown in Figure 5.15. Goldman [Goldman91] has developed a much more general form for a 3D shear, which is described in Case Study 5.4.

Rotations

Rotations in three dimensions are common in graphics, for we often want to rotate an object or a camera in order to obtain different views. There is a much greater variety of rotations in three than in two dimensions, since we must specify an axis about which the rotation occurs, rather than just a single point. One helpful approach is to decompose a rotation into a combination of simpler ones.

Elementary rotations about a coordinate axis The simplest rotation is a rotation about one of the coordinate axes. We call a rotation about the x-axis an "x-roll," a rotation about the y-axis a "y-roll," and a rotation about the z-axis a "z-roll." We present individually the matrices that produce an x-roll, a y-roll, and a z-roll. In each case, the rotation is through an angle β, about the given axis. We define positive angles using a "looking inward" convention:

> *Positive values of β cause a counterclockwise (CCW) rotation about an axis as one looks inward from a point on the positive axis toward the origin.*

The three basic positive rotations are illustrated in Figure 5.25.[7]

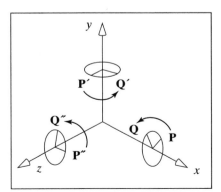

FIGURE 5.25 Positive rotations about the three axes.

---

[7] In a left-handed system, the sense of a rotation through a positive β would be CCW looking *outward* along the positive axis from the origin. This formulation is used by some authors.

This formulation is also consistent with our notion of 2D rotations: A positive rotation in two dimensions is equivalent to a z-roll as we look at the xy-plane from a point on the positive z-axis.

Notice what happens, according to the convention, in the particular case of a $90°$ rotation:

- For a z-roll, the x-axis rotates to the y-axis.
- For an x-roll, the y-axis rotates to the z-axis.
- For a y-roll, the z-axis rotates to the x-axis.

The following three matrices represent transformations that rotate points through an angle β about a coordinate axis [we use the suggestive notation $R_x(\ )$, $R_y(\ )$, and $R_z(\ )$ to denote x-, y-, and z-rolls, respectively; the parameter is the angle, in radians, through which points are rotated, and c stands for $\cos(\beta)$ and s for $\sin(\beta)$]:

1. An x-roll:

$$R_x(\beta) = \begin{pmatrix} 1 & 0 & 0 & 0 \\ 0 & c & -s & 0 \\ 0 & s & c & 0 \\ 0 & 0 & 0 & 1 \end{pmatrix}. \tag{5.27}$$

2. A y-roll:

$$R_y(\beta) = \begin{pmatrix} c & 0 & s & 0 \\ 0 & 1 & 0 & 0 \\ -s & 0 & c & 0 \\ 0 & 0 & 0 & 1 \end{pmatrix}. \tag{5.28}$$

3. A z-roll:

$$R_z(\beta) = \begin{pmatrix} c & -s & 0 & 0 \\ s & c & 0 & 0 \\ 0 & 0 & 1 & 0 \\ 0 & 0 & 0 & 1 \end{pmatrix}. \tag{5.29}$$

Note that 12 of the terms in each matrix are the zeros and ones of the identity matrix. They occur in the row and column that correspond to the axis about which the rotation is being made (e.g., the first row and column for an x-roll). These terms guarantee that the corresponding coordinate of the point being transformed will not be altered. The c and s terms always appear in a rectangular pattern in the other rows and columns.

Note that the $-s$ term appears in the lower row for the x- and z-rolls, but in the upper row for the y- roll. Is a y-roll inherently different in some way? This question is explored in the exercises.

■ **EXAMPLE 5.3.1 Rotating the barn**

Figure 5.26 shows a "barn" in its original orientation (a) and after a $-70°$ x-roll (b), a $30°$ y-roll (c), and a $-90°$ z-roll (d).

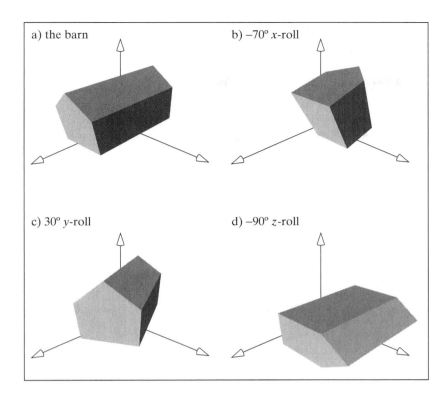

a) the barn

b) −70° x-roll

c) 30° y-roll

d) −90° z-roll

FIGURE 5.26 Rotating the basic barn.

EXAMPLE 5.3.2

Rotate the point $P = (3, 1, 4)$ through $30°$ about the y-axis.

SOLUTION:

Using Equation (5.28) with $c = .866$ and $s = .5$, we transform P into

$$Q = \begin{pmatrix} c & 0 & s & 0 \\ 0 & 1 & 0 & 0 \\ -s & 0 & c & 0 \\ 0 & 0 & 0 & 1 \end{pmatrix} \begin{pmatrix} 3 \\ 1 \\ 4 \\ 1 \end{pmatrix} = \begin{pmatrix} 4.6 \\ 1 \\ 1.964 \\ 1 \end{pmatrix}.$$

As expected, the y-coordinate of the point is not altered.

PRACTICE EXERCISES

5.3.1 Visualizing the 90° rotations

Draw a right-handed 3D system, and convince yourself that a $90°$ rotation (CCW looking toward the origin) about each axis rotates the other axes into one another. What is the effect of rotating a point on the x-axis about the x-axis?

5.3.2 Rotating the basic barn

Sketch the basic barn after each vertex has undergone a $45°$ x-roll. Repeat for y- and z-rolls.

5.3.3 Do a rotation

Find the image Q of the point $P = (1, 2, -1)$ after a $45°$ y-roll. Sketch P and Q in a 3D coordinate system, and show that your result is reasonable.

5.3.4 Testing 90° rotations of the axes

This exercise provides a useful trick for remembering the form of the rotation matrices. Using a 90° rotation, apply each of the three rotation matrices to each of the standard unit position vectors **i**, **j**, and **k**. In each case, discuss the effect of the transformation on the unit vector.

5.3.5 Is a y-roll indeed different?

The minus sign in Equation (5.28) seems to be in the wrong place: on the lower s rather than the upper one. Show that Equations (5.27)–(5.29) are in fact consistent; it's just a matter of how things are ordered. Think of the three axes x, y, and z as occurring cyclically: $x \rightarrow y \rightarrow z \rightarrow x \rightarrow y, \ldots$, etc. If we are discussing a rotation about some "current" axis (x y, or z), then we can identify the "previous" axis and the "next" axis. For instance, if x is the current axis, then the previous one is z, and the next is y. Show that with this naming, all three types of rotations use the same equations: $Q_{\text{curr}} = P_{\text{curr}}$, $Q_{\text{next}} = cP_{\text{next}} - sP_{\text{prev}}$, and $Q_{\text{prev}} = sP_{\text{next}} + cP_{\text{prev}}$. Write these equations out for each of the three possible "current" axes. ■

5.3.2 Composing 3D Affine Transformations

Not surprisingly, 3D affine transformations can be composed, and the result is another 3D affine transformation. The thinking is exactly parallel to that which led to Equation (5.17) in the 2D case. The matrix that represents the overall transformation is the product of the individual matrices M_1 and M_2 that perform the two transformations, with M_2 *premultiplying* M_1:

$$M = M_2 M_1. \tag{5.30}$$

Any number of affine transformations can be composed in this way, and a single matrix results that represents the overall transformation.

Figure 5.27 shows an example in which a barn is first transformed using some M_1, and then that transformed barn is again transformed using M_2. The result is the same as the barn transformed once using $M_2 M_1$.

FIGURE 5.27 Composing 3D affine transformations.

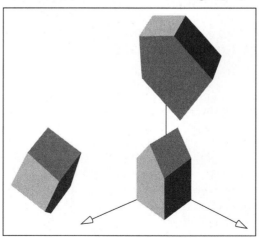

5.3.3 Combining Rotations

Results! Why, man, I have gotten a lot of results. I know several thousand things that won't work.

Thomas A. Edison

One of the most important distinctions between 2D and 3D transformations is the manner in which rotations combine. In 2D, two rotations, say, $R(\beta_1)$ and $R(\beta_2)$, combine to produce $R(\beta_1 + \beta_2)$, and the order in which the rotations are combined makes no difference. In 3D the situation is much more complicated, because rotations can be about different axes. The order in which two rotations about different axes are performed *does* matter: 3D rotation matrices do *not* commute. In this section, we explore some properties of 3D rotations, investigating different ways that a rotation can be represented, and see how to create rotations that do a certain job.

It is very common to build a rotation in 3D by composing three elementary rotations: an x-roll followed by a y-roll and then a z-roll. Using the notation of Equations (5.27)–(5.29) for each individual roll, we find that the overall rotation is given by

$$M = R_z(\beta_3)R_y(\beta_2)R_x(\beta_1). \tag{5.31}$$

In this context, the angles β_1, β_2, and β_3 are often called **Euler**[8] **angles**. One form of **Euler's theorem** asserts that *any* 3D rotation can be obtained by three rolls about the x-, y-, and z-axes, so any rotation can be written as a particular product of five matrices for the appropriate choice of Euler angles. (See later.) This statement implies that it takes three values to completely specify a rotation.

▪ EXAMPLE 5.3.3

What is the matrix associated with an x-roll of $45°$, followed by a y-roll of $30°$, followed by a z-roll of $60°$? Direct multiplication of the three component matrices (in the proper "reverse" order) yields

$$\begin{pmatrix} .5 & -.866 & 0 & 0 \\ .866 & .5 & 0 & 0 \\ 0 & 0 & 1 & 0 \\ 0 & 0 & 0 & 1 \end{pmatrix} \begin{pmatrix} .866 & 0 & .5 & .0 \\ 0 & 1 & 0 & 0 \\ -.5 & 0 & .866 & 0 \\ 0 & 0 & 0 & 1 \end{pmatrix} \begin{pmatrix} 1 & 0 & 0 & 0 \\ 0 & .707 & -.707 & 0 \\ 0 & .707 & .707 & 0 \\ 0 & 0 & 0 & 1 \end{pmatrix} = \begin{pmatrix} .433 & -.436 & .789 & 0 \\ .75 & .66 & -.047 & 0 \\ -.5 & .612 & .612 & 0 \\ 0 & 0 & 0 & 1 \end{pmatrix}.$$

Some people use a different ordering of "rolls" to create a complicated rotation. For instance, they might express a rotation as $R_y(\beta_1)R_z(\beta_2)R_x(\beta_3)$: first an x-roll, then a z-roll, and then a y-roll. Because rotations in 3D do not commute, this transformation requires the use of different Euler angles β_1, β_2, and β_3 to create the same rotation. There are 12 possible orderings of the three individual rolls, and each uses different values for β_1, β_2, and β_3.

Rotations about an Arbitrary Axis

When using Euler angles, we perform a sequence of x-, y-, and z-rolls—that is, rotations about a coordinate axis. But it can be much easier to work with rotations if we have a way to rotate about an axis that points in an arbitrary direction. Visualize the earth or a toy top spinning about a tilted axis. In fact, Euler's theorem states that *every* rotation can be represented as one of this type:

EULER'S THEOREM: Any rotation (or sequence of rotations) about a point is equivalent to a single rotation about some axis through that point.[9]

What is the matrix for such a rotation, and can we work with it conveniently?

---

[8] After Leonhard Euler, 1707–1783, a Swiss mathematician of extraordinary ability who made important contributions to all branches of mathematics.

[9] The theorem is sometimes stated as follows: Given two rectangular coordinate systems with the same origin and arbitrary directions of axes, one can always specify a line through the origin such that one coordinate system goes into the other by a rotation about that line [Gellert75].

FIGURE 5.28 Rotation about an axis through the origin.

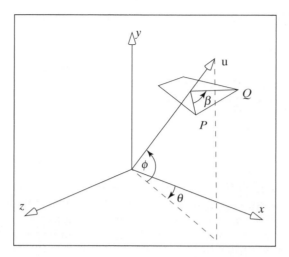

Figure 5.28 shows an axis represented by a vector **u** and an arbitrary point P that is to be rotated through angle β about **u** to produce point Q. Because **u** can have any direction, it would seem at first glance to be very difficult to find a single matrix that represents this rotation. But in fact, such a matrix can be found in two rather different ways, a classic way and a constructive way.

The Classic Way We decompose the required rotation into a sequence of known steps:

1. Perform two rotations so that **u** becomes aligned with the x-axis.
2. Do a z-roll through the angle β.
3. Undo the two alignment rotations to restore **u** to its original direction.

This method is reminiscent of rotating about a point in two dimensions: The first step prepares the situation for a simpler, known operation, the simple operation is then done, and, finally, the preparation step is undone. The result for the 3D case (discussed in the exercises at the end of the section) is that the transformation requires the multiplication of five matrices:

$$R_{\mathbf{u}}(\beta) = R_y(-\theta)R_z(\phi)R_x(\beta)R_z(-\phi)R_y(\theta). \tag{5.32}$$

Each multiplication is a rotation about one of the coordinate axes. The transformation is tedious to do by hand, but is straightforward to carry out in a computer program. However, expanding the product gives little insight into how the "ingredients" go together.

The Constructive Way Using some vector tools, we can obtain a more revealing expression for the matrix $R_{\mathbf{u}}(\beta)$. This approach has become popular recently, and versions of it are described by several authors in GEMS I [Glassner90]. We adapt the derivation of Maillot [Maillot90].

Figure 5.29 shows the axis of rotation, **u**, and we wish to express the operation of rotating point P through angle β into point Q. The method, spelled out in Case Study 5.5, effectively establishes a 2D coordinate system in the plane of rotation as shown. In the system, two orthogonal vectors **a** and **b** lie in the plane, and, as shown in Figure 5.29(b), point Q is expressed as a linear combination of those vectors. The expression for Q involves dot products and cross products of various "ingredients" in the problem. But because each of the terms is linear in the coordinates of P, it can be rewritten as P times a matrix.

FIGURE 5.29 P rotates to Q in the plane of rotation.

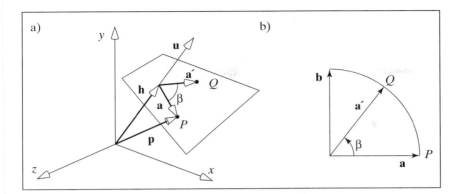

The final result is the matrix

$$R_\mathbf{u}(\beta) = \begin{pmatrix} c + (1-c)u_x^2 & (1-c)u_y u_x - su_z & (1-c)u_z u_x + su_y & 0 \\ (1-c)u_x u_y + su_z & c + (1-c)u_y^2 & (1-c)u_z u_y - su_x & 0 \\ (1-c)u_x u_z - su_y & (1-c)u_y u_z + su_x & c + (1-c)u_z^2 & 0 \\ 0 & 0 & 0 & 1 \end{pmatrix}, \quad (5.33)$$

where $c = \cos(\beta)$, $s = \sin(\beta)$, and (u_x, u_y, u_z) are the components of the unit vector $\mathbf{u}$. This matrix looks more complicated than it is. In fact, as we shall see later, there is so much structure in the terms, that, given an arbitrary rotation matrix, we can find the specific axis and angle that produces the rotation in question (which proves Euler's theorem).

Later, we shall learn that OpenGL provides a function to create a rotation about an arbitrary axis:

```
glRotated(angle, ux, uy, uz);
```

▪ EXAMPLE 5.3.4 Rotating about an axis

Find the matrix that produces a rotation through $45°$ about the axis $\mathbf{u} = (1, 1, 1)/\sqrt{3} = (0.577, 0.577, 0.577)$.

SOLUTION:

For a $45°$ rotation, $c = s = 0.707$, and filling in the terms in Equation (5.33), we obtain

$$R_\mathbf{u}(45^0) = \begin{pmatrix} .8047 & -.31 & .5058 & 0 \\ .5058 & .8047 & -.31 & 0 \\ -.31 & .5058 & .8047 & 0 \\ 0 & 0 & 0 & 1 \end{pmatrix}.$$

This matrix has a determinant of unity, as expected. Figure 5.30 shows the basic barn, shifted away from the origin, before it is rotated (dark), after a rotation through $22.5°$ (medium), and after a rotation of $45°$ (light).

Finding the Axis and Angle of Rotation

Euler's theorem guarantees that any rotation is equivalent to a rotation about some axis. When presented with some rotation matrix, it is often useful to determine the specific axis and angle. That is, given values m_{ij} for the matrix

$$R_\mathbf{u}(\beta) = \begin{pmatrix} m_{11} & m_{12} & m_{13} & 0 \\ m_{21} & m_{22} & m_{23} & 0 \\ m_{31} & m_{32} & m_{33} & 0 \\ 0 & 0 & 0 & 1 \end{pmatrix},$$

FIGURE 5.30 The basic barn rotated about axis **u**.

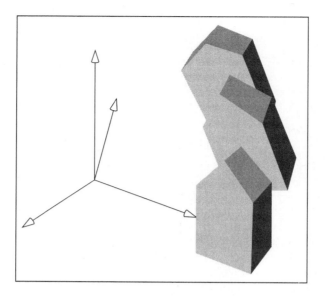

we seek to extract the angle β and the unit vector **u**. This is surprisingly easy to do by examining Equation (5.33) [Watt92]. First, note that the trace of $R_{\mathbf{u}}(\beta)$—that is, the sum of the three diagonal elements—is $3c + (1 - c)(u_x^2 + u_y^2 + u_z^2) = 1 + 2\cos(\beta)$. So we can solve for $\cos(\beta)$ directly:

$$\cos(\beta) = \tfrac{1}{2}(m_{11} + m_{22} + m_{33} - 1).$$

We take the arccosine of this value to obtain β and use it to find $s = \sin(\beta)$ as well. Now we see that pairs of elements of the matrix combine to reveal the individual components of **u**:

$$u_x = \frac{m_{32} - m_{23}}{2\sin(\beta)},$$

$$u_y = \frac{m_{13} - m_{31}}{2\sin(\beta)},$$

$$u_z = \frac{m_{21} - m_{12}}{2\sin(\beta)}. \tag{5.34}$$

■ **EXAMPLE 5.3.5 Find the axis and angle**

Pretend that you do not know the underlying axis and angle for the rotation matrix in Example 5.3.4, and solve for them. The trace is 2.414, so $\cos(\beta) = 0.707$, β must be 45°, and $\sin(\beta) = 0.707$. Now calculate each of the terms in Equation (5.34): They all yield the value 0.577, so $\mathbf{u} = (1, 1, 1)/\sqrt{3}$, just as we expected.

PRACTICE EXERCISES

5.3.6 Which ones commute?

Consider two affine transformations T_1 and T_2. Is $T_1 T_2$ the same as $T_2 T_1$ when

a. They are both pure translations?
b. They are both scalings?
c. They are both shears?
d. One is a rotation and one is a translation?
e. One is a rotation and one is a scaling?
f. One is a scaling and one is a shear?

5.3.7 Special cases of rotation about a general axis u

It always helps to see that a complicated result collapses to a familiar one in special cases. Check that this happens in Equation (5.33) when **u** is itself

a. the x-axis, **i**;
b. the y-axis, **j**;
c. the z-axis, **k**.

5.3.8 Classic approach to rotation about an axis

In this exercise, we suggest how to find the rotations that cause **u** to become aligned with the z-axis. (See Appendix 2 for a review of spherical coordinates.) Suppose the direction of **u** is given by the spherical coordinate angles ϕ and θ, as indicated in Figure 5.28. Then align **u** with the x-axis by a y-roll through θ; this swings **u** into the xy-plane to form the new axis, **u'**. (Sketch this axis.) Use Equation (5.28) to obtain $R_y(\theta)$. Second, a z-roll through $-\phi$ completes the alignment process. With **u** aligned along the x-axis, do the desired x-roll through angle β, using Equation (5.27). Finally, the alignment rotations must be undone to restore the axis to its original direction. To do this, use the inverse matrices of $R_y(\theta)$ and $R_z(-\phi)$, which are $R_y(-\theta)$ and $R_z(\phi)$, respectively. First, undo the z-roll and then the y-roll. Finally, multiply these five elementary rotations to obtain Equation (5.32). Work out the details, and apply them to find the matrix M that performs a rotation through an angle of $35°$ about the axis situated at $\theta = 30°$ and $\phi = 45°$. Show that the final result is

$$M = \begin{pmatrix} .877 & -.366 & .281 & 0 \\ .445 & .842 & -.306 & 0 \\ -.124 & .396 & .910 & 0 \\ 0 & 0 & 0 & 1 \end{pmatrix}.$$

5.3.9 Orthogonal matrices

A matrix is **orthogonal** if its columns are mutually orthogonal unit-length vectors. Show that each of the three rotation matrices given in Equations (5.27)–(5.29) is orthogonal. What is the determinant of an orthogonal matrix? A splendid property of an orthogonal matrix is that *its inverse is identical to its transpose.* (See also Appendix 2.) Show how the orthogonality of the columns guarantees this property. Find the inverse of each of the aforementioned three rotation matrices, and show that the inverse of a rotation is simply a rotation in the opposite direction.

5.3.10 The matrix is orthogonal

Show that the complicated rotation matrix in Equation (5.33) is orthogonal.

5.3.11 Structure of a rotation matrix

Show that, for a three-by-three rotation matrix M, the three rows are pairwise orthogonal, and the third is the cross product of the first two.

5.3.12 What if the axis of rotation does not pass through the origin?

If the axis of rotation does not pass through the origin, but instead is given by $S + \mathbf{u}t$ for some point S, then we must first translate to the origin through $-S$, apply the appropriate rotation, and then translate back through S. Derive the overall matrix that results. ▪

5.3.4 Summary of Properties of 3D Affine Transformations

The properties noted for affine transformations in Section 5.2.7 apply, of course, to 3D affine transformations. Stated in terms of any 3D affine transformation $T(.)$ having matrix M, these properties are as follows:

- **Affine transformations preserve affine combinations of points**. If $a + b = 1$, then $aP + bQ$ is a meaningful 3D point, and $T(aP + bQ) = aT(P) + bT(Q)$.
- **Affine transformations preserve lines and planes.** Straightness is preserved: The image $T(L)$ of a line L in 3D space is another straight line; the image $T(W)$ of a plane W in 3D space is another plane.
- **Parallelism of lines and planes is preserved.** If W and Z are parallel lines (or planes), then $T(W)$ and $T(Z)$ are also parallel.
- **The Columns of the Matrix Reveal the Transformed Coordinate Frame.** If the columns of M are the vectors $\mathbf{m}_1, \mathbf{m}_2$, and $\mathbf{m}_3$ and the point m_4, the transformation maps the frame $(\mathbf{i}, \mathbf{j}, \mathbf{k}, \vartheta)$ to the frame $(\mathbf{m}_1, \mathbf{m}_2, \mathbf{m}_3, m_4)$.
- **Relative Ratios Are Preserved.** If P is a fraction f of the way from point A to point B, then $T(P)$ is the same fraction f of the way from point $T(A)$ to $T(B)$.
- **Effect of Transformations on the Volumes of Figures.** If the 3D object D has volume V, then the image $T(D)$ of D has volume $|\det M|\, V$, where $|\det M|$ is the absolute value of the determinant of M.
- **Every Affine Transformation Is Composed of Elementary Operations.** A 3D affine transformation may be decomposed into elementary transformations, in several ways.

5.4 CHANGING COORDINATE SYSTEMS

There is another way to think about affine transformations. In many respects it is a more natural approach when modeling a scene. Instead of viewing an affine transformation as producing a different point in a fixed coordinate system, you think of it as producing a new coordinate system in which to represent points.

A word on notation: To make things fit better on the printed page, we shall sometimes use the notation $(P_x, P_y, 1)^T$ in place of $\begin{pmatrix} P_x \\ P_y \\ 1 \end{pmatrix}$. (See also Appendix 2.) The superscript T denotes the **transpose**, so we are simply writing the column vector as a transposed row vector.

Suppose, then, that we have a 2D coordinate frame #1 as shown in Figure 5.31, with origin ϑ and axes $\mathbf{i}$ and $\mathbf{j}$. Suppose further that we have an affine transformation $T(.)$ represented by the matrix M. So $T(.)$ transforms coordinate frame #1 into coordinate frame #2, with new origin $\vartheta' = T(\vartheta)$, and new axes $\mathbf{i}' = T(\mathbf{i})$ and $\mathbf{j}' = T(\mathbf{j})$.

FIGURE 5.31 Transforming a coordinate frame.

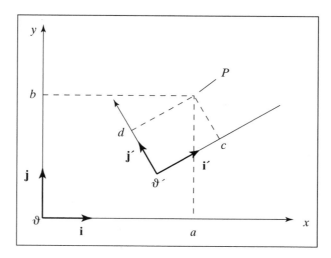

Now, let P be a point with representation $(c, d, 1)^T$ in the new system #2. What are the values of a and b in the representation of P, $(a, b, 1)^T$, in the original system #1? The answer is found just by multiplying $(c, d, 1)^T$ by M:

$$\begin{pmatrix} a \\ b \\ 1 \end{pmatrix} = M \begin{pmatrix} c \\ d \\ 1 \end{pmatrix}. \tag{5.35}$$

Summarizing, we have the following "theorem": Suppose coordinate system #2 is formed from coordinate system #1 by the affine transformation M. Suppose further that point $P = (P_x, P_y, 1)$ are the coordinates of a point P expressed in system #2. Then the coordinates of P expressed in system #1 are MP.

"Theorem" may seem obvious to some readers, but in case it doesn't, a proof is developed in the exercises at the end of the section. This result also holds for 3D systems, of course, and we use it extensively when calculating how 3D points are transformed as they are passed down the graphics "pipeline."

■ EXAMPLE 5.4.1 Rotating a coordinate system

Consider again the transformation of Example 5.2.5, which rotates points through $30°$ about the point $(-2, 3)$. (See Figure 5.22b.) This transformation maps the origin ϑ and axes $\mathbf{i}$ and $\mathbf{j}$ into system #2 as shown in that figure. Now consider the point P with coordinates $(P_x, P_y, 1)^T$ in the *new* coordinate system. What are the coordinates of this point, expressed in terms of the *original* system #1? The answer is simply MP. For instance, $(1, 2, 1)^T$ in the new system lies at $M(1, 2, 1)^T = (1.098, 3.634, 1)^T$ in the original system. (Sketch this in the figure.) Notice that the point $(-2, 3, 1)^T$, the center of rotation of the transformation, is a *fixed point* of the transformation: $M(-2, 3, 1)^T = (-2, 3, 1)^T$. Thus, if we take $P = (-2, 3, 1)^T$ in the new system, it maps to $(-2, 3, 1)^T$ in the original system. (Check this visually.)

Successive Changes in a Coordinate Frame

Now consider forming a transformation by making two successive changes of the coordinate system. What is the overall effect? As suggested in Figure 5.32, system #1 is converted to system #2 by the transformation $T_1(.)$, and system #2 is then transformed to system #3 by the transformation $T_2(.)$. Note that system #3 is transformed *relative* to #2.

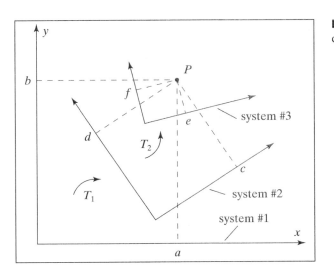

FIGURE 5.32 Transforming a coordinate system twice.

Again, the question is, If point P has the representation $(e, f, 1)^T$ with respect to system #3, what are the coordinates $(a, b, 1)^T$ of P with respect to the original system #1? To answer this question, just work backwards and collect the effects of each transformation. In terms of system #2, the point P has coordinates $(c, d, 1)^T = M_2(e, f, 1)^T$. And in terms of system #1, the point $(c, d, 1)^T$ has coordinates $(a, b, 1)^T = M_1(c, d, 1)^T$. Putting these together yields

$$\begin{pmatrix} a \\ b \\ 1 \end{pmatrix} = M_1 \begin{pmatrix} c \\ d \\ 1 \end{pmatrix} = M_1 M_2 \begin{pmatrix} e \\ f \\ 1 \end{pmatrix}. \tag{5.36}$$

The essential point is that, in determining the desired coordinates $(a, b, 1)^T$ from $(e, f, 1)^T$, we apply *first* M_2 and *then* M_1, just the *opposite* order as when we apply transformations to points. We summarize this fact for the case of three successive transformations (the result generalizes immediately to any number of transformations):

Transforming Points

To apply a sequence of transformations $T_1()$, $T_2()$, $T_3()$ (in that order) to a point P, form the matrix:

$M = M_3 \times M_2 \times M_1.$

Then P is transformed to MP. To compose each successive transformation M_i, you must *premultiply* by M_i.

Transforming the Coordinate System

To apply a sequence of transformations $T_1()$, $T_2()$, $T_3()$ (in that order) to the coordinate system, form the matrix

$M = M_1 \times M_2 \times M_3.$

Then a point P expressed in the transformed system has coordinates MP in the original system. To compose each additional transformation M_i, you must *postmultiply* by M_i.

How OpenGL Operates

We shall see in the next section that OpenGL provides tools for successively applying transformations in order to build up an overall "current transformation." In fact, OpenGL is organized so as to *postmultiply* each new transformation matrix in order to combine it with the current transformation. Thus, it will often seem more natural to the modeler to think in terms of successively transforming the coordinate system involved, since the order in which these transformations are carried out is the *same* as the order in which OpenGL computes them.

PRACTICE EXERCISES

5.4.1 How transforming a coordinate system relates to transforming a point

We wish to prove Equation (5.35). To do this, show each of the following:

a. Show why the point P with representation $(c, d, 1)^T$ used in system #2 lies at $c\mathbf{i}' + d\mathbf{j}' + \vartheta'$.
b. We want to find where P lies in system #1. Show that the representation (in system #1) of $\mathbf{i}'$ is $M(1, 0, 0)^T$, that of $\mathbf{j}'$ is $M(0, 1, 0)^T$, and that of ϑ' is $M(0, 0, 1)$.
c. Show that, therefore, the representation of the point $c\mathbf{i}' + d\mathbf{j}' + \vartheta'$ is $cM(1, 0, 0)^T + dM (0, 1, 0)^T + M(0, 0, 1)^T$.
d. Show that the representation in Part (c) is the same as $M(c, 0, 0)^T + M(0, d, 0)^T + M(0, 0, 1)$ and that this is $M(c, d, 1)^T$, as claimed.

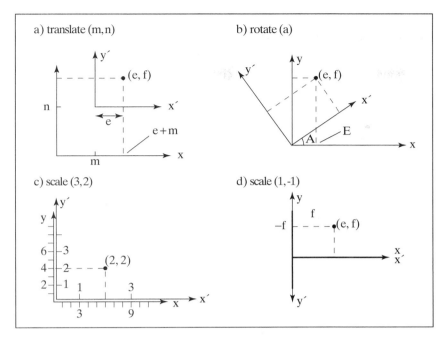

FIGURE 5.33 Elementary changes between coordinate systems.

5.4.2 Using Elementary Examples

Figure 5.33 shows the effect of four elementary transformations of a coordinate system. In each case, the original system with axes x and y is transformed into the new system with axes x' and y'.

a. Part (a) of the figure shows the effect of a translation through (m, n). Show that the point (e, f) in the new system lies at $(e + m, f + n)$ in the original system.

b. Part (b) of the figure shows the effect of a rotation about the origin through A degrees. Show that the point (e, f) in the new system lies at $(e \cos(a) - f \sin(a), e \sin(a) + f \cos(a))$, where $a = \pi A/180$ radians.

c. Part (c) of the figure shows the effect of a scaling of the axes by $(3, 2)$. To make the figure clearer, the new and old axes are shown slightly displaced. Show that a point (e, f) in the new system lies at $(3e, 2f)$ in the original system.

d. Part (d) of the figure shows a special case of scaling: a reflection about the x-axis. Show that the point (e, f) lies at $(e, -f)$ in the original system. ■

5.5 USING AFFINE TRANSFORMATIONS IN A PROGRAM

We want to see how to apply the theory of affine transformations in a program to carry out the scaling, rotating, and translating of graphical objects. We also investigate how that is done when OpenGL is used. We look at 2D examples first, as they are easier to visualize. Then we move on to 3D examples.

To set the stage, suppose you have a routine `house()` that draws house #1 in Figure 5.34. But you wish instead to draw house #2, shown rotated through −30° and then translated through (32, 25). This is a frequently encountered situation: An object is defined at a convenient size and position, but we want to draw it (perhaps many times) at different sizes, orientations, and locations.

As we discussed in Chapter 3, the routine `house()` would draw the various polylines of the figure. If it were written in "raw" OpenGL, it might consist of a large number of chunks such as the following:

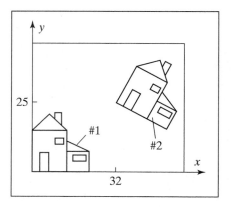

FIGURE 5.34 Drawing a rotated and translated house.

```
glBegin(GL_LINES);
      glVertex2d(V[0].x, V[0].y);
      glVertex2d(V[1].x, V[1].y);
      glVertex2d(V[2].x, V[2].y);
      .... // the remaining points
glEnd();
```

This code would be based on some array V[] of points. Or, if we use the Canvas class developed in Chapter 3 (and the global canvas object cvs), there would be a number of calls to moveTo() and lineTo(), as in the code

```
cvs.moveTo(V[0]);
cvs.lineTo(V[1]);
cvs.lineTo(V[2]);
...   // the remaining points
```

In either case, we would set up a world window and a viewport with calls like

```
cvs.setWindow(...);
cvs.setViewport(...);
```

and we would be assured that all vertex positions V[i] are "quietly" converted from world coordinates to screen window coordinates by the underlying window-to-viewport transformation.

But how do we arrange matters so that house #2 is drawn instead? There is the hard way, and there is the easy way.

The Hard Way

With this approach, we construct the matrix for the desired transformation, say, M, and build a routine, say, transform2D(), that transforms one point into another, such that

```
Q = transform2D(M, P);
```

The routine produces $Q = MP$. To apply the transformation to each point V[i] in house(), we must adjust the ealier source code, as in

```
cvs.moveTo(transform2D(M, V[0])); // move to the transformed point
cvs.lineTo(transform2D(M, V[1]));
cvs.lineTo(transform2D(M, V[2]));
...
```

so that the *transformed* points are sent to moveTo() and lineTo(). This adjustment is workable if the source code for house() is at hand. But it is cumbersome at best, and *not possible* at all, if the source code for house() is not available. Also, tools are required to create the matrix M in the first place.

The Easy Way

We cause the desired transformation to be applied automatically to each vertex. Just as we know that the window-to-viewport mapping is "quietly" applied to each vertex as part of `moveTo()` and `lineTo()`, we can have an additional transformation be quietly applied as well. We met this transformation earlier as the **current transformation**, CT. We enhance `moveTo()` and `lineTo()` in the Canvas class so that they first quietly apply CT to the argument vertex and then apply the window-to-viewport mapping. (Clipping is performed at the world window boundary as well.)

Figure 5.35 provides a slight elaboration of the graphics pipeline we introduced in Figure 5.7. When `glVertex2d()` is called with the argument V, the vertex V is first transformed by the CT to form point Q, which is then passed through the window-to-viewport mapping to form point S in the screen window. (As we shall see later, clipping is also performed, "inside" this last mapping process.)

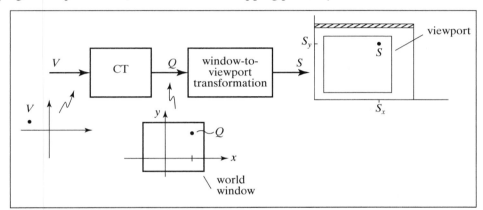

FIGURE 5.35 The current transformation is applied to vertices.

How do we extend `moveTo()` and `lineTo()` so that they quietly carry out this additional mapping? (That is, how do we rewrite these functions in the Canvas class?) If you are not using OpenGL, you must write code that actually performs the transformation; this code is described in Case Study 5.1. If you are using OpenGL, the transformation is done automatically! OpenGL maintains a so-called **modelview matrix,** and every vertex that is passed down the graphics pipeline is multiplied by this matrix. We need only set up the modelview matrix to embody the desired transformation.

OpenGL works entirely in 3D, so its modelview matrix produces 3D transformations. Here, we work with the modelview matrix in a restricted way to perform 2D transformations. Later, we use its full power. Figure 5.36 shows how we restrict the 3D transformations to carry out the desired 2D transformations. The main idea is that 2D drawing is done in the xy-plane: The z-coordinate is understood to be zero. Therefore,

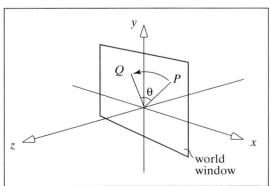

FIGURE 5.36 2D drawing takes place in the xy-plane.

when we transform 2D points, we set the part of the underlying 3D transformation that affects the z-coordinate so that it has no effect at all. For example, rotating about the origin in 2D is equivalent to rotating about the z-axis in 3D, as shown in the figure. Further, although a scaling in 3D takes three scale factors, Sx, Sy, and Sz, to scale in the x, y, and z dimensions, respectively, we set the scale factor $Sz = 1$.

The principal routines for altering the modelview matrix are `glRotated()`[10], `glScaled()`, and `glTranslated()`. These do not set the CT directly; instead, each *postmultiplies* the CT (the modelview matrix) by a particular matrix, say, M, and puts the result back into the CT. That is, each of the routines creates a matrix M required for the new transformation and performs the operation

$$CT = CT* M \qquad\qquad (5.37)$$

The order is important: As we saw earlier, applying CT* M to a point is equivalent to first performing the transformation embodied in M, followed by performing the transformation dictated by the previous value of CT. Or if we are thinking in terms of transforming the coordinate system, it is equivalent to performing one additional transformation to the current coordinate system.

The following are OpenGL routines for applying transformations in the 2D case:

- `glScaled(sx, sy, 1.0);` Postmultiply CT by a matrix that performs a scaling by sx in x and by sy in y; put the result back into CT. No scaling in z is done.
- `glTranslated(dx, dy, 0);` Postmultiply CT by a matrix that performs a translation by dx in x and by dy in y; put the result back into CT. No translation in z is done.
- `glRotated(angle, 0, 0, 1);` Postmultiply CT by a matrix that performs a rotation through *angle* degrees about the z-axis [indicated by $(0, 0, 1)$][11]. Put the result back into CT.

Since these routines only compose a transformation with the CT, we need some way to get started: to initialize the CT to the identity transformation. For that purpose OpenGL provides the routine `glLoadIdentity()`. And because the functions listed can be set to work on any of the matrices that OpenGL supports, we must inform OpenGL which matrix we are altering. This is accomplished using `glMatrix-Mode(GL_MODELVIEW)`.

Figure 5.37 shows suitable definitions of four new methods of the *Canvas* class that manage the CT and allow us to build up arbitrarily complex 2D transformations. Their pleasing simplicity is possible because OpenGL is doing the hard work.

We are now in a position to use 2D transformations. Returning to drawing version #2 of the house in Figure 5.34, we next show the code that first rotates the house through $-30°$ and then translates it through $(32, 25)$. Notice that, to get the ordering straight, the operations are called in opposite order to the way they are applied: *first* the translation operation and *then* the rotation operation.

```
cvs.setWindow(...);
cvs.setViewport(..);      // set the window to viewport mapping
cvs.initCT();             // get started with the identity
                          //   transformation
house();                  // draw the untransformed house first
cvs.translate2D(32, 25);  // CT now includes translation
cvs.rotate2D(-30.0);      // CT now includes translation and rotation
house();                  // draw the transformed house
```

---

[10] The suffix "d" indicates that the arguments of the function are `doubles`. There is also the version `glRotatef()`, which takes `float` arguments.

[11] Here, as always, positive angles produce CCW rotations.

```
//<<<<<<<<<<<<<<< initCT >>>>>>>>>>>>>>>>
void Canvas:: initCT(void)
{
      glMatrixMode(GL_MODELVIEW);
      glLoadIdentity();          // set CT to the identity matrix
}
//<<<<<<<<<<<<<<< scale2D >>>>>>>>>>>>>>>>>>>
void Canvas:: scale2D(double sx, double sy)
{
      glMatrixMode(GL_MODELVIEW);
      glScaled(sx, sy, 1.0); // set CT to CT * (2D scaling)
}
//<<<<<<<<<<<<<<< translate2D >>>>>>>>>>>>>>>>>
void Canvas:: translate2D(double dx, double dy)
{
      glMatrixMode(GL_MODELVIEW);
      glTranslated(dx, dy, 0); // set CT to CT * (2D translation)
}
//<<<<<<<<<<<<<<< rotate2D >>>>>>>>>>>>>>>>>>>>>
void Canvas:: rotate2D(double angle)
{
      glMatrixMode(GL_MODELVIEW);
      glRotated(angle, 0.0, 0.0, 1.0); // set CT to CT * (2D rotation)
}
```

FIGURE 5.37 Routines to manage the CT for 2D transformations.

Notice that we can scale, rotate, and position the house in any manner we choose, and never need to "go inside" the routine `house()` or alter it. (In particular, the source code for `house()` need not be available.)

Some people find it more natural to think in terms of transforming the coordinate system rather than the house itself. As shown in Figure 5.38, they would think of first translating the coordinate system through (32, 25) to form system #2 and then rotating *that* system through −30° to obtain coordinate system #3. Because OpenGL applies transformations in the order that coordinate systems are altered, the code for doing the overall transformation this way first calls `cvs.translate2D(32, 25)` and then calls `cvs.rotate2D(-30.0)`. This is, of course, *identical* to the code obtained by performing the transformation the other way, but it has been arrived at through a different thinking process.

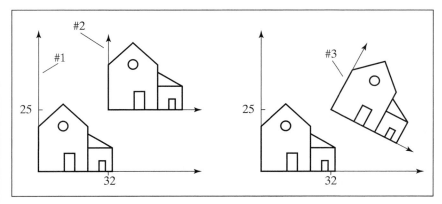

FIGURE 5.38 The same transformation viewed as a sequence of changes of coordinate systems.

Some further examples show how easily the CT is manipulated to produce various effects.

■ EXAMPLE 5.5.1 Capitalizing on rotational symmetry

Figure 5.39(a) shows a star made of stripes that seem to interlock with one another. The figure is easy to draw using `rotate2D()`. Suppose that routine `starMotif()` draws a part of the star—the polygon shown in Figure 5.39(b). (Determining the positions of this polygon's vertices is challenging and is addressed in Case Study 5.2.) Then, to draw the whole star, we just draw the motif five times, each time rotating it through an additional 72°:

FIGURE 5.39 Using successive rotations of the coordinate system.

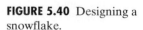

```
for(int count = 0; count < 5; count++)
{
    starMotif();
    cvs.rotate2D(72.0);   // concatenate another rotation
}
```

Visualize what is happening during each of these steps.

■ EXAMPLE 5.5.2 Drawing snowflakes

The beauty of a snowflake arises in large measure from its high degree of symmetry. A snowflake has six identical spokes oriented 60° apart, and each spoke is symmetrical about its own axis. It is easy to produce a complex snowflake by designing one half of a spoke and drawing it 12 times. Figure 5.40(a) shows a snowflake, based on the motif shown in Figure 5.40(b). The motif is a polyline that meanders around above the positive *x*-axis. (To avoid any overlap with other parts of the snowflake, the polyline is kept below the 30° line shown in the figure.) Suppose the routine `flakeMotif()` draws this polyline.

FIGURE 5.40 Designing a snowflake.

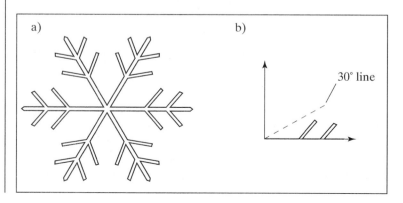

Each spoke of the snowflake is a combination of the motif and a reflected version of it. A reflection about the *x*-axis is achieved by the use of `scale2D(1,-1)` (why?), so the motif plus its reflection can be drawn using the following code:

```
flakeMotif();              // draw the top half
cvs.scale2D(1.0,-1.0);     // flip it vertically
flakeMotif();              // draw the bottom half
cvs.scale2D(1.0,-1.0);     // restore the original axis
```

To draw the entire snowflake, just execute this code six times, with an intervening rotation of 60°:

```
void drawFlake()
{
   for(int count = 0; count < 6; count++) // draw a snowflake
   {
      flakeMotif();
      cvs.scale2D(1.0, -1.0);
      flakeMotif();
      cvs.scale2D(1.0, -1.0);
      cvs.rotate2D(60.0);          // concatenate a 60-
                                   degree rotation

   }
}
```

▪ EXAMPLE 5.5.3 A flurry of snowflakes

A flurry of snowflakes like that shown in Figure 5.41 can be achieved by drawing the flake repeatedly at random positions. The OpenGL code is as follows:

FIGURE 5.41 A flurry of snowflakes.

```
while(!bored)
{
      cvs.initCT();
      cvs.translate2D(random amount, random amount);
      drawFlake();
}
```

Notice that the CT has to be initialized each time, to prevent the translations from accumulating.

■ EXAMPLE 5.5.4 Making patterns from a motif

Figure 5.42 shows two configurations of the dinosaur motif. The dinosaurs are distributed around a circle in both versions, but in one case each dinosaur is rotated so that its feet point toward the origin, and in the other all the dinosaurs are upright. In both cases, a combination of rotations and translations is used to create the pattern. It is interesting to see how the ordering of the operations affects the picture.

FIGURE 5.42 Two patterns based on a motif. (a) Each motif is rotated separately. (b) All motifs are upright.

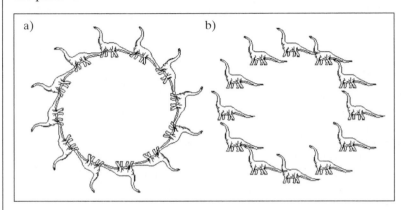

Suppose that `drawDino()` draws an upright dinosaur centered at the origin. In Figure 5.42(a), the coordinate system for each motif is first rotated about the origin through a suitable angle and then translated along its *y*-axis by *H* units. The following code does the job. (note that the CT is reinitialized each time through the loop, so that the transformations do not accumulate; Think through the transformations you would use if, instead, you took the point of view of transforming points of the motif):

```
const int numMotifs = 12;
for(int i = 0; i < numMotifs; i++)
{
        cvs.initCT(); // init CT at each iteration
        cvs.rotate2D(i * 360 / numMotifs); // rotate
        cvs.translate2D(0.0, H); // shift along the y-axis
        drawDino();
}
```

An easy way to keep the motifs upright, as in Part (b) of the figure is to rotate each motif before translating it. If a particular motif is to appear finally at 120°, it is first rotated (while still at the origin) through −120°, then translated up by *H* units, and then rotated through 120°. What adjustments to the preceding code will achieve this effect?

5.5.1 Saving the CT for Later Use

A program can involve rather lengthy sequences of calls to `rotate2D()`, `scale2D()`, and `translate2D()`. These functions make "additional" or "relative" changes to the CT, but sometimes we may need to "back up" to some prior CT in order to follow a different path of transformations for the next instance of a picture. To "remember" the desired CT, we make a copy of it and store it in a convenient location. Then, at a later point, we can restore the CT, effectively returning to the transformation that was in effect at that point. We may even want to keep a collection of

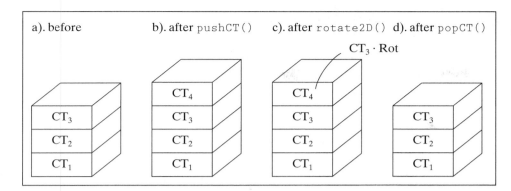

FIGURE 5.43 Manipulating a stack of CT's.

prior CT's, and return to selected ones at key moments. To do this, you can work with a **stack of transformations**, as suggested by Figure 5.43. The top matrix on the stack is the actual CT, and operations like `rotate2D()` compose their transformation with it in the manner described earlier. To save this CT for later use, a copy of it is made and "pushed" onto the stack using a routine `pushCT()`. This makes the top two items on the stack identical. The top item can now be altered further with additional calls to `scale2D()` and the like. To return to the previous CT, the top item is simply "popped" off the stack using `popCT()` and then discarded. That way, we can return to the most recent CT, the next most recent CT, and so forth, in a last-in, first-out order.

The implementation of `pushCT()` and `popCT()` is simple with OpenGL, which has routines `glPushMatrix()` and `glPopMatrix()` to manage several different stacks of matrices. Figure 5.44 shows the required functions. Note that each of them must inform OpenGL which matrix stack is being affected.

FIGURE 5.44 Routines to save and restore CT's.

```
void Canvas:: pushCT(void)
{
      glMatrixMode(GL_MODELVIEW);
      glPushMatrix();              // push a copy of the top matrix
}
void Canvas:: popCT(void)
{
      glMatrixMode(GL_MODELVIEW);
      glPopMatrix();               // pop the top matrix from the stack
}
```

■ **EXAMPLE 5.5.5 Tilings made easy**

Many beautiful designs called **tilings** appear on walls, pottery, and fabric. They are based on the repetition of a basic motif both horizontally and vertically. Consider tiling the window with some motif, as suggested in Figure 5.45. The motif is drawn centered in its own coordinate system, as shown in Part (a), with the use of some routine `motif()`. Copies of the motif are drawn L units apart in the x-direction and D units apart in the y-direction, as shown in Part (b).

FIGURE 5.45 A tiling based on a motif. (a) The motif. (b) The tiling.

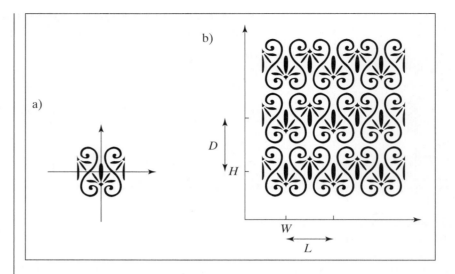

Figure 5.46 shows how easily the coordinate system can be manipulated in a double loop to draw the tiling. The CT is restored after drawing each row, so it returns to the start of that row, ready to move up to start the next row. In addition, the whole block of code is surrounded with a `pushCT()` and a `popCT()`, so that after the tiling has been drawn, the CT is returned to its initial value, in case more drawing needs to be done.

FIGURE 5.46 Drawing a hexagonal tiling.

```
cvs.pushCT();    // so we can return here
cvs.translate2D(W, H);        // position for the first motif
for(row = 0; row < 3; row++) // draw each row
{
   cvs.pushCT();
   for(col = 0; col < 4; col++)// draw the next row of motifs
   {
      motif();
      cvs.translate2D(L, 0);  // move to the right
   }
   cvs.popCT();     // back to the start of this row
   cvs.translate2D(0, D); // move up to the next row
}
cvs.popCT();    // back to where we started
```

■ **EXAMPLE 5.5.6 Using modeling transformations in a CAD program**

Some programs must draw many instances of a small collection of shapes. Figure 5.47 shows the example of a CAD program that analyzes the behavior of an interconnection of digital logic gates. The user can construct a circuit by "picking and placing" different gates at different places in the work area, possibly with different sizes and orientations. Each picture of the object in the scene is called an **instance** of the object. A single definition of the object is given in a coordinate system that is convenient for dealing with the shape of that particular object, called its **master coordinate system**. The transformation that carries the object from its own master coordinate system to world coordinates to produce an instance is often called a **modeling transformation**.

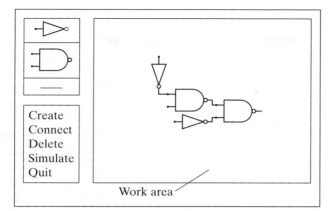

FIGURE 5.47 Creating instances in a pick-and-place application.

Figure 5.48 shows two logic gates, each defined once in its own master coordinate system. As the user creates each instance of one of these gates, the appropriate modeling transformation is generated that orients and positions the drawing. The transformation might be stored simply as a set of parameters, say, S, A, dx, and dy, with the understanding that the modeling transformation would always consist of

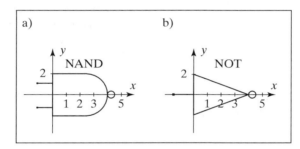

FIGURE 5.48 Each type of gate is defined in its own coordinate system.

1. a scaling by the factor S,
2. a rotation through angle A, and
3. a translation through (dx, dy),

performed in that order. A list is kept of the gates in the circuit, along with the transformation parameters of each gate.

Whenever the drawing must be refreshed, each instance is drawn in turn, with the proper modeling transformation applied. Code to do this might look like the following:

```
clear the screen
for(i = 0; i < numberOfGates; i++) // for each gate
{
        pushCT(); // remember the CT
        translate2D(dx[i], dy[i]); // apply the transformation
        rotate2D(A[i]);
        scale2D( S[i], S[i]);
        drawGate(type[i]); // draw one of the two types
        popCT(); // restore the CT
}
```

The CT is pushed before drawing each instance, so that it can be restored after the instance has been drawn. The modeling transformation for the instance is determined by its parameters, and then one of the two gate shapes is drawn. The necessary code has a simple organization, because the burden of sizing, orienting, and positioning each instance has been passed to the underlying tools that maintain the CT and its stack.

PRACTICE EXERCISES

5.5.1 Developing the transformations

Supposing that OpenGL were not available, detail how you would write the following routines that perform elementary coordinate system changes:

```
void scale2D(double sx, double  sy);
void translate2D(double dx, double  dy);
```

5.5.2 Implementing "pushing" and "popping" of the transformation stack

Define, in the absence of OpenGL, appropriate data types for a stack of transformations, and write the routines `pushCT()` and `popCT()`.

5.5.3 A hexagonal tiling

A hexagonal pattern provides a rich setting for tilings, since regular hexagons fit together neatly as in a beehive. Figure 5.49 shows nine columns of stacked hexagons. The hexagons are shown empty, but we could draw interesting figures inside them.

FIGURE 5.49 A simple hexagonal tiling.

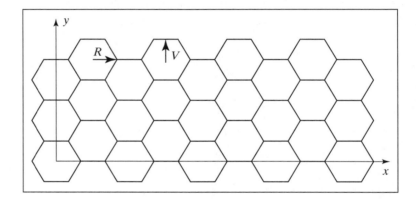

a. Show that the length of each edge of a hexagon with radius R is also R.
b. Show that the centers of adjacent hexagons in a column are separated vertically by $\sqrt{3} \cdot R$ and that adjacent columns are separated horizontally by $3R/2$.
c. Using `pushCT()` and `popCT()` and suitable transformations to keep track of where each row and column start, develop code that draws the hexagonal tiling shown in the figure. ■

5.6 DRAWING 3D SCENES WITH OPENGL

We introduced the drawing of 2D objects in Chapter 3, developing a simple class, *Canvas*. This class provides functions that establish a window and a viewport and that do line drawing by means of the functions `moveTo()` and `lineTo()`. So far in this chapter, we have added the notion of the CT and provided functions that perform 2D rotations, scalings, and translations. These 2D transformations are really just special cases of 3D transformations that ignore the third dimension.

In this section, we examine how 3D transformations are used in an OpenGL-based program. The main emphasis is on transforming objects in order to orient and position them as desired in a 3D scene. Not surprisingly, all the work is done with matrices, and OpenGL provides the necessary functions to build the required matrices. Further, the matrix stack maintained by OpenGL makes it easy to set up a transformation for one object and then "back up" to a previous transformation, in preparation for transforming another object.

It is very satisfying to build a program that draws different scenes using a collection of 3D transformations. Experimenting with such a program also improves your ability to visualize what the various 3D transformations do. OpenGL makes it easy to set up a "camera" that takes a "snapshot" of the scene from a particular point of view. The camera is created with a matrix as well, and in Chapter 7 we study in detail how this is done. Here we just use an OpenGL tool to set up a reasonable camera, so that attention can be focused on transforming objects. Granted that we are using a tool before seeing exactly how it operates, but the payoff is high: You can make impressive pictures of 3D scenes with just a few simple calls to OpenGL functions.

5.6.1 An Overview of the Viewing Process and the Graphics Pipeline

All of our 2D drawing so far has actually used a special case of 3D viewing, based on a simple "parallel projection." We have been using the "camera" suggested in Figure 5.50. The "eye" that is viewing the scene looks along the z-axis at the "window," a rectangle lying in the *xy*-plane. The **view volume** of the camera is a rectangular parallelepiped, whose four sidewalls are determined by the border of the window and whose other two walls are determined by a **near plane** and a **far plane**. Points lying inside the view volume are projected onto the window along lines parallel to the z-axis. This is equivalent to simply ignoring the *z*-components of those points, so that the 3D point (x_1, y_1, z_1) projects to $(x_1, y_1, 0)$. Points lying outside the view volume are clipped off. A separate **viewport transformation** maps the projected points from the window to the viewport on the display device.

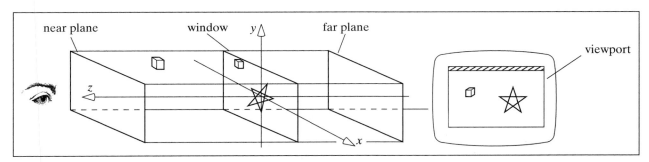

FIGURE 5.50 Simple viewing used in OpenGL for 2D drawing.

Now we move into 3D graphics and place 3D objects in a scene. For the examples here, we continue to utilize a parallel projection. (The more realistic perspective projection, in which remote objects appear smaller than nearby objects, is described in Chapter 7.) Therefore, we use the same camera as in Figure 5.50, but allow it to have a more general position and orientation in the 3D scene, in order to produce better views of the scene.

Figure 5.51 shows such a camera immersed in a scene, The scene consists of a block, part of which lies outside the view volume. The image produced by the camera is also shown.

We saw in the previous section that OpenGL provides the three functions `glScaled(..)`, `glRotated(..)`, and `glTranslated(..)` for applying modeling transformations to a shape. The block in Figure 5.51 is in fact a cube that has been stretched, rotated, and shifted as shown. OpenGL also provides functions for defining the view volume and its position in the scene.

FIGURE 5.51 A camera to produce parallel views of a scene.

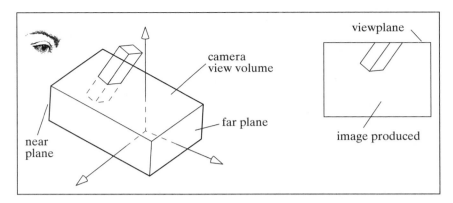

The graphics pipeline implemented by OpenGL does its major work through matrix transformations, so we first afford an insight into what each of the matrices in the pipeline does. At this point it is important only to grasp the basic idea of how each matrix operates; in Chapter 7 we shall give a detailed discussion. Figure 5.52 shows the pipeline (slightly simplified). Each vertex of an object is passed through this pipeline with a call such as `glVertex3d(x, y, z)`. The vertex is multiplied by the various matrices shown, it is clipped if necessary, and if it survives clipping, it is ultimately mapped onto the viewport. Each vertex encounters the following three matrices:

- The **modelview matrix;**
- The **projection matrix;**
- The **viewport matrix.**

FIGURE 5.52 The OpenGL pipeline (slightly simplified).

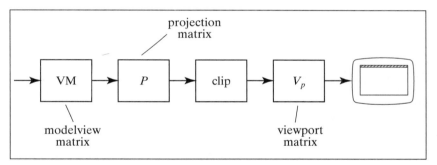

The **modelview matrix** basically provides what we have been calling the CT. It combines two effects: the sequence of modeling transformations applied to objects and the transformation that orients and positions the camera in space (hence its peculiar name *modelview*). Although the modelview matrix is a single matrix in the actual pipeline, it is easier to think of it as the product of two matrices: a modeling matrix M and a viewing matrix V. First the modeling matrix is applied and then the viewing matrix, so the modelview matrix is in fact the product VM. (Why?)

Figure 5.53 suggests what the M and V matrices do, for the situation introduced in Figure 5.51, in which a camera "looks down" on a scene consisting of a block. Part (a) shows a unit cube centered at the origin. A modeling transformation based on M scales, rotates, and translates the cube into the block shown in Part (b), which also shows the relative position of the camera's view volume. The V matrix is now used to rotate and translate the block into a new position. The specific transformation is that which would carry the camera from its position in the scene to its "generic" position, with the eye at the origin and the view volume aligned with the z-axis, as shown in Part (c) of the figure. The vertices of the block are now positioned (that

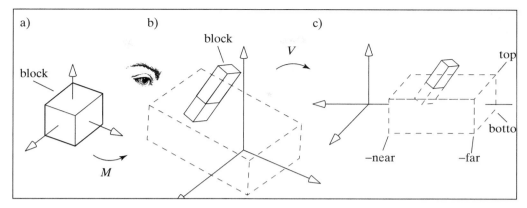

is, their coordinates have the proper values), so that projecting them onto a plane such as the near plane yields the proper values for displaying the projected image. So the matrix V in fact effects a change of coordinates of the scene's vertices into the camera's coordinate system. (Camera coordinates are sometimes also called **eye coordinates**.) In the camera's coordinate system, the edges of the view volume are parallel to the x-, y-, and z-axes. The view volume extends from *left* to *right* in x, from *bottom* to *top* in y, and from $-near$ to $-far$ in z. (We discuss the significance of the minus signs in front of *near* and *far* shortly.) When the vertices of the original cube have passed through the entire modelview matrix, they are located as shown in Part (c).

The **projection matrix** scales and shifts each vertex in a particular way, so that all those vertices that lie inside the view volume will lie inside a *standard cube* that extends from -1 to 1 in each dimension.[12] (When perspective projections are being used, this matrix does quite a bit more, as we shall see in Chapter 7.) The projection matrix effectively squashes the view volume into the cube centered at the origin, which is a particularly efficient boundary against which to clip objects. Scaling the block in this fashion might badly distort it, of course, but the distortion will be compensated for in the viewport transformation. The projection matrix also reverses the sense of the z-axis, so that increasing values of z now represent increasing values of the depth of a point from the eye. Figure 5.54 shows how the block is transformed into a different block by this transformation. (Notice that the view volume of the camera need never be created as an object itself; it is defined only as that particular shape which the projection matrix converts into the standard cube!)

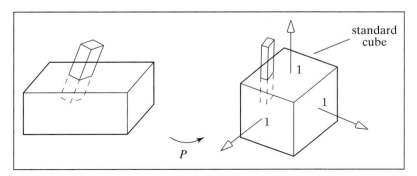

FIGURE 5.54 Effect of the projection matrix (for parallel projections).

---

[12] Coordinates in this system are sometimes called *normalized device coordinates*.

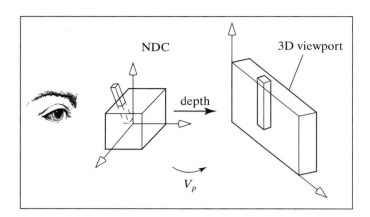

Clipping is now performed, which eliminates the portion of the block that lies outside the standard cube. And finally, the **viewport matrix** maps the surviving portion of the block into a "3D viewport." This matrix maps the standard cube into a block shape whose x and y values extend across the viewport (in screen coordinates) and whose z-component extends from 0 to 1 and retains a measure of the depth of point (the distance between the point and the eye of the camera), as shown in Figure 5.55.

The preceding overview has outlined how the whole OpenGL graphics pipeline operates, showing that transformations are a central ingredient. Each vertex of an object is subjected to a sequence of transformations that carry it from world coordinates into eye coordinates, into a neutral system specially designed for clipping, and finally, into the right coordinate system for proper display. Each transformation is effected by a matrix multiplication. Note that we have omitted some important details of the pipeline in this first overview. When perspective projections are used, we need to include a "perspective division" that capitalizes on a property of homogeneous coordinates. And of course, many interesting details lurk in the last step of actually rendering the image, such as computing the color of pixels "in between" vertices and checking for the proper removal of hidden surfaces. These details are all addressed in later chapters.

5.6.2 Some OpenGL Tools for Modeling and Viewing

We now examine what functions OpenGL provides for modeling and setting the camera.

Three Functions Are Used to Set Modeling Transformations

The following functions are normally used to modify the modelview matrix, which is first made "current" by executing: `glMatrixMode(GL_MODELVIEW)`:

- `glScaled(sx, sy, sz)`; Postmultiply the current matrix by a matrix that performs a scaling by sx in x, by sy in y, and by sz in z. Put the result back into the current matrix.
- `glTranslated(dx, dy, dz)`; Postmultiply the current matrix by a matrix that performs a translation by dx in x, by dy in y, and by dz in z. Put the result back into the current matrix.
- `glRotated(angle, ux, uy, uz)`; Postmultiply the current matrix by a matrix that performs a rotation through *angle* degrees about the axis that passes through the origin and the point (ux, uy, uz).[13] Put the result back in the current matrix. Equation (5.33) is the matrix that is used to perform the rotation.

---

[13] Positive values of *angle* produce rotations that are CCW as one looks along the axis from the point (ux, uy, uz) towards the origin.

Setting the Camera in OpenGL (for a Parallel Projection)

The function `glOrtho(left,right,bott,top,near,far);` establishes as a view volume a parallelipiped that extends from[14] `left` to `right` in x, from `bott` to `top` in y, and from $-near$ to $-far$ in z. (Since this definition operates in eye coordinates, the camera's eye is at the origin, looking down the negative z-axis.) The function creates a matrix and postmultiplies the current matrix by it. (We show in Chapter 7 precisely what values the new matrix contains.)

Notice the minus signs before `near` and `far`: Because the default camera is located at the origin looking down the negative z-axis, using a value of 2 for `near` means to place the near plane at $z = -2$, that is, 2 units in front of the eye. Similarly, using 20 for `far` places the far plane 20 units in front of the eye.

The following code sets the projection matrix:

```
glMatrixMode(GL_PROJECTION);  // make the projection matrix
                                       current
glLoadIdentity();             // set it to the identity matrix
glOrtho(left,right,bottom,top,near,far); // multiply it by the
                                       new matrix
```

Positioning and Aiming the Camera

OpenGL offers a function that makes it easy to set up a basic camera:

```
gluLookAt(eye.x, eye.y, eye.z, look.x, look.y, look.z, up.x,
up.y, up.z);
```

This function creates the view matrix and postmultiplies the current matrix by it. The function takes as parameters the eye position, `eye`, of the camera and the look-at point, `look`. It also takes an approximate upwards direction, `up`. Since the programmer knows where an interesting part of the scene is situated, it is usually straightforward to choose reasonable values for `eye` and `look` for a good first view. And `up` is most often set to $(0, 1, 0)$ to suggest an upwards direction parallel to the y-axis. Later we develop more powerful tools for setting up a camera and for interactively "flying it" in an animation.

We want this function to set the V part of the modelview matrix VM. So it is invoked before any modeling transformations are added, since subsequent such transformations will postmultiply the modelview matrix. So to use `gluLookAt()`, we employ the following sequence:

```
glMatrixMode(GL_MODELVIEW);      // make the modelview matrix
                                      current
glLoadIdentity();                // start with a unit matrix
gluLookAt(eye.x, eye.y, eye.z,   // the eye position
          look.x, look.y, look.z, // the "look at" point
          up.x, up.y, up.z);     // the upwards direction
```

We discuss how this function operates in Chapter 7, where we also develop more flexible tools for establishing the camera. Those who are curious about what values `gluLookAt()` actually places in the modelview matrix should consult the exercises at the end of the section.

---

[14] All parameters of `glOrtho()` are of the type `GLdouble`.

■ EXAMPLE 5.6.1 Set up a typical camera

Cameras are often set to "look down" on a scene from some nearby position. Figure 5.56 shows a camera with its eye situated at $eye = (4, 4, 4)$, looking at the origin with $look = (0, 1, 0)$. The upwards direction is set to $up = (0, 1, 0)$. Suppose we also want the view volume to have a width of 6.4 and a height of 4.8 (so that its aspect ratio is 640/480), and suppose we wish to set $near$ to 1 and far to 50. The camera could be established with the following code:

```
glMatixMode(GL_PROJECTION); // set the view volume
glLoadIdentity();
glOrtho(-3.2, 3.2, -2.4, 2.4, 1, 50);
glMatrixMode(GL_MODELVIEW); // place and aim the camera
glLoadIdentity();
gluLookAt(4, 4, 4, 0, 1, 0, 0, 1, 0);
```

FIGURE 5.56 Setting a camera with `gluLookAt()`.

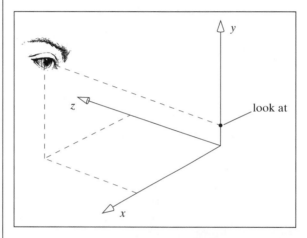

The exercises show the specific values that get placed in the modelview matrix.

PRACTICE EXERCISES

5.6.1 What does gluLookAt() do?

We know that `gluLookAt()` builds a matrix that converts world coordinates into eye coordinates. Figure 5.57 shows the camera as a coordinate system suspended in the world, with its origin at *eye* and oriented according to its three mutually perpendicular unit vectors $\mathbf{u}$, $\mathbf{v}$, and $\mathbf{n}$. The eye is "looking" in the direction $-\mathbf{n}$. `gluLookAt()`

FIGURE 5.57 Converting from world to camera coordinates.

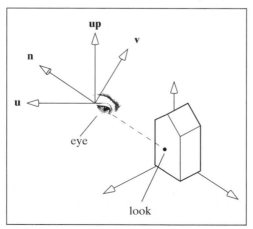

uses the parameters *eye*, *look*, and **up** to create **u**, **v**, and **n** according to the following relationships:

$$\mathbf{n} = eye - look$$
$$\mathbf{u} = \mathbf{up} \times \mathbf{n} \qquad\qquad (5.38)$$
$$\mathbf{v} = \mathbf{n} \times \mathbf{u}$$

`gluLookAt()` then normalizes all three of these vectors to unit length, building the matrix

$$V = \begin{pmatrix} u_x & u_y & u_z & d_x \\ v_x & v_y & v_z & d_y \\ n_x & n_y & n_z & d_z \\ 0 & 0 & 0 & 1 \end{pmatrix},$$

where the point d has components $(d_x, d_y, d_z) = (-eye \cdot \mathbf{u}, -eye \cdot \mathbf{v}, -eye \cdot \mathbf{n})$.

a. Show that **u**, **v**, and **n** are mutually perpendicular.
b. Show that the matrix V properly converts world coordinates to eye coordinates by demonstrating that it maps *eye* into the origin $(0, 0, 0, 1)^T$, **u** into **i** $= (1, 0, 0, 0)$, **v** into **j** $= (0, 1, 0)$, and **n** into **k** $= (0, 0, 1)$.
c. Show, for the case *eye* $= (4, 4, 4)$, *lookAt* $= (0, 1, 0)$, and **up** $= (0, 1, 0)$, that the resulting matrix is

$$V = \begin{pmatrix} .70711 & 0 & -.70711 & 0 \\ -.3313 & .88345 & -.3313 & -.88345 \\ .6247 & .4685 & .6247 & -6.872 \\ 0 & 0 & 0 & 1 \end{pmatrix}.$$

5.6.2 Inquiring about the values in a matrix in OpenGL

Print out the values in the modelview matrix to test some of the assertions made about how it is formed. To see what is stored in the modelview matrix in OpenGL, define an array `GLfloat mat[16]` and use `glGetFloatv(GL_MODELVIEW_MA-TRIX,mat)`, which copies into `mat[]` the 16 values in the modelview matrix. `M[i][j]` is copied into the element `mat[4j + i]`, for $i, j = 0, 1, \ldots, 3$. ■

5.6.3 Drawing Elementary Shapes Provided by OpenGL

We shall see in the next chapter how to create our own 3D objects, but at this point we need some 3D objects to draw, in order to experiment with setting and using cameras. The GLUT provides several ready-made such objects, including a sphere, a cone, a torus, the five Platonic solids (discussed in Chapter 6), and the famous teapot. Each is available as a wire-frame model and as a solid model with faces that can be shaded. The following list shows the functions used to draw some of these objects:

- **cube:** `glutWireCube(GLdouble size)`; Each side is of length `size`.
- **sphere:** `glutWireSphere(GLdouble radius, GLint nSlices, GLint nStacks)`
- **torus:** `glutWireTorus(GLdouble inRad, GLdouble outRad, GLint nSlices, GLint nStacks)`
- **teapot:** `glutWireTeapot(GLdouble size)`

There are also a `glutSolidCube()`, `glutSolidSphere()`, etc., which we use later. The shape of the torus is determined by the inner radius `inRad` and outer radius `outRad`. The sphere and torus are approximated by polygonal faces, and you can adjust the parameters `nSlices` and `nStacks` to specify how many faces to use in the approximation. `nSlices` is the number of subdivisions around the z-axis, and `nStacks` is the number of "bands" along the z-axis, as if the shape were a stack of `nStacks` disks.

The functions used to render four of the Platonic solids (the fifth is the cube, already presented) are as follows:

- **tetrahedron:**   `glutWireTetrahedron()`
- **octahedron:**   `glutWireOctahedron()`
- **dodecahedron:**   `glutWireDodecahedron()`
- **icosahedron:**   `glutWireIcosahedron()`

All of the preceding shapes are centered at the origin. We also have the following solids:

- **cone:** `glutWireCone(GLdouble baseRad, GLdouble height, GLint nSlices, GLint nStacks)`
- **tapered cylinder:** `gluCylinder(GLUquadricObj * qobj, GLdouble baseRad, GLdouble topRad, GLdouble height, GLint nSlices, GLint nStacks)`

The axes of the cone and tapered cylinder coincide with the z-axis. Their bases rest on the $z = 0$ plane and extend to $z = $ `height` along the z-axis. The radius of the cone and tapered cylinder at $z = 0$ is given by `baseRad`. The radius of the tapered cylinder at $z = $ `height` is `topRad`.

The **tapered cylinder** is actually a *family* of shapes, distinguished by the value of `topRad`. When `topRad` is 1, there is no taper, and we have the classic **right circular cylinder**. When `topRad` is 0, the tapered cylinder is identical to the **cone**.

Note that drawing the tapered cylinder in OpenGL requires some extra work, because it is a special case of a quadric surface, as we shall see in Chapter 6. To draw it, you must (1) define a new quadric object, (2) set the drawing style (`GLU_LINE` for a wire frame, `GLU_FILL` for a solid rendering), and (3) draw the object. The code shown in Figure 5.58 does all of this.

```
GLUquadricObj * qobj = gluNewQuadric();              // make a quadric object
gluQuadricDrawStyle(qobj,GLU_LINE);                  // set style to wireframe
gluCylinder(qobj, baseRad, topRad, height, nSlices, nStacks); // draw the cylinder
```

FIGURE 5.58 Shapes available in the GLU.

We next employ some of the foregoing shapes in two substantial examples that focus on using affine transformations to model and view a 3D scene. The complete program to draw each scene is given. A great deal of insight can be obtained if you enter these programs into the computer, produce the figures, and then see the effect of varying the parameters in the code.

■ **EXAMPLE 5.6.2 A scene composed of wire-frame objects**

Figure 5.59 shows a scene with several objects disposed at the corners of a unit cube, which itself has one corner at the origin. Seven objects appear at various corners of the cube, all drawn as wire frames.

The camera is given a view volume that extends from -2 to 2 in y, with an aspect ratio of 640/480. The near plane is at $N = 0.1$, the far plane at $F = 100$. This is accomplished using

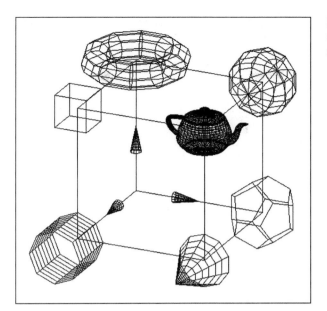

FIGURE 5.59 Wire-frame drawing of various primitive shapes.

```
glOrtho(-2.0* aspect, 2.0* aspect, -2.0, 2.0, 0.1, 100);
```

The camera is positioned with *eye* = (2, 2, 2), *lookAt* = (0, 0, 0), and *up* = (0, 1, 0) (parallel to the *y*-axis), using

```
gluLookAt(2.0, 2.0, 2.0, 0.0, 0.0, 0.0, 0.0, 1.0, 0.0);
```

Figure 5.60 shows the complete program to produce the drawing. The `main()` routine initializes a 640-by-480 pixel screen window, sets the viewport and background color, and specifies `displayWire()` as the display function to be called to perform the drawing. In `displayWire()`, the shape and position of the camera are established first. Then each object is drawn in turn. Most objects need their own modeling matrix in order to rotate and position them as desired. Before each modeling transformation is established, a `glPushMatrix()` is used to remember the current transformation, and after the object has been drawn, the current transformation is restored with a `glPopMatrix()`. Thus, the code to draw each object is imbedded in a `glPushMatrix()`, `glPopMatrix()` pair. Check each transformation carefully to see that it places its object at the proper place.

Also shown in the figure are the *x*-, *y*-, and *z*-axes, drawn with conical arrowheads. Displaying the underlying coordinate system can help to orient the viewer. To draw the *x*-axis, the *z*-axis is rotated 90° about the *y*-axis to form a rotated system, and the *x*-axis is redrawn in its new orientation. Note that this axis is drawn without immersing it in a `glPushMatrix()`, `glPopMatrix()` pair, so the next rotation to produce the *y*-axis takes place in the already rotated coordinate system. Check that this is the proper rotation.

Notice that the sides of the large cube that are parallel in 3D are displayed as parallel—a result of using a parallel projection. The cube looks slightly unnatural, because we are used to seeing the world in a perspective projection. As we shall see in Chapter 7, if a perspective projection were used instead, the parallel edges would not be drawn parallel.

```
#include <windows.h>   //suitable when using Windows 95/98/NT
#include <gl/Gl.h>
#include <gl/Glu.h>
#include <gl/glut.h>
//<<<<<<<<<<<<<<<<<<< axis >>>>>>>>>>>>>>
void axis(double length)
{ // draw a z-axis, with cone at end
     glPushMatrix();
     glBegin(GL_LINES);
        glVertex3d(0, 0, 0); glVertex3d(0,0,length); // along the z-axis
     glEnd();
     glTranslated(0, 0,length -0.2);
     glutWireCone(0.04, 0.2, 12, 9);
     glPopMatrix();
}
//<<<<<<<<<<<<<<<<<<<<<<<<<<<< displayWire >>>>>>>>>>>>>>>>>>>>>>>>
void displayWire(void)
{
     glMatrixMode(GL_PROJECTION); // set the view volume shape
     glLoadIdentity();
     glOrtho(-2.0*64/48.0, 2.0*64/48.0, -2.0, 2.0, 0.1, 100);
     glMatrixMode(GL_MODELVIEW); // position and aim the camera
     glLoadIdentity();
     gluLookAt(2.0, 2.0, 2.0, 0.0, 0.0, 0.0, 0.0, 1.0, 0.0);

     glClear(GL_COLOR_BUFFER_BIT); // clear the screen
     glColor3d(0,0,0: // draw black lines
     axis(0.5);        // z-axis
     glPushMatrix();
     glRotated(90, 0,1.0, 0);
     axis(0.5);       // y-axis
     glRotated(-90.0, 1, 0, 0);
     axis(0.5);       // z-axis
     glPopMatrix();

     glPushMatrix();
     glTranslated(0.5, 0.5, 0.5); // big cube at (0.5, 0.5, 0.5)
     glutWireCube(1.0);
     glPopMatrix();

     glPushMatrix();
     glTranslated(1.0,1.0,0); // sphere at (1,1,0)
     glutWireSphere(0.25, 10, 8);
     glPopMatrix();

     glPushMatrix();
     glTranslated(1.0,0,1.0); // cone at (1,0,1)
     glutWireCone(0.2, 0.5, 10, 8);
     glPopMatrix();

     glPushMatrix();
     glTranslated(1,1,1);
     glutWireTeapot(0.2); // teapot at (1,1,1)
     glPopMatrix();
```

FIGURE 5.60
Complete program
to draw Figure 5.59
using OpenGL.

FIGURE 5.60 (*Continued*)

```
     glPushMatrix();
     glTranslated(0, 1.0 ,0); // torus at (0,1,0)
     glRotated(90.0, 1,0,0);
     glutWireTorus(0.1, 0.3, 10,10);
     glPopMatrix();

     glPushMatrix();
     glTranslated(1.0, 0 ,0); // dodecahedron at (1,0,0)
     glScaled(0.15, 0.15, 0.15);
     glutWireDodecahedron();
     glPopMatrix();

     glPushMatrix();
     glTranslated(0, 1.0 ,1.0); // small cube at (0,1,1)
     glutWireCube(0.25);
     glPopMatrix();

     glPushMatrix();
     glTranslated(0, 0 ,1.0); // cylinder at (0,0,1)
     GLUquadricObj * qobj;
     qobj = gluNewQuadric();
     gluQuadricDrawStyle(qobj,GLU_LINE);
     gluCylinder(qobj, 0.2, 0.2, 0.4, 8,8);
     glPopMatrix();
     glFlush();
}
//<<<<<<<<<<<<<<<<<<<<<<<< main >>>>>>>>>>>>>>>>>>>>>>>>>>>>>
void main(int argc, char **argv)
{
     glutInit(&argc, argv);
     glutInitDisplayMode(GLUT_SINGLE | GLUT_RGB );
     glutInitWindowSize(640,480);
     glutInitWindowPosition(100, 100);
     glutCreateWindow("Transformation testbed - wire frames");
     glutDisplayFunc(displayWire);
     glClearColor(1.0f, 1.0f, 1.0f,0.0f);  // background is white
     glViewport(0, 0, 640, 480);
     glutMainLoop();
}
```

■ **EXAMPLE 5.6.3 A 3D Scene Rendered with Shading**

In this example, we develop a somewhat more complex scene to illustrate further the use of modeling transformations. We also show how easy OpenGL makes it to draw much more realistic drawings of solid objects by incorporating shading, along with the proper removal of hidden surfaces.

Two views of a scene are shown in Figure 5.61. Both views use a camera set by `gluLookAt(2.3, 1.3, 2, 0, 0.25, 0, 0.0,1.0,0.0)`. Part (a) uses a large view volume that encompasses the whole scene; Part (b) uses a small view volume that encompasses only a small portion of the scene, thereby providing a close-up view.

The scene contains three objects resting on a table in the corner of a "room." Each of the three walls is made by flattening a cube into a thin sheet

FIGURE 5.61 A simple 3D scene (a) using a large view volume and (b) using a small view volume.

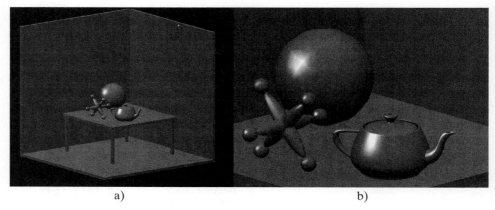

a)   b)

and moving it into position. (Again, the walls look somewhat unnatural due to the use of a parallel projection.) The jack is composed of three stretched spheres oriented at right angles to each other, plus six small spheres at their ends. The table consists of a tabletop and four legs. Each of the table's five pieces is a cube that has been scaled to the desired size and shape. The layout for the table is shown in Figure 5.62 and is based on four parameters that characterize the size of its parts: `topWidth`, `topThick`, `legLen`, and `legThick`. A routine `tableLeg()` draws each leg and is called four times within the routine `table()` to draw the legs in the four different locations. The different parameters used produce different modeling transformations within `tableLeg()`. As always, a `glPushMatrix()`, `glPopMatrix()` pair surrounds the modeling functions to isolate their effect.

FIGURE 5.62 Designing the table.

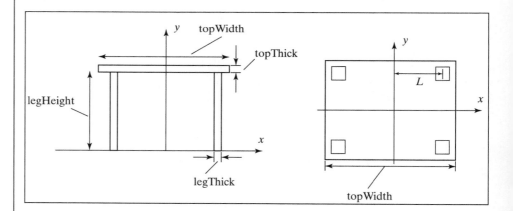

The complete code for this program is shown in Figure 5.63. Note that the solid version of each shape, such as `glutSolidSphere()`, is used here, rather than the wire-frame version. Check the assorted transformations used to orient and position each object in the scene. Check the model of the jack in particular. This example is designed to whet your appetite for trying out scenes on your own, practicing with transformations.

The code also shows the various things that must be done to create shaded images. The position and properties of a light source must be specified, along with certain properties of the objects' surfaces, in order to describe how they reflect light. Since we discuss the shading process in Chapter 8, we just present the various function calls here; using them as shown will generate shading.

FIGURE 5.63 Complete
program to draw the shaded
scene.

```
#include <windows.h>
#include <iostream.h>
#include <gl/Gl.h>
#include <gl/Glu.h>
#include <gl/glut.h>
//<<<<<<<<<<<<<<< wall >>>>>>>>>>>>>>>>
void wall(double thickness)
{ // draw thin wall with top = xz-plane, corner at origin
      glPushMatrix();
      glTranslated(0.5, 0.5 * thickness,  0.5);
      glScaled(1.0, thickness, 1.0);
      glutSolidCube(1.0);
      glPopMatrix();
}
//<<<<<<<<<<<<<<<<<<< tableLeg >>>>>>>>>>>>>>>>>>>>
void tableLeg(double thick, double len)
{
      glPushMatrix();
      glTranslated(0, len/2, 0);
      glScaled(thick, len, thick);
      glutSolidCube(1.0);
      glPopMatrix();
}
//<<<<<<<<<<<<<<<<<<<<<< jack part >>>>>>>>>>>>>
void jackPart()
{ // draw one axis of the unit jack - a stretched sphere
      glPushMatrix();
      glScaled(0.2,0.2,1.0);
      glutSolidSphere(1,15,15);
      glPopMatrix();
      glPushMatrix();
      glTranslated(0,0,1.2); // ball on one end
      glutSolidSphere(0.2,15,15);
      glTranslated(0,0, -2.4);
      glutSolidSphere(0.2,15,15); // ball on the other end
      glPopMatrix();
}
//<<<<<<<<<<<<<<<<<<<<<< jack >>>>>>>>>>>>>>>>>>>>>>>
void jack()
{ // draw a unit jack out of spheroids
      glPushMatrix();
      jackPart();
      glRotated(90.0, 0, 1, 0);
      jackPart();
      glRotated(90.0, 1,0,0);
      jackPart();
      glPopMatrix();
}
```

PRACTICE EXERCISES

5.6.3 Adjusting the Scene

What changes should be made in Figure 5.63 to place the jack on the floor and the
sphere perched on top of the teapot? ■

FIGURE 5.63
(*Continued*)

```
//<<<<<<<<<<<<<<<<<<<<<<<<<< table >>>>>>>>>>>>>>>>>>>>
void table(double topWid, double topThick, double legThick, double legLen)
{ // draw the table - a top and four legs
      glPushMatrix(); // draw the table top
      glTranslated(0, legLen, 0);
      glScaled(topWid, topThick, topWid);
      glutSolidCube(1.0);
      glPopMatrix();
      double dist = 0.95 * topWid/2.0 - legThick / 2.0;
      glPushMatrix();
      glTranslated(dist, 0, dist);
      tableLeg(legThick, legLen);
      glTranslated(0, 0, -2 * dist);
      tableLeg(legThick, legLen);
      glTranslated(-2 * dist, 0, 2*dist);
      tableLeg(legThick, legLen);
      glTranslated(0, 0, -2*dist);
      tableLeg(legThick, legLen);
      glPopMatrix();
}
//<<<<<<<<<<<<<<<<<<<<<<<< displaySolid >>>>>>>>>>>>>>>>>>>>>>
void displaySolid(void)
{
 //set properties of the surface material
      GLfloat mat_ambient[] = { 0.7f, 0.7f, 0.7f, 1.0f}; // gray
      GLfloat mat_diffuse[] = {0.6f, 0.6f, 0.6f, 1.0f};
      GLfloat mat_specular[] = {1.0f, 1.0f, 1.0f, 1.0f};
      GLfloat mat_shininess[] = {50.0f};
      glMaterialfv(GL_FRONT,GL_AMBIENT,mat_ambient);
      glMaterialfv(GL_FRONT,GL_DIFFUSE,mat_diffuse);
      glMaterialfv(GL_FRONT,GL_SPECULAR,mat_specular);
      glMaterialfv(GL_FRONT,GL_SHININESS,mat_shininess);
      // set the light source properties
      GLfloat lightIntensity[] = {0.7f, 0.7f, 0.7f, 1.0f};
      GLfloat light_position[] = {2.0f, 6.0f, 3.0f, 0.0f};
      glLightfv(GL_LIGHT0, GL_POSITION, light_position);
      glLightfv(GL_LIGHT0, GL_DIFFUSE, lightIntensity);
      // set the camera
      glMatrixMode(GL_PROJECTION);
      glLoadIdentity();
      double winHt = 1.0; // half-height of the window
      glOrtho(-winHt*64/48.0, winHt*64/48.0, -winHt, winHt, 0.1, 100.0);
      glMatrixMode(GL_MODELVIEW);
      glLoadIdentity();
      gluLookAt(2.3, 1.3, 2, 0, 0.25, 0, 0.0,1.0,0.0);
// start drawing
      glClear(GL_COLOR_BUFFER_BIT|GL_DEPTH_BUFFER_BIT); // clear the screen
      glPushMatrix();
      glTranslated(0.4, 0.4, 0.6);
      glRotated(45,0,0,1);
      glScaled(0.08, 0.08, 0.08);
```

FIGURE 5.63 *(Continued)*

```
jack();     // draw the jack
        glPopMatrix();
        glPushMatrix();
        glTranslated(0.6, 0.38, 0.5);
        glRotated(30,0,1,0);
        glutSolidTeapot(0.08);          // draw the teapot
        glPopMatrix();
        glPushMatrix();
        glTranslated(0.25, 0.42, 0.35);// draw the sphere
        glutSolidSphere(0.1, 15, 15);
        glPopMatrix();
        glPushMatrix();
        glTranslated(0.4, 0, 0.4);
        table(0.6, 0.02, 0.02, 0.3); // draw the table
        glPopMatrix();
        wall(0.02);                     // wall #1: in xz-plane
        glPushMatrix();
        glRotated(90.0, 0.0, 0.0, 1.0);
        wall(0.02);                     // wall #2: in yz-plane
        glPopMatrix();
        glPushMatrix();
        glRotated(-90.0,1.0, 0.0, 0.0);
        wall(0.02);                     // wall #3: in xy-plane
        glPopMatrix();
        glFlush();
}
//<<<<<<<<<<<<<<<<<<<<<< main >>>>>>>>>>>>>>>>>>>>>>>>>>>>>>
void main(int argc, char **argv)
{
        glutInit(&argc, argv);
        glutInitDisplayMode(GLUT_SINGLE | GLUT_RGB| GLUT_DEPTH);
        glutInitWindowSize(640,480);
        glutInitWindowPosition(100, 100);
        glutCreateWindow("shaded example - 3D scene");
        glutDisplayFunc(displaySolid);
        glEnable(GL_LIGHTING); // enable the light source
        glEnable(GL_LIGHT0);
        glShadeModel(GL_SMOOTH);
        glEnable(GL_DEPTH_TEST); // for removal of hidden surfaces
        glEnable(GL_NORMALIZE); // normalize vectors for proper shading
        glClearColor(0.1f,0.1f,0.1f,0.0f);  // background is light gray
        glViewport(0, 0, 640, 480);
        glutMainLoop();
}
```

5.6.4 Reading a Description of a Scene from a File

In the previous examples, the scene was described through specific OpenGL calls that transform and draw each object, as in the following code:

```
glTranslated(0.25, 0.42, 0.35);
glutSolidSphere(0.1, 15, 15); // draw a sphere
```

The objects in the scene were therefore "hardwired" into the program. This way of specifying a scene is cumbersome and prone to error. It is a boon when the designer can specify the objects in a scene through a simple language and place the description of the scene in a file. The drawing program then becomes a (much simpler) general-purpose program: It reads the file describing the scene at run time and draws whatever objects are encountered in the file.

The Scene Description Language (SDL) described in Appendix 5 provides such a tool. We define a `Scene` class—also described in Appendix 3 and available on the book's Web site—that supports the reading of an SDL file and the drawing of the objects described in the file. It is very simple to use the `Scene` class in an application: First a global `Scene` object is created via the code

```
Scene scn; // create a scene object
```

and the `read()` method of the class is called to read in a scene file by means of the function

```
scn.read("simple.dat");  // read the scene file & build an
                         object list
```

Figure 5.64 shows the data structure for the `scn` object, created by reading the following simple SDL file:

FIGURE 5.64 An object of the `Scene` class.

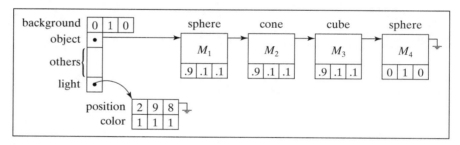

```
! simple.dat: a simple scene having one light and four shapes
background 0 0 1         ! give the scene a blue background
light 2 9 8 1 1 1       ! put a white light at (9, 9, 9)
diffuse .9 .1 .1         ! make the following objects reddish
translate 3 5 -2   sphere       ! put a sphere at 3 5 -2
translate -4 -6 8   cone ! put a cone in the scene
translate  1 1 1 cube    ! add a cube
diffuse 0 1 0            ! make the following objects green
translate 40 5 2 scale .2 .2 .2 sphere !add a tiny sphere
```

The first line is a comment; each comment extends to the end of the line. This scene has a bright blue background color (*red, green, blue*) = (0, 0, 1), a bright white (1, 1, 1) light situated at (2, 9, 8), and four objects: two spheres, a cone, and a cube. The `light` field points to the list of light sources, and the `obj` field points to the list of objects. Each differently shaped object has its own affine transformation *M* that describes how it is scaled, rotated, and positioned in the scene. Each object listed also contains various data fields that specify its material properties, which are important when we want to render the object faithfully, as discussed in Chapter 8. Only the diffuse field is shown in the figure.

Once the light list and object list have been built, the application can render the scene via the code

```
scn.makeLightsOpenGL();
scn.drawSceneOpenGL();  // render the scene using OpenGL
```

The first instruction passes a description of the light sources to OpenGL. The second uses the method `drawSceneOpenGL()` to draw each object in the object list. The code for this method is very simple:

```
void Scene :: drawSceneOpenGL()
{
        for(GeomObj* p = obj; p ; p = p->next)
             p->drawOpenGL(); // draw it
}
```

The function moves a pointer through the object list, calling `drawOpenGL()` for each object in turn. This is a nice example of using polymorphism, which is a cornerstone of object-oriented programming: Each different shape "knows" how to draw itself; it has a method, `drawOpenGL()`, that calls the appropriate routine for that shape. So when p points to a sphere, the `drawOpenGL()` routine for a sphere is called automatically, when p points to a cone, the `drawOpenGL()` routine for a cone is called, etc. Figure 5.65 shows the methods for the `Sphere` and `Cone` classes; they differ only in the final OpenGL drawing routine that is called. Each first passes the object's material properties to OpenGL and then updates the modelview matrix with the object's specific affine transformation. The original modelview matrix is pushed and later restored, to protect it from being affected after the object has been drawn.

```
void Sphere :: drawOpenGL()
{
   tellMaterialsGL();  //pass material data to OpenGL
   glPushMatrix();
   glMultMatrixf(transf.m); // load this object's matrix
   glutSolidSphere(1.0,10,12); // draw a sphere
   glPopMatrix();
}
void Cone :: drawOpenGL()
{
   tellMaterialsGL();//pass material data to OpenGL
   glPushMatrix();
   glMultMatrixf(transf.m); // load this object's matrix
   glutSolidCone(1.0,1.0, 10,12); // draw a cone
   glPopMatrix();
}
```

FIGURE 5.65 The `drawOpenGL()` methods for two shapes.

Figure 5.66 shows the program that reads an SDL file and draws the scene. The program is very short (but of course, the code for the classes `Scene`, `Shape`, etc., must be loaded as well). It reads the particular SDL file `myScene1.dat`, which re-creates the same scene as in Figure 5.61. Note that by simply changing the SDL file that is read, this program can draw *any* scene described in SDL, without any changes in its code.

The SDL file that describes the scene of Figure 5.61 is shown in Figure 5.67. The file defines the jack shape of nine spheres by first defining a `jackPart` and then using it three times, as explained in Appendix 5. Similarly, a leg of the table is first defined as a unit and then used four times.

With a scene description language like SDL available, along with tools to read and parse it, the designer can focus on creating complex scenes without having to work at the application code level. The scene being developed can be edited and tested again and again until it is right. The code developer puts the initial effort into constructing an application that can render any scene describable in SDL.

```
#include "SDL.h"
//########################## GLOBALS ##########################
Scene scn;  // construct the scene object
//<<<<<<<<<<<<<<<<<<<<<<<<< displaySDL >>>>>>>>>>>>>>>>>>>>>>>>>
void displaySDL(void)
{
    glMatrixMode(GL_PROJECTION); //set the camera
    glLoadIdentity();
    double winHt = 1.0; // half-height of the window
    glOrtho(-winHt*64/48.0, winHt*64/48.0, -winHt, winHt, 0.1, 100.0);
    glMatrixMode(GL_MODELVIEW);
    glLoadIdentity();
    gluLookAt(2.3, 1.3, 2, 0, 0.25, 0, 0.0,1.0,0.0);
    glClear(GL_COLOR_BUFFER_BIT|GL_DEPTH_BUFFER_BIT); // clear screen
    scn.drawSceneOpenGL();
} // end of display
//<<<<<<<<<<<<<<<<<<<<<<<<< main >>>>>>>>>>>>>>>>>>>>>>>>>>>>>>>
void main(int argc, char **argv)
{
    glutInit(&argc, argv);
    glutInitDisplayMode(GLUT_RGB |GLUT_DEPTH);
    glutInitWindowSize(640, 480);
    glutInitWindowPosition(100, 100);
    glutCreateWindow("read and draw an SDL scene");
    glutDisplayFunc(displaySDL);
    glShadeModel(GL_SMOOTH);
    glEnable(GL_DEPTH_TEST);
    glEnable(GL_NORMALIZE);
    glViewport(0, 0, 640, 480);
    scn.read("myScene1.dat"); //read the SDL file and build the objects
    glEnable(GL_LIGHTING);
    scn.makeLightsOpenGL(); // scan the light list and make OpenGL lights
    glutMainLoop();
}
```

FIGURE 5.66 Drawing a scene read in from an SDL file.

5.7 SUMMARY

Affine transformations are a staple in computer graphics, for they offer a unified tool for manipulating graphical objects in important ways. A designer always needs to scale, orient, and position objects in order to compose a scene, as well as an appropriate view of it, and affine transformations make this task simple to manage in a program.

Affine transformations convert one coordinate frame into another, and when homogeneous coordinates are used, an affine transformation is captured in a single matrix form. A sequence of such transformations can be combined into a single transformation whose matrix is simply the product of the individual transformation matrices. Significantly, affine transformations preserve straightness, so the image of a line is another line, and the image of a plane is a plane. This invariance vastly simplifies working with lines and planes in a program: One benefits from the simple representations of a line (by its two endpoints) and a plane (by three points or four coefficients). In addition, parallelism is preserved, so that parallelograms map to parallelograms, and in 3D parallelepipeds map to parallelepipeds. Again, this invariance makes it simpler to visualize the geometric effects of affine transformations.

Three-dimensional affine transformations are much more complex than their 2D counterparts, particularly when it comes to visualizing a combination of rotations. A given rotation can be viewed as three elementary rotations through Euler angles, or a rotation about some

```
! - myScene1.dat
light 20 60 30 .7 .7 .7 !put a light at (20,60,30),color:(.7, .7, .7)
ambient .7 .7 .7 ! set material properties for all of the objects
diffuse .6 .6 .6
specular 1 1 1
specularExponent 50

def jackPart{ push scale .2 .2 1 sphere pop
push translate  0 0 1.2 scale .2 .2 .2 sphere pop
push translate 0 0 -1.2 scale .2 .2 .2 sphere pop
}

def jack{ push use jackPart
rotate 90 0 1 0 use jackPart
rotate 90 1 0 0 use jackPart pop
}

def wall{push translate 1 .01 1 scale 1 .02 1 cube pop}
def leg {push translate 0 .15 0 scale .01 .15 .01 cube pop}

def table{
push translate  0  .3  0 scale .3 .01 .3 cube pop !table top
push
translate .275  0 .275 use leg
translate  0 0 -.55 use leg
translate -.55 0 .55 use leg
translate 0  0 -.55 use leg pop
}
!now add the objects themselves
push translate .4 .4 .6 rotate 45 0 0 1 scale .08 .08 .08 use jack pop
push translate .25 .42 .35 scale .1 .1 .1 sphere pop
push translate .6 .38 .5 rotate 30 0 1 0 scale .08 .08 .08 teapot pop
push translate 0.4 0 0.4 use table pop

use wall
push rotate 90 0 0 1 use wall pop
push rotate -90 1 0 0 use wall pop
```

FIGURE 5.67 The SDL file to create the scene of Figure 5.61.

axis, or simply as a matrix that has special properties (its columns are orthogonal unit vectors). It is often important to move between these different forms.

OpenGL and other graphics packages offer powerful tools for manipulating and applying transformations. In OpenGL, all points are passed through several transformations, and the programmer can exploit this fact to define and manipulate a "camera," as well as to size and position different objects into a scene. Two of the matrices used by OpenGL (the modelview and viewport transformations) define affine transformations, whereas the projection matrix normally defines a perspective transformation, to be examined thoroughly in Chapter 7. OpenGL also maintains a stack of transformations, which makes it easy for the scene designer to control the dependency of one object's position on that of another and to create objects that are composed of several related parts.

The SDL language, along with the Scene and Shape classes, make it much simpler to separate programming issues from scene design issues. An application is developed once that can draw any scene described by a list of light sources and a list of geometric objects. This application is then used over and over again with different scene files. A key task in the scene design process is applying the proper geometric transformations to each object. Since a certain amount of trial and error is usually required, it is convenient to be able to express these transformations in a concise and readable way.

The case studies that follow elaborate on the main ideas of the chapter and suggest ways to practice with affine transformations in a graphics program. These exercises range from plunging deeper into the theory of transformations to the actual modeling and rendering of objects such as electronic CAD circuits and robots.

5.8 CASE STUDIES

CASE STUDY 5.1 DOING YOUR OWN TRANSFORMING BY THE CT IN CANVAS

Level of Effort: II. It is easy to envision situations in which you must implement the transformation mechanism yourself, rather than rely on OpenGL to do it. In this case study, you add the support of a current transformation to the Canvas class for 2D drawing. This involves writing several functions to initialize and alter the CT itself:

```
void Canvas:: initCT(void);    // init CT to unit transformation
void Canvas:: scale2D(double sx, double sy);
void Canvas:: translate2D(double dx, double dy);
void Canvas:: rotate2D(double angle);
```

You must also write other functions that are incorporated into moveTo() and lineTo() so that all points sent to them are "silently" transformed before being used. For extra benefit, add the stack mechanism for the CT as well, along with the functions pushCT() and popCT(). Use your new tools on some interesting 2D modeling and drawing examples.

CASE STUDY 5.2 DRAW THE STAR OF FIGURE 5.39 USING MULTIPLE ROTATIONS

Level of Effort: I. Develop a function that draws the polygon in Figure 5.39(b) that is one fifth of the star of Figure 5.39(a). Use the polygon with rotation transformations to draw the whole star.

CASE STUDY 5.3 DECOMPOSING A 2D AFFINE TRANSFORMATION

Level of Effort: II. We have seen that some affine transformations can be expressed as combinations of others. Here we "decompose" any 2D affine transformation into a combination of scalings, rotations, and translations. We also show that a rotation can be performed by three successive shears, which gives rise to a very fast arc-drawing routine. Some results on what lurks in any 3D affine transformation are discussed as well.

Because an affine transformation is a linear transformation followed by an offset, we omit the translation part of the affine transformation and focus on what a linear transformation is. So we use two-by-two matrices here for simplicity.

Two 2D Linear Transformations

Consider the two-by-two matrix M that represents a 2D linear transformation. M can always be factored into a rotation, a scaling, and a shear. Call the four scalars in M by the names $a, b, c,$ and d for brevity. Verify by direct multiplication that M is the product of the three matrices [Martin82]:

$$\begin{pmatrix} a & b \\ c & d \end{pmatrix} = \begin{pmatrix} 1 & 0 \\ \dfrac{ac+bd}{R^2} & 1 \end{pmatrix} \begin{pmatrix} R & 0 \\ 0 & \dfrac{ad-bc}{R} \end{pmatrix} \begin{pmatrix} \dfrac{a}{R} & \dfrac{b}{R} \\ -\dfrac{b}{R} & \dfrac{a}{R} \end{pmatrix}, \tag{5.39}$$

where $R = \sqrt{a^2 + b^2}$. The leftmost matrix is recognized as a shear, the middle one as a scaling, and the rightmost one as a rotation. (Why?) Thus, *any* 2D affine transformation is a rotation, followed by a scaling, followed by a shear, followed by a translation.

An alternative decomposition is discussed in Case Study 5.6.

■ EXAMPLE 5.8.1

Decompose the matrix $M = \begin{pmatrix} 4 & -3 \\ 2 & 7 \end{pmatrix}$ into the product of shear, scaling, and rotation matrices.

SOLUTION:

Check the following, obtained by direct substitution into Equation (5.39):

$$M = \begin{pmatrix} 4 & -3 \\ 2 & 7 \end{pmatrix} = \begin{pmatrix} 1 & 0 \\ -13/25 & 1 \end{pmatrix} \begin{pmatrix} 5 & 0 \\ 0 & 34/5 \end{pmatrix} \begin{pmatrix} 4/5 & -3/5 \\ 3/5 & 4/5 \end{pmatrix}$$

A 2D Rotation Is Three Shears

Matrices can be factored in different ways. In fact, a rotation matrix can be written as the product of three shear matrices [Paeth90]. This leads to a particularly fast method for performing a series of rotations.

Consider the equation

$$\begin{pmatrix} \cos(a) & \sin(a) \\ -\sin(a) & \cos(a) \end{pmatrix} = \begin{pmatrix} 1 & \tan(a/2) \\ 0 & 1 \end{pmatrix} \begin{pmatrix} 1 & 0 \\ -\sin(a) & 1 \end{pmatrix} \begin{pmatrix} 1 & \tan(a/2) \\ 0 & 1 \end{pmatrix}, \qquad (5.40)$$

which shows a rotation represented as three successive shears. This equation can be verified by direct multiplication. It demonstrates that a rotation is a shear in y, followed by a shear in x, followed by a repetition of the first shear. Calling $T = \tan(a/2)$ and $S = \sin(a)$, show that we can write the sequence of operations that rotate point (x, y) as[15]

$x' = T*y + x,$ (first shear)
$y' = y;$

$x'' = x',$ (second shear)
$y'' = y' - S*x';$

$x''' = T*y'' + x',$ (third shear)
$y''' = y'';$

using primes to distinguish new values from old. But operations like $x'' = x'$ do nothing, so the primes are unnecessary, and the sequence reduces to

$x = x + T*y,$
$y = y - S*x,$ (actual operations for the three shears)
$x = x + T*y.$

If we have only one rotation to perform, there is no advantage to going about it this way. However, the process becomes more efficient if we need to do a succession of rotations through the same angle. Two places where we need to do this are in (1) calculating the vertices of an n-gon—which are equispaced points around a circle—and (2) computing the points along the arc of a circle.

Develop a program for calculating the positions of n points around a circle. The program loads the successive values $(\cos(2\pi i/n + b), \sin(2\pi i/n + b))$ into the array of points p [].

---

[15] Note that $\sin(a)$ may be found quickly from $\tan(a/2)$ by one multiplication and one division: $S = (2T)/(1 + T^2)$.

Figure 5.68 shows how to use shears to build a fast arc drawer. It does the same job as `drawArc()` in Chapter 3, but much more efficiently, since it avoids the repetitive computation of sin() and cos(). Develop a test program that uses this routine to draw arcs. Compare the efficiency of your program with arc drawers that compute each vertex using trigonometry.

Is a Shear "Fundamental"?

One sometimes reads in the graphics literature that the fundamental elementary transformations are the rotation, scaling, and translation; shears seem to be "second-class citizens." This attitude may stem from the fact that any shear can be decomposed into a combination of rotations and scalings. The following equation may be verified by multiplying out the three matrices on the right [Greene90]:

$$\begin{pmatrix} 1 & 0 \\ a - \dfrac{1}{a} & 1 \end{pmatrix} = \frac{1}{\sqrt{1 + a^2}} \begin{pmatrix} 1 & -a \\ a & 1 \end{pmatrix} \begin{pmatrix} a & 0 \\ 0 & 1/a \end{pmatrix} \begin{pmatrix} a & 1 \\ -1 & a \end{pmatrix} \frac{1}{\sqrt{1 + a^2}}. \tag{5.41}$$

FIGURE 5.68 A fast arc drawer.

```
void drawArc2(RealPoint c, double R,
        double startangle, double sweep) // in degrees
{
    #define n 30
    #define RadPerDeg .01745329
    double delang = RadPerDeg * sweep / n;
    double T = tan(delang/2);            // tan. of half angle
    double S = 2 * T/(1 + T * T);        // sine of half angle
    double snR = R * sin(RadPerDeg * startangle);
    double csR = R * cos(RadPerDeg * startangle);
    moveTo(c.x + csR, c.y + snR);
    for(int i = 1; i < n; i++)
    {
        snR += T * csR;       // build next snR, csR pair
        csR -= S * snR;
        snR += T * csR;
        lineTo(c.x + csR, c.y + snR);
    }
}
```

The middle matrix is a scaling, while the outer two matrices (when combined with the scale factors shown) are rotations. For the left-hand rotation, associate $1/\sqrt{1 + a^2}$ with $\cos(\alpha)$ and $-a/\sqrt{1 + a^2}$ with $\sin(\alpha)$ for some angle α. Thus, $\tan(\alpha) = -a$. Similarly, for the right-hand rotation, associate similar terms with $\cos(\beta)$ and $\sin(\beta)$ for angle β, where $\tan(\beta) = 1/a$. Note that α and β are related by $\beta = \alpha + \pi/2$. (Why?)

Using the decomposition of Equation (5.41), write the shear as a rotation, followed by a scaling, followed by a rotation, to conclude that

Any 2D affine transformation = Translation × Rotation
$$\times \text{ Scale} \times \text{ Rotation} \times \text{ Scale} \times \text{ Rotation}. \tag{5.42}$$

PRACTICE EXERCISES

5.8.1 A "golden" decomposition

Consider the special case of a "unit shear," where the term $a - 1/a$ in Equation (5.41) is equal to unity. What value must a have? Determine the two angles α and β associated with the rotations.

SOLUTION:

Since a must satisfy $a = 1 + 1/a$, a is the golden ratio ϕ! Thus,

$$\begin{pmatrix} 1 & 0 \\ 1 & 1 \end{pmatrix} = \begin{pmatrix} \cos(\alpha) & -\sin(\alpha) \\ \sin(\alpha) & \cos(\alpha) \end{pmatrix} \begin{pmatrix} \phi & 0 \\ 0 & \frac{1}{\phi} \end{pmatrix} \begin{pmatrix} \cos(\beta) & \sin(\beta) \\ -\sin(\beta) & \cos(\beta) \end{pmatrix}, \tag{5.43}$$

where $\alpha = \tan^{-1}(\phi) = 58.28°$ and $\beta = \tan^{-1}(1/\phi) = 31.72°$.

5.8.2 Unit shears

Show that any shear contains a unit shear within it. Decompose the shear given by

$$\begin{pmatrix} 1 & 0 \\ h & 1 \end{pmatrix}$$

into the product of a scaling, a unit shear, and another scaling.

5.8.3 Seeing it graphically

Drawing upon the ideas in Exercise 5.8.1, draw a rectangle on graph paper, rotate it through $-58.28°$, scale it by $(\phi, 1/\phi)$, and finally, rotate it through $31.72°$. Sketch each intermediate result, and show that the final result is the same parallelogram that is obtained when the original rectangle undergoes a unit shear.

5.8.4 Decompose a transformation

Decompose the transformation

$$Q_x = 3P_x - 2P_y + 5,$$
$$Q_y = 4P_x + P_y - 6,$$

into a product of rotations, scalings, and translations.

5.8.5 One reflection can always be in the x-axis

Show that a rotation through an angle A about the origin may always be effected by a reflection in the x-axis followed by a reflection in a line at an angle $A/2$.

5.8.6 Isometries

The **isometries** ("same measure") are a particularly important family of affine transformations in the study of symmetry, since they don't alter the distance between two points and their images. For any two points P and Q, the distance $|T(P) - T(Q)|$ is the same as the distance $|P - Q|$ when $T()$ is an isometry. Show that if $T()$ is affine with matrix M, then T is an isometry if and only if the first two rows of M, considered as vectors, are of unit length and the two rows are orthogonal.

SOLUTION:

Call $\mathbf{r} = P - Q$. Then $|T(P) - T(Q)| = |M\mathbf{r}| = |(r_x m_{11} + r_y m_{12}, r_x m_{21} + r_y m_{22})|$. Equating $|M\mathbf{r}|^2$ to $|\mathbf{r}|^2$ requires that $m_{11}^2 + m_{21}^2 = 1$, $m_{12}^2 + m_{22}^2 = 1$, and $m_{11}m_{12} + m_{22}m_{21} = 0$, as claimed.

5.8.7 Ellipses are invariant

Show that ellipses are invariant under an affine transformation. That is, if E is an ellipse and T is an affine transformation, then the image $T(E)$ of the points in E also makes an ellipse.

HINT TO SOLUTION:

Any affine transformation is a combination of rotations and scalings. When an ellipse is rotated, it is still an ellipse, so only the nonuniform scalings could destroy the ellipse. So it is necessary only to show that when an ellipse is subjected to a nonuniform scaling, it is still an ellipse.

5.8.8 What else is invariant?

Consider what class of shapes (perhaps a broader class than ellipses) is invariant under affine transformations. If the equation $f(x, y) = 0$ describes a shape, show that after transforming it with transformation T, the new shape is described by all points that satisfy $g(x, y) = f(T^{-1}(x, y)) = 0$. Then show the details of this form when T is affine. Finally, try to describe the largest class of shapes that is preserved under affine transformations.   ▪

CASE STUDY 5.4 GENERALIZED 3D SHEARS

Level of Effort: II. A shear can be more general than those discussed in Section 5.3.1. As suggested by Goldman [Goldman91], the ingredients of a shear are

- a plane through the origin having unit normal vector **m**;
- a unit vector **v** lying in the plane (and thus perpendicular to **m**); and
- an angle ϕ.

Then, as shown in Figure 5.69, point P is sheared to point Q by shifting it a certain amount in the direction **v**. The amount is proportional both to the distance at which P lies from the plane and to $\tan \phi$. Goldman shows that this shear has the matrix representation

$$M = I + \tan(\phi) \begin{pmatrix} m_x v_x & m_x v_y & m_x v_z \\ m_y v_x & m_y v_y & m_y v_z \\ m_z v_x & m_z v_y & m_z v_z \end{pmatrix}, \tag{5.44}$$

where I is the three-by-three identity matrix. Some details of the derivation of Equation (5.44) are given next.

FIGURE 5.69 Defining a shear in 3D.

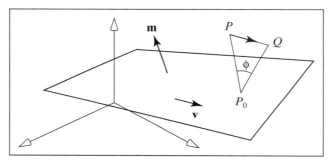

▪ EXAMPLE 5.8.2

Find the shear associated with the plane having unit normal vector $\mathbf{m} = (1, 1, 1)/\sqrt{3}$ $= (0.577, 0.577, 0.577)$, unit vector $\mathbf{v} = (0, 0.707, -0.707)$, and angle $\phi = 30°$.

SOLUTION:

Note that **v** lies in the plane, as required. (Why?) Applying Equation (5.44), we obtain

$$M = I + 0.577 \begin{pmatrix} 0 & 0.408 & -0.408 \\ 0 & 0.408 & -0.408 \\ 0 & 0.408 & -0.408 \end{pmatrix} = \begin{pmatrix} 1 & 0.235 & -0.235 \\ 0 & 1.235 & -0.235 \\ 0 & 0.235 & 0.764 \end{pmatrix}.$$

Now we derive the shear matrix. We want to express the point Q in Figure 5.69 in terms of P and the "ingredients" of the shear. The (signed) distance of P from the plane is given by $P \cdot \mathbf{m}$ (considering P as a position vector pinned to the origin). We put the ingredients together to obtain

$$Q = P + (P \cdot \mathbf{m}) \tan(\phi)\mathbf{v} \tag{5.45}$$

Note that points "on the other side" of the plane are sheared in the opposite direction, as we would expect.

Now we need to find the second term as P times some matrix. Use Appendix 2 to show that $P \cdot \mathbf{m}$ is $P\mathbf{m}^T$, and therefore that $Q = P(I + \tan(\phi)\mathbf{m}^T\mathbf{v})$. Then show that the shear matrix is $(I + \tan(\phi)\mathbf{m}^T\mathbf{v})$, where the matrix $\mathbf{m}^T\mathbf{v}$ has the form

$$\mathbf{m}^T\mathbf{v} = \begin{pmatrix} m_x \\ m_y \\ m_z \end{pmatrix}(v_x, v_y, v_z) = \begin{pmatrix} m_x v_x & m_x v_y & m_x v_z \\ m_y v_x & m_y v_y & m_y v_z \\ m_z v_x & m_z v_y & m_z v_z \end{pmatrix}. \tag{5.46}$$

This is called the **outer product** (or **tensor product**) of $\mathbf{m}$ with $\mathbf{v}$.

PRACTICE EXERCISES

5.8.9 Consistency with a simple shear

Express the matrix for the shear associated with the direction $\mathbf{v} = (1, 0, 0)$ and the plane having normal vector $(0, 1, 0)$. Show that this is a form of the elementary shear matrix given in Equation (5.45), for any angle ϕ.

5.8.10 Find the shear

Compute the shear matrix for the shear that uses a normal $\mathbf{m} = 0.577(1, -1, 1)$, direction vector $\mathbf{v} = 0.707(1, 1, 0)$, and angle $\phi = 45°$. Sketch the vectors and plane involved, and sketch how a cube centered at the origin with edges aligned with the coordinate axes is affected by the shear.

5.8.11 How is a three-dimensional shear like a two-dimensional translation in homogeneous coordinates?

Consider the specific shear

$$Q\begin{pmatrix} 1 & 0 & t & 0 \\ 0 & 1 & s & 0 \\ 0 & 0 & 1 & 0 \\ 0 & 0 & 0 & 1 \end{pmatrix}P, \tag{5.47}$$

which alters the 3D point P by shearing it along x with factor t, owing to z, and along y with factor s, also owing to z. If P lies in the $z = 1$ plane with coordinates $P = (P_x, P_y, 1)$, show that P is transformed into $(P_x + t, P_y + s, 1)$. Hence, it is simply shifted in x by the amount t and in y by the amount s. Show also that, for any point in the $z = 1$ plane, the shear is equivalent to a translation. Finally, show that the upper left three by three matrix in Equation (5.47) is identical to the homogeneous coordinate form for a pure translation in two dimensions. Understanding this identity helps reinforce how homogeneous coordinates operate. ■

CASE STUDY 5.5 ROTATION ABOUT AN AXIS: THE CONSTRUCTIVE APPROACH

Level of Effort: II. In this case study, you are asked to fill in the details of the following derivation of the rotation matrix $R_\mathbf{u}(\beta)$ of Equation 5.33. For simplicity, we assume that $\mathbf{u}$ is a unit vector: $|\mathbf{u}| = 1$. Denote the position vector based on P by the name $\mathbf{p}$, so that $\mathbf{p} = P - O$, where O is the origin of the coordinate system. Now project $\mathbf{p}$ onto $\mathbf{u}$ to obtain vector $\mathbf{h}$, as shown in Figure 5.29a.

a. Show that $\mathbf{h}$ has the form $(\mathbf{p} \cdot \mathbf{u})\mathbf{u}$. Define two perpendicular vectors $\mathbf{a} = \mathbf{p} - \mathbf{h}$ and $\mathbf{b} = \mathbf{u} \times \mathbf{a}$ that lie in the plane of rotation.
b. Show that $\mathbf{a}$ and $\mathbf{b}$ are perpendicular, they have the same length, that they both lie in the plane of rotation, and that $\mathbf{b} = \mathbf{u} \times (\mathbf{p} - \mathbf{h})$ simplifies to $\mathbf{u} \times \mathbf{p}$. This effectively establishes a 2D coordinate system in the plane of rotation. Now look onto the plane of rotation, as in Figure 5.29b. The rotation operation rotates $\mathbf{a}$ to $\mathbf{a}' = \cos\beta\,\mathbf{a} + \sin\beta\,\mathbf{b}$, so the rotated point

$Q = \mathbf{h} + \cos\beta\,\mathbf{a} + \sin\beta\,\mathbf{b},$

or, using the foregoing expressions for $\mathbf{a}$ and $\mathbf{b}$,

$$Q = \mathbf{p}\cos\beta + (1 - \cos\beta)(\mathbf{p}\cdot\mathbf{u})\mathbf{u} + \sin\beta(\mathbf{u}\times\mathbf{p}). \qquad (5.48)$$

This is a rather general result, showing how the rotated point Q can be decomposed into portions along $\mathbf{h}$ and along two orthogonal axes lying in the plane of rotation.

The form for Q shown in Equation (5.48) hardly looks like the multiplication of P by some matrix, but it is because each of the three terms is linear in $\mathbf{p}$. Convert each of the terms to the proper form as follows:

c. Replace $\mathbf{p}$ with P to immediately obtain $\mathbf{p}(\cos\beta) = I(\cos\beta)P$, where I is the three-by-three identity matrix.

d. Use the result (see Appendix 2) that a dot product $\mathbf{p}\cdot\mathbf{u}$ can be rewritten as P times a matrix: $(\mathbf{u}^T P)$ to show that $(\mathbf{p}\cdot\mathbf{u})\mathbf{u} = \mathbf{u}^T\mathbf{u}P$, where $\mathbf{u}^T\mathbf{u}$ is an outer product similar to Equation 5.46.

e. Use the fact developed in Appendix 2 that a cross product $\mathbf{u}\times\mathbf{p}$ can also be written as P times a matrix to show that $\mathbf{u}\times\mathbf{p} = \mathrm{Cross}(\mathbf{u})P$, where the matrix

$$\mathrm{Cross}(\mathbf{u}) = \begin{pmatrix} 0 & u_z & -u_y \\ -u_z & 0 & u_x \\ u_y & -u_x & 0 \end{pmatrix}. \qquad (5.49)$$

f. Put these terms together to obtain the matrix[16]

$$M = \cos\beta I + (1 - \cos\beta)\mathbf{u}^T\mathbf{u} + \sin\beta\,\mathrm{Cross}(\mathbf{u}) \qquad (5.50)$$

M is therefore the sum of three weighted matrices, which surely is easier to build than the product of five matrices, as in the classic route.

g. Write out Equation (5.50) to obtain Equation 5.33.

CASE STUDY 5.6 DECOMPOSING 3D AFFINE TRANSFORMATIONS

Level of Effort: III. This case study looks at several broad families of affine tansformations.

What Is in a 3D Affine Transformation?

Once again, we ignore the translation portion of an affine transformation and focus on the linear-transformation part represented by the 3×3 matrix M. What kind of transformations are "imbedded" in M? Goldman [Goldman92b] shows that every such M is the product of a scaling S, a rotation R, and two shears H_1 and H_2; that is,

$$M = SRH_1H_2. \qquad (5.51)$$

Every 3D affine transformation, then, can be viewed as this sequence of elementary operations, followed by a translation. In this case study, we explore the mathematics behind the form shown in Equation (5.51) and see how an actual decomposition might be carried out.

Useful Classes of Transformations

It is useful to categorize affine transformations according to what they do or do not do to certain properties of an object when it is transformed. We know that such transformations always preserve parallelism of the edges of an object, but which transformations also preserve the length of each edge, and which ones preserve the angles between each pair of edges?

Rigid-Body Motions It is intuitively clear that translating an object or rotating it will not change its shape or size. In addition, reflecting the object about a plane has no effect on its shape or size. Since the shape is not affected by any one of these transformations alone, it is also not affected by an arbitrary composition of them. We denote by

$T_{\mathrm{rigid}} = \{\text{rotations, reflections, translations}\}$

---

[16] Goldman [Goldman90] reports the same form for M and gives compact results for several other complex transformations.

the collection of all affine transformations that consist of any sequence of rotations, reflections, and translations. These are known classically as the **rigid-body motions**, since a rigid object is moved from one position and orientation to another. Such transformations have *orthogonal* matrices in homogeneous coordinates. These are matrices for which the inverse is the same as the transpose:

$$\tilde{M}^{-1} = \tilde{M}^T.$$

Angle-Preserving Transformations A uniform scaling (having equal scale factors $S_x = S_y = S_z$) expands or shrinks an object, but does so uniformly, so there is no change in the object's shape. Thus, the angle between any two edges is unaffected. We can denote such a class of transformations as

$$T_{\text{angle}} = \{\text{rotations, reflections, translations, uniform scalings}\}.$$

This class is larger than the class of rigid-body motions, since it includes uniform scaling. It is also an important class because, as we shall see in Chapter 8, calculations of lighting and shading depend on the dot products between various vectors. If a certain transformation does not alter angles, then it does not alter dot products, and lighting calculations can take place in either the transformed or the untransformed space.

Decomposing a 3D Affine Transformation Given a 3D affine transformation $\{M, \mathbf{d}\}$, we wish to see how it is composed of a sequence of elementary transformations. Following Goldman [Goldman92], we develop the steps required to decompose the three-by-three matrix M into the product of a scaling S, a rotation R, and two shears H_1 and H_2 [Equation (5.51)].

You are asked to verify each step along the way and to develop a routine that will produce the individual matrices S, R, H_1 and H_2.

Suppose the matrix M has rows $\mathbf{u}, \mathbf{v}$, and $\mathbf{w}$, each a 3D vector; that is,

$$M = \begin{pmatrix} \mathbf{u} \\ \mathbf{v} \\ \mathbf{w} \end{pmatrix}.$$

Goldman's approach is based on the classical Gram–Schmidt orthogonalization procedure, whereby the rows of M are combined in such a way that they become mutually orthogonal and of unit length. The matrix composed of these rows is therefore orthogonal and so represents a rotation (or a rotation with a reflection). Goldman shows that the orthogonalization process is in fact two shears. The rest is detail. Carefully perform each of the following of Goldman's steps, and do each of the tasks given in parentheses.

1. Normalize $\mathbf{u}$ to $\mathbf{u}^* = \mathbf{u}/S_1$, where $S_1 = |\mathbf{u}|$.
2. Subtract a piece of $\mathbf{u}^*$ from $\mathbf{v}$ so that what is left is orthogonal to $\mathbf{u}^*$. Let $\mathbf{b} = \mathbf{v} - d\mathbf{u}^*$, where $d = \mathbf{v} \cdot \mathbf{u}^*$. (Show that $\mathbf{b} \cdot \mathbf{u}^* = 0$.)
3. Normalize $\mathbf{b}$: Set $\mathbf{v}^* = \mathbf{b}/S_2$, where $S_2 = |\mathbf{b}|$.
4. Set up some intermediate values: $m = \mathbf{w} \cdot \mathbf{u}^*$, $n = \mathbf{w} \cdot \mathbf{v}^*$, $e = \sqrt{m^2 + n^2}$, and $\mathbf{r} = (m\mathbf{u}^* + n\mathbf{v}^*)/e$.
5. Subtract a piece of $\mathbf{r}$ from $\mathbf{w}$ so that what is left is orthogonal to both $\mathbf{u}^*$ and $\mathbf{v}^*$. Call $\mathbf{c} = \mathbf{w} - e\mathbf{r}$. (Show that $\mathbf{c} \cdot \mathbf{u}^* = \mathbf{c} \cdot \mathbf{v}^* = 0$.)
6. Normalize $\mathbf{c}$: Set $\mathbf{w}^* = \mathbf{c}/S_3$, where $S_3 = |\mathbf{c}|$.
7. The matrix

$$R = \begin{pmatrix} \mathbf{u}^* \\ \mathbf{v}^* \\ \mathbf{w}^* \end{pmatrix}$$

is therefore orthogonal and so represents a rotation. (Compute its determinant: If it is -1, then simply replace $\mathbf{w}^*$ with $-\mathbf{w}^*$.)

8. Define the shear matrix $H_1 = I + \left(\dfrac{d}{S_2}\right)(\mathbf{v}^* \otimes \mathbf{u}^*)$, where $(\mathbf{v}^* \otimes \mathbf{u}^*) = (\mathbf{v}^*)^T \mathbf{u}^*$ is the outer product of $\mathbf{v}^*$ and $\mathbf{u}^*$.

9. Define the shear matrix $H_2 = I + \left(\dfrac{e}{S_3}\right)(\mathbf{w}^* \otimes \mathbf{r})$, where $(\mathbf{w}^* \otimes \mathbf{r}) = (\mathbf{w}^*)^T \mathbf{r}$.

10. Show that $\mathbf{u}^*H_1 = \mathbf{u}^*, \mathbf{v}^*H_1 = \mathbf{v}^* + d\mathbf{u}^*/S_2 = \mathbf{v}/S_2$, and $\mathbf{w}^* H_1 = \mathbf{w}^*$. First show the property of the outer product that, for any vectors $\mathbf{a}, \mathbf{b}$, and $\mathbf{c}, \mathbf{a}(\mathbf{b} \otimes \mathbf{c}) = (\mathbf{a} \cdot \mathbf{b})\mathbf{c}$. Then use this property, along with the orthogonality of $\mathbf{u}^*, \mathbf{v}^*$, and $\mathbf{w}^*$, to show that the three relations hold.

11. Show that $\mathbf{u}^*H_2 = \mathbf{u}^*, \mathbf{v}^*H_2 = \mathbf{v}^*$, and $\mathbf{w}^*H_2 = \mathbf{w}^* + e\mathbf{r}/S_3 = \mathbf{w}/S_3$.

12. Put these intermediate results together to show that $M = SRH_1H_2$, where

$$S = \begin{pmatrix} S_1 & 0 & 0 \\ 0 & S_2 & 0 \\ 0 & 0 & S_3 \end{pmatrix}.$$

Note that the decomposition is not unique, since the vectors $\mathbf{u}, \mathbf{v}$, and $\mathbf{w}$ could be orthogonalized in a different order. For instance, we could first form $\mathbf{w}^*$ as $\mathbf{w}/|\mathbf{w}|$, then subtract a piece of $\mathbf{v}$ from $\mathbf{w}^*$ to make a vector orthogonal to $\mathbf{w}^*$, and then subtract a vector from $\mathbf{u}$ to make a vector orthogonal to the other two.

Write the routine

```
void decompose(DBL m[3][3],DBL S[3][3],DBL R[3][3],DBL
H1[3][3],DBL H2[3][3])
```

which takes matrix M and computes the matrices S, R, H_1 and H_2 as described in Goldman's 12 steps. `DBL` is defined as `double`. Test your routine on several matrices.

Other ways to decompose a 3D transformation have been found as well. See, for instance, [Thomas91 and Shoemake94].

CASE STUDY 5.7 DRAWING 3D SCENES DESCRIBED BY SDL

Level of Effort: II. Develop a complete application that uses the `Scene`, `Shape`, `Affine4`, etc., classes and supports reading in and drawing the scene described in an SDL file. To assist you, use any classes provided on the book's Web site. Flesh out any `drawOpenGL()` methods that are needed. Develop a scene file that contains descriptions of the jack, a wooden chair, and several walls.

5.9 FURTHER READING

Among the several excellent books on transformations that supplement the treatment given here are George Martin's superb *Transformation Geometry* [Martin82] and Yaglom's *Geometric Transformations* [Yaglom62]. Hogar also provides a fine chapter on vectors and transformations [Hoggar92]. Several of Blinn's engaging articles in *Jim Blinn's Corner: A Trip down the Graphics Pipeline* [Blinn96] provide excellent discussions of homogeneous coordinates and transformations in computer graphics.

6 Modeling Shapes with Polygonal Meshes

Try to learn something about everything and everything about something.

T. H. Huxley

Goals of the Chapter

▲ To develop tools for working with objects in 3D space.

▲ To represent solid objects using polygonal meshes.

▲ To draw simple wire-frame views of mesh objects.

PREVIEW

In this chapter, we examine ways to describe 3D objects by using polygonal meshes. Section 6.1 gives an overview of the 3D modeling process. Section 6.2 describes polygonal meshes that allow one to capture the shape of complex 3D objects in simple data structures. The properties of such meshes are reviewed, and algorithms are presented for viewing the associated objects.

Section 6.3 describes families of interesting 3D shapes, such as the Platonic solids, the buckyball, geodesic domes, and prisms. Section 6.4 examines the family of extruded or "swept" shapes and shows how to create 3D letters for flying logos, tubes, "snakes" that undulate through space, and surfaces of revolution.

Section 6.5 discusses building meshes to model solids that have smoothly curved surfaces. The meshes approximate some smooth "underlying" surface. A key ingredient is the computation of the normal vector to the underlying surface at any point. Several interesting families of smooth solids are discussed, including quadric and superquadric surfaces, ruled surfaces and Coons patches, explicit functions of two variables, and surfaces of revolution.

The case studies at the end of the chapter explore many ideas further and request that you develop applications to test things out. Some of the case studies are theoretical in nature, such as deriving the Newell formula for computing a normal vector and examining the algebraic form for quadric surfaces. Others are more practical— for example, reading mesh data from a file and creating beautiful 3D shapes like tubes and arches.

287

6.1 INTRODUCTION

Polygonal meshes are simply collections of polygons, or "faces," that together form the "skin" of an object. They have become a standard way of representing a broad class of solid shapes in graphics. We have seen several examples, such as the cube and the icosahedron, as well as approximations of smooth shapes like the sphere, cylinder, and cone. In this chapter, we shall see many more examples. Their prominence in graphics stems from the simplicity of using polygons, which are easy to represent (by a sequence of vertices) and transform, have simple properties (a single normal vector, a well-defined inside and outside, etc.), and are easy to draw (using a polygon-fill routine or by mapping texture onto the polygon).

Many rendering systems, including OpenGL, are based on drawing objects by drawing a sequence of polygons. Each polygonal face is sent through the graphics pipeline where its vertices undergo various transformations, until, finally, the portion of the face that survives clipping is colored in, or "shaded," and shown on the display device.

We want to see how to design complicated 3D shapes by defining an appropriate set of faces. Some objects can be perfectly represented by a polygonal mesh, whereas others can only be approximated. The barn of Figure 6.1(a), for example, naturally has flat faces, and in a rendering, the edges between the faces should be visible. But the cylinder in Figure 6.1(b) is supposed to have a smoothly rounded wall. This roundness cannot be achieved with polygons alone: The individual flat faces are quite visible, as are the edges between them. There are, however, rendering techniques that make a mesh like this *appear* to be smooth, as in Figure 6.1(c). We examine the details of so-called Gouraud shading in Chapter 8.

FIGURE 6.1 Various shapes modeled by meshes.

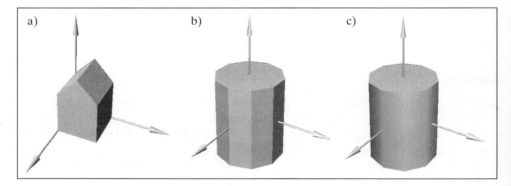

We begin by describing polygonal meshes in some generality and seeing how to define and manipulate them in a program (with or without OpenGL). We apply these ideas to modeling polyhedra, which inherently have flat faces, and study a number of interesting families of polyhedra. We then tackle the problem of using a mesh to approximate a smoothly curved shape and develop the necessary tools to create and manipulate such models.

6.2 INTRODUCTION TO SOLID MODELING WITH POLYGONAL MESHES

I never forget a face, but in your case I'll make an exception.

Groucho Marx

We shall use meshes to model both solid shapes and thin "skins." The object is considered to be **solid** if the polygonal faces fit together to enclose a space. In other cases the faces fit together without enclosing a space, so they represent an infinitesimally thick surface. In both cases, we call the collection of polygons a **polygonal mesh** (or simply **mesh**).

A polygonal mesh is given by a list of polygons, along with information about the direction in which each polygon is "facing." This directional information is often simply the **normal vector** to the plane of the face, and it is used in the shading process to determine how much light from a light source is scattered off the face. Figure 6.2 shows the normal vectors for various faces of a barn. As we examine the subject in detail in Chapter 8, we shall see that one component of the brightness of a face is assumed to be proportional to the cosine of the angle (shown as θ in the figure for the sidewall of the barn) between the normal vector to a face and the vector to the light source. Thus, the orientation of a surface with respect to light sources plays an important part in the final drawing.

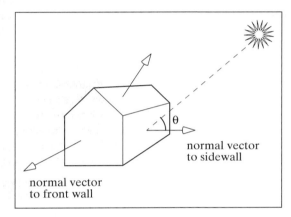

FIGURE 6.2 The normal direction to a face determines its brightness.

Vertex Normals Versus Face Normals

It turns out to be highly advantageous to associate a "normal vector" with each vertex of a face, rather than one vector to an entire face. As we shall see, this practice facilitates the clipping process, as well as the shading process for smoothly curved shapes. For flat surfaces such as the wall of a barn, each of the vertices V_1, V_2, V_3, and V_4 that define the sidewalls of the barn will be associated with the *same* normal $\mathbf{n}_1$, the normal vector to the sidewall itself. [See Figure 6.3(a).] But vertices of the front wall, such as V_5, will use normal $\mathbf{n}_2$. (Note that vertices V_1 and V_5 are located at the same point in space, but use different normals.)

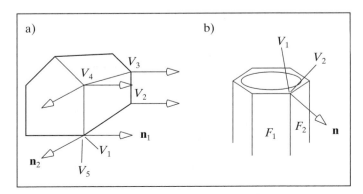

FIGURE 6.3 Associating a "normal" with each vertex of each face.

For a smoothly curved surface such as the cylinder in Figure 6.3(b), a different approach is used in order to permit shading that makes the surface appear smooth. Both vertex V_1 of face F_1 and vertex V_2 of face F_2 use the same normal **n**, which is the vector perpendicular to the underlying smooth surface. We see how to compute this vector conveniently in Section 6.2.2.

6.2.1 Defining a Polygonal Mesh

A polygonal mesh is a collection of polygons, along with a normal vector associated with each vertex of each polygon. We begin with an example.

■ **EXAMPLE 6.2.1 The "basic barn"**

Figure 6.4 shows a simple shape we call the "basic barn." It has seven polygonal faces and a total of 10 vertices (each of which is shared by three faces). For convenience, it has a square floor one unit on a side. (The barn would be scaled and oriented appropriately before being placed in a scene.) Because the barn is assumed to have flat walls, there are only seven distinct normal vectors involved: the normal to each face, as shown.

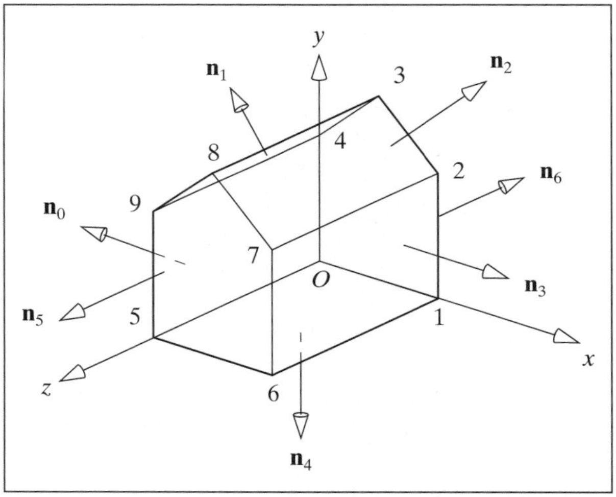

FIGURE 6.4 Introducing the "basic barn."

There are various ways to store information about a mesh in a file or program. For the barn, you could use a list of seven polygons and list, for each one, where its vertices are located and where the normal for each of its vertices is pointing (a total of 30 vertices and 30 normals). But this structure would be quite redundant and bulky, since there are only 10 distinct vertices and seven distinct normals.

A more efficient approach uses three separate lists: a **vertex list**, a **normal list**, and a **face list**. The vertex list reports the locations of the distinct vertices in the mesh. The list of normals reports the directions of the distinct normal vectors that occur in the model. The face list simply indexes into the other two lists. As we shall see next, the barn is thereby captured with 10 vertices, seven normals, and a list of seven simple face descriptors.

The three lists work together: The vertex list contains locational or **geometric** information, the normal list contains **orientation** information, and the face list contains connectivity or **topological** information.

The vertex list for the barn is shown in Figure 6.5. The list of the seven distinct normals is shown in Figure 6.6. The vertices have indices 0 through 9, and the nor-

vertex	x	y	z
0	0	0	0
1	1	0	0
2	1	1	0
3	0.5	1.5	0
4	0	1	0
5	0	0	1
6	1	0	1
7	1	1	1
8	0.5	1.5	1
9	0	1	1

FIGURE 6.5 Vertex list for the basic barn.

normal	n_x	n_y	n_z
0	−1	0	0
1	−0.707	0.707	0
2	0.707	0.707	0
3	1	0	0
4	0	−1	0
5	0	0	1
6	0	0	−1

FIGURE 6.6 The list of distinct normal vectors involved.

mals have indices 0 through 6. The vectors shown have already been normalized, since most shading algorithms require unit vectors. (Recall that a cosine can be found as the dot product between two unit vectors.)

Figure 6.7 shows the barn's face list: Each face has a list of vertices and the normal vector associated with each vertex. To save space, just the indices of the proper vertices and normals are used. (Since each surface is flat, all of the vertices in a face are associated with the same normal.) The list of vertices for each face begins with any vertex in the face and then proceeds around the face vertex by vertex, until a complete circuit has been made. There are two ways to traverse a polygon: clockwise and counterclockwise. For instance, face #5 could be listed as (5, 6, 7, 8, 9) or (9, 8, 7, 6, 5). Either direction could be used, but we follow a convention that proves handy in practice:

Traverse the polygon counterclockwise as seen from outside the object.

Using this order, if you traverse the face by walking on the outside surface from vertex to vertex, the interior of the face is on your left. We later design algorithms that exploit such an ordering. Because of it, the algorithms are able to distinguish with ease the "front" from the "back" of a face.

face	vertices	associated normal
0 (left)	0,5,9,4	0,0,0,0
1 (roof left)	3,4,9,8	1,1,1,1
2 (roof right)	2,3,8,7	2,2,2,2
3 (right)	1,2,7,6	3,3,3,3
4 (bottom)	0,1,6,5	4,4,4,4
5 (front)	5,6,7,8,9	5,5,5,5,5
6 (back)	0,4,3,2,1	6,6,6,6,6

FIGURE 6.7 Face list for the basic barn.

The barn is an example of a "data-intensive" model, in which the position of each vertex is entered (maybe by hand) by the designer. In contrast, later we shall see some models that are generated algorithmically. It isn't too hard to come up with the vertices for the basic barn: The designer chooses a simple unit square for the floor, decides to put one corner of the barn at the origin, and chooses a roof height of 1.5 units. By suitable scaling, these dimensions can be altered later (although the relative height of the wall to the barn's peak, 1:1.5, is forever fixed).

6.2.2 Finding the Normal Vectors

It may be possible to set vertex positions by hand, but it is not so easy to calculate the normal vectors. In general, each face will have three or more vertices, and a designer would find it challenging to jot down the normal vector. It is best to let the computer calculate the normal vectors during the creation of the mesh model.

If the face is considered flat, as in the case of the barn, we need only find the normal vector to the face itself and associate it with each of the face's vertices. One direct way to do this uses the vector cross product to find the normal, as in Figure 4.16. We take any three adjacent points on the face, say, V_1, V_2, and V_3, and compute the normal as the cross product $\mathbf{m} = (V_1 - V_2) \times (V_3 - V_2)$. The normal vector can then be normalized to unit length.

There are two problems with this simple approach: First, if the two vectors $V_1 - V_2$ and $V_3 - V_2$ are nearly parallel, the cross product will be very small (why?), and numerical inaccuracies may result. Second, as we shall see later, it may turn out that the polygon is not perfectly planar—that is, that not all of the vertices lie in the same plane. Thus, the surface represented by the vertices cannot be truly flat. In that case, we need to form some "average" value for the normal to the polygon, one that takes all of the vertices into consideration.

A robust method that solves both of these problems was devised by Martin Newell. The method computes the components m_x, m_y, and m_z of the normal $\mathbf{m}$ according to the formulas

$$m_x = \sum_{i=0}^{N-1} (y_i - y_{\text{next}(i)})(z_i + z_{\text{next}(i)}),$$

$$m_y = \sum_{i=0}^{N-1} (z_i - z_{\text{next}(i)})(x_i + x_{\text{next}(i)}), \tag{6.1}$$

and

$$m_z = \sum_{i=0}^{N-1} (x_i - x_{\text{next}(i)})(y_i + y_{\text{next}(i)}),$$

where N is the number of vertices in the face, (x_i, y_i, z_i) is the position of the ith vertex, and $\text{next}(j) = (j + 1) \bmod N$ is the index of the "next" vertex around the face after vertex j, in order to take care of the "wrap-around" from the $(N - 1)$st to the zeroth vertex. The computation requires only one multiplication per edge for each of the components of the normal, and no testing for collinearity is needed. This result is developed in Case Study 6.2, and C++ code is presented for it. The vector $\mathbf{m}$ computed by the Newell method could point toward the inside or toward the outside of the polygon. Accordingly, we also show in the case study that if the vertices of the polygon are traversed (as i increases) in a CCW direction as seen from outside the polygon, then $\mathbf{m}$ points toward the outside of the face.

■ **EXAMPLE 6.2.2**

Consider the polygon with vertices $P_0 = (6, 1, 4)$, $P_1 = (7, 0, 9)$, and $P_2 = (1, 1, 2)$. Find the normal to this polygon using the Newell method.

SOLUTION:

Direct use of the cross product gives $((7, 0, 9) - (6, 1, 4)) \times ((1, 1, 2) - (6, 1, 4)) = (2, -23, -5)$. Application of the Newell method yields the same result: $(2, -23, -5)$.

PRACTICE EXERCISES

6.2.1 Using the Newell method

For the three vertices $(6, 1, 4)$, $(2, 0, 5)$, and $(7, 0, 9)$, compare the normal found using the Newell method with that found using the usual cross product. Then use the Newell method to find (n_x, n_y, n_z) for the polygon having vertices $(1, 1, 2)$, $(2, 0, 5)$, $(5, 1, 4)$, and $(6, 0, 7)$. Is the polygon planar? If so, find its true normal using the cross product, and compare the true normal with the result of the Newell method.

6.2.2 What about a nonplanar polygon?

Consider the quadrilateral shown in Figure 6.8 with vertices $(0, 0, 0)$, $(1, 0, 0)$, $(0, 0, 1)$, and $(1, a, 1)$. When a is nonzero, the quadrilateral is a nonplanar polygon. Find the "normal" to the polygon by using the Newell method, and discuss how good an estimate it is for different values of a.

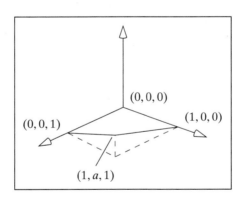

FIGURE 6.8 A nonplanar polygon.

6.2.3 Represent the "generic cube"

Make vertex, normal, and face lists for the "generic cube," which is centered at the origin, has its edges aligned with the coordinate axes, and has edges of length two. Thus, its eight vertices lie at the eight possible combinations of " + " and " − " in $(\pm1, \pm1, \pm1)$.

6.2.4 Faces with holes

Figure 6.9 shows how a face containing a hole can be captured in a face list. A pair of imaginary edges are added that bridge the gap between the circumference of the face and the hole, as suggested in the figure.

The face is traversed so that (when one walks along the outside surface) the interior of the face lies to the left. Thus, a hole is traversed in the CW direction. Assuming that we are looking at the face in the figure from its outside, the list of vertices would be 5, 4, 3, 8, 9, 6, 7, 8, 3, 2, 1. Sketch the face with an additional hole in it, and give the proper list of vertices for the face. What normals would be associated with each vertex?

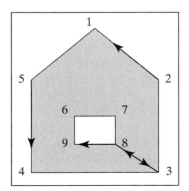

FIGURE 6.9 A face containing a hole.

6.2.3 Properties of Meshes

Given a mesh consisting of vertex, normal, and face lists, we might wonder what kind of an object the mesh represents. The following are some properties of interest:

- **Solidity.** As mentioned earlier, a mesh represents a solid object if its faces together enclose a positive and finite amount of space.
- **Connectedness.** A mesh is **connected** if an unbroken path along polygon edges exists between any two vertices. (If a mesh is not connected, it is usually considered to represent more than one object.)
- **Simplicity.** A mesh is **simple** if the object it represents is solid and has no holes through it; that is, the object can be deformed into a sphere without tearing. (Note that the term "simple" is being used here in quite a different sense than when it is applied to a polygon.)
- **Planarity.** A mesh is planar if every face of the object it represents is a **planar** polygon: The vertices of each face then lie in a single plane. Some graphics algorithms work much more efficiently if a face is planar. Triangles are inherently planar, and some modeling software takes advantage of that fact by using only triangles. Quadrilaterals, on the other hand, may or may not be planar. The quadrilateral in Figure 6.8, for instance, is planar if and only if $a = 0$.
- **Convexity.** The mesh represents a **convex** object if the line connecting any two points within the object lies wholly inside the object. Convexity was first discussed in Section 2.3.6 in connection with polygons. Figure 6.10 shows some convex and some nonconvex objects. For each nonconvex object, a sample line is shown whose endpoints lie in the object, but that is not itself contained within the object.

FIGURE 6.10 Examples of convex and nonconvex 3D objects.

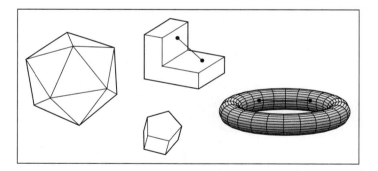

The basic barn happens to possess all of these properties. (Check this!) For a given mesh, some of these properties are easy to determine in a program, in the sense that a simple algorithm exists that does the job. (We discuss some of these algorithms later.) Other properties, such as solidity, are quite difficult to establish.

The polygonal meshes we choose to use to model objects in graphics may have some or all of the aforementioned properties: The choice depends on how one is going to use the mesh. If the mesh is supposed to represent a physical object made of some material, perhaps to determine its mass or center of gravity, we may insist that it be at least connected and solid. If we just want to draw the object, however, much greater freedom is available, since many objects can still be drawn, even if they are "nonphysical."

Figure 6.11 shows some examples of objects we might wish to represent by meshes. PYRAMID is made up of triangular faces, which are necessarily planar. Not only is PYRAMID convex; in fact, it has all of the foregoing properties. DONUT is con-

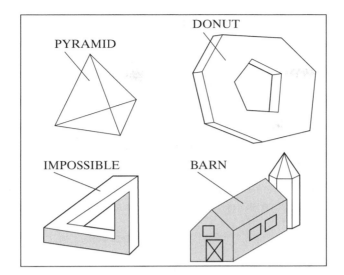

FIGURE 6.11 Examples of solids to be described by meshes.

nected and solid, but is neither simple (there is a hole through it) nor convex. Two of its faces themselves have holes. Whether or not donut's faces are planar polygons cannot be determined from the figure alone. Later we give an algorithm for determining planarity from the face and vertex lists.

IMPOSSIBLE cannot exist in space. Can it really be represented by a mesh? BARN seems to be made up of two parts, but it could be contained in a single mesh. Whether it is connected would then depend on how the faces were defined at the juncture between the silo and the main building. BARN also illustrates a situation often encountered in graphics: Some faces have been added to the mesh that represent windows and doors, to provide "texture" to the object. For instance, the side of the barn is a rectangle with no holes in it, but two squares have been added to the mesh to represent windows. These squares are made to lie in the same plane as the side of the barn. The mesh, then, is not connected, but it can still be displayed on a graphics device.

6.2.4 Mesh Models for Nonsolid Objects

Figure 6.12 shows examples of other objects that can be characterized by polygonal meshes. These objects are surfaces, and are best thought of as infinitesimally thick "shells."

BOX is an open box whose lid has been raised. In a graphics context, we might want to color the outside of BOX's six faces blue and their insides green. (What is obtained if we remove one face from PYRAMID in Figure 6.11?)

FIGURE 6.12 Some surfaces describable by meshes. [Part (c) is courtesy of the University of Utah.]

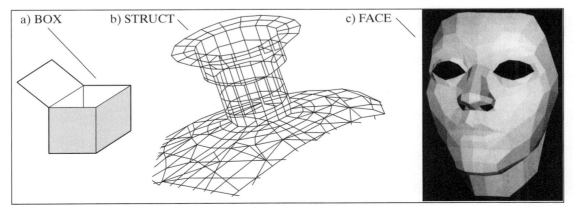

Two complex surfaces, STRUCT and FACE, are also shown. In these examples, the polygonal faces are being used to approximate a smooth underlying surface. In some situations the mesh may be all that is available for the object, perhaps from digitizing points on a person's face. If each face of the mesh is drawn as a shaded polygon, the picture will look artificial, as seen with FACE. Later we shall examine tools that attempt to draw the smooth underlying surface only on the basis of the mesh model.

Many geometric modeling software packages construct a model from some object—a solid or a surface—that tries to capture the true shape of the object in a polygonal mesh. The problem of composing the lists of vertices, normals, and faces can be difficult. As an example, consider creating an algorithm that generates vertex and face lists to approximate the shape of an engine block, a prosthetic limb, or a building. By using a sufficient number of faces, a mesh can approximate the "underlying surface" to any degree of accuracy desired. This property of **completeness** makes polygon meshes a versatile tool for modeling.

6.2.5 Working with Meshes in a Program

We want an efficient way to capture a mesh in a program that makes it easy to create and draw the object represented by the mesh. Since mesh data are frequently stored in a file, we also need simple ways to read and write "mesh files." It is natural to define a class *Mesh* and to imbue it with the desired functionality.

FIGURE 6.13 Proposed data type for a mesh.

```
//################## VertexID ##################
class VertexID{
   public:
      int vertIndex:      // index of this vertex in the vertex list
      int normIndex;      // index of this vertex's normal
};
//#################### Face ####################
class Face{
   public:
      int nVerts;      // number of vertices in this face
      VertexID * vert;      // the list of vertex and normal indices
      Face(){nVerts = 0; vert = NULL;}      // constructor
      -Face(){delete[] vert; nVerts = 0;}      // destructor
};
//###################### Mesh ######################
class Mesh{
   private:
      int numVerts;      // number of vertices in the mesh
      Point3* pt;      // array of 3D vertices
      int numNormals;      // number of normal vectors for the mesh
      Vector3 *norm;      // array of normals
      int numFaces;      // number of faces in the mesh
      Face* face;      // array of face data
      // ... others to be added later
   public:
      Mesh();      // constructor
      ~Mesh();      // destructor
      int readFile(char * fileName);      // to read in a filed mesh
      .. others ..
};
```

Figure 6.13 shows the declaration of the class `Mesh`, along with those of two simple helper classes: `VertexID` and `Face`.[1] A `Mesh` object has a vertex list, a normal list, and a face list, represented simply by the arrays `pt`, `norm`, and `face`, respectively. These arrays are allocated dynamically at run time, when it is known how large they must be. Their lengths are stored in `numVerts`, `numNormals`, and `numFaces`, respectively. Additional data fields can be added later that describe various physical properties of the object, such as its weight and the type of material it is made of.

The `Face` data type is basically a list of vertices and the normal vector associated with each vertex in the face. It is organized here as an array of index pairs: The `v`th vertex in the `f`th face has position `pt[face[f].vert[v].vertIndex]` and normal vector `norm[face[f].vert[v].normIndex]`. This arrangement appears cumbersome at first exposure, but the indexing scheme is quite orderly and easy to manage, and it has the advantage of efficiency, allowing rapid "random-access" indexing into the `pt[]` array.

■ **EXAMPLE 6.2.3 Data for the tetrahedron**

Figure 6.14 shows a tetrahedron with vertices at $(0, 0, 0)$, $(1, 0, 0)$, $(0, 1, 0)$, and $(0, 0, 1)$, together with the data representing it. Check the values reported in each field. (We discuss how to find the normal vectors later.)

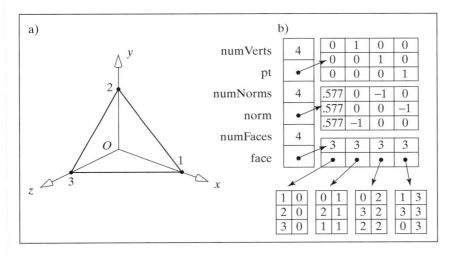

FIGURE 6.14 A tetrahedron and the data representing it.

The first task is to develop a method for drawing such a mesh object. It is a matter of drawing each of its faces, of course. An OpenGL-based implementation of the `Mesh::draw()` method must traverse the array of faces in the mesh object and, for each face, send the list of vertices and their normals down the graphics pipeline. In OpenGL, one specifies that subsequent vertices are associated with the normal vector **m** by executing `glNormal3f(m.x, m.y, m.z)`.[2] So the basic flow of `Mesh::draw()` is as follows:

---

[1] Definitions of the basic classes `Point3` and `Vertex3` have been given previously and also appear in Appendix 3.

[2] For proper shading, the normal vectors must be normalized. Otherwise, place `glEnable(GL_NORMALIZE)` in the `init()` function, which requests that OpenGL automatically normalize all normal vectors.

```
for (each face f in the mesh)
{
        glBegin (GL_POLYGON);
        for (each vertex v in face f)
        {
            glNormal3f (normal at vertex v);
            glVertex3f (position of vertex v);
        }
    glEnd();
}
```

FIGURE 6.15 Method for drawing a mesh using OpenGL.

The implementation of this algorithm is shown in Figure 6.15.

```
void Mesh:: draw()      // use OpenGL to draw this mesh
{
   for (int f = 0; f < numFaces; f++)      // draw each face
   {
      glBegin (GL_POLYGON);
         for (int v = 0; v < face[f].nVerts; v++)      // for each one..
         {
            int in = face[f].vert[v].normIndex;     // index of this normal
            int iv = face[f].vert[v].vertIndex;      // index of this vertex
            glNormal3f(norm[in].x, norm[in].y, norm[in].z);
            glVertex3f(pt[iv].x, pt[iv].y, pt[iv].z);
         }
      glEnd();
   }
}
```

We also need methods to create a particular mesh and to read a predefined mesh into memory from a file. Accordingly, we next examine a number of interesting families of shapes that can be stored in a mesh and see how to create them. (We consider reading from and writing to files in Case Study 6.1.)

Using SDL to Create and Draw a Mesh Object

It is convenient in a graphics application to read in mesh descriptions using the SDL language introduced in Chapter 5. To make this possible, we simply derive the Mesh class from Shape and add the method drawOpenGL(). Thus, Figure 6.13 is embellished to the following code:

```
class Mesh : public Shape {
      //same as in Figure 6.13
   virtual void drawOpenGL()
   {
        tellMaterialsGL(); glPushMatrix(); // load properties
        glMultMatrixf(transf.m);
        draw();   // draw the mesh
        glPopMatrix();
   }
}; //end of Mesh class
```

The Scene class that reads SDL files is already set to accept the keyword mesh, followed by the name of the file that contains the description of the mesh. Hence, to create and draw a pawn with a certain translation and scaling, we use

push translate 3 5 4 scale 3 3 3 mesh pawn.3vn pop

(A number of such files having suffix 3vn, are available on the book's Internet site.)

6.3 POLYHEDRA

It is frequently convenient to restrict the data in a mesh so that it represents a **polyhedron**. A very large number of solid objects of interest are indeed polyhedra, and algorithms for processing a mesh can be greatly simplified if they need only process meshes that represent a polyhedron.

Slightly different definitions for a polyhedron are used in different contexts [Coxeter69, Hilbert52, Foley90,], but we use the following one.

> **DEFINITION:** A **polyhedron** is a connected mesh of simple planar polygons that encloses a finite amount of space.

So, by definition, a polyhedron represents a single solid object. This entails that

- every edge is shared by exactly two faces;
- at least three edges meet at each vertex; and
- faces do not interpenetrate: Two faces either do not touch at all, or they touch only along their common edge.

In Figure 6.11, PYRAMID is clearly a polyhedron. DONUT evidently encloses a space, so it is a polyhedron if its faces are in fact planar. It is not a simple polyhedron, however, since there is a hole through it. In addition, two of its faces themselves have holes. Is IMPOSSIBLE a polyhedron? Why? If the texture faces are omitted, BARN might be modeled as two polyhedra—one for the main part and one for the silo.

Euler's Formula

Euler's formula (which is very easy to prove; see, for instance, [Courant 61]) provides a fundamental relationship between the number of faces, edges, and vertices (F, E, and V, respectively) of a simple polyhedron:

$$V + F - E = 2.$$

For example, a cube has $V = 8$, $F = 6$, and $E = 12$.

A generalization of this formula to a polyhedron that is not simple [Foley90] is

$$V + F - E = 2 + H - 2G, \tag{6.2}$$

where H is the total number of holes occurring in faces and G is the number of holes through the polyhedron. Figure 6.16(a) shows one parallelepiped constructed with a hole in the shape of another parallelepiped. The two ends are beveled off. For this object, $V = 16$, $F = 16$, $E = 32$, $H = 0$, and $G = 1$. Figure 6.16(b) shows a polyhedron having a hole A penetrating part way into it and a hole B passing through it. Here, $V = 24$, $F = 15$, $E = 36$, $H = 3$, and $G = 1$. Both sets of values satisfy Euler's formula.

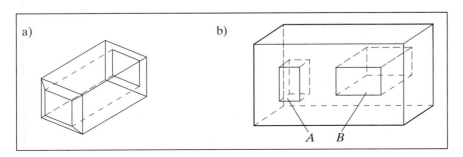

FIGURE 6.16 Polyhedron with holes.

The "structure" of a polyhedron is often nicely revealed by a **Schlegel diagram**, which is based on a view of the polyhedron from a point just outside the center of one of its faces, as suggested in Figure 6.17(a). Viewing a cube in this way produces the Schlegel diagram shown in Figure 6.17(b). The front face appears as a large polygon surrounding the rest of the faces.

FIGURE 6.17 The Schlegel diagrams for a cube.

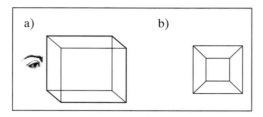

Figure 6.18 shows further examples. Part (a) is the Schlegel diagram of the object PYRAMID of Figure 6.11, and Parts (b) and (c) show two quite different Schlegel diagrams for the basic barn. (Which faces are closest to the eye?)

FIGURE 6.18 Schlegel diagrams for PYRAMID and the basic barn.

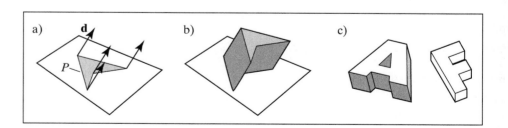

6.3.1 Prisms and Antiprisms

A prism is a particular type of polyhedron that embodies certain symmetries and therefore is quite simple to describe. As shown in Figure 6.19, a prism is defined by **sweeping** (or **extruding**) a polygon along a straight line, turning a 2D polygon into a 3D polyhedron. In Figure 6.19(a), polygon P is swept along vector $\mathbf{d}$ to form the polyhedron shown in Part (b). When $\mathbf{d}$ is perpendicular to the plane of P, the prism is a **right prism**. Figure 6.19(c) shows some block letters of the alphabet swept to form prisms.

FIGURE 6.19 Forming a prism.

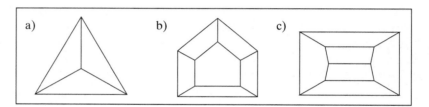

A **regular prism** has a regular polygon for its base and squares for its side faces. A hexagonal version is shown in Figure 6.20(a). A variation is the **antiprism**, shown in Figure 6.20(b). This is not an extruded object; instead, the top n-gon is rotated through $180/n$ degrees and connected to the bottom n-gon to form faces that are equilateral triangles. (How many triangular faces are there?) The regular prism and the antiprism are examples of "semiregular" polyhedra, which we examine further later.

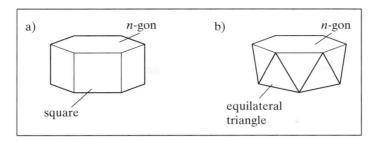

FIGURE 6.20 A regular prism and an antiprism.

PRACTICE EXERCISES

6.3.1 Build the lists for a prism

Give the vertex, normal, and face lists for the prism shown in Figure 6.21. Assume the base of the prism (face #4) lies in the xy-plane and that vertex 2 lies on the z-axis at $z = 4$. Assume further that vertex 5 lies three units along the x-axis and that the base is an equilateral triangle.

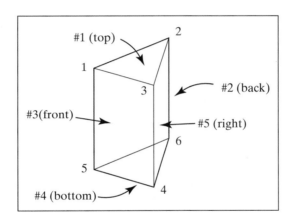

FIGURE 6.21 A sample polyhedral object.

6.3.2 The perched cube

Build vertex, normal, and face lists for any cube that has one vertex at $(0, 0, 0)$ and the opposite vertex at $(1, 1, 1)$.

6.3.3 An antiprism

Build vertex, normal, and face lists for an antiprism having a square as its top polygon.

6.3.4 Is this mesh connected?

Is the mesh defined by the list of faces $(4, 1, 3), (4, 7, 2, 1), (2, 7, 5), (3, 4, 8, 7, 9)$ connected? Try to sketch the object, choosing arbitrary positions for the nine vertices. What algorithm might be used to test a face list for connectedness?

6.3.5 Build meshes

For the DONUT, IMPOSSIBLE, and BARN objects in Figure 6.11, assign numbers to each vertex and then write a face list.

6.3.6 Schlegel diagrams

Draw Schlegel diagrams for the prisms of Figures 6.20 and 6.21.

6.3.2 The Platonic Solids

If all of the faces of a polyhedron are identical and each is a regular polygon, the object is a **regular polyhedron**. These symmetry constraints are so severe that only five such objects exist: the **Platonic solids**[3] shown in Figure 6.22 [Coxeter61]. The Platonic solids exhibit a sublime symmetry and a fascinating array of properties. They make interesting objects of study in computer graphics and often appear in solid-modeling CAD applications.

FIGURE 6.22 The five Platonic solids.

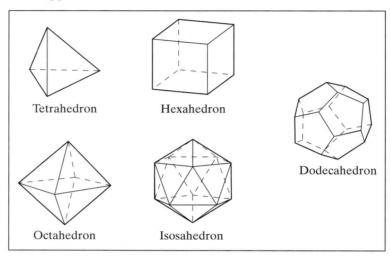

Tetrahedron   Hexahedron

Dodecahedron

Octahedron   Isosahedron

Three of the Platonic solids have equilateral triangles as faces, one has squares, and the dodecahedron has pentagons. The cube is a regular prism, and the octahedron is an antiprism. (Why?) The values of V, F, and E for each solid are shown in Figure 6.23. Also shown is the Schläfli[4] symbol (p, q) for each solid; it states that each face is a p-gon and that q of them meet at each vertex.

FIGURE 6.23 Descriptors for the Platonic solids.

Solid	V	F	E	Schläfli
Tetrahedron	4	4	6	$(3, 3)$
Hexahedron	8	6	12	$(4, 3)$
Octahedron	6	8	12	$(3, 4)$
Icosahedron	12	20	30	$(3, 5)$
Dodecahedron	20	12	30	$(5, 3)$

It is straightforward to build mesh lists for the cube and the octahedron. (See the exercises on p. 304.) We give sample vertex and face lists for the tetrahedron and icosahedron shortly and discuss how to compute normal lists. We also show how to derive the lists for the dodecahedron from those of the icosahedron, making use of the "duality" of these solids, which we define next.

---

[3]   Named in honor of Plato (427–347 B.C.), who commemorated them in his *Timaeus*. But they were known before Plato: A toy dodecahedron was found near Padua in Etruscan ruins dating from 500 B.C.

[4]   Named for L. Schläfli (1814–1895), a Swiss mathematician.

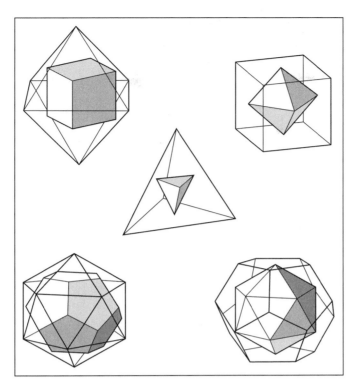

FIGURE 6.24 Dual Platonic solids.

Dual polyhedra

Each of the Platonic solids P has a **dual** polyhedron D. The vertices of D are the *centers* of the faces of P, so edges of D connect the midpoints of adjacent faces of P. Figure 6.24 shows the dual of each Platonic solid inscribed within it. The following list reports some solids that are duals:

- The dual of a tetrahedron is also a tetrahedron.
- The cube and octahedron are duals.
- The icosahedron and dodecahedron are duals.

Duals have the same number E of edges, and V for one is F for the other. In addition, if (p, q) is the Schläfli symbol for one dual, then (q, p) is the Schläfli symbol for the other.

If we know the vertex list of one Platonic solid P, we can immediately build the vertex list of its dual D, since vertex k of D lies at the center of face k of P. Building D in this way actually builds a version that inscribes P.

To keep track of vertex and face numbering, we use a **model**, which is fashioned by slicing along certain edges of each solid and "unfolding" it to lie flat, so that all the faces are seen from the outside. Models for three of the Platonic solids are shown in Figure 6.25.

Consider the dual pair of the cube and the octahedron. Face 4 of the cube is seen to be surrounded by vertices 1, 5, 6, and 2. So, by duality, vertex 4 of the octahedron is surrounded by faces 1, 5, 6, and 2. Note that since the tetrahedron is self-dual, the list of vertices surrounding the kth face is identical to the list of faces surrounding the kth vertex.

The position of vertex 4 of the octahedron is the center of face 4 of the cube. Recall from Chapter 4 that the center of a face is just the *average* of the vertices belonging to that face. So if we know the vertices V_1, V_5, V_6, and V_2 for face 4 of the cube, we immediately have

$$V_4 = \frac{1}{4}(V_1 + V_5 + V_6 + V_2). \tag{6.3}$$

FIGURE 6.25 Models for the tetrahedron, cube, and octahedron.

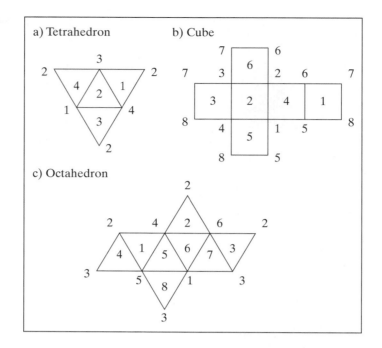

a) Tetrahedron   b) Cube

c) Octahedron

PRACTICE EXERCISES

6.3.7 The octahedron

Consider the octahedron that is the dual of the cube. Build vertex and face lists for this octahedron.

6.3.8 Check duality

Beginning with the face and vertex lists of the octahedron in the previous exercise, find the dual of this polyhedron, and check that the dual is a cube.   ■

Normal Vectors for the Platonic Solids

If we wish to build meshes for the Platonic solids, we must compute the normal vector to each face. This can be done in the usual way with Newell's method, but the high degree of symmetry of a Platonic solid offers a much simpler approach. Assuming that the solid is centered at the origin, we see that the normal vector to each face is the vector from the origin to the *center* of the face, which is formed as the average of the vertices. Figure 6.26 shows this normal vector for an octahedron; the normal to the face is simply

FIGURE 6.26 Using symmetry to find the normal to a face.

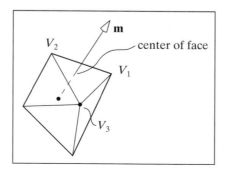

$$\mathbf{m} = \frac{V_1 + V_2 + V_3}{3} \qquad\qquad (6.4)$$

(Note that this vector is the same as that from the origin to the appropriate vertex on the dual Platonic solid.)

The Tetrahedron

The vertex list of a tetrahedron depends, of course, on the tetrahedron's position, orientation, and size. It is interesting that a tetrahedron can be inscribed in a cube (such that its four vertices lie in corners of the cube and its four edges lie in faces of the cube). Consider the unit cube having vertices $(\pm1, \pm1, \pm1)$, and choose the tetrahedron that has one vertex at $(1, 1, 1)$. Then this tetrahedron has vertex and face lists given in Figure 6.27 [Blinn87].

Vertex list				Face list	
Vertex	x	y	z	**Face number**	**Vertices**
0	1	1	1	0	1,2,3
1	1	−1	−1	1	0,3,2
2	−1	−1	1	2	0,1,3
3	−1	1	−1	3	0,2,1

FIGURE 6.27 Vertex list and face list for a tetrahedron.

The Icosahedron

The vertex list for the icosahedron presents more of a challenge, but we can exploit a remarkable fact to make it simple. Figure 6.28 shows that three mutually perpendicular **golden rectangles** inscribe the icosahedron, so that a vertex list may be read directly from this picture. We choose to align each golden rectangle with a coordinate axis. For convenience, we size the rectangles so that

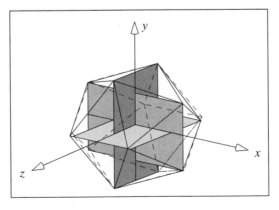

FIGURE 6.28 Golden rectangles defining the icosahedron.

their longer edge extends from −1 to 1 along its axis. The shorter edge then extends from $-\tau$ to τ, where $\tau = (\sqrt{5} - 1)/2 = 0.618\ldots$ is the reciprocal of the golden ratio ϕ. From here, it is just a matter of listing vertex positions, as shown in Figure 6.29.

FIGURE 6.29 Vertex list for the icosahedron.

Vertex	x	y	z
0	0	1	τ
1	0	1	$-\tau$
2	1	τ	0
3	1	$-\tau$	0
4	0	-1	$-\tau$
5	0	-1	τ
6	τ	0	1
7	$-\tau$	0	1
8	τ	0	-1
9	$-\tau$	0	-1
10	-1	τ	0
11	-1	$-\tau$	0

A model for the icosahedron is shown in Figure 6.30. The face list for the icosahedron can be read directly off of the figure. (Question: What is the normal vector to face #8?)

Some people prefer to adjust the model for the icosahedron slightly, making it into the form shown in Figure 6.31. This form makes it clearer that an icosahedron is made up of an antiprism (shown shaded) and two pentagonal pyramids on its top and bottom.

FIGURE 6.30 Model for the icosahedron.

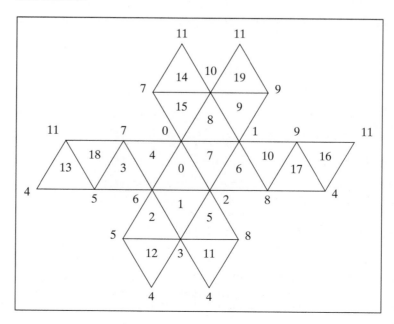

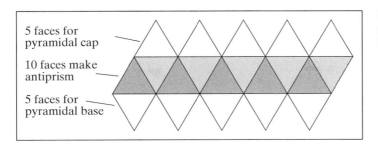

FIGURE 6.31 An icosahedron is an antiprism with a cap and base.

The Dodecahedron

The dodecahedron is dual to the icosahedron, so all the information needed to build lists for the dodecahedron is buried in the lists for the icosahedron. But it is convenient to see the model of the dodecahedron laid out, as in Figure 6.32.

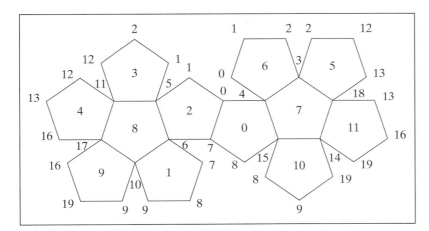

FIGURE 6.32 Model for the dodecahedron.

Using duality again, we know that vertex k of the dodecahedron lies at the center of face k of the icosahedron: we just average the three vertices of face k. *All* of the vertices of the dodecahedron are easily calculated in this fashion.

PRACTICE EXERCISES

6.3.9 Icosahedral distances

What is the radial distance of each vertex of the icosahedron from the origin?

6.3.10 Vertex list for the dodecahedron

Build the vertex list and normal list for the dodecahedron. ■

6.3.3 Other Interesting Polyhedra

There are endless varieties of polyhedra (see, for instance, [Wenninger 71] and [Coxeter63]), but one class is particularly interesting. Whereas each Platonic solid has the same type of n-gon for all of its faces, the **Archimedean** (also **semiregular**) solids have more than one kind of face, although they are still regular polygons. In addition, it is required for semiregularity that every vertex be surrounded by the same collection of polygons in the same order.

For instance, the "truncated cube," shown in Figure 6.33(a), has 8-gons and 3-gons for faces, and around each vertex one finds one triangle and two 8-gons. This pair of properties is summarized by associating the symbol $3 \cdot 8 \cdot 8$ with this solid.

FIGURE 6.33 The truncated cube.

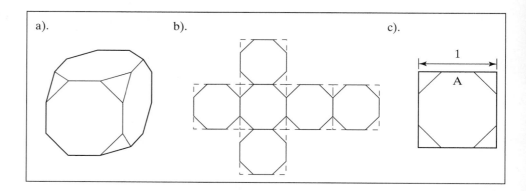

The truncated cube is formed by "slicing" off each corner of a cube in just the right fashion. The model for the truncated cube, shown in Figure 6.33(b), is based on that of the cube. Each edge of the cube is divided into three parts, the middle part is of length $A = 1/(1 + \sqrt{2})$ [Figure 6.33(c)], and the middle portion of each edge is joined to its neighbors. Thus, if an edge of the cube has endpoints C and D, two new vertices, V and W, are formed as the affine combinations

$$V = \frac{1 + A}{2} C + \frac{1 - A}{2} D$$

and

$$W = \frac{1 - A}{2} C + \frac{1 + A}{2} D.$$

(6.5)

On the basis of this equation, it is straightforward to build vertex and face lists for the truncated cube. (See the exercises at the end of the section and Case Study 6.10.)

Given the constraint that faces must be regular polygons and that they must occur in the same arrangement about each vertex, there are only 13 possible Archimedean solids, discussed further in Case Study 6.10. Archimedean solids still possess enough symmetry that the normal vector to each face is found using the center of the face.

One Archimedean solid that is of particular interest is the truncated icosahedron $5 \cdot 6^2$ shown in Figure 6.34, which consists of regular hexagons and pentagons. The pattern is familiar from soccer balls used around the world. More recently, this shape has been named the **buckyball**, after Buckminster Fuller, because of his interest in similar geodesic structures. Not long ago, crystallographers discovered that 60 atoms of carbon can be arranged at the vertices of the truncated icosahedron, producing a new kind of carbon molecule that is neither graphite nor diamond. The material has many remarkable properties, such as high-temperature stability and superconductivity [Browne90]; it has acquired the name **fullerene**.

The Buckyball is interesting to model and view on a graphics display. To build its vertex and face lists, we draw the model of the icosahedron given in Figure 6.30 and divide each edge into three equal parts. This produces two new vertices along each edge, whose positions are easily calculated. We number the 60 new vertices according to taste to build the vertex list of a buckyball. Figure 6.35 shows a partial model of the icosahedron with the new vertices connected by edges. Note that each old face of the icosahedron becomes a hexagon and that each old vertex of the icosahedron has been "snipped off" to form a pentagonal face. Building the face list is just a matter of listing what is seen in the model. Case Study 6.10 explores the Archimedean solids further.

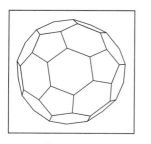

FIGURE 6.34 The Buckyball.

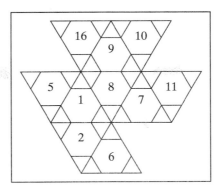

FIGURE 6.35 Building a buckyball.

Geodesic Domes

Few things are harder to put up with than a good example.

Mark Twain

Although Buckminster Fuller was a pioneer along many lines, he is best known for introducing geodesic domes [Fuller73]. These solids form an interesting class of poly-hedra having many useful properties. In particular, a geodesic dome constructed out of actual materials exhibits extraordinary strength for its weight.

There are many forms a geodesic dome can take, and they all approximate a sphere by an arrangement of faces, usually triangular in shape. Once the sphere has been approximated by such faces, the bottom half is removed, leaving the familiar dome shape. An example based on the icosahedron is shown in Figure 6.36.

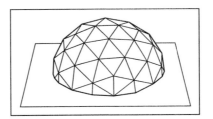

FIGURE 6.36 A geodesic dome.

To determine the faces, each edge of the icosahedron is subdivided into $3F$ equal parts, where F is what Fuller called the **frequency** of the dome. In the example, $F = 3$, so each icosahedral edge is trisected to form nine smaller triangular faces. [See Figure 6.37(a).]

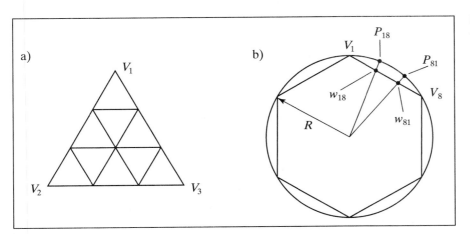

FIGURE 6.37 Building new vertices for the dome.

These faces do not lie in the plane of the original faces, however: First, the new vertices are "projected outward" onto the surrounding sphere. Figure 6.37(b) presents a cross-sectional view of the projection process. For example, the edge from V_1 to V_8 is subdivided to produce the two points W_{18} and W_{81}. The former is given by

$$W_{18} = \frac{2}{3} V_1 + \frac{1}{3} V_8. \tag{6.6}$$

(What is W_{81}?) Projecting W_{18} onto the enclosing sphere of radius R is simply a scaling; we have

$$P_{18} = R \frac{\mathbf{w}_{18}}{|\mathbf{w}_{18}|}, \tag{6.7}$$

where we write $\mathbf{w}_{18}$ for the position vector associated with point W_{18}. The old and new vertices are connected by straight lines to produce the nine triangular faces for each face of the icosahedron. (Why isn't the geodesic dome a new Platonic solid?) What are the values of E, F, and V for this polyhedron? Much more on geodesic domes can be found in [Fuller75] and [Kappraff91].

PRACTICE EXERCISES

6.3.11 Lists for the truncated icosahedron

Write the vertex, normal, and face lists for the truncated icosahedron.

6.3.12 Lists for a buckyball

Create the vertex, normal, and face lists for a buckyball. Because computing 60 vertices is tedious, it is perhaps easiest to write a small routine to form each new vertex by using the vertex list of the icosahedron of Figure 6.29.

6.3.13 Build lists for the geodesic dome

Construct vertex, normal, and face lists for a frequency-3 geodesic dome.   ■

6.4 EXTRUDED SHAPES

A large class of shapes can be generated by **extruding**, or **sweeping**, a 2D shape through space. The prism shown in Figure 6.19 is an example of a shape produced by sweeping linearly,—that is, in a straight line. As we shall see, the tetrahedron and octahedron of Figure 6.22 are also examples of extruding a shape through space in a certain way. And surfaces of revolution can also be approximated by extruding a polygon, once we slightly broaden the definition of extrusion.

In this section, we examine some ways to generate meshes by sweeping polygons in discrete steps. In Section 6.5, we develop similar tools for building meshes that attempt to approximate smoothly swept shapes.

6.4.1 Creating Prisms

We begin with the prism, which is formed by sweeping a polygon in a straight line. Figure 6.38(a) shows a prism based on a polygon P lying in the xy-plane. P is swept through a distance H along the z-axis, forming the ARROW prism shown in Figure 6.38(b). (More generally, the sweep could be along a vector $\mathbf{d}$, as in Figure 6.19.) As P is swept along, an edge in the z-direction is created for each vertex of P. This generates another 7 vertices, so the prism has 14 vertices in all. They appear in pairs: If $(x_i, y_i, 0)$ is one of the vertices of the base P, then the prism also contains the vertex (x_i, y_i, H).

What face list describes ARROW? The prism is "unfolded" into the model shown in Figure 6.38(c) to expose its nine faces, as seen from the outside. There are seven

FIGURE 6.38 A sample prism.

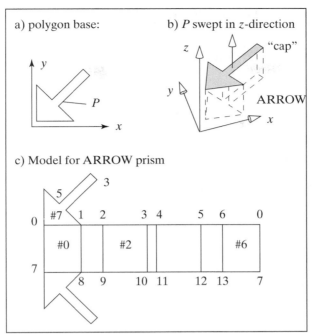

a) polygon base:

b) P swept in z-direction

c) Model for ARROW prism

rectangular sides, plus the bottom **base** P and the top **cap**. Face 2, for instance, is defined by vertices 2, 9, 10, and 3.

Because the prism has flat faces, we associate the same normal vector with every vertex of a face: the normal vector to the face itself.

Building a Mesh for the Prism

We want a tool to make a mesh for the prism, based on an arbitrary polygon. Suppose the prism's base is a polygon with N vertices (x_i, y_i). We number the vertices of the base $0, \ldots, N - 1$ and those of the cap $N, \ldots, 2N - 1$, so that an edge joins vertices i and $i + N$, as in Figure 6.38. The vertex list is then easily constructed to contain the points $(x_i, y_i, 0)$ and (x_i, y_i, H), for $i = 0, 1, \ldots, N - 1$.

The face list is also straightforward to construct. We first make the "side" faces, or "walls," and then add the cap and base. For the jth wall ($j = 0, \ldots, N - 1$), we create a face with the four vertices having indices $j, j + N$, $\text{next}(j) + N$, and $\text{next}(j)$, where $\text{next}(j)$ is $j + 1$, except if j equals $N - 1$, whereupon $\text{next}(j) = 0$. This takes care of the "wraparound" from the $(N - 1)$st to the zeroth vertex; we then have

$$\text{next}(j) = (j + 1) \text{ modulo } N, \qquad (6.8)$$

or, in terms of program code, `next = (j < (N-1)) ? (j + 1) : 0`. Each face is inserted in the face list as it is created. The normal vector to each face is easily found using the Newell method described earlier. We then create the base and cap faces and insert them in the face list. Case Study 6.3 provides more details for building mesh models of prisms.

6.4.2 Arrays of Extruded Prisms: "Bricklaying"

Some rendering tools, like OpenGL, can reliably draw only convex polygons. They might fail, for instance, to draw the arrow of Figure 6.38 correctly. If your software is of this variety, you can decompose (tessellate) the polygon into a set of convex polygons and extrude each one. Figure 6.39 shows some examples, including a few extruded letters of the alphabet.

FIGURE 6.39 Extruded objects based on a collection of convex prisms.

Objects like those shown in the figure are composed of an array of convex prisms. Some of the component prisms abut one another and therefore share all or parts of some walls. Because vertex positions are being computed with high precision, the crease where two walls adjoin will usually be invisible.

For this family of shapes, we need a method that builds a mesh out of an array of prisms, say,

```
void Mesh:: makePrismArray(...)
```

which would take as its arguments a suitable list of (convex) base polygons (assumed to lie in the *xy*-plane) and perhaps a vector **d** that describes the direction and amount of extrusion. The vertex list would contain the vertices of the cap and base polygons for each prism, and the individual walls, base, and cap of each prism would be stored in the face list. Drawing such a mesh would involve some wasted effort, since walls that abut would be drawn (twice), even though they are ultimately invisible.

Special Case: Extruded Quad-Strips

A simpler, but very interesting, family of prisms such as that just described can be built and manipulated more efficiently. These are prisms for which the base polygon can be represented by a *quad-strip*—an array of quadrilaterals connected in a chain (like bricks laid in a row), such that neighboring faces coincide completely, as shown in Figure 6.40(a). Recall from Figure 2.37 that the quad-strip is an OpenGL geometric primitive. A quad-strip is described by a sequence of vertices:

FIGURE 6.40 Quad-strips and prisms built upon quad-strips.

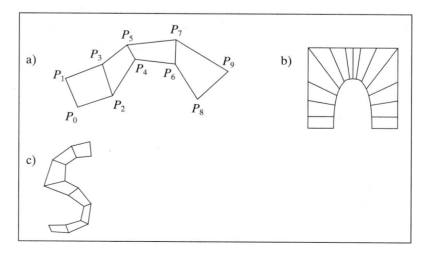

$$\text{quad-strip} = \{p_0, p_1, p_2, \ldots, p_{M-1}\}. \tag{6.9}$$

The vertices are understood to be taken in pairs, with the odd ones forming one "edge" of the quad-strip and the even ones forming the other edge. Not every polygon can be represented as a quad-strip. (Which of the polygons in Figure 6.39 are not quad-strips? What block letters of the alphabet can be drawn as quad-strips?)

When a mesh is formed as an extruded quad-strip, only $2M$ vertices are placed in the vertex list, and only the "outside walls" are included in the face list. There are $2M - 2$ faces in all. (Why?) Thus, no redundant walls are drawn when the mesh is rendered. A method for creating a mesh for an extruded quad-strip would take an array of 2D points and an extrusion vector as its parameters:

```
void Mesh:: makeExtrudedQuadStrip(Point2 p[], int numPts, Vector3 d);
```

Figure 6.41 shows an example of an interesting extruded quad-strip. Case Study 6.4 considers how to make such meshes in more detail.

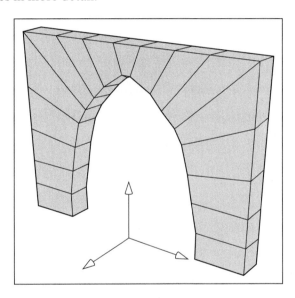

FIGURE 6.41 Extruded quad-strip formed into an arch.

6.4.3 Extrusions with a "Twist"

So far, an extrusion just shifts the base polygon to a new position to define the cap polygon. It is easy to generalize on this concept in a way that produces a much broader family of shapes: simply create the cap polygon as an enlarged or shrunken, and possibly rotated, version of the base polygon. Specifically, if the base polygon is P, with vertices $\{p_0, p_1, \ldots, p_{N-1}\}$, the cap polygon has vertices

$$P' = \{Mp_0, Mp_1, \ldots, Mp_{N-1}\}, \tag{6.10}$$

where M is some four-by-four matrix representing an affine transformation. Figure 6.42 shows some examples. Parts (a) and (b) show truncated pyramids or tapered cylinders (also truncated cones) such that the cap is a smaller version of the base. The transformation matrix for this type of object is

$$M = \begin{pmatrix} 0.7 & 0 & 0 & 0 \\ 0 & 0.7 & 0 & 0 \\ 0 & 0 & 1 & H \\ 0 & 0 & 0 & 1 \end{pmatrix},$$

based simply on a scaling factor of 0.7 and a translation by H along z. Part (c) shows a cylinder whose cap has been rotated through an angle θ about the z-axis before translation, using the matrix

$$M = \begin{pmatrix} \cos(\theta) & \sin(\theta) & 0 & 0 \\ -\sin(\theta) & \cos(\theta) & 0 & 0 \\ 0 & 0 & 1 & H \\ 0 & 0 & 0 & 1 \end{pmatrix},$$

and Part (d) shows in cross section how cap P' can be rotated arbitrarily before it is translated to the desired position.

Prisms such as these are just as easy to create as those that use a simple translation for M: The face list is identical to the original one; only the vertex positions (and the values for the normal vectors) are altered.

PRACTICE EXERCISES

6.4.1 The tapered cylinder

Describe in detail how to make vertex, normal, and face lists for a tapered cylinder having regular pentagons for its base and cap, where the cap is one-half as large as the base.

6.4.2 The tetrahedron as a tapered cylinder

Describe how to model a tetrahedron as a tapered cylinder with a triangular base. Is this an efficient way to obtain a mesh for a tetrahedron?

6.4.3 An antiprism

Discuss how to model the antiprism shown in Figure 6.20(b). Can it be modeled as a certain kind of extrusion?   ▪

FIGURE 6.42 Pyramids and twisted prisms.

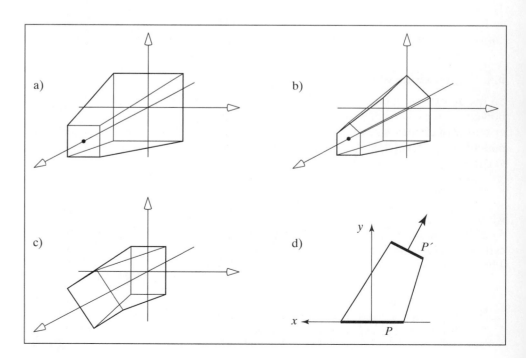

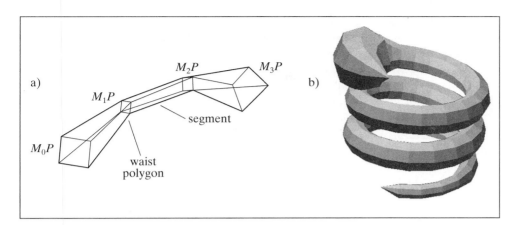

a)

M_2P M_3P

M_1P

segment

M_0P

waist
polygon

b)

FIGURE 6.43 A tube made
from successive extrusions of a
polygon.

6.4.4 Building Segmented Extrusions: Tubes and Snakes

Another rich set of objects can be modeled by employing a sequence of extrusions,
each with its own transformation, and laying them end to end to form a tube. Figure 6.43(a) shows a tube made by extruding a square P three times, in different directions with different tapers and twists. The first segment has end polygons M_0P
and M_1P, where the initial matrix M_0 positions and orients the starting end of the
tube. The second segment has end polygons M_1P and M_2P, etc. We shall call the various transformed squares the "**waists**" of the tube. In this example, the vertex list of
the mesh contains the 16 vertices M_0p_0, M_0p_1, M_0p_2, M_0p_3, M_1p_0, M_1p_1, M_1p_2,
$M_1p_3, \dots, M_3p_0, M_3p_1, M_3p_2, M_3p_3$. Figure 6.43(b) shows a "snake," so called because the matrices M_i cause the tube to grow and shrink to represent the body and
head of a snake.

Designing Tubes Based on 3D Curves

How do we design interesting and useful tubes and snakes? We could choose the
individual matrices M_i by hand, but this is awkward at best. It is much easier to
think of the tube as wrapped around a curve, which we shall call the **spine** of the
tube, that undulates through space in some organized fashion.[5] We shall represent
the curve parametrically as $C(t)$. For example, the helix (recall Section 3.8) shown
is stereo in Figure 6.44(a) has the parametric representation

$$C(t) = (\cos(t), \sin(t), bt), \tag{6.11}$$

for some constant b.

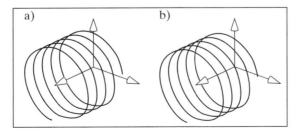

a)   b)

FIGURE 6.44 A stereo view of a
helix.

---

[5] The VRML 2.0 modeling language includes an "extrusion" node that works in a similar fashion, allowing the
designer to define a "spine" along which the polygons are placed, each with its own transformation.

To form the various waist polygons of the tube, we sample $C(t)$ at a set of t-values, $\{t_0, t_1, \ldots\}$, and build a transformed polygon in the plane perpendicular to the curve at each point $C(t_i)$, as suggested in Figure 6.45. It is convenient to think of erecting a local coordinate system at each chosen point along the spine: The local "z-axis" points along the curve, and the local "x- and y-axes" point in directions normal to the z-axis (and normal to each other). The waist polygon is set to lie in the local xy-plane. All we need is a straightforward way to determine the vertices of each waist polygon.

FIGURE 6.45 Constructing local coordinate systems along the spine curve.

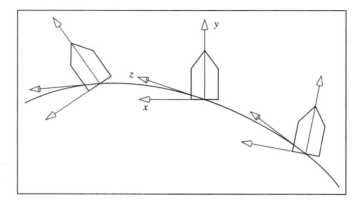

It is most convenient to let the curve $C(t)$ *itself* determine the local coordinate systems. A well-known method in differential geometry creates the **Frenet frame** at each point along the spine [Gray 93]. At each value t_i of interest, a vector $\boldsymbol{T}(t_i)$ that is tangent to the curve is computed. Then two vectors, $\mathbf{N}(t_i)$ and $\mathbf{B}(t_i)$, which are perpendicular to $\mathbf{T}(t_i)$ and to each other, are computed. These three vectors constitute the Frenet frame at t_i.

Once the Frenet frame is computed, it is easy to find the transformation matrix M that transforms the base polygon of the tube to its position and orientation in that frame. It is the transformation matrix that carries the world coordinate system into the new coordinate system. (The reasoning is very similar to that used in Practice Exercise 5.6.1 on transforming the camera coordinate system into the world coordinate system.) The matrix M_i must carry $\mathbf{i}, \mathbf{j}$, and $\mathbf{k}$ into $\mathbf{N}(t_i), \mathbf{B}(t_i)$, and $\mathbf{T}(t_i)$, respectively, and must carry the origin of the world into the spine point $C(t)$. Thus, the matrix has columns consisting directly of $\mathbf{N}(t_i), \mathbf{B}(t_i), \mathbf{T}(t_i)$, and $C(t_i)$ expressed in homogeneous coordinates:

$$M_i = (\mathbf{N}(t_i)|\mathbf{B}(t_i)\,|\,\mathbf{T}(t_i)|C(t_i)). \tag{6.12}$$

Forming the Frenet Frame

The Frenet frame at each point along a curve depends on how the curve twists and undulates. The frame is derived from certain derivatives of $C(t)$, and so it is easy to form if these derivatives can be calculated.

Specifically, if the formula that we have for $C(t)$ is differentiable, we can take its derivative and form the tangent vector to the curve at each point, $\dot{\mathbf{C}}(t)$. (If $C(t)$ has components $C_x(t)$, $C_y(t)$, and $C_z(t)$, the derivative is simply $\dot{\mathbf{C}}(t) = (\dot{C}_x(t), \dot{C}_y(t), \dot{C}_z(t))$. The vector $\dot{\mathbf{C}}(t)$ points in the direction the curve "is headed" at each value of t,—that is, in the direction of the **tangent** to the curve. We normalize $\dot{\mathbf{C}}(t)$ to unit length to obtain the **unit tangent vector** at t. For example, the helix of Equation (6.11) has the unit tangent vector given by

$$\mathbf{T}(t) = \frac{1}{\sqrt{1 + b^2}}(-\sin(t), \cos(t), b). \tag{6.13}$$

This tangent is shown for various values of t in Figure 6.46(a).

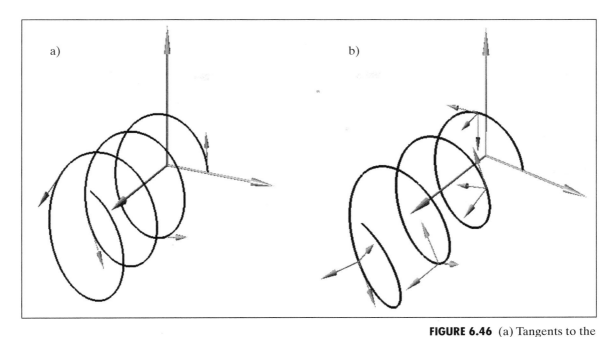

a)   b)

FIGURE 6.46 (a) Tangents to the helix. (b) Shows the Frenet frame at various values of t along the helix.

If we form the cross product of Equation (6.13) with any noncollinear vector, we must obtain a vector perpendicular to $\mathbf{T}(t)$ and therefore perpendicular to the spine of the curve. (Why?) A particularly good choice is the **acceleration**, based on the second derivative, $\ddot{C}(t)$. So we form $\dot{C}(t) \times \ddot{C}(t)$, and since it will be used for an axis of the coordinate system, we normalize it to obtain the "unit **binormal**" vector

$$\mathbf{B}(t) = \frac{\dot{\mathbf{C}}(t) \times \ddot{\mathbf{C}}(t)}{|\dot{\mathbf{C}}(t) \times \ddot{\mathbf{C}}(t)|}. \tag{6.14}$$

We then obtain a vector perpendicular to both $\mathbf{T}(t)$ and $\mathbf{B}(t)$ by using the cross product again:

$$\mathbf{N}(t) = \mathbf{B}(t) \times \mathbf{T}(t). \tag{6.15}$$

Convince yourself that these three vectors are mutually perpendicular and have unit length, thus constituting a local Frenet frame at $C(t)$. Also check that, in the case of a helix, the vectors are given by

$$\mathbf{B}(t) = \frac{1}{\sqrt{1 + b^2}} (b \sin(t), -b \cos(t), 1),$$
$$\mathbf{N}(t) = (-\cos(t), -\sin(t), 0). \tag{6.16}$$

Finding the Frenet Frame Numerically

If the formula for $C(t)$ is complicated, it may be awkward to form its successive derivatives in closed form such that formulas for $\mathbf{T}(t)$, $\mathbf{B}(t)$, and $\mathbf{N}(t)$ can be hardwired into a program. As an alternative, it is possible to approximate the derivatives numerically by using

$$\dot{\mathbf{C}}(t) \doteq \frac{C(t + \varepsilon) - C(t - \varepsilon)}{2\varepsilon},$$
$$\ddot{\mathbf{C}}(t) \doteq \frac{C(t - \varepsilon) - 2C(t) + C(t + \varepsilon)}{\varepsilon^2}. \tag{6.17}$$

This computation will usually produce acceptable directions for $\mathbf{T}(t)$, $\mathbf{B}(t)$, and $\mathbf{N}(t)$, although the user should beware that numerical differentiation is an inherently unstable process [Burden85].

Figure 6.47 shows the result of wrapping a decagon about the helix via the use of Frenet frames. The helix was sampled at 30 points, a Frenet frame was constructed at each point, and the decagon was erected in the new frame.

FIGURE 6.47 A tube wrapped along a helix.

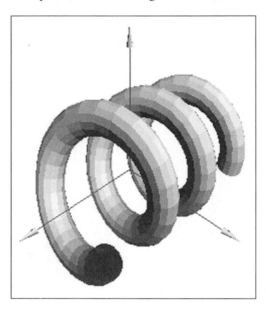

Figure 6.48 shows other interesting examples, based on the toroidal spiral (which we first saw in Section 3.8) [Gray93]. (The edges of the individual faces are drawn to clarify how the tube twists as it proceeds; drawing the edges of a mesh is considered in Case Study 6.7.) A toroidal spiral is formed when a spiral is wrapped about a torus. (Try to envision the underlying invisible torus here.) The toroidal spiral is given by

$$C(t) = \big((a + b\cos(qt))\cos(pt), (a + b\cos(qt))\sin(pt), c\sin(qt)\big), \qquad (6.18)$$

for some choice of constants a, b, p, and q. For Part (a) of the figure the parameters p and q were respectively chosen to be 2 and 5, and for Part (b) they were chosen to be 1 and 7.

FIGURE 6.48 Tubes based on toroidal spirals.

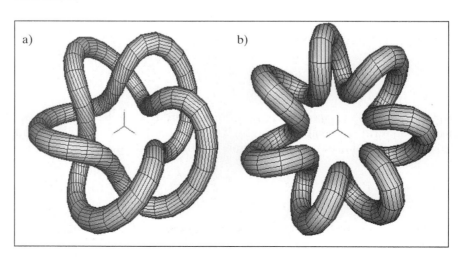

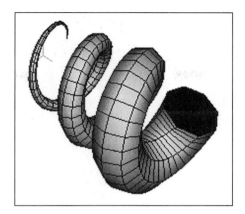

FIGURE 6.49 A "seashell."

Figure 6.49 shows a "seashell," formed by wrapping a tube with a growing radius about a helix. To accomplish this, the matrix of Equation (6.12) was multiplied by the scaling matrix.

$$M' = M \begin{pmatrix} g(t) & 0 & 0 & 0 \\ 0 & g(t) & 0 & 0 \\ 0 & 0 & 1 & 0 \\ 0 & 0 & 0 & 1 \end{pmatrix}.$$

Where the scale factors also depend on t. Here, $g(t) = t$. It is also possible to add a rotation to the matrix, so that the tube appears to twist more vigorously as one looks along the spine.

One of the problems with using Frenet frames to sweep out curves is that the local frame sometimes twists in such a way as to introduce undesired "knots" in the surface. Recent work, such as that of Wang [Wang97], finds alternatives to the Frenet frame that produce less twisting and, therefore, more graceful surfaces.

PRACTICE EXERCISES

6.4.4 What is N(*t*)?

Show that $\mathbf{N}(t)$ is parallel to $\ddot{\mathbf{C}}(t) - (\dot{\mathbf{C}}(t) \cdot \ddot{\mathbf{C}}(t)) \dot{\mathbf{C}}(t) / |\dot{\mathbf{C}}(t)|^2$, so it points in the direction of the acceleration when the velocity and acceleration at t are perpendicular.

6.4.5 The frame for the helix

Consider the circular helix treated in the text. Show that the formulas for the unit tangent, binormal, and normal vectors are correct. Show also that these vectors are of unit length and mutually perpendicular. Visualize how this local coordinate system orients itself as you move along the curve. ■

Figure 6.50 shows additional examples. Part (a) shows a hexagon wrapped about an elliptical spine to form a kind of elliptical torus, and Part (b) shows segments arranged into a knot along a Lissajous figure given by

$$C(t) = (r \cos(Mt + \phi), 0, r \sin(Nt)), \tag{6.19}$$

with $M = 2, N = 3$, and $\phi = 0$.

Case Study 6.5 examines more details of forming meshes that model tubes based on a parametric curve.

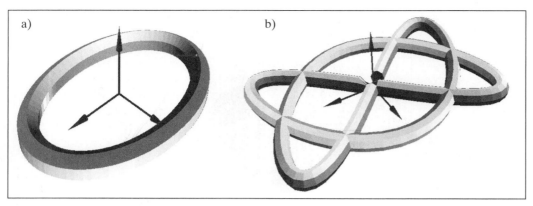

FIGURE 6.50 (a) A hexagon wrapped about an elliptical torus. (b) A 7-gon wrapped about a Lissajous figure.

6.4.5 "Discretely" Swept Surfaces of Revolution

The tubes presented in the previous section use affine transformations to fashion a new coordinate system at each spine point. If we employ pure rotations for the affine transformations and place all spine points at the origin, a rich set of polyhedral shapes emerges. Figure 6.51 shows an example in which a base polygon—now called the **profile**—is initially positioned three units out along the x-axis and then is successively rotated in steps about the y-axis to form an approximation of a torus. This operation is equivalent to **circularly sweeping** a shape about an axis, and the resulting shape is often called a **surface of revolution**. We examine true surfaces of revolution in Section 6.5; here we merely form a discrete approximation to them, since we are sweeping in discrete steps.

FIGURE 6.51 Rotational sweeping in discrete steps.

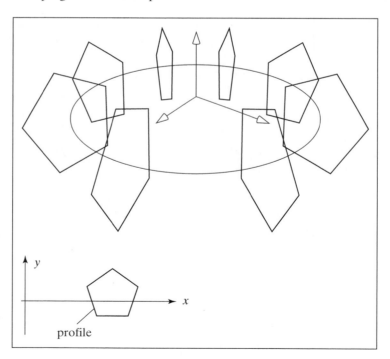

Figure 6.52 shows an example that produces pictures of a martini glass. The profile here is not a closed polygon, but a simple polyline based on points $P_j = (x_j, y_j, 0)$. If we choose to place this polyline at K equispaced angles about the y-axis, then the transformations have matrices

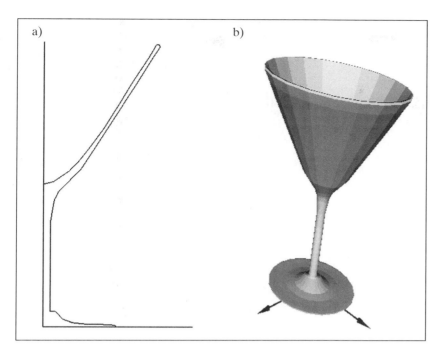

FIGURE 6.52 Approximating a martini glass with a discretely swept polyline. (a) The profile. (b) The swept surface.

$$M_i = \begin{pmatrix} \cos(\theta_i) & 0 & \sin(\theta_i) & 0 \\ 0 & 1 & 0 & 0 \\ -\sin(\theta_i) & 0 & \cos(\theta_i) & 0 \\ 0 & 0 & 0 & 1 \end{pmatrix},$$

where $\theta_i = 2\pi i / K$, $i = 0, 1, \ldots, K - 1$. Note that there is no translation involved. This transformation is simple enough that we can write the positions of the vertices directly. The rotation sets the points of the i-th "waist" polyline at

$$(x_j \cos(\theta_i), y_j, x_j \sin(\theta_i)). \tag{6.20}$$

Building meshes that model surfaces of revolution is treated further in Case Study 6.6.

6.5 MESH APPROXIMATIONS TO SMOOTH OBJECTS

So far, we have built meshes to represent polyhedra, wherein each shape is a collection of flat polygonal faces. These meshes tend to be "data intensive"—specified by listing the vertices of each face individually. Now we want to build meshes that attempt to approximate inherently smooth shapes, like a sphere or a torus. These shapes are normally defined by formulas rather than data. We also want to arrange matters so that the meshes we use can be *smoothly shaded*: Even though they are represented by a collection of flat faces, as before, the proper algorithm (Gouraud shading) draws them with smooth gradations in shading, and the individual faces are invisible. (Recall Figure 6.1.) All that this requires is that we find the proper normal vector at each vertex of each face; specifically, we compute the normal vector to the underlying smooth surface. We discuss the Gouraud shading algorithm in Chapter 8.

The basic approach for each type of surface is to "**polygonalize**" (also called **tesselate**) it into a collection of flat faces. If the faces are small enough and there is a graceful change in direction from one face to the next, the resulting mesh will provide a good approximation to the underlying surface. The faces have vertices that are found by evaluating the surface's parametric representation at discrete points. A mesh is created by building a vertex list and face list in the usual way, except here the vertices are computed from formulas. The same is true for the vertex normal vectors: They are computed by evaluating formulas for the normal to the surface at discrete points.

6.5.1 Representations of Surfaces

To set the stage, recall that in Section 4.5.5 we examined the planar **patch**, given parametrically by

$$P(u, v) = C + \mathbf{a}u + \mathbf{b}v, \tag{6.21}$$

where C is a point and $\mathbf{a}$ and $\mathbf{b}$ are vectors. The range of values for the parameters u and v is usually restricted to $[0, 1]$, in which case the patch is a parallelogram in 3D with corner vertices $C, C + \mathbf{a}, C + \mathbf{b}$, and $C + \mathbf{a} + \mathbf{b}$. (Recall Figure 4.34.)

Here we enlarge our interests to nonlinear forms, to represent more general surface shapes. We introduce three functions $X()$, $Y()$, and $Z()$ so that, in point form, the surface has the parametric representation

$$P(u, v) = \big(X(u, v), Y(u, v), Z(u, v)\big), \tag{6.22}$$

where u and v are restricted to suitable intervals. Different surfaces are characterized by different functions X, Y, and Z. The notion is that the surface is "at" $\big(X(0, 0), Y(0, 0), Z(0, 0)\big)$ when both u and v are zero, at $\big(X(1, 0), Y(1, 0), Z(1, 0)\big)$ when $u = 1$ and $v = 0$, and so on. Keep in mind that two parameters are required to represent a surface, whereas a curve in 3D requires only one. Letting u vary while keeping v constant generates a curve called a **v-contour**. Similarly, letting v vary while holding u constant produces a **u-contour**.

The Implicit Form of a Surface

Although we are mainly concerned with parametric representations of different surfaces, it will prove useful to keep track of an alternative way to describe a surface: through its **implicit form.** Recall from Section 3.8 that a curve in 2D has an implicit form $F(x, y)$ that must evaluate to zero for all and only those points (x, y) that lie on the curve. For surfaces in 3D, a similar function $F(x, y, z)$ exists that evaluates to zero if and only if the point (x, y, z) is on the surface. The surface therefore has an **implicit equation** given by

$$F(x, y, z) = 0 \tag{6.23}$$

that is satisfied for all and only those points that lie on it. The equation constrains the way that values of x, y, and z must be related to confine the point (x, y, z) to the surface in question. For example, recall (from Chapter 4) that the plane which passes through point B and has normal vector $\mathbf{n}$ is described by the equation $n_x x + n_y y + n_z z = D$ (where $D = \mathbf{n} \cdot B$), so the implicit form for this plane is $F(x, y, z) = n_x x + n_y y + n_z z - D$. Sometimes it is more convenient to think of F as a function of a point P, rather than a function of three variables x, y, and z, and we write $F(P) = 0$ to describe all points that lie on the surface. For the example of the plane we are describing here, we would define $F(P) = \mathbf{n} \cdot (P - B)$ and say that P lies in the plane if and only if $F(P) = \mathbf{n} \cdot (P - B)$ is zero. If we wish to work with coordinate frames (recall Section 4.5), so that $\widetilde{P}$ is the quadruple $\widetilde{P} = (x, y, z, 1)^T$, the implicit form for a plane is even simpler, viz., $F(\widetilde{P}) = \tilde{n} \cdot \widetilde{P}$, where $\tilde{n} = (n_x, n_y, n_z, -D)$ captures both the normal vector and the value $-D$.

It is not always easy to find the function $F(x, y, z)$ or $F(P)$ from a given parametric form. (Nor can you always find a parametric form when given $F(x, y, z)$.) But if both a parametric form and an implicit form are available, it is simple to determine whether they describe the same surface: Simply substitute $X(u, v)$, $Y(u, v)$, and $Z(u, v)$ for x, y, and z, respectively, in $F(x, y, z)$, and check that F is zero for all values of u and v that are of interest.

For some surfaces—like that of a sphere—which enclose a portion of space, it is meaningful to define an inside region and an outside region. Other surfaces, such as a plane, clearly divide 3D space into two regions, but one must refer to the context of the application to tell which half-space is the inside and which the outside. There are also many surfaces, such as a strip of ribbon candy, for which it makes little sense to name an inside and an outside.

When it is meaningful to designate an inside and an outside to a surface, the implicit form $F(x, y, z)$ of the surface is also called its **inside–outside function**. We then say that a point (x, y, z) is

inside the surface if	$F(x, y, z) < 0,$	
on the surface if	$F(x, y, z) = 0,$	(6.24)

and

outside the surface if	$F(x, y, z) > 0.$

This set of conditions provides a quick and simple test for the disposition of a given point (x', y', z') relative to the surface: Just evaluate $F(x', y', z')$, and test whether it is positive, negative, or zero. The test is useful in algorithms for removing hidden lines and hidden surfaces (see Chapter 13) and in Chapter 14 it is used in ray-tracing algorithms. There has also been vigorous recent activity in rendering surfaces directly from their implicit forms. (See [Bloomenthal97].)

6.5.2 The Normal Vector to a Surface

As mentioned earlier, we need to determine the direction of the normal vector to a surface at any desired point. In this section we present one way of doing so based on the parametric equation, and one based on the implicit form, of the surface. As each type of surface is examined later, we find suitable expressions for its normal vector at any point.

The normal direction to a surface can be defined at a point $P(u_0, v_0)$ on the surface by considering a very small region of the surface around $P(u_0, v_0)$. If the region is small enough and the surface varies "smoothly" in the vicinity, the region will be essentially flat. Thus, it behaves locally like a tiny planar patch and has a well-defined normal direction. Figure 6.53 shows a surface patch with the normal vector drawn at various points. The direction of the normal vector is seen to be different at different points on the surface.

We use the name $\mathbf{n}(u, v)$ for the normal at (u, v). We now examine how it can be calculated.

FIGURE 6.53 The normal vector to a surface.

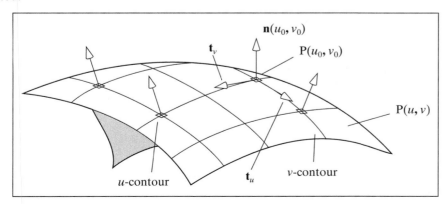

The Normal Vector for a Surface Given Parametrically

Not surprisingly, $\mathbf{n}(u_0, v_0)$ takes the form of a cross product between two vectors that lie in the tiny planar patch near (u_0, v_0). Being a cross product, it is guaranteed to be perpendicular to both vectors. The two vectors in the plane (indicated as $\mathbf{t}_u$ and $\mathbf{t}_v$ in Figure 6.53) are certain tangent vectors. Calculus texts show that they are simply related to partial derivatives of $\mathbf{p}(u, v)$ [the vector from the origin to the surface point $P(u, v)$],[6] evaluated at the point in question [Thomas53]. An expression for the normal vector is therefore

$$\mathbf{n}(u_0, v_0) = \left(\frac{\partial \mathbf{p}}{\partial u} \times \frac{\partial \mathbf{p}}{\partial v}\right)\Bigg|_{u=u_0, v=v_0}, \tag{6.25}$$

where the vertical bar indicates that the derivatives are evaluated at $u = u_0$ and $v = v_0$. Formed this way, $\mathbf{n}(u_0, v_0)$ is not automatically a unit-length vector, but it can be normalized if desired.

■ **EXAMPLE 6.5.1 Does equation (6.25) work for a plane?**

Consider the plane given parametrically by $P(u, v) = C + \mathbf{a}u + \mathbf{b}v$. The partial derivative of P with respect to u is just $\mathbf{a}$, and that with respect to v is $\mathbf{b}$. Thus, according to Equation (6.25), $\mathbf{n}(u, v) = \mathbf{a} \times \mathbf{b}$, which we recognize as the correct result.

More generally, the partial derivatives of $\mathbf{p}(u, v)$ exist whenever the surface is "smooth enough." Most of the surfaces of interest to us in modeling scenes have the necessary smoothness and have simple enough mathematical expressions so that finding the required derivatives is not difficult. Because $\mathbf{p}(u, v) = X(u, v)\mathbf{i} + Y(u, v)\mathbf{j} + Z(u, v)\mathbf{k}$, the derivative of a vector is just the vector of the individual derivatives:

$$\frac{\partial \mathbf{p}(u, v)}{\partial u} = \left(\frac{\partial X(u, v)}{\partial u}, \frac{\partial Y(u, v)}{\partial u}, \frac{\partial Z(u, v)}{\partial u}\right). \tag{6.26}$$

We apply these formulas directly to each surface type we examine later.

The Normal Vector for a Surface Given Implicitly

An alternative expression is used for a surface given by an implicit form, $F(x, y, z) = 0$. The normal direction at the surface point (x, y, z) is found using the **gradient**, ∇F, of F, which is given by [Thomas53]

$$\mathbf{n}(x_0, y_0, z_0) = \nabla F|_{x=x_0, y=y_0, z=z_0} = \left(\frac{\partial F}{\partial x}, \frac{\partial F}{\partial y}, \frac{\partial F}{\partial z}\right)\Bigg|_{x=x_0, y=y_0, z=z_0}, \tag{6.27}$$

where each partial derivative is evaluated at the desired point, (x_0, y_0, z_0). If the point (x_0, y_0, z_0) for the surface in question corresponds to the point $P(u_0, v_0)$ of the parametric form, then $\mathbf{n}(x_0, y_0, z_0)$ has the same direction as $\mathbf{n}(u_0, v_0)$ in Equation (6.25), but it may have a different length. Again, it can be normalized if desired.

■ **EXAMPLE 6.5.2 The plane again**

Consider once again a plane with normal $\mathbf{n}$ that passes through point A. Let the equation of this plane be given implicitly by $F(x, y, z) = \mathbf{n} \cdot ((x, y, z) - A) = 0$, or $n_x x + n_y y + n_z z - \mathbf{n} \cdot A = 0$.
  The plane has a gradient of $\nabla F = \mathbf{n}$, as expected.

---

[6] Since $\mathbf{p}(u, v)$ is simply the difference $P(u, v) - (0, 0, 0)$, the derivative of $\mathbf{p}()$ is the same as that of $P()$.

Note that the gradient-based form gives the normal vector as a function of x, y, and z, rather than of u and v. Sometimes we know *both* the inside–outside function $F(x, y, z)$ and the parametric form $\mathbf{p}(u, v) = X(u, v)\mathbf{i} + Y(u, v)\mathbf{j} + Z(u, v)\mathbf{k}$ of a surface. In such cases it may be easiest to find the parametric form $\mathbf{n}(u, v)$ of the normal at (u, v) by a two-step method: (1) Use Equation (6.27) to get the normal at (x, y, z) in terms of x, y, and z, and then (2) substitute the known functions $X(u, v)$ for x, $Y(u, v)$ for y, and $Z(u, v)$ for z. Some of the later examples illustrate this method.

6.5.3 The Effect of an Affine Transformation

On occasion, we shall need to work with the implicit and parametric forms of a surface after the surface has been subjected to an affine transformation. We will also want to know how the normal to the surface is affected by the transformation.

Suppose that the transformation is represented by a four-by-four matrix M and that the original surface has the implicit form (in terms of points in homogeneous coordinates) $F(\tilde{P})$ and the parametric form $\tilde{P}(u, v) = (X(u, v), Y(u, v), Z(u, v), 1)^T$. Then it is clear that the transformed surface has the parametric form $M\tilde{P}(u, v)$. (Why?) Also, it is easy to show (see the exercises that follow) that the transformed surface has the implicit form

$$F'(\tilde{P}) = F(M^{-1}\tilde{P}).$$

Further, if the original surface has normal vector $\mathbf{n}(u, v)$, then the transformed surface has normal vector $M^{-T}\mathbf{n}(u, v)$.

For example, suppose we transform the aforementioned plane, given by $F(\tilde{P}) = \tilde{n} \cdot \tilde{P}$ with $\tilde{n} = (n_x, n_y, n_z, -D)$. The transformed plane has the implicit form $F'(\tilde{P}) = \tilde{n} \cdot (M^{-1}\tilde{P})$. This can be written (see the exercises that follow) as $(M^{-T}\tilde{n}) \cdot \tilde{P}$, so the normal vector of the transformed plane involves the inverse transpose of the matrix, which is consistent with the form claimed for the normal to a general surface.

PRACTICE EXERCISES

6.5.1 The implicit form of a transformed surface

Suppose that all points on a surface satisfy the equation $F(P) = 0$ and that M transforms $\tilde{P}$ into $\tilde{Q}$; that is, $\tilde{Q} = M\tilde{P}$. Argue that any point $\tilde{Q}$ on the transformed surface comes from a point $M^{-1}\tilde{Q}$, and those points all satisfy the equation $F(M^{-1}\tilde{Q}) = 0$. Show that this argument proves that the implicit form for the transformed surface is $F(\tilde{Q}) = F(M^{-1}\tilde{Q})$.

6.5.2 How are normal vectors affected?

Let $\mathbf{n} = (n_x, n_y, n_z, 0)^T$ be the normal to a surface at a point P, and let $\mathbf{v}$ be any vector tangent to the surface at P. Then $\mathbf{n}$ must be perpendicular to $\mathbf{v}$, and we can write $\mathbf{n} \cdot \mathbf{v} = 0$.

a. Show that the dot product can be written as the matrix product $\mathbf{n}^T\mathbf{v} = 0$. (See Appendix 2.)
b. Show that $\mathbf{n} \cdot \mathbf{v}$ is still zero when the matrix product $M^{-1}M$ is inserted; that is, show that $\mathbf{n}^T M^{-1}M\mathbf{v} = 0$.
c. Show that $\mathbf{n}^T M^{-1}M\mathbf{v} = 0$ can be rewritten as $(M^{-T}\mathbf{n})(M\mathbf{v}) = 0$, so that $M^{-T}\mathbf{n}$ is perpendicular to $M\mathbf{v}$.

Now, since the tangent $\mathbf{v}$ transforms to $M\mathbf{v}$, which is tangent to the transformed surface, show that $M^{-T}\mathbf{n}$ must be normal to the transformed surface, which is what we wished to show.

d. The normal to a surface is also given by the gradient of the implicit form, so the normal to the transformed surface at point P must be the gradient of $F(M^{-1}P)$. Show, by the chain rule of calculus, that the gradient of the latter function is M^{-T} multiplied onto the gradient of $F()$.

6.5.3 The tangent plane to a transformed surface

To find how normal vectors are transformed, we can also find how the tangent plane to a surface is mapped to the tangent plane on the transformed surface. Suppose the tangent plane to the original surface at point P has the parametric representation $P + \mathbf{a}u + \mathbf{b}v$, where $\mathbf{a}$ and $\mathbf{b}$ are two vectors lying in the plane. The normal to the surface is therefore $\mathbf{n} = \mathbf{a} \times \mathbf{b}$.

a. Show that the parametric representation of the transformed plane is $MP + M\mathbf{a}u + M\mathbf{b}v$ and that this plane has normal $\mathbf{n}' = (M\mathbf{a}) \times (M\mathbf{b})$.
b. Referring to Appendix 2, show that the following identity holds:

$$(M\mathbf{a}) \times (M\mathbf{b}) = (\det M)M^{-T}(\mathbf{a} \times \mathbf{b}).$$

This equation relates the cross product of transformed vectors to the cross product of the vectors themselves.
c. Show that $\mathbf{n}'$ is therefore parallel to $M^{-T}\mathbf{n}$. ■

6.5.4 Three "Generic" Shapes: the Sphere, Cylinder, and Cone

In this section, we begin with three classic objects, "generic" versions of the sphere, cylinder, and cone. We develop the implicit form and parametric form for each of these and see how one might make meshes to approximate them. We also derive formulas for the normal direction at each point on the object. Note that we have already used OpenGL functions in Chapter 5 to draw these shapes. Adding our own tools has a couple of advantages, however, namely, that we have much more control over the detailed nature of the shape being created and that we have the object as an actual mesh that can be operated upon by methods of the `Mesh` class.

The Generic Sphere

We call the sphere of unit radius centered at the origin the "generic sphere." [See Figure 6.54(a).] It forms the basis for all other spherelike shapes we use. This sphere has the familiar implicit form

$$F(x, y, z) = x^2 + y^2 + z^2 - 1. \tag{6.28}$$

FIGURE 6.54 (a) The generic sphere. (b) A parametric form. (c) Parallels and meridians.

In the alternative notation $F(P)$, we obtain the more elegant $F(P) = |P|^2 - 1$. (What would these forms be if the sphere has radius R?)

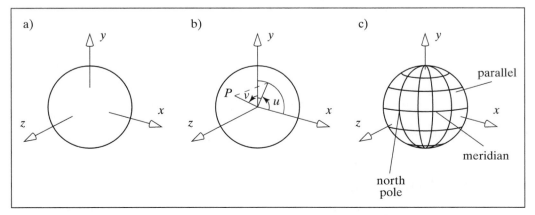

A parametric description of this sphere comes immediately from the basic description of a point in spherical coordinates. (See Appendix 2.) We choose to let u correspond to azimuth and v correspond to latitude. Then any point $P = (x, y, z)$ on the sphere has the representation $(\cos(v)\cos(u), \cos(v)\sin(u), \sin(v))$ in spherical coordinates. [See Figure 6.54(b).] We let u vary over $(0, 2\pi)$ and v vary over $(-\pi/2, \pi/2)$ to cover all such points. A parametric form for the sphere is therefore

$$P(u, v) = (\cos(v)\cos(u), \cos(v)\sin(u), \sin(v)). \tag{6.29}$$

It is easy to check that this is consistent with the implicit form: We merely substitute terms of Equation (6.29) into corresponding terms of Equation (6.28) and see that zero is obtained for *any* value of u and v.

(*Question:* What is the corresponding parametric form if the sphere instead has radius R and is centered at (a, b, c)?)

For geographical reasons, certain contours along a sphere are given common names: u-contours are called **meridians**, and v-contours are known as **parallels**, as suggested in Figure 6.54(c). (Note that this classical definition of spherical coordinates, parallels, and meridians causes the sphere to appear to lie on its side. That is simply a result of how we sketch 3D figures, with the y-axis pointing "up.")

Different parametric forms are possible for a given shape. An alternative parametric form for the sphere is examined in the exercises at the end of the section.

What is the normal direction $\mathbf{n}(u, v)$ to the sphere's surface at the point specified by the pair of parameters (u, v)? Intuitively, the normal vector is always aimed "radially outward," so it must be parallel to the vector from the origin to the point itself. This is confirmed by Equation (6.28): The gradient is simply $2(x, y, z)$, which is proportional to P. Working with the parametric form, we find that Equation (6.29) yields $\mathbf{n}(u, v) = -\cos(v)\mathbf{p}(u, v)$, so $\mathbf{n}(u, v)$ is parallel to $\mathbf{p}(u, v)$ as expected. The scale factor $-\cos(v)$ will disappear when we normalize $\mathbf{n}$. We must make sure to use $\mathbf{p}(u, v)$ rather than $-\mathbf{p}(u, v)$ for the normal, so that it does indeed point radially outward.

The Generic Cylinder

We adopt as the "generic" cylinder the cylinder whose axis coincides with the z-axis and that has a circular cross section of radius 1 and extends in z from 0 to 1, as pictured in Figure 6.55(a). It is convenient to view this cylinder as one member of the large family of **tapered cylinders**, as we did in Chapter 5. Figure 6.55(b) shows the "generic" tapered cylinder, having a "small radius" of s when $z = 1$.

The generic cylinder is simply a tapered cylinder with $s = 1$. Further, the generic cone, to be examined next, is simply a tapered cylinder with $s = 0$. We develop formulas for the tapered cylinder with an arbitrary value of s. These formulas provide other ones for the generic cylinder and cone by setting s to 1 or 0, respectively.

If we consider the tapered cylinder to be a thin hollow "shell," its **wall** is given by the implicit form

$$F(x, y, z) = x^2 + y^2 - (1 + (s - 1)z)^2 \text{ for } 0 < z < 1 \tag{6.30}$$

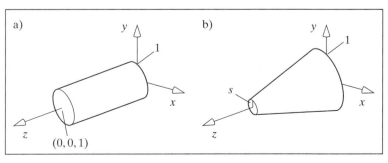

FIGURE 6.55 The generic cylinder and the tapered cylinder.

and by the parametric form

$$P(u, v) = ((1 + (s - 1)v) \cos(u), (1 + (s - 1)v) \sin(u), v) \qquad (6.31)$$

for appropriate ranges of u and v. (Which ones?) What are these expressions for the generic cylinder with $s = 1$?

When it is important to model the tapered cylinder as a solid object, we add two circular discs—a **base** and a **cap**—at its ends. The cap is that circular portion of the plane $z = 1$ characterized by the inequality $x^2 + y^2 < s^2$ or given parametrically by $P(u, v) = (v \cos(u), v \sin(u), 1)$ for v in $[0, s]$. (What is the parametric representation of the base?)

The normal vector to the wall of the tapered cylinder is found using Equation (6.27) (be sure to check this) and is

$$\mathbf{n}(x, y, z) = (x, y, -(s - 1)(1 + (s - 1)z)), \qquad (6.32)$$

or, in parametric form, $\mathbf{n}(u, v) = (\cos(u), \sin(u), 1 - s)$. For the generic cylinder, the normal is simply $(\cos(u), \sin(u), 0)$. This representation agrees with intuition: The normal is directed radially away from the axis of the cylinder. It is also directed radially away from the tapered cylinder, but is shifted by a constant z-component. (What are the normals to the cap and base?)

The Generic Cone

We take as the "generic" cone the cone whose axis coincides with the z-axis and that has a circular cross section of maximum radius 1 and extends in the z-direction from 0 to 1, as pictured in Figure 6.56. The generic cone is actually a tapered cylinder with a small radius of $s = 0$. Thus, its wall has the implicit form

FIGURE 6.56 The generic cone.

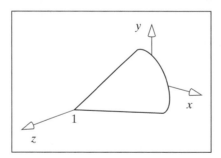

$$F(x, y, z) = x^2 + y^2 - (1 - z)^2 = 0 \quad \text{for} \quad 0 < z < 1 \qquad (6.33)$$

and the parametric form $P(u, v) = ((1 - v) \cos(u), (1 - v) \sin(u), v)$ for azimuth u in $[0, 2\pi]$ and v in $[0, 1]$. Using the results for the tapered cylinder again, we find that the normal vector to the wall of the cone is $(x, y, 1 - z)$. What is it parametrically?

For easy reference, Figure 6.57 shows the normal vector to the generic surfaces we have discussed.

FIGURE 6.57 Normal vectors to the generic surfaces.

Surface	$\mathbf{n}(u, v)$ at $\mathbf{p}(u, v)$	$F(x, y, z)$
Sphere	$\mathbf{p}(u, v)$	(x, y, z)
Tapered cylinder	$(\cos(u), \sin(u), 1 - s)$	$(x, y, -(s - 1)(1 + (s - 1)z))$
Cylinder	$(\cos(u), \sin(u), 0)$	$(x, y, 0)$
Cone	$(\cos(u), \sin(u), 1)$	$(x, y, 1 - z)$

PRACTICE EXERCISES

6.5.4 Alternative representation for the generic sphere

We can associate different geometric quantities with the parameters u and v and obtain a different parametric form for the sphere. We again employ the parameter u for azimuth, but use v for the height of the point above the xy-plane. All points at height v lie on a circle of radius $\sqrt{1 - v^2}$, so the alternative parametric form is given by

$$P_2(u, v) = (\sqrt{1 - v^2}\cos(u), \sqrt{1 - v^2}\sin(u), v) \qquad (6.34)$$

for u in $[0, 2\pi]$ and v in $[-1, 1]$. Show that P_2 lies unit distance from the origin for all u and v.

6.5.5 What's the surface?

Let A be a fixed point with position vector $\mathbf{a}$ and P be an arbitrary point with position vector $\mathbf{p}$. Describe in words and sketch the surface described by (a) $\mathbf{p} \cdot \mathbf{a} = 0$, (b) $\mathbf{p} \cdot \mathbf{a} = |\mathbf{a}|$, (c) $|\mathbf{p} \times \mathbf{a}| = |\mathbf{a}|$, (d) $\mathbf{p} \cdot \mathbf{a} = \mathbf{p} \cdot \mathbf{p}$, and (e) $\mathbf{p} \cdot \mathbf{a} = |\mathbf{a}||\mathbf{p}|/2$.

6.5.6 Finding the normal vector to the generic cylinder and cone

Derive the normal vector for the generic tapered cylinder and the generic cone in two ways:

a. Using the parametric representation.
b. Using the implicit form and then expressing the result parametrically.

6.5.7 Transformed spheres

Find the implicit form for a generic sphere that has been scaled in x by 2 and in y by 3 and then rotated $30°$ about the z-axis. ■

6.5.5 Forming a Polygonal Mesh for a Curved Surface

Now we examine how to make a mesh object that approximates a smooth surface such as the sphere, cylinder, or cone. The process is called "**polygonalization**," or, more formally, **tesselation**, and it involves replacing the surface by a collection of triangles and quadrilaterals. The vertices of these polygons lie in the surface itself, and they are joined by straight edges (which usually do not lie in the surface). One proceeds by choosing a number of values of u and v and "sampling" the parametric form for the surface at these values to obtain a collection of vertices. These vertices are then placed in a vertex list. Next, a face list is created: Each face consists of three or four indices pointing to suitable vertices in the vertex list. Associated with each vertex in a face is the normal vector to the surface. This normal vector is the normal direction to the true underlying surface at each vertex. (Note how this normal contrasts with that used in representing a flat-faced polyhedron: There, the vertex of each face is associated with the normal to the face.)

Figure 6.58 shows how the procedure works for the generic sphere. We think of slicing up the sphere along azimuth lines and latitude lines. Using OpenGL terminology of "slices" and "stacks" (see Section 5.6.3), we choose to slice the sphere into `nSlices` slices around the equator and `nStacks` stacks from the south pole to the north pole. The figure shows an example with 12 slices and 8 stacks. The larger `nSlices` and `nStacks` are, the better the mesh approximates a true sphere.

To make slices, we need `nSlices` values of u between 0 and 2π. Usually, these are chosen to be equispaced: $u_i = 2\pi i/\texttt{nSlices}, i = 0, 1, \ldots, \texttt{nSlices} - 1$. As for stacks, we put half of them above the equator and half below. The top and bottom stacks will consist of triangles; all other faces will be quadrilaterals. This requires that we define ($\texttt{nStacks} + 1$) values of latitude: $v_j = \pi/2 - \pi j/\texttt{nStacks}, j = 0, 1, \ldots, \texttt{nStacks}$.

FIGURE 6.58 (a) A mesh approximation to the generic sphere. (b) Numbering the vertices.

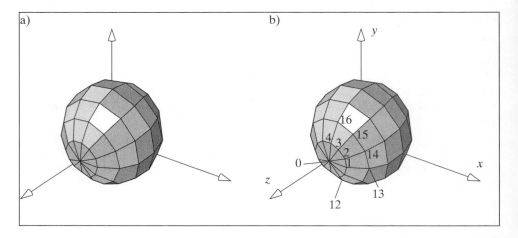

The vertex list can now be created. The figure shows how we might number the vertices (the ordering is a matter of convenience): We put the north pole in pt[0], the bottom points of the top stack into the next 12 vertices, etc. With 12 slices and 8 stacks, there will be a total of 98 points. (Why?)

The normal-vector list is also easily created: norm[k] will hold the normal to the sphere at vertex pt[k]. norm[k] is computed by evaluating the parametric form of $\mathbf{n}(u, v)$ at the same (u, v) used for the points. For the sphere, this computation is particularly easy, since norm[k] is the same as pt[k].

The face list will have 96 faces, of which 24 are triangles. We can put the top triangles in the first 12 faces, the 12 quadrilaterals of the next stack down in the next 12 faces, etc. The first few faces will contain the following data:

Number of vertices:	3	3	3	...
Vertex indices:	0 1 2	0 2 3	0 3 4	...
normal indices:	0 1 2	0 2 3	0 3 4	...

Note that the normIndex is always the same as the vertIndex for all meshes that try to represent smooth shapes, so the data structure holds redundant information. (Because of this, one could use a more streamlined data structure for such meshes. What would it be?) "Polygonalization" of the sphere in this way is straightforward, but it can be very tricky for more complicated shapes. (See the references for further discussions.)

Ultimately, we need a method, such as makeSurfaceMesh(), that generates these meshes for a given surface $P(u, v)$. We discuss the implementation of a function that does just that job in Case Study 6.13.

Note that some graphics packages have routines that are highly optimized when they operate on triangles. To exploit these routines, we might choose to "polygonalize" the sphere into a collection of triangles, subdividing each quadrilateral into two triangles.

A simple approach would use the same vertices as before, but alter the face list, replacing each quadrilateral with two triangles. For instance, a face that uses vertices 2, 3, 15, and 14 might be subdivided into two triangles, one using vertices 2, 3, and 15 and the other using 2, 15, and 14.

The sphere is a special case of a surface of revolution, which we treat in Section 6.5.7. The tapered cylinder is also a surface of revolution. It is straightforward to develop a mesh model for the tapered cylinder. Figure 6.59 shows the tapered cylinder approximated with nSlices = 10 and nStacks = 1. A decagon is used for the cap and base. [If you prefer to use only triangles in a mesh, the walls, the cap, and the base could be dissected into triangles. (How?)]

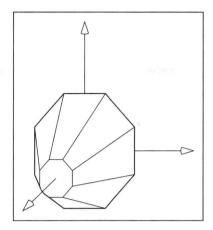

FIGURE 6.59 A mesh approximation to the tapered cylinder.

PRACTICE EXERCISES

6.5.8 The mesh for a given sphere

Choosing a convenient numbering scheme, write out the vertex, normal, and face lists for the sphere when $\texttt{nSlices} = 6$ and $\texttt{nStacks} = 4$.

6.5.9 Restricting the mesh to triangular faces

Adjust the lists in the previous exercise for the case where all faces are triangles.

6.5.10 The mesh for a cylinder and cone

Write out vertex, normal, and face lists for the generic tapered cylinder that uses $\texttt{nSlices} = 4$ and $\texttt{nStacks} = 2$. ▪

6.5.6 Ruled Surfaces

In this section, we resume an exploration of curved surfaces with the family of **ruled surfaces**. This family is simple to describe, yet it provides a wide variety of useful and interesting shapes. We study how to describe these shapes, "polygonalize" them, and compute the normal vector to them at each point.

Ruled surfaces (also called lofted surfaces) are swept out by moving a straight line along a particular trajectory. They are composed of a collection of straight lines in accordance with the following definition.

> **DEFINITION:** A surface is **ruled** if, through every one of its points, there passes at least one line that lies entirely on the surface.

Because ruled surfaces are based on a family of lines, it is not surprising to find buried in their parametric representations something akin to the familiar form for a line, $P(v) = (1 - v)P_0 + vP_1$, where P_0 and P_1 are points. But for ruled surfaces, the points P_0 and P_1 become functions of another parameter u: P_0 becomes $P_0(u)$, and P_1 becomes $P_1(u)$. Thus, the ruled surfaces that we examine have the parametric form

$$P(u, v) = (1 - v)P_0(u) + vP_1(u). \tag{6.35}$$

The functions $P_0(u)$ and $P_1(u)$ define curves lying in 3D space. Each is described by three component functions, as in $P_0(u) = \big(X_0(u), Y_0(u), Z_0(u)\big)$. Both $P_0(u)$ and $P_1(u)$ are defined on the same interval in u (commonly from 0 to 1). The ruled surface consists of one straight line joining each pair of corresponding points, $P_0(u')$ and $P_1(u')$,

FIGURE 6.60 A ruled surface as a family of straight lines.

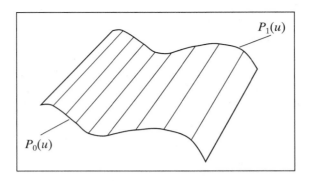

for each u' in $(0, 1)$, as indicated in Figure 6.60. At $v = 0$ the surface is "at" $P_0(u')$, and at $v = 1$ it is at $P_1(u')$. The straight line at $u = u'$ is often called the **ruling** at u'.

For a particular fixed value v', the **v'-contour** is an affine combination of the two curves $P_0(u)$ and $P_1(u)$, with the first weighted by $(1 - v')$ and the second by v'. When v' is close to zero, the shape of the v'-contour is determined mainly by $P_0(u)$, whereas when v' is close to unit, the curve $P_1(u)$ has the most influence.

If we restrict v to lie between 0 and 1, only the line segment between corresponding points on the curves will be part of the surface. On the other hand, if v is not restricted, each line will continue forever in both directions, and the surface will resemble an unbounded curved "sheet." A **ruled patch** is formed by restricting the range of both u and v, to values between, say, 0 and 1.

A ruled surface is easily "polygonalized" in the usual fashion: We choose a set of samples u_i and v_j and compute the position $P(u_i, v_j)$ and normal $\mathbf{n}(u_i, v_j)$ at each. Then we build the lists as we have done before.

Some special cases of ruled surfaces will reveal their nature as well as their versatility. We discuss three important families of ruled surfaces: the **cone**, the **cylinder**, and the **bilinear patch**.

Cones

A cone is a ruled surface for which one of the curves, say, $P_0(u)$, is a *single* point: the apex of the cone, as suggested in Figure 6.61. In Equation (6.35), this restriction produces the equation

FIGURE 6.61 A cone.

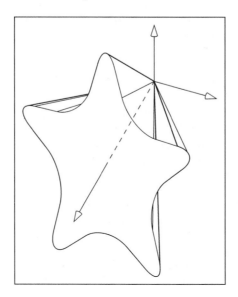

$$P(u, v) = (1 - v)P_0 + vP_1(u) \qquad \text{(a general cone)}, \qquad (6.36)$$

where P_0 is the apex. For this parameterization, all lines pass through P_0 at $v = 0$ and through $P_1(u)$ at $v = 1$. Certain special cases are familiar: A circular cone results when $P_1(u)$ is a circle, and a right circular cone results when the circle lies in a plane that is perpendicular to the line joining the circle's center to P_0. The specific example shown in Figure 6.61 uses $P_1(u) = \big(r(u) \cos u, r(u) \sin u, 1\big)$ where the "radius" curve $r(u)$ varies sinusoidally according to the equation $r(u) = 0.5 + 0.2 \cos(5u)$.

Cylinders

A cylinder is a ruled surface for which $P_1(u)$ is simply a translated version of $P_0(u)$: $P_1(u) = P_0(u) + \mathbf{d}$, for some vector $\mathbf{d}$, as shown in Figure 6.62(a). Sometimes one speaks of "sweeping" the line with endpoints $P_0(0)$ and $P_0(0) + \mathbf{d}$ (often called the *generator*) along the curve $P_0(u)$ (often called the *directrix*), without altering the direction of the line, to produce a cylinder.

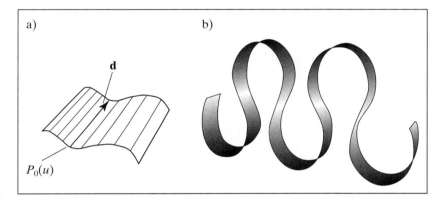

FIGURE 6.62 (a) A cylinder. (b) A ribbon candy cylinder.

The general cylinder therefore has the parametric form

$$P(u, v) = P_0(u) + \mathbf{d}v. \qquad (6.37)$$

To generate a true cylinder, the curve $P_0(u)$ is confined to lie in a plane. If $P_0(u)$ is a circle, the cylinder is a **circular cylinder**. The direction $\mathbf{d}$ need not be perpendicular to this plane, but if it is, the surface is called a **right cylinder**. This is the case for the generic cylinder. Figure 6.62b shows a "ribbon candy cylinder," where $P_0(u)$ undulates back and forth like a piece of ribbon. The ribbon shape is explored in the exercises at the end of the section.

Bilinear Patches

A bilinear patch is formed when both $P_0(u)$ and $P_1(u)$ are straight-line segments defined over the same interval in u, say, 0 to 1. Suppose the endpoints of $P_0(u)$ are P_{00} and P_{01} (so that $P_0(u)$ is given by $(1 - u)P_{00} + u P_{01}$) and the endpoints of $P_1(u)$ are P_{10} and P_{11}. Then, from Equation (6.35), the patch is given parametrically by

$$P(u, v) = (1 - v)(1 - u)P_{00} + (1 - v)u P_{01} + v(1 - u)P_{10} + uv P_{11}. \qquad (6.38)$$

This surface is called *bilinear*, because its dependence is linear in u and linear in v. Bilinear patches need not be planar; in fact, they are planar only if the lines $P_0(u)$ and $P_1(u)$ lie in the same plane. (See the exercises.) Otherwise there must be a twist in the surface as we move from one of the defining lines to the other.

An example of a nonplanar bilinear patch is shown in Figure 6.63. $P_0(u)$ is the line from $(2, -2, 2)$ to $(2, 2, -2)$, and $P_1(u)$ is the line from $(-2, -2, -2)$ to $(-2, 2, 2)$.

FIGURE 6.63 A bilinear patch.

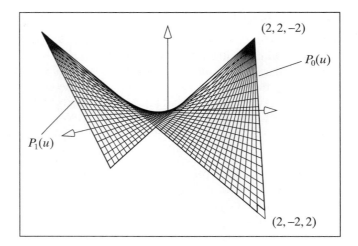

These lines are not coplanar; several u-contours are shown, and the twist in the patch is clearly visible.

The normal vector to a bilinear patch is easily found using Equation (6.25). If the patch is planar, the direction of the normal is constant, but its magnitude can vary with u and v. If the patch is nonplanar, both the magnitude and direction of the normal vector vary with position.

Other Ruled Surfaces

There are many other interesting ruled surfaces. Figure 6.64(a) shows a double helix formed when $P_0(u)$ and $P_1(u)$ are helices that wind around each other. Part (b) shows the intriguing Möbius strip, which has only one edge. The exercises explore the parametric representation of these surfaces. Part (c) shows a vaulted roof made up of four ruled surfaces. Case Study 6.8 examines modeling such vaulted domes of cathedrals.

FIGURE 6.64 (a) Double helix. (b) Möbius strip. (c) Vaulted roof.

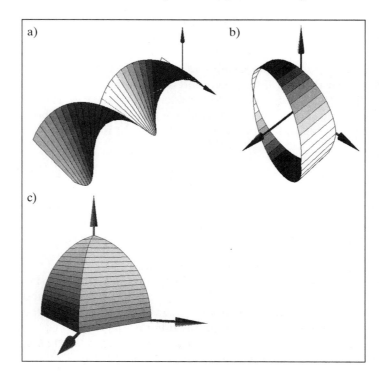

Bilinearly Blended Surfaces: Coons Patches

An interesting and useful generalization of a ruled surface that interpolates two boundary curves $P_0(u)$ and $P_1(u)$ is a bilinearly blended patch that interpolates to *four* boundary curves. This family was first developed by Steven Coons [Coons67] and is sometimes called a *Coons patch*.

Figure 6.65 shows four adjoining boundary curves, named $p_{u0}(u)$, $p_{u1}(u)$, $p_{0v}(v)$, and $p_{1v}(v)$. These curves meet at the corners of the patch that is depicted (where u and v are combinations of 0 and 1), but otherwise have arbitrary shapes. This example therefore generalizes the bilinear patch for which the boundary curves are straight lines. We want a formula $P(u, v)$ that produces a smooth transition from each boundary curve to the other as u and v vary.

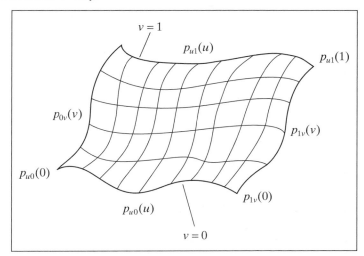

FIGURE 6.65 Four boundary curves determining a Coons patch.

A natural first guess is to somehow combine a ruled patch built out of $p_{u0}(u)$ and $p_{u1}(u)$ with a ruled patch built out of $p_{0v}(v)$ and $p_{1v}(v)$. But simply adding such surfaces doesn't work: It fails to interpolate the four curves properly (and it is invalid, resulting in a nonaffine combination of points!). The trick is to add these surfaces and then subtract the bilinear patch formed from the four corners of the curves. Figure 6.66 shows visually how this works [Heckbert94].

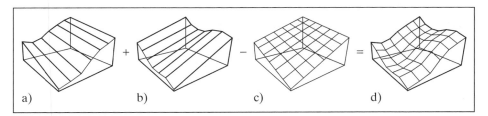

FIGURE 6.66 Combining patches to create the Coons patch.

The formula for the patch is therefore

$$P(u, v) = \left[p_{0v}(v)(1 - u) + p_{1v}(v)u \right] + \left[p_{u0}(u)(1 - v) + p_{u1}(u)v \right]$$
$$- \left[(1 - u)(1 - v)p_{0v}(0) + u(1 - v)p_{1v}(0)u + p_{0v}(1)v(1 - u) + p_{1v}(1)u\,v \right]. \quad (6.39)$$

Note that at each (u, v) this equation still represents an affine combination of points, as we insist: At $(u, v) = (0, 0)$ it evaluates to $p_{u0}(0)$, and similarly, it coincides with the other three corners at the other extreme values of u and v. Figure 6.67 shows a sample Coons patch bounded by curves that have a sinusoidal oscillation.

FIGURE 6.67 Example of a Coons patch.

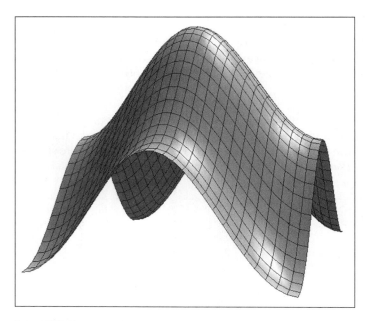

PRACTICE EXERCISES

6.5.11 A pyramid is a cone

What shape should $P_1(u)$ have in order to create a ruled surface that is a pyramid with a square base? Give specific expressions for the curve and the point P_0 so that the square base of the pyramid lies in the x, z-plane, centered at the origin, with sides of length 2. The pyramid should have height 1.5.

6.5.12 Ribbon candy cylinders

Find a parametric form for $P_0(u)$ that produces a good approximation to the ribbon candy cylinder shown in Figure 6.62(b). Assume that the ribbon is wrapped around a succession of abutting circular cylinders of radius 1. The center of the ith cylinder lies at $(x_i, y_i) = (i2d, \pm r)$, where the pluses and minuses alternate and $d^2 = 1 - r^2$. Choose some value of r between 0 and 1.

6.5.13 The double helix

The parametric form for a helix is $(\cos(t), \sin(t), t)$. Find expressions for two helices, $P_0(u)$ and $P_1(u)$, both of which wind around the z-axis, yet are 180° out of phase, so that they wind around each other. Write the parametric form for the ruled surface formed with the use of these two curves.

6.5.14 The Möbius strip

Find a parametric form for the Möbius strip shown in Figure 6.64(b). (*Hint*: Revolve a line about the z-axis, but put in a twist as the line goes around. Does the pair of equations $P_0(u) = (\cos(2pu), \sin(2pu), u)$ and $P_1(u) = (\cos(2pu), \sin(2pu), 1 - u)$ do the job?

6.5.15 Is it affine?

Show that the Coons patch $P(u, v)$ of Equation (6.39) is composed of an affine combination of points.

6.5.16 Does it really interpolate?

Check to make sure that $P(u, v)$ of Equation (6.39) interpolates each of the four boundary curves and therefore interpolates each of the four corners.   ■

6.5.7 Surfaces of Revolution

As described earlier, a surface of revolution is formed by a **rotational sweep** of a profile curve C around an axis. Suppose we place the profile in the xz-plane and represent it parametrically by $C(v) = (X(v), Z(v))$. To generate the surface of revolution, we sweep the profile about the z-axis under control of the u parameter, where u specifies the angle through which each point has been swept about the axis. As before, the different positions of the curve C around the axis are called **meridians**. When the point $(X(v), 0, Z(v))$ is rotated by u radians, it becomes $(X(v)\cos(u), X(v)\sin(u), Z(v))$. Sweeping the curve completely around generates a full circle, so contours of constant v are circles, called **parallels** of the surface.[7] The parallel at v has radius $X(v)$ and lies at a height $Z(v)$ above the xy-plane. Thus, the general point on the surface is

$$P(u, v) = (X(v)\cos(u), X(v)\sin(u), Z(v)) \qquad (6.40)$$

The generic sphere, tapered cylinder, and cone are all familiar special cases of the surface of revolution. (What are their profiles?)

The normal vector to a surface of revolution is easily found by directly applying Equation (6.40) to Equation (6.25) (See the exercises at the end of the section.) This yields

$$\mathbf{n}(u, v) = X(v)(\dot{Z}(v)\cos(u), \dot{Z}(v)\sin(u), -\dot{X}(v)), \qquad (6.41)$$

where the dot denotes the first derivative of the function. The scaling factor $X(v)$ disappears upon normalization of the vector. This result specializes to the forms we found for the simple generic shapes. (See the exercises.)

For example, the **torus** is generated by sweeping a displaced circle about the z-axis, as shown in Figure 6.68(a). The circle has radius A and is displaced along the x-axis by D, so that its profile is $C(v) = (D + A\cos(v), A\sin(v))$. Therefore, the torus [Figure 6.68(b)] has the representation

$$P(u, v) = ((D + A\cos(v))\cos(u), (D + A\cos(v))\sin(u), A\sin(v)). \qquad (6.42)$$

The normal vector is developed in the exercises.

FIGURE 6.68 A torus.

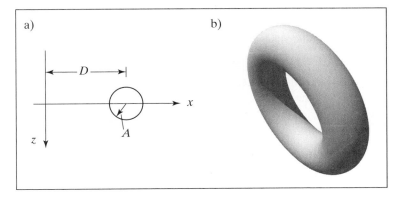

We usually sweep a curve lying in a plane about an axis that lies in that plane, but a surface of revolution can be formed by sweeping about any axis. Choosing different axes for a given profile can lead to interesting families of surfaces. The general form for $P(u, v)$ for the surface of revolution about an arbitrary axis is developed in the exercises.

A mesh for a surface of revolution is built into a program in the usual way. We choose a set of u and v values, $\{u_i\}$ and $\{v_j\}$, and compute a vertex at each from $P(u_i, v_j)$ and

---

[7] More formally, a **meridian** is the intersection of a surface with a plane that contains the axis of revolution of the surface, and a **parallel** is the intersection of the surface with a plane perpendicular to the axis of revolution.

a normal direction from $\mathbf{n}(u_i, v_j)$. Polygonal faces are built by joining four adjacent vertices with straight lines. A method for doing this is discussed in Case Study 6.13.

Figure 6.69(a) shows an example in which we try to model the dome of the exquisite Taj Mahal in Agra, India. Part (b) shows the profile curve in the xz-plane, and Part (c) shows the resulting surface of revolution. We describe the profile by a collection of data points $C_i = (X_i, Z_i)$, since no suitable parametric formula is available. (We rectify this shortcoming in Chapter 11 by using a B-spline curve to form a smooth parametric curve based on a set of data points.)

To build a surface of revolution when the profile consists of discrete points, we simply take as the ijth vertex the slightly different form of Equation (6.40):

$$P_{i,j} = (X_j \cos(u_i), X_j \sin(u_i), Z_j).$$

FIGURE 6.69 A surface of revolution - the dome of the Taj Mahal.

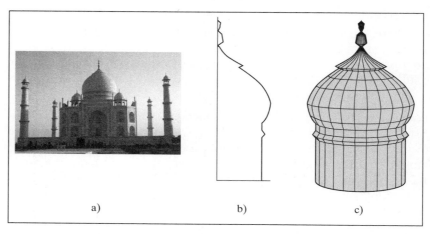

a)   b)   c)

PRACTICE EXERCISES

6.5.17 The generic shapes as surfaces of revolution

Describe the profiles of the generic sphere, cylinder, and cone parametrically, and then express them as surfaces of revolution.

6.5.18 Rotation about other axes

Consider a profile curve $C(v) = (X(v), Z(v))$, lying in the xz-plane, and an arbitrary axis through the origin given by the unit vector $\mathbf{r}$. We know from Equation (5.33) that the matrix $R_r(\theta)$ performs a rotation of a point through θ radians about the axis $\mathbf{r}$.

a. Show that the surface of revolution formed by sweeping $C(v)$ about axis $\mathbf{r}$ is

$$(X(u, v), Y(u, v), Z(u, v), 1) = R_r(u) \begin{pmatrix} X(v) \\ 0 \\ Z(v) \\ 1 \end{pmatrix}.$$

b. Check this equation for the special case of rotation about the z-axis.
c. Repeat Part (b) for rotations about the x-axis and about the y-axis.

6.5.19 Finding normal vectors

a. Apply Equation (6.40) to Equation (6.25) to derive the form in Equation (6.41) for the normal vector to a surface of revolution.
b. Use the result of Part (a) to find the normal to each of the generic sphere, cylinder, and cone, and show that the results agree with those found in Section 6.5.4. Show that the normal vector to the torus has the form

$$\mathbf{n}(u, v) = (\cos(v) \cos(u), \cos(v) \sin(u), \sin(v))(D + A \cos(v)).$$

Also, find the inside–outside function for the torus, and compute the normal using the gradient of the function.

6.5.20 An elliptical torus

Find the parametric representation for the following two surfaces of revolution: (a) the surface formed when ellipse given by $\left(a\cos(v), b\sin(v)\right)$ is first displaced R units along the x-axis and then revolved about the y-axis; (b) the surface formed when same ellipse is revolved about the x-axis.

6.5.21 A "Lissajous of revolution"

Sketch what the surface would look like if the Lissajous figure of Equation (6.19) with $M = 2, N = 3$, and $\phi = 0$ is rotated about the y-axis.

6.5.22 Revolved n-gons

Sketch the surface generated when a square having vertices $(1, 0, 0), (0, 1, 0), (-1, 0, 0), (0, -1, 0)$ is revolved about the y-axis. Repeat for a pentagon and a hexagon. ■

6.5.8 The Quadric Surfaces

An important family of surfaces, the quadric surfaces, are the 3D analogs of conic sections (the ellipse, parabola, and hyperbola, which we examined in Chapter 3). Some of the quadric surfaces have beautiful shapes and can be put to good use in graphics.

The six quadric surfaces are illustrated in Figure 6.70. We need only characterize the "generic" versions of these shapes, since we can obtain all the variations of interest

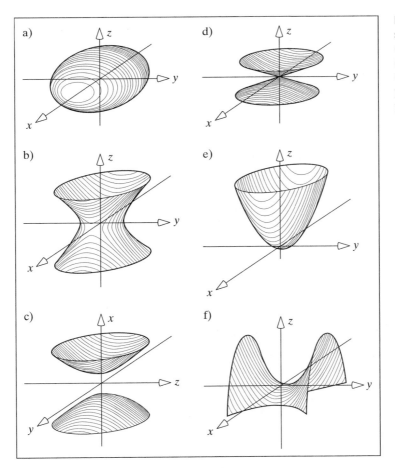

FIGURE 6.70 The six quadric surfaces: (a) Ellipsoid. (b) Hyperboloid of one sheet. (c) Hyperboloid of two sheets. (d) Elliptic cone. (e) Elliptic paraboloid. (f) Hyperbolic paraboloid.

by scaling, rotating, and translating the generic shapes. For example, the ellipsoid is usually said to have the inside–outside function

$$F(x, y, z) = \left(\frac{x}{a}\right)^2 + \left(\frac{y}{b}\right)^2 + \left(\frac{z}{c}\right)^2 - 1, \tag{6.43}$$

so that it extends from $-a$ to a in x, from $-b$ to b in y, and from $-c$ to c in z. This shape may be obtained from the form of the generic sphere by scaling it in x, y, and z by $a, b,$ and c, respectively, as we describe shortly. We can obtain rotated versions of the ellipsoid in a similar manner.

FIGURE 6.71 Characterization of the six "generic" quadric surfaces.

Figure 6.71 describes the six generic quadric surfaces, giving both their implicit and parametric forms. We discuss some interesting properties of each shape later.

Name of quadric	Implicit form	Parametric form	v-range, u-range
Ellipsoid	$x^2 + y^2 + z^2 - 1$	$(\cos(v)\cos(u), \cos(v)\sin(u), \sin(v))$	$(-\pi/2, \pi/2), (-\pi, \pi)$
Hyperboloid of one sheet	$x^2 + y^2 - z^2 - 1$	$(\sec(v)\cos(u), \sec(v)\sin(u), \tan(v))$	$(-\pi/2, \pi/2), (-\pi, \pi)$
Hyperboloid of two sheets	$x^2 - y^2 - z^2 - 1$	$(\sec(v)\cos(u), \sec(v)\tan(u), \tan(v))$	$(-\pi/2, \pi/2)$[a]
Elliptic cone	$x^2 + y^2 - z^2$	$(v\cos(u), v\sin(u), v)$	any real numbers, $(-\pi, \pi)$
Elliptic paraboloid	$x^2 + y^2 - z$	$(v\cos(u), v\sin(u), v^2)$	$v \geq 0, (-\pi, \pi)$
Hyperbolic paraboloid	$-x^2 + y^2 - z$	$(v\tan(u), v\sec(u), v^2)$	$v \geq 0, (-\pi, \pi)$

[a]The v-range for sheet # 1 is $(-\pi/2, \pi/2)$ and for sheet # 2 is $(\pi/2, 3\pi/2)$

Figure 6.71 also reports the parametric form for each of the generic quadric surfaces. It is straightforward to check that each of these forms is consistent with its corresponding implicit form: We simply substitute the parametric form for the x-, y-, and z- components and use trigonometric identities to obtain zero.

Note that a change of sign in one term of the inside–outside function causes a $\cos()$ to be changed to $\sec()$ and a $\sin()$ to be changed to $\tan()$ in the parametric forms. Both $\sec()$ and $\tan()$ grow without bound as their arguments approach $\pi/2$, so, in drawing u-contours or v-contours, the relevant parameter is restricted to a smaller range.

Some Notes on the Quadric Surfaces

We shall summarize briefly some significant properties of each quadric surface. One such property is the nature of traces of the surface. A **trace** is the curve formed when the surface is cut by a plane. All traces of a quadric surface are conic sections. (See the exercises at the end of the section.) The **principal traces** are the curves that are generated when the cutting planes are aligned with the axes: the planes $z = k, y = k$, or $x = k$, where k is some constant.

In the discussion that follows, we suppose that the generic surfaces have been scaled in $x, y,$ and z by the values $a, b,$ and c, respectively, to make it easier to talk about the dimensions of the surfaces and to distinguish cases in which the surface is a surface of revolution from cases in which it is not.

Ellipsoid Compare the implicit form and parametric form for the ellipse in Chapter 3 to see how they extend the 2D ellipse to the 3D ellipsoid. Parameters $a, b,$ and c give the extent of the ellipsoid along each axis. When two of the parameters are equal, the ellipsoid is a surface of revolution. (If $a = b$, what is the axis of revolution?)

When a, b, and c all are equal, the ellipsoid becomes a sphere. All traces of the ellipsoid are ellipses.

Hyperboloid of One Sheet When $a = b$, the hyperboloid becomes a surface of revolution formed by rotating a hyperbola about an axis. The principal traces for the planes $z = k$ are ellipses, and those for the planes $x = k$ and $y = k$ are hyperbolas. The hyperboloid of one sheet is particularly interesting, because it is a *ruled* surface, as suggested in Figure 6.72(a). If a thread is woven between two parallel ellipses, as shown, this surface will be created. Formulas for the rulings are discussed in the exercises.

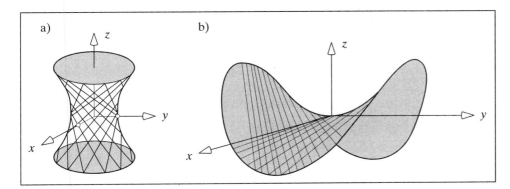

FIGURE 6.72 Two ruled quadric surfaces.

Hyperboloid of Two Sheets No part of this surface lies between $x = -a$ and $x = a$. (Why?) When $a = b$, the figure becomes a surface of revolution. The traces for planes $x = k$ when $|k| > a$ are ellipses, and the other principal traces are hyperbolas.

Elliptic Cone The elliptic cone is a special case of the general cone treated earlier: Its generator lines trace an ellipse. This cone is, of course, a ruled surface, and the principal traces for planes $z = k$ are ellipses. (What are traces for planes that contain the z-axis?) When $a = b$, this quadric is a surface of revolution: It becomes a right circular cone.

Elliptic Paraboloid The traces of an elliptic paraboloid for planes $z = k > 0$ are ellipses, and the other principal traces are parabolas. When $a = b$, the figure becomes a surface of revolution.

Hyperbolic Paraboloid The hyperbolic paraboloid is sometimes called a saddle-shaped surface. The traces for planes $z = k$ (when $k \neq 0$) are hyperbolas, and for planes $x = k$ or $y = k$, they are parabolas. (What is the intersection of this surface with the plane $z = 0$?) The hyperbolic paraboloid is also a ruled surface. [See Figure 6.72(b).]

Normal Vectors to Quadric Surfaces

Because the implicit form for each quadric surface is quadratic in x, y, and z, taking the gradient to find the normal presents no problem. Further, since each component of the gradient vector is linear in its own variable or is just a constant, it is straightforward to write the gradient in parametric form: We just substitute $X(u, v)$ for x, etc. For instance, the gradient of $F(x, y, z)$ for the ellipsoid is

$$F = (2x, 2y, 2z),$$

so, in parametric form and after deleting the 2, the normal is

$$n(u, v) = (\cos(v)\cos(u), \cos(v)\sin(u), \sin(v)). \tag{6.44}$$

Normals for the other quadric surfaces follow just as easily, so they need not be tabulated.

PRACTICE EXERCISES

6.5.23 The hyperboloid is a ruled surface

Show that the implicit form of a hyperboloid of one sheet can be written $(x + z)$ $(x - z) = (1 - y)(1 + y)$. Show also that, therefore, two families of straight lines lie in the surface: the family $x - z = A(1 - y)$ and the family $A(x + z) = 1 + y$, where A is a constant. Sketch these families for various values of A. Examine similar rulings in the hyperbolic paraboloid.

6.5.24 The hyperboloid of one sheet

Show that an alternative parametric form for the hyperboloid of one sheet is $p(u, v) = \big(\cosh(v)\cos(u), \cosh(v)\sin(u), \sinh(v)\big)$.

6.5.25 Traces of quadrics are conics

Consider any three noncollinear points lying on a quadric surface. They determine a plane that cuts through the quadric, forming the trace curve. Show that this curve is always a parabola, an ellipse, or a hyperbola.

6.5.26 Finding normals to the quadrics

Find the normal vector in parametric form for each of the six quadric surfaces.

6.5.27 The hyperboloid as a ruled surface

Suppose $(x_0, y_0, 0)$ is a point on the hyperboloid of one sheet. Show that the vector

$$R(t) = (x_0 + y_0 t, y_0 - x_0 t, t)$$

describes a straight line that lies everywhere on the hyperboloid and passes through the point $(x_0, y_0, 0.)$ Is this property sufficient to make the surface a ruled surface? Why or why not [Apostol61]?

6.5.28 The hyperbolic paraboloid as a ruled surface

Show that the intersection of any plane parallel to the line $y = \pm x$ cuts the hyperbolic paraboloid along a straight line.   ◼

6.5.9 The Superquadrics

Following the work of Alan Barr [Barr81], we can extend the quadric surfaces to a vastly larger family, in much the way we extended the ellipse to the superellipse in Chapter 3. This provides additional interesting surface shapes we can use as models in applications.

Barr defines four superquadric solids: the superellipsoid, superhyperboloid of one sheet, and superhyperboloid of two sheets, which together extend the first three quadric surfaces, and the supertoroid, which extends the torus. The extensions introduce two "bulge factors," m and n, to which various terms are raised. These bulge factors affect the surfaces much as n does for the superellipse. When both factors equal 2, the first three superquadrics revert to the quadric surfaces catalogued previously. Sample shapes for the four superquadrics are shown in Figure 6.73. The implicit forms and parametric forms[8] are given in Figure 6.74.

---

[8]   Keep in mind that it is illegitimate to raise a negative value to a fractional exponent. So expressions such as $\cos^{2/m}(v)$ should be evaluated as $\cos(v)|\cos(v)|^{2/m-1}$ or the equivalent.

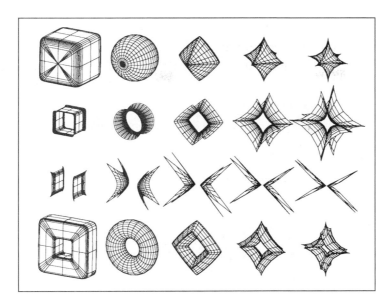

FIGURE 6.73 Samples of the four superquadrics. n_1 and n_2 are (left to right) 10, 2, 1.11, .77, and .514. (Courtesy of Jay Greco.)

Name of quadric	Implicit form	Parametric form	v-range, u-range
Superellipsoid	$(x^n + y^n)^{m/n} + z^m - 1$	$(\cos^{2/m}(v) \cos^{2/n}(u), \cos^{2/m}(v) \sin^{2/n}(u), \sin^{2/m}(v))$	$[-\pi/2, \pi/2], [-\pi, \pi]$
Superhyperboloid of one sheet	$(x^n + y^n)^{m/n} - z^m - 1$	$(\sec^{2/m}(v) \cos^{2/n}(u), \sec^{2/m}(v) \sin^{2/n}(u), \tan^{2/m}(v))$	$(-\pi/2, \pi/2), [-\pi, \pi]$
Superhyperboloid of two sheets	$(x^n - y^n)^{m/n} - z^m - 1$	$(\sec^{2/m}(v) \sec^{2/n}(u), \sec^{2/m}(v) \tan^{2/n}(u), \tan^{2/m}(v))$	$(-\pi/2, \pi/2)$
Supertoroid	$((x^n - y^n)^{1/n} - d)^m + z^m - 1$	$((d + \cos^{2/m}(v)) \cos^{2/n}(u), (d + \cos^{2/m}(v)) \sin^{2/n}(u), \sin^{2/m}(v))$	$[-\pi, \pi), [-\pi, \pi)$

FIGURE 6.74 Characterization of the four superquadric surfaces.

The superquadrics listed in the figure are "generic" ones, in the sense that they are centered at the origin, are aligned with the coordinate axes, and have unit dimensions. Like other shapes, they may be scaled, rotated, and translated as desired, using the current transformation to prepare them properly for a scene.

Normals to the Superellipsoid and Supertoroid

The normal vector $\mathbf{n}(u, v)$ can be computed for each superquadric in the usual ways. We shall give only the results here. The normal vectors for the superellipsoid and the supertoroid are the same:

$$\mathbf{n}(u, v) = \left(\cos^{2-2/m}(v) \cos^{2-2/n}(u), \cos^{2-2/m}(v) \sin^{2-2/n}(u), \sin^{2-2/m}(v)\right). \qquad (6.45)$$

(How can they be the same? The two surfaces surely do not have the same shape.)

The Superhyperboloid of One Sheet

The normal vector to the superhyperboloid of one sheet is the same as that of the superellipsoid, except that all occurrences of $\cos(v)$ are replaced with $\sec(v)$ and those of $\sin(v)$ are replaced with $\tan(v)$. Do not alter $\cos(u)$ or $\sin(u)$ or any other term.

The Superhyperboloid of Two Sheets

For the superhyperboloid of two sheets, the trigonometric functions in both u and v are replaced. We replace all occurrences of $\cos(v)$ with $\sec(v)$, those of $\sin(v)$ with $\tan(v)$, those of $\cos(u)$ with $\sec(u)$, and those of $\sin(u)$ with $\tan(u)$.

PRACTICE EXERCISES

6.5.29 Extents of superquadrics

What are the maximum x, y, and z values attainable for the superellipsoid and the supertoroid?

6.5.30 Surfaces of revolution

Determine the values of the bulge factors m and n for which each of the superquadrics is a surface of revolution, and find the axis of revolution. Describe any other symmetries in the surfaces.

6.5.31 Deriving the normal vectors

Derive the formula for the normal vector to each superquadric surface.   ■

6.5.10 Tubes Based on 3D Curves

In Section 6.4.4, we studied tubes that were based on a spine curve $C(t)$ meandering through 3D space. A polygon was stationed at each of a selection of spine points and was oriented according to the Frenet frame computed there. Then, corresponding points on adjacent polygons were connected to form a flat-faced tube along the spine.

Here we do the same thing, except we compute the normal to the surface at each vertex, so that smooth shading can be performed. Figure 6.75 shows a tube wrapped around a helical shape. Compare this shape with Figure 6.47.

FIGURE 6.75 A helical tube undulating through space.

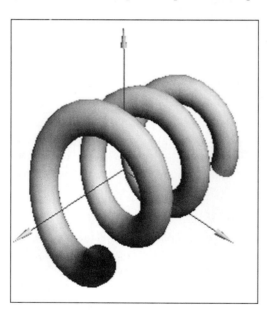

If we wish to wrap a circle given by $(\cos(u), \sin(u), 0)$ about the spine $C(t)$, the resulting surface has the parametric representation

$$P(u, v) = C(v) + \cos(u)\mathbf{N}(v) + \sin(u)\mathbf{B}(v), \qquad (6.46)$$

where the normal vector $\mathbf{N}(t)$ and the binormal vector $\mathbf{B}(t)$ are those given in Equations (6.15) and (6.14), respectively. Now we can build a mesh for this tube in the usual way, by taking samples of $P(u, v)$ and building the vertex, normal, and face lists, etc. (What would be altered if we wrapped a cycloid—recall Figure 3.98—about the spine instead of a circle?)

6.5.11 Surfaces Based on Explicit Functions of Two Variables

Many surface shapes are **single valued** in one dimension, so their position can be represented as an explicit function of two of the independent variables. For instance, there may be a single value of "height" of the surface above the xz-plane for each point (x, z), as suggested in Figure 6.76. We can then say that the height of the surface at (x, z) is some function $f(x, z)$. Such a function is sometimes called a **height field** [Bloomenthal97] and is often given by a formula such as

$$f(x, z) = e^{-ax^2 - bz^2} \tag{6.47}$$

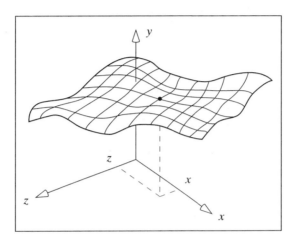

FIGURE 6.76 A single-valued height field above the xz-plane.

(where a and b are given constants) or by the circularly symmetric "sinc" function

$$f(x, z) = \frac{\sin(\sqrt{x^2 + z^2})}{\sqrt{x^2 + z^2}}. \tag{6.48}$$

Contrast this surface with surfaces such as the sphere, for which more than one value of y is associated with each point (x, z). Single-valued functions permit a simple parametric form,

$$P(u, v) = (u, f(u, v), v), \tag{6.49}$$

and their normal vector is $\mathbf{n}(u, v) = (-\partial f / \partial u, 1, -\partial f / \partial v)$. (Check this.) That is, u and v can be used directly as the dependent variables for the function. Thus, u-contours lie in planes of constant x, and v-contours lie in planes of constant z. Figure 6.77(a) shows a view of the surface described by Equation (6.47), and Figure 6.77(b) shows the function of Equation (6.48). Each line is a trace of the surface cut by a plane, $x = k$ or $z = k$, for some value of k. Plots such as these can help illustrate the behavior of a mathematical function.

PRACTICE EXERCISE

6.5.32 The quadrics as explicit functions

The elliptic paraboloid can be written as $z = f(x, y)$, so it has an alternative parametric form $(u, v, f(u, v))$. What is $f()$? In what ways is this form useful? What other quadrics can be represented this way? Can any superquadrics be represented explicitly that way? ■

FIGURE 6.77 Two height fields. (a) Gaussian. (b) sinc function.

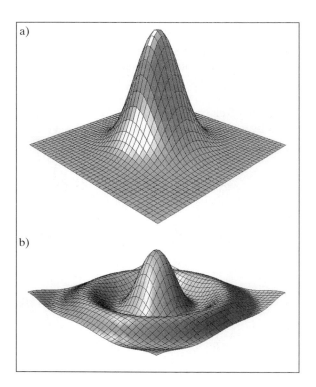

6.6 SUMMARY

This chapter is concerned with modeling and drawing a wide variety of surfaces of 3D objects. Doing so involves finding suitable mathematical descriptions for surfaces of various shapes and creating efficient data structures that hold sufficient detail about a surface to facilitate rendering it. We developed the Mesh class, whose data fields include three lists: the vertex, normal vector, and face lists. This structure can efficiently hold all relevant geometric data about a flat-faced object such as a polyhedron, and it can hold sufficient data to model a polygonal "skin" that approximates other smoothly curved surfaces.

We showed that once a mesh data structure has been built, it is straightforward to render it in an OpenGL environment. It is also easy to store a mesh in a file and to read it back again into a program. Modern shading algorithms use the normal vector at each vertex of each face to determine how light or dark the different points within a face should be drawn. If the face should be drawn flat, the same normal vector—the normal vector to the face itself—is used for every vertex. If the mesh is designed to represent an underlying smoothly curved surface, the normal vector at each vertex is set to the normal of the underlying surface at that point, and rendering algorithms use a form of interpolation to produce gracefully varying shades in the picture (as we shall discuss in Chapter 8). Thus, the choice of what normal vectors to store in a mesh depends on how the designer wishes the object to appear.

A wide variety of polyhedral shapes that occur in popular applications were examined, and techniques were developed that build meshes for several polyhedral families. Here, special care was taken to use the normal to the face at each of the face's vertices. We also studied large families of smoothly varying objects, including the classical quadric surfaces, cylinders, and cones, and discussed how to compute the direction of the normal vector at each point by suitable derivatives of the parametric form for the surface.

The case studies in the next section elaborate on some of these ideas and should not be skipped. Some of the case studies probe further into theory. A derivation of the Newell method to compute a normal vector is outlined, and you are asked to fill in various details. The family of quadric surfaces is seen to have a unifying matrix form that reveals its underlying structure, and a congenial method for transforming quadrics is described. Other case studies ask you to develop methods or applications for creating and drawing meshes for the more interesting classes of shapes described.

6.7 CASE STUDIES

CASE STUDY 6.1 MESHES STORED IN FILES

Level of Effort: II. We want the `Mesh` class to support writing `Mesh` objects to a file and reading filed mesh objects back into a program. We choose a simple format for such files. The first line lists the number of vertices, number of normals, and number of faces in the mesh. Then each vertex in the mesh is listed as a triple of floating-point values, (x_i, y_i, z_i). Several vertices are listed on each line. Next, each normal vector is listed, also as a triple of floating-point numbers. Finally, each face is listed, in the following format:

> number of vertices in the current face
> the list of indices in the vertex list for the vertices in the current face
> the list of indices in the normal list for the vertices in the current face

For example, the simple barn of Figure 6.4 would be stored in the following form:

```
10 7 7
0 0 0     1 0 0     1 1 0     .5 1.5 0     0 1 0
0 0 1     1 0 1     1 1 1     .5 1.5 1     0 1 1
-1 0 0     -0.707 0.707 0     0.707 0.707 0
1 0 0     0 -1 0     0 0 1     0 0 -1
4     0 5 9 4     0 0 0 0
4     3 4 9 8     1 1 1 1
4     2 3 8 7     2 2 2 2
4     1 2 7 6     3 3 3 3
4     0 1 6 5     4 4 4 4
5     5 6 7 8 9     5 5 5 5 5
5     0 4 3 2 1     6 6 6 6 6
```

Here, the first face is a quadrilateral based on the vertices numbered 0, 5, 9, and 4, and the last two faces are pentagons.

To read a mesh into a program from a file, you might wish to use the code in Figure 6.78. Given a file name, the routine opens and reads the file with that name into an existing mesh object and returns zero if it can do this successfully. A non-zero value is returned if an error occurs, as for example, when the designated file cannot be found. (The routine should employ additional testing to catch formatting errors, such as receiving a floating-point number when an integer is expected.) Note that, because no knowledge of the required mesh size is available before `numVerts`, `numNorms`, and `numFaces` are read, the arrays that hold the vertices, normals, and faces are allocated dynamically at run time with the proper sizes.

A number of files in the format shown are available on the Internet site for this book. (They have the suffix .3vn.) Also, it is straightforward to convert `IndexedFace` objects in VRML2.0 files to this format. It is equally straightforward to fashion the routine `int Mesh::writeFile(char* fileName)`, which *writes* a mesh object to a file.

Write an application that reads mesh objects from files and draws the objects. Let the program also allow the user to write a mesh object to a file. Have the application get started by creating meshes for a tetrahedron and the simple barn.

CASE STUDY 6.2 DERIVATION OF THE NEWELL METHOD

Level of Effort: II. This study develops the theory behind the **Newell method** for computing the normal to a polygon based on its vertices. The necessary mathematics is presented as needed as the discussion unfolds; you are asked to show several of the intermediate results. In the discussions, we work with the polygonal face

$$P = \{P_0, P_1, \ldots, P_{N-1}\} \tag{6.50}$$

given by the N 3D vertices. We want to show why the formulas in Equation (6.1) provide an exact computation of the normal vector $\mathbf{m} = (m_x, m_y, m_z)$ to P when P is planar and offer a good direction to use as an "average" normal when P is nonplanar.

FIGURE 6.78 Reading a mesh into memory from a file.

```
int Mesh:: readFile (char * fileName)
{
    fstream infile;
    infile.open (fileName, ios::in);
    if(infile.fail())return -1;      // error-can't open file
    if(infile.eof())return -1;       // error-empty file
    infile >> numVerts >> numNorms >> numFaces;
    pt = new Point3[numVerts] ;
    norm = new Vector3[numNorms] ;
    face = new Face[numFaces] ;
    // check that enough memory was found:
    if( !pt || !norm || !face)return -1;       // out of memory
    for(int p = 0; p < numVerts; p++)      // read the vertices
        infile >> pt[p].x >> pt[p].y >> pt[p].z;
    for(int n = 0; n < numNorms; n++)      // read the normals
        infile >> norm[n].x >> norm[n].y >> norm[n].z;
    for(int f = 0; f < numFaces; f++)      // read the faces
    {
        infile >> face[f].nVerts;
        face[f].vert = new VertexId[ face[f].nVerts];
        for(int i = 0; i < face[f].nVerts; i++)
            infile >> face[f].vert[i].vertIndex
                    >> face[f].vert[i].normIndex;
    }
    return 0;      // success
}
```

A. To begin, Figure 6.79 shows P projected orthographically (i.e., along the principal axes) onto each of the principal planes—the $x = 0$, $y = 0$, and $z = 0$ planes. Each projection is a 2D polygon. We first show that the components of **m** are proportional to the areas, A_x, A_y, and A_z, respectively, of these projected polygons.

FIGURE 6.79 Using projected areas to find the normal vector.

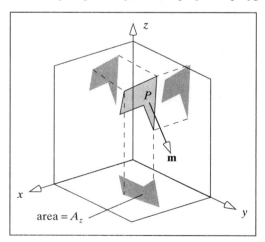

For simplicity, consider the case where P is a triangle, as shown in Figure 6.80. Call the triangle T, and suppose its unit normal vector is some **m**. Further, let T' be the projection of T onto the plane with unit normal **n**. We show that the area of T', denoted Area (T'), is a certain fraction of the area of T, denoted Area (T), and that the fraction is a simple dot product:

$$\text{Area}\,(T') = (\mathbf{m} \cdot \mathbf{n})\,\text{Area}\,(T).$$

Toward that end, suppose triangle T has edges defined by the vectors **v** and **w** as shown in the figure.

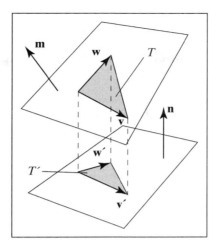

FIGURE 6.80 Effect of orthographic projection on area.

a. Show that $\text{Area}(T) = \frac{1}{2}|\mathbf{w} \times \mathbf{v}|$ and that $\mathbf{v} \times \mathbf{w} = 2\,\text{Area}(T)\mathbf{m}$.
   We now explore the projection of T onto the plane with normal vector $\mathbf{n}$. This projection, T', is defined by the projected vectors $\mathbf{w}'$ and $\mathbf{v}'$; its area is $\text{Area}(T) = \frac{1}{2}|\mathbf{w}' \times \mathbf{v}'|$, so
   $\mathbf{v}' \times \mathbf{w}' = 2\,\text{Area}(T)\mathbf{n}$. We now calculate $\mathbf{w}'$ and $\mathbf{v}'$ and form $\text{Area}(T')$.

b. Using ideas from Chapter 4, show that that $\mathbf{v}$ projects to $\mathbf{v}' = \mathbf{v} - (\mathbf{v} \cdot \mathbf{n})\mathbf{n}$ and, similarly, that $\mathbf{w}' = \mathbf{w} - (\mathbf{w} \cdot \mathbf{n})\mathbf{n}$.
   So we need only relate the sizes of the two cross products.

c. Use the forms of $\mathbf{u}'$ and $\mathbf{v}'$ to show that $\mathbf{v}' \times \mathbf{w}' = \mathbf{v} \times \mathbf{w} - (\mathbf{w} \cdot \mathbf{n})(\mathbf{v} \times \mathbf{n}) + (\mathbf{v} \cdot \mathbf{n})(\mathbf{w} \times \mathbf{n}) + (\mathbf{w} \cdot \mathbf{n})(\mathbf{v} \cdot \mathbf{n})(\mathbf{n} \times \mathbf{n})$, and explain why the last term vanishes. Thus, we have

   $$2\,\text{Area}(T')\mathbf{n} = \mathbf{v} \times \mathbf{w} - (\mathbf{w} \cdot \mathbf{n})(\mathbf{v} \times \mathbf{n}) + (\mathbf{v} \cdot \mathbf{n})(\mathbf{w} \times \mathbf{n}).$$

d. Dot both sides of the preceding equation with $\mathbf{n}$, and show that the last two terms drop out and that we have $2\,\text{Area}(T') = \mathbf{v} \times \mathbf{w} \cdot \mathbf{n} = 2\,\text{Area}(T)\mathbf{m} \cdot \mathbf{n}$, as claimed.

e. Show that the foregoing result generalizes to the areas of any planar polygon P and its projected image P'.

f. Recalling that a dot product is proportional to the cosine of an angle, show that $\text{Area}(T') = \text{Area}(T)\cos\phi$, and state what the angle ϕ is.

g. Show that the areas A_x, A_y, and A_z defined earlier are simply Km_x, Km_y, and Km_z, respectively, where K is some constant. Hence, the areas A_x, A_y, and A_z are in the same ratios as m_x, m_y, and m_z.

B. To find $\mathbf{m}$ now, we need only compute the vector (A_x, A_y, A_z) and normalize it to unit length. We next show how to compute the area of the projection of P of Equation (6.50) onto the xy-plane directly from the vertices of P. The other two projected areas follow similarly.

   Each 3D vertex $P_i = (x_i, y_i, z_i)$ projects onto the xy-plane as $V_i = (x_i, y_i)$. Figure 6.81 shows an example of a projected polygon P'. Each edge of P' defines a trapezoidal region lying between that edge and the x-axis.

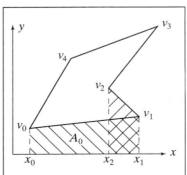

FIGURE 6.81 Computing the area of a polygon.

h. Show that the area of the aforesaid trapezoid is the width of the base times the height of the midpoint of the edge. For instance, the area A_0 in the figure is $A_0 = 0.5(x_0 - x_1)(y_0 + y_1)$. This quantity is negative if x_0 lies to the left of x_1 and is positive otherwise. We use this same form for each edge. For the ith edge, define

$$A_i = \frac{1}{2}(x_i - x_{\text{next}(i)})(y_i + y_{\text{next}(i)}),$$

where $\text{next}(i)$ is 0 if i is equal to $N - 1$ and is $i + 1$ otherwise.

i. Show that if two adjacent edges of the polygon are collinear (which would make a cross product based on them zero), the area contributed by these edges is still properly accounted for.

j. Show that the A_i sum either to the area, or to the negative of the area, of the polygon.

Now we ask which of the two basic directions **m** points in. That is, if you circle the fingers of your right hand around the vertices of the polygon, moving from P_0 to P_1, to P_2, etc. (the direction of the arrow in Figure 6.82), does **m** point along your thumb or in the opposite direction?

FIGURE 6.82 The direction of the normal found by the Newell method.

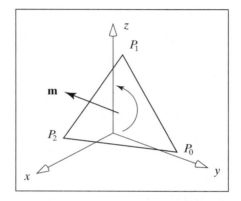

k. Show that **m** *does* point as shown in Figure 6.82. Thus, for a mesh that has a well-defined inside and outside, we can say that **m** is the outward-pointing normal if the vertices are labeled CCW as seen from the outside.

CASE STUDY 6.3 THE PRISM

Level of Effort: III. Write an application that allows the user to specify the polygonal base of a prism with the use of the mouse. The program then creates the vertex, normal, and face lists for the prism and displays the latter.

Figure 6.83(a) shows the user's "drawing area," a square presented on the screen. The user lays down a sequence of points in this square with the mouse, terminating the process with a click of the right-hand mouse button.

In 3D space, the corresponding square is considered to be a unit square lying in the xy-plane, as suggested in Figure 6.83(b), and the base of the prism lies within the square. This establish-

FIGURE 6.83 Designing and building a prism mesh.

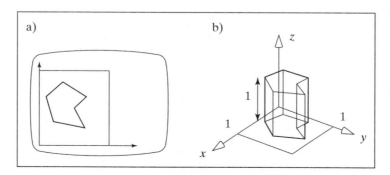

es the size of the base in the 3D "world." The prism is considered to be the base polygon after it is swept one unit in the direction of the z-axis. Execute your program on several prisms input by the user. See if your implementation of OpenGL properly draws nonconvex base polygons.

CASE STUDY 6.4 PRISM ARRAYS AND EXTRUDED QUAD-STRIPS

Level of Effort: III. Write the two routines described in Section 6.4.2 that create meshes for an array of prisms and for an extruded quad-strip:

```
void Mesh:: makePrismArray(...);
void Mesh:: makeExtrudedQuadStrip(...);
```

a. **Arrays of Prisms**. Choose an appropriate data type to represent an array of prisms. Note that makePrismArray() is similar to the routine that makes a mesh for a single prism. Execute makePrismArray() on at least the block letters K and W. (Try D also if you wish.)

b. **Extruded Quad-strips Used to Form Tubes**. The process of building the vertex, normal, and face lists of a mesh is really a matter of keeping straight the many indices for these arrays. To assist in developing a routine that does this, consider a quad-strip base polygon described as in Equation (6.9) by its vertices:

$$\text{quad-strip} = \{p_0, p_1, \dots, p_{M-1}\}.$$

Here, $p_i = (x_i, y_i, 0)$ lies in the xy-plane, as shown in Figure 6.84(a). When extruded, each successive pair of vertices forms a "waist" of the tube, as shown in Figure 6.84(b). The tube has num $= M/2 - 1$ segments.

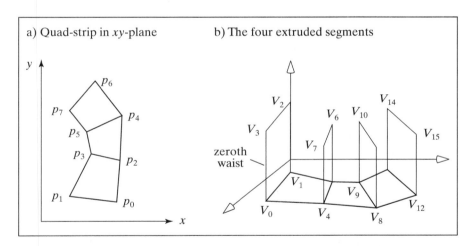

FIGURE 6.84 Building a mesh from a quad-strip base polygon.

The zeroth waist consists of vertices $p_0, p_1, p_1 + \mathbf{d}$, and $p_0 + \mathbf{d}$, where $\mathbf{d}$ is the extrusion vector. We add vertices to the vertex list as follows: pt[4i] $= p_{2i}$, pt[4i + 1] $= p_{2i+1}$, pt[4i + 2] $= p_{2i+1} + \mathbf{d}$, and pt[4i+3] $= p_{2i} + \mathbf{d}$, for $i = 0, \dots,$ num, as suggested in Figure 6.84(b).

Now we tackle the face list. First we add all of the "outside walls" of each segment of the tube. Then we append the "end walls" (i.e., the first end wall uses vertices of the first waist). Each of the num segments has four walls. For each wall, we list the four vertices in CCW order as seen from the outside. There are patterns in the various indices encountered, but they are complicated. Check that the following vertex indices are correct for each of the four walls of the kth segment: The jth wall of the kth segment has vertices with indices i_0, i_1, i_2, and i_3, where

$i_0 = 4k + j$,
$i_1 = i_0 + 4$,
$i_3 = 4k + (j + 3) \bmod 4$,
$i_2 = i_3 + 4$,
for $k = 0, 1, \dots,$ num and $j = 0, 1, 2, 3$.

What are indices of the two end faces of the tube?

Each face has a normal vector determined by the Newell method and is straightforward to calculate at the same time the vertex indices are placed in the face list. All vertex normals of a face use the same normal vector, `face[L].normindex = {L,L,L,L}`, for each L.

Experiment with the `makeExtrudedQuadStrip()` routine by modeling and drawing some arches, such as the one shown in Figure 6.39, as well as some block letters that permit the use of quad-strips for their base polygon.

CASE STUDY 6.5 TUBES AND SNAKES BASED ON A PARAMETRIC CURVE

Level of Effort: III. Write and test a routine

```
void Mesh:: makeTube(Point2 P[], int numPts, float t[], int numTimes)
```

that builds a flat-faced mesh based on wrapping the polygon with vertices $P_0, P_1, \ldots, P_{N-1}$ about the spine curve $C(t)$. The waists of the tube are formed on the spine at the set of instants $t_0, t_1, \ldots, t_{M-1}$, and a Frenet frame is constructed at each $C(t_i)$. The function $C(t)$ is "hardwired" into the code as a formula, and its derivatives are formed numerically.

Experiment with your routine by wrapping polygons taken from Example 3.6.3 that involve a line jumping back and forth between two concentric circles. Try at least the helix and a Lissajous figure as examples of spine curves.

CASE STUDY 6.6 BUILDING DISCRETE-STEPPED SURFACES OF REVOLUTION

Level of Effort: III. Write an application that allows the user to specify the "profile" of an object with the mouse, as in Figure 6.85. The program then creates the mesh for a surface of revolution and displays the mesh. The program also writes the mesh data to a file in the format described in Case Study 6.1.

FIGURE 6.85 Designing a profile for a surface of revolution.

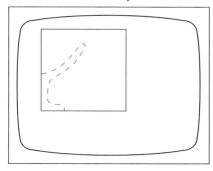

Figure 6.85 shows the user's "drawing area," a square presented on the screen. The user lays down a sequence of points in this square with the mouse. In 3D space, the corresponding square is considered to be a unit square lying in the *xy*-plane. This establishes the size of the profile in the 3D "world." The surface of revolution is formed by sweeping the profile about the *z*-axis in a user-defined number of steps.

Execute your program on several surfaces of revolution input by the user.

CASE STUDY 6.7 ON EDGE LISTS AND WIRE-FRAME MODELS

Level of Effort: II. A wire-frame version of a mesh can be rendered by drawing a line for each edge of the mesh. Write a routine `void Mesh:: drawEdges(void)` that does this for any given mesh. The routine simply traverses each face, connecting adjacent vertices with a line. This draws each line twice. (Why?) In some time-critical situations, this inefficiency might be intolerable. In such a case, an **edge list** can be built that contains each edge of the mesh only once. An edge list is an array of index pairs, where the two indices indicate the two endpoints of each edge. Describe an algorithm that builds an edge list for any mesh. The algorithm traverses each face of the mesh, noting each edge as it is found, but adding it only if that edge is not already on the list.

Note that one usually cannot build a face list from an edge list and a vertex list. Figure 6.86 shows the classic example. From an edge list alone, there is no way to tell where the faces are: Even a wire-frame model for a cube could be a closed box or an open one. A face list has more information, therefore, than does an edge list.

CASE STUDY 6.8 VAULTED CEILINGS

Level of Effort: III. Many classic buildings have arched ceilings or roofs shaped as a **vault**. Figure 6.87(a) shows a "domical vault" [Fleming66] built on a square base. Four "webs," each a ruled surface, rise in a circular sweep to meet at the peak. The shape of this arch is based on an ogee, as described in Figure 3.88. Part (b) of Figure 6.87 shows a domical vault built on an octagon and having eight webs. This arch is based on the pointed arch described in Figure 3.87. Write a function that creates a mesh model for a domical vault built on a cube and a domical vault built on a octagon.

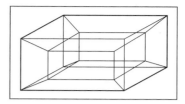

FIGURE 6.86 An ambiguous object.

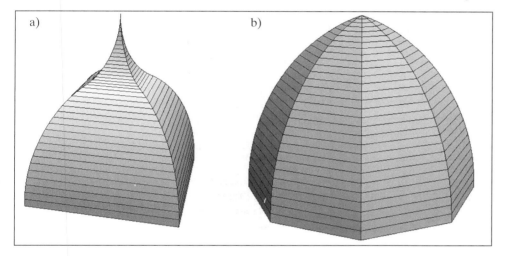

a)

b)

FIGURE 6.87 Examples of vaulted ceilings.

CASE STUDY 6.9 ON PLATONIC SOLIDS

Level of Effort: II. Create files (in the format described in Case Study 6.1) for each of the Platonic solids. Experiment by reading in each file into an application and drawing the associated object.

CASE STUDY 6.10 ON ARCHIMEDEAN SOLIDS

Level of Effort: II. Pictures of the 13 Archimedean solids may be found in many sources (e.g., [Kappraff91] and [Wenninger71]). Each Archimedean solid can be formed by truncating one of the Platonic solids as described in Section 6.3.3. Create files (in the format described in Case Study 6.1) for each of the following polyhedra:

a. the buckyball;
b. the truncated cube;
c. the cuboctahedron (a truncated cube with new vertices formed from the midpoints of each of its edges).

Test your files by reading each object into an application and drawing it.

CASE STUDY 6.11 ALGEBRAIC FORM FOR THE QUADRIC SURFACES

Level of Effort: I. The implicit equations for the quadric surfaces share a compact and useful form based on a matrix. For example, the implicit form $F(x, y, z)$ of the generic sphere is given in Figure 6.71 as $x^2 + y^2 + z^2 - 1$. By inspection, this equation can be written as the **quadratic form**

$$F(x, y, z) = (x, y, z, 1) \begin{pmatrix} 1 & 0 & 0 & 0 \\ 0 & 1 & 0 & 0 \\ 0 & 0 & 1 & 0 \\ 0 & 0 & 0 & -1 \end{pmatrix} \begin{pmatrix} x \\ y \\ z \\ 1 \end{pmatrix}, \tag{6.51}$$

or, more compactly, using the homogeneous representation of point (x, y, z) given by $P^T = (x, y, z, 1)$,

$$F(x, y, z) = P^T R_{\text{sphere}} P, \tag{6.52}$$

where R_{sphere} is the four-by-four matrix displayed in Equation (6.51). The point (x, y, z) is on the ellipsoid whenever F evaluates to zero. The implicit forms for the other quadric surfaces all have the same form; only the matrix R is different. For instance, the matrices for the hyperboloid of two sheets and the elliptic paraboloid are respectively given by

$$R_{\text{hyperboloid2}} = \begin{pmatrix} 1 & 0 & 0 & 0 \\ 0 & -1 & 0 & 0 \\ 0 & 0 & -1 & 0 \\ 0 & 0 & 0 & -1 \end{pmatrix} \quad \text{and} \quad R_{\text{ellipticParab}} = \begin{pmatrix} 1 & 0 & 0 & 0 \\ 0 & 1 & 0 & 0 \\ 0 & 0 & 0 & -\frac{1}{2} \\ 0 & 0 & -\frac{1}{2} & 0 \end{pmatrix}. \tag{6.53}$$

a. What the are matrices for the remaining three shapes?
   Now recall from Section 6.5.3 that when an affine transformation with matrix M is applied to a surface with implicit function $F(P)$, the transformed surface has the implicit function $F(M^{-1}P)$.

b. Show that when a quadric surface is transformed, its implicit function becomes $G(P) = (M^{-1}P)^T R(M^{-1}P)$, which is easily manipulated (as in Appendix 2) into the form $G(P) = P^1(M^{-1}RM^{-1})P$. Thus, the transformed surface *is also a quadric surface* with a different defining matrix that depends both on the original shape of the quadric and on the transformation.
   For example, to convert the generic sphere into an ellipsoid that extends from $-a$ to a in x, $-b$ to b in y, and $-c$ to c in z, use the scaling matrix

$$M = \begin{pmatrix} a & 0 & 0 & 0 \\ 0 & b & 0 & 0 \\ 0 & 0 & c & 0 \\ 0 & 0 & 0 & 1 \end{pmatrix}.$$

c. Find M^{-1}, and show that the matrix for the ellipsoid is

$$M^{-T}RM^{-1} = \begin{pmatrix} \frac{1}{a^2} & 0 & 0 & 0 \\ 0 & \frac{1}{b^2} & 0 & 0 \\ 0 & 0 & \frac{1}{c^2} & 0 \\ 0 & 0 & 0 & 1 \end{pmatrix}.$$

   Write the ellipsoid's implicit form.

d. Find the defining matrix for an elliptic cone that has been scaled by 2 in the x-direction and by 3 in the y-direction and then has been rotated through $30°$ about the y-axis.

e. Show that the matrix R in the implicit function $F(P) = P^T RP$ for a quadric surface can always be taken to be symmetric. (*Hint*: Write R as the sum of a symmetric and an antisymmetric part, and show that the antisymmetric part has no effect on the shape of the surface.

CASE STUDY 6.12 SUPERQUADRIC SCENES

Level of Effort: III. Write an application that can create generic superquadrics with user-selected bulge factors and that places several of these superquadrics in a scene in different sizes and orientations.

CASE STUDY 6.13 DRAWING SMOOTH PARAMETRIC SURFACES

Level of Effort: III. Develop a function that creates a mesh model of any well-behaved smooth surface given by $P(u, v) = (X(u, v), Y(u, v), Z(u, v))$. The function "samples" the surface at `numValuesU` uniformly spaced values in u between `uMin` and `uMax` and at `numValuesV` values in v between `vMin` and `vMax`. The functions $X()$, $Y()$, and $Z()$, as well as the normal com-

```
void Mesh:: makeSurfaceMesh()
{
  int i, j, numValsU = 40, numValsV = 40;// set these
  double u, v, uMin = -10.0, vMin = -10.0, uMax = 10.0, vMax = 10.0;
  double delU = (uMax - uMin)/(numValsU - 1);
  double delV = (vMax - vMin)/(numValsV - 1);

  numVerts = numValsU * numValsV + 1; // total # of vertices
  numFaces = (numValsU -1) * (numValsV - 1) ; // # of faces
  numNorms = numVerts; // for smooth shading - one normal per vertex
  pt    = new Point3[numVerts];  assert(pt   != NULL); // make space
  face = new Face[numFaces];     assert(face != NULL);
  norm = new Vector3[numNorms]; assert(norm != NULL);

  for(i = 0, u = uMin; i < numValsU; i++, u += delU)
     for(j = 0, v = vMin; j < numValsV; j++, v += delV)
     {
         int whichVert = i * numValsV + j; //index of the vertex and normal
         // set this vertex: use functions X, Y, and Z
         pt[whichVert].set(X(u, v),Y(u, v),Z(u, v));
         // set the normal at this vertex: use functions nx, ny, nz
         norm[whichVert].set(nx(u, v), ny(u, v), nz(u, v));
         normalize(norm[whichVert]);
         // make quadrilateral
         if(i > 0 && j > 0) // when to compute next face
         {
             int whichFace =(i - 1) * (numValsV - 1) + (j - 1);
             face[whichFace].vert = new VertexID[4];
             assert(face[whichFace].vert != NULL);
             face[whichFace].nVerts = 4;
             face[whichFace].vert[0].vertIndex = // same as norm index
             face[whichFace].vert[0].normIndex = whichVert;
             face[whichFace].vert[1].vertIndex =
             face[whichFace].vert[1].normIndex = whichVert - 1;
             face[whichFace].vert[2].vertIndex =
             face[whichFace].vert[2].normIndex = whichVert - numValsV - 1;
             face[whichFace].vert[3].vertIndex =
             face[whichFace].vert[3].normIndex = whichVert - numValsV;
         }
     }
}
```

FIGURE 6.88 Skeleton of a mesh creation routine for a smooth surface.

ponent functions are "hardwired" into the routine, which builds the vertex list and normal list on the basis of these sample values and creates a face list consisting of quadrilaterals. The only difficult part is keeping the indices of the vertices straight for each face in the face list. The suggested skeleton shown in Figure 6.88 may prove helpful.

Apply your function to the task of building an interesting surface of revolution and a height field.

CASE STUDY 6.14 TAPER, TWIST, BEND, AND SQUASH IT

Level of Effort: III. It is useful to have a method for **deforming** a 3D object in a controlled way. For instance, in an animation, a bouncing rubber ball is seen to deform as it hits the floor and then to regain its spherical shape as it bounces up again. Or a mound of jello bends and wiggles, or a flag waves in the breeze. In cases like these, it is important to have the deformations look natural by following laws of physics that take into account the conservation of mass, elasticity, and the like. **Physically based modeling**, which attempts to mirror how actual objects behave under various forces, is a large and fascinating subject that is described in many books and articles e.g., [Watt92,Bloomenthal97].

You can also produce purely geometrical deformations [Barr84], chosen by the designer for their visual effect. For instance, it is straightforward to **taper** an object along an axis, as suggested in Figure 6.89. This is achieved by scaling all points in the x and y dimensions by amounts that vary with z, according to some profile function, say, $g(z)$. The function defines a (non-affine) transformation that can be written as a scaling matrix

$$M = \begin{pmatrix} g(z) & 0 & 0 \\ 0 & g(z) & 0 \\ 0 & 0 & 1 \end{pmatrix}. \tag{6.54}$$

FIGURE 6.89 The pawn before and after tapering.

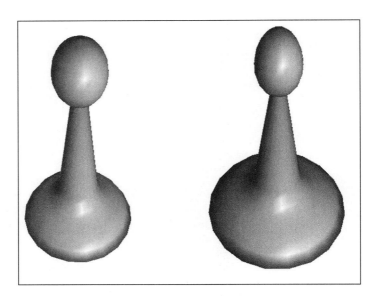

FIGURE 6.90 The pawn after twisting.

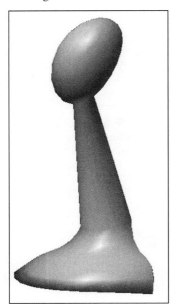

If the undeformed surface has the parametric representation $P(u, v) = (X(u, v), Y(u, v), Z(u, v))$, then the deformation given by Equation (6.54) converts it to

$$P'(u, v) = (X(u, v)g(Z(u, v)), Y(u, v) g(Z(u, v)), Z(u, v)) \tag{6.55}$$

To produce Figure 6.89, the mesh for the pawn was first created, and then each mesh vertex (x, y, z) was altered to (xF, yF, z), where $F = 1 - 0.04(z + 6)$. (Note that the pawn extends from 0 to −12 in z.)

Another useful deformation is **twisting**. To twist about the z-axis, for instance, one rotates all points on the object about that axis by an angle that depends on z, using the matrix

$$M = \begin{pmatrix} \cos(g(z)) & \sin(g(z)) & 0 \\ -\sin(g(z)) & \cos(g(z)) & 0 \\ 0 & 0 & 1 \end{pmatrix}. \tag{6.56}$$

Figure 6.90 shows the pawn after a linearly increasing twist is applied. The pawn is a surface of revolution about the z-axis, so it doesn't make much sense to twist it about that axis. Instead, the twist here is about the y-axis, with $g(z) = 0.02\pi|z + 6|$.

Apply these deformations to several mesh models, including the torus. (Note that you cannot use OpenGL's modelview matrix to perform any of the deformations, since the transformation here is not affine. The vertices in the actual vertex list must be transformed. Bending is another deformation treated by Barr. Refer to his paper [Barr84], and experiment with the bending deformation as well.

6.8 FURTHER READING

A number of books are available that treat the definition and generation of surfaces and solids. Rogers and Adams's *Mathematical Elements for Computer Graphics* [Rogers90] provides a clear introduction to curves and surfaces, as does Faux and Pratt's *Computational Geometry for Design and Manufacture* [Faux79]. Gray's *Modern Differential Geometry of Curves and Surfaces with Mathematica* [Gray93] offers a rigorous mathematical treatment of differently shaped curves and surfaces and gives Mathematica code for drawing them. Mortenson's *Geometric Modeling* [Mortenson85] is an excellent treatment of solid modeling used in the CAD industry.

7 *Three-Dimensional Viewing*

> I am a camera with its shutter open, quite passive, recording, not thinking.
> *Christopher Isherwood, A Berlin Diary*

Goals of the Chapter

▲ To develop tools for creating and manipulating a "camera" that produces pictures of a 3D scene.

▲ To see how to "fly" a camera through a scene interactively and to make animations.

▲ To learn the mathematics that describes various kinds of projections.

▲ To see how each operation in the OpenGL graphics pipeline operates and why it is used.

▲ To build a powerful clipping algorithm for 3D objects.

▲ To devise a means for producing stereo views of objects.

PREVIEW

This chapter examines 3D graphics both within and without OpenGL. Section 7.1 provides an overview of the additional tools that are needed to build an application that lets a camera "fly" through a scene. Section 7.2 defines a camera that produces perspective views and shows how to make such a camera using OpenGL. Aviation terminology helps to describe ways to manipulate a camera. Using matrices, the section develops some of the mathematics needed to describe a camera's orientation. Section 7.3 defines the Camera class to encapsulate information about a camera and develops methods that create and adjust a camera in an application.

Section 7.4 examines the geometric nature of perspective projections and uses mathematical tools to describe perspective. How to incorporate perspective projections into the graphics pipeline, both with and without the use of OpenGL, is described. An additional property of homogeneous coordinates is introduced to facilitate the discussion. The section also develops a powerful clipping algorithm that operates in homogeneous coordinate space; the algorithm's efficiency is a result of proper transformations applied to points before clipping begins. Code for the clipper is given for those programmers who wish to develop their own graphics pipeline.

Section 7.5 shows how to produce stereo views of a scene in order to make them more intelligible. Section 7.6 develops a taxonomy of the many kinds of projections used in art, architecture, and engineering and shows how to produce each kind of projection in a program. The chapter closes with a number of case studies which develop applications that test the techniques discussed.

7.1 INTRODUCTION

We are already in a position to create pictures of elaborate 3D objects. As we saw in Chapter 5, OpenGL provides tools for establishing a camera in a scene, for projecting the scene onto the camera's viewplane, and for rendering the projection in the viewport. So far, our camera produces only parallel projections. In Chapter 6 we described several classes of interesting 3D shapes that can be used to model the objects we want in a scene, and through the `Mesh` class we have ways of drawing any of them with appropriate shading.

So what's left to do? For greater realism, we want to create and control a camera that produces perspective projections. We also need ways to take more control of the camera's position and orientation, so that the user can "fly" the camera through the scene in an animation. This requires developing more control, however, than OpenGL provides. We also need to achieve precise control over the camera's view volume, which is determined in the perspective case as it was in forming parallel projections; namely, by a certain matrix. Because a deeper use of homogeneous coordinates than we have used so far is required, we develop the mathematics of perspective projections from the beginning and see how they are incorporated into the OpenGL graphics pipeline. We also describe how clipping is done against the camera's view volume, which again requires some detailed working with homogeneous coordinates. So we finally see how all of the operations are done, from start to finish! The discussion also provides the underlying theory for those programmers who must develop 3D graphics software without the benefit of OpenGL.

7.2 THE CAMERA REVISITED

It adds a precious seeing to the eye.

William Shakespeare, Love's Labours Lost

In Chapter 5, we used a camera that produces parallel projections. Its view volume is a parallelepiped bounded by six walls, including a near plane and a far plane. OpenGL also supports a camera that creates perspective views of 3D scenes. It is similar in many ways to the camera used before, except that its view volume has a different shape.

Figure 7.1 shows the general form of such a camera. It has an **eye** positioned at some point in space, and its **view volume** is a portion of a rectangular pyramid, whose apex is at the eye. The opening of the pyramid is set by the **viewangle** θ. [see Part (b) of the figure.] Two planes are defined perpendicular to the axis of the pyramid: the **near plane** and the **far plane**. Where these planes intersect the pyramid, they form rectangular windows. The windows have a certain **aspect ratio**, which can be set in a program. OpenGL clips off any parts of the scene that lie outside the view volume. Points lying inside the view volume are projected onto the **viewplane** to a corresponding point P' as suggested in Part (c). (We shall see that it doesn't matter which plane one uses as the viewplane, so for now, take it to be the near plane.) With a perspective projection, the point P' is determined by finding where a line from the eye to P intersects

FIGURE 7.1 A camera to produce perspective views of a scene.

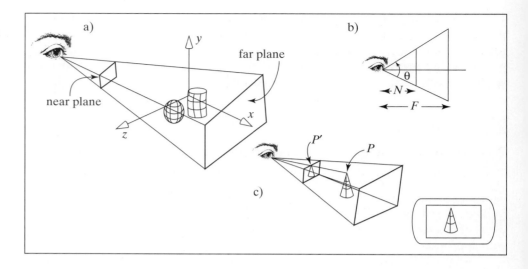

the viewplane. (Contrast this notion with how a parallel projection operates.) Finally, the image formed on the viewplane is mapped into the viewport as shown in Part (c), and it becomes visible on the display device.

7.2.1 Setting the View Volume

Figure 7.2 shows the camera in its default position, with the eye at the origin and the axis of the pyramid aligned with the z-axis. The eye is looking down the negative z-axis.

FIGURE 7.2 The camera in its default position.

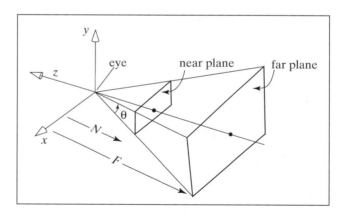

OpenGL provides a simple way to set the view volume in a program. Recall that the shape of the camera's view volume is encoded in the **projection matrix** that appears in the graphics pipeline. The projection matrix is set up using the function `glu-Perspective()` with four parameters. The following sequence is used:

```
glMatrixMode(GL_PROJECTION); // make the projection matrix
                                current
glLoadIdentity();             // start with a unit matrix
gluPerspective(viewAngle, aspectRatio, N, F); // load the
appropriate values
```

The parameter `viewAngle`, shown as θ in the figure, is given in degrees and sets the angle between the top and bottom walls of the pyramid. The parameter `aspectRa-`

tio sets the aspect ratio of any window parallel to the xy-plane. The value N is the distance from the eye to the near plane, and F is the distance from the eye to the far plane. N and F should be positive. For example, gluPerspective(60.0, 1.5, 0.3, 50.0) establishes the view volume to have a vertical opening of 60°, with a window that has an aspect ratio of 1.5. The near plane lies at $z = -0.3$, and the far plane lies at $z = -50.0$. We see later exactly what values this function places in the projection matrix.

7.2.2 Positioning and Pointing the Camera

In order to obtain the desired view of a scene, we move the camera away from its default position shown in Figure 7.2 and aim it in a particular direction. We do this by performing a rotation and a translation, and these transformations become part of the **modelview matrix**, as we discussed in Section 5.6.

We set up the camera's position and orientation in *exactly* the same way as we did for the parallel-projection camera. (The only difference between a parallel- and perspective-projection camera resides in the projection matrix, which determines the *shape* of the view volume.) The simplest function to use is again gluLookAt(), in the following sequence:

```
glMatrixMode(GL_MODELVIEW); // make the modelview matrix current
glLoadIdentity();           // start with a unit matrix
gluLookAt(eye.x, eye.y, eye.z, look.x, look.y, look.z, up.x,
up.y, up.z);
```

As before, this code moves the camera so that its eye resides at point eye and it looks towards the point of interest look. The "upward" direction is generally suggested by the vector up, which is most often set simply to $(0, 1, 0)$. We took these parameters and the whole process of setting the camera pretty much for granted in Chapter 5. In this chapter we will probe deeper, both to see, and to take finer control over, setting the camera. We also develop tools to make *relative* changes to the camera's direction, such as rotating it slightly to the left, tilting it up, or sliding it forward.

The General Camera with Arbitrary Orientation and Position

A camera can have any position in a scene and any orientation. Imagine a transformation that picks up the camera of Figure 7.2, moves it somewhere in space, and then rotates it around to aim it as desired. We need a way to describe this transformation precisely and to determine what the resulting modelview matrix will be.

It will serve us well to attach an explicit coordinate system to the camera, as suggested by Figure 7.3. This coordinate system has its origin at the eye and has three axes, usually called the u-, v-, and n-axes, that define its orientation. The axes are pointed in directions given by the vectors **u**, **v**, and **n** as shown in the figure. Because,

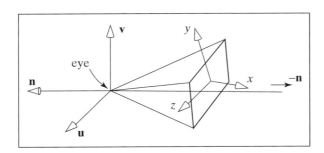

FIGURE 7.3 Attaching a coordinate system to the camera.

by default, the camera looks down the negative *z*-axis, we say in general that the camera looks down the negative *n*-axis, in the direction -**n**. The direction **u** points off "to the right of" the camera, and the direction **v** points "upward." Think of the *u*-, *v*-, and *n*-axes as clones of the *x*-, *y*-, and *z*-axes of Figure 7.2 that are moved and rotated as we move the camera into position.

FIGURE 7.4 A plane's orientation relative to the "world."

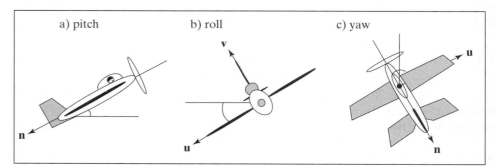

a) pitch　　　　b) roll　　　　c) yaw

Position is easy to describe, but orientation is difficult. It helps to specify orientation using the aviation terms **pitch**, **heading**, **yaw**, and **roll**, as suggested in Figure 7.4. The *pitch* of an air plane is the angle that its longitudinal axis (running from tail to nose and having direction -**n**) makes with the horizontal plane. An air plane *rolls* by rotating about its longitudinal axis; the *roll* is the amount of rotation relative to the horizontal. An air plane's *heading* is the direction in which it is headed. (Other terms are *azimuth* and *bearing*.) To find the heading and pitch, given **n**, simply express -**n** in spherical coordinates, as shown in Figure 7.5. (See Appendix 2 for a review of spherical coordinates.) The vector -**n** has longitude and latitude given by angles θ and ϕ, respectively. The heading of a plane is given by the longitude of -**n**, and the pitch is given by the latitude of -**n**. Formulas for roll, pitch, and heading in terms of the vectors **u** and **n** are developed in the exercises at the end of the section.

FIGURE 7.5. The heading and pitch of a plane.

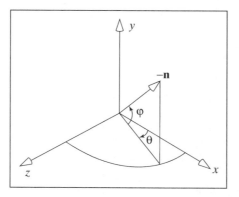

Pitch and *roll* are both nouns and verbs. When used as verbs, they describe a change in the airplane's orientation. You can say a airplane "pitches up" when it increases its pitch (rotates about its *u*-axis) and that it "rolls" when it rotates about its *n*-axis. The common term for changing heading is *yaw*: To yaw left or right the airplane rotates about its *v*-axis.

The same can be used with a camera as well. Figure 7.6(a) shows a camera with the same coordinate system attached: It has *u*-, *v*-, and *n*-axes, and its origin is at position *eye*. The camera In Part (b) has some nonzero roll, whereas the one in Part (c) has zero roll. We most often set a camera to have zero roll and call it a "**no-roll**" camera. The *u*-axis of a no-roll camera is horizontal—that is, perpendicular to the *y*-axis of the

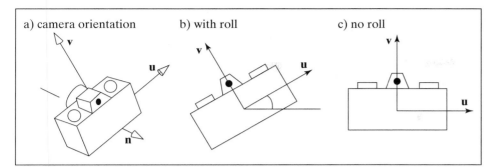

FIGURE 7.6 Various camera orientations.

"world." Note that a no-roll camera can still have an arbitrary **n** direction, so it can have any pitch or heading.

How do we control the roll, pitch, and heading of a camera? The function `glu-LookAt()` is handy for setting up an initial camera, since we usually have a good idea of how to choose *eye* and *look*. But it is harder to visualize how to choose **up** to obtain a certain roll, and it is quite difficult to make relative adjustments to the camera later using only `gluLookAt()`. (`gluLookAt()` works with Cartesian coordinates, whereas orientation deals with angles and rotations about axes.) OpenGL doesn't give direct access to the **u**, **v**, and **n** directions, so we shall maintain them ourselves in a program. This will make it much easier to describe and adjust the camera.

What `gluLookAt()` Does: Some Mathematical Underpinnings

What, then, are the directions **u**, **v**, and **n** when we execute `gluLookAt()` with given values for *eye*, *look*, and **up**? Let us see exactly what `gluLookAt()` does and why it does it.

As shown in Figure 7.7(a), we are given the locations of *eye* and *look*, as well as the **up** direction. We immediately know that **n** must be parallel to the vector *eye* − *look*, as shown in Figure 7.7(b), so we set **n** = *eye* − *look*. (We shall normalize **n** and the other vectors later as necessary.)

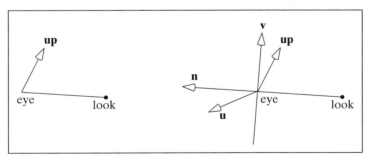

FIGURE 7.7 Building the vectors **u**, **v**, and **n**.

We now need to find a **u** and a **v** that are perpendicular to **n** and to each other. The **u** direction points "off to the side" of a camera, so it is (fairly) natural to make it perpendicular to **up**, which the user has said is the "upward" direction. This is the assumption `gluLookAt()` makes in any case, so the direction **u** is made perpendicular to **n** and **up**. An excellent way to build a vector that is perpendicular to two given vectors is to form their cross product, so we set **u** = **up** × **n**. (The user should not choose an **up** direction that is parallel to **n**, because **u** then would have zero length. Why?) We choose **u** = **up** × **n** rather than **n** × **up** so that **u** will point "to the right" as we look along −**n**.

With **u** and **n** in hand it is easy to form **v**: It must be perpendicular to both **u** and **n** so we use a cross product again: **v** = **n** × **u**. Notice that **v** will usually not be aligned with **up**: **v** must be aimed perpendicular to **n**, whereas the user provides **up** as a suggestion of "upwardness," and the only property of **up** that is used is its cross product with **n**.

To **summarize**, given *eye*, *look*, and **up**, we form

$$\mathbf{n} = eye - look,$$

$$\mathbf{u} = \mathbf{up} \times \mathbf{n},$$ (7.1)

and

$$\mathbf{v} = \mathbf{n} \times \mathbf{u}$$

and then normalize all three vectors to unit length.

Note how this scheme plays out for the common case where **up** $= (0, 1, 0)$. Convince yourself that in this case $\mathbf{u} = (n_z, 0, -n_x)$ and $\mathbf{v} = (-n_x n_y, n_x^2 + n_z^2, -n_z n_y)$. Notice that **u** does indeed have a y-component of zero, so it is "horizontal." Further, **v** has a positive y-component, so it is pointed more or less "upward."

■ **EXAMPLE 7.2.1 Find the camera coordinate system**

Consider a camera with $eye = (4, 4, 4)$ that "looks down" on a look-at point $look = (0, 1, 0)$. Suppose further that **up** is initially set to $(0, 1, 0)$. Find **u**, **v**, and **n**. Repeat for **up** $= (2, 1, 0)$.

SOLUTION:

From Equation 7.1, we find that $\mathbf{u} = (4, 0, -4)$, $\mathbf{v} = (-12, 32, -12)$, and $\mathbf{n} = (4, 3, 4)$, all of which are easily normalized to unit length. (Sketch this situation.) Note that **u** is indeed horizontal. Check that the vectors are mutually perpendicular. For the case of **up** $= (2, 1, 0)$ (try to visualize this camera before working out the arithmetic), $\mathbf{u} = (4, -8, 2)$, $\mathbf{v} = (38, 8, -44)$, and $\mathbf{n} = (4, 3, 4)$. Sketch this situation. Check that these vectors are mutually perpendicular.

■ **EXAMPLE 7.2.2 Building intuition with cameras**

To assist in developing geometric intuition when setting up a camera, Figure 7.8 shows two examples of cameras—each depicted as a coordinate system with a view volume—positioned above the world coordinate system, which is made more vis-

FIGURE 7.8 Two sample settings of the camera.

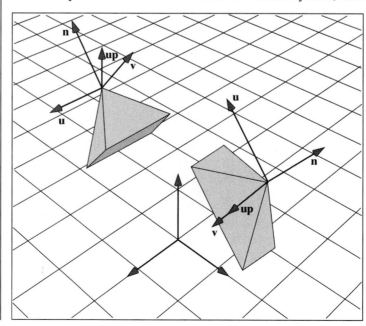

ible by grids drawn in the xz-plane. The view volume of both cameras has an aspect ratio of 2. One camera is set with $eye = (-2, 2, 0)$, $look = (0, 0, 0)$, and $\mathbf{up} = (0, 1, 0)$. For this camera, we find, from Equation (7.1), that $\mathbf{n} = (-2, 2, 0)$, $\mathbf{u} = (0, 0, 2)$, and $\mathbf{v} = (4, 4, 0)$. The figure shows these vectors, as well as the $\mathbf{up}$ vector. The second camera uses $eye = (2, 2, 0)$, $look = (0, 0, 0)$, and $\mathbf{up} = (0, 0, 1)$. In this case, $\mathbf{u} = (-2, 2, 0)$ and $\mathbf{v} = (0, 0, 8)$. The direction $\mathbf{v}$ is parallel to $\mathbf{up}$ here. Note that this camera appears to be on its side. (Check that all of these vectors appear to be oriented in the proper directions.)

Finally, we want to see what values $\texttt{gluLookAt()}$ places in the modelview matrix. From Chapter 5, we know that the modelview matrix is the product of two matrices: the matrix V that accounts for the transformation of world points into camera coordinates and the matrix M that embodies all of the modeling transformations applied to points. The function $\texttt{gluLookAt()}$ builds the V matrix and postmultiplies the current matrix by it. Because the job of the V matrix is to convert world coordinates to camera coordinates, it must transform the camera's coordinate system into the generic position for the camera, as shown in Figure 7.9. This means that V must transform eye into the origin, $\mathbf{u}$ into the vector $\mathbf{i}$, $\mathbf{v}$ into $\mathbf{j}$, and $\mathbf{n}$ into $\mathbf{k}$. There are several ways to derive what V must be, but it is easiest to check that the following matrix does the trick:

$$V = \begin{pmatrix} u_x & u_y & u_z & d_x \\ v_x & v_y & v_z & d_y \\ n_x & n_y & n_z & d_z \\ 0 & 0 & 0 & 0 \end{pmatrix}. \tag{7.2}$$

Here, $(d_x, d_y, d_z) = (-eye \cdot \mathbf{u}, -eye \cdot \mathbf{v}, -eye \cdot \mathbf{n})$.[1] (Check that, in fact,

$$V \begin{pmatrix} eye_x \\ eye_y \\ eye_z \\ 1 \end{pmatrix} = \begin{pmatrix} 0 \\ 0 \\ 0 \\ 1 \end{pmatrix},$$

as desired, where we have extended point eye to homogeneous coordinates. Also, check that

$$V \begin{pmatrix} u_x \\ u_y \\ u_z \\ 0 \end{pmatrix} = \begin{pmatrix} 1 \\ 0 \\ 0 \\ 0 \end{pmatrix}$$

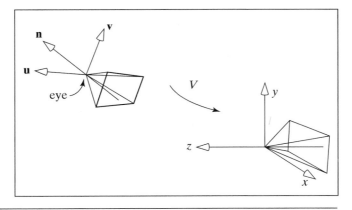

FIGURE 7.9 The transformation that $\texttt{gluLookAt()}$ sets up.

[1]   A technicality is that, since it is not valid to dot a point and a vector, eye should be replaced here by the vector $(eye - (0,0,0))$

and that V maps $\mathbf{v}$ into $(0,1,0,0)^T$ and maps $\mathbf{n}$ into $(0,0,1,0)^T$.) The matrix V is created by `gluLookAt()` and postmultiplies the current matrix. We shall have occasion to perform this same operation later when we maintain our own camera in a program.

PRACTICE EXERCISES

7.2.1 Finding the roll, pitch, and heading given vectors u, v, and n

Suppose a camera is based on a coordinate system with axes in the directions $\mathbf{u}, \mathbf{v}$, and $\mathbf{n}$, all unit vectors. The heading and pitch of the camera are found by representing $-\mathbf{n}$ in spherical coordinates. Using Appendix 2, show that

$$heading = \arctan(-n_z, -n_x)$$

and

$$pitch = \sin^{-1}(-n_y).$$

Further, the roll of the camera is the angle its u-axis makes with the horizontal. To find the roll, construct a vector $\mathbf{b}$ that is horizontal and that lies in the uv-plane. Show that $\mathbf{b} = \mathbf{j} \times \mathbf{n}$ has these properties. Show also that the angle between $\mathbf{b}$ and $\mathbf{u}$ is given by

$$roll = \cos^{-1}\left(\frac{u_x n_z - u_z n_x}{n_x^2 + n_z^2}\right).$$

7.2.2 Using up sets v to a "best approximation" to up

Show that using up as in Equation (7.1) to set $\mathbf{u}$ and $\mathbf{v}$ is equivalent to making $\mathbf{v}$ the closest vector to $\mathbf{up}$ that is perpendicular to vector $\mathbf{n}$. Follow these steps:

a. Show that $\mathbf{v} = \mathbf{n} \times (\mathbf{up} \times \mathbf{n})$.
b. Use a property of the "triple vector product", which states that
   $\mathbf{a} \times (\mathbf{b} \times \mathbf{c}) = (\mathbf{a} \cdot \mathbf{c})\mathbf{b} - (\mathbf{a} \cdot \mathbf{b})\mathbf{c}$.
c. Show that $\mathbf{v}$ is therefore the projection of $\mathbf{up}$ onto the plane with normal $\mathbf{n}$ (see Chapter 4) and, consequently, that $\mathbf{v}$ is the closest vector to $\mathbf{up}$ in this plane.   ■

7.3 BUILDING A CAMERA IN A PROGRAM

It is as interesting and as difficult to say a thing well as to paint it.

Vincent van Gogh

In order to have fine control over camera movements, we create and manipulate our own camera in a program. After each change to this camera is made, the camera "tells" OpenGL what the new camera is.

We create a `Camera` class that knows how to do all the things a camera does. Doing this is very simple and the payoff is high. In a program, we create a `Camera` object called, say, `cam`, and adjust it with functions such as the following:

```
cam.set(eye, look, up);   // initialize the camera
cam.slide(-1,0,-2);   // slide the camera forward and to the left
cam.roll(30); // roll it through 30°
cam.yaw(20); // yaw it through 20°
etc.
```

Figure 7.10 shows the basic definition of the Camera class. The definition contains fields for the *eye* and the directions $\mathbf{u}, \mathbf{v}$, and $\mathbf{n}$. (`Point3` and `Vector3` are the basic

```
class Camera{
  private:
      Point3 eye;
      Vector3 u,v,n;
      double viewAngle, aspect, nearDist, farDist; // view volume shape
      void setModelViewMatrix(); // tell OpenGL where the camera is

  public:
      Camera(); // default constructor
      void set(Point3 eye, Point3 look, Vector3 up); // like gluLookAt()
      void roll(float angle); // roll it
      void pitch(float angle); // increase the pitch
      void yaw(float angle); // yaw it
      void slide(float delU, float delV, float delN); // slide it
      void setShape(float vAng, float asp, float nearD, float farD);
};
```

FIGURE 7.10 The `Camera` class definition.

data types defined in Appendix 3.) It also has fields that describe the shape of the view volume: `viewAngle`, `aspect`, `nearDist`, and `farDist`.

The utility routine `setModelViewMatrix()` communicates the modelview matrix to OpenGL. It is used only by member functions of the class and needs to be called after each change is made to the camera's position or orientation. Figure 7.11 shows a possible implementation of this routine. It computes the matrix of Equation 7.2 on the basis of current values of *eye*, **u**, **v**, and **n** and loads the matrix directly into the modelview matrix via `glLoadMatrixf()`.

FIGURE 7.11 The utility routines `set()` and `set()ModelViewMatrix()`.

```
void Camera :: setModelViewMatrix(void)
{ // load modelview matrix with existing camera values
      float m[16];
      Vector3 eVec(eye.x, eye.y, eye.z); // a vector version of eye
      m[0]  =  u.x; m[4]  =  u.y; m[8]   =  u.z;  m[12] = -eVec.dot(u);
      m[1]  =  v.x; m[5]  =  v.y; m[9]   =  v.z;  m[13] = -eVec.dot(v);
      m[2]  =  n.x; m[6]  =  n.y; m[10]  =  n.z;  m[14] = -eVec.dot(n);
      m[3]  =  0;   m[7]  =  0;   m[11]  =  0;    m[15] = 1.0;
      glMatrixMode(GL_MODELVIEW);
      glLoadMatrixf(m); // load OpenGL's modelview matrix
}
void Camera:: set(Point3 Eye, Point3 look, Vector3 up)
{ // create a modelview matrix and send it to OpenGL
      eye.set(Eye); // store the given eye position
      n.set(eye.x - look.x, eye.y - look.y, eye.z - look.z); // make n
      u.set(up.cross(n)); // make u = up X n
      n.normalize(); u.normalize(); // make them unit length
      v.set(n.cross(u));  // make v =  n X u
      setModelViewMatrix(); // tell OpenGL
}
```

The method `set()` acts just like `gluLookAt()`: It uses the values of `eye`, `look`, and `up` to compute **u**, **v**, and **n** according to Equation 7.1. It places this information in the camera's fields and communicates it to OpenGL.

The routine `setShape()` is even simpler: It puts the four argument values into the appropriate camera fields and then calls `gluPerspective(viewangle,aspect,nearDist, farDist)` (along with `glMatrixMode(GL_PROJECTION)` and `glLoadIdentity()`) to set the projection matrix.

The central camera functions are `slide()`, `roll()`, `yaw()`, and `pitch()`, which make *relative* changes to the camera's position and orientation. (The whole reason for maintaining the `eye`, `u`, `v`, and `n` fields in our Camera data structure is so that we will have a record of the "current" camera and can therefore alter it.) We next examine how the camera methods operate.

7.3.1 "Flying" the Camera

The user "flies" the camera through a scene interactively by pressing keys or clicking the mouse. For instance, pressing *u* might slide the camera "up" some amount, pressing *y* might yaw the camera to the left, and pressing *f* might slide it forward. The user can see how the scene looks from one point of view and then change the camera to a better viewing spot and direction and produce another picture. Or the user can "fly" around a scene taking different snapshots. If the snapshots are stored and then played back rapidly, an animation is produced of the camera flying around the scene.

There are six degrees of freedom for adjusting a camera: It can be "slid" in three dimensions, and it can be rotated about any of three coordinate axes. We first develop the `slide()` function.

Sliding the Camera

Sliding a camera means to move it along one of its *own* axes—that is, in the **u**, **v**, or **n** direction—without rotating it. Since the camera is looking along the negative **n**-axis, movement along **n** is "forward" or "back." Similarly, movement along **u** is "left" or "right" and along **v** is "up" or "down."

It is simple to move the camera along one of its axes. To move it a distance D along its *u*-axis, set *eye* to $eye + D\mathbf{u}$. For convenience, we can combine the three possible slides in a single function: `slide(delU, delV, delN)` slides the camera amount `delU` along **u**, `delV` along **v**, and `delN` along **n**. The code is as follows:

```
void Camera:: slide(float delU, float delV, float delN)
{
        eye.x += delU * u.x + delV * v.x + delN * n.x;
        eye.y += delU * u.y + delV * v.y + delN * n.y;
        eye.z += delU * u.z + delV * v.z + delN * n.z;
        setModelViewMatrix();
}
```

Rotating the Camera

We want to roll, pitch, or yaw the camera. Each of these involves a rotation of the camera about one of its own axes. We look at rolling in detail; the other two types of rotation are similar.

To roll the camera is to rotate it about its own **n**-axis. This means that both the directions **u** and **v** must be rotated, as shown in Figure 7.12. We form two new axes **u**′ and **v**′ that lie in the same plane as **u** and **v**, yet have been rotated through the angle α radians.

So we need only form **u**′ as the appropriate linear combination of **u** and **v**, and similarly for **v**′:

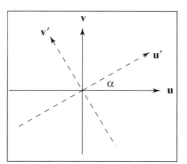

FIGURE 7.12 Rolling the camera.

$$\mathbf{u}' = \cos(\alpha)\mathbf{u} + \sin(\alpha)\mathbf{v};$$
$$\mathbf{v}' = -\sin(\alpha)\mathbf{u} + \cos(\alpha)\mathbf{v}. \tag{7.3}$$

The new axes **u'** and **v'** then replace **u** and **v**, respectively, in the camera. This function is straightforward to implement. For convenience, it measures angles in degrees.

```
void Camera :: roll(float angle)
{ // roll the camera through angle degrees
     float cs = cos(3.14159265/180 * angle);
     float sn = sin(3.14159265/180 * angle);
     Vector3 t = u; // remember old u
     u.set(cs*t.x - sn*v.x, cs*t.y - sn*v.y, cs*t.z - sn*v.z);
     v.set(sn*t.x + cs*v.x, sn*t.y + cs*v.y, sn*t.z + cs*v.z);
     setModelViewMatrix();
}
```

The functions `pitch()` and `yaw()` are implemented in a similar fashion. (See the exercises at the end of the section.

Putting It All Together

We show in Figure 7.13 how the `Camera` class can be used with OpenGL to "fly" a camera through a scene. The scene consists of a lone teapot. The camera is a global object and is set up in `main()` with a good starting view and shape. When a key is pressed, `myKeyboard()` is called, and the camera is slid or rotated, depending on which key was pressed. For instance, if *P* is pressed, the camera is pitched up by 1 degree. If CTRL F is pressed[2] (hold down the control key and press *F*), the camera is pitched down by 1 degree. After the keystroke has been processed, `glutPostRedisplay()` causes `myDisplay()` to be called again to draw the new picture.

Notice the call to `glutSwapBuffers()`.[3] This application uses **double buffering** to produce a rapid and smooth transition between one picture and the next. Two memory buffers are used to store the pictures that are generated. The display switches from showing one buffer to showing the other under the control of `glutSwapBuffers()`. Each new picture is drawn in the invisible buffer, and when the drawing is complete, the display switches to it. Thus, the viewer doesn't see the screen erased and the new picture slowly emerge line by line, which is visually annoying. Instead, the "old" picture is displayed steadily, while the "new" picture is being composed off-screen, and then the display switches very rapidly to the newly completed picture.

Drawing SDL Scenes Using a Camera

It is easy to incorporate a camera into an application that reads SDL files, as described in Chapter 5. There are then two global objects, viz.

```
Camera cam;
Scene scn;
```

and in main() an SDL file is read and parsed using `scn.read("myScene.dat")`. Finally, in `myDisplay(void)`, simply replace `glutWireTeapot(1.0)` with `scn.drawSceneOpenGL()`,

PRACTICE EXERCISES

7.3.1 Implementing `pitch()` and `yaw()`

Write the functions `void Camera:: pitch(float angle)` and `void Camera :: yaw(float angle)` which respectively pitch and yaw the camera. Arrange

---

[2] On most keyboards, pressing CTRL and a letter key returns an ASCII value that is 64 less than the ASCII value returned by the letter itself.

[3] `glutInitDisplayMode()` must have an argument of GLUT_DOUBLE to enable double buffering.

```
// the usual includes
#include "camera.h"

Camera cam; // global camera object

//<<<<<<<<<<<<<<<<<<<<<<<<< myKeyboard >>>>>>>>>>>>>>>>>>>>>>>>
void myKeyboard(unsigned char key, int x, int y)
{
  switch(key)
  {
      // controls for the camera
      case 'F':     cam.slide(0,0, 0.2); break; // slide camera forward
      case 'F'-64: cam.slide(0,0,-0.2); break; //slide camera back
      // add up/down and left/right controls
      case 'P':        cam.pitch(-1.0); break;
      case 'P' - 64: cam.pitch( 1.0); break;
      // add roll and yaw controls
  }
      glutPostRedisplay(); // draw it again
}
//<<<<<<<<<<<<<<<<<<<<<<<<< myDisplay >>>>>>>>>>>>>>>>>>>>>>>>>
void myDisplay(void)
{
      glClear(GL_COLOR_BUFFER_BIT||GL_DEPTH_BUFFER_BIT);
      glutWireTeapot(1.0); // draw the teapot
      glFlush();
      glutSwapBuffers(); // display the screen just made
}
//<<<<<<<<<<<<<<<<<<<<<<<<< main >>>>>>>>>>>>>>>>>>>>>>>>>>>>>>
void main(int argc, char **argv)
{
      glutInit(&argc, argv);
      glutInitDisplayMode(GLUT_DOUBLE | GLUT_RGB); // double buffering
      glutInitWindowSize(640,480);
      glutInitWindowPosition(50, 50);
      glutCreateWindow("fly a camera around a teapot");
      glutKeyboardFunc(myKeyboard);
      glutDisplayFunc(myDisplay);
      glClearColor(1.0f,1.0f,1.0f,1.0f);  // background is white
      glColor3f(0.0f,0.0f,0.0f);   // set color of stuff
      glViewport(0, 0, 640, 480);
      cam.set(4, 4, 4, 0, 0, 0, 0, 1, 0); // make the initial camera
      cam.setShape(30.0f, 64.0f/48.0f, 0.5f, 50.0f);
      glutMainLoop();
}
```

FIGURE 7.13 Application to "fly" a camera around a teapot.

matters so that a positive yaw yaws the camera to the "left" and a positive pitches the camera "up."

7.3.2 Building a universal `rotate()` function

Write the function `void Camera:: rotate(Vector3 axis, float angle)` which rotates the camera through `angle` degrees about `axis`. The function rotates all three axes **u**, **v**, and **n** about the eye.

7.4 PERSPECTIVE PROJECTIONS OF 3D OBJECTS

Treat them in terms of the cylinder, the sphere, the cone, all in perspective.

Ashanti proverb

With the Camera class in hand, we can navigate around 3D scenes and readily create pictures. Using OpenGL, we create each picture by passing vertices of objects (such as a mesh representing a teapot or chess piece) down the graphics pipeline, as we described in Chapter 5. Figure 7.14 shows the graphics pipeline again, with one new element.

FIGURE 7.14 The graphics pipeline revisited.

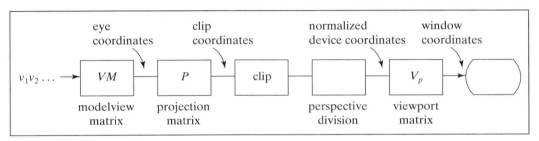

Recall that each vertex v is multiplied by the modelview matrix (VM). The modeling part (M) embodies all of the modeling transformations for the object; the viewing part (V) accounts for the transformation set by the camera's position and orientation. When a vertex emerges from this matrix, it is in **eye coordinates**—that is, in the coordinate system of the eye. Figure 7.15 shows this system, for which the eye is at the origin and the near plane is perpendicular to the z-axis, residing at $z = -N$. A vertex located at P in eye coordinates is passed through the next stages of the pipeline, where it is (somehow) projected onto a certain point (x^*, y^*) on the near plane, clipping is carried out, and finally, the surviving vertices are mapped to the viewport on the display.

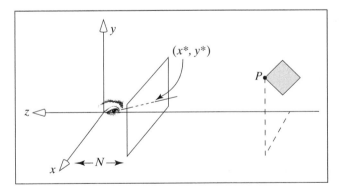

FIGURE 7.15 Perspectival projection of vertices expressed in eye coordinates.

At this point, we must look more deeply into the process of forming perspective projections. We need answers to a number of questions: What operations constitute forming a perspective projection, and how does the pipeline do these operations? What is the relationship between perspective projections and matrices. How does the projection map the view volume into a "canonical view volume" for clipping? How is clipping done? How do homogeneous coordinates come into play in the process? How is the "depth" of a point from the eye retained so that hidden surfaces may be properly removed?

We start by examining the nature of perspective projection, independently of looking at specific processing steps in the pipeline. Then we see how the steps in the pipeline are carefully crafted to produce the numerical values required for a perspective projection.

7.4.1 Perspective Projection of a Point

The fundamental operation in a perspective projection is projecting a 3D point to a 2D point on a plane. Figure 7.16 elaborates on Figure 7.15 to show the point $P = (P_x, P_y, P_z)$ projecting onto the near plane of the camera to a point (x^*, y^*). We erect a local coordinate system on the near plane, with its origin on the camera's z-axis. Then it is meaningful to talk about the point x^* units over to the right of the origin, and y^* units above the origin.

FIGURE 7.16 Finding the projection of a point P in eye coordinates.

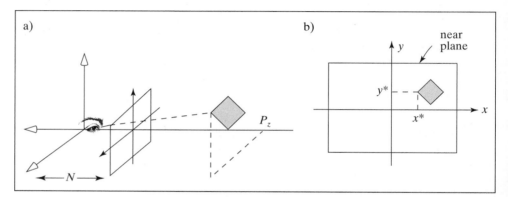

The first question is, then, what are x^* and y^*? It is simplest to use similar triangles and say that x^* is in the same ratio to P_x as the distance N is to the distance $|P_z|$. Since P_z is negative, we can say that

$$\frac{x^*}{P_x} = \frac{N}{-P_z}.$$

or $x^* = NP_x/(-P_z)$. Similarly, $y^* = NP_y/(-P_z)$. So P projects to the point

$$(x^*, y^*) = \left(N\frac{P_x}{-P_z}, N\frac{P_y}{-P_z} \right) \qquad \text{(the projection of } P\text{)} \tag{7.4}$$

on the viewplane. An alternative (analytical) method for arriving at this result is given in the exercises at the end of the section.

■ **EXAMPLE 7.4.1**

Where on the viewplane does $P = (1, 0.5, -1.5)$ lie for a camera having a near plane at $N = 1$?

SOLUTION:

The direct use of Equation (7.4) yields $(x^*, y^*) = (0.666, 0.333)$.

We can make some preliminary observations about how points are projected:

1. Note the denominator term $-P_z$ in Equation (7.4). It is larger for more remote points (those farther along the negative z-axis), which reduces the values of x^* and y^*. This introduces **perspective foreshortening** and makes remote parts of an object appear smaller than nearer parts.

2. Denominators have a nasty way of evaluating to zero, and P_z becomes zero when P lies in the "same plane" as the eye: the $z = 0$ plane. Normally, we use clipping to remove such offending points before trying to project them.
3. If P lies "behind the eye" the sign of P_z is reversed, which causes further trouble, as we shall see later. These points, too, are usually removed by clipping.
4. The effect of the near-plane distance N is simply to *scale* the picture. (Both $x*$ and $y*$ are proportional to N.) So if we choose some other plane (still parallel to the near plane) as the viewplane onto which to project pictures, the projection will differ only in size from the projection onto the near plane. Since we ultimately map this projection to a viewport of a fixed size on the display, the size of the projected image makes no difference. This shows that any viewplane parallel to the near plane would work just as well, so we might as well use the near plane itself.
5. Straight lines project to straight lines. Figure 7.17 provides the simplest proof. Consider the line in 3D space between points A and B. A projects to A' and B projects to B'. But do points between A and B project to points directly between A' and B'? The answer is yes: Just consider the plane formed by A, B, and the origin. Since any two planes intersect in a straight line, this plane intersects the near plane in a straight line. Thus, line segment AB projects to *line segment $A'B'$*.

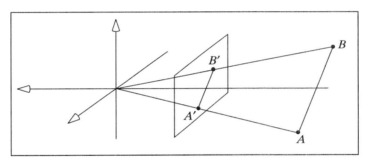

FIGURE 7.17 Proof that a straight line projects to a straight line.

■ **EXAMPLE 7.4.2 Three projections of the barn**

A lot of intuition can be acquired by seeing how a simple object is viewed by different cameras. In this example, we examine how the edges of the barn defined in Chapter 6 and repeated in Figure 7.18 are projected onto three cameras. The barn has 10 vertices, 15 edges, and seven faces.

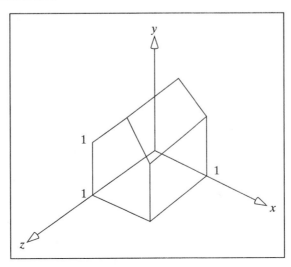

FIGURE 7.18 The basic barn revisited.

View #1 We first set the camera's *eye* at $(0, 0, 2)$ and have it look down the negative z-axis, with $\mathbf{u} = (1,0,0)$ and $\mathbf{n} = (-1, 0, 0)$. We set the near plane at a distance of unity from the eye. (The near plane happens, therefore, to coincide with the front of the barn.) In terms of camera coordinates, all points on the front wall of the barn have $P_z = -1$, and those on the back wall have $P_z = -2$. So, from Equation (7.4), any point (P_x, P_y, P_z) on the front wall projects to

$$P' = (P_x, P_y) \qquad \text{(projection of a point on the front wall)},$$

and any point on the back wall projects to

$$P' = (P_x/2, P_y/2). \qquad \text{(projection of a point on the back wall)}.$$

The foreshortening factor is 2 for those points on the back wall. Figure 7.19(a)

FIGURE 7.19 Projections of the barn for views #1 and #2.

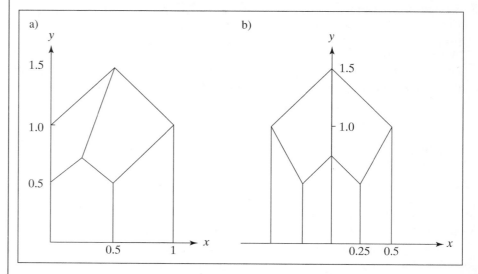

shows the projection of the barn for this view. Note that edges on the rear wall project at half their true length, and note that edges of the barn that are actually parallel in 3D *need not* project as parallel. (We shall see that parallel edges that are parallel to the viewplane do project as parallel, but parallel edges that are not parallel to the viewplane are not parallel: they recede to a "vanishing point.")

View #2 Here, the camera has been slid over so that *eye* = $(0.5, 0, 2)$, but $\mathbf{u}$ and $\mathbf{n}$ are the same as in view #1. Figure 7.19(b) shows the projection.

View #3 Here we use the camera with *Eye* = $(2, 5, 2)$ and *look* = $(0,0,0)$, resulting in Figure 7.20. The world axes have been added as a guide. This view shows the barn from an informative standpoint. From a wire-frame view, it is difficult to discern which faces are where.

FIGURE 7.20 A third view of the barn.

PRACTICE EXERCISES

7.4.1 Sketch a cube in perspective

Draw (by hand) the perspective view of a **cube** C (aligned with the axes and centered at the origin, with sides of length 2) when the eye is at $E = 5$ on the z-axis. Repeat when C is shifted so that its center is at $(1, 1, 1)$.

7.4.2 Where does the ray hit the viewplane? (Don't skip this one.)

We want to derive Equation (7.4) by finding where the ray from the origin to P intersects the near plane.

a. Show that if this ray is at the origin at time $t = 0$ and at P at $t = 1$, then it has the parametric representation $r(t) = Pt$.
b. Show that the ray hits the near plane at $t = N/(-P_z)$.
c. Show that the "hit point" is $(x^*, y^*) = (NP_x/(-P_z), NP_y/(-P_z))$.

7.4.2 Perspective Projection of a Line

We next develop some interesting properties of perspective projections by examining how straight lines project.

1. Lines that are parallel in 3D project to lines, but the two are not necessarily parallel. If they are not parallel, they meet at some "vanishing point."
2. Lines that pass behind the eye of the camera cause a catastrophic "passage through infinity." (Such lines should be clipped off.)
3. Perspective projections usually produce geometrically realistic pictures. But realism is strained for very long lines parallel to the viewplane.

Projecting Parallel Lines

Suppose a line in 3D passes (using camera coordinates) through the point $A = (A_x, A_y, A_z)$ and has direction vector $\mathbf{c} = (c_x, c_y, c_z)$. Then the line has the parametric form $P(t) = A + \mathbf{c}t$. Substituting this form into Equation (7.4) yields the parametric form for the projection of this line:

$$p(t) = \left(N\frac{A_x + c_x t}{-A_z - c_z t}, N\frac{A_y + c_y t}{-A_z - c_z t}\right). \tag{7.5}$$

(This may not look like the parametric form of a straight line, but it is; see the exercises.) Thus, the point A in 3D projects to the point $p(0)$, and as t varies, the projected point $p(t)$ moves across the screen (in a straight line). We can discern several important properties directly from this formula.

Suppose the line $A + \mathbf{c}t$ is parallel to the viewplane. Then $c_z = 0$ and the projected line is given by

$$p(t) = \frac{N}{-A_z}(A_x + c_x t, A_y + c_y t).$$

This is the parametric form of a line with slope c_y/c_x. The slope does not depend on the position of the line; rather, it is a function of its direction $\mathbf{c}$ alone. Thus, all lines in 3D with direction $\mathbf{c}$ will project with this slope, so their projections are parallel. We conclude that

*If two lines in 3D are parallel to each other **and** to the viewplane, they project to two parallel lines.*

Now consider the case where the direction $\mathbf{c}$ is not parallel to the viewplane. For convenience, suppose $c_z < 0$, so that as t increases, the line recedes further and further from the eye. At very large values of t, Equation (7.5) becomes:

$$p(\infty) = \left(N\frac{c_x}{-c_z}, N\frac{c_y}{-c_z}\right). \tag{7.6}$$

The value of this equation is called the **vanishing point** of the line; it is the point towards which the projected line moves as t gets larger and larger. Notice that it depends only on the direction $\mathbf{c}$ of the line and not on its position (which is embodied in A). Thus, all parallel lines share the same vanishing point. In particular, they project to lines that are *not* parallel.

FIGURE 7.21 The vanishing point for parallel lines.

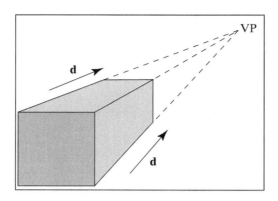

Figure 7.21 makes the last statement more vivid for the example of a cube. Several edges of the cube are parallel: There are those that are horizontal, those that are vertical, and those that recede from the eye. The picture was made with the camera oriented so that its near plane was parallel to the front face of the cube. Thus, in camera coordinates, the z-component of **c** for the horizontal and vertical edges is zero. The horizontal edges therefore project to parallel lines, and so do the vertical edges. The receding edges, however, are not parallel to the viewplane and hence converge onto a vanishing point (VP). Artists often set up drawings of objects this way, choosing the vanishing point and sketching parallel lines so that they point toward the VP. We shall discuss vanishing points more as we proceed.

Figure 7.22 suggests what a vanishing point is geometrically. Looking down onto the camera's xz-plane from above, we see the eye viewing various points on the line AB. A projects to A', B projects to B', etc. Very remote points on the line project to VP as shown. The point VP is situated so that the line from the eye through it is *parallel* to AB. (Why?)

Lines that Pass behind the Eye

Earlier, we saw that trying to project a point that lies in the plane of the eye ($z = 0$ in eye coordinates) results in a denominator of zero, and would surely spell trouble

FIGURE 7.22 The geometry of a vanishing point.

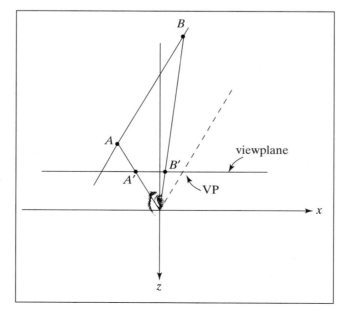

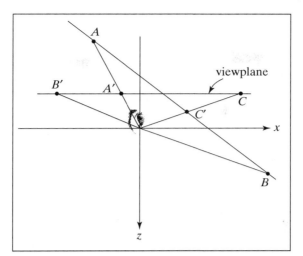

FIGURE 7.23 Projecting the line segment AB, with B "behind the eye."

if we tried to project that point. We now examine the projection of a line segment such that one endpoint lies in front of the eye and one endpoint lies behind it.

Figure 7.23 again looks down on the camera from above. Point A lies in front of the eye and projects to A' in a very reasonable manner. Point B, on the other hand, lies behind the eye, and projects to B', which seems to end up on the wrong side of the viewplane! Let us consider a point C that moves from A to B and sketch how its projection moves. As C moves back towards the plane of the eye, its projection slides further and further along the viewplane to the right. As C approaches the plane of the eye, its projection spurts off to infinity, and as C moves behind the eye, its projection reappears from far off to the left on the viewplane. You might say that the projection has "wrapped around infinity" and come back from the opposite direction [Blinn96]. If we tried to draw such a line, there would most likely be chaos. Therefore, all parts of the line closer to the eye than the near plane are clipped off before the projection is attempted.

■ EXAMPLE 7.4.3 The classic horizontal plane in perspective

A good way to gain insight into vanishing points is to view a grid of lines in perspective, as in Figure 7.24. Grid lines here lie in the xz-plane and are spaced one unit apart. The eye is perched one unit above the xz-plane, at $(0, 1, 0)$, and looks along $-\mathbf{n}$, where $\mathbf{n} = (0,0,1)$. As usual, we take **up** $= (0,1,0)$. N is chosen to be unity.

In eye coordinates, the grid lines of constant x have the parametric form $(i, -1, -t)$, where i takes on the values from $-M$ to M for some M, and t varies from zero to infinity. By Equation (7.4), the i-th line projects to $(i/t, -1/t)$, which is a line through the vanishing point $(0, 0)$, so all of these lines converge on the same vanishing point, as expected.

The grid lines of constant z are given by $(t, -1, -i)$, where $i = 1, 2, \ldots, N$ for some N and t varies from negative infinity to infinity. These grid lines project to $(t/i, -1/i)$, which appear as horizontal straight lines. (Check this.) Their projections are parallel, since the grid lines themselves are parallel to the viewplane. The more remote ones (larger values of i) lie closer together, providing a vivid example of perspective foreshortening. Many of the remote contours are not drawn here, as they become so crowded that they cannot be drawn clearly. The collection of them is shown as a gray region. The **horizon** consists of all the contours such that z is very large and negative; it is positioned at $y = 0$.

The Anomaly of Viewing Long Parallel Lines

Perspective projections seem to be a reasonable model for the way we see. But there

FIGURE 7.24 Viewing a horizontal grid on the xz-plane.

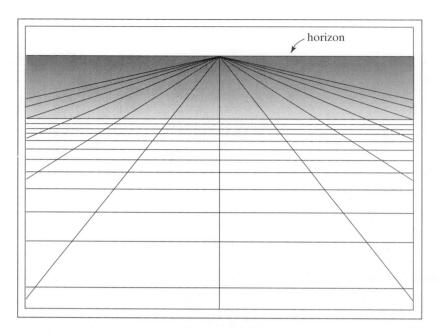

are some anomalies, mainly because our eyes do not have planar "view screens." One problem occurs with very long objects. Consider an experiment, for example, in which you look up at a pair of parallel telephone wires, as suggested in Figure 7.25(a).

For the perspective view, we know if we orient the viewplane to be parallel to the wires, the image will show two straight, parallel lines [Part (b)]. But what you see is quite different: The wires appear curved as they converge to "vanishing points" in both directions [part (c)]! In practice, this anomaly is barely visible, because the window or your eye limits the field of view to a reasonable region. (To see different parts of the wires, you have to roll your eyes up and down, which, of course, rotates your "viewplanes.")

FIGURE 7.25 Viewing very long parallel wires.

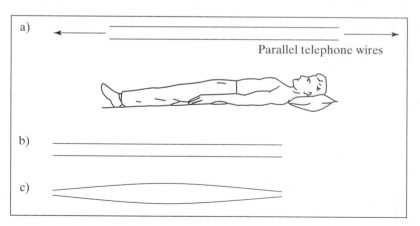

PRACTICE EXERCISES

7.4.3 Straight lines project as straight lines: the parametric form

Show that the parametric form in Equation (7.5) is that of a straight line. [*Hint*: For the x-component, divide the denominator into the numerator to get $-A_x N/A_z + Rg(t)$, where R depends on the x-components, but not the y-components, of A and $\mathbf{c}$ and $g(t)$ is some function of t that depends on neither the x nor the

y-components of A or $\mathbf{c}$. Repeat for the y-component, obtaining $-A_y N/A_z + Sg(t)$ with similar properties. Argue why this is the parametric representation of a straight line (albeit one for which the point does not move with constant speed as t varies)].

7.4.4 Derive results for horizontal grids

Derive the parametric forms for the projected grid lines in Example 7.4.3. ■

7.4.3 Incorporating Perspective into the Graphics Pipeline.

> *Only a fool tests the depth of the river with both feet. Paul Cezanne, 1925*

We want the graphics pipeline to project vertices of 3D objects onto the near plane and then map them to the viewport. After passing through the modelview matrix, the vertices are represented in the camera's coordinate system, and Equation (7.4) shows the values we need to compute for the proper projection. We also must do clipping and then map what survives to the viewport. But we need a little more as well.

Adding Pseudodepth

Taking a projection discards information on depth; that is, we lose information about how far the point is from the eye. But we mustn't discard this information completely, or it will be impossible to remove hidden surfaces later.

The actual distance of a point P from the eye, in camera coordinates, is $\sqrt{P_x^2 + P_y^2 + P_z^2}$, which would be cumbersome and slow to compute for each point of interest. All we really need is some measure of distance that tells, when two points project to the *same* point on the near plane, which point is the closer. Figure 7.26 shows points P_1 and P_2, which both lie on a line from the eye and therefore project to the same point. We must be able to test whether P_1 obscures P_2 or vice versa. So, for each point P that we project, we compute a value called the **pseudodepth** that provides an adequate measure of depth for P. We then say that P projects to (x^*, y^*, z^*), where (x^*, y^*) is the value obtained from Equation (7.4) and z^* is the pseudodepth of P.

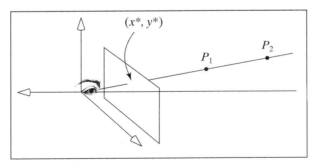

FIGURE 7.26 Is P_1 closer than P_2 or farther away?

What is a good choice for the pseudodepth function? Notice that if two points project to the same point, the farther one always has a more negative value of P_z, so we might use P_z itself for the pseudodepth. But it turns out to be both harmonious and efficient to choose a function with the *same denominator* $(-P_z)$ as occurs with x^* and y^*. So we try a function that has this denominator and a numerator that is linear in P_z, and we say that P "projects to"

$$(x^*, y^*, z^*) = \left(N \frac{P_x}{-P_z}, N \frac{P_y}{-P_z}, \frac{aP_z + b}{-P_z} \right) \qquad (7.7)$$

for some choice of the constants a and b. Although many different choices for a and b will do, we choose them so that the pseudodepth varies between -1 and 1. (Later we shall see why these are good choices.) Since depth increases as a point moves further down the negative z-axis, we decide that the pseudodepth is -1 when $P_z = -N$ and is $+1$ when $P_z = -F$. With these two conditions, we can easily solve for a and b, obtaining

$$a = -\frac{F + N}{F - N}, b = \frac{-2FN}{F - N}. \tag{7.8}$$

Figure 7.27 plots the pseudodepth versus $(-P_z)$. As we have stated, it grows from -1 for a point on the near plane up to $+1$ for a point on the far plane. As P_z approaches zero (so that the point is just in front of the eye), the pseudodepth plummets to negative infinity. For a point just behind the eye, the pseudodepth is large and positive. But we will clip off points that lie closer than the near plane, so this catastrophic behavior will never be encountered.

FIGURE 7.27 The pseudodepth grows as P_z becomes more negative.

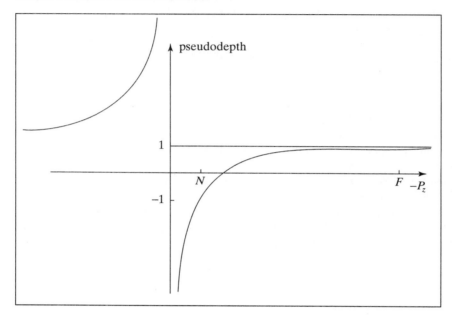

Notice that the pseudodepth values bunch together as $-P_z$ gets closer to F. Given the finite precision arithmetic of a computer, this crowding can cause a problem when you must distinguish the pseudodepth of two points during the removal of hidden surfaces: The points have different true depths from the eye, but their pseudodepths come out with the same value!

Note that defining the pseudodepth as in Equation (7.7) causes it to become more positive as P_z becomes more negative. This behavior seems reasonable, since the depth from the eye increases as P_z moves further along the negative z-axis.

■ **EXAMPLE 7.4.4 Pseudodepth varies slowly as $-P_z$ approaches F**

Suppose $N = 1$ and $F = 100$. Then $a = -101/99$ and $b = -200/99$, so we have

$$\text{pseudodepth}|_{N=1, F=100} = \frac{101P_z + 200}{99P_z}.$$

This function maps appropriately to -1 at $P_z = -N$ and to 1 at $P_z = -F$. But close to $-F$, it varies quite slowly with $-P_z$. For $-P_z$ values of 97, 98, and 99, for instance, the function evaluates to 0.9993752, 0.9995877, and 0.9997959, respectively.

A little algebra (see the exercises at the end of the section) shows that when N is much smaller than F, as it normally will be, the pseudodepth can be approximated by

$$\text{pseudodepth} \doteq 1 + \frac{2N}{P_z}. \tag{7.9}$$

Again this function varies more and more slowly as $-P_z$ approaches F. But its variation is increased by using large values of N. Thus, N should be set as large as possible (but, of course, not so large that objects nearest to the camera are clipped off!).

Using Homogeneous Coordinates

Why was consideration given to having the same denominator for each term in Equation (7.7)? As we now show, having the same denominator makes it possible to represent all of the steps so far in the graphics pipeline as matrix multiplications, offering both processing efficiency and uniformity. (Chips on some graphics cards can multiply a point by a matrix in hardware, making that operation extremely fast!) Doing it this way will also allow us to set things up for a highly efficient and reliable clipping step.

The new approach requires that we represent points in homogeneous coordinates. We have been doing that anyway, since such a representation makes it easier to transform a vertex by the modelview matrix. But we are going to expand the notion of the homogeneous coordinate representation beyond what we have needed up to now, and therein we shall find new power. In particular, a matrix will be able to perform not only an affine transformation, but also a "perspective transformation."

Up to now, we have said that a point $P = (P_x, P_y, P_z)$ has the representation $(P_x, P_y, P_z, 1)$ in homogeneous coordinates and that a vector $\mathbf{v} = (v_x, v_y, v_z)$ has the representation $(v_x, v_y, v_z, 0)$. In other words, we have simply appended a 1 to the original representation of the point and a 0 to that of the vector. This made it possible to use coordinate frames as a basis for representing the points and vectors of interest, and it allowed us to represent an affine transformation by a matrix.

Now we extend the idea and say that a point $P = (P_x, P_y, P_z)$ has a whole family of homogeneous representations (wP_x, wP_y, wP_z, w) for *any* value of w except 0. For example, the point $(1, 2, 3)$ has the representations $(1, 2, 3, 1), (2, 4, 6, 2), (0.003, 0.006, 0.009, 0.001), (-1, -2, -3, -1)$, and so forth. If someone hands you a point in this form—say, $(3, 6, 2, 3)$—and asks what point it is, just divide through by the last component to get $(1, 2, 2/3, 1)$, and then discard the last component: The point, in "ordinary" coordinates, is $1(, 2, 2/3)$. Thus,

- To convert a point from *ordinary coordinates* to *homogeneous coordinates*, append a 1;[4]
- To convert a point from *homogeneous coordinates* to *ordinary coordinates*, divide all of the components by the last component, and discard the fourth component.

The additional property of being able to scale all the components of a point without changing the point is really the basis for the name "homogeneous." Up until now, we have been working with the special case in which the final component is 1.

We examine homogeneous coordinates further in the exercises at the end of the section, but now we focus on how they operate when transforming points. Affine transformations work fine when homogeneous coordinates are used. Recall that the matrix for an affine transformation always has $(0, 0, 0, 1)$ in its fourth row. Therefore,

---

[4] And, if you wish, multiply all four components by any nonzero value.

if we multiply a point P in homogeneous representation by such a matrix M to form $MP = Q$ [recall Equation (5.24)], as in the example

$$\begin{pmatrix} 2 & -1 & 3 & 1 \\ 6 & .5 & 1 & 4 \\ 0 & 4 & 2 & -3 \\ 0 & 0 & 0 & 1 \end{pmatrix} \begin{pmatrix} wP_x \\ wP_y \\ wP_z \\ w \end{pmatrix} = \begin{pmatrix} wQ_x \\ wQ_y \\ wQ_z \\ w \end{pmatrix},$$

the final component of Q will always be unaltered: It is still w. Therefore, we can convert the Q back to ordinary coordinates in the usual fashion.

But something new happens if we deviate from a fourth row of $(0, 0, 0, 1)$. Consider the important example

$$\begin{pmatrix} N & 0 & 0 & 0 \\ 0 & N & 0 & 0 \\ 0 & 0 & a & b \\ 0 & 0 & -1 & 0 \end{pmatrix} \qquad \text{(the projection matrix, version 1)}, \qquad (7.10)$$

which has a fourth row of $(0, 0, -1, 0)$, (and which is close to what we shall later call the "projection matrix"), for any choices of N, a, and b. If we multiply this matrix by a point represented in homogeneous coordinates with an arbitrary w, that is,

$$\begin{pmatrix} N & 0 & 0 & 0 \\ 0 & N & 0 & 0 \\ 0 & 0 & a & b \\ 0 & 0 & -1 & 0 \end{pmatrix} \begin{pmatrix} wP_x \\ wP_y \\ wP_z \\ w \end{pmatrix} = \begin{pmatrix} wNP_x \\ wNP_y \\ w(aP_z + b) \\ -wP_z \end{pmatrix},$$

we obtain an ordinary point. But which one? To find out, we divide through by the fourth component and discard it. The result is

$$\left(N \frac{P_x}{-P_z}, N \frac{P_y}{-P_z}, \frac{aP_z + b}{-P_z} \right),$$

which is precisely what we need, according to Equation (7.7). Thus, using homogeneous coordinates allows us to capture perspective using a matrix multiplication! To make this approach work, however, we must always divide through by the fourth component, a step called **perspective division**.

A matrix that has values other than $(0, 0, 0, 1)$ for its fourth row does not perform an affine transformation. Instead, it performs a more general class of transformation called a **perspective transformation**. Note that this is a *transformation*, not a projection; a projection reduces the dimensionality of a point, to an ordered triple or pair, whereas a perspective transformation takes a quadruple and produces a quadruple.

Consider the algebraic effect of putting nonzero values, such as (A, B, C, D), in the fourth row of the matrix. When you multiply the matrix by $(P_x, P_y, P_z, 1)$ (or any multiple thereof), the fourth term in the resulting point becomes $AP_x + BP_y + CP_z + D$, making it linearly dependent on each of the components of P. After perspective division, this term appears in the denominator of the point. Such a denominator is exactly what is needed to produce the geometric effect of perspective projection onto a general plane, as we show in the exercises.

The perspective transformation therefore carries a 3D point P into another 3D point P', according to the mapping

$$(P_x, P_y, P_z) \rightarrow \left(N \frac{P_x}{-P_z}, N \frac{P_y}{-P_z}, \frac{aP_z + b}{-P_z} \right) \qquad \text{(the perspective transformation). (7.11)}$$

Where does the projection part come into play? Further along the pipeline, the first two components of this point are used for drawing, to locate, in screen coordinates, the position of the point to be drawn. The third component is "peeled off," to be used for depth testing. As far as locating the point on the screen is concerned, ignoring the third component is equivalent to replacing it by zero, as in

$$\left(N\frac{P_x}{-P_z}, N\frac{P_y}{-P_z}, \frac{aP_z + b}{-P_z} \right) \rightarrow \left(N\frac{P_x}{-P_z}, N\frac{P_y}{-P_z}, 0 \right) \qquad \text{(the projection).} \qquad (7.12)$$

This is just what we did in Chapter 5 to project a point orthographically (meaning perpendicularly to the viewplane) when setting up a camera for our first efforts at viewing a 3D scene. We will study orthographic projections in full detail later. For now, we can conclude that

(perspective projection) = **(perspective transformation)** + **(orthographic projection)**.

This decomposition of a perspective projection into a specific transformation followed by a (trivial) projection will prove very useful, both algorithmically and for understanding better what actually happens to each point as it passes through the graphics pipeline. OpenGL does the transformation step separately from the projection step; in fact, it inserts clipping, perspective division, and one additional mapping between them. We next look deeper into the transformation part of the process.

The Geometric Nature of the Perspective Transformation

The perspective transformation alters the 3D point P into another 3D point according to Equation (7.11), in order to "prepare" the point for projection. It is useful to think of the transformation as causing a "warping" of 3D space and to see how it warps one shape into another. Very importantly, it preserves straightness and flatness, so that lines transform into lines, planes into planes, and polygonal faces into other polygonal faces. It also preserves "in-between-ness," so if a point is inside an object, the transformed point will also be inside the transformed object. (Our choice of a suitable pseudodepth function was guided by the need to preserve these properties, the proof of which is examined in the exercises.)

Of particular interest is how the perspective transformation transforms the camera's view volume, because if we are going to do clipping in the warped space, we will be clipping against the warped view volume. The transformation shines in this regard: The warped view volume is a perfect shape for simple and efficient clipping! Figure 7.28 suggests how the view volume and other shapes are transformed. The near plane W at $z = -N$ maps into the plane W' at $z = -1$, and the far plane maps to the plane at $z = +1$. The top wall T is "tilted" into the horizontal plane T', so the latter is parallel to the z-axis. The bottom wall S becomes the horizontal S', and the two sidewalls become parallel to the z-axis. The camera's view volume is thus transformed into a parallelepiped!

It is easy to prove how these planes are transformed, because they all involve lines either that are parallel to the near plane or that pass through the eye. Check the following facts carefully:

Fact: Lines through the eye map into lines parallel to the z-axis. **Proof:** All points on a line through the eye project to a single point, say, (x^*, y^*), on the viewplane. So all of the points along the line transform to all of the points (x, y, z) with $x = x^*, y = y^*$, and z taking on all pseudodepth values between -1 and 1.

Fact: Lines perpendicular to the z-axis map into lines perpendicular to the z-axis. **Proof:** All points along such a line have the same z-coordinate, so they all map to points with the same pseudodepth value.

With the use of these facts, it is straightforward to derive the exact shape and dimensions of the warped view volume.

FIGURE 7.28 The view volume warped by the perspectival transformation.

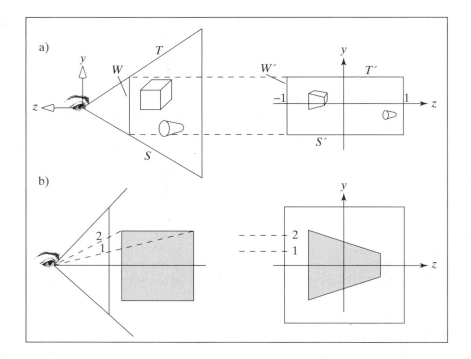

The transformation also warps objects into new shapes. Figure 7.28(b) shows a block being projected onto the near plane. Suppose the top edge of the front face of the block projects to $y = 2$ and the top edge of the back face projects to $y = 1$. Then, when the block is transformed, it becomes a truncated pyramid: The top edge of its front face lies at $y = 2$, and the top edge of its back face lies at $y = 1$. Things closer to the eye than the near plane become bigger, and things beyond the near plane become smaller. The transformed object is smaller at the back than the front because the original object projects that way. The x- and y-coordinates of the transformed object are the x- and y-coordinates of the *projection* of the original object—the coordinates you would encounter upon making an orthographic projection of the transformed object. In a nutshell,

> *The perspective transformation "warps" objects so that, when viewed with an orthographic projection, they appear the same as the original objects do when viewed with a perspective projection.*

So all objects are warped into properly foreshortened shapes according to the rules of perspective projection. Thereafter, they can be viewed with an orthographic projection, and the correct picture is produced.

We next look more closely at the specific shape and dimensions of the transformed view volume.

Details of the Transformed View Volume; Mapping into the Canonical View Volume

We want to put some numbers on the dimensions of the view volume before and after it is warped. Consider the top plane, and suppose it passes through the point (*left*, *top*, $-N$) at $z = -N$, as shown in Figure 7.29. Because it is composed of lines that pass through the eye and through points in the near plane, all of which have a y-coordinate of *top*, the top plane must transform to the plane $y = top$. Similarly,

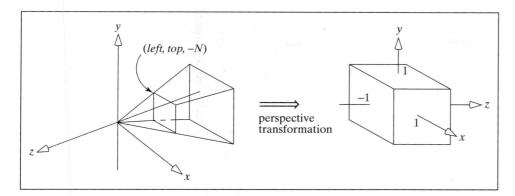

FIGURE 7.29 Details of the perspective transformation.

- the bottom plane transforms to the $y = bott$ plane;
- the left plane transforms to the $x = left$ plane;
- the right plane transforms to the $x = right$ plane.

We now know the transformed view volume precisely: a parallelepiped with dimensions that are related to the camera's properties in a very simple way. This is a splendid shape to clip against, as we shall see, because its walls are parallel to the coordinate planes. But it would be an even better shape for clipping if its dimensions didn't depend on the particular camera being used. OpenGL composes the perspective transformation with another mapping that scales and shifts this parallelepiped into the **canonical view volume**, a cube that extends from −1 to 1 in each dimension. Because this mapping scales things differently in the x- and y-dimensions as it "squashes" the scene into a fixed volume, it introduces some distortion, but the distortion will be eliminated in the final viewport transformation.

The transformed view volume already extends from −1 to 1 in z, so it only needs to be scaled in the other two dimensions. We therefore include a scaling and a shift in both x and y to map the parallelepiped into the canonical view volume. First we shift by -$(right + left)/2$ in x and by -$(top + bott)/2$ in y. Then we scale by $2/(right - left)$ in x and by $2/(top - bott)$ in y. When the matrix multiplications are done (see the exercises), we obtain the final matrix:

$$R = \begin{pmatrix} \dfrac{2N}{right - left} & 0 & \dfrac{right + left}{right - left} & 0 \\ 0 & \dfrac{2N}{top - bott} & \dfrac{top + bott}{top - bott} & 0 \\ 0 & 0 & \dfrac{-(F + N)}{F - N} & \dfrac{-2FN}{F - N} \\ 0 & 0 & -1 & 0 \end{pmatrix} \quad \text{(the projection matrix). (7.13)}$$

This is known as the **projection matrix**, and it performs the perspective transformation plus a scaling and shifting to transform the camera's view volume into the canonical view volume. It is precisely the matrix that OpenGL creates (and by which it multiplies the current matrix) when `glFrustum(left, right, bott, top, N, F)` is executed. Recall that `gluPerspective(viewAngle, aspect, N, F)` is usually used instead, as its parameters are more intuitive. The function `gluPerspective` sets up the same matrix, after computing values for top, $bott$, etc., using the formulas

$$top = N \tan\left(\frac{\pi}{180} viewAngle/2\right),$$

$bott = -top$, $right = top \times aspect$, and $left = -right$.

7.4.4 Clipping Faces against the View Volume

Recall from Figure 7.14 that clipping is performed after vertices have passed through the projection matrix. It is done in this warped space because the canonical view volume is particularly well suited for efficient clipping. Here we show how to exploit this feature, and we develop the details of the clipping algorithm.

Clipping in the warped space works because a point lies inside the camera's view volume if and only if its transformed version lies inside the canonical view volume. Figure 7.30(a) shows an example of clipping in action. A triangle has vertices v_1, v_2, and v_3, the last of which lies outside the canonical view volume CVV. The clipper works on edges: It first clips edge $v_1 v_2$ and finds that the entire edge lies inside the CVV. Then it clips edge $v_2 v_3$ and records the new vertex a formed where the edge exits from the CVV. Finally, it clips edge $v_3 v_1$ and records the new vertex where the edge enters the CVV. At the end of the process, the original triangle has become a quadrilateral with vertices $v_1 v_2 ab$. (We will see later that, in addition to identifying the locations of the new vertices, the pipeline also computes new color and texture parameters at these new vertices.)

FIGURE 7.30 Clipping against the canonical view volume (CVV).

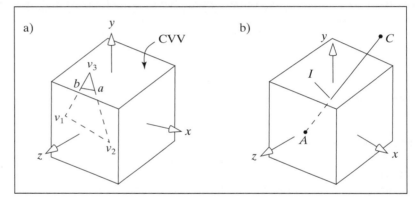

The clipping problem is basically the problem of clipping a line segment against the CVV. We examined such an algorithm, the Cyrus–Beck clipper, in Section 4.8.3. The clipper we develop here is similar to that one, but of course, it works in 3D rather than 2D.

Actually, it works in 4D: We will clip in the 4D homogeneous coordinate space called "clip coordinates" in Figure 7.14. This is easier than it might seem, and it will nicely distinguish between points in front of, and points behind, the eye.

Suppose we want to clip the line segment AC shown in Figure 7.30(b) against the CVV. This means that we are given two points in homogeneous coordinates, $A = (a_x, a_y, a_z, a_w)$ and $C = (c_x, c_y, c_z, c_w)$, and we want to determine which part of the segment lies inside the CVV. If the segment intersects the boundary of the CVV, we will need to compute the intersection point $I = (I_x, I_y, I_z, I_w)$.

As with the Cyrus–Beck algorithm, we view the CVV as six infinite planes and consider where the given edge lies relative to each plane in turn. We can represent the edge parametrically as $A + (C - A)t$. It lies at A when $t = 0$ and at C when $t = 1$. For each wall of the CVV, we first test whether A and C lie on the same side of a wall. If they do, there is no need to compute the intersection of the edge with the wall. If they lie on opposite sides, we locate the intersection point and clip off the part of the edge that lies outside the wall.

So we must be able to test whether a point is on the "outside" or "inside" of a plane. Consider the plane $x = -1$, for instance, which is one of the walls of the CVV. The point A lies to the right of it (on the "inside") if

$$\frac{a_x}{a_w} > -1, \quad \text{or} \quad a_x > -a_w, \quad \text{or} \left(a_w + a_x \right) > 0. \tag{7.14}$$

(When you multiply both sides of an inequality by a negative term you must reverse the direction of the inequality. But we are ultimately dealing with only positive values of a_w here; see the exercises.) Similarly, A is inside the plane $x = 1$ if

$$\frac{a_x}{a_w} < 1, \quad \text{or} \quad \left(a_w - a_x \right) > 0.$$

Blinn [Blinn96] calls these quantities the "boundary coordinates" (BC's) of point A, and he lists the six such quantities that we work with in Figure 7.31. We form these six quantities for A and again for C. If all six are positive, the point lies inside the CVV. If any are negative, the point lies outside. If both points lie inside, we have the same kind of trivial acceptance we had in the Cohen–Sutherland clipper of Section 3.3. If A and C lie outside on the same side (corresponding BC's are negative) the edge must lie wholly outside the CVV. We thus have the following criteria:

boundary coordinate	homogeneous value	clip plane
BC_0	$w + x$	$x = -1$
BC_1	$w - x$	$x = 1$
BC_2	$w + y$	$y = -1$
BC_3	$w - y$	$y = 1$
BC_4	$w + z$	$z = -1$
BC_5	$w - z$	$z = 1$

FIGURE 7.31 The boundary codes computed for each endpoint of an edge.

Trivial acceptance: Both endpoints lie inside the CVV. (All 12 BC's are positive.)
Trivial rejection: Both endpoints lie outside the same plane of the CVV.

If neither condition prevails, we must clip segment AC against each plane individually. Just as with the Cyrus–Beck clipper, we keep track of a **candidate interval** (CI) (see Figure 4.45)—an interval of time during which the edge might still be inside the CVV. Basically, we know the converse of this condition: If t is outside the CI, then the edge is *not* inside the CVV. Note that the CI extends from $t = t_{in}$ to $t = t_{out}$.

We test the edge against each wall in turn. If the corresponding boundary codes have opposite signs, the edge hits the plane at some time t_{hit}, which we then compute. If the edge "is entering" (is moving into the "inside" of) the plane as t increases, we update $t_{in} = \max\left(\text{old } t_{in}, t_{hit}\right)$, since the edge could not be entering at an earlier time than t_{hit}. Similarly, if the edge is exiting, we update $t_{out} = \min\left(\text{old } t_{out}, t_{hit}\right)$. If at any time the CI is reduced to the empty interval (i.e, if t_{out} becomes greater than t_{in}), the entire edge is clipped off and we have an "early out," which saves unnecessary computation.

It is straightforward to calculate the hit time of an edge with a plane. We write the edge parametrically in homogeneous coordinates:

$$\text{edge}(t) = \left(a_x + \left(c_x - a_x \right)t, a_y + \left(c_y - a_y \right)t, a_z + \left(c_z - a_z \right)t, a_w + \left(c_w - a_w \right)t \right)$$

If the edge is the $x = 1$ plane, for instance, the edge hits when the x-coordinate of $A + (C - A)t$ is 1, or

$$\frac{a_x + \left(c_x - a_x \right)t}{a_w + \left(c_w - a_w \right)t} = 1,$$

We solve for t, to get

$$t = \frac{a_w - a_x}{(a_w - a_x) - (c_w - c_x)}.$$

(7.15)

Note that t_{hit} depends on only two boundary coordinates. Intersections with other planes yield similar formulas.

The preceding mathematics is easily put into code, as shown in Figure 7.32. It is basically the Liang–Barsky algorithm [Liang84], with some refinements suggested by

FIGURE 7.32 The edge clipper (as refined by Blinn).

```
int clipEdge(Point4& A, Point4& C)
{
    double tIn = 0.0, tOut = 1.0, tHit;
    double aBC[6], cBC[6];
    int aOutcode = 0, cOutcode = 0;
    .. find BC's for A and C ..
    .. form outcodes for A and C ..

    if((aOutcode & cOutcode) != 0) // trivial reject
        return 0;
    if((aOutcode | cOutcode) == 0) // trivial accept
        return 1;

    for(int i = 0; i < 6; i++) // clip against each plane
    {
        if(cBC[i] < 0)  // exits: C is outside
        {
            tHit = aBC[i]/(aBC[i] - cBC[i]);
            tOut = MIN(tOut,tHit);
        }
        else if(aBC[i] < 0) //enters: A is outside
        {
            tHit = aBC[i]/(aBC[i] - cBC[i]);
            tIn = MAX(tIn, tHit);
        }
        if(tIn > tOut) return 0; //CI is empty: early out
    }
    // update the end points as necessary
    Point4 tmp;
    if(aOutcode != 0) // A is out: tIn has changed
    { // find updated A, (but don't change A yet)
        tmp.x = A.x + tIn * (C.x - A.x);
        tmp.y = A.y + tIn * (C.y - A.y);
        tmp.z = A.z + tIn * (C.z - A.z);
        tmp.w = A.w + tIn * (C.w - A.w);
    }
    if(cOutcode != 0) // C is out: tOut has changed
    { // update C (using original value of A)
        C.x = A.x + tOut * (C.x - A.x);
        C.y = A.y + tOut * (C.y - A.y);
        C.z = A.z + tOut * (C.z - A.z);
        C.w = A.w + tOut * (C.w - A.w);
    }
    A = tmp; // now update A
    return 1; // some of the edge lies inside the CVV
}
```

Blinn [Blinn96]. The routine `clipEdge(Point4& A, Point4& C)` takes two points in homogeneous coordinates (having fields x, y, z, and w) and returns 0 if no part of AC lies in the CVV, and 1 otherwise. It also alters A and C so that when the routine is finished, they are the endpoints of the clipped edge.

The routine finds the six boundary coordinates for each endpoint and stores them in `aBC[]` and `cBC[]`. For efficiency, it also builds an **outcode** for each point, which holds the *signs* of the six boundary codes for that point. Bit i of A's outcode holds a 0 if `aBC[i] > 0` (A is inside the ith wall) and a 1 otherwise. A trivial acceptance occurs when both `aOutcode` and `cOutcode` are zero. A trivial rejection occurs when the bitwise AND of the two outcodes is nonzero.

In the loop that tests the edge against each plane, at most one of the BC's can be negative. (Why?) If A has a negative BC, the edge must be entering at the hit point; if C has a negative BC, the edge must be exiting at the hit point. (Why?) (Blinn uses a slightly faster test by incorporating a mask that tests one bit of an outcode.) Each time `tIn` or `tOut` is updated, an early out is taken if `tIn` has become greater than `tOut`.

When all planes have been tested, one or both of `tIn` and `tOut` have been altered. (Why?) A is updated to $A + (i - A)tIn$ if `tIn` has changed, and C is updated to $A + (C - A)tOut$ if `tOut` has changed.

Blinn suggests precomputing the BC's and outcode for every point to be processed. This eliminates the need to recompute these quantities when a vertex is an endpoint of more than one edge, as is often the case.

Why Did We Clip against the Canonical View Volume?

Now that we have seen how easy it is to clip against the canonical view volume, we can see the value of having transformed all objects of interest prior to clipping. There are two important features here:

1. The CVV is parameter free: The algorithm needs no extra information to describe the clipping volume; it uses only the values -1 and 1. So the code itself can be highly tuned for maximum efficiency.
2. The planes of the CVV are aligned with the coordinate axes (after the perspective transformation is performed). This means that, using a single coordinate (as in $a_x > -1$) we can determine which side of a plane a point lies on. If the planes were not aligned, an expensive dot product would be needed.

Why Did We Clip in Homogeneous Coordinates, rather than after the Perspective Division Step?

Clipping in homogeneous coordinates isn't completely necessary, but it makes the clipping algorithm clean, fast, and simple. Doing the perspective division step destroys information: If you have the values a_x and a_w explicitly, you know, of course, the signs of both of them. But given just the ratio a_x/a_w, you can tell only whether a_x and a_w have the same or opposite signs. Keeping values in homogeneous coordinates and clipping points closer to the eye than the near plane automatically removes points that lie behind the eye, such as point B in Figure 7.23.

Some "perverse" situations that necessitate clipping in homogeneous coordinates have been described [Blinn96, Foley90]. These situations involve peculiar transformations of objects or the construction of certain surfaces such that the original point (a_x, a_y, a_z, a_w) has a negative fourth term, even though the point is in front of the eye. None of the objects we discuss modeling here involve such cases. We conclude that clipping in homogeneous coordinates, although usually not critical, makes the algorithm fast and simple at almost no cost.

Following the clipping operation, **perspective division** is finally done (as in Figure

7.14), and the ordered triple (x, y, z) is passed through the viewport transformation. As we discuss next, this transformation sizes and shifts the x- and y-values so that they are placed properly in the viewport and makes minor adjustments on the z-component (regarding pseudodepth) to make it more suitable for depth testing.

The Viewport Transformation

As we have seen, the perspective transformation "squashes" a scene into the canonical cube, as suggested in Figure 7.33. If the aspect ratio of the camera's view volume (that is, the aspect ratio of the window on the near plane) is 1.5, then, obviously, distortion is introduced when the perspective transformation scales objects into a window with aspect ratio 1. But the viewport transformation can undo this distortion by mapping a square into a viewport of aspect ratio 1.5. We normally set the aspect ratio of the viewport to be the same as that of the view volume.

FIGURE 7.33 The viewport transformation restores the aspect ratio of an object.

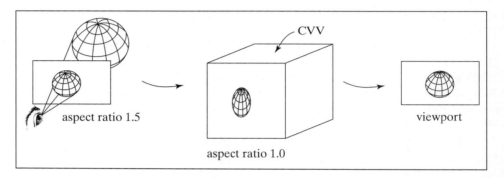

We have encountered the OpenGL function `glViewport(x, y, wid, ht)` often before. It specifies that the viewport will have lower left corner `(x,y)` in screen coordinates and will be `wid` pixels wide and `ht` pixels high. The function thus specifies a viewport with aspect ratio `wid/ht`. The viewport transformation also maps pseudodepth from the range -1 to 1 into the range 0 to 1.

Recall Figure 7.14, which reveals the entire graphics pipeline. Each point V (which is usually one vertex of a polygon) is passed through the following steps:

- V is **extended** to a homogeneous quadruple by appending a 1.
- The quadruple is multiplied by the **modelview matrix**, producing a quadruple giving the position in eye coordinates.
- The point is then multiplied by the **projection matrix**, producing a quadruple in clip coordinates.
- The edge having the projected point as an endpoint is **clipped**.
- **Perspective division** is performed, returning an ordered triple.
- The **viewport transformation** multiplies the preceding triple by a matrix; the result, (sx, sy, dz), is used for drawing and depth calculations. The point (sx, sy) is displayed in screen coordinates; dz is a measure of the depth of the original point from the eye of the camera.

PRACTICE EXERCISES

7.4.5 P projects where?

Suppose the viewplane is given in camera coordinates by the equation $Ax + By + Cz = D$. Show that any point P projects onto this plane at the point given in homogeneous coordinates by

$$P' = \left(DP_x, DP_y, DP_z, AP_x + BP_y + CP_z\right)$$

Use the following steps in your demonstration:

a. Show that the projected point is the point at which the ray between the eye and P hits the given plane.
b. Show that the ray is given by Pt and that it hits the plane at
$t^* = D/(AP_x + BP_y + CP_z)$.
c. Show that the projected point—the hit point—is therefore given properly by the expression for P'.
d. Show that, for the near plane we used earlier, we obtain (x^*, y^*) as given by Equation (7.4).

7.4.6 A revealing approximate form for the pseudodepth

Show that the pseudodepth $a + b/(-P_z)$, where a and b are as given in Equation (7.8), is well approximated by Equation (7.9) when N is much smaller than F.

7.4.7 Points at infinity in homogeneous coordinates

Consider the nature of the homogeneous coordinate point (x, y, z, w) as w becomes smaller and smaller. For $w = .01$ it is $(100x, 100y, 100z)$, for $w = 0.0001$ it is $(10,000x, 10,000y, 10,000z)$, etc. The point progresses out "toward infinity" in the direction (x, y, z). The point with representation $(x, y, z, 0)$ is, in fact, called a "point at infinity." One of the advantages of homogeneous coordinates is that such an idealized point has a perfectly finite representation that removes many awkward special cases in some mathematical derivations. For instance, two lines will always intersect, even if they are parallel [Ayers67; Semple52]. But other things don't work as well. For example, what is the difference of two points in homogeneous coordinates?

7.4.8 How does the perspective transformation affect lines and planes?

We must show that the perspective transformation preserves flatness and in-betweenness.

a. Argue that this is proven if we can show that a point P lying on the line between two points A and B transforms to a point P' that lies between the transformed versions of A and B.
b. Show that the perspective transformation does indeed produce a point P' with the property just stated.
c. Show that each plane that passes through the eye maps to a plane that is parallel to the z-axis.
d. Show that each plane that is perpendicular to the z-axis maps to a plane perpendicular to the z-axis.
e. Show that relative depth is preserved.

7.4.9 The details of the transformed view volume

Show that the warped view volume has the dimensions given in the subsection "Details of the Transformed View Volume". Use the facts developed in the preceding exercise.

7.4.10 Show the final form of the projection matrix

The projection matrix is basically that of Equation (7.10), followed by a shift and a scaling. If the matrix of that equation is denoted as M, and if T represents the shifting matrix and S the scaling matrix, show that the matrix product STM is that given in Equation (7.13).

7.4.11 What becomes of points behind the eye?

If the perspective transformation moves the eye off to minus infinity, what happens to points that lie behind the eye? Consider a line $P(t)$ that begins at a point in front of the eye at $t = 0$ and moves to a point behind the eye at $t = 1$.

a. Find the parametric form of this line in homogeneous coordinates.
b. Find the parametric representation after the line undergoes the perspective transformation.
c. Interpret the situation geometrically. Specifically, state what the fourth homogeneous coordinate is geometrically. A valuable discussion of this phenomenon is given by [Blinn78].

7.5 PRODUCING STEREO VIEWS

Let us digress briefly to use the camera controls developed earlier for producing stereo views of a scene. A stereo view can make a picture much more intelligible; when viewed properly, the picture offers a sense of depth that reduces visual ambiguity. All of the stereo figures in this book were made using the technique to be described.

We might call the camera used so far a "cyclops" camera, after the fabled one-eyed monster. To get a sense of its limitations, keep one eye closed as you walk around a room, and try to do simple tasks. Our natural stereoscopic eye–brain system gives us a tremendous amount of information by providing a visual sense of depth. We want to add this same capability to computer graphics pictures.

To make a stereo view, two pictures—a "left eye" and a "right eye" picture—are made using slightly different cameras, as suggested in Figure 7.34. The cameras are built using the same *LookAt* point, but different eye positions. Two viewports are created side by side on the display, as in Figure 7.34(b). The left-eye picture is displayed in the left viewport and the right-eye picture in the right viewport. To view a stereo picture, let your left eye look at the left picture and your right eye look at the right picture. Done properly, the two images fuse into a single image that appears to have depth. (The viewing procedure may take some practice; the preface describes a method for learning how to do it.)

FIGURE 7.34 Creating stereo views.

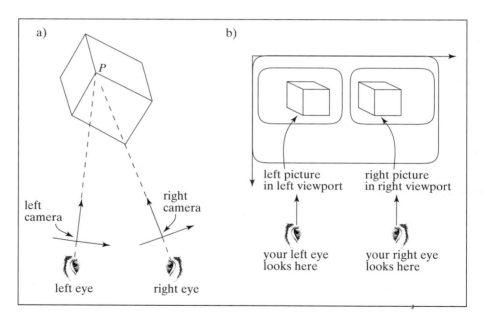

Figure 7.35 shows a stereo wire-frame view of the buckyball described in Chapter 6. The two pictures are evidently quite different, and there is significant visual ambiguity (which edges are in front, which behind?) when only one of the pictures is viewed. A stereo view, however, disambiguates the various edges, making the picture easily intelligible.

Figure 7.36 shows close-up stereo views of a barn. In Part (a), the camera is rolled by 40°. Note that the orientation of the barn is difficult to comprehend without the stereo effect. Part (b) shows a close-up of one corner of the barn, and the severe distortion produced by perspective is clearly visible.

To build the two cameras required for stereo viewing, we must decide where to put the left and right eyes. A simple approach begins with a regular camera based on a

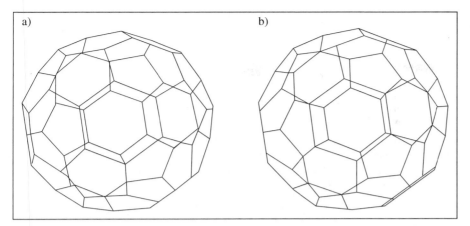

FIGURE 7.35 Stereo view of the buckyball.

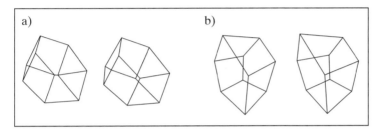

FIGURE 7.36 Close-up views of a barn.

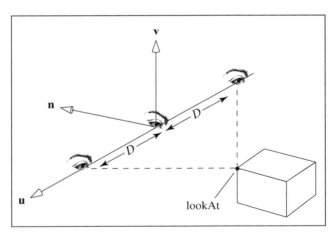

FIGURE 7.37 Setting the two eye positions for stereo viewing.

single `LookAt` point and a single initial "cyclops" eye, as suggested in Figure 7.37. Along with a choice of **up**, these two parameters establish the "cyclops camera," with its **u**, **v**, and **n** directions.

The left and right eyes are defined at slight displacements of the cyclops eye, at some distance D along $-\mathbf{u}$ and $\mathbf{u}$, respectively. The choice of D depends on the unit of measure being used in the application. If all lengths and distances are being thought of as inches, then the user will probably set up the camera at an appropriate number of inches from the desired *lookAt* point. Human eyes are about 3 inches apart, so a good first choice of D would be 1.5. If things were measured in meters instead, you might use the distance in meters between the eyes. In those cases in which a scene is fanciful and has no inherent scale, some experimentation would be needed to achieve the desired visual effect. Case Study 7.2 suggests a project to produce stereo views.

7.6 TAXONOMY OF PROJECTIONS

As lines, so loves oblique, may well
Themselves in every angle greet; But ours, so truly parallel,
Though infinite, can never meet. Andrew Marvell, The Definition of Love

Thus far, we have examined the basic ideas of "planar projections," wherein points are projected in one way or another onto a plane. We looked at parallel projections in Chapter 5, and we have examined perspective projections in this chapter. Many special cases of these projections have been used in art, architecture, and engineering drawings, and we now look at their characteristics and how they fit together.

Planar projections fall naturally into the tree structure shown in Figure 7.38. Each child of a particular type of projection represents a special case of its parent in the tree. The first fundamental split is between parallel and perspective projections. Let us begin by examining the latter class.

FIGURE 7.38 A taxonomy of popular projections.

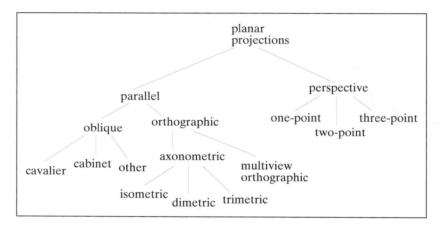

7.6.1 One-, Two-, and Three-Point Perspective

Perspective projections divide nicely into three classes: one-point, two-point, and three-point projections, distinguished by the orientation of the camera relative to the world coordinate system. The names derive from the situation of viewing the unit cube shown in Figure 7.39. The unit cube is nestled into the positive x-, y-, z-octant with one corner at the origin. Most important, its edges are aligned with the

FIGURE 7.39 The unit cube, the principal axes, and the principal planes.

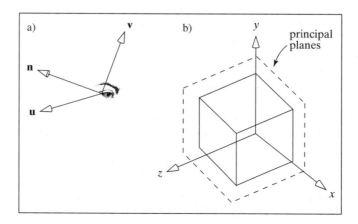

world coordinate axes, which in this discussion are called **principal axes**, lying in the directions of the unit vectors **i**, **j**, and **k**. Similarly, the three planes $x = 0$, $y = 0$, and $z = 0$ are called the **principal planes**, and the cube has its six faces aligned with them.

The camera can be oriented in an infinite number of ways relative to this coordinate system. For some of these, the n-axis of the camera is perpendicular to one principal axis or another. Traditionally, perspective projections are categorized by counting the number of **finite vanishing points** that the principal axes produce. Recall that if a line is perpendicular to **n**, its vanishing point is at infinity; otherwise its vanishing point is finite. So we can also count the number of principal axes that are *not* perpendicular to **n**. This is also the number of principal axes that **pierce** the viewplane of the camera. (Why?)

One point Perspective

In a one-point perspective projection, exactly one principal axis has a finite vanishing point. Thus, **n** is not perpendicular to exactly one of the three directions **i**, **j**, or **k**, but it is perpendicular to the other two directions, so it is perpendicular to one of the principal planes. Two of the three components of **n**—n_x, n_y, and n_z—must be zero.

Figure 7.40(a) shows a one-point perspective view, in which the camera has been oriented with its viewplane parallel to the xy-plane. The receding lines of the cube converge to a finite vanishing point (VP). The camera here has $\mathbf{n} = (0,0,1)$. In camera coordinates, the receding lines have direction $\mathbf{c} = (0,0,-1)$, so by Equation (7.6), the vanishing point lies at $(0,0)$. On the other hand, the lines parallel to the x- and y-axes have vanishing points "at infinity."

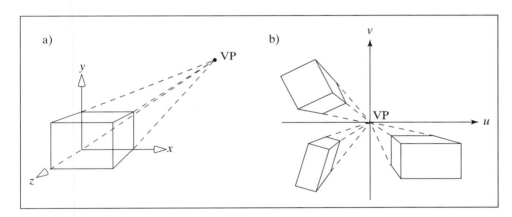

FIGURE 7.40 One-point perspective views.

The location of the vanishing point does not depend on the position of the camera relative to a cube. Figure 7.40(b) shows several blocks in one-point perspective. Each block may be considered to have its own principal axes, and in this picture the front face of each block is parallel to the viewplane. All receding lines share the same vanishing point, $(0,0)$.

Recall Figure 7.24, which shows two sets of grid lines on a horizontal plane. The grid lines run parallel to the principal axes (the world coordinate axes). Another set of grid lines, not shown, would run vertically, parallel to the world y-axis. The figure looks like a one-point perspective, since there seems to be a single finite vanishing point at the horizon. But the camera could be aimed "downward," making the view a two-point perspective, discussed next. You simply cannot tell from the figure alone. (If you are told that the horizon projects to $y = 0$, you could then conclude that the camera is level and that the figure is indeed a one-point perspective.)

FIGURE 7.41 A two-point perspective view.

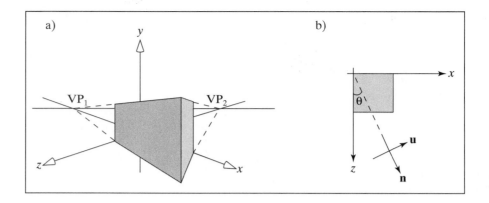

Two-point Perspective

In a two-point perspective, exactly two principal axes have finite vanishing points. Thus, the camera's **n** direction is not perpendicular to two of these axes; it is perpendicular to only one. Accordingly, one of the three components of **n** must be zero.

Figure 7.41(a) shows a cube in two-point perspective: There are two finite vanishing points, since both axes **i** and **k** pierce the viewplane. The camera was set up as suggested in Figure 7.41(b), with its **n** making an angle of θ with the z-axis, so that $\mathbf{n} = (\sin(\theta), 0, \cos(\theta))$. Here, **n** is perpendicular to **j**, so the vertical principal axis has an infinite vanishing point. It is not hard to compute where the finite vanishing points are located. (See the exercises at the end of the section.)

It is interesting to see what happens if we view the infinite-grid scene, first seen in Figure 7.24, in two-point perspective. Figure 7.42 shows the case where the eye is still at $y = 1$, looking horizontally, but the camera has been yawed to the left so that $\mathbf{n} = (.74, 0, .67)$. Now both sets of lines recede to the horizon, producing two widely separated vanishing points there. (What are the vanishing points numerically?) Many of the more remote lines are not drawn in the figure, as they are so crowded together that they cannot be plainly seen.

FIGURE 7.42 The infinite grid in two-point perspective.

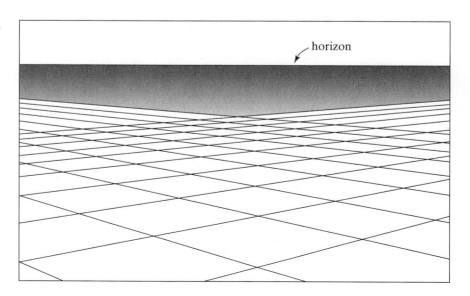

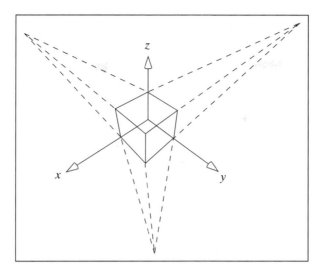

FIGURE 7.43 Three-point perspective.

Three-point Perspective

In three-point perspective drawings, all three principal axes have finite vanishing points: All three pierce the viewplane. The vector **n** is not perpendicular to any axes, so all of its components are nonzero.

Figure 7.43 shows the cube in three-point perspective. The three finite vanishing points are visible.

Artists often use vanishing points in perspective drawings, in order to highlight certain features or to increase the drawings' dramatic effect. The beguiling lithograph by M. C. Escher in Figure 7.44 shows the sense of scope afforded by a three-point perspective. (Where are the three vanishing points in this drawing?)

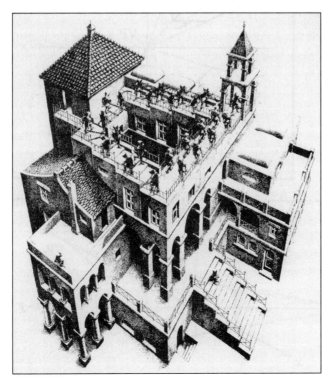

FIGURE 7.44 M.C. Escher's *Ascending and Descending*: a three-point perspective (© 1988 M. C. Escher Heirs/Cordon Art-Baarn-Holland. Used by permission).

PRACTICE EXERCISES

7.6.1 Setting up a one-point perspective

In an application, we choose `eye` and `look` to establish the desired camera, and **n** is determined from `eye` - `look`. Give three examples of `eye` and the corresponding `look` that produce interesting one-point perspectival views of the unit cube.

7.6.2 Position of the vanishing point

Draw by hand the unit cube and the world coordinate axes in one-point perspective for a camera with `eye` = (2, 3, 4).

7.6.3 Calculating vanishing points

Find the locations of the two vanishing points in Figure 7.41(a) for an arbitrary value of θ.

7.6.4 Creating two-point perspective views

Give three examples of `eye` and the corresponding `look` for a camera that produces interesting two-point perspective views of the unit cube. For each example, compute the actual positions of the vanishing points.　■

7.6.2 Parallel Projections

We next explore the various types of parallel projections. We introduced parallel projections in Chapter 5 as a simple way to get started viewing objects. The function `glOrtho()` was used to establish a view volume, and OpenGL did the rest. Now we shall look a little deeper at the nature of parallel projections and distinguish the various types that are used in practice.

We know that with a perspective projection, all points P in the scene are projected onto the viewplane along projectors that converge on the eye: Each projector is determined by P itself and the eye, and all the projectors have assorted directions. In contrast, with a parallel projection, all of the projectors are given the same direction, say, **d**. Figure 7.45 shows two arbitrary points being projected: P projects to p on the viewplane, and Q projects to q, both along vector **d**.

FIGURE 7.45 Parallel projections.

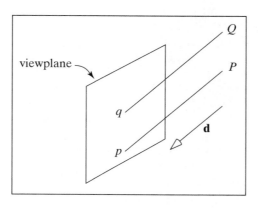

Some Theory concerning Parallel Projections

To what point p does P project? Suppose the plane has normal vector **n** and passes through some point B. Then p lies on the plane at the spot where a ray from P along **d** hits the plane. We have done this calculation in several places earlier. If the ray has the parametric form $P + \mathbf{d}t$, we substitute this for Q in the planar equation $\mathbf{n} \cdot (Q - B) = 0$ and solve for t. We then use this value of t in $P + \mathbf{d}t$ to obtain the hit point:

$$p = P + \mathbf{d}\frac{\mathbf{n} \cdot (B - P)}{\mathbf{n} \cdot \mathbf{d}}. \tag{7.16}$$

This is quite different from the expression we obtain when perspective projection is used. In particular, there is no foreshortening with distance; that is, there is no P term in the denominator. (Notice in addition that $\mathbf{d}$ can be replaced with $-\mathbf{d}$ with no effect on the resulting projection.)

We consider the familiar camera to see what Equation (7.16) reveals. We shall work in camera coordinates, so that $\mathbf{n} = (0, 0, 1)$, and project onto the xy-plane, for which $B = (0, 0, 0)$. (This makes things a little simpler than projecting onto the near plane.) Then

$$p = \left(P_x - d_x \frac{P_z}{d_z}, P_y - d_y \frac{P_z}{d_z}, 0 \right). \tag{7.17}$$

(Check the formula!) Parallel projections split into two principal types, as illustrated in Figure 7.46:

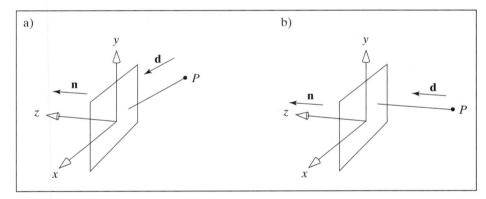

FIGURE 7.46 Parallel projections working in camera coordinates. (a) A general $\mathbf{d}$. (b) $\mathbf{d}$ parallel to $\mathbf{n}$.

1. *Oblique*: the projection direction $\mathbf{d}$ is not parallel to $\mathbf{n}$.
2. *Orthographic*: the projection direction $\mathbf{d}$ is parallel to $\mathbf{n}$.

Part (a) of the figure shows the case of a general direction $\mathbf{d}$, not necessarily parallel to $\mathbf{n}$. (We will, of course, never choose to make d_z equal to zero.) Part (b) shows the case where $\mathbf{d}$ is parallel to $\mathbf{n}$, so d_x and d_y are equal to zero. We look at each type in turn.

Orthographic Projections

In orthographic projections, both d_x and d_y are zero. Then p becomes $p = (P_x, P_y, 0)$. Thus, projecting orthographically is a matter of just dropping the third component of P in camera coordinates.

It is interesting to see how OpenGL carries out orthographic projection. Recall that OpenGL uses the projection matrix to describe the view volume of the camera. In particular, the projection matrix specifies how to transform vertices so as to "squash" them into the canonical view volume (CVV). Suppose the actual view volume extends from l to r (short for *left* and *right*) in x, from b to t (short for *bottom* and *top*) in y, and from $-n$ to $-f$ (short for *near* and *far*) in z. To transform the parallelepiped thereby formed into the CVV, we must shift and scale so that the CVV extends from −1 to 1 in each dimension. It is easy to check (see the exercises) that the matrix

$$\begin{pmatrix} \dfrac{2}{r-l} & 0 & 0 & -\dfrac{r+l}{r-l} \\[2ex] 0 & \dfrac{2}{t-b} & 0 & \dfrac{-t+b}{t-b} \\[2ex] 0 & 0 & \dfrac{-2}{f-n} & -\dfrac{f+n}{f-n} \\[2ex] 0 & 0 & 0 & 1 \end{pmatrix}$$

(OpenGL projection matrix for orthographic projection)   (7.18)

does indeed map the view volume into the CVV. This matrix is the one formed by `glOrtho()`. If you multiply it by P (expressed in homogeneous coordinates), you get the actual point p that OpenGL submits for clipping and mapping to the viewport. Notice that OpenGL does not set the z-component to zero, as we have done; it performs a transformation, not a projection. It ultimately does the actual projection by separating off the z-component at the very end, using the x- and y- components in screen coordinates for drawing and the z-component for depth testing.

Types of Orthographic Projections

There are various kinds of orthographic projections, distinguished by different orientations of the camera in the world. These projections are named according to how the camera's **n** direction is aimed relative to the world coordinate axes.

Multiview Orthographic Projections These are traditionally presented as the top, front, and side views of an object. The vector **n** is made parallel to **k**, **i**, and **j** in turn, and the object of interest is drawn. Figure 7.47 gives an example. Multiview orthographic projections are especially suited to engineering drawings, as you can measure the dimensions of an object directly, particularly when the object is cubelike, so that its various faces are aligned with the world axes.

Axonometric Views In an axonometric view, **n** is chosen to obtain a better 3D "sense" of the shape of the object. In such a view, **n** is usually not parallel to any principal axis; rather, it is oriented so that three adjacent faces of the (cubelike) object are visible.

FIGURE 7.47 A multiview orthographic drawing.

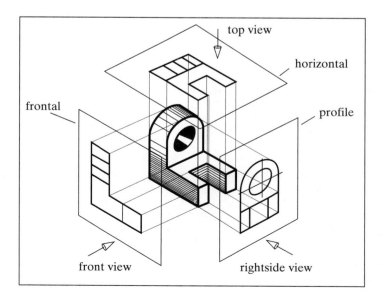

The choice of which faces to make visible depends on which faces of the object are important and should be emphasized. In addition, one of the principal axes is usually chosen to be vertical. Parallel lines in the object are, of course, viewed as parallel, but if a line recedes, it is **foreshortened** by some factor. Figure 7.48 shows **n** tilted to form an angle α with the x-axis.

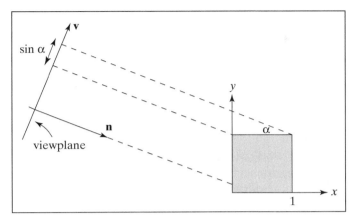

FIGURE 7.48 The foreshortening factor.

A line of unit length oriented α radians from the normal to the viewplane is viewed as having a length of $\sin(\alpha)$, the value assigned to the **foreshortening factor**.

Axonometric projections fall into three classes, depending on how many principal axes are *equally* foreshortened:

1. Isometric ("equal measure"): All three principal axes are foreshortened equally.
2. Dimetric ("two measures"): Two principal axes are foreshortened equally.
3. Trimetric ("three measures"): All three principal axes are foreshortened un-equally.

Isometric Views An **isometric** view of a cube is shown in Figure 7.49(a), in a direction along one of the cube's eight diagonals. All three axes are foreshortened by the same amount. As seen in Figure 7.49(b), an isometric view of a transparent cube is just a regular hexagon with three diagonal lines.

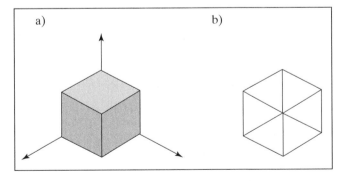

FIGURE 7.49 An isometric view of a cube.

The condition for an isometric view is $n_x = \pm n_y = \pm n_z$. In an isometric view, the angles between the projections of the principal axes are equal. The length of any line that lies in a principal plane can be measured directly from the drawing, and this length can then be scaled by a fixed amount (how much?) to obtain the true length of the line.

Dimetric Views When only two of the axes make the same angle with **n**, the view is called **dimetric**. In a dimetric view, two of the direction cosines must have the same

FIGURE 7.50 Several dimetric views of a cube.

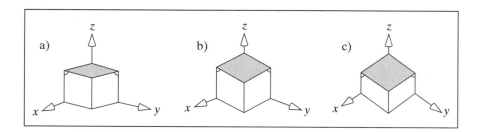

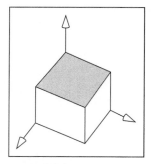

FIGURE 7.51 A trimetric view.

magnitude, so that $n_x = \pm n_y$, $n_x = \pm n_z$, or $n_y = \pm n_z$. A sequence of dimetric views is shown in Figure 7.50; the third one is almost isometric. For each view, $n_x = n_y$, and both are negative. (What is n_z, approximately, in the first figure? In the last one?) In each view, the angles indicated are equal. The different orientations place differing amounts of emphasis on the faces.

Trimetric Views Finally, if the three axes make different angles with **n**, the view is called **trimetric**. Figure 7.51 provides an example, in which there is almost complete freedom of choice for the components of **n**. When the proper orientation is chosen, a trimetric view can look the most natural.

Oblique Projections

Orthographic projections preserve the exact shape of one face of an object, but do not reveal its 3D nature very well. On the other hand, axonometric projections show a 3D quality, but do not yield the exact shape of any of the faces of the object. Oblique projections are an attempt to combine the useful properties of both orthographic and axonometric projections. They usually present the exact shape of one face of an object (the most important face), while simultaneously revealing the general 3D appearance of the object.

Equation (7.17) determines where the projection of any point P in a scene appears on the viewplane. If d_x is nonzero, x is altered by a term proportional to P_z. The value of y is offset similarly when d_y is nonzero. Recall that a perturbation of one coordinate by an amount proportional to another is a **shear**. Thus, the effect of obliqueness is a shearing of the image, which makes additional sides of a cubelike object visible.

If we write Equation (7.17) in matrix form, we obtain

$$
\begin{pmatrix} p_x \\ p_y \\ p_z \\ 1 \end{pmatrix} = \begin{pmatrix} 1 & 0 & -\dfrac{d_x}{d_z} & 0 \\ 0 & 1 & -\dfrac{d_y}{d_z} & 0 \\ 0 & 0 & 0 & 0 \\ 0 & 0 & 0 & 1 \end{pmatrix} \begin{pmatrix} P_x \\ P_y \\ P_z \\ 1 \end{pmatrix}. \tag{7.19}
$$

The two off-diagonal terms indicate the shearing. Figure 7.52 shows an example of viewing the barn with an oblique projection. The upper part shows the barn from directly above, and the viewplane is attached to the rear wall of the barn. For the vector **d** shown, A projects to a, B projects to b, etc. Of course, points on the rear wall of the barn project to themselves. This projection is equivalent to shearing the barn in x, described by an angle θ where $\tan(\theta) = d_x/d_z$. The lower part of the figure shows the projected image of the barn as seen from the front. The front wall of the barn is

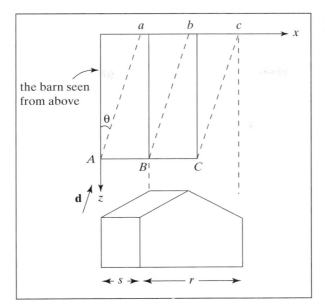

FIGURE 7.52 Shearing the barn to obtain a 3D view.

reproduced exactly, and a portion of the sidewall is visible due to the shear. Notice the lengths r and s. The barn has width r, which is matched in its image. But in addition, a sidewall of the barn has been made visible by the shear. The visible part has length s.

Figure 7.53 shows several views of the cube created by different values of **d**. The first and last views are popular and have been given names. The first is a **cavalier** projection; it uses $d_x = d_y = d_z$, so the shear makes the side and top of the cube project with the same length as the front. The last view is a **cabinet** projection and uses $d_x = d_y = d_z/2$, so that the side and top appear to have one-half the length of the front. Some people feel that the cavalier version looks too elongated and the cabinet a little too squat, but nonetheless, the numerical simplicity of these views makes them useful.

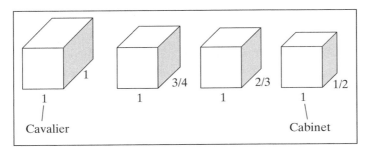

FIGURE 7.53 Several oblique projections of a cube.

OpenGL does not directly support making oblique projections. The routine `glOrtho()` sets up only an orthographic projection, but we can still create oblique views if we do the shearing ourselves.

We want to first shear the object and then map it into the canonical view volume. So we initialize the projection matrix to the form in Equation (7.18) by using `glOrtho()` and postmultiply it by a shearing matrix. Since we are defining a camera by doing this, it makes sense to add a function to the `Camera` class—say, `setOblique()`. This function takes as parameters the six parameters left, top, etc., needed by `glOrtho()`, plus a vector **d** that specifies the direction of the projectors. When

$\mathbf{d} = (0, 0, 1)$, the camera will produce the usual orthographic projections. The following code might be used:

```
void Camera:: setOblique(Vector3 d,..others..)
{ // establish camera for oblique projections
      glMatrixMode(GL_PROJECTION);
      glLoadIdentity();
      glOrtho(l,r,b,t,n,f);        // set the projection matrix
      if(d.z == 0.0) return;       // for orthographic projections
      float m[16]; // space for a 4-by-4 matrix
      for(int i = 0; i < 16; i++)// start with identity matrix
          m[i] = (i%5 == 0)? 1.0 : 0.0; // identity matrix
      m[8] = -d.x/d.z;             // add the shear terms
      m[9] = -d.y/d.z;
      glMultMatrixf(m);            // postmultiply it by m
}
```

This routine initializes the projection matrix to a parallel projection with `glOrtho()` and then postmultiplies that matrix with the shearing matrix. For the latter matrix, the program uses a slight variation of the matrix of Equation (7.19), replacing the 0 in the third row and column with a 1. This approach is more consistent with OpenGL's, and it retains information on depth so that OpenGL can remove hidden surfaces. Case Study 7.3 suggests ways to experiment with producing oblique projections.

PRACTICE EXERCISES

7.6.5 The projection matrix revealed

Show that Equation (7.18) correctly reports the projection matrix used by OpenGL. That is, check that the matrix maps each corner of the view volume into the proper corner of the canonical view volume.

7.6.7 Finding n

Determine the components of $\mathbf{n}$ that produce foreshortening ratios for the x-, y-, and z-axes of .6, .4, and .7, respectively. How many possible $\mathbf{n}$ directions produce these ratios?

7.6.8 The vector n in spherical coordinates

Find the three foreshortening ratios for the $\mathbf{n}$ having latitude 60° and azimuth 125°.

7.6.9 Sketch a cube

Sketch a sequence of dimetric views of the cube for which n_y is equal to $-n_z$ and n_x increases from 0 to 1.

7.6.10 The camera in spherical coordinates

What are the possible latitudes and azimuths for $\mathbf{n}$ in an isometric view?   ■

7.7 SUMMARY

In this chapter, we saw how to define and manipulate a "viewing system" in a program so that a user can make pictures of how a 3D scene "looks" from various points of view and "fly" a camera through a scene in an animation. The camera is modeled as an eye and a view volume residing in its own coordinate system. It generally resembles a "pinhole" camera and projects points onto a flat viewplane. Points lying inside the view volume are projected onto the viewplane; those lying outside are clipped away.

Much of the mathematics of the viewing process revolves around geometric transformations that relate the positions of points in different spaces. The graphics pipeline employed by OpenGL and many other systems performs a sequence of transformations on the vertices fed into it. Each transformation embodies separate properties of the camera and the projection mechanism. Through the use of homogeneous coordinates, all of these transformations can be performed by matrix multiplication. Points are ultimately mapped into a special space that is ideally suited for efficient clipping of edges, and in addition, a single clipping algorithm suffices for any camera.

The geometry of perspective projections is essentially one of similarity, and happily, it preserves flatness and "in-betweenness," so the projection of an entire line can be computed simply by projecting two points on the line. The central transformation that a point undergoes when being projected involves a division by the depth of the point, which makes more remote objects appear smaller. This division of spatial coordinates by a common divisor makes the transformation well suited for expression in homogeneous coordinates, where the fourth coordinate is the divisor. The transformation can therefore be implemented by a matrix multiplication followed by a division step, and so the geometric details that distinguish one projection from another simply determine the parameters of a matrix.

The full graphics pipeline can now be seen to be a matrix multiplication followed by a clip operation, then a perspective division step, and, finally, a matrix multiplication into screen coordinates. The first matrix is often separated into a modelview matrix and a projection matrix, as this allows the orientation and position of the camera to be specified independently of its view volume. Earlier, we learned that the modelview matrix combines two transformations: the transformation that places an object in the scene at the desired position and with the desired size, and the transformation that reflects the position and orientation of the camera in the scene.

It is useful to categorize the different kinds of projections one encounters in practice. The principal distinction is between perspective and parallel projections, both of which are valuable in different settings. Perspective projections correspond fairly well to what we see in daily life. By orienting the camera viewplane with respect to an object, one-, two-, or three-point perspective views can be achieved, each producing a specific visual effect. Parallel projections are useful when it is important to preserve the exact shape of a particular face. These projections are often used in CAD settings when measurements must be made from a drawing.

7.8 CASE STUDIES

CASE STUDY 7.1 "FLYING" A CAMERA THROUGH A SCENE

Level of Effort: II. Write an application that allows the user to "fly" a camera through some scene. (If you have previously developed a mesh viewer, as in Chapter 5, its viewing functions need only be replaced with the Camera class.) The user presses keys to control the camera. With each keystroke, the camera is slid in one of the three dimensions or is rotated about one of its axes (through function calls similar to those used in Figure 7.13), and the scene is redrawn from the point of view of the new camera. Also, allow the user to change the viewangle and aspect ratio of the camera with other keystrokes.

Experimentation with a camera is made much more intelligible if you cover the horizontal plane with a set of **grid lines**, as in Figure 7.24. This is easily done in a loop such as

```
for(int x = -100; x < 100; x++)
{
    glBegin(GL_LINES);
        glVertex3d(x,0,100); glVertex3d(x,0,-100);
    glEnd();
}
```

which draws a set of 200 x-contours. A similar loop draws the z-contours. Add a keystroke control so that the user can toggle the grid lines on and off.

OpenGL offers primitives that can be used to model interesting scenes. Use several of the objects described in Chapter 5, such as spheres, cones, dodecahedra, and a teapot, to make such a scene. Choose either the wire-frame or solid versions of these objects. If you select the solid versions, establish a light source and assign material properties to objects. Use the examples in Chapter 5 as guide.

CASE STUDY 7.2 STEREO VIEWS

Level of Effort: II. Extend your mesh viewer so that it can produce stereo views of objects, as shown in Figure 7.34. Three Camera objects are created. First the "cyclops" camera is created as a regular camera, and then the left- and right-eye cameras are constructed using information (the value of *eye*, the direction **u**, etc.) stored in the cyclops camera.

The images formed by the two cameras are placed side by side in two viewports within the screen window. Practice allowing your eyes to drift so that you can see the stereo effect.

Allow the user to move the left- and right-eye cameras (locked together) around the scene to obtain good views. Experiment to find the most natural interocular distance, both for objects close to the cameras and for those far away.

CASE STUDY 7.3 CREATING PARALLEL PROJECTIONS

Level of Effort: II. Add the setOblique() function discussed in Section 7.6.2 to the Camera class, so that you can produce orthographic and oblique views of objects. Experiment with this camera by using a scene composed of the grid lines discussed in Case Study 7.1, along with several cubes positioned on and above the horizontal plane. Notice that the grid lines project as parallel, and there are no (finite) vanishing points. Allow the user to move the camera through the scene, and examine how parallel the edges of a cube appear in different camera positions.

Allow the user to increase and decrease d_x/d_z and d_y/d_z with keystrokes, so that different oblique projections can be produced. Determine when a cabinet projection is being viewed and when a cavalier one is.

CASE STUDY 7.4 DO-IT-YOURSELF VIEWING (AS IF OPENGL WERE NOT AVAILABLE)

Level of Effort: III. Write an application that produces perspective views of 3D objects, using your own graphics pipeline instead of OpenGL's pipeline. This task is easier than it may appear; it requires fashioning your own modelview matrix (modViewMat[16]), projection matrix (projMat[16]), and clipping routine (perhaps using the code in Figure 7.32).

For actual rendering, you can still use OpenGL (if, indeed, it is available to you). Load identity matrices into both the OpenGL modelview and projection matrices to turn these matrices off. OpenGL will still clip against the canonical view volume. Execute your program on various mesh objects, "flying" around and through them, and observe the effect of clipping.

CASE STUDY 7.5 REMOVAL OF BACK FACES FOR GREATER EFFICIENCY

Level of Effort: II. When we render a mesh object, each of its faces is sent down the graphics pipeline, its vertices are transformed, and the face is then rendered. But in any orientation of the object, there are many faces that are "pointed away" from the viewer. These are called **back faces**, and there is no need to send them through the pipeline, since they will not be visible: There will be some other face that is closer to the eye and therefore obscures them. Figure 7.54 shows the classic barn being viewed by a certain camera. For any position of the camera, some of the barn's faces will be back faces; two are labeled in the figure.

FIGURE 7.54 (a) Back faces of a barn. (b) Definition of a back face.

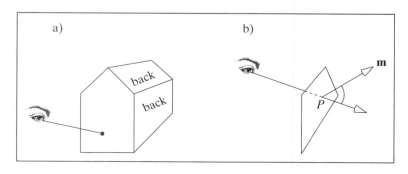

We call a face a back face if its outside surface is pointed away from the eye. This means that its outward-pointing normal vector, say, **m**, is pointing less than 90° away from the vector from the eye to any point P on the face. [See part (b) of the figure.] Now, if an angle between two vectors is less than 90°, the dot product between them is positive. So the test for a face to be a back face is as follows:

F is a *back face* if $(P - eye) \cdot \mathbf{m} > 0$.

This test is inexpensive to perform. Therefore, first testing whether a face is a back face and, if so, skipping it might speed up the drawing of a complex mesh object significantly.

The code that follows is adapted slightly from the `Mesh :: draw()` routine of Figure 6.15. The function draws only the front faces of a mesh object, skipping those which it determines are back faces by means of the test `if(isBackFace(f,...)) continue`. Develop the code for `int isBackFace()`, which returns a 1 if f is a back face and a 0 otherwise, using the simplest set of parameters that must be passed to it. Be alert, however: The mesh vertices are always transformed by the modelview matrix, so you must determine whether (and how) to work in world coordinates, eye coordinates, or something else. Here is the code:

```
void Mesh:: drawFrontFaces() // use OpenGL to draw this mesh
{
  for(int f = 0; f < numFaces; f++) // draw each face
  {
    if(isBackFace(f,...)) continue;
    glBegin(GL_POLYGON);
      for(int v = 0; v < face[f].nVerts; v++) // for each one...
      {
        int in = face[f].vert[v].normIndex ; // index of this normal
        int iv = face[f].vert[v].vertIndex ; // index of this vertex
        glNormal3f(norm[in].x, norm[in].y, norm[in].z);
        glVertex3f(pt[iv].x, pt[iv].y, pt[iv].z);
      }
    glEnd();
  }
}
```

Develop an application that draws meshes with an arbitrary camera, and test the speed of your program both with and without the removal of back faces.

7.9 FURTHER READING

As mentioned throughout this chapter, the *OpenGL Programming Guide* [Woo99] provides a clear introduction to setting up and controlling a viewing system for 3D graphics. Foley et al [Foley90] go into additional detail. An early paper by Carlbom and Paciorek [Carlbom78] develops many of the ideas of different types of parallel and perspective projections. And several articles in Blinn's *Jim Blinn's Corner: A Trip down the Graphics Pipeline* [Blinn96] offer clear and entertaining discussions of projections, viewing transformations, and clipping methods.

8

Rendering Faces for Visual Realism

Goals of the Chapter

▲ To add realism to drawings of 3D scenes.

▲ To examine ways to determine how light reflects off of surfaces.

▲ To render polygonal meshes that are bathed in light.

▲ To see how to make a polygonal mesh object appear smooth.

▲ To remove hidden surfaces by means of a depth buffer.

▲ To develop methods for adding textures to the surfaces of objects.

▲ To add shadows of objects to a scene.

PREVIEW

This chapter takes the objects we developed in previous chapters and seeks to make them visually appealing and realistic. Section 8.1 motivates the need for enhancing the realism of pictures of 3D objects. Section 8.2 introduces various shading models used in computer graphics and develops tools for computing the ambient, diffuse, and specular light contributions to an object's color. The section also describes how to set up light sources in OpenGL, how to characterize the material properties of surfaces, and how the OpenGL graphics pipeline operates when rendering polygonal meshes.

Section 8.3 focuses on rendering objects modeled as polygon meshes. Flat shading, as well as Gouraud and Phong shading, are examined. Section 8.4 develops a simple technique for removing hidden surfaces based on a depth buffer. Proper removal of hidden surfaces greatly improves the realism of pictures.

Section 8.5 develops methods for "painting" texture onto the surface of an object, to make it appear to be made of a real material such as brick or wood, or to wrap a label or picture of a friend around it. Procedural textures, which create texture through a routine, are also described. The thorny issue of the proper interpolation of texture is developed in detail. The section also (1) presents a complete program that uses OpenGL to add texture to objects, (2) discusses the mapping of texture onto curved surfaces, bump mapping, and environment mapping, and (3) provides more tools for making a 3D scene appear real.

Section 8.6 describes two techniques for adding shadows to pictures. The chapter finishes with a number of case studies that delve deeper into some of these topics and urges the reader to experiment with them.

8.1 INTRODUCTION

In previous chapters, we developed tools for modeling mesh objects and for manipulating a camera to view and make pictures of them. In this chapter, we want to add tools to make these objects and others look visually interesting, or realistic, or both. Some examples in Chapter 5 invoked a number of OpenGL functions to produce shiny teapots and spheres apparently bathed in light, but none of the underlying theory of how this is done was examined. Here we rectify this shortcoming and develop the lore of **rendering** a picture of the objects of interest. This is the business of *computing* how each pixel of a picture should look. Much of it is based on a **shading model**, which attempts to model how light that emanates from light sources would interact with objects in a scene. Due to practical limitations, one usually doesn't try to simulate all of the physical principles having to do with the scattering and reflection of light. These principles are quite complicated and would lead to very slow algorithms. But a number of models have been invented that use approximations and still do a good job producing various levels of realism.

We start by describing a hierarchy of techniques that provide increasing levels of realism, in order to show the basic issues involved. Then we examine how to incorporate each technique into an application and also how to use OpenGL to do much of the hard work for us.

At the bottom of the hierarchy, offering the lowest level of realism, is a **wire-frame** rendering. Figure 8.1 shows a flurry of 540 cubes as wire frames. Only the edges of each object are drawn, and you can see right through an object. With this technique, it can be difficult to see what's what. (A stereo view would help a little.)

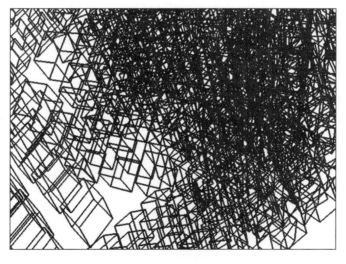

FIGURE 8.1 A wire-frame rendering of a scene.

Figure 8.2 makes a significant improvement by not drawing any edges that lie behind a face. We can call this a "wire-frame with hidden surface removal" rendering. Even though only edges are drawn, the objects now look solid, and it is easy to tell where one stops and the next begins. Notice that some edges simply end abruptly as they slip behind a face. (For the curious, this picture was made using OpenGL with its depth buffer enabled. For each mesh object, the faces were drawn in white using `drawMesh()`, and then the edges were drawn in black using `drawEdges()`. Both routines were discussed in Chapter 6.)

The next step in the hierarchy produces pictures in which objects appear to be "in a scene," illuminated by some light sources. Different parts of the object reflect different amounts of light, depending on the properties of the surfaces involved and on

FIGURE 8.2 Wire-frame view with hidden surfaces removed.

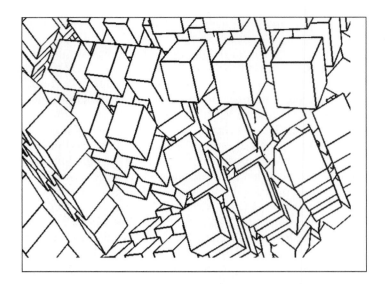

the positions of the sources and the camera's eye. This effect requires computing the brightness or color of each fragment rather than having the user choose it. The computation uses a shading model which determines the proper amount of light that is reflected from each fragment.

Figure 8.3 shows a scene modeled with polygonal meshes: A buckyball rests atop two cylinders, and a jack rests with it on a table. Part (a) shows the wire-frame version, and Part (b) shows a shaded version (with hidden surfaces removed). Those faces aimed toward the light source appear brighter than those aimed away from the source. This picture shows **flat shading**: A calculation of how much light is scattered from each face is computed at a single point, so all points on a face are rendered with the same gray level. The next step up is, of course, to use color. Plate 22 shows the same scene, except that the objects are given different colors.

In Chapter 6, we discussed building a mesh approximation to a smoothly curved object. A picture of such an object ought to reflect its smoothness, showing the smooth

FIGURE 8.3 A mesh approximation shaded with a shading model. (a) Wire-frame view. (b) Flat shading.

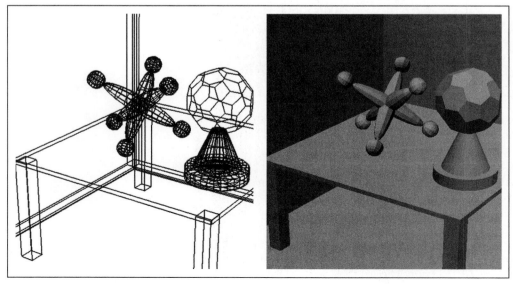

"underlying surface" rather than the individual polygons making up the object. Figure 8.4 depicts the scene of Figure 8.3, this time rendered with the use of **smooth shading**. (Plate 23 shows the colored version.) In the figures, different points of a face are drawn with different gray levels found through an interpolation scheme known as **Gouraud shading**. The variation in gray levels is much smoother than in Figure 8.3(b), and the edges of polygons disappear, giving the impression of an even, rather than a faceted, surface. We examine Gouraud shading in Section 8.3.

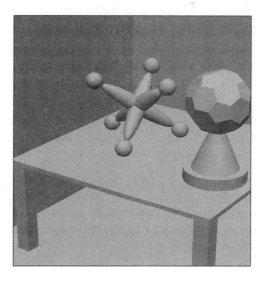

FIGURE 8.4 The scene of Figure 8.3, rendered with smooth shading.

Highlights can be added to make objects look shiny. Figure 8.5 shows the scene of Figure 8.4, but with **specular light** components added. (Plate 24 shows the colored version.) The shinier an object is, the more localized are its specular highlights, which often make an object appear to be made of plastic.

FIGURE 8.5 Adding specular highlights.

Another effect that improves the realism of a picture is shadowing. Figure 8.6 show the scene of Figure 8.5, but with shadows properly rendered. (One object casts a shadow onto a neighboring object.) We discuss how to do this in Section 8.6.

FIGURE 8.6 The scene rendered with shadows.

Adding texture to an object can produce a big step in realism. Figure 8.7 (and Plate 25) shows the scene of Figure 8.6, but now with different textures "painted" on each surface. These textures can make the various surfaces appear to made of some material such as wood, marble, or copper. And images can be "wrapped around" an object like a decal.

FIGURE 8.7 Mapping textures onto surfaces.

There are additional techniques that improve realism. In Chapter 14, we study ray tracing in depth. Although it is a computationally expensive approach, ray tracing is easy to program and produces pictures that show proper shadows, mirrorlike reflections, and the passage of light through transparent objects.

In this chapter, we describe a number of methods for rendering scenes with greater realism. We first look at the classical lighting models used in computer graphics that make an object appear bathed in light from some light sources, and we see how to draw a polygonal mesh so that it appears to have a smoothly curved surface. We then examine a particular method for removing hidden surfaces—the technique that

OpenGL uses—and see how it is incorporated into the rendering process. (Chapter 13 examines a number of other methods for removing hidden surfaces.) We then consider techniques for drawing shadows that one object casts upon another and for adding texture to each surface to make it appear to be made of some particular material or to have some image painted on it. We also examine chrome mapping and environment mapping to see how to make a local scene appear to be embedded in a more global scene.

8.2 INTRODUCTION TO SHADING MODELS

The mechanism of light reflection from an actual surface is very complicated and depends on many factors. Some of these are geometric, such as the relative directions of the light source, the observer's eye, and the normal to the surface. Others are related to the characteristics of the surface, such as its roughness, and to the color of the surface.

A shading model dictates how light is scattered or reflected from a surface. We shall examine some simple shading models, focusing on **achromatic** light, which has brightness, but no color. Achromatic light is only a shade of gray; hence, it is described by a single value: its intensity. We shall see how to calculate the intensity of the light reaching the eye of the camera from each portion of the object. We then extend these ideas to include colored lights and colored objects. The computations are almost identical to those for achromatic light, except that separate intensities of red, green, and blue components are calculated.

A shading model frequently used in graphics presupposes that two types of light sources illuminate the objects in a scene: point light sources and **ambient** light. These light sources "shine" on the various surfaces of the objects, and the incident light interacts with the surface in three different ways:

- Some is absorbed by the surface and is converted to heat.
- Some is reflected from the surface.
- Some is transmitted into the interior of the object, as in the case of a piece of glass.

If all of the incident light is absorbed, the object appears black and is known as a **blackbody**. If all of the light is transmitted, the object is visible only through the effects of refraction, which we shall discuss in Chapter 14.

Here, we focus on the part of the light that is reflected or scattered from the surface. Some amount of this reflected light travels in just the right direction to reach the eye, causing the object to be seen. The fraction that travels to the eye is highly dependent on the geometry of the situation. We assume that there are two types of reflection of incident light:

- **Diffuse scattering** occurs when some of the incident light penetrates the surface slightly and is re-radiated uniformly in all directions. Scattered light interacts strongly with the surface, so its color is usually affected by the nature of the material out of which the surface is made.
- **Specular reflections** are more mirrorlike and are highly directional: Incident light does not penetrate the object, but instead is reflected directly from its outer surface. This gives rise to highlights and makes the surface look shiny. In the simplest model of specular light, the reflected light has the same color as the incident light, which tends to make the material look like plastic. In a more complex model, the color of the specular light varies over the highlights, providing a better approximation to the shininess of metal surfaces. We discuss both models of specular reflection.

Most surfaces produce some combination of the two types of reflection, depending on the characteristics of the surfaces, such as roughness and the type of material from which the surface is made. We say that the total light reflected from the surface in a certain direction is the sum of the diffuse component and the specular component. For each point of interest on the surfaces, we compute the size of each component that reaches the eye. Algorithms are developed next that accomplish this task.

8.2.1 Geometric Ingredients for Finding Reflected Light

On the outside grows the furside, on the inside grows the skinside;
So the furside is the outside, and the skinside is the inside.
Herbert George Ponting-The Sleeping Bag

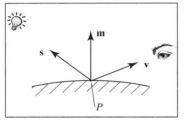

FIGURE 8.8 Important directions used in computing reflected light.

To compute the diffuse and specular components of light, we need to find three vectors. Figure 8.8 shows the three principal vectors required to find the amount of light that reaches the eye from a point P:

1. The normal vector **m** to the surface at P.
2. The vector **v** from P to the viewer's eye.
3. The vector **s** from P to the light source.

The angles between these three vectors form the basis for computing light intensities. These angles are normally calculated using world coordinates, because some transformations (such as the perspective transformation) do not preserve angles.

Each face of a mesh object has two sides. If the object is solid, one side is usually the "inside" and one is the "outside" of the object. The eye can then see only the outside (unless the eye is inside the object!), and it is this side for which we must compute light contributions. But for some objects, such as the open box of Figure 8.9, the eye might be able to see the inside of the lid. It depends on the angle between the normal to that side, $\mathbf{m}_2$, and the vector to the eye, **v**. If the angle is less than 90°, this side is visible. Since the cosine of the angle is proportional to the dot product $\mathbf{v} \cdot \mathbf{m}_2$, the eye can see that side only if $\mathbf{v} \cdot \mathbf{m}_2 > 0$.

FIGURE 8.9 Light computations are made for one side of each face.

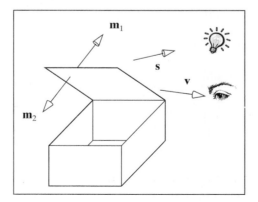

We shall develop the shading model for a given side of a face. If that side of the face is "turned away" from the eye, there is normally no light contribution. In an actual application, the rendering algorithm must be told whether to compute light contributions from one side or both sides of a given face. We shall see that OpenGL supports this feature.

8.2.2 Computing the Diffuse Component

Suppose that light falls from a point source onto one side of a facet (a small piece of a surface). A fraction of the light is reradiated diffusely in all directions from that side. Some fraction of the reradiated part reaches the eye, with an intensity denoted by I_d. How does I_d depend on the directions **m**, **v**, and **s**?

Because the scattering is uniform in all directions, the orientation of the facet relative to the eye is not significant. Therefore, I_d is independent of the angle between **m** and **v** (unless $\mathbf{v} \cdot \mathbf{m} < 0$, whereupon I_d is zero). On the other hand, the amount of light that illuminates the facet *does* depend on the orientation of the facet relative to the point source: It is proportional to the area of the facet that it "sees"—that is, the area subtended by a facet.

Figure 8.10(a) shows, in cross section, a point source illuminating a facet S when **m** is aligned with **s**. In Figure 8.10(b), the facet is turned partially away from the light source through an angle θ. The area subtended is now only the fraction $\cos(\theta)$ as much as before, so that the brightness of S is reduced by that same fraction. This relationship between brightness and surface orientation is often called **Lambert's law**. Notice that, for θ near zero, brightness varies only slightly with angle, because the cosine changes slowly around zero. As θ approaches 90°, however, the brightness falls rapidly to zero.

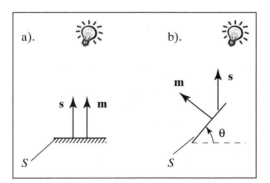

FIGURE 8.10 The brightness depends on the area subtended.

Now, we know that $\cos(\theta)$ is the dot product of normalized versions of **s** and **m**. Therefore, for the intensity of the diffuse component, we can adopt the expression

$$I_d = I_s \rho_d \frac{\mathbf{s} \cdot \mathbf{m}}{|\mathbf{s}||\mathbf{m}|},$$

where I_s is the intensity of the light source and ρ_d is the **diffuse reflection coefficient**. Note that if the facet is aimed away from the eye, this dot product is negative, and we want I_d to evaluate to zero. So a more precise computation of the diffuse component is

$$I_d = I_s \rho_d \max\left(\frac{\mathbf{s} \cdot \mathbf{m}}{|\mathbf{s}||\mathbf{m}|}, 0\right). \tag{8.1}$$

The last term might be implemented in code (using the `Vector3` methods `dot()` and `length()`; see Appendix 3) by

```
double tmp = s.dot(m); // form the dot product
double value = (tmp<0) ? 0 : tmp/ (s.length() * m.length());
```

Figure 8.11 shows how a sphere appears when it reflects diffuse light, for six reflection coefficients: 0, 0.2, 0.4, 0.6, 0.8, and 1. In each case, the source intensity is 1.0 and the background intensity is set to 0.4. Note that the sphere is totally black when ρ_d is

FIGURE 8.11 Spheres with
various reflection coefficients
shaded with diffuse light.

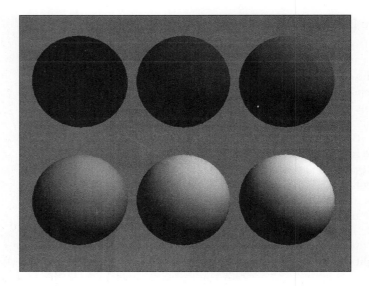

0.0, and the shadow in its bottom half (when the dot in Equation (8.1) is negative) is also black.

In reality, the mechanism behind diffuse reflection is much more complex than the simple model we have adopted here. The reflection coefficient ρ_d depends on the wavelength (color) of the incident light, the angle θ, and various physical properties of the surface. But for simplicity and to reduce computation time, these effects are usually suppressed in the rendering of images. A "reasonable" value for ρ_d is chosen for each surface, sometimes by trial and error according to the realism observed in the resulting image.

In some shading models the effect of distance is also included, although it is somewhat controversial. The light intensity falling on facet S in Figure 8.10 from the point source is known to fall off as the inverse square of the distance between S and the source. But experiments have shown that using this law yields pictures with exaggerated depth effects. (What is more, it is sometimes convenient to model light sources as if they lie "at infinity." Using an inverse-square law in such a case would quench the light entirely!) The problem is thought to be in the model: We model light sources as point sources for simplicity, but most scenes are actually illuminated by additional reflections from the surroundings, which are difficult to model. (These effects are lumped together into an ambient-light component.) It is not surprising, therefore, that strict adherence to a physical law based on an unrealistic model can lead to unrealistic results.

The realism of most pictures is enhanced rather little by the introduction of a distance term. Some approaches force the intensity to be inversely proportional to the distance between the eye and the object, but this relationship is not based on physical principles. It is interesting to experiment with such models, and OpenGL provides some control over this effect, as we shall see in Section 8.2.9, but we omit the distance term in the development that follows.

8.2.3 Specular Reflection

Real objects do not scatter light uniformly in all directions, so a specular component is added to the shading model. Specular reflection causes highlights, which can add significantly to the realism of a picture when objects are shiny. In this section, we discuss a simple model for the behavior of specular light due to Phong [Phong75]. The

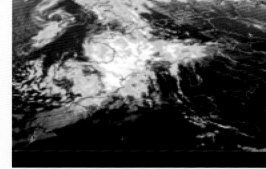

Plate 16.
Weather turbulence. *(Courtesy of AustroControl GmbH and Dept. of Communications and Wavepropagation, Graz University of Technology, Austria)*

Plate 17.
A Minimal Surface. *(Courtesy of Jim Hoffman)*

Plate 18.
The Mandelbrot set. *(Courtesy of Elwood Anderson)*

Plate 19.
A full-color image using 24 bits per pixel.

Plate 20.
The image with reduced color depth: 3 bits for red and green pixels, and two bits for blue pixels.

Plate 21.
The image with 256 carefully chosen colors.

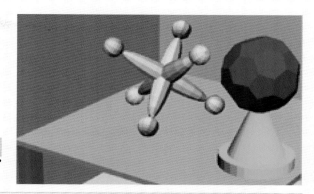

Plate 22.
A scene using flat shading.

Plate 23.
A scene using smooth shading.

Plate 24
A scene with specular highlights added.

Plate 25.
A scene with texture added.

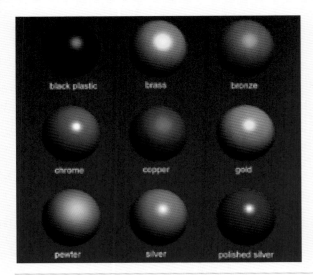

Plate 26.
Shiny spheres made of different materials.

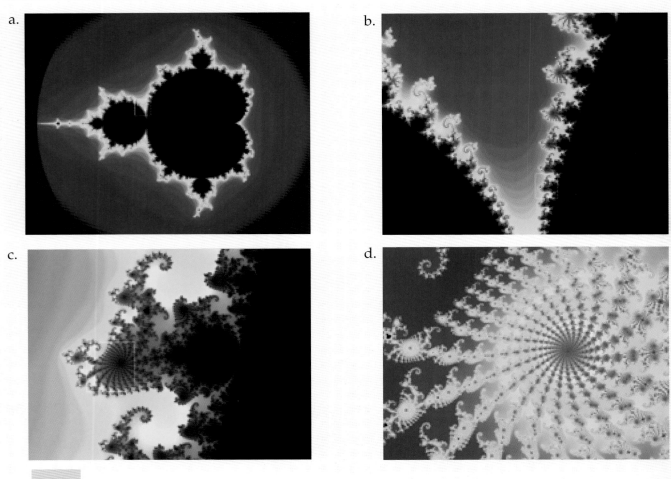

a.

b.

c.

d.

Plate 27.
Zooming in on a region. *(Courtesy of Bernie Freidin)*

model is easy to apply, and OpenGL supports a good approximation to it. Highlights generated by Phong specular light give an object a plasticlike appearance, so the Phong model is good when you intend the object to be made of shiny plastic or glass. The model is less successful with objects that are supposed to have a shiny metallic surface, although you can still approximate them with OpenGL by careful choices of certain color parameters, as we shall see. More advanced models of specular light have been developed that do a better job of modeling shiny metals. Because these models are not supported directly by OpenGL's rendering process, we defer a detailed discussion of them to Chapter 14 on ray tracing.

Figure 8.12(a) shows a situation in which light from a source impinges on a surface and is reflected in different directions. In the **Phong model**, the amount of light reflected is greatest in the direction of perfect mirror reflection, **r**, where the angle of incidence equals the angle of reflection. This is the direction in which all light would travel if the surface were a perfect mirror. At other nearby angles, the amount of light reflected diminishes rapidly, as indicated by the relative lengths of the reflected vectors. Part (b) shows this distribution in terms of a "beam pattern" familiar in radar circles. The distance from P to the beam envelope shows the relative strength of the light scattered in that direction.

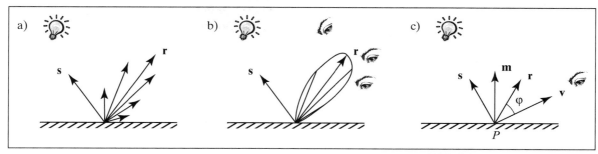

FIGURE 8.12 Specular reflection from a shiny surface.

Figure 8.12(c) shows how to quantify this beam-pattern effect. We know from Chapter 4 that the direction **r** of perfect reflection depends on both **s** and the normal vector **m** to the surface, according to the relationship

$$\mathbf{r} = -\mathbf{s} + 2\frac{(\mathbf{s} \cdot \mathbf{m})}{|\mathbf{m}|^2}\mathbf{m} \qquad \text{(the mirror-reflection direction)}. \tag{8.2}$$

For surfaces that are shiny, but still not true mirrors, the amount of light reflected falls off as the angle ϕ between **r** and **v** increases. The actual amount of falloff is a complicated function of ϕ, but in the Phong model it is said to vary as some power f of the cosine of ϕ—that is, according to $\cos^f(\phi)$, in which f is chosen experimentally and usually lies between 1 and 200. Figure 8.13 shows how this intensity function varies with ϕ for different values of f. As f increases, the reflection becomes more mirror-like and is more highly concentrated along the direction **r**. A perfect mirror could be modeled using $f = \infty$, but pure reflections are usually handled in a different manner, as described in Chapter 14.

Using the fact that $\cos(\phi)$ is equivalent to the dot product of **r** and **v** (after they are normalized), we can model the contribution I_{sp} due to specular reflection by

$$I_{sp} = I_s \rho_s \left(\frac{\mathbf{r}}{|\mathbf{r}|} \cdot \frac{\mathbf{v}}{|\mathbf{v}|} \right)^f, \tag{8.3}$$

where the new term ρ_s is the **specular reflection coefficient**. Like most other coefficients in the shading model, it is usually determined experimentally. (As with the diffuse term, if the dot product $\mathbf{r} \cdot \mathbf{v}$ is found to be negative, I_{sp} is set to zero.)

FIGURE 8.13 Falloff of specular light with angle.

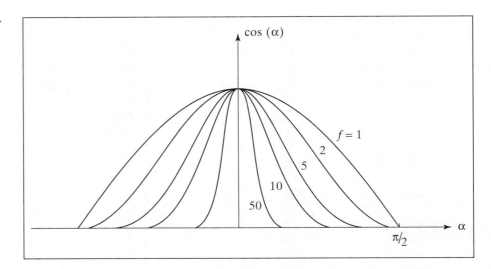

A boost in efficiency using the "halfway vector." It can be expensive to compute the specular term in Equation (8.3), since it requires first finding vector **r** and then normalizing it. In practice, an alternative term, apparently first described by Blinn [Blinn77], is used to speed up computation. Instead of using the cosine of the angle between **r** and **v**, one finds a vector halfway between **s** and **v**; that is, **h** = **s** + **v**, as suggested in Figure 8.14. If the normal to the surface were oriented along **h**, the viewer

FIGURE 8.14 The halfway vector.

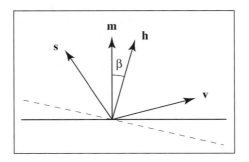

would see the brightest specular highlight. Therefore, the angle β between **m** and **h** can be used to measure the falloff of specular intensity that the viewer sees. The angle β is not the same as ϕ (in fact, β is twice ϕ if the various vectors are coplanar; see the exercises), but this difference can be compensated for by using a different value of the exponent f. (The specular term is not based on physical principles anyway, so it is at least plausible that our adjustment to it yields acceptable results.) It is common practice to base the specular term on $\cos(\beta)$, using the dot product of **h** and **m**:

$$I_{sp} = I_s \rho_s \max\left(0, \left(\frac{\mathbf{h}}{|\mathbf{h}|} \cdot \frac{\mathbf{m}}{|\mathbf{m}|}\right)^f\right) \quad \text{(adjusted specular term).} \tag{8.4}$$

Note that with this adjustment the reflection vector **r** need not be found, saving computation time. In addition, if both the light source and the viewer are very remote, then **s** and **v** are constant over the different faces of an object, so **b** need be computed only once.

Figure 8.15 shows a sphere reflecting different amounts of specular light. The reflection coefficient ρ_s varies from top to bottom with values 0.25, 0.5, and 0.75, and

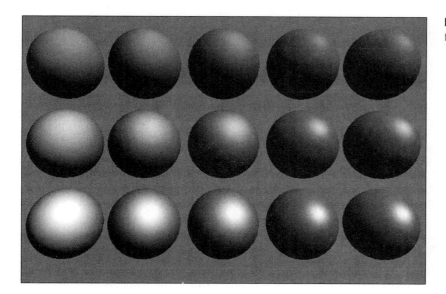

FIGURE 8.15 Specular reflection from a shiny surface.

the exponent f varies from left to right with values $3, 6, 9, 25,$ and 200. (The ambient and diffuse reflection coefficients are 0.1 and 0.4 for all spheres.)

The physical mechanism for specularly reflected light is actually much more complicated than the Phong model suggests. A more realistic model makes the specular reflection coefficient dependent on both the wavelength λ (i.e., the color) of the incident light and the angle of incidence, θ (the angle between vectors **s** and **m** in Figure 8.10), and it couples the coefficient to a "Fresnel term" that describes the physical characteristics of how light reflects off -certain classes of surface materials. As mentioned, OpenGL is not organized to include these effects, so we defer further discussion of them until Chapter 14 on ray tracing, where we compute colors on a point-by-point basis, applying a shading model directly.

PRACTICE EXERCISES

8.2.1 Drawing beam patterns

Draw beam patterns similar to that in Figure 8.12 for the cases $f = 1, f = 10,$ and $f = 100$.

8.2.2 On the halfway vector

By examining the geometry displayed in Figure 8.14, show that $\beta = 2\phi$ if the vectors involved are coplanar. Show that this is not so if the vectors are noncoplanar. (See also [Fisher94].)

8.2.3 A specular speedup

Schlick [Schick94] has suggested an alternative to the exponentiation required in computing the specular term. Let D denote the dot product $\mathbf{r} \cdot \mathbf{v}/|\mathbf{r}||\mathbf{v}|$ in Equation (8.3). Schlick suggests replacing D^f with $D/(f - fD + D)$, which is faster to compute. Plot these two functions for values of D in $[0, 1]$ for various values of f, and compare them. Pay particular attention to values of D near unity, since this is where specular highlights are brightest. ■

8.2.4 The Role of Ambient Light

The diffuse and specular components of reflected light are found by simplifying the "rules" by which physical light reflects from physical surfaces. Incorporating the dependence of these components on the relative positions of the eye, the object, and the light sources greatly improves the realism of a picture over renderings that simply fill a wire frame with a shade. But our desire for a simple reflection model leaves us with far from perfect renderings of a scene. As an example, shadows are seen to be unrealistically deep and harsh. To soften these shadows, we can add a third light component called "ambient light."

With only diffuse and specular reflections, any parts of a surface that are shadowed from the point source receive no light and so are drawn black! But this is not our everyday experience; the scenes we observe around us always seem to be bathed in some soft nondirectional light. This light arrives by multiple reflections from various objects in the surroundings and from light sources that populate the environment, such as light coming through a window, fluorescent lamps, and the like. But it would be computationally very expensive to model such light precisely.

Ambient Sources and Ambient Reflections

To overcome the problem of totally dark shadows, we imagine that a uniform "background glow" called **ambient light** exists in the environment. This ambient light source is not situated at any particular place, and it spreads in all directions uniformly. The source is assigned an intensity I_a. Each face in the model is assigned a value for its **ambient reflection coefficient** ρ_a (often this is the same as the diffuse reflection coefficient ρ_d), and the term $I_a\rho_a$ is simply added to whatever diffuse and specular light is reaching the eye from each point P on that face. I_a and ρ_a are usually arrived at experimentally, by trying various values and seeing what looks best. Too little ambient light makes shadows appear too deep and harsh; too much makes the picture look washed out and bland.

Figure 8.16 shows the effect of adding various amounts of ambient light to the diffuse light reflected by a sphere. In each case, both the diffuse and ambient sources have intensity 1.0, and the diffuse reflection coefficient is 0.04. From left to right, the ambient reflection coefficient takes on the values 0.0, 0.1, 0.3, 0.5, and 0.7. With only a modest amount of ambient light, the harsh shadows on the underside of the sphere are softened and look more realistic. Too much ambient reflection, on the other hand, suppresses the shadows excessively.

FIGURE 8.16 On the effect of ambient light.

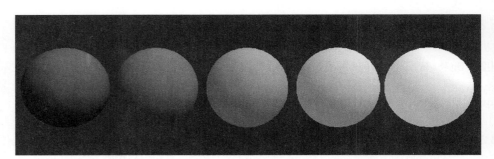

8.2.5 Combining Light Contributions

We can now sum the three light contributions—diffuse, specular, and ambient—to form the total amount of light I that reaches the eye from point P, namely,

$$I = I_a\rho_a + I_d\rho_d \times \text{lambert} + I_{sp}\rho_s \times \text{phong}^f, \tag{8.5}$$

where we define the values

$$\text{lambert} = \max\left(0, \frac{\mathbf{s} \cdot \mathbf{m}}{|\mathbf{s}||\mathbf{m}|}\right) \quad \text{and} \quad \text{phong} = \max\left(0, \frac{\mathbf{h} \cdot \mathbf{m}}{|\mathbf{h}||\mathbf{m}|}\right). \tag{8.6}$$

I depends on the various intensities of the sources and reflection coefficients of the object, as well as on the relative positions of the point P, the eye, and the point light source. Here we have given different names, I_d and I_{sp}, to the intensities of the diffuse and specular components of the light source, because OpenGL allows you to set them individually, as we shall see later. In practice, the two usually have the same value.

To gain some insight into the variation of I with the position of P, consider again Figure 8.12. I is computed for different points P on the facet shown. The ambient component exhibits no variation over the facet; $\mathbf{m}$ is the same for all points P on the facet, but the directions of both $\mathbf{s}$ and $\mathbf{v}$ depend on P. (For instance, $\mathbf{s} = S - P$, where S is the location of the light source. How does $\mathbf{v}$ depend on P and the eye?) If the light source is fairly far away (the typical case), $\mathbf{s}$ will change only slightly as P changes, so that the diffuse component will change only slightly for different points P. This is especially true when $\mathbf{s}$ and $\mathbf{m}$ are nearly aligned, as the value of the cosine function changes slowly for small angles. For remote light sources, the variation in the direction of the halfway vector $\mathbf{h}$ is also slight as P varies. On the other hand, if the light source is close to the facet, there can be substantial changes in $\mathbf{s}$ and $\mathbf{h}$ as P varies. Then the specular term can change significantly over the facet, and the bright highlight can be confined to a small portion of the facet. This effect is increased when the eye is also close to the facet—causing large changes in the direction of $\mathbf{v}$—and when the exponent f is very large.

PRACTICE EXERCISE

8.2.4 Effect of the distance of the eye from the facet

Describe how much the various light contributions change as P varies over a facet when (a) the eye is far away from the facet and (b) the eye is near the facet. ◼

8.2.6 Adding Color

It is straightforward to extend the shading model under consideration to the case of colored light reflecting from colored surfaces. Again, the more general model is an approximation born from simplicity, but it offers reasonable results and is serviceable.

Chapter 12 provides more detail and background on the nature of color, but as we have seen previously, light of any color can be constructed by adding certain amounts of red, green, and blue light. When dealing with colored sources and surfaces, we calculate each color component individually and simply add them to form the final color of reflected light. So, to compute the red, green, and blue components of reflected light, Equation (8.5) is applied three times:

$$I_r = I_{ar}\rho_{ar} + I_{dr}\rho_{dr} \times lambert + I_{spr}\rho_{sr} \times phong^f;$$
$$I_g = I_{ag}\rho_{ag} + I_{dg}\rho_{dg} \times lambert + I_{spg}\rho_{sg} \times phong^f;$$
$$I_b = I_{ab}\rho_{ab} + I_{db}\rho_{db} \times lambert + I_{spb}\rho_{sb} \times phong^f. \qquad (8.7)$$

[*Lambert* and *phong* are as given in Equation (8.6).]

Note that we say that the light sources have three "types" of color: ambient $= (I_{ar}, I_{ag}, I_{ab})$, diffuse $= (I_{dr}, I_{dg}, I_{db})$, and specular $= (I_{spr}, I_{spg}, I_{spb})$. Usually, the diffuse and specular light colors are the same. Note also that the *lambert* and *phong* terms do not depend on which color component is being computed, so they need be computed only once. To pursue this approach, we need to define nine reflection coefficients:

ambient reflection coefficients: ρ_{ar}, ρ_{ag}, and ρ_{ab};
diffuse reflection coefficients: ρ_{dr}, ρ_{dg}, and ρ_{db};
specular reflection coefficients: ρ_{sr}, ρ_{sg}, and ρ_{sb}.

The ambient and diffuse reflection coefficients are based on the color of the surface, itself. By the "color" of a surface, we mean the color that is reflected from it when the illumination is *white* light. Thus, a surface is red if it appears red when bathed in white light. If bathed in some other color, the surface can exhibit an entirely different color. The examples that follow illustrate this relativity of color.

■ **EXAMPLE 8.2.1 The color of an object**

If we say that the color of a sphere is 30% red, 45% green, and 25% blue, it makes sense to set the ambient and diffuse reflection coefficients of the sphere to $(0.3K, 0.45K, 0.25K)$, where K is some scaling value that determines the overall fraction of incident light that is reflected from the sphere. Now, if the sphere is bathed in white light having equal amounts of red, green, and blue $(I_{sr} = I_{sg} = I_{sb} = I)$, the individual diffuse components have intensities $I_r = 0.3KI$, $I_g = 0.45KI$, and $I_b = 0.25KI$, so, as expected, we see a color that is 30% red, 45% green, and 25% blue.

■ **EXAMPLE 8.2.2 A reddish object bathed in greenish light**

Suppose a sphere has ambient and diffuse reflection coefficients of $(0.8, 0.2, 0.1)$, so it appears mostly red when bathed in white light. We illuminate the sphere with a greenish light with $I_s = (0.15, 0.7, 0.15)$. The reflected light is then given by $(0.12, 0.14, 0.015)$, which is a fairly even mix of red and green. The sphere would then appear yellowish.

The Color of Specular Light

Because specular light is mirrorlike, the color of the specular component is often the same as that of the light source. For instance, it is a matter of experience that the specular highlight seen on a glossy red apple illuminated by a yellow light is yellow rather than red. This effect is also observed with shiny objects made of plasticlike material. To create specular highlights for a plastic surface, the specular reflection coefficients ρ_{sr}, ρ_{sg}, and ρ_{sb} used in Equation (8.7) are set to the same value, say, ρ_s, so that the reflection coefficients are "gray" in nature and do not alter the color of the incident light. The designer might choose $\rho_s = 0.5$ for a slightly shiny plastic surface and $\rho_s = 0.9$ for a highly shiny surface.

Objects Made of Different Materials

A careful selection of reflection coefficients can make an object appear to be made of a specific material, such as copper, gold, or pewter—at least approximately. McReynolds and Blythe [McReynolds97] have suggested using the reflection coefficients given in Figure 8.17. Plate 26 shows several spheres modeled with the use of these coefficients. The spheres do appear to be made of different materials. Note that the specular reflection coefficients have different red, green, and blue components, so the color of specular light is not simply that of the incident light. But McReynolds and Blythe caution users that, because OpenGL's shading algorithm incorporates a Phong specular component, the visual effects are not completely realistic. We shall revisit the issue in Chapter 14 and describe the more realistic Cook–Torrance shading approach then.

8.2.7 Shading and the Graphics Pipeline

At which step in the graphics pipeline is shading performed? And how is it done? Figure 8.18 shows the pipeline again. The key idea is that the vertices of a mesh are sent down the pipeline along with their associated normals, and all shading calcula-

Material	ambient: $\rho_{ar}, \rho_{ag}, \rho_{ab}$	diffuse: $\rho_{dr}, \rho_{dg}, \rho_{db}$	specular: $\rho_{sr}, \rho_{sg}, \rho_{sb}$	exponent: f
Black Plastic	0.0 0.0 0.0	0.01 0.01 0.01	0.50 0.50 0.50	32
Brass	0.329412 0.223529 0.027451	0.780392 0.568627 0.113725	0.992157 0.941176 0.807843	27.8974
Bronze	0.2125 0.1275 0.054	0.714 0.4284 0.18144	0.393548 0.271906 0.166721	25.6
Chrome	0.25 0.25 0.25	0.4 0.4 0.4	0.774597 0.774597 0.774597	76.8
Copper	0.19125 0.0735 0.0225	0.7038 0.27048 0.0828	0.256777 0.137622 0.086014	12.8
Gold	0.24725 0.1995 0.0745	0.75164 0.60648 0.22648	0.628281 0.555802 0.366065	51.2
Pewter	0.10588 0.058824 0.113725	0.427451 0.470588 0.541176	0.3333 0.3333 0.521569	9.84615
Silver	0.19225 0.19225 0.19225	0.50754 0.50754 0.50754	0.508273 0.508273 0.508273	51.2
Polished Silver	0.23125 0.23125 0.23125	0.2775 0.2775 0.2775	0.773911 0.773911 0.773911	89.6

FIGURE 8.17 Parameters for common materials [McReynolds97].

tions are done on *vertices*. (Recall that the `draw()` routine in the `Mesh` class sends a normal along with each vertex, as in Figure 6.15.)

Figure 8.18 shows a triangle with vertices v_0, v_1, and v_2 being rendered. Vertex v_i has the normal vector $\mathbf{m}_i$ associated with it. These quantities are sent down the pipeline with calls such as

FIGURE 8.18 The graphics pipeline revisited.

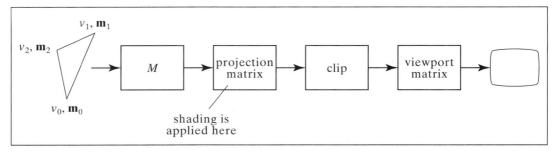

```
glBegin(GL_POLYGON);
    for(int i = 0; i < 3; i++)
    {
        glNormal3f(norm[i].x, norm[i].y, norm[i].z);
        glVertex3f(pt[i].x, pt[i].y, pt[i].z);
    }
glEnd();
```

The call to `glNormal3f()` sets the "current normal vector," which is applied to all vertices subsequently sent by using `glVertex3f()`. That vector remains current until changed with another call to `glNormal3f()`. In the preceding code, a new normal is associated with each vertex.

The vertices are transformed by the modelview matrix M, effectively expressing them in camera (eye) coordinates. The normal vectors are also transformed, but vectors transform differently from points. As shown in Section 6.5.3, transforming points of a surface by a matrix M causes the normal $\mathbf{m}$ at any point to become the normal $M^{-T}\mathbf{m}$ on the transformed surface, where M^{-T} is the transpose of the inverse of M. OpenGL automatically performs this calculation on normal vectors.

As we discuss in the next section, OpenGL allows you to specify various light sources and their locations. Lights are objects, too, and the positions of the light sources are also transformed by the modelview matrix.

So after the modelview transformation, all quantities end up being expressed in camera coordinates. At this point, the model of Equation (8.7) is applied, and a color is "attached" to each vertex. The computation of this color requires knowledge of the vectors $\mathbf{m}$, $\mathbf{s}$, and $\mathbf{v}$, but these are all available at this point in the pipeline. (Convince yourself of this fact.)

Progressing farther down the pipeline, the pseudodepth term is created, and the vertices are passed through the perspective transformation. The color information tags along with each vertex. The clipping step is performed in homogeneous coordinates, as described earlier. This step may alter some of the vertices. Figure 8.19 shows the case where vertex v_1 of the triangle is clipped off and two new vertices, a and b, are created. The triangle becomes a quadrilateral. The color at each of the new vertices must be computed, since it is needed in the actual rendering step.

FIGURE 8.19 Clipping a polygon against the (warped) view volume.

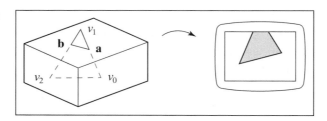

The color at each new vertex is usually found by interpolation. For instance, suppose that the color at v_0 is (r_0, g_0, b_0) and the color at v_1 is (r_1, g_1, b_1). If the point a is 40% of the way from v_0 to v_1, the color associated with a is a blend of 60% of (r_0, g_0, b_0) and 40% of (r_1, g_1, b_1). This relationship is expressed as

$$\text{color at point } a = (\text{lerp}(r_0, r_1, 0.4), \text{lerp}(g_0, g_1, 0.4), \text{lerp}(b_0, b_1, 0.4)), \qquad (8.8)$$

where we use the convenient function lerp() (short for "linear interpolation"; recall "tweening" in Section 4.5.4) defined by

$$\text{lerp}(G, H, f) = G + (H - G)f. \qquad (8.9)$$

The value of this function lies at a fraction f of the way from G to H.[1]

The vertices are finally passed through the viewport transformation, where they are mapped into screen coordinates (along with the pseudodepth, which now varies between 0 and 1). The quadrilateral is then rendered (with hidden surfaces removed), as suggested in Figure 8.19. We shall say much more about the actual rendering step in subsequent sections.

8.2.8 Using Light Sources in OpenGL

OpenGL provides a number of functions for setting up and using light sources, as well as for specifying the surface properties of materials. It can be daunting to absorb all of the many possible variations and details, so we describe only the basics here. In this section, we discuss how to establish different kinds of light sources in a scene. In the next section, we look at ways to characterize the reflective properties of the surfaces of an object.

Creating a Light Source

OpenGL allows you to define up to eight sources, which are referred to by the names GL_LIGHT0, GL_LIGHT1, etc. Each source is invested with various properties and must be enabled. Each property has a default value. For example, to create a source located at $(3, 6, 5)$ in world coordinates, we would use the following code:[2]

```
GLfloat myLightPosition[] = {3.0, 6.0, 5.0, 1.0};
glLightfv(GL_LIGHT0, GL_POSITION, myLightPosition);
glEnable(GL_LIGHTING); // enable
glEnable(GL_LIGHT0); // enable this particular source
```

The array myLightPosition[] (use any name you wish for this array) specifies the location of the light source and is passed to glLightfv() along with the name GL_LIGHT0, to attach it to the particular source denoted by GL_LIGHT0.

Some sources, such as a desk lamp, are "in the scene," whereas others, like the sun, are infinitely remote. OpenGL allows you to create both types by using homogeneous coordinates to specify the position of the source.

Thus, we have

$(x, y, z, 1)$: a local light source at the position (x, y, z)

and

$(x, y, z, 0)$: a vector to an infinitely remote light source in the direction (x, y, z).

Figure 8.20 shows a local source positioned at $(0, 3, 3, 1)$ and a remote source "located" along vector $(3, 3, 0, 0)$. Infinitely remote light sources are often called

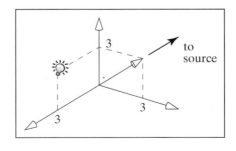

FIGURE 8.20 A local source and an infinitely remote source.

---

[1] In Section 8.5, we discuss replacing linear interpolation by "hyperbolic interpolation" as a more accurate way of generating the colors at the new vertices formed by clipping.

[2] Here and elsewhere, the type float would most likely serve as well as GLfloat. But using GLfloat makes your code more portable to other OpenGL environments.

"**directional**." There are computational advantages to using directional light sources, since the direction **s** in the calculations of diffuse and specular reflections is *constant* for all vertices in the scene. But directional light sources are not always the correct choice: Some visual effects are properly achieved only when a light source is close to an object.

You can also spell out different colors for a light source. OpenGL allows you to assign a different color to each of the three types of light that a source emits: ambient, diffuse, and specular. It may seem strange to say that a source emits ambient light. But this type of light is still treated as in Equation (8.7): a global, omnidirectional light that bathes the entire scene. The advantage of attaching ambient light to a source is that it can be turned on and off as an application proceeds. (OpenGL also offers a truly ambient light, not associated with any source, as we discuss later in connection with "lighting models.")

Arrays are defined to hold the colors emitted by light sources and are passed to glLightfv() via the following code:

```
GLfloat amb0[] = {0.2, 0.4, 0.6, 1.0}; // define some colors
GLfloat diff0[] = {0.8, 0.9, 0.5, 1.0};
GLfloat spec0[] = {1.0, 0.8, 1.0, 1.0};
glLightfv(GL_LIGHT0, GL_AMBIENT, amb0); // attach them to LIGHT0
glLightfv(GL_LIGHT0, GL_DIFFUSE, diff0);
glLightfv(GL_LIGHT0, GL_SPECULAR, spec0);
```

Colors are specified in so-called **RGBA** format, meaning red, green, blue, and "alpha." The alpha value is sometimes used for blending two colors on the screen; we discuss it in Chapter 10. For our purposes here, alpha is normally 1.0.

Light sources have various default values. For all sources;

default ambient $= (0, 0, 0, 1)$;   (dimmest possible = black)

For light source LIGHT0,

default diffuse $= (1, 1, 1, 1)$;   (brightest possible = white)

and

default specular $= (1, 1, 1, 1)$;   (brightest possible = white),

whereas for the other sources, the diffuse and specular values have defaults of black.

Spotlights

Light sources are *point sources* by default, meaning that they emit light uniformly in all directions. But OpenGL allows you to make them into spotlights, so that they emit light in a restricted set of directions. Figure 8.21 shows a spotlight aimed in a direction **d**, with a "cutoff angle" of α.

No light is seen at points lying outside the cutoff cone. For vertices such as P, which lie inside the cone, the amount of light reaching P is attenuated by the factor $\cos^\varepsilon(\beta)$, where β is the angle between **d** and a line from the source to P and ε is an exponent chosen by the user to give the desired falloff of light with angle.

The parameters for a spotlight are set by using glLightf() to set a single value and glLightfv() to set a vector:

```
glLightf(GL_LIGHT0, GL_SPOT_CUTOFF, 45.0); // a cutoff angle of 45°
glLightf(GL_LIGHT0, GL_SPOT_EXPONENT, 4.0); // ε = 4.0
GLfloat dir[] = {2.0, 1.0, -4.0}; // the spotlight's direction
glLightfv(GL_LIGHT0, GL_SPOT_DIRECTION, dir);
```

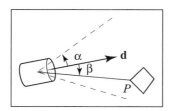

FIGURE 8.21 Properties of a spotlight.

The default values for these parameters are $\mathbf{d} = (0, 0, -1)$, $\alpha = 180°$, and $\varepsilon = 0$, which makes a source an omnidirectional point source.

Attenuation of Light with Distance

OpenGL also allows you to specify how rapidly light diminishes with distance from a source. Although we have downplayed the importance of this dependence, it can be interesting to experiment with different falloff rates and to fine-tune a picture. OpenGL attenuates the strength of a positional[3] light source by the attenuation factor

$$\text{atten} = \frac{1}{k_c + k_l D + k_q D^2},\qquad\qquad (8.10)$$

where k_c, k_l, and k_q are coefficients and D is the distance between the position of the light and the vertex in question. This expression is rich enough to allow you to model any combination of constant, linear, and quadratic (inverse square) dependence on distance from a source. The parameters are controlled by function calls

```
glLightf(GL_LIGHT0, GL_CONSTANT_ATTENUATION, 2.0);
```

and similarly for GL_LINEAR_ATTENUATION and GL_QUADRATIC_ATTENUATION. The default values are $k_c = 1$, $k_l = 0$, and $k_q = 0$, which eliminate any attenuation.

Lighting Model

OpenGL allows three parameters to be set that specify general rules for applying the lighting model. These parameters are passed to variations of the function glLightModel.

The Color of Global Ambient Light In any given scene, you can establish a global ambient light that is independent of any particular source. To create this light, specify its color with the statements

```
GLfloat amb[] = {0.2, 0.3, 0.1, 1.0};
glLightModelfv(GL_LIGHT_MODEL_AMBIENT, amb);
```

This code sets the ambient source to the color (0.2, 0.3, 0.1). The default value is (0.2, 0.2, 0.2, 1.0), so the ambient light is always present, unless you purposely alter it. Setting the ambient source to a non-zero value makes objects in a scene visible even if you have not invoked any of the lighting functions.

Is the Viewpoint Local or Remote? OpenGL computes specular reflections using the "halfway vector" $\mathbf{h} = \mathbf{s} + \mathbf{v}$ described in Section 8.2.3. The true directions $\mathbf{s}$ and $\mathbf{v}$ are normally different at each vertex in a mesh. (Visualize this configuration!) If the light source is directional, then $\mathbf{s}$ is constant, but $\mathbf{v}$ still varies from vertex to vertex. The rendering speed is increased if $\mathbf{v}$ is made constant for all vertices. As a default, OpenGL uses $\mathbf{v} = (0, 0, 1)$, which points along the positive z-axis in camera coordinates. You can force the pipeline to compute the true value of $\mathbf{v}$ for each vertex by executing the statement

```
glLightModeli(GL_LIGHT_MODEL_LOCAL_VIEWER, GL_TRUE);
```

Are Both Sides of a Polygon Shaded Properly?

Each polygonal face in a model has two sides. When modeling, we tend to think of these sides as the "inside" and "outside" surfaces. The convention is to list the vertices of a face in counterclockwise (CCW) order as seen from outside the object. Most mesh objects represent solids that enclose a space, so that there is a well-defined inside and outside. For such objects, the camera can see only the outside surface of

---

3   This attenuation factor is disabled for directional light sources, since they are infinitely remote.

each face (assuming that the camera is not inside the object!). With hidden surfaces properly removed, the inside surface of each face is hidden from the eye by some closer face.

OpenGL has no notion of "inside" and "outside"; it can distinguish only between "front faces" and "back faces." A face is a **front face** if its vertices are listed in CCW order as seen by the eye.[4] Figure 8.22(a) shows the eye viewing a cube, which we presume was modeled using the CCW ordering convention. Arrows indicate the order in which the vertices of each face are passed to OpenGL (in a `glBegin(GL_POLY-GON);...; glEnd()` block). For an object that encloses some space, all faces that are visible to the eye are front faces, and OpenGL draws them properly with the correct shading. OpenGL also draws the back faces,[5] but they are ultimately hidden by closer front faces.

FIGURE 8.22 OpenGL's definition of a front face.

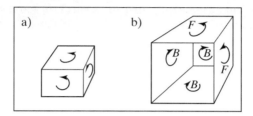

Things are different in Figure 8.22(b), which shows a box with a face removed. Again, arrows indicate the order in which vertices of a face are sent down the pipeline. Three of the visible faces are back faces. By default, OpenGL does not shade these properly. To instruct OpenGL to do proper shading of back faces, we use the statement

```
glLightModeli(GL_LIGHT_MODEL_TWO_SIDE, GL_TRUE);
```

When this statement is executed, OpenGL reverses the normal vectors of any back face so that they point toward the viewer, and then it performs shading computations properly. Replacing `GL_TRUE` with `GL_FALSE` (the default) will turn off this facility. (*Note*: Faces drawn by OpenGL do not cast shadows, so all the back faces receive the same light from a source, even though there may be some other face between some of them and the source.)

Moving Light Sources

Recall that light sources pass through the modelview matrix just as vertices do. Therefore, lights can be repositioned by suitable uses of `glRotated()` and `glTranslated()`. The array `position`, specified by using `glLightfv(GL_LIGHT0, GL_POSITION, position)`, is modified by the modelview matrix that is in effect at the time `glLightfv()` is called. So, to modify the position of the light with transformations and independently move the camera, we embed the light-positioning command in a push–pop pair, as in the following code:

```
void display()
{
    GLfloat position[] = {2, 1, 3, 1}; // initial light position
    clear the color and depth buffers
    glMatrixMode(GL_MODELVIEW);
```

[4] You can reverse this sense with `glFrontFace(GL_CW)`, which stipulates that a face is a front face only if its vertices are listed in clockwise (CW) order. The default is `glFrontFace(GL_CCW)`.

[5] You can improve your computer's performance by instructing OpenGL to skip the rendering of back faces. The code you use is `glCullFace(GL_BACK); glEnable(GL_CULL_FACE);`.

```
    glLoadIdentity();
    glPushMatrix();
       glRotated(...); // move the light
       glTranslated(...);
       glLightfv(GL_LIGHT0, GL_POSITION, position);
    glPopMatrix();

    gluLookAt(...); // set the camera position
    draw the object
    glutSwapBuffers();
}
```

On the other hand, to have the light move with the camera, we use the following code:

```
GLfloat pos[] = {0, 0, 0, 1};
glMatrixMode(GL_MODELVIEW);
glLoadIdentity();
glLightfv(GL_LIGHT0, GL_POSITION, position); // light at (0, 0, 0)
gluLookAt(...); // move the light and the camera
        draw the object
```

This code establishes the light to be positioned at the eye (as a miner's lamp is), and the light moves with the camera.

8.2.9 Working with Material Properties in OpenGL

You can see the effect of a light source only when light reflects off an object's surface. OpenGL provides ways to specify the various reflection coefficients that appear in Equation (8.7). These coefficients are set with variations of the function glMaterial, and they can be specified individually for front faces and back faces. (Recall the discussion concerning Figure 8.22.) For instance, the code

```
GLfloat myDiffuse[] = {0.8, 0.2, 0.0, 1.0};
glMaterialfv(GL_FRONT, GL_DIFFUSE, myDiffuse);
```

sets the diffuse reflection coefficient $(\rho_{dr}, \rho_{dg}, \rho_{db})$ equal to $(0.8, 0.2, 0.0)$ for all subsequently specified front faces. Reflection coefficients are specified as a quadruple in RBGA format, just as a color is. The first parameter of glMaterialfv() can take on the following values:

GL_FRONT: Set the reflection coefficient for front faces.
GL_BACK: Set the reflection coefficient for back faces.
GL_FRONT_AND_BACK: Set the reflection coefficient for both front and back faces.

The second parameter can take on the following values:

GL_AMBIENT: Set the ambient reflection coefficients.
GL_DIFFUSE: Set the diffuse reflection coefficients.
GL_SPECULAR: Set the specular reflection coefficients.
GL_AMBIENT_AND_DIFFUSE: Set both the ambient and the diffuse reflection coefficients to the same values. This setting is for convenience, since the ambient and diffuse coefficients are so often chosen to be the same.
GL_EMISSION: Set the emissive color of the surface.

The last choice sets the **emissive color** of a face, causing it to "glow" in the specified color, independently of any light source.

Putting It All Together

We now extend Equation (8.7) to include the additional contributions that OpenGL actually calculates. The total red component is given by

$$I_r = e_r + I_{mr}\rho_{ar}$$

$$+ \sum_i \text{atten}_i \times \text{spot}_i \times \left(I^i_{ar}\rho_{ar} + I^i_{dr}\rho_{dr} \times \text{lambert}_i + I^i_{spr}\rho_{sr} \times \text{phong}^f_i\right). \qquad (8.11)$$

Expressions for the green and blue components are similar. The emissive light is e_r, and I_{mr} is the global ambient light introduced into the lighting model. The summation denotes that the ambient, diffuse, and specular contributions of all light sources are summed. For the ith source, atten_i is the attenuation factor as in Equation (8.10), spot_i is the spotlight factor (see Figure 8.21), and lambert_i and phong_i are the familiar diffuse and specular dot products, respectively. All of these terms must be recalculated for each source. (*Note*: If I_r turns out to have a value larger than 1.0, OpenGL clamps it to that value: The brightest any light component can be is 1.0.)

8.2.10 Shading of Scenes Specified by SDL

The scene description language SDL introduced in Chapter 5 supports the loading of material properties into objects so that they can be shaded properly. For instance, the code

```
light 3 4 5 .8 .8 .8 ! bright white light at (3, 4, 5)
background 1 1 1 ! white background
globalAmbient .2 .2 .2 ! a dark gray global ambient light
ambient .2 .6 0
diffuse .8 .2. 1 ! red material
specular 1 1 1 ! bright specular spots - the color of the source
specularExponent 20 !set the Phong exponent
scale 4 4 4 sphere
```

describes a scene containing a sphere with the following material properties [see Equation (8.7)]:

- ambient reflection coefficients: $\left(\rho_{ar}, \rho_{ag}, \rho_{ab}\right) = (.2, 0.6, 0)$;
- diffuse reflection coefficients: $\left(\rho_{dr}, \rho_{dg}, \rho_{db}\right) = (0.8, 0.2, 1.0)$;
- specular reflection coefficients: $\left(\rho_{sr}, \rho_{sg}, \rho_{sb}\right) = (1.0, 1.0, 1.0)$;
- Phong exponent $f = 20$.

The light source is given a color of $(0.8, 0.8, 0.8)$ for both its diffuse and its specular component. There is a global ambient term $\left(I_{ar}, I_{ag}, I_{ab}\right) = (0.2, 0.2, 0.2)$.

The current material properties are loaded into each object's `mtrl` field at the time the object is created. (See the end of `Scene :: getObject()` in `SDL.cpp` of Appendix 3.) When an object is drawn by using `drawOpenGL()`, it first passes its material properties to OpenGL (see `Shape:: tellMaterialsGL()`), so that at the moment the object is actually drawn, OpenGL has those properties in its current state.

In Chapter 14, when tracing rays, we shall use each object's material field in a similar way to acquire the material properties and do proper shading.

8.3 FLAT SHADING AND SMOOTH SHADING

Different objects require different shading effects. In Chapter 6, we modeled a variety of shapes by using polygonal meshes. For some, like the barn or buckyball, we want to see the individual faces in a picture, but for others, like the sphere or chess pawn, we want to see the "underlying" surface that the faces approximate.

In the modeling process, we attached a normal vector to each vertex of each face. If a certain face is to appear as a distinct polygon, we attach the *same* normal vector to all of its vertices; the normal vector chosen is that indicating the direction normal to the plane of the face. On the other hand, if the face is supposed to approximate an underlying surface, we attach to each vertex the normal to the underlying surface at that point.

We now examine how information obtained from the normal vector at each vertex is used to perform different kinds of shading. The main distinction is between a shading method that accentuates the individual polygons (flat shading) and a method that blends the faces to de-emphasize the edges between them (smooth shading). We shall discuss the two kinds of smooth shading there are: Gouraud and Phong shading.

In both kinds of shading, the vertices are passed down the graphics pipeline, shading calculations are performed to attach a color to each vertex, and, ultimately, the vertices of the face are converted to screen coordinates and the face is "painted" pixel by pixel with the appropriate color.

Painting a Face

A face is colored using a polygon-fill routine. Filling a polygon is very simple, although fine-tuning the fill algorithm for highest efficiency can get complex. (See Chapter 10.) Here, we look at the basics, focusing on how the color of each pixel is set.

A polygon-fill routine is sometimes called a **tiler**, because it moves over the polygon pixel by pixel, coloring each pixel as appropriate, as one would lay down tiles on a parquet floor. The pixels in a polygon are visited in a regular order, usually scan line by scan line from the bottom to the top of the polygon and across each scan line from left to right.

We assume that the polygons of interest are *convex*. A tiler designed to fill only convex polygons can be made highly efficient, since, at each scan line, there is a single unbroken "run" of pixels that lie inside the polygon. Most implementations of OpenGL exploit this property and always fill convex polygons correctly; in contrast, they do not guarantee to fill nonconvex polygons properly. (See the exercises for more thoughts on convexity.)

Figure 8.23 shows a convex quadrilateral whose face is being filled with color. The screen coordinates of each vertex are noted. The lowest and highest points on the face are y_{bott} and y_{top}, respectively. The tiler first fills in the row at $y = y_{bott}$ (in this case a single pixel), then the one at $y_{bott} + 1$, etc. At each scan line, say, y_s in the figure, there is a leftmost pixel x_{left} and a rightmost pixel x_{right}. The tiler moves from x_{left} to x_{right}, placing the desired color in each pixel. So the tiler is implemented as a simple double loop:

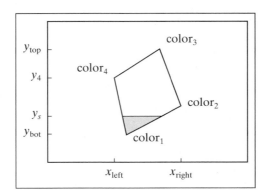

FIGURE 8.23 Filling a polygonal face with color.

```
for (int y = y_bott ; y <= y_top ; y++)  // for each scan line
{
   find x_left and x_right
   for (int x = x_left ; x <= x_right ; x++)// fill across the scan line
   {
   find the color c for this pixel
   put c into the pixel at (x, y)
   }
}
```

(We shall see later how hidden surfaces are easily removed within this double loop as well.) The principal difference between flat and smooth shading is the manner in which the color c is determined at each pixel.

8.3.1 Flat Shading

When a face is flat (like the roof of a barn) and the light sources are quite distant, the diffuse light component varies little over different points on the roof. (The lambert term in Equation 8.6 is nearly the same at each vertex of the face.) In such cases, it is reasonable to use the same color for every pixel "covered" by the face. OpenGL offers a rendering mode in which the entire face is drawn with the same color. In this mode, although a color is passed down the pipeline as part of each vertex of the face, the painting algorithm uses only one color value (usually that of the first vertex in the face). So the preceding command, `find the color c for this pixel`, is not inside the loops, but instead appears just prior to the loops, setting c to the color of one of the vertices. (Using the same color for every pixel tends to make flat shading quite fast.)

Flat shading is established in OpenGL by using the command

```
glShadeModel(GL_FLAT);
```

Figure 8.24 shows a buckyball and a sphere rendered by means of flat shading. The individual faces are clearly visible on both objects. The sphere is modeled as a smooth object, but no smoothing takes place in the rendering, since the color of an entire face is set to that of only one vertex.

Edges between faces actually appear more pronounced than they would be on an actual physical object, due to a phenomenon in the eye known as **lateral inhibition**, first described by Ernst Mach.[6] When there is a discontinuity in intensity across an object, the eye manufactures a **Mach band** at the discontinuity, and a vivid edge is seen. This band exaggerates the polygonal "look" of mesh objects rendered with flat shading.

FIGURE 8.24 Two meshes rendered using flat shading.

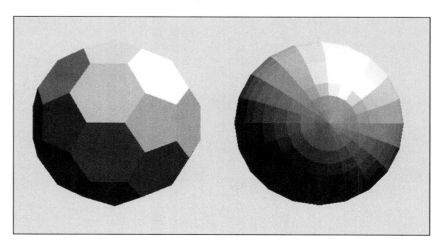

Specular highlights are rendered poorly with flat shading, again because an entire face is filled with a color that was computed at only one vertex. If there happens to be a large specular component at the representative vertex, that brightness is drawn uniformly over the entire face. If a specular highlight doesn't fall on the representative point, it is missed entirely. For this reason, there is little incentive to include the specular reflection component in the computation of shading.

8.3.2 Smooth Shading

Smooth shading attempts to de-emphasize edges between faces by computing colors at more points on each face. The two principal types of smooth shading are Gouraud shading [Gouraud71] and Phong shading [Phong75]. OpenGL does only Gouraud shading, but we describe both varieties.

Gouraud Shading

Gouraud shading computes a different value of c for each pixel. For the scan line at y_s in Figure 8.23, it finds the color at the leftmost pixel, $color_{left}$, by linear interpolation of the colors at the top and bottom of the left edge of the polygon.[7] For the same scan line, the color at the top is $color_4$, and that at the bottom is $color_1$, so $color_{left}$ would be calculated as [recall Equation (8.9)]

$$color_{left} = lerp(color_1, color_4, f),\qquad (8.12)$$

where the fraction

$$f = \frac{y_s - y_{bott}}{y_4 - y_{bott}}$$

varies between 0 and 1 as y_s varies from y_{bott} to y_4. Note that Equation (8.12) involves three calculations, since each color quantity has a red, green, and blue component.

Similarly, $color_{right}$ is found by interpolating the colors at the top and bottom of the right edge. The tiler then fills across the scan line, linearly interpolating between $color_{left}$ and $color_{right}$ to obtain the color at pixel x:

$$c(x) = lerp\left(color_{left}, color_{right}, \frac{x - x_{left}}{x_{right} - x_{left}}\right).\qquad (8.13)$$

To increase the efficiency of the fill, this color is computed incrementally at each pixel. That is, there is a constant difference between $c(x + 1)$ and $c(x)$, so that

$$c(x + 1) = c(x) + \frac{color_{right} - color_{left}}{x_{right} - x_{left}}.\qquad (8.14)$$

The increment is calculated only once outside of the innermost loop. The code looks like the following:

```
for (int y = ybott ; y <= ytop ; y++)        // for each scan line
{
      find xleft and xright
      find colorleft and colorright
      colorinc = (colorright - colorleft) / (xright - xleft);
      for (int x = xleft , c = colorleft ; x <= xright ; x++, c+=colorinc )
                put c into the pixel at (x, y)
}
```

---

[6] Ernst Mach (1838–1916) was an Austrian physicist whose early work strongly influenced the theory of relativity.

[7] We shall see later that, although colors are usually interpolated *linearly*, as we interpolate them here, better results can be obtained by using so-called *hyperbolic interpolation*. For Gouraud shading, the distinction is minor; for texture mapping, it is crucial.

Computationally speaking, Gouraud shading is modestly more expensive than flat shading. Gouraud shading is established in OpenGL with the use of the function

```
glShadeModel(GL_SMOOTH);
```

Figure 8.25 shows a buckyball and a sphere rendered by means of Gouraud shading. The buckyball looks the same as when it was rendered with flat shading in Figure 8.24, because the same color is associated with each vertex of a face, so interpolation changes nothing. But the sphere looks much smoother: There are no abrupt jumps in color between neighboring faces, and the edges of the faces (and the Mach bands) are gone, replaced by a smoothly varying color across the object. Along the silhouette, however, you can still see the bounding edges of individual faces.

FIGURE 8.25 Two meshes rendered by using smooth shading.

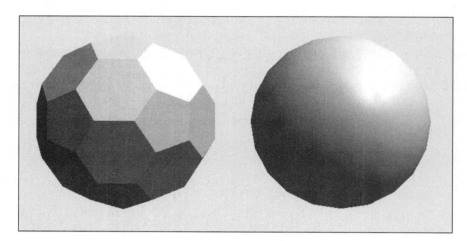

Why do the edges disappear with this technique? Figure 8.26(a) shows two faces, F and F', that share an edge. In rendering F, the colors c_L and c_R are used, and in rendering F', the colors c_L' and c_R' are used. But since c_R equals c_L', there is no abrupt change in color at the edge along the scan line.

Figure 8.26(b) suggests how Gouraud shading reveals the "underlying" surface approximated by the mesh. The polygonal surface is shown in cross section, with vertices V_1, V_2, etc., marked. The imaginary smooth surface that the mesh supposedly represents is suggested as well. Properly computed vertex normals $\mathbf{m}_1, \mathbf{m}_2$, etc., point perpendicularly to this imaginary surface so that the normal for "correct" shading will be used at each vertex and the color thereby found will be correct. The color is then made to vary smoothly between vertices, not obeying any physical law, but instead following a simple mathematical one.

Because colors are formed by interpolation rather than computing them at every pixel, Gouraud shading does not picture highlights well. Therefore, when Gouraud

FIGURE 8.26 Continuity of color across a polygonal edge.

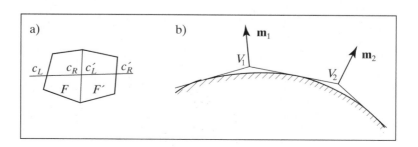

shading is used, one normally suppresses the specular component of intensity in Equation (8.11). Highlights are better reproduced using Phong shading, discussed next.

Phong Shading

Greater realism can be achieved, particularly with regard to highlights on shiny objects, by a better approximation of the normal vector to the face at each pixel. This type of shading is called **Phong shading**, after its inventor Phong Bui-tuong [Phong75].

When computing Phong shading, we find the normal vector *at each point* on the face of the object, and we apply the shading model there to find the color. We compute the normal vector at each pixel by interpolating the normal vectors at the vertices of the polygon.

Figure 8.27 shows a projected face, with the normal vectors $\mathbf{m}_1$, $\mathbf{m}_2$, $\mathbf{m}_3$, and $\mathbf{m}_4$ indicated at the four vertices. For the scan line y_s, the vectors $\mathbf{m}_{\text{left}}$ and $\mathbf{m}_{\text{right}}$ are found by linear interpolation. For instance,

$$\mathbf{m}_{\text{left}} = \text{lerp}\left(\mathbf{m}_4, \mathbf{m}_3, \frac{y_s - y_4}{y_3 - y_4}\right).$$

This interpolated vector must be normalized to unit length before it is used in the shading formula. Once $\mathbf{m}_{\text{left}}$ and $\mathbf{m}_{\text{right}}$ are known, they are interpolated to form a normal vector at each x along the scan line. That vector, once normalized, is used in the shading calculation to form the color at the pixel in question.

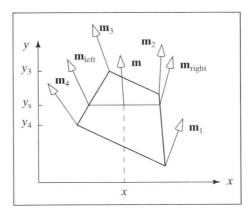

FIGURE 8.27 Interpolating normals.

Figure 8.28 shows an object rendered by using Gouraud shading and the same object rendered by using Phong shading. Because, with Phong shading, the direction of the normal vector varies smoothly from point to point and more closely approximates that of an underlying smooth surface, the production of specular highlights is much more faithful than with Gouraud shading, and more realistic renderings are produced. The principal drawback of Phong shading is its relatively slow speed: A

FIGURE 8.28 Comparison of Gouraud and Phong shading (*Courtesy of Bishop and Weimar [Bishop86]*).

great deal more computation is required per pixel, so that Phong shading can take six to eight times longer than Gouraud shading to perform. A number of approaches have been taken to speed up the process [Bishop86, Claussen90].

OpenGL is not set up to do Phong shading, because it applies the shading model once per vertex right after the modelview transformation and because normal vector information is not passed to the rendering stage following the perspective transformation and division. We will see in Section 8.5, however, that an approximation to Phong shading can be created by mapping a "highlight" texture onto an object with the use of the environment mapping technique.

PRACTICE EXERCISES

8.3.1 Filling your face

Discuss the details of how the polygon fill algorithm operates for the polygon with vertices $(x, y) = (23, 137), (120, 204), (200, 100)$, and $(100, 25)$, for scan lines $y = 136$, $y = 137$, and $y = 138$. Specifically, write the values of x_{left} and x_{right} in each case.

8.3.2 Clipped convex polygons are still convex

Prove that if a convex polygon is clipped against the camera's view volume, the clipped polygon is still convex.

8.3.3 Retaining edges with gouraud shading

In some cases, we may want to show specific creases and edges in a model. Discuss how this feature can be controlled by the choice of the vertex normal vectors. For instance, to retain the edge between faces F and F' in Figure 8.26, what should the vertex normals be? Other tricks and issues can be found in the references [e.g., Rogers90].

8.3.4 Faster phong shading with fence shading

To increase the speed of Phong shading, Behrens [Behrens94] suggests interpolating normal vectors between vertices to get $\mathbf{m}_L$ and $\mathbf{m}_R$ in the usual way at each scan line, but then computing colors only at these left and right pixels, interpolating them along a scan line as in Gouraud shading. This so-called fence shading speeds up rendering dramatically, but does less well in rendering highlights than does true Phong shading. Describe general directions for the vertex normals $\mathbf{m}_1, \mathbf{m}_2, \mathbf{m}_3$, and $\mathbf{m}_4$ in Figure 8.27 such that

a. Fence shading produces the same highlights as Phong shading.
b. Fence shading produces very different highlights than does Phong shading.

8.3.5 The phong shading algorithm

Make the necessary changes to the tiling code to incorporate Phong shading. Assume that the vertex normal vectors are available for each face. Also, discuss how Phong shading can be approximated by OpenGL's smooth-shading algorithm. (*Hint*: Increase the number of faces in the model.)   ■

8.4 REMOVING HIDDEN SURFACES

It is very simple to incorporate the removal of hidden surfaces into the rendering process described in the previous section if enough memory is available to have a "depth buffer" (also called a "z-buffer"). Because such a buffer fits so easily into the rendering mechanisms we are discussing, we examine it next. Other (more efficient and less memory-hungry) algorithms for the removal of hidden surfaces are described in Chapter 13.

8.4.1 The Depth Buffer Approach

The depth buffer (or z-buffer) algorithm is one of the simplest and most easily implemented methods for removing hidden surfaces. Its principal limitations are that it requires a large amount of memory and that it often renders an object that is later obscured by a nearer object (so that the time spent rendering the first object is wasted).

Figure 8.29 shows a depth buffer associated with the frame buffer. For every pixel $p[i][j]$ on the display, the depth buffer stores a b-bit quantity $d[i][j]$. The value of b is usually in the range from 12 to 30 bits. During the rendering process, the depth buffer value $d[i][j]$ contains the pseudodepth of the closest object encountered (so far) at pixel $[i]$ $[j]$. As the tiler proceeds pixel by pixel across a scan line, filling the current face, it tests whether the pseudodepth of the current face is less than the depth $d[i][j]$ stored in the depth buffer at that point. If so, the color of the closer surface replaces the color $p[i][j]$, and this smaller pseudodepth replaces the old value in $d[i][j]$. Faces can be drawn in any order. If a remote face is drawn first, the colors of some of the pixels that show the face will later be replaced by the colors of the pixels of a nearer face. The time spent rendering the more remote face is therefore wasted. Note that this algorithm works for objects of any shape, including curved surfaces, because it finds the closest surface, based on a point-by-point test.

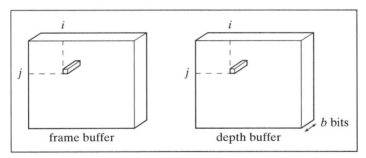

FIGURE 8.29 Conceptual view of the depth buffer.

The array $d[\ ][\ ]$ is initially loaded with the value 1.0, the greatest pseudodepth value possible. The frame buffer is initially loaded with the background color.

Finding the Pseudodepth at Each Pixel

We need a rapid way to compute the pseudodepth at each pixel. Recall that each vertex $P = (P_x, P_y, P_z)$ of a face is sent down the graphics pipeline and passes through various transformations. The information available for each vertex after the viewport transformation is the value of the ordered triple that is a scaled and shifted version of

$$(x, y, z) = \left(\frac{P_x}{-P_z}, \frac{P_y}{-P_z}, \frac{aP_z + b}{-P_z} \right).$$

[See also Equation (7.11).] The third component is the pseudodepth. The constants a and b have been chosen so that the third component equals zero if P lies in the near plane and unity if P lies in the far plane. For the most efficiency, we would like to compute the pseudodepth at each pixel incrementally, which implies using linear interpolation, as we did for color in Equation (8.14).

Figure 8.30 shows a face being filled along the scan line y. The pseudodepth values at various points are marked. The pseudodepths d_1, d_2, d_3, and d_4 at the vertices are known. We want to calculate d_{left} at scan line y_s as $\text{lerp}(d_1, d_4, f)$ for the fraction $f = (y_s - y_1)/(y_4 - y_1)$ and, similarly, d_{right} as $\text{lerp}(d_2, d_3, h)$ for the appropriate h. And we want to find the pseudodepth d at each pixel (x, y) along the scan line as $\text{lerp}(d_{\text{left}}, d_{\text{right}}, k)$ for the appropriate k. (What are the values of h and k?) The

FIGURE 8.30 Incremental computation of pseudodepth.

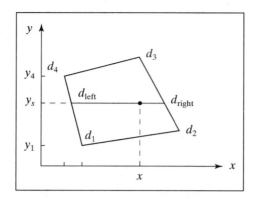

question is whether this calculation produces the "true" pseudodepth of the corresponding point on the 3D face. The answer is that it works correctly. We prove this later, after developing some additional algebraic artillery, but the key idea is that the original 3D face is flat, and perspective projection preserves flatness, so the pseudodepth varies linearly with the projected x and y coordinates. (See Exercise 8.5.2 on page 451.)

Figure 8.31 shows the nearly trivial additions to the Gouraud-shading tiling algorithm that accomplish the removal of hidden surfaces. Values of d_{left} and d_{right} are found (incrementally) for each scan line, along with d_{inc}, which is used in the innermost loop. For each pixel, d is found, a single comparison is made, and $d[i][j]$ is updated if the current face is found to be the closest one to the viewer.

```
for(int y = ybott; y <= ytop; y++)        // for each scan-line
{
    find xleft and xright
    find dleft and dright, and dinc
    find colorleft and colorright, and colorinc
    for (int x = xleft, c = colorleft, d = dleft; x <= xright; x++, c+=colorinc, d+= dinc)
            if(d < d[x][y])
            {
                put c into the pixel at (x, y)
                d[x][y] = d; // update the closest depth
            }
}
```

FIGURE 8.31 Doing depth computations incrementally.

Depth Compression at Greater Distances

Recall from Example 7.4.4 that the pseudodepth of a point does not vary linearly with the actual depth of the point from the eye, but instead approaches an asymptote. This means that small changes in the true depth map into extremely small changes in the pseudodepth when the depth is large. Since only a limited number of bits are used to represent the pseudodepth, two nearby values can easily map into the same value, which can lead to errors in the comparison d < d[x][y]. Using a larger number of bits to represent the pseudodepth helps, but requires more memory. It also helps to place the near plane as far away from the eye as possible.

OpenGL supports a depth buffer and uses the algorithm described in Figure 8.31 to remove hidden surfaces. You must instruct OpenGL to create a depth buffer when it initializes the display mode by means of the command

```
glutInitDisplayMode(GLUT_DEPTH | GLUT_RGB);
```

and you enable depth testing with

```
glEnable(GL_DEPTH_TEST);
```

Then, each time a new picture is to be created, the depth buffer must be initialized by using the function

```
glClear(GL_COLOR_BUFFER_BIT | GL_DEPTH_BUFFER_BIT);
```

PRACTICE EXERCISES

8.4.1 The increments

Fill in the details of how d_{left}, d_{right}, and d are found from the pseudodepth values known at the vertices of the polygon.

8.4.2 Coding depth values

Suppose b bits are allocated for each element in the depth buffer. These b bits must record values of pseudodepth between 0 and 1. A value between 0 and 1 can be expressed in binary in the form $d_1\, d_2\, d_3 \ldots d_b$, where d_i is 0 or 1. For instance, a pseudodepth of 0.75 would be coded as $1100000000\ldots$ Is this a good use of the b bits? Discuss alternatives.

8.4.3 Reducing the size of the depth buffer

Even if there is not enough memory to implement a full depth buffer, one can still generate a picture in pieces. With this technique, depth buffer is established for only a fraction of the scan lines, and the algorithm is repeated for each fraction. For instance, in a 512-by-512 display, one can allocate memory for a depth buffer of only 64 scan lines and execute the algorithm eight times. Each time the entire face list is scanned, depths are computed for faces covering the scan lines involved, and comparisons are made with the reigning depths so far. Having to scan the face list eight times, of course, makes the algorithm operate more slowly. Suppose that a scene involves F faces and each face covers, on the average, L scan lines. Estimate how much more time it takes to use the depth buffer method when memory is allocated for only $nRows/N$ scan lines.

8.4.4 A depth buffer for a single scan line

The fragmentation of the frame buffer of the previous exercise can be taken to the extreme where the depth buffer records depths for only *one* scan line. This approach appears to require more computation, as each face is "brought in fresh" to the process many times, once for each scan line. Discuss how the previous algorithm is modified to handle a single scan line, and estimate how much longer it takes to execute the new algorithm compared with the old one that uses a full-screen depth buffer. ■

8.5 ADDING TEXTURE TO FACES

I found Rome a city of bricks and left it a city of marble

Augustus Caesar-Suetonius

The realism of an image is greatly enhanced by adding surface texture to the various faces of a mesh object. Figure 8.32 shows some examples. In Part (a), images have been "pasted onto" each of the faces of a box. In Part (b), a label has been wrapped around a cylindrical can, and the wall behind the can appears to be made of bricks. (See also Plate 25, for an assortment of textured objects.)

FIGURE 8.32 Examples of
texture mapped onto surfaces.

The basic technique begins with some texture function, texture (s, t), in "**texture space**," which is traditionally marked off by parameters named s and t. The function texture (s, t) produces a color or intensity value for each value of s and t between 0 and 1. Figure 8.33 shows two examples of texture functions, where the value of texture (s, t) varies between 0 (dark) and 1 (light). Part a shows a bit-map texture, and part b shows a procedural texture, discussed next.

FIGURE 8.33 Examples of
textures. a) image texture, b)
procedural texture.

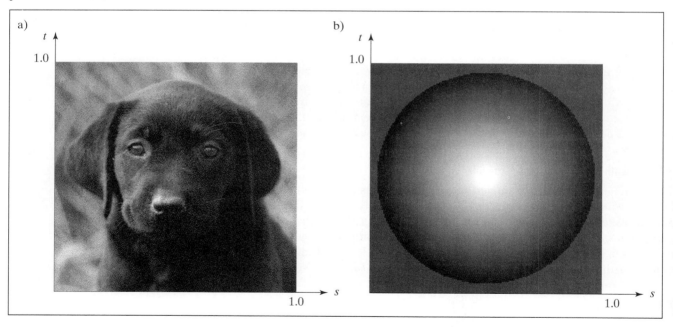

There are numerous sources of textures. The most common are bitmaps and computed functions.

Bitmap Textures

Textures are often formed from bitmap representations of images (such as a digitized photo, clip art, or an image computed previously in some program). Such a representation consists of an array, say, `txtr[c][r]`, of color values (often called **texels**). If the array has C columns and R rows, the indices `c` and `r` vary from 0 to $C - 1$ and

$R - 1$, respectively. In the simplest case, the function texture (s, t) accesses "samples" in the array, as in the code

```
Color3 texture(float s, float t)
{
     return txtr[(int)(s * C)][(int)(t * R)];
}
```

where `Color3` holds an RGB triple. For example, if $R = 400$ and $C = 600$, then texture $(0.261, 0.783)$ evaluates to `txtr[156][313]`. Note that a variation in s from 0 to 1 encompasses 600 pixels, whereas the same variation in t encompasses 400 pixels. To avoid distortion during rendering, this texture must be mapped onto a rectangle with aspect ratio 6/4.

Procedural Textures

Alternatively, we can define a texture by a mathematical function or procedure. For instance, the spherical shape that appears in Figure 8.33(b) could be generated by the function

```
float fakeSphere(float s, float t)
{
   float r = sqrt((s-0.5)*(s-0.5)+(t-0.5)*(t-0.5));
   if(r < 0.3) return 1 - r/0.3; // sphere intensity
   else return 0.2; // dark background
}
```

This function varies from 1 (white) at the center to 0 (black) at the edges of the apparent sphere. Another example that mimics a checkerboard is examined in the exercises that follow. Anything that can be computed can provide a texture: smooth blends and swirls of color, the Mandelbrot set, wire-frame drawings of solids, etc.

We shall see later that the value texture (s, t) can be used in a variety of ways: as the color of the face itself as if the face is "glowing," as a reflection coefficient to "modulate" the amount of light reflected from the face, and as a means of altering the normal vector to the surface to give it a "bumpy" appearance.

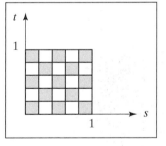

FIGURE 8.34 A classic checkerboard pattern.

PRACTICE EXERCISE

8.5.1 The classic checkerboard texture

Figure 8.34 shows a checkerboard consisting of five-by-five squares with brightness levels that alternate between 0 (for black) and 1 (for white).

a. Write the function `float texture(float s, float t)` for this texture. (See also Exercise 2.3.1.)
b. Write `texture()` for the case where there are M rows and N columns in the checkerboard.
c. Repeat Part (b) for the case where the checkerboard is rotated 40° relative to the s and t axes.

With a texture function in hand, the next step is to map it properly onto the desired surface and then to view it with a camera. Figure 8.35 shows an example that illustrates the overall problem. A single example of texture is mapped onto three different objects: a planar polygon, a cylinder, and a sphere. For each object, there is some transformation, say, T_{tw} (for "texture to world") that maps texture values (s, t) to points (x, y, z) on the object's surface. The camera takes a snapshot of the scene from some angle, producing the view shown. We call the transformation from points in 3D to points on the screen T_{ws} ("from world to screen"), so a point (x, y, z) on a surface is

FIGURE 8.35 Drawing texture on several objects of different shape.

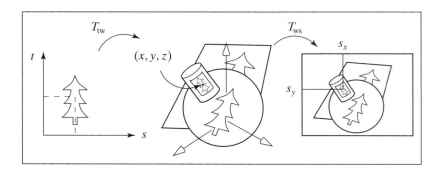

"seen" at pixel location $(sx, sy) = T_{ws}(x, y, z)$. Overall, then, the value (s^*, t^*) of the texture finally arrives at pixel $(sx, sy) = T_{ws}(T_{tw}(s^*, t^*))$.

The rendering process actually goes the other way: For each pixel at (sx, sy), we apply the following sequence of questions:

a. What is the closest surface "seen" at (sx, sy)? The answer to this question determines which texture is relevant.
b. To what point (x, y, z) on the surface does (sx, sy) correspond?
c. To which texture coordinate pair (s, t) does the point (x, y, z) correspond?

So we need the inverse transformation, something like $(s, t) = T_{tw}^{-1}(T_{ws}^{-1}(sx, sy))$, which reports (s, t) coordinates, given pixel coordinates. This inverse transformation can be hard to obtain or easy to obtain, depending on the shape of the surface.

8.5.1 Pasting the Texture onto a Flat Surface

We first examine the most important case: mapping texture onto a flat surface. This is a modeling task. In Section 8.5.2, we tackle the viewing task to see how the texture is actually rendered. We then discuss mapping textures onto more complicated surface shapes.

Pasting Texture onto a Flat Face

Since texture space itself is flat, it is simplest to paste texture onto a flat surface. Figure 8.36 shows a texture image mapped to a portion of a planar polygon F. We must specify how to associate points on the texture with points on F. In OpenGL, we use the function `glTexCoord2f()` to associate a point in texture space, $P_i = (s_i, t_i)$, with each vertex V_i of the face. The function `glTexCoord2f(s, t)` sets the "current texture coordinates" to (s, t), and they are attached to subsequently defined vertices. Normally, each call to `glVertex3f()` is preceded by a call to `glTexCoord2f()`, so each vertex gets a new pair of texture coordinates. For example, to define a quadri-

FIGURE 8.36 Mapping texture onto a planar polygon.

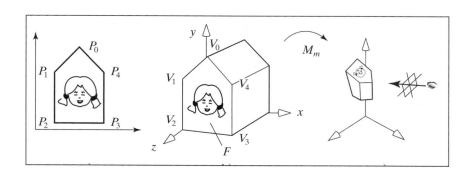

lateral face and to position a texture on it, we send OpenGL four texture coordinates and four 3D points, as follows:

```
glBegin(GL_QUADS); // define a quadrilateral face
      glTexCoord2f(0.0, 0.0); glVertex3f(1.0, 2.5, 1.5);
      glTexCoord2f(0.0, 0.6); glVertex3f(1.0, 3.7, 1.5);
      glTexCoord2f(0.8, 0.6); glVertex3f(2.0, 3.7, 1.5);
      glTexCoord2f(0.8, 0.0); glVertex3f(2.0, 2.5, 1.5);
glEnd();
```

Attaching a P_i to each V_i is equivalent to prescribing a polygon P in texture space that has the same number of vertices as F. Usually, P has the same shape as F as well; then the portion of the texture that lies inside P is pasted without distortion onto the whole of F. When P and F have the same shape, the mapping is clearly affine: It is a scaling, possibly accompanied by a rotation and a translation.

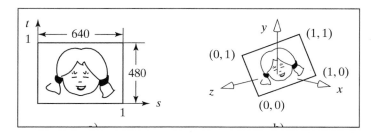

FIGURE 8.37 Mapping a square to a rectangle.

Figure 8.37 shows the common case in which the four corners of the texture square are associated with the four corners of a rectangle. (The texture coordinates (s, t) associated with each corner are noted on the 3D face.) In this example, the texture is a 640-by-480-pixel bit map, and it is pasted onto a rectangle with aspect ratio 640/480, so it appears without distortion. (Note that the texture coordinates s and t still vary from 0 to 1.) Figure 8.38 shows the use of texture coordinates that **tile** the texture, making it repeat. To do this, some texture coordinates that lie outside of the interval $[0, 1]$ are used. When the rendering routine encounters a value of s and t outside of the unit square, such as $s = 2.67$, it ignores the integral part and uses only the fractional part, 0.67. Thus, the point on a face that requires $(s, t) = (2.6, 3.77)$ is textured with texture $(0.6, 0.77)$. By default, OpenGL tiles texture this way; if desired, it may be set to "clamp" texture values instead. (See the exercises.)

Thus, a coordinate pair (s, t) is sent down the pipeline along with each vertex of the face. As we shall see in the next section, the notion is that points inside F will be filled with texture values lying inside P, by finding the internal coordinate values

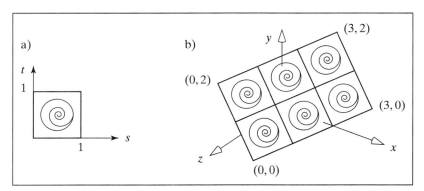

FIGURE 8.38 Producing repeated textures.

(s, t) through the use of interpolation. This interpolation process is described in the next section.

Adding Texture Coordinates to Mesh Objects

Recall from Figure 6.13 that a mesh object has three lists: the vertex list, the normal vector list, and the face list. We must add to these a "texture coordinate" list, which stores the coordinates (s_i, t_i) to be associated with various vertices. We can add an array of elements of the type

```
class TxtrCoord{public: float s, t;};
```

to hold all of the coordinate pairs of interest for the mesh. There are several different ways to treat texture for an object, and each has implications for how information on texture is organized in a model. The two most important techniques are as follows:

1. The mesh object consists of a small number of flat faces, and a different texture is to be applied to each. Here, each face has only a single normal vector, but its own list of texture coordinates. So the following would be the data associated with each face:
   - the number of vertices in the face.
   - the index of the normal vector to the face.
   - a list of indices of the vertices.
   - a list of indices of the texture coordinates.
2. The mesh represents a smooth underlying object, and a single texture is to be "wrapped" around it (or a portion of it). Here, each vertex has associated with it a specific normal vector and a particular texture coordinate pair. A single index into the vertex, normal vector, and texture lists is used for each vertex. The data associated with each face would then be the following:
   - the number of vertices in the face.
   - list of indices of the vertices.

The exercises at the end of Section 8.5.2 take a further look at the required data structures for these types of meshes.

8.5.2 Rendering the Texture

Rendering texture in a face F is similar to Gouraud shading: It proceeds across the face pixel by pixel. For each pixel, it must determine the corresponding texture coordinates (s, t), access the texture, and set the pixel to the proper texture color. We shall see that finding the coordinates (s, t) must be done very carefully.

Figure 8.39 shows the camera taking a snapshot of a face F with texture pasted onto it and the rendering in progress. The scan line y is being filled from x_{left} to x_{right}. For each x along this scan line, we must compute the correct position (shown as $P(x, y)$) on the face and from that, obtain the correct position $(s*, t*)$ within the texture.

FIGURE 8.39 Rendering a face in a camera snapshot.

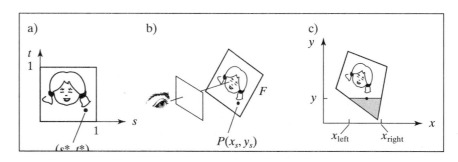

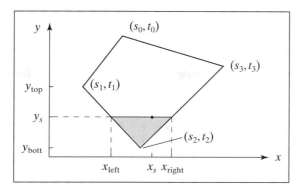

FIGURE 8.40 Incremental calculation of texture coordinates.

Having set up the texture-to-object mapping, we know the texture coordinates at each of the vertices of F, as suggested in Figure 8.40. The natural thing is to compute $(s_{\text{left}}, t_{\text{left}})$ and $(s_{\text{right}}, t_{\text{right}})$ for each scan line in a rapid incremental fashion and to interpolate between these values, moving across the scan line. But we must be careful: Simple increments from s_{left} to s_{right} as we march across scan line y from x_{left} to x_{right} will not work, since equal steps across a projected face do *not* correspond to equal steps across the 3D face.

Figure 8.41 illustrates the problem. Part (a) shows face F, viewed so that its left edge is closer to the viewer than its right edge. Part (b) shows the projection F' of this face on the screen. At scan line $y = 170$, we mark points equally spaced across F', suggesting the positions of successive pixels on the face. The corresponding positions of these marks on the actual face are shown in Part (a). They are seen to be more closely spaced at the farther end of F, simply the effect of perspective foreshortening.

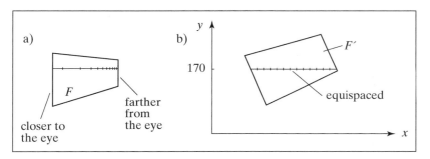

FIGURE 8.41 Spacing of samples with linear interpolation.

If we use simple linear interpolation and take equally spaced steps in s and t to compute texture coordinates, we "sample" into the texture at the wrong spots, and a distorted image results. Figure 8.42 shows what happens with a simple checkerboard texture mapped onto a rectangle. Linear interpolation is used in Part (a), producing palpable distortion in the texture. This distortion is particularly disturbing in an animation which the polygon is rotating, as the texture appears to warp and stretch dynamically. Correct interpolation is used in Part (b), and the checkerboard looks as it should. In an animation, this texture would appear to be firmly attached to the moving or rotating face.

Several approaches that develop the proper interpolation method have appeared in the literature. Heckbert and Moreton [Heckbert91] and Blinn [Blinn96] describe an elegant development based on the general nature of affine and projective mappings. Segal et al. [Segal92] arrive at the same result, using a more algebraic derivation based on the parametric representation for a line segment. We follow the latter approach here.

FIGURE 8.42 Images formed using linear interpolation and correct interpolation.

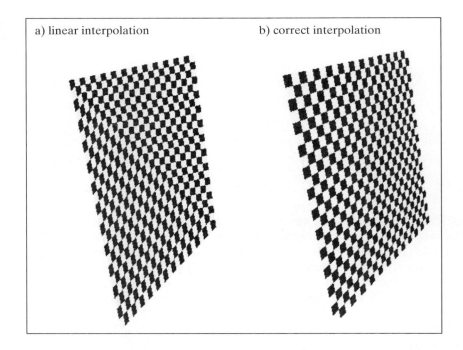

Figure 8.43 shows the situation to be analyzed. We know that affine and projective transformations preserve straightness, so line L_e in eye space projects to line L_s in screen space, and similarly, the texels we wish to draw on line L_s lie along the line L_t in texture space, which maps to L_e. The key question is this: If we move in equal steps across L_s on the screen, how should we step across texels along L_t in texture space? We develop a general result next that summarizes how interpolation works: It all has to do with the effect of perspective division. Then we relate the general result to the transformations performed in the graphics pipeline and see precisely where extra steps must be taken to map texture properly.

FIGURE 8.43 Lines in one space map to lines in another.

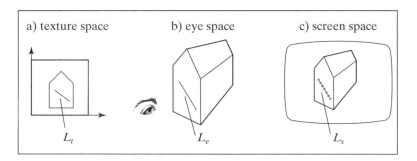

Figure 8.44 shows the line AB in 3D being transformed into the line ab in 3D by the matrix M. (M might represent an affine transformation or a more general perspective transformation.) A maps to a, and B maps to b. Consider the point $R(g)$ that

FIGURE 8.44 How does motion along corresponding lines operate?

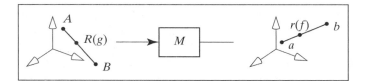

lies a fraction g of the way between A and B. This point maps to some point $r(f)$ that lies a fraction f of the way from a to b. The fractions f and g are *not* the same, as we shall see. The question is, As f varies from 0 to 1, how exactly does g vary? That is, how does motion along ab correspond to motion along AB?

Deriving How g and f Are Related

We denote the homogeneous coordinate version of a by $\tilde{a} = (a_1, a_2, a_3, a_4)$. (We use the subscripts $1, 2, 3$, and 4 instead of x, y, etc., to avoid ambiguity, since there are so many different "x, y, z" spaces.) So point a is found from $\tilde{a}$ by perspective division: $a = (a_1/a_4, a_2/a_4, a_3/a_4)$. Since M maps $A = (A_1, A_2, A_3)$ to a, we know that $\tilde{a} = M(A, 1)^T$, where $(A, 1)^T$ is the column vector with components A_1, A_2, A_3, and 1. Similarly, $\tilde{b} = M(B, 1)^T$. (Check each of these relations carefully.) Now, using lerp() notation to keep things succinct, we have defined $R(g) = \text{lerp}(A, B, g)$, which maps to $M(\text{lerp}(A, B, g), 1)^T = \text{lerp}(\tilde{a}, \tilde{b}, g) = (\text{lerp}(a_1, b_1, g), \text{lerp}(a_2, b_2, g), \text{lerp}(a_3, b_3, g), \text{lerp}(a_4, b_4, g))$. (Check these, too.) The latter equation is the homogeneous coordinate version $\tilde{r}(f)$ of the point $r(f)$. We recover the actual components of $r(f)$ by perspective division. For simplicity, we write just the first component,

$$r_1(f) = \frac{\text{lerp}(a_1, b_1, g)}{\text{lerp}(a_4, b_4, g)}. \tag{8.15}$$

But since, by definition, $r(f) = \text{lerp}(a, b, f)$, we have another expression for the first component:

$$r_1(f) = \text{lerp}\left(\frac{a_1}{a_4}, \frac{b_1}{b_4}, f\right). \tag{8.16}$$

Expressions for $r_2(f)$ and $r_3(f)$ follow similarly. (What are they?) We equate these two formulas for $r_1(f)$ and do a little algebra to obtain the desired relationship between f and g:

$$g = \frac{f}{\text{lerp}\left(\frac{b_4}{a_4}, 1, f\right)}. \tag{8.17}$$

Therefore, the point $R(g)$ maps to $r(f)$, but g and f are not the same fraction. g matches f at $f = 0$ and at $f = 1$, but its growth with f is tempered by a denominator that depends on the ratio b_4/a_4. If a_4 equals b_4, then g is identical to f. (Check this.) Figure 8.45 shows how g varies with f, for different values of b_4/a_4.

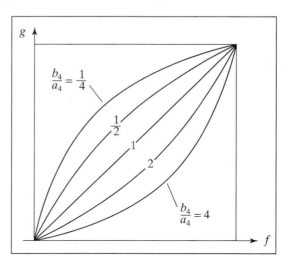

FIGURE 8.45 How g depends on f.

We can go the final step and show where the point $R(g)$ is on the 3D face that maps into $r(f)$: we merely use Equation (8.17) in $R(g) = A(1 - g) + Bg$ and simplify algebraically (check this out) to obtain, for the first component,

$$R_1 = \frac{\text{lerp}\left(\dfrac{A_1}{a_4}, \dfrac{B_1}{b_4}, f\right)}{\text{lerp}\left(\dfrac{1}{a_4}, \dfrac{1}{b_4}, f\right)}, \tag{8.18}$$

with similar expressions resulting for the components R_2 and R_3 (which have the *same* denominator as R_1). This is a key result; it tells which 3D point (R_1, R_2, R_3) corresponds (in eye coordinates) to a given point that lies (a fraction f of the way) between two given points a and b in screen coordinates. So any quantity (such as texture) that is "attached" to vertices of the 3D face and that varies linearly between them will behave the same way.

The two cases of interest for the transformation with matrix M are as follows:

- The transformation is affine.
- The transformation is the perspective transformation.

Let us consider each of these in turn.

When the transformation is affine, a_4 and b_4 are both unity (why?), so the foregoing formulas simplify immediately. The fractions f and g become identical, and R_1 becomes $\text{lerp}(A_1, B_1, f)$. We can summarize this conjunction of events as follows:

Fact

If M is *affine*, equal steps along the line ab *do* correspond to equal steps along the line AB.

When M represents the perspective transformation from eye coordinates to clip coordinates, the fourth components, a_4 and b_4, are no longer unity. We developed the matrix M in Chapter 7; its basic form, given in Equation (7.10), is

$$M = \begin{pmatrix} N & 0 & 0 & 0 \\ 0 & N & 0 & 0 \\ 0 & 0 & c & d \\ 0 & 0 & -1 & 0 \end{pmatrix},$$

where c and d are constants that make the pseudodepth work properly. What is M $(A, 1)^T$ for this matrix? It is $\tilde{a} = (NA_1, NA_2, cA_3 + d, -A_3)$, the crucial part being that $a_4 = -A_3$. This is the position of the point along the z-axis in camera coordinates— that is, the depth of the point in front of the eye.

So the relative sizes of a_4 and b_4 lie at the heart of perspective foreshortening of a line segment: They report the "depths" of A and B, respectively, along the camera's viewplane normal. If A and B have the same depth (i.e., if they lie in a plane parallel to the camera's viewplane), there is no perspective distortion along the segment, so g and f are indeed the same. Figure 8.46 shows in cross section how rays from the eye through evenly spaced spots (those with equal increments in f) on the viewplane correspond to unevenly spaced spots on the original face in 3D. For the case shown, A is closer than B, causing $a_4 < b_4$, so the g-increments grow in size as one traverses the face from A to B.

Rendering Images Incrementally

We now put the preceding ingredients together and find the proper texture coordinates (s, t) at each point on the face being rendered. Figure 8.47 shows a face of a

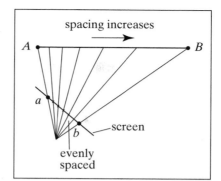

FIGURE 8.46 The values of a_4 and b_4 are related to the depths of points.

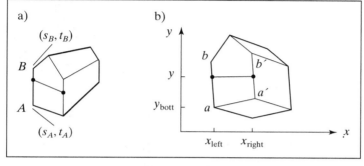

FIGURE 8.47 Rendering the texture on a face.

barn. The left edge of the projected face has endpoints a and b. The face extends from x_{left} to x_{right} across scan line y. We need to find appropriate texture coordinates $(s_{\text{left}}, t_{\text{left}})$ and $(s_{\text{right}}, t_{\text{right}})$ to attach to x_{left} and x_{right}, respectively, which we can then interpolate across the scan line. Consider finding $s_{\text{left}}(y)$, the value of s_{left} at scan line y. We know that texture coordinate s_A is attached to point a and s_B is attached to point b, since these values have been passed down the pipeline along with the vertices A and B. If the scan line at y is a fraction f of the way between y_{bott} and y_{top} so that $f = (y - y_{\text{bott}})/(y_{\text{top}} - y_{\text{bott}}))$, then we know from Equation (8.18) that the proper texture coordinate to use is

$$s_{\text{left}}(y) = \frac{\text{lerp}\left(\dfrac{s_A}{a_4}, \dfrac{s_B}{b_4}, f\right)}{\text{lerp}\left(\dfrac{1}{a_4}, \dfrac{1}{b_4}, f\right)} \tag{8.19}$$

and similarly for t_{left}. Notice that s_{left} and t_{left} have the same denominator: a linear interpolation between the values $1/a_4$ and $1/b_4$. The numerator terms are linear interpolations of texture coordinates that have been divided by a_4 and b_4. This technique is sometimes called "rational linear" rendering [Heckbert91] or "hyperbolic interpolation" [Blinn96]. To calculate (s, t) efficiently as f advances, we need to store values of $s_A/a_4, s_B/b_4, t_A/a_4, t_B/b_4, 1/a_4$, and $1/b_4$, as these remain constant from pixel to pixel. Both the numerator and denominator terms can be found incrementally for each y, just as we did for Gouraud shading. [See Equation (8.14).] But to find s_{left} and t_{left}, we must still perform an explicit division at each value of y.

The pair $(s_{\text{right}}, t_{\text{right}})$ is calculated in a similar fashion. The two components have denominators that are based on values of a_4' and b_4' that arise from the projected points a' and b'.

Once $(s_{\text{left}}, t_{\text{left}})$ and $(s_{\text{right}}, t_{\text{right}})$ have been found, the scan line can be filled. For each x from x_{left} to x_{right}, the values s and t are found, again by hyperbolic interpolation. (What is the expression for s at x?)

Implications for the Graphics Pipeline

What are the implications of having to use hyperbolic interpolation to render texture properly? And does the clipping step need any refinement? As we shall see, we must send certain additional information down the pipeline and calculate slightly different quantities than we have supposed so far.

Figure 8.48 shows a refinement of the pipeline. Various points are labeled with the information that is available at that point. Each vertex V is associated with a texture pair (s, t), as well as a vertex normal. The vertex is transformed by the modelview matrix (and the normal is multiplied by the inverse transpose of this matrix), producing vertex $A = (A_1, A_2, A_3)$ and a normal $\mathbf{n}'$ in eye coordinates. Shading calculations are done using this normal, producing the color $\mathbf{c} = (c_r, c_g, c_b)$. The texture coordinates (s_A, t_A) (which are the same as (s, t)) are still attached to A. Vertex A then undergoes the perspective transformation, producing $\tilde{a} = (a_1, a_2, a_3, a_4)$. The texture coordinates and color $\mathbf{c}$ are not altered.

FIGURE 8.48 Refinement of the graphics pipeline that includes hyperbolic interpolation.

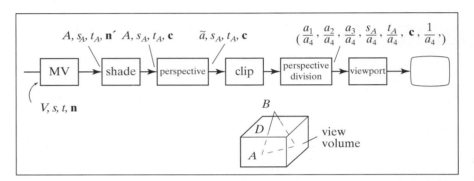

Next, clipping against the view volume is done, as discussed in Chapter 7. As the figure suggests, this can cause some vertices to disappear and others to be formed. When a vertex such as D is created, we must determine its position (d_1, d_2, d_3, d_4) and attach to it the appropriate color and texture point. By the nature of the clipping algorithm, the position components d_i are formed by linear interpolation: $d_i = \text{lerp}(a_i, b_i, t)$, for $i = 1, \ldots, 4$, for some t. Notice that the fourth component, d_4, is also formed this way. It is natural as well to use linear interpolation here to form both the color components and the texture coordinates. (The rationale for this is discussed in the exercises at the end of the Section.) Therefore, after clipping, the face still consists of a number of vertices, to each of which is attached a color and a texture point. For point A, the information is stored in the array $(a_1, a_2, a_3, a_4, s_A, t_A, \mathbf{c}, 1)$. A final term of 1 has been appended; we will use it in the next step.

Now perspective division is done. Since, for hyperbolic interpolation, we need terms such as s_A/a_4 and $1/a_4$ [see Equation (8.19)], we divide *every* item in the array that we wish to interpolate hyperbolically by a_4 to obtain the array $(x, y, z, 1, s_A/a_4, t_A/a_4, \mathbf{c}, 1/a_4)$. (We could also divide the color components, in order to obtain slightly more realistic Gouraud shading; see the exercises.) The first three components of the array, $(x, y, z) = (a_1/a_4, a_2/a_4, a_3/a_4)$, report the position of the point in normalized device coordinates. (The third component is the pseudodepth, and the first two are scaled and shifted by the viewport transformation.) To simplify notation, we shall continue to call the screen coordinate point (x, y, z).

So, finally, the rendering routine receives the array $(x, y, z, 1, s_A/a_4, t_A/a_4, \mathbf{c}, 1/a_4)$ for each vertex of the face to be rendered. Now it is simple to render texture by using hyperbolic interpolation as in Equation (8.19): The required values s_A/a_4 and $1/a_4$ are available for each vertex.

PRACTICE EXERCISES

8.5.1 Data structures for mesh models with textures

Discuss the specific data types needed to represent mesh objects in the following two cases:

a. A different texture is to be applied to each face.
b. A single texture is to be "wrapped" around the entire mesh.

Draw templates for the two data types required, and, for each, show sample data in the various arrays when the mesh holds a cube.

8.5.2 Pseudodepth calculations are correct

Show that it is correct, as claimed in Section 8.4, to use linear (rather than hyperbolic) interpolation in finding the pseudodepth of a point. Assume that point A projects to a and B projects to b. With linear interpolation, we compute the pseudodepth at the projected point $\text{lerp}(a, b, f)$ as the third component of this point. This is the correct thing to do only if the resulting value equals the true pseudodepth of the point that $\text{lerp}(A, B, g)$ (for the appropriate g) projects to. Show that it is in fact correct. (*Hint*: Apply Equations (8.15) and (8.16) to the third component of the point being projected.

8.5.3 Wrapping and clamping textures in OpenGL

To make the pattern "wrap" or "tile" in the s direction, use `glTexParameteri(GL_TEXTURE_2D, GL_TEXTURE_WRAP_S, GL_REPEAT)`. Similarly, use `GL_TEXTURE_WRAP_T` for wrapping in the t-direction. This is actually the default, so you needn't do it explicitly. To turn off tiling, replace `GL_REPEAT` with `GL_CLAMP`. Refer to the OpenGL documentation for more details, and experiment with different OpenGL settings to see their effect.

8.5.4 Rationale for linear interpolation of texture during clipping

New vertices are often created when a face is clipped against the view volume. We must then assign texture coordinates to each vertex. Suppose a new vertex V is formed that is a fraction f of the way from vertex A to vertex B on a face. Suppose further that A is assigned texture coordinates (s_A, t_A) and similarly for B. Argue why, if a texture is considered to be "pasted" onto a flat face, it makes sense to assign texture coordinates $(\text{lerp}(s_A, s_B, f), \text{lerp}(t_A, t_B, f))$ to V.

8.5.5 Computational Burden of Hyperbolic Interpolation

Compare the amount of computation required to perform hyperbolic interpolation versus linear interpolation of texture coordinates. Assume that multiplication and division each require 10 times as much time as addition and subtraction. ■

8.5.3 What Does the Texture Modulate?

How are the values in a texture map "applied" in the rendering calculation? We examine three common ways to use such values in order to achieve different visual effects. We do this for the simple case of the gray-scale intensity calculation of Equation (8.5). For full color, the same calculations are applied individually for the red, green, and blue components.

Creating a Glowing Object

This is the simplest method computationally. The visible intensity I is set equal to the texture value (or to some constant multiple of it) at each spot:

$$I = \text{texture}(s, t).$$

The object then appears to emit light, or glow. Lower texture values emit less light, and higher texture values emit more light. No additional lighting calculations need be done. (For colored light, the red, green, and blue components are set separately; for instance, the red component is $I_r = \text{texture}_r(s,t)$.) To cause OpenGL to do this type of texturing, we specify[8]

```
glTexEnvf(GL_TEXTURE_ENV, GL_TEXTURE_ENV_MODE, GL_REPLACE);
```

Painting the Texture by Modulating the Reflection Coefficient

We noted earlier that the color of an object is the color of its diffuse light component (when the object is bathed in white light). Therefore, we can make the texture appear to be painted onto the surface by varying the diffuse reflection coefficient (and perhaps the ambient reflection coefficient as well). We say that the texture function "modulates" the value of the reflection coefficient from point to point. Thus, we replace Equation (8.5) with

$$I = \text{texture}(s,t)\left[I_a \rho_a + I_d \rho_d \times \text{lambert}\right] + I_{\text{sp}} \rho_s \times \text{phong}^f,$$

for appropriate values of s and t. Since Phong specular reflections are the color of the source rather than the object, highlights do not depend on the texture. To cause OpenGL to do this type of texturing, we specify

```
glTexEnvf(GL_TEXTURE_ENV, GL_TEXTURE_ENV_MODE, GL_MODULATE);
```

Simulating Roughness by Bump Mapping

Bump mapping is a technique developed by Blinn [Blinn78a] to give a surface a wrinkled (like a raisin) or dimpled (like an orange) appearance without struggling to model each dimple itself. The texture function is used to perturb the surface normal vector, which causes perturbations in the amount of diffuse and specular light. Figure 8.49 shows an example. One problem associated with applying bump mapping to a surface like a teapot is that, since the model itself does not contain the dimples, the object's silhouette does not show dimples either, but is perfectly smooth along each face.

The goal is to make a scalar function texture (s,t) perturb the normal vector at each spot in a controlled fashion. In addition, the perturbation should depend only on the shape of the surface and the texture itself, and not on the orientation of the object or position of the eye. If the perturbation depended on orientation, the dimples would change as the object moved in an animation, contrary to the desired effect.

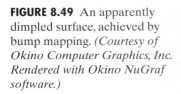

FIGURE 8.49 An apparently dimpled surface, achieved by bump mapping. *(Courtesy of Okino Computer Graphics, Inc. Rendered with Okino NuGraf software.)*

Figure 8.50 shows in cross section how bump mapping works. Suppose the surface is represented parametrically by the function $P(u,v)$ and has unit normal vector $\mathbf{m}(u,v)$. Suppose further that the 3D point at (u^*, v^*) corresponds to the texture at (u^*, v^*). Blinn's method simulates perturbing the position of the true surface in the direction of the normal vector by an amount proportional to texture (u^*, v^*); that is,

---

[8]   Use either `GL_REPLACE` or `GL_DECAL` as the last parameter.

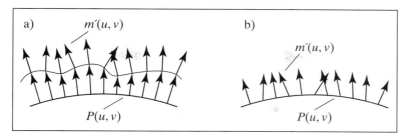

FIGURE 8.50 On the nature of bump mapping.

$$P'(u^*, v^*) = P(u^*, v^*) + \text{texture}(u^*, v^*)\mathbf{m}(u^*, v^*). \tag{8.20}$$

Figure 8.50(a) shows how this technique adds undulations and wrinkles to the surface. The perturbed surface has a new normal vector $\mathbf{m}'(u^*, v^*)$ at each point. The idea is to use this perturbed normal as if it were "attached" to the original unperturbed surface at each point, as shown in Figure 8.50(b). Blinn has demonstrated that a good approximation to $\mathbf{m}'(u^*, v^*)$ (before normalization) is given by

$$\mathbf{m}'(u^*, v^*) = \mathbf{m}(u^*, v^*) + \mathbf{d}(u^*, v^*), \tag{8.21}$$

where the perturbation vector $\mathbf{d}$ is given by

$$\mathbf{d}(u^*, v^*) = (\mathbf{m} \times P_v)\,\text{texture}_u - (\mathbf{m} \times P_u)\,\text{texture}_v,$$

in which $texture_u$ and $texture_v$ are partial derivatives of the texture function with respect to u and v, respectively. Further, P_u and P_v are partial derivative of $P(u, v)$ with respect to u and v, respectively. All functions are evaluated at (u^*, v^*). Derivations of this result may also be found in [Watt92 and Miller98]. Note that the perturbation function depends only on the partial derivatives of texture(), not on texture() itself.

If a mathematical expression is available for texture(), you can form its partial derivatives analytically. For example, texture() might undulate in two directions by combining sine waves, as in $\text{texture}(u, v) = \sin(au)\sin(bv)$, for some constants a and b. If the texture comes instead from an image array, linear interpolation can be used to evaluate it at (u^*, v^*), and finite differences can be used to approximate the partial derivatives.

8.5.4 A Texturing Example Using OpenGL

To illustrate how to invoke the texturing tools that OpenGL provides, we show an application that displays a rotating cube having different images painted on its six sides. Figure 8.51 shows a snapshot from the animation created by this program.

FIGURE 8.51 The textured cube generated by the sample code.

The code for the application is shown in Figure 8.52. It uses a number of OpenGL functions to establish the six textures and to attach them to the walls of the cube.

FIGURE 8.52

An application of a rotating textured cube.

```
#include "RGBpixmap.h"
//######################## GLOBALS #########################
RGBpixmap pix[6];      // make six (empty) pixmaps
float xSpeed = 0, ySpeed = 0,  xAngle = 0.0, yAngle = 0.0;
//<<<<<<<<<<<<<<<<<<<<<<<<<<<< myinit >>>>>>>>>>>>>>>>>>>>>>>>>>.
void myInit(void)
{
    glClearColor(1.0f,1.0f,1.0f,1.0f);  // background is white
    glEnable(GL_DEPTH_TEST);
    glEnable(GL_TEXTURE_2D);

    pix[0].makeCheckerboard();          // make pixmap procedurally
    pix[0].setTexture(2001);                 // create texture
    pix[1].readBMPFile("Mandrill.bmp");  // make pixmap from image
    pix[1].setTexture(2002);  // create texture
    …similarly for other four textures …

    glViewport(0, 0, 640, 480); // set up the viewing system
    glMatrixMode(GL_PROJECTION);
    glLoadIdentity();
    gluPerspective(60.0, 640.0/ 480, 1.0, 30.0); // set camera shape
    glMatrixMode(GL_MODELVIEW);
    glLoadIdentity();
    glTranslated(0.0, 0.0, -4); // move camera back
}
//<<<<<<<<<<<<<<<<<<<<<<<<<<<< display >>>>>>>>>>>>>>>>>>>>>>>>
void display(void)
{
    glClear(GL_COLOR_BUFFER_BIT | GL_DEPTH_BUFFER_BIT);
    glTexEnvf(GL_TEXTURE_ENV, GL_TEXTURE_ENV_MODE, GL_DECAL);
    glPushMatrix();
    glRotated(xAngle, 1.0,0.0,0.0);  glRotated(yAngle, 0.0,1.0,0.0); // rotate

    glBindTexture(GL_TEXTURE_2D,2001);  // top face: 'fake' checkerboard
    glBegin(GL_QUADS);
    glTexCoord2f(-1.0, -1.0); glVertex3f(-1.0f, 1.0f, -1.0f);
    glTexCoord2f(-1.0, 2.0); glVertex3f(-1.0f, 1.0f,  1.0f);
    glTexCoord2f(2.0, 2.0); glVertex3f( 1.0f, 1.0f,  1.0f);
    glTexCoord2f(2.0, -1.0); glVertex3f( 1.0f, 1.0f, -1.0f);
    glEnd();

    glBindTexture(GL_TEXTURE_2D,2002);  // right face: mandrill
    glBegin(GL_QUADS);
    glTexCoord2f(0.0, 0.0); glVertex3f(1.0f, -1.0f,  1.0f);
    glTexCoord2f(0.0, 2.0); glVertex3f(1.0f, -1.0f, -1.0f);
    glTexCoord2f(2.0, 2.0); glVertex3f(1.0f,  1.0f, -1.0f);
    glTexCoord2f(2.0, 0.0); glVertex3f(1.0f,  1.0f,  1.0f);
    glEnd();

    … similarly for other four faces …
    glFlush();
    glPopMatrix();
    glutSwapBuffers();
}
```

```
//<<<<<<<<<<<<<<<<<<<<<<<<<<<<<<<<< spinner >>>>>>>>>>>>>>>>>>>>
void spinner(void)
{ // alter angles by small amount
    xAngle += xSpeed;  yAngle += ySpeed;
    display();
}
//<<<<<<<<<<<<<<<<<<<<<<< main >>>>>>>>>>>>>>>>>>>>>>>>>>>>>>>>
void main(int argc, char **argv)
{
    glutInit(&argc, argv);
    glutInitDisplayMode(GLUT_DOUBLE | GLUT_RGB | GLUT_DEPTH);
    glutInitWindowSize(640,480);
    glutInitWindowPosition(10, 10);
    glutCreateWindow("rotating textured cube");
    glutDisplayFunc(display);
    myInit();
    glutIdleFunc(spinner);
    glutMainLoop();
}
```

FiGURE 8.52 (*continued*).

There are many variations of the parameters shown that one could use to map textures. The version depicted works well, but careful adjustment of some parameters (using the OpenGL documentation as a guide) can improve the images or increase the algorithm's performance. We discuss only the basics of the key routines.

In adding texture to pictures, one of the first tasks is to create a "pixel map," **pixmap**, of the texture in memory. Pixmaps are discussed in depth in Chapter 10, and the class RGBpixmap, which provides tools for creating and manipulating pixmaps, is developed there. Here, we view a pixmap as a simple array of pixel values, each being a triple of bytes to hold the red, green, and blue color values:

```
class RGB{ // holds a color triple—each with 256 possible values
    public: unsigned char r,g,b;
};
```

The RGBpixmap class stores the number of rows and columns in the pixmap, as well as the address of the first pixel in memory:

```
class RGBpixmap{
  public:
    int nRows, nCols; // dimensions of the pixmap
    RGB* pixel;       // array of pixels
    int readBMPFile(char * fname); // read BMP file into
                                   // this pixmap
    void makeCheckerboard();
    void setTexture(GLuint textureName);
};
```

Here we show the class as having only three methods that we need for mapping textures. Other methods and details are discussed in Chapter 10. The function readBMP- File() reads a BMP file[9] and stores the pixel values in its pixmap object; this function is detailed in Appendix 3. The other two methods are discussed next.

---

[9] This is a standard device-independent image file format from Microsoft. Many images are available on the internet in BMP format, and tools are readily available on the internet to convert other image formats to BMP files.

Our sample OpenGL application will use six textures. To create them, we first make an RGBpixmap object for each via the function

```
RGBpixmap pix[6]; // create six (empty) pixmaps
```

and then load the desired texture image into each one. Finally, each object is passed to OpenGL to define a texture.

Making a Procedural Texture

We first create a checkerboard texture using the method makeCheckerboard(). The checkerboard pattern is familiar and easy to create, and its geometric regularity makes it a good texture for testing correctness. The application generates a checkerboard pixmap in pix[0], using

```
pix[0].makeCheckerboard().
```

The method itself is as follows:

```
void RGBpixmap:: makeCheckerboard()
{   // make checkerboard pattern
    nRows = nCols = 64;
    pixel = new RGB[3 * nRows * nCols];
    if(!pixel) {cout << "out of memory!";return;}
    long count = 0;
    for(int i = 0; i < nRows; i++)
        for(int j = 0; j < nCols; j++)
        {
            int c = (((i/8) + (j/8)) %2) * 255;¹⁰
            pixel[count].r = c;      // red
            pixel[count].g = c;      // green
            pixel[count++].b = 0;    // blue
        }
}
```

The routine creates a 64-by-64 pixel array, where each pixel is an RGB triple. OpenGL requires that texture pixel maps have a width and height that are both some power of two. The pixel map is laid out in memory as one long array of bytes: row by row from bottom to top, left to right across a row. Each pixel is loaded with the value $(c, c, 0)$, where c jumps back and forth between 0 and 255 every 8 pixels. (We used a similar "jumping" method in Exercise 2.3.1.) The two colors of the checkerboard are black and yellow; represented by $(0, 0, 0)$ and $(255, 255, 0)$, respectively. The function returns the address of the first pixel of the pixmap, which is later passed to glTexImage2D() to create the actual texture for OpenGL.

Once the pixel map has been formed, we must bind it to a unique integer "name" so that it can be referred to in OpenGL without ambiguity. We arbitrarily assign the names $2001, 2002, \ldots, 2006$ to our six textures in this example.[11] The texture is created by making certain calls to OpenGL, which we encapsulate in the following method:

```
void RGBpixmap :: setTexture(GLuint textureName)
{
    glBindTexture(GL_TEXTURE_2D,textureName);
    glTexParameteri(GL_TEXTURE_2D,
```

---

[10] A faster way that uses C++'s bit-manipulation operators is c = ((i&8)^(j&8))*255;.

[11] To avoid overlap in (integer) names in an application that uses many textures, it is better to let OpenGL supply unique names for textures with the function glGenTextures(). If we need six unique names, we can build an array GLuint name[6] to hold them and then call glGenTextures(6,name). OpenGL places six heretofore unused integers in name[0],...,name[5], and we subsequently refer to the ith texture using name[i].

```
GL_TEXTURE_MAG_FILTER,GL_NEAREST);
   glTexParameteri(GL_TEXTURE_2D,
GL_TEXTURE_MIN_FILTER,GL_NEAREST);
   glTexImage2D(GL_TEXTURE_2D, 0, GL_RGB,nCols,nRows,0, GL_RGB,
               GL_UNSIGNED_BYTE, pixel);
}
```

The call to `glBindTexture()` binds the given name to the texture being formed. When this call is made at a later time, it will make that texture the "active" texture, as we shall see.

The calls to `glTexParameteri()` specify that a pixel should be filled with the texel whose coordinates are nearest the center of the pixel, whenever the texture needs to be magnified or reduced in size. This routine is fast, but can lead to aliasing effects. We discuss filtering of images and antialiasing further in Chapter 10. Finally, the call to `glTexImage2D()` associates the pixmap with the current texture. This call describes the texture as 2D and consisting of RGB byte triples and gives the width, height, and the address in memory (`pixel`) of the first byte of the bit map.

Making a Texture from a Stored Image

OpenGL offers no support for reading an image file and creating the pixel map in memory. The method `readBMPFile()`, given in Appendix 3, provides a simple way to read a BMP image into a pixmap. For instance,

```
pix[1].readBMPFile("mandrill.bmp");
```

reads the file `mandrill.bmp` and creates the pixmap in `pix[1]`.

Once the pixmap has been created, `pix[1].setTexture()` is used to pass it to OpenGL to make a texture.

Texture mapping must also be enabled with `glEnable(GL_TEXTURE_2D)`. In addition, the routine `glHint(GL_PERSPECTIVE_CORRECTION_HINT,GL_NICEST)` is used to request that OpenGL render the texture properly (via hyperbolic interpolation), so that it appears correctly attached to faces even when a face rotates relative to the viewer in an animation.

Texture creation, enabling, and binding need to be done only once, in an initialization routine. Then, each time through the display routine, the texture is actually applied. In `display()`, the cube is rotated through the angles `xAngle` and `yAngle`, and the six faces are drawn. This requires simply that the appropriate texture be bound to the face and that within a `glBegin()/glEnd()` pair, the texture coordinates and 3D positions of the face's vertices be specified, as shown in the code.

Once the rendering (off screen) of the cube is complete, `glutSwapBuffers()` is called to make the new frame visible. The animation is controlled by using the callback function `spinner()` as the "idle function." Whenever the system is idle–that is, when it is not responding to user input—`spinner` is called automatically. This routine alters the rotation angles of the cube slightly and calls `display()` once again. The effect is an ongoing animation showing the cube rotating, so that its various faces come into view and rotate out of view again and again.

8.5.5 Wrapping Texture on Curved Surfaces

Now that have seen how to paste a texture onto a flat surface, we can examine how to wrap texture onto a curved surface, such as a beer can or a chess piece. As before, we assume that the object is modeled by a mesh, so it consists of a large number of small, flat faces. As discussed at the end of Section 8.5.1, each vertex of the mesh has an associated texture coordinate pair (s_i, t_i). The main task is finding the proper texture coordinate (s, t) for each vertex of the mesh.

The next four examples show how to map textures onto "cylinderlike" objects and "spherelike" objects and discuss how a modeler might deal with each case.

■ EXAMPLE 8.5.1 Wrapping a label around a can

Suppose that we want to wrap a label around a circular cylinder, as suggested in Figure 8.53(a). It is natural to think in terms of cylindrical coordinates. The label is to extend from θ_a to θ_b in azimuth and from z_a to z_b along the z-axis. The cylinder is modeled as a polygonal mesh, so its walls are rectangular strips, as shown in Part (b). For vertex V_i of each face, we must find suitable texture coordinates (s_i, t_i), so that the correct "slice" of the texture is mapped onto the face.

The geometry is simple enough that a solution is straightforward. There is a direct linear relationship between (s, t) and the azimuth and height (θ, z) of a point on the cylinder's surface:

$$s = \frac{\theta - \theta_a}{\theta_b - \theta_a}, \qquad t = \frac{z - z_a}{z_b - z_a}. \tag{8.22}$$

So if there are N faces around the cylinder, the ith face has its left edge at azimuth $\theta_i = 2\pi i / N$, and its upper left vertex has texture coordinates $(s_i, t_i) = ((2\pi i / N - \theta_a)/(\theta_b - \theta_a), 1)$. Texture coordinates for the other three vertices follow in a similar fashion. This association between (s, t) and the vertices of each face is easily put in a loop in the modeling routine. (See the exercises at the end of the section.)

FIGURE 8.53 Wrapping a label around a cylinder.

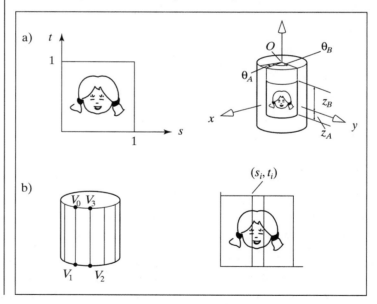

Things get more complicated when the object isn't a simple cylinder. We see next how to map texture onto a more general surface of revolution.

■ EXAMPLE 8.5.2 "Shrink-wrapping" a label onto a surface of revolution

Recall from Chapter 6 that a surface of revolution is defined by a profile curve $(x(v), z(v))$,[12] as shown in Figure 8.54(a), and is given parametrically by $P(u, v) = (x(v) \cos u, x(v) \sin u, z(v))$. The shape—here a vase—is modeled as a collection of faces with sides along contours of constant u and v. [See Figure 8.54(b).]

---

[12] We revert to calling the parameters u and v in the parametric representation of the shape, since we are using s and t for the texture coordinates.

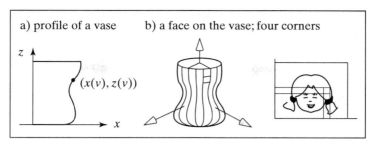

a) profile of a vase   b) a face on the vase; four corners

$(x(v), z(v))$

FIGURE 8.54 Wrapping a label around a vase.

So a given face F_i has four vertices: $P(u_i, v_i)$, $P(u_{i+1}, v_i)$, $P(u_i, v_{i+1})$, and $P(u_{i+1}, v_{i+1})$. We need to find the appropriate (s, t) coordinates for each of these vertices.

One natural approach is to proceed as before and to make s and t vary linearly with u and v in the manner of Equation (8.22). This is equivalent to wrapping the texture about an imaginary rubber cylinder that encloses the vase [see Figure 8.55(a)] and then letting the cylinder collapse, so that each texture point slides radially (and horizontally) until it hits the surface of the vase. This method is called "shrink-wrapping" by Bier and Sloane [Bier86], who discuss several possible ways to map texture onto different classes of shapes. These authors view shrink-wrapping in terms of the imaginary cylinder's normal vector [see Figure 8.55(b)]: texture point P_i is associated with the object point V_i that lies along the normal from P_i. Shrink-wrapping works well for cylinderlike objects, although the texture pattern will be distorted if the profile curve has a complicated shape.

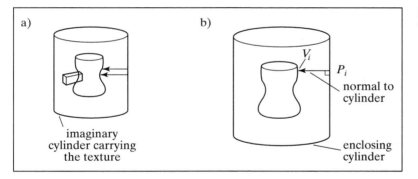

a)

imaginary
cylinder carrying
the texture

b)

V_i

P_i

normal to
cylinder

enclosing
cylinder

FIGURE 8.55 Shrink-wrapping texture onto the vase.

Bier and Sloane suggest some alternative ways to associate texture points on the imaginary cylinder with vertices on the object. Figure 8.56 shows two other possibilities. In Part (a), a line is drawn from the object's centroid C, through the vertex V_i, until it intersects with the cylinder P_i. In Part (b), the normal vector to the object's surface at V_i is used: P_i is at the intersection of this normal from V_i with the cylinder. Notice that these three ways to associate texture points with object points can lead to very different results, depending on the shape of the object. (See the exercises at

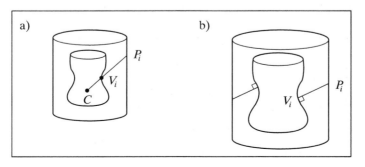

a)

P_i

V_i

C

b)

P_i

V_i

FIGURE 8.56 Alternative mappings from the imaginary cylinder to the object.

the end of the Section.) The designer must choose the most suitable method, based on the object's shape and the nature of the texture image being mapped. (What would be appropriate for a chess pawn?)

■ **EXAMPLE 8.5.3 Mapping texture onto a sphere**

It is easy to wrap a texture rectangle around a cylinder: Topologically, the cylinder can be sliced open and laid flat without distortion. A sphere is a different matter: As all mapmakers know, there is no way to show accurate details of the entire globe on a flat piece of paper. If you slice open a sphere and lay it flat, some parts always suffer serious stretching. (Try to imagine a checkerboard mapped over an entire sphere!)

It is not hard to paste a rectangular texture image onto a *portion* of a sphere, however. To map the texture square to the portion lying between azimuth θ_a to θ_b and latitude ϕ_a to ϕ_b, we just perform the mapping linearly, as in Equation (8.22): If vertex V_i lies at (θ_i, ϕ_i), we associate it with texture coordinates $(s_i, t_i) = ((\theta_i - \theta_a)/(\theta_b - \theta_a), (\phi_i - \phi_a)/(\phi_b - \phi_a))$. Figure 8.57(a) shows an image pasted onto a band around a sphere. Only a small amount of distortion is seen. Figure 8.57(b) shows how one might cover an entire sphere with texture: Merely map eight triangular texture maps onto the eight octants of the sphere.

FIGURE 8.57 Mapping texture onto a sphere.

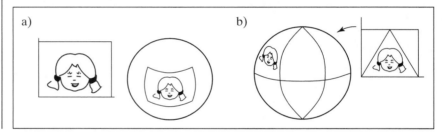

■ **EXAMPLE 8.5.4 Mapping texture to spherelike objects**

Some objects are more spherelike than cylinderlike. Figure 8.58(a) shows the buckyball, whose faces are pentagons and hexagons. One could devise a number of pentagonal and hexagonal textures and manually paste one on each face, but for some scenes, it may be desirable to wrap the whole buckyball in a single texture.

It is natural to surround a spherelike object with an imaginary sphere (rather than a cylinder) that has texture pasted to it and use one of the association methods discussed earlier. Figure 8.58(b) shows the buckyball surrounded by such a sphere, in cross section. The three ways of associating texture points P_i with object vertices V_i are sketched:

FIGURE 8.58 Spherelike objects.

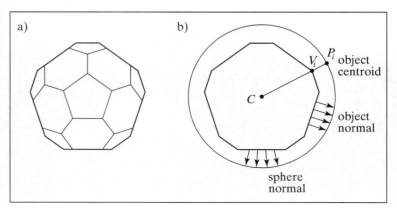

object centroid: P_i is on a line from the centroid C through the vertex V_i.

object normal: P_i is the intersection of a ray from V_i in the direction of the face normal.

sphere normal: V_i is the intersection of a ray from P_i in the direction of the normal to the sphere at P_i.

An interesting question is, Are the object-centroid and sphere-normal methods the same if the centroid of the object coincides with the center of the sphere? The object-centroid method is most likely the best and is easy to implement. As Bier and Sloane argue, the other two methods usually produce unacceptable final renderings.

Bier and Sloane also discuss using an imaginary box, rather than a sphere, to surround the object in question. Figure 8.59(a) shows the six faces of a cube spread out over a texture image, and Figure 8.59(b) shows the same texture wrapped around the cube, which in turn encloses an object. Vertices on the object can be associated with texture points in the three ways just discussed; the object-centroid and cube-normal approaches are probably the best choices.

a)

b)

FIGURE 8.59 Using an enclosing box.

PRACTICE EXERCISES

8.5.6 How to associate P_i and V_i

The surface of revolution shown in Figure 8.60 consists of a sphere resting on a cylinder. The object is surrounded by an imaginary cylinder having a checkerboard texture pasted on it. Sketch how the texture will look for each of the following methods of associating texture points with vertices:

a. shrink-wrapping.
b. object centroid.
c. object normal.

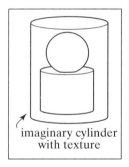

FIGURE 8.60 A surface of revolution surrounded by an imaginary cylinder.

8.5.7 Wrap a texture onto a torus

A torus can be viewed as a cylinder that bends around and closes on itself. The torus shown in Figure 8.61 has the parametric representation $P(u, v) = ((D + A\cos(v)) \cos(u), (D + A\cos(v)) \sin(u), A\sin(v))$. Suppose you decide to "polygonalize" the torus by taking vertices based on the samples $u_i = 2\pi i/N$ and $v_j = 2\pi j/M$, and you wish to wrap some texture from the unit texture space around this torus. For each of the faces, write code that generates each vertex and its associated texture coordinates (s, t). ■

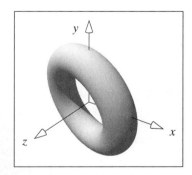

FIGURE 8.61 Wrapping texture about a torus.

8.5.6 Reflection Mapping

The class of techniques known as reflection mapping can significantly improve the realism of pictures, particularly animations. The basic idea is to see reflections in an object that suggest the "world" surrounding that object.

The two main types of reflection mapping are called chrome mapping and environment mapping. In **chrome mapping**, a rough and usually blurry image that suggests the surrounding environment is reflected in the object, as you would see in a surface coated with chrome. Television commercials abound with animations of shiny letters and logos flying around in space, for which the chrome map includes occasional spotlights for dramatic effect. Figure 8.62 offers an example. The reflection provides a rough suggestion of the world surrounding the object.

FIGURE 8.62 Example of chrome mapping. *(Courtesy of Okino Computer Graphics, Inc.)*

In the case of **environment mapping** (first introduced by Blinn and Newell [Blinn 76]), a recognizable image of the surrounding environment is seen reflected in the object. We get valuable visual cues from such reflections, particularly when the object moves about. Everyone has seen the classic photographs of an astronaut walking on the moon with the moonscape reflected in his face mask. And in the movies, you sometimes see close-ups of a character's reflective dark glasses, in which the world about her is reflected. Figure 8.63 shows two examples, in which a cafeteria is reflected in a sphere and a torus. The cafeteria texture is wrapped around a large sphere that surrounds the object, so that the texture coordinates (s, t) correspond to azimuth and latitude, respectively, about the enclosing sphere.

FIGURE 8.63 Example of environment mapping (courtesy of Haeberli and Segal [Haeberli93]).

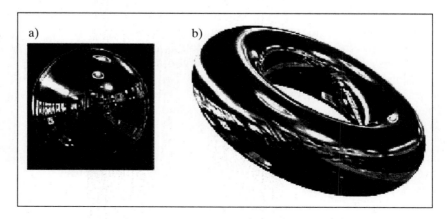

a)

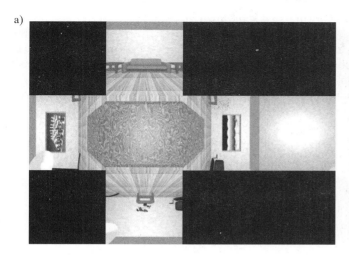

b)

FIGURE 8.64 Environment mapping based on a surrounding cube. *(Courtesy of Yoshihiro Mizutani, Kurt Reindel, and Tom Dawson.)*

Figure 8.64 shows the use of a surrounding cube rather than a sphere. Part (a) shows the map, consisting of six images of various views of the interior walls, floor, and ceiling of a room. Part (b) shows a shiny teapot reflecting different parts of the room. The use of an enclosing cube was introduced by Greene [Greene86] and generally produces less distorted reflections than are seen with an enclosing sphere. The six maps can be generated by rendering six separate images from the point of view of the object (with the object itself removed, of course). For each image, a synthetic camera is set up and the appropriate window is set. Alternatively, the textures can be digitized from photos taken by a real camera that looks in the six principal directions inside an actual room or scene.

Chrome and environment mapping differ most dramatically from normal texture mapping in an animation when a shiny object is moving. The reflected image will "flow" over the moving object, whereas a normal texture map will be attached to the object and move with it. And if a shiny sphere rotates about a fixed spot, a normal texture map spins with the sphere, but a reflection map stays fixed.

How is environment mapping done? What you see at point P on the shiny object is what has arrived at P from the environment in just the right direction to reflect into your eye. To find that direction, trace a ray from the eye to P, and determine the direction of the reflected ray. Then trace that ray to find where it hits the texture (on the enclosing cube or sphere). Figure 8.65 shows a ray emanating from the eye to point P. If the direction of this ray is $\mathbf{u}$ and the unit normal at P is $\mathbf{m}$, then, from Equation (8.2), the reflected ray is in the direction $\mathbf{r} = \mathbf{u} - 2(\mathbf{u} \cdot \mathbf{m})\mathbf{m}$. The reflected ray continues in that direction until it hits the hypothetical surface with its attached texture. Computationally, it is easiest to suppose that the shiny object is centered in, and is much smaller than, the enclosing cube or sphere. Then the reflected ray emanates approximately from the object's center, and its direction $\mathbf{r}$ can be used directly to index into the texture.

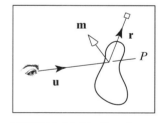

FIGURE 8.65 Finding the direction of the reflected ray.

OpenGL provides a routine to perform approximate environment mapping for the case where the texture is wrapped about a large enclosing sphere. The routine is invoked by setting a mapping mode for both s and t, using the following code:

```
glTexGenf(GL_S,GL_TEXTURE_GEN_MODE, GL_SPHERE_MAP);
glTexGenf(GL_T,GL_TEXTURE_GEN_MODE, GL_SPHERE_MAP);
glEnable(GL_TEXTURE_GEN_S);
glEnable(GL_TEXTURE_GEN_T);
```

When a vertex P with its unit normal $\mathbf{m}$ is sent down the pipeline, OpenGL calculates a texture coordinate pair (s, t) suitable for indexing into the texture attached to the surrounding sphere. This calculation is done for each vertex of the face on the object, and the face is drawn, as always, through the use of interpolated texture coordinates (s, t) for points in between the vertices.

How does OpenGL rapidly compute a suitable coordinate pair (s, t)? As shown in Figure 8.66(a), first it finds (in eye coordinates) the reflected direction $\mathbf{r}$ (using the aforementioned formula), where $\mathbf{u}$ is the unit vector (in eye coordinates) from the eye to the vertex V on the object and $\mathbf{m}$ is the normal at V. Then it simply uses the expression

$$(s, t) = \left(\frac{1}{2} \left(\frac{r_x}{p} + 1 \right), \frac{1}{2} \left(\frac{r_y}{p} + 1 \right) \right), \tag{8.23}$$

FIGURE 8.66 OpenGL's computation of the texture coordinates.

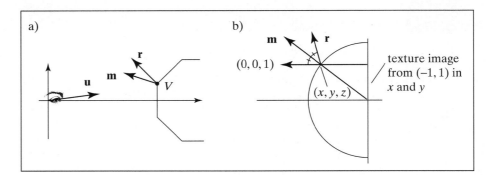

where $p = \sqrt{r_x^2 + r_y^2 + (r_z + 1)^2}$ is a mysterious scaling factor. (The derivation of this term is developed in the exercises that follow.) To carry out this procedure, we must precompute a texture that shows what you would see of the environment in a perfectly reflecting sphere, from an eye position far removed from the sphere [Haeberli93]. The procedure maps the part of the environment that lies in the hemisphere behind the eye into a circle in the middle of the texture and maps the part of the environment in the hemisphere in front of the eye into an annulus around this circle (Visualize this configuration). The texture must be recomputed if the eye changes position. The pictures in Figure 8.63 were made with the use of this method.

Simulating Highlights by Means of Environment Mapping

Reflection mapping can be used in OpenGL to produce specular highlights on a surface. A texture map is created that has an intense, concentrated bright spot. Reflection mapping "paints" this highlight onto the surface, making it appear to be an actual light source situated in the environment. The highlight that is created can be more concentrated and detailed than those created using the Phong specular term with Gouraud shading. Recall that the Phong term is computed only at the vertices of a face, and it is easy to "miss" a specular highlight that falls between two vertices. With reflection mapping, the coordinates (s, t) into the texture are formed at each vertex and then interpolated in between. So if the coordinates indexed by the vertices happen to surround the bright spot, the spot will be properly rendered inside the face.

PRACTICE EXERCISE

8.5.8 OpenGL's computation of texture coordinates for environment mapping

Derive Equation (8.23). Figure 8.66(b) shows, in cross-sectional view, the vectors involved (in eye coordinates). The eye is looking from a remote location in the direction $(0, 0, 1)$. A sphere of radius unity is positioned on the negative z-axis. Suppose light comes in from the direction $\mathbf{r}$, hitting the sphere at the point (x, y, z). The normal to the sphere at this point is (x, y, z), which also must be just right so that light coming along $\mathbf{r}$ is reflected to the direction $(0, 0, 1)$. This means that the normal must be halfway between $\mathbf{r}$ and $(0, 0, 1)$, or else it must be proportional to their sum, so $(x, y, z) = K(r_x, r_y, r_z + 1)$ for some K.

a. Show that the normal vector has unit length if K is $1/p$, where p is as given in Equation (8.23).
b. Show that, therefore, $(x, y) = (r_x/p, r_y/p)$.
c. Suppose for the moment that the texture image extends from -1 to 1 in x and from -1 to 1 in y. Argue that what we want to see reflected at the point (x, y, z) is the value of the texture image at (x, y).
d. Show that if, instead, the texture uses coordinates from 0 to 1—as is true in OpenGL—then we want to see at (x, y) the value of the texture image at (s, t) given by Equation (8.23). ■

8.6 ADDING SHADOWS OF OBJECTS

Shadows make an image much more realistic. From everyday experience, we know that the way one object casts a shadow on another object gives important visual cues as to how the two objects are positioned with respect to each other. Figure 8.67 shows two images involving a cube and a sphere suspended above a plane. Shadows are absent in Part (a), and it is impossible to see how far above the plane the cube and sphere are floating. By contrast, the shadows seen in Part (b) give useful hints as to the positions of the objects. A shadow conveys a lot of information; it is as if you are getting a second look at the object (from the viewpoint of the light source).

FIGURE 8.67 The effect of shadows.

a)   b)

In this section, we examine two methods for computing shadows, one based on "painting" the shadows as if they were texture and the other an adaptation of the depth-buffer approach for removing hidden surfaces. In Chapter 14, we shall see that a third method arises naturally in ray tracing. There are many other techniques, well surveyed in [watt92, crow77, woo90, bergeron86].

8.6.1 Shadows as Texture

The technique of "painting" shadows as a texture works for shadows that are cast onto a flat surface by a point light source. The problem is to compute the shape of the shadow that is cast. Figure 8.68(a) shows a box casting a shadow onto the floor. The shape of the shadow is determined by the projections of each of the faces of the box

FIGURE 8.68 Computing the shape of a shadow.

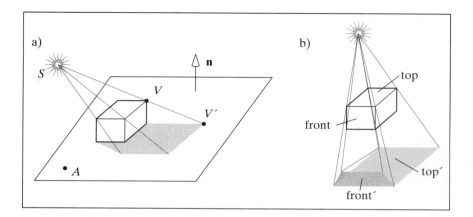

onto the plane of the floor, using the light source as the center of projection. In fact, the shadow is the union[13] of the projections of the six faces. Figure 8.68(b) shows the superposed projections of two of the faces: The top face projects to *top'* and the front face to *front'*. (Sketch the projections of the other four faces, and verify that their union is the required shadow.[14])

This provides the key to drawing the shadow: After drawing the plane by the use of ambient, diffuse, and specular light contributions, draw the six projections of the box's faces on the plane, using only ambient light. This technique will draw the shadow in the right shape and color. Finally, draw the box. (If the box is near the plane, parts of it might obscure portions of the shadow.)

Building the "Projected" Face

To make the new face F' produced by F, we project each of the vertices of F onto the plane in question. We need a way to calculate the positions of these vertices on the plane. Suppose, as in Figure 8.68(a), that the plane passes through point A and has normal vector $\mathbf{n}$. Consider projecting vertex V, producing point V'. The mathematics here is familiar: V' is the point where the ray from the source at S through V hits the plane. As is developed in the exercises, this point is

$$V' = S + (V - S)\frac{\mathbf{n} \cdot (A - S)}{\mathbf{n} \cdot (V - S)}. \tag{8.24}$$

The exercises show how this equation can be written in homogeneous coordinates as V times a matrix, which is handy for rendering engines, like OpenGL, that support convenient matrix multiplication.

PRACTICE EXERCISES

8.6.1 Shadow shapes

Suppose a cube is floating above a plane. What is the shape of the cube's shadow if the point source lies (a) directly above the top face? or (b) along a main diagonal of the cube (as in an isometric view)? Sketch shadows for a sphere and for a cylinder floating above a plane for various positions of the source.

---

[13] We mean the set-theoretic union: A point is in the shadow if it is in one or more of the projections.

[14] You need to form the union of the projections of only the three "front" faces—those facing toward the light source. (Why?)

8.6.2 Making the "shadow" face

a. Show that the ray from a source point S through a vertex V hits the plane $\mathbf{n} \cdot (P - A) = 0$ at $t^* = [\mathbf{n} \cdot (A - S)]/[\mathbf{n} \cdot (V - S)]$.

b. Show that the intersection of the point and plane in Part (a) defines the hit point V' as given in Equation (8.24).

8.6.3 It's equivalent to a matrix multiplication

a. Show that the expression for V' in Equation (8.24) can be written as the matrix multiplication $V' = M(V_x, V_y, V_z, 1)^T$, where M is a four-by-four matrix

b. Express the terms of M in terms of A, S, and $\mathbf{n}$.

8.6.2 Creating Shadows with the Use of a Shadow Buffer

A rather different method for drawing shadows uses a variant of the depth buffer that performs the removal of hidden surfaces. In this method, an auxiliary second depth buffer, called a **shadow buffer**, is employed for each light source. This requires a lot of memory, but the approach is not restricted to casting shadows onto planar surfaces.

The method is based on the principle that any points in a scene that are "hidden" from the light source must be in shadow. On the other hand, if no object lies between a point and the light source, the point is not in shadow. The shadow buffer contains a "depth picture" of the scene from the point of view of the light source: Each of the elements of the buffer records the distance from the source to the *closest* object in the associated direction.

Rendering is done in two stages:

1. **Loading the Shadow Buffer**

   The shadow buffer is initialized with 1.0 in each element, the largest pseudodepth possible. Then, via a camera positioned at the light source, each of the faces in the scene is rasterized, but only the pseudodepth of the point on the face is tested. Each element of the shadow buffer keeps track of the smallest pseudodepth seen so far.

   To be more specific, Figure 8.69 shows a scene being viewed by the usual "eye camera," as well as a "source camera" located at the light source. Suppose that point P is on the ray from the source through shadow buffer "pixel" $d[i][j]$ and that point B on the pyramid is also on this ray. If the pyramid is present, $d[i][j]$ contains the pseudodepth to B; if the pyramid happens to be absent $d[i][j]$ contains the pseudodepth to P.

   Note that the shadow-buffer calculation is independent of the eye position, so in an animation in which only the eye moves, the shadow buffer is loaded only once. The shadow buffer must be recalculated, however, whenever the objects move relative to the light source.

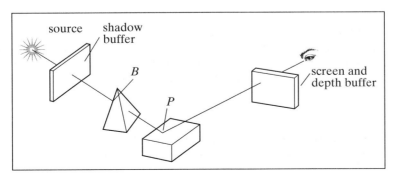

FIGURE 8.69 Using the shadow buffer.

2. Rendering the Scene

Each face in the scene is rendered using the eye camera as usual. Suppose the eye camera "sees" point P through pixel $p[c][r]$. When rendering $p[c][r]$, we must find[15]

- the pseudodepth D from the source to P;
- the index location $[i][j]$ in the shadow buffer that is to be tested; and
- the value $d[i][j]$ stored in the shadow buffer.

If $d[i][j]$ is less than D, the point P is in shadow, and $p[c][r]$ is set using only ambient light. Otherwise P is not in shadow, and $p[c][r]$ is set using ambient, diffuse, and specular light.

How are these steps done? As described in the exercises that follow, to each point on the eye camera viewplane, there corresponds a point on the source camera viewplane.[16] For each screen pixel, this correspondence is invoked to find the pseudodepth from the source to P, as well as the index $[i][j]$ that yields the pseudodepth stored in the shadow buffer.

PRACTICE EXERCISES

8.6.4 Finding the pseudodepth from the source

Suppose the matrices M_c and M_s map the point P in a scene to the appropriate (3D) spots on the eye camera's viewplane and the source camera's viewplane, respectively.

a. Describe how to establish a "source camera" and how to find the resulting matrix M_s.
b. Find the transformation that, given position (x, y) on the eye camera's viewplane, produces the position (i, j) and pseudodepth on the source camera's viewplane.
c. Once (i, j) are known, how are the index $[i][j]$ and the pseudodepth of P on the source camera determined?

8.6.5 Extended light sources

We have considered only point light sources in this chapter. Greater realism is provided by modeling extended light sources. As suggested in Figure 8.70(a), such sources cast more complicated shadows, having an **umbra** within which no light from the source is seen, and a lighter **penumbra**, within which a part of the source is visible. In Part (b) of the figure, a glowing sphere of radius 2 shines light on a unit cube, thereby casting a shadow on the wall W. Make an accurate sketch of the umbra and penumbra that are observed on the wall. As you might expect, algorithms for rendering shadows due to extended light sources are complex. (See [Watt92] for a thorough treatment of the subject.) ■

FIGURE 8.70 Umbra and penumbra for extended light sources.

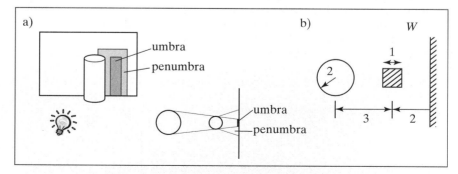

---

[15] Of course, this test is made only if P is closer to the eye than the value stored in the normal depth buffer of the eye camera.

[16] Keep in mind that these are 3D points, with two position coordinates on the viewplane and the pseudodepth as the third coordinate.

8.7 SUMMARY

Since the beginning of computer graphics, there has been a relentless quest for greater realism in rendering 3D scenes. Wire-frame views of objects can be drawn very rapidly, but are difficult to interpret, particularly if several objects in a scene overlap. Realism is greatly enhanced when the faces of the objects are filled with some color and surfaces that should be hidden are removed, but pictures rendered this way still do not give the impression of objects residing in a scene, illuminated by light sources.

What is needed is a shading model that describes how light reflects off a surface, depending on the nature of the surface and its orientation to both light sources and the camera's eye. The physics of the reflection of light is highly complex, so programmers have developed a number of approximations and "tricks" that do an acceptable job most of the time and are reasonably efficient computationally. The model for the diffuse component is the one most closely based on reality, and it becomes extremely complex as more and more ingredients are considered. Specular reflections are not modeled on physical principles at all, but can do an adequate job of re-creating highlights on shiny objects. And ambient light is purely an abstraction—a shortcut that avoids dealing with multiple reflections from object to object and that prevents shadows from being too deep.

Even simple shading models involve several parameters, such as reflection coefficients, descriptions of a surface's roughness, and the color of light sources. OpenGL provides ways to set many of these parameters. There is little guidance for the designer, however, in choosing the values of these parameters; they are often determined by trial and error until the final rendered picture "looks right".

In this chapter, we focused on the rendering of polygonal mesh models, so the basic task was to render a polygon. Polygonal faces are particularly simple and are described by a modest amount of data, such as vertex positions, vertex normals, surface colors, and surface materials. In addition, there are highly efficient algorithms for filling a polygonal face with calculated colors, especially if it is known to be convex. And algorithms can capitalize on the flatness of a polygon to interpolate depth in an incremental fashion. In this manner, the depth-buffer algorithm for removing hidden surfaces is simple and efficient.

When a mesh model is supposed to approximate an underlying smooth surface, the appearance of a face's edges can be objectionable. Gouraud and Phong shading provide ways to draw a smoothed version of the surface (except along silhouettes). Gouraud shading is very fast, but does not reproduce highlights very faithfully; Phong shading produces more realistic renderings, but is computationally quite expensive.

The realism of a rendered scene is greatly enhanced by the appearance of texturing on the surfaces of objects. With texturing, an object can appear to be made of some material such as brick or wood, and labels or other figures can be pasted onto surfaces. Texture maps can be used to modulate the amount of light that reflects from an object, or they can be used as "bump maps," which give a surface a bumpy appearance. Environment mapping shows the viewer an impression of the environment that surrounds a shiny object, and this can make scenes more realistic, particularly in animations. Texture mapping must be done with care, however, using proper interpolation and antialiasing (which we discuss in Chapter 10).

The chapter closed with a description of some simple methods for producing shadows of objects. This is a complex subject, and many techniques have been developed. The two algorithms described provide simple, but only partial, solutions to the problem.

Greater realism can be attained with more elaborate techniques, such as ray tracing. Chapter 14 develops the key ideas of this technique.

8.8 CASE STUDIES

CASE STUDY 8.1 CREATING SHADED OBJECTS WITH THE USE OF OPENGL

Level of Effort: II, but beyond that of Case Study 7.1. Extend Case Study 7.1, which flies a camera through space looking at various polygonal mesh objects, by establishing a point light source in the scene and assigning various material properties to the meshes. Include ambient, diffuse, and specular light components. Provide a keystroke that switches between flat and smooth shading.

CASE STUDY 8.2 THE DO-IT-YOURSELF GRAPHICS PIPELINE

Level of Effort: III. Write an application that reads the characteristics of a polygonal mesh model from a file as described in Chapter 6, defines a camera and a point light source, and renders the mesh object by using flat shading with ambient and diffuse light contributions. Only gray-scale intensities need be computed. For this project, do *not* use OpenGL's pipeline; instead, create your own. Define modelview, perspective, and viewport matrices. Arrange things so that vertices can be passed through the first two matrices and have the shading model applied, followed by perspective division (no clipping need be done) and the viewport transformation. Each vertex emerges as the array $\{x, y, z, b\}$, where x and y are screen coordinates, z is the pseudodepth, and b is the gray-scale brightness of the vertex. Use a tool that draws filled polygons to do the actual rendering; if you use OpenGL, use only its 2D drawing (and depth-buffer) components. Experiment with different mesh models, camera positions, and light sources to ensure that lighting is done properly.

CASE STUDY 8.3 ADD POLYGON FILL AND DEPTH-BUFFER REMOVAL OF HIDDEN SURFACES

Level of Effort: III, but beyond that needed for Case Study 8.2. Implement your own depth buffer, and use it in the application you developed in Case Study 8.2. You will need to develop a polygon fill routine as well. (See Chapter 10.)

CASE STUDY 8.4 RENDERING TEXTURE

Level of Effort: II, but beyond that of Case Study 8.1. Enhance the program you wrote in Case Study 8.1 so that textures can be painted on the faces of mesh objects. Assemble a routine that can read a BMP image file and attach it to an OpenGL texture object. Experiment by putting five different image textures and one procedural texture on the sides of a cube and arranging to have the cube rotate in an animation. Provide a keystroke that lets the user switch between linear interpolation and correct interpolation for rendering textures.

CASE STUDY 8.5 APPLYING PROCEDURAL 3D TEXTURES

Level of Effort: III. An interesting effect is achieved by making an object appear to be carved out of some solid material, such as wood or marble. 3D textures are discussed in detail in Chapter 14 in connection with ray tracing, but it is also possible to map "slices" of a 3D texture onto the surfaces of an object, to achieve a convincing effect.

Suppose you have a texture function $B(x, y, z)$ that attaches different intensities or colors to different points in 3D space. For instance, $B(x, y, z)$ might represent how "inky" the sea is at position (x, y, z). As you swim around, you encounter a varying inkiness right before your eyes. If you freeze a block of water and carve some shape out of the block, the surface of the shape will exhibit a varying inkiness. $B()$ can be vector valued as well, providing three values at each (x, y, z) that might represent the diffuse reflection coefficients for red, green, and blue light of the material at each point in space. It is not hard to construct interesting functions $B()$:

a. A 3D black-and-white checkerboard with 125 blocks is formed by using

$$B(x, y, z) = \big((\text{int})(5x) + (\text{int})(5y) + (\text{int})(5z)\big) \,\% \,2 \text{ as } x, y, \text{ and } z \text{ vary from 0 to 1}.$$

b. A cube has six different colors at its vertices, with a continuously varying color at points in between. Just use $B(x, y, z) = (x, y, z)$, where x, y, and z vary from 0 to 1. The vertex at $(0, 0, 0)$ is black, that at $(1, 0, 0)$ is red, etc.

c. All of space can be filled with cubes such as those described in (b), stacked upon one another, by using $B(x, y, z) = \big(\text{fract}(x), \text{fract}(y), \text{fract}(z)\big)$, where $\text{fract}(x)$ is the fractional part of the value x.

Methods for creating wood grain and turbulent marble are discussed in Chapter 14; they can be used here as well.

In the present context, we wish to paste such texture onto surfaces. To do this, a bit map is computed by using $B()$ for each surface of the object. If the object is a cube, for instance, six different bit maps are computed, one for each face of the cube. Suppose a certain face of the cube is characterized by the planar surface $P + \mathbf{a}t + \mathbf{b}s$, for s, t in 0 to 1. Then use as texture $B(P_x + a_x t + b_x s, P_y + a_y t + b_y s, P_z + a_z t + b_z s)$. Notice that if there is any coherence to the pattern $B()$ (so that nearby points enjoy somewhat the same inkiness or color), then nearby points on adjacent faces of the cube will also have nearly the same color. This makes the object truly look like it is carved out of a single solid material.

Extend Case Study 8.4 to include pasting texture like this onto the faces of a cube and an icosahedron. Use a checkerboard texture, a color cube texture, and a wood-grain texture (as described in Chapter 14).

Form a sequence of images of a textured cube that moves slightly through the material from frame to frame. The object will appear to "slide through" the texture in which it is embedded, giving a very different effect from an object moving with its texture attached. Experiment with such animations.

CASE STUDY 8.6 DRAWING SHADOWS

Level of Effort: III. Extend the program you developed in Case Study 8.1 to produce shadows. Make one of the objects in the scene a flat planar surface, on which is seen shadows of other objects. Experiment with the "projected-faces" approach. If time permits, develop as well the shadow-buffer approach.

CASE STUDY 8.7 EXTENDING SDL TO INCLUDE TEXTURING

Level of Effort: III. Scene Description Language (SDL) does not yet include a means to specify the texture that one wants applied to each face of an object. The keyword `texture` is in the language, but nothing is done when it is encountered in a file. Do a careful study of the code in the `Scene` and `Shape` classes, available on the book's Internet site, and design an approach that permits a syntax such as

```
texture giraffe.bmp p1 p2 p3 p4
```

to create a texture from a stored image (here, `giraffe.bmp`) and paste the texture onto certain faces of subsequently defined objects. Determine how many parameters `texture` should require and how they should be used. Extend `drawOpenGL()` for two or three shapes so that it properly pastes such texture onto the objects in question.

8.9 FURTHER READING

Jim Blinn's two books, *A Trip down the Graphics Pipeline* [Blinn96] and *Dirty Pixels* [Blinn98], from the series titled "Jim Blinn's Corner," offer several articles that lucidly explain the issues involved in drawing shadows and the hyperbolic interpolation used in rendering texture. Heckbert's "Survey of Texture Mapping" [Heckbert86] gives many interesting insights into this difficult topic. The papers "Fast Shadows and Lighting Effects Using Texture Mapping," by Segal et al. [Segal92], and "Texture Mapping as a Fundamental Drawing Primitive," by Haeberli and Segal [Haeberli93] (also available on-line at *http://www.sgi.com/grafica/texmap/*) provide excellent background and context.

9 Approaches to Infinity

So, naturalists observe, a flea
Hath smaller fleas that on him prey;
And these have smaller still to bite 'em;
And so proceed ad infinitum.

Jonathan Swift, "On Poetry, a Rhapsody"

The earthworm burrowing through the soil encounters another earthworm
and says "Oh, you're beautiful! Will you marry me?"
and is answered: "Don't be silly! I'm your other end."

Robert Heinlein

Goals of the Chapter

▲ To examine the effective use of repetition and recursion in creating figures.

▲ To extend the ability to visualize complex patterns.

▲ To use recursion to draw space-filling curves.

▲ To construct fractal curves and trees.

▲ To examine fractal image compression.

▲ To examine the nature, and construct pictures of, the Mandelbrot and Julia sets.

▲ To develop methods for "fractalizing" a curve using random fractals.

PREVIEW

In this chapter we "move toward" infinity in various ways, exploiting the power of computer graphics to reveal what is encountered along the way. We examine three approaches to the infinite: to the infinitely small, zooming in on ever greater detail or adding ever finer levels of detail to a figure; to the infinitely large, examining patterns that can be reproduced in certain ways to form larger patterns; and to the "infinitely often," studying what happens when a process is repeated again and again, conceptually forever.

Section 9.2 introduces the notion of fractals and self-similarity—the property of a shape that has the same degree of roughness no matter how much it is magnified. Methods are presented for refining the shape of a curve, moving towards the infinitely small to achieve ever greater levels of detail. Section 9.3 develops a method for drawing very complex curves, based on a small set of rules for replacing one string of characters with another. Each generation replaces its predecessor with a more complex curve.

Section 9.4 discusses moving from the small to the infinitely large by covering the entire plane with replicas of a single shape that fit together exactly. Extensions of this technique to a small set of shapes are discussed, and the fascinating class of "reptiles" is described, along with methods for drawing them.

Section 9.5 describes how to draw complex images known as "strange attractors" by the repeated application of a set of affine transformations to some starting image. The "Chaos Game" is introduced as an alternative method for drawing such objects. The inverse problem is then addressed: how to find a set of affine transformations whose attractor is a given image. This leads to a discussion of fractal image compression that exploits the technique used to solve that problem.

Section 9.6 introduces the celebrated Mandelbrot set, discusses its mathematical underpinnings, and develops some tools to draw the set. Section 9.7 describes the family of Julia sets and relates them to the Mandelbrot set. Methods for drawing the two kinds of Julia sets are developed.

Section 9.8 discusses how to "fractalize" a given curve or polyline, "roughening" it to create the texture of a rugged coastline or fur. The chapter closes with eight case studies that explore these topics further.

9.1 INTRODUCTION

Computers are particularly good at repetition: They will do something again and again without complaint. In addition, the high precision with which modern computers can do calculations allows an algorithm to take closer and closer "looks" at an object, effectively "zooming in" to ever greater levels of detail.

We have seen in previous chapters how computer graphics can produce pictures of things that do not yet exist in nature or, perhaps, could never exist. This is especially true of the objects we study in this chapter, and computer graphics provides a powerful tool for investigating them. But here we go further, and we will bump up against the inherent finiteness of any computer-generated picture: It has finite resolution and finite size, and it must be made in a finite amount of time. Thus, the pictures we make can only be approximations to the creatures being studied, and the observer of such a picture uses it just as a hint of what the underlying object really looks like.

9.2 FRACTALS AND SELF-SIMILARITY

It seems that nobody is indifferent to fractals. In fact, many view their first encounter with fractal geometry as a totally new experience from the viewpoint of aesthetics as well as science. Benoit Mandelbrot, The Beauty of Fractals.

We want methods that allow us to "approach infinity"—more precisely, the infinitesimal—in an organized way. The methods will feature recursion, which modern computer languages manage very effectively. Recursion often makes a difficult geometric task extremely simple. Among other things, it lets one decompose or refine shapes into ever smaller ones, conceptually *ad infinitum*. Recursive algorithms can give rise to shapes that are both lovely and intriguing, or that have useful applications in science and engineering.

Many of the curves and pictures we describe here have a particularly important property: they are **self-similar**. Intuitively, this means that they appear "the same" at every scale: No matter how much one enlarges a picture of the curve, it has the same level of detail. Some curves are **exactly self-similar**, whereby if a region is enlarged, the enlargement looks exactly like the original (except for a possible rotation and shift). Other curves are only **statistically self-similar**, such that the wiggles and irregularities in the curve are the same "on the average," no matter how many times the picture is enlarged.

Nature provides examples that mimic statistical self-similarity. The classic example is a coastline. Seen from a satellite, it has a certain level of ruggedness, caused by bays, inlets, and peninsulas. As one flies in for a closer look, more details emerge. A bay takes on a certain ruggedness of its own that was not visible before. Zooming further, one finds that individual boulders and undulations in a beach give a similar roughness to the view. When one zooms in still further, smaller rocks and pebbles seem to produce about the same level of ruggedness. The process continues as one looks at individual grains of sand, as through a microscope. Other natural phenomena appear self-similar, as well, such as the branches of a tree, the surface of a sponge, cracks in a pavement, and blood vessel systems in animals. Clouds are also roughly self-similar, and provide an interesting example: While flying in an airplane, one encounters difficulty in judging how large a cloud is. Is it small and close by, or large and distant?

During the 1970s, Benoit Mandelbrot of Yale University (then at the IBM Research Center) brought together and popularized investigations into the nature of self-similarity (e.g., [Mandelbrot83]). He called various forms of self-similar curves **fractals**.[1] A line is one dimensional and a plane is two dimensional, but there are "creatures" in between. For instance, we shall define curves that are infinite in length, yet lie inside a finite rectangle: Their dimension lies somewhere between 1 and 2.

The work of Mandelbrot and others has spawned an enormous amount of investigation into both the mathematical and computer-graphics nature of fractallike objects, and the excitement continues in many centers around the world.

9.2.1 Successive Refinement of Curves

Very complex curves can be fashioned recursively by repeatedly "refining" a simple curve. The simplest example perhaps is the **Koch** curve, discovered in 1904 by the Swedish mathematician Helge von Koch. This curve stirred great interest in the mathematical world because it produces an infinitely long line within a region of finite area [Gardner78].

Successive generations of the Koch curve are denoted $K_0, K_1, K_2, \ldots$ here. The zeroth-generation shape K_0 is just a horizontal line of length unity. The curve K_1 is shown in Figure 9.1. To create K_1, divide the line K_0 into three equal parts, and replace the middle section with a triangular "bump" having sides of length $1/3$. The total length of the line is evidently $4/3$. The second-order curve K_2, also shown, is formed by building a bump on each of the four line segments of K_1.

FIGURE 9.1 Two generations of the Koch curve.

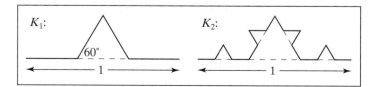

---

[1] Mandelbrot coined this term from the Latin *fractus*, meaning "fragmented" or "irregular," but it also suggests "fractional dimensional."

To form K_{n+1} from K_n;

Subdivide each segment of K_n into three equal parts, and replace the middle part with a bump in the shape of an equilateral triangle.

In this process, each segment is increased in length by a factor of 4/3, so the total length of the curve is 4/3 larger than that of the previous generation. Thus, K_i has total length $(4/3)^i$, which increases as i increases. As i tends to infinity, the length of the curve becomes infinite.

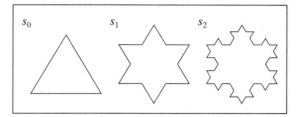

FIGURE 9.2 The first few generations of the Koch snowflake.

The Koch snowflake of Figure 9.2 is formed out of three Koch curves joined together. The perimeter of the ith-generation shape S_i is three times the length of a simple Koch curve and so is $3(4/3)^i$, which, of course, grows forever as i increases. But the area inside the Koch snowflake grows quite slowly, and in fact, in the limit (see the exercises on page 477), the area of S_∞ is only 8/5 the area of S_0 ! So the edge of the Koch snowflake gets rougher and rougher and longer and longer, but the area remains bounded. Figure 9.3 shows the third, fourth, and fifth-generation Koch snowflakes.

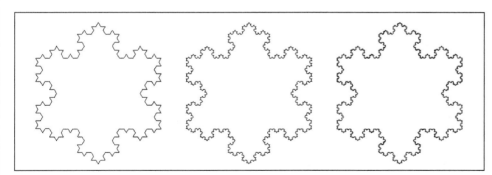

FIGURE 9.3 Koch snowflake, s_3, s_4, and s_5.

The Koch curve K_n is self-similar in the following sense: Place a small window about some portion of K_n, and observe its ragged shape. Now choose a window a billion times smaller, and observe its shape blown up to visibility. If n is very large, the curve still appears to have the same shape and roughness. Indeed, the portion could be enlarged another billion times, and still the shape would be the same. Only the limiting case K_∞ is truly self-similar, but the effect of self-similarity can be approximated in a computer graphics setting: Just make n so large that, even at the biggest blowup to be used, the smallest line segments are shorter than the spacing between pixels.

9.2.2 Drawing Koch Curves and Snowflakes

We can view Koch curves another way: Each generation consists of four versions of the previous generation. For instance, K_2 shown in Figure 9.1 consists of four versions of K_1, tied end to end with certain angles between. We call n the **order** of the curve K_n, and we say the order-n Koch curve consists of four versions of the order-$(n - 1)$ Koch curve. It is natural here to think in terms of turtle graphics (recall Chapter 3): To draw K_2, we draw a smaller version of K_1, then turn left 60°, draw K_1 again, turn right 120°, draw K_1 a third time, etc. For the snowflake, this routine is performed just three times, with a 120° turn in between.

So we have a natural recursive method for drawing any order Koch curve, shown in pseudocode as follows:

```
To draw Kₙ:
    if (n equals 0)  Draw a straight line;
    else{
        Draw Kₙ₋₁;
        Turn left 60°;

        Draw Kₙ₋₁;
        Turn right 120°;
        Draw Kₙ₋₁;
        Turn left 60°;
        Draw Kₙ₋₁;
    }
```

The routine `drawKoch()` in Figure 9.4 draws K_n on the basis of a "parent" line of length *len* that extends from the current position in the direction *dir*. We can think of *Koch()* as a way of **refining** the parent line into a Koch curve, and we invent the verb "Koch" to describe the procedure. To keep track of the direction of each "child" generation, the parameter *dir* is passed to subsequent calls to *Koch()*.

FIGURE 9.4 Drawing a Koch curve.

```
void drawKoch(double dir, double len, int n)
{ // "Koch" to order n the line of length len
       // from CP in the direction dir

    double dirRad = 0.0174533 * dir; // in radians
    if(n == 0)
        lineRel(len * cos(dirRad), len * sin(dirRad));
    else{
        n--;        // reduce the order
        len /= 3;       // and the length
        drawKoch(dir, len, n);
        dir += 60;
        drawKoch(dir, len, n);
        dir -= 120;
        drawKoch(dir, len, n);
        dir += 60;
        drawKoch(dir, len, n);
    }
}
```

PRACTICE EXERCISES

9.2.1 "Koching" an arbitrary line

Define the steps needed to draw a Koch curve of order n between the points A and B.

9.2.2 The length of a Koch curve

Show that when a line of length L is "Koched" to order n, the length of each smallest line segment is $(L/3)^n$, and the length of the total Koch curve is $(4L/3)^n$.

9.2.3 The area of the Koch snowflake

Consider the family of Koch snowflakes, S_k, introduced in Figure 9.2.

a. Show by simple geometry that the area of S_0 is $a_0 = L^2\sqrt{3}/4$, where L is the length of one side of S_0. Adding "bumps" always increases the area.
b. Show that each of the bumps added to make S_1 has area $a_0/9$, so the area of S_1 is
$a_1 = a_0(1 + 1/3)$.
c. Now show that for each subsequent generation, there are four times as many bumps, and each bump has one-ninth the area of those in the previous generation.
d. Write the area of S_k as a geometric series, and find the limit as k goes to ∞. ■

9.2.3 Fractional Dimension

In the limit, the Koch curve has infinite length, yet occupies a finite region in the plane. What is its dimension? It seems to be more complicated than that of a line (one dimension), yet it still has a topological dimension of one.

The mathematician Felix Hausdorff (1868–1942) built up the notion of fractional dimensions on the basis of considerations of simple self-similar objects such as lines, squares, and cubes. For instance, suppose we subdivide a straight line of length 1 into N equal segments. Each segment is clearly only $r = 1/N$ times as long as the original line. So far, so good. Now we do the same for a square: Divide it into N identical squares, and note that the side of each small square is smaller by the ratio $r = 1/N^{1/2}$. Finally, we perform the procedure on a three-dimensional object such as a cube. We divide it into N congruent pieces and find that the side of each subcube is smaller by the ratio $r = 1/N^{1/3}$. A pattern is taking shape here: The dimension of the object appears in the exponent of N. So we say that an object has dimension D if, when it is subdivided into N equal parts, each part must be made smaller on each side by $r = 1/N^{1/D}$. Taking logarithms (using any base) on both sides of this equation simplifies it to (check this)

$$D = \frac{\log(N)}{\log\left(\dfrac{1}{r}\right)}. \tag{9.1}$$

What, then, is the fractional dimension of the Koch curve? As we proceed from one generation to the next, $N = 4$ segments are created from each parent segment, but their lengths are $r = 1/3$ as long, so

$$D = \log(4)/\log(3) = 1.26.$$

The dimension of the Koch curve is indeed between 1 and 2. If curve A has a larger value of D than curve B does, curve A is fundamentally more "wiggly" than B; that is, it is less "linelike" and more "plane filling." A fractal curve can in fact "fill the plane" and therefore have a dimension of 2, as we shall see later. Such curves are called **Peano curves**.[2]

There are many other ways in which each generation of a curve can be refined to create the next generation. Figure 9.5 shows three examples: the quadratic Koch curve, the "dragon," and the Gosper curve, named for David Gosper, an American mathematician born in 1943. For the quadratic Koch curve, the segments are refined at each generation to eight segments that are one fourth as long as the original segment, so $D = \log(8)/\log(4) = 1.5$. (The dashed line shows the previous generation superposed with the new generation.) For the dragon curve, each line is replaced by two lines $1/\sqrt{2}$ long, so $D = \log(2)/\log(\sqrt{2}) = 2$. For the Gosper curve, each line

---

[2] Named after Giuseppe Peano (1858–1932), Italian logician and mathematician.

FIGURE 9.5 Other examples of refining lines.

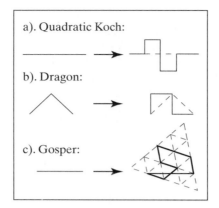

segment AB is replaced by seven segments $1/\sqrt{7}$ as long, so again, $D = 2$. Specific techniques to draw these curves are discussed next.

9.3 STRING PRODUCTION AND PEANO CURVES

There is no excellent beauty that hath not some strangeness in the proportion. Francis Bacon

A large number of interesting curves can be generated by refining line segments. A particularly simple approach to generating these curves uses so called **L-Systems** to draw complex curves based on a simple set of rules [Smith84, Prusinkiewicz80].

We saw in Chapter 3 how a turtle can be "driven" by a string of characters. It "reads" the string and interprets each character as a command to perform some operation. We give the turtle the following repertoire:

'F' means `forward(1, 1)`   (go forward visibly a distance 1 in the current direction).

'+' means `turn(A)`   (turn right through angle A degrees).

'-' means `turn(-A)`   (turn left through angle A degrees).

If given the string "F-F++F-F", for example, with angle A equal to 60°, the turtle would draw the first-generation Koch curve K_1 shown in Figure 9.1.

How do we turn a simple string like "F-F++F-F" into a longer one that will generate a richer curve? The process is based on a set of **string-production** rules, which we embed in a routine `produceString()`, to be defined. The rule for the Koch curve is simply

'F' → "F-F++F-F"

where "→" means that each "F" is replaced by "F-F++F-F" as it is encountered. There is no rule given for either '+' or '-', so these are just passed along unchanged. Figure 9.6(a) shows two stages of the string-production process. In the first stage, an initial string called the **atom**, in this case "F", "produces" the first-generation string, $S_1 = $ "F-F++F-F". S_1 then is input into the same process, and it produces the second generation string,

$S_2 = $ F-F++F-F-F-F++F-F++F-F++F-F-F-F++F-F

which is seen to be four clusters of "F-F++F-F" separated by '-', then '++', and finally,'-'. If the turtle now interprets this string, it draws the second-generation Koch curve K_2!

One way to draw one of these curves is to have each call to `produceString()` read a string from an input file and ultimately write the "produced" string to an output file. The output file of each `produceString()` becomes the input file to the next stage. (The files quickly become very long.) The first file holds just the atom. When the desired number of calls to `produceString()` has been made, the turtle reads the final file and responds to each command. In pseudocode, this approach would be implemented in two routines:

For each stage of `produceString()`:

```
for(each character ch in the input file)
    if(ch == '+' || ch == '-') write it to the output file;
    else if(ch == 'F') write "F-F++F-F" to the output file;
```

and the turtle then performs

```
for(each character ch in the input file)
    if(ch== '+') turn(A);
    else if(ch == '-') turn(-A);
    else if(ch == 'F') forward(1,1);
```

Note that this process is yet another example of an *iterated function system* (IFS; recall Chapter 2), wherein each string is repeatedly fed back into the same function to produce the next higher order object. (What is the production rule for the quadratic Koch curve of Figure 9.5(a)?) Figure 9.6(b) shows the equivalent IFS. A recursive version of `produceString()` is developed later, after we enrich the routine with more capabilities.

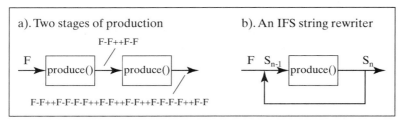

a). Two stages of production

F-F++F-F

F → produce() → produce() →

F-F++F-F-F-F++F-F++F-F++F-F-F-F++F-F

b). An IFS string rewriter

F S_{n-1} → produce() → S_n

FIGURE 9.6 (a) String production applied twice to the atom "F". (b) The IFS machine.

Extending the Language

A richer set of curves can be generated by adding more rules to the string-production process. We can use other characters, such as 'X' and 'Y', and give them rules as well. For instance, consider the set of rules that generates "**dragon curves**":

```
'F' -> 'F'
'X' -> "X+YF+"        ← "dragon" rules
'Y' -> "-FX-Y"
atom = "FX"
```

Here, 'F' just reproduces itself, whereas 'X' produces a five-character string containing a mix of 'F', 'X', 'Y' and '+'.

Using the atom "FX", we find that the order-1 string is "FX+YF+" and the order-2 string is

S_2 = FX+YF++-FX-YF+

(What is the order-3 string? What would it be if the atom were 'F' instead?)

We also must specify how the turtle interprets the new characters for purposes of drawing. The rule is that any 'X' and 'Y' characters are ignored, whereas 'F', '+', and '-' are interpreted as before.

As regards the dragon rules, the turtle draws the 1st-order dragon by ignoring the 'X' and 'Y' in "FX+YF+" and just responds to "F+F+", so the curve consists of two line segments forming an "elbow" with angle A. (An angle of 90° is most often used.) For the 2nd-order dragon, the turtle responds to "F+F++-F-F+", or equivalently, "F+F+F-F+", which is two elbows with a switch in direction: "F+F" then "F-F". Figure 9.7(a) shows the 3rd-order dragon, with a second-order dragon superimposed with dashed lines. Figure 9.7(b) shows a 12th-order dragon.

FIGURE 9.7 Dragons of order 3 and 12.

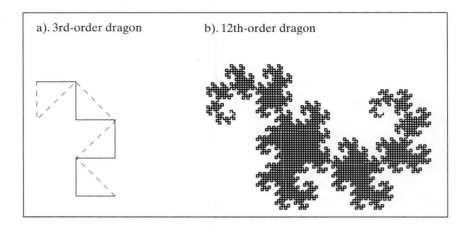

a). 3rd-order dragon   b). 12th-order dragon

9.3.1 Producing Strings Recursively and Drawing in a Program

Mathematics is the only infinite human activity. It is conceivable that humanity could eventually learn everything in physics and biology. But humanity certainly won't ever to able to find out everything about mathematics, because the subject is infinite. Numbers themselves are infinite. Paul Erdös.

Instead of filing the successive strings generated by produceString(), we can reorganize the routine to operate recursively, such that it generates strings on the fly and drives the turtle directly.

To do this, we store, in a variable called order, the number of times to apply the rule to the string; for example, S_2 is the order-2 string based on the atom 'F'.

The function produceString() shown in Figure 9.8 scans an input string character by character. If the character is '+' or '-', the turtle turns accordingly. If it is 'F', 'X', or 'Y', produceString() calls itself with the corresponding string, but at the next lower value of order. If order is 0, the function interprets 'F' as a turtle command and draws a line in the current direction. The function uses the

FIGURE 9.8 The string-production routine.

```
void produceString(char *st,int order)
{
   for(;st; st++)  // scan through each character
     switch(*st)
      {
         case '+': CD -= angle; break; // right turn
         case '-': CD += angle; break;  // left turn
         case 'F': if(order > 0)
             produceString(Fstr, order - 1);
             else forward(length, 1); break;
         case 'X': if(order > 0)
             produceString(Xstr, order - 1); break;
         case 'Y': if(order > 0)
             produceString(Ystr, order - 1);
      }
}
```

globally available strings Fstr, Xstr, and Ystr, as well as the variables angle and length.

Note that the turtle uses a fixed step size of length here. Because higher order curves involve more steps than lower order curves, their pictures will be larger. Before doing any drawing, we want to set up a window of the proper size and position to surround the desired curve, but it is very difficult to predict analytically what region a given curve will occupy. Case Study 9.1 at the end of the chapter describes a method that solves this problem: The turtle first "walks invisibly" over the curve in a preprocessing step, building a window as it goes.

■ **EXAMPLE 9.3.1 Curves based on string production.**

Data for seven classes of curves are given in Figure 9.9. The five key ingredients for each curve are given in the order (atom, F-string, X-string, Y-string, angle in degrees); "nil" indicates an empty string. Examples of four of these curves are shown in Figure 9.10.

FIGURE 9.9 Data for several string production curves.

```
Koch curve:
(F, F-F++F-F, nil, nil, 60)
Quadratic Koch Island:
(F+F+F+F, F+F-F-FF+F+F-F, nil, nil, 90)
Hilbert curve: 3
(X, F, -YF+XFX+FY-,  +XF-YFY-FX+, 90)
Dragon curve:
(X, F, X+YF+, -FX-Y, 90)
Gosper hexagonal curve:
( XF, F,  X+YF++YF-FX--FXFX-YF+,  -FX+YFYF++YF+FX--FX-Y, 60)
Sierpinski gasket:
(FXF--FF--FF, FF, --FXF++FXF++FXF--, nil, 60)
Sierpinski arrowhead:
(YF, F, YF+XF+Y, XF-YF-X, 60)
```

Some of the curves shown in Figure 9.10 are in fact **space-filling**, or **Peano, curves.** As mentioned earlier, such curves have a fractal dimension of 2, and they completely fill a region of space. The two most famous are the Hilbert[3] and Sierpinski curves. (A more recent discovery is the Mandelbrot "snowflake," discussed in the Case Study 9.2.) Some low-order Hilbert curves are shown in Figure 9.11.

Hilbert proved that as the order tends toward infinity, the infinitely thin, continuous line of the Hilbert curve passes through every point in the unit square! In addition to the string production method described here there are several different methods for drawing Hilbert curves. (See [Wirth76 and Griffith83].)

---

[3] This curve is named after the great mathematician David Hilbert (1862–1943).

FIGURE 9.10 Examples of curves generated using string production rules.

a). Fifth-order Gosper curve:

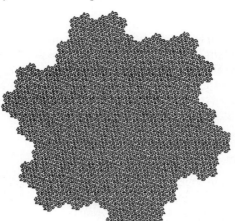

b). Third-order quadratic Koch island:

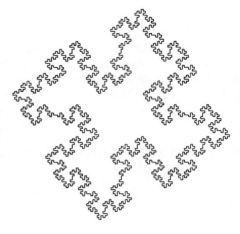

c). Sixth-order Hilbert curve:

d). Seventh-order Sierpinski arrowhead:

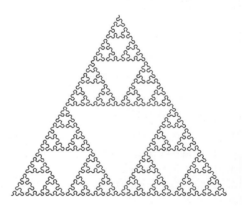

FIGURE 9.11 First few generations of the Hilbert curve.

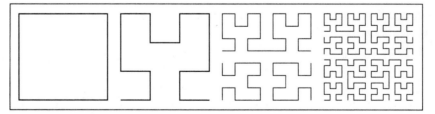

PRACTICE EXERCISES

9.3.1 How large is a dragon?

Consider a dragon curve of order n based on the line segment from $(0,0)$ to $(1,0)$. The dragon lies in a rectangular bounding box, which grows as the order increases. What are the coordinates of the corners of this rectangle as n increases to infinity? What is the length of this order-n dragon curve?

9.3.2 A dragon is a folded strip of paper

It is interesting to note that a dragon curve is produced by successively folding a thin strip of paper. Lay the strip flat, and then fold one end over to meet the other end. Repeat this process indefinitely, always folding over in the same direction. (Only about seven folds are possible in practice.) When the paper is unfolded so that all angles are 90°, a dragon curve emerges. Show that this process does indeed produce dragon curves for orders 1 through 4.

9.3.3 What curves are these?

Two additional curves are defined by the rules that follow. The first is a variation on a closed Sierpinski curve, and the second is the original Peano curve [Wagon91]. Sketch the first three generations of each curve.

a. Sierpinski-bis: (F+XF+F+XF,F, XF-F+F-XF+F+XF-F+F-X, nil, 90);
b. Original Peano (space filling): (X, F, XFYFX+F+YFXFY-F-XFYFX,
   YFXFY-F-XFYFX+F+YFXFY, 90)

9.3.4 Find the strings (Polya's Peano curve.)

What string-production rule or rules govern the generation of Polya's space-filling curve shown in Figure 9.12? The curve associated with the previous generation is shown with dashed lines in each case. Each segment of one generation is replaced by a right-angled elbow, but the directions of the elbows alternate in a L, RL, LRLR,...fashion. (That is, if we were to move along the segments of one generation, we would see the segments of the next generation lying to the left, then to the right, then to the left, etc., of the current segments.) ■

FIGURE 9.12 Polya's space-filling curve.

9.3.2 Allowing Branching

We add a final capability to the string-production rules that allows the turtle to "pick up where it left off" at some earlier point in a drawing. This capability permits the turtle to draw branchlike figures, like the branches of a tree, wherein several shapes emanate from the same point. The tools to do this are simple: We need a character that commands the turtle to "save its current state" for later use and a character that causes the turtle to return to that state.

Accordingly, we add the characters '[' and ']' to the language, with the following meanings:

    '[': saveTurtle()   ← store the current state of the turtle.
    ']': restoreTurtle()   ← set the turtle's state to a previously stored value.

What is the "state" of a turtle, anyway? A turtle has a position and points in some direction, so its state simply consists of the values of the current position (CP) and current direction (CD):

State of the turtle = {CP, CD}

A convenient method for storing recent turtle states is on a stack, so we maintain a **turtle stack**, which might look like

    (1.3, 5.22), 45 ← top of turtle stack
    (0.7, −2.7), 30
    (6.0, 4.3), 180

This code means that the most recent state pushed onto the stack was the current position (1.3, 5.22) and current direction 45°, and the state saved before that involved a CP = (0.7, −2.7) and a CD = 30°. The result of encountering a '[' in a string is to "push" the current turtle state onto the stack, to save it for later use. The result of encountering a ']' is to "pop" the top value off of the stack and set the turtle state to the

FIGURE 9.13 A fourth-order "bush."

FIGURE 9.14 First two orders of a bush.

value "popped." We need only add two lines to the `switch` statement of `produceString()` shown in Figure 9.8:

```
'[': saveTurtle();  break;       ← push the current turtle state
'[': restoreTurtle(); break;     ← pop the turtle state from the stack
```

(The exercises at the end of the section suggest ways to implement this stack in program code.)

■ **EXAMPLE 9.3.2 Fractal trees**

So-called fractal trees provide an interesting family of shapes that resemble actual trees, as suggested in Figure 9.13. Such shrubbery can be used to ornament various drawings, and they form excellent objects of study in themselves. These "bushes" have several "branches" that shoot out from various places, and often each branch is like a scaled-down version of the whole tree. (If this self-similarity is carried to arbitrary depths, the figure becomes a fractal.)

The bush in Figure 9.14 is based on the atom 'F', an angle of 22°, and the F-string,

```
F →   "FF-[-F+F+F]+[+F-F-F]"
```

Here, a "branch" 'F' is replaced at each level of recursion by three things, as suggested in Figure 9.14(a)

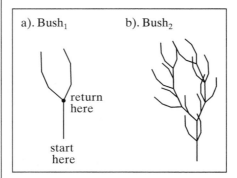

- a long straight line "FF", the branch's "trunk";
- a left branch consisting of three short lines; and
- a right branch consisting of three short lines.

The turtle returns to the point labeled "return here" each of the two times it encounters the ']' command. It has a slightly different current direction the second time. (Why?) This point is also the starting point for the next generation, since each 'F' is replaced by the string shown, which ends in ']'. It is very illuminating to check that the second-order bush of Figure 9.14(b) does in fact arise from producing the F-string at each occurrence of 'F' in the previous string.

PRACTICE EXERCISES

9.3.5 Other bushes

Analyze what the following rules [PrusinKiewicz80] produce, and incorporate the rules into a routine that draws what they produce:

a. (X, F → FF, X → F[+X]F[-X]+X, 20°) (a bush).
b. (X, F → FF, X → F-[[X]+X]+F[+FX]-X, 22.5°) (another bush).

c. $(X, F \rightarrow F, X \rightarrow [-F+F[Y]+F][+F-F[X]-F], Y \rightarrow [-F+F[Y]+F][+F-F-F], 60°)$ (hexagonal tiling).

d. $(X+X+X+X+X+X+X+X+X+X+X+X+X+X+X+X+X+X+X+X+X+X+X+X, F \rightarrow F,$
   $X \rightarrow [F+F+F+F[--X-Y]+++++F+++++++++F-F-F-F],$
   $Y \rightarrow [F+F+F+F[- -Y]+++++F+++++++++F-F-F-F], 15°)$
   (aperiodic tiling)

9.3.6 Implementing turtle stacks

a. Implement a turtle stack as a linked list of nodes of type `tTurtleStack`, where each node contains two fields, one of type `tTurtle` (containing a CP and a CD), and the other a pointer to type `tTurtleStack`.

b. Write a routine called `SaveTurtle()`, that allocates new memory for a node, loads the current turtle state into this memory, and pushes the node on top of the stack.

c. Write a function `RestoreTurtle()` that pops the top node from the stack, uses the data retrieved to update the current turtle state, and then disposes of the node's memory.

d. Test your routines developed in Parts (a)–(c) in a program that draws each of the objects discussed in this section that involve branching.

9.3.7 Adding randomness and tapering

Branching objects such as bushes can look more natural if they are made less regular. A slight amount of randomness can be incorporated into the string-production rules (e.g., by adding a small random offset to each angle turned when '+' or '-' is encountered in a string.) Further, if lines can be given thickness, it is often pleasing to display "tapering" of the branches to ever thinner widths. Figure 9.15 shows some pleasing examples based on these improvements. Experiment with various types of randomness in `produceString()`, and find some combinations of parameters that give the best results. ▪

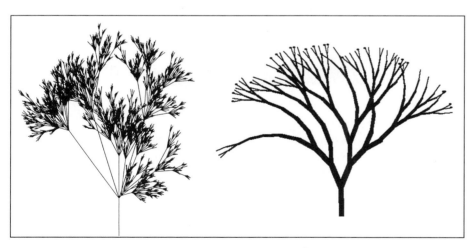

FIGURE 9.15 Adding randomness and tapering to trees. [Courtesy of Bill McQuaid and Adam Lavine.]

9.4 TILING THE PLANE[4]

Many of the brightly colored tile-covered walls and floors of the Alhambra in Spain show us that the Moors were masters in the art of filling a plane with similar interlocking figures, bordering each other without gaps. What a pity that their religion forbade them to make images! M. C. Escher

Another way to move towards infinity is to repeat a shape again and again, ultimately covering the entire plane with different versions of it. We examined some ways to

---

[4] This section may be omitted on a first reading without loss of continuity.

arrange such infinite ripetitions in Chapter 3 through wallpaper patterns that repeat forever in two directions. With wallpaper patterns, no restriction is placed on the nature of the figure that is repeated; any "motif" at all can be repeated. In this section, we examine an interesting special case of wallpaper patterns: the periodic **tilings** (or **tesselations**) of the plane with a simple figure. The notion is to take many copies of some shape, such as a polygon, and to "fit" them together like a jigsaw puzzle so that they cover the entire plane with no gaps.

The artist M. C. Escher created many intriguing tesselations, two of which are shown in Figure 9.16. A figure of a single horseman is used in the first example. The repeated horsemen form perfectly interlocking rows, and these rows also interlock with reversed horsemen in adjacent rows. Two figures are used in the fish-and-bird tesselation, but again the whole plane is perfectly tiled. The foreground and background of these figures keep reversing as the eye is drawn from one detail to the next.

FIGURE 9.16 Two tesselations by M. C. Escher. (1988, M. C. Escher Heirs/Cordon Art-Baarn-Holland)

There is an extensive theory of tesselations which is well covered in the encyclopedic work of Grunbaum and Shephard [Grunbaum89], although many questions remain unanswered. We look here at the basic ideas, focusing on tilings whose regions consist of polygons.

9.4.1 Monohedral Tilings

First we shall examine **monohedral** tilings—those based on a single polygon. The polygon in question is called the **prototile** of the tesselation. If we insist further that the polygon be regular, there are only the three possible **regular tilings** shown in Figure 9.17. Only a triangle, a square, and a hexagon can tile the plane.

FIGURE 9.17 The three possible tilings with *n*-gons.

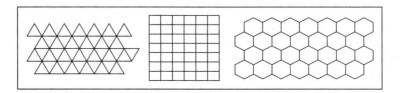

Note that the equilateral triangles must have alternating orientations in order to fit together. Note also that the triangular tiling can be made to overlay the hexagonal tiling perfectly, since groups of six triangles form a hexagon.

Hexagonal tesselations appear in beehives and in crystallography (see, for example, [Coxeter69], and the game Hex, invented by Piet Hein, is played on a portion of a hexagonal tiling [Berlchamp82].

All three tesselations are conveniently named according to their **Schläfli symbol**, $\{p, q\}$, which specifies that each is a tesselation of p-gons, q of which surround each vertex. Thus, the three tilings in Figure 9.17 are given $\{3, 6\}$, $\{4, 4\}$, and $\{6, 3\}$.

Some simple variations of these tilings are possible: Rows of squares can be shifted horizontally in the square tesselation to form layers of "bricks" or other patterns, and bands of triangles can be shifted in one of three directions (which ones?) in the triangle tesselation. But to keep things simple, we consider here only **edge-to-edge** tilings: those for which two tiles touch only along an entire common edge, at a common vertex, or not at all. The edge-to-edge restriction removes all variations, leaving only the three patterns in Figure 9.17.

If we allow prototiles that are not regular, the possibilities increase dramatically. Any parallelogram certainly tiles the plane. (Why?) (Keep in mind that the statement "object X tiles the plane" means that copies of X, and only X, can be laid down in such a fashion as to completely cover the infinite plane with no gaps.) And further, each of the following polygons tiles the plane:

a. Any triangle.
b. Any hexagon with a point of symmetry.
c. Any quadrilateral.

Let us demonstrate these statements one at a time:

a. To show that any triangle tiles the plane, just rotate it about the midpoint of one of its sides to form a parallelogram, which tiles the plane.
b. If a hexagon has a point of symmetry (i.e., if the hexagon is unchanged by a half-turn about its center), then its opposite sides are parallel and equal in length. As shown in Figure 9.18(a), such hexagons always "fit together" without a gap just by an appropriate translation.
c. Finally, one can build a hexagon with a point of symmetry out of *any* quadrilateral, just by rotating the quadrilateral about a midpoint of one of its sides, as shown in Figure 9.18(b). Since such a hexagon tiles the plane, so does any quadrilateral!

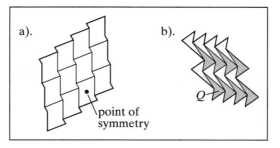

FIGURE 9.18 Any hexagon tiles the plane.

A 5-gon can't tile the plane, but an equilateral pentagon can, as shown in Figure 9.19. The pentagon in Figure 9.19(a) has equal sides, but does not have equal interior angles. Four such pentagons fit together to form a hexagon, which tiles the plane. This is called a **Cairo tiling**, because many streets in Cairo, Egypt, are paved in that pattern.

FIGURE 9.19 The Cairo tiling.

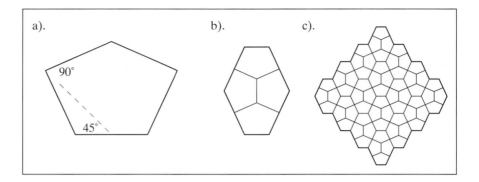

Some other polygons that may or may not tile the plane are shown in Figure 9.20. Those in Figure 9.20(a) are some of Solomon Golomb's [Golomb65] famous **polyominoes**, formed by connecting unit squares edge to edge. Polyominoes generalize the domino, which is just two squares connected edge to edge. **Polyiamonds** are formed by connecting congruent equilateral triangles together [Gardner88]; some examples are shown in Figure 9.20(b). The exercises on page 490 ask that you determine which of these polygons tile the plane?

FIGURE 9.20 Polyominoes and polyiamonds.

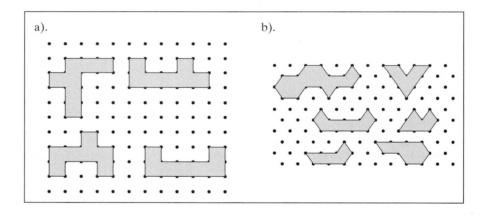

Deforming a Prototile

A variety of interesting tilings can be generated by deforming the n-gon prototiles of Figure 9.17. For example, an edge of the square prototile can be converted into a zigzag as long as the opposite edge is similarly deformed, as shown in Figure 9.21. The example of Pegasus shown in Figure 9.22 was formed in this way, as suggested by McGregor and Watt [McGregor86]. Does Escher's horseman in Figure 9.16 fit this model?

9.4.2 Dihedral Tilings

Dihedral tilings permit the use of two prototiles and therefore offer many more possibilities. For example, the hexagonal network shown in Figure 9.23 is based on two prototiles. (Which ones?) It also is a variation of the $\{6, 3\}$ tiling of Figure 9.17: we simply draw each hexagon of the tesselation in the same position, but reduced in size, and connect adjacent hexagons with links. This arrangement has been studied in such diverse fields as computer networks, cellular communication systems for mobile radios, and the design of memory architectures. In computer networking, for example,

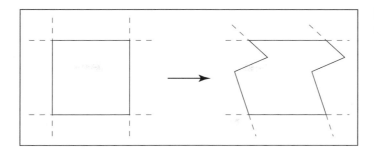

FIGURE 9.21 Deforming an edge into a zigzag.

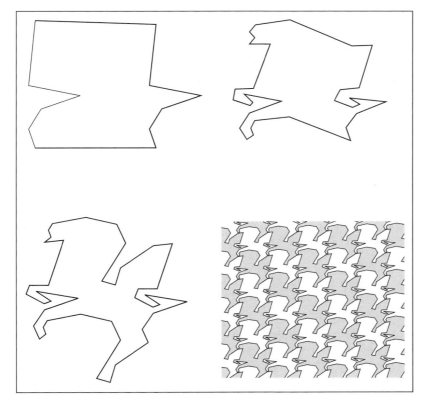

FIGURE 9.22 Creating the Pegasus tesselation.

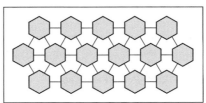

FIGURE 9.23 A hexagonal network.

the hexagons represent processors, and the lines represent links over which the processors share data.

The most famous dihedral tilings are the **semiregular**, or **Archimedean**, tilings, of which there are eight [McGregor86], [Steinhaus69]. As shown in Figure 9.24, each tiling is based on two *n*-gons and has the property that every vertex has the same **type**: It is surrounded by the same sequence of *n*-gons in the same order. In the first example presented, for instance, each vertex is surrounded by a triangle, and then a hexagon, then a triangle, then a hexagon, which we write in shorthand as 3.6.3.6, an extension

FIGURE 9.24 The Archimedean tilings.

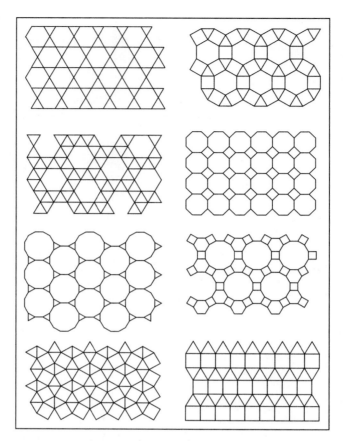

of the Schläfli symbol used earlier, where {6, 3} means 6.6.6 (i.e., three hexagons surround each vertex). It turns out [Martin82] that stating the sequence of *n*-gons about each vertex is sufficient to specify the nature of the tiling, as long as we consider only edge-to-edge tilings. In this notation the Archimedean tilings are as follows:

3.6.3.6	4.6.4.3	3.3.3.3.6	4.8.8
3.12.12	4.6.12	3.3.4.3.4	3.3.3.4.4

(Which symbol belongs to which tiling?)

PRACTICE EXERCISES

9.4.1 Which ones tile the plane?

Which polyominoes and which polyiamonds in Figure 9.20 tile the plane?

9.4.2 Do these tile the plane?

Which of the polygons in Figure 9.25 tile the plane?

FIGURE 9.25 Two polygons.

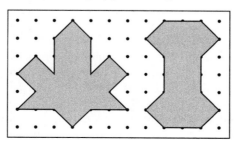

9.4.3 The Cairo tile

What are the interior angles of the pentagon in the Cairo tile? What are the relative lengths of the sides of the hexagons involved?

9.4.4 Constraints on deformations

In deforming a square, as shown in Figure 9.21, the 90° angles of each corner may be altered into new angles. What relationship must be maintained among the angles of the four corners?

9.4.5 Which group is it?

Find the symmetry group of each of the Archimedean tilings. ◼

9.4.3 Drawing Tilings

It is usually straightforward to draw periodic tilings in a graphics program: Simply set up a large window, and then draw the prototile again and again, displacing each copy by the proper amount in x and y and clipping each figure to the window. (See Figure 3.14.) For some tilings, it is simplest to first group several prototiles together into a single figure and then draw the group again and again. For example, four copies of the Cairo tile in Figure 9.19 would be combined to form a hexagon, which would be drawn repetitively.

There are also many interesting **nonperiodic tilings**, which are not as easily drawn. We examine one class of nonperidoic tilings next, drawn by going from the very large to the very small, drawing a large number of small figures inside a single large figure. Other kinds of nonperiodic tilings, such as Penrose tilings, are examined in Case Study 9.7.

9.4.4 Reptiles

Reptiles are a class of nonperiodic tilings that are most easily described recursively. Different replicas of a reptile fit together to form a large reptile of the same shape. Thus, a large tile can be defined recursively in terms of smaller versions of itself.

A **k-rep** tile is any polygon P that can be dissected into k congruent parts, each of which is similar to P [McGregor 86]. (We also say that such a polygon is "k-rep.") Figure 9.26 shows five simple examples. The **triomino** is a 4-rep polyomino and the sphinx is a polyiamond. The sphinx is the only known 4-rep pentagon.

Reptiles are "self-replicating" in two opposite directions: toward the infinitely large and toward the infinitely small. We can paste together four sphinxes to get a larger

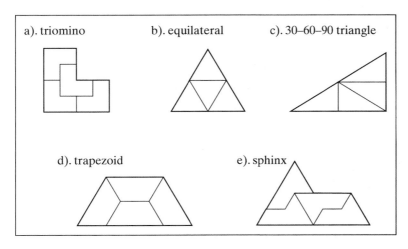

a). triomino   b). equilateral   c). 30–60–90 triangle

d). trapezoid   e). sphinx

FIGURE 9.26 Examples of reptiles.

sphinx and repeat this forever to obtain an arbitrarily large sphinx. Similarly, we can draw small sphinxes inside each sphinx and repeat in an infinite regression to ever smaller sphinxes. (Check these statements out for each of the five examples shown.)

Note that *every* triangle is a 4-rep reptile: Just join the midpoints of the three sides. This shows that any *n*-gon is also a reptile, since it can always be decomposed into *n* triangles. Also, for any given k, there exists a k-rep tile: A parallelogram with sides in the ratio 1 to $\sqrt{k}$ does the trick. (What does it look like?) It turns out that such a parallelogram is the only known 7-rep tile.

Drawing Reptiles

It is convenient to think in terms of "generations" of reptiles: A k-rep tile can be thought of as the "parent" of k "children," and each reptile has one parent. To draw a reptile, we simply draw its children, a process that is naturally recursive. We can stop the recursion either by testing its depth—the number of generations that have been spawned—or by stopping when the size of the children becomes "small enough."

Figure 9.27 shows the routine `doTrio()` for drawing the triomino in Figure 9.26. If `depth` is 1 the outer boundary of the triomino is drawn. If `depth > 1`, the routine calls itself four times, to draw the four half-sized children of the next lower order.

FIGURE 9.27 Skeleton for drawing triominos.

```
void doTrio(double size, int depth)
{
    int i;
    if(depth == 1) drawTrio();
    else for(i = 0; i < 4; i++) // draw four children
    {
        set up for the i-th child;
        doTrio(size / 2, depth - 1);     // draw child
    }
}
```

The actual drawing in `doTrio()`, as well as the processing in `set up for the ith child`, can be carried out in several ways. For some shapes, turtle graphics is most convenient; we shall examine these next. For other shapes, it is simpler to alter the coordinate system by manipulating the current transformation, as in Case Study 9.2.

Figure 9.28 shows a triomino with its four children labeled for convenience. (The tree embellishment simply helps to orient the eye.) The turtle approach is illustrated in the figure: The "shell" of the triomino is drawn by a series of `forward()` and `turn()` instructions, starting at the lower right corner, as suggested by the shaded turtle icon. If, instead, the children must be drawn, `set up for the ith child` first moves the turtle invisibly to one of the four starting points and then turns it to the proper direction. You are requested to implement this routine in the exercises that follow.

Figure 9.29 shows examples of the triomino generated by the code of Figure 9.27. For the case of `depth = 6`, the window was chosen to lie totally within the object, so the window appears tessellated.

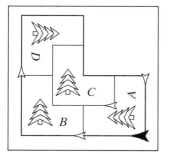

FIGURE 9.28 Drawing the triomino.

PRACTICE EXERCISES

9.4.6 Finding reptiles

As a good way to become familiar with reptiles, prove each of the following assertions (adapted from Clason90):

a. Every square, rectangle, and parallelogram is a 4-rep tile.
b. A rectangle (or a parallelogram) with base twice its height is a 4-rep tile in four ways.
c. A rectangle (or a parallelogram) with sides proportional to unity and $\sqrt{k}$ is a k-rep tile.

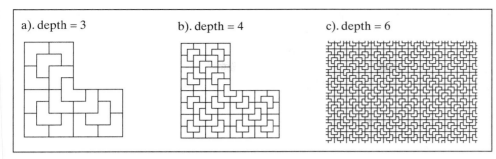

FIGURE 9.29 Examples of the triomino.

d. There are two different trapezoids, each with two right angles, that are 4-rep tiles. (*Hint*: Each has angles 90, 90, 60, 120).
e. A 30–60–90 triangle is a 3-rep tile.
f. A right triangle, the lengths of whose legs are in the ratio 1:2, is a 5-rep tile.

9.4.7 The Sierpinski gasket as a reptile

Figure 9.30 shows the Sierpinski gasket, a reptile based on the equilateral triangle. A large triangle is drawn by drawing three smaller inner ones, leaving a hole congruent to them. (Is this tile therefore 3-rep or 4-rep?) Using the preceding ideas, show how the triangle is drawn.

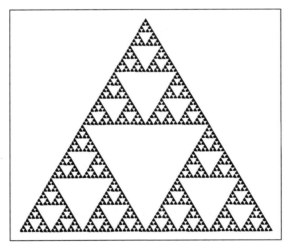

FIGURE 9.30 A Sierpinski gasket reptile (of depth 5).

9.4.8 Embellishments of reptiles

Interesting variations are possible by altering what is actually drawn at the lowest level (i.e., by altering how the deepest child is drawn). For the triomino, this is the triomino hexagon itself; for Sierpinski's gasket, it is the triangle shown in Figure 9.31(a). The figure shows two variations on what is drawn, suggested by Clason [Clason90]. The motif in Part (b) produces the intriguing mesh shown in Figure 9.32, suggesting overlapping strips. Here, all four children triangle motifs are drawn inside each parent, and in addition, the children are rotated different amounts to construct the overall pattern. Explain in detail how the children must be rotated. ■

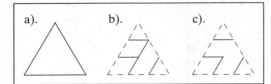

FIGURE 9.31 Variations on the basic shape.

FIGURE 9.32 Reptile mesh based on a variation.

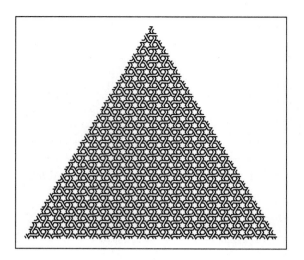

9.5 CREATING AN IMAGE BY MEANS OF ITERATED FUNCTION SYSTEMS

Another way to approach infinity is to apply a transformation to a picture again and again and examine what results. We shall see that this technique provides another fascinating way to create fractal shapes. The idea has also been developed by Barnsley [Barnsley93] into a way of compressing images to an extraordinary degree, so that an entire image can be represented by a handful of numbers.

9.5.1 An Experimental Copier

In this section, the IFSs first described in Chapter 2 are again brought into play. We take an initial image I_0, and put it through a special "photocopier" that produces a new image I_1, as suggested in Figure 9.33(a).[5] I_1 is not just a simple copy of I_0; rather, it is a superposition of several reduced versions of I_0, as we shall see. We then take I_1 and feed it back into the copier again, to produce image I_2. We repeat this process forever, obtaining a sequence of images $I_0, I_1, I_2, \ldots$, called the **orbit of I_0**. (Recall the same in Chapter 2.) We ask whether these images "converge" to some image and, if so, which one.

FIGURE 9.33 Making new "copies" from old.

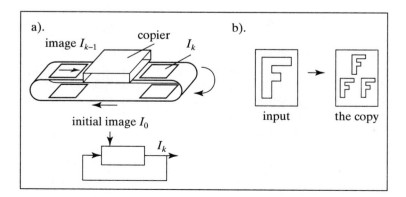

---

[5]   This description is based on the 1990 article by Jurgens, Peitgen, and Saupe. [Jurgens90]

■ EXAMPLE 9.5.1 The "Sierpinski copier"

Consider a specific example of a copier that we might call the supercopier, "S-copier." It superimposes three smaller versions of whatever image is fed into it. Figure 9.33(b) shows what one pass through S-copier produces when the input is the letter F. These three smaller images could just as well overlap, although they don't in this example. Figure 9.34 shows the first few "iterates" that the S-copier produces. The figure suggests that the iterates converge to the Sierpinski triangle seen earlier, and indeed, they do! At each iteration the individual component Fs become one-half as large, and they triple in number. As more and more iterations are made, the Fs approach dots in size, and these dots are arranged on the Sierpinski triangle. The "final" image doesn't depend on the shape of the F at all, but only on the nature of the supercopier.

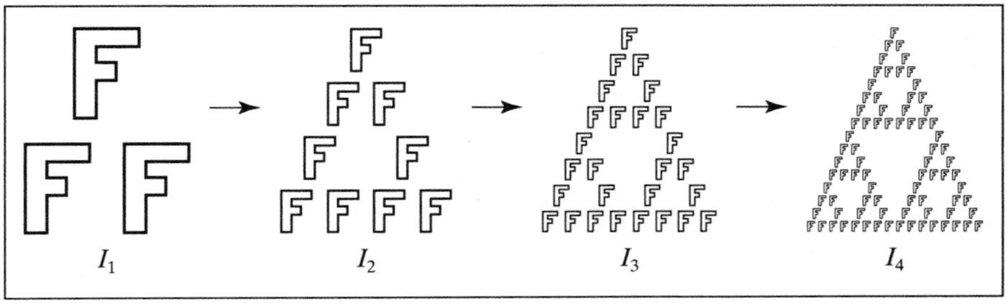

FIGURE 9.34 The first part of the orbit of I_0 for the S-copier.

How might the S-copier make its images? Think of it as containing three lenses, each of which reduces the input image to one-half its size and moves it to a new position. These three reduced and shifted images are superposed on the printed output. Scaling and shifting are easily done by an affine transformation. Each lens therefore performs its own affine transformation (or, more briefly, "affine map") $T_1(P)$, $T_2(P)$, or $T_3(P)$ on every point P of the input image, and the output of the S-copier is the superposition of all these transformed points.

Suppose map T_i uses matrix M_i. This particular machine uses the matrices:

$$M_1 = \begin{pmatrix} \frac{1}{2} & 0 & 0 \\ 0 & \frac{1}{2} & 0 \\ 0 & 0 & 1 \end{pmatrix}$$

$$M_2 = \begin{pmatrix} \frac{1}{2} & 0 & 0 \\ 0 & \frac{1}{2} & \frac{1}{2} \\ 0 & 0 & 1 \end{pmatrix}$$

$$M_3 = \begin{pmatrix} \frac{1}{2} & 0 & \frac{1}{4} \\ 0 & \frac{1}{2} & \frac{1}{2} \\ 0 & 0 & 1 \end{pmatrix}$$

so each performs a scaling by 0.5 and a certain translation. (Sketch the output image when the input is the triangle with vertices $(-1, 0)$, $(1\ 0)$, and $(0, 2)$.)

It will be convenient to list the ingredients of an affine map in the form of a six-tuple: (recall Equation 5.4):

$$T = \{m_{11}, m_{12}, m_{21}, m_{22}, m_{13}, m_{23}\} \tag{9.2}$$

The first four terms contain the elements that perform scaling and rotation; the final two terms perform translation. Thus the three maps of the S-copier are:

$$T_1 = \{0.5, 0, 0, 0.5, 0, 0\}$$
$$T_2 = \{0.5, 0, 0, 0.5, 0.5, 0\}, \tag{9.3}$$
$$T_3 = \{0.5, 0, 0, 0.5, 0.25, 0.25\}.$$

In general, the copier will have N lenses, each of which performs an affine mapping and then adds its image to the output. Following Barnsley [Barnsley93], the collection of the N affine transformations is called an "iterated function system" (IFS):

> **DEFINITION:** An **iterated function system** is a collection of N affine transformations T_i, for $i = 1, 2, \ldots, N$.

Note that this definition represents a restriction on our previous use of the term "IFS," in which *any* function could be employed to perform the iteration, not just an affine transformation or a collection of such transformation.

9.5.2 Some Underlying Theory of the Copying Process

In order to describe how an image is formed by the S-copier, we introduce a few terms. Each lens in the copier builds an image by transforming every point in the input image and drawing it on the output image. A black-and-white image I can be described simply as the set of its black points:

I = set of all black points = $\{(x, y)$ such that (x, y) is colored black$\}$

Suppose I is the image input to the copier. Then the i-th lens, characterized by transformation T_i, builds a new set of points we denote as $T_i(I)$ and adds them to the image being produced at the current iteration. Each added set $T_i(I)$ is the set of all transformed points I:

$T_i(I) = \{(x', y')$ such that $(x', y') = T_i(P)$ for some point P in $I\}$.

Upon superposing the three transformed images, we obtain the output image as the union of the outputs from the three lenses:

$$\text{output image} = T_1(I) \cup T_2(I) \cup T_3(I). \tag{9.4}$$

We define the overall mapping from input image to output image (for one pass through the copier) as $W(.)$. It maps one set of points—one image—into another and is given by

$$W(.) = T_1(.) \cup T_2(.) \cup T_3(.). \tag{9.5}$$

So, for instance, the "copy" of the first image I_0 is the set $W(I_0)$.

Now, what happens when we iteratively cycle copies back through the copier an infinite number of times? That is, to what image does the orbit of images $I_0, I_1, I_2, \ldots$ converge? Barnsley shows that under mild conditions on the IFS—roughly speaking, that each affine map "reduces" the size of its image at least slightly[6]—the orbit does indeed converge to a unique image called the **attractor** of the IFS.[7] (The attractor of the sample IFS of Example 9.5.1 is the Sierpinski gasket.) We denote the attractor by the set A, some of whose important properties are the following:

1. The attractor set A is a **fixed point** of the mapping $W(.)$, which we write as $W(A) = A$. That is, putting A through the copier again produces exactly the same image A. Roughly speaking, the iterates have already converged to the set A, so iterating once more makes no difference.

2. Starting with *any* input image B, and iterating the copying process enough times, we find that the orbit of images *always* converges to the same A. Thus, if

---

[6] More precisely, each affine transformation must be a **contraction mapping**. This is guaranteed if the matrix of each T_i has a determinant whose size is less than unity.

[7] Often called a "strange attractor" when it is a very complex image.

$I_k = W^{[k]}(B)$ is the k-th iterate of image B, then as k goes to infinity, I_k becomes indistinguishable from the attractor A. What is remarkable is that the choice of initial image B makes no difference [Barnsley93].

9.5.3 Drawing the kth Iterate

We can use graphics to display each of the iterates along the orbit. The initial image I_0 can be any set, but two choices are particularly suited to the tools we have already developed:

- I_0 is a polyline (like the letter F of Figure 9.34). Then successive iterates are collections of polylines.
- I_0 is a single point. Then successive iterates are collections of points.

Using a polyline for I_0 has the advantage that you can see how each polyline is reduced in size in each successive iterate. But more memory and time are required to draw each polyline, and we know that ultimately each polyline is so reduced as to be indistinguishable from a point.

Using a single point for I_0 causes each iterate to be a set of points, so it is straightforward to store these in a list. Then, if the IFS consists of N affine maps, the first iterate I_1 consists of N points, image I_2 consists of N^2 points, I_3 contains N^3 points, etc.

■ **EXAMPLE 9.5.2 The fern**

Figure 9.35 shows an example based on the well-known fern IFS.
   The fern uses four affine maps, given in the following equations [Barnsley93]:

$$T_1 = \{0, 0, 0, .16, 0, 0\};$$
$$T_2 = \{.2, .23, -.26, .22, 0, 1.6\}; \qquad (9.6)$$
$$T_3 = \{-.15, .26, .28, .24, 0, .44\};$$
$$T_4 = \{.85, -.04, .04, .85, 0, 1.6\}.$$

Note in this example that the first matrix scales by zero in the x-direction, forming a vertical stem for the fern. The last matrix performs a small rotation and then reduces its image only slightly (by about 85%), so iterates of it get smaller very slowly. For high enough values of k, the kth iterate drawn will be close to the attractor A of the IFS.

What routine actually draws (an approximation to) the attractor? We give a recursive version in Figure 9.36. This routine takes a list of points `pts` and does the following:

FIGURE 9.35 The Fern.

FIGURE 9.36 Mimicking the copier operation (pseudocode).

```
void superCopier(RealPolyArray pts, int k)
{// Draw k-th iterate of input point list pts for the IFS
  int i;
  RealPolyArray newpts;               // reserve space for new list
  if(k == 0) drawPoints(pts);
  else for(i = 1; i <= N; i++)        // apply each affine
  {
     newpts.num = N * pts.num;        // the list size grows fast
     for(j = 0; j < newpts.num; j++)  // transform the j-th pt
        transform(affines[i], pts.pt[j], newpts.pt[j]);
     superCopier(newpts, k - 1);
  }
}
```

- If k = 0 it draws the points in the list.
- if k > 0 it applies each of the affine maps T_i, in turn, to all of the points, creating a new list of points, newpts, and then calls superCopier(newpts, k-1).

To implement the algorithm, we suppose that the affine maps are stored in the global array Affine affines[N].

This method works, but it has some shortcomings. One is inefficiency: There are *many* recursive calls, each with some computational overhead. More troubling, however, is the huge amount of memory required: The kth iterate must draw N^k points, and each call to superCopier() allocates memory for a new list of points. All of the currently active recursive calls need to keep a whole list of points. (Typically, they store them on the system stack!) Fortunately, there is a nonrecursive way known as the "Chaos Game" to draw the attractor for an IFS.

9.5.4 The Chaos Game

Perhaps an angel of the Lord surveyed an endless sea of chaos, then troubled it gently with his finger. In this tiny and temporary swirl of equations, our cosmos took shape.

Martin Gardner

The "Chaos Game" (also known as the "Random Iteration Algorithm") offers a simple nonrecursive way to produce a picture of the attractor of an IFS [Barnsley 99, Barnsley93]. We have already seen an example of this in Chapter 2 (see Case Study 2.2) in drawing the Sierpinski gasket. Figure 9.37 summarizes, in pseudocode, how we did it there.

FIGURE 9.37 Review of the process for drawing the Sierpinski gasket (pseudocode).

```
Set corners of triangle: p[0]=(0,0),p[1]=(1,0),p[2]=(.5,1)
Set P to one of these, chosen randomly ;
do{
    Draw a dot at P ;
    Choose one of the 3 points at random ;
    Set newPt to the midpoint of P and the chosen point ;
    Set P = newPt ;
}while(!bored);
```

A point called P is transformed to the midpoint of itself and one of the three fixed points: $p[0]$, $p[1]$, or $p[2]$ (chosen at random). The new point is then drawn as a dot, and the process repeats (forever). The picture slowly fills in as the sequence of dots is drawn.

The key is that forming a midpoint based on P is in fact applying an affine transformation. That is,

$$P = \tfrac{1}{2}(P + p[..])   \text{(find the midpoint of } P \text{ and } p[..])$$

can be written as

$$P = P\begin{pmatrix} \tfrac{1}{2} & 0 \\ 0 & \tfrac{1}{2} \end{pmatrix} + \tfrac{1}{2}p[..],$$

so that P is subjected to the affine map, and then the transformed version is written back into P. The offset for this map depends on which point $p[i]$ is chosen.

Figure 9.38 shows the process schematically. One of three affine maps is chosen at random each time, and the previous point P is subjected to it. The new point is drawn and becomes the next point to be transformed.

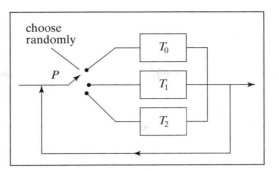

FIGURE 9.38 Drawing the Sierpinski gasket.

For the Sierpinski gasket, the three maps are given by [see also Equation 9.3)]

$$T_1 = \{0.5, 0, 0, 0.5, 0.5 \; p[0].x, 0.5 \; p[0].y\}, \mathrm{pr}_1 = 0.33;$$
$$T_2 = \{0.5, 0, 0, 0.5, 0.5 \; p[1].x, 0.5 \; p[1].y\}, \mathrm{pr}_2 = 0.33; \qquad (9.7)$$
$$T_3 = \{0.5, 0, 0, 0.5, 0.5 \; p[2].x, 0.5 \; p[2].y\}, \mathrm{pr}_3 = 0.33.$$

Also listed with each map is the probability pr_i that that map is chosen at each iteration; here, the three maps are equally likely.

Starting with a point P_0, the sequence of iterations through this system produces a sequence of points $P_0, P_1, \ldots$, which we might call the **orbit** of the system with starting point P_0. This is a random orbit, however: Different points are visited, depending on the random choices made at each iteration. The question is, What does the set of dots look like?

Remarkably, this system draws the same picture that the supercopier in Figure 9.34 produces! That is, given a sufficiently large number of iterations, the orbit will cover the entire attractor of the IFS of Equation (9.3). The idea behind this approach is that the attractor consists of all points that are "reachable" by applying a long sequence of affine maps in the IFS to one of the points in the starting image. And the Chaos Game lays down points that are in fact the result of a long sequence of affines in the IFS. The randomness is invoked to ensure that the system is "fully exercised": that every combination of affine maps is used somewhere in the process.

We can generalize to any IFS and say that the Chaos Game will produce the same picture as the supercopier.[8] This is true for any starting point and any reasonable set of probabilities, although the attractor will fill in more quickly with certain choices of probabilities. For example, the fern of Figure 9.35 was produced using the Chaos Game and the transformations of Equation (9.6). The probabilities used were

$$\mathrm{pr}_1 = 0.01, \mathrm{pr}_2 = 0.07, \mathrm{pr}_3 = 0.07, \text{ and } \mathrm{pr}_4 = 0.85. \quad \{\text{probabilities for the fern}\}. \quad (9.8)$$

Figure 9.39 shows an outline of the function chaosGame() that plays the Chaos Game. The function draws the attractor of the IFS whose N transforms are stored in the array aff[]. The probabilities to be used are stored in an array pr[]. At each iteration, one of the N affine maps is chosen randomly by the function chooseAffine() and is used to transform the previous point into the next point. The details of chooseAffine() are discussed in Case Study 9.3, which outlines a project to draw a number of interesting attractors.

---

[8] This result is known as *Elton's ergodic theorem*. Its proof requires some rather subtle mathematics and is presented in [Barnsley93].

FIGURE 9.39 Pseudocode for playing the Chaos Game

```
void chaosGame(Affine aff[], double pr[], int N)
{
  RealPoint P = {0.0,0.0};  // set some initial point
  int index;
  do{
      index = chooseAffine(pr, N); // choose the next affine
        P = transform(aff[index], P);
          drawRealDot(P); // draw the dot
  } while(!bored);
}
```

Figure 9.40 shows some additional examples. Figure 9.40(a) shows the attractor of the dragon IFS:

$T_1 = \{.824074, .281482, -.212346, .864198, -1.882290, -0.110607\}, \mathrm{pr}_1 = .787473;$
$T_2 = \{.088272, .520988, -.463889, -.377778, 0.785360, 8.095795\}, \mathrm{pr}_2 = .212527.$

Figure 9.40(b) shows the attractor of the spiral IFS:

$T_1 = \{.787879, -.424242, .242424, .859848, 1.758647, 1.408065\}, \mathrm{pr}_1 = .895652;$
$T_2 = \{-.121212, .257576, .151515, .053030, -6.721654, 1.377236\}, \mathrm{pr}_2 = .052174;$
$T_3 = \{.181818, -.136364, .090909, .181818, 6.086107, 1.568035\}, \mathrm{pr}_3 = .052174$

These and many other examples may be found as part of the superb FRACTINT program available on the Internet [Fractint96].

FIGURE 9.40 Further examples of attractors. (a) The dragon. (b) The spiral.

a) dragon

b) spiral

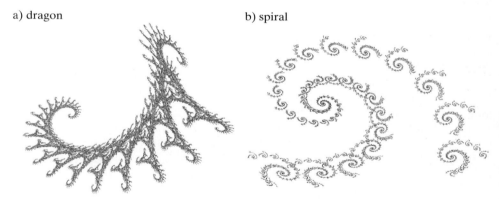

Adding Color

So far, the pictures formed playing the Chaos Game are bilevel: black dots on a white background. It is easy to extend the method so that it draws gray-scale and color images of objects. The image, as always, is viewed as a collection of pixels, and at each iteration the transformed point lands in one of the pixels. A counter is kept for each pixel, and at the completion of the game, the number of times each pixel has been visited is converted into a color according to some appropriate mapping. This extension is discussed in Case Study 9.3.

PRACTICE EXERCISE

9.5.1 Using FRACTINT

Download a copy of the freeware FRACTINT program from the Internet, and explore the program's capabilities. In particular, execute the various examples under IFS. Also, explore the newsgroup alt.fractals on the Internet.   ■

9.5.5 Finding the IFS; Fractal Image Compression

The Chaos Game makes it easy to generate an image, given an IFS. But can we go the other way: Given an image, can we assert that it is the attractor for some IFS? And if so, can we find the IFS and therefore generate the image using a method like the Chaos Game?

The promise of dramatic levels of image compression provides strong motivation for finding an IFS whose attractor is the given image. A typical image may contain a million bytes of data, but it takes only hundreds or thousands of bytes to store the co-efficients of the affine maps in the IFS. Figure 9.41 illustrates the process of **fractal image compression**. The original image is processed to create the list of affine maps, resulting in a greatly compressed representation of the image.

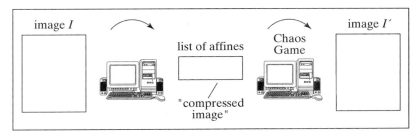

FIGURE 9.41 Fractal Image Compression and regeneration.

In the "decompression" phase, the list of affine maps is used, and an algorithm such as the Chaos Game reconstructs the image. Notice that this compression scheme is **lossy**: The image I' that is generated by the game during "decompression" is not a perfect replica of the original image I.

Finding the List of Affine Maps

The real trick is to find the list of affine maps in a reasonable amount of computer time. Given an image I (think of it as the set of all dots in the image), we want to find an IFS (i.e., a set of affine maps $T_1(.), T_2(.), \ldots, T_N(.)$) such that I is the attractor of the IFS. One way to proceed is to choose some affine maps that "seem right," use the Chaos Game to generate the attractor, and then compare I with the attractor to see if it's "close enough." If it isn't, we adjust the IFS and try again. This approach, how-ever, is doomed to failure: The "search space" of possible IFSs is much too big for the technique to be practical.

For a more promising approach, recall that the attractor of an IFS is the fixed point of the transformation

$$W(.) = T_1(.) \cup T_2(.) \cup \ldots \cup T_N(.). \tag{9.9}$$

Each IFS has an associated function $W(.)$, and applying $W(.)$ to an image I is the same as passing I once through the special copying machine described earlier. So we seek an IFS such that the given I is the fixed point of $W(.)$. That is, we must have

$$I = W(I) \qquad (I \text{ is a fixed point}). \tag{9.10}$$

Barnsley developed the **collage theorem**, which states that if $W(I)$ is "close to" I, then the attractor of the IFS is also "close to"[9] I. So we do not have to work with the attractor directly. Instead, we search over a family of IFSs, looking for one whose $W(.)$, when applied to our given I, produces an image close to I itself. That is, we seek to express I as a "collage" (union) of reduced, rotated, and shifted versions of itself.

---

[9] Some complicated mathematics is contained in this theorem, as Barnsley is using a certain notion of "dis-tance" between two sets to measure how much one image is like another.

(The whole is made up of its parts; the parts are reduced replicas of the whole.) For the Sierpinski gasket, the underlying IFS can be seen immediately; for most images, it is not even clear whether there *exists* an underlying IFS.

The search space is still much too big for a fully automated approach. Early algorithms depended on human intervention to guide the search. To get started, the user tries to partition I into segments, each of which looks like a reduced (and perhaps rotated and reflected) copy of the whole image. The transformation that carries the whole into a given segment is added to the list of affine transformations. With an initial set of transformations selected, the user observes I and $W(I)$, and adjusts the coefficients of the affine maps with the use of some input device, to make $W(I)$ closer to I. Although finding the IFS this way required very fast computers and was still rather slow, the company Iterated Systems, Inc. (`http://www.iterated.com/`), was successfully launched by Barnsley to provide fractal image compression. Initially, Barnsley was able to compress by a factor of between 10 and 100. Then a breakthrough was made by Barnsley's student Jacquin, who developed the partitioned iterated function system (PIFS). This system finally made it possible to completely automate the compression process in a reasonable amount of computer time. Figure 9.42 shows how a particular version of the system works. The original image I is partitioned into a number of nonoverlapping four-by-four pixel ranges $R_0, R_1, \ldots$. For each such range R_i, a search is made for some eight-by-eight pixel domain D_i in the image itself that, when suitably transformed, matches R_i. The chosen domains may overlap. Each mapping involves a scaling by one-half in both directions (since the domain is eight by eight, and the range is four by four) and a translation that positions the domain on the range. A mapping might also involve a rotation and a reflection.

FIGURE 9.42 Finding the affine maps in a PIFS.

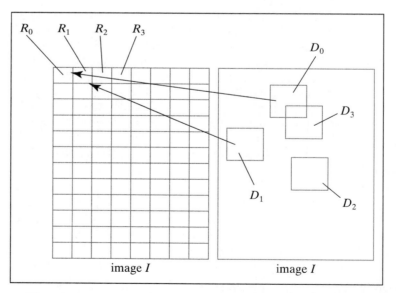

The pixel pattern in a mapped domain might resemble the pixel pattern in the range reasonably well, except for being too bright or too dark. So the search algorithm also looks for the best linear mapping from domain pixel levels to range pixels levels.[10] This effectively makes the affine maps 3D instead of 2D:

---

[10] For color images, this process is done three times independently, once each for the red, green, and blue components.

$$\begin{pmatrix} x' \\ y' \\ b' \\ 1 \end{pmatrix} = \begin{pmatrix} m_{11} & m_{12} & 0 & d_x \\ m_{21} & m_{22} & 0 & d_y \\ 0 & 0 & g & h \\ 0 & 0 & 0 & 1 \end{pmatrix} \begin{pmatrix} x \\ y \\ b \\ 1 \end{pmatrix} \qquad (9.11)$$

Here, (x, y) is mapped into (x', y') in the usual way, and the brightness b is mapped into the brightness b' by using the coefficients g and h. (g must be chosen to be less than unity to ensure that the mapping is contractive.) The encoded image thus consists of a list of 3D affine maps, along with information on the domain of each map, such as the location of its upper left-hand corner.

Now, in the reconstruction phase, we no longer play the pure Chaos Game. Instead, we start with an arbitrary image I_0, perhaps all black pixels. Then, at each iteration, each one of the maps is applied to all of the pixels *in its domain*. Because the ranges do not overlap, each such mapping alters the pixel values in one block of ranges. Because the mapping is contractive, the sequence $I_0, I_1, \ldots$ is guaranteed to converge to the fixed point of the mapping—in practice, usually in 8 to 10 iterations.

A fine discussion of this method, along with C code to implement it, may be found in Mark Nelson's *Data Compression*. [Nelson96]. Figure 9.43 shows an original image (requiring 64,000 bytes) with two domains and two ranges (here larger than four by four or eight by eight) marked. There is a strong similarity between one range and one domain and a strong similarity between the other range and domain. (Which ones?) Fractal compression reduces the space needed to 2,849 bytes!)

FIGURE 9.43 A gray-scale image with two domains and two ranges marked. (Courtesy of Jean-Loup Gailly.)

Figure 9.44 shows the image of Figure 9.43 filling in during the decoding phase. Beginning with an all-black image for I_0, the figure successively exhibits the images I_1, I_2, I_3, and I_8. Even I_1 is highly recognizable, and I_8 is very close to the attractor.

One aspect of fractal image compression is **resolution independence**. Basically, this means that you can zoom in on the reconstructed image and see more detail. Suppose the original image is 256 by 256 pixels in size. Normally, you would reconstruct it from the affine maps by starting with I_0 as an all-black image of 256 by 256. But if you start with I_0 as a 1,024-by-1,024 image and run through the iterations, the reconstructed image is much larger. Four times as much detail will appear in the reconstruction, avoiding any "blockiness" that would normally be seen from zooming in too far into an image. Of course, there is no additional information in this image: The extra detail is just "self-similarity" detail added to the image. It makes the image look more natural, but keep in mind that the added detail is artificial.

FIGURE 9.44 Reconstructing the image from its affine maps. (Courtesy of Jean-Loup Gailly.)

9.6 THE MANDELBROT SET

Where the world ceases to be the stage for personal hopes and desires, where we, as free beings, behold it in wonder, to question and to contemplate, there we enter the realm of art and of science. If we trace out what we behold and experience through the language of logic, we are doing science; if we show it in forms whose interrelationships are not accessible to our conscious thought but are intuitively recognized as meaningful, we are doing art. Common to both is the devotion to something beyond the personal, removed from the arbitrary.

Albert Einstein

In principle … [the Mandelbrot Set] could have been discovered as soon as men learned to count. But even if they never grew tired, and never made a mistake, all the human beings who have ever existed would not have sufficed to do the elementary arithmetic required to produce a Mandelbrot Set of quite modest magnification.

Arthur F. Clarke, The Ghost from the Grand Banks

Graphics provides a powerful tool for studying a fascinating collection of sets that are thought by some to be the most complicated objects seen in mathematics. Julia sets and the Mandelbrot set are based on a few surprisingly simple definitions, yet are astonishingly rich in their structure and, when displayed with the help of computer graphics, can yield awe-inspiring pictures of great beauty. Julia sets are studied in Section 9.7.

Julia and Mandelbrot sets arise from a branch of analysis known as iteration theory (also, dynamical systems theory), which asks what happens when one iterates a function endlessly. Many of the key results of iteration theory were developed early in the 20th century (without the assistance of computers, of course) by Gaston Julia (1893–1978) and Pierre Fatou (1878–1929). Their ideas lay fallow for a long time, until they were revived and extended by Benoit Mandelbrot in the 1970s. As part of his research, Mandelbrot used computer graphics to perform essential experiments, which stimulated conjectures along very fruitful lines, leading to further analysis and discoveries.

Several excellent accounts of the story behind these discoveries are available (e.g., in [Mandelbrot83, Peitgen86, and Peitgen88]), along with beautiful images generated by techniques we describe in the rest of the chapter.

9.6.1 Mandelbrot Sets and Iterated Function Systems

We begin by discussing aspects relevant to both Mandelbrot and Julia sets. There is one Mandelbrot set and an infinity of Julia sets, and they are intimately related. A view of the **Mandelbrot set** is shown in Figure 9.45. It is the black inner portion, which ap-

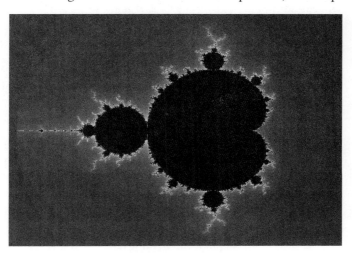

FIGURE 9.45 The Mandelbrot set.

pears to consist of a cardioid along with a number of wartlike circles glued to it. In actuality, its border is astoundingly complicated, and this complexity can be explored by zooming in on a portion of the border and computing a close-up view. In theory, the zooming can be repeated forever—the border is "infinitely complex." (In fact, it is a fractal curve!) Each point in the figure is shaded or colored according to the outcome of an experiment run on an IFS. The IFS of interest is shown in Figure 9.46. It uses the particularly simple function

$$f(z) = z^2 + c, \tag{9.12}$$

where c is some constant. That is, the system produces each "output" by squaring its "input" and adding c. We assume that the process begins with the **starting value** s, so the system generates the sequence of values, or **orbit** (recall Chapter 2);

$$
\begin{aligned}
d_1 &= (s)^2 + c \\
d_2 &= \left((s)^2 + c\right)^2 + c \\
d_3 &= \left(\left((s)^2 + c\right)^2 + c\right)^2 + c \\
d_4 &= \left(\left(\left((s)^2 + c\right)^2 + c\right)^2 + c\right)^2 + c, \\
&\vdots
\end{aligned}
\tag{9.13}
$$

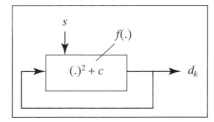

FIGURE 9.46 The Iterated function system for Julia and Mandelbrot sets.

Note that the orbit depends on two ingredients: the starting point s and the given value of c.

Orbits of s are the principal objects of interest for both Julia sets and the Mandelbrot set. The basic question is, Given the two values s and c, how do points d_k along the orbit behave as k gets larger and larger? Specifically, does the orbit remain **finite** (wherein *all* points on it are a finite distance from 0), or does it **explode** (shoot off to infinity)? As we shall define more precisely next, orbits that remain finite lie in their corresponding Julia or Mandelbrot set, whereas those that explode lie outside the set.

■ **EXAMPLE 9.6.1 Orbits with $c = 0$**

Let $c = 0$. Then the machine just squares its input value at each iteration. Check each of following assertions:

- The orbit of $s = 1$ is $1, 1, 1, 1, 1, 1, \ldots$, which is, of course, finite. (What is the orbit of $s = -1$?)
- The orbit of $s = 1/2$ is $1/2, 1/4, 1/8, 1/16, \ldots,$, which converges to the value 0.
- If $|s| < 1$, the orbit is finite; if $|s| > 1$, the orbit explodes.

■ **EXAMPLE 9.6.2 Orbits of 0 for different c values**

Now consider orbits with starting value 0:

- Let $c = -1$. Then the orbit is $0, -1, 0, -1, 0, -1, 0, -1, \ldots$, which cycles endlessly between two values. Thus, the orbit is finite.
- Let $c = 1$. Then the orbit of $s = 0$ is $0, 1, 2, 5, 26, 677, \ldots$, which explodes.
- Let $c = -1.3$. Then the orbit of $s = 0$ is $0, -1.3, \ldots$, which, after 50 steps or so, gets caught in a **periodic** sequence of the four values -1.148665, $.019430, -1.299622, .389018, \ldots$ forever.

We can try to map out these results to see what range of values for c leads to finite orbits. Figure 9.47 shows a first attempt. It is very illuminating to experiment with other c's. For instance, as we increase c from 0 what's the largest value having a finite orbit?

FIGURE 9.47 What does the orbit of 0 do for each value of c?

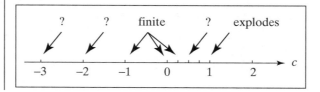

ESSENTIAL PRACTICE EXERCISES

9.6.1 What are the orbits of 0?

Compute (by hand or with a calculator) the orbits of 0 for the following values of c:

a. $c = 0.5$; b. $c = -0.8$; c. $c = -1$; d. $c = -2$; e. $c = -1.2$.

9.6.2 What are the orbits?

Let $c = -1$. Compute the orbits of s for the following values of s.

a. $s = 0$; b. $s = -1$; c. $s = 1$; d. $s = 2$.

This system already exhibits intriguing "dynamics." But things get incredibly richer when s and c are chosen to be *complex numbers* and complex arithmetic is used each time the function is applied. The Mandelbrot and Julia sets "live" in the complex plane—the plane of complex numbers. Recall that in graphics we display complex numbers using a diagram in which each complex number $z = x + yi$ is displayed at position (x, y).[11]

The system of Figure 9.46 works just as well with complex numbers as with real numbers. Both c and s are complex, and at each iteration we square the previous result and add c. Recall (see Appendix 2) that squaring a complex number $z = x + yi$ yields the new complex number

$$(x + yi)^2 = (x^2 - y^2) + (2xy)i, \qquad (9.14)$$

having real part equal to $x^2 - y^2$ and imaginary part equal to $2xy$. We continue to ask about the "finiteness" of orbits of s: whether the "size" of successive iterates on the orbit get arbitrarily large. By "size," we mean the usual magnitude: $|x + yi| = \sqrt{x^2 + y^2}$.

■ **EXAMPLE 9.6.3 What is the orbit of 0 for $c = -.2 + .5i$?**

Consider the orbit of 0 for $c = -.2 + .5i$. A hand calculator can be used to perform the iterations, but various tools available on many computers make the job a lot easier[12]. We get the following orbit:

$d_1 = -.2 + .5i,$
$d_2 = -.41 + .3i,$
$d_3 = -.1219 + .254i,$
$d_4 = -.2497 + .4381i,$
$\vdots$

After about 80 iterations, the d_k's converge to $d_k = -0.249227 + 0.333677i$. This is called a **fixed point** of the function, because squaring it and adding c yields exactly the same value. (Try it!) Of course, any orbit that converges to a fixed point remains finite. We conclude that the orbit of $-.2 + .5i$ remains finite.

Some Notes on the Fixed Points of the System

In studying the Mandelbrot and Julia sets, it is useful to examine the fixed points of the system $f(.) = (.)2 + c$. The behavior of orbits depends strongly on these fixed points—that is, those complex numbers z that map into themselves, so that $z^2 + c = z$. This gives us the quadratic equation $z^2 - z + c = 0$, and the **fixed points** of the system are the two solutions of this equation, given by

$$p_+, p_- = \frac{1}{2} \pm \sqrt{\frac{1}{4} - c}. \qquad (9.15)$$

(Note that because we are dealing with complex numbers, there is no problem with taking the square root of $(1/4) - c$, even if it is negative or complex. Appendix 2 shows how to take such square roots in a program.) In the preceding example, we

---

[11] The reader who is unfamiliar with complex arithmetic can still use computer graphics to create pictures of the Mandelbrot set. Read lightly the material that follows, and proceed to the discussion of the algorithms, which work entirely with points (x, y) having real coordinates.

[12] One such tool is Mathematica. In Mathematica's language $f[x\_] := N[x*x + c]$ defines the iterating function, $c = -.2 + .5I$ defines c, and $NestList[f, 0, 80]$ displays a list of the first 80 values on the orbit. In fact, this can all be put into the compact single command $NestList[N[\#\wedge2-.2 + .5I\&],0,80]$.

obtained the fixed point $p_- = -0.249227 + 0.333677i$. The other fixed point is $p_+ = 1.249323 - 0.333677i$. If an orbit ever reaches a fixed point p, it gets trapped there forever. The two fixed points are positioned symmetrically at the same distance (what is it?) from the point $1/2 + 0i$.

We can gain further insight by characterizing a fixed point as **attracting** or **repelling**. Roughly speaking, if an orbit "flies" close to a fixed point p, the next point along the orbit will be forced

- closer to p if p is an attracting fixed point;
- farther away from p if p is a repelling fixed point.

If an orbit gets close enough to an attracting fixed point, it is "sucked into" the point. In contrast, a repelling fixed point keeps the orbit away from it. It is not hard to show (see the next exercise) that a fixed point is attractive only if it lies within a distance of $1/2$ from the origin—that is, inside a circle of radius $1/2$ centered at the origin.

PRACTICE EXERCISES

9.6.3 On attractive fixed points

As a "hand-waving" calculation, let p be a fixed point of $f()$, and pick a $z = p + \varepsilon$ near p, where ε is a small complex number. Consider how far $f(z)$ is from p—that is, how large $|f(p + \varepsilon) - p|$ is. Expanding $f(p + \varepsilon)$ in a Taylor series results in $f(p + \varepsilon) = f(p) + f'(p)\varepsilon +$ higher order terms, so, for small ε, we have $|f(p + \varepsilon) - p| = |f'(p)||\varepsilon|$. But $|\varepsilon| = |z - p|$, so $|f(z) - p|$ is approximately $|f'(p)||z - p|$. Thus, p is attracting (i.e., $|f(z) - p|$ is smaller than $|z - p|$) if $|f'(p)| < 1$, and repelling if $|f'(p)| > 1$. For this function, $f'(z) = 2z$, so p is attracting if $|2p| < 1$. If $|f'(p)| = 1$, the fixed point is neither attracting more repelling, but is "indifferent." Orbits near indifferent points can also be rather complicated [Peitgen88]. ■

9.6.2 Defining the Mandelbrot Set

The Mandelbrot set considers different values of c, always using the starting point $s = 0$. For each value of c, the set reports on the nature of the orbit of 0, whose first few values are as follows:

orbit of 0: $\qquad 0, \quad c, \quad c^2 + c, (c^2 + c)^2 + c, ((c^2 + c)^2 + c)^2 + c, \ldots$ (9.16)

For each complex number c, either this orbit is **finite**, so that no matter how far along the orbit one goes, the values remain finite, or the orbit **explodes**—that is, the values get ever larger without limit. The Mandelbrot set, denoted M, contains just those values of c that result in finite orbits:

- The point c is in M if 0 has a finite orbit.
- The point c is not in M if the orbit of 0 explodes.

> **DEFINITION:** The **Mandelbrot set** M is the set of all complex numbers c that produce a finite orbit of 0.

(Note that for a given value of c, the orbit of 0 becomes the orbit of c after one iteration, so we get the same orbital behavior starting at either 0 or c.)

Figure 9.48 shows some sample orbits for different values of c, superimposed on a crude rendition of the Mandelbrot set to help orient the eye. Each orbit is shown as a polyline, beginning at its private value of c, which is shown as a dot. (We could have drawn each orbit beginning at 0, but that would have cluttered the picture.) Note carefully that each dot shows the relevant value of c used in the system $f(.) = (.)^2 + c$ that is being iterated, as well as the starting point for the orbit.

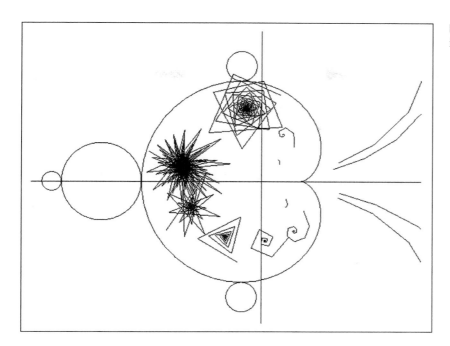

FIGURE 9.48 Examples of orbits in the *c*-plane.

If *c* is chosen *outside* of *M*, the resulting orbit explodes. Four exploding orbits are shown in the figure. If *c* is chosen just beyond the border of *M*, the orbit usually thrashes wildly around the plane and finally blasts off to infinity. Such orbits would confuse the picture beyond recognition and are not shown. Case Study 9.4 at the end of the chapter outlines a program that draws orbits for any value of *c*. This case study is an excellent test bed for developing one's intuition about iterates of $(.)^2 + c$.

If the value of *c* is chosen *inside M*, the corresponding orbit can do a variety of things. For some *c*'s, it plunges immediately to a fixed point or spirals into such a point (quite slowly if *c* is near the boundary of *M*).

To see what the orbit might do, think of each *c* as determining two fixed points according to Equation (9.15). If one of the fixed points is attracting (that is, if it lies within a radius of 1/2 of the origin), the orbit of 0 will plunge into it. Several examples are shown in Figure 9.48. (Note that the point *c* is *not* the same as the fixed point.) On the other hand, if neither fixed point is attracting, the orbit does not converge to a fixed value at all. Instead, it gets caught in a cyclic sequence of values that "orbits" about one of the repelling fixed points. For instance, orbits for *c*-values lying in the small circles at the top and bottom of *M* happen to have period 3.

PRACTICE EXERCISES

9.6.4 On fixed points

What are the fixed points for the following values of *c*, and which, if any, of the fixed points is attracting?
a. $c = 0$; b. $c = 1 + i$; c. $c = -2$; d. $c = -2 + i$.

9.6.5 When is there an attracting fixed point?

Characterize the shape of the region in the *c*-plane such that the system $(.)^2 + c$ has an attracting fixed point. Are all these values of *c* inside the Mandelbrot set?

9.6.6 Why is the Mandelbrot set symmetrical

The mirror image of $c = x + yi$ about the real axis is the **conjugate** $c^* = x - yi$ of c. How is the orbit found by using c^* related to that found by using c? (*Hint*: $(z^*)^2 = (z^2)^*$.) Use this relation to show that c^* is in M if and only if c is in M.   ■

9.6.3 Computing whether Point c is in the Mandelbrot Set

We need a routine that determines whether or not a given complex number c lies in M. With a starting point of $s = 0$, the routine must examine the size of the numbers d_k of Equation (9.13) along the orbit. As k increases, the value of $|d_k|$ either explodes (so that c is not in M) or does not explode (so c is in M). A theorem from complex analysis states that if $|d_k|$ ever exceeds the value 2, then the orbit will definitely explode at some point. The number of iterations $|d_k|$ takes to exceed 2 is called the **dwell** of the orbit (a term perhaps arising from how long the orbit "dwells" in a region.)

But if c lies in M, the orbit has an infinite dwell, and we can't know this without iterating forever. The best we can do is to set some upper limit *Num* on the maximum number of iterations we are willing to wait for. A typical value is *Num* = 100. If $|d_k|$ hasn't exceeded 2 after *Num* iterations, we assume that it never will, and we conclude that c is in M. It turns out that orbits for values of c just outside the boundary of M often have an extremely large dwell, and if their dwell exceeds *Num*, we wrongly decide that they lie inside M. (Are values of c *inside* M ever wrongly interpreted?) A drawing based on too small a value of *Num*, therefore, will show a Mandelbrot set that is slightly too large.

We encapsulate these calculations in the routine `dwell()` shown in Figure 9.49. For a given value of $c = c_x + c_y i$, the routine returns the number of iterations required for $|d_k|$ to exceed 2, or it returns *Num* if 2 has not been exceeded after *Num* iterations. For convenience, `dwell()` defines a data type for its parameter.

At each iteration, the current d_k resides in the pair (dx, dy), which is squared by using

FIGURE 9.49 Estimating the dwell.

```
int dwell(double cx, double cy)
   { // return true dwell or Num, whichever is smaller
     #define Num 100    // increase this for better pictures

     double tmp, dx = cx, dy = cy, fsq = cx * cx + cy * cy;
     for(int count = 0; count <= Num && fsq <= 4; count++)
     {
         tmp = dx;                        // save old real part
         dx = dx * dx - dy * dy + cx;   // new real part
         dy = 2.0 * tmp * dy + cy;       // new imag. part
         fsq = dx * dx + dy* dy;
     }
     return count;                       // number of iterations used
   }
};
```

Equation (9.14) and then added to (cx, cy) to form the next d-value. The value $|d_k|^2$ is kept in *fsq* and compared with 4. This comparison is equivalent to comparing $|d_k|$ with 2, yet saves having to take a square root.

The function `dwell()` plays a key role in drawing the Mandelbrot set.

9.6.4 Drawing the Mandelbrot Set

Suppose we want to display M on a raster graphics device. To do this, we set up a cor-

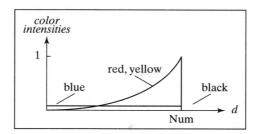

FIGURE 9.50 Assigning colors according to the orbit's dwell.

respondence between each pixel on the display and a value of c, and the dwell for that c-value is found. A color is assigned to the pixel, depending on whether the dwell is finite or has reached its limit.

The simplest pictures of the Mandelbrot set just assign black to points inside M (where the dwell has reached its maximum) and white to those outside (where the dwell is smaller than its maximum). But pictures are much more appealing to the eye if a *range* of colors is associated with points outside M. Such points all have dwells less than the maximum, and we can assign different colors to them on the basis of the dwell size. For example, you might assign a bright yellow to points just outside M, and a dimmer yellow to points farther away from M. This will make the boundary of M very distinct and dramatic. Figure 9.50 shows how color might be assigned to a point having dwell d. For very small values of d only a dim blue component is used. As d approaches *Num* the red and green components (which together form yellow) are increased up to a maximum of unity. This could be implemented in OpenGL using:

```
float v = d/(float)Num;
glColor3f(v * v, v*, v, 0.2); // red & green at level v-squared
```

The only thing remaining is to see how to associate a pixel with a specific complex

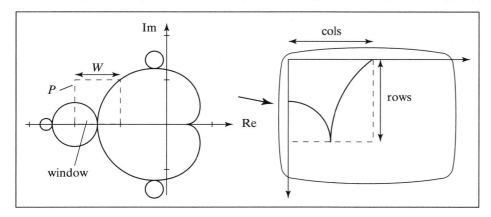

FIGURE 9.51 Establishing a window on M and a correspondence between points and pixels.

value of c. A simple approach is suggested in Figure 9.51. The user specifies how large the desired image is to be on the screen—that is,

- the number of rows, `rows`   (example: `rows=80`) and
- the number of columns, `cols`   (example: `cols=120`).

This specification determines the aspect ratio of the image: $R =$ `cols/rows`. The user also chooses a portion of the complex plane to be displayed: a rectangular region having the same aspect ratio as the image. To do this, the user simply specifies the region's upper left-hand corner P and its width W. (For example, we might have $P = -1 + .5i$, or put another way, $P = (-1, .5)$ and $W = 0.5$.) The computer does the rest. The rectangle's height is set by the required aspect ratio. We decide to display the image in the upper left corner of the display, as suggested in the figure.

Now, to what complex value $c = c_x + c_y i$ does the center of the i, jth pixel correspond? Combining the ingredients, we see that it must be

$$c_{ij} = \left(P_x + \frac{i + \frac{1}{2}}{cols} W, P_y - \frac{j + \frac{1}{2}}{cols} W \right), \tag{9.17}$$

for $i = 0, \ldots, \text{cols} - 1$ and $j = 0, \ldots, \text{rows} - 1$. (Check this out!)

The chosen region of the Mandelbrot set is drawn pixel by pixel. For each pixel, the corresponding value of c is passed to `dwell()`, and the appropriate color associated with the dwell is found. The pixel is then set to this color. Figure 9.52 gives the algorithm in pseudocode.

FIGURE 9.52 Pseudocode for drawing a region of the Mandelbrot set.

```
for(j = 0; j < rows; j++)
    for(i = 0; i < cols; i++)
    {
        find the corresponding c-value in Equation 9.17
        estimate the dwell of the orbit
        find Color determined by estimated dwell
        setPixel(j, k, Color);
    }
```

A practical problem is that, to study close-up views of the Mandelbrot set, numbers must be stored and manipulated with great precision. Double- (or higher) precision arithmetic should be employed. Also, when working close to the boundary of the set, you should use a larger value of *Num*, as discussed before. Therefore, the calculation times for each image will increase as you zoom in on a region of the boundary of M. But images of modest size can easily be created on a microcomputer in a reasonable amount of time, and the results are well worth the wait. (See Case Study 9.5.)

9.6.5 Some Notes on the Mandelbrot Set

What are the properties of the Mandelbrot set and its fiery extensions? The set has been studied by a number of mathematicians, and many fascinating facts are known about it. (See [Mandelbrot83, Peitgen86, and Peitgen88] for a wealth of ideas: these books contain many stunning pictures that were computed in the manner we have described.) The following are some of those facts:

1. The points $c = -1$ and $c = -2$ are in M (why?), and, as mentioned earlier, M is symmetrical about the real axis.
2. The largest "blobs" of the Mandelbrot set have been carefully scrutinized [Peitgen and Richter, 1986]:
   - The boundary of the center blob of M is the cardioid having the parametric representation
     $$c.x = .25 + .5(1 - \cos(t)) \cos(t); \tag{9.18}$$
     $$c.y = .5(1 - \cos(t)) \sin(t).$$

   Orbits inside this cardioid are attracted to a fixed point, given by one of the two solutions to $z^2 + c = z$. (Why?)
   - The circle to the left of the cardioid has radius $1/4$ and center at $c = -1$; Orbits inside this circle become periodic with period 2.
   - The smaller circle to the left of the circle just mentioned has radius 0.0607 and center at $c = -1.3107$. Orbits inside this circle become periodic with period 4.
   - The circles above and below the cardioid have radius 0.0954 and centers at $c = -0.1226 \pm 0.7449i$. Orbits inside this circle become periodic with period 3.

3. The boundary of the Mandelbrot set is the most interesting place to look and in fact turns out to be a fractal curve. As one zooms in ever closer on a region of interest—by using smaller and smaller windows—new details continually emerge. Plate 27 shows three successive zooms into the region centered at $c = -0.744271 + 0.14858i$. The last picture in the sequence uses the window with the lower left corner at $(-0.746778, 0.14647)$ and the top right corner at $(-0.743351, 0.149950)$. At each zoom, a new world of detail becomes visible. For example, what was a single black dot at one zoom becomes an entire new "wart" at the next zoom ("a flea hath smaller fleas that on him prey;...and so proceed ad infinitum"). It turns out that no two of the miniature warts are exactly alike. Another astonishing fact, proved by John H. Hubbard of Cornell University, is that the Mandelbrot set is connected [Dewdney88]: Even though the tiny warts seem to float freely in the plane, there is always a wispy tendril of points in the Mandelbrot set that connects the warts to the parent set.

9.7 JULIA SETS

Like the Mandelbrot set, Julia sets are extremely complicated sets of points in the complex plane. There is a different Julia set, denoted J_c, for each value of c. A closely related variation is the **filled-in Julia set**, denoted K_c, which is easier to define, so we begin with that.

9.7.1 The Filled-in Julia Set K_c

We consider again the iterated function system of Figure 9.46, but now we set c to some *fixed* chosen value and examine what happens for *different starting points s*. As before, we ask how the orbit of starting point s behaves. Either it explodes or it doesn't. If it is finite, we say the starting point s is in K_c, otherwise s lies outside of K_c. We thus have the following definition:

DEFINITION: The **filled-in Julia set at c**, K_c, is the set of all starting points whose orbits are finite.

Note how this definition differs from that of the Mandelbrot set: When studying M, one considers different values of c and always uses the starting point 0; when studying K_c, one chooses a single value for c and considers different starting points. It is not obvious that there is any deep connection between the two sets, in spite of the tantalizing similarity of their definitions. But in fact, the connection between them runs deep.

Note that K_c must always be **symmetrical** about the origin, since the orbits of s and $-s$ become identical after one iteration. (By contrast, the Mandelbrot set is symmetrical only about the real axis.)

9.7.2 Drawing Filled-in Julia Sets

Because a starting point s is in K_c depending on whether its orbit is finite or explodes, the process of drawing a filled-in Julia set is almost identical to that for the Mandelbrot set. We again choose a window in the complex plane and associate pixels with points in the window. Here, however, pixels correspond to different values of the starting point s. A single value of c is chosen, and then the orbit for each pixel position is examined to see whether it explodes and, if so, how quickly it does. So in Figure 9.52 we, simply replace

find the corresponding c-value in Equation 9.17

with

find the corresponding s-value in Equation 9.17

Of course, `dwell()` in Figure 9.49 must be passed the starting point s as well as c now, and the line $d = c$ must be replaced with $d = s$ to get the orbit started properly.

Plate 28 shows examples for $c = -0.5 + 0.58i$ and $c = -0.76 + 0.147i$. The first value of c lies within M so its K_c is a connected region. The second value of c lies outside M, and its K_c is so-called Fatou dust. Many other pictures may be seen in [Peitgen86].

Just as in the case of the Mandelbrot set, making a high-resolution image of a K_c requires a great deal of computer time, since a complex calculation is associated with every pixel. Accordingly, we next discuss an alternative method for getting a quick picture of the boundary of K_c.

9.7.3 Some Notes on Fixed Points and Basins of Attraction

Let us look again at the nature of fixed points of $f(.) = (.)^2 + c$ to gain further insight into the behavior of different orbits. It is easier to see what is happening here than with the Mandelbrot set, since only one value of c is operative; instead of varying c, we are watching orbits unfold from different starting points.

■ **EXAMPLE 9.7.1**

To warm up, it is interesting to do some hand calculations for the Julia set associated with $c = -1$. The question is, What starting points are in K_{-1}? Certainly, the two fixed points must be starting points (why?), so we first find these. From Equation (9.15), we obtain the pleasant fact that the fixed points are related to the golden ratio

$$\phi = (1 + \sqrt{5})/2 = 1.618\ldots:$$
Fixed points for $c = -1$: $p_+ = \phi$ and $p_- = -1/\phi = -0.618\ldots$.   (9.19)

Consider some "common" starting points:

a. $s = 0$. The orbit is $0, -1, 0, -1, 0, \ldots$, which cycles forever, so 0 is in K_{-1}. Incidentally, so is -1. (Why?)
b. $s = \sqrt{\phi}$. The orbit is (check this) $\sqrt{\phi}, 1/\phi, -1/\phi, -1/\phi, \ldots$,
   which gets trapped at the fixed point after just a few iterations. So this s, as well as $1/\phi$, is in K_{-1}.
c. $s = .5$. A hand calculator yields the orbit $.5, -0.75, -0.4375, -0.809, -0.346, \ldots$, which ultimately gets caught in the cycle $0, -1, 0, -1, \ldots$, which is, of course, finite. Therefore *all* of the numbers in this orbit are also in K_{-1}.

Things look quite "regular" here, but see below that K_{-1} is in fact extremely complicated!

PRACTICE EXERCISES

9.7.1 Which of these points lie in K_{-1}?

For $c = -1$, which of the following starting points lie in the filled-in Julia set?
a. $s = -0.5$ b. $s = \pm1$ c. $s = \pm2$ d. $s = \pm1.5$.   ■

More generally, if an orbit starts close enough to an attracting fixed point, it is "sucked into" that point. If it starts too far away, it explodes. The set of points that are sucked in forms a so-called **basin of attraction** for the fixed point p. The set is precisely the filled-in Julia set K_c. It is not hard to show that the fixed point which lies inside the circle $|z| = 1/2$ (centered at the origin with radius $1/2$) is the attracting point.

Figure 9.53 shows a rough sketch of the Julia set for $c = 0.32019 + 0.25694i$. (To simplify the picture, only the boundary of K_c is shown.) The given value of c and the two fixed points (at $0.18681 + 0.41021i$ and $0.81319 - 0.41021i$) are also shown. All points outside K_c have orbits that explode; one example is shown. All points inside K_c have orbits that spiral or plunge into the attracting fixed point; two examples are shown.

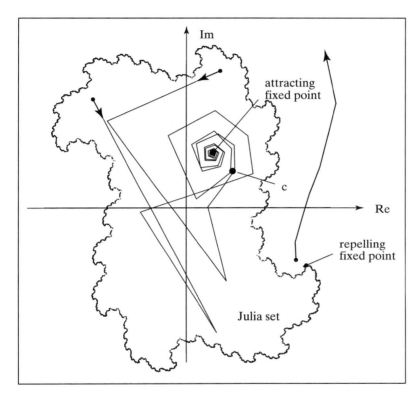

FIGURE 9.53 Some orbits with $c = 0.32019 + 0.25694i$.

Note that if the starting point is inside K_c, then *all* of the points on the orbit must also be inside K_c, since they are legitimate starting points themselves and they all produce a finite orbit. Note also that the repelling fixed point is on the boundary of K_c. This is always the case.

K_c for Two Simple Cases

It turns out that the set K_c is simple for two values of c (but only for these values):

1. $c = 0$: Starting at any point s, the orbit is simply $s, s^2, s^4, \ldots, s^{2k}, \ldots$, so the orbit spirals into 0 if $|s| < 1$ and explodes if $|s| > 1$. Thus, K_0 is the set of all complex numbers lying inside the **unit circle**, the circle of radius 1 centered at the origin. (What are the two fixed points here?)

2. $c = -2$: In this case, it turns out that the filled-in Julia set consists of all points lying on the real axis between -2 and 2. This is not at all easy to prove [Peitgen88], but it is illuminating to hand calculate orbits (at least the first few dozen points) for different starting values between -2 and 2.

For all other values of c, the set K_c is extraordinarily complex. (In fact, it is a fractal!) It has been shown that each K_c is one of two types [Peitgen86]:

- K_c is connected (it consists of a single "piece"), or
- K_c is a Cantor set (it consists of "dust").[13]

A remarkable theoretical result is that K_c is connected for precisely those values of c that lie in the Mandelbrot set! Hence, in Example 9.7.1, where $c = -1$ which lies in M, the set K_{-1} is connected, but is still a fractal.

9.7.4 The Julia Set J_c

It is easy to say loosely what the Julia set J_c is for any given value of c: it is the **boundary** of K_c. Because K_c is the set of all starting points that have finite orbits, every point outside K_c has an exploding orbit. We might say that the points just along the boundary of K_c are "on the fence": Just inside the boundary, all orbits remain finite; just outside it, all orbits shoot off to infinity. If s is in J_c, then any perturbation of s, no matter how tiny, will alter its orbit in a fundamental way. This is very similar to the notion of chaos discussed in Case Study 3.1: Infinitesimal changes in a system result in grossly different behavior.

Preimages and Fixed Points

The key to developing intuition about these matters is to examine the orbit of s in Equation (9.13). What if the process started instead at $f(s)$, the **image** of s? Then the two orbits would be

$$s, f(s), f^2(s), f^3(s), \ldots \qquad \text{(orbit of } s)$$

or

$$f(s), f^2(s), f^3(s), f^4(s) \ldots \qquad \text{(orbit of } f(s))$$

which have the same values forever afterward. Thus, as mentioned earlier, if the orbit of s is finite, then so is the orbit of its image $f(s)$. In fact, all of the points in the orbit, if considered as starting points on their own, have orbits with the same behavior: They all are finite or they all explode.

And we can go the other way "in time" and say that any starting point whose orbit passes through s has the same behavior as the orbit that starts at s: The two orbits are identical forever afterward. The point "just before" s in the sequence is called the **preimage** of s and is the inverse of the function $f(.) = (.)^2 + c$. The inverse of $f(.)$ is $\pm\sqrt{z - c}$, so we have

$$\text{two preimages of } z \text{ are given by } \pm\sqrt{z - c}. \qquad (9.20)$$

To check that Equation (9.20) is correct, note that if either preimage is passed through $(.)^2 + c$, the result is z. This test is illustrated in Figure 9.54(a), where the orbit of s is shown with black dots and the two preimages of s are as marked. The two orbits of these preimages "join up" with that of s. As a matter of fact, each of these preimages has two preimages, and each of those has two, so there is a huge collection of orbits that join up with the orbit of s, and thereafter are committed to the same path. The "tree" of preimages of s is suggested in Figure 9.54(b): s has two parent preimages, 4 grandparents, etc. Going back k "generations," we find that there are 2^k preimages.

---

[13] The classical Cantor set is based on the real interval $[0, 1]$. Remove the middle third of it, so there remains $[0, 1/3]$ and $[2/3, 1]$. Now remove the middle third of each of these, then the middle third of each of those, etc. In the limit, an infinity of points remains, but there are no intervals. (If ternary notation is used to represent each point, as in .012100201, then the points that remain have no 1's in their representation.)

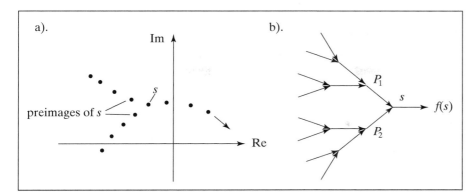

FIGURE 9.54 Orbits that coincide at s.

■ **EXAMPLE 9.7.2**

Suppose $c = -1$. We saw in an earlier example that the orbit of 0 is $0, -1, 0, -1, \ldots$, which is trapped forever in a cycle of period 2. If we examine the preimages of 0 and each of their preimages, etc., we can see that there are many other values which have orbits that are "attracted" into this 2-cycle:

The preimages of 0 are ± 1;
the preimages of $+1$ are $\pm\sqrt{2}$;
both preimages of -1 are 0;
the preimages of $+\sqrt{2}$ are $\pm\sqrt{\sqrt{2} + 1} = \pm 1.553$;
the preimages of $-\sqrt{2}$ are $\pm(\sqrt{\sqrt{2} + 1})i = \pm 1.6435i$;
etc.

What are the preimages of ± 1.553?

Figure 9.55 uses arrows to show how certain complex numbers map into others when $c = -1$. The point $1.6435i$ reaches -1 after four steps. (Is $1.6435i$ in the filled-in Julia set K_{-1}?)

What significance do preimages have for defining a Julia set? The Julia set Jc can be characterized in many ways that are more precise than simply saying it is the "bound-

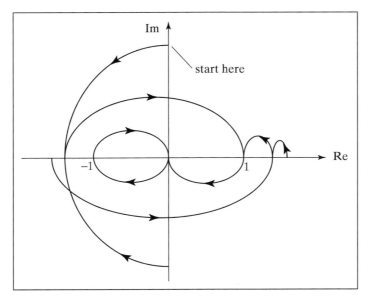

FIGURE 9.55 Some paths that lead to -1.

ary" of K_c. One such characterization [Peitgen86] that suggests an algorithm for drawing J_c is the following:

The collection of all preimages of any point in J_c is dense in J_c.

That is, starting with any point z in J_c, we simply compute its two parent preimages, their four grandparent preimages, their eight great-grandparent ones, etc. So we draw a dot at each such preimage, and the display fills in with a picture of the Julia set. To say that these dots are "dense" in J_c means that for every point in J_c, there is some preimage that is arbitrarily close by. No claim is made as to how many "generations" back one must explore to reach a satisfactory number of points on J_c.

Drawing the Julia set J_c

To draw J_c, we need only find a point in it and place a dot at all of the point's preimages. There are two problems with this methodology, however: (1) finding a point in J_c and (2) keeping track of all the preimages (2^k of them for k generations). An approach known as the **backward-iteration method** works around both of these obstacles and usually produces good results. The idea is simple: Choose some point z in the complex plane. The point may or may not be in J_c. Now begin to iterate backwards: At each iteration choose one of the two square roots randomly, to produce a new z-value. The following pseudocode is illustrative:

```
do{
    if(coin flip is heads z = + √z − c ;
    else z = - √z − c ;
        draw dot at z;
}while (not bored);
```

Remarkably a picture of J_c will emerge! The idea is that, for any reasonable starting point, iterating backwards a few times will produce a z that *is* in J_c. It is as if the backward orbit is "sucked" into the Julia set [Peitgen88]. Once it is in the Julia set, all subsequent backward iterations must stay there, so point after point builds up inside J_c, and a picture emerges. Because the preimages are dense in J_c, we know that iterating long enough will produce a set of plotted points arbitrarily close to "all" of the points in J_c. (An unlucky choice of starting point may cause some patterns to fill in more-slowly than others.)

Plates 29 and 30 show Julia sets produced by the blackward-iteration method.

PRACTICE EXERCISES

9.7.2 Alternative Julia sets

Julia sets are based on iterations of the function $(.)^2 + c$, but other functions can be iterated as well [Peitgen88, Pickover92]. Write a program that draws the Julia sets for the following functions:

a. $f(.) = \cosh(.) + c$, where $\cosh(z) = \frac{1}{2}(e^z + e^{-z})$. (Find out how to compute e^z when z is a complex number.)

b.

$$f(z) = z - \frac{z^3 - 1}{3z^2}$$

which happens to be the iteration function for Newton's method when one is trying to solve the equation $z^3 - 1 = 0$ [Barnsley88].

Obtain other examples from the FRACTINT program [Fractint96].

9.8 RANDOM FRACTALS

Chaos and chance are words to describe phenomena of which we are ignorant. Sven G. Carlson

The fractal shapes described so far are completely deterministic: No random elements are used in generating them, and their shapes are completely predictable (although very complicated). In graphics, the term *fractal* has become widely associated with randomly generated curves and surfaces that exhibit a degree of self-similarity. These curves are used to provide "naturalistic" shapes for representing objects such as coastlines, rugged mountains, grass, and fire.

9.8.1 Fractalizing a Segment

Perhaps the simplest random fractal is formed by recursively roughening or "fractalizing" a line segment. At each step, each line segment is replaced with a "random elbow." Figure 9.56 shows this process applied to the line segment S having endpoints A and B. S is replaced by the two segments from A to C and from C to B. For a fractal curve, point C is randomly chosen along the perpendicular bisector L of S. The elbow lies randomly on one or the other side of the "parent" segment AB.

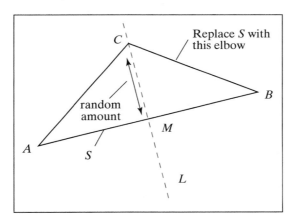

FIGURE 9.56 Fractalizing with a random elbow.

Three stages in the fractalization of a segment are shown in Figure 9.57. In the first stage, the midpoint of AB is perturbed to form point C. In the next stage, each of the two segments has its midpoint perturbed to form points D and E. In the final stage, the new points $F \ldots I$ are added. (How many points are there in total after k stages?)

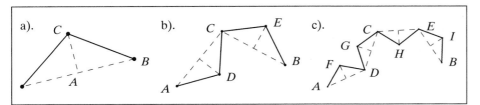

FIGURE 9.57 Steps in the fractalization process.

How do we actually perform fractalization in a program? In Figure 9.56, Line L passes through the midpoint M of segment S and is perpendicular to it. We saw in Chapter 4 that any point C along L has the parametric form

$$C(t) = M + (B - A)^{\perp} t, \qquad (9.21)$$

for some value of t, where the midpoint $M = (A + B)/2$. The distance of C from M is $|B - A||t|$, which is proportional to both t and the length of S. So, to produce a point C on the random elbow, we let t be computed randomly. If t is positive, the elbow lies to one side of AB; if t is negative, it lies to the other side.

For most fractal curves, t is modeled as a Gaussian random variable with a zero mean and some standard deviation. Using a mean of zero causes, with equal probability, the elbow to lie above or below the parent segment.

The routine `fract()` shown in Figure 9.58 generates curves that approximate actual fractals. The routine recursively replaces each segment in a random elbow with a smaller random elbow. A simple stopping criterion is used: When the length of the segment is small enough (specifically, when the square of its length is smaller than some global value *minLenSq* set by the user), the segment is drawn using `cvs.lineTo()`, where `cvs` is a Canvas object (see Chapter 3). The variable t is made to be approximately Gaussian in its distribution by summing together 12 uniformly distributed random values lying between 0 and 1 [Knuth98] The result has a mean value of 6 and a variance of 1. The mean value is then shifted to 0, and the variance is scaled as necessary.

FIGURE 9.58 Fractalizing a line segment.

```
d fract(Point2 A, Point 2 B, double stdDev)
/ generate a fractal curve from A to B.
   double xDiff = A.x - B.x, yDiff = A.y - B.y;
   Point2 C;
   if(xDiff * XDiff + YDiff * yDiff < minLenSq)
         cvs.lintTo(B.x, B.y);
   else
   {
         stdDev *= factor;      // scale stdDev by factor
         double t = 0;
         // make a gaussian variate t lying between 0 and 12.0
         for(int i = 0; i , 12; i++)
              t += rand()/32768.0;
         t = (t - 6) * stdDev;    // shift the mean to 0 and sc
         C.x = 0.5 * (A.x + B.x) - t * (B.y - A.y);
         C.y = 0.5 * (A.y + B.y) + t * (B.x - A.x);
         fract(A, C, stdDev);
         fract(C, B, stdDev);
   }
```

Note that because the offset expressed in Equation (9.21) is proportional to the length of the parent segment, fractal curves are indeed (statistically) self-similar. At each successive level of recursion, the standard deviation `stdDev` is scaled by a global factor `factor`, which is discussed next.

The depth of recursion in `fract()` is seen to be controlled by the length of the line segment. Often this length is chosen so that recursion will continue to the limit of the display device's resolution. For a graphics application, there is no need to go any further.

PRACTICE EXERCISES

9.8.1 Controlling the recursion depth

An alternative method for stopping the recursive calls in `fract()` is to pass it a parameter `depth`, giving the maximum depth of recursion. Show how to alter `fract()` in order to stop the recursion when a certain depth is reached.

9.8.2 Fractalize to the resolution of the device

Lines are to be fractalized and displayed on a 512-by-512-pixel display. If you want to fractalize lines so that any horizontal or vertical lines will be fractalized to the resolution of the display, what is the maximum depth of recursion that needs to be used? ■

9.8.2 Controlling the Spectral Density of the Fractal Curve

Peitgen [Peitgen88] shows that the fractal curves generated by using the algorithm of Figure 9.58 have a "power spectral density" given by

$$S(f) = 1/f^\beta \qquad (9.22)$$

where β, the power (exponent) of the "noise process," is a parameter the user can set to control the "jaggedness" of the fractal noise. When β is 2, the process is known as **Brownian motion**, and when β is 1, the process is called "$1/f$ noise." $1/f$ noise is *self-similar* in a statistical sense, and has been shown to be a good model for many physical processes, such as clouds, the sequence of tones in music from many cultures, and certain crystal growth. Peitgen et al. also show that the fractal dimension of such processes is:

$$D = \frac{5 - \beta}{2} \qquad (9.23)$$

In the routine `fract()` of Figure 9.58, the scaling factor `factor` by which the standard deviation is scaled at each level is based on the exponent β of the fractal curve, which determines how jagged the curve is. β varies between 1 and 3: Values larger than 2 lead to smoother ("persistent") curves, and values smaller than 2 lead to more jagged, "antipersistent" curves. The value of *factor* is given by [Peitgen88]:

$$\text{factor} = 2^{(1-\beta/2)} \qquad (9.24)$$

Thus, factor decreases as β increases. Some sample values are shown in Figure 9.59.

Note that `factor` $= 1$ when $\beta = 2$, in which case the relative standard deviation does not change from level to level. This provides a model of **Brownian motion**. For persistent curves in which $\beta > 2$, we see that `factor` < 1, so the standard deviation diminishes from level to level: The offsets of the elbows become less and less pronounced statistically. On the other hand, when $\beta < 2$, antipersistent curves are formed: `factor` is greater than 1, so the standard deviation increases from level to level, and the elbows tend to become more and more pronounced.

factor	β	D	
1.4	1	2	1/f noise
1.1	1.6	1.7	
1.0	2	1.5	Brownian motion
0.9	2.4	1.3	
0.7	3	1	

FIGURE 9.59 How factor and D depend on β.

A fractal can be drawn as shown in Figure 9.60. In this routine, `factor` is computed using the C++ library function `pow(.,.)`.

---

[14] In some papers, the family of "noises" having spectral density $1/f^\beta$ for any β between .5 and 1.5 are *all* referred to as $1/f$ noise [Peitgen88].

FIGURE 9.60 Drawing a fractal curve (pseudocode).

```
double MinLenSq, factor; // global variables

void drawFractal(Point2 A, Point2 B)
{
    double beta, StdDev;
    user inputs beta, MinLenSq, and the initial StdDev
    factor = pow(2.0,(1.0 - beta)/2.0);
    cvs.moveTo(A);
    fract(A, B, StdDev);
}
```

Some examples fractal curves are shown in Figure 9.61 for various values of β based on a line segment of unit length. (minLenSq was set to .05 and stdDev to .1 for these figures.) In each case, five fractal curves were generated between the same endpoints to show the possible variations. Note the pronounced effect of changing the exponent β of the fractals.

FIGURE 9.61 Examples of fractal curves. (a) $\beta = 2.4$; (b) $\beta = 2$; (c) $\beta = 1.6$.

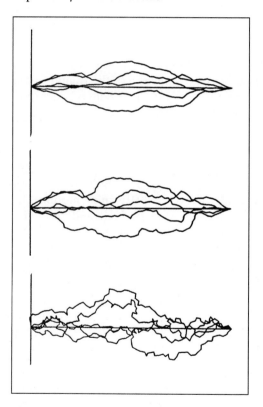

Arbitrary polylines can be fractalized, as shown in Figure 9.62, providing a simple means of roughening a shape to make it look naturally rugged. In the figure, the coastline of Florida was crudely digitized, so that the state is approximated by only 20 points [Figure 9.62(a)]. Then each of the segments of the coastline of Florida was fractalized, whereas the inland state borders that should be straight were left unfractalized. It is fascinating to fractalize polygons that represent known geographic entities such as islands, countries, or continents, to see how natural their various borders can be made to look. One can also fractalize other shapes, such as animals and the top of a person's head, to give them a natural appearance.

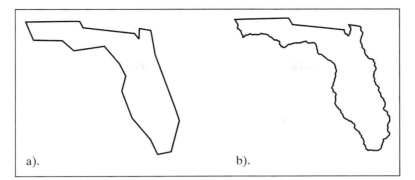

FIGURE 9.62 Generating realistic coastlines.

a).

b).

One of the features of fractal curves generated by pseudorandom-number generators is that they are completely repeatable. All that is required is to use the same seed each time the curve is fractalized. Each of the three sets of fractals in Figure 9.61 used the same starting seed, so they are based on exactly the same sequence of random values (except for a scaling factor based on their different variances). In this manner, a complicated shape such as the fractalized coastline can be completely described in a database by storing only

- the polypoint that describes the original line segments,
- the values of `minLenSq` and `stdDev`, and
- the seed.

From this modest amount of data, an extract replica of the fractalized curve can be regenerated at any time.

Fractal Surfaces

Surfaces, as well as lines, can be fractalized in order to generate realistic-looking mountainous terrain. Plate 31 shows some spectacular examples. Methods for generating such scenes are discussed in Case Study 9.9.

9.9 SUMMARY

This chapter examined some approaches to the infinite, using repetition and recursion. With certain figures, we can move "outward" toward infinity by placing the figures side by side forever, thus tiling the entire infinite plane. It is also possible to go "inward" toward the infinitely small, at least in principle. Recursion provides a simple mechanism for drawing ever smaller "child" versions of a figure inside the "parent" figure, down to the resolution of the display. If the proper class of figures is chosen, the patterns will become self-similar fractals: No matter how closely they are scrutinized, they will exhibit the same level of detail. Randomness can be used to provide an automatic roughness for drawing coastlines, trees, and other natural features.

An iterated function system (IFS) is a set of affine transformations that can be used to generate complex images. Playing the Chaos Game, you can generate the "strange attractor" of an IFS through a simple process of repetitively choosing one of the affine maps at random and mapping a single point. The process can be turned around, and a given image can be analyzed to produce an IFS having the image as its attractor. Since it takes so many fewer bytes to represent an IFS than to store an image, the approach has generated a great deal of interest in the field of image compression.

We explored the beguiling Mandelbrot set, whose boundary is itself a fractal curve. As one zooms in on a region near the boundary, new details emerge, and the wart pattern seems to reproduce itself over and over again. Because this process can continue forever, the Mandelbrot set is "infinitely complicated." Computer graphics provides a simple and powerful tool for exploring phenomena such as these. The pictures are generated simply, yet they can reveal enormous complexity. We also looked at how the Julia sets are formed and can be drawn algorithmically and how the Mandelbrot set is a "map" into the entire family of Julia sets.

9.11 CASE STUDIES

CASE STUDY 9.1 DRAWING STRING PRODUCTIONS

Level of Effort: II. Build and test an application that draws curves based on string production, as discussed in Section 9.3. Your application should be able to draw each of the curves specified in Figure 9.9, at a variety of orders. Test the program further on the following string rules of Herb Savage, said to generate a collection of Penrose aperiodic tiles (see Case Study 9.7; the rules were obtained from the FRACTINT program available on the Internet [Fractint96]):

```
Angle = 10 degrees,
Axiom = +WF--XF--YF--ZF,
W=YF++ZF----XF[-YF----WF]++,
X=+YF-ZF[--WF--XF]+,
Y=-WF++XF[+++YF++ZF]-,
Z=--YF++++WF[+ZF++++XF]--XF,
F= empty
```

To achieve automatic sizing of the window that encloses each curve, adjust `produceString()` so that if a variable `visible` is 0, it does no drawing, but instead calculates a window border `window=(w.l, w.t, w.r, w.b)` that completely surrounds the curve being produced. If `visible` is 1, the routine draws the curve. An easy way to do this is to add a test to `forward()` so that when `visible` is 0, the program tests whether the latest value of CP has moved out of the window formed so far. The code should look like the following:

```
if(CP.x < w.l) w.l = CP.x;
if(CP.x > w.r) w.r = CP.x;    etc.
```

How is the window first initialized?

Optional extension. Extend the application so that it can draw fractal trees, such as the "bush" in Figure 9.13.

CASE STUDY 9.2 DRAWING SNOWFLAKES AND REPTILES

Level Effort: II
Part A. The Mandelbrot Snowflake
Mandelbrot invented a fascinating self-similar fractal curve that fits exactly inside a Koch snowflake. The cover of the April 1978 issue of *Scientific American*, shows the third-order Mandelbrot curve M_3. The k-th-order curve M_k is built up in the following manner, based on subdivisions of an equilateral triangle [Gardner78]: An equilateral triangle, *ABC*, as shown in Figure 9.63(a), has its three sides trisected by points *D* through *I*.

FIGURE 9.63 Development of the Mandelbrot snowflake.

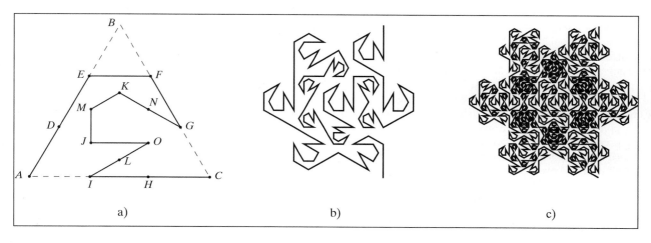

a)   b)   c)

Further, points K and N trisect EG, points M and J trisect EI, and points L and O trisect IG. The Mandelbrot curve M_1 consists of the 13 segments of the polyline ADE-$FGNKMJOLIHC$. This curve is said to be "built on" segment AC. It also has a "left sense," because, when one looks from A to C, it starts off with a turn to the left. To form the next generation, M_2, build a curve of the same shape on each of the 13 segments, as shown in Figure 9.63(b). The size of each segment determines the size of the curve. Some of the curves have a left (L) sense, and some have a right (R) sense. Beginning at S, the L–R sequence is $RLLLLRRRLLRRL$. Notice that M_2 fits inside a Koch snowflake of the second order. Write a routine that draws the Mandelbrot curve M_i for $i = 1, 2, 3$. (Figure 9.63c shows M_3.)

Part B. Section 9.4 presented one way to draw reptiles: using a function like `doTrio()` that calls itself recursively with size information in order to draw smaller reptiles inside a large one. Alternatively, we can draw each child by manipulating the coordinate system and properly managing the CT. As shown in Figure 9.64, to draw each child of a triomino, we alter the coordinate system appropriately and draw the child in the new system. Call the corner labeled p in the figure the pivot. Draw each child by translating the coordinate system to its own pivot and rotating the axes properly. Also, scale the system by 0.5, since children are half as large as their parents.

Each call to `drawTrio()` saves a copy of the CT and restores it at the end (so `drawTrio()` has no overall effect on the coordinate system). But note that the children "feel" the effects of changes to the system—as is desired—since the recursive calls to `drawTrio()` occur *before* the CT is restored.

Code for `drawTrio()` is suggested in Figure 9.65. The maximum depth of recursion that is desired is controlled by passing `depth` as a parameter to `drawTrio()` and testing it against a global value `maxdepth`; Each child has a depth one greater than its parent. The initial call is `drawTrio(1)`. As a matter of efficiency, `scale(0.5, 0.5)` is called only once rather than for each child. Therefore, the translation amounts are all adjusted to twice what one might expect. Trace the changes in the coordinate system carefully through the various calls.

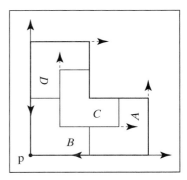

FIGURE 9.64 Changing the coordinate system to draw the triomino.

FIGURE 9.65 Drawing the triomino.

```
void drawTrio(int depth)
{ // Draw a triomino manipulating the CT
    if(depth >= maxDepth)     // draw the outline
    {
        moveTo(0, 0); lineTo(0, 4);
        lineTo(2, 4); lineTo(2, 2);
        lineTo(4, 2); lineTo(4, 0);
        lineTo(0, 0);
        return;
    }
    saveCT();                 // make a copy for later
    depth++;                  // update for the next generation
    scale(0.5, 0.5);
    drawTrio(depth);          // Draw B
    translate(2,2);           // to pivot of C
    drawTrio(depth);          // Draw C
    translate(6,-2);
    rotate(90);
    drawTrio(depth);          // Draw A
    translate(8,8);
    rotate(180);
    drawTrio(depth);          // Draw D
    restoreCT();              // restore the original CT
}
```

Write and execute an application that draws reptiles using this method. Arrange matters so that the application can draw all of the reptiles shown in Figure 9.26. In addition, it should be able to draw interesting reptiles from Practice Exercise 9.4.6, as well as draw the Sierpinski gasket.

Optional Extensions

1. Extend your application so it can fill the lowest level "children" polygons with a pattern [Clason90]. Experiment with each of the patterns shown in Figure 9.66, and draw patterns to depth 4 or more.

FIGURE 9.66 Filling regions of reptiles.

2. Extend the reptile tool so that it can draw lines such as those shown in Figure 9.31 inside the lowest level polygons, in order to produce interesting variations such as the one in Figure 9.32. Experiment with various "inner lines."

CASE STUDY 9.3 PLAYING THE CHAOS GAME

Level of Effort: II. Build and test an application that draws the attractor of a given iterated function system. The application might flow as follows:

```
read the IFS from a file into arrays affine[] and prob[]
set the window and viewport
chaosGame(affine,prob,N);
```

Here, chaosGame() is outlined in Figure 9.39. Your program should read in (from a file) data for an IFS, enter graphics mode, and begin the iteration shown in chaosGame(). To set the window so that it encloses the attractor, you may wish to use the method suggested in Case Study 9.1.

Because it can take several iterations before points begin to get close to the actual attractor, the first handful of points in the iteration should be discarded rather than drawn. Then, each iteration, the function int chooseAffine (double pr[], int N) chooses one of the N affine maps of the IFS, picking the i-th map with probability pr[i]. The method of doing this is most easily described through the following example:

Suppose N is 4 and the elements of the array pr[] are {.41, .29, .04, .26}. These elements, of course, sum to unity. The following code will select the numbers 0, 1, 2, 3 with the associated probabilities:

```
val = rand() % 10000;       // random value in the range 0..9999
if(val < 4100) return 1;
else if(val < 4100 + 2900) return 2;
else if(val < 4100 + 2900 + 400) return 3;
else return 4;
```

Here, rand()%10000 returns a value that is equally likely to be anywhere in the range 0..9999. This range is broken up by the if() statements so that the proper fraction of outcomes from rand()%10000 land in each subinterval. Such an approach is easily generalized to any array pr[].

Test your program on each of the IFS's given in Section 9.5.4, and also obtain others from the FRACTINT program on the Internet [Fractint96].

Optional Extension: The Chaos Game in Color

Extend your application so that it draws colored dots. The window-to-viewport mapping is set up as usual so that each point (x, y) corresponds to a pixel location (col, row). (See Chapter 3.) Now when the Chaos Game is played, as each new point is computed, a counter in the corresponding pixel is incremented. At the end there is a value in each pixel indicating how many times the pixel was "visited" by the dot as it moved around on the attractor. To display these values with colors, associate a color with each "visit count" value, and draw the picture.

CASE STUDY 9.4 DRAWING ORBITS IN THE MANDELBROT SET

Level of Effort: II. Write and execute an application that draws the orbit of c for the system $f(.) = (.)^2 + c$ for any value of c input by the user. The flow of the program is as follows:

1. A crude rendition of the Mandelbrot set is drawn on the screen. (See Figure 9.48.) Equation (9.18) may be of help here.
2. The user clicks the mouse somewhere on the figure, to specify a particular complex number c.
3. The orbit of 0 is drawn for the value of c that is selected. To prevent clutter in the picture, start drawing the orbit from c rather than from 0. Draw the path of an exploding orbit only until it leaves some prescribed rectangle on the screen.
4. Go to step 2.

CASE STUDY 9.5 CREATING PICTURES OF THE MANDELBROT SET

Level of Effort: II. Write a program that draws selected portions of the Mandelbrot set in full color. Base your program on the discussion in Section 9.6.4. After each Mandelbrot set is drawn, the user can zoom in on any rectangular region or press a key to exit from the program. To describe the desired zoom, the user clicks twice with the mouse to indicate two opposite corners of a rectangle, and this portion of the Mandelbrot set is drawn next at full screen size.

CASE STUDY 9.6 CREATING PICTURES OF JULIA SETS

Level of Effort: II. Generate the Julia set $J(-0.7448185 + 0.1050935)$. Experiment with other values of c. (See [Peitgen88].)

CASE STUDY 9.7 NONPERIODIC TILINGS; PENROSE TILES

> *Although it is possible to construct Penrose patterns with a high degreee of symmetry, most patterns, like the universe, are a mystifying mixture of order and unexpected deviations from order.* Martin Gardner

Estimate of time required: five hours. Periodic and nonperiodic tilings were discussed in Section 9.4. The tiling shown in Figure 9.67 is nonperiodic. The pattern extends to infinity by adding more "rings," but is clearly not periodic. The figure is based on the so-called versatile by B. Grünbaum and G.C.Shephard [Grünbaum86], shown in Figure 9.68(a). (Its nine sides have the same length, and all successive sides are $\beta = 15°$ apart, except for the two angles of 5β and 8β shown.) Figure 9.68(b) shows that this shape can in fact tile the plane periodically. (Why does the figure provide a proof of that?) So we have a polygon that tiles the plane *both* periodically and non-periodically, depending on how the tiles are laid down relative to each other. It turns out that many different shapes can do this, like some of the reptiles examined in Section 9.4.4.

The preceding discussion leads to a much deeper question: Is there a set of shapes that will tile the plane *only* nonperiodically? This means that no subset of the collection can be made to tile the plane periodically, but that all of the tiles in the set will tile it nonperiodically. (It is permissible to use rotations and reflections of the tiles.) It was believed for many years that such a set could not exist, but in 1964 Robert Berger, a graduate student at Harvard, discovered a set consisting of more than 20,000 tiles. More work followed, reducing the number required to 6, and then in 1974 Roger Penrose at the University of Oxford found a set of two tiles that tile the plane only nonperiodically. (It is still unknown today whether there is a *single* tile of some shape that tiles only nonperiodically.) Fascinating discussions of the problem and the route to its solution can be found in [Gardner89] and [Penrose89].

Figure 9.69(a) shows the most familiar versions of the Penrose tiles, known as the **kite** and the **dart**. As seen in Figure 9.69(b) their shape is fundamentally connected to the golden ratio! If allowed to fit together as shown, these shapes make a rhombus, which we know tiles the

FIGURE 9.67 A nonperiodic
tiling.

FIGURE 9.68 The "versatile"
and a partial tiling.

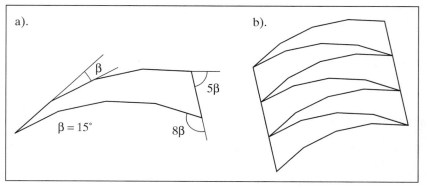

plane periodically (why?), so this configuration must be forbidden if we wish only nonperiodic tilings. One way to forbid it is to insert appropriate "bumps" and "dents" in each tile as
shown in Figure 9.69(c), so that the kite and dart can fit together only in certain ways. Alternatively, the various corners can be labeled with H and T for heads and tails as shown, and we
allow only corners with the same letter to meet. A prettier method was proposed by John Conway: Arcs are drawn in black and gray on the kite and dart as shown in Figure 9.69(d), and the
pieces can be laid down so that abutting edges join arcs of the same color. (See the exercises
at the end of this case study.) As shown in Plate 32, the joined arcs make lovely undulating patterns in the tiling.

Penrose has shown that with these restrictions, kites and darts can be laid down in infinitely
many ways to tile the plane, but that each such tiling must be nonperiodic. (It is well worth the

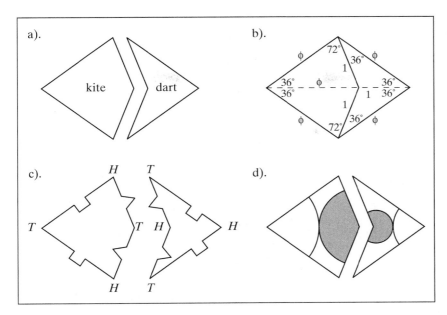

FIGURE 9.69 The Penrose kite and dart.

effort to cut out 100 or so kites and 50 or so darts, color them, and experiment with laying down tilings.) He proved that the proportion of kites to darts in any infinite tiling is exactly the golden ratio ϕ. Because ϕ is an irrational number, he had his proof that any tiling must be non-periodic; in a periodic tiling, the ratio would have to be rational.

Penrose and Conway have gone on to develop striking theorems about these tilings, described wonderfully, as always, by Martin Gardner [Gardner89]. For instance, whenever a black or gray curve closes, it must have a pentagonal symmetry, and the entire region inside the curve must have a fivefold symmetry. Further, in most tilings, all curves close: A pattern can have at most two curves of each color that do not close.

Develop an algorithm for drawing Penrose tilings, and execute it. (*Note:* This can be done with string productions also; see Case Study 9.1.

PRACTICE EXERCISES

9.11.1 The shape of the versatile

Show that the versatile is closed. That is, given the angles as shown in Figure 9.68, show that the versatile is indeed a closed polygon if all of the sides have equal length.

9.11.2 Arcs drawn on the kite and dart

Figure 9.69(d) shows black and gray arcs drawn on the Penrose tiles. The arcs just graze each other. Each arc is centered on a vertex and has just the right radius to "match" the same-colored arc of a valid piece placed next to it. Show that the arcs cut the sides of the kite and dart in the ratio $\phi:1$.

9.11.3 Out of triangles... .

Figure 9.70 shows how an isosceles triangle can be deformed into an "enneagon," which has the property that it fits perfectly with a half-turned version of itself, forming an octagon [Gardner89].

a. Show that the octagon always tiles the plane periodically.
b. What are the constraints on edges A and B that make the figure into a true enneagon?
c. Show that there are infinitely many different ennagon shapes.

FIGURE 9.70 An "enneagon" and a pair that tiles periodically.

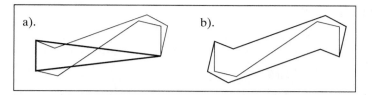

a).   b).

CASE STUDY 9.8 FRACTALIZING CURVES

Level of Effort: II. Write and execute an application that draws "fractalized" lines. The user lays down a polyline with the mouse in the usual way, and each line of the polyline is drawn fractalized. Allow the user to enter values for the various parameters involved. (See Figure 9.59) While executing your program, experiment with different values. Experiment with various polylines that represent islands, states, or countries, and see if fractalizing gives them a natural appearance.

CASE STUDY 9.9 MODELING FRACTALIZED MOUNTAINS

Level of Effort: III. A fractalization process similar to that used for fractalizing a line can be used to build very complex "fractal mountains." (See Plate 31). Figure 9.71 suggests the process. Begin with a triangle, ABC, resting on the x, y-plane, and vertically displace the three edge midpoints, a, b, and c, by a random amount, to form "pins" rising from the floor. Now join the pinheads to one another and to the original vertices to form four triangular "facets" (small faces), $a'b'c'$, $a'b'C$, etc. Repeat the process. Each facet is then replaced by four new facets by vertically displacing the midpoints of its edges a random amount and then connecting them. The process is repeated until the facets are "small enough."

FIGURE 9.71 Fractalizing a surface.

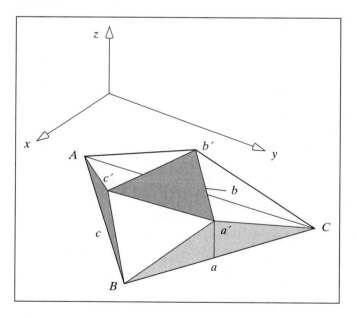

The user can provide a "seed" for the pseudo-random number generator (for instance, using the standard function `srand(29)` sets the seed for `rand()` to 29) and thereby make the mountain perfectly repeatable. You may choose to have each facet be drawn (filled in with some color) as it is created or to build the entire mountain as a large face list and then to draw its facets all at once.

Write an application that accepts the initial triangle ABC and suitable information about the average height of the "displacements", and creates a mesh model (as discussed in Chapter 6) of a fractalized mountain. The application then sets up a camera and a light source and draws the fractal mountain.

9.12 FURTHER READING

J. McGregor and A. Watt's *The Art of Graphics for the IBM* [Mcgregor86] offers a number of illuminating discussions of patterns and methods to form them with the use of graphics. Several books discuss fractals from the appreciator's point of view including Pickover's *Computers, Pattern, Chaos, and Beauty* [Pickover90] and *Mazes for the Mind* [Pickover92]. For a rigorous investigation of the mathematics behind fractals, as well as many useful insights into fractals in general, see Barnsley's *Fractals Everywhere* [Barnsley93]. The books *Chaos and Fractals, and New Frontiers of Science* [Peitgen96] and *The Science of Fractal Images* [Barnsley99] have many beautiful illustrations of fractals, as well as a clear exposition of the underlying mechanisms.

10 Tools for Raster Displays

"A Designer knows he has achieved perfection
not when there is nothing left to add,
but when there is nothing left to take away."

Antoine de Saint-Exupéry

Goals of the Chapter

▲ To describe pixmaps and useful operations on them.

▲ To develop tools for copying, scaling, and rotating pixmaps.

▲ To discuss different drawing modes, such as XOR mode.

▲ To develop tools for compositing images.

▲ To develop ways to define and manipulate regions.

▲ To develop Bresenham's line-drawing algorithm.

▲ To build tools for filling regions—particularly polygon-defined ones.

▲ To discuss aliasing and to develop antialiasing methods.

▲ To develop dithering and error-diffusion tools for creating more gray levels.

PREVIEW

In this chapter, we examine details of how an image is formed from graphics primitives and how an image can be manipulated to achieve an assortment of visual effects. Sections 10.1 and 10.2 revisit the pixmap as a fundamental object for storing and manipulating images, and several operations on pixmaps are developed. Section 10.3 describes ways to combine pixmaps and ways to use drawing modes such as "exclusive-or" mode. Section 10.4 develops Bresenham's line-drawing algorithm, and the next three sections examine ways to describe "regions" in a pixmap, fill them with a color or pattern, and manipulate them. Particular attention is given to filling a polygonal region. Section 10.8 discusses the phenomenon of aliasing (known fondly as the "jaggies") that is inherent in pictures displayed on a raster device and develops techniques for ameliorating its visual effect.

Section 10.9 describes ways to make a raster display appear to have more colors than it really has, by using dithering and error diffusion. The case studies elaborate on these topics and suggest several important programming projects.

[10.1] INTRODUCTION

Images are composed of arrays of pixels and are commonly viewed on a raster display. There are two main ways to create an image:

1. Scan (and digitize) an existing photograph or television image.
2. Compute pixel values procedurally, as in rendering a scene.

In previous chapters we focused on the second route: we generated graphics primitives such as lines or polygons, and we saw how to attach colors and texture coordinates to each. Using openGL, we simply "sent them" to the viewport, whence they were displayed on the screen. In doing this, however, we glossed over the key step of determining the proper colors of the individual pixel values "inside" the line or polygon. This process of taking high-level information such as the positions and colors of vertices and determining the colors of many pixels in a region of the frame buffer is called **scan conversion**, or **rasterization**. Figure 10.1 shows a "back end" portion of the graphics pipeline where rasterization is performed. When vertices emerge from the viewport transformation, OpenGL "assembles" them into the appropriate primitive (as determined by `glBegin(GL_POLYGON)` or the like) and then rasterizes the primitive, determining the properties of those pixels that "lie inside" it. In this chapter, we examine how this is done, showing ways to draw lines and to fill polygons with colors and textures.

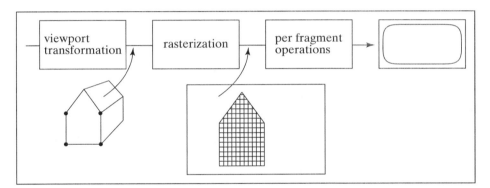

FIGURE 10.1 The rasterization step in the graphics pipeline.

Actually, the rasterization process doesn't produce just simple pixels; rather, it produces **fragments**, which consist of a color, a depth, and a texture coordinate pair. A number of steps and tests (denoted in the figure as "per fragment operations") are performed on fragments before they are written into the frame buffer as simple pixel values. We describe various possibilities for these operations and discuss how the operations are useful.

We also describe how to perform various operations on an image once it has been created. Doing this involves calculating new pixel values based on certain related pixel values in an existing image (or in several images that are being combined). OpenGL performs these manipulations in the "per fragment operations" portion of the pipeline.

Chapter 1 introduced raster images and some of the devices that display them. Recall that an image is stored in memory in the form of a **pixmap** (short for "pixel map")—a rectangular array of numerical values. Pixmaps can be stored in arbitrary regions of a computer's memory and copied from one place to another. When a pixmap is copied to the frame buffer, the scan controller orchestrates the conversion of pixel values to "dots" of colored light, and the pixmap becomes visible on the display. What you see on the screen is a "picture" of what is stored in the frame buffer. The term "pixels" often refers both to the numerical values stored in the pixmap and to the dots of light themselves.

Recall also that each pixel location in a pixmap consists of a fixed number of bits, called the **color depth** of the pixel. If a pixel has a color depth of b bits, then it can take on 2^b different values and thus can represent a maximum of 2^b different colors. If b is 1, only two colors are possible; two-color pixmaps are often called **bitmaps**.

Raster images and displays therefore deal with data that are **discrete**, both spatially and in color value. This discreteness, coupled with the ability of a program to operate directly on pixel values in memory, leads to a special collection of tools for generating and processing images.

10.2 MANIPULATING PIXMAPS

Things equal to nothing else are equal to each other.

One of *Murphy's laws of computers*

In this section, we examine a number of tools for manipulating pixmaps, both on-screen (when they reside in the frame buffer) and off-screen (when they are located in regular memory), and describe the visual effects these manipulations produce. We also see what tools OpenGL provides for working with pixmaps.

10.2.1 Operations of Interest for Pixmaps

We first outline the things you can do with pixmaps. Then, in subsequent sections, we discuss how to do each of them and how well they work in different situations.

Drawing a Picture

Rendering operations that draw into the frame buffer change the particular pixmap that is visible on the display.[1] So, for instance, when OpenGL is used to render a scene, the "writing" is done directly into the frame buffer's pixmap.

Copying a Pixmap from One Place to Another

You can copy a pixmap from one section of memory to another. Figure 10.2 shows four kinds of copying. Four pixmaps are illustrated, along with their copies. The *copy* operation copies an image from one place on the display to another. The *read* operation copies a portion of the displayed image to off-screen memory. The *draw* operation copies a pixmap from off-screen memory onto the display. And an operation we shall call *memCopy* makes a second copy of an image within off-screen memory.

As we shall see in more detail later, OpenGL offers several functions for performing these copying operations:

- `glReadPixels();` ← reads a region of the frame buffer into off-screen memory
- `glCopyPixels();` ← copies a region of the frame buffer into another part of the frame buffer
- `glDrawPixels();` ← draws a given pixmap into the frame buffer

Scaling and Rotating a Pixmap

It is often necessary to magnify or reduce an image, as well as to rotate it. Doing this can be a simple or rather complex process, depending on the magnification factor and the rotation angle involved.

Comparing Two Pixmaps

Another important task is to compare two pixmaps to see how they differ. For instance, two digitized X rays can be compared to see whether a tumor has changed over time. Usually, the two pixmaps are compared pixel by pixel, and some mathematical operation is performed on pairs of corresponding pixels.

---

[1] Frame-buffer memory is sometimes called "on-screen" memory, due to the close connection between pixel values and what is seen on the screen.

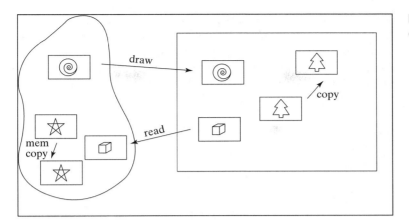

FIGURE 10.2 Varieties of copy operations for a pixmap.

Representing and Coloring Regions in a Pixmap

Some pixmaps contain clearly identifiable objects, such as circles, polygons, or certain **regions** of pixels that are in some way homogeneous. We need ways to describe regions in a pixmap and to represent them in a "higher level," more abstract or symbolic form. In addition, we often want to color all of the pixels that lie inside some region with a given color or pattern, a process known as **region filling**.

10.2.2 Useful Data Types for Pixmaps

Measuring software productivity by lines of code is like measuring progress on an airplane by how much it weighs. Bill Gates

It is natural to design some classes to support pixmap manipulations. A pixmap has a certain number of rows and columns, and each of its pixels contains data stored in a certain manner:

- The **bitmap**: Each pixel is stored in a single bit, so each pixel is either "on" or "off."
- The **gray-scale** pixmap: Each pixel is stored in a single byte, representing levels of gray from 0 for black up to 255 for white.
- **LUT indices**: Each pixel contains a number that represents an index into a color lookup table (LUT), as described in Chapter 1. Very often, the LUT contains 256 entries, so an index value can be stored in a single byte.
- The **RGB pixmap**: Each pixel consists of three bytes, one each for the red, green, and blue components of the pixel. Such pixels are considered to represent "true color."
- The **RGBA pixmap**: Each pixel consists of four bytes: the same three as in the RGB pixmap and a fourth byte that contains an "alpha value," which represents opacity. We discuss the use of the "alpha channel" in Section 10.3.

In order to work with pixmaps, we fashion a class that holds a pixmap's data and provides methods to manage the images derived therefrom. We develop the details for RGB pixmaps and extend them as needed to other types of pixmaps. To capitalize on OpenGL's image manipulation tools, we store the pixmap data in the same way that OpenGL does.[2]

We first define a type called RGB that holds a single pixel value as an RGB triple:

```
class RGB{
    public: unsigned char r,g,b;
};
```

---

[2] OpenGL actually offers a number of ways to "pack" data for a pixmap in memory. We work with the most commonly used format.

Figure 10.3 shows the beginning of our `RGBpixmap` class. We follow OpenGL and represent a pixmap as a simple array `pixel` of pixel values, stored row by row from bottom to top and across each row from left to right.

Several methods are outlined in the figure. The default `RGBpixmap` constructor makes an empty pixmap, and the other constructor creates a pixmap having *r* rows and *c* columns. The methods `setPixel()` and `getPixel()` respectively set and read a specific pixel value.

The methods `draw()`, `read()`, and `copy()` are implemented directly in terms of OpenGL functions:

- `draw()` copies the pixmap to the frame buffer, placing the lower left corner of the map at the "current raster position," a variable that can be set using `glRasterPos2i(x, y)`.

FIGURE 10.3 The `RGBpixmap` class for manipulating RGB images.

```
class RGBpixmap{
    private:
        int nRows, nCols; // dimensions of the pixmap
        RGB* pixel; // array of pixels
    public:
        RGBpixmap() {nRows = nCols = 0; pixel = 0;}
        RGBpixmap(int r, int c) //constructor
        {
            nRows = r;
            nCols = c;
            pixel = new RGB[r*c];
        }
        void setPixel(int x, int y, RGB color)
        {
            if(x >= 0 && x < nCols && y >= 0 && y < nRows)
                pixel[nCols * y + x] = color;
        }
        RGB getPixel(int x, int y)
        {
                return pixel[nCols * y + x];
        }
    //*** draw this pixmap at the current raster position
    void draw(){
        glDrawPixels(nCols, nRows, GL_RGB, GL_UNSIGNED_BYTE,pixel);
    }
    //*** read a rectangle of pixels into this pixmap
    void read(int x, int y, int wid, int ht){
        nRows = ht;
        nCols = wid;
        pixel = new RGB[nRows *nCols]; if(!pixel)exit(-1);
        glReadPixels(x, y, nCols, nRows, GL_RGB,
        GL_UNSIGNED_BYTE, pixel);
    }
    //*** copy a region of the display back onto the display
    void copy(int x, int y, int wid, int ht){
        glCopyPixels(x, y, wid, ht, GL_COLOR);
    }
    //*** read BMP file into this pixmap
    int readBmpFile(char * fname);
    //*** write this pixmap to a BMP file
    void writeBmpFile(char * fname);

    // …others …
};
```

- `read()` copies in the other direction, from a rectangular region in the frame buffer into the pixmap. The lower left corner of this region lies at point `pt`, and `wid` and `ht` specify the size of the region. `read()` allocates the memory necessary to hold the pixels, and `glReadPixels()` does the actual copying.
- `copy()` copies one region of the frame buffer into another, effectively performing both a `read()` and a `draw()`, but without creating an intermediate pixmap. The region has lower left corner at point `(x, y)`, and a size given by `wid` and `ht`. The region is copied to a new position in the frame buffer, whose lower left corner lies at the current raster position. This is a form of the "**bitBLT**" operation we examine in Section 10.3.4.

The utilities `readBmpFile()` and `writeBmpFile()` allow easy creation and storage of pixmaps. `readBmpFile()` reads an image stored as a BMP file into the pixmap, allocating storage as necessary. `writeBmpFile()` creates a BMP file that contains the pixmap. Code for both of these functions is given in Appendix 3.

The class `RGBpixmap` is simple, yet quite powerful. In the next example, we show how it may be used.

■ **EXAMPLE 10.2.1 A test bed for manipulating pixmaps**

Figure 10.4 shows an application that uses the `pixmap` class to control the reading and drawing of pixmaps with the mouse and keyboard. It is very informative to experiment with this program. Two pixmaps, `Pic[0]` and `Pic[1]`, are created at the start of the routine and are loaded with two BMP images. One of the images is dis-

FIGURE 10.4 A test-bed application for manipulating pixmaps.

```
RGBpixmap pic[2]; // create two (empty) global pixmaps
 int screenWidth = 640, screenHeight = 480;
IntPoint rasterPos(100,100);
int whichPic = 0; // which pixmap to display
//<<<<<<<<<<<<<<<<<<<<<<<<<< myMouse >>>>>>>>>>>>>>>>>>>>>>>>
void myMouse(int button, int state, int mx, int my)
{ // set raster position with a left click
  if(button == GLUT_LEFT_BUTTON)
  {
      rasterPos.x = mx; rasterPos.y = screenHeight - my;
      glRasterPos2i(rasterPos.x, rasterPos.y);
      glutPostRedisplay();
  }
  else glClear(GL_COLOR_BUFFER_BIT); // clear with right click
}
//<<<<<<<<<<<<<<<<<<<<<<<<<< mouseMove >>>>>>>>>>>>>>>>>>>
void mouseMove(int x, int y)
{// set raster position with mouse motion
    rasterPos.x = x; rasterPos.y = screenHeight - y;
    glRasterPos2i(rasterPos.x, rasterPos.y);
    glutPostRedisplay();
}
//<<<<<<<<<<<<<<<<<<<<<<<<<< myReshape >>>>>>>>>>>>>>>>>>>>
void myReshape(int w, int h)
{
    screenWidth = w; screenHeight = h;
}
//<<<<<<<<<<<<<<<<<<<<<<<<<< myDisplay >>>>>>>>>>>>>>>>>>>>>>>>
void myDisplay(void)
{
    pic[whichPic].draw(); //draw it at the raster position
}
```

FiGURE 10.4 (*continued*)

```
//<<<<<<<<<<<<<<<<<<<<<<<< myKeys >>>>>>>>>>>>>>>>>>>>>>>
void myKeys(unsigned char key, int x, int y)
{
 switch(key)
 {
    case 'q': exit(0);
    case 's': whichPic = 1 - whichPic; break; // switch pixmaps
    case 'r': pic[0].read(0,0,200,200); break; //grab a piece
 }
 glutPostRedisplay();
}
//<<<<<<<<<<<<<<<<<<<<<<<< main >>>>>>>>>>>>>>>>>>>>>>>>>
void main(int argc, char **argv)
{
 glutInit(&argc, argv);
 glutInitDisplayMode(GLUT_SINGLE | GLUT_RGB);
 glutInitWindowSize(screenWidth, screenHeight);
 glutInitWindowPosition(30, 30);
 glutCreateWindow("Experiment with images");
 glutKeyboardFunc(myKeys);
 glutMouseFunc(myMouse);
 glutMotionFunc(mouseMove);
 glutDisplayFunc(myDisplay);
 glutReshapeFunc(myReshape);
 glClearColor(0.9f, 0.9f, 0.9f, 0.0); //background color
 glClear(GL_COLOR_BUFFER_BIT);
 pic[0].readBmpFile("CokeCan2.bmp"); //make a pixmap
 pic[1].readBmpFile("Mandrill.bmp"); // make another one
 glutMainLoop();
}
```

played at the initial raster position. A left mouse click `draw()`'s it again at the mouse position. If the left button is held down, the pixmap is drawn again and again as the mouse is swept around the screen window. Pressing the 's' key toggles between the two pixmaps that are drawn in this way. Pressing 'r' `read()`'s whatever has been drawn in a 200-by-200-pixel region in the screen window and places the data in `pic[0]`, destroying its previous contents. A right mouse click clears the screen.

We show in subsequent examples how variants of the `draw()`, `read()`, and `copy()` functions can be used to carry out frequently needed tasks. These utility routines are applied in Case Study 10.1.

■ EXAMPLE 10.2.2 Writing text to the screen

One common way to draw text characters on a raster display is to build a different pixmap for each possible character. Figure 10.5 shows several examples. These pixmaps provide "pictures" of characters defined in a cell of a certain size, say, 12 pixels by 8 pixels, typically by making some pixels 0 and the rest 1. A large cell size allows more freedom in creating the shape of each character, and more pleasing fonts can be fashioned.

When a workstation is initialized, a variety of fonts can be loaded from disk into off-screen memory to make them readily available. To draw a string of characters, each character is `draw()`'n into the frame buffer at the proper spot. After each character is drawn, the *x*-position is incremented by the width of that character. With a **proportionally spaced** font, each character has a specific width. ("i" usually has the narrowest width, "W" the widest.)

FIGURE 10.5 Characters defined as pixmaps.

■ EXAMPLE 10.2.3 Window scrolling

In applications such as word processors, the screen usually fills with text, line by line. To make room for a new line of text at the bottom, all of the text above the bottom must be scrolled up one line (discarding the top line of text, of course), as suggested in Figure 10.6. To do this, the rectangle containing all but the top line is `copy()`'d up one line, overwriting what was previously there. Then a blank line is `draw()`'n into the position of the last row.

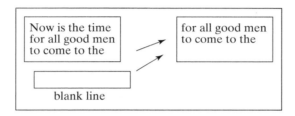

FIGURE 10.6 Scrolling text in a window.

■ EXAMPLE 10.2.4 Pop-up and pull-down menus; dialog boxes

Most interaction with a computer today is through a graphical user interface (GUI). Among other things, the interface presents menus and dialog boxes, and the user uses the mouse to choose each action desired.

When a menu is activated, it pops into view, temporarily covering some part of the screen. Figure 10.7(a) shows a part of the screen obscured by a **pull-down menu**. After the user makes a choice, the menu disappears, and the portion that was hidden by it is again revealed [Figure 10.7(b)]. This hidden portion must first be stored in off-screen memory, so that it can later be restored. Menu management is done as follows:

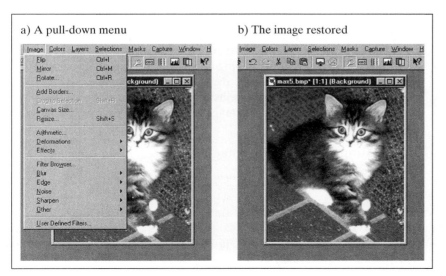

FIGURE 10.7 A pull-down menu.

1. The user selects a menu header.
2. The program determines the rectangular region about to be obscured.
3. A copy of the region to be obscured is `read()` to a pixmap off-screen.
4. The picture of the menu is `draw()`'n in its appropriate place.
5. The user moves the cursor to the desired menu item and releases the button.
6. The application restores the obscured portion by copying the off-screen pixmap to its original position.

■ EXAMPLE 10.2.5 Maintaining multiple windows

It is common today to have a number of applications running simultaneously in overlapping windows. Figure 10.8 shows a display with several windows. Because portions of one window overlap and obscure portions of another, the program must properly restore areas of the screen when a window is moved or closed. For instance, suppose we wish to draw another window at the position indicated in the figure. Then, as before, we must

FIGURE 10.8 Opening and moving a new window.

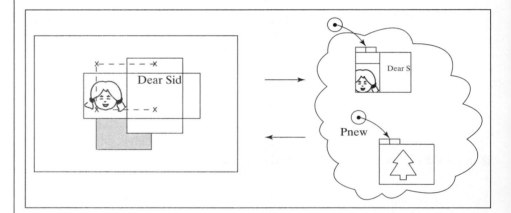

- `read()` a copy of the region about to be obscured and
- `draw()` the new window, obscuring the original image in the region.

Later, if the covering window is removed, it is first stored for subsequent use if necessary, and the original rectangle is restored by a `draw()`.

The preceding scheme works well when the image in an underlying obscured window is "frozen" while the window is covered. Things become considerably more complicated, on the other hand, when the information in a covered window changes. The problem is how to handle the parts of images that change while they are obscured. When the underlying window is later uncovered, its image must be up to date. Several schemes are discussed in the literature [OReilly88; Pike83]. Often, it is the application's responsibility to keep track of what happens in these windows and to regenerate the image whenever the window becomes uncovered.

10.2.3 Scaling and Rotating Images

Never wear earmuffs in a bed full of rattlesnakes. Another of Murphy's laws of computers

Images often must be scaled or rotated. For instance, a satellite image of the earth might show Europe in a 1,200-by-1,600-pixel pixmap, and we may wish to compare this image with a previously scanned 1,540-by-1,880-pixel image. Before the pixmaps can be compared, however, the smaller one must be enlarged to make corresponding parts of the images "line up" properly. Similarly, we may be compiling a collection of digitized fingerprints, but find that some fingerprint images are rotated slightly relative to the others. To compare different fingerprints, the images must be rotated into the same alignment. We look briefly at some of the simple types of scaling and rotation.

In scaling a pixmap by some factor, say, s, the idea is to create a pixmap that has s times as many pixels in both x and y. In photography parlance, when s is larger than unity, the pixmap is **enlarged**; otherwise it is **reduced**. The pixels themselves, of course, don't change size. When s is an integer, it is easy to scale a pixmap by **pixel replication**. Figure 10.9 shows an example of pixel doubling of a character bitmap. Each pixel in the smaller character produces a two-by-two array of pixels. For other integer values of s, each pixel produces an s-by-s array of pixels.

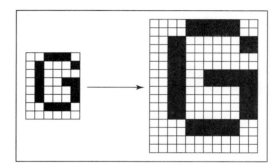

FIGURE 10.9 Pixel doubling to scale characters.

It is also straightforward to reduce a pixmap by some integer factor (i.e., $s = 1/n$, where n is an integer). For $s = 1/3$, for instance, we could build the reduced pixmap simply by retaining only every third row and column of the original. "Sampling" the original pixmap in this way usually loses information, so the reduced image may be far inferior to the original. It is usually better, if possible, to compute the average color of the nine pixels and place it in the remaining representative pixel. We discuss this and other antialiasing techniques in Section 10.8.

OpenGL provides a simple mechanism for scaling the picture drawn by a pixmap through either `glDrawPixels()` or `glCopyPixels()` (so the methods `draw()` and `copy()` will show the effects of the scaling). The function

```
glPixelZoom(float sx, float sy);
```

sets scale factors in x and y by which pixmaps are subsequently drawn. The pixmaps themselves are not scaled; rather, the pictures produced from the pixmaps are scaled. Any floating-point values are allowed for `sx` and `sy`—even negative ones. The default values are 1.0.

The scaling takes place about the current raster position, pt. Consider the pixel in row r and column c of the pixmap. Roughly speaking, it will be drawn as a rectangle of width `sx` and height `sy` screen pixels, with lower left corner at screen pixel $(pt.x + sx*r, pt.y + sy*c)$. More precisely, any screen pixels whose centers lie in that rectangle are drawn in the color of this pixmap pixel. For example, if `sx` is 2 and `sy` is 3, the pixmap is drawn with true pixel replication and will be twice as wide and three times as high as the unscaled pixmap. Its lower left corner remains at the current raster position. If `sx` or `sy` (or both) has a fractional value, the image will be correspondingly reduced and may suffer a loss in quality, since the color of each screen pixel is simply the color of the "rectangular" pixel in which its center lies.

If `sx` or `sy` is negative, the image is flipped about the current raster position. Flipping can be useful for presenting a pixmap upside down (using `glPixelZoom`

$(1.0, -1.0))$ and for producing special visual effects. Figure 10.10 shows four scaled versions of an image placed side by side (by using the sequence of scale factors $sx = 1$, $-1, 0.5$ and 1.5). To produce each image, the new value of sx was set, and `glPixel-Zoom(sx, 1); glutPostRedisplay();` was executed.

FIGURE 10.10 Multiple versions of a pixmap formed by scaling in x.

Quarter-turn Rotations

The process of rotating a pixmap through 90°, 180°, or 270° is very simple: A new pixmap is created, and pixels are copied from one map to the other with the use of `getPixel()` and `setPixel()`. (See the exercises at the end of the section.)

More General Scaling and Rotations

Things are more complicated when an *arbitrary* scaling or rotation is desired. Suppose, for example, that we wish to create a pixmap that contains a transformed version of some original pixmap? Figure 10.11 shows a pixmap S (the source) that we wish to alter with a transformation T, perhaps an affine transformation that involves some mix of scalings and rotations. The result will be the pixmap D (the destination). The task is to compute the proper pixel color at each point p in D. The simplest approach finds, for the center point p of each pixel in D, the color of the pixel in S that covers the point $T^{-1}(p)$. This color is then used for the pixel at p in D. However, using just these "samples" can lead to poor results with severe aliasing. It is usually far better to find the average color in the region of S that transforms to the square pixel in D and use that average instead. This approach is again a form of antialiasing.

FIGURE 10.11 Computing the transformed image.

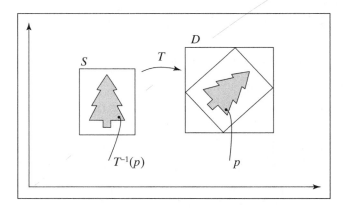

PRACTICE EXERCISES

10.2.1 Design the letter *R*

Design and sketch an 8-by-16 bilevel image that displays the letter R. Show both the pattern of 1's and 0's and the picture that results when 0 stands for white and 1 for black.

10.2.2 Designing characters

Design the most pleasing-looking characters, $a, A, r, R, ?$, and 3, inside cells of r rows and c columns. Do this for each of the following cell sizes:

a. $(r, c) = (6, 4)$;
b. $(r, c) = (10, 8)$;
c. $(r, c) = (14, 12)$.

10.2.3 Too small to be recognizable?

A cell size of $(5, 3)$ contains 15 pixels and so permits 2^{15} different bilevel pixel patterns. Can all of the printable ASCII characters be drawn in such a cell so that they are distinguishable (and recognizable)?

10.2.4 Reducing characters

One way to reduce the size of a character defined in a rectangular pixmap is to cut the cell size in half in both dimensions. Then each pixel in the reduced pixmap must mimic what was a 2-by-2 array of pixels in the original cell. Develop an algorithm that produces a 6-row-by-5-column pixel pattern from a 12-row-by-10-column pixmap. One approach sets each new pixel to unity if two or more pixels in the 2-by-2 array are unity. Is this a good rule?

10.2.5 Rotation through 90°

Consider the square pixmap represented by the array `A[i][j]`, where `i` and `j` vary from 0 to N-1. Express the value `B[col][row]` of the pixmap formed by rotating A through 90° counterclockwise. ■

10.3 COMBINING PIXMAPS

In certain circumstances, we wish to combine two pixmaps to produce a third. Combining pix maps is useful for such things as moving cursors around a screen, comparing two images, and morphing one image into another. We look at several examples of practical importance.

Pixmaps are usually combined *pixelwise*—that is, by performing some operation between corresponding pixels in the old and new maps. Specifically, two pixmaps A and B are combined to form a third pixmap C according to the formula

$$C[i][j] = A[i][j] \otimes B[i][j], \quad \text{for each } i, j$$

where $\otimes$ denotes some operation. Following are some examples of different operations:

- Averaging two images. Here, $\otimes$ means to form the sum of one-half of A and one-half of B:

$$C[i][j] = \frac{1}{2}(A[i][j] + B[i][j]).$$

- Taking the difference of two images. To determine how different two images are, $\otimes$ now means subtraction:

$$C[i][j] = A[i][j] - B[i][j].$$

- Finding where one image is brighter than another. Here, $\otimes$ means "is greater than":

$$C[i][j] = A[i][j] > B[i][j].$$

  This formula gives each pixel in C the value unity if the corresponding pixel in A is brighter than that in B and gives the value zero otherwise.

A generalization of averaging two images is to form their **weighted average**. Pixmap A is weighted by $(1 - f)$ and B is weighted by f, for some fraction f:

$$C[i][j] = (1 - f)A[i][j] + fB[i][j]. \tag{10.1}$$

For instance, if the RGB components of $A[i][j]$ are $(14, 246, 97)$ and those of $B[i][j]$ are $(82, 12, 190)$, then for $f = 0.2$, we have $C[i][j] = (27, 199, 115)$. A weighted average of two `RGBpixmaps` can be achieved using the `setPixel()` and `getPixel()` tools developed earlier.

■ **EXAMPLE 10.3.1 Dissolving one image into another**

An interesting application of a weighted average occurs when one image is to be **dissolved** into another. First, image A is fully displayed, but as time passes, A slowly fades, and image B emerges superimposed on A, until finally, only B is displayed. If t represents time, then at time t the image

$$A(1 - t) + Bt$$

is displayed, as t moves smoothly from 0 to 1. This technique is similar to "tweening," described in Chapter 4. Figure 10.12 shows five stages of the displayed image, for values of $t = 0, 0.25, 0.5, 0.75$, and 1. Case Study 10.2 discusses an easy way to dissolve an image, by using the "alpha channel" facility of OpenGL, which we shall describe in Section 10.3.2.

FIGURE 10.12 Dissolving between two images.

PRACTICE EXERCISES

10.3.1 Forming a weighted average of two `RGBpixmaps`

Write code that forms `RGBpixmap` C according to Equation (10.1), using the class' methods `getPixel()` and `setPixel()`.

10.3.2 Research on numerical considerations

Blinn [Blinn98] talks about the round-off error involved in performing averaging of pixmaps. Read his text.   ■

10.3.1 The Read–Modify–Write Cycle

In forming a new pixmap C as a combination of two pixmaps, say, D (for destination) and S (for source), a special case occurs when C is the same as D, so that the result is placed back into D. This case can be represented as $D = D \otimes S$: The pixels in pixmap D are combined with those in S, and the result is put back into D. This operation is called a **read–modify–write** cycle, because first the pixels in D are read from memory, then they are modified by combining them with the pixels of S, and finally, the result is written back into D. Figure 10.13 suggests symbolically how the cycle

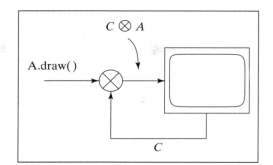

FIGURE 10.13 A read–modify–write cycle applied to the frame buffer.

works when D is the frame buffer itself. The cycle is applied for each pixel of D in turn. Some hardware configurations make this a very efficient operation. OpenGL provides tools to perform a read–modify–write cycle to an entire pixmap in one instruction, as we shall see.

10.3.2 The Alpha Channel and Image Blending

Forming a weighted sum of two images is actually a special case of a more general operation that is variously called **blending** or **compositing** of images. Blending allows you to draw a partially transparent image over another image. The key is to add a fourth component, the so-called **alpha value**, to *each* RGB color. In terms of data types to hold pixels, we extend the previous RGB type to the RGBA type,

```
class RGBA{
public: unsigned char r, g, b, a;
};
```

and assign each pixel an alpha value a between 0 and 255. The usual interpretation is that the alpha value specifies how "opaque" each pixel is: A value of 0 indicates complete transparency, and a value of 255 indicates total opacity. Note that it takes four-thirds as much memory to store an RGBA pixmap as it does to store an RGB pixmap. Taken together, the collection of alpha values present in a pixmap is often called the **alpha channel**.

As we shall see next, the alpha component is most frequently used as a scaling factor that lies between 0 and 1, so the actual value used is the fraction $a/255$.

■ **EXAMPLE 10.3.2 Overlaying an image with a partially transparent image**

Figure 10.14 shows an example of overlaying an image S of a mask and a dragon onto a background image D. When the source image S is created, the dragon pixels are given alpha values of 255 (totally opaque), the mask pixels are given alpha values of 128 (half opaque), and all other pixels are given alpha values of 0. When S is blended with D, the result shows the dragon in the foreground on top of the background D, and some of the background color "seeps through" the mask.

FIGURE 10.14 Compositing image S onto image D.

Alpha blending can be accomplished in a read–modify–write cycle by forming a weighted average of the source and destination pixels and putting this average back into the destination. Symbolically, $D = aS + (1 - a)D$, where a is the alpha value of the source, considered as some fraction between 0 and 1. But the alpha value varies from pixel to pixel, and both S and D have red, green, and blue components, so a more precise formula for, say, the green component of the final destination pixel at row j and column i is

$$D[i][j].g = aS[i][j].g + (1 - a)D[i][j].g, \tag{10.2}$$

where the fraction

$$a = \frac{S[i][j].a}{255}.$$

Note particularly the dependence of a on i and j: The alpha value varies from pixel to pixel. Similar expressions hold for the red and blue components.

To do this kind of blending in a program, we would first extend the `RGBpixmap` class described earlier to the class `RGBApixmap` (see the exercises at the end of the section) and then add a method `blend()` that performs the overlaying in a read–modify–write cycle. Then, blending pixmap S with pixmap D would be carried out using the code

```
D.draw(); //draw D opaquely, as usual
S.blend(); //use alpha values in S: form a weighted average with D
```

OpenGL offers tools that make it easy to implement `blend()`: You simply set a "blend mode" that specifies how `blend()` determines the "source scaling factor" and the "destination scaling factor." To set a to the source's alpha value, simply specify

```
glBlendFunc(GL_SRC_ALPHA, GL_ONE_MINUS_SRC_ALPHA);
```

This command sets the source scale factor to the alpha value of the source itself and the destination scale factor to 1 minus the source's alpha value, as desired. Figure 10.15 shows a simple implementation of `blend()`.

FIGURE 10.15 Blending a source and destination image using the source's alpha channel.

```
void RGBApixmap :: blend()
{
    glBlendFunc(GL_SRC_ALPHA, GL_ONE_MINUS_SRC_ALPHA);
    glEnable(GL_BLEND); // enable blending
    draw(); // draw this pixmap blended with the destination
}
```

■ **EXAMPLE 10.3.3 Simulating ChromaKey: forcing certain colors to be transparent**

A familiar sight on television is the weatherperson standing in front of a map pointing at various weather conditions. In fact, the person is standing in front of a blue background [Figure 10.16(a)], and a separate weather map is filmed simultaneously. The television signal switches between the image of the person and that of the map on the fly: When the blue color is encountered during a line scan, the map is shown; otherwise the person is shown.

We can simulate this effect with pixmaps and make a specific color in the source pixmap transparent by setting its alpha value to zero. The following routine scans through a pixmap and sets the alpha value of each pixel to zero if the pixel's color matches the chosen color and to unity otherwise:

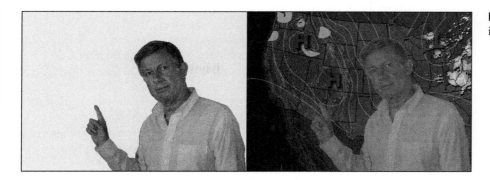

FIGURE 10.16 ChromaKey used in television.

```
void RGBApixmap::setChromaKey(RGB c)
{     long count = 0;
      for(int row = 0; row < nCols; row++)
       for(int col = 0; col < nRows; col++)
       {
      RGBA p = pixel[count];
      if(p.r == c.r && p.g == c.g && p.b == c.b)
               pixel[count++].a = 0;
           else pixel[count++].a = 255;
       }
}
```

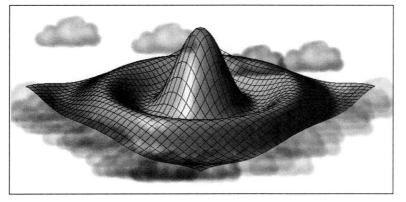

FIGURE 10.17 Painting with a "cloud" paintbrush.

■ EXAMPLE 10.3.4 Applying paint with a paintbrush

In a painting program, the mouse cursor acts like a paintbrush, and you can lay down a swatch of color with each "brush stroke." This can be done in OpenGL by blend()-ing the pixmap of the paintbrush with the destination image, using an alpha of 10% or so for the paintbrush pixels. At each brush stroke, a little more of the paintbrush's color is blended into the destination. (See the exercises for an estimate of how the amount of the new color grows with each brush stroke.) Pixels near the center of the brush can be given a higher value of alpha than those near the edges, so that color is added more rapidly near the center. Figure 10.17 shows the use of a "cloud" brush that is applied various times to get varying amounts of coverage.

■ **EXAMPLE 10.3.5 Cursor management**

When the user moves the mouse, the cursor is swept across the display. At each position the cursor occupies, it obscures the part of the display that it covers. When the mouse moves on, that part must be restored. The process for doing this is similar to that required for a pull-down menu, as we show in Figure 10.18. Before the cursor is drawn on the screen, a copy (shown as pix map *Pix1*) is made of the rectangular piece of the image that is about to be covered by the cursor. The cursor pixmap is then blended at that spot. This pixmap has an alpha of unity in the opaque part of the cursor arrow and an alpha of zero elsewhere, so, when the two pixmaps are blended, the arrow appears to float over the background image. When the cursor is moved to a new position, three things happen:

FIGURE 10.18 Managing the moving cursor.

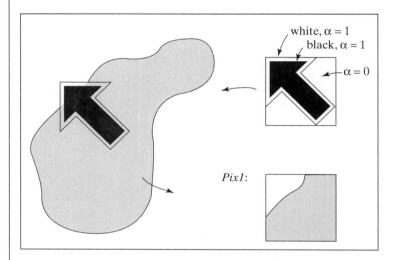

1. *Pix1* is `draw()`'n (with an alpha of unity) to cover the current cursor image and to restore the original image.
2. A copy of the part about to be obscured is `read()` into off-screen memory.
3. The cursor is again blended at the new position.

Note that this procedure works even if the cursor is moved only a very small distance.

Extensions Available in OpenGL

OpenGL offers a couple of tools for setting and using the alpha channel.

Setting Alpha Values While rendering a scene, you can explicitly set alpha values of subsequently drawn graphics objects by specifying these objects' fourth color component with the use of `glColor4f(r,g,b,a)`, where *a* ranges from 0.0 (total transparency) to 1.0 (total opacity). The default alpha value is 1.0. You can also give a 3D object a semitransparent look, in which all pixels drawn for the object have specific alpha values. This is done by specifying an alpha value in the diffuse reflection coefficient for each vertex of the object, using the code

```
glMaterialfv(GL_FRONT, GL_DIFFUSE, refl);
```

where `refl` is an ordered quadruple giving the color of the diffuse component, as in `float refl[4] = {0.5, 0.3, 0.8, 0.4}`. This statement assigns an alpha value of 0.4 to subsequently defined vertices.

Setting Blending Methods We saw the use of `glBlendFunc(GL_SRC_ALPHA, GL_ONE_MINUS_SRC_ALPHA)` to produce the weighted average $D = aS + (1 - a)D$ of the source and destination pixmaps. OpenGL allows the source and destination scaling factors to be set to different values by choosing different parameters for `glBlendFunc()`, such as `GL_ZERO`, `GL_ONE`, `GL_DST_ALPHA`, `GL_SRC_COLOR`, etc. For example, `glBlendFunc(GL_DST_ALPHA,GL_ONE_MINUS_DST_ALPHA)` weights the source and destination pixels by a_D and $(1 - a_D)$, respectively, where a_D is now the alpha value of the destination rather than of the source. And `glBlendFunc(GL_DST_COLOR, GL_ZERO)` modulates (multiplies) each color component of a source pixel by the level of the corresponding component in the destination.

PRACTICE EXERCISES

10.3.3 Extend the RGBpixmap class to include an alpha component

Make adjustments to the `RGBpixmap` class defined in Section 10.2.2 so that pixmaps support an alpha channel. Add the `blend()` and `setChromaKey()` methods, and test them by (a) reading a BMP image into a pixmap (this is most interesting if the image has a uniform background of some color), (b) making a certain color transparent by using `setChromaKey()`; and (c) blending the pixmap with some other one to see the transparency in action.

10.3.4 Applying new color with brush strokes

Consider a paintbrush pixmap that has small alpha values near the center of the brush and alpha values of zero elsewhere. Each time the paintbrush is applied, it blends the brush color C with whatever image D is in the destination, so D becomes $aC + (1 - a)D$. Repeated applications increase the amount of paintbrush color. Show that after the ith application, the destination color is $D_i = aC + (1 - a)D_{i-1}$. Solve for the fraction of the destination color that is due to the source color C after eight applications. ■

10.3.3 Logical Combinations of Pixmaps

There are other ways of combining pixmaps that treat each pixel value simply as a collection of bits, paying no attention to the numerical value that the bits represent. The pixmaps are combined pixel by pixel as before, but the bits in a pixel are combined **logically**, bit by bit. For instance, they might be OR-ed, AND-ed, or EXCLUSIVE OR-ed together.

Suppose, for example, that pixel A has RGB components $(21, 127, 0)$. Writing the components in binary form, we have $A = (00010101, 01111111, 00000000)$. Suppose further that pixel B is $(01010101, 11110000, 10000101)$ in binary. If these two triples are OR-ed together, the result is C, given by

$(01010101, 11111111, 10000101)$ ← the OR of A and B.

Each bit of C is a 1 if either (or both) of the corresponding bits in A and B is a 1. If, on the other hand, A and B are EXCLUSIVE OR-ed (XOR-ed) together, we get

$C = (01000000, 10001111, 10000101)$ ← the XOR of A and B.

In this case, each bit of C is a 1 if exactly one of the corresponding bits in A and B is a 1—that is, if one bit, but not both, is a 1. The color $C = A$ XOR B depends on both A and B in a complex manner. [See the exercises at the end of the section; also, (what is A XOR B if B is $(0,0,0)$ (black)? What is A XOR B if B is $(255, 255, 255)$ (white)?] An interesting property of the XOR operation is that applying it twice is equivalent to not applying it at all; that is, if we form $C = A$ XOR B and then XOR C with B to form $(A$ XOR $B)$ XOR B, the result is A again! (See the exercises.) We exploit this property later when doing rubber banding.

Languages like C++ directly support executing bitwise logical operations, so it is straightforward to perform them in a routine. To OR the green components of A and B, for instance, we simply execute `C.g = A.g | B.g`. Similarly, to XOR the red bytes, we execute `C.r = A.r ^ B.r`.

Other operators include AND, NOT, and combinations of these. If two values are AND-ed, represented in C++ for the green component as `C.g = A.g & B.g`, each bit in `C.g` is a 1 only if both the corresponding bits in A and B are a 1. If a value is NOT-ed or complemented, represented in C++ as `C.g = ~A.g`, each bit in C is 1 if and only if the corresponding bit in A is 0.

We could use these logical operators in C++ to combine two pixmaps pixel by pixel, but happily, OpenGL provides a mechanism for combining two pixmaps all at once. Once a logical operation is chosen and enabled, all subsequent drawing performs a read–modify–write cycle of the source pixels with the pixels currently stored in the frame buffer.

The use of logical operations is enabled via the command `glEnable` `(GL_COLOR_LOGIC_OP)`. The operator is selected by using `glLogicOp()` with one of the arguments shown in Figure 10.19, where S stands for the source pixel and D for the destination pixel. The default is `GL_COPY`, which simply replaces the destination with the source.

FIGURE 10.19 Possible logical operations in OpenGL.

parameter value	value written to destination
GL_CLEAR	0
GL_COPY	S
GL_NOOP	D
GL_SET	1
GL_COPY_INVERTED	NOT S
GL_INVERT	NOT D
GL_AND_REVERSE	S OR NOT D
GL_AND	S AND D
GL_OR	S OR D
GL_NAND	NOT(S AND D)
GL_NOR	NOT(S OR D)
GL_XOR	S XOR D
GL_EQUIV	NOT(S XOR D)
GL_AND_INVERTED	NOT S AND D
GL_OR_INVERTED	NOT S OR D

Figure 10.20 shows examples of logically combining two pixmaps A and B in the case of binary-valued pixels. The association of pixel value with color here is black for 0 and white for 1. (What do the pixmaps look like for the GL_AND and GL_EQUIV operators?)

We describe the classic application of XOR by drawing "rubber rectangles" next and show how it is implemented in OpenGL. The operation exploits the fact that two successive drawings of an object in XOR mode erases the object, leaving the original image untouched. Other examples are considered in the exercises.

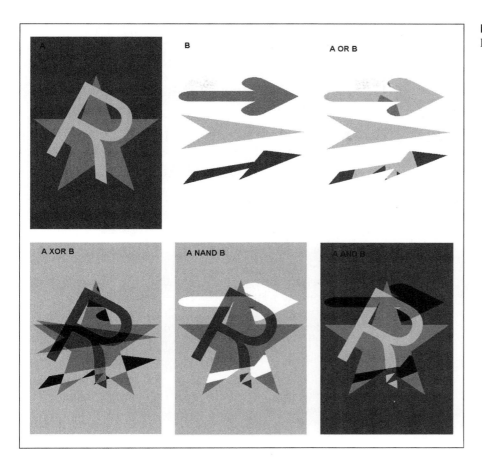

FIGURE 10.20 Effect of various logical operations.

■ EXAMPLE 10.3.6 Drawing "rubber rectangles"

"Rubber rectangles" and "rubber-band lines" provide valuable feedback to a user who wishes to draw precise figures on the display with the mouse. Figure 10.21 shows examples. When drawing a rubber rectangle as in Part (a), the user first points the mouse at the spot where one corner of the rectangle is desired and presses a mouse button. This action defines a pivot point. Then, as the user moves the mouse away from the pivot (with the button depressed), an "elastic" rectangle is seen that always has one corner at the pivot and the opposite corner at the current mouse position. As the rectangle changes, it appears to pass over whatever is drawn on the screen without altering it. The user can adjust the rectangle back and forth until it covers exactly the region desired. When the button is released, the final rectangle remains visible, and its coordinates can be used by the program to do further drawing. A rubber band [Part (b)] is an elastic line that extends from the pivot to the mouse position, growing and shrinking as the mouse is moved. It is just a variation of the rubber rectangle, produced by drawing only the diagonal of the rectangle.

A rubber rectangle (or rubber-band line) must be continually erased and redrawn at slightly different positions. The rectangle cannot simply be erased by redrawing it in the background color, as that would destroy the image lying beneath the line. Drawing in XOR mode provides the solution. To erase the rectangle, it is simply drawn a second time, which restores the original image.

FIGURE 10.21 Rubber rectangles and rubber-band lines.

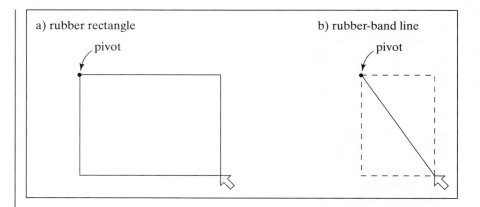

a) rubber rectangle   b) rubber-band line

pivot   pivot

Figure 10.22 shows mouse routines that create and manage a rubber rectangle. These callback routines are registered in `main()` in the usual way, with `glut-MouseFunc(myMouse)` to make `myMouse()` the callback for pressing or releasing the mouse button and `glutMouseMotionFunc(mouseMove)` to make `mouseMove()` the callback for a move event with the button down. A global rectangle object `rr` is used and referred to by both routines. The initial rectangle (of zero size) is established by `myMouse()`. Be sure not to draw the rectangle using black (all zeros) for the drawing color! (Why?)

FIGURE 10.22 Mouse routines for a rubber rectangle.

```
IntRect rr; // global rectangle

//<<<<<<<<<<<<<<<< myMouse >>>>>>>>>>>>>>>>
void myMouse(int button, int state, int mx, int my)
{
  if(button == GLUT_LEFT_BUTTON && state == GLUT_DOWN)
  {
        glEnable(GL_COLOR_LOGIC_OP); //enable logical operations
        glLogicOp(GL_XOR);            // set it to XOR mode
        rr.left = rr.right = mx; //set the pivot
        rr.top = rr.bott = screenHeight - my;
  }
  if(button == GLUT_LEFT_BUTTON && state == GLUT_UP)
    glDisable(GL_COLOR_LOGIC_OP); // disable logical operations
}
//<<<<<<<<<<<<<<<< mouseMove >>>>>>>>>>>>>>>>
void mouseMove(int mx, int my)
{
    rr.draw(); //erase the old: works only in XOR mode
    rr.right = mx; // set the new opp. corner
    rr.bott = screenHeight - my; // flip y-coord.
    rr.draw(); // draw the new
}
```

Notice that in XOR drawing mode the rubber rectangle does not have a uniform color. Instead, each pixel along the rectangle is drawn in the color that results from XOR-ing the "true" rectangle color with the background color at that point. This lack of uniformity is usually not too annoying. Indeed, it can even be useful, because any objects "under" the rectangle are plainly visible.

PRACTICE EXERCISES

10.3.5 Drawing multiple colors in XOR mode

Suppose that the frame buffer supports three bits per pixel and that colors are displayed according to the scheme in Figure 1.31. Describe what color is observed when the pixel value 110 is XOR-ed with each of the possible pixel values.

10.3.6 Drawing twice in XOR mode equals drawing not at all

Show, for any pixel colors A and B, that drawing B twice in XOR mode leaves A unchanged; that is, show that $(A \text{ XOR } B) \text{ XOR } B$ is A itself.

10.3.7 Symmetric operators

Note that the OR operator is symmetric: $A \text{ OR } B$ is the same as $B \text{ OR } A$. Which of the 16 operators $\oplus$ is "symmetric" in the sense that $a \oplus b = b \oplus a$?

10.3.8 Swapping two images in place

Show that two pixmaps A and B may be interchanged by performing the following three XOR combinations (when the process is complete, A contains the pixel values originally held by B, and vice versa):

$A = A \text{ XOR } B$;
$B = A \text{ XOR } B$;
$A = A \text{ XOR } B$.

10.3.9 Reverse-mode drawing

Drawing a pattern in reverse mode can also be used to erase a line and restore the original pixel values. A b-bit frame buffer has $N = 2^b$ possible pixel values, ranging from 0 to $2^b - 1$. Drawing a pixel in reverse mode means replacing the current pixel value d with the value $f(d) = N - d$. Note that this drawing function is an "involution": Drawing twice restores the original, because $f(f(d)) = N - f(d) = N - (N - d) = d$. Describe how this technique operates for rubber-band drawing and what colors are seen along the rubber-band line as it crosses pixels of various colors. Is it the same as drawing in XOR mode? For a single bit plane ($b = 1$), what is the difference between reverse mode and XOR drawing? ■

10.3.4 The BitBLT Operation

The routines `draw()`, `read()`, and `copy()` can be integrated into a single function with some added capabilities that vastly increase their power and applicability. The operation has become known as **BitBLT** (pronounced "bitblit"), which stands for *bit* boundary *bl*ock *t*ransfer. It is also called a **raster op** [Ingalls78; Newman79]. BitBLTs are sometimes called **pixelBLTs** when more than one bit per pixel is involved. We use "BitBLT" to denote either possibility.

A BitBLT is sometimes performed in software, but it has become such a pervasive operation, that specially designed VLSI chips have been crafted to perform BitBLTs at very high speeds (hundreds of millions of pixels per second). A few parameters are written to the BitBLT chip, which then takes over and interacts directly with the system bus to move data.

Definition of the BitBLT Operation

There are several versions of the BitBLT that differ in various details. In its simplest form, BitBLT copies a **source rectangle** of pixels to a **destination rectangle** of the same height and width. The source and the destination may reside in either on- or off-screen memory. The BitBLT processor keeps track of the two rectangles in a simple manner: It stores the x- and y-coordinates of the upper left corner of each rectangle and also records their height and width (in pixels). The processor makes all necessary conversions between an (x, y) pair and the corresponding address in memory.

The BitBLT copies source pixels S to the destination rectangle D using the logical combination method described earlier: $D = D \otimes S$. Various choices for $\otimes$ are available.

Some versions of BitBLT allow the user to "premix" the image in the source rectangle with some other predefined pixmap referred to as a **halftone pattern**, and this premixed version becomes the source S that is copied to the destination. The halftone pattern is stored in a pixmap of some size, such as 16 by 16 pixels. It might be, for instance, a checkerboard pattern of 0's and 1's that simulates a shade of gray. If the mask is smaller than the source, it is replicated (tiled) until it attains the size of the source. The user has four choices for the source pixmap S:

- the AND of the source and the halftone pattern.
- the source alone (so that the halftone pattern is ignored).
- the halftone pattern alone.
- solid black.

Most BitBLT processors also maintain a **clipping** rectangle. Before each pixel in the destination is drawn, its coordinates are compared with the boundaries of the clipping rectangle, and the pixel is drawn only if it lies within the boundaries. This can be done rapidly in hardware within the processor. The clipping rectangle effectively limits the region of the destination in which drawing can take place.

10.4 DO-IT-YOURSELF LINE DRAWING: BRESENHAM'S ALGORITHM

Most graphics environments come with a built-in tool that draws straight lines. Every environment has at least some form of `line()` or `lineto()`. OpenGL, of course, goes much further. We usually aren't concerned, therefore, with the details of how such a tool works—how it determines which pixels to turn on between the two endpoints of the line.

But line drawing is fundamental to computer graphics, and it is enlightening to see how such a routine operates. In fact, programmers still need to write a line-drawing routine when they are developing or optimizing new commercial graphics packages.

We start with a straightforward, but dreadfully inefficient, method in order to set forth the main ideas. Then we present a much faster method known as **Bresenham's line-drawing algorithm**.

Suppose we want to set pixel values so that a line appears on the screen between the integer coordinates (a_x, a_y) and (b_x, b_y). Figure 10.23 shows that certain pixels along the mathematical ideal line from (a_x, a_y) to (b_x, b_y) are set to "on". Hopefully, these pixels can be chosen efficiently, and together they will give the appearance of a straight line (albeit with some inevitable "jaggies").

From elementary algebra, the ideal line satisfies the equation

$$y = m(x - a_x) + a_y,$$ (10.3)

where x varies between a_x and b_x and

$$m = \frac{b_y - a_y}{b_x - a_x}$$ (10.4)

is the **slope** of the line. For example, given $(a_x, a_y) = (23, 41)$ and $(b_x, b_y) = (125, 96)$, it follows that $m = 55/102 = 0.5392$. The slope is meaningful only for nonvertical lines, for which a_x and b_x are different. If a line is horizontal or vertical, it is

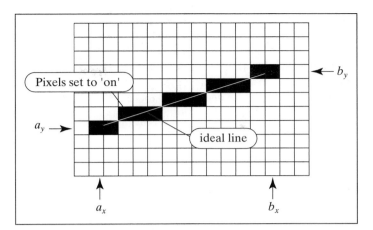

FIGURE 10.23 Drawing a straight-line-segment.

clear which pixels to turn on, but for other lines we need an algorithm that computes which ones to turn on.

The simple, but inefficient, first approach just steps across in x from a_x to b_x in steps of one unit and at each step **rounds** the corresponding value of $m(x - a_x) + a_y$ to the nearest integer. In the case where a_x is less than b_x, this leads to the code

```
float y = a.y;      // initial value
for (int x = a.x; x <= b.x ; x++, y += m)
        setPixel(x, round(y));
```

where, as before, `setPixel(x, y)` writes the current color into the pixel in column x and row y in the frame buffer. Note that the y-value must be rounded to the nearest integer value, a fairly expensive operation.

10.4.1 Bresenham's Line-Drawing Algorithm

Bresenham's algorithm offers a significant advantage over the method just set out, as it avoids floating-point arithmetic and rounding. The ideas behind it are important also because they appear in other types of utilities, such as circle- and ellipse-drawing algorithms. Bresenham's algorithm is a classic example of an **incremental algorithm** that computes the location of each pixel along a line, based on information about the previous pixel.[3] It uses only integer values, avoids any multiplications, and has a tight and efficient innermost loop that generates the proper pixels.

There are several variations of Bresenham's algorithm that do the job in slightly different ways. We describe the version known as the **midpoint algorithm**. This algorithm produces the same pixels as Bresenham's algorithm for straight lines, and its approach can be extended directly to the drawing of more complex shapes such as circles and ellipses.

Suppose that, as before, we are given the integer-valued endpoints (a_x, a_y) and (b_x, b_y) of a line. We want to determine the best sequence of intervening pixels.

To simplify our discussion, we shall examine the special case in which $a_x < b_x$ (i.e., b lies to the right of a) and the slope of the line lies between 0 and 1. (We remove these restrictions later.) For convenience, we define the extents of the segment in x and y, say, W for "width" and H for "height":

$$W = b_x - a_x;$$
$$H = b_y - a_y. \tag{10.5}$$

---

[3] The algorithm is sometimes called a **digital differential analyzer** (DDA) algorithm, after a mechanical device used to solve differential equations in an incremental fashion.

Under the assumptions we have set out, H and W are positive, with $H < W$. Therefore, as x increases from a_x to b_x, the corresponding y increases from a_y to b_y, but y increases less rapidly than does x. As x steps across in unit increments from a_x to b_x, the best integer y value will sometimes stay the same and sometimes increase by 1. The midpoint algorithm quickly determines which of these should occur. (Note that y never needs to either decrease or increase by more than 1. Why?)

From Chapter 4, we know that the equation of the ideal line through (a_x, a_y) and (b_x, b_y) is

$$-W(y - a_y) + H(x - a_x) = 0.$$

The left-hand side of this equation is zero for all points (x, y) that lie on the ideal line. We give a name to this expression for later use. Actually, it is strategic to double the expression first and then give it a name. (As we shall see, this prevents an awkward factor of $1/2$ from appearing in key formulas). So we define the function

$$F(x, y) = -2W(y - a_y) + 2H(x - a_x). \tag{10.6}$$

The important property of $F(x, y)$ is that its sign tells whether (x, y) lies above or below the ideal line:

- If $F(x, y) < 0$ then (x, y) lies above the line;
- If $F(x, y) > 0$ then (x, y) lies below the line.

NOTE *Hint at the reasoning:* Suppose (x, y) is on the line, so that we know that $F(x, y) = 0$. Adjust y upward slightly, keeping x the same. This makes the value of $F(., .)$ smaller. Hence, increasing y above the line makes F negative.)

PRACTICE EXERCISE

10.4.1

For the line segment between $(3, 7)$ and $(9, 11)$,

$$F(x, y) = (-12)(y - 7) + (8)(x - 3),$$

and points on the line, such as $(7, 29/3)$, satisfy $F(x, y) = 0$. What is the sign of $F(x, y)$ for the points $A = (4, 4)$ and $B = (5, 9)$, and where do these points lie relative to the line segment? **Answer**: A lies below the line and F is 44 there. B lies above the line and F is -8 there. ■

Now, how do we decide which pixels to turn on? Figure 10.24 shows some pixels near the ideal line. The circle at each intersection in the grid represents the center of a pixel. Suppose we somehow know that at p_x the best y-value is p_y, and we want to determine the best y-value at the next x-value, given by $p_x + 1$. We wish to know whether the line at $p_x + 1$ is closer to the point L (for "lower") given by $L = (p_x + 1, p_y)$ or to U (for "upper") given by $U = (p_x + 1, p_y + 1)$. The figure shows one possible position of the ideal line, but it could also pass slightly below L or slightly above U. (Why?)

We decide to turn on pixel U or L according to whether the ideal line lies above or below the midpoint $M = (p_x + 1, p_y + 1/2)$ between U and L. If we evaluate the function $F(,)$ at M, its sign will tell whether the ideal line lies above or below M:

- If $F(M_x, M_y) < 0$, then M lies above the ideal line, so we choose L.
- If $F(M_x, M_y) > 0$, then M lies below the ideal line, so we choose U.

Thus, if $F(M_x, M_y) > 0$, the pixel to be turned on is one higher than before, so we increment y. Otherwise we don't increment y. The rest is algebra: determining how

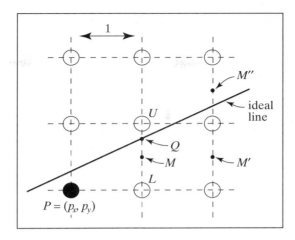

FIGURE 10.24 The configuration for deriving the midpoint technique.

to compute $F()$ quickly. The key is to compute it incrementally, according to how much its value must *change* from one step to the next.

For later reference, we note that at M,

$$F(M_x, M_y) = -2W\left(p_y + \frac{1}{2} - a_y\right) + 2H(p_x + 1 - a_x). \qquad (10.7)$$

Consider how $F(,)$ changes as we move from $x = p_x + 1$ to the next x-value, $p_x + 2$. The M in question is either M' or M'', as shown in Figure 10.24. It is $M' = (p_x + 2, p_y + 1/2)$ if we did not increment y in the previous step, whereas it is $M'' = (p_x + 2, p_y + 3/2)$ if we did increment y in that step.

Case 1: If F was negative in the previous step (so that y was not incremented in that step), then

$$F\left(p_x + 2, p_y + \frac{1}{2}\right) = -2W\left(p_y + \frac{1}{2} - a_y\right) + 2H(p_x + 2 - a_x).$$

We subtract Equation (10.7) to find out how much bigger the preceding equation is than $F(M_x, M_y)$:

$$F\left(p_x + 2, p_y + \frac{1}{2}\right) = F(M_x, M_y) + 2H.$$

Case 2: If F was positive on the previous step (i.e., if y *was* incremented in that step), then

$$F\left(p_x + 2, p_y + \frac{3}{2}\right) = -2W\left(p_y + \frac{3}{2} - a_y\right) + 2H(p_x + 2 - a_x)$$
$$= F(M_x, M_y) - 2(W - H).$$

In either case, the value of the "test quantity" has a constant added to it: $2H$ if we did not increment y and $-2(W - H)$ if we did.

The only question remaining is how to start the process. We know that when $x = a_x, y = a_y$. The first instance of M is therefore $M = (a_x + 1, a_y + 1/2)$, so

$$F(x, y) = -2W\left(a_y + \frac{1}{2} - a_y\right) + 2H(a_x + 1 - a_x) \qquad (10.8)$$
$$= 2H - W.$$

NOTE If we hadn't doubled the function earlier, this result would be $H - 0.5W$, preventing the use of integer values for all quantities involved!)

Summarizing, then, we initialize F to $2H - W$, x to a_x, and y to a_y. Then, at each step, we

1. set the pixel at (x, y) to the desired color value,
2. increment x by 1, and,
3. if $F < 0$, just update F by adding $2H$; otherwise we increment y by 1 and update F by adding $-2(W - H)$.

Putting all this together, we get Bresenham's algorithm (for this special case; see Figure 10.25). Because the algorithm reinitializes itself for each new line and depends only on the endpoint data, it is *repeatable*: Redrawing a line in a different color completely replaces the first line, pixel by pixel; for instance, drawing in the background color totally erases a previously drawn line.

FIGURE 10.25 The midpoint algorithm (special case).

```
bresenham(IntPoint a, IntPoint b)
{ // restriction: a.x < b.x and 0 < H/W < 1
    int y = a.y, W = b.x - a.x, H = b.y - a.y;
    int F = 2 * H - W;      // current error term
    for(int x = a.x; x <= b.x; x++) // inner loop
    {
            setPixel(x, y);
            if(F< 0)
                    F += 2 * H;       // set up for next pixel
            else{
                    y++;
                    F += 2 * (H - W);
            }
    }
}
```

Bresenham's algorithm is extremely simple, with an inner loop that has only a few comparisons and a few additions. It can be easily implemented in assembly language to achieve the greatest speed. Special-purpose graphics hardware is often available that implements the algorithm in a manner so as to achieve even higher performance.

■ EXAMPLE 10.4.1

It is instructive to watch how F varies in a specific example. Let $(a_x, a_y) = (4, 1)$ and $(b_x, b_y) = (16, 4)$. Then $W = 12$ and $H = 3$. Because this line has a slope of $1/4$, we expect the y-value to be incremented only every fourth step or so in x. F is initialized to -6. Each time x is incremented, we do one of two things: If F is negative, we add 6 to it; otherwise we subtract 18 and increment y.

The resulting sequence of values (viewed just after the setPixel(x,y) command is executed) is as follows:

```
x:  4    5    6    7    8    9    10   11   12   13   14   15   16
y:  1    1    2    2    2    2    3    3    3    3    4    4    4
F:  -6   0   -18  -12  -6    0   -18  -12  -6    0   -18  -12  -6
```

The behavior of the algorithm, as it is applied to this example, is shown in Figure 10.26, which illustrates both the resulting line and the variation in F. The "jaggies" are clearly visible in the line, where each short horizontal line segment breaks to the next higher one.

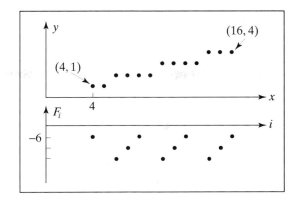

FIGURE 10.26 An example of the midpoint algorithm in action.

Removing the Restrictions on Bresenham's Algorithm

Bresenham's algorithm copes only with the special case in which $a_x < b_x$ and the line has a slope between zero and unity. The remaining cases are easily handled as well, by adding code that deals with each case as it arises.

To Get the Same Line when $a_x > b_x$. The midpoint algorithm sets whichever pixel is on the proper side of the midpoint between the two choices at each step. Thus, we need only adjust the code in Figure 10.25 so that it carries out the midpoint algorithm in the case where $a_x > b_x$. The adjustments are actually slight (See the exercises at the end of the section.) One detail to note is that the code shown in the figure distinguishes between the cases of $F < 0$ and $F \geq 0$, so the case of $F = 0$ is "lumped in" with that of $F > 0$ (in which y is incremented). So we must make sure, when tracing the line in the other direction, that we include the case of $F = 0$ together with the case in which y is decremented.

An alternative method just tests whether $a_x > b_x$ and, if so, swaps a_x with b_x and a_y with b_y, thereafter using the steps in Figure 10.25. In effect, this alternative approach never draws "towards the left"; instead, it redefines the endpoints so that it doesn't have to. The technique is not very successful, however, if the algorithm is to be used to draw connected line segments, as in rendering a polyline. Swapping endpoints would obliterate the natural order in which the segments of the polyline are drawn, and the order can be important when the lines are drawn dotted or dashed.

Lines Having Slope Greater than Unity In this case, we simply interchange the roles of x and y, step in y from a_y to b_y, and use the same test to determine when to increment (the less rapidly changing) x.

Lines with Negative Slopes If the slope of the line we are using is between 0 and −1, H automatically takes on the proper sign. We step in x using exactly the same tests, but decrement the dependent variable rather than increment it. If the slope is more negative than −1, we replace W with −W and interchange the roles of x and y, as in the case where the slope is greater than unity.

Horizontal and Vertical Lines These occur so frequently in graphics, that testing for them (e.g., via the code `if(a.x == b.x)`...) and using a simplified algorithm when they occur may improve the performance of one's routine. The improvement for a vertical line would be marginal; most of the time is spent in `setPixel()`, anyway. For a horizontal line, a routine may be used that writes many bits along a scan line at once, thereby significantly increasing the drawing speed.

(See the exercises to learn how to implement these generalizations.)

Summary of Properties a Drawn Line Should Have

What properties should we require of a line drawn by our algorithm? First, the line should be as straight as possible and should reliably pass through both of the given endpoints. Second, the line should be "smooth" and have uniform brightness along its length. (Lines of different slopes should have the same brightness.) Third, the line should be drawn so that it is repeatable: If, at a later time, we apply the algorithm to the same data specifying the endpoints of the line, it should turn exactly the same pixels on or off, as the case may be. This is important for erasing the line, which is accomplished by redrawing it in the background color or in XOR drawing mode. Finally, it shouldn't matter in which direction the line is drawn: If the line is drawn from (b_x, b_y) to (a_x, a_y), exactly the same pixels should be turned on as when it is drawn from (a_x, a_y) to (b_x, b_y). If this is so, the application can erase a previously drawn line without regard for how it was originally drawn.

Drawing Lines in Patterns

You may have occasion to draw lines in a pattern of dots or dashes. As mentioned in Chapter 2, the pattern for a dash is stored as a sequence of bits, such as 0011111100111111.

It is simple to incorporate such patterns into Bresenham's algorithm. Each time x is incremented, a pointer into the pattern can be incremented as well, and the corresponding bit value can be utilized to set the current drawing color used by `setPixel()`. For long lines, the pattern is used repeatedly by incrementing cyclically from the end of the pattern back to its beginning.

When a polyline is to be drawn dashed, you may want the pattern to be continuous from segment to segment. To do this, the pattern and the pointer into it are made globally available to Bresenham's algorithm so that they can be accessed during successive calls to the algorithm. (See the exercises for other issues concerning the drawing of patterns.)

PRACTICE EXERCISES

10.4.2 Removing restrictions on Bresenham's algorithm

Work out the variations of Bresenham's algorithm for the cases of (a) $a_x > b_x$, (b) lines with slopes greater than unity, and (c) lines with negative slopes, and combine your separate treatments of these cases into a single algorithm that works for any line segment. Try to make the routine as efficient as possible. Test it (at least) by hand.

10.4.3 Numerical example

For endpoints $(8, 23)$ and $(21, 11)$ show the sequences of x, y, and F that evolve as Bresenham's algorithm is applied. Demonstrate that the same pixels are illuminated when the algorithm is started from the opposite endpoint.

10.4.4 Bresenham's algorithm in assembly language

Implement a complete Bresenham's algorithm in machine language for an available host/graphics display. Make the code for the innermost loops as efficient as possible. Test the speed of the machine-language version against that of the C++ version. Also, test whether special code for horizontal and vertical lines improves the algorithm's speed.

10.4.5 Drawing in patterns

Extend Bresenham's algorithm to draw lines using a pattern of 16 bits. Arrange things so that if a polyline is drawn, the pattern will continue uninterrupted from one line segment to the next.   ■

10.5 DEFINING AND FILLING REGIONS OF PIXELS

A raster display can show regions of pixels **filled** with a solid color or a pattern of colors. By a **region**, we mean a collection of pixels lying "next to" one another in some fashion or being associated with each other by some common property. Figure 10.27 shows an image having a number of regions filled with various gray-scale patterns or color.

"Paint programs" are widely available today that allow one to create pictures interactively. All of these programs include a tool that allows the user to point with a mouse at a region and then select a new pattern, whereupon the region is instantly flooded with that pattern. In this section, we discuss how that is done.

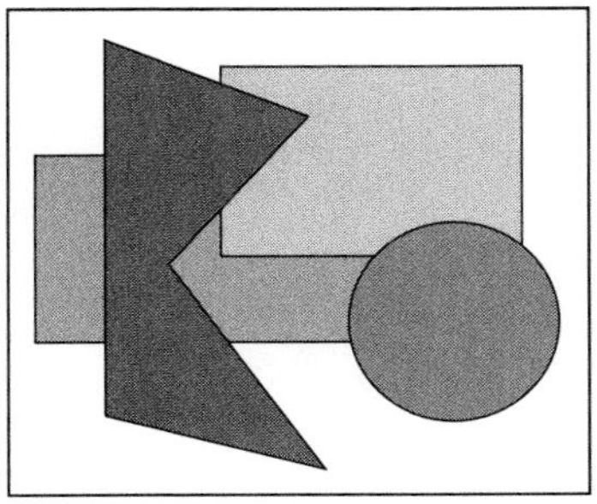

FIGURE 10.27 Several Regions filled with patterns.

10.5.1 Defining Regions

There are various ways to define a region. One important distinction is whether the description is "pixel defined" or "symbolic":

- A **pixel-defined** region is characterized by the actual colors of the pixels in a pixmap. The description of a region R might list each pixel considered to lie in R: $(34, 12), (34, 13), (34, 14)$, etc. Or R could be defined as consisting of all pixels having the value 77 that are "connected" in some way to pixel $(43, 129)$. The notion of connectedness has to be spelled out carefully. To see what the region R is, you must scrutinize the pixmap and observe just which pixels are in R according to this definition.
- A **symbolic** description does not enumerate the pixels, but rather provides some property that all the pixels in region R possess. Such descriptions tend to be "higher level," or more abstract, than pure pixel enumeration. The following are some possible ways to describe regions symbolically:
  - all pixels that are closer to a given point $(23, 47)$ than to any of the given points $(12, 14), (22, 56)$, or $(35, 45)$;
  - all pixels lying within a circle of radius 8 centered at $(5, 23)$;
  - all pixels inside the polygon with vertices at $(32, 56), (120, 546), (345, 1,129)$, and $(80, 87)$. This **polygon-defined** region is a particularly important case, which we discuss in detail later.

  The programmer who wishes to manipulate or analyze regions would most likely choose quite different data structures and algorithms, depending on how the regions of interest are described.

We first examine methods for dealing with pixel-defined regions. Then we discuss various methods for manipulating symbolically defined regions, particularly those defined by polygons.

10.5.2 Pixel-Defined Regions

One way to characterize a pixel-defined region is as follows:

Region R is the set of all pixels having color C that are "connected" to a given pixel S.

Region R is called **interior defined** in this case, since we are specifying the nature of all pixels lying "inside" R. But what might "connected" mean? We say two pixels are **connected** if there is an unbroken path of "adjacent" pixels between them. So the meaning of "connected" depends on the meaning of "adjacent," which has two common definitions in graphics:

- **4-adjacent.** Two pixels are 4-adjacent if they lie next to each other horizontally or vertically. For example, the pixel at $(23, 35)$ is 4-adjacent to the one at $(23, 36)$, but not to the one at $(24, 36)$.
- **8-adjacent.** Two pixels are 8-adjacent if they lie next to one another horizontally, vertically, or diagonally. Thus, pixels at $(23, 35)$ and $(24, 36)$ are 8-adjacent. Clearly, if two pixels are 4-adjacent, they are also 8-adjacent.

We then say that two pixels are **4-connected** if there is an unbroken path of 4-adjacent pixels that connects them. Similarly, they are **8-connected** if there is an unbroken path of 8-adjacent pixels that leads from one to the other.

Figure 10.28 shows a pixmap consisting of black, white, and gray pixels, one of which is designated S. Give the name R to the region whose interior consists of all gray pixels that are 4-connected to S. Then R consists of 20 pixels in the figure. (Locate them.) Call by R' the region whose interior consists of all gray pixels that are 8-connected to S. Then R' consists of all the pixels of R, plus eight others. (Which ones?)

FIGURE 10.28 Regions defined through pixel colors.

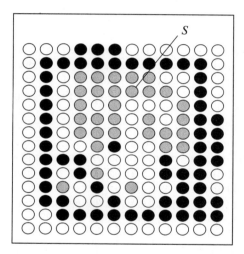

We can also define a region by a boundary, in which case the region is called **boundary defined**. The boundary consists of pixels having a certain boundary color. We might define a region B, for example, as all pixels that are 4-connected to a starting pixel S and do *not* have the boundary color black. The interior of B extends up to, but does not include, pixels of the boundary color. With this definition, region B in Figure 10.28 has 62 nonblack pixels that are 4-connected to S. The 5 nonblack pixels in the southwest corner are not 4-connected to S and so are not in R. Note that the boundary is thicker than one pixel in various places. Such thick boundaries are fine for many algorithms, but will throw others into confusion, as we shall see later.

If we switch "connected" to mean 8-connected, then region B has 67 nonblack pixels 8-connected to S, since the 5 pixels in the southwest corner are now part of the region.

10.5.3 A Recursive Flood-Fill Algorithm

We next describe two simple filling algorithms that work with pixel-based regions. The first operates on interior-defined, 4-connected regions. It changes every interior pixel of color `intColor` to a new color, `newColor`. It is called a **flood-fill** algorithm because it "floods" the region with `newColor`, "feeling its way" out from the "seed" at (x, y), "looking for" pixels of `intColor`, and changing each one it finds to `newColor`. This algorithm is sometimes used in interactive paint systems because the user can specify the seed by pointing to the interior of the region and then initiating the flood operation.

The idea of the algorithm is this: If the pixel at (x, y) is part of the interior (i.e., if it has color `intColor`), change it to `newColor`, and apply the same process recursively to each of its four neighbors. Otherwise do nothing. Figure 10.29 shows how simple the algorithm is. Note that `getPixel(x,y)` is used to interrogate the color of the pixel at (x, y).

FIGURE 10.29 Recursive flood fill for interior-defined regions.

```
void floodFill(short x ,short y, short intColor)
// Start at (x, y); change all pixels of intColor to newColor.
// assume drawing color is newColor
// 4-connected version
{
    if(getPixel(x,y) == intColor)
    {
        setPixel(x, y);   // change its color
        floodFill(x - 1, y, intColor);   // fill left
        floodFill(x + 1, y, intColor);   // fill right
        floodFill(x, y + 1, intColor);   // fill down
        floodFill(x, y - 1, intColor)    // fill up
    }
}
```

The process starts anew at each pixel address that appears in a call to `floodFill()`. The algorithm proceeds blindly, testing nearest neighbors regardless of what has already been tested. Thus, there is no account taken of **region coherence**—the likelihood that a pixel adjacent to an interior pixel is also an interior pixel. For this reason, many pixels are tested several times, requiring a very large number of procedure calls.

■ **EXAMPLE 10.5.1**

Consider the interior-defined region shown in Figure 10.30, consisting of only five pixels. Suppose that the seed is at $(4, 2)$, marked S. When `floodFill(4, 2, white)` is called, the sequence of addresses with which it is called begins with

$(3, 2), (2, 2), (1, 2), (3, 2), (2, 3), (2, 1), (4, 2), (3, 3), (2, 3), (4, 3), \ldots$

In all, there are 21 calls to the procedure, involving many repeated tests of the same pixel, such as $(2, 3)$.

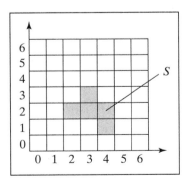

FIGURE 10.30 A sample interior-defined region for filling.

Because the flood-fill algorithm is highly recursive, the recursion stack can become very deep, even for a simple region. Hence, there is a chance that the algorithm will cause a stack overflow and fail even on regions of modest size. In addition, overhead is required to manage the recursion, which can slow the filling process substantially. More efficient (but more complex) methods that capitalize on coherence are discussed later.

To extend the algorithm to an 8-connected version, we simply add four instructions that test the four diagonal neighbors, such as `floodFill(x+1, y-1, intColor)`. This recursive method can also be adapted to boundary-defined regions. (See the exercises.)

10.5.4 Filling Regions with Patterns

The flood-fill algorithm fills regions with a solid color. We might instead wish to fill a region with a pattern, as in Figure 10.27. Suppose the desired pattern is stored in an array

```
RGB pattern[Width][Height];
```

The pixmap in `pattern[][]` might be an entire image that we want to "paint" into a given region, or it might be a small **tiling pattern** that is to be laid down repeatedly. Figure 10.31 shows an eight-by-eight tiling pattern and the result of **tiling** it over a larger region. It is a simple matter to take values from the `pattern` array and to "lay down" the pattern. To draw the pixel at (x, y), we set the drawing color to `pattern[x][y]`, and to cause the pattern to be tiled, we set the drawing color to `pattern [x % Width][y % Height]`. Here, the modulo function % restricts the indices in the pattern array to the proper ranges and replicates the pattern over a region of any size.

FIGURE 10.31 Example of a tiling pattern and the resulting tiling.

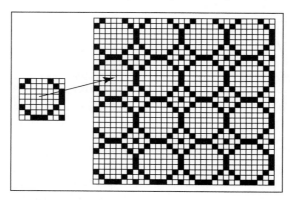

PRACTICE EXERCISES

10.5.1 Boundary-defined flood fill

a. Adapt the algorithm of Figure 10.29 so that it fills boundary-defined, 4-connected regions. Suppose that the boundary color is stored as `boundaryColor` and that the seed lies in the interior of the region, not on its boundary.
b. Does this method work when `boundaryColor` equals `newColor`?
c. If `boundaryColor` is not the same as `newColor`, and if some interior pixels happen to be of color `newColor`, show some geometrical patterns on which the algorithm can get hung up and terminate before the entire region is filled.

10.5.2 Hand simulation of flood fill

Exercise by hand the algorithm of Figure 10.29 on a region whose interior is defined by the pixels $(1, 1), (2, 1), (2, 2), (3, 2), (2, 3),$ and $(1, 3)$. The seed is taken to be $(2, 2)$. Repeat when the algorithm is adapted to 8-connected regions in which the additional four calls are taken in the order $(x - 1, y - 1), (x + 1, y - 1), (x - 1, y + 1), (x + 1, y + 1)$.

10.5.3 Recursive region filling

For the interior-defined region shown in Figure 10.30,

a. Display the "tree of procedure calls" that results when a seed beginning at $(4, 2)$ is used. That is, draw a tree, each node of which contains the address of the pixel being tested by the `if(getPixel()...)` statement in Figure 10.29. When the test succeeds, four subtrees of procedure calls are spawned.
b. What is the depth of this call tree?
c. What is the worst arrangement of four interior pixels for the algorithm, in the sense that the largest number of recursive calls to the procedure is made?

10.5.4 Using a tiling pattern

Sketch the patterns created by the bit sequences:

```
11110101     1000
01101010     1100
01100101     1110
11111010     1111
```

as each is tiled over a large region. Invent three other four-by-four tiling patterns that create interesting patterns.

10.5.5 Dragging a region

Some paint systems allow the user to shift the position of a region by using a mouse. When the mouse button is released, the region is redrawn at the new position. If the region is filled with a tiling pattern, will the pattern always appear the same inside the region? Explain. ■

10.5.5 Using Coherence: Region Filling Based on Runs of Pixels

In order to improve the performance of the previous algorithms and to prevent stack overflows, we shall examine a more sophisticated approach that fills a region, not pixel by pixel, but by groups of pixels situated in runs. A **run** is a group of adjacent pixels lying on the same scan line. If we can identify and fill a whole run at once in a region, we can speed up the filling process dramatically.

To see how this run-oriented filling method operates, consider the boundary-defined, 4-connected region shown in Figure 10.32(a). The s marks the initial seed pixel. The run from a to b that contains s is filled first. Then the row above that one is scanned from a to b, looking for additional runs of interior pixels. One is found, and its rightmost pixel, c, is saved (its address is placed on a stack), to be dealt with later. Then the row below is scanned from a to b; an interior run is found, and its rightmost pixel, d, is saved on the stack. Figure 10.32(b) shows the situation at this point.

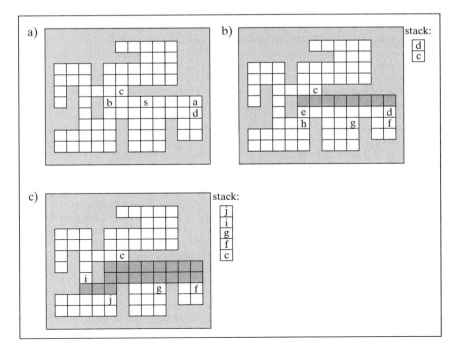

FIGURE 10.32 A sample region to be filled using runs.

Now the stack is popped to produce the new seed, d, and the process is repeated. The run from d to e is filled; the row above that is scanned—finding no interior run—and the row below is scanned between d and e, finding three interior runs. Pixels f, g, and h are pushed onto the stack. Pixel h is then popped, its run is filled, and the two additional runs i and j are identified. At this stage, the situation is as shown in Figure 10.32(c). The process continues until the stack is empty, at which point all interior pixels reachable from the initial seed will have been filled. It is revealing to follow through this example to develop an understanding of the algorithm. (How can it be extended to 8-connected regions? See the exercises at the end of the section.)

The main flow of this "run-fill" algorithm is shown in Figure 10.33. The algorithm will run most efficiently if the region exhibits **span coherence**, wherein many pixels along a scan line have the same value, and **scan-line coherence**, in which what is found on one scan line is likely to be found on the next scan line as well. Because runs are horizontal, the filling process for each run is orderly and can be done efficiently, perhaps filling groups of pixels at once. The left and right ends of the run are found by detecting pixels of the boundary color, and then the whole run is filled with the new color without having to read its pixel values again.

FIGURE 10.33 Skeleton of run-fill region-filling algorithm.

```
Push address of seed pixel on the stack;
while (stack not empty)
{
   Pop the stack to provide the next seed;
   Fill in the run defined by the seed;
   In the row above find interior runs reachable from this run;
   Push the addresses of the rightmost pixels of each such run;
   Do the same for the row below the current run;
}
```

PRACTICE EXERCISES

10.5.6 Simulating the run-fill algorithm

On a sheet of graph paper, lay out a region that approximates the shape of the letter B and contains at least 14 interior pixels. Hand simulate the operation of the run-fill algorithm described in this section, noting the contents of the stack before each pop.

10.5.7 Worst-case regions

What shape of a region of 20 interior pixels is the worst for the run-fill algorithm, in the sense that the most pops of the stack are required? Is the count of pops a reasonable measure of how long the algorithm takes to execute? Discuss other measures.

10.5.8 Filling 8-connected regions

Extend the run-fill algorithm so that it fills 8-connected regions.   ■

10.6 MANIPULATING SYMBOLICALLY DEFINED REGIONS

The flood-fill and run-fill algorithms read the frame buffer pixel by pixel in order to identify each pixel's color and thus "feel their way" across a region. One might suspect that a fill algorithm would be much better if it had access to a higher level, more symbolic, description of the region than a pixel-by-pixel enumeration. Accordingly, we examine some ways to capture a region symbolically, each with its own advantages and disadvantages. The most widely used method in graphics defines a region as the interior of a **polygon**, and this approach is described in detail. The methods fall into two classes: The first represents a region by a collection of **rectangles**, and the second captures a region by a **path** that defines the boundary of the region.

10.6.1 Rectangle-defined Regions

This method of capturing a region describes the region as a list of rectangles. The rectangles may be as small as a single pixel or as large as an entire pix map. The region may have holes and even isolated "blobs."

Figure 10.34 shows a simple example in which each pixel value is black or white. We decompose the region into a collection of aligned rectangles. The representation is just a list of the various rectangles found. (A quick scan of the figure by eye shows that about 11 rectangles will do the job and that the decomposition can be done in different ways.)

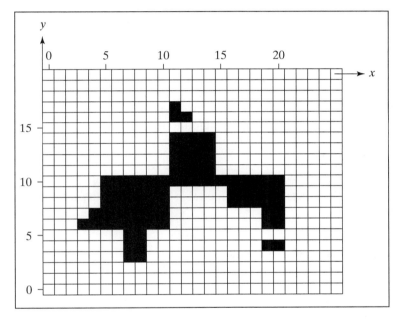

FIGURE 10.34 A region to be represented by rectangles.

We describe an organized way of decomposing the region that is simple and efficient: It allows the rapid building of a shape from a pix map and the rapid filling of a region described by the shape. To apply this technique, we start at the top of the map and move down scan line by scan line, identifying rectangles. Whenever the set of runs in a scan line differs from those in the scan line above, a "new" set of rectangles begins. The y-value of the bottom of each rectangle is not given explicitly, since it is one less than the y-value of the next rectangle. This requires that the bottom of the region be specified explicitly as "empty." (Why?)

In the figure, the topmost rectangle is just a single pixel that is captured by the three values $(17, 11, 1)$, meaning that this rectangle starts at $y = 17$ and extends from $x = 11$ for 1 pixel. The next rectangle contains only two pixels and is given by $(16, 11, 2)$. The third scan line has no pixels, so would be represented as an empty list. The fourth rectangle, given by $(14, 11, 4)$, extends for four scan lines. The complete pix map for this example is represented by the following "shape table" (some scan lines require a list of runs, such as the rectangles that begin at $y = 9$; the table lists 14 rectangles, slightly more than we would expect, due to the requirement that runs such as 19,2 be repeated):

y	Run 1	Run 2
17	11,1	
16	11,2	
15	empty	
14	11,4	
10	5,16	
9	5,6	16,5
7	4,7	19,2
6	3,8	19,2
5	7,2	
4	7,2	19,2
3	7,2	
2	empty	

This representation of a pix map is sometimes called its **shape** representation [Steinhart91; Atkinson86]. It is also sometimes characterized as a "*y*-sorted list of *x*-sorted rectangles." Note that such a representation can describe any set of pixels in a pixmap, including a collection of separate regions. Although it would be inefficient to do so, it can even capture a constellation of isolated pixels.

Regions represented by means of this method are most compact when they exhibit span coherence and scan line coherence, as described earlier. Regions that exhibit high degrees of coherence require fewer data per pixel to characterize them.

What if pixels can have more than two values? One approach would be to identify all the rectangles of uniform color and store them along with their color value. (As before, the background would not have to be stored explicitly.)

Given a pointer to the data structure, the region is filled by traversing the lists and filling each run as it is encountered. Both of these routines are considered further in Case Study 10.4.

Scaling and Translating Regions

The "shape" representation can also be useful when we want to manipulate regions in other ways. For example, to shift a region represented in "shape" form by 30 pixels in *x* and 55 pixels in *y*, we simply traverse the list, incrementing all *x*-values by 30 and all *y*-values by 55. And to double the size of a region, first we translate it so that the initial run is at the origin, $(0, 0)$, and then we double all values in the data structure. Finally, we translate the region to the desired position.

PRACTICE EXERCISES

10.6.1 Write out the lists

Write out the lists of the "shape table" for each of the following pix maps:

a. The arrow cursor in Figure 1.26.
b. The happy-face pix map of Figure 1.20.

10.6.2 Defining the data structures

Define suitable types for the ingredients of the data structure needed for the "shape" representation. ■

10.6.2 Path-defined Regions

It is natural to specify a region by its boundary, which we usually take to be a path of some sort. There are many ways to describe a path. Some useful ones are as follows:

- **By a mathematical formula.** The formula $(x - 122)^2 + (y - 36)^2 = 25$, for instance, defines a circular path 10 pixels in diameter. PostScript (see Appendix 4) allows one to build very complex paths in a frame buffer.
- **By a polypoint.** A sequence of pixel locations $(x_1, y_1), (x_2, y_2), \ldots, (x_n, y_n)$ defines a polyline path that, if closed $((x_1, y_1) = (x_n, y_n))$ specifies a polygon. Section 10.7 discusses methods to fill polygons.
- **By a sequence of adjacent pixels.** We have already seen that a boundary-defined pixel-based region is specified by a collection of pixels of some boundary color. The region is most meaningful if the boundary pixels together form a connected, closed path. This path could be stored in the frame buffer itself, or it could be stored separately as a list of pixel locations, such as $(23, 47), (24, 46), (24, 45), \ldots$ $<$ many others $>$ $, \ldots, (22, 46), (23, 47)$. If each pair of successive pixels in the path is 4-adjacent, we say that the path is "**4-connected**," and similarly for an "**8-connected**" path. (*Question*: Does an 8-connected boundary path define a 4-connected region?).

One particularly appealing way to represent a path of adjacent pixels is by a **chain code** [Freeman74]. The path is specified by a starting pixel, say, (34, 67), and a sequence of "moves" from pixel to pixel, such as "go up, go right, go down,...." The set of possible moves can be encoded in various ways. Figure 10.35 shows two versions. The first, shown in Part (a) of the figure, admits moves in the four "compass" directions, and each direction is associated with a number between 0 and 3. Thus, a sequence of such steps defines a 4-connected path. For example, path A is specified by the sequence shown in the figure, beginning at its lower right. This path happens to be closed, but in general, it need not be. (What is a condition on the numbers of '0', '1', '2', and '3's for a path to be closed?) Note that, since only four possible direction values are used, each can be represented by only two bits.

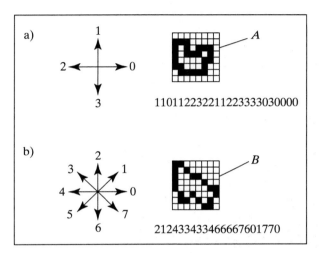

FIGURE 10.35 Defining a path by chain codes.

The version given in Figure 10.35(b) permits eight directions and so can represent 8-connected paths. A '1' indicates that the next pixel on the path is "up one" and "over one to the right," with similar combinations for the other three diagonal directions. (Where is the starting point of the sequence shown?) Chain codes are reminiscent of *relative* draws we saw in Chapter 3, except that they move pixel by pixel.

Figure 10.36 shows a possible data structure for storing a path. The first two elements give the starting pixel of the path and are followed by the number of steps and a list of the steps themselves. Chain codes can offer a very compact representation for certain paths and regions. (How many bits per step are needed for the eight-way code?) In addition, some processing tasks are easily performed:

1. **Translate** a path. This is trivial: Just change the starting pixel.
2. **Scale** a path by scale factor k: Repeat each symbol k times.
3. **Rotate** a path 90° CCW: For the four-direction chain code, increment each step value by 1, properly incrementing 3 to the value 0. Specifically, use `step=(step+1)%3`. For the eight-direction code, add 2 to each step.

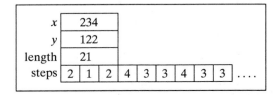

FIGURE 10.36 Suitable data structure for a chain-encoded path.

On the other hand, some operations are difficult. For instance, filling a region defined by a chain code is complicated, since runs of pixels along scan lines are not easily identified. One would most likely first convert the chain code representation into a "shape table."

10.7 FILLING POLYGON-DEFINED REGIONS

Regions are often defined by polygons, and efficient algorithms have been developed for filling them with a solid color or a pattern. Some graphics packages provide their own efficient filling routines. We examine how to perform a fill in one's own package.

Suppose that the region to be filled is a polygon P described by a set of pixel addresses $p_i = (x_i, y_i)$, for $i = 1, \ldots, N$, that specifies the sequence of P's vertices. Figure 10.37 shows an example having seven vertices. To fill P, we progress through the frame buffer scan line by scan line, filling in the appropriate portions of each line. As shown in the figure, the proper portions are determined by finding the intersections of the scan line, say, $y = 3$, with all the edges of P. The runs of pixels that lie between pairs of edges must lie inside P and are filled with the desired color.

FIGURE 10.37 Filling proper portions of a scan line.

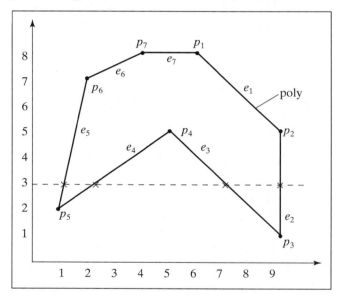

The following pseudocode suggests the filling process:

```
for(each scan line L)
{
        Find intersections of L with all edges of P
        Sort the intersections by increasing x-value
        Fill pixel runs between all pairs of intersections
}
```

For example, in the figure, the scan line at $y = 3$ intersects the four edges e_2, e_3, e_4, and e_5. The four x-values of the intersection are rounded up or down to integers, as described next, and are sorted to yield the sequence 1, 2, 7, 9. Then two runs are filled: the first from column 1 to 2 and the second from column 7 to 9.

Note that taking the sorted edge intersections in pairs uses a form of **inside–outside** test. Moving along a scan line, we pass either into or out of P at each intersection, the "inside-ness" of which changes. (Inside-ness is sometimes called **parity** in this context, and we say that the parity changes at each intersection.) If we pass to the inside, the subsequent pixels will be filled; if we pass to the outside, they will not. If P lies wholly to the right of the start of each scan line, the parity is initially *out*. Note that the algorithm exploits **span coherence**, the tendency for several consecutive pixels along a scan line to lie next to an interior pixel. Hence, an entire run can be filled with minimal calculation.

10.7.1 Which Pixels on an Edge Belong to a Polygon?

It is common for a scene to consist of several polygons and for some (say, two) of the polygons to lie next to one another and therefore share an edge. Such polygons are said to *abut* one another. If we are not careful, the algorithm we are considering could set pixels on the common edge first to the color of one polygon and then to the color of the other. Drawing the edge twice in this fashion could lead to a visually disturbing result: The edge could have a bizarre color if the application happened to be drawing in XOR mode, or it could be drawn twice too bright if the drawing is sent to a photorecorder. The algorithm must therefore decide which polygon "owns" each edge, so that each edge belongs to only one of the two polygons.

A rule that works well is that a polygon owns its left edges (or, in the case of horizontal edges, its bottom ones). So when two polygons abut, as in Figure 10.38, the edge belongs to the right-hand polygon and is drawn only once, in that polygon's color. If a shared edge is horizontal, it is drawn in the upper polygon's color. The figure uses simple triangles to show the four possible ways that two polygons can share an edge. In each case, the shared edge should be drawn in the color of polygon B.

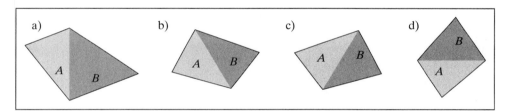

FIGURE 10.38 The shared edge belongs to polygon B.

How do we apply this rule in executing the command to "fill pixel runs between all pairs of intersections"? Figure 10.39 shows a sample polygon P with nine vertices. Pixels whose centers lie in the interior of P are colored, but which pixels with centers lying *on* the edges should be colored? Since the left and bottom edges are owned by P, pixels lying on these edges are colored, while those lying on the right and top edges are not. Thus, in filling each span along a scan line between two intersections, the span includes its leftmost pixel if that pixel lies on an edge, but not its rightmost pixel. This leaves unaffected any pixels that are owned by other polygons above and to the right of P. (Check to make sure that Figure 10.39 shows this property.)

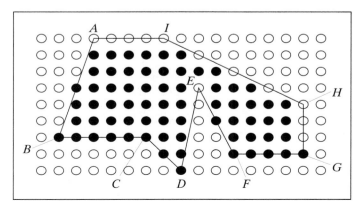

FIGURE 10.39 Filling in spans of internal pixels.

Since intersections will normally occur at some x that lies between integer values, we round up or down to the proper pixel to start and end each span. For example, suppose that the left intersection of a run lies at the real value xLeft and the right intersection at xRight. We want to compute the first and last pixels in the run, xFirst and xLast, respectively. By the preceding rule, xFirst is the smallest integer that is greater than or equal to xLeft. Similarly, xLast is the largest integer strictly less than xRight. The computation can be implemented in C++ using a tiny offset, eps, as follows:

```
#define eps 0.000001
xFirst = (short)(xLeft + 1 - eps); // on xLeft or the next up
xLast = (short)(xRight - eps);      // one smaller than xRight
for(x = xFirst; x <= xLast; x++) setPixel(x, y);
```

Handling Intersections with Edge Endpoints

It often happens that a scan line passes directly through an endpoint (since endpoints of an edge are integers). In order to achieve the correct change in parity, we must count this kind of passage as an intersection.

For instance, the scan line that passes through vertex H in Figure 10.39 "sees" two intersections (one with edge GH and one with edge HI), so the parity on both sides of H seems to be the same. But this sameness would cause us to fill to the right of H, which is clearly wrong. Further, the polygon owns its bottom horizontal edge BC, so we want to see one intersection at B. (Why?) However, the polygon doesn't own its top horizontal edge AI, so we want to see an even number of intersections at A. Apparently, there are so many different cases that it appears that a complex set of rules is required!

However, one simple rule that works well in every case is to ignore intersections of a scan line with the *upper* endpoint of an edge and to ignore horizontal edges altogether in calculations of intersections. Thus, in Figure 10.39, there are no intersections at A and I, and there is one at B and one at H, just as we hoped. Figure 10.40 illustrates other situations that can occur and shows a count of the number of intersections that are "seen" by scan lines that pass through the vertices of the polygon drawn. In each case, the parity to the right of the intersection has the proper value for filling. (Check this out.) Note that one inconsequential effect of this rule is that the pixel at E in Figure 10.39 is not drawn, being at the upper end of both edges. We therefore adjust the instruction in the fill algorithm, *Find intersections of L with all edges of P*, to include the following refinement:

FIGURE 10.40 Number of intersections seen with edges of a polygon.

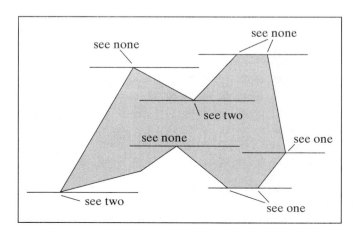

Find the intersections of the scan line with all edges of P.

Discard intersections with horizontal edges and with the upper endpoint of any edge.

PRACTICE EXERCISE

10.7.1 Testing the method

Consider the sample polygon Q of Figure 10.41, which has the following 16 vertices:

$A: (52, 30)$, $B: (74, 43)$, $C: (60, 60)$, $D: (38, 60)$, $E: (30, 50)$,
$F: (10, 50)$, $G: (10, 28)$, $H: (22, 41)$, $I: (33, 10)$, $J: (50, 10)$,
$K: (39, 30)$, $L: (40, 44)$, $M: (54, 44)$, $N: (46, 34)$, $O: (45, 42)$,
$P: (33, 34)$.

Note that the last five vertices constitute a hole in Q. Sketch this polygon on graph paper, and, using the method set forth in this section, determine that the polygon is filled properly.   ■

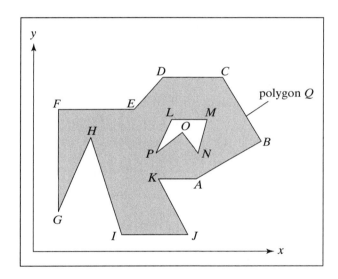

FIGURE 10.41 Sample polygon to be filled.

10.7.2 Improving the Algorithm's Performance

To improve the performance of the method of the preceding section, we look for the most time-consuming part. Here it is the large number of calculations pertaining to intersections between scan lines and edges. To reduce this burden, we build and maintain a simple list so that we can locate intersections rapidly. The list, called the *active-edge list* (AEL), allows the algorithm to capitalize on **edge coherence**, which has two parts:

- the tendency for many of the edges intersected by scan line y to be intersected as well by scan line $(y + 1)$.
- the property (of a straight line) that the x-value of the intersection migrates *in uniform increments* from scan line to scan line.

During the filling process, the appropriate runs of pixels along each scan line are filled simply by referring to the AEL, which contains the x-values of all the edge intersections for the current scan line (the line currently being filled). The x-values are maintained in sorted order, so that, according to the parity rule, the first two x-values define the first run, the next two define the next run, and so on.

For example, suppose we are filling the polygon shown in Figure 10.42 and have reached scanline $y = 50$. This scan line intersects four edges of the polygon. The x-values of the intersections are easily calculated to be 45, 56.66, 70, and 100, in sorted order. The two spans from 45 to 56 and from 70 to 99 are now easily filled in.

FIGURE 10.42 Example of filling a polygon.

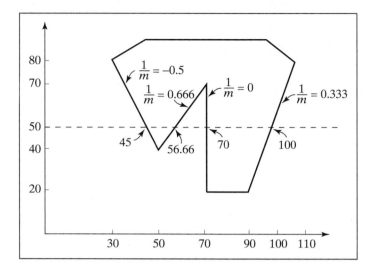

A linked-list form of the AEL for this situation is suggested in Figure 10.43, showing the four current intersections stored in order, along with some other data that lets the algorithm quickly update the AEL for use on the next scan line. The AEL contains three items for each currently intersected edge:

1. the x-value, x_{int}, of the intersection of the edge with the current scan line.
2. The reciprocal, $1/m$, of the edge's slope m.
3. The y-value, y_{high}, of the upper endpoint of the edge.

The second item is used to locate the intersections that scan line $y = 51$ makes with each edge. Note that if an edge has slope m, then moving up by 1 unit causes the x-value of the intersection to increase by $1/m$. (Check this out). The value $1/m$ is stored directly in the AEL for each edge, as shown in the figure. (For instance, the leftmost edge spans 20 units in x and 40 in y, so its inverse slope is 20/40; check the other values shown in the figure.) Thus, a single addition of x_{int} and $1/m$ finds the point of intersection of the edge with the next scan line above, capitalizing on edge coherence.

Note that incrementing by $1/m$ and rounding is basically what Bresenham's line algorithm does to migrate from point to point along a line. In fact, Bresenham's method (incrementing on the basis of the sign of an error term and then updating that term) would most likely be used at this juncture to maximize efficiency.

FIGURE 10.43 The AEL for scan line $y = 50$.

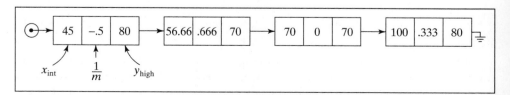

As we move to the next scan line in the filling process, several things can happen in addition to an incremental move along an edge:

1. The new scan line may now lie just beyond (above) an edge represented in the AEL. The y-value of the top endpoint of each edge is kept in the AEL to make this situation easy to identify. If the new value of y exceeds the upper value, the edge is deleted from the AEL.
2. One or more new edges may be encountered as y becomes equal to the y-value of the lower endpoint of some edges in the polygon. Edge records for such edges are added to the AEL by referring to a separate table, which we shall describe next.
3. For nonsimple polygons, the order of x-values of edge intersections may become reversed if two edges cross. The list of intersections must be resorted if this happens.

So after the runs have been filled for the current scan line, y is incremented, x-intersections are updated, some edges are dropped off the AEL, others are added, and the x-intersections are sorted if necessary. The runs along this next scan line can now be filled in a similar manner.

The Edge Table

To find which edges must be added as we procced to the next scan line, we could test each vertex of P to determine which edges have been reached as y is incremented, but this approach is inefficient. Instead, information is gathered about each edge in P ahead of time and cleverly placed in an **edge table** (ET). The ET provides rapid access to the required information while the AEL is updated.

The ET is fashioned as an array of lists, edgetable[], one list for each scan line. A portion of the ET for polygon Q in Figure 10.41 is shown in Figure 10.44. This part of the ET is formed while initially traversing the polygon to eliminate horizontal edges and shorten others.

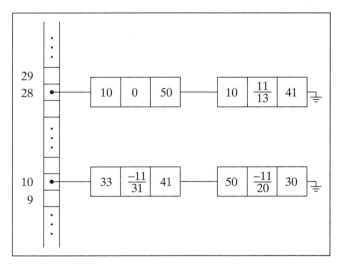

FIGURE 10.44 Edge table characterizing the polygon Q.

The list for each scan line contains information about any edge of Q that has its *lower* endpoint at that scan line. (This effectively sorts the edges of Q by their lower y-values; one says that the ET performs a **bucket sort** of the polygon's edges.) Thus, many of the lists in the ET are empty.

Each edge is characterized by a record of the same type as used in the AEL. The y_{high} and $1/m$ fields are loaded with the proper values, and the x_{int} field is loaded with the x-value of the lower endpoint of the edge in question.

The edge table makes it simple to identify those edges that must be added to the AEL during updating. For the new current scan line at row y, all edges pointed to by `edgetable[y]` have been reached and are added to the AEL. The x_{int} value automatically contains the initial intersection value, and the other fields are already properly loaded. Therefore, only a few pointers must be adjusted to insert the new edge records. Before filling pixel runs, the AEL is re-sorted into ascending x_{int} values to maintain parity.

A skeleton of the overall algorithm is shown in Figure 10.45. The algorithm begins with an empty AEL and successively fills each scan line, starting at $y = 0$. It moves quickly through the main loop, drawing nothing until the first edges are added to the AEL. More details on this algorithm are given in Case Study 10.7.

FIGURE 10.45 Skeleton of the polygon fill algorithm.

```
AEL = NULL;
for(y = 0; y <= maxRow; y++)
{       // AEL is initially empty
        add all edges in edgetable[y] to AEL
        if( AEL != NULL)  // any edges to process?
        {
                sort AEL by xInt value
                fill pixel values along y using AEL info
                delete from AEL any records for which yupper == y
                update each xInt value by its inverse slope
        }
}
```

A Simplification: Filling "Horizontally Convex" Polygons

The algorithm of Figure 10.45 can be substantially simplified if it is known that the polygon which is to be filled has only one left edge and one right edge at each scan line. Such polygons might be called "horizontally convex."[4] Clearly, every convex polygon is also horizontally convex. Triangles are horizontally convex, and some quadrilaterals are, while others are not. (Sketch some polygons that are horizontally convex.)

The main simplification in the algorithm is that, with horizontally convex polygons, the AEL always contains exactly two edges. This makes processing the list much simpler. Details are discussed in Case Study 10.7.

OpenGL can render complex 3D scenes much faster when the rendering routine will be presented only with horizontally convex polygons. Fortunately, most modeling software produces only convex polygons to represent the shapes we want to render.

PRACTICE EXERCISES

10.7.2 Table-fill algorithm

The table-fill algorithm fills a certain class of polygons very rapidly. Each edge of the polygon is first scan converted (perhaps using Bresenham's algorithm), pixel by pixel, to generate the (x, y) pairs that occur along its edges. As each pair (x, y) is formed, it is tested against two arrays, $\min[y]$ and $\max[y]$, that contain, for each y-value, the minimum and maximum x-values encountered so far. If $x < \min[y]$, then $\min[y]$ is updated to contain the new x-value, and similarly for $\max[y]$. The polygon is then

---

4   A polygon is horizontally convex if the straight line between any two points in the polygon *having the same y-value* lies entirely within the polygon.

filled by drawing in the run of pixels from min[y] to max[y] for each scan line y. No sorting is required, so the algorithm is fast.

What are the geometric conditions on a polygon which guarantee that it will be filled correctly? Give several examples of polygons for which the method works and several for which it fails.

10.7.3 Fence-fill algorithm

The fence-fill method for polygonal regions uses the notion of "complementing" or "reversing" certain pixels in the picture. For a bilevel display, a pixel of 1 (white) is set to 0 (black), and vice versa. The essential property of complementing is that doing it twice restores the original value of whatever is being complemented.

Complementing works as follows: Erect a vertical "fence"—perhaps through some vertex of the polygon to be filled. Set all pixels to 0. Now, for each edge of the polygon, do the following: On each scan line through the edge, complement all pixels from the edge to the fence. Pixels along a scan line that lie outside the polygon are complemented an even number of times and so are 0. Those that lie inside are complemented an odd number of times and so are 1 (filled). This property is independent of where the fence lies.

Draw sample polygons on paper, and use the fence-fill method to fill the polygons by hand. Show that the method works for multiple polygons and for polygons with holes. What will happen if the method is used on a single line rather than on a polygon having a true inside and outside? ■

10.8 ALIASING; ANTIALIASING TECHNIQUES

The notion of the "jaggies" has appeared in various earlier discussions. The pheomenon is a form of **aliasing**, which is an inherent property of raster displays. Aliasing occurs because of the discrete nature of pixels; that is, pixels occur on a display in a fixed rectangular array. As an example, a black rectangle is shown in Figure 10.46(a). If this rectangle covers a large number of pixels, its border will appear relatively smooth, although still somewhat jagged. But if it covers only a few pixels, as in Part (b), the "jaggies" will be very prominent and disturbing to the eye. In the figure, each pixel is set to black, based on whether the rectangle covers one particular spot: the pixel's center. Effectively, each pixel "samples" the rectangle at a single point, its center, asking whether the rectangle is present there. On the basis of this sample, the color of the entire pixel area is set to white or black.

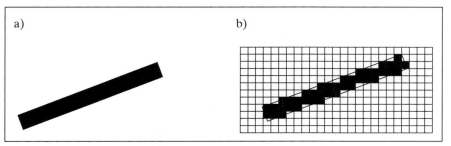

a)   b)

FIGURE 10.46 Aliasing of a rectangle.

Sampling in this manner can cause small objects (e.g., distant objects in a 3D scene) to disappear entirely, as suggested in Figure 10.47(a). If the object lands between the centers of two or more pixels, it will not be displayed at all. Part (b) of the figure shows how an object can "blink" on and off in an animation. The object might cover the center of a pixel in one frame, but miss it in the next, which would be rather objectionable to the viewer.

FIGURE 10.47 Small objects missed by aliasing.

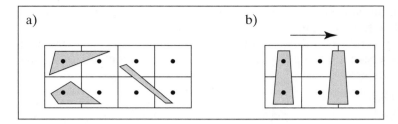

The term *aliasing* comes from sampling theory in signal processing [Oppenheim83]. Roughly speaking, if a rapidly varying signal is sampled too infrequently, the samples appear to represent a signal that varies at a lower frequency: The frequency of the original signal appears to be replaced by its lower "alias" frequency. Figure 10.48(a) shows a rapidly varying square wave, which is sampled uniformly at the instants shown by dots. On the basis of these samples alone, the signal appears to be a square wave with lower frequency, as shown in Part (b) of the figure.

FIGURE 10.48 Sampling too slowly makes a signal look like its alias.

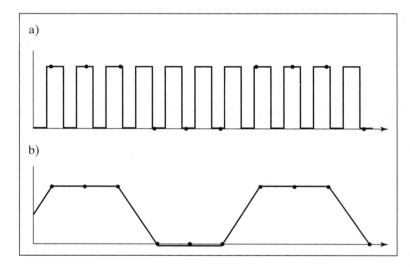

10.8.1 Antialiasing Techniques

How can one reduce the aliasing produced by insufficient sampling? A display with a higher resolution helps, because the jags are then smaller in size relative to the object. But both current technology and price place a limit on how much one can increase the resolution of a display. We must therefore look for other ways to deal with aliasing.

Antialiasing techniques involve one form or another of "blurring" to smooth an image. In the case of a black rectangle against a white background, the sharp transition from black to white is softened by using a mixture of gray pixels near the rectangle's border. When the picture is looked at from afar, the eye blends the gracefully varying shades together and sees a smoother edge.

Three approaches to antialiasing are commonly used: **prefiltering**, **supersampling**, and **postfiltering**.

Prefiltering

Prefiltering techniques compute pixel colors based on an object's *coverage*: the fraction of the pixel area that is covered by the object. Consider scan converting a white polygon on a black background, as in Figure 10.49(a). Suppose the intensity values are 0 for black and 1 for white. The polygon is situated in a square grid in which the center of each square corresponds to the center of a pixel on the display. A pixel that is half-covered by the polygon should be given the intensity 1/2; one that is one-third covered should be given the intensity 1/3; and so forth. If the frame buffer has 4 bits per pixel, so that black is represented by 0 and white by 15, a pixel that is one-quarter covered by the polygon should be given the value of $(1/4)15$, which rounds up to 4. Figure 10.49(b) shows the values that result when the coverage of each pixel is calculated. (What would this array of pixel values be if we instead just sampled the polygon at the center of each pixel, using level 15 when the rectangle covers the center and 0 otherwise?)

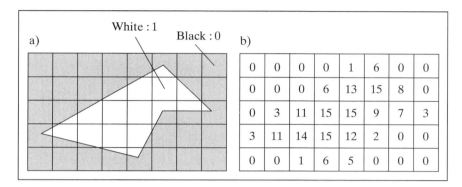

FIGURE 10.49 Using the fraction of the pixel area covered by the object.

The geometric computations required to find the coverage for each pixel can, of course, be very time consuming. A number of efficient approaches have been developed. We describe a modification of Bresenham's line algorithm that was developed by Pitteway and Watkinson [Pitteway80]. As with Bresenham's algorithm, its computations are incremental and based on integer arithmetic.

We have seen how a polygon fill routine progresses scan line by scan line, using the AEL to determine which runs of pixels to fill. The intersection points x_{int} stored in the AEL are updated after each scan line is filled, using a Bresenham-based cycle: (Increment if an error term is negative, and update the error term.) The values of the error term can also be used to keep track of the coverage of the first and last pixels in each run. So the pixels along the edges of the polygon are colored according to the polygon's coverage there, thereby achieving antialiasing.

Figure 10.50 shows Pitteway and Watkinson's approach through an example. The edge of the polygon has a slope of 4/10. The pixels identified by the standard Bresenham algorithm are shown dotted, and the shaded region for each of these pixels indicates the area inside the polygon. The numerical amount of this area is shown for each pixel: 0.5, 0.9, 0.3, and so forth. The first pixel is assumed to be 50 percent covered.

One can see from geometric considerations that as we move pixel by pixel to the right, the shaded area either increases by $m = 0.4$, if the y-value stays the same, or decreases by $1 - m = 0.6$, if the y-value is incremented. (See the exercises at the end of the section.) Hence, it is simple to update this area incrementally as part of the Bresenham algorithm.

Suppose, then, that the frame buffer supports the maximum intensity value `MaxLevel`. For an edge of slope m, we find the closest integer, `inc1` = `MaxLevel` * `m,` and either increment the intensity of each pixel by `inc1` or decrement it by `inc2` = `MaxLevel` - `inc1`. The main loop of Bresenham's algorithm (see Figure 10.25) needs only slight adjustments: If $F < 0$, then, in addition to updating the error term F += 2 * H, we update the intensity `colval` += `inc1`. Similarly, if $F \geq 0$, the

FIGURE 10.50 Example of scan conversion with antialiasing.

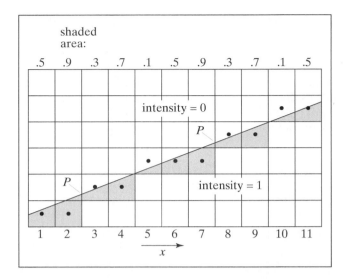

error is updated by $2*(H - W)$, and the intensity is updated by `-inc2`. In their original paper, Pitteway and Watkinson improved the efficiency of their routine further by adjusting matters so that `colval` itself could replace F as the test variable.

Prefiltering operates on the detailed geometric shape of the object(s) being scan converted and computes an average intensity for each pixel, based on the objects found lying within each pixel's area. For shapes other than polygons, prefiltering can be an expensive technique computationally, so we shall seek alternative approaches to antialiasing.

Supersampling

Since aliasing arises from sampling an object at too few points, we can try to reduce its effects by sampling more often than one sample per pixel. This technique is called **supersampling**: taking more intensity samples of the scene than are displayed. Each display pixel value is then formed as the average of several samples.

Figure 10.51 shows an example of double sampling: The object (in this case a tilted bar) is sampled two times more densely in both x and y than it is displayed. The squares indicate display pixels, and the x's denote spots at which the scene is sampled. Each final display pixel can be formed as the average of the nine "neighboring" samples: the center pixel and the eight surrounding ones. Some samples are reused in several pixel calculations. (Which ones?) The display pixel at A is based on six samples within the bar and three samples of the background. Its color is thus set to the sum of two-thirds the bar's color and one-third the background's color. The pixel at B is based on all nine samples within the bar: Its color is set to that of the bar.

Figure 10.52(a) shows a scene displayed at a resolution of 300-by-400 pixels. The "jaggies" are readily apparent. Figure 10.52(b) shows the benefits of double sampling. The same scene was sampled at a resolution of 600-by-800 samples, and each of the 300-by-400 display pixels is an average of nine neighbors. The "jaggies" have been softened considerably.

In general, supersampling computes N_s samples of a scene in both x and y for each display pixel, averaging some number of neighboring samples to form each display pixel value. Supersampling with $N_s = 4$, for example, averages 16 samples for each display pixel. (Sketch this situation.)

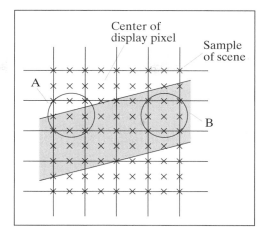

FIGURE 10.51 Antialiasing using supersampling.

FIGURE 10.52 Examples of antialiasing by supersampling.

One can achieve antialiasing even with no supersampling $(N_s = 1)$. In Figure 10.53, the scene shown is sampled at the corner of each display pixel. The intensity of each such pixel is set to the average of the four samples taken at its corners. Some softening of the "jaggies" is observed, even though there is no supersampling.

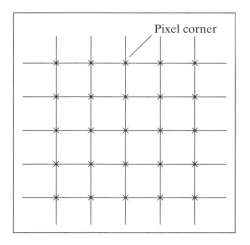

FIGURE 10.53 Antialiasing by corner sampling.

Postfiltering

In the double-sampling method, nine neighboring samples are averaged to compute each display pixel's intensity, giving each neighbor equal importance. This form of blurring or filtering might be improved by giving the center sample more weight and the eight neighbors less weight. Or it may help to include more neighbors in the averaging computation.

Postfiltering computes each display pixel as a **weighted average** of an appropriate set of neighboring samples of the scene. Figure 10.54 shows the situation in relation to double sampling. Each value represents the intensity of a sample of the scene, with the ones in gray indicating the centers of the various display pixels. The square **mask** or **window function** of weights is laid over each gray square in turn. Then each window weight is multiplied by its corresponding sample, and the nine products are summed to form the intensity of the display pixel. For example, when the mask shown is laid over the sample of intensity 30, the weighted average is found to be

$$\frac{30}{2} + \frac{28 + 16 + 4 + 42 + 17 + 53 + 60 + 62}{16} = 32.625,$$

which rounds to intensity 33. This mask gives eight times as much weight to the center as to the other eight neighbors. The weights always sum to unity.

FIGURE 10.54 Postfiltering a graphics image.

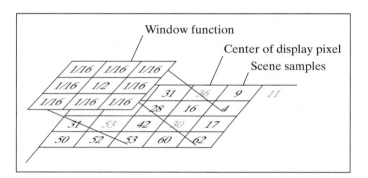

Note that as we have described it, supersampling is just a special case of postfiltering in which all the weights have the value 1/9. Sampling and filter theory [Gonzalez87; Oppenheim83] provide analytical methods for determining how different classes of window functions perform as postfilters. Sometimes larger masks, five by five or even seven by seven, are used. These "look farther" into the neighborhood of the center sample and can provide additional smoothing. Figure 10.55 shows some examples of masks that are often used in practice [Crow81]. The fraction next to each mask gives the common factor that scales each mask element so that, together, they sum to unity. In the first mask, the center is weighted four times as heavily as the 4-connected neighbors are, and the corners have no weight at all. The third example is a five-by-five mask that gives weight to the second ring of neighbors around each sample. Examples (b) and (c) are approximations to the "Bartlett window": The weights grow linearly from the edges toward the center.

FIGURE 10.55 Examples of window functions.

a)
$$\frac{1}{8}$$

0	1	0
1	4	1
0	1	0

b)
$$\frac{1}{16}$$

1	2	1
2	4	2
1	2	1

c)
$$\frac{1}{81}$$

1	2	3	2	1
2	4	6	4	2
3	6	9	6	3
2	4	6	4	2
1	2	3	2	1

Postfiltering can be performed for any value N_s of oversampling. If $N_s = 4$ is used, a five-by-five, seven-by-seven, or even nine-by-nine mask is appropriate [Crow81]. If $N_s = 1$, as in the case of corner sampling, one might use a three-by-three mask that weights the center pixel most heavily. This blurring may or may not pay off, depending on the scene being rendered.

More advanced techniques for antialiasing are discussed in Chapter 14 in connection with ray tracing. A great deal of further information is also available in [Foley90, Blinn96].

PRACTICE EXERCISES

10.8.1 Checking the incremental area

Show, for the case where the slope m of an edge lies between 0 and 1, that the area of an edge pixel covered by a polygon either increases by m or decreases by $1 - m$ as one moves along the edge pixel by pixel. Include in your calculation of pixel areas the small triangular areas (labeled P in Figure 10.50) belonging to the next higher pixels, as in the pixels at $x = 2$ and $x = 7$ in the figure.

10.8.2 The Pitteway–Watkinson algorithm in other quadrants

Our discussion of this algorithm restricted the slope of the polygon's edge to lie between 0 and 1. Extend the method to edges of arbitrary slope.

10.8.3 Antialiasing a polygon

For a frame buffer that holds values from 0 to 15, apply the antialiasing scan conversion to each edge of a white polygon with vertices $(1, 3), (6, 7), (15, 4), (11, 15)$, and $(1, 8)$. Assume a black background. Then fill the polygon with white, using a boundary-fill algorithm. Is there any chance that, if a hole appeared in the polygon's edge, the fill routine would fail? If so, how could this shortcoming be fixed?

10.8.4 Corner sampling

For a raster having R rows and C columns, how many samples of a scene must be computed when corner sampling is used? That is, how many corners does the raster have? Compare this kind of sampling with "center-of-pixel" sampling and with double sampling.

10.8.5 Other windows

Based on the patterns of the Bartlett windows in Figures 10.55(b) and (c), what are the elements of a seven-by-seven Bartlett window? What is the common scaling factor? ▪

10.8.2 Antialiasing of Texture

In Chapter 8, we examined how to map textures onto surfaces in order to achieve greater realism. Mapped textures are particularly prone to aliasing effects, because we usually expect the texture to represent some pattern or image faithfully. In addition, the texture itself is usually defined as a pixmap, and there is often a complex geometric relationship between pixels on the display and pixels in the map. We describe the specific issues that arise when drawing textures and examine some solutions.

Figure 10.56(a) shows a classic case of aliasing: texture painted onto a tilted plane. The checkerboard squares that are far away are severely aliased, giving rise to various moiré patterns. In Figure 10.56(b), the image has been antialiased, and the result is substantially better.

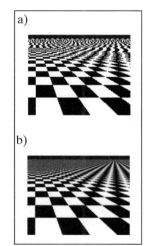

FIGURE 10.56 Example of aliasing and improvement due to antialiasing. (Courtesy of Paul Heckebert)

Recall that the texture is defined as a function *texture*(s, t) in texture space and that it undergoes a complex sequence of mappings before it is finally depicted on the display. The rendering task is to work the other way, and, for each given display pixel at coordinates (x, y), find the corresponding color in the *texture*() function.

Figure 10.57 shows a particular pixel at (x, y) being rendered and the corresponding value (s^*, t^*) in texture space that is accessed. For convenience, we will give the name $T()$ to the overall mapping from pixel space to texture space, so $(s^*, t^*) = T(x, y)$. (The components of this mapping were developed in Chapter 8.)

FIGURE 10.57 Cause of aliasing in rendering texture.

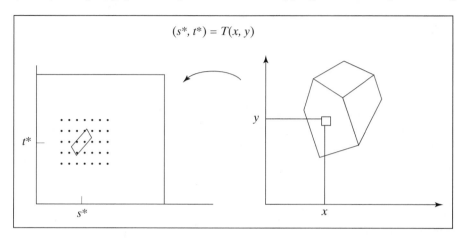

Because pixels are not single points, but have area, we should more properly think of how the whole square pixel centered at (x, y) maps to texture space. This pixel is also shown in Figure 10.57 as a quadrilateral.[5] We will call such a quadrilateral the *texture quad* corresponding to the screen pixel in question. Think of the texture space as being covered with such quads, each arising from a screen pixel. The size and shape of each texture quad depends on the nature of $T()$ and can be costly to find. If *texture*(,) varies inside the quad, yet the screen pixel is colored using only the single sample *texture*(s^*, t^*), significant information is missed, and substantial aliasing occurs.

To reduce the effects of aliasing, we should color each screen pixel with some form of average of the colors lying in the corresponding texture quad. Figure 10.58 shows a texture quad superimposed on the individual texture elements, or *texels*, of the pix map `txtr[][]` that defines the *texture*(s, t). If there were a simple way to find the area of each texel that lies inside this texture quad, the average would be easy to find: We would merely weight each `txtr[r][c]` by this area, sum the results, and divide by the area of the quad. This procedure is analogous to the prefiltering technique used earlier for antialiasing. Unfortunately such a calculation is costly, because it is hard to find the area of each texel covered by the quad.

Heckbert has surveyed the various methods researchers have developed to approximate this kind of prefiltering [Heckbert86]. One method in particular, the elliptical weighted-average (EWA) filter [Greene86], is recommended. As suggested in Figure 10.59, the method supposes each screen pixel to be covered by a circularly symmetric filter function (the concentric circles indicate different weighting levels, as in a topographic map) and maps the filter function into texture space, where it becomes a form of ellipse that roughly resembles the shape of the texture quad. Samples of the filter function, stored in an LUT, are used to weight different points within

---

[5]   If the 3D surface being viewed were curved, the sides of this quadrilateral would be curved. (Visualize this.)

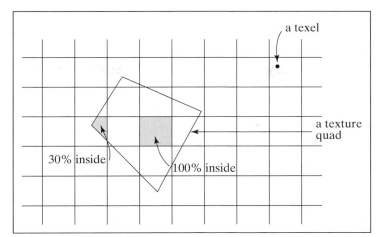

FIGURE 10.58 Finding the area-weighted average color.

the ellipse, and these weighted values are summed to form the average. This can all be done incrementally and very efficiently (capitalizing on the controlled transformation of the filter function from one space to the other) at the cost of a few arithmetic operations per texel. Figure 10.56(b) shows the receding checkerboard rendered using an EWA filter.

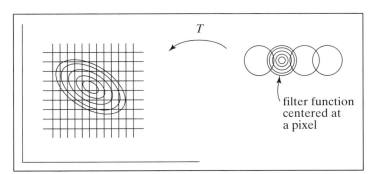

FIGURE 10.59 Elliptical weighted-average filtering.

A second approach, known as **stochastic sampling** and fully described in [Watt92], avoids difficult geometric calculations in forming an average texture color by sampling texels in a randomized pattern. Figure 10.60 shows the texture quad with center (s^*, t^*) associated with a particular screen pixel. The quad itself is not used directly; instead, the region around (s^*, t^*) is sampled at a number of points, and the texel colors are averaged to form the color:

$$\text{average} = \frac{1}{N_k} \text{texture}\left(s^* + \alpha_k, t^* + \beta_k\right)$$

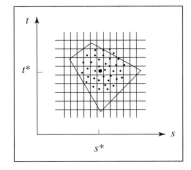

FIGURE 10.60 Antialiasing using stochastic sampling.

The values α_k and β_k are small random quantities that are easy to create using a random-number generator, and their distribution can be tuned to the general size of the texture quad if desired.

We will see stochastic sampling appear again in Chapter 14, where it offers a powerful tool for ray tracing.

10.8.3 Antialiasing Using OpenGL

OpenGL provides some tools to perform antialiasing. The simplest to use employs an **accumulation buffer**, which is an extra storage area similar to the frame buffer that OpenGL can create and draw into. The antialiasing method resembles stochastic sampling. It draws a scene multiple times at slightly different positions (which differ by just fractions of a pixel) and adds the results into the accumulation buffer. When all of the slightly perturbed drawings have been added to the accumulation buffer, the results are copied over into the frame buffer, and the antialiased drawing is displayed. Thus, for each pixel, the method forms an average value based on colors in the projected scene that lie in the immediate vicinity of the pixel.

The code that follows shows how this can be done when a camera is taking a picture of a 3D scene. The accumulation buffer is created at start-up[6] and is initially zeroed out (using `glClear(GL_ACCUM_BUFFER_BIT)`. Then the scene is drawn eight times, each time "sliding" the camera by a small displacement stored in an array `jitter[]` of vectors. Each new drawing is scaled by one-eighth and added, pixel by pixel, to the accumulation buffer by using `glAccum(GL_ACCUM, 1/8.0)`. When the eight renditions have been drawn, the accumulation buffer is copied into the frame buffer via `glAccum(GL_RETURN, 1.0)`. The following is the relevant code:

```
glClear(GL_ACCUM_BUFFER_BIT);
for(int i=0; i < 8; i++)
{
    cam.slide(f * jitter[i].x, f * jitter[i].y,0);
    display(); // draw the scene
    glAccum(GL_ACCUM, 1/8.0);
}
glAccum(GL_RETURN, 1.0);
```

Factor f controls the overall amount of camera sliding. The jitter vector contains eight points that lie in x and y between −0.5 and 0.5. The header file `jitter.h`[7] uses the values (−0.3348, 0.4353), (0.2864, −0.3934), (0.4594, 0.1415), (−0.4144, −0.1928), (−0.1837, 0.0821), (−0.0792, −0.3173), (0.1022, 0.2991), and (0.1642, −0.0549). These points mimic eight randomly chosen offsets from a circularly symmetric probability distribution, reminiscent of the EWA method described earlier. `jitter.h` also contains other jitter vectors, both shorter and longer, that can be used to try different levels of antialiasing.

Figure 10.61 shows a 3D scene rendered two ways: Part (a) shows the scene without antialiasing; Part b shows the improvement afforded by averaging eight "jittered" versions in the accumulation buffer. The "jaggies" in the antialiased version are noticeably reduced. This method is fairly costly in time, since the scene is rendered eight times for each frame.

FIGURE 10.61 A scene rendered (a) without antialiasing and (b) with antialiasing.

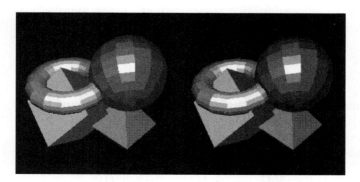

---

[6] By including GL_ACCUM in the initialization: `glutInitDisplayMode(GLUT_SINGLE| GLUT_RGB| GLUT_ACCUM| GLUT_DEPTH);`.

[7] Available as part of the download package of the GLUT.

10.9 CREATING MORE SHADES AND COLORS

Often, a graphics display supports an inadequate number of colors or shades of gray for a particular set of images. For example, bilevel displays produce only black and white, and many low-cost terminals permit only four or eight colors. How can one produce the visual effect of many shades or colors on such terminals?

One method is via **halftones**, which trade spatial resolution for color resolution [Ulichney87; Knuth87]. Newspapers provide a familiar example. Only black ink is used, yet an image seen in a newspaper appears to have many levels of gray. This is achieved by using smaller or larger "blobs" of black ink spaced closely together. Areas over which most of the blobs are large appear darker to the eye, because the average level of blackness is higher. Places where the blobs are smaller appear as a lighter shade of gray. The eye combines the blobs and perceives an average darkness over small regions. The spatial resolution of a newspaper picture is much less than that of a photograph, however, because the newspaper picture is made up of distinct blobs that cannot be arbitrarily small.

In a computer graphics context, the use of **digital halftones**, or patterning, employs arrays of small dots instead of variable-sized blobs. Figure 10.62(a) shows an example in which two-by-two arrays of dots (each dot having a value of 0 or 1) are used to simulate larger "blobs" having five possible intensity levels. For the purposes of this discussion, we adopt the printing analogy and associate level 0 with white (no ink) and 4 with black. The notion is that the eye sees the average intensity in each two-by-two "blob", so we can perceive five levels.

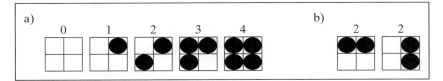

FIGURE 10.62 Two-by-two patterns.

To provide a concrete context for this discussion, suppose the original gray-scale image uses a 100-by-100 array of pixels whose intensity values range from 0 to 4. Suppose also that we have only a bilevel display available, so we display the image by using a 200-by-200-pixel area. We shade each 2-by-2 block of pixels appropriately to create a semblance of one of the gray shades $0, \ldots, 4$. Again, spatial resolution is exchanged for intensity resolution.

The positions of the black elements in the cell in Figure 10.62(a) were chosen to be as "irregular" as possible so as to avoid streaks or other artifacts in the image. If, instead, either of the patterns shown in Figure 10.62(b) were used for level 2, the image might exhibit horizontal or vertical stripes in certain patterns.

Figure 10.63a shows an example 872-by-599 grayscale image, and part b shows the 1744×1198 bilevel image when two-by-two patterning is used. The five effective gray levels are clearly visible. Larger cell sizes can be used to create a larger number of gray levels. Figure 10.64 shows a pattern using a three-by-three cell, which achieves 10 gray levels. In general, an n-by-n cell of zeros and ones can produce $n^2 + 1$ gray levels. (Why?) Patterning is most applicable when the original image is of lower resolution than the display device to be used.

10.9.1 Ordered Dither

Often, we do not have the luxury of using several display pixels to mimic a single larger gray pixel. For instance, we might need to display a 100-by-100-pixel image using only 100-by-100 bilevel pixels on the display. How can we still arrange the black

FIGURE 10.63 Example of using two-by-two patterning.
(a) grayscale image.
(b) patterned on a bilevel display.

FIGURE 10.64 Three-by-three patterns.

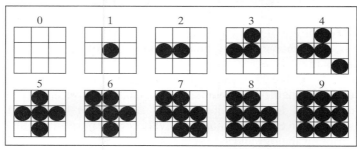

and white pixels to produce an apparent multilevel image to the eye? That is, what is a good way to decide when to use a 0 and when a 1, and how faithful will the image that is displayed be to the original?

The easy way to choose the pixel value is by **thresholding**. For each pixel, we define a threshold value: For the pixel at (x, y), the threshold value $t[x][y]$ is somehow specified. Suppose the image value in row y and column x is $p[x][y]$. If $p[x][y]$ is "above the threshold"—that is, if $p[x][y] >= t[x][y]$—we set the display pixel to 1. Otherwise we set it to 0.

The *same* threshold value could be used for every pixel, but that would create severe **contouring** in the image, with "islands" of black and white. (An example is given later.) Instead, an array of different thresholds is constructed by choosing a **dither pattern**, and the array is used to tile the image with varying threshold values.

For example, consider a 16-level image whose true pixel values range from 0 to 15. We choose the following two-by-two dither pattern:

$$\begin{pmatrix} 3 & 9 \\ 12 & 6 \end{pmatrix}. \tag{10.9}$$

(The values are chosen as four equispaced values between 0 and 15.) Imagine this pattern being laid down on top of the original image in a repeating checkerboard fashion, as shown in Figure 10.65. If the pattern is placed in a two-by-two matrix $D[2][2]$, the tiling process is accomplished by setting $t[x][y] = D[x \% 2][y \% 2]$. That is, we need not build the whole array $t[][]$ at once: Each value is calculated as needed by indexing into $D[][]$. The final bilevel image is formed pixel by pixel as stated earlier: 0 or 1, depending on the relative sizes of $p[x][y]$ and $t[x][y]$. The use of the dither pattern makes the threshold vary from pixel to pixel, as is illustrated in the figure.

What is the effect of this varying threshold? It produces additional *perceived* gray levels. To see this, consider a region of *constant* intensity in the original image, such as the region of 8's in the upper left corner of Figure 10.65. Since 8 exceeds 3 and 6, but is less than 9 and 12, each two-by-two block in this region is given the values

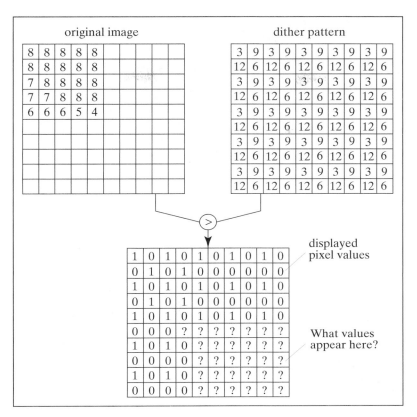

FIGURE 10.65 Thresholding an image with a dither pattern.

$\begin{pmatrix} 1 & 0 \\ 0 & 1 \end{pmatrix}$ in the displayed image. This matrix denotes an average of intensity 0.5, which is halfway between black and white. This corresponds well to the original halfway value between black and white: a pixel value of 8. So the pattern of 0's and 1's in the two-by-two array produces an average intensity that matches the average intensity of the original image more closely than if simple thresholding were used.

More generally, over regions where the image has constant intensity, the displayed image will exhibit one of the two-by-two patterns $\begin{pmatrix} 0 & 0 \\ 0 & 0 \end{pmatrix}, \begin{pmatrix} 1 & 0 \\ 0 & 0 \end{pmatrix}, \begin{pmatrix} 1 & 0 \\ 0 & 1 \end{pmatrix}, \begin{pmatrix} 1 & 1 \\ 0 & 1 \end{pmatrix}$

and $\begin{pmatrix} 1 & 1 \\ 1 & 1 \end{pmatrix}$, corresponding to average intensities of 0, 0.25, 0.5, 0.75, and 1, respectively. Figure 10.66 shows the correspondence between the averaged observed intensity and the constant pixel values of the original image. Dithering, therefore, enables a bilevel display to exhibit five levels of brightness over regions of constant intensity. This range, of course, is far short of the original 16 levels in the image, but still is far superior to only 2 levels. In regions of varying pixel values, the effect is more complicated, but an approximation to five different brightness levels is still perceived.

Figure 10.67 shows two dithered versions of the image of Figure 10.36a. Part (a) shows the original image after two-by-two dithering. All pixel values are 0 or 1, but even so, the original pattern is still well reproduced. Part (b) shows the original image after three-by-three dithering using the pattern of Equation 10.10, to be discussed next.

Larger dither patterns can be used to generate more levels. An n-by-n pattern can produce $n^2 + 1$ levels, since the number of pixels lying under such a pattern that are

FIGURE 10.66 Correspondence of input and output levels.

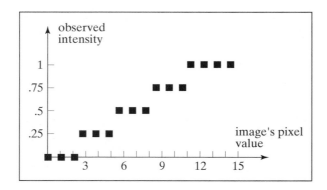

FIGURE 10.67 Example of two-by-two dithering.

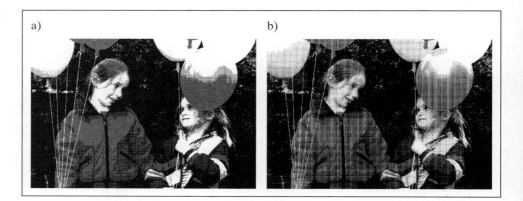

1 in the displayed image always has one of the values $0, 1, \ldots, n^2$. The n^2 entries in the pattern should be equispaced between 0 and the highest pixel value in the original image. For instance, if the pixel values range from 0 to 255, a three-by-three dither pattern would contain 10 equispaced values between 0 and 255, found by rounding the values $k \times 255/10$ to the nearest integer, for $k = 1, 2, \ldots, 9$. This results in the nine values $25, 51, 76, 102, \ldots, 229$, which can be arranged randomly within the matrix or according to a "growth sequence" [Foley90]. One acceptable arrangement is

$$\begin{pmatrix} 178 & 229 & 127 \\ 51 & 25 & 102 \\ 153 & 76 & 204 \end{pmatrix}. \tag{10.10}$$

Matrices of size four by four, eight by eight, and so on can be generated from the two-by-two matrix D [] [] by using a recursive relation. (See the exercises at the end of the section.)

Dithering trades spatial resolution for intensity resolution and also gives the impression of "noise" being added to an image. Many alternative dithering techniques attempt to overcome these artifacts. A good survey is presented along with some extensions in [Knuth87].

Dithering for Multilevel and color displays

Dithering can also be applied when the display supports more than two levels of gray [Schumaker91], or when it supports color. A number of variations are possible, but we give the main idea with a concrete example. Suppose that the original image has pixel values between 0 and 255, representing 256 gray levels. Suppose also that we want to display this image on a device that supports only 8 gray levels: $0, 1, \ldots, 7$. One way to do this is with simple thresholding: We find the closest display value D to each "true" pixel value P and then, basically, just divide by 32 and discard the remainder. The code is as follows:

```
D = (int)(P/32);      // get the closest value below
if(P - 32 * D >= 16)  // Is error too big for this D?
    D++;              // yes: use the next biggest
```

The second line tests whether the next displayable value up is a better approximation than the current value, by testing the "error" term `P - 32 * D` with a threshold of 16. If so, D is incremented by one.

Another way to improve the perceived image is with the use of dithering. The previous threshold of 16 is replaced with a set of four thresholds by indexing into a matrix M that tiles the image just as we saw before. The code is

```
D = (int)(P/32);
if(P - 32 * D >= M[col % 2][row % 2])
    D++;
```

where

$$M = \begin{pmatrix} 0 & 16 \\ 24 & 8 \end{pmatrix} \tag{10.11}$$

(using four equispaced values between 0 and 31). If the error term is larger than the corresponding matrix value, then D is incremented.

Consider what dithering does in regions of constant intensity within the image. Suppose $P = 178$ over such a region. Since 178 lies between $5 \times 32 = 160$ and $6 \times 32 = 192$, some of the pixels in each two-by-two area will be 5 and some will be 6. These areas will be displayed with the patterns given in the matrix

$$\text{displayed} = \begin{pmatrix} 6 & 6 \\ 5 & 6 \end{pmatrix}.$$

The average intensity is therefore 5.75, or three-fourths of the way from 5 to 6. Now, three-fourths of the way from 160 to 192 is 184, so the average intensity perceived in this region is 184, not too far from the "truth" of 178. Once again, dithering makes the image appear to have additional gray levels.

Colored Images

Colored images can be dithered in a manner similar to the way black-and-white images are dithered. The easiest approach is to dither the red, green, and blue components separately, using the same dither matrix. This technique produces additional "average" levels over regions of constant color, and the red, green, and blue averages combine to produce some average color value that approximates the true color in the region.

PRACTICE EXERCISES

10.9.1 Three-by-three dithering

Suppose the original image uses pixel values ranging from 0 to 16. Calculate the three-by-three dither matrix that corresponds to the arrangement in Equation (10.10).

10.9.2 Larger dither matrices

Jarvis developed a recursion relation for generating dither matrices of sizes $2n$ by $2n$ [Jarvis76]. Hawley provided an alternative version [Hawley90]. As discussed earlier, an n-by-n dither matrix should contain all the values $1, 2, \ldots, n^2$ in a suitable arrangement, scaled by an appropriate scale factor determined by the number of pixel values. The two-by-two case is a scaled version of

$$D_2 = \begin{pmatrix} 1 & 3 \\ 4 & 2 \end{pmatrix}.$$

The following matrix shows how to build D_4, D_8, etc., from D_2:

$$D_k = \begin{pmatrix} D_{k/2} & D_{k/2} + 2 \cdot 2^{k/2} \\ D_{k/2} + 3 \cdot 2^{k/2} & D_{k/2} + 1 \cdot 2^{k/2} \end{pmatrix}.$$

So D_4 is a four-by-four matrix built up of four versions of D_2.

a. Find the four-by-four dither matrix D_4. (*Hint*: The first row turns out to be 1 3 9 11.)
b. How must D_4 be scaled so that it provides a dithering matrix for the case of 256 pixel levels?

10.9.3 Dithering with multilevel displays

Use the three-by-three dithering matrix of Equation (10.10), suitably scaled, to dither an image whose pixel values range from 0 to 255 onto a display that supports the levels $0 \ldots 15$.   ■

10.9.2 Error Diffusion

Error diffusion provides another thresholding technique for displaying multilevel pixmaps on a bilevel display. Again, suppose each pixel of the original pixmap has intensities between 0 and 255 and that we need to replace each pixel by 0 or 1 in a judicious fashion. Then, if a pixel has intensity A, pure thresholding dictates that we replace it by 0 if $A < 128$ and by 1 if $A \geq 128$. If A is anything other than exactly 0 or 255, this method produces some error between the "true" and the "displayed" values. If $A = 42$, for instance, we set the display pixel to 0, which is too low by the amount 42. If $A = 167$, we display a 1 (the highest intensity, corresponding to a pixel value of 255), which is too high by the amount $255 - 167 = 88$. What is to be done with this error?

With error diffusion, we try to compensate for unavoidable errors by subtracting them from some neighboring pixels in the pix map. We pass portions of the error on to neighboring pixels that haven't been thresholded yet, so that when they get thresholded later, it is the *new*, adjusted value that is tested against the threshold. In this way, the error "diffuses" through the image, maintaining proper values of average intensity.

Figure 10.68 shows a portion of an original (multilevel) pixmap, which we assume is processed in the usual order from top to bottom and left to right. Suppose the shaded pixels have been processed; pixel p has just been compared with 128, and either a 0 or a 1 has been output. Let A denote the value of this pixel. If A is less than 128, the display pixel is set to 0 and the error E is $-A$. (We are displaying a value of A that is too low.) If A is greater than or equal to 128, the display pixel is set to 1 and the error E is $255 - A$. (We are now displaying a value that is too high by the amount $255 - A$).

Fractions of the resulting error E are then passed to pixels a, b, c, and d, as suggested in the figure. Old values of a, b, c, and d are replaced, respectively, with

$$a = a - f_a E \quad \text{(adjust pixel to the right),}$$
$$b = b - f_b E \quad \text{(adjust pixel at lower left),} \quad\quad (10.12)$$
$$c = c - f_c E \quad \text{(adjust pixel below),}$$

and

$$d = d - f_d E \quad \text{(adjust pixel at lower right),}$$

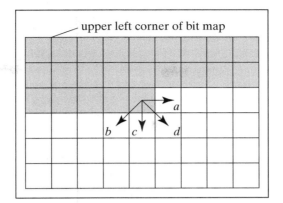

FIGURE 10.68 The error diffusion process.

where f_a, f_b, etc., are constants. A typical choice of the fractions is $(f_a, f_b, f_c, f_d) = (7/16, 3/16, 5/16, 1/16)$. These values sum to unity, so the entire amount of error has been passed off to neighbors of p, which tends to preserve the average intensity of a region.

When the end of a scan line is reached, the errors that would go to a and d do not get passed on to the start of the next scan line. (Why?) Instead, they might be discarded, or the algorithm could diffuse the entire error to pixels b and c. Experience shows that it is best to alternate the direction in which successive scan lines are processed—first left to right and then right to left, so the pattern in Figure 10.68 reverses on the next line, (e.g., a is to the left). The snakelike shape of this type of scanning has caused it to be called a **serpentine raster pattern**.

Figure 10.69 shows a 512-by-512 pix map after error diffusion. The error diffusion method used the serpentine raster and the coefficients cited in Equation (10.12). Extending this technique to displays that support more than two levels is trivial. At each pixel, the closest displayable level is found, and the resulting error is passed on exactly as just described. For color images, each of the three color components is error diffused independently.

FIGURE 10.69 A pix map viewed on a bilevel display after error diffusion.

The techniques of dithering and error diffusion have been combined by Knuth [Knuth87] into a method he calls "dot diffusion," which is only slightly more complex than either method alone and can produce better images.

PRACTICE EXERCISES

10.9.4 Doing it by hand

Carry out the error diffusion process on the top scan line of an image in which all pixels in the top scan line have the value 130 and all those on the next scan line have the value 132. Discuss what happens.

10.9.5 Diffusing other amounts of error

Explain the effect of error diffusion when all of the error is diffused to the right pixel. Explain the case where half is diffused to the right pixel and half is diffused down.

10.9.6 Trashing some error

Explain what happens if the coefficients in Equation (10.12) fail to add to unity. Does the average value of the bilevel image still match that of the original?   ■

10.10 SUMMARY

In this chapter, we looked at problems and opportunities that arise when you use a raster display to view an image. The fundamental property of a raster display is **discreteness**: The image that is viewed consists of many glowing pixels arranged in discrete rows and columns, and each pixel glows in one of several discrete colors. The image is discrete in three dimensions: the horizontal, the vertical, and the color value. But since the pixel dots are very close together, and there are (usually) many possible color values, your eye–brain system blends neighboring dots and tends to see "average" values, thereby fusing the array of glowing dots into recognizable patterns. This blending argues for making use of a fundamental property of raster displays: Regions of the image can appear to be "filled" in a solid color or pattern, something that is very difficult to do using a line-drawing device such as a pen plotter. We discussed a number of methods to fill regions, paying particular attention to those described by a polygon.

Discreteness is both good and bad. Discreteness in space (horizontal and vertical) gives rise to aliasing (the "jaggies"): A diagonal line appears to jerk abruptly along its path, which can be disturbing to the eye. So antialiasing methods have been developed to ameliorate the visual effect of aliasing. Excessive discreteness in color—as when a display has only two color values—produces images with artificial "bands" or "islands" of color, and much of the information in the intended image is lost. So dithering techniques have been developed that exploit the nature of the eye to blend closely spaced dots, tricking it into "seeing" more colors than are really there.

Raster display systems have another fundamental property: Pixels are represented by numbers, and numbers are stored in memory. A raster display is almost literally a "window" into a huge array of system memory and hence into a huge array of numbers: a **pixmap**. The display maps numbers into colors, making the pixmap palpable. Computer instructions manipulate numbers easily, which opens the door to a host of techniques: Cursors can be "swept" across the screen with a mouse, windows can scroll, images can be flipped back and forth from on-screen to off-screen memory, and so forth.

A characteristic of modern raster displays is that there are very many pixels to deal with, sometimes even millions. This plenitude allows rich images, but also increases the time required to perform certain operations. Copying large numbers of pixel values is often facilitated with specialized hardware, as with bitBlit chips. And people have been compelled to invent ever more efficient algorithms in an attempt to improve the performance of raster operations. Many of these algorithms capitalize on **coherence**, a notion that pervades much of graphics. **Span coherence**, for example, is the tendency of many adjacent pixels on a scan line to be of the same color. And **scan-line coherence** is the tendency for pixels on neighboring scan lines to be similar.

The various techniques discussed in the chapter operate at the pixel level to fashion or enhance a picture viewed on a raster display. They all work either to exploit the positive effects of the discreteness of the raster or to counteract its negative effects. Because there are so many pixels in a given image, the efficiency of each algorithm is important.

10.11 CASE STUDIES

CASE STUDY 10.1   READING AND DISPLAYING BMP IMAGE FILES

Write an application that fills in the details of the RGBpixmap methods draw(), read(), copy(), readBmpFile(), and writeBmpFile() and allows the user to read an image stored as a BMP file and display the image using OpenGL. Further, allow the user to designate a rectangle on the display with the mouse, upon which action the portion of the pixmap inside the rectangle is written to a BMP file. And if the user presses the key 'f', the pix map that is displayed is "flipped" about its horizontal centerline, thereby appearing upside down. Pressing 'v' flips the image about its vertical centerline.

CASE STUDY 10.2 DISSOLVING BETWEEN TWO PIXMAPS WITH OPENGL

Level of Effort: II. As discussed in Section 10.3, it is straightforward to have one image dissolve into another. Figure 10.12 showed an example. If the two images are stored in pixmaps A and B we need only draw the weighted averages $A(1 - t) + Bt$ of the pixmaps for a succession of t-values.

In this case study, we use the alpha-blending capability of OpenGL and the method `blend()` of Figure 10.15 to form the weighted averages. The basic steps are as follows:

a. Read two image files to create two pixmaps, A and B, of the same size.
b. Set the proper blending function, `glBlendFunc()`.
c. Erase the display.
d. Then for each of a set of t-values, say, 0, 0.2, 0.4, 0.6, 0.8, and 1.0,
e. Set the alpha of A to the value t.
f. Draw B, fully opaque.
g. Blend in A.
h. Pause to admire the latest blended image.

We need to set a "global" alpha value in one of the images; that is, we must set the alpha for every pixel to the *same* value. This is easily done by adding a method `setAlpha(float alph)` to the `RGBApixmap` class.

1. Write the method `setAlpha(float alpha)`. It simply traverses all the pixel values in the pixmap, setting the a component of each to the fraction `alpha` of its maximum value (of 255).
2. Using Example 10.3.2 as a guide, write a program that dissolves between images A and B. Arrange matters so that pressing the key 'd' begins a dissolve from A to B and pressing the key 'b' begins a dissolve from B to A. Execute your program on several pairs of images.

CASE STUDY 10.3 REGION FILLING BASED ON RUNS

Level of Effort: II. Implement the region-fill algorithm of Section 10.5.5 that scans for runs of pixels and fills them, for the case of a 4-connected, boundary-defined region. Test the routine on several sample regions.

NOTE *Extra benefit:* Show how to adjust the fill routine for 8-connected regions.

CASE STUDY 10.4 WORKING WITH THE "SHAPE" DATA STRUCTURE

Level of Effort: II. Section 10.6.1 described a data structure that represents a region in terms of a collection of rectangles. In this case study, you are asked to work out the programming details for actually dealing with such "creatures":

1. **Creating a shape.** Write the routine

```
void pixmap2Shape(RGBpixmap& pixmap,Shape& shape, Color3 color);
```

which creates a shape data structure from a pixmap. The shape structure accurately represents all of the regions described by the pixels having color `color` in the pixmap.
2. **Making pixmaps from shapes.** The inverse of the previous operation is to create a pix map that "contains" the regions described by a shape. Write

```
void shape2Pixmap(Shape& shape, RGBpixmap& pixmap, Color3 fore,
Color3 back);
```

which creates a pixmap of sufficient size to hold the regions described by `shape`. The pix map fills all pixels inside the shape in the color `fore` and all the remaining pixels in the color `back`.

CASE STUDY 10.5 CHAIN CODING OF SHAPES

Level of Effort: II. Chain coding of paths was discussed in Section 10.6.2. Design a suitable data type to hold a chain code, such as that in Figure 10.35, that can capture an 8-connected path contained in a pixmap. Write the routine

```
void makeChain(RGBpixmap& pmap, IntPoint startPt, Chain& chain);
```

which builds the chain by tracing over a path (a string of 8-connected pixels having the same color) located in a pixmap, starting at `startPt`. The routine need only work on a legitimate path. Also, write `void drawChainPath(Chain& chn)`, which draws the path described by a chain `chn`.

CASE STUDY 10.6 FILLING "HORIZONTALLY CONVEX" POLYGONS

Level of Effort: III. As discussed in Section 10.7, it is much easier to fill horizontally convex polygons than general polygons. Horizontally convex polygons have only one left and one right edge at each scan line, so only a single run of pixels is involved. The AEL becomes a simple pair of edges: `leftActive` and `rightActive`. The ET can be a simple array of edges that is easy to sort by the lower endpoints y-value. Updating the AEL is also simpler, since no local extrema are found in the polygon, and edges never cross. Therefore, the AEL need not be sorted after each update.

   Write a program that uses this approach to fill sample polygons input by the user. Each polygon is input with the mouse. (Pressing the left button adds a point to the polygon; pressing the right button closes the polygon and starts the filling process.) For variety, fill the polygons with a checkerboard pattern with each square four pixels wide.

CASE STUDY 10.7 GENERAL POLYGON FILLING

Level of Effort: III. Write the routine

```
short fillPoly(IntPolyArray& poly)
```

which fills the polygon `poly`. The routine returns -1 if the polygon is degenerate or ill formed or if the filling process is unsuccessful; it returns 0 otherwise. The routine uses the fill algorithm described in Section 10.7, and for efficiency, it employs an ET and an AEL.

   Test polygons are easily generated randomly: The user inputs the desired number of vertices, and the vertices are generated randomly.

CASE STUDY 10.8 ERROR DIFFUSION

Level of Effort: II. Write the routine `errorDiffuse(IntRect r)`, which performs error diffusion, as described in Equation (10.12), on the portion of the screen image lying inside rectangle `r`. The routine uses the serpentine pattern for scanning adjacent scan lines. Results will be most noticeable if the display supports only a few intensities or colors. Test the routine on several pictures.

10.12 FURTHER READING

Jim Blinn provides a very readable discussion of several of the topics introduced here in JIM BLINN's CORNER: DIRTY PIXELS [Blinn98], including antialiasing, dithering, and compositing. Ulichney's DIGITAL HALFTONING [Ulichney87] provides a thorough treatment of dithering, and Knuth offers a broad perspective on the topic as well [Knuth87]. And the OpenGL "Red Book" provides a lot of detail on how to control in applications many of the effects discussed in the chapter [Woo97].

11

Curve and Surface Design

You appear in splendid shape today, m'dear.

Anonymous

On the outside grows the furside, on the inside grows the skinside;
So the furside is the outside, and the skinside is the inside.

Herbert George Ponting, The Sleeping Bag

Goals of the Chapter

▲ To develop tools for representing and designing curves.

▲ To determine key properties of curves, such as their "smoothness".

▲ To develop the mathematical properties of Bezier and B-spline curves.

▲ To develop tools to design Bezier, B-spline, and NURBS surface patches.

PREVIEW

So far we have dealt mainly with simple geometric objects made up of collections of points or straight lines. In this chapter we set forth an organized way to describe and represent a much richer set of shapes that occur in computer graphics programs. Section 11.1 reviews important properties of parametric representations for curves and develops ways to measure the "smoothness" of such curves. Section 11.2 focuses on representing curves by polynomials and ratios of polynomials and describes the classes of shapes one can obtain from them. Section 11.3 introduces the main ideas of interactive curve design, wherein a designer specifies a set of "control points" with a mouse, uses a curve-generation algorithm to preview a curve, and then edits the control points in order to improve the curve's shape. Emphasis is placed on the distinction between curves that interpolate the points and those that only approximate the points. Section 11.4 introduces Bezier curves in this context, and Section 11.5 discusses the properties of Bezier curves that have made them so popular in computer-aided geometric design (CAGD). Section 11.6 examines the limitations of Bezier curves and begins the search for better methods for curve design, focusing on piecewise polynomials. This leads to a discussion of spline functions.

B-splines are introduced in Section 11.7, and their useful properties are developed in Section 11.8. Section 11.9 describes curves based on nonuniform rational B-splines (NURBS). Section 11.10 discusses some methods for finding curves that interpolate control points. Section 11.11 addresses the design of complex surface shapes and

597

extends the treatment in Chapter 6 to surfaces that are built upon Bezier, B-spline, and NURBS curves. The discussion confronts the issue of joining two surface patches together seamlessly and uses the classical teapot as an example of blending such patches. Several examples of surface designs are presented. Finally, the case studies present projects for describing and drawing a variety of parametric curves and surfaces. The Elliptipool game is described, as well as projects for drawing Bezier, B-spline, and NURBS curves and surfaces.

11.1 INTRODUCTION

Certain shapes are of particular interest to us because they are aesthetically pleasing to behold or because they represent the shape of some actual object found in nature. Other shapes are computed by some analysis program as the best possible for a particular job, such as the sweep of an airplane wing to give maximum lift. Still other shapes, like the curve of a car fender, are designed by a person, on the basis of a complex combination of engineering utility, ease of manufacture, and an intuitive sense of what is appealing to customers.

Some shapes, such as logarithmic spirals, superellipses, and cycloids, have a concise mathematical formulation that makes them easy to analyze, but is of little help when we want to write a routine to draw them. Thus, we need ways to convert these shapes from one kind of representation to another form more suited to certain tasks. Other kinds of shapes are more "free form" and are based on data rather than mathematical expressions. Those, too, we want to be able to handle in a program, perhaps to find where one such curve intersects another.

11.1.1 Parametric Curves as Trajectories

An important application of representing curves parametrically arises in describing the path that an object takes as it moves in time. For instance, in designing an animation, the trajectory of the camera through the scene must be specified at each instant. Figure 11.1 shows a camera, located at $P(t)$ at time t, moving through a scene. The designer chooses a suitable function $P(t)$ so that the camera moves as desired, perhaps taking snapshot #1 at $t = 0.1$, snapshot #2 at $t = 0.2$, etc. The view direction of the camera must also be specified at each instant.

In addition to having the camera be at specific positions at specific times, the designer must ensure that the camera moves smoothly as it progresses along $P(t)$,

FIGURE 11.1 Specifying the path of a camera in an animation.

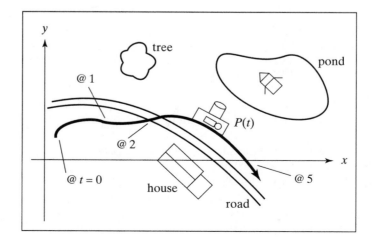

without any disturbing jerks that would show up when the animation is played back. This provision imposes certain conditions on the velocity $\mathbf{P}'(t)$ that we shall consider next.

Other objects might be moving in the animation as well: In Figure 11.1 a car might move along the road, the boat might change its course, and a person might come out of the house. As discussed in Chapter 5, the legs and arms of the person might have their own motions as well. The movement of each of these objects must be described by specifying appropriate parametric functions $F(t), G(t)$, etc.

Animations usually take place in a 3D world, of course, where the camera moves along a 3D path $P(t) = (x(t), y(t), z(t))$ and each snapshot is formed by projecting the scene onto the film of the camera.

11.1.2 Smoothness of Motion

Suppose the parameter t indicates the passage of time and the point $P(t)$ moves along the curve as t increases. It is then natural to ask what the velocity of $P(t)$ is along the curve at each instant. The **velocity** $\mathbf{v}(t)$ is a vector that describes the speed and direction of $P(t)$ as it traverses the curve. From elementary calculus, we have

$$\mathbf{v}(t) = \frac{dP(t)}{dt} = \left(\frac{dx(t)}{dt}, \frac{dy(t)}{dt} \right). \tag{11.1}$$

For example, at any time t, the ellipse given by $P(t) = (W\cos(t), H\sin(t))$ has the velocity $\mathbf{v}(t) = (-W\sin(t), H\cos(t))$. The magnitude of $\mathbf{v}(t)$ is often called the **speed** at t. Figure 11.2 shows the velocity at several points along the ellipse. Both the magnitude and direction of $\mathbf{v}$ change as t varies. (Where is the speed the greatest?)

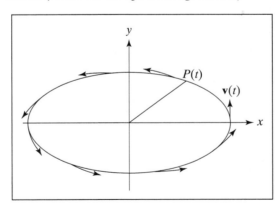

FIGURE 11.2 The velocity of $P(t)$ along a curve.

The **tangent line** to the curve $P(t)$ at $t = t_0$ can be given in parametric form $L(u)$ having parameter u as follows: Clearly, the line passes through $P(t_0)$ "at" $u = 0$ and "moves" in the direction $\mathbf{v}(t_0)$. So it is given by

$$L(u) = P(t_0) + \mathbf{v}(t_0)u. \tag{11.2}$$

These formulas make it straightforward to compute and draw tangent lines to curves in various applications.

The **normal** direction to a curve may also be found at each point. The normal is defined as the direction perpendicular to the tangent line at the point of interest. Thus, if the tangent line has direction $\mathbf{v}(t_0)$ at time t_0, as before, the normal direction at t_0 is any multiple of the vector

$$\mathbf{n}(t_0) = \mathbf{v}_\perp(t_0) = \left(\frac{-dy}{dt}, \frac{dx}{dt} \right)\bigg|_{t=t_0}. \tag{11.3}$$

The ellipse given by $P(t)$, for example, has normal vector $(-H \cos(t), -W \sin(t))$ or any multiple thereof. In the special case of a circle, $\mathbf{n}(t)$ is a multiple of $P(t)$ itself, so the normal points in the same direction as the radius vector from $\mathbf{0}$ to the point $P(t)$. (Note that this is *not* the case for an ellipse.)

When a curve $P(t)$ is used to describe how an object, such as a camera, moves in time, the following issue arises: Does the object move jerkily or smoothly along its trajectory? The object can move in an infinite variety of ways along a given path, starting, stopping, accelerating, temporarily retracing a portion of the curve, etc. If we are only drawing the curve, this motion is irrelevant: All trajectories have the same picture. But it is a very different story when the parametric function represents the motion of a camera: The details of movement along the trajectory are recorded in the sequence of snapshots taken. Abrupt accelerations or jumps have a distinctive visual effect that is normally undesirable.

As an example, consider a camera that moves along an elliptical trajectory, but with an altered parametric representation: At $t = a$, the camera's speed suddenly increases by a factor of three. The equation describing the motion is

$$P(t) = (x(t), y(t)) = \begin{cases} (W \cos(t), H \sin(t)) \text{ for } 0 < t < a \\ (W \cos(3t - 2a), H \sin(3t - 2a)) \text{ for } a < t < \dfrac{2(\pi + a)}{3} \end{cases}. \quad (11.4)$$

The situation is shown in Figure 11.3. The trajectory is still elliptical, but at $t = a$ both $x(t)$ and $y(t)$ start to oscillate three times faster, so there is a discontinuity in their derivatives at $t = a$. It is as if the time axis were suddenly compressed by a factor of three starting at that instant.

FIGURE 11.3 A trajectory with a sudden shift in speed of the motion described.

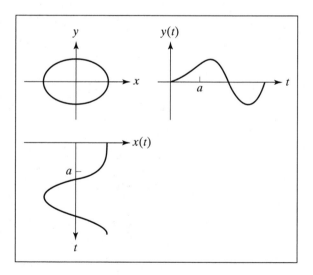

The velocity vectors at $t = a-$ ("just before" $t = a$) and at $t = a+$ ("just after" $t = a$) are, respectively,

$$\mathbf{P}'(a-) = (-W \sin(a), H \cos(a))$$

and   (11.5)

$$\mathbf{P}'(a+) = (3W \sin(a), 3H \cos(a)),$$

so the *direction* of the velocity is the same before and after the shift, but the *magnitude* of the velocity (the speed) suddenly jumps by a factor of three. The parametric curve is unaffected by this jump, but the nature of the motion of the point $P(t)$ along the curve is dramatically different before versus after $t = a$.

As we study the smoothness of curves and of a camera's motion, it will be handy to have notation that describes different kinds of continuity associated with derivatives of a curve. We will be interested in two kinds of smoothness, often called **parametric continuity** and **geometric continuity**.

Parametric Continuity (C^k-continuity or "k-smoothness")

> We say that a curve $P(t)$ has *kth-order parametric continuity* everywhere in the t-interval $[a, b]$ if all derivatives of the curve, up through the kth, exist and are continuous at all points inside $[a, b]$. To express this succinctly, we say that
>
> $P()$ is k-smooth in $[a, b]$. $(11.6)^1$

As an example, the ellipse in Figure 11.4 is 0-smooth everywhere, since the function $P(t)$ itself is continuous everywhere. But it is not 1-smooth everywhere, because there is a discontinuity in $\mathbf{P}'(t)$ at $t = a$. (It *is* 1-smooth everywhere except at $t = a$.) To avoid jerky animations, we usually insist that camera motion be 1-smooth.

A curve with a continuous velocity and a continuous acceleration is 2-smooth. Note that a k-smooth function $[a, b]$ is necessarily $(k - 1)$-smooth. A k-smooth function may or may not also be $(k + 1)$-smooth.

Geometric Continuity (G^k-continuity)

Geometric continuity is a more relaxed form of continuity that describes the visual smoothness of a curve rather than the smoothness of motion along a curve. Basically, G^k-continuity requires that the derivative vector have a continuous direction, even though it is allowed to have discontinuities in speed. The ellipse in Equation (11.4) is G^1-continuous, because its velocity has a continuous direction everywhere. For instance, at $t = a$, we know that $\mathbf{P}'(a+) = 3\mathbf{P}'(a-)$.

The example in Equation (11.4) suggests that it is the strange parametrization that causes 1-smoothness to fail and yet G^1-continuity to succeed, and this is true. In the exercises we explore the more formal definition of G^k-continuity, which is based on the existence of a reparametrization that removes the offending discontinuities. For our purposes in this book, the following definitions suffice:

- G^0 continuity is the same as 0-smoothness; it simply means that $P(t)$ is continuous with respect to t throughout the interval $[a, b]$ of interest.
- G^1 continuity in $[a, b]$ means that $\mathbf{P}'(c-) = k\mathbf{P}'(c+)$ for some constant k and for every c in the interval $[a, b]$.
- G^2 continuity in $[a, b]$ means that both the first and second derivatives of a curve have continuous directions: $\mathbf{P}'(c-) = k\mathbf{P}'(c+)$ and $\mathbf{P}''(c-) = m\mathbf{P}''(c+)$ for constants k and m and for each c in the interval $[a, b]$.

PRACTICE EXERCISES

11.1.1 Drawing tangent lines to an ellipse

Write a routine that draws the ellipse of Figure 11.2 and a short line segment tangent to the ellipse for any value of the parameter value t entered by the user.

---

[1] This terminology is borrowed from [Shikin95]. It is equivalent to saying that the function "is in $C^1[a, b]$," the set of functions, all of whose derivatives up through order k exist and are continuous over $[a, b]$.

11.1.2 Find Tangents to the ellipse

Calculate parametric forms for the tangent lines to the ellipse of Equation (3.13) for the times $t = 0, t = \pi/4, t = \pi/2$, and $t = \pi$. Sketch the ellipse and the four tangent lines on graph paper. Also, compute and sketch the normal directions at the given points.

11.1.3 Tangents and normals

Find an expression for the tangent vector and the normal vector to the superellipse of Equation (3.18) for each value of t.

11.1.4 Tangents and normals to the conic sections

Find expressions for the tangent line and the normal vector at any value of t for the parabola and for the hyperbola.

11.1.5 Find the parametric representation

Find a parametric representation $P(t)$ for the curve shown in Figure 11.4. The curve starts at point A at $t = 0$ and moves at *constant speed* over the entire shape shown, reaching point B at $t = 20$.

FIGURE 11.4 What is the parametric representation?

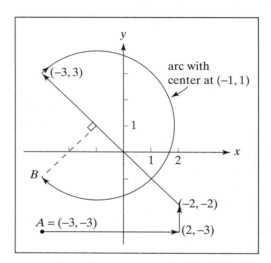

11.1.6 Another parametric form for the circle

In addition to the variety of representations that is produced by "time warps," some curves permit simple representations that differ greatly in character, such as this next one. Show that the following form generates part of a circle as t varies from 0 to infinity:

$$x(t) = a\frac{1-t}{1+t};$$ (11.7)

$$y(t) = 2a\frac{\sqrt{t}}{1+t}.$$

What are the center and radius of the curve? What portion is generated as t varies from 0 to 1? *Hint*: Recall the relations $T = \tan(b/2)$ for some parameter b. Then $\sin(b) = 2T/(1 + T^2)$ and $\cos(b) = (1 - T^2)/(1 + T^2)$.

11.1.7 On G^k-continuity

Farin gives the following definition of G^k-continuity [farin 90]: "The curve $P(t)$ is G^k-continuous if there exists a regular reparametrization after which it is k-smooth."

That is, if we can find a monotonically increasing function $g(.)$ such that the reparametrized version $P(g(t))$ is k-smooth, the original curve $P(t)$ is G^k-continuous. To be regular, $g(t)$ must ensure that the curve $P(g(t)) = (f(t), h(t))$ "never stops." That is, $f'(t)$ and $h'(t)$ must never be zero. We examine the ramifications of this definition here.

For the example of Equation (11.4), we seek a function $g(t)$ that will make the jump in the speed of the curve disappear.

a. Show that the choice

$g(t) = t$ for $t \le a$,
$g(t) = (t + 2a)/3$ for $t > a$,

removes the discontinuity in the parametrization, leaving a 1-smooth curve.

b. More generally, show that the velocity of a G^1-continuous curve $P(t)$ has a continuous direction. That is, given that there exists a $g(t)$ such that $d/dt P(g(t))$ is continuous, then the direction of $P'(.)$ is also continuous. *Hint*: The chain rule for derivatives might prove useful; that is, $P'(g(t)) = (x'(g(t))g'(t), y'(g(t))g'(t)) = g'(t)(x'(g(t)), y'(g(t)))$, whereby the term $g'(t)$ affects both components in the same way.

c. The issue here is why there is mention of a "regular" reparametrization. Consider an example that uses a non-regular parametrization [Bartels 87]:

$$P(t) = \begin{cases} (2t - t^2, 2t - t^2) & \text{for } 0 \le t \le 1 \\ (2 - 2t + t^2, 2t - t^2) & \text{for } 1 \le t \le 2 \end{cases}. \tag{11.8}$$

Plot the curve, and plot the velocity at each value of t. Note that the velocity has an abrupt change in direction at $t = 1$, but that it is continuous everywhere! Thus, if nonregular parametrizations are included in the definition of G^1-continuous curves, we could have a situation in which a 1-smooth curve is not G^1-continuous. Argue why this would be undesirable. ■

11.2 DESCRIBING CURVES BY MEANS OF POLYNOMIALS

Polynomials are fundamental mathematical objects and are frequently used in computer graphics because they are well behaved and efficient to compute. We will focus on particular forms of polynomials in the rest of the chapter; here we examine the interplay between implicit forms and parametric forms that are simple polynomials.

First, a reminder: An **L-th-degree polynomial in t** is a function given by

$$a_0 + a_1 t + a_2 t^2 + \cdots + a_L t^L, \tag{11.9}$$

where the constants $a_0, a_1, \ldots, a_L$ are the **coefficients** of the polynomial, each of which is associated with one of the powers of t. The **degree** of the polynomial is the highest power to which t is raised. For this to be of the Lth degree, we insist that a_L not equal zero. The **order** of the polynomial is the number of coefficients it has ($L + 1$ here). The order is always one greater than the degree.

Polynomial Curves of Degree 1

We have already examined **linear** polynomials and know that a linear parametric form for $x(t)$ and $y(t)$ yields a **straight line**, and the corresponding implicit form is linear in x and y.

Polynomial Curves of Degree 2

We naturally ask what shapes of curves are attainable by using the quadratic polynomials

$x(t) = at^2 + 2bt + c$

and

$y(t) = dt^2 + 2et + f, \tag{11.10}$

where a, b, etc., are constants. The answer is simple (but perhaps disappointing): This curve is always a **parabola**, for any choice of constants $a, b, \dots, f$. So there is no way to generate an ellipse or hyperbola using Equation (11.10).

Implicit Forms of Degree Two

Going the other way, we look at quadratic implicit forms—that is, polynomials of degree 2 in both x and y. Recall from analytic geometry that the general second-degree implicit form is

$$F(x,y) = Ax^2 + 2Bxy + Cy^2 + Dx + Ey + F, \tag{11.11}$$

for constants $A, \dots, F$, and that the shape of the curve $F(x, y) = 0$ thereby described is a conic section (as long as it is not degenerate; see the exercises at the end of the section.) Which conic is represented depends on the value of the **discriminant**, $AC - B^2$:

If $AC - B^2 > 0$, the curve is an **ellipse**.
If $AC - B^2 = 0$, the curve is a **parabola**.   (11.12)
If $AC - B^2 < 0$, the curve is a **hyperbola**.

Thus, $x^2 + xy + y^2 - 1$ is the implicit function for an ellipse $\left(AC - B^2 = 0.5\right)$, $x^2 + 2xy + y^2 + 3x - 6y - 7$ is the implicit function for a parabola $\left(AC - B^2 = 0\right)$, and $x^2 + 4xy + 2y^2 - 4x + y - 3$ is the implicit function for a hyperbola $\left(AC - B^2 = -1\right)$.

The Common-Vertex Equations of the Conics A special case of the general quadratic form of Equation (11.11) gives a useful perspective on how the three conic sections are related. It uses the so-called called common-vertex equation

$$y^2 = 2px - \left(1 - \varepsilon^2\right)x^2. \tag{11.13}$$

The curve represented by this equation passes through $(0, 0)$ and has an overall scale proportional to the constant p. The conic that it describes depends on the value of the **eccentricity** ε, as suggested in Figure 11.5. The exercises explore possible choices of parametrization for drawing this set of curves.

FIGURE 11.5 The common-vertex equations of the conics.

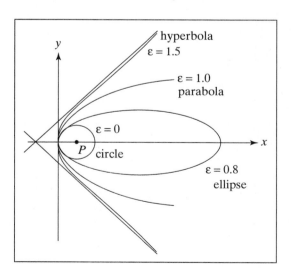

Polynomial Curves of Degree Three and Higher

Curves parametrized with first- and second-degree polynomials are well understood. Things get more complicated when the polynomials are of higher degree, however.

Sederberg has shown that it is always possible to find an implicit form given polynomial functions for $x(t)$ and $y(t)$, but that a parametric form can in general be found, given an implicit form that is of degree one or two [Sederberg85].

In the discussion that follows, our main workhorse with Bezier and B-spline curves will be the cubic polynomial, and it will be seen to provide a powerful approach to curve design. But the methods won't start with an implicit form and try to parametrize it. Rather, they will start with a collection of "control points" laid down by the designer, allow a specific algorithm to generate points along the curve, and accept the curve regardless of the implicit function it satisfies. In many ways, this is a more natural approach to curve design than a purely mathematical one.

Before leaving the current analytical approach to curve design, however, we preview briefly the class of **rational polynomial** functions, which we examine more fully later. (These functions are the basis for NURBS, as we shall see subsequently.) This first look at rational polynomials shows how the definition of a few *points* can determine the shape of a curve. It also produces an important result: The conic sections can be represented *exactly* by a ratio of two quadratic polynomials.

Rational Parametric Forms

Consider parametrizations in which $x(.)$ and $y(.)$ are each defined as a **ratio** of two polynomials. The linear case is explored in the exercises. We look here at the quadratic polynomial case, focusing on the particular parametric form

$$P(t) = \frac{P_0(1-t)^2 + 2wP_1t(1-t) + P_2t^2}{(1-t)^2 + 2wt(1-t) + t^2}, \tag{11.14}$$

where $P_0, P_1,$ and P_2 are any three points in the plane. These points are called **control points** in this context, because they control the shape of the curve. Equation (11.14) is actually two equations, of course, being shorthand for

$$(x(t), y(t)) = \left(\frac{x_0(1-t)^2 + 2x_1wt(1-t) + x_2t^2}{(1-t)^2 + 2wt(1-t) + t^2}, \frac{y_0(1-t)^2 + 2y_1wt(1-t) + y_2t^2}{(1-t)^2 + 2wt(1-t) + t^2} \right), \tag{11.15}$$

where x_0 and y_0 are the components of P_0, and similarly for the other two points. The coefficients of the quadratic polynomials in the numerators are the components of the control points. The denominator polynomials are the same for $x(.)$ and $y(.)$ and are also quadratic, but do not depend on the points. They do depend on a "weight" parameter w, however.

Note that $P(t)$ is a linear combination of control points. As we saw in Section 4.5.2, in order to make sense as a point, $P(t)$ must be an affine combination of these points. Happily this is so, as is discussed in the exercises.

Note that if we evaluate Equation (11.15) at $t = 0$, the right-hand side collapses simply to (x_0, y_0), so the curve given thereby passes through, or **interpolates**, the point P_0. Similarly, at $t = 1$, the curve passes through P_2. For t in between $t = 0$ and $t = 1$, $P(t)$ depends on all three points in a complicated way.

Figure 11.6(a) shows the three control points and illustrates how the curve emerges from P_0 as t increases from 0 and ends up at P_2 as t approaches 1. In effect, the figure asks what the shape in between is. Part (b) gives the answer: The curve is one of the conic sections, and the type depends on the value of w:

If $w < 1$, the curve is an **ellipse**.
If $w = 1$, the curve is a **parabola**. (11.16)
If $w > 1$, the curve is a **hyperbola**.

So we have a way of generating the conic sections parametrically, without recourse to the trigonometric functions needed earlier. The exercises show how to generate the

FIGURE 11.6 Generating conics
with rational quadratics.

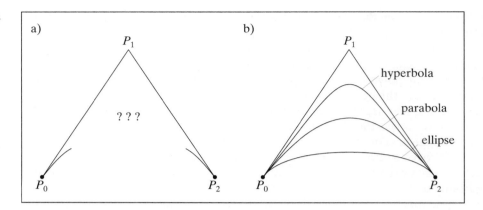

"other half" of each of these curves and also how to generate a circle using this parametric form.

PRACTICE EXERCISES

11.2.1 Degenerate quadratics
Give examples of the coefficients $A, B, \ldots, F$ in Equation (11.11) such that the curve $F(x, y) = 0$ is

a. nonexistant (i.e., no points satisfy $F(x, y) = 0$);
b. a single point;
c. a straight line;
d. two parallel lines.

11.2.2 Parametrization of the common-vertex equation
The simplest parametrization of Equation (11.13) would just use $x = t$ and $y = \pm\sqrt{2pt - (1 - \varepsilon^2)t^2}$, necessitating drawing the "upper half" and "lower half" of the associated curve separately. Will equidistant samples in t provide a good drawing of the curves? What might be a better set of t's to use?

11.2.3 Linear rational parametrizations
Discuss the class of curves that can be generated by the parametrizations

$$x(t) = \frac{a + bt}{e + ft},$$

$$y(t) = \frac{c + dt}{g + ht}, \tag{11.17}$$

for constants $a, b, \ldots, h$. Can curves that are not straight be generated? Give some examples that show how "rich" this class is.

11.2.4 Is it straight?
From Figure 11.6 it appears that if P_0, P_1, and P_2 lie in a straight line, the whole curve should be a straight line. Show whether this is true or not.

11.2.5 Using rational quadratics to draw conic sections
Figure 11.7(a) shows a circle inscribed in an equilateral triangle. One-third of the circle can be drawn using the parametric form of Equation (11.14), based on the points P_0, P_1, and P_2 as shown. Thus, the whole circle can be drawn as three arcs, each generated using three points. It can be shown [Farin90] that the proper weight to use for

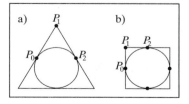

FIGURE 11.7 A circle viewed as
three or four arcs.

a circle is $w = \cos(a)$, where a is the angle $P_2 P_0 P_1$. The angle is 60° for the equilateral triangle.

a. Plot by hand the point $P(t)$ of Equation (11.14) for five values of t, such that the points are approximately equispaced along the arc from P_0 to P_2.
b. Is your hand plot in Part (a) a more efficient way to draw a circle than using samples of $(\cos(.), \sin(.))$? Discuss.
c. Repeat Parts (a) and (b) for one of the four arcs shown in Figure 11.7(b). What is angle $P_2 P_0 P_1$ in this case?

11.2.6 Generating the "other half" of the conics

The parametric form in Equation (11.13) draws only a portion of each conic as t varies from 0 to 1.

a. Is the rest of each curve drawn if you use values of t less than 0 or greater than 1—say, the whole range from negative infinity to infinity ? If not, what curve is drawn for t in this range?
b. Farin [Farin90] shows that each point $P'(t)$ on the other portion of the conic, called the "complementary segment," is generated by reversing the sign of w in Equation (11.14), and that, geometrically, P_1, $P(t)$, and $P'(t)$ are collinear, as shown in Figure 11.8. For $w = .6$ (an ellipse) and a suitable choice of three points, plot by hand the points $P(t)$ and $P'(t)$ for the t-values 0, .2, .4, .6, .8, and 1.

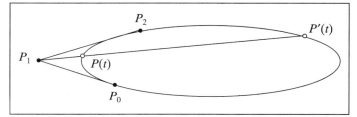

FIGURE 11.8 The complementary segment of a conic [Farin90].

c. Repeat Part (b) for $w = 1$ (a parabola).
d. Repeat Part (b) for $w = 2$ (a hyperbola).

11.2.7 Is it an affine combination?

Show that the curve $P(t)$ given by Equation (11.14) is an affine combination of the points P_0, P_1, and P_2. That is, show that the coefficients that weight those points sum to unity for any w and every value of t. ■

11.3 ON INTERACTIVE CURVE DESIGN

I could never make out what those damned dots meant.
Lord Randolph Churchill

The curves considered so far have been based on relatively simple mathematical formulas. Now we want to broaden the task and develop more complex curves that serve a certain purpose. In particular, we want to develop tools that allow a designer to fashion a large variety of shapes simply by specifying a small collection of "control points."

Suppose, for example, that the designer wishes to create a computer representation of the curve of Figure 11.9(a). This curve might be a part of an emerging design for a car fender, a turbine blade, or the casing of an electric drill. Or it might be the trajectory of a camera as it sweeps through a scene taking snapshots. The goal is to

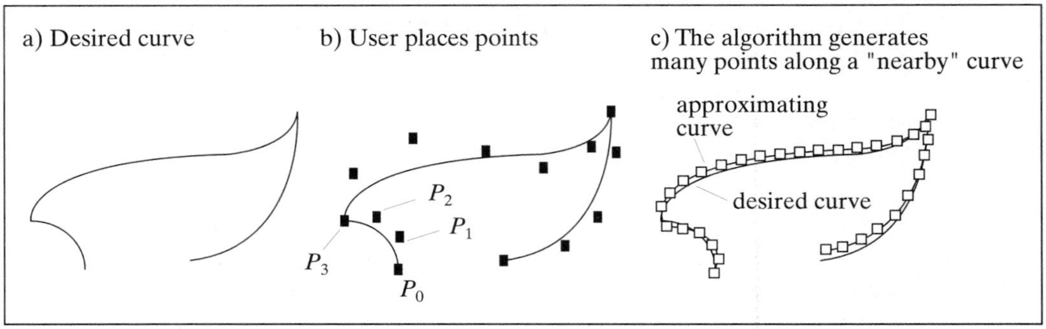

a) Desired curve   b) User places points   c) The algorithm generates many points along a "nearby" curve

approximating curve

desired curve

P_2

P_1

P_3

P_0

FIGURE 11.9 A curve-design scenario.

capture the shape of the curve in a form that permits it to be reproduced at will, adjusted in shape and size as desired, sent to a machine for automatic cutting or molding, etc. Most likely, no simple formula matches the curve exactly.

To "enter" the curve, the designer tapes a sketch of the figure onto a drawing tablet and then moves the pointer along the curve, clicking at a set of **control points** P_0, $P_1,\ldots$ close to the curve, as shown in Figure 11.9(b). The sequence of control points is often called the **control polygon**.[2] The designer enters the control polygon on the basis of a lot of experience, along with a clear understanding of the characteristics of the curve-generation algorithm—the algorithm that will later be used to regenerate the curve from the data points.

As suggested in Figure 11.10, the role of the algorithm is to produce a point $P(t)$ for any value of t given to it. The "data" for the algorithm is the set of control points, which together determine the curve along which the points $P(t)$ will fall. The algorithm is usually implemented as a function

FIGURE 11.10 The curve-generation algorithm.

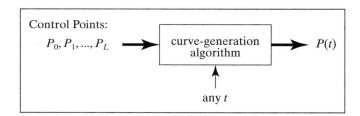

Control Points: $P_0, P_1, ..., P_L$ → curve-generation algorithm → $P(t)$

any t

```
Point2 curvePt(double t, RealPointArray pts)
```

that returns a point for any value of t in a certain interval. To draw the curve, the user can choose a sequence of t-values, evaluate `curvePt()` at each of them, and connect the points with line segments to form a polyline. Figure 11.9(c) shows a collection of small squares indicating the points that might be returned by a reasonable algorithm that is given the set of control points in Figure 11.9(b).

Hopefully, the polyline defined by these points will closely approximate the original curve the designer had in mind when entering the control points. If the curve that is generated does not provide an adequate approximation to the original curve, the designer will "edit" the control points, presumably with the mouse, shifting them this way and that and generating the curve again with many calls to `curvePt()`. This iterative process continues until the designer is satisfied. Interactive design therefore consists of the following steps:

---

[2] The term "polygon" suggests a closed figure bordered by lines, which is imprecise, since we are dealing with just a sequence of points, but the terminology has become common.

1. Lay down the initial control points.
2. Use the algorithm to generate the curve.
3. If the curve is satisfactory, stop.
4. Adjust some control points.
5. Go to step 2.

Interpolation versus Approximation

Figure 11.11 distinguishes between two main classes of curve-generation algorithms. Part (a) shows a curve $P(t)$ generated by an algorithm that **interpolates** the control points: The algorithm returns points along a curve $P(t)$ that passes exactly through the control points at specific instants and forms a smooth curve for points in between. Part (b) uses an algorithm that generates a curve $R(t)$ that **approximates** the control points: The points this algorithm returns form a curve that is attracted towards each control point in turn, but $R(t)$ doesn't actually pass through all of them. In our upcoming study of various algorithms, we shall see that each kind of algorithm has advantages and disadvantages.

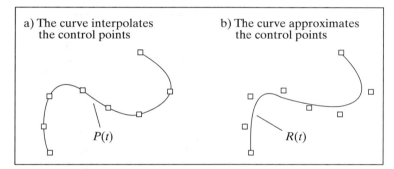

a) The curve interpolates the control points

$P(t)$

b) The curve approximates the control points

$R(t)$

FIGURE 11.11 Interpolating versus approximating curve-generation methods.

This scenario of iterative curve design is a staple in the field of computer-aided geometric design (CAGD) and is often used when one is designing an item to be manufactured. In the next few sections, we shall build up a set of techniques for designing curves as well as surfaces. Choosing from the many approaches one might take (see, for instance, Bartels87, Farin 1988, and Faux79), we emphasize interactive curve design using Bezier and B-spline curves. These families of curves have become very popular in CAGD applications. Our presentation will necessarily be brief, but we shall provide enough detail to enable you to write programs that perform interactive curve design and that create drawings of the objects so designed.

We first examine some techniques for approximating curves (whereby the curve $P(t)$ does not necessarily interpolate the control points), focusing on Bezier curves and B-spline curves. Although it might seem that a designer would always want to interpolate the control points, we shall see that there are advantages to the approximation approach. We then study how to adjust algorithms to ensure interpolation of the control points.

11.4 BEZIER CURVES FOR CURVE DESIGN

We begin with the simple and elegant de Casteljau algorithm that produces Bezier curves, which are fundamental to CAGD. Bezier curves were developed by Paul de Casteljau in 1959 and independently by Pierre Bezier around 1962. They were formulated as ingredients in CAGD systems at two automobile companies, Citroen and Renault, to help design shapes for automobile bodies.

11.4.1 The de Casteljau Algorithm

The de Casteljau algorithm uses a sequence of points, $P_0, P_1, P_2, \ldots$, to construct a well-defined value for the point $P(t)$ at each value of t from 0 to 1. Thus, it provides a way to generate a curve from a set of points. Changing the points changes the curve. The construction is based on a sequence of familiar "tweening" steps (recall Chapter 4) that are easy to implement. Because tweening is such a well-behaved procedure, it is possible to deduce many valuable properties of the curves that it generates.

Tweening Three Points to Create a Parabola

We start with three points, P_0, P_1, and P_2, as shown in Figure 11.12(a). We choose some value of t between 0 and 1, say, $t = 0.3$, and locate the point A that is a fraction t of the way along the line from P_0 to P_1. Similarly, we locate a point B at a fraction t between the endpoints P_1 and P_2 (using the same t). From Chapter 4, we know that the new points can be expressed as

$$A(t) = (1 - t)P_0 + tP_1 \tag{11.18}$$

FIGURE 11.12 The de Casteljau algorithm for three points.

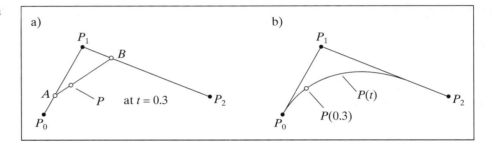

and

$$B(t) = (1 - t)P_1 + tP_2.$$

Now we repeat the linear interpolation step on these points (again using the same t): We find the point $P(t)$ that lies a fraction t of the way between *them*:

$$P(t) = (1 - t)A + tB. \tag{11.19}$$

As an example, for $t = .5$, $P(0.5)$ is simply the midpoint of the midpoints of the three given points. If this process is carried out for *every* t between 0 and 1, the curve $P(t)$ shown in Figure 11.12(b) will be generated. What is the parametric form for this curve? By direct substitution of Equation (11.18) into Equation (11.19), we obtain

$$P(t) = (1 - t)^2 P_0 + 2t(1 - t)tP_1 + t^2 P_2. \tag{11.20}$$

Equation (11.20) can be expressed in terms of the `Tween()` function of Chapter 4. (See the exercises at the end of the Section.)

The parametric form for $P(t)$ is quadratic in t, so we know from Section 11.2 that the curve is a parabola. It will still be a parabola even if t is allowed to vary from negative infinity to infinity. Clearly, the curve passes through P_0 at $t = 0$ and through P_2 at $t = 1$. (Why?) We thus have a well-defined process that can generate a smooth parabolic curve based on three given points.

What if more than three control points are used? The most commonly used family of Bezier curves are those based on four control points. Figure 11.13(a) shows how the de Casteljau algorithm is applied to the points P_0, P_1, P_2, and P_3. For a given value of t, point A is placed a fraction t of the way from P_0 to P_1, and similarly for points B and C. Then D is placed a fraction t of the way from A to B, and similarly for point E. Finally, the desired point P is located a fraction t of the way from D to E. If this is done for every t between 0 and 1, the curve $P(t)$ that starts at P_0, is "attracted" toward P_1 and P_2, and ends at P_3 is formed. $P(t)$ is the Bezier curve determined by the four points. Figure 11.13(b) shows the Bezier curves defined by different configurations of four points.

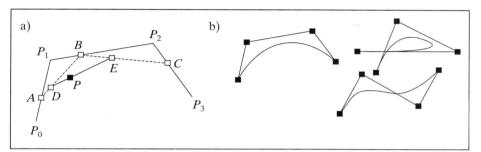

FIGURE 11.13 The Bezier curve based on four points.

It is easy to show (see the exercises) that the Bezier curve based on four points has the parametric form

$$P(t) = P_0(1 - t)^3 + P_1 3(1 - t)^2 t + P_2 3(1 - t)t^2 + P_3 t^3, \tag{11.21}$$

which is a cubic polynomial in t. Each control point P_i is weighted by a cubic polynomial, and the weighted points are added. The terms involved are known as **Bernstein polynomials**. The four cubic Bernstein polynomials are

$$B_0^3(t) = (1 - t)^3,$$
$$B_1^3(t) = 3(1 - t)^2 t, \tag{11.22}$$
$$B_2^3(t) = 3(1 - t)t^2,$$

and

$$B_3^3(t) = t^3.$$

The cubic Bernstein polynomials are easily remembered as the terms one gets by expanding the expression $\left[(1 - t) + t\right]^3$ and then collecting terms in the various powers of $(1 - t)$ and t. The resulting equation is

$$\left((1 - t) + t\right)^3 = (1 - t)^3 + 3(1 - t)^2 t + 3(1 - t)t^2 + t^3.$$

This equation immediately yields an important property of these polynomials: They add to unity at *every* t. (Why?) Mathematically,

$$\sum_{k=0}^{3} B_k^3(t) = 1. \tag{11.23}$$

For this reason, $P(t)$ of Equation (11.21) is clearly an affine combination of points, so it is legitimate to add the weighted points together. (Recall the issue of adding points in Chapter 4.)

Figure 11.14 plots the shapes of the four Bernstein polynomials of degree 3 as t varies between 0 and 1. These polynomials are seen to undulate smoothly with t. Later we see just how "smooth" they are.

Figure 11.15 illustrates geometrically how the four points $P_0, \ldots, P_3$ in Equation (11.21) are blended together to form $P(t)$. If we view the points as vectors bound to the origin (so that we write P_0 as $\mathbf{p}_0$, etc.) and let $t = 0.3$, we see that that equation becomes

$$\mathbf{p}(0.3) = 0.343\mathbf{p}_0 + 0.441\mathbf{p}_1 + 0.189\mathbf{p}_2 + 0.027\mathbf{p}_3.$$

FIGURE 11.14 The Bernstein polynomials of degree 3.

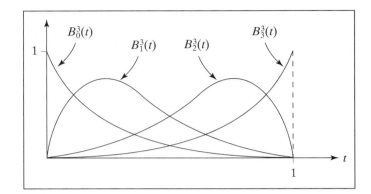

FIGURE 11.15 Blending four vectors with Bernstein polynomials.

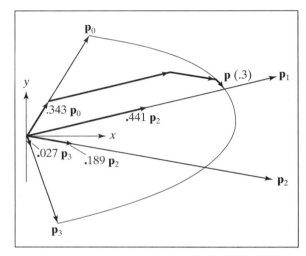

In the figure, the four vectors are weighted and the results are added by using the parallelogram rule to form the vector $\mathbf{p}(0.3)$. It is seen that at $t = 0.3$ the main contributors are $\mathbf{p}_0$ and $\mathbf{p}_1$, although the effect of $\mathbf{p}_2$ is also apparent, since $\mathbf{p}_2$ is such a "big" vector.

As t varies, the relative weights on the four vectors change, and $\mathbf{p}(t)$ shifts to different positions. Try to visualize how the vectors would be weighted at $t = 0.5$ and how each would contribute to form the resulting vector $\mathbf{p}(0.5)$.

Extending the de Casteljau Algorithm to Any Number of Points

We have seen that the de Casteljau algorithm employs tweening to produce quadratic parametric representations when three points are used and cubic representations when four points are used. The algorithm generalizes gracefully to the case in which $L + 1$ control points $P_0, P_1, \ldots, P_L$ are used. For each value of t, a succession of "generations" is built up, each one by tweening adjacent points produced in the previous generation. We obtain

$$P_i^4(t) = (1 - t)P_i^3(t) + tP_{i+1}^3(t)$$
$$\vdots$$
$$P_i^L(t) = (1 - t)P_i^{L-1}(t) + tP_{i+1}^{L-1}(t),$$

(11.24)

for $i = 0, \ldots, L$. The superscript k in $P_i^k(t)$ denotes the generation. The process starts with $P_i^0(t) = P_i$ and ends with the final Bezier curve $P(t) = P_i^L(t)$. The resulting Bezier curve can be written in terms of Bernstein polynomials as

$$P(t) = \sum_{k=0}^{L} P_k B_k^L(t),$$

(11.25)

where the kth Bernstein polynomial of degree L is defined as[3]

$$B_k^L(t) = \binom{L}{k}(1 - t)^{L-k}t^k, \qquad (11.26)$$

where

$$\binom{L}{k} = \frac{L!}{k!(L - k)!}, \qquad \text{for } L \geq k, \qquad (11.27)$$

is the binomial coefficient function. The value of this term is zero if $L < k$. Each of the Bernstein polynomials is seen to be of degree L. As before, the Bernstein polynomials are the terms one gets when expanding $\left[(1 - t) + t\right]^L$, so we are assured that

$$\sum_{k=0}^{L} B_k^L(t) = 1 \qquad \text{for all } t \qquad (11.28)$$

and that $P(t)$ is a legitimate affine combination of points.

PRACTICE EXERCISES

11.4.1 Generate the curve by hand

Using the de Casteljau method with the three points $(0, 0)$, $(2, 4)$, and $(6, 1)$, locate $P(t)$ on graph paper for the t-values $0, .2, .4, .6, .8$, and 1.

11.4.2 Quadratic curves must be planar

Justify the assertion that there is a unique quadratic curve that passes through a set of three (distinct) points. Remembering that three (noncollinear) points determine a plane, show that the quadratic they determine never leaves that plane. Thus, a parabola can never deviate from a plane. For extra benefit, show that a cubic curve *can* be nonplanar.

11.4.3 A Bezier curve in terms of `Tween()`

Recall the function `Tween()` in Section 4.5.3. The function takes two points as arguments and returns the tween of these points at a given value of t. Show that $P(t)$ of Equation (11.20) can be written as `Tween(Tween(P0,P1,t),Tween (P1,P2,t),t)`. Write a similar expression for the cubic version.

11.4.4 The cubic Bezier curve

By writing out a succession of tweens as in the previous exercise, show that the parametric form of the Bezier curve given in Equation (11.21) is correct.

11.4.5 Building intuitions about Bezier curves

Using Equation (11.21), compute the position of $P(t)$ at the times $t = 0.2, 0.5$, and 0.9, when the four control points are $(2, 3)$, $(6, 6)$, $(8, 1)$, and $(4, -3)$. Sketch the weighted vectors, as in Figure 11.15, that contribute to the final value of $P(t)$.

11.4.6 The quartic and quintic Bezier curves

Write out the Bernstein functions in Equation (11.26) for the case of $L = 4$. Show that these functions are the terms one gets upon expanding $\left[(1 - t) + t\right]^4$. Repeat for $L = 5$.

11.4.7 Recursion relation for the Bernstein polynomials

Show that the nth-order Bernstein polynomial can always be formed from $(n - 1)$th-order versions by using the equation

$$B_i^n(t) = (1 - t)B_i^{n-1}(t) + tB_{i-1}^{n-1}(t), \qquad (11.29)$$

---

[3] Readers who are familiar with probability theory will notice a strong resemblance between this form and the binomial probability distribution.

where $B_0^0(t) = 1$ and where $B_j^n(t) = 0$ when j is not in the range $0, \ldots, n$. (*Hint:* $\dbinom{n}{i} = \dbinom{n-1}{i} + \dbinom{n-1}{i-1}$.)

11.4.8 Bezier curves interpolate at both ends

Show that the general L-degree Bezier curve passes through the two outermost control points $P(0) = P_0$ and $P(1) = P_L$. Do this by examining the values of the Bernstein polynomials at $t = 0$ and $t = 1$ and showing that all but one term vanishes at these endpoints.   ■

11.5 PROPERTIES OF BEZIER CURVES

Bezier curves have some important properties that make them well suited for CAGD. Later, we shall see that these properties apply to B-splines as well. Exploring the various properties and their proofs provides a great deal of insight into Bezier curves.

Endpoint Interpolation

The Bezier curve $P(t)$ based on control points $P_0, P_1, \ldots, P_L$ does not generally pass through, or interpolate, all of the control points. But we have seen that it always interpolates P_0 and P_L. This is a very useful property, because a designer who is inputting a sequence of points thereby knows precisely where the Bezier curve will begin and end.

Affine Invariance

It is often necessary to subject a Bezier curve to an affine transformation in order to scale it, orient it, or position it for subsequent use. Suppose we wish to transform point $P(t)$ on the Bezier curve given by Equation (11.25) to the new point $Q(t)$, using the affine transformation T (represented by a three-by-three matrix in the 2D case and by a four-by-four matrix in the 3D case). So $Q(t) = T\big(P(t)\big)$. It appears that, to find $Q(t)$ at any given value of t, we must first evaluate $P(t)$ and then transform it, effectively starting over fresh for each new t. But this, in fact, is not so; we need only transform the control points (once) and then use the new control points in the same Bernstein form to re-create the transformed Bezier curve at any t! That is,

$$Q(t) = \sum_{k=0}^{L} T(P_k) B_k^L(t). \tag{11.30}$$

Affine invariance means that the transformed curve is identical to the curve that is based on the transformed control points.

Figure 11.16 shows a Bezier curve based on four control points $P_0, \ldots, P_3$. These points are rotated, scaled, and translated to the new control points Q_k, and the Bezier curve determined by them is drawn. The curve is identical, point by point, to the result of transforming the original Bezier curve.

FIGURE 11.16 Showing affine invariance.

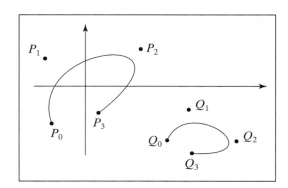

Bezier curves are affine invariant for a very simple reason: They are formed as an affine combination of points, and from Section 5.2.7, we know that an affine transformation preserves affine combinations.

Invariance under Affine Transformations of the Parameter

So far, we have defined Bezier curves on the parametric interval $t\varepsilon[0, 1]$. Sometimes it is convenient, however, to use a different interval. Suppose we wish to define the Bezier curve $R(u)$ (based, as before, on the control points $P_0, P_1, \ldots, P_L$) that is swept out as a parameter u varies over the interval from a to b. To do this, we simply replace each occurrence of t with

$$\frac{u - a}{b - a}.$$

The Bezier curve is now given by

$$R(u) = \sum_{k=0}^{L} P_k B_k^L\left(\frac{u - a}{b - a}\right). \tag{11.31}$$

Notice that as u varies from a to b, the argument of each Bernstein polynomial varies from 0 to 1, as intended. The mapping from u to t given by $t = (u - a)/(b - a)$ is clearly affine: It is a scaling followed by a translation. The Bezier curve is invariant to this mapping in the sense that the same path is swept out by $R(u)$ for $u\varepsilon[a, b]$ as is swept out by $P(t)$ for $t\varepsilon[0, 1]$.

Convex-hull Property

Another property designers often rely on is that a Bezier curve $P(t)$ never wanders outside its convex hull. The convex hull of a set of points $P_0, P_1, \ldots, P_L$ is the set of all *convex combinations* of the points—that is, the set of all points given by

$$\sum_{k=0}^{L} \alpha_k P_k, \tag{11.32}$$

where each α_k is nonnegative and $\sum \alpha_k = 1$.

But $P(t)$ of Equation (11.25) *is* a convex combination of its control points for every t, since no Bernstein polynomial is ever negative and they sum to unity. Thus, every point on the Bezier curve is a convex combination of its control points, so it must lie within the convex hull of the control points.

The convex-hull property also follows immediately from the fact that each point on the curve is the result of tweening two points that are themselves tweens, and the tweening of two points forms a convex combination of them. Figure 11.17 illustrates how the designer can use the convex-hull property. Even though the eight control points form a jagged control polygon, the designer knows that the Bezier curve will flow smoothly between the two endpoints, never extending outside the convex hull.

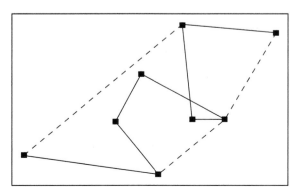

FIGURE 11.17 Using the convex hull property.

Linear Precision

Can a Bezier curve be a simple straight line? The convex-hull property shows that it can: If all of the control points are placed in a straight line, their convex hull collapses to a line. The Bezier curve is therefore "trapped" inside this hull and so must also be a straight line. The property of achieving a straight portion of a curve by properly positioning the control points is called **linear precision**.

Variation-diminishing Property

Roughly speaking, Bezier curves can't "fluctuate" more than their control polygon does. More precisely, no straight line (or, in three dimensions, no plane) can have more intersections with a Bezier curve than it has with the curve's control polygon. Figure 11.18 shows a Bezier curve based on the control polygon P. Line L cuts through P five times, but through the Bezier curve only three times. No line can be found that cuts the curve more often than it cuts P, a property that can be proved in general for Bezier curves. (See, for instance, [Farin90].) This is a useful property for curve designers as they lay down a control polygon: They can predict with confidence that the resulting Bezier curve will not undulate wildly or exhibit extra bends and curves. (On the other hand, some alternative curve-design techniques, such as certain interpolation schemes, do produce unruly fluctuations; see [Acton70].)

FIGURE 11.18 The variation-diminishing property of Bezier curves.

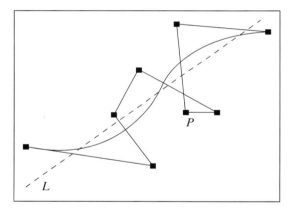

Derivatives of Bezier Curves

Because a curve can exhibit corners and other abrupt changes when its derivatives with respect to t have discontinuities, we must investigate the various derivatives of $P(t)$ in Equation (11.25).

For a Bezier curve, one can show that the first derivative is

$$\mathbf{p}'(t) = L \sum_{k=0}^{L-1} \Delta P_k B_k^{L-1}(t), \tag{11.33}$$

where

$$\Delta P_k = P_{k+1} - P_k. \tag{11.34}$$

(See the exercises that follow.) So the velocity is another Bezier curve, built on a new set of control vectors ΔP_k. We simply take the difference of the original control points, in pairs, to form the control vectors of the velocity. Note from the form $B_k^{L-1}(t)$ that taking the derivative lowers the order of the curve by one: For instance, the derivative of a cubic Bezier curve is a quadratic Bezier curve. The "smoothness" of Bezier curves is addressed in the exercises.

Creating and Drawing Bezier Curves

Suppose we wish to build an application that draws a Bezier curve from a sequence of control points. How might such an application be organized? The Bezier curve $P(t)$ of Equation (11.25) will be drawn by an approximating polyline. The function $P(t)$ is sampled at closely spaced values of t—say, at $t_i = i/N$ for $i = 0, 1, \ldots, N$—and the points $P(t_i)$ are connected by straight lines. The only issue is the evaluation of $P(t)$ at each desired value of t, which we suppose is performed in the following function:

```
Point2 bezier(RealPointArray poly, double t);
// compute position P(t) of the Bezier curve based on a
control polygon
```

This routine uses the array of points (called the **control polygon**) stored in `poly` to evaluate Equation (11.25) for the given value of t and returns the resulting point. Notice that the degree of the Bernstein polynomials is stored in `poly.num`. Implementing the routine is left as a (valuable) exercise. A great deal of insight is gained by experimenting with a Bezier curve design application, to see the effect of using different control polygons.

PRACTICE EXERCISES

11.5.1 A matrix form for the Bezier curve

Some formulations express Bezier curves in terms of matrices, which can be advantageous when they are manipulated within a computer (for instance, if matrix multiplier hardware is available [Faux79; Foley90]). Toward that end, it is convenient to define two arrays of now-familiar quantities: the Bernstein polynomial array, defined as

$$\mathbf{B}^L(t) = \left(B_0^L(t),\, B_1^L(t), \ldots, B_L^L(t) \right), \tag{11.35}$$

and the control-point array

$$\mathbf{P} = \left(P_0, P_1, \ldots, P_L \right). \tag{11.36}$$

a. Equation (11.25) expresses $P(t)$ as a sum of products. Show that this is formally the dot product; that is,

$$P(t) = \mathbf{B}^L(t) \cdot \mathbf{P}. \tag{11.37}$$

b. Use Appendix 2 to show that $P(t)$ can also be expressed as the product of a row array with a column array. Mathematically, $P(t) = \mathbf{B}^L(t)\mathbf{P}^T$, where T denotes the transposition.

c. Show that, because each Bernstein polynomial in turn is a polynomial of the form of Equation (11.26), each such polynomial can be written as a dot product. For instance, we might have

$$B_2^3(t) = 3(1 - t)t^2 = \left(t^0, t^1, t^2, t^3 \right) \cdot (0, 0, 3, -3). \tag{11.38}$$

d. Each polynomial $B_k^L(t)$, requires a different array of coefficients. What is this array for $B_0^3(t)$?

e. An array of the powers of t, such as $\left(t^0, t^1, t^2, t^3 \right)$, is often called the **power basis**. So the Bernstein array $\mathbf{B}^L(t)$ can be expressed by placing the various coefficient arrays for the different $B_k^L(t)$ terms side by side into a matrix $\mathbf{Bez}^L$. Show that, for the case $L = 3$,

$$\mathbf{B}^3(t) = \left(t^0, t^1, t^2, t^3 \right)\mathbf{Bez}^3, \tag{11.39}$$

where

$$\mathbf{Bez}^3 = \begin{pmatrix} 1 & 0 & 0 & 0 \\ -3 & 3 & 0 & 0 \\ 3 & -6 & 3 & 0 \\ -1 & 3 & -3 & 1 \end{pmatrix} \tag{11.40}$$

f. Putting all of the preceding ingredients together for the general Lth-order case, show that the Bezier curve may be expressed as

$$P(t) = \mathbf{Pow}^L(t)\mathbf{Bez}^L\mathbf{P}^T, \tag{11.41}$$

where

$$\mathbf{Pow}^L(t) = (1, t, t^2, \ldots, t^L) \tag{11.42}$$

represents the power basis and the matrix $\mathbf{Bez}^L$ has ijth term

$$m_{ij} = (-1)^{j-i} \binom{n}{i}\binom{i}{j}. \tag{11.43}$$

Note that when you want to fashion curves from points by using polynomials other than Bernstein polynomials, you obtain the same expression as in Equation (11.41), but some other matrix replaces $\mathbf{Bez}^L$. (See examples and details in [Faux79] and [Foley90].) This uniformity makes the process of changing from one type of curve generation to another much more understandable.

11.5.2 Draw the velocity

Plot four points on graph paper, sketch the Bezier curve for these points, and carefully sketch its velocity and acceleration vectors as functions of t.

11.5.3 Deriving the velocity of a Bezier curve (this is a challenging exercise)

Show that the velocity given in Equation (11.37) is correct. *Hint*: Show that the derivative of $t^k(1-t)^{L-k}$ is $kt^{k-1}(1-t)^{L-k} - (L-k)t^k(1-t)^{L-k-1}$, so $\mathbf{p}'(t)$ may be written as the difference of two Bezier curves. Manipulate the two Bezier forms (e.g., by shifting the index of summation) so that they depend on the same Bernstein polynomials, and then combine the two terms into one.

11.5.4 The acceleration of Bezier curves

Because taking the derivative of a Bezier curve simply requires building a Bezier curve on the first differences of its control points, the second derivative must be a Bezier curve formed by taking the difference of the differences. Show that the acceleration for a Bezier curve is given by

$$\mathbf{p}''(t) = L(L-1) \sum_{k=0}^{L-2} \Delta^2 P_k B_k^{L-2}(t), \tag{11.44}$$

where

$$\Delta^2 P_k = \Delta P_{k+1} - \Delta P_k \tag{11.45}$$

are the second differences of the control points. Express the second difference, $\Delta^2 P_k$, in terms of the original control points. Find a general form for the rth difference of the control points, and form an expression for the rth derivative of a Bezier curve.

11.5.5 How differentiable are Lth-order Bezier curves?

Is a Bezier curve based on L control points L-smooth? If so, prove it. If not, what is the highest order of derivative that is continuous for such a curve?

11.5.6 The quadratic and quartic cases

Find the matrix $\mathbf{Bez}^L$ for the cases $L = 2$ and $L = 4$.

11.5.7 Derive the terms in Bez^L

Show that the ijth term of the matrix $\mathbf{Bez}^L$ is as given in Equation (11.43).   ■

11.6 FINDING BETTER BLENDING FUNCTIONS

I was gratified to be able to answer promptly.
I said I didn't know.

Mark Twain

It might appear that Bezier curves provide the ultimate tool for designing curves. An endless variety of smooth curves can be fashioned by placing control points judiciously in the plane. But we see next that Bezier curves by themselves do not provide enough flexibility in curve design. One problem is that the degree of the Bernstein polynomials used is coupled to the number of control points: A Bezier curve based on $L + 1$ control points is a combination of L-degree polynomials. Polynomials of high degree are expensive to compute and are vulnerable to numerical round-off errors. We want the designer to be free to use as many control points as desired—even 40 or more.

11.6.1 The Problem of Local Control

An even more significant problem than their relative inflexibility is that Bezier curves do not offer enough **local control** over the shape of the curve. Figure 11.19 shows a situation in which five control points are used to fashion a Bezier curve (shown solid), which deviates somewhat from the desired curve (dashed) near $t = 1$. To correct this deviation, the user would move P_2 and P_3 up somewhat to force the Bezier curve closer to the desired curve. But, as shown in the figure, that also affects the shape of the first half of the curve, forcing it away somewhat from the desired version.

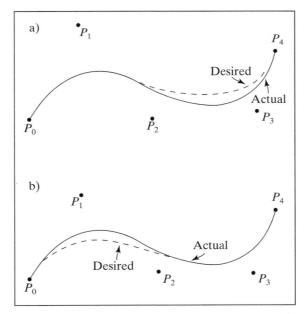

FIGURE 11.19 Editing portions of a curve.

The problem is that a change to any control point alters the *entire* curve. This relationship arises from the nature of Bernstein polynomials (recall Figure 11.14): Each one is "active" (meaning nonzero) over the entire interval $[0, 1]$. The interval over which a function is nonzero is often called its **support**. Because every Bernstein polynomial has support over the entire interval $[0, 1]$, and because the curve is a blend of these functions, it follows that each control point has an effect on the curve at all t-values between 0 and 1. Therefore, adjusting any control point affects the shape of the curve everywhere, with no local control.

Contrast that situation with the more favorable set of blending functions illustrated in Figure 11.20. Six blending functions $R_0(t), R_1(t), \ldots, R_5(t)$ (to be defined)[4]

---

[4] These are in fact quadratic B-splines, to be developed later.

FIGURE 11.20 Blending functions having concentrated support.

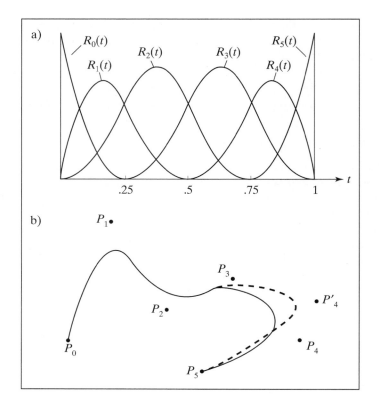

are shown, each having support that is only a part of the interval $[0, 1]$. For instance, the support of $R_0(t)$ is $[0, .25]$ and that of $R_3(t)$ is $[.25, 1.0]$. In fact, at any value of t, no more than three of the blending functions are active.

Consider using these blending functions to build a curve $V(t)$ based on six given control points $P_0, P_1, \ldots, P_5$. We use the same kind of parametric form as for Bezier curves:

$$V(t) = \sum_{k=0}^{5} P_k R_k(t). \tag{11.46}$$

Figure 11.20(b) shows the curve for a sample set of control points. At each t, the position $V(t)$ depends on no more than three of the control points. In particular, for all t in $[0.75, 1.0]$, only the points P_3, P_4, and P_5 control the shape of the curve. If the single control point P_4 is moved to P'_4, only that portion of the curve shown dashed will change. Thus, this set of blending functions does give some local control to the control points.

11.6.2 Wish List for a Set of Blending Functions

The shapes of the blending functions in Figure 11.20 were apparently concocted just to illustrate the property of local control. But they are in fact based on "real" functions that are often used to design curves. Their detailed nature is described later, but we scrutinize them further here to get a sense of what properties a set of blending functions should have.

As always, we suppose that the curve-generation algorithm to be used blends the control points $P_0, \ldots, P_L$ according to the formula

$$V(t) = \sum_{k=0}^{L} P_k R_k(t), \quad \text{for } t \text{ in } [a, b], \tag{11.47}$$

where the blending functions $R_0(t), \ldots, R_L(t)$ have certain properties that either produce "better" curves or make the design process more intuitive. We construct a wish list of such properties. The blending functions should

- be easy to compute and numerically stable.
- sum to unity at every t in $[a, b]$.
- have support only over a small portion of $[a, b]$, to offer local control;
- interpolate certain control points, chosen by the designer;
- be smooth enough to produce a desirable shape.

We consider each of these properties individually.

The Functions Should Be Easy to Compute and Numerically Stable

To generate curves rapidly, we want the blending functions to be computationally simple. We also want them to be minimally susceptible to numerical round-off error. These considerations lead one to choose polynomials for the blending functions, and the degree of the polynomials should be fairly small. Other kinds of functions, such as sines and cosines, would be too expensive to use.

The Functions Must Sum to Unity at Every t in $[a, b]$

$V(t)$ is a weighted sum of points at each t, and this makes sense only if $V(t)$ is an *affine* sum of points at every t in $[a, b]$. Thus, we insist that

$$\sum_{k=0}^{L} R_k(t) = 1. \tag{11.48}$$

You can see that the candidate functions in Figure 11.20 appear to enjoy this property.

The Functions Should Have Support Only over a Small Portion of $[a, b]$

To achieve local control, we want each blending function to be concentrated in t, having support over only a small portion of the interval $[a, b]$.

The Functions Should Interpolate Certain Control Points

The designer may want $V(t)$ to pass through some of the control points, but only be attracted towards others. The shapes in Figure 11.20 cause the first and last control points to be interpolated. We will see shortly how to provide a mechanism that adjusts the blending functions so that specific points are interpolated.

The Functions Should Have Sufficient Smoothness

The designer normally wants $V(t)$ to be a smooth curve for any set of control points. Typically, $V(t)$ should be at least 1-smooth, maybe even 2-smooth, to produce curves of desirable shapes. The smoothness of $V(t)$ depends on the smoothness of the blending functions; specifically, if every blending function is 1-smooth in $[a, b]$, then $V(t)$ will also be 1-smooth in $[a, b]$.

Notice that the blending functions in Figure 11.20 appear to be smooth in their interior. It is also important that they "start" and "stop" gracefully. Figure 11.21 shows a blending function along with its first derivative. The derivative of the function varies continuously from zero at $t = c$, where the function starts. But where it ends at d, its derivative is discontinuous, jumping abruptly from A to zero. This function is 1-smooth everywhere, except at $t = d$. A curve that used this blending function would not be 1-smooth at $t = d$. Thus, it is desirable for blending functions to be smooth internally and also to start and end where their derivative is zero.

Some of the shapes in Figure 11.20 start and stop where their derivative is zero, while others do not. The shapes that begin and end inside the interval $[0, 1]$ do so with a derivative of zero, so the curve $V(t)$ will be 1-smooth inside $(0, 1)$. It is acceptable

FIGURE 11.21 A candidate blending function and its derivative.

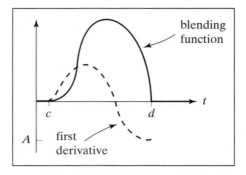

for derivatives to be discontinuous at the ends of the interval $[0, 1]$ because we never use values of t that are less than zero or greater than unity.

11.6.3 Piecewise Polynomial Curves and Splines

Let us start looking for good candidate blending functions, say, polynomials of low degree. For instance, is there some cubic polynomial with the shape suggested in Figure 11.22 that will satisfy all our needs? To explore this question, we define the function

$$R(t) = at^3 + bt^2 + ct + d$$

FIGURE 11.22 Can we find a cubic polynomial like this?

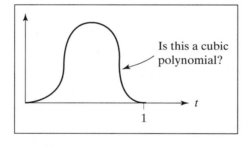

and see whether there is a choice of coefficients that makes $R(t)$ and its first derivative both zero at $t = 0$ and $t = 1$. This leads to four conditions on the coefficients:

$$R(0) = d = 0;$$
$$R(1) = a + b + c + d = 0;$$
$$R'(0) = c = 0;$$
$$R'(1) = 3a + 2b + c = 0.$$

Unfortunately, these conditions force $a = b = c = d = 0$, so there is no such shape. There just isn't enough flexibility in a cubic to do the "bending" we need. (The exercises on page 625 ask whether a quartic polynomial would work.)

To attain more flexibility, we can try "piecing" together several low-degree polynomials. Such curves are defined by different polynomials in different t-intervals and are called **piecewise polynomials**. The sample shape $g(t)$ shown in Figure 11.23 helps establish some nomenclature. We see that $g(t)$ consists of three polynomial **segments**, defined as

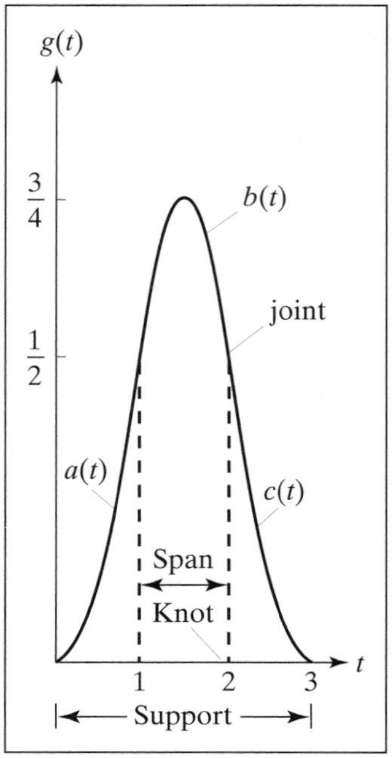

$$a(t) = \frac{1}{2}t^2,$$

$$b(t) = \frac{3}{4} - \left(t - \frac{3}{2}\right)^2, \qquad (11.49)$$

FIGURE 11.23 Ingredients of a piecewise polynomial.

and

$$c(t) = \frac{1}{2}(3 - t)^2.$$

The support of $g(t)$ is $[0, 3]$; $a(t)$ is defined on the **span** $[0, 1]$, $b(t)$ on the span $[1, 2]$, and $c(t)$ on the span $[2, 3]$. The points at which a pair of the individual segments meet are called **joints**, and the values of t at which this happens are called **knots**. There are four knots in this example: 0, 1, 2, and 3.

Is $g(t)$ continuous everywhere over its support? Because it is built from polynomials, it is certainly continuous inside each span, so we need only check that the segments meet properly at the joints. This, in fact, is easily checked from Equation (11.49); we obtain $a(1) = b(1) = 1/2$ and $b(2) = c(2) = 1/2$.

Going further, the derivative of $g(t)$ is continuous everywhere, so $g(t)$ is 1-smooth in $[0, 3]$. To see this, note that the derivative is necessarily continuous inside each span (why?), so we need to check its continuity only at the knots. Direct calculation shows that $a'(1) = b'(1) = 1$ and $b'(2) = c'(2) = -1$. Thus, as we move from one polynomial piece to the next, the slope does not jump abruptly. By contrast, the second derivative is not continuous, but does jump abruptly between two values (which ones?) at the knots.

The shape $g(t)$ is an example of a **spline function**, a piecewise polynomial function that possesses "enough" smoothness. Specifically, we have the following definition:

> **DEFINITION: Definition of a Spline Function**
>
> An Mth-degree spline function is a piecewise polynomial of degree M that is $(M - 1)$-smooth at each knot.

Evidently, our sample $g(t)$ is a quadratic spline: It is a piecewise polynomial of degree 2 and has a continuous first derivative everywhere.

11.6.4 Building a Set of Blending Functions out of $g(t)$

How can we use the foregoing spline function $g(t)$ as a blending function to represent a curve? One way is to use shifted versions of $g(t)$, where each blending function $g_k(t)$ is formed by translating the basic shape of $g(t)$ by a certain amount. Figure 11.24 shows the following seven blending functions, $g_0(t), \ldots, g_6(t)$, formed by shifting $g(.)$ by integer amounts:

$$g_k(t) = g(t - k), \qquad \text{for } k = 0, 1, \ldots. \tag{11.50}$$

(Since the knots of the various versions of $g(.)$ occur at integers, shifting $g(.)$ in this manner is equivalent to shifting so that knots of one translation "line up" with knots

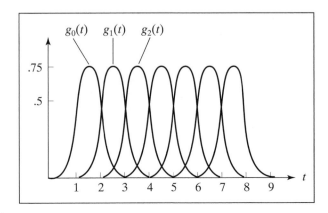

FIGURE 11.24 Closed curves based on splines.

of the next translation.) These shifted versions will form a legitimate set of blending functions only if they add up exactly to unity at every t. But in fact, they *do* for all t between 2 and 7! (See the exercises at the end of the section.) That is,

$$\sum_{k=0}^{6} g(t - k) = 1, \qquad \text{for } t \text{ in } [2, 7]. \tag{11.51}$$

This shifting may seem like magic, but we will see that it is a general property of the blending functions we ultimately develop. Here it is crucial that we translate each function by an integer, to make the shapes "line up" properly so that they sum to unity.

So the designer chooses seven control points and generates the curve by using the algorithm

$$V(t) = \sum_{k=0}^{6} P_k g(t - k). \tag{11.52}$$

Only values of t between 2 and 7 can be utilized. (Why?) In that range, note that exactly three of the blending functions are active at any value of t, so there is good local control of the curve's shape. In addition, note that at times $t = 2, 3, \ldots, 7$ only two of the functions are active and they both have the value 0.5. Therefore, at these t-values $V(t)$ will lie at the *midpoint* of the line between two of the control points.

Figure 11.25 shows an example of the placement of the seven control points, together with the resulting curve. The curve begins at $t = 2$ at the midpoint of $P_0 P_1$ and fluctuates smoothly, passing through subsequent midpoints of the edges of the control polygon. As t increases, the various blending functions rise and fall, and the major influence on the curve is "passed on" from point to point.

FIGURE 11.25 Curve design using translates of $g(.)$.

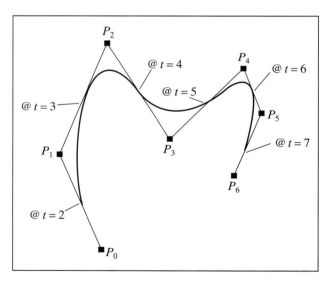

What are some properties of curves based on this set of blending functions?

- The designer has some local control over shape of the curve, because the interval of support for each blending function is limited to length 3.
- The designer will lay down points exploiting the knowledge that the curve must pass through midpoints of the edges of the control polygon. So the algorithm has some intuitive geometric properties.
- Because each blending function is 1-smooth, the whole curve is 1-smooth.
- No points on the curve are interpolated.

- All polynomials are of degree two, so they are fast and stable to compute. The degree of the polynomials does not depend on the number of control points; the technique works for any number of control points.

The preceding curve-generation algorithm can easily be implemented in the routine

```
Point2 curvePt(double t, RealPointArray pts)
```

which returns the point $V(t)$ for each value of t input into it. This algorithm is further discussed in Case Study 11.4.

■ **EXAMPLE 11.6.1 Extension to drawing closed curves**

It is not difficult to extend the technique just set forth to the generation of closed curves such as those shown in Figure 11.26(a). Figure 11.26(b) shows the closed version of the curve in Figure 11.25. All that is involved is adding two more terms to the sum in Equation 11.52, with two additional control points that *duplicate* P_0 and P_1. (So $P_7 = P_0$ and $P_8 = P_1$.) We know that at $t = 7$ the previous curve passed through the midpoint of leg $P_5 P_6$. Thus, at $t = 8$ the curve passes through the midpoint of $P_6 P_7$, and at $t = 9$ it passes through the midpoint of $P_7 P_8$, closing the curve. An alternative method is given in the exercises.

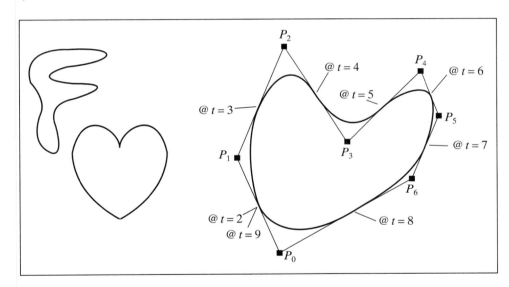

FIGURE 11.26 Generating closed curves.

PRACTICE EXERCISES

11.6.1 Is there a quartic polynomial blending function?

Consider the quartic polynomial $r(t) = at^4 + bt^3 + ct^2 + dt + e$. Are there values of a, b, c, d, and e that cause this function to pass through the point zero and have a first derivative equal to zero at both $t = 0$ and $t = 1$? If so, find suitable values and sketch the curve.

11.6.2 Show that the $g(.)$ translates add to unity at every t

Consider the sum of translates $g(t) + g(t - 1) + g(t - 2)$, where $g(t)$ is the piecewise polynomial defined in Equation (11.49). Show that this sum is equal to unity for every t between 2 and 3.

11.6.3 Are Bernstein polynomials splines?

Show that the Bernstein polynomials $B_k^L(t)$ are indeed splines. How many polynomials are pieced together to form each one? Where are the knots? What degree is the spline? Is it sufficiently continuously differentiable?

11.6.4 Develop intuitions about quadratic spline curves

Draw 12 control points in some complex pattern, and sketch the curve that is generated by means of the quadratic spline functions of Equation (11.49). Use the fact that the curve passes through the midpoint of certain edges of the control polygon.

11.6.5 Building closed curves with no extra control points

Show that a slight variation on Equation (11.52), viz.,

$$V(t) = \sum_{k=0}^{6} P_k g\big((t - k)\bmod 7\big), \tag{11.53}$$

creates a closed curve based on seven (distinct) control points as t varies from 0 to 7. No duplicate control points are required. The modulo function mod effectively "folds" the blending functions into the interval $[0, 7]$, making them active in different parts of the interval. To see how this works, sketch, for $L = 4$, the five functions $g\big((t - k)\bmod(L + 1)\big)$ for $k = 0, 1, 2, 3, 4$ as t varies from 0 to 5. ■

11.6.5 Spline Curves and Basis Functions

The method involving translates of the quadratic $g(t)$ seems to give us a fine curve-design tool. So why go further? The issue is that we need more control over the shape of the curve: it must "bend" more and be smoother than just 1-smooth. This requirement suggests moving to cubic polynomials. We also want the designer to be able to specify which control points are interpolated. And it would be beneficial to have a single algorithm that encompasses all of the design techniques we have described, including Bezier curves.

Thus, we seek to develop more general families of blending functions that meet all the properties discussed in the earlier wish list. We continue to use the same parametric form

$$P(t) = \sum_{k=0}^{L} P_k R_k(t) \tag{11.54}$$

based on $L + 1$ control points and $L + 1$ blending functions $R_0(t), \dots, R_L(t)$. We continue to require that $P(t)$ be an affine sum of points. We also continue to use piecewise polynomials for the blending functions, but now they are defined on a more general sequence of knots, called the **knot vector**,

$$\mathbf{T} = (t_0, t_1, t_2, \dots), \tag{11.55}$$

which is simply a list of knot values $t_0, t_1, \dots$ that are assumed to be nondecreasing; that is $t_i \le t_{i+1}$. Some of the knots might have the same value, but are still given distinct names. The number of knots involved in $\mathbf{T}$ is discussed later.

Figure 11.27 illustrates the situation. Each blending function $R_k(t)$ is a piecewise polynomial that is zero up to time t_k, is nonzero over several spans in the knot vector, and then returns to zero again. We insist further that each $R_k(t)$ be a spline function, so that it enjoys a certain level of smoothness at all t in its support.

Notice that both the Bezier curve formulation and the formulation involving the translates of $g(t)$ fit into this more general scheme:

• *Bezier.* There is one span from 0 to 1, all the Bernstein polynomials are of degree L, and there are $L + 1$ knots at $t = 0$ and $L + 1$ more knots at $t = 1$. The Bernstein polynomials are splines, since they have continuous derivatives of order L.

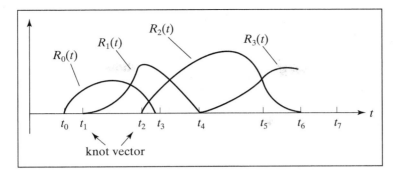

FIGURE 11.27 Generalizing on the knot vector and blending functions.

- *Translates of $g(t)$.* The knot values are the integers $0, 1, \ldots, L + 2$, and each translate $g(t - k)$ is a spline consisting of three polynomials of degree 2 and covering a span of 3.

Because each $R_k(t)$ is a piecewise polynomial, the whole curve $P(t)$ is a sum of piecewise polynomials, weighted by the control points. For instance, in some span, the curve might be given by

$$P(t) = P_0(3t^2 - 4t + 2) + P_1(8t^2 - 7.3t - 7.99) + \ldots. \tag{11.56}$$

In an adjacent span, the curve is given by a different sum of polynomials, but we know that all segments meet to make the curve continuous. Such a curve is known as a **spline curve** [Farin90].[5]

The following question can now be posed: Given a knot vector, is there some family of blending functions that can be used to generate every possible spline curve that can be defined on that knot vector? Such a family is called a **basis** for the splines, meaning that any spline curve whatsoever can be matched by the sum in Equation (11.54) by choosing the proper control polygon. The answer is that there are many such families, but there is one basis in particular whose blending functions have the smallest support and therefore offer the greatest local control: the **B-splines**, where B is derived from the word *basis*.

11.7 THE B-SPLINE BASIS FUNCTIONS

When the going gets tough, the smart get lost.

Robert Byrne

We wish to define the B-spline blending functions, $R_k(t)$, in a way that lends some intuition to them and, in addition, leads to a straightforward computer implementation. Although the literature offers many different approaches to formulating B-splines, there is a single formula that defines all the B-spline functions of any order. It is a recursive relation that is easy to implement in a program and is numerically well behaved. (Some other methods are more computationally efficient—see the exercises at the end of Section 11.7.1.)

Each B-spline function is based on polynomials of a certain order m. If $m = 3$, the polynomials will be of order 3 and thus of degree 2, so they will be quadratic B-splines. If $m = 4$, the underlying polynomials will be of degree 3, or cubic. These

---

[5] Note the difference between a *spline function*, defined in Section 11.6.3, and a *spline curve*. A spline function is simply a piecewise polynomial having a certain level of smoothness. A spline curve is an affine blend of points using piecewise polynomial blending functions. A spline curve must be continuous at its knots, but might have discontinuous derivatives there.

are the two most important cases, although the formulation allows us to construct B-splines of any order.

11.7.1 Definition of B-spline Functions

It is useful to make the order of a B-spline function explicit in the notation, so, instead of saying simply $R_k(t)$, we denote the kth B-spline blending function of order m by $N_{k,m}(t)$. Hence, for B-spline curves, Equation (11.54) becomes

$$P(t) = \sum_{k=0}^{L} P_k N_{k,m}(t). \tag{11.57}$$

Summarizing the ingredients to this point, we have

- a knot vector $\mathbf{T} = (t_0, t_1, t_2 \dots)$;
- $(L + 1)$ control points P_k; and
- the order m of the B-spline functions.

The fundamental formula for the B-spline function $N_{k,m}(t)$ is

$$N_{k,m}(t) = \left(\frac{t - t_k}{t_{k+m-1} - t_k}\right) N_{k,m-1}(t) + \left(\frac{t_{k+m} - t}{t_{k+m} - t_{k+1}}\right) N_{k+1,m-1}(t), \tag{11.58}$$

for $k = 0, 1, \dots, L$. This is a recursive definition, specifying how to construct the mth-order function from two B-spline functions of order $(m - 1)$. To get things started, the first-order function must be defined. It is simply the constant function 1 within its span:

$$N_{k,1}(t) = \begin{cases} 1 & \text{if } t_k < t \le t_{k+1} \\ 0 & \text{otherwise} \end{cases}. \tag{11.59}$$

Note that this set of functions automatically sums to unity at every t, so it is legitimate to use such functions in forming combinations of points.

■ **EXAMPLE 11.7.1 Linear B-splines**

What shape does $N_{0,2}(t)$, which is the first ($k = 0$) B-spline function of order $m = 2$, have when the knots are equispaced (i.e., $\mathbf{T} = (t_0{=}0, t_1{=}1, t_2{=}2, \dots)$)? With these parameters, Equation (11.58) becomes

$$N_{0,2}(t) = \frac{t}{1} N_{0,1}(t) + \frac{2 - t}{1} N_{1,1}(t). \tag{11.60}$$

We see that a linear "up ramp" (given by the term t) multiplies $N_{0,1}(t)$ and that a linear "down ramp" $(2 - t)$ multiplies $N_{1,1}(t)$, as shown in Figure 11.28(a). When these ramps are summed, the result is a triangular pulse [Figure 11.28(b)]. Notice the similarity to tweening here: $N_{0,2}(t)$ is an affine combination of $N_{0,1}(t)$ and $N_{1,1}(t)$. So $N_{0,2}(t)$ is equal to t for $0 \le t \le 1$, is $2 - t$ for $1 \le t \le 2$, and is zero otherwise.

FIGURE 11.28 Construction of linear B-splines.

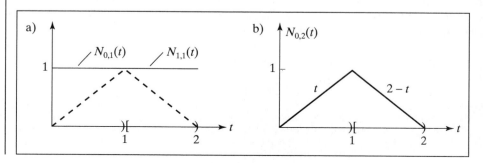

The construction of other linear B-splines follows similarly. For instance, $N_{1,2}(t)$ is a triangular pulse beginning at $t = 1$ and ending at $t = 3$: just a shifted version of the previous pulse. More generally, every linear spline is a shifted version of the zeroth one when equispaced knots are used; that is, $N_{i,2}(t) = N_{0,2}(t - i)$.

By drawing several of the functions $N_{k,2}(t)$, it is easily seen that the pulses overlap in just the right way to ensure that they sum to unity at all t. (Try it!)

Note that the curve built on linear B-splines is the control polyline itself. (Is this also true if the knots are not equi-spaced?) Because linear splines offer nothing beyond simple straight lines, they are normally not used for curve design. But they arise, of course, in the process of constructing higher order B-splines.

▪ EXAMPLE 11.7.2 Quadratic B-splines

Suppose we wish to determine the shape of the quadratic $(m = 3)$ B-spline functions $N_{i,3}(t)$ based on the same equispaced knots as in the previous example. Then we need build only $N_{0,3}(t)$, as the other functions are simple translations of this one. Equation (11.58) shows that

$$N_{0,3}(t) = \frac{t}{2} N_{0,2}(t) + \frac{3 - t}{2} N_{1,2}(t). \tag{11.61}$$

(Notice again the tweening of the two lower order spline functions.) The first term is an up ramp times the first triangular pulse, and the second term is a down ramp times the second pulse. As shown in Figure 11.29(a), a ramp times a triangular pulse produces two parabolas that meet at a corner. But when the two terms in Equation (11.61) are summed, the corners vanish and the resulting pulse, $N_{0,3}(t)$ [Figure 11.29(b)], has a continuous derivative.

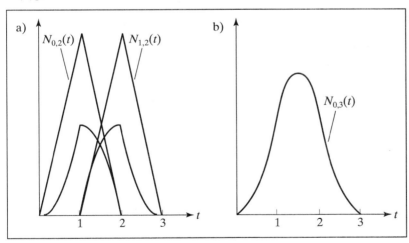

FIGURE 11.29 The first quadratic B-spline shape.

Equation 11.61 can be used to determine the algebraic form of the quadratic spline for each segment. The middle segment involves the sum of two quadratics, and the result is

$$N_{0,3}(t) = \begin{cases} \dfrac{1}{2} t^2, & \text{for } 0 \leq t \leq 1 \\[2mm] \dfrac{3}{4} - \left(t - \dfrac{3}{2}\right)^2, & \text{for } 1 \leq t \leq 2 \\[2mm] \dfrac{1}{2}(3 - t)^2, & \text{for } 2 \leq t \leq 3 \\[2mm] 0, & \text{otherwise} \end{cases} \tag{11.62}$$

Note that $N_{0,3}$ depends on the four knots $0, 1, 2,$ and 3 and that its support is the interval $[0, 3]$.

Comparing $N_{0,3}(t)$ with $g(t)$ of Equation (11.49), we see that they are precisely the same. This is because $g(t)$ was (secretly) chosen to be a B-spline function. Its first derivative has already been checked and found to be continuous. Its second derivative is not. Thus, quadratic B-splines (at least on equispaced knots) are in fact splines.

The other quadratic spline shapes, $N_{k,3}(t)$, are obtained easily when the knots are equispaced. Because the first-order splines are simple translations of one another, and because all the ramp terms in Equation (11.58) involve only differences among knot values, the quadratic B-splines must be simple translations of one another also. In fact, this is true for a B-spline of any order on equally spaced knots:

If knot $t_k = k$, then $N_{k,m}(t) = N_{0,m}(t - k)$.   (11.63)

This form can be substituted directly into Equation (11.57) when the knots are equispaced.

Earlier, we claimed that the quadratic splines of Equation (11.58) sum to unity at all t. This is true even if the knots are not equispaced, as we show in the exercises at the end of the section.

■ EXAMPLE 11.7.3 Cubic B-splines

The cubic B-spline is perhaps the most frequently used B-spline. $N_{0,4}(t)$ for equally spaced knots is shown in Figure 11.30(a). Its form is found in the same fashion as before. (See the exercises.) $N_{0,4}(t)$ is symmetrical about $t = 2$ and can be written compactly as

$$N_{0,4}(t) = \begin{cases} u(1 - t) & \text{for} \quad 0 \le t \le 1 \\ v(2 - t) & \text{for} \quad 1 \le t \le 2 \\ v(t - 2) & \text{for} \quad 2 \le t \le 3, \\ u(t - 3) & \text{for} \quad 3 \le t \le 4 \\ 0 & \text{otherwise} \end{cases}$$ (11.64)

FIGURE 11.30 The cubic B-spline on equispaced knots.

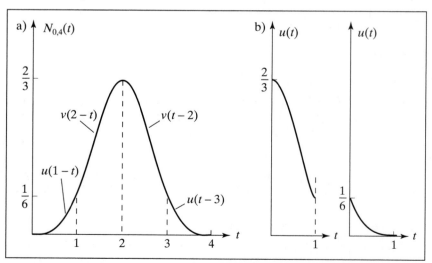

where the two segments $u(\ )$ and $v(\ )$ are shown in Figure 11.30(b) and are given by

$$u(t) = \frac{1}{6}(1 - t)^3$$

and

$$v(t) = \frac{1}{6}(3t^3 - 6t^2 + 4).$$

(11.65)

Direct calculation of derivatives shows that the first and second derivatives of the cubic spline are everywhere continuous, so cubic spline curves are 2-smooth, at least on equispaced knots.

Based on the reasoning here, one can show (see the exercises) that, in general, the function $N_{k,m}(t)$ begins at t_k and ends at t_{k+m}, so support is $[t_k, t_{k+m}]$. The function is also never negative.

One must always be alert to a potential division by zero: One or both denominators in Equation (11.58) might become zero for certain choices of knots. But whenever this happens, the corresponding lower order function, $N_{k,m-1}(t)$ or $N_{k+1,m-1}(t)$, is also always zero. So we can adopt the rule that any term having a zero denominator is evaluated as zero.

It is easy to implement the recursive formulation of the function $N_{k,m}(t)$ in computer code and therefore to compute its value at any t for any given knot vector. The fragment of code shown in Figure 11.31 is a direct translation of Equation (11.58).

```
float bSpline(int k, int m, float t, float knot[])
{
    float denom1, denom2, sum = 0.0;
    if(m == 1)
        return (t >= knot[k] && t < knot[k+1]); // 1 or 0
    // m exceeds 1.. use recursion
    denom1 = knot[k + m -1] - knot[k];
    if(denom1 != 0.0)
        sum = (t - knot[k]) * bSpline(k,m-1,t, knot) / denom1;
    denom2 = knot[k + m] - knot[k+1];
    if(denom2 != 0.0)
        sum += (knot[k+m] - t) * bSpline(k+1,m-1,t,knot) / denom2;
    return sum;
}
```

FIGURE 11.31 Computing B-spline blending functions.

PRACTICE EXERCISES

11.7.1 Potential division by zero

Show that when two knots have the same value, a denominator term in Equation (11.58) has the value zero. Show that in this case the term in which the denominator of zero appears also is always zero.

11.7.2 B-spline support

Show that, in general, $N_{k,m}(t)$ is zero outside the interval $[t_k, t_{k+m}]$, so the support of an mth order B-spline is m spans in the knot vector. Show also that $N_{k,m}(t)$ is nonnegative for all t.

11.7.3 Quadratic B-spline functions always sum to unity

We have already shown that the linear B-spline functions sum to unity. Show that this is true as well for the quadratic B-splines. (*Hint*: The following sequence of steps might help: You want to show that

$$\sum_{k=-\infty}^{\infty} N_{k,3}(t) = \sum_{k=-\infty}^{\infty} \frac{t - t_k}{t_{k+2} - t_k} N_{k,2}(t) + \sum_{k=-\infty}^{\infty} \frac{t_{k+3} - t}{t_{k+3} - t_{k+1}} N_{k+1,2}(t) = 1$$

for all t (note we sum from $-\infty$ to ∞), where we have just applied Equation (11.58) directly. Simply make a change of variable on the second sum ($k \rightarrow k - 1$), and then combine the sums into one and note that the coefficient of $N_{k,2}(t)$ is always unity. Since the second-order B-splines add to unity everywhere, you are done.)

11.7.4 Computation of the cubic B-spline

Verify the formulas in Equation (11.64) for the cubic B-spline based on equispaced knots. Also, calculate the first and second derivatives for the cubic B-spline, and show that they are continuous everywhere.

11.7.5 Hand simulation

Simulate by hand the algorithm in Figure 11.31 to calculate the value of $N_{3,2}(2.6)$ for the case of equispaced knots where $t_i = i$.

11.7.6 Periodic B-spline curves

Show that the curve

$$P(t) = \sum_{k=0}^{L} P_k N_{0,m}((t - k)\bmod(L + 1)), \qquad (11.66)$$

based on $L + 1$ control points and mth-order B-splines, closes on itself and is therefore periodic in t.   ■

11.7.2 Using Multiple Knots in the Knot Vector

Up to this point, we have used only B-splines based on equispaced knots. By varying the spacing between knots, the curve designer acquires much greater control of the shape of the final curve. A central question is, What happens to the shapes of the blending functions when two knots are set very close to one another? Figure 11.32 shows the situation when the knot vector is $\mathbf{T} = (0, 1, 2, 3, 3 + \varepsilon, 4 + \varepsilon, \dots)$, where ε is a small positive number. Now the "piece" of each piecewise polynomial lying in the interval $[3, 3 + \varepsilon]$ has been "squeezed'" into a very narrow span. The blending functions will clearly no longer be translations of one another. If ε is set to zero, this span will vanish altogether, and a **multiple knot** will occur at $t = 3$. This knot is said to have a "multiplicity of 2." Figure 11.33 shows the resulting blending functions. Now two of the linear B-spline shapes are discontinuous [Part (b) of the figure], and the quadratic shapes have a discontinuous derivative at $t = 3$ [Part (c)]. In general, an i-smooth curve is reduced to an $(i - 1)$-smooth curve at the multiple knot value. The cubic B-spline curves [Part (d)] are 1-smooth everywhere, but not 2-smooth at $t = 3$. But notice in Part (c) that if quadratic B-splines are used, the curve will interpolate control point P_2, because the blending function $N_{2,3}(t)$ reaches unity at $t = 3$ and all the other blending functions are zero there. In general, when t approaches a knot of multiplicity greater than unity, there is a stronger attraction to the governing control point. (Which one?)

FIGURE 11.32 Moving knots close together.

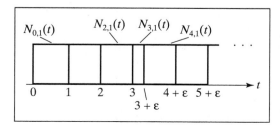

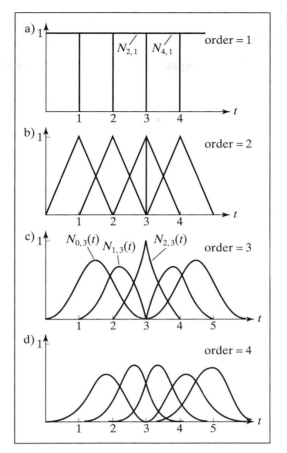

FIGURE 11.33 B-spline shapes near a knot of multiplicity 2.

Going further, quadratic splines become discontinuous near a knot of multiplicity 3. Cubic splines exhibit a discontinuous derivative near a knot of multiplicity 3, but they also interpolate one of the control points. By adjusting the multiplicity of each knot, the designer can therefore change the shape of the curve. Neither Equation (11.58) nor the fragment of code in Figure 11.31 need be altered to account for a knot vector that contains multiple knots. As we mentioned, some of the denominators in that equation become zero, but the code automatically handles this situation, and no adjustments need be made.

11.7.3 Open B-spline Curves: Standard Knot Vector

One special choice of knot vector has become a standard for curve design. With this arrangement, the curve interpolates the first and last control points, thus better enabling the designer to predict where the computed curve will lie.

The **standard knot vector** for a B-spline of order m begins and ends with a knot of multiplicity m and uses unit spacing for the remaining knots. We start with an example and then see how it arises. Suppose there are eight control points and we want to use cubic ($m = 4$) B-splines. The standard knot vector turns out to be

$$\mathbf{T} = (0, 0, 0, 0, 1, 2, 3, 4, 5, 5, 5, 5).$$

[The eight blending functions $N_{0,4}(t), \ldots, N_{7,4}(t)$ are defined on these knots by using Equation (11.58) and are shown in Figure 11.34(a). $N_{0,4}(t)$ and $N_{7,4}(t)$ are discontinuous and have a support of just one unit span. Only $N_{3,4}(t)$ and $N_{4,4}(t)$ have the usual span of four units. The remaining blending functions have two or three unit spans, and their shapes become more distorted as they approach the first and last knots. The specific polynomial functions that make up the blending functions are requested in the exercises. Notice that, taken together, these functions always ensure the first and last control points are interpolated. For example, at $t = 0$, all blending functions are zero except for $N_{0,4}(t)$, which is unity. It is also not hard to show that the initial direction of the B-spline curve at $t = 0$ is along the first segment of the control polygon, and similarly for the final direction. (See the exercises at the end of the section.)

FIGURE 11.34 Eight cubic B-spline blending functions.

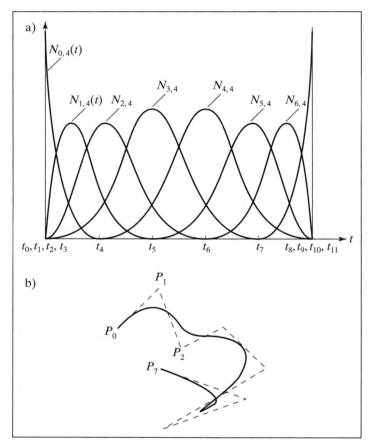

Figure 11.34(b) shows an example of a curve based on eight control points. Clearly, the first and last points are interpolated, and the directions of the curve at these points are as promised.

Note that a B-spline curve can cross itself when the control polygon does.

The standard knot vector for $L + 1$ control points and B-splines of order m is described as follows (comments about the corresponding blending functions appear in parentheses):

1. There are $L + m + 1$ knots altogether, denoted as $t_0, \ldots, t_{L+m}$.
2. The first m knots, $t_0, \ldots, t_{m-1}$, all share the value zero. (The first m blending functions start at $t = 0$.)
3. Knots $t_m, \ldots, t_L$ increase in increments of 1, from 1 through the value $L - m + 1$. (The final blending function, $N_{L,m}(t)$, begins at $t_L = L - m + 1$ and has a support of width 1.)
4. The final m knots, $t_{L+1}, \ldots, t_{L+m}$, all equal $L - m + 2$.

From these rules, it is easy to compose a procedure that generates the standard knot vector for given values of m and L, as shown by the following fragment of code:

```
void buildKnots(int m, int L, double knot[])
{
  // Build the standard knot vector for L + 1 control points
  // and B-splines of order m
  int i;
  if(L < (m - 1)) return;         // too few control points
  for(i = 0; i <= L + m; i++)
    if (i < m) knot[i] = 0.0;
    else if (i <= L) knot[i] = i - m + 1;// i is at least m here
    else knot[i] = L - m + 2;       // i exceeds L here
}
```

Note the error condition based on the values of m and L. For a given m, there must be a sufficient number of control points so that there will be " room" for at least one span of width 1. This leads to the following constraint:

> The order m cannot exceed the number of control points, $L + 1$.

Bezier Curves Are B-spline Curves

Bezier curves were introduced earlier through two approaches: the de Casteljau algorithm and Bernstein polynomials. We can now state a third approach: Bezier curves are also a special case of B-splines. This is so because the B-spline blending functions defined on the standard knot vector are in fact Bernstein polynomials when $m = L + 1$! That is,

$$N_{k, L+1}(t) = B_k^L(t),$$

for $k = 0, \ldots, L$. (Note that, by convention, the upper parameter of $B()$ is **degree**, while the second parameter of $N()$ is **order**.) To see this, note what happens to the standard knot vector as the order m is increased up to $L + 1$. (See the exercises.) The first m knots have the value 0, the last m have the value 1, and t varies only over $[0, 1]$. For example, if $L = 5$ and $m = 6$, we obtain $\mathbf{T} = (0, 0, 0, 0, 0, 0, 1, 1, 1, 1, 1, 1)$. Thus, each piecewise polynomial has only a single span, and each is a polynomial of order $m = L + 1$. This is precisely how the Bernstein polynomials behave. In fact, one can derive the Bernstein polynomials directly from Equation (11.58).

Recall that the prime motivation for going beyond Bezier curves to B-spline curves was the desire to obtain local control over the curve's shape. When the order of the B-spline polynomials is increased by 1, the support of each B-spline blending function extends one span further, reducing the amount of local control. When m reaches the bound of $L + 1$, the Bezier case is obtained, and local control is at a minimum. Figure 11.35 shows how B-spline curves become more "taut," thereby permitting less local control, as their order increases. There are eight control points, so the curve of order $m = 8$ is the Bezier curve. All of these curves were generated using the fragment of code shown in Figure 11.31. (What is the $m = 2$ curve?)

PRACTICE EXERCISES

11.7.7 Standard knots for quadratic B-spline curves

Show that the standard knot vector for a B-spline curve of order $m = 3$ based on eight control points is $\mathbf{T} = (0, 0, 0, 1, 2, 3, 4, 5, 6, 6, 6)$.

FIGURE 11.35 Curves based on splines of different orders.

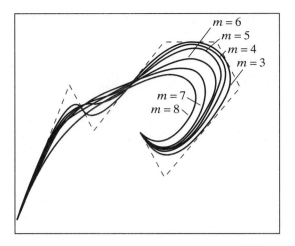

11.7.8 Knot vectors as the order m is increased

What is the standard knot vector when seven control points are used for B-splines of order (a) $m = 3$, (b) $m = 4$, (c) $m = 5$, (d) $m = 6$, and (e) $m = 7$?

11.7.9 Quadratic B-splines on standard knot vectors

Using Equation (11.58), find explicit expressions for the piecewise polynomials that describe the quadratic B-spline blending functions defined on the standard knot vector.

11.7.10 Cubic B-splines

Find analytically the first four cubic B-splines defined on a standard knot vector. Find also their derivatives at $t = 0$, and show that the initial direction of the B-spline curve is along the first segment of the control polygon.

11.7.11 Deriving the Bernstein polynomials

Show that, when $m = L + 1 = 4$, the B-spline functions of Equation (11.58) are the Bernstein polynomials.

11.7.12 On the efficient computation of B-splines

In drawing a B-spline curve, many points have to be formed, so that values $N_{k,m}(t)$ must be computed at a large number of t-values. Using the recursive form of Equation (11.58) at each t makes many redundant calls to lower order B-spline functions. It is much more efficient, therefore, to compute values of each $N_{k,m}(t)$ once and store the values in arrays, such as the array $N[k, i]$, which holds $N_{k,m}(t)$ evaluated at $t_i = i\Delta t$, where Δt is the fixed difference between the t-values desired. Samples of each $N[k, i]$ need only be formed over the support of the corresponding B-spline function. Furthermore, just a few different shapes $N[k, i]$ are needed, since many are just translations of one another and have the same shape. If there are 55 control points, how many different cubic B-spline functions will be needed?

Once stored, each point on the curve can be fashioned by accessing the proper samples of the functions: $P(t_i)$ is formed as the vector sum of the terms $C[k]N[n, j]$, where $C[k]$ is a control point and proper values of n and j are selected. Determine, for the case of cubic splines, the proper values of n and j to be used, for each k and t_i. Note that when j is outside a certain region, the function $N[k, j]$ is certainly zero, so the array is not accessed. ■

11.8 USEFUL DESIGN PROPERTIES OF B-SPLINE CURVES

It is useful to summarize the principal properties of B-splines and the curves they generate. We shall also see that many of the desirable properties attributed to Bezier curves carry over intact to B-spline curves.

1. The mth-order B-spline functions are piecewise polynomials of order m. They are splines that are $(m - 2)$-smooth: They exhibit $(m - 2)$ orders of continuous derivatives at every point in their support. They form a basis for any spline of the same order defined on the same knots; that is, any spline can be represented as a linear combination of B-splines. Of all spline bases, the B-splines are the most concentrated, having the shortest supports.

2. The B-spline blending function, $N_{k,m}(t)$, begins at t_k and ends at t_{k+m}. Its support is $[t_k, t_{k+m}]$. The support of the family of functions $N_{k,m}(t)$, for $k = 0,\ldots,L$, is the interval $[t_0, t_{m+L}]$.

3. A closed B-spline curve based on $L + 1$ control points may be obtained using Equation (11.66) (assuming evenly spaced knots in the definition of $N_{0,m}(.)$).

4. If the standard knot vector is used, the B-spline curve will interpolate the first and last control points. Its initial and final directions are along the first and last edges of the control polygon, respectively.

5. Each B-spline function $N_{k,m}(t)$, is nonnegative for every t, and the family of such functions sums to unity; that is,

$$\sum_{k=0}^{L} N_{k,m}(t) = 1 \tag{11.67}$$

for every $t\varepsilon[t_0, t_{m+L}]$. As we have seen for the low-order cases, this assertion can be proved by induction from Equation (11.58).

6. Curves based on B-splines are affine invariant. To transform a B-spline curve, we simply transform each control point and generate the new curve on the basis of the transformed control points. To prove this, simply note that a B-spline curve is an affine sum of points and that affine transformations preserve affine combinations.

7. According to property 5, a B-spline curve is a convex combination of its control points and so lies in their convex hull. A stronger statement is possible: At any t, only m B-spline functions are " active" (nonzero). Thus, at each t, the curve must lie in the convex hull of at most m consecutive active control points. Figure 11.36 shows a quadratic B-spline curve based on the standard knot vector. At most three control points are active at each t, so the relevant convex hulls are triangles. As t increases, $P(t)$ progressively passes out of each convex hull and into the next one as each new blending function becomes active in turn. At which t-value does the curve enter and exit the shaded convex hull?

   Convex hulls based on m control points are typically smaller regions than the hull based on all the control points. The curve is therefore "trapped" in a smaller region than is the case for a Bezier curve. The narrow support of the B-splines not only gives local control to the designer, but also provides more insight into the nature of the curve.

8. B-spline curves exhibit linear precision: If m consecutive control points are collinear, their convex hull will be a straight line, and the curve will be trapped inside it.

9. B-spline curves are variation diminishing: A B-spline curve does not pass through any line more times than does its control polygon [Farin90].

FIGURE 11.36 Convex hulls for
the quadratic B-spline curve.

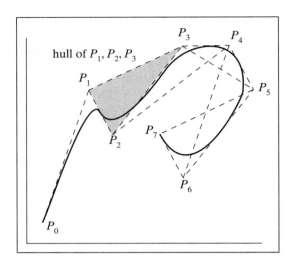

FIGURE 11.36 Convex hulls for
the quadratic B-spline curve.

11.8.1 Using Multiple Control Points

The designer can usefully alter the shape of a B-spline curve by placing several control points at the same spot, producing a **multiple control point**, which attracts the curve more strongly to itself.

Figure 11.37 shows an example that uses cubic B-spline curves. The curve based on control points A, B, C, D, E, F, and G exhibits the usual behavior for cubic splines. When a double point is used at D, so that the control polygon is A, B, C, D, D, E, F, G, the curve is pulled more strongly toward D. When a triple point is placed at D, making the control polygon $A, B, C, D, D, D, E, F, G$, the curve must actually interpolate the point!

The interpolation effect is easily explained from Figure 11.34(a). Note that at t-values such as t_5 and t_6, exactly three B-spline functions are nonzero and that they sum to unity. If they are all weighted by the same control point, the weighted sum will be the control point itself. More generally, recall that a cubic B-spline is always trapped within some convex hull based on four consecutive control points. When a triple point is used at D, the convex hulls that surround D consist

FIGURE 11.37 Curve control
using multiple control points.

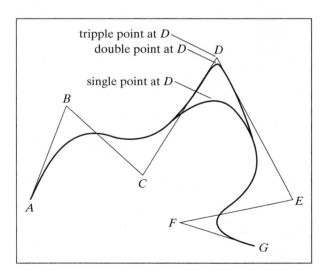

of edges of the control polygon, so the curve is trapped "in" this edge for one span of the polynomials.

Notice that the use of multiple control points is not the same as the use of multiple knots, although the effects are similar. It is usually easier for a designer to increase the multiplicity of a control point than that of a knot, because control points are plainly visible and can be pointed to. (The designer could click on a point multiple times to specify its multiplicity.)

PRACTICE EXERCISES

11.8.1 Sketching the convex hull property

Draw several different control polygons of eight points. Consider quadratic B-splines based on the standard knot vector. Draw the successive convex hulls, and determine the values of t for which the curve enters and exits each hull. Sketch the resulting B-spline curve, labeling various t-values along it. Be sure that the curve also passes through the midpoints of each inner edge of the control polygon.

11.8.2 Multiple control points with quadratic B-splines

Explain the effect of a double control point on a quadratic B-spline curve. Sketch an interesting control polygon having no multiple control points, show the sequence of convex hulls that trap the curve, and sketch the curve. Then increase the multiplicity of one of the control points and repeat. ■

11.9 RATIONAL SPLINES AND NURBS CURVES

Whose afraid of NURBS, anyway?

overheard on a bus at SIGGRAPH '98

In Section 11.2, we looked briefly at rational parametric forms and noted that conic sections (the ellipse, hyperbola, and parabola) can be generated exactly by the ratio of polynomials in Equation (11.14). In the current section, we take a more detailed look at rational polynomial forms based specifically on B-splines.

A rational spline curve is very similar to its B-spline counterpart and is formed as the familiar blending of control points,

$$P(t) = \sum_{k=0}^{L} P_k R_k(t), \tag{11.68}$$

but uses a slightly different set of blending functions. The designer conjures up a set of **weights**, $\{w_0, w_1, \ldots, w_L\}$, and creates the following blending functions:

$$R_k(t) = \frac{w_k N_{k,m}(t)}{\sum_{k=0}^{L} w_k N_{k,m}(t)}. \tag{11.69}$$

The weights are often called "shape parameters" and are usually set by the designer to be nonnegative to ensure that the denominator is never zero. Each $R_k(t)$ is evidently a ratio of polynomials (hence the term "rational B-splines"). Because the knot vector used to define the B-spline functions is usually nonuniform (i.e., not equispaced), this family of curves has come to be called the **nonuniform rational B-splines**, or simply **NURBS**.

Note carefully that if all the weights are made the *same*, the denominator becomes a constant (why?), and this form collapses to the earlier B-spline form of Equation (11.57). So Equation (11.69) is a true extension of Equation (11.57) and differs from it only when the weights are unequal.

It helps to see where these blending functions come from. As requested in Exercise 11.9.3 to follow, work in homogeneous coordinates and use each weight w_k to give a weight to the kth control point. Then convert back into ordinary coordinates, and you have the NURBS curve. NURBS curves attain their desirable properties through the weighting of points in a higher dimensional space.

Two Principal Advantages to NURBS Curves

An advantage of NURBS curves is that, with properly chosen control points and weights, $P(t)$ is *exactly* a conic section. (See Example 11.9.2.) This property is in direct contrast to the nonrational B-spline curves, which can only approximate a true conic.

A second advantage is that NURBS curves are invariant under so-called **projective transformations**. These transformations are like the perspective transformation of Chapter 7, which produces a perspective view of a scene. They are generalizations of affine transformations. The matrix for an affine transformation has a fourth row of $(0, 0, 0, 1)$, but a projective transformation can have a more general fourth row. Recall that normal B-spline curves are invariant under only affine transformations, so NURBS curves are invariant under a larger class of transformations.

Among other things, this invariance means that you can draw a perspective projection of a NURB curve simply by finding the perspective projection of each of its control points and then fashioning the curve with the use of the *same* algorithm given in Equation (11.68). (The weights must be adjusted as well.) This method is far more efficient than finding the perspective projection of "every" point on the curve individually. By contrast, nonrational B-spline curves are invariant under affine transformations, but not under projective transformations.

Projective Invariance

We fill in some details of the projective invariance property for NURB curves (in 2D or 3D). A derivation is given in Case Study 11.9. The main idea is that when a NURB curve is transformed by a general four-by-four matrix (which may produce perspective distortion), the result is another NURB curve, and its control points are simply transformed versions of the original control points. To make things work, the weights must also be adjusted.

Specifically, consider the case of 3D points, and let T be the transformation represented by the general four-by-four matrix M. Denote the rows of M by $\mathbf{m}_1, \mathbf{m}_2, \mathbf{m}_3$, and $\mathbf{m}_4$, so that in partitioned form $M = (\mathbf{m}_1 | \mathbf{m}_2 | \mathbf{m}_3 | \mathbf{m}_4)^T$. ($T$, as always, represents the transpose.) If the last row is $(0, 0, 0, 1)$ the transformation specializes to an affine transformation (and so produces no perspective distortion). The result is [Piegl91] that the curve $T(P(t))$ obtained by applying $T()$ to the NURB curve of Equation (11.68) is identical to the NURB curve based on transformed control points $T(P_k)$, viz.,

$$T(P(t)) = \frac{\sum_{k=0}^{L} \bar{w}_k T(P_k) N_{k,m}(t)}{\sum_{k=0}^{L} \bar{w}_k N_{k,m}(t)}, \tag{11.70}$$

where the adjusted weights are

$$\bar{w}_k = w_k(\widetilde{P}_k \cdot \mathbf{m}_4), \tag{11.71}$$

in which $\widetilde{P}_k = (P_x, P_y, P_z, 1)^T$ is the usual extension of P to homogeneous coordinates. Note that the weights depend on the positions of the control points, as well as on the fourth row of the matrix. If the transformation is affine, so that $(P_k \cdot \mathbf{m}_4) = 1$, the weights need no adjustment.

PRACTICE EXERCISES

11.9.1 Fashioning generic surfaces

Discuss how you could create each of the following surfaces using NURBS curves:

a. a circular cylinder;
b. a circular cone;
c. a planar patch;
d. a sphere.

See Case Study 11.10 for more details. Can an arbitrary Coon's patch be created?

11.9.2 What if the weights are equal?

Suppose a NURB curve $q(t)$ happens to have all its weights equal (so that it is a B-spline curve). Is it still a NURB curve after it has been transformed by M? Is it still a B-spline curve?

11.9.3 Forming NURBS curves in homogeneous coordinates

Consider forming a B-spline curve based on control points P_k that have been weighted by a chosen set of weights $\{w_k\}$. This B-spline curve is formed in homogeneous coordinates as

$$\widetilde{R}(t) = \sum_{k=0}^{L} w_k \widetilde{P}_k N_{k,m}(t), \tag{11.72}$$

where $\widetilde{P}_k$ denotes the homogeneous coordinate form of P_k (i.e., $\widetilde{P}_k = (x_k, y_k, z_k, 1)^T$ for a 3D point).

a. Write out the individual components $x(t)$, $y(t)$, $z(t)$, and $w(t)$ of $\widetilde{R}(t) = (x(t), y(t), z(t), w(t))^T$, paying particular attention to the form of $w(t)$.
b. Convert Equation (11.72) to ordinary coordinates by dividing through by $w(t)$. Show that this produces the equation

$$P(t) = \frac{\sum\limits_{k=0}^{L} w_k P_k N_{k,m}(t)}{\sum\limits_{k=0}^{L} w_k N_{k,m}(t)}. \tag{11.73}$$

c. Show that Equation (11.73) is the same form as Equations (11.68) and (11.69). ■

■ EXAMPLE 11.9.1 Getting the conics

To see the special case of Equation (11.14) emerge, let $m = 3$ (quadratic B-splines), and choose the knot vector so that we obtain the Bernstein polynomials. (How?) Now set $w_0 = w_2 = 1$ and $w_1 = w$, and the result is Equation (11.14).

■ EXAMPLE 11.9.2 Making a perfect circle

There are several ways to create an exact circle with a NURB curve [Piegl89]. We examine a basic method founded on quadratic B-splines using seven control points. Figure 11.38(a) shows the control points $P_0, \ldots, P_6$ situated about a square, along with the full circle that is generated. The proper weights are also labeled; note that they are either 1 or $1/2$. The knot vector is given by

$$T = \left\{0, 0, 0, \frac{1}{4}, \frac{1}{4}, \frac{1}{2}, \frac{1}{2}, \frac{3}{4}, \frac{3}{4}, 1, 1, 1\right\}.$$

Note the double knots. Figure 11.38(b) shows the seven basis functions that weight the control points. The shape of the common denominator curve of each $R_k(t)$ is

FIGURE 11.38 Making a perfect circle.

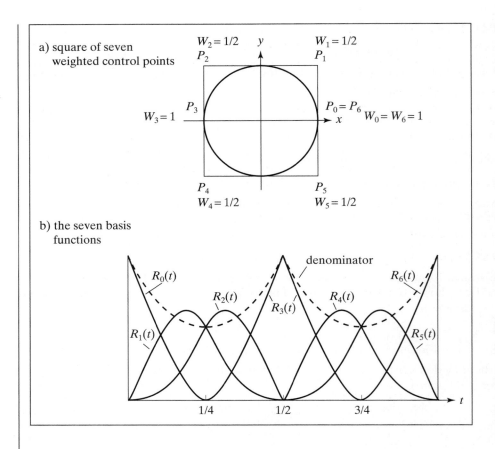

a) square of seven weighted control points

b) the seven basis functions

shown dotted. See Exercise 11.9.4 at the end of the section for a process for determining the actual formulas for each of the basis functions in each knot interval and to assure yourself that $x^2(t) + y^2(t) = 1$ for all t.

■ **EXAMPLE 11.9.3 Seeing the effect of weight factors**

Figure 11.39(a) shows a cubic B-spline curve based on six control points (with equispaced knots). This curve is the usual nonrational B-spline (or, equivalently, a NURB with equal weights w_i). Figure 11.39(b) shows what happens when the weights are made unequal: The curve is more attracted to those points with higher weights. (What if some point has zero weight?)

FIGURE 11.39 Effect of unequal weights in the NURB curve.

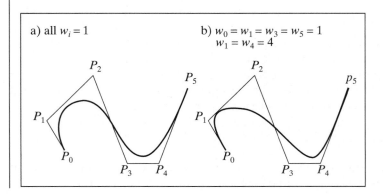

a) all $w_i = 1$

b) $w_0 = w_1 = w_3 = w_5 = 1$
   $w_1 = w_4 = 4$

NURBS have become popular with curve designers due to their generality and flexibility. Because they include B-splines as a special case, a single curve-creation algorithm can be used to create a broad family of shapes, including the conic sections. Thus, a designer does not need a toolbox containing many different curve algorithms; a single method is available.

A number of other curve-design techniques are available, some of which give the user even greater control over the shape of the curve. For example, one can vary the separation between knots (here taken to be the same) in the knot vector or add extra "ghost" points to the given data in order to control the curve's behavior at its endpoints. The reader interested in the various generalizations should consult one of the many sources on B-splines, such as [Bartels87, Farin90].

PRACTICE EXERCISES

11.9.4 Is it really a circle?

Show that the NURB curve described in Example 11.9.2 is truly a circle. Do this by finding expressions for the basis function polynomials in each knot interval, evaluating $x^2(t) + y^2(t)$ and showing that it is unity at all t. ◼

11.10 A GLIMPSE AT INTERPOLATION

Sometimes the designer wants the curve-design algorithm to produce a curve that passes through all of the control points. This might seem more natural than using an algorithm that just "attracts" the curve to the control points, but we will see that constraining a curve to pass through a set of points can result in shapes with too little local control or with undesired extra "wiggles" between control points. In spite of such limitations, we want to provide the designer with an interpolating tool for those situations that benefit from interpolation.

The designer already has one way of achieving interpolation: using B-splines; if the designer lays down control points of sufficient multiplicity, the B-spline curve is guaranteed to interpolate them. In Case Study 11.6, we shall see another method based on B-splines. In that method, the designer lays down points, and the algorithm calculates a *different* set of points such that a B-spline curve generated by them happens to pass through the designer's points.

In this section, we look briefly at curve-generation algorithms that directly interpolate all of the control points laid down by the user. This is a broad topic with a long history; we examine only a restricted class of methods. Farin [Farin90] discusses interpolation in a more general setting and provides many details.

11.10.1 Interpolation by Means of Piecewise Cubic Polynomials

We next describe the interpolation of a set of control points by using piecewise cubic polynomials. We restrict ourselves to piecewise cubics because they offer sufficient richness and flexibility for our needs, yet are simple enough that they can be used effectively.

Figure 11.40(a) shows the basic design problem. The user places a sequence of control points $P_0, P_1, \ldots, P_L$ (here, $L = 4$) and desires a "sufficiently smooth" curve to be generated that passes through all of them in turn. Figure 11.40(b) shows one such curve $R(t)$. The curve consists of four segments, each a cubic polynomial

$$R_k(t) = A_k t^3 + B_k t^2 + C_k t + D_k, k = 0, 1, \ldots, L - 1, \text{ for } t \text{ in } [0, 1]. \qquad (11.74)$$

Each of the terms has both an x- and a y-component, of course. The question is, What should the coefficients A_k, B_k, C_k, and D_k be?

FIGURE 11.40 Interpolating with piecewise cubic polynomials.

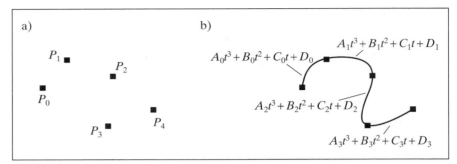

Notice that we are employing a slightly different formulation than earlier, to simplify the notation: Each segment uses the same t-interval, 0 to 1. Thus, to draw this curve, we would draw four separate curves, as are produced by the following pseudocode:

```
for(k = 0; k < L; k++)
{
    retrieve the coefficients A[k], B[k],C[k],D[k]
    Draw the curve R_k(t) , using these coefficients in short line segments, as t goes from 0 to 1
}
```

The segment $R_k(t) = (x(t), y(t))$ is a 2D curve as always. If $R(t)$ interpolates a point $P = (x, y)$, then $x(t)$ must interpolate x and $y(t)$ must interpolate y. So we can consider how interpolation works separately for the x- and the y-components. The notation is simplified by doing this, and it is easier to visualize what is happening.

Figure 11.41(a) shows the interpolation problem for the y-coordinate alone. A sequence of y-values $y_0, y_1, \ldots, y_L$ is given, and we want $y(t)$ to be a piecewise cubic polynomial that passes through the y-values and is 1-smooth. (In some cases we will force it to be 2-smooth as well—i.e., to be a spline.) The kth cubic segment of the curve is shown in Figure 11.41(b) and is given by

$$y_k(t) = a_k t^3 + b_k t^2 + c_k t + d_k, \quad k = 0, 1, \ldots, L - 1, \quad \text{for } t \text{ in } [0, 1]. \quad (11.75)$$

We denote the value of the derivative of this function at y_k by s_k (i.e., $y_k'(0) = s_k$). As we shall see, in some cases the values s_k are given (i.e., input by the user), and in others they are computed from other required properties of the curve. Again we ask, What are the coefficients?

FIGURE 11.41 The y-component of the interpolating curve.

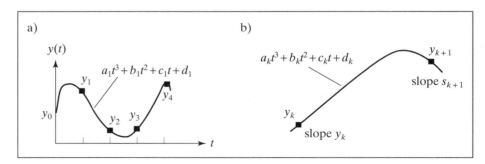

11.10.2 Hermite Interpolation

We develop conditions on the coefficients a_k, b_k, c_k, and d_k so that each segment interpolates the given value y_k at $t = 0$ and the value y_{k+1} at $t = 1$. We have, for $k = 0, \ldots, L - 1$,

at $t = 0$, $d_k = y_k$,

and

at $t = 1$, $\quad a_k + b_k + c_k + d_k = y_{k+1}$.

These two equations provide $2L$ conditions. We also force the derivative of $y_k(t)$ to equal the given values s_k and s_{k+1} at $t = 0$ and $t = 1$, respectively. Since the derivative is $y'_k(t) = 3a_k t^2 + 2b_k t + c_k$, this yields the following conditions for $k = 0, \ldots, L - 1$:

At $t = 0$, $\quad c_k = s_k$;
At $t = 1$, $\quad 3a_k + 2b_k + c_k = s_{k+1}$.

These two equations provide another $2L$ conditions, so we have a total of $4L$ conditions on the $4L$ unknown coefficients. Notice that setting the derivatives to the given values of the slope in this fashion automatically forces the slope to be continuous at the joints, so the curve is 1-smooth.

On the basis of these equations, it is straightforward to solve for the coefficients symbolically in terms of the values y_k and s_k. (Check this out.) We have, for $k = 0, \ldots, L - 1$,

$$a_k = s_{k+1} + s_k - 2(y_{k+1} - y_k);$$
$$b_k = 3(y_{k+1} - y_k) - 2s_k - s_{k+1};$$
$$c_k = s_k;$$
$$d_k = y_k.$$

These equations specify the components of $y_k(t)$ for each segment. A similar process yields equations that specify the coefficients of $x_k(t)$, and the cubic curve segments can be drawn as before to produce the piecewise cubic curve.

The solution would now be complete if we knew the slope values s_k at each y_k. There are several approaches to determining these values. We first see what effect s_k has on the shape of the curve. We then examine what it takes to make the curve 2-smooth. This leads to the "natural" cubic spline.

■ EXAMPLE 11.10.1 On tangents and slopes

In order to gain insight into how the many ingredients we have just examined fit together, consider a curve consisting of two cubic segments, $R_0(t)$ and $R_1(t)$, with the following properties:

Segment 0. $R_0(t)$ passes through $(1, 1)$ at $t = 0$ and through $(4, 3)$ at $t = 1$. In addition, its velocity is $(1, 0)$ at $t = 0$ and is $(0, S)$ at $t = 1$, where S is some value we will vary to see the effect of changes in the slope of the curves.

Segment 1. $R_1(t)$ passes through $(4, 3)$ at $t = 0$ and through $(0, 3)$ at $t = 1$. Its velocity is $(0, S)$ at $t = 0$ and $(0, 1)$ at $t = 1$. The resulting curve for the specific case $S = 1$ is shown in Figure 11.42. The parametric segments are shown in the xy-plane, and in addition, the figure shows the components $x_0(t)$, $x_1(t)$, $y_0(t)$, and $y_1(t)$ that make up the curve.

Carefully trace the curve and note how its shape derives from the shapes of the individual components. Observe that the curve makes a smooth transition from one segment to the next, since its velocity is continuous there. This results because both $x(t)$ and $y(t)$ are continuous and have continuous slopes at the joint, so the curve is 1-smooth. The slope of $x(t)$ is zero at the joint for both segments, so both segments are level just to the left and to the right of the joint. $y(t)$ also moves smoothly from one segment to the other: Its slope is $S = 1$ just to the left and to the right of the joint.

FIGURE 11.42 Two cubic segments meeting with a prescribed velocity.

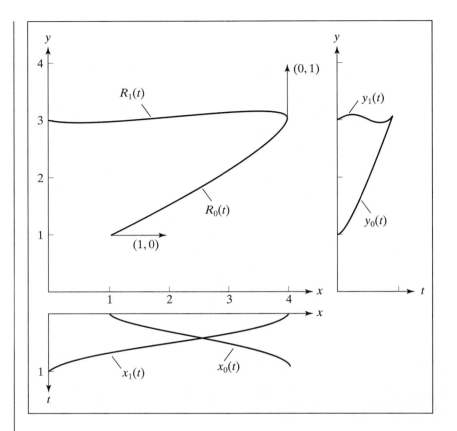

To see the exact nature of the segments, we apply Equation (11.74) to the data. For the y-component, we have the following values:

Segment 0. $y_0 = 1$, $y_1 = 3$, $s_0 = 0$, and $s_1 = S$, which leads to the cubic equation

$$y_0(t) = (S - 4)t^3 + (6 - S)t^2 + 1.$$

Segment 1. $y_1 = 3$, $y_2 = 3$, $s_1 = S$, and $s_2 = 1$, which leads to the cubic equation

$$y_1(t) = (S + 1)t^3 - (2S + 1)t^2 + St + 3.$$

Similarly, for the x-component, we have the following values:

Segment 0. $x_0 = 1$, $x_1 = 4$, $s_0 = 1$, and $s_1 = 0$, which leads to the cubic equation

$$x_0(t) = -5t^3 + 7t^2 + t + 1.$$

Segment 1. $x_1 = 4$, $x_2 = 0$, $s_1 = 0$, and $s_2 = 0$, which leads to the cubic equation

$$x_1(t) = 8t^3 - 12t^2 + 4.$$

Thus, the two segments have the shape given by the following equations:

$$R_0(t) = \left(-5t^3 + 7t^2 + t + 1, (S - 4)t^3 + (6 - S)t^2 + 1\right);$$
$$R_1(t) = \left(8t^3 - 12t^2 + 4, (S + 1)t^3 - (2S + 1)t^2 + St + 3\right).$$

It is illuminating to observe the effect of changing the slope S of the $y()$ component at the joint. This alters only the *magnitude* of the velocity at the joint, not its direction. From the formulas, it is evident that S affects the coefficients of $y_0(t)$ and $y_1(t)$, but has no effect on the x-component functions. Figure 11.43 shows the $y(t)$ functions and the parametric curve for various values of S.

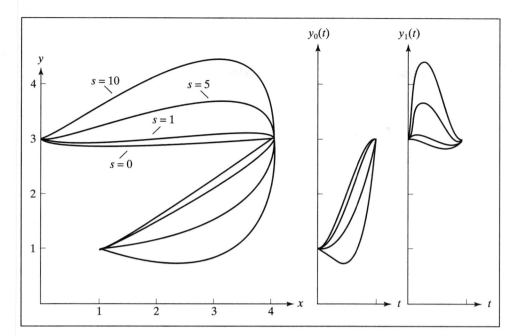

FIGURE 11.43 The effect of varying the size of the slope.

For large values of S, the curve has a high speed at the joint. To accommodate this speed, the curve has to bulge out before and after the joint to "prepare" for the rapid passage through the joint in the vertical direction. This illustrates how "elastic" a cubic curve is: It can't bend arbitrarily rapidly—there just aren't enough degrees of freedom—so its shape throughout the interval adjusts to meet the slope constraint at one end.

The case of $S = 0$ produces a corner at the joint. (See the exercises that follow.) The speeds of both $R_0(t)$ and $R_1(t)$ go to zero as they approach the joint, so even though the velocity of the curve changes direction abruptly at the joint, it is still continuous and the curve is 1-smooth. (Is the curve G^1-continuous?)

PRACTICE EXERCISES

11.10.1 When the speed is zero

Suppose a cubic curve segment has a speed of zero at both ends. Show that the segment is a straight line.

11.10.2 Scrutinize the curves

Write a short program that generates the curves shown in Figures 11.42 and 11.43, and execute the program with different values of S. To assist in executing the program, it is convenient to define the function

```
Point2 y(float t, float S, int seg)
{
    double t2 = t * t, t3 = t2 * t;
    return (seg == 0)?
        (S-4) * t3 + (6 - S) * t2 + 1:
        (S+1) * t3 - (2 * S + 1) * t2 + S * t + 3;
}
```

and a similar one for $x(.)$.

11.10.3 Make a loop

Show that if $S = -1$, the curve in Figure 11.42 has a loop in it.   ■

11.10.3 The Natural Cubic Spline

As one approach to setting the values s_k of the derivative in the Hermite formulation, we find the specific values of the s_k that will cause the *second* derivative of $y(t)$ to be continuous at each of the "inner" joints, where $k = 1, 2, \ldots, L - 1$. (At the "ends" of the whole curve, there is no need for the derivatives to be continuous.) The second derivative in each segment is $y''(t) = 6a_k t + 2b_k$, so matching the second derivative $y''_{k-1}(1)$ with $y''_k(0)$, we get

$$6a_{k-1} + 2b_{k-1} = 2b_k \tag{11.76}$$

for $k = 1, \ldots, L - 1$. Using the values of the coefficients in Equation (11.74) and simplifying imposes the following condition on the slopes:

$$s_{k-1} + 4s_k + s_{k+1} = 3(y_{k+1} - y_{k-1}) \tag{11.77}$$

for $k = 1, \ldots, L - 1$. This equation shows how the various neighboring slopes must be related to ensure a continuous second derivative at the inner joints. We still need to fix the first and last slopes, s_0 and s_L. A classic approach chooses them so that the second derivatives are zero at the two ends of the curve; that is, $y''_0(0) = 0$ and $y''_{L-1}(1) = 0$. The first of these sets b_0 to zero, and the second sets $3a_{L-1} + b_{L-1}$ to zero. (Why?) Again using Equation (11.74), we obtain the final two conditions:

$$2s_0 + s_1 = 3(y_1 - y_0);$$
$$2s_L + s_{L-1} = 3(y_L - y_{L-1}). \tag{11.78}$$

Together, Equations (11.76) and (11.77) provide $L + 1$ linear equations in the unknown slopes s_k. As is shown in the exercises that follow, the nature of these equations makes them rather easy to solve.

Figure 11.44 shows a set of control points and the natural cubic spline that interpolates them. Note that visually the curve is smooth everywhere and that at its ends the curve straightens out so that the second derivative vanishes. The dashed line shows the effect of moving one of the control points. The shape of the curve is affected everywhere: There is no local control with natural splines, since the constraint of a continuous second derivative "couples" together the first-order derivatives at the knots, making a change in one derivative ripple through all of the others.

FIGURE 11.44 Natural cubic splines interpolating control points.

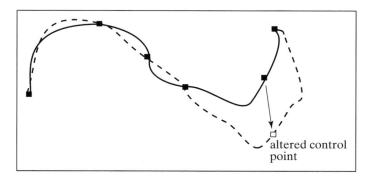

altered control
point

PRACTICE EXERCISES

11.10.4 Solving the equations for the natural-spline slopes

It is revealing to write Equations (11.76) and (11.77) in matrix form. For the case $L = 4$, we have

$$(s_0, s_1, s_2, s_3, s_4) \begin{pmatrix} 2 & 1 & 0 & 0 & 0 \\ 1 & 4 & 1 & 0 & 0 \\ 0 & 1 & 4 & 1 & 0 \\ 0 & 0 & 1 & 4 & 1 \\ 0 & 0 & 0 & 1 & 2 \end{pmatrix} = 3(y_1 - y_0, y_2 - y_0, y_3 - y_1, y_4 - y_2, y_4 - y_3).$$

This matrix is **tridiagonal**: Its nonzero terms are confined to three diagonals. This allows the set of equations to be solved in two easy steps, which we now outline.

a. First, perform a **forward-elimination** pass through the set of equations to eliminate the upper strip of 1's. To do this, divide the first equation through by 2 so that its leading term is 1. Then, beginning with the second equation, subtract, from each equation in turn, the proper amount of the previous equation to eliminate the 1, and then scale the equation so a 1 appears in the diagonal term. Show that doing this converts the set of equations into the " lower triangular" form (having all zeros above the major diagonal):

$$(s_0, s_1, s_2, s_3, s_4) \begin{pmatrix} 1 & 0 & 0 & 0 & 0 \\ v_0 & 1 & 0 & 0 & 0 \\ 0 & v_1 & 1 & 0 & 0 \\ 0 & 0 & v_2 & 1 & 0 \\ 0 & 0 & 0 & v_3 & 1 \end{pmatrix} = (q_0, q_1, q_2, q_3, q_4). \tag{11.79}$$

Also, show how the v_i and q_i terms are easily computed.

b. Show that Figure 11.45 properly represents the code to perform forward elimination, based on the arrays $v[\,]$ and $q[\,]$.

```
v[0] = 0.25;
q[0] = 3.0  * (y[1] - y[0]) * v[0];
for(i = 1; i < L; i++)
{
    v[i] = 1.0 / (4.0 - v[i - 1]);
    q[i] = (3.0 * (y[i]-y[i-1]) - q[i - 1]) * v[i];
}
```

FIGURE 11.45 The forward-elimination step.

c. To obtain the desired $s[\,]$ terms, perform a **backward-substitution** step. The matrix in equation (11.79) has a single term in the rightmost column, so $s_4 = g_4$. Using the following fragment of code, show that you can work back up through the equations to obtain each s_i:

```
s[L] = q[L];
for(i = L - 1; i > 0; i --) s[i] = q[i] - v[i] * s[i+1]; ■
```

11.10.4 Computing the Slopes in Cubic Interpolation

Several other approaches can be used to fix the slopes of curves at the joints. We look briefly at one of the most popular, the **Catmull–Rom**[6] family of splines [Bartels87; Farin90], along with its variations. We still want the curve to be 1-smooth at the "inner"

---

[6] These are also called **cardinal** splines by some and **Overhauser** splines by others. They are in fact special cases of a larger family of Catmull–Rom curves.

joints, but now forfeit the requirement that it be 2-smooth there. The hope is that giving up this extra level of smoothness will afford the designer greater local control over the shape of the curve. In contrast with setting the slope values s_k in order to force a continuous second derivative, here we set them based on the positions of their neighboring control points.

The (simplest) Catmull–Rom approach is to force the velocity vector at P_k to be a value $\mathbf{P}'(t_k)$ based on the positions of the two neighboring points. As shown in Figure 11.46, that vector is simply made proportional to the vector from P_{k-1} to P_{k+1}. This influences the curve at P_k to move parallel to the direction between the previous and next points, so we insist that

$$\mathbf{P}'(t_k) = m(P_{k+1} - P_{k-1}), \tag{11.80}$$

FIGURE 11.46 Determining slopes based on neighboring data values.

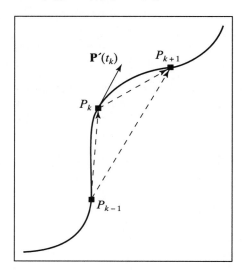

for some scalar m. (Shortly, we will examine the effect of the coefficient m; $m = 1/2$ is often used.) In terms of previous quantities, this condition sets the slope of the y-component s_k to $m(y_{k+1} - y_{k-1})$, and similarly for the x-component.

At this point we have set the values of the slopes s_k for each inner joint, so that the coefficients of the various cubic polynomials in Equation (11.74) can be determined for $k = 1, \ldots, L - 2$. We still need two additional conditions to set the unspecified end slopes s_0 and s_{L-1}. To do this, we can use the same condition of vanishing second derivatives at the ends that leads to Equation (11.78). Other possibilities are considered in the exercises. Figure 11.47 shows an example of the curve that is generated by using this method.

Adding Tension Control

To give the designer greater control over the shape of the curve at each joint, the Catmull–Rom method introduces a "tension" parameter v_k. This parameter gives the designer control over the constant m in Equation (11.80), adjusting the magnitude of the velocity $\mathbf{P}'(t)$ at a joint without altering its direction. In this method, the velocity at the kth joint is set to

$$\mathbf{P}'(t_k) = \frac{1}{2}(1 - v_k)(P_{k+1} - P_{k-1}), \tag{11.81}$$

for $k = 1, \ldots, L - 1$. (What value does this cause s_k to have?)

Although the tension v_k is normally set between -1 and 1, it can have any value. The case $v_k = 0$ corresponds to $m = 1/2$ in Equation (11.80). Figure 11.48 shows the

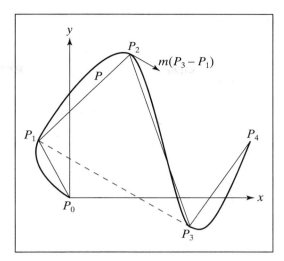

influence the tension at vertex P_2 has on the shape of the curve. In part (a) the tension v_2 is 1, so the speed is made zero at the joint. This straightens out the curve as it approaches the joint. (Why?) In part (b) v_2 is −1 and the curve is more "slack" at the joint.

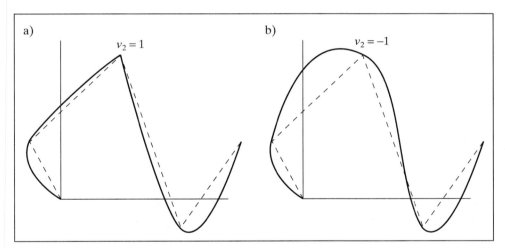

FIGURE 11.48 Effect of tension at vertex 2. (a) tension = 1, (b) tension = −1.

Adding Bias Control

The class of curves known as the **Kochanek–Bartels splines** adds more parameters to further assist in controlling the shape of the curve [Kochanek84]. One of these parameters is "bias". Notice that we can rewrite Equation (11.80) (using $m = 1/2$) as

$$\mathbf{P}'(t_k) = \tfrac{1}{2}(P_k - P_{k-1}) + \tfrac{1}{2}(P_{k+1} - P_k), \tag{11.82}$$

which is the average of the two neighboring vectors $P_k - P_{k-1}$ and $P_{k+1} - P_k$. (Observe these in Figure 11.46.) The **bias** parameter b_k weights these two contributions unequally via the formula

$$\mathbf{P}'(t_k) = \tfrac{1}{2}(1 - b_k)(P_k - P_{k-1}) + \tfrac{1}{2}(1 + b_k)(P_{k+1} - P_k), \tag{11.83}$$

so the actual velocity specified at the joint is determined more by one of these neighboring vectors than by the other. When $b_k = 0$, the two vectors are weighted equally. Figure 11.49 shows the effect of bias at vertex P_2 for the curve of Figure 11.47.

FIGURE 11.49 Effect of bias at vertex 2. (a) bias = −0.8, (b) bias = 0.8.

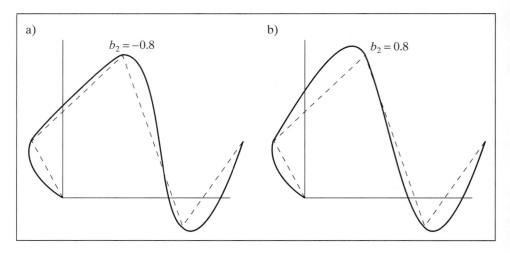

Adding Continuity Control

Instead of forcing the velocity to be continuous at P_k, Kochanek and Bartels introduce another parameter to let the designer make the velocity "just before" a joint differ from that "just after" the joint. Consider the joint at P_k. The $(k − 1)$st segment, $R_{k−1}(t)$ [recall Equation (11.74)], reaches P_k at $t = 1$. We set the velocity of this segment at $t = 1$ to

$$\mathbf{R}'_{k−1}(1) = \tfrac{1}{2}(1 − c_k)(P_k − P_{k−1}) + \tfrac{1}{2}(1 + c_k)(P_{k+1} − P_k), \qquad (11.84)$$

using some value for c_k, the "continuity parameter." (At this point, it looks like the bias parameter: Larger values of c_k bias the velocity toward $P_{k+1} − P_k$.) Similarly, the kth segment, $R_k(t)$, leaves P_k at $t = 0$. We set its velocity at that time to

$$\mathbf{R}'_k(0) = \tfrac{1}{2}(1 + c_k)(P_k − P_{k−1}) + \tfrac{1}{2}(1 − c_k)(P_{k+1} − P_k), \qquad (11.85)$$

using the same value c_k. Again, this is like a bias: Larger values of c_k bias the velocity toward $P_k − P_{k−1}$. If $c_k = 0$, the two velocities are equal and the curve is 1-smooth at the joint. As c_k deviates from zero, the two velocities have different magnitudes and directions. Figure 11.50 shows the effect of varying the continuity parameter.

In practice, the three parameters of tension, bias, and continuity are used together (see the exercises that follow), and the designer can set them individually for each joint. In a typical scenario, the designer might follow these steps:

FIGURE 11.50 Effect of continuity parameter. (a) $c_2 = 1$. (b) $c_2 = −1$.

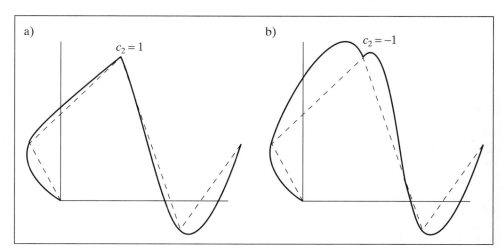

1. Lay down initial choices for the control points with the mouse.
2. Examine the resulting curve. If it is satisfactory, stop.
3. Edit the control points, and adjust tension, bias, and continuity for each. (The designer might click on a control point and drag it to a new position. Then, to adjust the various parameters at that point, a sequence of keystrokes could be made. For instance, the key 'b' might be pressed to reduce the bias, or 'B' to increase it.)
4. Go to step 2.

PRACTICE EXERCISES

11.10.5 Putting the Kochanek–Bartels splines together

Put the three influences of tension, bias, and continuity together to write a formula for $\mathbf{R}'_{k-1}(1)$ and $\mathbf{R}'_k(0)$ for the Kochanek–Bartels splines.

11.10.6 Choosing the end conditions

Recall that when cubic interpolation is to be performed on $L + 1$ control points, we must set $4L$ coefficients. Since $4L - 2$ are set by interpolation and slope constraints, two must still be fixed. In Equation (11.77) they were fixed by requiring the second derivative at the end segments to vanish, but other conditions can be used to fix them. We just need to derive two equations that are linear in the coefficients and independent of the other $4L - 2$ equations. Determine the equations that arise for each of the following conditions:

a. Set the first derivatives at the endpoints P_0 and P_L to zero.
b. Require that the third derivatives at P_1 and at P_{L-1} be continuous. (This is known as de Boor's "not-a-knot" constraint; it makes the first two segments into a single polynomial and the last segments also.)
c. Add two "ghost" points (effectively, P_{-1} and P_{L+1}) at the ends of the control polygon. The curve is still drawn starting at P_0, and it ends at P_L, but we can derive velocity values at these two points.

11.10.7 Pass a parabola through the control points

To find the slope at P_k, we can find the unique parabola that passes through P_{k-1}, P_k, and P_{k+1} and compute its velocity at P_k. For any three such control points, find the formula for this velocity. ◾

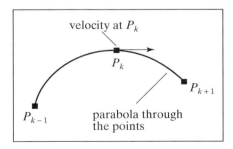

FIGURE 11.51 Setting the velocity by the parabola through three points.

11.10.5 Specifying the Tangent Vectors Interactively

Some CAGD drawing programs offer the designer visual "handles" for setting the tangent vectors, as suggested in Figure 11.52. The user lays down the control points, and an initial interpolating curve is drawn. Then, as the user drags different handles with the mouse, the corresponding tangent vectors are altered and the new curve instantly replaces the old. This visual feedback allows the user to edit a curve to its desired shape rapidly.

FIGURE 11.52 Interactive design of the cubic segments.

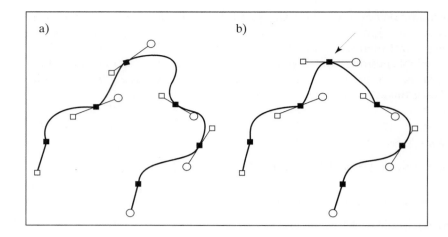

11.11 MODELING CURVED SURFACES

So far, we have been examining how to represent and generate 2D and 3D curves. It is straightforward to extend these ideas to the generation of curved surfaces. In Chapter 6 we examined a variety of different types of surfaces, such as ruled surfaces, bilinear and Coons patches, and surfaces of revolution. Now we consider how to use Bezier and B-spline curves to design these surfaces, thereby developing powerful tools for creating a rich set of curved surfaces.

11.11.1 Ruled Surfaces Based on B-splines

It is particularly easy to work with ruled surfaces. Recall from Section 6.5.6 that a ruled surface is defined by two "end curves" $P_0(u)$ and $P_1(u)$, that are connected by a straight line at each value of u. Therefore, the parametric expression for a ruled surface is just a linear interpolation (or a "tweening") between corresponding points on the two curves. Repeating Equation (6.35) for convenience, we have

$$P(u, v) = (1 - v)P_0(u) + vP_1(u). \tag{11.86}$$

The extension here is to choose $P_0(u)$ and $P_1(u)$ to be B-spline (or Bezier) curves. Figure 11.53 shows a ruled surface both of whose end curves $P_0(u)$ and $P_1(u)$ are cubic Bezier curves. $P_0(u)$ is based on the four control points P_0^0, P_1^0, P_2^0, P_3^0, and $P_1(u)$ is based on the four control points P_0^1, P_1^1, P_2^1, P_3^1. Using Equation (11.25) for a Bezier curve, we can write this surface as

$$P(u, v) = \sum_{k=0}^{3} ((1 - v)P_k^0 + vP_k^1)B_k^3(u). \tag{11.87}$$

FIGURE 11.53 A ruled surface based on Bezier curves.

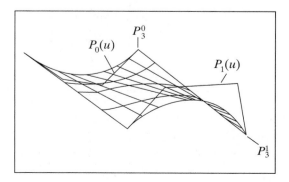

Visualize how this shape behaves. Its u-contours are straight lines joining corresponding points on the two Bezier curves. Its v-contours are Bezier curves whose control points are "tweens," $(1 - v)P_k^0 + vP_k^1$, of the control points of the two Bezier curves. B-spline or NURBS curves could be used just as well for the end curves; they can even be defined on different knot vectors, as long as their u parameter varies over the same interval.

All of the special cases of ruled surfaces, such as cones and cylinders, are also easily obtained. For instance, what does the surface become if $P_0(u)$ is a version of $P_1(u)$ that has been translated through space?

11.11.2 Surfaces of Revolution Based on B-splines

Recall from Section 6.5.7 that a surface of revolution is formed when a **profile** $C(v) = (X(v), Z(v))$ is swept about the z-axis. The resulting surface has the parametric form

$$P(u, v) = (X(v) \cos(u), X(v) \sin(u), Z(v)). \qquad (11.88)$$

It is often convenient to express the profile using Bezier or B-spline curves. We do this by selecting $L + 1$ control points (X_k, Z_k) and using them to create the curve

$$(X(v), Z(v)) = \sum_{k=0}^{L} (X_k, Z_k)N_{k,m}(v). \qquad (11.89)$$

Figure 11.54(a) shows a profile of a goblet defined by a cubic B-spline curve. The control polygon is also shown. Figure 11.54(b) shows the resulting surface of revolution. (A mesh object for the surface of revolution was created as discussed in Chapter 6, and the mesh was drawn using the `Mesh :: draw()` method.)

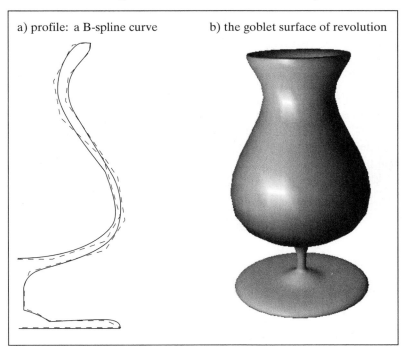

a) profile: a B-spline curve   b) the goblet surface of revolution

FIGURE 11.54 The profile as a B-spline curve.

■ EXAMPLE 11.11.1 The classic teapot

Bezier curves may also be used to design profiles. Figure 11.55(a) shows a profile of the body of a "teapot" originally designed by Martin Newell [Blinn96; Crow87] The teapot body is shown in Figure 11.55(b). The body profile consists of three

i	x	z
0	1.4	2.25
1	1.3375	2.38125
2	1.4375	2.38125
3	1.5	2.25
4	1.75	1.725
5	2	1.2
6	2	0.75
7	2	0.3
8	1.5	0.075
9	1.5	0

FIGURE 11.56 Data for the profile of the body of a teapot.

FIGURE 11.55 Bezier-based profiles for the body of a teapot.

Bezier curves, based on the 10 points displayed in Figure 11.56. The first Bezier curve is defined by points 0, 1, 2, and 3, the second by points 3, 4, 5, and 6, and the third by points 6, 7, 8, and 9. Notice that the last segment of each curve is collinear with the first segment of the next curve. This condition ensures that the different Bezier curves blend together with G^1 continuity. (Recall Section 11.1.2.) The lid of the teapot is also a surface of revolution and is described in Case Study 11.8.

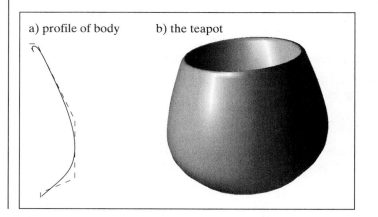

a) profile of body   b) the teapot

11.11.3 Bezier Surface Patches

Figure 11.53 showed a ruled patch based on two Bezier curves. For greater design flexibility, we can replace the linear u-contours in Equation (11.87) with Bezier or B-spline curves. A Bezier patch uses Bezier curves for both the u- and v-contours. For example, if the u-contours are quadratic Bezier curves and the v-contours are cubic Bezier curves, the Bezier patch has the representation

$$P(u, v) = \sum_{k=0}^{3} P_k(v)B_k^3(u) = \sum_{k=0}^{3} \left(\sum_{i=0}^{2} P_{i,k} B_i^3(v) \right) B_k^3(u), \tag{11.90}$$

where u and v vary as usual between 0 and 1. Figure 11.57 shows an example Each v-contour, such as the one at v_0, is a Bezier curve in u based on the four control "points" $P_k(v_0)$, which themselves lie along a quadratic Bezier curve. (How would you describe each u-contour?) The 12 control points $P_{i,k}$ together constitute the **control polyhedron**, which determines the shape of the patch. This form for a surface is called the **tensor product** form.

FIGURE 11.57 An example of a Bezier patch.

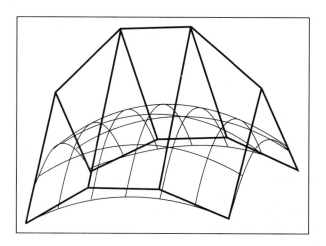

In general, the control polyhedron is a network of $(M + 1)(L + 1)$ vertices, and the surface is given by

$$P(u, v) = \sum_{k=0}^{L} \sum_{i=0}^{M} P_{i,k} B_i^M(u) B_k^L(v). \qquad (11.91)$$

To create a patch, the designer carefully specifies the positions of these vertices and then applies Equation (11.91) to define the shape of the surface. An alternative matrix-based form for a Bezier surface is discussed in the exercises that follow.

Figure 11.58 shows an example of a **bicubic** Bezier patch (for which L and M are both 3), along with its control polyhedron. For more detail on Bezier surfaces, see [Rogers90].

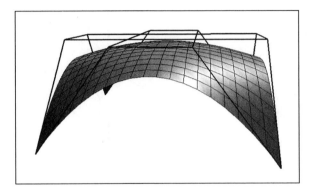

FIGURE 11.58 A bicubic Bezier patch with its control polyhedron.

PRACTICE EXERCISES

11.11.1 Regaining the in-betweening form

How must the control polyhedron used in Equation (11.91) be configured to produce linear interpolation between two control polygons?

11.11.2 Normals to Bezier patches

Apply the parametric form for a Bezier patch to Equation (6.25) to obtain a (complicated) expression for the normal vector to the patch. Simplify the expression analytically as much as possible. Does the normal vector vary continuously at all (u, v)?

11.11.3 An alternative form for a Bezier patch

The following form for a bicubic $(L = M = 3)$ Bezier surface helps to reveal how its ingredients work together:

$$p(u, v) = (u^3, u^2, u, 1) \begin{pmatrix} -1 & 3 & -3 & 1 \\ 3 & -6 & 3 & 0 \\ -3 & 3 & 0 & 0 \\ 1 & 0 & 0 & 0 \end{pmatrix} \begin{pmatrix} P_{0,0} & P_{0,1} & P_{0,2} & P_{0,3} \\ P_{1,0} & P_{1,1} & P_{1,2} & P_{1,3} \\ P_{2,0} & P_{2,1} & P_{2,2} & P_{2,3} \\ P_{3,0} & P_{3,1} & P_{3,2} & P_{3,3} \end{pmatrix} \begin{pmatrix} -1 & 3 & -3 & 1 \\ 3 & -6 & 3 & 0 \\ -3 & 3 & 0 & 0 \\ 1 & 0 & 0 & 0 \end{pmatrix} \begin{pmatrix} v^3 \\ v^2 \\ v \\ 1 \end{pmatrix}. \qquad (11.92)$$

The outer pairs of vectors and matrices create the Bernstein polynomials, and the inner matrix captures the geometry of the patch.

a. Compare Equation (11.92) with the similar form for Bezier curves of Equation (11.41).
b. Show that Equation (11.92) is identical to Equation (11.91). Which equation is easier to organize in a computer program, and why? ■

11.11.4 Patching Together Bezier Patches

The designer might want to model a complex shape out of several Bezier surface patches and have the patches meet smoothly at their common boundaries. Figure 11.59 shows two control polyhedra, one in black and one in gray, that define two Bezier patches. Equation (11.91) is used for both patches, and u and v each vary from 0 to 1 to generate each patch. Only the control polyhedra differ. What conditions must the designer impose on the two control polyhedra so that the two patches will meet "seamlessly"? It is simple to make the two patches meet at all points along a common boundary: Just make their control polyhedra coincide at the boundary. This is so because the shape of the "boundary" Bezier curve depends only on the boundary polygon of the control polyhedron. [See what happens when $u = 0$ in Equation (11.91).] So the designer chooses these boundary control polygons to be identical for the two patches.

FIGURE 11.59 Two Bezier patches meeting continuously.

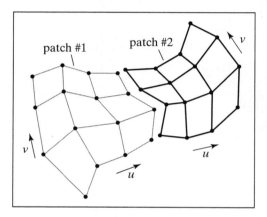

It is more difficult to achieve tangent continuity at the join of the two patches. (But once achieved, it will also guarantee continuity of the normal vector to the surface at the join.) One sufficient condition [Faux79] is illustrated in Figure 11.60: Each pair of polyhedron edges that meet at the boundary, such as E and E^1, must be collinear. This condition, however, can be awkward for a designer to satisfy. Other slightly different conditions are discussed in [Faux79] as well.

FIGURE 11.60 Achieving tangent continuity across the boundary.

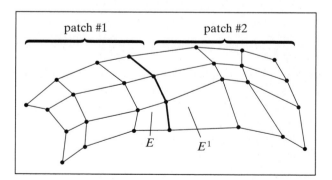

■ **EXAMPLE 11.11.2 Designing the handle of the teapot**

We have seen that the body and the lid of the teapot shown in Figure 11.55 are surfaces of revolution based on Bezier curves. The handle and the spout, on the other hand, each consist of four Bezier patches. In this example, we show how the handle is constructed [Blinn96]; the spout is described in Case Study 11.8.

Figure 11.61(a) shows a 3D view of the handle of the teapot. Part (b) shows the handle in cross section. The handle's surface is symmetrical about the xz-plane. An upper and a lower patch are on the positive y-side of the xz-plane and mirror upper and lower patches on the negative y-side of the same plane. The control polyhedron for the upper "positive y" patch consists of four rectangles erected on the xz-plane that extend a distance 0.3 into the positive xzy-octant. The first such rectangle uses point A_0 once with $y = 0$ and once with $y = 0.3$, and similarly, it uses point B_0 once with $y = 0.3$ and once with $y = 0$.

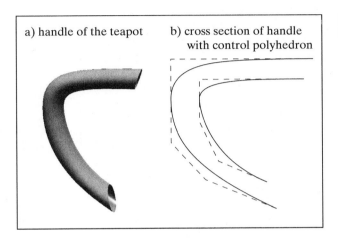

a) handle of the teapot   b) cross section of handle with control polyhedron

FIGURE 11.61 Design of the handle of the teapot.

The entire upper positive-y patch has the following 16 control points:

based on A_0, B_0: $(-1.6, 0.0, 1.875)$, $(-1.6, 0.3, 1.875)$, $(-1.5, 0.3, 2.1)$, $(-1.5, 0.0, 2.1)$;
based on A_1, B_1: $(-2.3, 0.0, 1.875)$, $(-2.3, 0.3, 1.875)$, $(-2.5, 0.3, 2.1)$, $(-2.5, 0.0, 2.1)$;
based on A_2, B_2: $(-2.7, 0.0, 1.875)$, $(-2.7, 0.3, 1.875)$, $(-3.0, 0.3, 2.1)$, $(-3.0, 0.0, 2.1)$;
based on A_3, B_3: $(-2.7, 0.0, 1.65)$, $(-2.7, 0.3, 1.65)$, $(-3.0, 0.3, 1.65)$, $(-3.0, 0.0, 1.65)$.

Similarly, the lower positive-y patch has the following 16 control points:

based on A_3, B_3: $(-2.7, 0.0, 1.65)$, $(-2.7, 0.3, 1.65)$, $(-3.0, 0.3, 1.65)$, $(-3.0, 0.0, 1.65)$;
based on A_4, B_4: $(-2.7, 0.0, 1.425)$, $(-2.7, 0.3, 1.425)$, $(-3.0, 0.3, 1.2)$, $(-3.0, 0.0, 1.2)$;
based on A_5, B_5: $(-2.5, 0.0, 0.975)$, $(-2.5, 0.3, 0.975)$, $(-2.65, 0.3, 0.7875)$, $(-2.65, 0.0, 0.7875)$;
based on A_6, B_6: $(-2.0, 0.0, 0.75)$, $(-2.0, 0.3, 0.75)$, $(-1.9, 0.3, 0.45)$, $(-1.9, 0.0, 0.45)$.

Case Study 11.8 exhorts you to write a program to draw the teapot from different points of view using these data.

11.11.5 B-spline Patches

B-spline functions can be used in place of Bernstein polynomials in the tensor-product form to achieve greater local control in surface design. The equation is

$$P(u, v) = \sum_{i=0}^{M} \sum_{k=0}^{L} P_{i,k} N_{i,m}(u) N_{k,n}(v), \tag{11.93}$$

where $N_{i,m}(u)$ and $N_{k,n}(v)$ are B-spline basis functions (possibly of different order) as defined in Equation (11.58). Usually, the standard knot vector is chosen for both B-spline forms, so that the corners of the polyhedron are properly interpolated. Closed surfaces (in u or v or both) will be formed if control points are duplicated or if a periodic form like that in Equation (11.66) is used. The control polyhedron consists of

$(L + 1)(M + 1)$ control points, and u and v each vary from zero to the maximum knot value in their respective knot vectors. Cubic B-splines (for which $m = n = 4$) are again a popular choice, and because there is no limit on the number of control points (since this number does not affect the order of the polynomials, as it does for Bezier curves), one can fashion extremely complex surfaces. As before, the designer must choose the knot polyhedron to create a surface having the desired shape.

Figure 11.62 shows an example of a B-spline surface, periodic in one of the parameters. (See the exercise that follows.) The control polyhedron is shown, as are the u, v contours on the surface. A different view is provided in part (b), from which it is clear this surface is not a surface of revolution. The NURBS surface discussed next is required to achieve a surface of revolution.

FIGURE 11.62 Example of a B-spline surface.

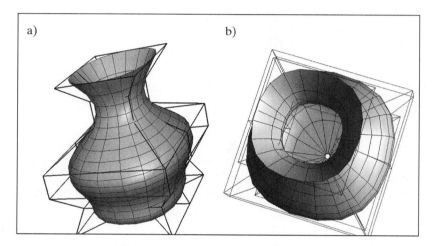

a)   b)

PRACTICE EXERCISES

11.11.4 Periodic B-spline surfaces

Specialize Equation (11.93) to the case where the surface is periodic in u. You may find Equation (11.66) helpful for this task. What would useful knot vectors for the two kinds of B-splines be here?   ■

11.11.6 NURBS Surfaces

In Section 11.9, we looked briefly at curves based on rational parametric B-splines. As seen in Equation (11.68), the shape of such curves depends both on a set of control points and a set of weights w_i. These parameters are set by the designer to achieve the desired shape for the curve in question.

We can extend NURBS curves to NURBS surfaces by forming the tensor product just as we did for B-splines in Equation (11.93) [Tiller83, Piegl97]:

$$P(u, v) = \frac{\sum_{i=0}^{M} \sum_{k=0}^{L} w_{i, k} P_{i, k} N_{i, m}(u) N_{k, n}(v)}{\sum_{i=0}^{M} \sum_{k=0}^{L} w_{i, k} N_{i, m}(u) N_{k, n}(v)}. \tag{11.94}$$

The control polyhedron based on the control points $P_{i, k}$ and the weights $w_{i, k}$ are chosen by the designer to control the shape of the surface. As in the case of B-spline curves, if all of the weights are equal, this surface simplifies to the B-spline surface of Equation (11.93). (Check this!)

As discussed earlier, there are two principal advantages to NURBS surfaces:

1. With properly chosen control points and weights, the contours of $P(u, v)$ are exactly quadric surfaces. This is in contrast to the nonrational B-spline patches, whose contours can only approximate true quadrics.
2. NURBS surfaces are invariant under **projective transformations**. This invariance means that you can draw a perspective projection of a NURBS patch simply by finding the perspective projection of each of its control points, adjusting the weights somewhat, and then using Equation (11.94). By contrast, nonrational B-spline patches are invariant under affine transformations, but not under projective transformations.

Because of their generality and flexibility, NURBS surfaces have become popular with curve and surface designers. Since NURBS surfaces include B-splines as a special case, a *single* surface-creation algorithm can be used to create a broad family of surface shapes. Thus, a designer does not need a toolbox containing many different curve algorithms; a single method is available.

Fashioning Commonly Used NURBS Surfaces

The NURBS family of surfaces offers a tremendous variety of shapes, including as special cases some discussed earlier in the chapter.

Example families are:

- *Ruled surfaces*. The two edge curves are NURBS curves in u; the rulings are first order NURBS curves in v. Figure 11.63(a) shows a wireframe example.
- *Extruded surfaces*. The prism shape is determined by a NURBS curve in para-

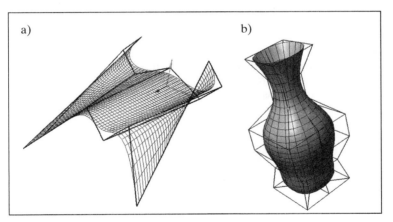

a)   b)

FIGURE 11.63 Example of NURBS surfaces.

meter u; the straight sides are produced by a first order NURBS curve in v. This is a special case of a ruled surface where the two edge curves have the same shape.
- *Surfaces of revolution*. The profile is a NURBS curve lying in the xz-plane; the circular cross sections parallel to the $z = 0$ plane exploit the ability of NURBS curve to create true conic sections. Figure 11.63(b) shows an example.
- *Quadric surfaces*. Quadrics that are surfaces of revolution use conic sections for their profiles. To distort such a surface so that it no longer is circularly symmetric, use an affine transformation on the NURBS surface.

We emphasize that the single NURBS design tool offers enough flexibility to create all of the various surfaces. Case Study 11.10 addresses the details of designing and building such surfaces.

Many other techniques have been developed for defining surfaces and operating on them. Several books that discuss such approaches are [Bartels87, Coons67, Farin90, Faux79, Mortenson85].

PRACTICE EXERCISES

11.11.5 Fashioning generic surface shapes

Discuss how you could create each of the following surfaces using NURBS surfaces:

a. a circular cylinder.
b. a circular cone.
c. a planar patch.
d. a sphere.

See Case Study 11.10 for more details. Can an arbitrary Coon's patch be created? ■

11.12 SUMMARY

In this chapter, we discussed several techniques for representing and manipulating complex curves and surfaces. The two principal uses of such curves are rendering them in a graphics application and modeling the motion of objects such as a camera in an animation. We based most of our designs on the parametric representation for a curve, first described in Chapter 3. Parametric forms are more natural than implicit equations when one has to manipulate and draw curves that cross over themselves at certain points or that have a vertical portion.

Some important properties that we examined are the velocity of a curve and the normal vector to a curve at each point. The property of the "smoothness" of a curve was defined and shown to be rather subtle. For instance, a 1-smooth curve has a continuous velocity (the derivative with respect to the parameter t) everywhere along its path, but if the parametrization happens to reduce the velocity to zero at some point where its direction changes abruptly, the curve is still 1-smooth, but, geometrically, has a corner. The notion of G^1-continuity was developed to describe curves that have no corners. A number of different families of curves were examined. The conic sections were discussed, and curves based on polynomials, as well as ratios of polynomials, were presented.

The chapter also discussed how to generate smoothly varying curves by means of a set of control points. This approach is a staple in the field of computer-aided geometric design (CAGD). A designer can specify a small set of points that act as data to control the shape of a curve as they are blended numerically. The distinction between curves that interpolate these control points and those that only approximate the control points was emphasized. In either case, the small set of control points, along with an algorithm, produces an infinite set of points along the curve, one for each value of the parameter t.

Bezier curves were defined first because of their simplicity. These curves arise from the iterative de Casteljau process of tweening, which lends a great deal of intuition to their properties. They were shown to have an assortment of desirable properties that make their shape predictable, thereby guiding the designer when he or she is laying down control points.

Bezier curves are useful in many design situations, but they do not allow local control, because the Bernstein polynomials on which they are based have support over the entire parametric interval. Another complication is that the order of the underlying polynomials increases as the number of control points is increased. This characteristic tends to "quench" the intended variation and can make the curves more expensive and less stable computationally. We therefore examined a richer class of blending functions based on splines, which are piecewise polynomials that come together in such a way that various orders of derivatives are everywhere continuous. A particular family of basis functions, the B-splines, can generate any spline and are the most concentrated of such shapes. They therefore offer the designer the strongest measure of local control, and they also exhibit the same desirable properties seen in Bezier functions. When the order of the B-spline polynomials is increased to the number of control points being used, the B-splines become identical to Bernstein polynomials.

Additional control over the shape of a curve is attained by using NURBS curves. These curves are more complicated than Bezier or B-spline curves, but include B-splines as a special case and can represent conic sections perfectly. A CAGD environment that supports the NURBS algorithm gives the designer a single unified tool for creating a very large variety of curves of different shapes.

We examined algorithms for forcing a curve to interpolate the given control points, instead of only being attracted to them. We focused on piecewise cubic polynomial curves and developed conditions on the various coefficients so that the curve not only interpolates the points, but also has a prescribed velocity at each joint. The velocity can be fixed by the user, by a constraint of greater smoothness at the joints, or by local geometric information based on neighboring control points. Additional parameters such as tension and bias can be introduced that afford the designer a great deal of control over the final shape of the curve.

Another approach to interpolation uses B-splines, which do not usually cause the curve to interpolate any but the first and last control points. The trick here is to compute a second set of control points cleverly positioned so that the B-spline curve based on them passes through every one of the original control points. This approach is discussed in Case Study 11.6.

We extended the curve-design techniques to the design of different families of surfaces, including ruled surfaces, surfaces of revolution, and quadric surfaces. We also considered surface design using Bezier, B-spline, and rational B-spline functions. One may think of generating a Bezier patch by sweeping a Bezier curve of changing shape through space. Each point on the moving Bezier curve travels along a trajectory that is itself a Bezier curve. Bezier patches may be pieced together if certain conditions on their control polyhedra are met. B-spline surfaces offer more flexibility to the designer: Because the order of the polynomials involved does not increase as the number of control points increases, very complex surface shapes can be fashioned.

The final extension was to the family of NURBS surfaces, which provide an additional degree of design flexibility by allowing the designer to vary a set of weights to alter the shape of the patch. NURBS surfaces are invariant under both affine and projective transformations. In addition, NURBS surfaces specialize to many other families of surfaces, so a designer armed with a NURBS surface algorithm can fashion many types of surfaces.

The chapter only touched on the fundamentals of surface design. Many variations of these techniques have been developed, and large computer-aided design packages often include an assortment of methods. The designer can choose from among these methods and iteratively fine-tune the shapes he or she produces until the design goals are met. Some shapes, such as the wing of an airplane or the hull of a sailboat, are fashioned from a complex mixture of principles, aesthetics, intuition, and experience.

11.13 CASE STUDIES

CASE STUDY 11.1 A POTPOURRI OF INTERESTING PARAMETRIC CURVES

Level of Effort: II. **A Generalization of the Ellipse.** An ellipse is formed by using a single sine and cosine for its parametric representation. An interesting family of curves may be generated by superimposing several ellipses that are traversed at different speeds. The summing of "harmonics" in this way is similar to the Fourier series plots seen in Chapter 3, but now it is done in two dimensions. We start with two terms and then generalize. Consider the family of curves described by

$$x(t) = X_1 \cos(2\pi t) + X_2 \cos(2\pi k t);$$
$$y(t) = Y_1 \sin(2\pi t) + Y_2 \sin(2\pi k t). \tag{11.95}$$

The first term in each formula represents an ellipse, to which is added a second, "piggyback" ellipse that is traced out k times as fast. As t varies from 0 to 1, the first ellipse is traced out once, whereas the other is traced out k times. If k is an integer, the figure will close exactly. Write a program that draws such periodic figures, using the values of X_1, X_2, Y_1, Y_2, and k as input. Generalize further by adding more terms to $x(t)$ and $y(t)$.

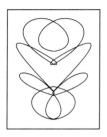

FIGURE 11.64 Genie rising.

The Involute of the Circle. Grab a point P on a piece of thread wound around a broomstick. Keeping the thread taut, unwrap it by circling the broomstick with your hand. The path taken by P is a spiral known as the "involute of a circle." The thread connecting the circle (broomstick) to P forms a tangent to the circle. Evidently, this tangent is always perpendicular to the spiral. In addition, successive coils of the spiral are parallel and separated by the same distance. (What distance?) A family of such spirals is formed by rotating the figure (or by choosing different points P on the thread). Each spiral is orthogonal to all lines tangent to the circle. The parametric form for this curve is

$$x(t) = \cos(2\pi t) + 2\pi t \sin(2\pi t);$$
$$y(t) = \sin(2\pi t) - 2\pi t \cos(2\pi t). \tag{11.96}$$

Write a program that draws involutes of a circle.

Other Sinusoidal Curves. Slight adjustments to $x(t)$ and $y(t)$ in the previous exercises can produce remarkably different shapes. For instance, the curve in Figure 11.64 (contributed by Professor Robert Weaver of Mount Holyoke College, South Hadley, Massachusetts) results from the following functions:

$$x(t) = \cos(t) + \sin(8t);$$
$$y(t) = 2\sin(t) + 7\sin(7t). \tag{11.97}$$

Write a routine that produces this curve, and try other variations as well. Under what conditions on the arguments of the trigonometric functions does the curve always form a closed (periodic) figure?

Lissajous Figures. A variation on the ellipse is provided if the frequencies of the two sinusoids are allowed to differ. For example, let

$$x(t) = \cos(2\pi M t + angle)$$

and

$$y(t) = \sin(2\pi N t), \tag{11.98}$$

where M and N are the new frequencies and *angle* is a "phase offset" between the two components. These shapes are called Lissajous figures and are sometimes viewed on an oscilloscope while one is testing electrical circuits. Write a program that takes M, N, and *angle* as parameters and displays the resulting Lissajous figures. Experiment with large increments in t between points chosen on the curves to see the variety of shapes that result. Interesting symmetries can be observed if the values of the x and y variables are interchanged after each line is drawn.

CASE STUDY 11.2 "ELLIPTIPOOL"

Level of Effort: III. In Case Study 4.4, we examined how rays bounce off the walls of a polygonal chamber. It is interesting to consider chambers of other shapes. Elliptical pool tables went on sale in the United States in 1964 under the name "Elliptipool" [Gardner71, Steinhaus69]. We can simulate Elliptipool by tracing rays bouncing inside an elliptical chamber, as suggested in Figure 11.65. An initial ray $S + \mathbf{c}t$ is given, with starting point S inside the ellipse. The point P where the ray hits the ellipse is determined, and the direction $\mathbf{r}$ of the reflected ray is also found. A line is drawn from S to P to "trace" the ray. Then the next ray is set as $P + \mathbf{r}t$, and the process repeats. Suppose the ellipse has the implicit form

$$F(P) = \left(\frac{x}{a}\right)^2 + \left(\frac{y}{b}\right)^2 - 1 = 0$$

FIGURE 11.65 Simulation of Elliptipool.

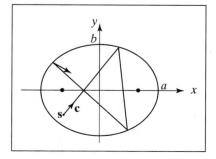

and that a ray is given by $S + \mathbf{c}t$. We seek to intersect the ray with an ellipse. If the ray intersects the ellipse at all, it must happen at some value of t that produces a point $S + \mathbf{c}t$ lying on the curve $F(P) = 0$. This produces a condition on t: $F(S + \mathbf{c}t) = 0$. So, for the ellipse, we obtain the equation

$$\left(\frac{S_x + c_x t}{a}\right)^2 + \left(\frac{S_y + c_y t}{b}\right)^2 - 1 = 0,$$

which is a *quadratic* equation in t. Quadratic equations are easily solved and have zero, one, or two solutions, the upshot of which is us follows:

- No solutions: The ray misses the ellipse.
- One solution: The ray grazes the ellipse.
- Two solutions: The ray enters the ellipse and later exits from it.

If the ray starts out in the interior of the chamber, one of the solutions is positive and one is negative. (Why?) Use the positive one, and call it t_{hit}. We must find the direction of the reflected ray at the hit point. Use $x(t) = a \cos(t)$ and $y(t) = b \sin(t)$ in Equation (11.3) to obtain the normal vector $(-b \cos(t), -a \sin(t))$, which can be written in terms of x and y as $(-bx/a, -ay/b)$. Since only the direction of the normal is important, it is convenient to scale it to $(-b^2 x, -a^2 y)$. Now, we want the inner normal, as the ray bounces off the inside wall of the ellipse. By inspection of Figure 11.65, we see that both the x- and y-components of the inner normal are negative when x and y are positive, so the form

$$\mathbf{n} = (-b^2 x, -a^2 y) \qquad\qquad (11.99)$$

does indeed have the direction of the inner normal. The reflected ray $\mathbf{r}$ may be obtained by substituting Equation (11.99) into Equation (4.27).

A simulation of Elliptipool reveals some fascinating behavior: There are only three types of paths that rays can take [Steinhaus69]:

- If the ray passes over either focus, it will rebound and pass over the other focus. This is due, of course, to the reflection property of ellipses: that a ray leaving one focus always bounces off the elliptical wall and goes to the other focus. The ray will pass over alternating foci forever. After a few passes, the path will become indistinguishable from the x-axis.
- If the ray does not pass between the foci on its initial path, it will never pass between them thereafter. Instead, it will move along paths that are tangent to a smaller ellipse having the same foci, as shown in Figure 11.66.

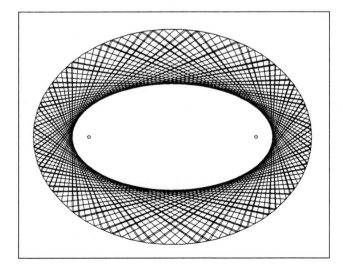

FIGURE 11.66 Rays tangent to a second ellipse.

- If the ray starts off passing between the foci, it will trace out an endless path that will never get closer to the foci than a hyperbola with the same foci, as shown in Figure 11.67.

FIGURE 11.67 Rays tangent to a hyperbola.

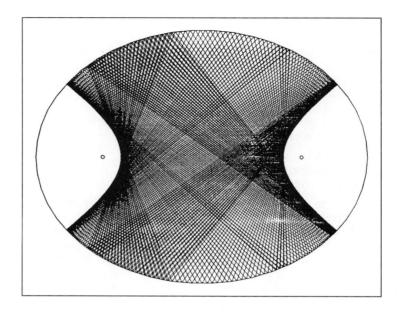

Write and exercise a program that simulates Elliptipool. The user indicates the starting position and direction of the ray in some fashion, and the ray is traced for a large number of bounces. Allow the user to specify the case of the ray passing through a focus. (Beware that for this situation, an arithmetic round-off error may cause some unpredicted effects. How can such an error be counteracted?) Have the ray change color occasionally so that its current path remains apparent as the display fills in with paths. Experiment with ellipses of different eccentricity, including circular pool tables.

(Optional). Enhance the experiment by placing circles or other barriers (ellipses?) inside the elliptical pool table. Do any recognizable patterns emerge in the paths of the rays in this case?

(Optional). Repeat this experiment, except make the shape of the pool table a superellipse. Determine how to compute ray–wall intersections and the inner normal vector to the wall at any point on it.

CASE STUDY 11.3 BEZIER CURVES

Level of Effort: II. Write a program that takes as input a sequence of control points laid down by the user with the mouse and draws the Bezier curve based on these points. Points along the curve are computed at closely spaced values of *t* and are joined by straight-line segments. Execute your program with different numbers of control points. Notice how the computation slows down for larger numbers of control points, since the polynomials are then of higher degree.

CASE STUDY 11.4 A QUADRATIC SPLINE-CURVE GENERATOR

Level of Effort: II. Equation (11.52) represents a curve as a weighted sum of blending functions $g(t - k)$, viz.,

$$V(t) = \sum_{k=0}^{6} P_k g(t - k),$$

where $g(t)$ is the quadratic spline function defined in Equation (11.49). Write and execute a program that lets the user lay down a sequence of control points P_k with the mouse and then draws the curve $V(t)$. The task may be aided by developing a function `double g(double t)` that returns the value of $g(t)$, in particular returning 0 if t lies outside of the interval $[0, 3]$.

CASE STUDY 11.5 BUILDING A SPLINE-CURVE EDITOR

Level of Effort: III. Design and execute a program that allows the user to create a control polygon **P** by using the mouse. On request, the program draws the B-spline curve determined by **P**. The program should implement the following commands, which are executed by pressing suitable keys on the keyboard ('b' for begin, 'd' for delete, etc.):

- b)egin: begin a new control polygon **P**
- d)elete: delete the closest point in **P** that is pointed to
- m)ove: drag the point of **P** pointed at to a new location
- r)efresh: draw **P**
- o)rder ('1'..'9') draw the spline curve of the specified order, based on **P**
- c)losed ('-1',...,'-9') draw the *closed* B-spline curve, based on **P**
- e)rase: erase the screen
- q)uit: exit from the program

1. **(Optional). Having several control polygons.** Extend your program so that you can have up to 10 different control polygons on the display at one time, and edit each one at will.
2. **(Optional). Can B-splines make circles?** Experiment with four and eight control points that lie on a circle to see how closely a closed cubic B-spline curve based on these points approximates a circle. Develop a reasonable numerical measure of the error between the curve and the circle, and try different configurations to determine the best curve.
3. **(Optional). Transforming B-spline curves.** Extend your program so that the user can specify an affine transformation (perhaps from a menu of prestored versions) and point to a control polygon, after which the B-spline curve is drawn on the basis of the transformed polygon.

CASE STUDY 11.6 INTERPOLATION OF CONTROL POINTS WITH B-SPLINES

Level of Effort: III. A curve based on B-spline blending functions and the standard knot vector interpolates only the first and last control point. However, a preprocessing step can be applied to the control points so that the B-spline curve interpolates all of them. During preprocessing, a new set of control points is carefully fashioned out of the given set. This new set has the property that when a B-spline curve is formed from it, the curve passes through all of the points in the original set.

We develop the central idea through a specific example, interpolating a set of six data points, $y_0, \ldots, y_5$, at equispaced values of t with cubic B-splines, as shown in Figure 11.68(a). Instead of using the standard knot vector, knots are made equispaced, so that $N_{0,4}(t)$ begins at $t = 0$ and "bulges up" at $t = 2$, $N_{1,4}(t)$ begins at $t = 1$ and "bulges up" at $t = 3$, etc. Thus, we attempt to interpolate y_0 at $t = 2$, y_1 at $t = 3$, and so forth.

As shown in Figure 11.68(b), the sum

$$y(t) = \sum_{i=0}^{5} y_i N_{i,4}(t)$$

does not pass through the data points. The reason is that, because the B-spline functions overlap, the various terms in the sum interact in such a way that $y(t)$ falls short of the points. To correct this shortfall, a different set of values, $c_0, \ldots, c_5$, is used instead of the y_i, so that the curve based on them, viz.,

$$p(t) = \sum_{i=0}^{5} c_i N_{i,4}(t), \tag{11.100}$$

does indeed interpolate the y_i's, as shown in Figure 11.68(b). We must find just the right set of c_i values to accomplish the task. We can do that by solving a set of linear equations. The conditions for interpolating the six points are $p(2) = y_0$, $p(3) = y_1$, $p(4) = y_2, \ldots, p(7) = y_5$. Because the only values taken on by the B-spline functions at integer values of t are $0, 1/6$, and $4/6$, these six conditions have the form

$$4c_0 + c_1 = 6y_0,$$
$$c_0 + 4c_1 + c_2 = 6y_1,$$
$$c_1 + 4c_2 + c_3 = 6y_2, \tag{11.101}$$
$$\vdots$$
$$c_4 + 4c_5 = 6y_5.$$

These equations are nearly identical to Equations (11.76) and (11.77), so they can be solved using the techniques described in Section 11.10.3.

FIGURE 11.68 Attempt to interpolate six points with cubic B-splines.

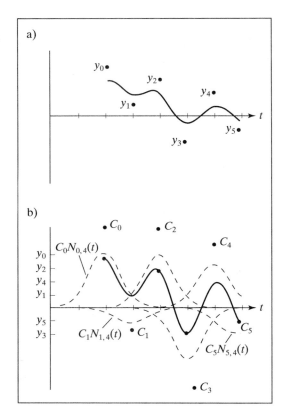

FIGURE 11.69 Example of 2D interpolation with B-splines. (Courtesy of Tuan Le Ngoc.)

The preceding ideas extend immediately to any number of data points, $y_0, y_1, \ldots, y_L$, simply by choosing the proper L. Write a function, `void adjust(double y[], double c[], int L)` that produces the array `c[]`, given the array `y[]`.

To interpolate points $p_i = (x_i, y_i)$, the process we have just described is performed once for the x-components and once for the y-components, producing the two arrays `x_new[]` and `y_new[]`. Then the interpolating curve is given by

$$P(t) = \sum_{i=0}^{L} W_i N_{i,4}(t),$$

where $W_i = ($ `x_new[i]`, `y_new[i]` $)$. An example is shown in Figure 11.69.

Write a program that allows the user to lay down a sequence of $(L + 1)$ control points with the mouse and then draws the interpolating curve based on cubic B-splines. Experiment with different values of L.

(Optional). Extend your program so that it draws *closed* curves that interpolate the control points. What adjustments are needed in Equation (11.101) to do this?

CASE STUDY 11.7 INTERPOLATING WITH CUBIC POLYNOMIALS

Level of Effort: III. Write a program that allows the user to lay down a sequence of $L + 1$ control points with the mouse and then draws the interpolating curve based on cubic polynomials. The velocities at the inner joints are set using the Kochanek–Bartels approach, with specified values of tension, bias, and continuity. The remaining two conditions on the cubic coefficients are set by forcing the second derivatives at the end control points to zero.

Allow the user to adjust the tension, bias, and continuity at each inner control point by using keystrokes. For instance, the user might click on the control point in question and tap the key 'v' to decrease the tension there by some small fixed amount or 'V' to increase it. Similarly, 'b' or 'B' is tapped to change the bias and 'c' or 'C' to adjust the continuity.

CASE STUDY 11.8 THE VENERABLE TEAPOT

Level of Effort: II. Write a program that uses OpenGL to draw the classical teapot from different points of view. Do not use the GLUT version of the teapot; fashion your own teapot out of surface patches.

The teapot has four major parts. The **body** is a surface of revolution whose profile consists of three Bezier curves in the xz-plane, as described in Section 11.11.2. The **handle** consists of four Bezier patches, as described in Section 11.11.3. The **lid** is a surface of revolution whose profile is described by two Bezier curves as shown in Figure 11.70, with data points given in

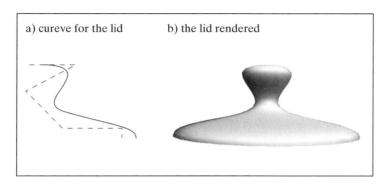

a) cureve for the lid   b) the lid rendered

FIGURE 11.70 The lid of the teapot.

Figure 11.71. The **spout** is similar to the handle, also consisting of four Bezier patches. Figure 11.72(a) shows the spout in cross section, along with a cross-sectional view of the control polyhedron for the patches. Similar to the handle, the spout's surface is symmetrical about the xz-plane. The entire upper positive-y patch has the following 16 control points:

based on C_0, D_0: (1.7, 0.0, 0.45), (1.7, 0.66, 0.45), (1.7, 0.66, 1.275), (1.7, 0.0, 1.275);
based on C_1, D_1: (3.1, 0.0, 0.675), (3.1, 0.66, 0.675), (2.6, 0.66, 1.275), (2.6, 0.0, 1.275);
based on C_2, D_2: (2.4, 0.0, 1.875), (2.4, 0.25, 1.875), (2.3, 0.25, 1.95), (2.3, 0.0, 1.95);
based on C_3, D_3: (3.3, 0.0, 2.25), (3.3, 0.25, 2.25), (2.7, 0.25, 2.25), (2.7, 0.0, 2.25).

The lower positive-y patch has the following 16 control points:

based on C_3, D_3: (3.3, 0.0, 2.25), (3.3, 0.25, 2.25), (2.7, 0.25, 2.25), (2.7, 0.0, 2.25);
based on C_4, D_4: (3.525, 0.0, 2.34375), (3.525, 0.25, 2.34375), (2.8, 0.25, 2.325), (2.8, 0.0, 2.325);
based on C_5, D_5: (3.45, 0.0, 2.3625), (3.45, 0.1, 2.3625), (2.9, 0.1, 2.325), (2.9, 0.0, 2.325);
based on C_6, D_6: (3.2, 0.0, 2.25), (3.2, 0.15, 2.25), (2.8, 0.15, 2.25), (2.8, 0.0, 2.25).

i	x	z
0	0	3
1	0.8	3
2	0	2.7
3	0.2	2.55
4	0.4	2.4
5	1.3	2.4
6	1.3	2.25

FIGURE 11.71 Data for the lid profile of the teapot.

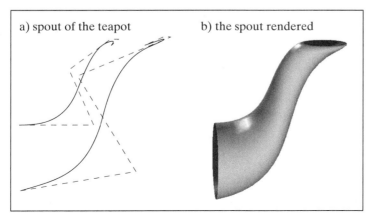

a) spout of the teapot   b) the spout rendered

FIGURE 11.72 Design of the spout of the teapot.

CASE STUDY 11.9 INVARIANCE TO PROJECTIVE TRANSFORMATIONS

Level of Effort: I. This case study provides a step-by-step demonstration that NURBS curves are invariant under a projective transformation, T. Show the details leading to each of the steps. Suppose the NURBS curve is given by Equation (11.68) and the transformation has the four-by-four matrix M whose rows are the vectors $\mathbf{m}_1, \mathbf{m}_2, \mathbf{m}_3$, and $\mathbf{m}_4$, respectively.

a. Show that when it is transformed by T, the homogeneous coordinate version $\widetilde{P}(t)$ of the curve in Equation (11.68) becomes the curve

$$M\widetilde{P}(t) = \sum_{k=0}^{L} w_k (\widetilde{P}_k \cdot \mathbf{m}_1, \widetilde{P}_k \cdot \mathbf{m}_2, \widetilde{P}_k \cdot \mathbf{m}_3, \widetilde{P}_k \cdot \mathbf{m}_4)^T N_{k,m}(t), \qquad (11.102)$$

where $\widetilde{P}_k = (P_x, P_y, P_z, 1)^T$ is the homogeneous coordinate version of P_k.

b. Show that, in ordinary coordinates, Equation (11.102) becomes

$$T(P(t)) = \frac{\displaystyle\sum_{k=0}^{L} w_k (\widetilde{P}_k \cdot \mathbf{m}_1, \widetilde{P}_k \cdot \mathbf{m}_2, \widetilde{P}_k \cdot \mathbf{m}_3)^T N_{k,m}(t)}{\displaystyle\sum_{k=0}^{L} w_k (\widetilde{P}_k \cdot \mathbf{m}_4) N_{k,m}(t)}. \qquad (11.103)$$

c. Show that each control point P_k is transformed to

$$T(P_k) = \left(\frac{\widetilde{P}_k \cdot \mathbf{m}_1}{\widetilde{P}_k \cdot \mathbf{m}_4}, \frac{\widetilde{P}_k \cdot \mathbf{m}_2}{\widetilde{P}_k \cdot \mathbf{m}_4}, \frac{\widetilde{P}_k \cdot \mathbf{m}_3}{\widetilde{P}_k \cdot \mathbf{m}_4}, \right)^T.$$

d. Show that building a NURBS curve with weights, say, v_k, on the transformed control points yields the curve

$$\frac{\displaystyle\sum_{k=0}^{L} v_k \left(\frac{\widetilde{P}_k \cdot \mathbf{m}_1}{\widetilde{P}_k \cdot \mathbf{m}_4}, \frac{\widetilde{P}_k \cdot \mathbf{m}_2}{\widetilde{P}_k \cdot \mathbf{m}_4}, \frac{\widetilde{P}_k \cdot \mathbf{m}_3}{\widetilde{P}_k \cdot \mathbf{m}_4}, \right)^T N_{k,m}(t)}{\displaystyle\sum_{k=0}^{L} v_k N_{k,m}(t)}.$$

e. Show that the preceding equation agrees with Equation (11.70) for the choice of v_k equal to the $\bar{w}_k$ of Equation (11.71).

Why B-splines aren't projectively invariant. Show where the derivation in the previous exercise fails for B-splines.

Extension to surfaces. Work through steps similar to the preceding ones to show that NURBS surfaces are also projectively invariant.

CASE STUDY 11.10 DRAWING NURBS PATCHES

Level of Effort: II.

a. Write and experiment with an application that draws u- and v-contours of NURBS surfaces. The core of such an application is a function that evaluates points on the surface $P(u, v)$. The prototype of the function might look something like the following:

```
Point3 nurbsPoint(Point3 P[][],  // matrix of control points
          int L, int M,          // # of control pts = (L+1)(M+1)
          float w[][],           // vector of weights
          float knot[],          // knot vector
          int m, int n,          // orders of B-splines
          float u,  v);          // values of parameters u and v
```

b. Experiment with the control polyhedron shown in a planar view in Figure 11.73, where the label 0, a, or b gives the height of each point above the xy-plane. The figure shows an example of the **domelike** shape produced by a NURBS patch for certain choices of weights and heights a and b. Build and draw patches formed this way for user-specified values of a and b. Try various ways of selecting weights:

   i. All weights are equal.

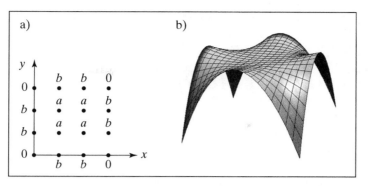

FIGURE 11.73 Designing a dome.

ii. Points at a height of zero each have weight W, and all the others have weight sW, where the user enters values of s.

iii. Use other interesting arrangements of weights.

Does any combination you come upon produce a dome that is nearly a hemisphere? What adjustments might produce a more hemispherical dome?

c. Build and draw various **surfaces of revolution**. As we have seen, a surface of revolution is created by rotating a profile curve about an axis. Suppose the profile curve lies in the xz-plane and is defined as the NURBS curve

$$C(u) = \frac{\sum_{k=0}^{L} w_k Q_k N_{k,m}(u)}{\sum_{k=0}^{L} w_k N_{k,m}(u)} \qquad (11.104)$$

built upon the set of $L + 1$ control points Q_k. We make this curve into a surface of revolution (with the z-axis as its axis of revolution) by combining it with circles that lie perpendicular to the z-axis. The circles are also defined as NURBS curves, capitalizing on the ability of those curves to form perfect conic sections. Here we use the NURBS circle described in Example 11.9.2 that is based on quadratic splines with seven control points.

The final matrix of control points is formed as the outer product of the control-point values for the profile and for the circle, so that the control polyhedron is a collection of squares parallel to the xy-plane, at different heights and of different sizes according to the positions of the control points Q_k. Try a weight matrix that is also the outer product of the individual weight vectors. Experiment with different profile curves to create a variety of surfaces of revolution. In at least one case, make the profile a conic section, so the surface is a quadric surface.

Experiment with creating extruded (linearly swept) surfaces by using NURBS surfaces. A contour $C(u)$, described as a NURBS curve, is swept in a direction perpendicular to the plane in which it lies. The straight sides are produced by a first-order NURBS curve in v. Also, experiment with a ruled surface, where the two edge curves are NURBS curves in u and the rulings are first-order NURBS curves in v.

11.14 FURTHER READING

An excellent early book by Faux and Pratt [Faux79] develops the mathematical foundations of curve and surface design. The book by Rogers and Adams [Rogers90] provides a wealth of techniques and examples for designing surfaces, and Farin [Farin90] offers a lucid treatment of the underlying mathematics of surfaces. Bartles, Beatty, and Barsky [Bartles87] discuss the many varieties of splines that you can use in curve and surface design, and describe their different properties. The recent book edited by Bloomenthal [Bloomenthal97] has several fine chapters on surface design, including one by Blinn on second order surfaces, and one by Bajaj on implicitly-defined surface patches.

12

Color Theory

> Colors and textures will become important to you.
>
> *Found in fortune cookie, Amherst, Massachusetts*

Goals of the Chapter

▲ To study the nature of color and its numerical description.

▲ To examine some standards for representing color.

▲ To define and use various color spaces.

▲ To describe different methods for reducing the number of colors in an image.

▲ To develop methods for programming the color lookup table

PREVIEW

In this chapter, we examine the nature of color and how to represent it in computer graphics.

Section 12.1 describes some of the intricacies of the human color vision system and introduces the problem of describing colors numerically in a reliable and reproducible way. Section 12.2 discusses the process of color matching and representing any color as a linear combination of three primary colors. The issue of choosing "good" primary colors is addressed. Section 12.3 develops central ideas of the standard chromaticity diagram devised by the International Commission on Illumination and shows how the diagram is useful in color calculations. The notion of a gamut of colors is also discussed. Section 12.4 describes different color spaces and gives some tools for converting a color between spaces. Section 12.5 discusses methods used for color quantization: reducing the number of different colors in an image without destroying its visual quality. The octree quantization method is developed in some detail.

12.1 INTRODUCTION

The shading models discussed in the previous chapter computed colors by working separately with three basic primaries: red, green, and blue. This simple approach is serviceable and is consistent with the most common graphics displays used today, which generate color by mixing amounts of some built-in red, green, and blue colors. But the subject of color is much more complex than that; color depends on subtle interactions between the physics of light radiation and the eye–brain system. (See [Feynman63] for a superb discussion.) From the point of view of writing computer graphics applications, we must be able to answer several questions:

- How are colors described accurately in numerical terms?
- How do the numerical descriptions relate to everyday ways of describing color?
- How does one compare colors?
- What range of colors can a CRT display or a printed page reveal?
- How can color lookup tables be loaded to produce the colors required?
- How do we deal with color palettes when a device can display only, say, 256 colors?

Computer-generated pictures should be able to provide this extra dimension as well, so we need tools to describe and control color in applications.

Light itself is an electromagnetic phenomenon, like television waves, infrared radiation, and X rays. By light, we mean those waves that lie in a narrow band of wavelengths in the so-called visible spectrum. Figure 12.1 shows the location of the visible spectrum (for humans) within the entire electromagnetic spectrum, along with the spectra of some other common phenomena. The frequency of vibration, f, increases to the right, whereas the wavelength λ increases to the left.[1] The eye responds to light with wavelengths between approximately 400 and 700 nanometers (nm).

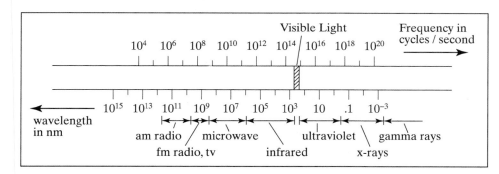

FIGURE 12.1 Electromagnetic spectrum.

An Aside on the Eye

The retina of the eye is a light-sensitive membrane. It lines the posterior portion of the eye's wall and contains two kinds of receptor cells: cones and rods. The **cones** are the color-sensitive cells, each of which responds to a particular color—red, green, or blue. According to the tristimulus theory, the color we see is the result of our cones' relative responses to red, green, and blue light. The human eye can distinguish about 200 intensities each of red, green, and blue. Each eye has 6 to 7 million cones, concentrated in a small portion of the retina called the **fovea**. Each cone has its own nerve cell, thereby allowing the eye to discern tiny details. To see an object in detail, the eye looks directly at it in order to bring the image onto the fovea.

By contrast, the **rods** can neither distinguish colors nor see fine detail. Seventy-five million to 150 million rods are crowded onto the retina surrounding the fovea. Moreover, many rods are attached to a single nerve cell, preventing them from discriminating fine detail [Gonzalez87]. What do rods do then? They are very sensitive to low levels of light and can see things in dim light that the cones miss. At night, for instance, it is best to look slightly away from an object, so that the image falls outside the fovea. Detail and color are lost, but at least the general form of the object

---

[1] The wavelength of a wave is the distance light travels during one cycle of its vibration. The wavelength λ and the frequency f are inversely related by $\lambda = v/f$, where v is the speed of light in the medium of interest. In air (or a vacuum), $v = 300{,}000$ km/sec; in glass light travels about 65 percent as fast.

(a predator?) is visible. Indeed, the sensitivity of our peripheral vision to dim light was probably instrumental in our evolution.

Some light sources, such as lasers, emit light of essentially a single wavelength, or "pure spectral" light. We perceive 400-nm light as violet and 620-nm light as red, with the other pure colors lying in between these extremes. Figure 12.2 shows some sample **spectral densities** $S(\lambda)$ (power per unit wavelength) for pure light and the common names given to their perceived colors.

FIGURE 12.2 Spectra for some pure colors.

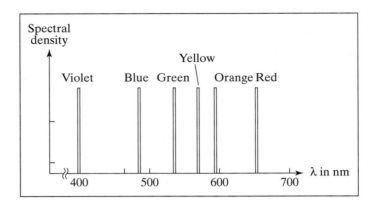

The light from most sources does not consist of only one wavelength; instead, it contains power of various amounts over a continuous set of wavelengths, and their spectral densities (or "spectra") cover a band of wavelengths. The total power of the light in any band of wavelengths is calculated as the *area* under the density curve over that band. Figure 12.3 shows several example spectra for lights. The label for each indicates the color that we perceive when we look at such light. Note that white light contains approximately equal amounts of all frequencies, whereas reds tend to have more power concentrated at the longer wavelengths. Gray light also exhibits a "flat" spectral density, but at a lower intensity. These examples highlight one of the difficulties of trying to describe color numerically; that is, an enormous variety of spectral density functions is perceived by the eye as having the same color. For example, a given color sample can be "matched" by many different spectral density shapes such that the colors of the sample and any of the spectral densities are indistinguishable when placed side by side.

12.2 DESCRIBING COLORS

Suppose that we want to describe a color precisely over the telephone, perhaps to a dye manufacturer or a production manager in a publishing company. It isn't enough to say "a bright robin's egg blue"; we must make sure that the listener receives a precise characterization of the color we have in mind. If we knew the spectral density curve of the color, as in Figure 12.3, we could try to describe its level at a dozen or so wavelengths, but that is clearly awkward and seems too specific, as many different spectral shapes produce the same color. Ideally, we would be able to recite a few numbers, such as "the target color is 3.24, 1.6, 85, and 1.117," and we would be assured that exactly the same color could be reproduced every time from this description.

How many numbers are required, and what do they mean? Remarkably, the answer is just three numbers: color perception is three dimensional. But we still must agree on what "coding" scheme is to be used to map colors into numbers and vice versa. We shall examine several conventions in the following sections and then discuss the ideas behind the current international standard.

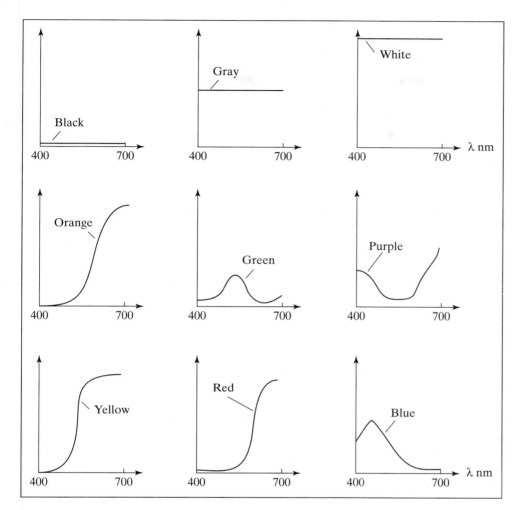

FIGURE 12.3 Sample spectra for light and their perceived colors.

12.2.1 Dominant Wavelength

One simple way to describe a color capitalizes on the variety of spectra that produce the same (perceived) color. This approach specifies a spectrum having the very simple shape shown in Figure 12.4 by stating three numbers: the dominant wavelength, the saturation, and the luminance. The spectrum consists of a "spike" located at a dominant wavelength, 620 nm in the example. The location of the **dominant wavelength** specifies the **hue** of the color, in this case red. In addition, a certain amount of white light is present, represented by the rectangular "pedestal" that "desaturates" the red light, making it appear pink.

The total power in the light, known as its **luminance**, is given by the area under the entire spectrum: $L = (D - A)B + AW$, where D is the strength of the spike and B is its bandwidth, and A is the strength of the white light spectrum (What is W?) The **saturation** (or purity) of the light is defined as the percentage of luminance that resides in the dominant component [Billmeyer81]:

$$\text{purity} = \frac{(D - A)B}{L} \times 100\%. \qquad (12.1)$$

If $D = A$, the purity is 0, and white light is observed without any trace of red. If $A = 0$, no white light is present, and a pure red light is seen. Pastel colors contain a large amount

FIGURE 12.4 Spectrum of a
color using a dominant
wavelength.

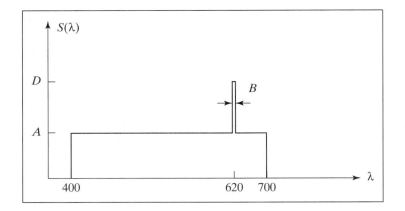

of white and are said to be **unsaturated**. When two colors differ only in hue, the eye can
distinguish about 128 different hues. When two colors differ only in saturation, the eye
can distinguish about 20 different saturations, depending on the hue.

The notions of saturation, luminance, and dominant wavelength are useful for describing colors, but when one is presented with a sample color, it is not clear how to
measure these values. We shall thus consider some more effective ways to describe
color. To get started, we need a way of testing when two colors are the "same." This
leads to the area of *color matching*, which is the basis for specifying all colors.

12.2.2 Color Matching

Colors are often described by comparing them with a set of standard color samples
and finding the closest match. Many such standard sets have been devised and are
widely used in the dyeing and printing industry [Munsell41]. One can also try to produce a sample color by matching it to the proper combination of some test lights, as
shown in Figure 12.5.

The sample color with spectral density $S(\lambda)$ is projected onto one part of a screen,
and the other part is bathed in the superposition of three test lights with spectral densities $A(\lambda), B(\lambda)$, and $C(\lambda)$. The observer adjusts the intensities $(a, b, $ and $c)$ of the
test lights until the test color $T(\lambda) = aA(\lambda) + bB(\lambda) + cC(\lambda)$ is indistinguishable
from the sample color, even though the two spectra, $S(\lambda)$ and $T(\lambda)$, may be quite dif-

FIGURE 12.5 Color matching
using superposition of test
lights.

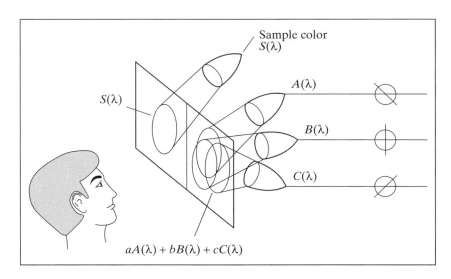

ferent. The temptation is then to say that the sample color consists of a "sum" of the "amounts" a, b, and c of the three test colors. But in what sense is this meaningful?

There is a remarkable "algebra" of color superposition [Feynman63]. Suppose that two spectral shapes, $S(\lambda)$ and $P(\lambda)$, have the same (perceived) color, a fact that we denote as $S = P$. Now add a third color, N, to both of these, by superposing light with spectrum $N(\lambda)$ on both. It is an experimental fact that these two new colors will still be indistinguishable!

Along with the symbol $=$, which means that two colors are indistinguishable, we define the meaning of $+$ for colors so that $S + N$ denotes the color observed when the spectra $S(\lambda)$ and $N(\lambda)$ are added. This experimental fact can then be written as

$$\text{If } (S = P), \text{then } (N + S = N + P). \tag{12.2}$$

The same goes for *scaling* colors, or scaling their spectral densities or overall brightness: If $S = P$, then $aS = aP$, for any scalar a. And it is meaningful to write *linear combinations* of two colors A and B, as in $T = aA + bB$, where a and b are scalars. (Recall Chapter 4.) Thus, there is an experimentally verified *vector algebra* of colors, in which we treat colors as vectors, add them, scale them, decompose them into their components, and so forth.

As we have mentioned, another remarkable fact of human color perception is that it is three dimensional:[2] Any color C can be constructed as the superposition of just three primary colors, say, R, G, and B, according to the formula

$$C = rR + gG + bB, \tag{12.3}$$

where r, g, and b are scalars describing the amounts of each of the primary colors contained in C. The symbols R, G, and B are suggestive of red, green, and blue, which are often used as the primary colors in a discussion. (The reason for stressing red, green, and blue stems from the sensitivity of our cones to these three colors). But Equation (12.3) works with any choice of primaries, as long as one of them is not just a combination of the other two.

Given a set of three primary colors, R, G, and B, then, we can represent any other color, $C = rR + gG + bB$, in three-dimensional space by the point (r, g, b). For instance, if R, G, and B correspond to some versions of what we normally call red, green, and blue, $(0, 1, 0)$ will represent a pure green of unit brightness, and $(.2, .3, .5)$ will represent a yellow. If we double each component, we will obtain a color that is twice as bright, but appears as the same color.

Experiments have been run to see how people match colors. Of particular interest is one experiment that combines three specific choices of R, G, and B in order to produce a (perceived) "pure spectral color"—that is, a totally saturated monochromatic color having its power concentrated at a single wavelength. (In dominant-wavelength terms, this color is 100-percent saturated and has dominant wavelength λ.) Figure 12.6 shows the results of experiments run on a large number of observers. The primary colors that were used were pure monochromatic red, green, and blue lights at wavelengths of 700 nm, 546 nm, and 436 nm, respectively. The functions $r(\lambda), g(\lambda)$, and $b(\lambda)$ show how much of these red, green, and blue lights are needed to match the pure spectral color at λ. We shall call this pure spectral color mono (λ). So we have

$$\text{mono}(\lambda) = r(\lambda)R + g(\lambda)G + b(\lambda)B. \tag{12.4}$$

For example, a pure orange color mono (600) looks (to the average observer) identical to the combination $0.37R + .08G$. Obviously, the spectrum of the orange light is not the same as the spectrum of this sum, but the two lights still look exactly the same.

---

[2] Another way of saying this is that any four colors are always linearly related; that is, any one of them can be represented as a combination of the other three.

FIGURE 12.6 Color-matching functions for RGB primaries.

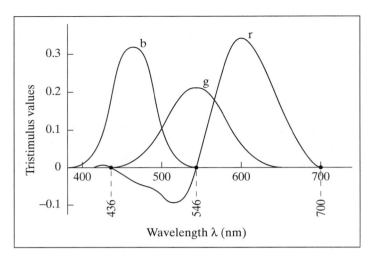

But there is a rub: For this set of choices of R, G, and B, some of the scalars r, g, and b must be *negative* in order to make Equation (12.4) correct! For instance, $r(\lambda)$ is negative at $\lambda = 520$. What is the physical meaning of the minus sign in a color such as $C = 0.7R + 0.5G - 0.2B$? One cannot remove light that isn't there. Fortunately, this contradiction disappears if we rewrite the equation as $C + 0.2B = 0.7R + 0.5G$. Whereas C alone cannot be constructed as the superpositions of positive amounts of the primary colors, the color $C + 0.2B$ can be matched by positive amounts of R and G. This is in fact what happens with any choice of visible primary colors R, G, and B. Many colors can be fabricated (using positive coefficients r, g, and b), but some cannot, and one primary must be "put on the other side of the equation." Roughly speaking, the problem is that when two colors are added, the result is a less saturated color, so it is impossible to form a highly saturated color by superposing two others. This is particularly obvious for any of the pure spectral colors, which are themselves saturated.

It is useful to scale the color-matching functions so that they add to unity, so we define

$$\bar{r}(\lambda) = \frac{r(\lambda)}{r(\lambda) + g(\lambda) + b(\lambda)}, \bar{g}(\lambda) = \frac{g(\lambda)}{r(\lambda) + g(\lambda) + b(\lambda)}, \bar{b}(\lambda) = \frac{b(\lambda)}{r(\lambda) + g(\lambda) + b(\lambda)}$$

and therefore know that $\bar{r}(\lambda) + \bar{g}(\lambda) + \bar{b}(\lambda) = 1$. These relative weights are called "chromaticity values" for $\text{mono}(\lambda)$. They give the amounts of each of the primary colors that are required to match a unit brightness of light at λ. Removing variations in brightness allows us to specify colors with only two numbers, say, $(\bar{r}(\lambda), \bar{g}(\lambda))$, as we can always determine $\bar{b}(\lambda)$ from the equation $\bar{b}(\lambda) = 1 - \bar{r}(\lambda) - \bar{g}(\lambda)$. We can plot the position of the 3D point $(\bar{r}(\lambda), \bar{g}(\lambda), \bar{b}(\lambda))$ as λ varies across the visible spectrum, as shown in Figure 12.7. Because of the normalization we have applied, all points on this curve lie on the $r + g + b = 1$ plane as shown. Notice that because some coordinates are negative at certain values of λ, the curve does not lie totally inside the positive octant in this space. The standard to be discussed next provides a variation of this curve that does lie totally inside the positive octant, with all three coordinates everywhere positive.

12.3 THE INTERNATIONAL COMMISSION ON ILLUMINATION STANDARD

How can colors be specified precisely in a way that everyone agrees on? Because color perception is three dimensional, we need only agree on three primary colors and describe any other color desired by the proper 3-tuple, as in (r, g, b). But what pri-

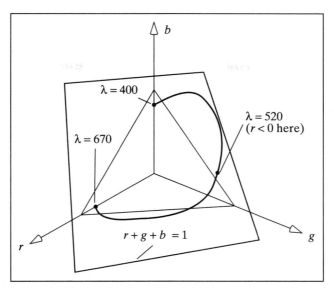

FIGURE 12.7 The pure-spectral-color curve for the RGB primaries.

maries are to be used? Unfortunately, all physically realizable primaries require negative coefficients for at least some visible colors.

To circumvent this awkwardness, a standard was devised in 1931 by the International Commission on Illumination (Commission Internationale de l'Éclairage, or CIE). The CIE defined three special "supersaturated" primary colors $X, Y,$ and Z that do not correspond to real colors, but that have the property that all real colors can be represented as *positive* combinations of them. These primary colors are defined through color-matching functions like those in Figure 12.6.

Figure 12.8 shows the color-matching functions adopted by the CIE. The idea is the same as that behind Equation (12.4): A monochromatic light at wavelength λ is matched by the specified linear combination of the special primary colors. The resulting equation is

$$\text{mono}(\lambda) = x(\lambda)X + y(\lambda)Y + z(\lambda)Z. \tag{12.5}$$

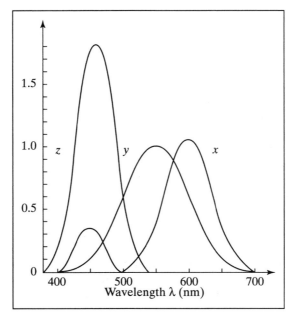

FIGURE 12.8 Color-matching functions for primary $X, Y,$ and Z.

Notice that all three functions are positive at every λ, so mono(λ) is always a positive linear combination of the primary colors.

How were the primary colors X, Y, and Z determined? They were defined by means of an affine transformation applied to color-matching functions such as $r(\lambda)$, $g(\lambda)$, and $b(\lambda)$ in Equation (12.4): $x(\lambda)$ is a particular linear combination of these shapes, and so are $y(\lambda)$ and $z(\lambda)$. (For convenience, $y(\lambda)$ was chosen to have the same shape as the "luminous efficiency function," which is the eye's measured response to monochromatic light of fixed strength at different wavelengths. This causes the amount of the Y primary color present in a light to equal the overall intensity of the light.)

It is useful to work again with normalized chromaticity values to maintain unit brightness, so we define

$$\bar{x}(\lambda) = \frac{x(\lambda)}{x(\lambda) + y(\lambda) + z(\lambda)}, \bar{y}(\lambda) = \frac{y(\lambda)}{x(\lambda) + y(\lambda) + z(\lambda)}, \bar{z}(\lambda) = \frac{z(\lambda)}{x(\lambda) + y(\lambda) + z(\lambda)}$$

and, of course, $\bar{z}(\lambda) = 1 - \bar{x}(\lambda) - \bar{y}(\lambda)$. Figure 12.9 shows the parametric form $\mathbf{s}(\lambda) = \left(\bar{x}(\lambda), \bar{y}(\lambda), \bar{z}(\lambda)\right)$, which describes a curve that now lies in the positive octant of the xyz-plane. (The specific nature of the original primaries used and the details of deriving the transformation can be found in various references [Billmeyer81, Conrac85]. However, you need not know this in order to understand and use the CIE standard.)

FIGURE 12.9 Building the CIE standard.

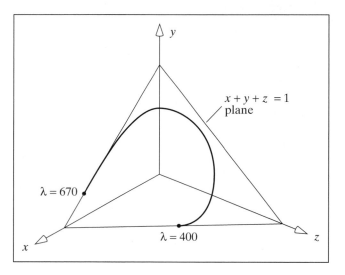

12.3.1 Constructing the CIE Chart

The spectral color curve $\mathbf{s}(\lambda)$ lies in three-dimensional space, but because it lies in the plane $x + y + z = 1$, it is easy to represent its shape in a two-dimensional chart that can be printed on a page for reference. Only x and y are needed to specify a (unit intensity) color, because, given (x, y), we can find z trivially. (How?)

Thus, the standard *CIE chromaticity diagram* is the curve $\mathbf{s}'(\lambda) = \left(\bar{x}(\lambda), \bar{y}(\lambda)\right)$, shown in Figure 12.10. (Think of viewing the 3D curve of Figure 12.9 in an orthographic projection, looking along the z-axis.) The diagram displays the horseshoe-shaped locus of all pure spectral colors, labeled according to wavelength. Inside the horseshoe lie all other visible colors. Points that are outside the horseshoe region do not correspond to visible light.

Various regions are labeled in the figure with names that people commonly use to describe the colors found there; for example, points near $(0.6, 0.3)$ are perceived as red. Unfortunately, equal distances between points in the chart do not correspond to

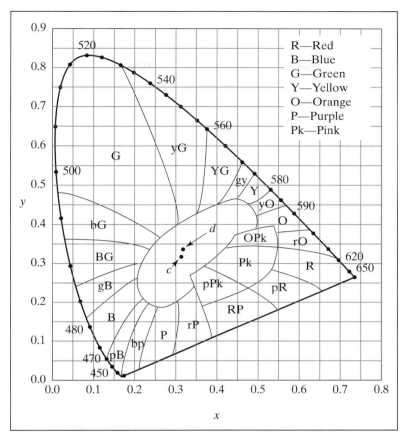

FIGURE 12.10 The CIE chromaticity diagram.

equal differences in perceived color. For instance, small changes in position in the *G* region cause only slight changes in perceived color. On the other hand, rather small changes in position in the *B* or *Y* region cause large changes in perceived color.

The CIE chromaticity diagram defines certain special points. Point *c* at $(x, y) = (0.310, 0.316)$ is a white color known as "Illuminant C," which is taken to be the "fully unsaturated" color. It is often used as the reference color "white" in aligning some graphics monitors. Illuminant C has the color of an overcast sky at midday. Point *d* at $(0.313, 0.329)$ is the color that an ideal blackbody radiator emits when raised to the "white-hot" temperature of 6,504° K. This color is a little "greener" than Illuminant C. Many other colors, such as those emitted by a tungsten filament lightbulb, by moonlight, by red-hot steel at certain temperatures, and so on, have been carefully measured [Conrac85: Rogers98].

The great value of the CIE chromaticity diagram is that it provides a worldwide standard for describing any color. Instruments have been devised that can generate the color represented by any (x, y, z) inside the horseshoe, so, by careful matching, one can measure the "value" for any color desired. (Instruments also exist that automatically measure (x, y, z) for a given color sample.) In addition, the chart permits important calculations to be performed on colors, as we shall see next.

12.3.2 Using the CIE Chromaticity Diagram

The CIE chromaticity diagram has many uses. Several of them stem from the ease with which we can interpret straight lines on the chart, as suggested in Figure 12.11.

Consider line *l*, between the two colors *a* and *b*. All points on *l* are convex combinations (recall Chapter 4) of *a* and *b*, having the form $(\alpha)a + (1 - \alpha)b$ for

FIGURE 12.11 Uses for the CIE chromaticity diagram.

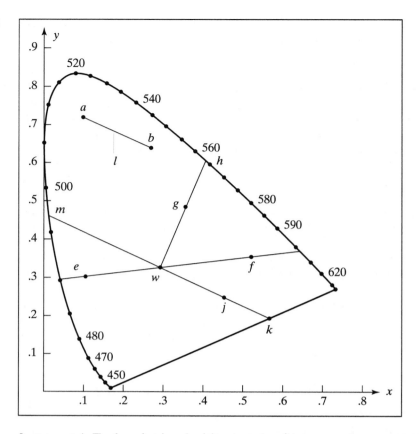

red   ⇔   cyan

green   ⇔   magenta

blue   ⇔   yellow

FIGURE 12.12 Complementary colors.

$0 \le \alpha \le 1$. Each point is a legitimate color (its x, y, and z components sum to 1; why?), so we can assert that any colors on the straight line (and only those colors) can be generated by shining various amounts of colors a and b onto a screen.

When two colors are added and their sum turns out to denote white, we say that the colors are **complementary** (with respect to the choice of white). Thus, in Figure 12.10, e (blue green) and f (orange pink) are seen to be complementary colors with respect to w (white), because proper amounts of them added together form white. Some familiar pairs of complementary colors, to be discussed further, are listed in Figure 12.12.

The CIE chromaticity diagram can also be used to measure the dominant wavelength and purity of a given color, such as g in Figure 12.11. Accordingly, g must be the linear combination of some pure spectral color (found on the edge of the horseshoe) and a standard white, w. To find which spectral color is involved, just draw a line from w through g (and on to h here), and measure the wavelength at h—in this case, 564 nm, a yellowish green. Similarly, the saturation, or purity, is just the ratio of distances gw/hw. The color at j has no dominant wavelength, because extending line wj hits k on the so-called purple line, which does not correspond to a single pure spectral color. (Colors along this line are combinations of red and violet.) In such a case, the dominant wavelength is specified by finding the complement of j at m and using its wavelength with a c suffix—that is, 498_c.

12.3.3 Color Gamuts

The CIE diagram is especially useful in defining *color gamuts*, the range of colors that can be produced on a device. For instance, a CRT monitor can produce combinations of only the basic red, green, and blue primary colors that its three phosphor types can generate. Plate 33 shows the locations of phosphor colors r, g, and b for a typical color CRT monitor. Figure 12.13 shows the positions of these colors. (See [Stone88]).

The three points define the triangular region shown in the figure. Any color within this triangle is a convex combination of the three primary colors and can be displayed.[3] Colors outside this triangle are not in the gamut of the display and thus cannot be displayed. White falls within the gamut, reflecting the well-known fact that appropriate amounts of red, green, and blue yield white.

Also shown is the gamut for a color printing process. (Because of the mechanism by which color is placed on paper, colors are not directly additive, so the gamut is not a simple triangle.) This gamut is somewhat smaller than the gamut for a CRT monitor, so some colors that can be reproduced on this monitor cannot be displayed by a printer. On the other hand, some points that the printer gamut can reach lie outside the monitor gamut. Therefore, some colors can be printed, but not observed on the CRT monitor.

Note that for any choice of three primaries—even the pure spectral colors on the edge of the horseshoe—a triangular gamut can never encompass all visible colors, because the horseshoe "bulges" outside any triangle whose vertices are within it. Red, green, and blue are natural choices for primary colors, as they lie far apart in the CIE chart and therefore produce a gamut that "covers" a large part of the chart's area. If, instead, yellow, cyan, and magenta were used as primary colors, the gamut would be much smaller. (Could white still be produced?)

Primary	x	y
red	.628	.330
green	.258	.590
blue	.1507	.060

FIGURE 12.13 CIE coordinates for typical CRT monitor primaries.

PRACTICE EXERCISE

12.3.1. Why red, green, and blue?

Provide physical and philosophical arguments why the cones in our eyes have peak sensitivities to red, green, and blue lights. ■

12.4 COLOR SPACES

The CIE's specification of color is precise and standard, but it is not necessarily the most natural one. In computer graphics particularly, it is most natural to think of combining red, green, and blue to form the colors that are desired. Other people, however, are more comfortable thinking in terms of hue, saturation, and lightness, and artists frequently refer to tints, shades, and tones to describe color. These all are examples of **color models**, choices of three "descriptors" used to describe colors. If one can quantify the three descriptors, one can then describe a color by means of a triple of values, such as (tint, shade, tone) = (.125, 1.68, .045). This establishes a 3D coordinate system in which to describe color. The different choices of coordinates then give rise to different **color spaces**, and we need ways to convert color descriptions from one color space to another.

12.4.1 The RGB and CMY Color Spaces

The RGB (short for "red, green, blue") color model describes colors as positive combinations of three appropriately defined red, green, and blue primary colors, as in Equation (12.3). If the scalars r, g, and b are confined to values between 0 and 1, all definable colors will lie in the cube shown in Figure 12.14.

---

[3] The National Television Standards Committee (NTSC) defines the following standard primary colors in CIE coordinates: red = (.670, .330), green = (.210, .710), and blue = (.140, .080) [Rogers98].

FIGURE 12.14 The RGB color cube.

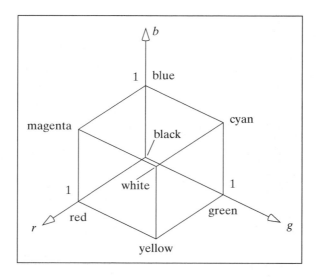

Unlike the CIE diagram, the RGB model does not normalize the intensity of the color: Points close to $(0, 0, 0)$ are dark, and those farther out are lighter. For example, $(1, 1, 1)$ corresponds to pure white. This color space is the most natural for computer graphics, in which a color specification such as $(.3, .56, .9)$ can be directly translated into values stored in a color lookup table (LUT). Note that the corner marked magenta properly signifies that red light plus blue light produces magenta light, and similarly for yellow and cyan. Colors at diagonally opposite corners are complementary.

When normalized to unit intensity, all of the colors that can be defined in this model will, of course, lie in the CIE chromaticity diagram once suitable positions of red, green, and blue have been identified. (What shape is the gamut?) It is not hard to convert a color that is specified in CIE coordinates (x, y, z) into (r, g, b) space, and vice versa. Because the R, G, B primaries are linear combinations of the X, Y, and Z CIE primaries, a linear transformation suffices. The mapping depends on the definition of the primaries R, G, and B and on the definition of white. For the primaries given in Figure 12.13 and white given by point d in Figure 12.10, the transformation is (see [Rogers98] for details)

$$(r, g, b) = (x, y, z) \begin{pmatrix} 2.739 & -1.110 & .138 \\ -1.145 & 2.029 & -.333 \\ -.424 & .033 & 1.105 \end{pmatrix}. \tag{12.6}$$

Naturally, the conversion from RGB to XYZ uses the inverse of this matrix.

PRACTICE EXERCISE

12.4.1. Converting from RGB to CIE space

Find the inverse of the matrix in Equation (12.6) to provide the transformation from RGB coordinates to CIE space. An important property of CIE space is that all colors can be expressed as positive linear combinations of the primary colors X, Y, and Z. What condition does this impose on the inverse matrix? Does the inverse you calculate satisfy that condition?

12.4.2 Additive and Subtractive Color Systems

So far, we have considered summing contributions of colored light to form new colors, an *additive* process. An **additive color system** expresses a color, say, D, as the sum of certain amounts of primary colors, usually red, green, and blue. [Thus, $D = (r, g, b)$.] An additive system can use any three primary colors, but because red, green, and blue are situated far apart in the CIE chart, they provide a large gamut.

Subtractive color systems are used when it is natural to think in terms of removing colors. When light is reflected (diffusely) from a surface or is transmitted through a partially transparent medium (as when photographic filters are used), certain colors are absorbed by the material and thus removed. This is a *subtractive* process.

A **subtractive color system** expresses a color—again, say D—by means of an ordered triple, just as an additive system does, but each of the three values specifies how much of a certain color (the complement of the corresponding primary) to *remove* from white in order to produce D. To clarify this statement, consider the most common subtractive system—the CMY system, which uses the subtractive primaries cyan, magenta, and yellow. If we say that $D = (c, m, y)_{CMY}$, we are saying that D is formed from white by subtracting amount c of the complement of cyan (i.e., red), amount m of the complement of magenta (green), and amount y of the complement of yellow (blue). Thus, we immediately have the following relationship between the RGB and CMY systems:

$$(r, g, b)_{RGB} = (1, 1, 1) - (c, m, y)_{CMY}. \tag{12.7}$$

That is, the amount of blue b in a color is reduced by increasing y, since y specifies the amount of yellow's complement to remove from white.

Figure 12.15 illustrates the subtractive process. The three glass slides are described in the CMY system by $(.4, .5, .2)_{CMY}$. When white light, given by $(1, 1, 1)_{RGB}$ in the RGB additive system, penetrates the cyan-colored slide, 40 percent of the red component is absorbed, and a "cyanish" light containing $(.6, 1, 1)_{RGB}$ emerges. When this light penetrates the magenta slide, 50 percent of the green light is removed, and the color $(.6, .5, 1)_{RGB}$ emerges. (What color is it now?) Finally, this light penetrates the yellow slide, whereupon 20 percent of the blue component is absorbed and the color $(.6, .5, .8)_{RGB}$ emerges.

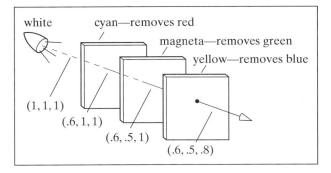

white   cyan—removes red
magneta—removes green
yellow—removes blue
$(1, 1, 1)$
$(.6, 1, 1)$
$(.6, .5, 1)$
$(.6, .5, .8)$

FIGURE 12.15 The subtractive process.

A similar description applies to light scattering from a colored surface. In a three-color printing process, for instance, cyan, magenta, and yellow pigments are suspended in a colorless paint. Each color subtracts a portion of the complementary component of its incident light. For example, if magenta particles are mixed into a colorless paint, the particles will subtract the green portion of the white light and reflect only the red and blue components. The subtractive system is used for color hard-copy devices to fashion colors by mixing the three CMY primaries.

Figure 12.16 shows the additive and subtractive primary colors and their interaction. (Plate 34 shows the same thing in color). In Part (a), red, green, and blue beams of light shine on a white surface. Where the two beams overlap, their lights combine to form a new color. For instance, red and green add to form yellow light. Where all three overlap, white light is formed.

FIGURE 12.16 Additive and subtractive color systems.

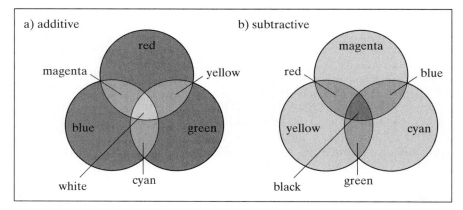

Part (b) shows a different situation. Each circle is formed by laying down ink in the color shown. If we view Plate 34 in white light, one disk will appear yellow, because its pigment subtracts the complement (blue) from the incident white light. When the yellow and cyan pigments are blended, one sees green, since both the blue and the red components have been removed. The center is black, because all the components have been removed.

12.4.3 The HLS Color Model

A more intuitive color model uses coordinates hue (H), lightness (L), and saturation (S) to describe colors, because these are qualities that the human eye easily recognizes and can distinguish. The model arises from a distortion of the RGB cube into a double cone, as shown in Figure 12.17. By looking along the diagonal of the RGB cube from $(1, 1, 1)$ to $(0, 0, 0)$, the six principal hues (R, G, B, and their three complements) are seen to lie on the vertices of a hexagon. Thus, hue can be associated with an angle between 0 and 360 degrees. Convention puts 0 degrees at red. Lightness varies from 0, when all the RGB components are 0, to 1, when they all are 1. This arrangement corresponds nicely to the distance along the diagonal of the RGB cube from black to white. Saturation, which is roughly the distance a color lies away from the diagonal of the RGB cube, is mapped into radial distance from the lightness axis of the HLS cones.

The HLS color space is based on a distortion of the RGB space, leading us to seek an algorithm that maps elements from one system to the other. The distortion is quite complex, so we do not insist on an exact geometric transformation. The principal algorithm converting from RGB into HLS coordinates is shown in Figure 12.18. Note that the algorithm pays the most attention to the largest and smallest of the R, G, and B components, but it provides a useful conversion and is invertible. (See the exercises at the end of the section.). Some examples follow the fragment of code.

Worked-out Examples of the Conversion

1. Find H, L, and S for a pure green: $(r, g, b) = (0, 1, 0)$. From the algorithm shown in Figure 12.18, we see that $mx = 1$ and $mn = 0$, so the lightness $hls.l = 0.5$.

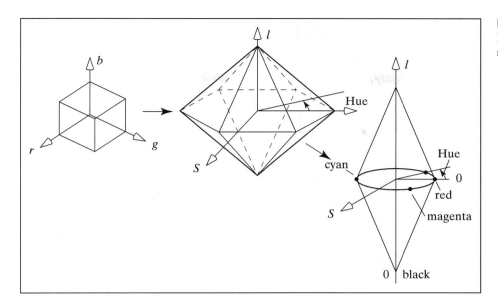

FIGURE 12.17 Warping the RGB system to the HLS system.

FIGURE 12.18 Conversion from the RGB into the HLS color system.

```
class RGBColor{public: double r, g, b;};
class HLSColor{public: double h, l, s;};

RGB_to_HLS (RGBColor rgb, HLSColor& hls)
{// convert (r, g, b), each in [0, 1], to h, l, s
    double mx, mn;
    RGBColor tmp;
    mx = MAX(rgb.r, rgb.g, rgb.b);
    mn = MIN(rgb.r, rgb.g, rgb.b);
    hls.l =(mx + mn) / 2.0;    // compute lightness
    if (mx == mn) // compute saturation
     hls.s = 0.0;  // color is gray
    else {     // color is chromatic
     if(hls.l <= 0.5)   hls.s = (mx - mn)/(mx + mn);
     else hls.s = (mx - mn)/(2 - mx + mn);
     // compute hue
     tmp.r =(mx - rgb.r)/(mx - mn);
     tmp.g =(mx - rgb.g)/(mx - mn);
     tmp.b =(mx - rgb.b)/(mx - mn);
     if (rgb.r == mx) hls.h = tmp.b - tmp.g;
     else if (rgb.g == mx) hls.h  = 2 + tmp.r - tmp.b;
     else if (rgb.b == mx) hls.h = 4 + tmp.g - tmp.r:
     hls.h * = 60;
     if(hls.h < 0.0)
     hls.h += 360;
     }
}
```

Based on this *hls.l*, we get a saturation of *hls.s* = 1.0, which is reasonable, as this is a pure color. Finally, *tmp.r* = *tmp.b* = 1, and *rbg.g* is the largest, so *hls.h* = 2, yielding *hls.h* = 120°, as expected. Thus, $(r, g, b) = (0, 1, 0)$ implies that $(H, L, S) = (120°, 0.5, 1.0)$.

2. Find H, L, S for a shade of gray: $(r, g, b) = (.4, .4, .4)$. Here, $mx = 0.4$ and $mn = 0.4$, so $hls.l = 0.4$. Because $mx = mn$, the light is achromatic, with saturation $hls.s = 0$. In this case, the hue is not defined.

PRACTICE EXERCISES

12.4.2. Perform some conversions

Find (H, L, S) for each of the following cases, and explain why the result is reasonable:

$(r, g, b) = (.2, .8, .1)$;
$(r, g, b) = (0, 0, .8)$;
$(r, g, b) = (1, 1, 1)$;
$(r, g, b) = (0, .7, .7)$.

12.4.3. HLS-to-RGB conversion

Work out an algorithm, $HLS\_to\_RGB(\ )$, that converts from HLS into RGB coordinates. It should provide an inverse transformation to the RBG-to-HLS conversion that we discussed, in that it recovers the original R, G, B values when applied to the H, L, S values obtained by using the preceding algorithm.

12.4.4. The HSV color model

Another color model, the hue (H), saturation (S), and value (V) system, is also based on a warped version of the RGB cube, but is a single cone rather than a double one, as suggested in Figure 12.19. In this model, hue is again mapped to angle (with the hexagon distorted into a circle, as in the HLS system, and the saturation having the same interpretation as in the HLS system). The light's intensity is captured in the value V, which varies from 0 to 1 as shown. Develop an algorithm that converts from RGB into HSV coordinates. ■

FIGURE 12.19 The HSV color model.

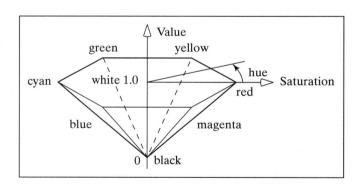

12.5 COLOR QUANTIZATION

In rendering a scene, an enormous number of floating-point color triples (I_r, I_g, I_b) are generated, one for each pixel in the image. Chapter 10 discussed strategies for converting such color triples to binary values that can be sent to a display or placed in a file for later use. A common approach is to convert each floating-point value to a single byte, so the image is represented by "true-color" pixel values, with 24 bits per pixel. It is also common for scanners to produce true-color image files in digitizing a photograph.

But two serious problems must be dealt with:

• Some displays are unable to handle 24-bit colors. Although plummeting memory costs are making 24-bit displays more affordable, many displays are much more limited. They might be built to handle only five bits each for red, green, and blue, or they might be built with an LUT that has only 256 entries, each of which allows, say, six bits each for red, green, and blue.

- True-color images can be very large, requiring considerable amounts of disk space or taking inordinate amounts of time to transmit over a network. (Designers of Web pages want to use only small images that will download quickly; otherwise customers won't visit their pages.)

We therefore need methods for reducing the size of color images and for reducing the number of colors contained in them. For instance, we need a way of choosing the "best" 256 colors found in a true-color image and replacing all of the other colors in the image by "good" substitutes from the list of 256. This process is commonly known as **color quantization.** The problem is as follows: Given N color triples, find K colors that do the best job of representing the original colors. (Normally, K is much smaller than N.) For each original color, find the closest *representative*. If desired, replace the original color triple by the index $0, 1, \ldots, K - 1$ of its best representative.

There are many questions to be answered in tackling this problem, such as what "best" and "closest" mean. Also, since N is so large, any worthwhile algorithm must be efficient. We look at four different methods for reducing the colors in an image. In each case, we assume that the original image is stored in a file of RGB color triples[4]—either floating-point triples or byte triples.

A useful first preprocessing step is to scan the file of triples in order to determine the range of pixel triples residing in the image. In particular, we look for the extreme values of each of the three color components: r_{min} and r_{max} for the r component, g_{min} and g_{max} for the green, and so forth. These values define a parallelepiped in RGB-space, as suggested by Figure 12.20. The entire **color population** resides within this block.

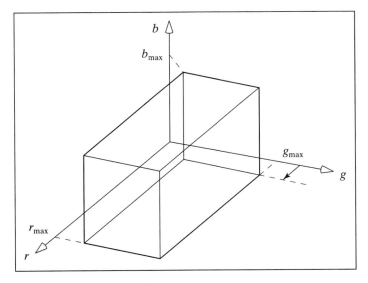

FIGURE 12.20 A color population residing in a color block.

Think of a large number of dots, each representing a color, scattered in different regions of the block. Some colors may be repeated many times; others might lie in tight clusters; still others might be "loners," with no neighbors over a significant portion of

---

[4] Alternatively, it might improve things to convert the RGB colors into some other system, such as HSV or CIE, and then to quantize values in this new system.

the block. Questions abound: If many dots lie in a compact region, should we replace them all by a color near the center of the cluster? If a color occurs many times, but has no nearby neighbors, should we attempt to represent it with high precision?

12.5.1 Uniform Quantization

The simplest approach is to subdivide the color block along color axes into a number of non-overlapping subblocks and to choose as the representative of each subblock a color value near its center. But how should the color block be subdivided? The block is subdivided by "slicing" it along each of the three axes, as shown in Figure 12.21. This allows the red, green, and blue components of the color representatives to be chosen independently. For instance, if $K = 256$, the red range $r_{min}, \ldots, r_{max}$ might be divided into eight slices, the green into eight, and the blue into four, creating exactly 256 subblocks. Alternatively, we might break both the red and blue into six slices and the green into seven slices, to produce a total of 252 subregions. (If an LUT is being loaded, four entries could go unused, or they could be loaded with colors for some border or text annotation.)

FIGURE 12.21 Slicing the color block.

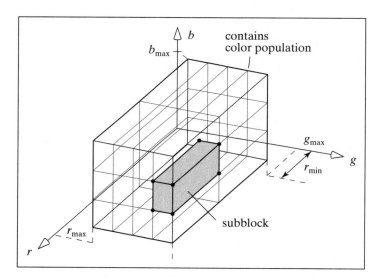

An equally important consideration is where to locate the color representatives, which are digital values that must "fit" in the LUT entries. For instance, suppose there are four bits in each entry for the green value, permitting green intensities from 0 to 15 (0000 to 1111 in binary). If we decide on six slices for green, which six values between 0 and 15 should we select? Note that the actual green brightness that corresponds to level 15 can be set independently on most raster displays by adjusting a control knob on the front panel of the display. For such terminals, only the relative intensities must be encoded. An example will help clarify how the various ingredients interact.

■ EXAMPLE 12.5.1.

Consider a typical case in which the LUT has $K = 256$ entries, each of which contains four bits for each of the red, green, and blue intensities. The image file of ordered triples is scanned, and it is found that r_{min}, g_{min}, and b_{min} all are very close to 0 and that $r_{max} = 4.0$, $g_{max} = 7.0$, and $b_{max} = 3.0$. How can we map triples into LUT values?

We decide to use seven representatives for green and six each for red and blue. We also choose, for simplicity, to space the representative values as evenly as we can over the 16 possible LUT values. For the red and blue colors, the six values 0, 3, 6, 9, 12, and 15 do a fine job. For green, we can't achieve an equal spacing, but the values 0, 3, 5, 8, 11, 13, and 15 provide a reasonable choice.

Now how are these values stored in LUT entries? An array `int r[6]` is created to store the six red values, and similarly for the arrays `g[]` and `b[]`. For instance, `r[]` holds the six values 0, 3, 6, 9, 12, and 15. As shown in Figure 12.22, three embedded loops cycle through all combinations of the values stored in these arrays, and for each combination, a single 12-bit number is created and stored in the `LUT[ ]` array.

```
#define numRed 6
#define numGreen 7
#define numBlue 6
#define pack(r,g,b) (256 * (r)+ 16 * (g) + (b))

for(rd = 0; rd < numRed; rd++)
  for(grn = 0; grn < numGreen; grn++)
    for(blu = 0; blu < numBlue; blu++)
    {
        index = numRed * numGreen * rd + numBlue * grn + blu;
        LUT[index] = pack(r[rd],g[grn],b[blu]);
    }
```

FIGURE 12.22 Loading the LUT.

The macro `pack` multiplies the red value by 256 to shift it into the upper four most significant bits of the LUT entry. It shifts the green value similarly. For instance, when `rd`, `grn`, and `blu` are 3, 2, and 5, respectively, the index into the LUT is 133, and the value composed from `r[3] = 9`, `g[2] = 5`, and `b[5] = 15` is 2,399, which is 95F in hexadecimal, as desired.

Now when the pixel list of triples (r_i, g_i, b_i) for the image file is rescanned, each r_i is compared with the six red representatives, and the nearest one is identified: Find j_r such that r_i is closest to $r[j\_r]$. For instance, if $r_i = 8.23$, the closest value will be 9, so $j\_r = 3$. The same steps are followed to identify index values j_g and j_b. Then the index value into the LUT itself is computed as $j = 42*j\_r + 6*j\_g + j\_b$.

This uniform quantization approach is rather hapless; it takes no account of the color population and learns nothing from scanning the original file of colors (except for the values of r_{max}, g_{max}, and b_{max}). It can work adequately for some images, however, particularly if the number of bits per pixel is large and the LUT offers a large palette.

Plate 35 shows an original true color image, and Plate 36 shows the result of quantizing that image as we have described. Notice large amounts of **banding** in regions of the image where there is a color gradient (a smooth variation of color across the image): Many slightly different color neighbors are replaced by a single representative, leading to regions of a fixed color when there should be a smooth variation in color.

PRACTICE EXERCISE

12.5.1. Trying out some values

Show the first 20 entries of the LUT in example 12.5.1. Does this seem like an orderly arrangement? What is stored in `LUT[29]`? What about `LUT[231]`? ■

12.5.2 The Popularity Algorithm

The popularity algorithm [Heckbert82] at least tries to determine which colors occur often in the file. It gives those colors greater priority, even if many of the most popular colors lie very close together. The basic method is to form a list of the number of times each color occurs in the file and to sort this list. Then the first K colors in the sorted list are the K most popularly occurring colors.

Because there are so many possible values for a true-color three-byte value (2^{32} of them), the problem is simplified by first truncating each red, green, and blue byte to five bits, leaving $2^{15} = 32K$ possible color values. An array of length 32K is then allocated and its elements are set to zero. The file is scanned, and as each color is read, the corresponding element in the array is incremented. When all N color values have been read, the array is sorted and the K most frequent colors are accepted as the color representatives.

Now when the file is rescanned, each color encountered (rd, grn, blu) must be replaced by the closest representative $(r, g, b)[i]$ in the popularity list. The minimum mean squared distance is often taken as a measure of "closest":

Find that value of *i* for which $(rd - r[i])^2 + (grn - g[i])^2 + (blu - b[i])^2$ is the smallest.

This can be an expensive operation.

12.5.3 The Median-cut Algorithm

The median-cut algorithm was introduced by Heckbert [Heckbert82]. It subdivides the color block into K subblocks such that each subblock has approximately the same number of color dots. Figure 12.23 shows the basic process, in 2D for clarity. (Suppose that colors have only a red and green component.) In Figure 12.23(a), the original color cube is first subdivided along its longest dimension: The *median* value r_1 is found such that $N/2$ dots occur in one subblock and $N/2$ occur in the other. Then each of these subblocks is processed similarly: sliced at the median along its longest dimension. The process continues until there are K subblocks. The color representative for each subblock is taken as the center of the subblock. Figure 12.23(b) shows some sample subblocks after seven cuts have been made.

FIGURE 12.23 The median-cut process at work (for 2D colors).

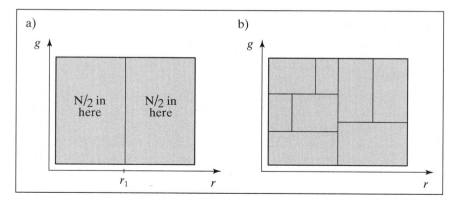

One simple way to organize the process is to use a queue of subblocks. An appropriate data structure is defined that holds the dimensions of the block and a pointer to the list of colors the block contains. At each stage, one subblock is dequeued and split into two subblocks at the median of the longest dimension. Each of these is then enqueued for later processing. (The procedure is reminiscent of a "breadth-first" creation of a tree.) The following pseudocode suggests how the median-cut algorithm works:

```
numBlocks = 1;                    // have one block so far
put original color block on the queue
while(numBlocks < K)
{
     thisBlock = delQueue();  // dequeue a block
     if(thisBlock contains more than one color)
     {
         find the median along the longest side
         make two blocks B₁, B₂ : split at the median
         addQueue(B₁); addQueue(B₂); // enqueue them
         numBlocks++;                 // have a net gain of one block
     }
     else addQueue(thisBlock); // just put it back in queue
}
```

At this juncture we have K subblocks, which can be numbered $0, 1, \ldots, K - 1$. Now the file is read again, and each color is tested to see which subblock it lies within. Heckbert [Heckbert82] suggests efficient ways to do this.

Plate 37 shows the same image as Plate 35, after the median-cut algorithm has been used to reduce the number of colors to 256. Some banding is still is visible.

12.5.4 Octree Quantization

Gervautz and Purgathofer[Gervautz90] suggested an efficient method based on an octree (a tree data structure in which each node has up to eight children) for reducing the number of colors in a file to K. In essence, the method reads the color file and builds an octree of colors, representing colors perfectly until K different colors have been encountered. Then, as each additional new color is read, it is added to the octree, but the octree is then "reduced," so it again contains no more than K different colors. The reduction process forces certain colors to be "lumped together" (into their color representative) and thus replaces colors by some nearby approximation. When all N colors in the file have been read, the octree contains K (or slightly fewer) color representatives. The octree is traversed and an index is assigned to each color representative.

The file is then read again, and as each color is encountered, it is inserted back into the tree and quickly "finds it place"—either its perfect representation at the bottom of the tree or at some intermediate node where its best color representative resides. The index of this node is then returned, denoting which color the current one is.

It is interesting to see how the octree structure is exploited to make this process efficient without excessive demands for memory. Figure 12.24 shows a portion of the octree: Each node contains some information about the colors that have been added to the octree. Each node also contains eight pointers to its children. When a color is inserted into the tree, its existence is recorded by "growing" a path down to level eight. Figure 12.25 shows a specific example in which the $R, G,$ and B bytes are displayed (in binary notation). Examine individual bits of the (R, G, B) triple, starting at the most significant bit each of $R, G,$ and B, here given by 101. This represents five in binary, so the path follows child number 5. If that child is so far empty, a new node is created and attached. The process then repeats with the next most significant bit triple (011), so the path looks at child number 3. After five more iterations, the least significant bits (110) of the color are examined, and the path follows child number 6. If a leaf node is present there (because this color has been encountered before in the file), the number of colors (which is one of the fields of a node) is incremented. Otherwise a leaf node is created, with a color count of 1. Note that the depth of the octree

FIGURE 12.24 The octree
containing four colors.

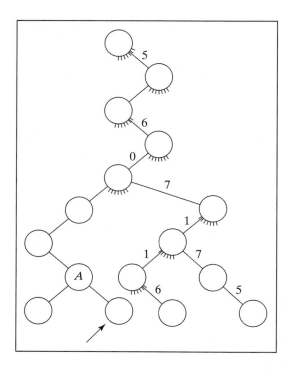

never exceeds eight, and inserting a color is fast, requiring no more than eight calculations of a child index.

Each node at depth 8 represents a color perfectly (to 24 bits of precision), whereas interior nodes represent subblocks of colors. For instance, a node at level 3 represents all colors having a specific set of three most significant bits for R, G, and B, but
arbitrary succeeding bits.

FIGURE 12.25 A sample path
from the root to the color's leaf.

R =	1	0	1	0	1	0	0	1
G =	0	1	1	0	1	0	0	1
B =	1	1	0	0	1	1	1	0
child:	5	3	6	0	7	1	1	6

When the octree contains more than K colors, it is reduced. A "reducible" node
(one with at least two children) is found at the lowest level possible. (The node marked
A in Figure 12.24 is a reducible node.) To reduce the octree, the children of the reducible node are deleted (which releases storage for use by future nodes), and the
node is marked as a leaf. The node already contains summary information about the
color occurrences that resided in its children. Each reduction reduces the number of
different colors in the octree by one less than the number of children deleted. (Why?)
Now additional colors can be inserted into the octree.

As described more fully in Case Study 12.7, each node keeps track of certain information, which includes the following, in code:

```
long numTimes;                   // # colors seen in this sub-block
long rSum, gSum, bSum;           // sum of color values accumulated
int isLeaf;                      // 1 if this node is a leaf
```

As each color (R, G, B) is inserted into the octree, every node in its path gets updated information:

```
numTimes++;     // encountered another color in this sub-block
rSum += R;      // total amount of red encountered
gSum += G;
bSum += B;
```

Therefore, when a node is reduced (i.e., when its children are deleted), it already contains the required information about everything that "happened" in the subtree below it. Later, when the tree is scanned to associate an index with each leaf, the color representative of the leaf is simply the average color:

$$\text{color representative} = \left(\frac{rSum}{numTimes}, \frac{gSum}{numTimes}, \frac{bSum}{numTimes} \right)$$

Finally, when the N colors are read from the file a second time, each color is traced down its path until it encounters a leaf, and the index is retrieved. Since each path is no longer than eight nodes, the process is fast.

Case Study 12.7 describes more details of the octree quantization method and urges you to experiment with it.

Gervautz and Purgathofer [Gervantz90] provide some opinions and estimates of the computer resources required for each method. They claim that the octree method produces results that are comparable in quality to those formed using the median-cut algorithm, but with much less processing time and memory required.

Plate 38 shows the same image as Plate 35, after the octree quantization method has been used to reduce the number of colors to 256. Some banding is still visible.

12.6 SUMMARY

The eye–brain system perceives colors in a complex way. The color of a light may be specified precisely according to its spectral density function, but this is an inconvenient format for communicating information about color, and in addition, the same perceived color can arise from myriad different spectral densities. In fact, our perception of color is three dimensional, so we need methods for describing color through a triple of numbers.

The CIE standard provides a precise approach to specifying colors. Any color S of unit brightness is described by two numbers (x, y). The notion is that S is created by adding the proper amounts of three special primary lights, X, Y, and Z, as defined by the standard. Specifically, $S = xX + yY + (1 - x - y)Z$. The special primary colors—which are supersaturated and cannot actually be seen—are chosen so that any pure spectral color (based on a single wavelength of light) can be formed by using positive amounts of x and y. The CIE chromaticity diagram provides a useful worldwide standard for describing colors and calculating the ingredients of a given color. The diagram is also used to display the gamut of colors that can be formed by adding together various amounts of available primary colors.

Some methods convert the colors described in one color system into those of another system, so that one can convert from CIE coordinates into more familiar RGB coordinates. Other color spaces are commonly used as well, such as hue, saturation, and lightness.

When computing colored images (based, for instance, on an illuminated 3D scene), the range of colors that the renderer produces is not known until rendering is finished, so it is difficult to display an image while rendering is underway. A good approach is to file all of the pixel 3-tuples as they are calculated, and then to scan this file to determine the color population of the image. Once the color population is known, one can set up appropriate mappings between color 3-tuples and values that a display device can handle. This may involve choosing a set of colors to load into a LUT. Because many devices can display only a limited number of colors, it is often necessary to reduce the number of colors found in an image. Several methods for color quantization have been developed. They vary in the difficulty of programming them, their computational efficiency, and the quality of the final image they can produce.

12.7 CASE STUDIES

CASE STUDY 12.1 DRAWING THE CIE CHART

Level of Effort: II. Write a program that draws the CIE chart, and illuminates each point (x, y) in the chart with an approximation to the color represented by (x, y). Draw the triangle that (approximately) designates the color gamut of the display being used. For those (x, y) that lie outside the color gamut of the display, draw in black.

CASE STUDY 12.2 DRAWING RGB SPACE

Level of Effort: II. Write a program that displays a "slice" through the RGB color cube of Figure 12.14. Points on the slice are shown in their proper color. Arrange so the user can choose the slicing plane (i.e. choose the constants a, b, c, and d of the plane $aR + bG + cB = d$) with the mouse.

CASE STUDY 12.3 HSV TO RGB

Level of Effort: II. Write a program that allows the user to choose values of H, S, and V with the mouse, displays the resulting color in a square on the screen, and prints out the corresponding RGB values for the color.

CASE STUDY 12.4 UNIFORM COLOR QUANTIZATION

Level of Effort: III. Write a program that lets you experiment with uniform color quantization. An image is read in from a file and two versions are displayed side by side on the screen: the full color on the left and the quantized version on the right. The user chooses the allowed number of red, green, and blue values (e.g. 8, 7, and 4, respectively), and the program computes the quantized colors and recalculates the image to be displayed.

CASE STUDY 12.5 POPULARITY COLOR QUANTIZATION

Level of Effort: III. Write a program that lets you experiment with the popularity color quantization method. A true color image is read in from a file. The user then chooses the allowed number K of different colors. The program scans the image, quantizing RGB triples to 15 bits, computes the histogram of color values, sorts the array, and uses the most popular K values. The image is then rescanned and for each pixel the best match of the K representatives is displayed. Two versions of the image are displayed side by side on the screen: the full color on the left and the quantized version on the right.

CASE STUDY 12.6 MEDIAN CUT COLOR QUANTIZATION

Level of Effort: III. Write a program that lets you experiment with the median cut color quantization algorithm. Obtain code that performs the algorithm either from the internet or from a book such as [lindley92]. A true color image is read in from a file. The user then chooses the allowed number K of different colors. The program scans the image, and finds the K representatives determined by the median cut method. The image is then rescanned and for each pixel the best match of the K representatives is displayed. Two versions are displayed side by side on the screen: the full color on the left and the quantized version on the right.

CASE STUDY 12.7 OCTREE COLOR QUANTIZATION

Level of Effort: III. Write a program that lets you experiment with the octree color quantization algorithm. Either write the algorithm yourself, or obtain code that performs the algorithm either from the internet or from a book such as [lindley92]. A true color image is read in from a file. The user then chooses the allowed number K of different colors. The program scans the image, builds the octree with K representatives, and then traverses the octree to attach an index to each leaf. The image is then rescanned, and for each pixel the appropriate index is found in the octree and that color is displayed. Two versions are displayed side by side on the screen: the full color on the left and the quantized version on the right.

A useful data type for an octree node is:

```
class Node{
  public:
  int isLeaf;          // 1 if this node is a leaf
  int whichLevel;      // the level this node is at
  int index;           // its LUT index — assigned in pass 2
  int numChildren;     // number of children this node has
  long numTimes;       // # colors seen in this sub-block
  long Rsum, Gsum, BSum;// sum of color values accumulated
  Node* nextCand;// candidate for reducing at this level
  Node* child[8];// the 8 children of this node
};
```

Skeletons of some of the key routines are given below.

```
insertTree(Node& node, BYTE rgb[])
{ // insert 24-bit color rgb into subtree
     if(node == NULL)
          makeNewNode(node); // make & initialize a new node
     if(node.isLeaf)
     {
          node.numTimes++;   // inc # of pixels represented
          addColors(node, rgb); // sum the color values
     }
     else
          childIndex = 4 * rgb[0] + 2 * rgb[1] + rgb[2];
          insertTree(childIndex, rgb);
}
```

How to find a reducible node? Maintain an array, reducible[], of seven stacks, one for each level of the tree. reducible[i] contains pointers to tree nodes at level i that are known to be reducible (they have more than one child). As each color is inserted into the octree it follows a specific path and/or builds new nodes in the path towards a leaf. At each node visited (except the final leaf node) the number of children is incremented by one and then tested: if the number of children is exactly 2 the node has just become reducible and a pointer to it is pushed onto the appropriate stack.

When the tree must be reduced the stacks are tested working back from $i = 7$ to smaller i: the first non-empty stack reducible[i] points to a reducible node, which is popped from that stack and reduced.

```
void reduceTree(void)
{
     thisNode = findReducibleNode();
     thisNode.isLeaf = 1;
     numLeaves -= (thisNode.numChildren - 1);
     freeChildren(thisNode);
}
```

12.8 FURTHER READING

The Feynman chapter on color [Feynman63] is beautifully written and is a classic introduction to color theory. Billmeyer gives a very thorough discussion of the technology of color [Billmeyer81]. And Rogers [Rogers90] provides a solid introduction to color and its management in computer graphics.

13 Elimination of Hidden Surfaces

Why hidest thou thy face from me?

Psalms 88:14

Behind a frowning providence he hides a shining face.
William Cowper, "Light Shining Out of Darkness," 1779

Goals of the Chapter

▲ To add greater realism to pictures by eliminating hidden surfaces on solid objects.

▲ To survey several techniques for removing hidden surfaces.

▲ To develop, in detail, some fundamental methods for removing hidden surfaces.

▲ To develop a method for removing hidden lines.

PREVIEW

Rendering 3D scenes requires overcoming the twin problems of hidden-surface removal (HSR) and hidden-line removal (HLR). Section 13.1 discusses the importance and difficulty of dealing with these probelms. The section describes the difference between "image precision" and "object precision" algorithms and develops a useful data structure for holding all of the polygonal faces in a scene, preprocessed for rapid HSR. Section 13.2 revisits the depth-buffer algorithm developed in Chapter 8 to see how it fits in with other HSR methods.

Section 13.3 describes three HSR methods based on sorting the list of faces of the object in clever ways so that a renderer can draw the faces in a new order, properly hiding those faces that lie behind other faces. Successful methods, such as the binary-space partition tree approach, require that certain faces be split into two pieces. Section 13.4 describes a scan-line HSR method that determines which of the many possible faces in a scene is closest to the eye "at a given pixel" and then draws the pixel, once for each pixel.

Section 13.5 discusses "divide-and-conquer" HSR methods based on subdividing the viewport into a (large) number of regions, inside of which the HSR problem is easy to solve. Section 13.6 introduces an HLR method that draws all of the visible edges of objects in a scene. The method need not do any erasing or painting over; it completely determines the visibility of each part of each edge before drawing that part.

Section 13.7 describes the issues, surrounding the HSR problem for scenes made up of curved surfaces when one does not want to approximate the surfaces with polygons. A number of solutions to this problem are offered. The chapter closes with several case studies designed to fix the various ideas of the algorithms and to produce working rendering programs that correctly remove hidden surfaces.

13.1 INTRODUCTION

Any program that attempts to render 3D scenes realistically must cope with the **hidden surface-removal** (HSR) problem. Most objects in a scene are opaque, and the program should not draw any portion of an object that lies "behind" an opaque object, as seen from the camera's point of view. This is a problem even when only a single object is involved. Figure 13.1(a) shows an object whose faces have been shaded in haphazard order, with each face drawn on top of those previously drawn. The results are unintelligible. Figure 13.1(b) is a correct rendering: Only the portions of each face actually visible to the eye have been shaded. Algorithms must be employed that remove the hidden parts of each surface.

FIGURE 13.1 Drawing faces in different orders.

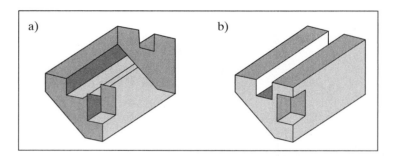

We have already examined two approaches to dealing with the HSR problem. "Back-face removal" was described in Chapter 7. The method works reliably only when the scene consists of a single object, and it can fail if the object is not convex. Though simple and useful in some situations, back-face removal would not be classified as a true HSR method. In Chapter 8, we developed a very serviceable HSR method based on a depth buffer. This method works for a wide variety of scenes and is very simple to program.

Why bother looking at any other methods? Either a hidden-surface algorithm works, or it doesn't. This is in contrast to shading and antialiasing algorithms, wherein one approach can produce better looking results than another. Some HSR methods work "perfectly" on scenes made up of any kind of objects, whereas others are designed to work only with particular classes of objects (such as polygonal meshes having convex faces). The issue with HSR algorithms is the usual one of time and space: Within a class of methods, what distinguishes one method from another is how long it takes to execute and how much extra memory is required.

In the case of the depth-buffer algorithm, a significant amount of time is "wasted" rendering surfaces that are later covered by other surfaces: The algorithm carefully renders each surface and is oblivious to the possibility that some other surface will later obscure the current one. The algorithm also requires a great deal of memory to maintain a depth buffer of sufficient precision. Its hunger for memory is becoming less of a limitation as memory gets ever cheaper. But memory is always a finite resource, and rendering programs seem to constantly need more of it, in order to manipulate, for instance, a large number of images with texture. The depth-buffer approach also must struggle with aliasing effects, as we discussed in Chapter 10.

So, over the history of computer graphics, people have been searching for different approaches to the HSR problem that demand less memory or that are particularly efficient with regard to certain classes of scenes. There is a long tradition in computer graphics for trying to come up with yet one more "better" HSR scheme. A large number of them are surveyed in [Sutherland74].

A problem closely related to HSR is **hidden-line removal** (HLR). This problem applies to line drawings in which the edges of each face are drawn. Figure 13.2(a) shows a wire-frame view of an object: All edges are drawn in their entirety. In Part (b), only the portion of each edge that is in fact visible to the eye has been drawn. Some edges, such as E_1, have not been drawn at all, whereas others, such as E_2, have been drawn only in part: E_2 is effectively clipped at the point where it intersects edge E_3.

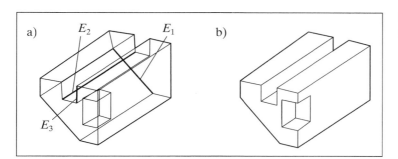

FIGURE 13.2 Hiding occluded edges.

In this chapter, we examine various HLR and HSR algorithms, lumping them together under the name *hidden-surface-removal* algorithms owing to their similarity. The goal of these algorithms is to identify efficiently which parts of one surface or edge are occluded by some other surface. The means of doing this lie in a complex interaction between the positions of the viewer and the various objects in the scene.

The focus in this chapter is on scenes composed of polygonal mesh objects, but other classes of object are discussed as well. In Chapter 14 we will see that ray tracing offers a very different approach to the HSR problem. With ray tracing, hidden surfaces of any shape are automatically removed, although at the expense of a great deal of computation.

13.1.1 Object-Precision versus Image-Precision Approaches

Algorithms to remove hidden lines or surfaces take different forms, depending on the following distinction, described in [Sutherland74]:

- *Object Precision.*[1] The algorithm computes, to the precision of the machine, the coordinates of each visible edge of each face. Algorithms of this type are implemented in the physical coordinate system in which the objects are described. This kind of precision is useful for engineering drawings. With the use of an object-precision approach, a picture can be enlarged many times, and the results will still be accurate.
- *Image Precision*. For each display pixel, the algorithm determines which element of which face is the closest to the viewer and draws the pixel in the appropriate shade. Image-precision algorithms are implemented only to the precision of the screen window coordinate system.

HSR algorithms should operate as rapidly as possible. We are interested in how the computation time depends on the complexity of the objects in a scene, as well as on the number of such objects. If we informally denote the number of elements—edges

---

[1] The terms "object space" and "image space" are also commonly used to mark this distinction.

or faces—in a scene by n, we might expect that an object-precision HSR algorithm would take time $O(n^2)^2$, since every element must be tested against every other element to see which of them obscures which.

On the other hand, an image-precision algorithm might well grow in a different way. If there are N pixels in the display, we might expect such an algorithm to be $O(nN)$, since, for each of the N pixels, we must test each of n scene elements. In practice, N is much larger than n.

As we shall see, one goes to great lengths to use *coherence* in developing an HSR algorithm, in order to reduce the number of tests that must be conducted. The purpose is to reduce the growth of computations from $O(n^2)$ or $O(nN)$ to a more manageable growth, such as $O(n \log(n)), O(N \log(n))$, or even $O(n)$. An extensive study in [Sutherland74] provides useful time estimates for many popular HSR algorithms.

13.1.2 Description of the Polygon Mesh Data

To set the stage for an examination of different HSR methods, recall from Chapter 8 the processing that each face of a polygonal mesh undergoes as it moves down the graphics pipeline. (See Figure 13.3.) (We think in terms of using a pipeline like that of OpenGL because it is a natural way to "preprocess" vertices. We are, of course, considering ways to do HSR alternative to that provided by OpenGL, so we would not use the OpenGL pipeline directly.) The vertices of the face are subjected to the modelview and projection transformations and are clipped against the canonical view volume—a unit cube with pseudodepths ranging from 0 to 1. Clipping may cause some vertices to vanish and others to appear. Attributes such as the pseudodepth, texture coordinates, and vertex normals are computed for these new vertices by interpolation. Perspective division from homogeneous coordinates is then performed, and the x- and y-components of each vertex are mapped from the unit cube to the actual viewport on the screen. The values of x and y are in screen coordinates now, but not truncated to integers, since an object-precision HSR algorithm needs high-precision information on the positions of objects.

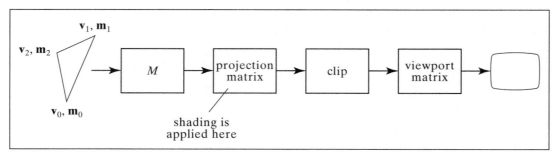

FIGURE 13.3 The graphics pipeline for polygonal faces.

At this point, therefore, the entire population of faces is contained in the "3D viewport" suggested in Figure 13.4. We denote the axes as (x, y, z) because those variables are so familiar, but keep in mind that the axes are not world coordinate axes, but those of a space prewarped by the perspective transformation. The z-axis measures pseudodepth, so points farther from the eye lie farther "into the screen." Depths vary from 0 to 1.

---

2   This is "big-Oh" notation often used to describe how complexity grows with the size of the task. Complexity is $O(n^2)$ if the time required is no more that some constant multiple of n^2, for very large values of n.

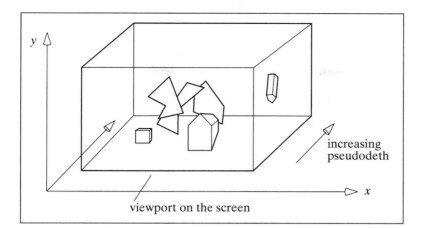

FIGURE 13.4 The 3D viewport containing the entire scene.

The prewarping produced by the projection matrix provides an important benefit for HSR algorithms: It separates information on position (x, y) from information on depth (z). If two points (x, y, z_1) and (x, y, z_2) have the same x- and y-components, so that one might occlude the other, we need only test the sizes of z_1 and z_2 to see which point is closer. (In world coordinates, depth is a complicated function of x, y, and z.)

In Chapter 8, we saw that each face was rendered as it was sent down the pipeline. But an HSR algorithm may need to examine all the faces before any rendering can be done. So we suppose that the faces are stored in the array

```
Face faces[maxNumFaces];
```

The type `Face` is an extension of that used in Chapter 6. It contains data that characterize the face in a form that can be conveniently accessed by the HSR routine and renderer. Figure 13.5 suggests how it might be organized. There are `nVerts` vertices in the face, and vertex data are stored in the arrays `pt[]` and `depth[]`. `pt[i]` holds the x and y coordinates of the `i`th vertex (in floating-point precision), and `depth[i]` holds the vertex's pseudodepth. Other fields can be included to increase the efficiency of the algorithm. For some HSR algorithms, the faces are inserted into a linked list or a binary tree, so some links to the next face in a list could be added.

```
class Face{
    int nVerts;         // number of vertices in vert array
    Point* pt;          // array of vertices in real screen coord's
    float* depth;       // array of vertex depths
    Plane plane;        // data for the plane of the face
    Cuboid extent;      // the extent of the face
    // other properties
};
```

FIGURE 13.5 Possible data type to hold face data.

The `plane` field holds data (m_x, m_y, m_z, D) for the plane equation $(m_x x + m_y y + m_z z = D)$ of the face, to be used as described later. Vector **m** is the outward-pointing normal vector to the face. Because this information is used to determine when one face is closer than another, we need the version of **m** and D for the plane expressed in the prewarped 3D viewport coordinate system.

The `extent` field describes the extent of the face. The **extent** (or *bounding box*) is a rectangular parallelepiped, with six walls aligned with the coordinate axes, that fits snugly about the polygon. Figure 13.6 shows a face enclosed in its extent. A suitable data type is `class Cuboid{float left, top, right, bott, near, far;}`. No point on the face lies closer to the eye than `near` or farther than `far`. The extent is usually a simpler geometric object than a polygon, so comparing the extents of two faces is quick and may make it unnecessary to do a complete comparison of the polygons themselves. The extent is easily computed. (See the exercises that follow.)

FIGURE 13.6 The extent of a face in three dimensions (stereo view).

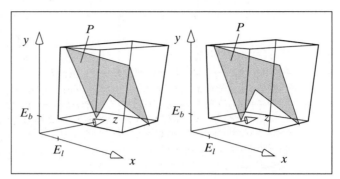

Other fields describe vertex normals, texture coordinates, surface properties of the face, reflection coefficients, etc.

PRACTICE EXERCISES

13.1.1

Given a face described in a `Face object`, write code that computes its extent. (Scan the vertices of the face to identify the largest and smallest x-, y-, and z-coordinates.)

13.1.2

Given a face described in a `Face` object, write code that computes its plane equation in `plane`. Is it better to compute the outward normal vector directly as a cross product (recall Chapter 4) or to transform the face's world coordinate plane? ■

13.2 THE DEPTH-BUFFER ALGORITHM REVISITED

To set the stage for a study of different HSR methods, recall from Chapter 8 the basic approach of the **depth buffer** (or "z-buffer") algorithm. The algorithm requires a depth buffer `d[x][y]` that records the closest thing seen so far at (x, y). It renders each face in turn and does not draw a pixel if the face has a depth greater than that encountered in the depth buffer (i.e., if a closer face obscures this one at (x, y)). The essential steps of the algorithm are shown in Figure 13.7.

FIGURE 13.7 Basic flow of the depth-buffer algorithm (pseudocode).

```
for (each face F)
      for (each pixel (x,y) covering the face)
      {
          depth = depth of F at (x,y);
          if(depth < d[x][y])        //F is closest so far
          {
              c = color of F at (x, y);
              set the pixel color at (x, y) to c
              d[x][y] = depth; // update the depth buffer
          }
      }
```

The depth-buffer algorithm has some welcome features in addition to simplicity:

- The faces can be drawn in any order from the `faces[]` list: No presorting of the list is needed. Unlike most HSR methods, which rely on one kind of sorting or another, there is no explicit sorting anywhere in depth-buffer approach—only a search for the closest face per pixel.
- The algorithm makes good use of **depth coherence** (the tendency for the depth of a face at one pixel to be close to, and easily computed from, the depth at nearby pixels) by calculating depths along a scan line incrementally, as described in Chapter 8. (Since it draws each face separately in scan-line order, the algorithm can also exploit **face coherence**—the tendency for certain properties, such as light intensity and the direction of the normal vector, to change slowly and predictably along a face.)
- Although we stress rendering polygonal meshes here, the depth-buffer method works just as well in the rendering of other classes of objects, such as Coons patches or quadric surfaces. The method requires only that the depth of the surface at each (x, y) can be found, for comparison with `d[][]`.
- If the depth buffer is saved in a file along with the image, it can be used another day to add new objects to a scene. Each new object is rendered using the most suitable technique, and pixels are drawn or are not drawn, depending on the depth of the object at different pixels.

But, as noted in Chapter 8, the algorithm has several properties that limit its use:

- It may draw a pixel many times. Each time a face is found to be closer at (x, y), an expensive shading calculation is done. This calculation is wasted if some face is found to be even closer later. (Some renderers perform a rough sort of the array `faces[]` such that the faces closest to the eye are drawn first. Then, as subsequent, more remote faces are rendered, the depth test `if(depth d[x][y])` fails most of the time, so little redrawing of pixels occurs.)
- A large amount of memory (one storage cell for each pixel) is needed to maintain the depth buffer. Each cell needs high precision (16 to 32 bits). (Bending terminology a little, we can say that the method works with "image precision" in depth as well as x and y.) Whatever precision is chosen may not be enough. When the depth buffer cannot resolve two slightly different depths, the wrong face may be drawn.[3] This is most problematic for remote faces having pseudodepths near their upper limit, due to the depth compression inherent in pseudodepth.

13.3 LIST-PRIORITY HSR METHODS

There is a large class of HSR algorithms that sort the `faces[]` array and draw the faces "back to front," so that nearer faces are drawn over more remote (and possibly occluded) faces. These algorithms constitute what are called *list-priority* methods, because the list `faces[]` is rearranged in ascending or descending priority, using a definition of priority that involves the depth of certain vertices. As we shall see, there may not be any arrangement of the array that produces the correct final picture. A successful algorithm must detect this conflict and adjust accordingly, usually by splitting a face into two pieces that separately do not produce any conflict.

---

[3] Suppose face A has depth 0.89485 at a certain pixel and tests as the closest face, but its depth is rounded to 0.895 in `d[][]`. Later, face B is found to have depth 0.89492 at this pixel and, when tested against the value 0.895, is calculated to be closer, so B is erroneously drawn!

706 **Chapter 13** ■ Elimination of Hidden Surfaces

In this section, we look at the following three algorithms:

- The "heedless painter's algorithm," which is simple, but faulty: It just paints whole faces in a back-to-front order.
- The binary-space partition tree algorithm, which is elegant and effective, but requires a preprocessing step to build a tree of faces. However, the same tree can be used many times to draw the scene from different viewpoints, as in an animation in which the camera moves through a fixed scene.
- The depth-sort algorithm, which is a classic HSR method based on sorting `faces[]`, with additional complex testing to fix the shortcomings of the painter's algorithm.

13.3.1 The Heedless Painter's Algorithm

The first attempt at producing an alternative to the depth-buffer approach is very simple, but often produces erroneous images, some as bad as that in Figure 13.1! Each face of the object is filled in turn *in its entirety*. This is a form of the *painter's algorithm*: As each face is painted into the frame buffer, its color paints over whatever was drawn there before, just as a painter covers old layers of paint with new ones. Thus, the color shown at each pixel is the most recently drawn color, and if two faces overlap in x and y, the last one drawn will obscure the first one, even if it is not closer.

To give this method at least a chance of drawing the scene properly, we use the `extent.far` field in the `face` array to determine which face has the most remote vertex, the second most remote, and so forth. The array `faces[]` is sorted using `extent.far` as the sort key, and the faces are then painted into the frame buffer, beginning with the farthest one, until finally the closest one is painted. A skeleton version of the algorithm therefore looks like the following:

Sort the `faces[]` list on the basis of the `extent.far` values;
paint entire faces, in order, from the farthest to the closest.

Note the presence of a sort routine in this algorithm. Sorting in one form or another is an integral part of most every HSR algorithm, since objects that are presented to the algorithm must be ordered in some way. (A variety of sort routines is readily found in any text on data structures and algorithms.)

When does the heedless painter's algorithm work? Figure 13.8 shows various situations involving two faces A and B. Each situation uses two orthographic views in concert. One view looks at the 3D viewport as a viewer would look at the screen, so the x- and y- axes are seen. The other looks down onto the 3D viewport from above, so depth increases in the upward, positive z- direction. (Forming a 3D picture in your mind from these two representations is challenging, but very useful.)

In Figure 13.8(a) the x-extents X_A and X_B of A and B overlap, as do the y-extents Y_A and Y_B, so we suspect that one face partially occludes the other. In the case shown, one face does occlude the other. But because their z-extents happen not to overlap, the heedless painter's algorithm works properly. Face A has the larger `extent.far` and so is drawn first, and then face B is drawn. There is no way, therefore, that A can partially obscure B.

In Figure 13.8(b) the faces are in slightly different positions, and the situation is quite different. Face A is the more remote according to the `extent.far` criterion, and so it is painted first, producing the result marked *error*. But in fact, because of its orientation, A is closer where it overlaps B, and so it should obscure B, thereby producing the result marked *truth*. (It is helpful to cut out some test faces from stiff paper and experiment with various orientations.) The situation in Figure 13.8(c) is even more complex: B interpenetrates with A. Here, the heedless painter's algorithm would mindlessly paint B over A.

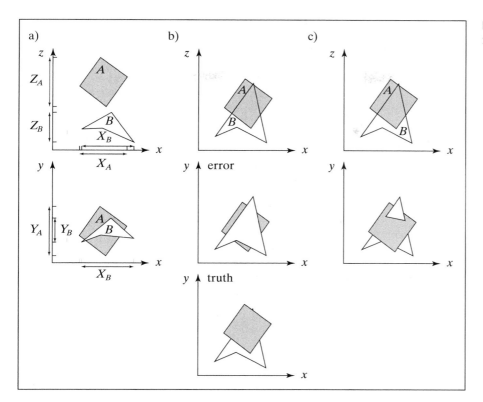

FIGURE 13.8 Depth ordering of faces.

The heedless painter's algorithm therefore fails to distinguish correctly which *portions* of one face overlap another. We cannot simply paint entire faces over one another on the basis of a single criterion such as maximum depth. We shall fix the painter's algorithm in Section 13.3.3 by performing additional tests on the faces involved. The resulting algorithm works correctly, but is significantly more complicated than the original.

PRACTICE EXERCISES

13.3.1 Occlusion?

Show that one face need not occlude another even when their x- and y-extents overlap.

13.3.2 When does the heedless painter's algorithm work?

What is the class of meshes for which this algorithm works for any view of a single object? (For instance, does it work for convex objects?) For objects not in this class, what condition causes the algorithm to fail? ■

13.3.2 HSR Using Binary-Space Partition Trees

An elegant method for removing hidden surfaces uses binary-space partition (BSP) trees [Fuchs80,Fuchs83]. In a preprocessing step, the polygons in `faces[]` are rearranged into a binary-tree data structure in a clever way, and certain faces are split into two pieces, so that the tree can be "traversed" in a systematic way to draw the scene with hidden surfaces properly removed. The BSP tree is **traversed** by visiting each of its nodes in turn (in some order) and drawing the face found in the node.

Building a BSP Tree

For ease of visualization, we introduce BSP trees using a 2D example involving edges. Because the organization of the tree does not depend on the dimensionality of the objects contained in the tree, the extension to a BSP of 3D polygons is immediate.

Figure 13.9 shows three polygons in the plane and an "eye" positioned at a certain point. The question is, What does the eye see? (If you prefer to think in 3D, imagine an observer standing in front of three large stone "pillars" rising out of the ground. The pillars have the cross-sectional shapes shown in the figure. Again, which parts of the walls of the pillars are visible, and which are obscured? Sketch the resulting scene for this example.) Each edge is given a number, and its outward-pointing normal vector is indicated. We wish to insert each edge into a tree in such a way that the plane is partitioned (or tesselated) into nonoverlapping polygonal regions.

FIGURE 13.9 A set of edges in 2D to be arranged in a BSP.

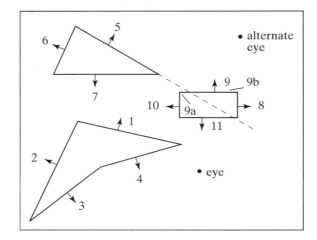

To begin building the tree for this set of edges, we take an edge, say, number 1. We extend this edge in both directions, whereupon it splits the plane into two half-spaces: the "outside" (the side pointed to by the outward-pointing normal to the edge) and the "inside." We put edge 1 into the root of the tree, as shown in Figure 13.10(a). Now we insert each of the other edges into the tree one by one: Those that lie in the outside half-space of edge 1 will go into the right subtree (labeled `outsideOnes`), and those that lie in the inside of edge 1 will go into the left subtree (labeled `insideOnes`). As each edge is inserted, it "finds its way" down the tree, comparing itself with each node it reaches. It goes to the `outsideOnes` subtree of the node if it lies on the outside of that node and to the `insideOnes` subtree otherwise, until it becomes attached to the tree as a new leaf.

FIGURE 13.10 Building the BSP tree.

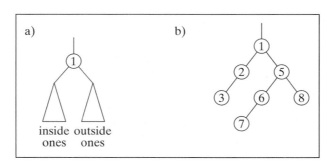

Figure 13.10(b) shows the status after seven more edges, numbered 2 through 8, have been inserted. Edge 2 lies on the inside half-space of edge 1, so it is placed in the `insideOnes` subtree. Edge 3 lies on the inside of both edge 1 and edge 2, so it finds its way to the position shown. (Check this!) Edge 4 is not shown; where does it go?

When we insert edge 9, something new happens. That edge lies on the outside of edge 1, but lies in both half spaces of edge 5. It is therefore **split** by edge 5 into two edges, 9a and 9b, as shown in Figure 13.9, and each of the pieces finds its way further down in the tree. Edge 9a lies on the inside of edge 5, so it goes down to the left and is tested against edges 6 and 7; edge 9b lies on the outside of edge 5, but on the inside of edge 8. Edges 10 and 11 are inserted in like manner and do not require splitting. (What does the final tree look like?)

The BSP tree lists the edges in a particular way, so that for any edge, you can quickly tell (by its position in the tree) in which "part" of space it lies (e.g., edge 6 lies on the outside of edge 1 and on the inside of edge 5). The tree's structure does not depend in any way on the position of the eye.

Notice that the order in which edges are inserted in the tree has a profound effect on the "shape" of the final tree. Some choices of ordering make the tree full and "shallow" (a small number of nodes from the root to the deepest leaf), while others make it scrawny and "deep." Shallow trees are more efficient to deal with. The worst case is a BSP tree in the shape of a single chain from top to bottom.

BSP Trees for 3D Scenes

The preceding ideas extend immediately to scenes composed of 3D polygon meshes. Consider the block shown in Figure 13.11(a). Each of its eight faces is numbered, and the outer-pointing normal vector is indicated. Part (b) shows another view of the same block. If the faces are inserted into a BSP tree in the order 1, 2, ..., 8, the tree shown in Part (c) is formed. (A face finds its way down the tree in the same way as in the 2D case: If it lies in the outside half-space of the node face, it goes to the `outsideOnes` subtree, etc.) Face 7 is split into faces 7a and 7b by the plane of face 3, as the dashed line in the figure indicates. Face 8 is also split. (Is there an order for inserting these faces such that *no* splits are necessary?) Case Study 13.2 presents more details on how to split a face.

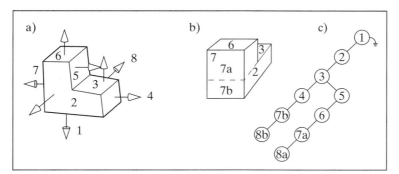

FIGURE 13.11 Building the BSP tree.

We examine how to build a BSP tree in a program in Case Study 13.3. In what follows next, we see how the BSP tree is used to draw a scene flawlessly.

Traversing the Tree (to Draw All the Faces)

To draw all of the faces of a scene in proper order, each node is visited in turn in a certain order, and the face contained in the node is rendered. (If it is a back face, the drawing can be skipped.)

How is the order of face drawing determined? It depends on the position of the camera's eye. Consider any face F in the tree, and suppose that the eye lies in the outside half-space of F. This means that all the faces in the `insideOnes` subtree of F lie on the other side of F from the eye, so none of them can possibly obscure F. We therefore draw all the faces in the `insideOnes` subtree of F and then draw F (which might paint over some of them). Now we can draw all the faces in the `outsideOnes` subtree of F, resting assured that they do not lie behind any face already drawn.

On the other hand, if the camera's eye lies in the inside half-space of F, we first draw all the faces in the `outsideOnes` subtree, then draw F, and then draw all the faces in the `insideOnes` subtree of F. But note that in this case F is always a "back face" (why?), so it is not actually drawn (unless there is a need to draw back faces).

The preceding discussion essentially constitutes the rule for drawing each subtree of the tree, so we obtain a recursive recipe for drawing the whole scene: To draw the entire scene, draw one subtree of the root (the choice being determined by the location of the eye), then draw the root, and finally, draw the other subtree of the root. Following is pseudocode corresponding to this rule:

```
To draw the faces stored in the BSP tree with root F,
if (the eye is in the "outside" half-space of face F )
{
      draw all faces in the inside subtree of F ;
      draw F ;
      draw all faces in the outside subtree of F ;
}
else   // the eye is on the "inside" of F
{     draw all faces in the outside subtree of F ;
      if (you want to draw back faces), draw F ;
      draw all faces in the inside subtree of F ;

}
```

This pseudocode can be recognized as a form of "inorder traversal" of the binary tree [Kruse91], where the order of traversing each subtree is determined by the position of the eye relative to the face of the subtree.

For the 3D scene in Figure 13.11(a), the tree in Part (c) can be traversed using this scheme, and the block will be drawn properly. Figure 13.12(a) shows arrows to indicate the order in which nodes of the BSP tree of Figure 13.11(c) are visited, for the particular view of the block shown in Figure 13.11(a). The order for drawing the faces is listed in Part (b). The underlined faces are back faces and are not actually drawn. (Check to make sure that the faces are drawn properly.)

If the eye is moved to another position, the same tree can be used to draw the scene, and the algorithm is unchanged. Figure 13.12(c) shows the order for drawing

FIGURE 13.12 Order for drawing the faces, given the position of the eye.

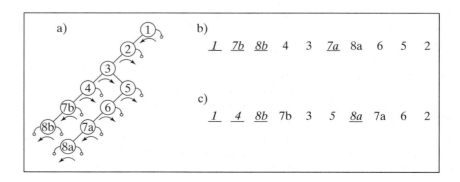

a)

b)   *1*   *7b*   *8b*   4   3   *7a*   8a   6   5   2

c)   *1*   *4*   *8b*   7b   3   5   *8a*   7a   6   2

the block when the eye is positioned to see it as in Figure 13.11(b). (See the exercises that follow for other examples.) The BSP algorithm is very attractive when many images must be formed in an animation as the camera moves around within a fixed scene. The preprocessing step that builds the tree is done only once. If the scene changes, however, a new BSP must be formed.

Case Study 13.2 discusses how to split a face with a plane. Case Study 13.3 examines routines for building a BSP tree in a program, and for drawing a scene stored in a BSP tree.

PRACTICE EXERCISES

13.3.3 Build a BSP tree in a different order

Draw the BSP tree formed when the edges of Figure 13.9 are inserted in the order 3, 6, 2, 7, 9, 10, 1, 11, 8, 5, 4.

13.3.4. BSP trees for convex polygons

What is the shape of the BSP tree for a convex polygon?

13.3.5 Drawing the pillars

Find the drawing order of the edges in Figure 13.9, using the BSP tree of Figure 13.10(b) (after completing the tree), for the position shown for the eye. Which edges are "back edges"? Is the scene drawn correctly? Repeat for the case where the eye is moved to the location labeled "alternative eye." Check that the scene is again drawn properly. ■

13.3.3 The Depth-Sort Algorithm

The depth-sort algorithm fixes the painter's algorithm by determining which parts of one face are in front of another face when the faces overlap in depth [Newell72]. The algorithm detects ambiguous situations and splits a face to resolve the ambiguity. Its basic steps are as follows:

- Sort the `faces[]` array according to `extent.far`, as in the painter's algorithm.
- Resolve ambiguities, rearranging the list and splitting faces as necessary.
- Render each face on the rearranged list, in order of decreasing `extent.far` (i.e., from back to front).

The new part is the second step, which does a thorough analysis of any polygons whose z-extents (the interval `extent.near` to `extent.far`) overlap.

Figure 13.13 shows various ambiguous cases that must be resolved. In Part (a), faces P and Q interpenetrate: Neither is completely in front of the other. The same is true in Part (b), in which Q is non-convex; the dashed line indicates where P will be split by the algorithm. And Part (c) shows two examples of cyclical overlap of three or four faces. A usable HSR algorithm must be able to resolve any of these situations, by properly splitting faces until, for any pair of faces, one lies entirely behind or entirely in front of the other.

The list `faces[ ]` is initially sorted by `extent.far`. Suppose P is the last polygon in the list (the farthest away). The painter's algorithm would just draw it outright. Instead, with the depth-sort algorithm, we test to see whether that polygon can obscure any other faces in `faces[ ]`. P can obscure another face only if its z-extent overlaps with that of the face. Therefore, for each face Q having a z-extent that overlaps P's we do a sequence of geometric tests to see whether we can determine definitively that P doesn't obscure any part of Q. If these tests show that P cannot obscure any of the Q's, P is removed from the list and drawn, and the next P is tested.

FIGURE 13.13 Ambiguous cases that must be resolved by the depth-sort algorithm.

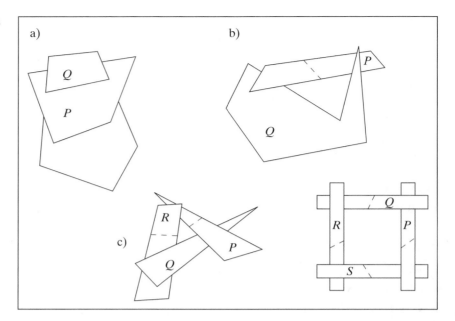

If we encounter a Q that P might obscure, we go to work on it. First, we see if it is "marked" as "previously moved" (as we shall see, faces are often moved around in the face list, and in order to avoid infinite looping, we allow a face to be moved only once.)

a. If the face is so marked, we do not test Q any further: We just split Q against the plane of P and put the pieces back into the list in the right places (according to `extent.far`).

b. If the face is not marked, we test whether Q can or cannot obscure P. If it cannot, Q is apparently behind P, so it is a good candidate to be drawn next. Accordingly, we put it at the end of the list, so that it is the first face tried next time, and mark it as moved, of course. If the test fails to prove that Q cannot obscure P, it appears that P and Q are hopelessly geometrically involved with one another, so we split Q against the plane of P and reinsert the pieces in the list.

Pseudocode for this algorithm is given in Figure 13.14, which clarifies the rather involved flow of tests. The flag `hopeful` is 1 as long as we can be hopeful that the current P won't obscure any of the Q's it overlaps in z. This is the pleasant situation, because then P can be drawn and is not considered again. When this hope is dashed, which occurs for a variety of reasons, other Q's are not tested; instead, a face either gets split or gets put at the end of the list.

Notice the bank of tests to see whether P can or cannot obscure Q. The tests are executed in order of increasing difficulty (processing time), and when any one of them is found to be true, it is known definitively that P does not obscure Q. The tests are as follows:

1. Are the x-extents of P and Q disjoint? (fast)
2. Are the y-extents of P and Q disjoint? (fast)
3. Is P entirely on the opposite side of Q's plane from the eye? (pretty fast)
4. Is Q entirely on the same side of P's plane as the eye? (pretty fast)
5. Are the projections of P and Q on the screen disjoint? (expensive)

The last test is the most demanding. Instead of just testing extents or the positions of vertices relative to a plane, a complete polygon-versus-polygon test must be made (in 2D, using just the x and y coordinates). The faces are disjoint only if no edges of

FIGURE 13.14 The depth-sort routine (pseudocode).

```
void depthSort(Face faces[])
{
  for(P = last face in list; list not empty; P = next face in list)
  {
    hopeful = 1;              // have definite action to take
    for((each Q overlapping P in z) && hopeful == 1)
    {
      if(   (x-extents of P and Q are disjoint)
         ||(y-extents of P and Q are disjoint)
         ||(P is on opposite side of Q's plane)
         ||(Q is on the same side of P's plane)
         ||(the projected faces P and Q don't overlap))
             continue; //try next Q
      // P might obscure this Q; see if Q is marked or behind P
      if (Q is marked)
        {
          split Q by plane of P;
          mark and insert pieces of Q;
          hopeful = 0;
        }
      else if(Q on opposite side of P's plane ||
              P on same side as Q's plane)
      {
          mark Q, put Q at end of list;
          hopeful = 0;
      }
      else // can't tell: They overlap too much
        {
          split Q by plane of P;
          mark and insert pieces of Q;
          hopeful = 0;
        }
    }// end.. for each q..
    if(hopeful)
       drawAndRemove(P);
  } // end of for each P
}
```

P intersect any edges of Q and neither face is contained inside the other. These tests are examined in further detail in Case Study 13.4.

The depth-sort method requires neither extra memory for a tree nor a preprocessing step (except for the initial sort on extent.far). The algorithm can begin to draw faces as soon as P on the end of the list has been shown to obscure nothing else in the list. It still must do face splitting, however, and must do insertions into a list, so faces[] would most likely be implemented as a linked list rather than a simple array. Note that this method suffers, as do the depth-buffer and the BSP tree methods, from the problem of redrawing faces on top of previously drawn faces. In effect, the effort taken to render the earlier faces is wasted.

13.4 A SCAN-LINE HSR METHOD

In this section, we discuss an image-precision approach that renders a scene scan line by scan line. Along each scan line, it considers all of the faces in the scene that are "involved" with that scan line and determines which one lies closest to the eye. It then fills in pixels with the color of that face. Thus, this approach does shading calculations only once for each pixel, and it does no redrawing.

The general flow of the algorithm is shown in Figure 13.15. It is similar to that of the polygon fill algorithm of Chapter 10, except that there is more than one polygon to consider at each pixel. Different versions of this algorithm [Bouknight70; Watkins70] are distinguished mainly by the way the closest face is determined and by the order in which the ingredients of the problem are processed.

```
for (each scan line, y)
  for(each pixel, x, on scan line y)
  {
      find the closest face that "covers" the pixel;
      c = color at (x, y) of the closest face;
      set the pixel at(x, y) to color c
  }
```

Runs of pixels are filled along a scan line with the color of the polygon that covers the run. If more than one polygon covers a pixel, the one with the smallest depth determines the color to be used. To do this efficiently, the algorithm creates and manages various lists in order to exploit the high degree of coherence along a scan line. That is, if one pixel is covered by some polygons, it is highly likely that its neighboring pixels will also be covered by them. The algorithm also capitalizes on edge coherence by preprocessing the edges of all faces and storing them in sorted order in a list.

The example in Figure 13.16 shows how the fill algorithm of Section 10.7.2 is adapted to perform HSR. The projections of three overlapping 3D planar faces A, B, and C are seen. The active-edge list shows the x-values at which an edge of some face intersects the current scan line L. The list holds these intersections in sorted order. Each node in the list points to the face responsible for the intersection: `numCovered` reports the number of faces that cover a given pixel, and the array `covered[ ]` contains *true* for the covering faces.

At the start of the scan in z across the line, all elements of `covered[ ]` are initialized to *false*, and `numCovered` is set to zero. In the example, no face covers the pixels between $x = 0$ and $x = x_1$, so the background color is applied. At x_1, face B is reached, so `covered[B]` is set to *true* and `numCovered` is set to 1. The depth of each covering face at the current pixel is maintained in a new `thisDepth` field in the face nodes. This field is initialized according to the depth of the point at the first intersection with the scan line. At each successive x-value, the depth need only be incremented by a constant, `depthInc`, just as was done with the depth-buffer approach in Chapter 8. This incremental computation of depth exploits depth coherence, the tendency for the depth at one point on a face to be easily computed from the depth at nearby points on the face.

In moving from $x = x_1$ to $x = x_2$, face B is the only covering face, so each of its pixels can be filled using the applicable shading rule. Depending on the rule, the entire run from x_1 to x_2 might be filled at once.

At x_2, face A is entered, and its depth is determined; `numCovered` becomes 2; and `covered[A]` is set to *true*. By "looking ahead" in the active-edge list, the routine knows that from x_2 to x_3 there are only two faces covering the pixels, so the closer face at each pixel is found by a simple comparison, of depths. If face A starts out being closer than face B, there is no guarantee that it will remain so; that is, the faces may interpenetrate. This can be checked by finding the two depths at x_3. If the depth

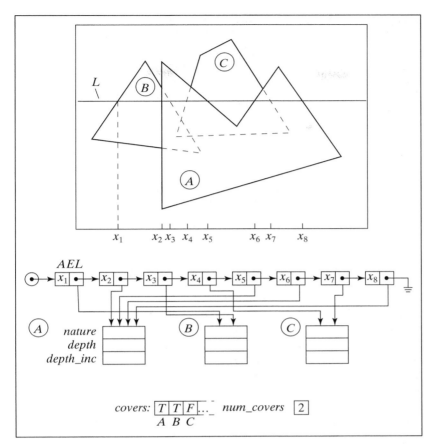

FIGURE 13.16 A example of a scan line and the active-edge list.

ordering is maintained over the run to x_3, the run can be filled as if there were only one covering face. At x_3, face B no longer covers, so the pixel color is easy to determine. (How?) At x_4, face C begins to cover, so the relative depths of faces A and C must be resolved.

In general, at each successive pixel across the scan line, the depth of each covering face is incremented. At each edge crossing, `covered[ ]` is set to true for a face if it is being entered or to *false* if it is being exited, and `numCovered` is adjusted accordingly. Whenever more than one face covers a pixel, the closest one is identified, and the shade or color of the face is computed. Because edges are crossed relatively infrequently, scan-line coherence is being exploited.

When scan line L has been traversed, the current scan line is incremented, all `covered[ ]` elements are reinitialized to *false*, and the active-edge list is updated so that it faithfully represents the edge crossings that are encountered along the new scan line. Updating the list is the same as for the polygon fill, using an edge table for efficiency.

Various modifications of this algorithm have been made to increase its efficiency or to enlarge the class of objects it can render. (See [Foley90].)

PRACTICE EXERCISES

13.4.1 Objects that do not interpenetrate

Often one knows some properties of the objects being rendered, and this knowledge can allow a simpler HSR algorithm to be used. What simplifications in the scan-line algorithm become available if it is known that no two faces ever interpenetrate?

13.4.2 Testing depth over a run

Show how the algorithm discussed in this section, "knowing" the depths of all covering faces at the beginning of a run, can "look ahead" to the end of the run and determine, with a simple calculation, the depths of the covering faces there. If the algorithm detects a reversal in the depth ordering of faces, can it find the pixel at which the reversals occur? How?

13.4.3 Do convex polygons help?

Discuss what simplifications are possible if the scan-line HSR algorithm can assume that all faces are convex.   ■

13.5 AREA SUBDIVISION APPROACHES

A rather different approach to HSR can be constructed that exploits the *area coherence* of a scene. As we have used the term, scan-line coherence is the notion that many neighboring pixels along a scan line share the same property of being covered or not covered by a face: There is coherence along x for a given y. **Area coherence**, on the other hand, is the notion that many pixels that are neighbors in either x or y share the same property. Hence, there is symmetry between the x and y directions.

Area subdivision methods are based on partitioning a picture into subregions and testing each subregion for visible surfaces. Whereas the scan-line method asks questions relating to depth at each pixel or, at most, along runs, area subdivision methods use a "divide-and-conquer" approach. They ask when a subregion is "simple" enough to be drawn in its entirety without further depth testing. If a region is simple in this way, it is drawn immediately; otherwise it is subdivided into a collection of smaller subregions, and the tests are repeated for each subregion. If the size of a subregion reduces to some predetermined minimum (often that of a single pixel), the subdivision is terminated, and explicit depth tests are performed to resolve the closest surface. The region is then drawn with the proper color.

There are several variations of area subdivision algorithms, which have generally become known as *Warnock algorithms*, after John Warnock, who first developed the approach [Warnock69]. They differ mainly in the definition of *simple* and in the way a region is partitioned.

13.5.1 Quadrant Subdivision

We shall focus on a quadrant subdivision method that is particularly easy to implement. Other approaches are considered in the exercises at the end of Section 13.5.2.

Figure 13.17 presents an example that uses a quadrant subdivision of a rectangular region. Figure 13.17(a) shows the projections of two 3D faces in region R, with no clue given as to which face is closer to the viewer.

Figure 13.17(b) shows the true arrangement that must finally be drawn: The faces are seen to interpenetrate. To begin the quadrant subdivision approach, suppose we decide that a region is simple enough to draw immediately if at most one face is "involved" with the region. Face F is **involved** with region R if any part of F overlaps any part of R. When only a single face is involved, the HSR problem is automatically solved, and the region is rendered easily by using a routine that draws the face clipped to the region. If no faces are involved, just the background color will be drawn.

Because two faces are involved with region R in the figure, that region is not simple enough and must therefore be subdivided. We choose to subdivide regions into four quadrants, labeled as in a map: northwest (NW), northeast (NE), southwest (SW), and southeast (SE). [See Figure 13.17(c).] In the figure, both the NW and SW quadrants are involved with only a single face, so the portions of the relevant faces

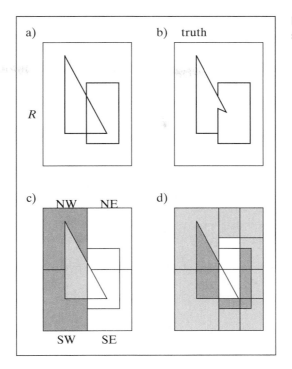

FIGURE 13.17 Quadrant subdivision of a region.

are drawn. (Suppose, for convenience, that at the outset we have flooded the entire screen with the background color.) On the other hand, both the NE and SE quadrants have two involved faces and must be subdivided, yielding Figure 13.17(d). All but two of the new subregions can now be rendered. The subdivision process continues with these two remaining subregions.

Regions can become extremely small in the subdivision process. How do we decide that a region is small enough that further subdivision is unwarranted? Regions are defined in the viewport, so we adopt the simple image-precision strategy that when a region has been subdivided so finely that it contains only one pixel center, we do not subdivide it any further, even if it is not simple. Instead, we determine which face to draw by testing the depths of all faces involved with the region and finding the closest face. The pixel is then set to the color of that face. If a region is so small that it contains no pixel center at all, it is ignored.

To implement the Warnock algorithm, we define a class `Region` as suggested in Figure 13.18 and give it various methods. The principal method is `draw(FaceList& faces)`, which draws the region in question. Its parameter is a list of all the faces in the scene, represented in some suitable data type, `Facelist`. The routine `draw()` uses `getSize()` to test how many pixel centers lie within `region`. If none is present, nothing is done. If exactly one pixel center is present, `drawClosestFace()` tests the depths of all involved faces at the pixel center and sets the pixel to the color of the closest face. If more than one pixel is present, `isSimple_drawIt()` tests whether the region is simple and, if so, draws it. Otherwise four subregions are constructed, and `draw()` calls itself for each subregion.

The meat of the Warnock algorithm lies in the geometric analysis performed by `isSimple_drawIt()`. The region must be tested against each face in the face list to determine how many faces are involved with the region. We encapsulate this testing in a method `isInvolved(Face & face)` that returns `true` if face `face` is involved with the region and `false` otherwise. The more clever this test is, the faster

```
class Region{
public:
  Rect r; // a region is a rectangle
  int getSize();   / how big is it?
  bool isSimple_DrawIt(FaceList& faces); // if it's simple, draw it
  void drawClosestFace(FaceList& faces);
  bool isInvolved(Face& face); //is the region involved with face?
  int buildQuadrants(Region& nw, Region& ne, Region& sw, Region& se);
  void draw(FaceList& faces) //the main drawing method
  {
      int size = getSize(); // how big is it?
      if(size < 1)return; // nothing to draw
      if(size == 1) drawClosestFace(faces); // covers one pixel center
      else if(isSimple_drawIt(faces))return; // draw it and exit
      else // it's not simple enough
      {
          Region NW, NE, SW, SE;
          buildQuadrants(NW, NE, SW, SE); / make subregions
          NW.draw(faces); // draw each of them
          NE.draw(faces);
          SW.draw(faces);
          SE.draw(faces);
      }
  }
};
```

FIGURE 13.18 Skeleton of a class to support the Warnock algorithm.

the HSR algorithm will operate. What tests might be required in this function? There are various ways that a face F can be involved or not involved with a rectangular region R, as suggested in Figure 13.19:

FIGURE 13.19 Varieties of involvement of a face and a region.

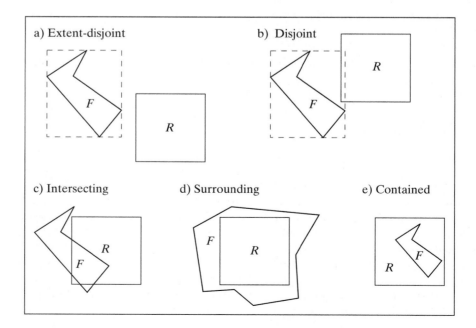

- *Extent disjoint.* Face F is extent disjoint from region R if the extent of F has no overlap with R [Figure 13.19(a)]. If F is extent disjoint from R, then F must lie entirely outside R. This is the simplest of the geometric situations to detect.
- *Disjoint.* Face F may be disjoint from R, even though its extent overlaps R [Figure 13.19(b)]. To test for this condition, clip each of the edges of F against region R. If all edges of F are clipped out, they must lie entirely outside R, and thus, F is disjoint from R. This is a more complex test than the extent-disjoint test, so it is performed only when the extent-disjoint test fails.
- *Intersecting.* At least one edge of F intersects a boundary of R [Figure 13.19(c)]. We shall see later how to combine the test for *intersecting* with that for *disjoint*. Note that there can be an intersection even if no vertex of F actually lies inside R. (How?)
- *Surrounding.* Region R is completely surrounded by F [Figure 13.19(d)]. After many subdivisions, the subregions of R are very small, so this condition occurs often.
- *Contained.* F is totally contained within region R [Figure 13.19(e)]. This situation obtains if, and only if, all vertices of F lie inside R.

Face F is seen to be involved with R if it is intersecting, surrounding, or contained. So our definition of a "simple" region is that

> R is **simple** if at most one face is intersecting, surrounding, or contained.

So `isInvolved(face)` must determine whether or not `face` intersects, surrounds, or is contained in region R. How can this be done efficiently? First, the routine does the simplest test: Is face `face` extent disjoint from R? If not, the best bet is to traverse the vertices of polygon `face`, testing each vertex and edge against the region. Since R is convex, it is easy to test whether a vertex lies within R. (How?) It is also easy to test whether an edge intersects one of the horizontal or vertical edges of R. (How?)

As `face` is traversed, as soon as a vertex is found to be inside R or an edge is found to intersect R, the testing terminates, and `isInvolved()` returns *true*. On the other hand, if all vertices are outside R and no edges intersect, then the face is disjoint or it is a *surrounder* of R. To distinguish these two situations, the routine tests whether a vertex of R lies inside the face. This can be done using a parity-type test, as discussed in Section 10.7.

13.5.2 Other Definitions of a Simple Region

So far, we have considered only one definition of *simple* for a region: A region is simple if no face or one face is involved. Other criteria can be used, however, that trade speed for simplicity.

When *Simple* Means *Empty*

The most primitive definition of *simple* is that the region in question is empty—that exactly zero faces are involved. Many more subregions are found to be nonsimple with this criterion, of course, so many more subdivisions are performed. In fact, for each pixel covered by any face, the subdivisions must proceed down to the single-pixel level, as this is the only way to stop the subdivisions! When only one face is involved, this approach is unable to detect it and continues to perform subdivisions. In effect, the approach gives many "false alarms," asserting that a region is too complex for the hidden-surface question to be answered when in fact the region is simple according to the previous definition. An advantage of the approach is that it needs no scan conversion; the only drawing tool required (after flooding with the background color) is a means to set a pixel.

Using Surrounders

Another widely used definition of *simple* requires somewhat more complex testing, but is very good at identifying simple regions and so necessitates far fewer subdivisions. This definition does not insist that at most one face be involved in a region. Instead, many faces may be involved, as long as one **dominates**. Face F dominates region R if F is a surrounder that is everywhere closer than are all other involved faces. A situation for which this meaning of *simple* saves many subdivisions is shown in Figure 13.20. Region A is simple after only the two levels of subdivision shown, even though more than one face is involved, because the single surrounding face is closest and masks off the others. If the first definition of simple were used, this region would be subdivided to the pixel level, since the more remote house has a face that overlaps the visible face entirely within A. (*Question*: Under which of the definitions of *simple* is region B simple?)

FIGURE 13.20 A surrounding face lies closest.

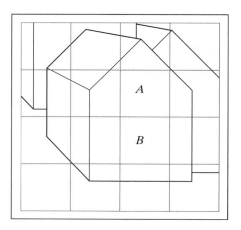

How is a surrounder tested to see whether it is everywhere closest within a subregion R? Its depth need be tested only at the four corners of R and compared with the depths of the planes of all other involved faces at those corners. If the surrounder is closest at all four corners, no other involved face can occlude it.

As the face list `faces` is scanned, we flag all surrounders before placing them in the `outFaces` list. When all faces have been tested, we test the depths of the surrounders to see whether one surrounder is closer than all the others. (It needn't be–why?) If it is, we test this winner against the planes of all the remaining faces in `faces`. If there is a "winning" surrounder, region R is rendered according to its surface color, and no further subdivisions are performed. Otherwise `outFaces` is passed recursively, as before. Note that when the surrounders have been flagged in `outFaces`, they need not be retested after the next subdivision, as they will certainly still be surrounders.

In using this definition of *simple*, there is a clear trade-off between the complexity involved in testing each face and the need for additional cycles of subdivision. Much more testing must be done on each region, in the hope that many fewer regions will have to be tested (because fewer subdivisions will be performed).

PRACTICE EXERCISES

13.5.1 Hand simulation of the warnock algorithm

For a situation in which an isosceles right triangle fits snugly into a square region, hand simulate the operation of `Region :: draw( )`, showing the creation of various face lists. Carry out the simulation until all necessary subregions of one-sixteenth of the original area have been tested.

13.5.2 Another meaning of *simple*

The first definition of *simple* required that at most one face be involved in a region. But if several *non overlapping* faces are involved, no depth calculations need be performed to solve the HSR problem. In this case, isSimple_drawIt() would build a list of the faces involved with the region and test whether they are nonoverlapping. If they are, the routine would simply draw each of these faces in turn. Discuss the complexity of this approach. In particular, how does one test whether a collection of faces known to be involved with the region do or do not overlap? Is this definition of *simple* likely to be worth the effort to implement it?

13.5.3 Alternative subdivision approaches

When edges of faces run diagonally across the display (as in Figure 13.17), many levels of subdivision may have to be performed, because the borders of the regions never "line up" with the edges. Figure 13.21 suggests a different way to subdivide a region: at a vertex A of a prominent face in the scene. The two edges E_1 and E_2 are extended to the borders of the region, thus defining four subregions $R_1, \ldots, R_4$. The triangle is now disjoint from three of these new regions, vastly simplifying them. The same tests as before are applied to each subregion, simple regions are rendered, and non-simple ones are subdivided further. Discuss the changes required in the quadrant subdivision method in order to implement this approach. Sketch a scene with several polygonal faces, and show how the subdivisions would be carried out to determine the visible surfaces.

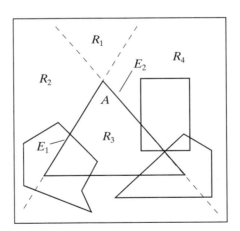

FIGURE 13.21 Subdividing a region along an edge.

13.5.4 Incorporating antialiasing

How can one incorporate antialiasing while performing HSR using area subdivision? Consider subdividing below the pixel level and then averaging. Discuss how this is to be done and how effective the technique is. ■

13.6 ON HIDDEN-LINE-REMOVAL METHODS

Sometimes you want to produce a line drawing of a scene, as in Figure 8.2. Only the visible portions of each edge are drawn, so the objects still look solid and opaque. A line drawing may be preferred for artistic reasons, or because it is much faster to produce than a shaded rendering, or because the available devices can make only line drawings.

If the device allows "painting over," so that edges can be drawn and then later covered by solid areas of background, we can apply earlier HSR techniques. We simply render (the visible parts of) each polygonal face in the solid background color and draw its edges in black. This technique paints each face over those farther away, suitably obscuring them, so that only the visible edges remain. The list-priority, Warnock, and depth-buffer algorithms can be used for the purpose.

If the device does not support "painting over," we need to apply different methods for HLR. For instance, once a pen plotter has drawn a line, it cannot be "undrawn." Also, some raster devices, such as photorecorders, do not permit rewriting lines, because overwriting blends colors instead of painting over them.

In this section, we examine approaches in which each element is drawn only after a complete test of its visibility has been performed, so that no part of it needs to be erased or painted over. We focus on drawing the visible edges of a mesh object. A direct approach clips each edge of the object against all faces that occlude it. As shown in Figure 13.22, some edges are not affected (e_1), some are entirely removed from the scene (e_2), some are clipped at one end, and others are broken into several pieces (e_3).

FIGURE 13.22 Performing hidden-line removal.

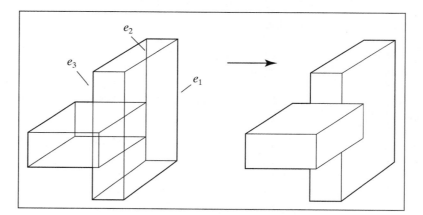

Must every edge be tested against every face? No, because, for a closed, solid object, we know two important facts: (1) If a back face obscures an edge, surely some front face must also obscure it (why?), and (2) every edge "belongs" to two faces. The first fact implies that we need to clip edges only against front faces and that back faces can be deleted at the start, just as they were in previous algorithms. The second fact implies that if an edge belongs to two back faces, it must be invisible and so need not be considered further.

A face can split an edge into many segments. (Show a situation in which a face with eight edges breaks an edge of another face into five pieces.) The algorithm must keep track of all the "surviving" pieces (those still potentially visible), and each survivor must be tested against the remaining faces in the face list.

The model is first processed to identify all of its potentially visible edges, which are placed into a list of edges. A cycle then begins in which an edge is removed from the edge list and processed. The edge is clipped against every (front) face, and if it survives, it is drawn. If a clip breaks the edge into pieces, one of the survivors is tested against the remaining faces, and the other pieces are put back in the edge list. If at any point the whole edge is clipped out, the cycle starts again by removing the next edge from the list. The cycles continue until the list is empty.

Figure 13.23 shows an example in which edge E, extending from vertex A to vertex B, is tested against face F and split into four visible parts. The first survivor is placed in edge E, and the remaining survivors are added to the edge list.

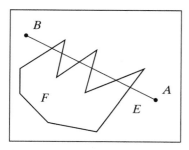

FIGURE 13.23 Effect of splitting an edge into visible pieces.

A Data Type for Edges

Figure 13.24 shows a skeleton of a class Edge that represents each edge to be tested. Besides the obvious need to store the endpoints of the edge (or indices into the vertex list if a vertex list is used) extra information is stored with each edge for greater efficiency. This information consists of the following items:

```
class Edge{
    Point3 first, second; // end points of the edge
    Face *face1, *face2;  // pointers to its two faces
    Cuboid extent;        // 3D extent of edge
    Face *nextFace;       // next face for testing
};
```

FIGURE 13.24 Skeleton of a Data Type for an Edge.

1. `extent`: the edge's extent—a parallelepiped, aligned with the coordinate axes, that just encloses the edge.
2. `face1`, `face2`: pointers to the two faces associated with the edge. Because neither of these faces can obscure the edge, they needn't be included in the test and so are skipped.
3. `nextFace`: a pointer to the next face in the face list that must be tested. When an edge is split and part of it is put back into the edge list, it has already been tested against some of the faces. Therefore, when it is removed later, we need test it only against the remaining faces in the list.

To build the initial edge list, the face list is scanned, and the edges of each front face are pushed onto the edge list. Duplicate edges are removed from the list as needed, and the fields in each Edge object are filled.

Note that there might be some benefit in reordering the face list so that "prominent" faces (large faces near the camera's eye) appear near the front of the list. In this way, the edges are tested first against those faces that are most likely to eliminate them.

It is convenient to isolate the geometric testing of an edge against a face in a routine such as

```
bool edgeTest(Edge& E, Face& F);
```

which tests edge E against face F and returns true if and only if there are any survivors. The routine sets E to the first survivor and places all other survivors in the edge list.

These ideas lead to the skeleton of the algorithm shown in Figure 13.25.

FIGURE 13.25 Skeleton of the HLR algorithm.

```
void drawVisibleEdges(FaceList faces)
{
    EdgeList edges; // the edge list
    build the edge list of all potentially visible edges
    while (edges is not empty)
    {
        Edge E = getNext(edges); // remove the next edge
        bool isVis = true;    // suppose it's visible
        for(F = E.nextFace; isVis && F != NULL; F is next face)
        {
            if(E belongs to F)continue; // no need to test this face
            isVis = edgeTest(E,F); //put survivors on edge list
        }
        if (isVis) E.draw(); // E is visible; draw it
    }
}
```

PRACTICE EXERCISE

13.6.1 Hand simulation of the HLR

For the objects in Figure 13.22, label each front face and each edge that belongs to at least one front face. List the front faces that occlude each back face. Show what happens to each edge as it is clipped against all of the front faces.

13.6.2 Situation for sorting the face list

For what kind of scene is it particularly advantageous to presort the face list? Does the scene consist of many faces or just a few? What about faces that contain many sides? Draw some examples for which presorting is worth the trouble and some for which it is not.

13.6.3 Hand simulation

For the objects in Figure 13.22, hand simulate the algorithm in Figure 13.25. Draw an appropriate face and edge list, and show the state of the lists when edge e_3 has just been clipped against the closest face to the eye. ■

13.6.1 The Geometric Testing in edgeTest( )

The main work of the HLR algorithm whose skeleton is given in Figure 13.25 lies in the function `edgeTest(E,F)`. The easiest tests should be performed first, in the hope of deciding about E as quickly as possible. If one test is inconclusive, the next test should be performed. Although many variations are possible, the following tests form a reasonable sequence:

- *Extent testing.* The extent in x of edge E is tested against that of face F. If there is no overlap, F cannot obscure E. If there is an overlap, the extents in y are then tested, and E will again survive if there is no overlap. These are very fast tests.
- *Edge on the near side.* If both endpoints, say, V_1 and V_2, of E are closer than the plane of face F, the edge cannot be occluded by F and therefore survives. If the plane of F has the equation $\mathbf{m} \cdot P = D$, where $\mathbf{m}$ is the outward-pointing normal vector, we form the two quantities $s_1 = (\mathbf{m} \cdot V_1 - D)$ and $s_2 = (\mathbf{m} \cdot V_2 - D)$. If both are positive, E lies on the near side of the plane (the same side as the eye). (Why?) We saw a similar test against the plane of a face in the depth-sort method of Figure 13.14.
- *Edge penetrates plane.* If the quantities s_1 and s_2 differ in sign, the edge must pierce the plane of the face. It is then convenient to split the edge into two pieces, one on the near side and one on the far side of the face plane. The near one is a clear survivor and so goes in the survivor list to be returned by `edgeTest( )`. The fate of the far one is still unknown. Similarly, if both s_1 and s_2 are negative, then all of E lies on the far side, and further testing is required.

To find where edge E with endpoints V_1 and V_2 penetrates the plane, we write the usual parametric form, $V_1(1 - t) + V_2 t$, and substitute it into the plane equation for the face. Then we solve for the hit time t_{hit} in the usual way. We use t_{hit} in the parametric form to compute the piercing point of E.

Only an edge that lies wholly on the far side of the plane of F will reach this stage of testing. The face may or may not occlude the edge. If the edge was split in the previous step, it is wise to retest the x- and y-extents of the remaining piece, in the hope that there is now no overlap. Assuming that the extents do overlap, there is little choice but to compute the intersections of the edge (call it E still) with each of the edges of F. We use the parametric form for E as in the previous paragraph and calculate the time for each intersection of E with some edge of the face. This provides a list of t-values. For the case shown in Figure 13.26, the list is $t_1, t_2, t_3, t_4, t_5, t_6$ (supposing that the list is formed starting with the edge between vertices v_1 and v_2). We the sort the t-values and analyze the list to determine where the portions that lie outside the face are situated. (see the exercise that follows). Finally, we place these outside portions on the survivor list to be returned by `edgeTest( )`.

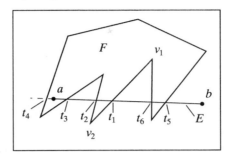

FIGURE 13.26 Finding the intersection of E and the edges of F.

PRACTICE EXERCISE

13.6.4 Analyzing the t-value list

Testing edge E for intersections with the sides of face F yields a list of t-values, as just discussed. Suppose the list is .6, .4, .1, -.3, -.8, 1.4. What else must be known in order to tell which intervals in t correspond to pieces of E lying outside the face? Devise a general method for analyzing such a list and building the desired t-intervals. ■

13.7 HSR METHODS FOR CURVED SURFACES

We have been taking the approach that curved surfaces, such as those discussed in Chapter 6, are usually "polygonalized" before they are rendered. (See Section 6.5.5) A surface given parametrically by $P(u, v)$ is divided into planar polygons along lines of constant u and v. But this can result in very large numbers of polygons to deal with and a heavy demand on memory. In addition, the final picture may show artefacts such as silhouettes that look disturbingly polygonal.

Sometimes it is preferable to render the curved surfaces directly. A number of methods have been developed [Catmull75; Blinn78b, Lane 80; Clark79; Blinn80] for solving the HSR and rendering problems for parametrically defined patches. We examine the issues here and describe one approach that has proven very successful.

Figure 13.27 shows a collection of patches blending together to form a curved surface. A particular scan line at $y = y_1$ is seen to intersect the highlighted patch at some point along its silhouette.

Catmull [Catmull75] developed a method that recursively divides a patch into four patches until a patch has a projection that covers at most one pixel. A depth buffer determines whether that patch is the closest surface yet seen at the pixel, and if so, it is drawn. Pseudocode for this method is shown in Figure 13.28.

All of the patches in the scene (except those whose extents lie wholly outside the camera's view volume) are loaded into a stack. The patches are then removed one by one, and their projected size is determined. If this size is larger than a pixel, the patch is subdivided (in parameter space u and v), and the four new patches are pushed back on to the stack for later processing. If the size is small enough, the depth of the surface at the pixel is found and compared with that in the depth buffer. If the patch is the closest yet seen, its color is determined and it is drawn.

Catmull suggests ways to improve the efficiency of the method. Measuring the size of a patch's projection is expensive, so the polygon formed from the patch's four corner points is projected and its size is tested instead. Also, before each patch is pushed on to the stack, it can be flagged as being wholly inside the view volume or not. When

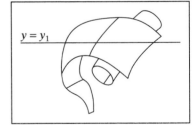

FIGURE 13.27 Rendering some patches.

FIGURE 13.28 Catmull's patch subdivision method (pseudocode).

```
push all patches onto a stack;
initialize the depth buffer;
while(stack not empty)
{
    pop patch from stack;
    if(patch covers at most one pixel)
    {
        if(patch is the closest yet in z)
                get its color, draw it, and update the depth buffer;
    }
    else
    {
        subdivide patch into 4 subpatches;
        push subpatches onto stack;
    }
}
```

it is later popped, it needs no further clipping, and if it is subdivided, its four pieces are known to be wholly inside as well.

Blinn and Whitted [Blinn80] each developed similar scan-line algorithms that keep track of the visible pieces of patches from one scan line to the next. Both methods require tricky numerical techniques to find the parameter values (u, v) for which the patch $P(u, v)$ has the given scan-line's y-coordinate.

FIGURE 13.29 The Lane–Carpenter scan-line method (pseudocode).

```
void LaneCarpenter(...)
{
    add all patches to the patch table;
    initialize the active patch list (APL);
    for(each scan line y)
    {
        update the APL;
        for(each patch P in the APL)
        {
            if(P is "planar enough")
            add P to the polygon list;
            else
            {
                split the patch into subpatches;
                for(each new subpatch S)
                    if(S still intersects the scan line)
                        add S to the APL;
                    else
                        add S to the patch table;
            }
        }
        do scan line HSR process for this scan line for
        the polygons in the polygon list;
    }
}
```

A different and quite successful approach subdivides patches until they are deemed to be "flat enough" to be treated as planar quadrilaterals, whereupon they are rendered in a scan-line HSR algorithm. If the patches involved are Bezier or B-spline patches, there are efficient techniques (described in [Foley90]) for subdividing a patch by forming new control polyhedra. Lane and Carpenter and Clark devised similar methods along these lines [Clark79; Lane79]. The Lane–Carpenter approach subdivides a patch only when a scan line begins to intersect the patch; the Clark method subdivides all patches in a preprocessing step. The former method requires a larger number of subdivisions, but the latter requires more memory.

Figure 13.29 shows pseudocode for the Lane–Carpenter method. The routine first places all patches in a patch table much like the edge table used for edges in Chapter 10. There is also an active-patch list that contains all of the patches that intersect the current scan line, as well as a polygon list that contains those "flat enough" quadrilaterals that are ready for rendering.

Each patch in the active-patch list is tested in turn; if it is flat enough, its approximating planar quadrilateral is placed in the polygon list for rendering (since the patch does intersect the current scan line). If it is not flat enough, it is subdivided into four patches, and those that intersect the current scan line are added to the active-patch list. Those that do not intersect the current scan line (because they lie above it) are put back in the patch list, to become active later. When all the patches in the list have been duly processed for this scan line, the scan-line HSR process is invoked on the polygon list to draw the proper polygons along the scan line.

13.8 SUMMARY

Removing hidden surfaces and lines is a fundamental problem in computer graphics, and a large number of techniques have been developed to do the job properly. Hidden-surface-removal (HSR) algorithms tend to be complex, with long execution times, and a great deal of effort has been devoted to increasing their efficiency. It is useful to separate the various methods into two categories. Some algorithms operate at the "object-precision" level, which means that the geometric calculations they use to examine the relative positions of points, edges, and planes work at the highest precision naturally available on the machine at hand. Others work at the "image-precision" level, which means that they ask questions on a discrete pixel-by-pixel basis or compare distances using an indicator that has finite precision.

In this chapter, we examined various HSR approaches for the important class of objects modeled as polygonal meshes. To set things up properly for efficient HSR, all of the faces in the scene are preprocessed: Back faces are removed, and front faces are clipped to the view volume. The surviving faces are mapped to the 3D viewport by using the perspective transformation and perspective division, so that each vertex in the viewport has its final (x, y) position and a value of pseudodepth. This preprocessing was also done in preparation for applying the depth-buffer algorithm, described in Chapter 8. The depth-buffer algorithm was revisited in this chapter for purposes of comparison. It is a very successful image-precision HSR method that is particularly easy to implement. But its speed is limited by the large amount of pixel redrawing it must do. In addition, the large amount of extra memory required for the depth buffer can seriously limit the memory available for other tasks in a program, and the fixed precision of the depth buffer causes the method to have trouble distinguishing fine differences in the depth of remote objects.

Because HSR methods are based on deciding which element is "closer" than another, or which of a number of elements is "closest," each HSR algorithm is built around a core of re-ordering and sorting. (This point is made particularly vivid in the excellent survey of HSR methods by Sutherland et al. [Sutherland74].) Because sorting can be expensive, the key to efficiency is to do no more sorting than is absolutely necessary. Methods such as the depth-buffer algorithm use vast amounts of memory to reduce the sorting burden (essentially converting it to a search for the closest element).

Different algorithms do the sorting in x, y, and z in different orders, according to the order in which they process data, as in the pseudocode

```
for (each pixel) {
    for (each face) {  ...}  }
```

versus

```
for (each face) {
    for (each pixel) {...}
```

All these algorithms also make different trade-offs among speed, storage space, and simplicity.

Clever methods have been developed that capitalize on coherence to reduce the computational burden of an HSR method. Coherence is the tendency for some aspect of a scene to change only slightly in some direction of motion, so that a property that obtains at one point very likely obtains at a nearby point. The methods discussed here exploit various kinds of coherence, such as area coherence, depth coherence, scan-line coherence, and edge coherence.

We examined three "list-priority" HSR algorithms—techniques based on sorting the list of faces in clever ways so that a renderer can draw the faces in a new order, properly hiding those faces that lie behind other faces. Successful methods, such as the binary-space partition tree approach, require that certain faces be split into two pieces. Like the depth-buffer approach, the list-priority methods suffer from large amounts of redrawing of pixels.

A scan-line HSR method was discussed that does no redrawing of pixels, but instead determines, for each pixel, which of the many faces in the scene is closest to the eye "at that pixel" and draws that face once. This method also capitalizes on face coherence and scan-line coherence (since the same face tends to be the closest over a portion of each scan line) to fill in "spans" of pixels at once, which speeds up the drawing process substantially.

The area subdivision approach of Warnock algorithms carries the preceding idea to two dimensions, by seeking regions over which a single face is easily identified as being the closest. If the region contains faces that still need depth sorting, the algorithm simply subdivides the region into smaller ones, with the aim of finding a simpler answer in each such smaller region. This method requires no redrawing of pixels.

We also looked at a hidden-line-removal method that is particularly suited for devices that are unable to erase or paint over lines. This algorithm tests the visibility of each edge against all of the front faces in the model. Because the geometric testing of an edge against a face can be complicated, a series of tests of increasing complexity is performed until an answer is found. An edge that lies partly behind a face can be fractured into several pieces, each of which must be processed in turn. To organize this process, we used the familiar technique of saving "those things yet to be processed" on a stack.

Finally, we glimpsed the issue of drawing 3D scenes made up of curved surfaces in situations where one does not want to approximate the surfaces with polygons. Some solutions involve scan-line algorithms that determine, at each pixel along a scan line, the surface element that is closest to the eye. Others work patch by patch, subdividing patches into smaller and smaller—hence, flatter and flatter—subpatches until a clear decision can be made as to what is closest to the eye and what its color is.

Many other HSR and HLR methods have been invented and scrutinized. Some (e.g., [Foley90; Rogers98]) explore additional ways to improve efficiency at the expense of simplicity. Others [Butland79; Rogers98] work on mathematical functions or larger classes of surface shapes.

13.9 CASE STUDIES

CASE STUDY 13.1 TESTING THE PAINTER'S ALGORITHM

Level of Effort: II. Write the routine `HeedlessPainter()`, which executes the heedless painter's algorithm. Faces in the `faces[]` array are sorted by the pseudodepth of their farthest vertex, and the list is then scanned and each face is drawn in its entirety, painting over any previously drawn faces. To assist in testing this and other HSR algorithms, write a routine that generates face lists for a collection of N cubes having randomly selected sizes, positions, and orientations in space. Test the Heedless Painter routine on scenes made up of N random cubes.

CASE STUDY 13.2 TEST AND SPLIT

Level of Effort: I. Write and test the routine `FaceWithPlane()` which tests whether a given convex polygonal face lies entirely on one side of a plane or the other. If it does not, the routine splits the face into two polygons, one of which lies entirely on the inside, and one on the outside, of the plane. You might find the following prototype useful (or choose your own):

```
int FaceWith Plane(Face& face,   // face to be tested
                   Face& node,    // with the plane of this face
                   Face& inFace,  // the inside piece when split
                   Face& outFace); // the outside piece when split
```

The routine returns the following values:

−1 if `face` lies on the inside of the plane of `node`.
+1 if `face` lies on the outside of the plane of `node`.
0 if `face` is split into two faces, `inFace` and `outFace`.

How might the routine operate? Figure 13.30 shows an example of splitting a convex face with a plane. Suppose face F has vertices $V_0, V_1, \ldots, V_{N-1}$ and the plane has the equation $\mathbf{m} \cdot P = D$, where $\mathbf{m}$ is the normal vector to the plane that points to its *outside*. The routine traverses the vertices of F, putting each of them, $V[i]$, onto an *outside list* or an *inside list* of vertices according to the following test:

$V[i]$ lies outside the plane if $\mathbf{m} \cdot V[i] \geq D$ {put it in *outside list*};

$V[i]$ lies inside the plane if $\mathbf{m} \cdot V[i] < D$ {put it in *inside list*}.

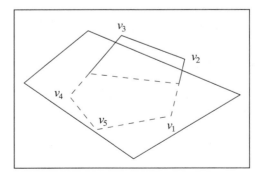

FIGURE 13.30 Splitting a convex face with a plane.

When the sign of $\mathbf{m} \cdot V[i] - D$ changes from one vertex to the next, the relevant edge straddles the two sides of the plane. Therefore, the routine finds the intersection of the edge with the plane, putting it onto both lists. (Why?) In the example of Figure 13.30, a pentagon is split into a pentagon and a quadrilateral. These pieces are created, and any other information that was in the original face is copied to both pieces. (Vertex normals and texture coordinates, if included, are found at the new vertices by interpolation.)

Discuss the extensions that must be made to this routine if the polygon is not convex.

CASE STUDY 13.3 USING BSP TREES TO REMOVE HIDDEN SURFACES

Level of Effort: III, if a routine to render a 3D scene (with no HSR) is already available. Write an application that renders the faces in `faces[]`, using a BSP tree to solve the hidden-surface problem. Test the program on interesting scenes containing several objects, such as a random collection of cubes.

The `Face` data type is extended to include two pointers, `Face *insideOnes` and `Face *outsideOnes`, which are properly set to NULL when the `faces[]` array is built. Before rendering begins, the faces are inserted into a BSP tree by means of a routine such as

```
Face *tree = NULL;        // create an empty BSP tree
for(i = 0; i < NumFaces; i++)
    tree = insertBSP(&faces[i], &tree);
```

When `faces[i]` is inserted into the tree (without splitting), only its children pointers are set; `faces[i]` still resides in the array `faces[]`, as well as residing simultaneously in the tree. If `faces[i]` must be split, two new faces are created (as discussed in Case Study 13.2) and inserted into the tree.

Figure 13.31 suggests a routine to insert a face into a BSP tree; the routine should be adjusted as necessary to correct any deficiencies. `FaceWithPlane()` (as described in Case Study 13.2) is used to test which side of a plane a face lies on, and it splits the face if necessary, inserting the two pieces farther down the tree.

FIGURE 13.31 Routine to insert a face into a BSP tree.

```
void insertBSP(Face& *Root, Face* face)
{ // insert face into subtree whose root is *Root.
  if(!face) return;      // nothing to insert
  Face inFace, outFace; // hold the two pieces of the face
  if(tree is empty so far)
  {
      attach the face to the tree
      return;
  }
  switch(FaceWithPlane(face, Rott, inFace, outFace)
  {
   case -1: // face lies inside plane
      insertBSP(face into insideOnes subtree);break;
   case 1: // face lies outside plane
      insertBSP(face into outsideOnes subree); break;
   case 0: // face was split
      insertBSP(inFace into the  insideOnes subtree);
      insertBSP(outFace into the outsideOnes subtree);break;
   }
}
```

The scene stored in the BSP tree is then drawn using a routine such as the one suggested by the pseudocode in Section 13.3.2.

CASE STUDY 13.4 USING DEPTH SORTING FOR HSR

Level of Effort: III, if a routine to render a 3D scene (with no HSR) is already available. Write an application that renders a scene using the depth-sort method of Section 13.3.3 to remove hidden surfaces. Test the program on interesting scenes containing several objects, such as N random cubes, as discussed in Case Study 13.1.

CASE STUDY 13.5 WORKING WITH A SCAN-LINE HSR APPROACH

Level of Effort: III, if a routine to render a 3D scene (with no HSR) is already available. Write an application that renders a scene using the scan-line algorithm of Section 13.4 to remove hidden surfaces. Test the program on interesting scenes containing several objects.

CASE STUDY 13.6 DRAWING WITH THE WARNOCK ALGORITHM

Level of Effort: III, if a routine to render a 3D scene (with no HSR) is already available. Write an application that renders a scene using the Warnock algorithm to remove hidden surfaces. Use the first definition of a simple region: that at most one face is intersecting, surrounding, or contained in the region. Then develop the necessary routines that were discussed in Section 13.5, such as `isSimple_drawIt()`, `drawFace()`, `isInvolved()`, `regionSize()`, `buildQuadrants()`, and `drawClosestFace()`. Test the program on interesting scenes containing several objects, such as a collection of random cubes.

Note that after a subdivision, subsequent testing of the "child" subregions needs to consider only those faces that were found to be involved with the "parent" region. Any faces that are disjoint from the parent region are surely disjoint from the subregions. We shall discuss later how to eliminate from further consideration those faces known to be disjoint from a region.

With this enhancement, `isSimpleRegion()` operates as follows: It is initialized to *false*, and *faces* is set to NULL. Each face in `faces` is tested for involvement with the region. (Because this list is tested by four instances of `drawRegion`, it must be preserved until all four scans are complete.) The involvement is determined by a function, `int isInvolved(Rect region, Face * f)`, that returns *true* if face `f` is involved with `region` and *false* otherwise. A copy of a pointer to each involved face is pushed onto `outFaces`, and a count is kept of the number of pushes. When `faces` has been traversed, the count is examined, and if it is 0 or 1, the routine returns *true*. Note that this version of `isSimpleRegion()` must test every face in its input list, regardless of involvement: It does not terminate as soon as two involved faces are identified.

CASE STUDY 13.7 THE EDGE STACK ALGORITHM FOR HLR

Level of Effort: II. Write an application that produces a line drawing of a 3D scene using the `drawVisibleEdges` algorithm of Section 13.6, wherein edges are drawn only when their visibility has been completely determined. Test the program on interesting scenes containing several objects, such as *N* random cubes, as discussed in Case Study 13.1.

To load the initial edge stack, write a routine `makeEdgeStack()`, which scans each face in `faces[]`, analyzes each edge of the face, and loads into a record of type `Edge` the edge data for all potentially visible edges (with no duplicates). Decide how to deal with edges that belong to only one back face.

13.10 FURTHER READING

The classic paper by Sutherland et al provides an excellent overview of the hidden surface removal problem, as well as lucid explanations of numerous HSR algorithms and their expected performance [Sutherland74]. Rogers discusses a large number of HSR algorithms in fine detail and gives many useful examples. Foley et al also present a valuable survey of the HSR problem and outline a number of solutions [Foley90].

14 Introduction to Ray Tracing

We attempt to abstract from the complexity of phenomena some simple systems whose properties are susceptible of being described mathematically. This power of abstraction is responsible for the amazing mathematical description of nature.

Morris Kline

For tribal man space was the uncontrollable mystery.
For technological man it is time that occupies the same role.

Marshall McLuhan

Full many a gem of purest ray serene
The dark, unfathomed caves of ocean bear.

Thomas Gray, Elegy, stanza 14

Ye little stars! hide your diminish'd rays.

Alexander Pope

Goals of the Chapter

▲ To develop the fundamental concepts of ray tracing.

▲ To set up the mathematics and algorithms to perform ray tracing.

▲ To build and render scenes of spheres, cones, cylinders, convex polyhedra, and other solids.

▲ To create highly realistic images that exhibit the effects of transparency and refraction of light.

▲ To develop tools for working with solid 3D texture and bit-mapped images.

PREVIEW

Because of its effectiveness, ray tracing is a widely used drawing technique. Section 14.1 introduces the technique, and Section 14.2 establishes the camera and geometry needed for ray tracing. Section 14.3 shows how an application performs ray tracing. Section 14.4 describes various primitive shapes that are easy to trace, and develops the heart of the technique of intersecting an object with a ray. The advantages accrued by transforming the ray into the generic coordinate system of the object are discussed.

Section 14.5 develops various classes and routines that make up a ray tracer with the use of an object-oriented approach and discusses how the various ingredients interact. A complete, albeit primitive, ray tracer is produced. Section 14.6 considers how to intersect rays with an extended set of shapes, including tapered cylinders and convex polyhedra.

Section 14.7 uses the shading models of Chapter 8 to develop a full-color ray tracer that handles ambient, diffuse, and specular reflections from surfaces. Physically based models of light reflection, such as the Cook–Torrance reflection model, are also developed. Section 14.8 explores techniques for "painting" texture onto surfaces during rendering. The painting of both 2D textures, derived from images, and 3D textures, such as marble or wood grain, is examined. The issue of antialiasing ray tracings is also addressed. Section 14.9 discusses how to speed up ray tracing dramatically through the judicious use of bounding boxes and other kinds of extents to eliminate many costly ray intersections.

Section 14.10 discusses how to "spawn" secondary rays in order to enhance the realism of a ray tracer. A method for the faithful generation of shadows is described. Section 14.11 examines the details of generating secondary rays to simulate both the reflection of light from a shiny surface and the refraction of light as it passes through a transparent object.

Section 14.12 extends the class of objects that can be ray traced to compound objects defined through constructive solid geometry. Methods are developed for ray tracing objects with arbitrarily complex shapes. The chapter closes with a number of case studies that guide the development and testing of working ray tracers.

14.1 INTRODUCTION

In Chapters 6 through 8 we described methods for rendering scenes composed of polygonal meshes, including shading models that represent—at least approximately— how light reflects from the surface of a polygon. In addition, the Gouraud and Phong interpolation schemes were applied to suppress the "faceted" nature of the mesh model. Pictures formed in this way show a smooth surface (except along the edges of silhouettes), even though the model consists of discrete faces.

Ray tracing (sometimes called *ray casting*) provides a related, but even more powerful, approach to rendering scenes. Figure 14.1 shows the basic idea. Think of the frame buffer as a simple array of pixels positioned in space, with the eye looking through it into the scene. For each pixel in the frame buffer, the question "What does the eye 'see' through this pixel?" is asked. One can think of a ray of light arriving at the eye through the pixel from some point P in the scene. The color of the pixel is set to that of the light which emanates along the ray from point P in the scene.

In reality, the process is reversed. A ray is cast from the eye through the center of the pixel and out into the scene. Its path is traced to see what object it hits first and

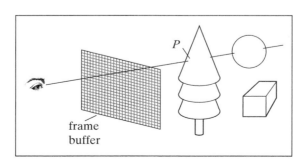

FIGURE 14.1 Viewing a point in a scene through a pixel.

at what point. (This process automatically solves the hidden-surface problem, since the first surface hit by the ray is the closest object to the eye; more remote surfaces are never reached.) Armed with a description of light sources in the scene, the same shading model as before is applied to the point first hit, and the ambient, diffuse, and specular components of light are computed. The resulting color is then displayed at the pixel. Because the path of a ray is traced through the scene, interesting visual effects, such as shadowing, reflection, and refraction, are easy to incorporate, producing images of dazzling realism that are difficult to create by any other method.

Another feature of ray tracing is its ability to work comfortably with a richer class of geometric objects than polygonal meshes. Solid objects are constructed out of various geometric primitives, such as spheres, cones, and cylinders. Each shape is represented exactly through a mathematical expression; it is not approximated as a faceted body. The shapes can also be subjected to transformations to alter their size and orientation before they are added to the scene, providing more modeling power for complex scenes.

In this chapter, we shall describe the algorithmic artillery needed to produce high-quality ray-traced images of complex scenes. Our development will be incremental, so that we can produce simple images with little programming after only a few sections. Additional tools are developed as needed to build up a repertoire of more advanced techniques.

14.2 SETTING UP THE GEOMETRY OF RAY TRACING

O Life! how pleasant is thy morning,
Young Fancy's rays the hills adorning!
Cold-pausing Caution's lesson scorning,
We frisk away,
Like schoolboys at th' expected warning,
To joy and play.

Robert Burns

In order to trace rays, we need a convenient representation for the ray that passes through a particular pixel. For easy reference, we gather together the required ingredients of the viewing process from Chapters 6 and 7. We use the same camera as in Chapter 7: Its eye is at point *eye*, and the axes of the camera are along the vectors $\mathbf{u}$, $\mathbf{v}$, and $\mathbf{n}$ as shown in Figure 14.2. The near plane lies at a distance N in front of the eye, and the frame buffer lies in the near plane. The shape of the camera is also the same as in Chapter 7, as shown in Figure 14.3: It has a viewangle of θ, and the window in the near plane has aspect ratio *aspect*. Thus, the camera extends from $-H$ to H in the $\mathbf{v}$-direction and from $-W$ to W in the $\mathbf{u}$-direction, where

$$H = N \tan(\theta/2) \qquad\qquad (14.1)$$

and

$$W = H \cdot aspect.$$

FIGURE 14.2 Setting up the camera for ray tracing.

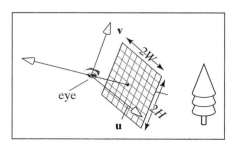

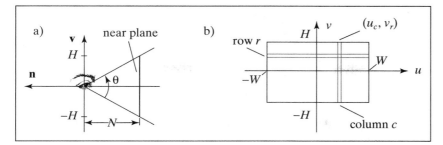

FIGURE 14.3 The shape of the camera.

Recall from Chapter 7 that the viewport transformation sets up a correspondence between points on the near plane and pixels in the viewport. Here we use the same correspondence, but without an explicit viewport transformation. In fact, it is simplest to think of the viewport as being "pasted onto" the window in the near plane, so that the eye is "looking through" individual pixels out into the scene. Suppose there are $nCols$ by $nRows$ of pixels in the viewport, and consider the pixel at row r and column c, where r varies from 0 to $nRows - 1$ and c varies from 0 to $nCols - 1$. We call that pixel the rcth pixel; it is shown in Part (b) of Figure 14.3. Where on the near plane does this pixel appear?

The lower left corner of the pixel lies at (u_c, v_r) given by (see the exercises at the end of the section)

$$u_c = -W + W \frac{2c}{nCols}, \qquad \text{for} \quad c = 0, 1, \ldots, nCols - 1;$$

$$v_r = -H + H \frac{2r}{nRows}, \qquad \text{for} \quad r = 0, 1, \ldots, nRows - 1. \tag{14.2}$$

In order to develop an expression for a ray that passes through this point, we will need to express where it lies in 3D: the actual point on the near plane. But this is easy: We merely find how far this point is from the eye. To do this, we start at eye and determine how far we must go in each of the directions $\mathbf{u}$, $\mathbf{v}$, and $\mathbf{n}$ to reach the corner of the pixel. We find that we must go a distance N in the negative $\mathbf{n}$-direction, u_c along $\mathbf{u}$, and v_r along $\mathbf{v}$. Thus, the 3D point is

$$eye - N\mathbf{n} + u_c\mathbf{u} + v_r\mathbf{v} \quad \text{(location of the corner of the pixel in space).}$$

The basic operation of ray tracing is to compute where a ray that starts at the eye and passes through a given pixel on the near plane goes—specifically, which objects it hits. Suppose the ray lies at eye at $t = 0$ and passes through the rcth corner of the pixel at $t = 1$. Its parametric form is then

$$r(t) = eye(1 - t) + (eye - N\mathbf{n} + u_c\mathbf{u} + v_r\mathbf{v})t.$$

(Check this carefully!) It is useful to isolate the starting point and direction of this ray as $r(t) = eye + \mathbf{dir}_{rc}t$. Simple manipulation of the previous expression gives the ray through the rcth pixel as

$$r(t) = eye + \mathbf{dir}_{rc}t;$$

$$\mathbf{dir}_{rc} = -N\mathbf{n} + W\left(\frac{2c}{nCols} - 1\right)\mathbf{u} + H\left(\frac{2r}{nRows} - 1\right)\mathbf{v}. \tag{14.3}$$

Let us call this the **rcth ray**. Note an important property of each ray in this family: As t increases from 0, the ray point moves farther and farther from the eye. If the ray strikes two objects in its path, say, at times t_a and t_b, the object lying closer to the eye will be the one hit at the lower value of t. Therefore, sorting the objects by depth from the eye corresponds to sorting the hit times at which the objects are intersected by the ray. Also, any objects that are hit at a negative t must lie behind the eye and so are ignored.

PRACTICE EXERCISES

14.2.1 Work out the details

Develop Equations (14.1)–(14.3) in detail, and prove that the rcth ray truly has the direction shown. Where is this ray at $t = 2$ and at $t = -1$?

14.2.2 Numerical calculation of a ray

Suppose the camera has $eye = (0, 0, -5)$, $\mathbf{u} = (1, 0, 0)$, and $\mathbf{v} = (0, 1, 0)$. Suppose further its viewangle is 30° and its *aspect* is 1.5. For $nRows = 480$ and $nCols = 640$, find the parametric expression for the rcth-ray when $r = 100$ and $c = 200$.

14.2.3 Where are the pixel corners?

Find formulas for the (u, v) coordinates corresponding to the center of the rcth pixel rather than its lower left corner.

14.2.4 Incremental calculation of rays

Note from Equation (14.3) that along a scan line, one ray can be found incrementally from the previous one by means of a single (vector) addition, found by expressing $\mathbf{dir}_{r,c+1}$ in terms of $\mathbf{dir}_{r,c}$. ■

14.3 OVERVIEW OF THE RAY-TRACING PROCESS

In Tracings of Eternal Light,....

J. C. F. von Schiller

We first develop an overview of a ray tracer to describe the basic operations required. Later we describe how to implement the key operations in a program.

Figure 14.4 shows the basic steps in a ray tracer. The scene to be traced is inhabited by various geometric objects and light sources. A typical scene may contain spheres, cones, boxes, cylinders, and the like, each having a specified shape, size, and position. These objects are described in some fashion and stored in an object list. The camera, as described earlier, is also created. Then, for each pixel in turn, we construct a ray that starts at the eye and passes through the lower left corner of the pixel. This involves simply evaluating the direction $\mathbf{dir}_{rc}$ for the rcth ray.

FIGURE 14.4 Pseudocode skeleton of a ray tracer.

```
define the objects and light sources in the scene
set up the camera
for(int r = 0; r < nRows; r++)
  for(int c = 0; c < nCols; c++)
  {
    1. Build the rc-th ray
    2. Find all intersections of the rc-th ray with objects in the scene
    3. Identify the intersection that lies closest to, and in front of, the eye
    4. Compute the "hit point" where the ray hits this object, and the normal vector at that point
    5. Find the color of the light returning to the eye along the ray from the point of intersection
    6. Place the color in the rc-th pixel.
  }
```

Steps 3–5 are new and are described in detail in the sections that follow. We first find whether the rcth ray intersects each object in the list, and if so, we note the "hit time"—the value of t at which the ray $r(t)$ coincides with the object's surface. When all objects have been tested, the object with the smallest hit time is the closest to the eye. The location of the "hit point" on the object is then found, along with the normal vector to the object's surface at the hit point. Next, the color of the light that reflects off the object, in the direction of the eye, is computed and stored in the pixel.

Figure 14.5 shows a simple scene consisting of some cylinders and spheres, as well as three cones. The snowman consists mainly of spheres. (What are the ingredients of his hat?) Two light sources are also shown. Notice that the objects in the scene can interpenetrate. As far as a picture is concerned, however, we are interested only in the outermost surfaces.

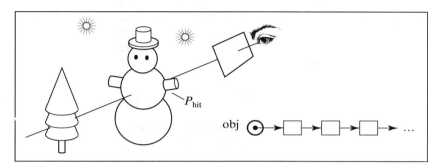

FIGURE 14.5 Ray tracing a scene.

Descriptions of all the objects are stored in an **object list**, suggested in the figure by the linked list of descriptive records. The ray that is shown intersects a sphere, a cylinder, and two cones. All the other objects are missed. The object with the smallest hit time—a cylinder in the scene—is identified. The hit spot, P_{hit}, is then easily found *from the ray itself* by evaluating the ray of Equation (14.3) at the hit time t_{hit}:

$$P_{hit} = eye + \mathbf{dir}_{r,c} t_{hit} \quad \text{(hit spot).} \tag{14.4}$$

14.4 INTERSECTION OF A RAY WITH AN OBJECT

Time is nature's way of keeping / everything from happening at once.

unknown

Nothing puzzles me more than time and space;
and yet nothing troubles me less, as I never think of them.

Charles Lamb

In Chapter 5 we introduced the `Scene` class, which can read a file in the SDL language and build a list of objects in a scene. We will use this tool for ray tracing as well, building the scene with the following code:

```
Scene scn;              // create a scene
scn.read("myScene.dat"); // read the SDL scene file
```

The objects in the scene are created and placed in a list. Each object is an instance of a "generic" shape such as a sphere or cone, along with an affine transformation that specifies how the object is scaled, oriented, and positioned in the scene. We introduced several generic shapes in Chapter 6. Figure 14.6 shows some of the generic shapes we shall be ray tracing.

FIGURE 14.6 Some common generic shapes used in ray tracing.

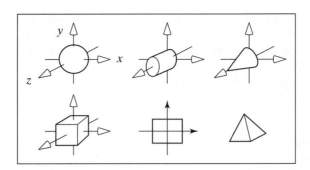

Whereas in Chapter 5 we used OpenGL to draw objects (via the method `drawOpenGL()` that we developed for each type of shape), here we will be ray tracing them. This involves finding where a ray intersects each object in a scene. As we shall see next, that is most easily accomplished by using the *implicit form* for each shape, discussed in Section 6.5.1. For example, the **generic sphere** has the implicit form

$$F(x, y, z) = x^2 + y^2 + z^2 - 1 \quad \text{(generic sphere)}. \tag{14.5}$$

If, for convenience, we use the notation $F(P)$, where the argument of the implicit function is a point, the implicit form for the generic sphere becomes

$$F(P) = |P|^2 - 1 \quad \text{(generic sphere)}. \tag{14.6}$$

Similarly, the **generic cylinder** has the implicit form

$$F(x, y, z) = x^2 + y^2 - 1 \quad \text{for } 0 < z < 1 \quad \text{(generic cylinder)}. \tag{14.7}$$

In a real scene, each generic shape is transformed by its affine transformation into a shape that has a quite different implicit form. But, as we see shortly, it turns out that we need only figure out how to intersect rays with generic objects! Thus, the implicit form of each generic shape will be of fundamental importance in ray tracing.

How do we find the intersection of a ray with a shape whose implicit form is $F(P)$? Suppose the ray has starting point S and direction $\mathbf{c}$. (This is simpler notation to use at first than a starting point *eye* and a direction $\mathbf{dir}_{rc}$.) The ray is therefore given by

$$r(t) = S + \mathbf{c}t. \tag{14.8}$$

It is easy to state the general theory. All points on the surface of the shape satisfy $F(P) = 0$, and the ray hits the surface whenever the point $r(t)$ coincides with the surface. A condition for $r(t)$ to coincide with a point on the surface is therefore $F(r(t)) = 0$. This will occur at the "hit time" t_{hit}, which we find by solving the equation

$$F(S + \mathbf{c}t_{\text{hit}}) = 0. \tag{14.9}$$

Much of the effort in ray tracing lies in trying to solve this equation efficiently for interesting objects. The equation is easy to solve for simple shapes such as a plane or a sphere, as we show next.

14.4.1 Intersection of a Ray with the Generic Plane

A scene often includes the floors and walls of some room. These are easily modeled as planes. They sometimes have a uniform color, or they might be covered with "texture" such as a checkerboard pattern or a digitized image.

The generic plane is the xy-plane, or $z = 0$, so its implicit form is $F(x, y, z) = z$. The ray $S + \mathbf{c}t$ intersects the generic plane when $S_z + \mathbf{c}_z t_h = 0$. This is a simple linear equation in t_h with solution

$$t_h = -\frac{S_z}{c_z}. \tag{14.10}$$

If $c_z = 0$, the ray is moving parallel to the plane, and there is no intersection (unless, of course, S_z is also zero, in which case the ray hits the plane end on and cannot be seen anyway). Otherwise the ray hits the plane at the point $P_{hit} = S - \mathbf{c}(S_z/c_z)$. (Why?)

■ **EXAMPLE 14.4.1 Where does a certain ray hit a certain plane?**

Where does the ray $r(t) = (4, 1, 3) + (-3, -5, -3)t$ hit the generic plane?

SOLUTION:

Equation (14.10) yields $t_h = -3/-3 = 1$. The hit point is found to be $S + \mathbf{c} = (1, -4, 0)$. Note that this point does indeed lie in the plane $z = 0$.

14.4.2 Intersection with a Generic Sphere

Where, then, does the ray $S + \mathbf{c}t$ intersect the generic sphere whose implicit form is given in Equation (14.6)? Substituting $S + \mathbf{c}t$ in $F(P) = 0$, we obtain $|S + \mathbf{c}t|^2 - 1 = 0$, or [using Equation (4.13)],[1]

$$|\mathbf{c}|^2 t^2 + 2(S \cdot \mathbf{c})t + (|S|^2 - 1) = 0. \tag{14.11}$$

This is a *quadratic* equation in t, of the form $At^2 + 2Bt + C = 0$, where

$$A = |\mathbf{c}|^2,$$
$$B = S \cdot \mathbf{c}, \tag{14.12}$$

and

$$C = |S|^2 - 1.$$

We solve the equation using the quadratic formula:

$$t_h = -\frac{B}{A} \pm \frac{\sqrt{B^2 - AC}}{A}. \tag{14.13}$$

If the *discriminant* $B^2 - AC$ is negative, there are no solutions, and the ray **misses** the sphere. If the discriminant is zero, the ray **grazes** the sphere at one point, and the hit time is $-B/A$. If the discriminant is positive, there are two hit times, t_1 and t_2, obtained with the plus and minus sign, respectively, in Equation (14.13).

The pleasant aspect of intersecting a ray with a plane or a sphere is that a simple linear or quadratic equation in t results and is easily solved. Some other simple shapes also yield reasonable equations in t, but many do not. We explore several such shapes in Section 14.6.

■ **EXAMPLE 14.4.2 Where does a sample ray hit the generic sphere?**

Where does the ray $r(t) = (3, 2, 3) + (-3, -2, -3)t$ hit the generic sphere?

SOLUTION:

From Equation (14.12), $A = 22$, $B = -22$, and $C = 21$. Then Equation (14.13) yields $t_1 = 0.7868$ and $t_2 = 1.2132$. The two hit points are $S + \mathbf{c}t_1 = (3, 2, 3)(1 - 0.7868) = (0.6393, 0.4264, 0.6396)$ and $S + \mathbf{c}t_2 = (3, 2, 3)(1 - 1.2132) = (-0.6393, -0.4264, -0.6396)$. Both of these points are easily seen to be exactly a unit distance from the origin, as expected. Notice the pleasant symmetry of points here; it arises because this ray goes through the origin and the generic sphere is centered at the origin.

---

[1] Notice some abuse of notation here for compactness. S is a point, not a vector, so technically we cannot use it in a dot product. Think of the notation $|S|^2$ simply as shorthand for $S_x^2 + S_y^2 + S_z^2$.

14.4.3 Intersection of the Ray with Transformed Objects

If I wish to explain what it is to him who asks me, I do not know.

St. Augustine on the nature of time

Each object in a scene has an associated affine transformation T that places it in the scene with the desired size, orientation, and position. What does transforming an object do to the equations and the results we obtained in the previous section?

Figure 14.7 illustrates the issue: Transformation T maps a generic sphere W' into an ellipsoid W. We ask, When does the ray $S + \mathbf{c}t$ hit W? Suppose we can find the implicit form, say, $G()$, for the transformed object W. We must solve $G(S + \mathbf{c}t) = 0$ for the the hit time.

FIGURE 14.7 Intersecting a ray with an ellipsoid.

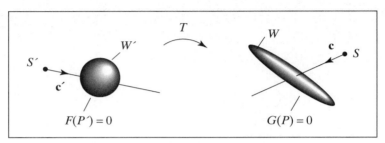

So it comes down to finding the implicit form for a transformed object. But we saw in Section 6.5.3 that if the original generic object has the implicit function $F(P)$, the transformed object has the implicit function $F(T^{-1}(P))$, where T^{-1} is the inverse transformation of T (i.e., the matrix of T^1 is M^{-1} if T has the matrix M). We therefore must solve the equation

$$F(T^{-1}(S + \mathbf{c}t)) = 0 \qquad (14.14)$$

for the hit time t. This could be a very messy equation. But in fact, it simply says, solve for the time at which the *inverse transformed ray* $T^{-1}(S + \mathbf{c}t)$ hits the original generic object! Because the transformation T is linear, the inverse transformed ray is

$$T^{-1}(S + \mathbf{c}t) = (T^{-1}S) + (T^{-1}\mathbf{c})t$$

which we denote as $S' + \mathbf{c}'t$ in Figure 14.7. (Not surprisingly, the inverse transformed ray is still a ray—a straight line emanating from S' in the direction $\mathbf{c}'$.) Now, suppose the matrix associated with the transformation T is M. Then, with the use of homogeneous coordinates, the inverse transformed ray is

$$\tilde{r}(t) = M^{-1}\begin{pmatrix} S_x \\ S_y \\ S_z \\ 1 \end{pmatrix} + M^{-1}\begin{pmatrix} c_x \\ c_y \\ c_z \\ 0 \end{pmatrix}t = \tilde{S}' + \tilde{\mathbf{c}}'t \qquad \text{(inverse transformed ray)}. \qquad (14.15)$$

Note that M^{-1} multiplies a point in one case and a vector in the other. S' is formed from $\tilde{S}'$ by dropping the 1; $\mathbf{c}'$ is formed from $\tilde{\mathbf{c}}'$ by dropping the 0.

Thus, instead of trying to intersect a ray with a transformed object, we intersect an "inverse transformed" ray with the generic object. The technique is this:

Each object in the object list has its own affine transformation. To intersect ray $S + \mathbf{c}t$ with the transformed object, we

- Inverse transform the ray (obtaining $S' + \mathbf{c}'t$),
- Find the intersection time t_h of the ray with the generic object, and
- Use the *same* t_h in $S + \mathbf{c}t$ to identify the actual hit point.

The beauty of this approach is that we need only work up code that intersects a ray with a *generic* object. It's a win–win situation (the programmer wins and the computer wins): We can apply affine transformations to objects for modeling purposes (in order to create interesting scenes), yet not pay the price of more complex code in the intersection routines. The "affine transformation burden" is shifted simply to transforming the ray.

■ **EXAMPLE 14.4.3 Where does a specific ray hit a transformed sphere?**

Suppose the ellipsoid W is formed from the generic sphere by using the following SDL commands:

```
translate 2 4 9
scale 1 4 4
sphere
```

Thus, the generic sphere is first scaled and then translated. Its transformation and inverse transformation have the matrices

$$M = \begin{pmatrix} 1 & 0 & 0 & 2 \\ 0 & 4 & 0 & 4 \\ 0 & 0 & 4 & 9 \\ 0 & 0 & 0 & 1 \end{pmatrix} \quad \text{and} \quad M^{-1} = \begin{pmatrix} 1 & 0 & 0 & -2 \\ 0 & \frac{1}{4} & 0 & -1 \\ 0 & 0 & \frac{1}{4} & -\frac{9}{4} \\ 0 & 0 & 0 & 1 \end{pmatrix},$$

respectively. (Check these!) Find where the ray $(10, 20, 5) + (-8, -12, 4)t$ intersects W.

SOLUTION:

The inverse transformed ray is $(8, 4, -1) + (-8, -3, 1)t$. (Check this, too!) Use this in Equation (14.12) to obtain $(A, B, C) = (74, -77, 80)$, so the discriminant is 9. Hence, there are two intersections. From Equation (14.13), we obtain the hit times 1.1621 and 0.9189. The hit spot is found by using the smaller hit time in the representation of the ray: $(10, 20, 5) + (-8, -12, 4)0.9189 = (2.649, 8.97, 8.67)$. (How would you check that this point lies on the sphere?)

PRACTICE EXERCISES

14.4.1 Find the intersection points

Find the times and points of intersection of the ray $(3, 5, 8) + (-4, -2, -6)t$ with the sphere of radius 5 centered at $(1, 2, 1)$.

SOLUTION:

$t = .41751$ or $t = 1.58248$, and the two intersections occur at $(1.33, 4.165, 5.495)$ and $(-3.33, 1.835, -1.495)$.

14.4.2 Hitting a plane

When and where does the ray $(10 - t, 8 - 2t, 3 + t)$ hit the plane created in SDL by the command `translate 4 5 6 rotate 90 1 0 0 plane`? ■

14.5 ORGANIZING A RAY TRACER APPLICATION

With the theory now in hand, we can construct an acual ray tracer based on the skeleton of Figure 14.4. We will use the Scene class and the SDL language first encountered in Chapter 5, since they provide convenient tools for describing a complex scene. Thus, we begin with an already constructed object list for the scene, in which each object has an associated affine transformation.

A ray tracer has to deal with several different interacting objects: the camera that is viewing the scene, the screen on which the image is created, rays that emanate from the camera and migrate through the scene, and the scene itself, which contains many geometric objects and light sources. An object-oriented approach should carefully define what types of objects are involved and decide which actions each data type must perform, as well as what information each object must have in order to perform the desired actions. We define one top-down approach here, but you could choose to divide up the tasks in a different manner.

In this approach, the camera is given the task of doing the ray tracing, for which we add a method to the existing `Camera` class:

```
void Camera :: raytrace(Scene& scn, int blockSize);
```

The camera is passed a scene to ray trace (and a certain "block size," to be described). The camera generates a ray from its eye through each pixel corner into the scene and determines the color of the light coming back along that ray. It then draws the pixel in that color.

We will use OpenGL to do the actual pixel drawing, and will have `raytrace()` set up the modelview and projection matrices to draw directly on the display, as explained later. This makes the `display()` function in the main loop of the application very simple: It need only clear the screen and tell the camera object `cam` to ray trace. We can use the following code:

```
void display(void)
{
    glClear(GL_COLOR_BUFFER_BIT);    // clear the screen
    cam.raytrace(scn, blockSize);    // ray trace the scene
}
```

A slight variation of this approach will make a big difference while developing your ray tracer. We already have in place a tool that draws an SDL scene using OpenGL's drawing functions, so there is no harm in drawing a "preview" of the scene just before ray tracing it each time. The preview quickly appears to reassure us that the camera is aimed properly and the objects are in their proper places. Then the tracing proceeds, and the preview scene is painted over, pixel by pixel, with the "true" colors the pixels should have according to ray tracing. If things are set up correctly, the ray-traced objects will line up exactly with the previewed objects. Any bugs in the ray tracer are immediately apparent.

To add a preview of the scene, simply extend `display()` to encompass the following code:

```
void display(void)
{
    //clear the screen and reset the depth buffer
    glClear(GL_COLOR_BUFFER_BIT|GL_DEPTH_BUFFER_BIT);
    cam.drawOpenGL(scn); // draw the preview
    cam.raytrace(scn, blockSize); // ray trace over the preview
}
```

Figure 14.8 shows an example of ray tracing in progress: The preview has been drawn, and the lower half of the screen has been ray traced. The important point here is that the ray tracing overlays the preview scene exactly.

FIGURE 14.8 A ray tracing in progress over a previewed scene.

The Ingredients of `raytrace()`

The `Camera` class' `raytrace()` method implements the steps of Figure 14.4. For each row r and column c, a ray object is created that emanates from the eye and passes through the lower left corner of the rcth pixel into the scene. We need a `Ray` class for this, the beginnings of which are shown in Figure 14.9. It has a field to hold the starting point of the ray and a field to hold its direction. We shall add other fields later. Two methods set the starting point and direction of a given ray.

```
class Ray{
public:
    Point3 start;
    Vector3 dir;
    void setStart(point3& p){start.x = p.x; etc..}
    void setDir(Vector3& v){dir.x = v.x; etc..}
    // other fields and methods
};
```

FIGURE 14.9 Beginning of the `Ray` class.

A skeleton of `raytrace()` is shown in Figure 14.10. It sets the start point of `theRay` once to the camera's eye, and then, for each pixel, it computes and sets the direction of the rcth ray [according to Equation (14.3)]. Next, the `Scene` object `scn` is told to find the color coming back along this ray: `clr = scn.shade(theRay)`. The method `shade()` does the hard work: It casts the ray into the scene, determines intersections, computes the color of the light coming back along the ray, and returns the value of the color. We develop this method in the remainder of the chapter.

Drawing "Pixel Blocks"

The `blockSize` parameter determines the size of the block of pixels being drawn at each step. Displaying pixel blocks is simply a time-saver for the viewer during the development of a ray tracer: The images formed are rough, but they appear rapidly; instead of tracing a ray through every pixel, wherein the picture emerges slowly, pixel by pixel, rays are traced only through the lower left corner of each block of pixels.

Figure 14.11(a) shows how the procedure works for a simple display that has 16 rows and 32 columns of actual pixels and wherein `blockSize` is set to 4. Each block consists of 16 pixels. The color of the ray through the corner of the block is determined, and the entire block (all 16 pixels) is set to this uniform color. The image would appear as a raster of 4-by-8 blocks, giving only a very rough approximation to

FIGURE 14.10 Skeleton of `raytrace()`.

```
void Camera :: raytrace(Scene& scn, int blockSize)
{
     Ray theRay;
     Color3 clr;
     theRay.setStart(eye);
     // set up OpenGL for simple 2D drawing
     glMatrixMode(GL_MODELVIEW);
     glLoadIdentity();
     glMatrixMode(GL_PROJECTION);
     glLoadIdentity();
     gluOrtho2D(0,nCols,0,nRows); // whole screen is the window
     glDisable(GL_LIGHTING); // so glColor3f() works properly
     // begin raytracing
     for(int row = 0; row < nRows; row += blockSize)
     for(int col = 0; col < nCols; col += blockSize)
     {
       compute the ray's direction
       theRay.setDir(<direction>); //set the ray's direction
       clr.ser(scn.shade(theRay)); // find the color
       glColor3f(clr.red, clr.green, clr.blue);
       glRecti(col,row,col + blockSize, row + blockSize);
     }
}
```

the full-resolution ray tracing. But it would be drawn very quickly. If this rough image suggests that everything is working correctly, the viewer can retrace the scene at full resolution by setting `blockSize` to 1. Figure 14.11(b) shows a simple scene ray traced with a block size of 4, 2, and 1. The first version is rendered 16 times faster than the last.

Note that `raytrace()` sets up OpenGL matrices for drawing the pixel blocks. The modelview matrix is set to the identity matrix, and the projection matrix does simple scaling of the window to the viewport with no projection. These steps effectively make the openGL pipeline "transparent," so that a square can be drawn directly into the viewport using `glRecti()`. (We assume that the viewport has already been set to the full screen window with a `glViewport(0,0,nCols,nRows)` command when the program is first started.) OpenGL's lighting must also be disabled so that `glColor3f()` will work properly.

FIGURE 14.11 (a) Ray tracing with blocks of pixels. (b) Ray tracings with different block sizes.

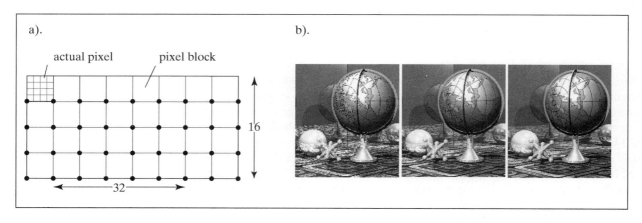

a).

actual pixel   pixel block

16

32

b).

The Basics of `shade(ray)`

The meat of a ray tracer resides in `shade()`, a skeleton of which is shown in Figure 14.12. The first job of the tracer is to determine whether the ray hits some object and, if so, which one. To do this, it uses a routine `getFirstHit(ray,best)`, which puts data concerning the first hit into an *intersection record* named `best`. Once information about the first hit is available, `shade()` proceeds to find the "color of the ray." If no object was hit, this is simply the background color, which `shade()` returns. On the other hand, if the ray did hit an object, `shade()` accumulates the various contributions in the variable `color`. These consist of the color emitted by the object if it is glowing, the ambient, diffuse, and specular components that are part of the classical shading model described in Chapter 8, and the light reflected from a shiny surface and refracted through a transparent surface.

```
Color3 Scene :: shade(Ray& ray)
{       // return the color of this ray
  Color3 color;     // total color to be returned
  Intersection best;  //data for the best hit so far
  getFirstHit(ray, best);  //fill the 'best' record
  if(best.numHits == 0)  //did the ray miss every object?
      return background;
  color.set(the emissive color of the object);
  color.add(ambient, diffuse and specular components); //add more contributions
  color.add(reflected and refracted components);
  return color;
}
```

FIGURE 14.12 Skeleton of `shade()`.

The routine `getFirstHit()` finds the object hit first by the ray and returns the information in the intersection record `best`. We implement intersection records using the class `Intersection`:

```
class Intersection{
 public:
   int numHits;     // # of hits at positive hit times
   HitInfo hit[8];  // list of hits - may need more than 8 later
   ... various methods ...
};
```

This class has two fields: the number of times the ray hits the object and an array holding data about each hit. We shall consider as legitimate only those intersections that occur at positive hit times (in front of the ray's starting point); hits "behind the eye" are of no interest. We are particularly interested in the first hit of the ray with an object. If `inter` is an intersection record and `inter.numHits` is greater than zero, information concerning the first hit is stored in `inter.hit[0]`.

Why keep information on *all* of the hits the ray makes with an object (at positive hit times), rather than just the first? One of the powerful advantages of the ray-tracing approach is its ability to render *Boolean* objects. (See Section 14.12.3.) To handle these objects, we must keep a record of all the hits a ray makes with an object, so we take pains now to set things up properly. Normally, the eye is outside of all objects and a ray hits just twice—once upon entering the object and once upon exiting it. In such cases, `inter.numHits` is 2, `inter.hit[0]` describes where the ray enters the object, and `inter.hit[1]` describes where it exits. But some objects, like the torus and the Boolean objects shown in Figure 14.13, can have more than two hits. In Part (a) of the figure, there are four hits with positive hit times (so inter.numHits is 4), and we store information regarding hits in inter.hit[0],..., inter.hit[3]. In Part (b), the ray hits the object eight times, but the eye is inside the object (assumed to be transparent), and only three of the hits occur with positive hit times (so inter.numHits is 3).

FIGURE 14.13 Multiple hits with an object, some occurring at negative hit times.

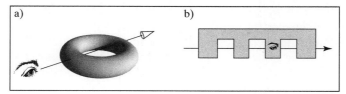

Information about each hit is stored in a record of type HitInfo:

```
class HitInfo { // data for each hit with a surface
    public:
    double hitTime;        // the hit time
    GeomObj* hitObject;    // the object hit
    bool isEntering;       // is the ray entering or exiting?
    int surface;           // which surface is hit?
    Point3 hitPoint;       // hit point
    Vector3 hitNormal;     // normal at hit point
    ... other fields and methods ...
};
```

A hit record contains several fields that describe the hit: the hit time, a pointer to the object that was hit, whether or not the ray was entering or exiting the object at the hit, the location of the hit point, and the normal vector to the surface at that point. All of these fields will be important at various points in the ray-tracing process.

The routine getFirstHit() is shown in Figure 14.14. It scans through the entire object list (starting at obj, a pointer to the first object in the list—see the Scene class in Appendix 3), testing whether the ray hits the object. To do this, it uses each object's own hit() method, which we describe starting in the next section. Each hit() method returns true if there is a legitimate hit and false otherwise. If there is a hit, the method builds an entire intersection record describing all of the hits with the object in question and places the record in inter. Then getFirstHit() compares the (first positive) hit time in inter with that of best, the record of the "best hit so far." If an earlier hit time is found, the data in inter are copied into best. The value of best.numHits is initialized to zero so that the first real hit will be counted as pObj scans through the object list.

Notice that getFirstHit() passes the burden of computing intersections of rays

FIGURE 14.14 The method getFirstHit().

```
void Scene:: getFirstHit(Ray& ray, Intersection& best)
{
    Intersection inter;                // make intersection record
    best.numHits = 0;                  // no hits yet

    for(GeomObj* pObj = obj; pObj != NULL; pObj = pObj->next)
    {        // test each object in the scene
        if(!pObj->hit(ray, inter))      //does the ray hit pObj?
            continue;                   // miss: test the next object
        if(best.numHits == 0 ||         // best has no hits yet
            inter.hit[0].hitTime < best.hit[0].hitTime)
                best.set(inter);        // copy inter into best
    }
}
```

onto the hit() routine that each object possesses. We shall develop a hit() method for each type of object. For the sake of efficiency, it will be finely tuned to exploit special knowledge of the shape of the generic object. This is an excellent example of using polymorphism to simplify code and make it more robust and efficient. The routine hit() is a virtual method of the GeomObj class from which all actual Shape classes are derived.

The job of hit() in a given class is to take a ray and build an intersection record, loading the record with all the details of the hits that the ray makes with the object. We develop hit() for a sphere next to show what is involved.

14.5.1 A Routine to Compute Ray–Sphere Intersections

Figure 14.15 shows the hit() method for the Sphere class. First, it transforms the ray r into the generic coordinates of the given sphere, using that sphere's

```
bool Sphere:: hit(Ray &r, Intersection& inter)
{
  Ray genRay; // need to make the generic ray
  xfrmRay(genRay,invTransf,r);
  double A, B, C;
  A = dot3D(genRay.dir, genRay.dir);
  B = dot3D(genRay.start, genRay.dir);
  C = dot3D(genRay.start, genRay.start) - 1.0;
  double discrim = B * B - A * C;
  if(discrim < 0.0) // ray misses
     return false;
  int num = 0;    // the # of hits so far
  double discRoot = sqrt(discrim);
  double t1 = (-B - discRoot)/A;         // the earlier hit
  if(t1 > 0.00001) // is hit in front of the eye?
  {
     inter.hit[0].hitTime = t1;
     inter.hit[0].hitObject = this;
     inter.hit[0].isEntering = true;
     inter.hit[0].surface = 0;
     Point3 P(rayPos(genRay, t1));//hit spot
     inter.hit[0].hitPoint.set(P);
     inter.hit[0].hitNormal.set(P);
     num = 1;    // have a hit
  }
  double t2 = (-B + discRoot)/A;  //the later hit
  if( t2 > 0.00001)
  {
     inter.hit[num].hitTime = t2;
     inter.hit[num].hitObject = this;
     inter.hit[num].isEntering = false;
     inter.hit[num].surface = 0;
     Point3 P(rayPos(genRay, t2));// hit spot
     inter.hit[num].hitPoint.set(P);
     inter.hit[num].hitNormal.set(P);
     num++;     // have another hit
  }
  inter.numHits = num;
  return (num > 0); // true or false
}
```

FIGURE 14.15 The hit() method for the Sphere class.

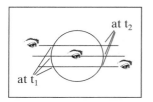

FIGURE 14.16 Which hits are in front of the eye?

particular inverse transformation. `xfrmRay()` transforms the ray according to Equation (14.15). (See the exercises at the end of the section.) Next, the coefficients A, B, and C of the quadratic equation (14.12) are found, and the discriminant $B^2 - AC$ is tested. If it is negative, there are no real solutions to the equation, and we know that the ray must miss the sphere. Therefore, `hit()` returns `false`, and `inter` is never used.

On the other hand, if the discriminant is positive, the two hit times are computed as in Equation (14.13). Call the earlier hit time t_1 and the later one t_2. As shown in Figure 14.16, there are three possibilities: The sphere can be in front of the eye, in which case both hit times are positive; the eye can be inside the sphere, in which case t_1 is negative, but t_2 is positive; and the sphere can be behind the eye, so that both times are negative. If t_1 is strictly positive, data for the first hit are placed in `inter.hit[0]`, and the variable `num` is set to unity to indicate that there has been a hit. If t_2 is positive, data for the next hit is placed in `inter.hit[num]`. (If the first hit time is negative, the second hit-time datum is automatically placed in `hit[0]`.)

The data that are placed in each hit record use information about a sphere. For instance, because the sphere is a convex object, the ray must be entering at the earlier hit time and exiting at the later hit time. The value of `surface` is set to zero, as a sphere has only one surface. (We address this notion later.) The points (in generic coordinates) where the ray hits the sphere are also recorded in the `hitPoint` field. The hit spot is always (by definition) the same as the position of the ray at the given hit time, which is found by the following function (see the exercises):

```
Point3 rayPos(Ray& r, float t);//returns the ray's location at
time t
```

The calculation of the normal vector at the hit spot is also simple for a sphere: Because the normal points radially outward from the center of the sphere, its coordinates are *identical* to those of the hit point itself.

PRACTICE EXERCISES

14.5.1 Convert a ray from scene to generic coordinates

Write the routine `xfrmRay()` that `hit()` uses to transform a ray into the generic coordinates of a sphere. Give careful attention to the difference between transforming a point and a vector.

14.5.2 The function `rayPos()`

Implement the function `rayPos()` described earlier. The function is given a ray and a time and returns the position of the ray at that time.

14.5.3 When the ray grazes the sphere

Discuss what values will be computed and stored for the case where the ray just grazes the sphere.

14.5.4 On computational complexity

How costly is it to intersect a ray with a sphere? How many multiplications, divisions, and square roots are required when the ray hits the sphere?   ■

14.5.2 A Complete Ray Tracer for Emissive-sphere Scenes

In full-orbed glory, yonder moon divine
Rolls through the dark blue depths;
Beneath her steady ray
The desert circle spreads
Like the round ocean, girdled with the sky.
How beautiful is night!

Robert Southey

We have enough tools in place to put together a simple ray tracer for scenes composed of spheres (and, of course, ellipsoids). It is very useful to get this much working before things get more complicated, to see how all of the ingredients discussed go together. Nothing is wasted in the process, as all of these tools are needed later.

So far we can make an object glow in some color only by setting its emissive component in the SDL file to some nonzero color, as in the command `emissive 0.3 0.6 0.2`. It is simple to adjust `Scene::shade()` of Figure 14.12 so that it handles only emissive light: Just remove the `color.add()` lines that find other light contributions. The result is as follows:

```
Color3 Scene :: shade(Ray& ray)
{
    Color3 color;
    Intersection best;
    getFirstHit(ray, best);
    if(best.numHits == 0) return background;
    Shape* myObj = (Shape*)best.hit[0].hitObject; //the hit object
    color.set(myObj->mtrl.emissive);
    return color;
}
```

The only parts of `Camera :: raytrace()` of Figure 14.10 that need fleshing out are the computation of the ray's direction for each pixel block:[2]

```
for(int row = 0; row < nRows; row += blockSize)
    for(int col = 0; col < nCols; col += blockSize)
    {
        float x = -W + col * 2 * W / (float)nCols;
        float y = -H +  row * 2 * H / (float)nRows;
        theRay.setDir( -nearDist * n.x + x * u.x + y * v.x,
                       -nearDist * n.y + x * u.y + y * v.y,
                       -nearDist * n.z + x * u.z + y * v.z);
        Color3 clr = scn.shade(theRay);  //color of this ray
        glColor3f(clr.red, clr.green, clr.blue);
        glRecti(col, row, col + blockSize, row + blockSize);
    }
```

Case Study 14.1 discusses in more detail the implementation of a simple ray tracer for scenes with spheres.

---

[2] Note that the computation of several of these variables can be removed from the inner loop for efficiency. (Which ones?)

14.6 INTERSECTING RAYS WITH OTHER PRIMITIVES

We need to develop the `hit()` method for other shape classes. All the `hit()` methods are similar: First the ray is transformed into the generic coordinates of the object in question, and then the various intersections with the generic object are computed. We need only work out the specific details of intersection for each generic shape.

14.6.1 Intersecting with a Square

A square is a useful generic shape. The generic square lies in the $z = 0$ plane and extends from -1 to 1 in both x and y. (The implicit form of the equation of the square is $F(P) = P_z$ for $|P_x| \leq 1$ and $|P_y| \leq 1$.) The square can be transformed into any parallelogram positioned in space, so it is often used in scenes to provide thin, flat surfaces such as walls and windows. The function `hit()` first finds where the ray hits the generic plane and then tests whether this hit spot also lies within the square, as suggested in Figure 14.17.

FIGURE 14.17 The `hit()` method for the Square class.

```
//<<<<<<<<<<<<<<<<<< hit for Square >>>>>>>>>>>>>>>>>.
bool Square:: hit(Ray &r, Intersection& inter)
{
    Ray genRay; // need to make the generic ray
    inter.numHits = 0; // initial assumption
    xfrmRay(genRay, invTransf, r);
    double denom = genRay.dir.z; //denominator
    if(fabs(denom) < 0.0001) return false; //ray parallel to plane: miss
    double time = -genRay.start.z/denom; //hit time
    if(time <= 0.0) return false; // it lies behind the eye
    double hx = genRay.start.x + genRay.dir.x * time;//x at hit
    double hy = genRay.start.y + genRay.dir.y * time;// y at hit
    if((hx > 1.0) || (hx < -1.0)) return false; // misses in x-direction
    if((hy > 1.0) || (hy < -1.0)) return false; // misses in y-direction
    inter.numHits = 1;   // have a hit
    inter.hit[0].hitObject = this;
    inter.hit[0].hitTime = time;
    inter.hit[0].isEntering = true;
    inter.hit[0].surface = 0;
    inter.hit[0].hitPoint.set(hx,hy,0);
    inter.hit[0].hitNormal.set(0,0,1);
    return true;
}
```

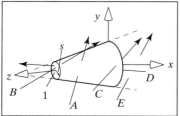

FIGURE 14.18 The generic tapered cylinder.

14.6.2 Intersecting with a Tapered Cylinder

The generic tapered cylinder is shown in Figure 14.18, along with several rays. The side of the cylinder is part of an infinitely long "wall" with a radius of 1 at $z = 0$ and a "small radius" of s at $z = 1$. From Equation (6.30), we know that this wall has the implicit form

$$F(x, y, z) = x^2 + y^2 - (1 + (s - 1)z)^2, \text{ for } 0 < z < 1.$$

If $s = 1$, the shape becomes the generic cylinder; if $s = 0$, it becomes the generic cone. We develop a `hit()` method for the tapered cylinder, which also provides a `hit()` method for the cylinder and cone.

Several rays are also shown in the figure, illustrating the variety of ways in which a ray can hit or miss this object. Ray A hits the wall twice on the actual cylinder (for brevity, we will often refer to a tapered cylinder simply as a "cylinder"), whereas ray B passes through the infinite wall before entering the cylinder through its cap and then exits through the side. Ray C hits the wall first and then exits through the base, and ray D enters through the base and exits through the cap. Ray E hits the infinite wall, but outside the extent of the cylinder and so misses the object. Not shown is a ray that misses the cylindrical wall entirely. (What other cases are not shown?)

With this many possibilities, we need an organized approach that avoids an unwieldy number of `if()..else` tests. The solution is to identify hits in whatever order is convenient and to put them in the `inter.hit[]` list regardless of order. At the end, if `inter.hit[]` holds two hits out of order, the two items are swapped. It's handy that we already have a list available to put these hits in.

The individual tests are straightforward. To determine whether the ray strikes the infinite wall, we merely substitute $S + \mathbf{c}t$ into the implicit form for the tapered cylinder to obtain the quadratic equation $At^2 + 2Bt + C = 0$. It is straightforward to show that

$$A = c_x^2 + c_y^2 - d^2,$$

$$B = S_x c_x + S_y c_y - Fd,$$

and

$$C = S_x^2 + S_y^2 - F^2, \tag{14.16}$$

where $d = (s - 1)c_z$ and $F = 1 + (s - 1)S_z$. (What do these equations become for the cylinder and the cone?)

We use the coefficients in the same manner as for a sphere. If the discriminant $B^2 - AC$ is negative, the ray passes by the tapered cylinder's wall. If the discriminant is not negative, the ray does strike the wall, and the hit times can be found by solving the quadratic equation. To test whether each hit is on the actual cylinder wall, find the z-component of the hit spot. The ray hits the cylinder only if the z-component lies between 0 and 1.

To test for an intersection with the base, intersect the ray with the plane $z = 0$. Suppose the ray hits at the point $(x, y, 0)$. The hit spot lies within the cap if $x^2 + y^2 < 1$. (Why?) Similarly, to test for an intersection with the cap, intersect the ray with the plane $z = 1$. Suppose it hits at the point $(x, y, 1)$. The hit spot lies within the cap if $x^2 + y^2 < s^2$.

A cylinder has more than one surface, and we will later want to know which surface is hit. (For instance, we may want to paste a different texture on the wall than on the cap.) Therefore, we adopt the following numbering: The wall is surface 0, the base is surface 1, and the cap is surface 2. The appropriate value is placed in the `surface` field of each hit record.

Figure 14.19 brings these ideas together with a skeleton of the code appropriate for the generic tapered cylinder. (As before, expressions in italics are pseudocode.) Note that each surface of the cylinder is tested in turn, and legitimate hits are added to the "hit list," including data about which surface is involved.

Note that the normal vector must be found at the two hit points. As we discussed in Chapter 6, the normal to the cylinder wall at point (x, y, z) is simply $(x, y, -(s - 1)(1 + (s - 1)z))$. The normal to the cap and base are $(0, 0, 1)$ and $(0, 0, -1)$, respectively. The `hitNormal` fields are filled with the appropriate values by `hit()`.

```
bool TaperedCylinder::hit(Ray &r, Intersection &inter)
{
 Ray genRay; //generic ray
 xfrmRay(genRay,invTransf,r);
 double A, B, C, discrim, disc_root, t1,t2,tb,tc;
 double sm = smallRadius - 1;
 double fDir = sm * genRay.dir.z; //handy short names
 double fStart = sm * genRay.start.z + 1;
 get A, B, and C as in Equation 14.16
 discrim = B*B - A*C;
 int num = 0; // no hits yet

 if(discrim > 0.0) //can take square root
 {
    disc_root = (double)sqrt(double(discrim));
    t1 = (-B - disc_root)/A;          // earlier hit
    float zHit = genRay.start.z + genRay.dir.z * t1; //z component of ray
    if(t1 > 0.00001 && zHit <= 1.0 && zHit >= 0)
    {
       inter.hit[num].hitTime = t1;
       inter.hit[num++].surface = 0; //hit is with wall
    }
    t2 = (-B + disc_root)/A;    // second hit
    zHit = genRay.start.z + genRay.dir.z * t2;
    if(t2 > 0.00001 && zHit <= 1.0 && zHit >=0)
    {
       inter.hit[num].hitTime = t2;
       inter.hit[num++].surface = 0; //hit is with wall
    }
 } // end if(discrim > 0)

 //test the base at z = 0
 tb = -genRay.start.z/genRay.dir.z; //hit time at z = 0 plane
 if(tb > 0.00001 && SQR(genRay.start.x + genRay.dir.x * tb) +
    SQR(genRay.start.y + genRay.dir.y * tb) < 1) //within disc of base
 {
    inter.hit[num].hitTime = tb;
    inter.hit[num++].surface = 1; //1 for the base
 }
 //test the cap at z = 1
 tc = (1 - genRay.start.z)/genRay.dir.z; //hit time at z = 1 plane
 if(tc > 0.00001 && SQR(genRay.start.x + genRay.dir.x * tc) +
    SQR(genRay.start.y + genRay.dir.y * tc) < SQR(smallRadius)) //within disc
 {
    inter.hit[num].hitTime = tc;
    inter.hit[num++].surface = 2; // 2 for the cap
 }
 if(num == 0) return false; // missed everything, or behind the eye
 inter.numHits = num;
```

FIGURE 14.19 Skeleton of the hit() method for the TaperedCylinder class.

PRACTICE EXERCISES

14.6.1 Implementation of hit() for the tapered cylinder

Check Equation (14.16) to verify that the coefficients of the quadratic equation of the tapered cylinder are correct. Flesh out the code for TaperedCylinder ::hit(Ray& r, Intersection& inter).

```
if(num == 1) // eye inside cylinder, only have the exiting hit
{
    inter.hit[0].isEntering = false;
    inter.hit[0].hitObject = this;
}
  else // have two hits - first must be entering
{    //now sort the two hits
      if(inter.hit[0].hitTime > inter.hit[1].hitTime) // must reverse them
      {// need only swap the hitTime and surface fields
            double tmpT = inter.hit[0].hitTime; //swap times
            inter.hit[0].hitTime = inter.hit[1].hitTime;
            inter.hit[1].hitTime = tmpT;
            int tmpS = inter.hit[0].surface; //swap surfaces
            inter.hit[0].surface = inter.hit[1].surface;
            inter.hit[1].surface = tmpS;
      }
      inter.hit[0].isEntering = true; inter.hit[1].isEntering = false;
      inter.hit[0].hitObject = inter.hit[1].hitObject = this;
}
// now set the hit point and normal for the hit or hits
for(int i = 0; i < num; i++)
{
    Point3 P0(rayPos(genRay, inter.hit[i].hitTime));// position of first hit
    inter.hit[i].hitPoint.set(P0);
    int surf = inter.hit[i].surface;
    if(surf == 0) // wall
        inter.hit[i].hitNormal.set(P0.x, P0.y, -sm * (1 + sm * P0.z));
    else if(surf == 1) // base
        inter.hit[i].hitNormal.set(0,0,-1);
    else inter.hit[i].hitNormal.set(0,0,1); //cap
}
return true;
}
```

FIGURE 14.19 (*continued*)

14.6.2 Implementation of `hit()` for intersecting a cone

If you wanted to have a `hit()` routine specially crafted for a `Cone` class, how would it differ from that for the `TaperedCylinder` class? Show which lines of code would be changed to increase the efficiency of the routine.

14.6.3 On computational complexity

How many additions/subtractions and multiplications/divisions are required to intersect a ray with a square and a tapered cylinder?

14.6.4 Other quadric surfaces

In Chapter 6 we examined the representation of various quadric surfaces, such as the hyperboloid and elliptic cone.

a. What is a reasonable definition of the *generic* version of each type of quadric surface?
b. For each generic quadric surface, show that intersecting it with a ray results in a quadratic equation, and provide the equation. ■

14.6.3 Intersecting with a Cube (or any Convex Polyhedron)

Convex polyhedra prove useful in many graphics situations and have been treated in several places in the book. (See, for example, the discussion of the Platonic solids in Chapter 6.) Because convex polyhedra are defined in terms of bounding planes, it is easy to develop an intersection routine for a ray with any convex polyhedron. We do this later in the section.

One particular convex polyhedron, the **generic cube**, deserves special attention. It is centered at the origin and has corners at $(\pm 1, \pm 1, \pm 1)$, using all eight combinations of $+1$ and -1. Thus, its edges are aligned with the coordinate axes, and its six faces lie in the planes specified in Figure 14.20. (To aid in visualizing the generic cube, a suggestive name is given to each plane according to how it is viewed from a point such as $(0, 0, 10)$.) The figure also shows the outward-pointing normal vector to each plane and a typical point, *spot*, that lies in the plane.

FIGURE 14.20 The six planes that define the generic cube.

Plane	name	Equation	outward normal	spot
0	top	y = 1	$(0, 1, 0)$	$(0, 1, 0)$
1	bottom	y = -1	$(0, -1, 0)$	$(0, -1, 0)$
2	right	x = 1	$(1, 0, 0)$	$(1, 0, 0)$
3	left	x = -1	$(-1, 0, 0)$	$(-1, 0, 0)$
4	front	z = 1	$(0, 0, 1)$	$(0, 0, 1)$
5	back	z = -1	$(0, 0, -1)$	$(0, 0, -1)$

The generic cube is important for two reasons:

- A large variety of interesting "boxes" can be modeled and placed in a scene by applying an affine transformation to a generic cube. Then, in ray tracing, each ray can be inverse transformed into the generic cube's coordinate system, and we can use a ray-with-generic-cube intersection routine (which can be made very efficient).
- The generic cube can be used as an **extent** for the other generic primitives in the sense of a **bounding box**: Each generic primitive, such as the cylinder, fits snugly inside the cube. As we shall see later, it is often efficient to test whether a ray intersects the extent of an object before testing whether it hits the object itself, particularly if the ray-with-object intersection routine is computationally expensive. If a ray misses the extent, it *must* miss the object. So there is a strong advantage in having available a highly efficient algorithm for intersecting a ray with the generic cube.

The Intersection Algorithm for the Generic Cube

The process of intersecting a ray with a cube is essentially the Cyrus–Beck algorithm described in Section 4.8.3, in which a line is clipped against a convex window in 2D space. The algorithm was also used for clipping a line against the camera's view volume in Chapter 8. The basic idea is that each plane of the cube defines an "inside" half-space and an "outside" half-space and that a point on a ray lies inside the cube if and only if it lies on the "inside" of every half-space of the cube. So intersecting a ray with a cube is a matter of finding the interval of time in which the ray lies inside all of the planes of the cube.

Call the cube P. We test the ray against each of the planes of P in turn, computing the time at which the ray either enters or exits the inside half-space for that plane. We keep track of a "candidate interval" CI: the interval of time in which, on the basis of our tests so far, the ray could be inside the object. This interval is bracketed by the values t_{in} and t_{out}; that is, CI $= [t_{in}, t_{out}]$. As each plane of P is tested, we "chop away" at that interval, either increasing t_{in} or reducing t_{out}. If at any point the CI becomes empty, the ray must miss the object, giving an "early out." If, after testing all of the planes of P, we find that the remaining CI is nonempty, the ray enters the object at t_{in} and exits at t_{out}.

To assist in visualizing this process, Figure 14.21(a) shows an example of a ray entering the generic cube at $t = 3.6$ and exiting at $t = 4.1$. So when testing is complete, the remaining CI is $[3.6, 4.1]$. Part (b) shows a 2D version of the same process as in Part (a), for simplicity; we wish to find the intersection of a ray with a square. From our omniscient vantage point, we see that the ray first hits the top plane of the square at $t = 1.6$ and is entering the square's inside half-space. Then it hits the right plane at $t = 1.8$, also entering. The ray hits the left plane at $t = 2.7$ and is exiting, and finally, it exits the bottom plane at $t = 2.9$.

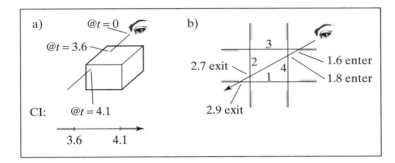

FIGURE 14.21 (a) A ray pierces the generic cube. (b) The 2D version.

Suppose we test the planes (sides) of the square in the order shown, beginning with plane 1 and proceeding to plane 4. Initially, we set CI $= (-\infty, \infty)$. The hit with plane 1 shows an exit time of 2.9, so we know that the ray must be outside the square after that time, and the CI becomes $(-\infty, 2.9]$. The test with plane 2 reveals that the ray actually exits earlier, at 2.7, so we set t_{out} to 2.7. The test with plane 3 shows that the ray cannot possibly enter earlier than $t = 1.6$, so we set t_{in} to that value. Finally, the test with plane 4 indicates that t_{in} is actually 1.8. The final CI is thus $[1.8, 2.7]$. At each step, t_{in} and t_{out} are adjusted according to the following code:

```
if(the ray is entering at t_hit)
       t_in = max(t_in, t_hit)
  else if(the ray is exiting at t_hit)
       t_out = min(t_out, t_hit)
```

As for the details, let the ray be $S + \mathbf{c}t$, and suppose the plane in question has outward-pointing normal $\mathbf{m}$ and contains the point B. The implicit form for this plane is $F(P) = \mathbf{m} \cdot (P - B)$, so the ray hits it when $\mathbf{m} \cdot (S + \mathbf{c}t - B) = 0$, or at the hit time

$$t = \frac{numer}{denom},$$

where

$$numer = \mathbf{m} \cdot (B - S)$$

and

$$denom = \mathbf{m} \cdot \mathbf{c}. \tag{14.17}$$

The ray is passing into the outside half-space of the plane if denom > 0 (since $\mathbf{m}$ and $\mathbf{c}$ are then less than 90° apart) and passing into the inside half-space if denom < 0. If denom $= 0$, the ray is parallel to the plane, and the value of numer determines

FIGURE 14.22 Interaction of a ray and a plane's inside half-space.

Situation	Condition
Pass to inside	denom < 0
Pass to outside	denom > 0
Wholly inside	denom $= 0$, numer > 0
Wholly outside	denom $= 0$, numer < 0

whether it lies wholly inside or wholly outside, as discussed in Section 4.8.3. The four possibilities are summarized in Figure 14.22. All of these ideas work just as well in 3D as 2D. For the generic cube, the quantities numer and denom can be computed very quickly: The dot products are trivial to find, because each vector **m** has two components of zero. The planes in Figure 14.20 yield the following values (check them):

Plane	numer	denom
0	$1 - S_y$	c_y
1	$1 + S_y$	$-c_y$
2	$1 - S_x$	c_x
3	$1 + S_x$	$-c_x$
4	$1 - S_z$	c_z
5	$1 + S_z$	$-c_z$

Figure 14.23 shows the routine `hit()` for the `Cube` class, which implements the required tests. As with the other `hit()` routines, the ray is converted to the object's generic coordinates, and all testing is done using the generic ray. The six planes are then tested in a loop, using the proper values of numer and denom. The initially infinite CI is chopped down to its final value, (`tIn`, `tOut`), unless it becomes empty after one of the tests, indicating that the ray misses the cube. Because it is important to keep track of which plane is associated with the current values of `tIn` and `tOut`, this information is stored in the variables `surfIn` and `surfOut`.

When all planes have been tested, we know the hit times `tIn` and `tOut`. If `tIn` is positive, the data for the hit at `tIn` is loaded into `inter.hit[0]`, and the data for the hit at `tOut` is loaded into `inter.hit[1]`. If only `tOut` is positive, the data for its hit are loaded into `inter.hit[0]`.

The normal vector to each hit surface is set using a helper function `cubeNormal(i)`, which returns the outward normal vector given in Figure 14.20. For instance, `cubeNormal(0)` returns $(0, 1, 0)$, and `cubeNormal(3)` returns $(-1, 0, 0)$. (See the exercises at the end of the section.)

The Intersection Algorithm for any Convex Polyhedron

The extension of `hit()` to any convex polyhedron is straightforward. Suppose there are N bounding planes and the ith plane contains point B_i and has (outward) normal vector $\mathbf{m}_i$. Everything in `hit()` for the cube remains the same, except that Equation (14.17) is used for the calculation of `numer` and `denom`. Now two expensive dot products must be calculated, and the `for` loop becomes

```
for (int i = 0; i < N; i++) //for each plane of the polyhedron
{
    numer = dot3 (m_i, B_i - S);
    denom = dot3 (m_i, c);
    if(fabs(denom) < eps) ... as before
    ... same as before ... .
}
```

```
bool Cube:: hit(Ray& r, Intersection& inter)
{
    double tHit, numer, denom;
    double tIn = -100000.0, tOut = 100000.0;// plus-minus infinity
    Ray genRay;
    int inSurf, outSurf; // which of the six surfaces
    xfrmRay(genRay, invTransf, r);
    for (int i = 0; i < 6; i++)
    {
      switch(i)  // which plane of cube to test
      {
      case 0: numer = 1.0 - genRay.start.y; denom = genRay.dir.y; break;
       case 1, case 2, case 3, case 4 similarly
      case 5: numer = 1.0 + genRay.start.z; denom = -genRay.dir.z; break;
      }
     if(fabs(denom) < 0.00001)     // ray is parallel
        {
          if(numer < 0) return false; //ray is out;
          else;                      // ray inside, no change to tIn,tOut
        }
        else                        // ray is not parallel
      {
        tHit = numer / denom;
        if(denom > 0){  // exiting
          if(tHit < tOut){ // a new earlier exit
              tOut = tHit; outSurf = i;
          }
        }
        else {  // denom is negative: entering
          if(tHit > tIn){  // a new later entrance
              tIn = tHit; inSurf = i;
          }
        }
      }
    }
    if(tIn >= tOut) return false; // it's a miss - early out
  } // end of the for loop
    int num = 0; // no positive hits yet
    if(tIn > 0.00001) //is first hit in front of the eye?
    {
        inter.hit[0].hitTime = tIn;
        inter.hit[0].surface = inSurf;
        inter.hit[0].isEntering = 1; // is entering
        inter.hit[0].hitObject = this;
        inter.hit[0].hitPoint.set(rayPos(genRay.start, genRay.dir,tIn));
        inter.hit[0].hitNormal.set(cubeNormal(inSurf));
        num++; //have a hit
    }
    if(tOut > 0.00001)
    {
        inter.hit[num].hitTime = tOut;
        inter.hit[num].surface = outSurf;
        inter.hit[num].isEntering = 0; // is exiting
        inter.hit[num].hitObject = this;
        inter.hit[num].hitPoint.set(rayPos(genRay.start,genRay.dir,tOut));
        inter.hit[num].hitNormal.set(cubeNormal(outSurf));
        num++;
    }
    inter.numHits = num; //number of hits in front of eye
    return (num > 0);
}
```

The Intersection Algorithm for a Mesh Object

Since we have a rich assortment of mesh objects to use from Chapter 6, and we already have a `drawOpenGL()` method for any mesh, it is natural to consider ray-tracing meshes. We use the previous approach to develop a `hit()` method for meshes. Recall that `Mesh` objects are described by a list of faces, and each face is a list of vertices along with a normal vector at each vertex. We shall take each face of the mesh in turn and treat it as a bounding plane. Call the plane associated with each face its "face plane." The object that is ray traced is the shape that is the intersection of the inside half-spaces of each of the object's face planes.

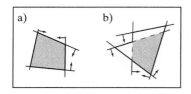

FIGURE 14.24 Objects (in 2D) and their face planes. (a) Convex. (b) Nonconvex.

Figure 14.24 shows two shapes (in 2D for simplicity) with their face planes marked. The object in Part (a) is convex, so its face planes are the same as its bounding planes. This shape will be ray traced correctly. Part (b) shows a nonconvex object. The portion that is inside all of its face planes is shown shaded. This is what the ray tracer will display! (Draw a nonconvex object that will be completely invisible when ray traced.) So using this method for a mesh will work only if the mesh represents a truly convex object. To build `hit()` for a mesh, we form `numer` and `denom` for each face in turn. We use as the representative point on the face plane the zeroth vertex of the face, viz., `pt[face[f].vert[0].vertIndex]`, and use as the normal to the face plane the normal associated with this vertex: `norm[face[f].vert[0].normIndex]`. So the code becomes

```
for(int f = 0; f < numFaces; f++){
    Vector3 diff;
    Vector3 normal(norm[ face[ f].vert[ 0].normIndex] ); //use
        constructors
    Point3 point(pt[ face[ f] .vert[ 0] .vertIndex] );
    form diff = point - genRay.start
    numer = dot3D(normal,diff);
    denom = dot3D(normal,genRay.dir);
    if(fabs(denom) < eps) ... as before
    ... same as before .... 
}
```

PRACTICE EXERCISES

14.6.5 Setting the normal vector for a cube intersection

Write the function `Vector3 cubeNormal(int which)`, which returns the outward normal vector to face `which` of a cube, according to Figure 14.20. Probably, the most readable code will use a single six-way switch statement that sets the vector to one of six hardwired values. A slightly briefer approach recognizes a pattern in the normals and computes them using the following instructions:

```
int m = which/2,n = (which%2)? -1:1;
if(m == 0)v.set( 0, n, 0);
else if(m == 1) v.set( n, 0, 0);
else v.set( 0, 0, n);
```

Determine how this method works, and rewrite the `cubeNormal` function so that it employs the method.

14.6.6 The planes of a tetrahedron

Using Figure 6.27 as a guide, show the ingredients of the list of planes for the regular tetrahedron.

14.6.7 Fine-tuning of `hit()` for a convex polyhedron

Fill in the details of the `ConvexPolyhedron :: hit()` method for intersecting a ray with a convex polyhedron. (See the `Shapes` class in Appendix 3 for more details on the `ConvexPolyhedron` class.)

14.6.8 Hand calculation of pierce times for the generic cube

For the ray $(4, 5, 6) + (-8, -8, -10)t$, find the six pierce times, plot them as in Figure 14.21(a), and determine the t-interval for which the ray is inside the cube. Repeat for the ray $(4, 5, 6) + (-12, -8, -10)t$. Does this ray intersect the cube?

14.6.9 Intersection with a tetrahedron

Find the t-interval for which the ray $(0, 0, 0) + (1, 2, 3)t$ is inside the tetrahedron with vertices $(1, 0, 0)$, $(-1, 0, -1)$, $(-1, 0, 1)$, and $(0, 1, 0)$.

14.6.10 On computational complexity

How many multiplications/divisions are required to test each plane of a convex polyhedron? Sometimes `tIn` exceeds `tOut` after only a few planes have been tested. What is a good rule of thumb for the average number of tests that are made for an N-plane convex polyhedron when a randomly chosen ray is tested? Compare this level of complexity with that for determining the intersection of a ray and a sphere. ■

14.6.4 Adding More Primitives

One can go beyond the generic primitives considered so far and include other kinds of shapes. We only need to have in hand the implicit form $F(P)$ of the shape. Then, as before, to find where the ray $S + \mathbf{c}t$ intersects the surface, we substitute $S + \mathbf{c}t$ for P in $F(P)$, forming the following function of time t:

$$d(t) = F(S + \mathbf{c}t). \tag{14.18}$$

This function is

- positive at those values of t for which the (point on the) ray is outside the object,
- zero when the ray coincides with the surface of the object, and
- negative when the ray is inside the surface.

In seeking intersections, we look for values of t that make $d(t) = 0$, so intersecting a ray is equivalent to solving this equation. We have seen that, for the sphere and other quadric surfaces, $d(t)$ is a simple quadratic equation.

A *torus* is a different matter. The generic torus has the implicit function (see Figure 6.74)

$$F(P) = \left(\sqrt{P_x^2 + P_y^2} - d\right)^2 + P_z^2 - 1, \tag{14.19}$$

so the resulting equation $d(t) = 0$ is quartic (fourth order). This equation is much harder to solve, although closed-form solutions may be found in various mathematical handbooks.

More generally, consider the overall shape of $d(t)$ as t increases. If the ray is aimed towards the object in question, and the start point S lies outside the object, we get shapes similar to those in Figure 14.25. The value of $d(0)$ is positive, since the ray starts outside the object. As the ray approaches the surface, $d(t)$ decreases, reaching zero if the ray intersects the surface (at t_1 in the figure). Then there is a period of time during which the ray is inside the object and $d(t) < 0$. When the ray emerges again, $d(t)$ passes through zero and increases thereafter. (For an object like a torus, the ray might reenter the object, so sketch a typical shape for $d(t)$ in such a case.) If, instead, the ray misses the object (an event represented by the dashed curve in the figure), $d(t)$ decreases for a while, but then increases forever without reaching zero.

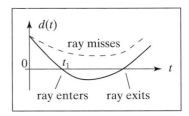

FIGURE 14.25 The function $d(t)$ versus t for a given ray and a given object.

For quadrics such as the sphere, $d(t)$ has a parabolic shape; for the torus, it has a quartic shape. For other surfaces, $d(t)$ may be so complicated that we have to search numerically to locate t's for which $d(.)$ equals zero. For instance, consider the super-ellipsoid of Figure 6.74. This surface yields the function

$$d(t) = ((S_x + c_x t)^n + (S_y + c_y t)^n)^{m/n} + (S_y + c_y t)^m - 1, \tag{14.20}$$

where n and m are constants that govern the shape of the surface. To find the smallest positive value of t that yields zero, we evaluate $d(t)$ at a sequence of t-values, searching for one that makes $d(t)$ very small. Techniques such as Newton's method [Acton70, Conte and deBoor 80] provide clever ways to progress towards better and better t-values, but in general, these numerical techniques require many iterations, which, of course, significantly slow down the ray-tracing process.

Techniques also have been developed for ray tracing a variety of other objects, notable among which are fractal surfaces, surfaces of revolution, and prismlike cylinders [Kajiya83]. (See Case Study 14.7 for approaches to ray tracing these objects.) The search for efficient algorithms to ray trace ever-larger collections of shapes is an ongoing subject of research in graphics.

PRACTICE EXERCISES

14.6.11 Intersections with a torus

Determine, from a mathematical handbook, how to find the solutions to a quartic equation, and set up the steps necessary to find the intersection(s) of a ray, $S + \mathbf{c}t$, with the torus in Equation (14.19).

14.6.12 Ray tracing the saddle: the hyperbolic paraboloid

Set up the steps required to find the intersections of the ray $S + \mathbf{c}t$ with the hyperbolic paraboloid of Figure 6.71.   ■

14.7 DRAWING SHADED PICTURES OF SCENES

A ray tracer that draws emissive objects provides a good way to get started with ray tracing, but is soon found to be inadequate when what you want are pictures that are stunningly realistic. To produce such pictures, we must determine the nature of the light that is reflected toward the eye from the hit point. To guide our calculations, we begin with the shading model of OpenGL discussed in Chapter 8. We then discuss how the model can be refined to achieve greater realism.

OpenGL draws scenes by combining the ambient, diffuse, and specular components of light that illuminate a vertex of an object. It uses the Phong model to calculate the specular light component. Figure 14.26 summarizes the main ingredients. The

FIGURE 14.26 Applying the shading model.

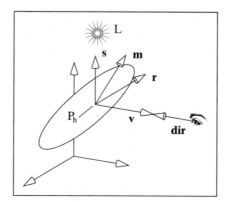

rcth ray is seen intersecting a spheroid at the hit point P_h. A light source is located at L. We wish to compute the amount of light that travels back from P_h to the eye. The principal vectors of interest are $\mathbf{s}$, $\mathbf{v}$, and $\mathbf{m}$. Vector $\mathbf{s}$ points to the light source and is therefore given by $\mathbf{s} = L - P_h$; vector $\mathbf{v}$ points to the viewer and so is just the negative of the ray's direction $\mathbf{dir}$; $\mathbf{m}$ is the normal to the surface at P_h.

As first set out in Chapter 8, the total light intensity observed by the eye, consisting of the ambient, diffuse, and specular components, is

$$I = I_a \rho_a + I_d \rho_d \times \text{lambert} + I_{sp} \rho_s \times \text{phong}^f, \tag{14.21}$$

where I_a is the ambient intensity and I_s is the intensity of the light source and where we define

$$\text{lambert} = \max\left(0, \frac{\mathbf{s} \cdot \mathbf{m}}{|\mathbf{s}||\mathbf{m}|}\right) \text{ and phong} = \max\left(0, \frac{\mathbf{h} \cdot \mathbf{m}}{|\mathbf{h}||\mathbf{m}|}\right). \tag{14.22}$$

The quantities ρ_a, ρ_d, and ρ_s are reflection coefficients, and f is the specular exponent. Vector $\mathbf{h}$ is the "halfway vector" given by $\mathbf{h} = \mathbf{s} + \mathbf{v}$.

If several light sources are present in the scene, there will be a diffuse and a specular contribution from each, and these are summed to form I. Recall that the ambient term is an approximation that lumps together diverse contributions from multiple reflections off neighboring bodies throughout the scene. We shall see later that we must trace some rays individually through multiple reflections when an object is shiny enough. The ambient term still helps approximate the effect of all the less prominent rays circulating about the scene, which are too numerous to trace individually.

As we did in Chapter 8, we extend this formulation to colored lights and objects. The light that reaches the eye will then have red, green, and blue components given by

$$I_r = I_{ar} \rho_{ar} + I_{dr} \rho_{dr} \times \text{lambert} + I_{spr} \rho_{sr} \times \text{phong}^f,$$
$$I_g = I_{ag} \rho_{ag} + I_{dg} \rho_{dg} \times \text{lambert} + I_{spg} \rho_{sg} \times \text{phong}^f,$$

and

$$I_b = I_{ab} \rho_{ab} + I_{db} \rho_{db} \times \text{lambert} + I_{spb} \rho_{sb} \times \text{phong}^f, \tag{14.23}$$

where the various I's and ρ's are intensities and reflection coefficients for the individual color components. Note in particular that the *same* terms *lambert* and *phong* (and the same vectors $\mathbf{m}$, $\mathbf{s}$, and $\mathbf{h}$) are used for the three color contributions, so a ray need only be traced once, and the *lambert* and *phong* terms need be evaluated only once.

Shading calculations require that we know the hit point P_h, as well as the vectors $\mathbf{h}$, $\mathbf{s}$, and $\mathbf{m}$. We next address the problem of computing $\mathbf{m}$, which requires several pieces of information, all of which are stored in the intersection record.

14.7.1 Finding the Normal at the Hit Spot

The vector $\mathbf{m}$ is the normal vector to the hit surface at the hit spot. How is it determined? We first find $\mathbf{m}$ most easily in generic coordinates and then transform it into world coordinates. In Section 6.5.3 we showed that if one object is transformed into another with the matrix M, the normal vector $\mathbf{m}'$ is transformed into the normal vector

$$\mathbf{m} = M^{-T}\mathbf{m}', \tag{14.24}$$

where M^{-T} denotes the transpose of the inverse of M. The desired normal $\mathbf{m}$ is therefore found by computing the normal vector to the surface of the generic object at the hit spot and then multiplying that vector by M^{-T}.

Happily, we have already computed and stored the normal vector at the hit point in generic coordinates; it resides in the `hitNormal` field of the intersection record for the hit in question. So it is available to be transformed into world coordinates. (See the exercise at the end of Section 14.7.2.)

14.7.2 Coloring Objects according to their Surface Materials

The color seen at the hit point depends on the combination of the ambient, diffuse, and specular light contributions. The reflection coefficients ρ_{ar}, ρ_{dg}, and so forth are stored with the object that is hit and are available in the `mtrl.ambient`, `mtrl.diffuse`, and `mtrl.specular` fields. These fields are loaded up when the SDL file is first read.

A common practice is to make the Phong specular light the same color as the light source. To do that, the `mtrl.specular` reflection coefficient is given equal red, green, and blue components, as in (0.9, 0.9, 0.9), so the product of that coefficient with the source color reproduces the source color, albeit slightly diminished. This effect tends to make the material look like a shiny plastic.

If `mtrl.specular` is chosen more carefully, Phong highlights can be made somewhat more realistic. The coefficients reported in Figure 8.17, due to McReynolds and Blythe, provide more realistic views of different materials. Plate 39 shows several ray-traced spheres "made of" different materials and illuminated with white light. All spheres use the McReynolds and Blythe ambient and diffuse coefficients. The spheres on the left show white Phong highlights. Those on the right use the McReynolds and Blythe specular coefficients for the Phong highlights. The designer of a scene will choose one set of coefficients over another to produce different effects.

The reflection coefficients are easily added to an SDL scene file. The different materials are first specified with code such as

```
def Copper{   ambient 0.19125 0.0735 0.0225
              diffuse 0.7038 0.27048 0.0828
              specular 0.256777 0.137622 0.086014 exponent 12.8}

def Gold{     ambient 0.24725 0.1995 0.0745
              diffuse 0.75164 0.60648 0.22648
              specular 0.628281 0.555802 0.366065 exponent 51.2}
```

and are then used to set the properties of various objects in the scene, with code like the following:

```
use Gold
sphere  ! make the sphere out of gold
translate 1 2 1
use Copper cube ! and the cube out of copper
```

It is not difficult to add ambient, diffuse, and specular light computations in a ray tracer. Figure 14.27 shows a skeleton of what needs to be added in the `shade()` method of Figure 14.12. The best intersection record, `best`, formed in `getFirstHit()` is examined in order to collect data for the first hit of the ray with an object. A convenient copy of `best.hit[0]` is put into the `HitInfo` record `h`. The position of the hit point `hitPoint` is computed using the ray and `h.hitTime`. The generic coordinate normal vector at the hit point, stored in `h.hitNormal`, is then converted to world coordinates by using Equation (14.24). The various contributions to the total color returning along the ray are then computed in `color`. The emissive and ambient components are found, and, for each light source, the diffuse and specular contributions arising from it are found and added into the growing `color`. If the light source is shadowed by some object at the hit point, there is no contribution from that source. (We discuss shadowing in Section 14.10; for now, simply omit the line "`if(isInShadow(...)) continue;`" to remove any shadow testing.) The spec-

```
Color3 Scene :: shade(Ray& r)
{
  Get the first hit using getFirstHit(r, best);
  Make handy copy h = best.hit[0]; //data about the first hit
  Form hitPoint based on h.hitTime
  Form v = - ray.dir; // direction to viewer
  v.normalize();
  Shape* myObj = (Shape*)h.hitObject; //point to the hit object
  Color3 color(myObj->mtrl.emissive)  ; //start with emissive part
  color.add(ambient contribution); // compute ambient color
  Vector3 normal;
  // transform the generic normal to the world normal
  xfrmNormal(normal, myObj->invTransf, h.hitNormal);
  normal.normalize(); //normalize it
  for(each light source, L)// sum over all sources
  {
      if(isInShadow(…)) continue; // skip L if it's in shadow
      Form s = L.pos - hitPoint; // vector from hit point to source
      s.normalize();
      float mDotS = s.dot(normal); // the Lambert term
      if(mDotS > 0.0) // hit point is turned toward the light
      Form diffuseColor = mDotS * myObj->mtrl.diffuse * L.color;
      color.add(diffuseColor);  //add the diffuse part
      Form h  = v + s; // the halfway vector
      h.normalize();
      float mDotH = h.dot(normal);// part of phong term
      if(mDotH <= 0) continue; // no specular contribution
      float phong = pow(mDotH, myObj->mtrl.specularExponent);
      specColor = phong * myObj->mtrl.specular * L.color;
      color.add(specColor);
  }
  return color;
}
```

FIGURE 14.27 Adding shading calculations to `shade()` (pseudocode).

ular component is found according to Equation (14.21), which requires computing the vector **h** and using the specular reflection coefficient (and exponent f) stored in `myObj->mtrl.specular`.

Figure 14.28 shows a scene in which objects have been rendered using ambient, diffuse, and specular light, but with no shadows computed. The specular highlights make the objects appear to be composed of a shiny plastic material.

PRACTICE EXERCISE

14.7.1 Transforming the normal vector

Write a routine `void xfrmNormal(Vector3& res, Affine4& aff, Vector3& v)` that multiplies the vector `v` by the *transpose* of the matrix stored in `aff` and produces the vector `res`. The routine is used in the ray tracer by calling `xfrmNormal(normal, myObj->invTransf, h.hitNormal)`. That is, the nor-

FIGURE 14.28 Objects illuminated with ambient, diffuse, and specular light.

---

[3] We assume that some handy constructors have been added to the `Vector3` and `Color3` classes: `Vector3 s(A,B)` constructs a vector as the difference of two points A and B, and `Color3 color(c)` constructs a color having the same components as color c.

mal vector `h.hitNormal` in generic coordinates is transformed using the *inverse* matrix `myObj-> invTransf` stored in the hit object, to product the normal vector `normal` in world coordinates.   ■

14.7.3 Physically Based Shading Models: Cook–Torrance Shading

Phong highlights are easy to generate, but tend to give objects a shiny plastic look. If OpenGL is used for shading, one is forced to settle for Phong highlights, but if we render an object by ray tracing, we have more options and can consider different algorithms for computing specular highlights.

In a quest for greater realism, many researchers have developed more elaborate shading models. These models start from physical principles that characterize how light reflects from an actual surface and develop mathematical expressions for the intensity and color of the reflected light that reaches the viewer. The models pay attention to the "balance" of light energy at the surface: The incident light energy is divided into a part that is absorbed in the material as heat, a part that interacts with the surface and is scattered back as diffuse light, and a part that reflects from the surface as specular light. Different materials split the incident light up differently; for example, a rough surface produces more diffuse light and less specular light than a smooth, shiny surface.

In early contributions by Torrance and Sparrow[Torrance67] and Trowbridge and Reitz[Trowbridge75], a rough surface was modeled conceptually as a collection of shiny "microfacets" oriented in different directions, as suggested in Figure 14.29. Incident light arrives at angle ϕ from the average normal direction **m** and reflects in different directions, depending on the microfacets that it hits. A fraction of the light reflects towards the viewer. Blinn used this model to develop an algorithm suitable for computer graphics and showed that it produced specular highlights quite different from Phong highlights[Blinn77]. Cook and Torrance[Cook82] extended and refined Blinn's model, showing that there is a "color shift" in the specular highlights, which does a better job of matching how light reflects off of real materials.

FIGURE 14.29 Modeling a rough surface as a collection of randomly oriented microfacets.

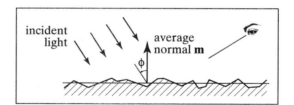

We describe the major ingredients of the Cook–Torrance model and show how it can be incorporated into a ray tracer. We discuss the three principal aspects of this model and the effects they have on the amount of specular light that is reflected. Each aspect attempts to represent accurately a physical phenomenon involved in the reflection of light in a way that can be built into an algorithm.

The Distribution of Facet Orientations

The Cook–Torrance model assumes that each microfacet acts as a tiny perfect mirror and that only those facets which are oriented perfectly contribute to the light that is reflected in a particular direction. As suggested in Figure 14.30(a), only those oriented with their normal in the direction **h** = **s** + **v** contribute to the light seen in the direction **v**. It is necessary, therefore, to know what fraction of the microfacets have this orientation. Statistical studies have been made of how randomly oriented microfacets might actually arrange themselves on a surface made of a certain material.

The studies yield a distribution function $D(\delta)$ that reports the fraction of microfacets that are aimed with their normals at angle δ relative to the surface normal **m**. As shown in Figure 14.30(b), if the incident angle is ϕ and the viewer lies at angle θ, then only facets lying at angle $\delta = (\theta - \phi)/2$ have the right orientation to reflect light to the viewer. (See the exercises at the end of the section.) The fraction of facets having this orientation is $D(\delta)$.

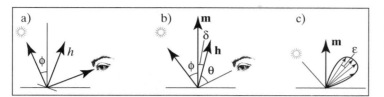

Various distribution functions have been developed. Cook and Torrance use the Beckmann [1963] distribution [Beckmann63] given by

$$D(\delta) = \frac{1}{4m^2 \cos^4(\delta)} e^{-\left(\frac{\tan(\delta)}{m}\right)^2}, \tag{14.25}$$

which has been shown to be a good mathematical fit for many actual rough surfaces. This distribution has its peak value at $\delta = 0$ and falls off as δ moves away from zero. (What *is* the peak value?) The parameter m is a measure of the roughness of the surface. (Specifically, it is the root-mean-square slope of the microfacets.) Its value would be around 0.2 for a nearly smooth surface and around 0.6 for a rough surface. $D(\delta)$ falls off more rapidly with δ at smaller values of m.

Cook and Torrance incorporate $D(\delta)$ as a scaling factor on the specular contribution in different directions with δ set equal to the angle between **h** and **m**. Figure 14.30(c) shows how the specular intensity varies at different viewing directions for $m = 0.3$. The figure shows a "beam pattern" similar to that in Figure 8.12. The relative size of the specular component in each direction is shown by the length of the arrow. It is strongest in the direction of perfect reflection (at an angle ϕ), because the facets are most likely to have normals parallel to **m**. It is smaller in the direction, say, ε, away from this perfect-mirror direction, because the facet would have to have a normal $\varepsilon/2$ away from **m** and the distribution function dictates that, on average, fewer facets do. (See the exercises at the end of the section.)

Shadowing and Masking

Torrance and Sparrow also considered the effects of "masking" and "shadowing" that would occur on a microfaceted surface. These result in a "geometry term" G that scales the strength of the specular component. Figure 14.31 suggests how this effect is related to the geometry of a typical facet. In Part (a), light arrives at the facet at such an angle that the entire facet is illuminated and all of the reflected light "escapes" from the facet. G would be equal to unity in this case. In Part (b), the direction of reflection relative to **h** is such that part of the light leaving the facet is masked off by the neighboring edge of the facet. This effect reduces the value of G accordingly. And in Part (c), only a portion of the facet is illuminated, the rest being shadowed by the edge of the neighboring facet. This effect makes G less than unity.

Blinn related these geometric phenomena to simple terms involving only dot products. The geometric factor uses the smallest of the three values 1, G_s, and G_m. Mathematically,

$$G = \min\left(1, G_m, G_s\right) \tag{14.26}$$

FIGURE 14.31 Masking and shadowing of light at the facet level.

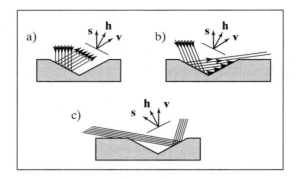

where

$$G_m = \frac{2(\mathbf{m} \cdot \mathbf{h})(\mathbf{m} \cdot \mathbf{s})}{\mathbf{h} \cdot \mathbf{s}}, G_s = \frac{2(\mathbf{m} \cdot \mathbf{h})(\mathbf{m} \cdot \mathbf{v})}{\mathbf{h} \cdot \mathbf{s}} \tag{14.27}$$

are, respectively, the fraction of light that is not masked out and the fraction of light that is not shadowed.

The Fresnel Coefficient

The third factor in the Torrance–Sparrow model also modulates the amount of specular light. The shiny microfacets are not perfect mirrors, but, like real materials, reflect only a fraction of the incident light that is upon them, with the remainder being transmitted into the surface. The fraction that is reflected is given by the Fresnel coefficient[4] $F(\phi, \eta)$, where ϕ is the angle of incidence, as in Figure 14.30 (the angle between $\mathbf{m}$ and $\mathbf{s}$), and η is the index of refraction of the material. Later, in ray tracing transparent materials[5] in Section 14.11, we will work with the index of refraction, but it comes into play also with opaque materials such as metals.

The Fresnel coefficient $F(\phi, \eta)$ can be derived from first principles of electromagnetic reflection applied to a surface having index of refraction η. Mathematically, it is given by

$$F = \frac{1}{2} \frac{(g - c)^2}{(g + c)^2} \left\{ 1 + \left(\frac{c(g + c) - 1}{c(g - c) + 1} \right)^2 \right\}, \tag{14.28}$$

where $c = \cos(\phi) = \mathbf{m} \cdot \mathbf{s}$ and $g^2 = \eta^2 + c^2 - 1$. Note that the intermediate term g depends on the index of refraction of the material. For many materials, the index of refraction varies with the wavelength of the light in a complex way, making the dependence of F on wavelength complicated indeed.

Figure 14.32 shows the basic shape of F versus ϕ for various values of η. The Fresnel coefficient is seen to have some material-dependent value at "normal incidence" ($\phi = 0$) and to vary smoothly up to the value 1.0 at a "grazing angle" ($\phi = \pi/2$). Also,

- At normal incidence, $F(0, \eta) < 1$.
- At grazing incidence, $F(\pi/2, \eta) = 1$.

---

[4]   Augustin Jean Fresnel (1788–1827), a French physicist, developed a number of basic results for the reflection, refraction, and polarization of light.

[5]   The index of refraction of a material is the ratio of the speed of light in air to the speed of light in the material. Typically, it depends on the wavelength of the light. The relationship between the wavelength and the color of light was described in Chapter 12.

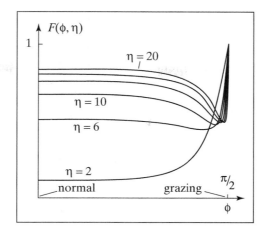

FIGURE 14.32 Fresnel coefficient versus angle of incidence.

Torrance and Sparrow[Torrance67] put these factors together for the microfacet model and formed a physically based model of specular reflections. They found that the relative amount of specular light reflected was the product of the three terms F, D, and G, divided by $\mathbf{m} \cdot \mathbf{v}$; that is,

$$\text{spec} = \frac{F(\phi, \eta)DG}{(\mathbf{m} \cdot \mathbf{v})}. \tag{14.29}$$

The denominator term $\mathbf{m} \cdot \mathbf{v}$ [which is $\cos(\theta)$; see Figure 14.30(b)] arises from the following argument: In viewing a surface at a grazing angle (large θ and therefore small cosine), more of the microfacets are seen within a given solid angle than is the case with a view having a small angle θ. Seeing more facets produces more light, so a smaller value of $\mathbf{m} \cdot \mathbf{v}$ produces a larger intensity.

Blinn adapted this model to computer graphics and compared it with Phong specular highlights[Blinn77]. Of particular interest was the different way the specular light behaved at different angles of incidence ϕ. With Phong shading, the specular highlight is always strongest in the direction of "perfect reflection" and falls off rapidly at viewing angles slightly away from that direction. Figure 14.33(a) shows the "beam pattern" that describes how the strength of Phong highlights fall off with angle. Beam patterns are shown for the two angles of incidence. The shape of the beam pattern is the same regardless of the angle of incidence ϕ. The beam patterns

FIGURE 14.33 A contrast of how specular intensity varies with incident angles.

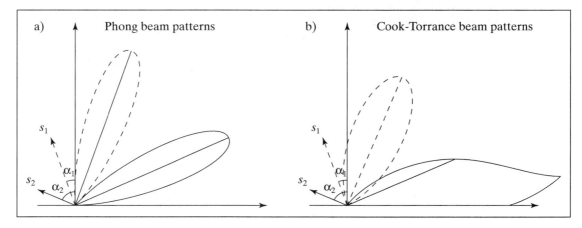

for the microfacet model are shown in Part (b) of the figure. (The exercises at the end of the section develop the expression for these beam patterns.) When ϕ is small (dashed lines), the shape of the beam is similar to that of Phong highlights. But for grazing incidence angles (solid lines), not only does the beam have a different shape, but the direction of greatest intensity is no longer the direction of mirrorlike reflection! This causes the "halo" of light around a specular glint to vary quite differently from the one seen about a Phong glint and is a phenomenon observed with light reflecting off of real surfaces.

Cook and Torrance[Cook82] extended the model in two directions. First, they took into account how incident light energy is divided into ambient, diffuse, and specular portions. Second, they took into account the variation of the index of refraction with the wavelength of incident light in real materials. This variation causes the Fresnel coefficient to vary as well with wavelength, which in turn causes the specular light to *change* color at different angles of incidence. This variation of color with angle, or "color shift," is also observed in real materials.

When suitable expressions for each of these phenomena are combined appropriately, the model takes the general form

$$I_r = I_{ar}k_aF(0, \eta_r) + I_{sr}\,d\omega\,k_dF(0, \eta_r) \times \text{lambert} + I_{sr}k_s\,d\omega\,\frac{F(\phi, \eta_r)DG}{(\mathbf{m} \cdot \mathbf{v})}. \quad (14.30)$$

This equation gives only the strength of the red color component; the green and blue components are the same, except that η_g and η_b are respectively used. The ambient source and light source have red strengths I_{ar} and I_{sr}, respectively, and the three contributions—from ambient, diffuse, and specular light—are recognizable. I_{ar} is usually taken to be a small fraction of I_{sr}. (If there is more than one light source, there is a similar diffuse and specular term for each source, and all contributions are summed.)

The ambient and diffuse reflection coefficients are based on the Fresnel coefficient $F(0, \eta_r)$ at normal incidence. This is an approximation that Cook and Torrance use for simplicity, noting that $F(\phi, \eta_r)$ varies only slightly over a range of values of ϕ near zero, so a reasonable approximation uses just the value at $\phi = 0$. Notice that this coefficient *is* different at different wavelengths (it "has a color"): The green and blue components depend on $F(0, \eta_g)$ and $F(0, \eta_b)$, respectively, and these values are different because the index of refraction is different at different colors.

The diffuse term contains the familiar Lambert term [see Equation (14.22)], along with two other factors. The term $d\omega$ is the solid angle subtended at the hit point by the light source. (See Figure 14.34.) For simplicity, this term is assumed to be constant at all points in the scene and is usually chosen as a small constant, such as 0.0001. (The sun subtends a solid angle of 0.000068 steradian.) The factor k_d (and its mate k_s in the specular term) report how the incident light is divided between diffuse and specular reflections. The two factors are a property of the material and sum to unity: $k_d + k_s = 1$. The specular term is the same as spec of Equation (14.29), with the explicit dependence of the Fresnel coefficient on wavelength.

To use these formulas, we must know the index of refraction of the material in question at different wavelengths. This information is generally not available. What is available are measurements of the "normal reflectance" of different materials—that is, values for $F(0, \eta)$ at different wavelengths. Cook and Torrance infer the index of refraction from these measured values by means of the following argument: If we evaluate $F(\phi, \eta)$ in Equation (14.28) at $\phi = 0$, then $c = 1$ and $g = \eta$. (Check this!) Therefore, the whole expression collapses to

$$F_0 = \frac{(\eta - 1)^2}{(\eta + 1)^2},$$

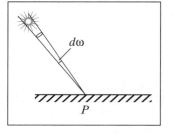

FIGURE 14.34 The source subtends a solid angle $d\omega$.

where F_0 denotes the value of the normal reflectance $F(0, \eta)$. This equation is easily inverted to expose η:

$$\eta = \frac{1 + \sqrt{F_0}}{1 - \sqrt{F_0}}. \tag{14.31}$$

So, given values F_0, we can solve for the corresponding index of refraction. Figure 14.35 shows some measured values of F_0 for four polished metals[Touloukian70].

	F_0 at red	F_0 at green	F_0 at blue
gold	0.989	0.876	0.399
silver	0.95	0.93	0.88
copper	0.755	0.49	0.095
iron	0.53	0.505	0.480

FIGURE 14.35 Measured normal reflectances at different wavelengths.

Plate 40 shows a comparison of the Cook–Torrance and Phong shading methods for spheres made of the four metals listed in Figure 14.35. Two light sources illuminate each sphere. The sources are arranged so that one specular highlight occurs at a grazing angle. The left spheres show Phong highlights and the right ones Cook–Torrance highlights. Note how the brightness and color of the highlight change at points farther from its center and how different the shape of the highlight is in the case of the grazing angle.

The Cook–Torrance shading model is computationally more expensive than the Phong model, but many people are willing to accept this cost in order to achieve the greater realism it offers. For even greater realism, scenes should be rendered at many more than three wavelengths, and the colors should be combined. Using only the red, green, and blue colors that more or less match those of a CRT display places an inherent limitation on the ultimate realism of computer-generated images.

PRACTICE EXERCISES

14.7.2 What angle is right for specular reflection?

Show that the angle δ in Figure 14.30(b) must be $\delta = (\theta - \phi)/2$ to cause light to be reflected from the source at angle ϕ to the viewer at angle θ.

14.7.3 Beam patterns for the microfacet model

Since incident and reflected lights lie in the same plane, the terms G, D, F, etc., used in Equation (14.29) can all be expressed in terms of the incident angle θ and the viewer angle ϕ.

a. Show that G of Equation (14.26) can be written as

$$G(\phi, \theta) = \min\left(1, \frac{\cos\left(\frac{\theta - \phi}{2}\right)\cos(\phi)}{\cos\left(\frac{\theta + \phi}{2}\right)}, \frac{\cos\left(\frac{\theta - \phi}{2}\right)\cos(\theta)}{\cos\left(\frac{\theta + \phi}{2}\right)}\right).$$

b. Show that spec of Equation (14.29) is therefore given by

$$\text{spec} = \frac{F(\phi, \eta)D\left(\frac{\theta - \phi}{2}\right)G(\phi, \theta)}{\cos(\theta)}.$$

c. Make your own plots of spec vs. θ for various values of ϕ, the roughness m, and the index of refraction.

■

FIGURE 14.36 A scene with several textured surfaces.

14.8 ADDING SURFACE TEXTURE

As we saw in Chapter 8, computer-generated images can be made much more lively and realistic by painting textures on various surfaces. Figure 14.36 shows a ray-traced scene with several examples of textures. In Chapter 8, the surfaces were polygons and OpenGL was used to render each face. For each face F, a pair of texture coordinates was attached to each vertex of F, and OpenGL "painted" each pixel inside the face by using the color of the corresponding point within a texture image.

We want to see how to incorporate texturing into a ray tracer. Two principal kinds of texture are used:

- With *image texture*, a 2D image is "pasted" onto each surface of the object.
- With *solid texture*, the object is considered to be carved out of a block of some material that itself has texturing. The ray tracer reveals the color of the texture at each point on the surface of the object.

We begin with solid texture, which is simple to work with. We discussed a method to apply solid texture in Case Study 8.5 when using OpenGL to draw polygonal faces, but it was somewhat contrived. Happily, that method fits very naturally within a ray-tracing framework.

14.8.1 Solid Texture

Solid texture is sometimes called "3D texture." It was first reported simultaneously by Perlin [Perlin 1985] and Peachey [Peachey85]. We view an object as being carved out of some textured material such as marble or wood. The texture is represented by a function texture (x, y, z) that produces an (r, g, b) color value at every point in space. Think of this texture as a color or "inkiness" that varies with position; if you look (with X-ray vision) at different points (x, y, z), you see different colors. When an object of some shape is defined in this space, and all the material outside of the shape is chipped away to reveal the object's surface, the point (x, y, z) on the surface is revealed and has the specified texture.

We first elaborate on some interesting examples that were mentioned in Case Study 8.5 and then show how to incorporate such texture into a ray tracer. Finally, we develop some richer types of materials, such as wood grain and marble.

FIGURE 14.37 Ray tracing of some objects with checkerboard solid texture.

▪ EXAMPLE 14.8.1 A 3D checkerboard that fills space

Imagine a 3D checkerboard made up of alternating red and black cubes stacked up throughout all of space. We position one of the "cubelets" with a vertex at $(0, 0, 0)$ and size it so that its diagonally opposite vertex lies at point $S = (S.x, S.y, S.z)$. All other cubes have this same size (a width of $S.x$, a height of $S.y$, etc.) and are placed adjacent to one another in all three dimensions. It is easy to write an expression for such a checkerboard texture: Add together the integer parts of $x/S.x$, $y/S.y$, and $z/S.z$, and reduce the sum modulo 2:

$$\text{jump}(x, y, z) = ((\text{int})(A + x/S.x) + (\text{int})(A + y/S.y) + (\text{int})(A + z/S.z)) \% 2. \tag{14.32}$$

We then set texture(x, y, z) to return black if jump$() = 0$ and red if jump$() = 1$. Because truncation through (int) acts peculiarly around 0, all arguments are offset by some constant A (e.g., 100) to avoid arguments near 0.

Figure 14.37 shows a generic sphere and a generic cube "composed" of material with this solid texture. The color of the material is the color of the texture. Notice that the sphere and the cube are clearly made up of solid "cubelets." Contrast how these objects would look if a 2D checkerboard image were "pasted" onto them.

■ **EXAMPLE 14.8.2 A stack of cubes of smoothly varying colors**

You can also stack up copies of a single cube. One interesting cube exhibits a smoothly varying color over the entire spectrum as you move around inside it. All eight corners are black, and the center point, $(0.5, 0.5, 0.5)$, of the cube is white. In between the color varies smoothly. To make the red component rise to unity and then fall back to zero along the x dimension, use red $= 1 - |2x - 1|$. The green component is similarly driven by y and the blue component by z. To stack an infinite number of copies of this cube together in space, use the fractional part of x, y, and z, giving, finally,

$$\text{texture}(x, y, z) = (1 - |2\text{fract}(x) - 1|, 1 - |2\text{fract}(y) - 1|, 1 - |2\text{fract}(z) - 1|),$$
$$(14.33)$$

where fract(x) is $1 - (\text{int})x$. (Visualize what a sphere of radius 100 would look like if made of this material.)

Ray Tracing Objects Composed of Solid Texture

Once the function texture() is available, almost nothing else is required to incorporate solid texture into a ray tracer. There are a couple of ways that the texture can alter the light coming from a surface point:

1. The light can be set equal to texture() itself, as if the object were "glowing" with that color.
2. The texture can modulate the ambient and diffuse reflection coefficients, so that

$$I = \text{texture}(x, y, z)(I_a \rho_a + I_s \rho_d(u_s \cdot u_n)) + I_s \rho_s(u_b \cdot u_m)^f, \qquad (14.34)$$

where texture(x, y, z) is evaluated at the hit point (x, y, z) of the ray. The latter is the most common use of texture: The surface looks as if its inherent color were lighter or darker at different points, according to the fluctuations in texture(). Here the specular highlight has the color of the source and is not affected by the texture. This makes the textured object appear to be shiny, as if it were made of plastic.

The hit point (x, y, z) used in Equation (14.34) could be either in generic coordinates or in world coordinates. Usually it is in generic coordinates, in which case the object "carries" the texture along with it when it is rotated or moved to its final position in the scene. In an animation in which the object is rotating or moving from frame to frame, the texture will be solidly attached to the object.

If, on the other hand, (x, y, z) is the world coordinate version, the texture is fixed in space. Now when the object rotates or moves in an animation, the texture will "sweep" over it, making it appear to be carved out of new material at each new position. This can produce an interesting visual effect, albeit not based on physical reality.

Rich and varied solid textures are easy to create, and some can faithfully model actual materials. The two classic examples are wood grain and marble.

Wood Grain Texture

The grain in a log of wood is due to concentric cylinders of varying color, corresponding to the "rings" seen when a log is cut. As the distance of points from some axis varies, the function jumps back and forth between two values. This effect can be simulated with the modulo function

```
rings(r) = ((int)r) % 2
```

where, for rings about the z-axis, the radius $r = \sqrt{x^2 + y^2}$. The value of the function rings() jumps between zero and unity as r increases from zero. The texture can be made to jump between two preset values, say, D and $D + A$, by using the function

```
simple_wood(x, y, z) = D + A * rings(r/M));
```

where, again, $r = \sqrt{x^2 + y^2}$. This produces rings of thickness M that are concentric about the z-axis.

Things get more interesting if we "wobble," "skew," and rotate the rings[Watt92]. To wobble the rings, we add a component that varies with the azimuth θ about the z-axis:

$$\text{rings}\left(\frac{r}{M} + K\sin\left(\frac{\theta}{N}\right)\right).$$

Now even when the radius is held constant, there is a fluctuation of the rings as θ varies, making the rings wobble in and out N times as you look around the axis. Note that we are nesting functions within functions to add more effects: The argument of rings() is not just r, but is the sum of r/M and a sinusoid, which is itself the quotient of an angle and N. Perlin [Perlin85] made powerful use of this functional composition to create many interesting visual effects. We can go further and add a "twist" to the wobbling wood grain by using the formula

$$\text{rings}\left(\frac{r}{M} + K\sin\left(\frac{\theta}{N} + Bz\right)\right), \qquad (14.35)$$

FIGURE 14.38 Objects "carved" out of wood.

so that the phase of the sinusoid varies with z, effectively rotating the wobble as z varies. And if we want to "tilt" this grain so that it is concentric about some axis other than the z-axis, we apply a rotation before evaluating r and θ. For instance, we form r as $\sqrt{x'^2 + y'^2}$, where $(x', y', z') = T(x, y, z)$ for some rotational transformation $T()$. Figure 14.38 shows some objects "carved" out of wood grain defined in these ways. Plate 41 shows a lovely example.

3D Noise and Marble Texture

The grain in materials such as marble is quite chaotic, as suggested in Figure 14.39. Turbulent rivulets of dark material course through the stone, with random whirls and blotches, as if the stone was formed out of some violently stirred molten material. We can simulate turbulence by building a "noise" function that produces an apparently random value at each point (x, y, z) in space. This "noise field" is then stirred up in a well-controlled way to give the appearance of turbulence.

FIGURE 14.39 Objects carved out of marble.

The noise field itself is easy to program. Imagine defining a random value at each *integer* position in space—that is, at $(x, y, z) = (i, j, k)$ for every combination of integers i, j, and k. Such an arrangement of points is called an **integer lattice**. Figure 14.40(a) shows a 2D version, in which various points in a 2D integer lattice are labeled with noise values between zero and unity. For instance, the point $(1, 2)$ has noise value 0.653 and the point $(3, 1)$ has noise value 0.129. Part (b) of the figure shows a 3D integer lattice. Visualize every integer point having some fixed noise value, such as 0.7341 at $(2, 2, 1)$.

FIGURE 14.40 Defining noise values at each point in a 3D integer lattice.

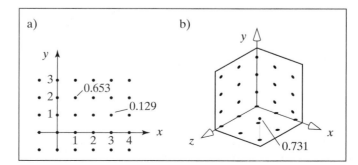

The collection of noise values could be stored in a huge array `float N[10000][10000][10000]`, but this would require an unacceptable amount of memory. It is far simpler to generate each noise value each time it is needed. For this approach, we need a function, say, `float latticeNoise(int i, int j, int k)`, that returns an apparently random value, given the integers i, j, and k that specify the position of the particular noise value in the lattice. The function must be efficient and completely repeatable, always returning the same noise value for a given (i, j, k). Several of the authors in the excellent text *Texturing and Modeling*[Ebert98] describe suitable approaches. We focus on the one introduced by Perlin and elaborated on by Peachey.

Generating Repeatable Random Values

The trick is to set up a fixed array, say, `noiseTable[]`, of pseudorandom noise values in an initialization step. Arrays of length 256 have been found to be quite adequate, so we use that length.

Now the main function, `latticeNoise(i, j, k)`, simply indexes into `noiseTable[]` in a repeatable way. To ensure that there is little or no pattern in the noise values as i, j, or k varies, the indexing function effectively scrambles or "hashes" the (i, j, k) combination into a value between 0 and 255. This is easy to accomplish using a second array, `index[]`, that contains the values 0 through 255, randomly permuted. (If we were instead dealing with arrays of length, say, 8, `index[]` might contain something like $\{3, 7, 0, 1, 6, 5, 4, 2\}$.) Peachey suggests defining the following two macros:

```
#define PERM(x) index[ (x) & 255]
#define INDEX(ix, iy,  iz) PERM( (ix) + PERM((iy) + PERM(iz)) )
```

The `PERM` macro takes an integer value of x and performs a "bitwise AND" operation on it with the number 255, effectively retaining only the low-order eight bits of x, which is thus hashed into a value between 0 and 255. The value of `PERM` is therefore one of the values selected from the index array. The `INDEX` macro uses `PERM` to dip into the index array three times, in each case choosing an element of `index[]` on the basis of one of the values `ix`, `iy`, and `iz`. Note that this is a repeatable and efficient operation and that plenty of scrambling takes place. The `latticeNoise()` function is then simply

```
float latticeNoise(int i, int j, int k)
{
    return noiseTable[ INDEX(i,j,k)];
}
```

Developing the `Noise` Class

It is convenient to encapsulate all of the action just described into a class `Noise` that we will use to generate marble and other noiselike textures. Figure 14.41 shows the declaration of this class. (See also Appendix 3.)

The method of greatest interest in the class is `marble()`, which returns a position-dependent value of brightness between zero and unity that mimics the rivulets of dark and light stone in marble. We develop the details of this method later. It would be used to generate a greenish marble by constructing a noise object at the start of the ray tracing with the command

```
Noise n; // create and construct a noise object
```

and thereafter obtaining the texture(x, y, z) value at each point (x, y, z) desired simply as `n.marble(x, y, z);`

The method `marble()` uses `noise()` and `turbulence()`, which we shall develop shortly, as well as the "helper" function `latticeNoise()`. The class

```
class Noise{
public:
        Noise()// a constructor
        {
                int i;
                index = new unsigned char[256];
                for(i = 0; i < 256; i++) index[i] = i; //fill array with indices
                for(i = 0; i < 256; i++) // shuffle it
                {
                        int which = rand() % 256; // choose random place in array
                        unsigned char tmp = index[which]; // swap them
                        index[which] = index[i];
                        index[i] = tmp;
                }
                noiseTable = new float[256];
                for(i = 0; i < 256; i++) noiseTable[i] = rand()/32767.99;
        } // end of constructor

        float noise(float x, float y, float z);
        float noise(float scale, Point3& p);
        float turbulence(float s, Point3& p);
        float marble(float x, float y, float z);
        float marble(float strength,Point3& p);

private:
        float* noiseTable;       // array of noise values
        unsigned char * index;   // pseudo random indices
        float mySpline(float x);  // used for marble
        float latticeNoise(int i, int j, int k)
        { // return noise value on an integer lattice
                #define PERM(x) index[(x) & 255]
                #define INDEX(ix, iy, iz) PERM( (ix) + PERM((iy) + PERM(iz)) )
                return noiseTable[INDEX(i,j,k)];
        }
};
```

FIGURE 14.41 Generating
repeatable noise values.

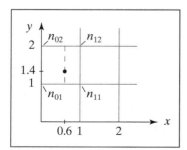

FIGURE 14.42 Linear
interpolation of noise values,
2D case.

constructor creates and fills the arrays `noiseTable[]` and `index[]`. The random values that are put into `noiseTable[]` are created by using the standard C function `rand()`, scaling the values to lie between 0.0 and 1.0. The array `index[]` is first loaded with values 0 to 255 in order and then "shuffled" by swapping each of its elements in turn with some randomly selected element.

With the function `latticeNoise()` in hand, which produces random values at integer lattice points, we want a function noise(x, y, z) that produces randomlike values at points in between—in fact, at *any* point in space. We also want the noise to vary smoothly as x, y, and z vary.

Simple linear interpolation between the lattice values gives acceptable results.[6] Figure 14.42 shows interpolation in 2D; the 3D case is similar. Here we wish to eval-

---

[6]   Perlin and Peachey argue that cubic interpolation gives more realistic results[Ebert98].

uate noise at $(x, y) = (0.6, 1.4)$, given the noise values on the four surrounding corners of the lattice. We first interpolate in x along $y = 1$ and $y = 2$ to form the values[7]

$$n(0.6, 1) = \text{lerp}(0.6, n_{01}, n_{11})$$

and

$$n(0.6, 2) = \text{lerp}(0.6, n_{02}, n_{12})$$

and then interpolate these in y to form

$$n(0.6, 1.4) = \text{lerp}(0.4, n(0.6, 1), n(0.6, 2)).$$

Figure 14.43 shows a possible implementation of the function `noise()` for the 3D case. It has an extra parameter `scale` that scales the given 3D point (x, y, z); this will prove handy when we are creating turbulence. The scaled point is first offset by 1000 in x, y, and z so that all components will be positive. (Since the lattice values are random anyway, this shift doesn't change the statistical nature of the noise generated.) Then noise values are generated at the eight lattice vertices that surround the point. Finally seven *lerp*'s are used to find the interpolated noise value.

```
float Noise:: noise(float scale, Point3& p)
{ // linearly interpolated lattice noise
  #define lerp(f, A, B) A + f * (B - A)
    float d[2][2][2];
    Point3 pp;
    pp.x = p.x * scale + 10000; //offset avoids negative values
    pp.y = p.y * scale + 10000;
    pp.z = p.z * scale + 10000;
    long ix = (long)pp.x; long iy = (long)pp.y; long iz = (long)pp.z;
    float tx,ty,tz, x0,x1,x2,x3, y0,y1;
    tx = pp.x - ix; ty = pp.y - iy; tz = pp.z - iz; // fractional parts
    float mtx = 1.0 - tx, mty = 1.0 - ty, mtz = 1.0 - tz;

    for(int k = 0; k <= 1; k++) // get noise at 8 lattice points
    for(int j = 0; j <= 1; j++)
    for(int i = 0; i <= 1; i++)
        d[k][j][i] = latticeNoise(ix + i, iy + j,iz + k);

    x0 = lerp(tx, d[0][0][0],d[0][0][1]);
    x1 = lerp(tx, d[0][1][0],d[0][1][1]);
    x2 = lerp(tx, d[1][0][0],d[1][0][1]);
    x3 = lerp(tx, d[1][1][0],d[1][1][1]);
    y0 = lerp(ty, x0, x1);
    y1 = lerp(ty, x2, x3);
    return lerp(tz, y0, y1);
}
```

FIGURE 14.43 A function to generate noise at any point p.

Figure 14.44(a) shows a plot of the function $\text{noise}(20, x, y, 0)$, using black for 0.0 and white for 1.0. In the figure, both x and y range from -1 to 1. Some structure is apparent

---

[7] Recall the lerp() function introduced in Chapter 4: $\text{lerp}(f, A, B) = A + (B - A)f$ is the value that lies a fraction f of the way from A to B.

FIGURE 14.44 Sample plots of (a) noise( ) and (b) turb( ).

a)

b)

in the noise field, due to the vagaries of the random-number generation process, but it is not excessive.

Turbulence

Perlin [Perlin85; Ebert98] devised a method for generating more interesting noise than that just described. The idea is to mix together several noise components: one that fluctuates slowly as you move slightly through space, one that fluctuates twice as rapidly, one that fluctuates four times as rapidly, etc. The more rapidly varying components are given progressively smaller strengths. The function

$$\text{turb}(s, x, y, z) = \frac{1}{2}\,\text{noise}(s, x, y, z) + \frac{1}{4}\,\text{noise}(2s, x, y, z) + \frac{1}{8}\,\text{noise}(4s, x, y, z) \quad (14.36)$$

adds three such components, each half as strong, and varying twice as rapidly, as its predecessor. The parameter s scales distances just as it does in `noise()`. Figure 14.45 suggests a way in 2D to see how turb( ) fluctuates. Think of the xy-plane covered with fixed values of noise$(1, x, y, 0)$. For each point $P = (x, y)$, turb$(1, x, y, 0)$ sums together three noise values, at the points (x, y), $(2x, 2y)$, and $(4x, 4y)$ shown. At nearby P' the value noise$(1, x', y', 0)$ is very similar to noise$(1, x, y, 0)$, but noise$(2, x', y, 0')$ will be quite different from noise$(2, x, y, 0)$, and noise$(4, x', y', 0)$ will be still more different. Features in the first noise component will appear at half size in the next component and at quarter size in the one after that. We can add more terms to turb( ), obtaining

$$\text{turb}(s, x, y, z) = \frac{1}{2}\sum_{k=0}^{M} \frac{1}{2^k}\,\text{noise}(2^k\, s, x, y, z), \quad (14.37)$$

for some M. The size of each component is one-half as large as its predecessor at each level of detail, but its frequency (or rate of fluctuation) is twice that of the previous component. This set of circumstances gives rise to the kind of **self-similarity** we

FIGURE 14.45 On the behavior of turb( ).

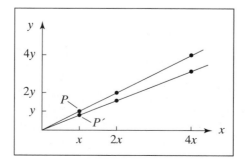

studied in Chapter 9, and in fact, under certain conditions turb( ) produces a useful approximation to so-called $1/f$ noise (see Section 9.8.2), which seems to show up in various naturalistic shapes. Figure 14.44(b) shows a plot of turb( ) generated from the noise( ) field of Part (a) when $M = 3$. The greater level of detail is apparent, and the fluctuations seem softer and more cloudlike. The turbulence that is provided by a function like turb( ) can be used to perturb some attribute of a shape or texture to give it a more realistic appearance, as we see next in the case of marble.

Marble Texture

Marble shows veins of dark and light material that have some regularity, but that also exhibit strongly chaotic irregularities. (See Plate 42 for an exquisite example.) Following Watt and Watt [Watt92], we can build up a marblelike 3D texture by giving the veins a smoothly fluctuating behavior in, say, the z-direction and then perturbing it chaotically using turb( ). We start with a texture that is constant in x and y and smoothly varying in z:

marble(x, y, z) = undulate$(\sin(z))$.

Here, undulate( ) is the spline-shaped function shown in Figure 14.46 [Watt92] that varies between some dark and some light value as its argument varies from -1 to 1. (The spline function is discussed in the exercises at the end of the section.) Using $\sin(z)$ for the argument of undulate( ) produces a periodic "ripple" in z that moves back and forth across the spline curve, once each period, producing the fluctuation in intensity shown in Figure 14.46(b). The vertical veins of color in the marble are, of course, much too regular, so the argument of sin( ) is modulated with some turbulence:

marble(x, y, z) = undulate$(\sin(z + A \text{ turb}(s, x, y, z)))$.

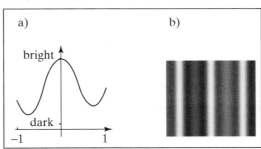

FIGURE 14.46 Constructing marble texture. (a) A spline curve. (b) Unperturbed marble texture.

The phase of sin( ) is offset different amounts at different positions in the marble, producing much more realistic veins. The parameter s makes the turbulence vary more or less rapidly at different points; the parameter A changes the amount of the perturbation. Watt demonstrated that if undulate( ) were replaced by a simple straight line, the effect would be much less satisfactory.

Figure 14.47 shows the marble texture seen on the face of a cube. The function plotted is

$g = $ undulate$(\sin(2\pi z + A \times \text{turb}(5, x, y, z)))$,

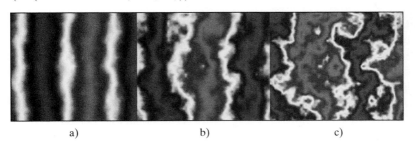

FIGURE 14.47 Marble texture. (a) $A = 1$. (b) $A = 3$. (c) $A = 6$.

where z moves from zero at the right to unity at the left and y points upward. The amplitude $A = 1$ in Part (a), so only a little turbulence is present. In Parts (b) and (c), A is 3 and 6, respectively, and the turbulence is much more profound.

The value of marble( ) would be used as a reflection coefficient in Equation (14.34) to modulate the amount of light returning from different points in the object hit by different rays. It is straightforward to extend marble( ) to return red, green, and blue components for full-color ray tracers. Figure 14.48 shows a scene containing a number of marble objects. The effect is quite convincing.

FIGURE 14.48 A scene with marble objects.

PRACTICE EXERCISES

14.8.1 A suitable spline function for producing a marble texture

The function

```
float Noise:: undulate(float x)
{
        if(x <-0.4) return 0.15 +  2.857 * SQR(x + 0.75);
        else if(x < 0.4) return 0.95 - 2.8125 * SQR(x);
        else return 0.26 + 2.666 * SQR(x - 0.7);
}
```

describes a smooth curve in y as x varies from -1 to 1. The function is composed of three polynomials defined in three different portions of this domain. Plot this function carefully to see its shape (SQR(x) forms the square of x), and then alter the coefficients to add another undulation to the curve.

14.8.2 Experimenting with random-noise generators

The noise constructor of Figure 14.41 relies on the properties of the standard C function rand( ), which is known to be flawed as a random-number generator (RNG), failing certain statistical tests. (A search for RNGs on the World Wide Web leads quickly to pages such as http://stat.fsu.edu/~geo/, maintained by George Marsaglia, for testing RNGs.) Better RNGs have been developed, but tend to be much more complicated. Explore the Web for sources and discussions of better RNGs.   ■

14.8.2 Pasting Images onto Surfaces

In Chapter 8, we examined how to paste images onto polygonal surfaces with the use of OpenGL. In this section, we examine how to paste images onto arbitrary curved surfaces in a ray tracer. The routines for doing so are simple, and results can be excellent, but more execution time is usually required than with OpenGL. Each pixel is computed individually, and no scan-line coherence can be exploited.

As in Chapter 8, we assume that a 2D texture function texture(u, v) has been defined, with u and v each varying from zero to unity, that produces an intensity or color at each point (u, v). The function texture(u, v) might be a procedural texture such as the checkerboard or a Mandelbrot set, or it might be an "image" texture stored in a pix map. Suppose the pix map is arranged as an N-by-M array of pixel values called `txtr[] []`. Then, given values for u and v between zero and unity, we can index into the appropriate pixel of `txtr` simply by using

```
txtr[ (int) (u*N)] [ (int) (v*M)].
```

It is simplest to paste a texture onto a generic object, rather than onto its transformed version in scene coordinates. The designer associates texture coordinates with coordinates on the generic object in such a way that, when the object is transformed into the scene, the texture appears correctly (and with the proper aspect ratio) on the transformed object.

Wrapping Texture onto Surfaces

We need a way to associate points (x, y, z) on a generic object's surface with texture coordinates (u, v). Different mappings are needed for different generic shapes.

▪ **EXAMPLE 14.8.3 Textures for the square and plane**

The generic plane is the xy-plane, and the generic square lies in this plane. Thus, there is a natural association between the image plane of texture(u, v) and the generic square or plane. As shown in Figure 14.49, the designer simply chooses a "window" on the plane (left, top, right, bottom), and if the ray hits the plane within this window, it is easy to compute which point (u, v) in the texture is to be used. Specifically, given the hit point $(x, y, 0)$ in generic coordinates, the corresponding texture coordinates are

$$u = \frac{x - \text{left}}{\text{right} - \text{left}}, v = \frac{y - \text{bottom}}{\text{top} - \text{bottom}}. \qquad (14.38)$$

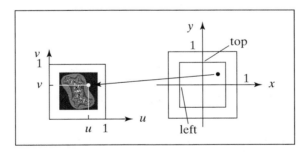

FIGURE 14.49 Mapping textures onto the square or plane.

The designer must also decide how to handle hit points that fall outside the window. A common approach is to specify some fixed value that is used for the texture when this occurs.

▪ **EXAMPLE 14.8.4 Textures for the cylinder**

Wrapping a texture around a generic cylinder is almost as easy as wrapping one around a square or plane. (Recall the discussion in Section 8.5.5.) The generic tapered cylinder is shown in Figure 14.50, with a "window" specified on its surface. The window extends in azimuth from a_1 to a_2 and in z from z_1 to z_2. When a ray hits a cylinder at (x, y, z), we simply compute the azimuth as $\theta = \arctan(y, x)$ and compute the texture coordinates (u, v) using

$$u = \frac{\theta - a_1}{a_2 - a_1} \text{ and } v = \frac{z - z_1}{z_2 - z_1}. \qquad (14.39)$$

FIGURE 14.50 Wrapping a texture about a cylinder.

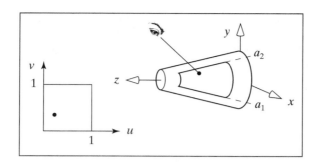

If the hit point lies outside of the designated window, the designer must choose the color to use for the texture. Notice that if the cylinder is highly tapered, the mapped texture image will be distorted. Pasting texture onto the cap or base of a cylinder is addressed in the exercises that follow. Also addressed is the problem of wrapping a texture about a sphere or cone.

PRACTICE EXERCISES

14.8.3 Wrapping a texture on the cap and base of a cylinder

Discuss in detail how to paste a texture onto the cap and base of a cylinder. A portion of a bit map is to be pasted so that it covers the cap or base completely.

14.8.4 Wrapping a texture about a sphere

Discuss in detail how to wrap a texture about a portion of a generic sphere. The texture "window" extends in azimuth from a_1 to a_2 and in latitude from l_1 to l_2. Discuss the severity of the distortion a bit map will suffer if l_1 or l_2 is set too close to $\pm 90°$. If a texture function is used instead of a bit map, can the function be defined so that it produces no distortion even near the poles of the sphere?

14.8.5 Wrapping the world around a sphere

Suppose you have a geographical database for the borders of all the countries of the world. The file consists of a large number of polylines whose endpoints are given as (longitude, latitude). Can this database be used to wrap a geographically accurate map of the world about the generic sphere? If so, describe how to do it.

14.8.6 Wrapping a texture about a cone

Discuss in detail how to wrap a texture about a portion of the wall of a generic cone. What is a natural interpretation of the "window" parameters? Discuss the nature of the distortion a bit map will suffer in various situations. Describe how to map a texture onto the base of the cone.   ■

14.8.3 Antialiasing Ray Tracings

Ray tracing is inherently a point-sampling process: taking discrete "looks" at a scene along individual rays. So it is not surprising that aliasing effects often degrade the quality of ray-traced images. As we saw in Chapter 10, aliasing effects can be reduced by sampling a scene at more points, often called **supersampling**. This is true for ray tracing, too: Several rays per pixel are traced into the scene, and the intensities that are returned along the ray are averaged. The cost is, of course, much more execution time.

Figure 14.51(a) shows a sampling pattern in which rays are shot through the corners of a group of pixels. The final color given to each pixel is the average of the colors found at its four corners. This level of antialiasing is easy to do (what changes are needed in the code of Figure 14.10?) and costs only a little in time (for an R-row-by-

C-column image, how many rays have to be traced?). Supersampling can involve many more rays per pixel. An example of shooting nine rays through parts of a pixel is shown in Figure 14.51(b). The light returned along all nine rays is averaged to form the final pixel value.

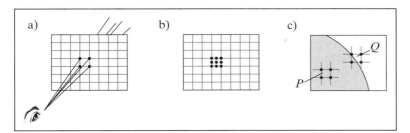

FIGURE 14.51 Supersampling techniques for antialiasing.

Several more sophisticated techniques have been developed that do a better job than those just described. Whitted [Whitted80] suggested an adaptive procedure that shoots more rays into regions where antialiasing is needed more: where there are abrupt changes in the image. In Whitted's method, rays are shot through the four corners of each pixel and the average intensity is formed, but then this average is compared with the four individual intensities; if the intensity at a corner differs too much from the average, the pixel is subdivided into quadrants (as in the Warnock HSR algorithm), and additional rays are sent through the corners of the quadrant. This approach is illustrated in Figure 14.51(c). The four rays for pixel *P* return nearly the same intensity because the scene is not changing in that region, but one of the rays for pixel *Q* sends back an intensity very different from the others. Therefore, three new rays are shot through the corners of the lower left-hand quadrant of *Q*, and again the intensity from each is compared with the average. Subdivision is performed recursively until either a prefixed recursion level has been reached or the four intensities are sufficiently close to the average to accept the intensity as "close enough." When this procedure has been done to the four quadrants of a pixel as needed, the final pixel value is formed as a weighted average of the quadrant averages.

Another technique, based on distributed sampling [Cook84], uses a form of stochastic sampling, which we saw in Chapter 10 in connection with antialiasing of texture. A random pattern of rays is shot into the scene for each pixel, and the resulting intensities are averaged. For instance, a pixel can be subdivided into a regular four-by-four grid. But instead of having rays shot exactly through these grid points, a ray is shot through displaced or "jittered" grid points. Jittering the sample points adds a measure of "noise" to the image (the intensities that are observed are from slightly offset locations in the image), but this noise can be less intrusive to the eye than aliasing errors. A smaller grid of samples can be used with jittering than without it.

14.9 USING EXTENTS

Ray tracing is very repetitive, performing the same set of functions again and again for a very large number of rays. Each ray must be intersected with every object, amounting to an enormous number of calculations of intersections. (And matters get much worse when we incorporate shadows, reflections, and refractions.) We welcome any technique that reduces the number of objects that must be completely scrutinized and processed. The use of extents can speed up the ray-tracing process significantly.

An **extent** of an object is a shape that encloses the object. An extent accelerates the ray-tracing process by quickly revealing when the current ray *could not possibly hit* a particular object. The notion is that if a ray misses the extent, it must perforce miss the object. If the extent has a simple shape, it may be inexpensive to intersect a ray with it, whereas it may be very expensive to intersect a ray with the enclosed object.

Figure 14.52 shows an example in which a torus (expensive to intersect) is enclosed in a boxlike extent (inexpensive to intersect). When the ray is tested against the extent, three things can happen:

FIGURE 14.52 Enclosing a torus in a box extent.

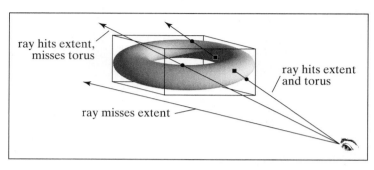

ray hits extent, misses torus

ray hits extent and torus

ray misses extent

- The ray misses the box. Therefore, the test against the torus is skipped.
- The ray hits the box, so the full test against the torus is performed, revealing that the ray misses the torus. (This might be called a "false alarm": The first test indicated that the ray hit the torus, but in fact it did not.)
- The ray hits the box, so the full test against the torus is performed, revealing that the ray hits the torus.

If the cost of the full hit test is much greater than that of the extent test, it is well worth making the extra test for those frequent cases wherein the ray does miss the extent.

A Brief Analysis of the Cost Saving

Suppose it costs T time units to test a ray against the extent and mT time units to test it against the torus. Suppose further that N rays are cast to create the image, and only a fraction f of them hit the box. It follows that N tests are made against the extent at a cost of NT, and fN tests are made against the torus at a cost of $fNmT$. So the total cost is $NT(1 + fm)$. On the other hand, if extents are not used, all N rays must be tested against the torus, at a total cost of mNT. This analysis yields the ratio

$$\text{comp time} = \frac{\text{cost without extents}}{\text{cost with extents}} = \frac{m}{1 + f \cdot m}. \tag{14.40}$$

For example, if $m = 20$ and $f = 1/40$ (each object in a typical scene covers only a small fraction of the image area), the speed ratio is about 13, so it would take 13 times as long to trace this scene if extent testing is disabled.

Note that we want f to be as small as possible. That is, we want each extent to be such that the fewest rays will hit it. This agrees with our intuition that extents should be as "tight fitting" about their parent objects as possible.

Where does extent testing fit into the ray-tracing process? Arvo and Kirk [Arvo89] made an excellent survey of possible approaches, including the use of hierarchical extents that enclose whole groups of objects within an extent. We focus on improving the basic `hit()` method that every object in the scene possesses. Recall the routine `getFirstHit()` of Figure 14.14, which tests the current ray against every object, using the specific `hit()` method for the object:

```
for(each object, obj)
{
    if(!obj->hit(ray,inter)) continue;
        compare this hit time with the best so far, etc.
}
```

We shall use extent testing inside `hit()` to accelerate each individual test. If we can quickly determine that the ray does *not* hit the object before we perform the entire calculation of the intersection, the overall speed of the ray tracer will increase significantly. One advantage of putting extent testing inside each `hit()` method is that the testing can be fine-tuned to the specific geometric shape in question.

There are several ways to create and use extents in ray tracing. Some are easy to implement, while others require more programming, but yield better performance. We examine a handful of different simple methods and show how they fit into the logical flow of a ray tracer. Other methods are described in the exercises at the end of Section 14.9.1.

14.9.1 Box and Sphere Extents

The two shapes most often used for extents are the sphere and an "aligned box":

> **Sphere extent**. A sphere that completely encloses the given object is specified by (C, r)—its center point C and radius r.
>
> **Box extent**. A rectangular parallelepiped whose sides are aligned with the coordinate axes is specified by six numbers: (left, top, right, bottom, front, back).

We have seen that intersecting each of these shapes with a ray is reasonably fast. For the sphere, we must form a quadratic equation and test whether the discriminant is positive. (See Figure 14.15.) For an aligned box, we must intersect the ray with six planes and test whether the "candidate interval" (t_{in}, t_{out}) vanishes. (See Figure 14.23.) Each of the plane intersections is very fast, since no dot products need to be formed. In addition, an "early out" frequently occurs, in which the candidate interval vanishes after only a few planes have been tested.

There are two spaces in which we can do extent testing: world coordinates and generic coordinates. Recall that each object is transformed from some generic shape into the scene by an affine transformation. To intersect the ray with the object, we first inverse transform the ray into generic coordinates and intersect the generic ray with the generic object. But we can place an extent about the object in the scene itself and test the current ray against it. If the ray misses this extent, the generic ray need not be computed, which saves a transformation. We can also place an extent about the generic object and test the inverse-transformed ray against it. If the ray misses this extent, a full intersection test is avoided.

Extents in world coordinates might not fit about their objects particularly well. Figure 14.53(a) shows two tapered cylinders positioned in some scene being ray traced surrounded by a sphere and a box extent. Part (b) shows the cylinder in 2D for simplicity. If the cylinder is long and thin, the sphere extent doesn't fit particularly closely, and using it would lead to many "false alarms." The box extent fits closely about the cylinder even if it is long and thin, unless the cylinder is rotated away from alignment with the coordinate axes. (The exercises at the end of the section ask you to estimate the likelihood of false alarms for various cases.)

Extents in generic coordinates usually fit more snugly. Figure 14.53(c) shows the generic tapered cylinder, surrounded by a sphere extent and a box extent. The sphere extent fits reasonably snugly, and the box extent fits very tightly about the cylinder.

There is a trade-off to consider in deciding whether to do extent testing in world coordinates or in generic coordinates. Testing in world coordinates is fast, because there is no need to compute the inverse-transformed ray. But extents may not fit very tightly about their objects. Testing in generic coordinates requires finding the generic ray, but extents fit more tightly. It is difficult to say in general which kind of test is superior. It is also difficult to generalize about the advantage of sphere extents over box extents. Using one or more of the methods, people do elaborate timing tests on

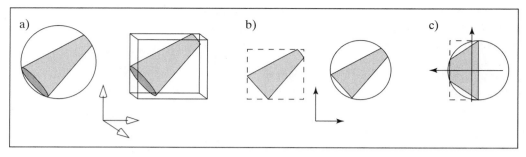

FIGURE 14.53 Extents formed in world and generic coordinates.

sample scenes and decide on the best combination to use in their ray tracers. One informal test on a scene of 100 randomly scaled and oriented tapered cylinders showed that the use of sphere extents in world coordinates reduced the ray-tracing time by 27%, whereas the use of any other combination of extents increased the ray-tracing time. But as we shall see later, when we incorporate more features in a ray tracer, the results can be quite different.

Figure 14.54 shows how extent testing fits into a `hit()` method in the case of the tapered cylinder. Sphere extent testing is shown, and the test is done in both world and generic coordinates to indicate where the testing code occurs. (Probably only one of the tests would be used in an actual ray tracer.) The routine `rayHitsSphereExtent()` is called to see whether the ray hits the sphere extent, and if not, there is an "early out" from `hit()`. The routine is called first with the ray in world coordinates and tested against a `worldSphereExtent`. If the ray hits this extent, it is inverse transformed. The routine is then called a second time to see whether the generic ray hits the generic sphere extent. Again, if it misses, there is an early out, and the elaborate intersection test of a ray with the generic cylinder is skipped. If it were felt that box extents would be more efficient than sphere extents for the tapered cylinder, we could replace the `rayHits-SphereExtent()` routine with a `rayHitsBoxExtent()` routine. We could even put *both* extent tests inside `hit()`, although this would most likely produce a net loss in speed.

FIGURE 14.54 Testing against sphere extents within the `hit()` method for the cylinder.

```
bool TaperedCylinder::hit(Ray &r, Intersection &inter)
{
  if(!rayHitsSphereExtent(r,worldSphereExtent)) return false;

  Ray genRay; //make the generic ray
  xfrmRay(genRay,invTransf,r);  //expensive

  if(!rayHitsSphereExtent(genRay,genSphereExtent)) return false;
  ...Do expensive full testing with the generic cylinder...
}
```

We must choose which tests to include in each `hit()` method for the different shape classes. Some choices are obvious: For a `Sphere` object, there is no sense in doing a sphere extent test in generic coordinates. (Why?) And similarly, you would never do a box extent test in generic coordinates for a `Cube` object. There are no extents for a `Plane`, so no tests are included in `Plane :: hit()`. For a `Square`, it is meaningful to build an extent, but the intersection test is so simple anyway that there is no gain achieved in using an extent test. A `Mesh` object, on the other hand, has a large number of bounding planes and is expensive to intersect, so extent testing can yield significant gains.

Implementing Extent Testing

How are extents formed for each geometric shape, and how is each extent test carried out? It is natural to store the extent information of an object inside the object itself, so we add some fields to the `GeomObj` class. (See Appendix 3.) We may want to do any one of the four types of extent testing, so we add fields for each:

```
SphereInfo genSphereExtent, worldSphereExtent;
Cuboid genBoxExtent, worldBoxExtent;
```

The `SphereInfo` class (see Appendix 3) holds a description of a sphere in two fields: `center`, which holds the location of the center of the sphere extent, and `radSq`, which holds the square of the radius of the sphere. (It could instead hold the radius, but only the square of the radius is required for the extent test.) The `Cuboid` class has six fields: `left`, `top`, `right`, `bottom`, `front`, and `back`. The box extent is understood to extend from `left` to `right` along the x-axis, from `bottom` to `top` along the y-axis, and from `back` to `front` along the z-axis.

After the object list has been built, but before ray tracing begins, data are placed in these fields for each object in the object list. Then, during ray tracing, some combination of the routines `rayHitsSphereExtent()` and `rayHitsBoxExtent()` is called inside each `hit()` method. The test of a ray with a sphere extent is particularly easy (see the exercises at the end of the section) and is realized by the function

```
bool rayHitsSphereExtent(Ray & ray, SphereInfo& sph)
{
        double A = dot3D(ray.dir, ray.dir);
        Vector3 diff = ray.start − sph.center;
        double B = dot3D(diff, ray.dir);
        double C = dot3D(diff,diff) - sph.radSq;
        return(B * B >= A * C);
}
```

This function tests whether the discriminant of the appropriate quadratic equation is positive. Eleven multiplications are required to compute the discriminant, so the test is not entirely without cost.

The `rayHitsBoxExtent()` test is an adaptation of the `hit()` method of the `Cube` class to work with a box extent described in a `Cuboid` data structure. It should be finely tuned for maximum speed. (See the exercises.)

Building the Sphere and Box Extents

We need to create the sphere and box extents for each given object. The generic extents need only be made once for each type of shape, but the world extents must be made for each instance of an object, taking into account the affine transformation associated with the instance. The involvement of a transformation makes the computation of the extent much more difficult. For instance, how do we find a sphere extent for a cylinder that has been scaled and rotated in a complex way?

A particularly straightforward method associates a **point cluster** with each shape. This is a set of points whose convex hull encloses the object. (Recall an intuitive way to envision the convex hull of a set of points fixed in space: Place a balloon about the points and let the balloon collapse onto the points. The resulting polyhedron is the convex hull.) With a point cluster in hand, it is easy to construct a sphere that just encloses the cluster. And certainly, such a sphere would enclose the original object. (By transitivity, if shape A encloses shape B and B encloses shape C, then A encloses C.) We can also obtain a convex hull for the object after it is transformed: We just transform each point in the point cluster and use the new points to define the transformed convex hull. Since affine transformations preserve "inside-ness," if object A lies inside the convex hull B, then the transformed object $T(A)$ must lie inside the convex hull $T(B)$ built on the transformed points.

We therefore need to build a point cluster for each type of shape. This is easy for the `Cube` and the `Square`: Their own vertices provide the points. It is also simple for a `Mesh`: We just use the vertex list itself as the point cluster.

The `Sphere` and the `TaperedCylinder` present more of a problem, since they are defined by various symmetry properties rather than by points. A reasonable approach wraps each shape in a tightly enclosing polyhedron and uses the vertices of the polyhedron as the point cluster. Figure 14.55(a) shows the generic tapered cylinder wrapped in a prism based on a hexagon at each end. The hexagon at the base must have a radius of 4/3 in order to fit snugly about the circular base. (See the exercises.) The hexagon at the cap has a radius of 4/3 times the radius of the cap. Note that this point cluster is constructed individually for each instance of a tapered cylinder and that it is designed specially for the specific shape of the cylinder. Figure 14.55(b) shows the generic sphere wrapped in an icosahedron, whose 12 vertices make up the point cluster. The vertices of the icosahedron must be placed at a radius of about 1.26 to ensure that the unit sphere is properly enclosed. (See the exercises.)

FIGURE 14.55 Defining point clusters for the cylinder and the sphere.

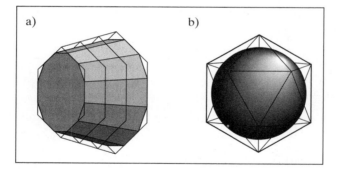

The point clusters for each type of shape can be stored in a simple `PointCluster` data structure containing a field `num` for the number of points in the cluster and an array `pt[]`. (See Appendix 3.) A method `makeExtentPoints(PointCluster& clust)` is developed for each shape class and is called once during a preprocessing step for each object in the scene. (See the exercises.)

Once the point cluster is available for a generic object, it is easy to find the box and sphere extents. Each field of the box extent holds the largest or smallest coordinate found among the cluster points $p[i]$: left = $\min_i p[i].x$, top = $\max_i p[i].y$, etc., so all fields can be found within a single loop over the cluster points. This would be done in a routine `void makeBoxExtent(PointCluster& clust,Cuboid& cub)`, which takes a point cluster and generates a `Cuboid` data structure that is then stored in the object. (See the exercises.)

Building the sphere extent takes only a little more work. The center of the extent is chosen to be the *centroid* of the point cluster, since this is a nice centralized point. (See Section 4.5.2.) (To find the centroid, just add up all of the points, componentwise, and divide by the number of points.) Then the radius of the enclosing sphere is found as the largest distance from the center of the extent to any one of the points in the cluster. On the basis of this approach, the routine `void makeSphereExtent (Point-Cluster& clust, SphereInfo& sph)` is easily fashioned. (See the exercises.)

Finally, it is easy to form the world box extent and world sphere extent: Simply transform each of the points of the generic object's point cluster to form a point cluster in world coordinates, and then use the same routines as before to form the desired extents.

PRACTICE EXERCISES

14.9.1 Estimating the false-alarm rate

Figure 14.53(b) shows the silhouette of a tapered cylinder surrounded by a circle. Calculate the "emptiness ratio" for various elongations and rotations of the cylinder within the circle. The emptiness ratio is defined as (area of circle − area of cylinder)/(area of circle), and it gives a rough measure of the probability of a false alarm: the case where the extent test suggests a hit, but the full test reveals a miss. Repeat for box extent testing.

14.9.2 Developing the sphere extent test

Adapt the ray–sphere intersection algorithm of Figure 14.15 to the case where the sphere is centered at *center* and has radius r.

14.9.3 Testing a ray with a sphere extent

a. Show that the smallest enclosing sphere about the generic cylinder with small radius of unity is centered at $(0,0 0.5)$ and has a radius of $\sqrt{1.25}$.
b. Show that the equation of this sphere therefore has the implicit form
$F(x, y, z) = x^2 + y^2 + (z - \frac{1}{2})^2 - 1.25.$
c. Show that solving $F(S + \mathbf{c}t) = 0$ as usual results in the quadratic equation
$At^2 + 2Bt + C = 0$, where $A = |\mathbf{c}|^2$, $B = \mathbf{c} \cdot S'$, and $C = |S'|^2 - 1.25$ and where we have defined $S' = (S_x, S_y, S_z - 0.5)$.

14.9.4 Implementing the generic box extent test

Adjust the `Cube :: hit()` method to develop the routine `bool rayHitsBox-Extent(Ray& ray, Cuboid& cub)`, which tests whether the given ray intersects the extent described in `cub`. This entails simplifying `hit()` without altering its logic. Show how the `numer` and `denom` values needed for each plane of the box depend on the data in `cub`. (The top plane, for instance, uses `numer = cub.top - ray.start.y; denom = ray.dir.y`.) As each of the planes of the box is intersected by the ray, the candidate interval (t_{in}, t_{out}) is updated, and if the interval vanishes, an "early out" occurs and the test returns *false*.

14.9.5 The point cluster for the tapered cylinder

Show that a hexagon that just encircles a circle with unity radius must have a radius of 4/3. Determine formulas for the 12 vertices of the point cluster for a cylinder. Write the method `makeExtentPoints(PointCluster& clust)` for the `Tapered-Cylinder` class.

14.9.6 The point cluster for the sphere

Using the vertex list of the icosahedron given in Figure 6.29, determine how much the icosahedron must be scaled so that it just encloses the generic sphere. (Is a scale factor of $f = 1.071$ sufficient?) Write the method `makeExtentPoints(PointCluster& clust)` for the Sphere class. Three double `for` loops do the trick. For instance, four of the vertices lie at $(0, \pm f, \pm f\tau)$, where $\tau = 0.618034$.

14.9.7 Routines to create the sphere and box extents

Write the routines `void makeSphereExtent(PointCluster& clust,Sphere-Info& sph)` and `void makeBoxExtent(PointCluster& clust,Cuboid& cub)`, which build a sphere extent and a box extent from a given point cluster.   ■

14.9.2 Using Projection Extents

There is another kind of extent whose use provides a dramatic gain in the speed of a ray tracer. In contrast with box and sphere extents, which operate in 3D space, this extent is a rectangular region on the screen.

The **projection extent** of an object is an aligned rectangle on the screen that encloses the projection of the object, as suggested in Figure 14.56(a). Part (b) of the figure shows the projection extent in more detail. The projection extent is captured by four numbers: {*left*, *top*, *right*, *bottom*}.

FIGURE 14.56 The projection extent of an object.

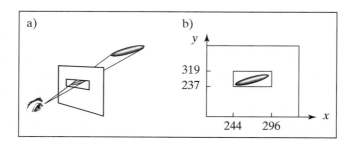

It is very easy to use projection extents while ray tracing. Each ray passes through the screen at a certain row and column value, say, (r, c). If (r, c) lies outside of the projection extent of an object, the ray cannot possibly intersect the object. For the example in Figure 14.56(b), if c is less than 244 or larger than 296, or if r is less than 237 or larger than 319, the ray definitely misses the object.

Because projection extents are intimately coupled to the geometry of the camera and the position of the eye, they can be used only for "eye rays"—rays that emanate from the eye. In later sections we will be generating rays for shadowing, reflection, and refraction, and since these emanate from arbitrary points in the scene, there is no screen on which to place a projection. But the technique works superbly for eye rays and can speed up ray tracing by a substantial factor.

We construct the projection extent for each object in a scene in a preprocessing step and store the extent with the object, just as we did with the box and sphere extents. To accommodate this storage feature, we add an `IntRect screenExtent` field to the `GeomObj` class. We also extend the `Ray` class so that a ray "knows" which row and column on the display it is passing through. And we give the ray one more piece of information: its so-called "recursion level," which will play a big part later when we work with reflection and refraction. Here the level simply keeps track of whether the ray in question is an eye ray. Eye rays are given a level of zero.

During ray tracing, a new test is performed at the start of the `hit()` method for each object type, before any sphere or box extent tests. Figure 14.57 shows where the new test is located for the `TaperedCylinder` class. (This same test is used for all object types, except the plane.) Compare the figure with Figure 14.54. The test checks whether the given ray is an eye ray, and if so, it compares the ray's row and column against the projection extent stored in the object. If the row or column is outside of the projection extent, the ray must miss the object, and `hit()` immediately returns `false`. The test is very fast indeed.

```
bool TaperedCylinder::hit(Ray &r, Intersection &inter)
{
   if(r.recurseLevel == 0 &&
      r.col < projExtnt.left ||
      r.col > projExtnt.right||
      r.row < projExtnt.bottom ||
      r.row > projExtnt.top )   return false;   //misses screen extent
      if(!rayHitsSphereExtent(r,worldSphereExtent)) return false;
      make, and inverse transform, the generic ray
      if(!rayHitsSphereExtent(genRay,genSphereExtent)) return false;
      ...do expensive full testing with the generic cylinder...
}
```

FIGURE 14.57 Testing against sphere extents within the hit() method for the cylinder.

Computing Projection Extents

The preprocessing step must compute the projection extent for each object in the scene. The extent is easily computed, given the point cluster of the object. The point cluster of the generic object is transformed into world coordinates by using the object's transformation, just as we did for world sphere and box extents, and so becomes a "cloud" of points, $p[0]$, $p[1]$, ... positioned in the scene. Figure 14.58 shows the 12 points of the cluster for a transformed cylinder.

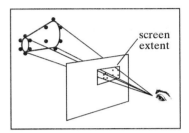

FIGURE 14.58 Building the projection extent.

Now each of the points $p[i]$ is projected onto the near plane of the camera. Given a general point p in the scene, we can find its projection p' by a calculation based on the location of p and the geometry of the camera. The projected point p' is associated with a particular row r and column c; the association is derived in the exercises at the end of the section. The result is that p projects to the pixel at row r and column c, where

$$r = \frac{nRows}{2}\left(1 - \frac{NP_v}{HP_n}\right)$$

and   (14.41)

$$c = \frac{nCols}{2}\left(1 - \frac{NP_u}{WP_n}\right).$$

(The expressions on the right side must be rounded to integers before being stored in r and c.) Here, P_u, P_v, and P_n are formed as dot products with the axes $\mathbf{u}$, $\mathbf{v}$, and $\mathbf{n}$ of the camera:

$$P_u = (p - eye) \cdot \mathbf{u};$$
$$P_v = (p - eye) \cdot \mathbf{v};$$ (14.42)
$$P_n = (p - eye) \cdot \mathbf{n}.$$

So each $p[i]$ is projected and the pair (r_i, c_i) is computed. A search is made through the list of (r_i, c_i)'s for the smallest and largest r-value and the smallest and largest c-value, which, when found, are stored in the projection extent data structure {*left, top, right, bottom*}.

Figure 14.59 shows a ray-traced scene, with each object's projection extent superimposed on the object. (For debugging purposes, some programmers like to draw the projection extents of every object before ray tracing starts. These rectangles disappear when the final pixel colors are painted in during ray tracing.)

FIGURE 14.59 A ray-traced scene with projection extents made visible.

PRACTICE EXERCISES

14.9.8 Finding the projection of a point

Show that Equations (14.41) and (14.42) are correct. Do this by "inverting" Equation (14.3), which gives a direction for a ray through the r, cth pixel: Start with a direction, and deduce the values of r and c. The ray from the eye to point p has direction $K(p - eye)$ for some scaling multiplier K. This direction must be equal to **dir** in Equation (14.3). To isolate some terms, take the dot product of both sides with respect to **u**, to obtain

$$K(p - eye) \cdot \mathbf{u} = W\left(\frac{2c}{nCols} - 1\right).$$

Dot the same expression successively with **v** and **n** to obtain two other equalities, one of which yields the value of K in terms of known quantities. Then show that this equality produces

$$\frac{NP_u}{WP_n} = 1 - \frac{2c}{nCols},$$

from which we can solve for c to obtain one of the results in Equation (14.41). Derive the other result similarly.

14.9.9 Union Extents for further time savings

Some scenes contain large areas that show only background and contain no objects at all. To save additional time during ray tracing, we can form the **union extent**, the smallest aligned rectangle that encloses *all* of the individual extents of the objects in the scene. Each ray is first tested against this extent. If it lies outside, it will be set immediately to the background color. Otherwise the object list will be scanned as always. Show how to form the union extent and how to use it in your ray tracer.

14.9.10 Lists for clustered objects

Another refinement can save significant computation time whenever it is applicable. When groups of objects appear in fairly isolated "clusters" in a scene, each cluster of objects can be placed in a separate object list—call it a **cluster list**. A union extent is computed for each cluster. So the object list becomes a list of cluster lists. During ray tracing, each ray is tested against the union extent of each cluster list, and only if it passes this test will the ray be tested against the objects in the cluster. Show how to organize the data types and the ray-tracing algorithm in order to implement this approach. ■

14.10 ADDING SHADOWS FOR GREATER REALISM

Misled by fancy's meteor ray,
By passion driven;
But yet the light that led astray
Was light from heaven.

Robert Burns

The presence of shadows of the proper shape and darkness adds a great deal of realism to computer-generated images. We saw in Chapter 8 that OpenGL offers some rudimentary mechanisms to produce shadows, but it is awkward at best to use these

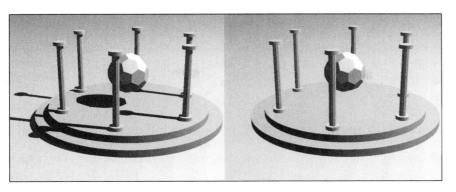

FIGURE 14.60 Rendering with and without shadows.

tools, and they produce shadows only in limited situations. Ray tracing, on the other hand, produces shadows with very little programming effort. (Unfortunately, producing shadows dramatically slows down the ray-tracing process.) Figure 14.60 shows a scene rendered with and without shadows.

The light intensities we have calculated up to now have assumed that the hit point, P_h, of the ray with the first object hit is in fact bathed in light from the various light sources. But this is not the case if some other object happens to lie between P_h and a light source. In that case, P_h is in shadow with respect to that source, and thus, both the diffuse and specular contributions are absent. This leaves only the ambient light component.

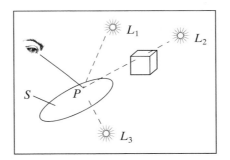

FIGURE 14.61 Various cases of shadowing the hit point.

Figure 14.61 shows various shadowing situations. Point P has no object between it and light source L_1, so P is not in shadow with respect to L_1. But P *is* in the shadow of the cube with respect to source L_2. Further, source L_3 is so positioned that the hit object itself hides the source from P; this is called "self-shadowing." In the configuration shown, therefore, the only light without anything between it and P is the light from source L_1.

Spawning Additional Rays: "Shadow Feelers"

In order to compute shadows accurately, we need to know when a hit point is in shadow with respect to a light source. So we need a routine, say, `isInShadow()`, that returns `true` if any part of *any* object lies between the hit point and a given source and `false` otherwise. To devise such a routine, we "spawn" a new ray, often called a **shadow feeler**, that emanates from P_h at $t = 0$ and reaches L at $t = 1$. The shadow feeler thus has the parametric representation $P_h + (L - P_h)t$. To see if it hits anything, the entire object list is scanned, and each object is tested for an intersection with the shadow feeler. If any intersection is found to lie between $t = 0$ and $t = 1$, `isInShadow()` returns `true`.

But a thorny problem lurks in a naïve use of this approach: the problem of "self-shadowing." If the shadow feeler really starts at P_h, then there is *always* an intersection between the feeler ray and the object itself: at $t = 0$! Thus, isInShadow() would always return true, which is clearly wrong. Some people try to cope with this difficulty by accepting intersections only if they occur at some t strictly greater than 0. But as shown in Figure 14.62(a), this approach will miss a true intersection with the square or plane if the source is on the opposite side of the square from the eye. The feeler from P to source L_1 correctly reports no intersection, but the feeler from P to L_2 would also report no intersection (why?), whereas the square itself shadows point P. (Why does this anomaly not arise for other shapes, such as spheres and cones?)

FIGURE 14.62 Shadow-feeler strategies.

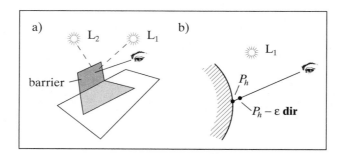

A strategy that works reliably sends an adjusted shadow feeler to isIn-Shadow(), as shown in Figure 14.62(b). The start point of the shadow feeler is shifted toward the eye by a small amount. If the ray has direction **dir** and has hit at point P_h, the start point of the shadow feeler is offset to $P_h - \varepsilon$ **dir**, where ε is a small positive number. This puts the starting point slightly "in front of" ("on the eye side of") the object that is hit by the ray. Using this start point for the shadow feeler, we find that there is no intersection with the object at $t = 0$, and the problem is solved.

The shadow feeler approach fits into the Scene :: shade(ray) method in the following way: When getFirstHit() has returned the best intersection record, the hit point and the normal vector at the hit point are determined. The ambient light color is found for the associated ray. Next, a feeler ray is constructed, and its start point is set to $P_h - \varepsilon$ **dir**. Its recurseLevel is set to unity, so that projection extents will be disabled in the various hit() methods. Then, for each light source L, the feeler direction is computed as L.pos - feeler.start, and isInShadow(feeler) is called to see if the feeler hits any object. If it does, the computation of the diffuse and specular light contributions is skipped for this light source. The shadow-related part of the process takes the following form in pseudocode:

```
feeler.start = hitPoint − ε ray.dir;
feeler.recurselevel = 1;
color = ambient part;
for(each light source, L)
{
     feeler.dir = L.pos-hitPoint;
     if(isInShadow(feeler))continue;
     color.add(diffuse light);
     color.add(specular light);
}
```

The following code shows one possible implementation of `isInShadow()` itself:

```
bool Scene :: isInShadow(Ray& f)
{
   for(GeomObj* p = obj; p; p = p->next)
      if(p->hit(f))return true;
   return false;
}
```

Note that the routine simply scans through the object list looking for a hit, and if one is found, it returns `false`. If no hits are found, it returns `true`. The routine uses a simplified version of `hit()` for each object type that takes only one argument—it doesn't need to build an intersection record. This version of `hit()` differs in three ways from the version we have been using up to now:

1. It only accepts a hit for which the hit time lies between zero and unity, since an object lying beyond the light source does not cast a shadow.
2. If it detects such a hit, it returns immediately, without computing any data about the hit itself.
3. It cannot use projection extents, since shadow feelers can originate anywhere in the scene. Therefore, it should perform some carefully selected combination of sphere or box extent tests (or both) for each object type.

14.11 REFLECTIONS AND TRANSPARENCY

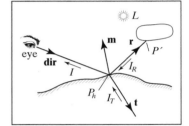

FIGURE 14.63 Including reflected and refracted light.

One of the great strengths of the ray-tracing method is the ease with which it can handle both reflection and refraction of light. This allows one to build scenes of exquisite realism,[8] containing mirrors, fishbowls, lenses, and the like. There can be multiple reflections in which light bounces off several shiny surfaces before reaching the eye, or elaborate combinations of refraction and reflection. Each of these processes requires the spawning and tracing of additional rays.

Figure 14.63 shows a ray emanating from the eye in the direction **dir** and hitting a surface at the point P_h. (The figure shows the key ingredients in 2D, which is acceptable because the nature of reflection and refraction causes all vectors to lie in the same plane. All formulas we develop operate in 3D.) When the surface is mirrorlike or transparent (or both), the light I that reaches the eye may have five components:

$$I = I_{amb} + I_{diff} + I_{spec} + I_{refl} + I_{tran}. \tag{14.43}$$

The first three are the familiar ambient, diffuse, and specular contributions. The diffuse and specular parts arise from light sources in the environment that are visible at P_h. I_{refl} is the reflected light component, arising from the light, I_R, that is incident at P_h along the direction $-\mathbf{r}$. This direction is such that the angles of incidence and reflection are equal, so, from Equation (4.27),

$$\mathbf{r} = \mathbf{dir} - 2(\mathbf{dir} \cdot \mathbf{m})\mathbf{m} \tag{14.44}$$

(where we assume that the normal vector **m** at P_h has been normalized).

Similarly, I_{tran} is the transmitted light component, arising from the light I_T that is transmitted through the transparent material to P_h along the direction $-\mathbf{t}$. A portion of this light passes through the surface and in so doing is "bent," continuing its travel along $-\mathbf{dir}$. The refraction direction **t** depends on several factors, and its details are developed in the next section.

Just as I is a sum of various light contributions, I_R and I_T each arise from their own five components—ambient, diffuse, and so on. As Figure 14.63 shows, I_R is the light

---

[8] Some people say "superrealistic" [Watt92].

that would be seen by an eye at P_h along a ray from P' to P_h. To determine I_R, we do in fact spawn a secondary ray from P_h in the direction **r**, find the first object it hits, and then repeat the same computation of light components as in Equation (14.43). This in turn may require spawning additional rays. Similarly, I_T is found by casting a ray in the direction **t** and seeing what surface is hit first, then computing the light contributions there, and so forth.

Figure 14.64(a) shows how the number of contributions of light grows at each contact point. I is the sum of three components: the reflected component R_1, the transmitted component T_1 from the refraction, and the "local" component L_1. The local component is simply the sum of the usual ambient, diffuse, and specular reflections at P_h. (Local components depend only on actual light sources; they are not computed on the basis of casting secondary rays. Recall that the role of the ambient term is to approximate the effect of diffuse and specular reflections off other surfaces.) R_1 is in turn the sum of R_3, T_3, and the local L_3. And T_3 is itself a sum of three other contributions. (Which ones?) Each contribution is the sum of three others, possibly ad infinitum. All this suggests a recursive approach to computing light intensity.

FIGURE 14.64 The tree of light.

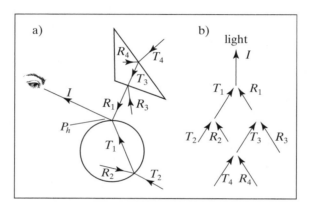

Figure 14.64(b) abstracts the various light components into a "tree" of light contributions, with the transmitted components arriving on the left branches and the reflected components arriving on the right branches [Whitted80]. At each node a local component must also be added, but for simplicity, it is not shown.

To incorporate these visual effects, `Scene :: shade()` is extended so that it can call itself recursively. Figure 14.65 shows a skeleton of `shade()`, emphasizing what is added to the version of `shade()` of Figure 14.12. Under the right conditions, `shade()` calls itself twice to accumulate reflected and transmitted light contributions. If the hit object is "shiny enough" to warrant the effort of "deeper" ray tracing, then a reflected ray is spawned, and `shade()` is used to compute how much light comes back along the direction of reflection. The amount of light `shade()` finds is tempered by the reflection coefficient, `reflectivity`, of the hit object. This reflection coefficient is stored in one of the fields of the object. (The user specifies it in an SDL file, using, say, `reflectivity 0.8`, as described in Appendix 5.) The coefficient is used for the "if shiny enough" test, as in `if(reflectivity > 0.6)`....

Similarly, if the hit object is "transparent enough" to warrant further ray tracing, then a transmitted ray is spawned, and `shade()` is used to compute how much light comes back along the direction of the transmission. The amount of light found is scaled by the transmission coefficient, `transparency`, of the hit object. This coefficient is also stored with the object, and it is used for the "if transparent enough" test, as in `if(transparency > 0.5)`....

```
Color3 Scene :: shade(Ray& r)
{
    Get the first hit, and build hitInfo h
    Shape* myObj = (Shape*)h.hitObject; //pointer to the hit object
    Color3 color.set(the emissive component);
    color.add(ambient contribution);
    get the normalized normal vector m at the hit point
    for(each light source)
        add the diffuse and specular components
    // now add the reflected and transmitted components

    if(r.recurseLevel == maxRecursionLevel)
        return color; // don't recurse further

    if(hit object is shiny enough) // add any reflected light
    {
        get reflection direction
        build reflected ray, refl
        refl.recurseLevel = r.recurseLevel + 1;
        color.add(shininess * shade(refl));
    }
    if(hit object is transparent enough)
    {
        get transmited direction
        build transmitted ray, trans
        trans.recurseLevel = r.recurseLevel + 1;
        color.add(transparency * shade(trans));
    }
    return color;
}
```

FIGURE 14.65 Skeleton of recursive shade().

Because, under certain conditions, rays might keep spawning new reflected or transmitted rays forever (e.g., consider a scene consisting of four perfect mirrors set at such angles that a ray perpetually bounces around them), some limit must be imposed on the depth of recursion. This is easily done by letting each ray keep track of "how deep" it is: The recurseLevel field mentioned in connection with shadowing is part of each ray. Rays that emanate from the eye have a recurseLevel of zero. This level is incremented each time a reflected or transmitted ray is formed. If the level of a ray is already at the limit maxRecursionDepth (which is stored in a field in the Scene object and specified in an SDL file as maxRecursionDepth 5), no further reflected or transmitted rays are spawned. Usually, a maximum recursion depth of 4 or 5 gives very realistic images.

14.11.1 The Refraction of Light

Be thou the rainbow to the storms of life,
The evening beam that smiles the clouds away,
And tints tomorrow with prophetic ray!

Lord Byron

When a ray of light strikes a transparent object, a portion of the ray penetrates the object, as shown in Figure 14.66. The ray will change direction from **dir** to **t** if the speed of light is different in medium 1 than in medium 2. (Vector **t** still lies in the same

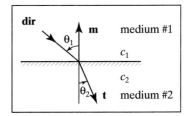

FIGURE 14.66 The refraction of light in a transparent medium.

plane as **dir** and the normal **m**.) If the angle of incidence of the ray is θ_1, **Snell's law** states that the angle of refraction θ_2 will be [Halliday70]

$$\frac{\sin(\theta_2)}{c_2} = \frac{\sin(\theta_1)}{c_1}, \tag{14.45}$$

where c_1 is the speed of light in medium 1 and c_2 is the speed of light in medium 2, as shown in the figure. Only the ratio c_2/c_1 is important. It is often called the **index of refraction** of medium 2 with respect to medium 1.[9] Note that if θ_1 equals zero, so does θ_2: Light hitting an interface at right angles is not bent.

■ **EXAMPLE 14.11.1 Find the angle**

Suppose medium 2 is some form of glass, in which light travels only 54% as fast as in a vacuum. Suppose further that the angle of incidence of the impinging light is 60° from the vertical. What is the angle of the transmitted light?

SOLUTION:

Evaluate $\sin(\theta_2)$ in Equation (14.45), using $c_2/c_1 = 0.54$, and $\sin(\theta_1) = 0.866$, to get $\sin(\theta_2) = (0.54)(0.866) = 0.4676$, so that $\theta_2 = 27.88°$. Accordingly, light is bent *closer* to the normal as it moves from a medium in which it travels faster into a medium in which it travels more slowly.

Figure 14.67 shows the speed of light in various media relative to that in a vacuum. The speeds listed are something of a simplification, because the speed of light generally varies with the wavelength of the light. For instance, the relative speed in fused quartz varies from 0.680 at $\lambda = 400$ nm (red), to 0.685 at $\lambda = 520$ nm (green), to 0.687 at $\lambda = 680$ nm (blue) [Halliday70]. This variation causes the familiar effect in which a beam of white light is split into its "rainbow" of spectral colors when the beam is passed through a glass prism. (See the exercises at the end of the section.)

FIGURE 14.67 Relative speed of light in various media.

in air: 99.97%
in glass: 52.2% to 59%
in water: 75.19%
in a 30% sugar solution: 72.46%
in acetone and ethyl alcohol: 73.5%
in sodium chloride: 64.93%
in benzene: 55.5%
in sapphire: 56.50%
in diamond: 41.33%

The Critical Angle

Example 14.11.1 noted that rays of light are bent more toward the normal direction when light enters a medium in which it travels more slowly than in the medium from which it came (i.e., $c_2/c_1 < 1$). This is clear from Equation (14.45), because $\sin(\theta_2)$, which equals $(c_2/c_1)\sin(\theta_1)$, is less than $\sin(\theta_1)$, so θ_2 must be less than θ_1.

The reverse is true when light increases its speed upon going from one medium to another: The light is bent further away from the normal. Snell's law is completely sym-

---

[9] Since the index of refraction is defined by some as c_1/c_2 and by others as c_2/c_1, we will avoid using it by name in formulas and will explicitly use c_2/c_1.

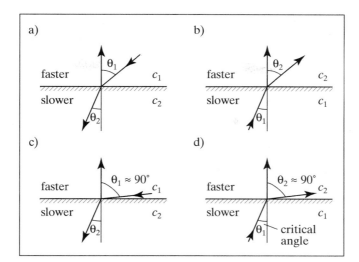

FIGURE 14.68 Symmetry of light transmission and the critical angle.

metrical when the subscripts 1 and 2 are interchanged. Figure 14.68(a) shows light moving from a medium in which it travels faster to one in which it travels more slowly, and Part (b) shows the reverse motion. The angles pair together in the same way in both cases: Just the names change. Parts (c) and (d) show similar situations, but the larger angle has become nearly 90°. The smaller angle is near the so-called **critical angle**. When the smaller angle (associated with the medium in which light travels more slowly) gets large enough, it forces the larger angle to 90°. A larger value is impossible, so no light is transmitted into the second medium. This phenomenon is called **total internal reflection**. In Part (d), in which the light increases its speed upon moving from one medium to the other, since $\sin(\theta_1)$ equals $(c_1/c_2)\sin(\theta_2)$, the angle $\theta_1 = \sin^{-1}(c_1/c_2)$ takes on its largest possible value when $\theta_2 = 90°$. For example, when light moves from water into air, we have $c_1/c_2 = 0.7519$, so the critical angle for water is 48.75°.

The critical angle appears in an interesting setting. When you are underwater in a pond, looking up at the surface, you can see the whole world above water within a limited solid angle from the vertical. If you look up at about 48°, you see the edge of the pond. (Sketch this.) On the other hand, if you are in a boat looking down into the pond, through what range of angles can you see? Is there a limited cone of view, outside of which you can't see objects? (See the exercises at the end of the section.)

■ **EXAMPLE 14.11.2 What is the shape of a rainbow?**

The speed of light in water varies with the light's wavelength, and this is the genesis of rainbows. Figure 14.69(a) shows several spherical droplets suspended in air. A ray of sunlight coming from the left is refracted slightly as it enters a droplet and experiences a total internal reflection before exiting. The angle between the incident and exiting rays is about 42°. Red light is refracted a little less than blue light, so the directions of the exiting rays are slightly different. Thus, red rays pour out of the myriad raindrops in one direction and blue rays in a slightly different direction.

In 1637, Descartes used a simple ray-tracing argument to explain the shape of a rainbow. Figure 14.69(b) shows an observer with his back to the sun, looking at a mist of raindrops. When the observer looks about 42° off the sun's direction, he sees rings of light. Raindrops situated along a cone of a certain angle reflect back light of one color; change the angle slightly, and the color is slightly different. Thus, a rainbow is a collection of circular rings, and each observer has his or her own private rainbow.

FIGURE 14.69 The genesis of a rainbow.

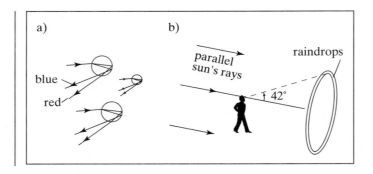

Finding the Direction of Transmission, **t**

For ray-tracing purposes, we must find the direction **t** (see Figure 14.66), given the surface normal **m** and the ray direction **dir**. We shall do this in a coordinate-free form using only dot products, so that our result applies to any directions **dir** and **m**. As we shall see in the exercises, the vector **t** that results is a linear combination of **m** and **dir** (assuming that both have been normalized to unit length). In particular,

$$\mathbf{t} = \frac{c_2}{c_1}\mathbf{dir} + \left(\frac{c_2}{c_1}(\mathbf{m} \cdot \mathbf{dir}) - \cos(\theta_2)\right)\mathbf{m}, \tag{14.46}$$

where $\cos(\theta_2)$ is found from Snell's law, viz.,

$$\cos(\theta_2) = \sqrt{1 - \left(\frac{c_2}{c_1}\right)^2 (1 - (\mathbf{m} \cdot \mathbf{dir})^2)}. \tag{14.47}$$

You can check that **t** has the correct value when either the speed of light is the same in the two media or the incident angle is $0°$.

There will be total internal reflection if the quantity under the square-root sign in Equation (14.47) becomes negative, in which case **t** becomes irrelevant. This happens at and beyond the critical angle. The exercises request an implementation of the routine `transmitDirection()`, which computes **t**. Note that, because the derivation of **t** uses only dot products, it is equally applicable to a 2D situation. Case Study 14.8 asks you to write a program demonstrating refraction in two dimensions.

In developing a ray tracer, it is simplest to model transparent objects so that their index of refraction does not depend on the wavelength of light. In that case, the same rays are used to trace the red, green, and blue color components. To do otherwise would require tracing separate rays for each of the color components, as they would be refracted in somewhat different directions. Such separate tracing would be expensive computationally and would still provide only an approximation, because an accurate model of refraction should take into account a large number of colors, not just the three primaries.

PRACTICE EXERCISES

14.11.1 On the effects of refraction

Figure 14.70(a) shows an eye at height H looking from air into a pool of water. A fish at a horizontal distance L is located at depth D. Where does the eye see the fish if light travels twice as fast in air as in water?

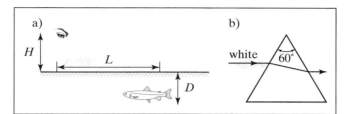

FIGURE 14.70 Some experiments with refraction.

14.11.2 Making a rainbow

Figure 14.70(b) shows a beam of white light entering a prism having an internal angle of 60°. The prism is made of fused quartz. Calculate and sketch the paths of the red, green, and blue components of light as they pass through and emerge from the prism. If the white beam passes instead through a slab of fused quartz having parallel walls, will a rainbow be seen as the light emerges?

14.11.3 Deriving the direction of refraction

Figure 14.71 shows a clever way to derive the transmission direction $\mathbf{t}$ of a ray of light that also results in an efficient algorithm (after Heckbert [Heckbert89]). The unit vectors $\mathbf{dir}$ and $\mathbf{m}$ together determine a plane in which both the reflected ray and the transmitted ray lie. The figure shows a unit circle drawn in this plane. Because all vectors are unit vectors, their various components along $\mathbf{m}$ and perpendicular to $\mathbf{m}$ have lengths that are simple sines and cosines of the angles θ_1 and θ_2.

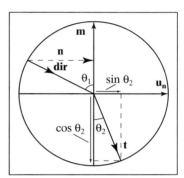

FIGURE 14.71 Deriving the transmission direction $\mathbf{t}$.

a. Show that the vector named $\mathbf{n}$ in the figure is

$$\mathbf{n} = \cos(\theta_1)\mathbf{m} + \mathbf{dir}$$

and that its length is $\sin(\theta_1)$, so that its normalized version $\mathbf{u}_n$ is $\mathbf{n}/\sin(\theta_1)$. Prove (with dot products) that $\mathbf{n}$ lies in the plane of $\mathbf{m}$ and $\mathbf{dir}$ and is perpendicular to $\mathbf{m}$.

b. Show that

$$\mathbf{t} = \sin(\theta_2)\mathbf{u}_n - \cos(\theta_2)\mathbf{m} = \frac{c_2}{c_1}\mathbf{dir} + \left(\frac{c_2}{c_1}\cos(\theta_1) - \cos(\theta_2)\right)\mathbf{m}$$

and that this is the same as Equation (14.46).

c. Using Snell's law, show that

$$\cos(\theta_2) = \sqrt{1 - \left(\frac{c_2}{c_1}\right)^2 \sin^2(\theta_1)}$$

and that Equation 14.47 follows immediately.

14.11.4 A routine to compute the direction of transmission

Write the routine `Vector3 transmitDirection(Vector3 m, Vector3 dir, float c1, float c2)`, which computes the direction $\mathbf{t}$, given the unit normal vectors $\mathbf{m}$ and $\mathbf{dir}$ and the speed of light in the two media. ■

14.11.2 Dealing with Refraction in `shade()`

In ray tracing scenes that include transparent objects, we must keep track of the medium through which a ray is passing, so that we can determine the value c_2/c_1 at the next intersection where the ray either exits from the current object or enters another one. This tracking is most easily accomplished by adding a field to the ray that holds a pointer to the object within which the ray is traveling.

How does `shade()` deal with rays that are inside objects? The answer depends on how much freedom is given to the modeler to describe scenes. We can think of several "design policies" the modeler might agree to.

Design Policy 1: No Two Transparent Objects May Interpenetrate

Suppose first that the modeler promises never to let two transparent objects inter-penetrate. Thus, there can be no glass marble placed inside another, nor a cube of water inside a glass box. Then each ray either is in air alone or is inside a *single* object.

a. Suppose the current ray in `shade()` is outside of all objects, and upon the ray's hitting an object, say, A, we find that A is "transparent enough." Then `shade()` computes the direction **t** of the transmitted ray from Equation (14.46), using $c_1 = 1$ (for air) and obtaining c_2 from the properties of A. The new ray is accordingly built, with its `recurseLevel` duly incremented and the ray containing a pointer to A. The routine `shade()` is then called recursively and ultimately returns a color, which is scaled by the `transparency` of A and added to the colors accumulated so far.

b. Suppose, on the other hand, that the current ray is inside some object A and hits another surface. Since it must be a surface of A (why?), the ray is exiting into air. (The routine can check that the ray hits the same object that it is currently in.) Because the ray is inside the object, the normal at the hit point must be reversed in sign: We want it to be pointing *into* the medium in which the ray is traveling. When a ray is inside an object, it is usually considered not to be bathed in light, so no local ambient, diffuse, or specular intensities are computed. (Is this a reasonable approximation to make?) The inside wall of A might be considered "shiny enough" to warrant casting a reflected ray back into A. (Is it reasonable to use the same value for the shininess of the outside of a surface as for its inside?) In that case, the reflected ray is created and cast as usual. As for the refracted ray, A is obviously transparent enough (why?), so the value of c_1 is taken from the properties of A, and c_2 is set to unity for air. If the angle of incidence is less than the critical angle, a new ray is spawned (with its pointer set to `NULL`, since it is not inside any object now) and sent on its way, to gather more light contributions.

Design Policy 2: Transparent Objects May Interpenetrate

Things get a little more complicated if we allow the modeler to place transparent objects in the scene so that they interpenetrate. Figure 14.72(a) shows a glass cube with several objects embedded in it: a quartz spherical marble, a cylindrical "airhole," a cube filled with water, and a partially embedded glass cone. Light travels at a different speed in each object. Figure 14.72(b) shows, in cross section, a ray traveling through a set of transparent objects. The ray enters and exits from objects in a complex sequence. A list of objects is shown with each segment of the ray, reporting which objects the ray is traveling in. As you read along the ray's path, notice the complicated sequence of additions and deletions from the list. This is admittedly a contrived scene, but it is worth seeing what it costs to ensure that `shade()` will always handle it correctly. (The extra feature could then be included or left out of a particular ray tracer.)

FIGURE 14.72 Several interpenetrating transparent objects.

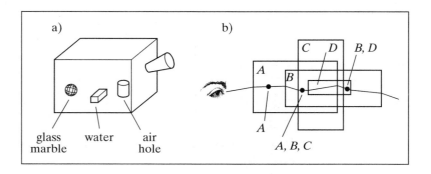

a.

b.

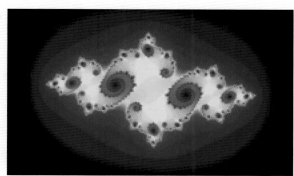

Plate 28.
Filled in Julia Sets. *(Courtesy of Bernie Freidin)*

Plate 29.
Julia set for c = -0.5 + 0.58i.

Plate 30.
Julia set for c = -0.76 + 0.147i.

Plate 31.
Realistic terrain based on fractal surfaces.
(Courtesy of Renzo and Adriano Del Fabbro.)

Plate 32.
A Penrose pattern.

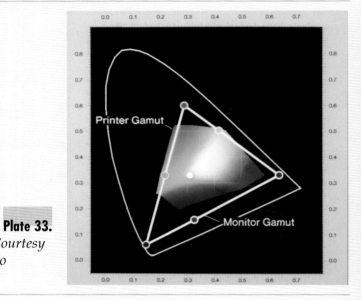

Plate 33.
Gamut for typical CRT monitor. *(Courtesy of Maureen Stone and Xerox Palo Alto Research Center)*

a.

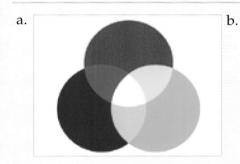

b.

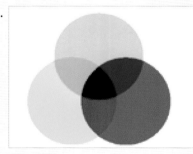

Plate 34.
The additive and subtractive primaries.

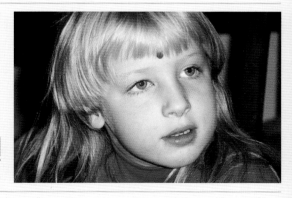

Plate 35.
Original true color image.

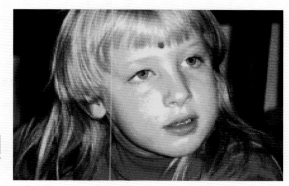

Plate 36.
The image after uniform quantization to 256 colors.

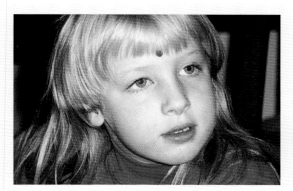

Plate 37.
The image after quantization to 256 colors by the
by the median cut algorithm.

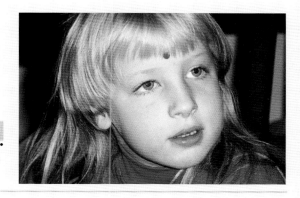

Plate 38.
The image after quantization to 256 colors
by the octree quantization method.

Plate 39.
A scene showing many reflections.

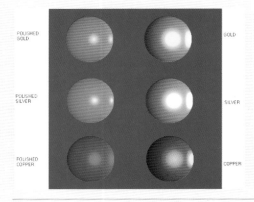

Plate 40.
Cook Torrance versus Phong shading.
(Courtesy of XiongZi Li)

Plate 41.
An example of chess pieces made from wood.
(Renzo and Adriano Del Fabbro)

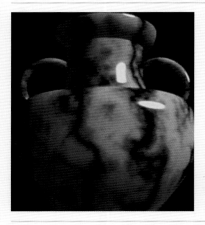

Plate 42.
An example of marble 3D texture. *(Courtesy of Ken Perlin)*

Plate 43.
Examples of shiny and transparent objects.
(Courtesy of Renzo and Adriano Del Fabbro)

What does it mean to be inside two transparent objects at once, such that certain points in space are "owned" by the two objects? In the modeling phase, you have to decide what the nature of the material is inside each joint region. If a green marble is completely enclosed in a blue marble, it makes sense to say that the joint region belongs to the green marble and assign it the color green. But if objects partially interpenetrate, as in Figure 14.72(b), there is no obvious way to decide which properties to use in the joint regions. The designer must assign a priority to each object, with the understanding that the color of the object with the highest priority dominates in each joint region.

One way to handle this situation is to add a field to each instance of an object, providing its priority, and to augment the pointer in the Ray data structure so that it becomes a list of pointers. At any instant, the ray is inside a certain set of objects, and the list reports this set. If the list is empty, the ray is outside of all objects. So we might enhance the Ray type as shown in Figure 14.73. (The list is implemented as an array rather than a linked list in order to facilitate copying the whole object at once when one is making a new ray.)

```
class Ray{
public:
      Point3 start;
      Vector3 dir;
      int recurseLevel;
      int row, col; // to assist with screen extents
      int numInside; // number of objects on the list
      GeomObj* inside[8]; // array of object pointers
      Ray(){recurseLevel = numInside = 0;} //constructor
      ...other methods ...
};
```

FIGURE 14.73 Augmenting the Ray type.

How is this "inside list" used in shade()? At any moment the current ray is inside some collection of objects, as reported by the list. When the ray hits the next surface of some object, say, B, we take different actions, depending on whether the ray is entering or exiting B (which is determined from the isEntering field of the hit record):

a. Suppose the ray is entering B. If B is not transparent enough, we stop spawning refracted rays, but spawn a reflected ray if B is shiny enough. If B is transparent enough, we use for c_1 the speed of light of the highest priority object currently on the list. If B has a higher priority, then we use its speed of light for c_2; otherwise we set c_2 equal to c_1. Then we add B to the list. Next, we make a new transmitted ray, copying the current list (with B added) into it. Finally, we call shade() recursively.

b. Suppose the ray is exiting B. Then, for c_1, we use the speed of light of the highest priority object in the list. Next, we remove B from the list, and for c_2, we use the speed of light of the highest priority object still on the list. We then make a new transmitted ray and copy the current "inside list" into it. Finally, we call shade() recursively.

Figure 14.74(a) shows a scene containing several transparent objects. The bending of light produced when light is refracted through a transparent object are apparent. (Plate 43 shows a beautiful example).

FIGURE 14.74 Scenes with and without refraction.

PRACTICE EXERCISES

14.11.5 Another possible design policy: if two transparent objects interpenetrate, one must contain the other

Suppose the modeler promises not to position two transparent objects so that they partially overlap: Either they are disjoint, or one encloses the other. (In set-theoretic terms, their intersection is empty or is identical to one of the objects.) Discuss what implications this has on the logic of `shade()`. Specifically, show that the list processing becomes simpler: No priorities are needed, and the list can be treated like a stack. Describe how this is done.

14.11.6 Light transmission through colored glass

Discuss how to include the effect of refracted light that passes through an orange glass sphere.   ■

14.12 COMPOUND OBJECTS: BOOLEAN OPERATIONS ON OBJECTS

So far, we can ray trace only a limited variety of shapes: transformed spheres, planes, cones, etc. But if a way can be found to combine these simple shapes into more complex ones and to develop a ray-tracing method for them, much richer and more interesting scenes can be ray traced. The technique known as **constructive solid geometry** (CSG) provides such a method. According to CSG, arbitrarily complex shapes are defined by set operations (also called Boolean operations) on simpler shapes [Ballard82, Mortenson85]. Objects such as lenses and hollow fishbowls, as well as objects with holes, are easily formed by combining the generic shapes treated thus far. Such objects are variously called **compound**, **Boolean**, or **CSG** objects. The ray-tracing method extends in a very organized way to compound objects: It is one of the great strengths of ray tracing that it "fits" so naturally with CSG models.

We look at examples of the three Boolean operators: **union**, **intersection**, and **difference**. Figure 14.75 shows two compound objects built from spheres. Figure 14.75(a) is a lens shape constructed as the **intersection** of two spheres. That is, a point is in the lens if and only if it lies in both spheres. Symbolically, "L is the intersection of the spheres S_1 and S_2" is written as

$$L = S_1 \cap S_2. \tag{14.48}$$

Part (b) of the figure shows a bowl, constructed using the difference operation. A point is in the **difference** of sets A and B, denoted $A - B$, if it is in A and not in B.

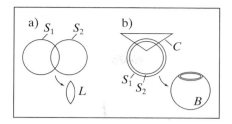

FIGURE 14.75 A lens and a fishbowl.

Applying the difference operation is analogous to removing material—to cutting or carving. The bowl is specified by

$$B = (S_1 - S_2) - C. \tag{14.49}$$

The solid globe, S_1, is "hollowed out" by removing all the points of the inner sphere, S_2, forming a hollow spherical shell. The top is then opened by removing all points in the cone C.

A point is in the **union** of two sets A and B, denoted $A \cup B$, if it is in A or in B or in both. Forming the union of two objects is analogous to gluing them together. Figure 14.76 shows a rocket constructed as the union of two cones and two cylinders; that is,

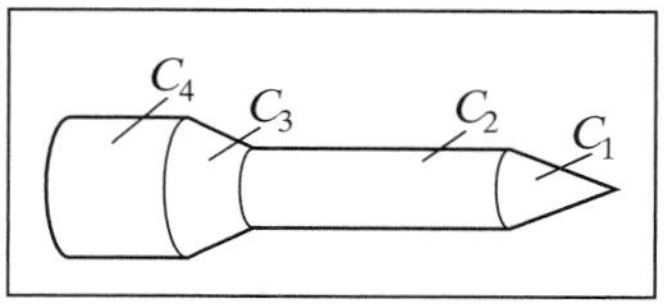

$$R = C_1 \cup C_2 \cup C_3 \cup C_4. \tag{14.50}$$

FIGURE 14.76 A union of four primitives.

Cone C_1 rests on cylinder C_2. Cone C_3 is partially embedded in C_2 and rests on the fatter cylinder C_4.

PRACTICE EXERCISES

14.12.1 Decomposing compound shapes

Give an equation that expresses each of the objects shown in Figure 14.77 in terms of set operations on spheres, cones, cylinders, and rectangular parallelepipeds. Notice that different expressions are possible for some objects. ■

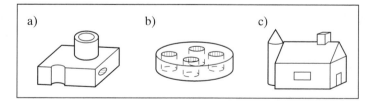

FIGURE 14.77 Various shapes made from primitives.

14.12.1 Ray Tracing CSG Objects

How do we ray trace objects that are Boolean combinations of simpler objects? First, consider the preceding examples. Figure 14.78 shows a ray entering and exiting the spheres S_1 and S_2 at the times indicated. The ray is therefore inside lens L from t_3 to t_2, and the hit time is t_3. If the lens is opaque, the familiar shading rules will be applied to find what color the lens is at the hit spot. If the lens is mirrorlike or transparent, spawned rays are generated with the proper directions and are traced farther.

The situation is similar for the bowl in Figure 14.78(b). Ray 1 first strikes the bowl at t_1, the smallest of the times for which it is in S_1, but not in either S_2 or C. Ray 2, on the other hand, first hits the bowl at t_5. Again, this is the smallest time for which the ray is in S_1, but in neither the other sphere nor the cone. The hits at earlier times are hits with component parts of the bowl, but not with the bowl itself.

FIGURE 14.78 Ray tracing the lens and fishbowl.

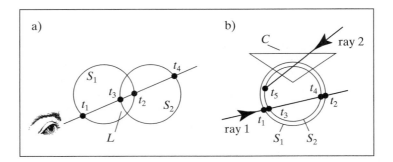

We organize these ideas into an algorithm to ray trace any compound object [Roth82]. Consider two objects A and B, together with a ray. We build a list of times at which the ray enters into and exits from A, ordered so that the times are increasing. Because the object is solid, the entry and exit times alternate. We build a similar list of entry and exit times for B. Two such lists are shown in Figure 14.79. The interval between each entry time and the next exit time is shown darkened: The ray is inside the object throughout each darkened interval. Call the set of t-values for which the ray is inside the object its **inside set**. An inside set is specified by an ordered list that contains the alternating entry and exit times of the ray, $(t_1, t_2, \dots)$, where t_1 is an entry time, t_2 is an exit time, t_3 is an entry time, t_4 is an exit time, and so forth. This list is sometimes called a "t-list."

FIGURE 14.79 Lists of t-values for a ray with two objects.

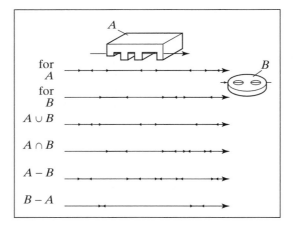

Given the inside sets for a ray with objects A and B, we want to find the inside set for the ray with a compound object built from A and B. The four new objects we can build are obtained by using $A \cup B$, $A \cap B$, $A - B$, and $B - A$. Consider $A \cup B$. The ray is inside the union of the objects if it is inside either of the objects. Thus, the inside set for $A \cup B$ is simply the union of the individual inside sets. The same thinking applies to the other three objects: The inside set for $A \cap B$ is the intersection of the individual inside sets, the inside set for $A - B$ is composed of the difference of the inside set for A and that for B, and similarly for $B - A$ (just reversing the roles of A and B). In general, if we denote by $T(A)$ and $T(B)$ the inside sets of two objects, A and B, then

$$T(A \text{ op } B) = T(A) \text{ op } T(B), \tag{14.51}$$

where op is one of the Boolean operators $\cup, \cap,$ or $-$. Therefore, finding inside sets for compound objects is equivalent to performing Boolean operations on lists of intervals.

Notice that although we are ultimately interested in only the first item in the inside set—the first hit time—we must retain *entire lists* for inside sets during the list-building process, because the ultimate first hit time may reside deep within one of the intermediate lists. Happily, we already have the "artillery" in place for creating inside sets in a ray tracer: The `hit()` method for each type of shape carefully collects all of the hits that a ray experiences with an object in the `inter.hit[]` array, in time-sorted order. Up to this point, we have made use only of the first hit time in the list. As we begin to ray trace Boolean objects, however, we will utilize the entire list.

■ **EXAMPLE 14.12.1 Forming inside sets**

Consider the following two lists that represent inside sets:

A_list: 1.2   1.5   2.1   2.5   3.1   3.8
B_list: 0.6   1.1   1.8   2.6   3.4   4.0

We apply the preceding rules to build four new inside sets (check their accuracy):

$A \cup B$ = 0.6, 1.1, 1.2, 1.5, 1.8, 2.6, 3.1, 4.0;
$A \cap B$ = 2.1, 2.5, 3.4, 3.8;
$A - B$ = 1.2, 1.5, 3.1, 3.4;
$B - A$ = 0.6, 1.1, 1.8, 2.1, 2.5, 2.6, 3.8, 4.0.

To construct new inside sets, we need a function `combineLists()` that takes an operator and two *t*-lists as arguments and creates a new list of *t*-values according to one of the preceding four Boolean operations. We discuss how this routine works later.

The ray-tracing process for a compound object boils down to ray tracing the object's components, building inside sets for each, and finally combining them. The first positive hit time on the combined list yields the point on the compound object that is hit first by the ray. The usual shading is then done, including the casting of secondary rays if the surface is shiny or transparent.

PRACTICE EXERCISES

14.12.2 Find the inside sets

Suppose that, for a given ray, the objects C and D have the following *t*-lists:

C_list: 0.8   1.7   2.2   2.9   4.7   5.55
D_list: 1.2   1.5   2.1   2.5   3.1   3.8   4.7   8.3

Find the *t*-list for each of the four possible Boolean combinations of C and D.   ■

14.12.2 Data Structure for Boolean Objects

So, naturalists observe, a flea
Hath smaller fleas that on him prey;
And these have smaller still to bite 'em;
And so proceed ad infinitum.

Jonathan Swift, "On Poetry, a Rhapsody"

How do we represent a compound object such as $((A \cap B) - C) - D$ in a program? Since a compound object is always the combination of two other (possibly themselves compound) objects, say, Obj_1 op Obj_2, a binary tree structure provides a natural description. Figure 14.80 shows the tree corresponding to the object

FIGURE 14.80 A compound
object and its CSG tree.

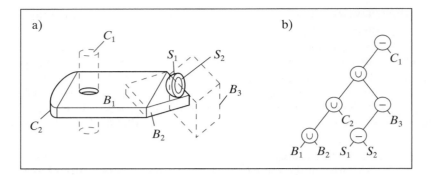

$(((B_1 \cup B_2) \cup C_2) \cup ((S_1 - S_2) - B_3)) - C_1$. Each internal node (circle) represents an operator, and each leaf (square) is a primitive shape. A tree is made up by combining subtrees, which are in turn primitive objects or subtrees ("and so proceed *ad infinitum*"). When a node contains the difference operator, it is understood that the node produces the (left subtree) − (right subtree) (as opposed to (right subtree) − (left subtree)).

The expression for a compound object may be rearranged to some degree without altering the ultimate shape of the object being represented. Each rearrangement gives rise to a different tree. (See the exercises at the end of the section.) Therefore, for a given compound object, there is no unique tree.

Currently, all the object types we have discussed, such as `Sphere` and `Cube`, are derived from the `Shape` class, which is in turn derived from the basic `GeomObj` class. (See the inheritance hierarchy in Appendix 3.) It seems natural to derive a new class, `Boolean`, from `GeomObj`, so that the object list (which is a list of `GeomObj`'s) can "hold" a `Boolean` object. In turn, a `Boolean` object must be able to hold a binary tree, so we give the `Boolean` pointers `left` and `right` to point to its child subtrees. These pointers must point to `GeomObj`'s, since in some places they point to geometric shapes and in others to `Boolean` trees. So a first cut at the `Boolean` class is as follows:

```
class Boolean: public GeomObj{
public:
      GeomObj *left, *right; //pointers to the children
      Boolean() {left = right = NULL;}// constructor
      virtual bool hit(Ray &r, Intersection &inter);
      ... other methods ... .
   };
```

Because `GeomObj`'s have sphere and box extents, so do `Boolean`s, which is useful, since `Boolean`s are expensive to ray trace and anything that speeds ray tracing up is a blessing. We shall design a special `hit()` routine for `Boolean`s that "knows" how to intersect a ray with a `Boolean`; thereby, we capitalize again on polymorphism to simplify code. As a matter of fact, since `hit()` must operate differently for unions, intersections, and differences, it will improve matters to derive separate classes for the three kinds of `Boolean`s. Accordingly, we form the classes `UnionBool`, `IntersectionBool`, and `DifferenceBool`. The definition of `UnionBool` is simply

```
class UnionBool : public Boolean{
public:
      UnionBool() {Boolean();} //constructor
      virtual bool hit(Ray &r, Intersection &inter);
      ... other methods ... .
   };
```

The other definitions are nearly identical. Each type will have a `hit()` routine that is finely tuned to handle its specific nature.

Notice that `Booleans` do not have their own affine transformation; only `Shapes` do. This causes a Boolean tree to have transformations only at its leaves. This is a design decision that offers both advantages and disadvantages, and in fact, some modeling systems and ray tracers operate differently. To understand the distinction, consider Figure 14.81(a), which shows a tree for a Boolean object that *does* have a transformation at each internal node, as well as one at each leaf. The effect of each transformation is "felt" by all nodes "beneath it" in its subtrees. As discussed in the exercises, this tree is equivalent geometrically to the tree in Part (b) of the figure (in the sense that both trees represent the same shape), where the transformations have "percolated down" to the leaf nodes and combined to form a single transformation at each leaf.

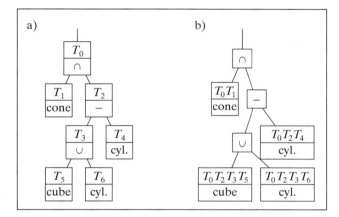

FIGURE 14.81 Including transformations at internal nodes of compound objects.

One advantage of keeping explicit transformations in internal nodes is that the designer can separately alter a particular transformation deep within a tree to adjust the shape of a CSG object after it has been created. It is also possible to have more control over the tightness of various extents for Boolean objects. A significant disadvantage, on the other hand, is the slow speed of ray tracing, since a ray must be inverse transformed at every node of the tree, not just at the leaves.

The way to specify a Boolean in an SDL file is to use one of the key words `union`, `intersection`, and `difference`, followed by the specification of the "left" geometric object and then the specification of the right one (which can themselves be Booleans). As an example, the fishbowl shape of Figure 14.75(b), given by $(S_1 - S_2) - C$, can be specified by the following code:

```
!make a fish bowl
rotate -90 1 0 0
difference
    difference
        sphere   ! outer sphere
        push scale 0.9 0.9 0.9 sphere pop !inner sphere
    push translate 0 0 1.3 rotate 180 1 0 0 cone pop
```

The first transformation rotates the whole bowl about the *x*-axis. The difference is then formed between the left object (which is itself a difference of two spheres) and the cone. Because transformations given to SDL postmultiply the current transformation and the current transformation is placed in a shape object at the time it is created, transformations are automatically percolated "down the tree."

PRACTICE EXERCISES

14.12.3 Rearranging expressions for booleans

Because there is some flexibility in writing expressions for a compound object, more than one tree can represent such an object. For instance, both ∩ and ∪ commute, so that, for example, $A \cup B = B \cup A$. Prove or disprove the following assertions:

a. $(A - B) - C = A - (B \cup C)$.
b. $(A \cup B) - (A \cup C) = A \cup (B - C)$.
c. $(A \cup B) \cap (A \cup C) = A \cap (B \cup C)$.

14.12.4 How transformations percolate down a Boolean tree

Consider the tree of Figure 14.81(a), which supports a transformation at each internal node.

a. Prove or disprove that the geometric shape represented by this tree is the same as that represented by the tree in Part (b) of the figure. Does the proof depend on the transformations being affine?
b. If transformation T_i in Figure 14.81 is represented in homogeneous coordinates by matrix M_i, is the combined matrix for the cube in Part (b) equal to $M_0 M_2 M_3 M_5$ or $M_5 M_3 M_2 M_0$?

Hint: Prove that, in general, $T(A \text{ opr } B) = T(A) \text{ opr } T(B)$, where $T()$ represents a one-to-one transformation, A and B are sets of points, and opr represents one of the operators ∩, ∪, and −.

14.12.5 Why does ray tracing handle unions automatically?

Explain why ray tracing the union, $A \cup B$, of two objects A and B (whether or not they interpenetrate) is equivalent to ray tracing them individually in a scene.

14.12.6 The whole scene as one CSG object

Discuss the pros and cons of modeling an entire scene as one compound object, rather than using a list of simpler (possibly compound) objects. ■

14.12.3 Intersecting Rays with Boolean Objects

We need to develop a `hit()` method to work with each type of Boolean object. The method must form the inside set for the ray with the left subtree, the inside set for the ray with the right subtree, and then combine the two sets appropriately. A skeleton of `hit()` is shown in Figure 14.82 for the case of an intersection operation. Extent tests are first made to see if there is an early out (as discussed in the next section). Then the proper `hit()` routine is called for the left subtree (which might itself be a Boolean), and unless the ray misses this subtree, the hit list `lftInter` is formed. If there is a miss, `hit()` returns the value *false* immediately (an "early out"), because the ray must hit both subtrees in order to hit their intersection. Then the hit list `rtInter` is formed.

FIGURE 14.82 A skeleton of `hit()` for Boolean intersection.

```
bool IntersectionBool:: hit(Ray &r, Intersection &inter)
{
    Intersection lftInter, rtInter;
    if (ray misses the extents) return false;
    if((!left->hit(r,lftInter))||(!right->hit(r,rtInter)))
        return false; // early out
    make the combined list: place it in inter
    return(inter.numHits > 0); // true if inter is not empty
}
```

The code is similar for the `UnionBool` and `DifferenceBool` classes. For `Union-Bool:: hit()`, the two hit lists are formed using

```
if((!left->hit(r,lftInter))&&(!right->hit(r,rtInter)))
    return false;
```

which provides an early out only if both hit lists are empty. For `Difference-Bool::hit()`, we use the code

```
if((!left->hit(r,lftInter)) return false; // a miss
if(!right->hit(r,rtInter))
{
    inter = lftInter;
    return true;
}
```

which gives an early out if the ray misses the left subtree, since it must then miss the whole object. If there are hits with the left subtree, but none with the right subtree, the final hit list is the same as that for the left subtree. (Why?)

Combining *t*-lists

Combining *t*-lists is intricate, but logical. Consider the two sample hit lists L and R (standing for "left" and "right," respectively) shown in Figure 14.83(a). (For brevity, we call the left list simply L[], rather than `leftInter.theHit[]`, and similarly for the right list. In addition, the `hitObject` and `surface` fields are not shown.) L shows eight hits for its object, and R shows five hits. Each list contains the positive hit times and is ordered in time, and the entering field of the zeroth element shows whether the first hit (that has a positive hit time—that is, "in front of the eye") occurs with the ray entering or exiting the object. (Since all objects are solid, the `entering` values alternate after the zeroth.)

The lists are combined by scanning through both of them, noting at each step which "next" item in the two lists has the smaller hit time and keeping track of whether the ray is inside or outside the object just before this next hit. These pieces of information are combined in a manner appropriate to the operator involved: *union, intersection,* or *difference.* Figure 14.83(b) shows the resulting *t*-list after combination, for each of the Boolean operators.

Consider a specific example of the logic used in combining the lists. Suppose that the operator is *difference*—that just before the next hit time, the ray is inside the left object and outside the right object, so it must be inside the difference of the objects. The next hit time on each list is examined; suppose the right one is found to be smaller. This means that just after this next hit time, the ray is inside the right object, so it must now be outside the difference. At this instant, the state of the ray in the combined object changes from inside to outside.

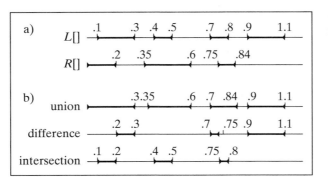

FIGURE 14.83 Sample intersection records.

We keep track of the state of the ray (whether it is inside or outside the object at the current time) as it progresses through the subtrees with the following variables:

```
bool lftInside;    // true if ray is inside left object;
bool rtInside;     // true if ray is inside right object;
bool combInside;   // true if ray is inside combined object;
```

These are the states of the ray *between* hits—that is, just before the next hit to be considered. lftInside is initialized according to whether the ray enters or exits the left object at the first hit—that is, according to L[0].isEntering. Specifically, lftInside is false if the first hit is entering (because before the hit, the ray must be outside) and is true if the first hit is exiting. So we can initialize lftInside to ! L[0].isEntering, and similarly for rtInside. Then combInside is found as a logical combination of lftInside and rtInside: If the operator is *union*, combInside is true if lftInside or rtInside or both are true. This is nicely captured using the logical operators combInside = lftInside || rtInside. Similarly, if the operator is *intersection*, we use combInside = lftInside && rtInside; if it is *difference*, we use combInside = lftInside && !rtInside.

The algorithm proceeds by moving through both the L[] and R[] lists, at each step, noting the smaller of the hit times and using it to update lftInside, rtInside, and combInside. If combInside *changes* at any point, the latest hit event is added to the C[] list.

When either L[] or R[] has been consumed (i.e., when its final hit time has been examined), the other unconsumed list may be considered as follows:

- For **intersection**, ignore the unconsumed list.
- For **union**, move through the unconsumed list, adding hit events as appropriate.
- For **difference**, if the left list is the unconsumed one, move through it, adding hit events as appropriate. If the right list is unconsumed, ignore it.

Figure 14.84 shows pseudocode for DifferenceBool :: hit(), to illustrate the process of combining lists.

Note that when combining lists, we must take care to put the all necessary information into each new hit[] record. Specifically, the isEntering and hitObject fields must be properly filled, because if a hit ever becomes the first hit of the ray, we will be gleaning properties about the surface hit from the hitObject itself. When an exiting hit on the right object causes the ray to be entering the object itself, we must be sure the hit information points to the left object, so that what we see in the "hole" are the properties of the left object.

We also must make sure that the logic of hit() for CSG objects works properly when the object is transparent and the ray is traveling inside the Boolean (as when the ray passes through a martini glass). Check that, for the aforementioned difference object, the correct hit information is placed on the hit list even when rays begin inside an object.

Figure 14.85 shows black-and-white examples of various compound objects that have been ray traced using these techniques, and Plate 43 shows some full-color examples. Try to identify the specific shapes out of which each Boolean object was formed.

PRACTICE EXERCISES

14.12.7 Hand simulate the algorithm

Hand simulate the list-combining algorithm of Figure 14.82 for the lists in Example 14.12.1.

```
bool DifferenceBool:: hit(Ray &r, Intersection &inter)
{
    Intersection lftInter, rtInter;
    lftInter.numHits = rtInter.numHits = 0;//initially
    if(ray misses extents) return false; // early out?
    if(!left->hit(r,lftInter))return false;
    GeomObj* leftObject = lftInter.hit[0].hitObject; // may need this later
    if(!right->hit(r,rtInter))
    {
        inter = lftInter; // right tree has no effect
        return true; // early out
    }
    //combine the lists. Initial states:
    bool lftInside = !(lftInter.hit[0].isEntering); // initial insideness
    bool rtInside = !(rtInter.hit[0].isEntering);
    bool combInside = lftInside && !rtInside // for the difference
    // go through lists until one has been consumed
    int iL = 0, iR = 0, iC = -1;
    HitInfo nextHit;
    while((iL < lftInter.numHits) && (iR < rtInter.numHits))
    {    //while both lists are nonempty
        bool newInside; // the new result state
        if(lftInter.hit[iL].hitTime <= rtInter.hit[iR].hitTime)
        {
            nextHit = lftInter.hit[iL++];    // grab left item;
            lftInside = !lftInside;          // state is reversed by hit
    newInside = lftInside && !rtInside;   // state after the hit
    leftObject = nextHit.hitObject;  //needed when exiting right tree
    if(newInside != combInside)     // has result state changed?
    {
            inter.hit[++iC] = nextHit; // put hit data on combined list
            combInside = newInside;
            inter.hit[iC].isEntering = combInside;
    }
}
```

FIGURE 14.84 hit() for the DifferenceBool class.

14.12.8 Writing the hit() methods

Implement the hit() methods for the UnionBool and IntersectionBool classes. Each should be fine-tuned to the specific requirements of its Boolean operator. ▪

14.12.4 Building and Using Extents for CSG Objects

One issue remaining is the creation of projection, sphere, and box extents for CSG objects. During a preprocessing step, the tree for the CSG object is scanned and extents are built for each node and stored within the node itself. Later, during ray tracing, the ray can be tested against each extent encountered, with the potential benefit of an "early out" in the intersection process if it becomes clear that the ray cannot hit the object. This procedure can save the cost of combining lists further up the CSG tree.

Extents are tested, as always, inside the hit() method of the object's class, as suggested in Figure 14.82. If the ray hits the extent for a given node of the tree, it is intersected with the left and right subtrees in the usual manner.

```
        else                       // smaller hit time is on right list
        {
        nextHit = rtInter.hit[iR++];  // grab right item; inc to next
        rtInside = !rtInside;         // reverse the inside-ness
        newInside = lftInside && !rtInside;  // new combined state
        if(newInside != combInside)         // has result state changed?
        {
            inter.hit[++iC] = nextHit;
            combInside = newInside;
            inter.hit[iC].isEntering = combInside;
            if(combInside)
            {
                nextHit.hitNormal.flip(); //reverse normal on right object
                inter.hit[iC].hitObject = leftObject; // point to left object
            }
        }
        } //end else
    } //end of for - while both lists nonempty
    while(iL < lftInter.numHits)// gobble rest of left list
    {
        nextHit = lftInter.hit[iL++];
        lftInside = !lftInside;
        inter.hit[++iC] = nextHit;
        inter.hit[iC].isEntering = lftInside;
    }
    inter.numHits = iC + 1;
    return (inter.numHits > 0);
}
```

FIGURE 14.84 (*continued*)

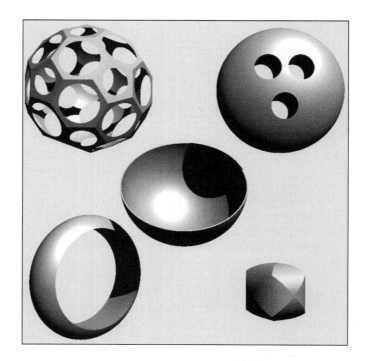

FIGURE 14.85 Black-and-white examples of ray-traced compound objects.

Making Box Extents

What is a reasonable definition of a box extent for a CSG node? (We mean, of course, world box extents, since a Boolean object doesn't have a generic version.) Suppose the node represents the object A opr B, where A and B are shapes and opr is one of the Boolean operators. The box extent for this object must enclose the object, so that we can rest assured that the ray misses the object if it misses the box. The shape of the object might be quite complicated (e.g., the intersection of a rotated torus with a skewed cube), so it will be very difficult to find the tightest aligned box automatically without an inordinate amount of processing.

We take the simplest approach and create the box extent of L opr R out of the box extent $E(L)$ of L and the box extent $E(R)$ of R. We define the box extent differently for the different operators:

a. **Union**. Take as the box extent the aligned box that fits about both $E(L)$ and $E(R)$ simultaneously. This is equivalent to $E(E(L) \cup E(R))$. (*Questions*: Is this always the same as $E(L \cup R)$? Would it be much more efficient to test $E(L)$ and $E(R)$ separately? If the ray misses both extents separately, does it necessarily miss $L \cup R$?)

b. **Intersection**. Take as the box extent the intersection of $E(L)$ and $E(R)$. The intersection of two aligned boxes is always an aligned box, and it is easy to compute its (*left, top, right, bottom, front, back*) components. (How?) (*Question*: Are you sure the ray will miss $L \cap R$ if it misses $E(L) \cap E(R)$?) The extent $E(L) \cap E(R)$ will most likely be reasonably tight if the extents of L and R are tight. (Why?)

c. **Difference**. Take as the box extent simply $E(L)$. This approach is very conservative, as we are failing to take advantage of the possibility that $L - R$ may be considerably smaller than L: R may have chopped out a lot of space from L. But to do a more thorough analysis would be very costly.

Box extents would be formed recursively, because the box extent for an internal node of a Boolean tree would be constructed out of the box extents of its children nodes. For shapes, the box extent would be constructed nonrecursively as we discussed earlier, by finding the "cloud of points" for the object in world coordinates and building an aligned box around it. Each type of shape would have its own `makeBoxExtent()` method. Each method would build the box extent, store it within the object, and return it for use by other objects. The `UnionBool` class, for example, might use the following routine:

```
Cuboid UnionBool :: makeBoxExtent()
{
    Cuboid lft = left->makeBoxExtent();
    Cuboid rt = right->makeBoxExtent();
    Cuboid tmp;
    tmp.left = min(lft.left,rt.left);//form the union
    tmp.top = max(lft.top,rt.top);
    etc. for the other four values
    worldBoxExtent = tmp; //store it in the object
    return tmp;
}
```

The preprocessing step would call `makeBoxExtent()` for each object in the object list. When this method is called for a Boolean object, it creates and stores a box extent at the root node of the tree, as well as at each internal node.

Making Sphere Extents

World sphere extents would be built in a manner similar to the way box extents are built. As discussed earlier, for shapes, the cloud of points is found in world coordinates, and the sphere extent is the closest fitting sphere about this cloud. For Boolean objects, we must decide how to form the sphere extent for a union, a difference, and an intersection of two objects.

The difference is easy: We use the sphere extent for the left object itself. This extent won't be very tight, but it is serviceable. The same choice could be made for intersections, as it is very difficult to compute the true sphere extent for an intersection. For unions, it is probably simplest to combine the clouds of points for the left and right objects and form a single sphere about it.

Making Projection Extents

There is a strong motivation to use projection extents for CSG objects, due to the cost of ray tracing them. A projection extent can be built for each node of a CSG object in much the same way as we built box extents: The projection extent of a node is formed by a combination of the projection extents of the left and right subobjects. Using $P(object)$ to mean the projection extent of *object*, we have, according to the rules set forth earlier,

$$P(L \cup R) = P(P(L) \cup P(R)),$$
$$P(L \cap R) = P(L) \cap P(R),$$

and

$$P(L - R) = P(L).$$

As before, each class has its own `makeProjectionExtent()` method.

14.13 SUMMARY

Ray tracing offers a conceptually simple and uniform approach to creating dazzlingly realistic images. A large collection of relevant rays of light is traced through a scene composed of various objects, each of which is analyzed to find how much light it returns to the observer's eye. This mechanism makes possible many visual effects. In addition to the usual simulation of ambient, diffuse, and specular light components, ray tracing can, with relative ease, simulate shadows, reflections from mirrorlike surfaces, and the transmission of refracted light through transparent objects. Ray tracing also provides a natural approach to applying both 2D and 3D texture to objects.

The heart of a ray-tracing application is the routine that finds the intersections between a ray and an object. A huge number of rays is cast to create a high-resolution image, and many of these rays spawn several secondary rays, so that much of the computation time is spent in finding intersections. Because each ray is tested against each object in the scene, the time required for ray tracing grows nearly linearly with the complexity of the scene. The judicious use of extents can produce many "early outs" and relieve a large number of objects from requiring a more complete intersection test, vastly speeding up the ray-tracing process.

Ray tracing automatically solves the problem of removing hidden surfaces, because the hit times that various objects make with a ray is a direct measure of their distance from the observer. Thus, the object with the smallest hit time is the closest one and cannot be obscured by any other object.

This same principle also makes it straightforward to calculate shadows: If there is an object positioned between a point of interest and a light source, that point is in the shadow of the object with respect to the source. Hence, to determine such shadowing is equivalent to determining whether any object has a hit time with a "shadow feeler" between zero and unity.

Some shapes are easy to ray trace, because finding their intersection with a ray is equivalent to solving a linear or quadratic equation. Typical among these shapes are planes, spheres, cylinders, and cones. The scene designer starts with generic versions of each of these and transforms them into their desired sizes, orientations, and positions, using an affine transformation. This can change spheres into ellipsoids, cubes into parallelepipeds, and so forth, thereby enlarging the class of objects that appears in a scene. It is also simple to model and ray trace any convex polyhedron, because its interior is merely the intersection of a number of half-spaces.

Rays are simple things that are easy to work with, and it is therefore not difficult to carry out the spawning of new rays from a given start point in some new direction and then to test what objects in the scene they hit. This provides a direct way to gather light contributions from reflections off shiny surfaces and from transmission through transparent bodies. The programming effort to implement these techniques is very modest.

Adding methods to ray trace CSG objects dramatically increases the variety of scenes that can be rendered. Highly complex shapes can be modeled and ray traced. The internal logic of a ray-tracing algorithm for CSG objects is straightforward and easy to manage in a program.

Ray tracing offers one of the most powerful approaches to computer-synthesized images today. Although the enormous amount of computation involved makes it one of the slower methods for generating images, the resulting images offer a degree of realism that is hard to match with other techniques.

14.14 CASE STUDIES

CASE STUDY 14.1 AN EMISSIVE RAY TRACER

Level of Effort: II. Write and execute an application that ray traces a scene described in SDL. This ray tracer properly handles emissive objects that glow with their own light. (The ray tracer need not handle ambient, diffuse, or specular light contribution.) Your routine should properly ray trace at least a sphere, tapered cylinder, cube, square, and plane. Other shapes noted in the SDL scene file are simply ignored. A preview of the scene is drawn before ray tracing begins, using the `Scene::drawOpenGL()` method.

Keystrokes are used to control the action. The key strokes '1', '2', '4', and '8' set the size of pixel blocks, as discussed in Section 14.5, permitting experimentation with different resolutions. Other keystrokes adjust the position and orientation of the camera.

Also, create a scene in SDL that contains several "jacks" and "octos," and arrange matters so that you can ray trace these objects. A jack consists of three mutually perpendicular "bars," where a bar is an elongated sphere with a small sphere at each end. An octo consists of a small sphere, positioned at the six vertices of an octohedron, and 12 edges between the vertices made up of elongated spheres.

CASE STUDY 14.2 A RENAISSANCE RAY TRACER

Level of Effort: II, given that the emissive ray tracer of Case Study 14.1 is available. Enhance the ray tracer of Case Study 14.1 so that it properly handles ambient and diffuse reflections, as well as Phong specular highlights. It need not handle reflections, refractions, or shadowing. It properly ray traces all of the generic primitives, as well as meshes that represent convex polyhedra. As with the previous ray tracer, a preview of the scene is drawn before each ray tracing.

For extra control, write code so that the user can indicate a rectangular region of the display with the mouse, after which the designated region is ray traced at full resolution (block size = 1). This is a boon to a user who wants rapid ray tracing, but needs full resolution only at limited places in a scene.

CASE STUDY 14.3 IMPLEMENTING SHADOWS IN A RAY TRACER

Level of Effort: I, given that the ray tracer of Case Study 14.2 is available. Enhance the ray tracer of Case Study 14.2 so that it properly displays shadows.

CASE STUDY 14.4 USING EXTENTS TO SPEED UP RAY TRACING

Level of Effort: II, given that the ray tracer of Case Study 14.3 is available. Implement the use of sphere extents, box extents, and projection extents in the ray tracer of Case Study 14.3, and make a study of the relative speedup the use of each type of extent provides. Allow the user to turn each kind of extent on and off with individual keystrokes and to see the elapsed time that each ray tracing requires.

CASE STUDY 14.5 RAY TRACING WITH 3D TEXTURES

Level of Effort: II, given that the ray tracer of Case Study 14.2 is available. Enhance the Renaissance ray tracer of Case Study 14.2 to support the display of several 3D textures, including a checkerboard pattern, wood grain, and marble. The user can choose which texture to employ by using different keystrokes, and all objects in the scene are rendered with the chosen texture.

Determine a way to extend SDL and the `Scene :read()` method so that parameters can be specified in an SDL file and attached to subsequently defined objects. Use the parameters to choose which texture each object is composed of and to specify some of the numerical parameters inherent in the definition of these textures. For instance, the SDL lines

```
parameter 3 12.6 -91
cube
```

might attach the three parameters shown to the cube, assigning texture 3 to this object.

CASE STUDY 14.6 ANTIALIASING

Level of Effort: II, given that the ray tracer of Case Study 14.2 is available. Extend the ray tracer of Case Study 14.2 so that it antialiases a ray-traced scene. For each major ray, it shoots N rays in slightly altered directions and averages the colors that return along the rays. Experiment with different amounts of jitter in the ray directions and with different values of N.

CASE STUDY 14.7 RAY TRACING OTHER PRIMITIVES

Level of Effort: III, given that the ray tracer of Case Study 14.2 is available. Study the paper by Jim Kajiya [Kajiya83] on ray tracing complex shapes such as prisms, fractal mountains, and surfaces of revolution. Implement at least the fractal mountain technique, and extend SDL with the keyword `mountain`, followed by some parameters that specify the nature of the mountain that is to be ray traced.

CASE STUDY 14.8 A 2D RAY TRACER TO EXPLORE REFRACTION

Level of Effort: II. Because the formula for the refracted direction **t** in Equation (14.46) uses only dot products, it is as correct for two-dimensional vectors as for three-dimensional vectors. Write and execute a program that generates pictures such as that in Figure 14.69. The user gives the index of refraction and the angle of incidence, and the program draws the incident and refracted rays.

CASE STUDY 14.9 REFLECTED AND REFRACTED LIGHT

Level of Effort: III, given that the ray tracer of Case Study 14.2 is available. Extend the ray tracer of Case Study 14.2 so that it properly handles both reflections from shiny surfaces and the refraction of light through transparent objects. Experiment with different transparent shapes and different indices of refraction to explore the basic properties of refraction.

CASE STUDY 14.10 RAY TRACING BOOLEAN COMBINATIONS OF OBJECTS

Level of Effort: III, given that the ray tracer of Case Study 14.2 is available. Extend the ray tracer of Case Study 14.2 so that it properly ray traces Boolean objects of any complexity. Build an interesting scene that includes several such objects, including

- an object with a cylindrical hole through it,
- a spherical lens $A \cap (B - C)$ (formed as the intersection of two spheres), and
- an object given by $A \cap (B - C)$, where A, B, and C are shapes.

Arrange so that you can see some object through the holes in other objects and some objects through the lens.

14.15 FURTHER READING

"An Introduction to Ray Tracing," edited by Andrew Glassner[Glassner89], provides an excellent collection of survey papers that explore the essential algorithms for ray tracing, along with methods for speeding up the ray-tracing process. Watt and Watt[Watt92] offer a broad perspective on ray tracing and different ray-tracing methods. The book by Lindley[Lindley92] has many code examples on an accompanying diskette.

APPENDIX

1

Graphics Tools: Obtaining OpenGL

Most of the code discussed in this book is based on using OpenGL as the application programming interface (API). In this appendix we describe how to acquire the OpenGL tools that you will need to build your own applications using OpenGL.

A1.1 OBTAINING AND INSTALLING OPENGL

It is straightforward and cost free to obtain the necessary OpenGL software for almost any computer platform in common use today. We discuss how to access the software for each of the major platforms. Also, an enormous amount of supplementary information about OpenGL is available through the Internet.[1]

Information Repositories for OpenGL.

A rich source of general information on OpenGL and a starting point for downloading software is *http://www.opengl.org/*. A great deal of information, including some on-line manuals, also is available at Silicon Graphics' site: *http://www.sgi.com/software/opengl/manual.html*. The Internet site (see the Preface) for this book provides additional information and links on OpenGL. The excellent book *OpenGL Programming Guide*, by Mason Woo, Jackie Neider, and Tom Davis (1999), currently in its third edition, is an essential source of information about using OpenGL, and gives pointers on obtaining and installing the software.

What You Need

With any system, you start with a good C/C++ compiler and install appropriate OpenGL header files and libraries. Three libraries with associated files are required to use OpenGL as it is described in this book:

> OpenGL (the basic API tool);
> GLU (the OpenGL Utility Library);
> GLUT (the OpenGL Utility Toolkit, a windowing tool kit that handles window system operations).

Typically, several files are associated with each library: a header file (`.h`), a library file (`.lib`), and in some systems, a dynamically linked library file (`.dll`).

Adding Header Files. Place the three files `Gl.h`, `Glu.h`, and `Glut.h` in a `gl` subdirectory of the `include` directory of your compiler. In each application you write the following include statements:

```
#include <gl/Gl.h>
#include <gl/Glu.h>
#include <gl/glut.h>
```

---

[1]   World Wide Web addresses are correct at the time of writing, but, of course, are subject to change.

Linking Library Files. Each application will be part of a project that is compiled and linked. In addition to the (`.c` or `.cpp`) files that you write, add the appropriate OpenGL library (`.lib`) files to your project so that the linker can find them.

We next discuss the individual requirements for each major type of system.

Microsoft Windows 95/98/NT

Much of OpenGL comes already installed on a Windows NT machine. (At the time of writing, OpenGL also comes installed on Windows 95 OSR 2 release and Windows 98 Second Edition machines.) For these systems, some of the steps we shall describe are not necessary.

A suitable environment for using OpenGL on Windows systems is Microsoft's Visual C++ 5.0 or later. (If you declare the application to be a "win32 console application", there is no need to build a graphical user interface: input from the keyboard and output of text take place through the separate console window.)

See "Downloads" at *http://www.opengl.org/Downloads/Downloads.html* for the latest information on OpenGL for windows. The libraries are also available as the self-extracting archive file on the Microsoft ftp site at *ftp://ftp.microsoft.com/softlib/mslfiles/opengl95.exe.* Included are `gl.h`, `glu.h`, `glu32.lib`, `opengl32.lib`, `glu32.dll`, and `opengl32.dll`. (Do not use older `.aux` files.)

The glut library is available at *http://reality.sgi.com/opengl/glut3/glutdlls.zip.* Included are `glut.h`, `glut32.lib`, and `glut32.dll`. (Do not use the `glut.lib` and `glut.dll` files.)

When these files have been downloaded and extracted, place the `.lib` files in some convenient directory from which you will add them to each of your projects. Place the `.dll` files in the `Windows/System` directory (if they aren't already there).

Write the following include statements to include the designated files in your applications:

```
#include <windows.h>
#include <gl/Gl.h>
#include <gl/Glu.h>
#include <gl/glut.h>
```

Macintosh

The principal source for OpenGL for Macintosh systems is *http://www.apple.com/opengl/.* Follow the directions bundled with the software.

Unix, Linux Systems

Mesa is an OpenGL look-alike library that is available for free. Currently, the best place to obtain it is at *http://www.mesa3d.org/.* Follow the directions bundled with each downloadable version; also, see the linux3d page *http://www.linux3d.org/ software.html* for other sources of Mesa.

Since the libraries run under Xwindows, write the following include statement:

```
#include <X11/X11.h>
```

APPENDIX

2

Some Mathematics for Computer Graphics

Mathematics, rightly viewed, possess not only truth,
but supreme beauty—a beauty cold and austere, like that of sculpture.

Bertrand Russell

This appendix draws together and summarizes various mathematical results that are referred to throughout the book. In some cases a brief derivation of a result is given, but that material is mainly for convenient reference.

A2.1 SOME KEY DEFINITIONS PERTAINING TO MATRICES AND THEIR OPERATIONS

In this appendix, we review some fundamental concepts of matrices and ways to manipulate them. More general treatments are available in many other books (for instance, [Birkhoff76, Faux79]).

A **matrix** is a rectangular array of elements, most commonly numbers. A matrix with m rows and n columns is said to be an **m-by-n matrix**. For example,

$$A = \begin{pmatrix} 3 & 2 & -5 \\ -1 & 8 & 0 \\ 6 & 3 & 9 \\ 1 & 21 & 2 \end{pmatrix} \tag{A2.1}$$

is a four-by-three matrix of integers, and

$$B = [1.34, -6.275, 0.0, 81.6]$$

is a one-by-four matrix, also called a "**quadruple**" or a vector. In common parlance, a 1-by-n matrix is a **row vector**, and an n-by-1 matrix is a **column vector**.

The individual elements of a matrix are conventionally given lowercase symbols and are distinguished by subscripts: The ijth element of matrix B is denoted as b_{ij}. This is the element in the ith row and jth column, so for matrix A of Equation (A2.1), $a_{32} = 3$.

A matrix is **square** if it has the same number of rows as columns. In graphics, we frequently work with two-by-two, three-by-three, and four-by-four matrices. Two common square matrices are the **zero matrix** and the **identity matrix**. All of the elements of the zero matrix are zero. All are zero for the identity matrix, too, except those along the **main diagonal** (those elements a_{ij} for which $i = j$), which have the value unity. The three-by-three identity matrix is therefore given by

$$I = \begin{pmatrix} 1 & 0 & 0 \\ 0 & 1 & 0 \\ 0 & 0 & 1 \end{pmatrix}.$$

A2.1.1 Manipulations with Matrices

A matrix B of numbers may be **scaled** by a number s. Each element of B is multiplied by s. The resulting matrix is denoted sB. Using matrix A of Equation (A2.1), for instance, we may have

$$6A = \begin{pmatrix} 18 & 12 & -30 \\ -6 & 48 & 0 \\ 36 & 18 & 54 \\ 6 & 126 & 12 \end{pmatrix}.$$

Two matrices C and D having the same number of rows and columns are said to have the same **shape** and may be added together. The ijth element of the sum $E = C + D$ is simply the sum of the corresponding elements: $e_{ij} = c_{ij} + d_{ij}$. Thus,

$$\begin{pmatrix} 3 & 2 & -5 \\ -1 & 8 & 0 \\ 6 & 3 & 9 \\ 1 & 21 & 2 \end{pmatrix} + \begin{pmatrix} 0 & 5 & -1 \\ 9 & 8 & -3 \\ 2 & 6 & 18 \\ 4 & 2 & 7 \end{pmatrix} = \begin{pmatrix} 3 & 7 & -6 \\ 8 & 16 & -3 \\ 8 & 9 & 27 \\ 5 & 23 & 9 \end{pmatrix}.$$

Since matrices can be scaled and added, it is meaningful to define **linear combinations** of matrices (of the same shape), such as $2A - 4B$. The following facts about three matrices A, B, and C of the same shape result directly from these definitions:

$$A + B = B + A;$$
$$A + (B + C) = (A + B) + C;$$
$$(f + g)(A + B) = fA + fB + gA + gB.$$

The **transpose** of a matrix M, denoted M^T, is formed by interchanging the rows and columns of M: The ijth element of M^T is the jith element of M. Thus, the transpose of matrix A of Equation (A2.1) is

$$A^T = \begin{pmatrix} 3 & -1 & 6 & 1 \\ 2 & 8 & 3 & 21 \\ -5 & 0 & 9 & 2 \end{pmatrix}.$$

The transpose of a row vector is a column vector. For example,

$$(3, 2, -5)^T = \begin{pmatrix} 3 \\ 2 \\ -5 \end{pmatrix}.$$

A matrix is **symmetric** if it is identical to its own transpose. Only square matrices can be symmetric. Thus, an n-by-n matrix M is symmetric if $m_{ij} = m_{ji}$ for i and j between 1 and n.

A2.1.2 Multiplying Two Matrices

The transformations initially discussed in Chapter 5 involve multiplying a vector by a matrix and multiplying two matrices together. The first is a special case of the second.

The **product** AB of two matrices A and B is defined only if the matrices **conform**. That means that the number of columns of the first matrix, A, equals the number of rows of the second one, B. Thus, if A is 3 by 5 and B is 5 by 2, then AB is defined, but BA is not. Each term of the product $C = AB$ of A with B is simply the dot product of some row of A with some column of B. Specifically, the ijth element c_{ij} of the product is the dot product of the ith row of A with the jth column of B. Thus, the product of an n-by-m matrix with an m-by-r matrix is an n by r matrix. For example, we might have

$$\begin{pmatrix} 2 & 0 & 6 & -3 \\ 8 & 1 & -4 & 0 \\ 0 & 5 & 7 & 1 \end{pmatrix} \begin{pmatrix} 6 & 2 \\ -1 & 1 \\ 3 & 1 \\ -5 & 8 \end{pmatrix} = \begin{pmatrix} 45 & -14 \\ 35 & 13 \\ 11 & 20 \end{pmatrix}.$$

Here, for instance, $c_{12} = -14$, since $(2, 0, 6, -3) \cdot (2, 1, 1, 8) = -14$. A routine to multiply square matrices is given in Appendix 3 and is easily extended to find the product of any two matrices that conform.

We list some useful properties of matrix multiplication. Suppose that matrices A, B, and C conform properly. Then

$$(AB)C = A(BC),$$
$$A(B + C) = AB + AC,$$
$$(A + B)C = AC + BC,$$
$$(AB)^T = B^T A^T,$$

and

$$A(sB) = sAB,$$

where s is a number.

In forming a product of two matrices A and B, the order in which the matrices are taken makes a difference. For the expression AB, we say "A **premultiplies** B" or "A is **postmultiplied** by B." If A and B are both square matrices of the same size, they conform both ways, so AB and BA are both well defined, but the two products may contain different elements. If $AB = BA$ for two matrices, we say that they **commute**. (Do two symmetric matrices always commute?)

Multiplying a Vector by a Matrix

A special case of matrix multiplication occurs when one of the matrices is a row vector or column vector. In graphics, we often see a column vector $\mathbf{w}$ being premultiplied by a matrix M in the form $M\mathbf{w}$. For example, let

$$w = \begin{pmatrix} 2 \\ 5 \\ -3 \end{pmatrix} = (2, 5, -3)^T$$

and

$$M = \begin{pmatrix} 2 & 0 & 6 \\ 8 & 1 & -4 \\ 0 & 5 & 7 \end{pmatrix}.$$

Then $\mathbf{w}$ conforms with M, and we can form

$$M\mathbf{w} = \begin{pmatrix} 2 & 0 & 6 \\ 8 & 1 & -4 \\ 0 & 5 & 7 \end{pmatrix} \begin{pmatrix} 2 \\ 5 \\ -3 \end{pmatrix} = \begin{pmatrix} -14 \\ 33 \\ 4 \end{pmatrix}.$$

By the same rules as those given previously, each component of $M\mathbf{w}$ is the dot product of the appropriate row of M with $\mathbf{w}$. One can also premultiply a matrix by a row vector $\mathbf{v}$, as in

$$\mathbf{v}M = (3, -1, 7) \begin{pmatrix} 2 & 0 & 6 \\ 8 & 1 & -4 \\ 0 & 5 & 7 \end{pmatrix} = (-2, 34, 71).$$

The Dot and Cross Products Revisited

It is useful in some analytical derivations to write the dot product $\mathbf{a} \cdot \mathbf{b}$ of two n-tuples as a vector times a matrix. Simply view vector $\mathbf{b}$ as a row matrix, and transpose it to form the n-by-1 column matrix $\mathbf{b}^T$. Then

$$\mathbf{a} \cdot \mathbf{b} = \mathbf{a}\mathbf{b}^T.$$

By the same reasoning, $\mathbf{a} \cdot \mathbf{b} = \mathbf{b}\mathbf{a}^T$.

Similarly, the cross product of two triples $\mathbf{a} \times \mathbf{b}$ (see Section 4.4) may be written as the product

$$\mathbf{a} \times \mathbf{b} = (a_1 \ a_2 \ a_3) \begin{pmatrix} 0 & -b_3 & b_2 \\ b_3 & 0 & -b_1 \\ -b_2 & b_1 & 0 \end{pmatrix}.$$

The cross product also is some matrix (which one?) postmultiplied by column vector $\mathbf{a}^T$. One other form, the **outer product,** or **tensor product,** of two vectors, provides the useful notation

$$\mathbf{a} \otimes \mathbf{b} = \mathbf{a}^T \mathbf{b} = \begin{pmatrix} a_1 \\ a_2 \\ a_3 \end{pmatrix} (b_1, b_2, b_3) = \begin{pmatrix} a_1 b_1 & a_1 b_2 & a_1 b_3 \\ a_2 b_1 & a_2 b_2 & a_2 b_3 \\ a_3 b_1 & a_3 b_2 & a_3 b_3 \end{pmatrix},$$

from which it follows that $\mathbf{b} \otimes \mathbf{a} = (\mathbf{a} \otimes \mathbf{b})^T$. (Why?) An easily proved property is

$$\mathbf{a}(\mathbf{b} \otimes \mathbf{c}) = (\mathbf{a} \cdot \mathbf{b})\mathbf{c}.$$

A2.1.3 Partitioning a Matrix

It is sometimes convenient to subdivide a matrix into blocks of elements and to give names to the various blocks. For example,

$$M = \begin{pmatrix} 2 & 0 & 6 \\ 8 & 1 & -4 \\ 3 & 2 & 7 \end{pmatrix} = \left(\begin{array}{c|c} M_1 & M_2 \\ \hline M_3 & M_4 \end{array} \right),$$

where the blocks are identified as

$$M_1 = \begin{pmatrix} 2 & 0 \\ 8 & 1 \end{pmatrix}, M_2 = \begin{pmatrix} 6 \\ -4 \end{pmatrix}, M_3 = (3 \ \ 2),$$

and M_4, consisting of the single element 7. This is called a **partition** of M into the four blocks shown. Note that when one block is positioned above another, the two blocks must have the same number of columns. Similarly, when two blocks lie side by side, they must have the same number of rows. Two matrices that have been partitioned in the same way (corresponding blocks have the same shape) may be added by adding the blocks individually. To transpose a partitioned matrix, transpose each block individually, and then transpose the arrangement of blocks. Thus,

$$\left(\begin{array}{c|c} M_1 & M_2 \\ \hline M_3 & M_4 \end{array} \right)^T = \left(\begin{array}{c|c} M_1^T & M_3^T \\ \hline M_2^T & M_4^T \end{array} \right).$$

You can also multiply two partitioned matrices by multiplying their submatrices in the usual way, as long as the submatrices conform:

$$\left(\begin{array}{c|c} M_1 & M_2 \\ \hline M_3 & M_4 \end{array} \right) \left(\begin{array}{c|c} M_5 & M_6 \\ \hline M_7 & M_8 \end{array} \right) = \left(\begin{array}{c|c} M_1 M_5 + M_2 M_7 & M_1 M_6 + M_2 M_8 \\ \hline M_3 M_5 + M_4 M_7 & M_3 M_6 + M_4 M_8 \end{array} \right).$$

A2.1.4 The Determinant of a Matrix

Every square matrix M has a number associated with it called its **determinant** and denoted by $|M|$. The determinant describes the volume of certain geometric shapes and provides information concerning the effect that a linear transformation has on areas and volumes of objects.

For a two-by-two matrix M, the determinant is simply the difference of two products:

$$|M| = \begin{vmatrix} m_{11} & m_{12} \\ m_{21} & m_{22} \end{vmatrix} = m_{11}m_{22} - m_{12}m_{21}.$$

If M is a three-by-three matrix, its determinant has the form

$$|M| = \begin{vmatrix} m_{11} & m_{12} & m_{13} \\ m_{21} & m_{22} & m_{23} \\ m_{31} & m_{32} & m_{33} \end{vmatrix} = m_{11}\begin{vmatrix} m_{22} & m_{23} \\ m_{32} & m_{33} \end{vmatrix} - m_{12}\begin{vmatrix} m_{21} & m_{23} \\ m_{31} & m_{33} \end{vmatrix} + m_{13}\begin{vmatrix} m_{21} & m_{22} \\ m_{31} & m_{32} \end{vmatrix}.$$

Accordingly,

$$\begin{vmatrix} 2 & 0 & 6 \\ 8 & 1 & -4 \\ 0 & 5 & 7 \end{vmatrix} = 294.$$

Note that $|M|$ here is the sum of three terms, $m_{11}M_{11} + m_{12}M_{12} + m_{13}M_{13}$, so it has the form of a dot product: $|M| = (m_{11}, m_{12}, m_{13}) \cdot (M_{11}, M_{12}, M_{13})$. What are the M_{ij} terms? M_{ij} is called the **cofactor** of element m_{ij} for matrix M. Since we shall see cofactors emerging when we seek the inverse of a matrix, it is convenient to define them formally.

> **DEFINITION:** Each element m_{ij} of a square matrix M has a corresponding **cofactor** M_{ij} that is $(-1)^{i+j}$ times the determinant of the matrix formed by deleting the ith row and the jth column from M.

Note that as one moves along a row or column, the value of $(-1)^{i+j}$ alternates between 1 and -1. One can visualize a checkerboard pattern of 1's and -1's distributed over the matrix.

The general rule for finding the determinant $|M|$ of any n-by-n matrix M is as follows: Pick any row of M, find the cofactor of each element in the row, and take the dot product of the row and the n-tuple of cofactors. Alternatively, pick a column of M and do the same thing. (Does this rule hold for a two-by-two matrix as well?)

Following are some useful properties of determinants:

- $|M| = |M^T|$.
- If two rows (or two columns) of M are identical, then $|M| = 0$.
- If M and B are both square, then $|MB| = |M| |B|$.
- If B is formed from M by interchanging two rows (or columns) of M, then $|B| = -|M|$.
- If B is formed from M by multiplying one row (or column) of M by a constant k, then $|B| = k |M|$.
- If B is formed from M by adding a multiple of one row (or column) of M to another, then $|B| = |M|$.

A2.1.5 The Inverse of a Matrix

An n-by-n matrix M is said to be **nonsingular** whenever $|M|$ is not equal to 0. In this case, M has an **inverse**, denoted M^{-1}, that has the property

$$MM^{-1} = M^{-1}M = I,$$

where I is the n-by-n identity matrix. Also, the inverse of a product of square matrices is

$$(AB)^{-1} = B^{-1}A^{-1}.$$

It is simple to specify the elements of M^{-1} in terms of cofactors of M. Let A be the inverse of M. Then A has ijth element

$$a_{ij} = \frac{M_{ji}}{|M|}.$$

That is, we find the cofactor of the term m_{ji} and divide it by the determinant of the whole matrix. Carefully note the subscripts here: The cofactor of m_{ji} is used when determining a_{ij}. An equivalent procedure is as follows:

1. Build an intermediate matrix C of cofactors $c_{ij} = M_{ij}$;
2. Find $|M|$ as the dot product of any row of C with the corresponding row of M;
3. Transpose C to get C^T;
4. Scale each element of C^T by $1/|M|$ to form M^{-1}.

■ **EXAMPLE**

Find the inverse of

$$M = \begin{pmatrix} 2 & 0 & 6 \\ 8 & 1 & -4 \\ 0 & 5 & 7 \end{pmatrix}.$$

SOLUTION:

Build the matrix C of cofactors of M:

$$\begin{pmatrix} 27 & -56 & 40 \\ 30 & 14 & -10 \\ -6 & 56 & 2 \end{pmatrix}.$$

Next, find $|M|$ as $(2,0,6)\cdot(27,-56,40) = 294$. Then transpose C and scale each element by $1/|M|$ to obtain

$$M^{-1} = \frac{1}{294}\begin{pmatrix} 27 & 30 & -6 \\ -56 & 14 & 56 \\ 40 & -10 & 2 \end{pmatrix}.$$

Check this answer by multiplying out MM^{-1} and $M^{-1}M$.

The inverse is often used to solve a **set of linear equations**

$$N\begin{pmatrix} x_1 \\ x_2 \\ \vdots \\ x_n \end{pmatrix} = \begin{pmatrix} b_1 \\ b_2 \\ \vdots \\ b_n \end{pmatrix},$$

where an n-by-n matrix N is given along with the column vector $\mathbf{b}$ and where it is necessary to find the vector $\mathbf{x}$ such that all n of the equations are satisfied simultaneously. If N is nonsingular, the solution may be found as

$$\mathbf{x} = N^{-1}\mathbf{b}.$$

There are numerical techniques for solving such a system of equations that are faster and more numerically stable than computing $N^{-1}\mathbf{b}$ directly.

Note that although the use of column vectors is prevalent in graphics, in certain fields it is more common to use row vectors and to write the preceding set of equations as

$$(x_1, x_2, \ldots, x_n)M = (b_1, b_2, \ldots, b_n).$$

It is not difficult to show that this is the same set of equations as the previous ones when $M = N^T$ and that the solution is given by $\mathbf{x} = \mathbf{b}M^{-1}$.

Orthogonal Matrices

For some transformations, such as rotations (see Chapter 5), the associated matrix has an inverse that is particularly easy to find. A matrix M said to be **orthogonal** if simply transposing it produces its inverse—that is, if $M^T = M^{-1}$. Therefore, $MM^T = I$. If M is orthogonal, $MM^T = I$ implies that each row of M is a unit length vector and that the rows are mutually orthogonal. The same is true for the columns of M. (Why?) For instance, if M is three by three, partition it into three rows as follows:

$$M = \begin{pmatrix} \mathbf{a} \\ \mathbf{b} \\ \mathbf{c} \end{pmatrix}$$

Then the triples $\mathbf{a}, \mathbf{b}$, and $\mathbf{c}$ are each of unit length and $\mathbf{a} \cdot \mathbf{b} = \mathbf{a} \cdot \mathbf{c} = \mathbf{b} \cdot \mathbf{c} = 0$.

A2.2 SOME PROPERTIES OF VECTORS AND THEIR OPERATIONS

A2.2.1 The Perp of a Vector; the Perp Dot Product

The perp and perp dot product apply only to two-dimensional vectors.

The Perp of a Vector. Let vector $\mathbf{a} = (a_x, a_y)$. Then the **counterclockwise** perpendicular, or "perp", of $\mathbf{a}$, denoted by $\mathbf{a}^\perp$, is given by $\mathbf{a}^\perp = (-a_y, a_x)$, and the following properties hold:

a. Vectors $\mathbf{a}$ and $\mathbf{a}^\perp$ have the same length: $|\mathbf{a}| = |\mathbf{a}^\perp|$.
b. Linearity: $(\mathbf{a} + \mathbf{b})^\perp = \mathbf{a}^\perp + \mathbf{b}^\perp$ and $(A\mathbf{a})^\perp = A\mathbf{a}^\perp$ for any scalar A;
c. Two perps make a negation: $\mathbf{a}^{\perp\perp} = (\mathbf{a}^\perp)^\perp = -\mathbf{a}$.

The Perp Dot Product $\mathbf{a}^\perp \cdot \mathbf{b}$.

a. The perp dot product $\mathbf{a}^\perp \cdot \mathbf{b} = a_x b_y - a_y b_x$.
b. $\mathbf{a}^\perp \cdot \mathbf{a} = 0$. ($\mathbf{a}^\perp$ is perpendicular to $\mathbf{a}$.)
c. $|\mathbf{a}^\perp|^2 = |\mathbf{a}|^2 \cdot$ ($\mathbf{a}^\perp$ and $\mathbf{a}$ have the same length.)
d. $\mathbf{a}^\perp \cdot \mathbf{b} = -\mathbf{b}^\perp \cdot \mathbf{a}$. (The perp dot product is antisymmetric.)
e. $\mathbf{a}^\perp \cdot \mathbf{b}$ can be written as the determinant

$$\mathbf{a}^\perp \cdot \mathbf{b} = \begin{vmatrix} a_x & a_y \\ b_x & b_y \end{vmatrix}.$$

f. $(\mathbf{a}^\perp \cdot \mathbf{b})^2 + (\mathbf{a} \cdot \mathbf{b})^2 = |\mathbf{a}|^2|\mathbf{b}|^2$.
g. If $\mathbf{a} + \mathbf{b} + \mathbf{c} = 0$, then $\mathbf{a}^\perp \cdot \mathbf{b} = \mathbf{b}^\perp \cdot \mathbf{c} = \mathbf{c}^\perp \cdot \mathbf{a}$.
h. $\mathbf{a}^\perp \cdot \mathbf{b} > 0$ if and only if there is a CCW turn from $\mathbf{a}$ to $\mathbf{b}$.
i. $\mathbf{a}^\perp \cdot \mathbf{b} = 0$ if $\mathbf{b}$ is parallel or antiparallel to $\mathbf{a}$
j. $|\mathbf{a}^\perp \cdot \mathbf{b}|$ is the area of the parallelogram determined by vectors $\mathbf{a}$ and $\mathbf{b}$.

A2.2.2 The Scalar Triple Product

For the three dimensional vectors $\mathbf{a}, \mathbf{b}$, and $\mathbf{c}$ a very useful quantity combines the cross product with the dot product. To derive this quantity, given three vectors $\mathbf{a}, \mathbf{b}$, and $\mathbf{c}$, we create the scalar

$$S = \mathbf{a} \cdot (\mathbf{b} \times \mathbf{c}) = a_x(b_y c_z - b_z c_y) + a_y(b_z c_x - b_x c_z) + a_z(b_x c_y - b_y c_x).$$

This can also be written conveniently as the determinant

$$S = \begin{vmatrix} a_x & a_y & a_z \\ b_x & b_y & b_z \\ c_x & c_y & c_z \end{vmatrix}.$$

Interchanging the rows of a determinant causes only a change in sign, so interchanging twice produces no change at all. Hence, a cyclic permutation in the vectors has no effect on the value of S, which accordingly has the following three equivalent forms:

$$S = \mathbf{a} \cdot (\mathbf{b} \times \mathbf{c}) = \mathbf{b} \cdot (\mathbf{c} \times \mathbf{a}) = \mathbf{c} \cdot (\mathbf{a} \times \mathbf{b})$$

The scalar triple product has a simple geometric interpretation (it plays the same role in 3D as the perp dot product $\mathbf{b}^\perp \cdot \mathbf{c}$ plays in 2D):

- Its *magnitude* $|S|$ is the volume of the parallelepiped formed by the vectors $\mathbf{a}, \mathbf{b}$, and $\mathbf{c}$, all bound to the same point.
- The *sign* of the triple scalar product follows that of $\cos(\phi)$: positive if $|\phi| < 90°$ and negative if $|\phi| > 90°$. (*Question*: If we express $\mathbf{a}, \mathbf{b}$, and $\mathbf{c}$ instead in a left-handed coordinate system, does S change?).

Note that if the three vectors lie in the same plane, the scalar triple product will be zero, as the volume of the parallelepiped then degenerates to zero. Suppose that none of $\mathbf{a}, \mathbf{b}$, or $\mathbf{c}$ is the zero vector. Then the scalar triple product $\mathbf{a} \cdot (\mathbf{b} \times \mathbf{c}) = 0$ if, and only if, the three vectors are coplanar. (*Corollary*: The three vectors are coplanar if any two of them are parallel.) This property can be used to determine how nearly planar a polygon is.

The Intersection of Three Planes

Two planes intersect in a line, and a third plane intersects this line at a single point. The scalar triple product provides a closed-form expression for this point. If the planes are given by $\mathbf{n}_i \cdot \mathbf{r} = D_i$, for $i = 1, 2, 3$, their point of intersection is

$$\mathbf{r} = \frac{D_1(\mathbf{n}_2 \times \mathbf{n}_3) + D_2(\mathbf{n}_3 \times \mathbf{n}_1) + D_3(\mathbf{n}_1 \times \mathbf{n}_2)}{\mathbf{n}_1 \cdot (\mathbf{n}_2 \times \mathbf{n}_3)},$$

provided that the denominator is not zero.

The expression for $\mathbf{r}$ can be checked by seeing that $\mathbf{r}$ lies in each of the three planes: we merely substitute the expression for each plane into the formula for $\mathbf{r}$ and use the properties of the triple scalar product to show that an equality results.

A Useful Identity for Cross Products

In studying normal vectors to surfaces, it is necessary to work with the cross product of two transformed 3D vectors, as in $(M\mathbf{a}) \times (M\mathbf{b})$, where $\mathbf{a}$ and $\mathbf{b}$ are 3D vectors and M is a three-by-three matrix. The question is how this cross product is related to the cross product $\mathbf{a} \times \mathbf{b}$ of $\mathbf{a}$ and $\mathbf{b}$ alone. The answer is

$$(M\mathbf{a}) \times (M\mathbf{b}) = (\det M)M^{-T}(\mathbf{a} \times \mathbf{b}),$$

so $\mathbf{a} \times \mathbf{b}$ is scaled by the determinant of M and multiplied by the inverse transpose of M. To establish this result, the following steps may prove helpful (can you find a more immediate derivation?):

Denote the rows of M by the vectors $\mathbf{r}_1, \mathbf{r}_2$, and $\mathbf{r}_3$. First show that

$$(M\mathbf{a}) \times (M\mathbf{b}) = \begin{pmatrix} \mathbf{r}_2 \times \mathbf{r}_3 \\ \mathbf{r}_3 \times \mathbf{r}_1 \\ \mathbf{r}_1 \times \mathbf{r}_2 \end{pmatrix} (\mathbf{a} \times \mathbf{b}).$$

Then show that

$$M^{-T}(M\mathbf{a}) \times (M\mathbf{b}) = \begin{pmatrix} \mathbf{r}_2 \times \mathbf{r}_3 \\ \mathbf{r}_3 \times \mathbf{r}_1 \\ \mathbf{r}_1 \times \mathbf{r}_2 \end{pmatrix} (\mathbf{r}_1^T | \mathbf{r}_2^T | \mathbf{r}_3^T)(\mathbf{a} \times \mathbf{b}).$$

Finally, show that the product of the first two matrices on the right-hand side is a diagonal matrix with each diagonal term equal to the determinant of M. (*Hint*: Use properties of the scalar triple product such as $\mathbf{a} \cdot \mathbf{c} \times \mathbf{a} = 0$.)

A2.2.3 The Triple Vector Product and Products of Four Vectors

The triple vector product of three 3D vectors $\mathbf{a}$, $\mathbf{b}$, and $\mathbf{c}$ is TVP $= \mathbf{a} \times (\mathbf{b} \times \mathbf{c})$. It often arises during pencil-and-paper calculations involving cross products. The triple vector product can be written as the difference of the two scaled vectors: TVP $= (\mathbf{a} \cdot \mathbf{c})\mathbf{b} - (\mathbf{a} \cdot \mathbf{b})\mathbf{c}$ [Faux79].

Products of Four Vectors

For any four 3D vectors $\mathbf{a}$, $\mathbf{b}$, $\mathbf{c}$, and $\mathbf{d}$,

$$(\mathbf{a} \times \mathbf{b}) \cdot (\mathbf{c} \times \mathbf{d}) = (\mathbf{a} \cdot \mathbf{c})(\mathbf{b} \cdot \mathbf{d}) - (\mathbf{a} \cdot \mathbf{d})(\mathbf{b} \cdot \mathbf{c}).$$

A2.3 THE ARITHMETIC OF COMPLEX NUMBERS

It is not essential to bring complex numbers into play in studying geometric methods in computer graphics. However, because complex numbers and their manipulations lend considerable insight into various facts, a study of them is well worth while. This appendix collects the elementary facts of complex arithmetic in one place, as a refresher for readers who have some familiarity with them.

A complex number such as $z = 3 + 4i$ has two parts. Its **real** part, denoted Re(z), is equal to 3, and its so-called **imaginary** part, denoted Im(z), is 4. The quantity i, defined by $i^2 = -1$, is usually written $i = \sqrt{-1}$. There is nothing either complex or imaginary about these objects; they are simply defined according to a set of rules by which they operate. In performing arithmetic, the usual operations apply:

- addition: $(a + bi) + (c + di) = (a + c) + (b + d)i$;
- multiplication: $(a + bi)*(c + di) = (ac - bd) + (ac + cd)i$,

where the term bdi^2 has been replaced by $-bd$ according to the rule $i^2 = -1$. For instance, $(3 + 2i) + (1 + i) = 4 + 3i$, and $(3 + 2i)(1 + i) = 1 + 5i$.

It is in their correspondence to points in the plane that complex numbers, together with their operations, take on a rich geometric character. The complex number $x + yi$ is associated with the point (x, y) in the usual rectangular coordinate system. The x-coordinate is the real part of the number and the y-coordinate is the imaginary part. Thus, $3 + 4i$ corresponds to $(3, 4)$. Any complex number may be "plotted" in the plane. Such a representation is called an **Argand diagram.**[1] Figure A2.1(a) shows the

FIGURE A2.1 The Argand diagram.

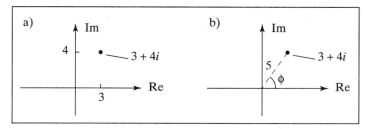

---

[1]   Named after Jean Robert Argand, a Swiss bookkeeper, who described such a diagram in 1806. The Norwegian surveyor Casper Wessel had actually described it nine years earlier, and Gauss used it at about the same time.

complex number $3 + 4i$ plotted as $(3,4)$. The usual x-axis is often called the real axis, and the y-axis the imaginary axis, to reinforce the association.

Just as the point $(3, 4)$ is at a distance $5 = \sqrt{3^2 + 4^2}$ from the origin, a complex number $c = a + bi$ is said to have a **magnitude** or **modulus**,

$$|c| = \sqrt{a^2 + b^2}.$$

Not surprisingly, the **angle,** or **argument,** of $c = a + bi$ is the angle ϕ shown in Figure A2.1(b). The argument of z is often denoted $\text{Arg}(z)$, so $\text{Arg}(z) = \phi$. Thus, the real part of c is $|c| \cos \phi$, and the imaginary part is $|c| \sin \phi$, so we can write the "polar" form

$$c = |c| \cos \phi + i|c| \sin \phi.$$

More generally, suppose that z has the polar form $z = |z|(\cos \theta + i \sin \theta)$ (i.e., magnitude $|z|$ and argument θ). Now multiply c by z and simplify the result to get

$$cz = |c|(\cos \phi + i \sin \phi)|z|(\cos \theta + i \sin \theta)$$
$$= |c||z|(\cos(\phi + \theta) + i \sin(\phi + \theta)) \qquad\qquad (A2.2)$$

We conclude that

- the magnitude of the product of two complex numbers is the product of their magnitudes and
- the argument of the product of two complex numbers is the sum of their arguments.

Figure A2.2 illustrates the geometric meaning of adding and multiplying complex numbers. Addition of complex numbers (part a) follows the same rules as vector addition. Multiplication of complex numbers is shown in part b. Note that the triangle formed by $0, 1$, and c is similar to that formed by $0, z$, and cz, so multiplying by a complex number converts a triangle into a similar triangle.

Letting $z = c$ in Equation (A2.2), we obtain $z^2 = |z|^2 (\cos 2\phi + i \sin 2\phi)$, which generalizes immediately to an expression for z^n. (Which one?) Setting $|z| = 1$, we get DeMoivre's renowned formula,

$$(\cos \phi + i \sin \phi)^n = \cos(n\phi) + i \sin(n\phi).$$

Let us examine the function $\cos \phi + i \sin \phi$ more closely. Call it $f(\phi)$. De Moivre's formula says that $f^n(\phi) = f(n\phi)$: Raising a function to a power n is the same as multiplying its argument by n. This is highly suggestive of an exponential function and, in fact, can be proven rigorously to be so. It produces **Euler's formula**:

$$e^{i\phi} = \cos \phi + i \sin \phi.$$

(*Proof*: Both sides have the same infinite series expansion.) As special cases, note that $e^{i0} = 1$, $e^{i\pi/2} = i$, and $e^{i\pi} = -1$. (This last equation relates in a remarkable way the four fundamental mathematical values e, i, π, and 1.) Euler's formula provides us with an alternative and very compact polar form for a complex number c having magnitude $|c|$ and angle ϕ:

$$c = |c|e^{i\phi}.$$

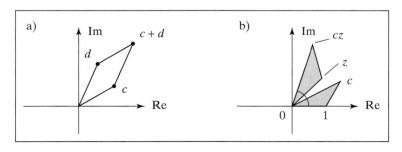

FIGURE A2.2 Adding and multiplying complex numbers.

For example, the n vertices of an n-gon of radius R are given by the n complex numbers

$$p_k = Re^{i2\pi k/n}, \quad k = 1, 2, \ldots, n.$$

Each complex number z also has a **conjugate**, denoted z^*. If $z = x + iy$, then, by definition, $z^* = x - iy$. Thus, $|z^*| = |z|$ and $\text{Arg}(z^*) = -\text{Arg}(z)$. Taking the conjugate is equivalent to effecting a reflection about the x-axis. (What are the magnitude and argument of $(z^*)^n$?)

The Square Root $\sqrt{z}$ of a complex number z

If the complex number z has the polar form $z = |z|e^{i\phi}$, then, clearly,

$$\sqrt{z} = \sqrt{|z|}e^{i\phi/2}.$$

Thus, taking the square root takes the square root of the magnitude and halves the argument of z. This relationship can also be written without recourse to the polar form. If $z = x + iy$, then

$$\begin{aligned} \sqrt{z} &= a + ib & \text{if } y \geq 0 \\ \sqrt{z} &= -a + ib & \text{if } y < 0, \end{aligned} \tag{A2.3}$$

where

$$a = \sqrt{\frac{|z| + x}{2}}$$

and

$$b = \sqrt{\frac{|z| - x}{2}}.$$

Check: Square $a + ib$ and $-a + ib$ directly and work out the algebra, to see that the result is z itself.

PRACTICE EXERCISES

A2.3.1. The division operation

Show that if z and w are complex numbers, then

$$\frac{z}{w} = \frac{|z|}{|w|}e^{i(\text{Arg}(z) - \text{Arg}(w))} = \frac{zw^*}{ww^*} = \frac{zw^*}{|w|^2}.$$

A2.3.2. A ratio that always has unit magnitude

Show that $(a + ib)/(a - ib)$ has a magnitude of unity for any a and b.

A2.3.3 When must four complex numbers lie on a circle?

Show that $\text{Arg}((z_3 - z_1)/(z_2 - z_1)) = \text{Arg}((z_4 - z_1)/(z_4 - z_2))$ if and only if $z_1, \ldots, z_4$ lie on a circle or straight line if and only if $[(z_3 - z_1)/(z_3 - z_2)]/[(z_4 - z_1)/(z_4 - z_2)]$ is real. ■

A2.4 SPHERICAL COORDINATES AND DIRECTION COSINES

In this section, we review the notion of spherical coordinates and summarize how to convert back and forth from spherical coordinates to Cartesian coordinates.

Figure A2.3 shows how a point U is defined in spherical coordinates. R is the radial distance of U from the origin, and ϕ is the angle that U makes with the xz-plane, known as the **latitude** of point U. θ is the **azimuth** of U, the angle between the xy-plane and the plane through U and the y-axis. ϕ lies in the interval $-\pi/2 \leq \phi < \pi/2$, and θ lies in the range $0 \leq \theta < 2\pi$.

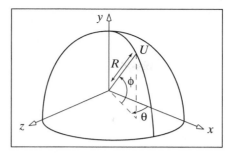

FIGURE A2.3 Spherical coordinates.

With the use of simple trigonometry, it is straightforward to work out the relationships between these quantities and the Cartesian coordinates (u_x, u_y, u_z) for U. The equations are

$$u_x = R\cos(\phi)\cos(\theta),$$

$$u_y = R\sin(\phi),$$

(A2.4)

and

$$u_z = R\cos(\phi)\sin(\theta).$$

One can also invert these relations to express (R, ϕ, θ) in terms of (u_x, u_y, u_z):

$$R = \sqrt{u_x^2 + u_y^2 + u_z^2};$$

$$\phi = \sin^{-1}\left(\frac{u_y}{R}\right);$$

(A2.5)

$$\theta = \arctan(u_z, u_x).$$

The function arctan(,) is the two-argument form of the arctangent, defined as

$$\arctan(y, x) = \begin{cases} \tan^{-1}(y/x) & \text{if } x > 0 \\ \pi + \tan^{-1}(y/x) & \text{if } x < 0 \\ \pi/2 & \text{if } x = 0 \text{ and } y > 0 \\ -\pi/2 & \text{if } x = 0 \text{ and } y < 0 \end{cases}.$$

(A2.6)

This function can distinguish between the case where both x and y are positive and the case where both of them are negative, unlike the usual form $\tan^{-1}(x/y)$, which always produces angles between $-\pi/2$ and $\pi/2$.

■ EXAMPLE A2.4.1

Suppose that point U is at a distance 2 from the origin, is 60° up from the xz-plane, and is along the negative x-axis. Hence, U is in the xy-plane. Then U is expressed in spherical coordinates as $(2, 60°, 180°)$. Using Equation (A2.4) to compute U in Cartesian coordinates, we obtain $U = (-1, 1.732, 0)$.

Direction Cosines

The direction of point U in the preceding example is given in terms of two angles: the azimuth and the latitude. Directions are often specified in an alternative useful way through direction cosines. The direction cosines of a line through the origin are the cosines of the three angles it makes with the x-, y-, and z-axes, respectively.

Recall that the cosine of the angle between two unit vectors is given by their dot product. Using the given point U, we form the position vector (u_x, u_y, u_z). From the preceding discussion, we see that the length of this vector is R, so it must be normalized to the unit-length vector $\mathbf{m} = (u_x/R, u_y/R, u_z/R)$. Then the cosine of the angle it makes with the x-axis is given by the dot product $\mathbf{m} \cdot \mathbf{i} = u_x/R$, which is simply the first component of **m**. Similarly, the second and third components of **m** are the second and third direction cosines, respectively. Calling the angles made with the x-, y-, and z-axes α, β, and γ, respectively, we have, for the three direction cosines for the line from 0 to U,

$$\cos(\alpha) = \frac{u_x}{R}$$
$$\cos(\beta) = \frac{u_y}{R}$$

(A2.7)

and

$$\cos(\gamma) = \frac{u_z}{R}.$$

Note that the three direction cosines are related, since the sum of their squares is always unity.

PRACTICE EXERCISES

A2.4.1

Convert the point $(x, y, z) = (2, 4, -3)$ to spherical coordinates.

A2.4.2

Convert the point $(r, \phi, \theta) = (5, 35°, -67°)$ to rectangular coordinates.

A2.4.3

Find the direction cosines of the vector **n**, where

 i. $\mathbf{n} = (1, 1, 1)$;
 ii. $\mathbf{n} = (2, 3, 4)$.

APPENDIX

3

Some Useful Classes and Utility Routines

This appendix defines some data types and algorithms that may prove useful in developing graphics applications. The basic types are set forth through various classes, some of which are fully defined and others of which have a number of methods declared, but are not defined. It is up to the reader to flesh latter out. Some classes are given only in a skeletal form, to suggest what might be developed in an actual application.

With most classes, a relaxed approach to encapsulation is taken: Most data fields are declared `public` rather than `private`, as a matter of brevity and to avoid the need to define a large number of accessor and mutator functions.

Another excellent source of classes and utilities may be found in the "Graphics Gems" series, whose on-line repository is *http://www.acm.org/tog/GraphicsGems/index.html*.

The classes defined in this appendix are collected in various header (`.h`) and source (`.cpp`) files, which are also available on the book's Internet site. (See the preface.)

The Collections of Classes Described Here

1. Classes for **2D Graphics**. These classes provide some support for drawing 2D figures and include `IntPoint`, `Point2`, `Polyline`, `IntRect`, `Vector2`, and `Canvas`.
2. **RGBpixmap**. These classes (e.g., `mRGB` and `RGBpixmap` provide support for creating and drawing pix maps, including reading an image stored in the BMP format.
3. **SDL**. These classes support the manipulation and drawing of 3D scenes, including scenes described in the SDL. (See Appendix 5.) The supporting classes include `Point3`, `Vector3`, `Color3`, `Light`, `Affine4`, `AffineStack`, `Material`, `GeomObj`, `Boolean`, `UnionBool`, `IntersectionBool`, `DifferenceBool`, `Shape`, `Cube`, `Sphere`, `TaperedCylinder`, `Square`, `Plane`, `Face`, `Mesh`, `Torus`, `Teapot`, and `Scene`.
4. **Noise**. Among these classes are the `Noise` class for creating 3D noise and turbulence for solid texturing.
5. **Ray-tracing** classes. Includes: `PointCluster`, `SphereInfo`, `Cuboid`, `Ray`, `HitInfo`, and `Intersection`.

CLASSES FOR 2D GRAPHICS

```
// graphics2d.h  // A collection of classes to support 2D
classes
#ifndef _GRAPHICS2D
#define _GRAPHICS2D
#include <string>
#include <iostream>
```

```cpp
#include <fstream>
#include <strstream>
using namespace std;
#include <windows.h> //change if using xWindows or other
platform
#include <assert.h>
#include <math.h>
#include <stdlib.h>
#include <gl/Gl.h>
#include <gl/Glu.h>
#include <gl/glut.h>
//@@@@@@@@@@@@@@@@@ IntPoint class @@@@@@@@@@@@@@@
class IntPoint{ // for 2D points with integer coordinates
public:
 int x,y;
 void set(int dx, int dy){x = dx; y = dy;}
 void set(IntPoint& p){ x = p.x; y = p.y;}
 IntPoint(int xx, int yy){x = xx; y = yy;}
 IntPoint(){ x = y = 0;}
};
//@@@@@@@@@@@@@@@@@ Point2 class @@@@@@@@@@@@@@@
class Point2{ // for 2D points with real coordinates
public:
 float x,y;
 void set(float dx, float dy){x = dx; y = dy;}
 void set(Point2& p){ x = p.x; y = p.y;}
 Point2(float xx, float yy){x = xx; y = yy;}
 Point2(){x = y = 0;}
};
//<<<<<<<<<<<<<<<<<<<<< PolyLine >>>>>>>>>>>>>>>>>>>>>>>>
class PolyLine{ // a polyline is a num plus an array of points
public:
 int num;
 Point2 pt[80]; //may need larger arrays in some circumstances
 PolyLine(){num = 0;}
};
// @@@@@@@@@@@@@@@@@@@@@@@@ IntRect class @@@@@@@@@@@@@@@@@@@@@@@@
class IntRect{ // a rectangle with integer border values
public:
 int left, top, right, bott;
 IntRect(){left = top = right = bott = 0;}
 IntRect(int l, int t, int r, int b)
 {left = l; top = t; right = r; bott = b;}
 void set(int l, int t, int r, int b)
 {left = l; top = t; right = r; bott = b;}
 void set(IntRect& r)
 {left = r.left; top = r.top; right = r.right; bott = r.bott;}
};

//@@@@@@@@@@@@@@@@@ Vector2 class @@@@@@@@@@@@@@@
class Vector2{
public:
 float x,y;
 void set(float dx, float dy){ x = dx; y = dy; }
 void set(Vector2& v){ x = v.x; y = v.y;}
 void setDiff(Point2& a, Point2& b)//set to difference a - b
 {x = a.x - b.x; y = a.y - b.y;}
```

```
  void normalize()//adjust this vector to unit length
  {    double sizeSq = x * x + y * y;
    if(sizeSq < 0.0000001)
    {
      cerr << "\nnormalize() sees vector (0,0)!";
      return; // does nothing to zero vectors;
    }
    float scaleFactor = 1.0/(float)sqrt(sizeSq);
    x *= scaleFactor; y *= scaleFactor;
  }
  Vector2(float xx, float yy){x = xx; y = yy; }
  Vector2(Vector2& v){x = v.x; y = v.y; }
  Vector2(){x = y = 0;} //default constructor
  float dot(Vector2 b) // return this dotted with b
  {return x * b.x + y * b.y;}
  void perp() // perp this vector
  {float tmp = x; x = -y; y = tmp;}
  float perpDot(Vector2& v) // return perp of this dotted with v
  {return x *v.x - y * v.y;}
};


//<<<<<<<<<<<<<<<<<<<<<<<< Canvas class >>>>>>>>>>>
// a global Canvas object (described in Chapter 3) knows how
//to draw lines in world coordinates and to perform
turtlegraphics
class Canvas {
 private:
   Point2 CP;      // current position in world
   float CD; // current direction in degrees
 public:
   float windowAspect;
   Canvas(int width, int height, char* title);
   void setWindow(float l, float r, float b, float t);
   void setViewport(int l, int r, int b, int t);
   float getWindowAspect(void) { return windowAspect;}
   void lineTo(float x, float y);
   void moveTo(float x, float y){CP.x = x; CP.y = y;}
   void turn(float ang) {CD += ang;}
   void turnTo(float ang) {CD = ang;}
   void forward(float dist, int vis);
   void initCT() // initialize the CT (model view matrix)
 {
    glMatrixMode(GL_MODELVIEW); glLoadIdentity();
 }
 void rotate2D(double angle)
 {
    glMatrixMode(GL_MODELVIEW); glRotated(angle, 0.0, 0.0, 1.0);
 }
 void translate2D(double dx, double dy)
 {
    glMatrixMode(GL_MODELVIEW); glTranslated(dx, dy, 0.0);
 }
 void scale2D(double sx, double sy)
 {
    glMatrixMode(GL_MODELVIEW); glScaled(sx, sy, 1.0);
 }
```

```cpp
    void pushCT(void)
    {
        glMatrixMode(GL_MODELVIEW); glPushMatrix();
    }
    void popCT(void)
    {
        glMatrixMode(GL_MODELVIEW); glPopMatrix();
    }
    void ngon(int n, float cx, float cy, float radius);
    };
#endif
// end of graphics2d.h
```

// graphics2d.cpp - use #include "graphics2d.h"
```cpp
// Some methods for the classes defined in graphics2d.h
#include "graphics2d.h"
Canvas :: Canvas(int width, int height, char* title)
{
 char* list; //dummy list for glutInit
 int numArgs = 1;//dummy value for glutInit
 glutInit(&numArgs, &list);
 glutInitDisplayMode(GLUT_SINGLE | GLUT_RGB);
 glutInitWindowSize(width, height);
 glutInitWindowPosition(100, 100);
 glutCreateWindow(title);
 CP.x = CP.y = 0.0;
 windowAspect = 1.0;
}
void Canvas :: setWindow(float l, float r, float b, float t)
{
 glMatrixMode(GL_PROJECTION);
 glLoadIdentity();
 gluOrtho2D((GLdouble)l, (GLdouble)r, (GLdouble)b, (GLdouble)t);
 if(t == b) return;
 windowAspect = (r - 1)/(t - b);
}
void Canvas :: setViewport(int l, int r, int b, int t)
{glViewport((GLint)l, (GLint)b, (GLint)(r-1), (GLint)(t-b));}
void Canvas :: lineTo(float x, float y)
{
  glBegin(GL_LINES);
  glVertex2f((GLfloat)CP.x, (GLfloat)CP.y);
  CP.x = x; CP.y = y;
  glVertex2f((GLfloat)CP.x, (GLfloat)CP.y);
  glEnd();    glFlush();
}
void Canvas :: forward(float dist, int vis)
{
#define RadPerDeg 0.017453393 //radians per degree
  float x = CP.x + dist * cos(RadPerDeg * CD);
  float y = CP.y + dist * sin(RadPerDeg * CD);
  if(vis) lineTo(x, y);
  else moveTo(x, y);
  CP.x = x; CP.y = y;
}
```

```
void Canvas::ngon(int n,float cx, float cy, float radius)
{
#define RadPerDeg 0.017453393 //radians per degree
  if(n < 3) return; // bad number of sides
  double angle = 0, angleInc = 2 * 3.14159265 /n;  //angle
increment
  moveTo(cx + radius, cy);
  for(int k = 1; k <= n; k++)
  {
    angle += angleInc;
    lineTo(radius * cos(angle) + cx, radius * sin(angle) + cy);
  }
}
// end of graphics2d.cpp
```

RGBPixmap CLASS

```
// RGBpixmap.h: a class to support working with RGB pix maps.
#ifndef _RGBPIXMAP
#define _RGBPIXMAP
#include <fstream>
// Needs the IntPoint and IntRect classes to be defined

typedef unsigned char uchar;

class mRGB{    // the name RGB is already used by Windows
public: uchar r,g,b;
     mRGB(){r = g = b = 0;}
     mRGB(mRGB& p){r = p.r; g = p.g; b = p.b;}
     mRGB(uchar rr, uchar gg, uchar bb){r = rr; g = gg; b = bb;}
     void set(uchar rr, uchar gg, uchar bb){r = rr; g = gg; b = bb;}
};
//$$$$$$$$$$$$$$$$$$$ RGBPixmap class $$$$$$$$$$$$$$$$$$
class RGBpixmap{
private:
 mRGB* pixel; // array of pixels

public:
 int nRows, nCols; // dimensions of the pix map
 RGBpixmap() {nRows = nCols = 0; pixel = 0;}
 RGBpixmap(int rows, int cols) //constructor
 {
    nRows = rows;
    nCols = cols;
    pixel = new mRGB[rows*cols];
 }
 int readBMPFile(string fname); // read BMP file into this pix map
 void freeIt() // give back memory for this pix map
 {
    delete []pixel; nRows = nCols = 0;
 }
 //<<<<<<<<<<<<<<<<<< copy >>>>>>>>>>>>>>>>>>>
 void copy(IntPoint from, IntPoint to, int x, int y, int width,
    int height)
 { // copy a region of the display back onto the display
```

```
        if(nRows == 0 || nCols == 0) return;
        glCopyPixels(x, y, width, height,GL_COLOR);
    }
    //<<<<<<<<<<<<<<<<<<<< draw >>>>>>>>>>>>>>>>>
     void draw()
    { // draw this pix map at current raster position

        if(nRows == 0 || nCols == 0) return;
        //tell OpenGL: don't align pixels with 4-byte boundaries in
    memory
        glPixelStorei(GL_UNPACK_ALIGNMENT,1);
        glDrawPixels(nCols, nRows,GL_RGB, GL_UNSIGNED_BYTE,pixel);
    }
    //<<<<<<<<<<<<<<<<<<< read >>>>>>>>>>>>>>>>>
     int read(int x, int y, int wid, int ht)
    { // read a rectangle of pixels into this pixmap
        nRows = ht;
        nCols = wid;
        pixel = new mRGB[nRows *nCols]; if(!pixel) return -1;
        //tell OpenGL: don't align pixels with 4-byte boundaries in
    memory

        glPixelStorei(GL_PACK_ALIGNMENT,1);
        glReadPixels(x, y, nCols, nRows,
    GL_RGB,GL_UNSIGNED_BYTE,pixel);
        return 0;
    }
    //<<<<<<<<<<<<<<<<<< read from IntRect >>>>>>>>>>>>>>>>>
     int read(IntRect r)
    { // read a rectangle of pixels into this pix map
        nRows = r.top - r.bott;
        nCols = r.right - r.left;
        pixel = new mRGB[nRows *nCols]; if(!pixel) return -1;
        //tell OpenGL: don't align pixels with 4-byte boundaries in
    memory
        glPixelStorei(GL_PACK_ALIGNMENT,1);
        glReadPixels(r.left,r.bott, nCols, nRows, GL_RGB,
    GL_UNSIGNED_BYTE, pixel);
        return 0;
    }
    //<<<<<<<<<<<<<<<<< setPixel >>>>>>>>>>>>>
    void setPixel(int x, int y, mRGB color)
    {
        if(x>=0 && x <nCols && y >=0 && y < nRows)
            pixel[nCols * y + x] = color;
    }
    //<<<<<<<<<<<<<<<<<< getPixel >>>>>>>>>>>>

    mRGB getPixel(int x, int y)
    {
        mRGB bad(255,255,255);
        assert(x >= 0 && x < nCols);
        assert(y >= 0 && y < nRows);
        return pixel[nCols * y + x];
    }
}; //end of class RGBpixmap
#endif
```

```
// RGBpixmap.cpp - routines to read a BMP file
#include "RGBpixmap.h"
typedef unsigned short ushort;
typedef unsigned long ulong;
fstream inf; // global in this file for convenience
//<<<<<<<<<<<<<<<<<<<<<<< getShort >>>>>>>>>>>>>>>>>>>>>>
ushort getShort() //helper function
{ //BMP format uses little-endian integer types
 // get and construct in memory a 2-byte integer stored in
little-endian form
    char ic;
    ushort ip;
    inf.get(ic); ip = ic;  //first byte is little one
    inf.get(ic);  ip |= ((ushort)ic << 8); // or in high order
byte
    return ip;
}
//<<<<<<<<<<<<<<<<<<<<<< getLong >>>>>>>>>>>>>>>>>>>>
ulong getLong() //helper function
{  //BMP format uses little-endian integer types
    // get and construct in memory a 4-byte integer stored in
little-endian form
    ulong ip = 0;
    char ic = 0;
    unsigned char uc = ic;
    inf.get(ic); uc = ic; ip = uc;
    inf.get(ic); uc = ic; ip |=((ulong)uc << 8);

    inf.get(ic); uc = ic; ip |=((ulong)uc << 16);

    inf.get(ic); uc = ic; ip |=((ulong)uc << 24);
    return ip;
 }
//<<<<<<<<<<<<<<<<<<<<<< RGBPixmap:: readBmpFile>>>>>>>>>>>>>>
int RGBpixmap:: readBMPFile(string fname)
{  // Read into memory an mRGB image from an uncompressed BMP
file.
  // return 0 on failure, 1 on success
  inf.open(fname.c_str(), ios::in|ios::binary); //read binary
char's
  if(!inf){ cout << " can't open file: " << fname << endl;
return 0;}
  int k, row, col, numPadBytes, nBytesInRow;
  // read the file header information
  char ch1, ch2;
  inf.get(ch1); inf.get(ch2); //type: always 'BM'
  ulong fileSize =     getLong();
  ushort reserved1 =  getShort();  // always 0
  ushort reserved2=   getShort();  // always 0
  ulong offBits =      getLong();  // offset to image -
unreliable
  ulong headerSize =   getLong();        // always 40
  ulong numCols =      getLong();  // number of columns in image
  ulong numRows =      getLong();  // number of rows in image
  ushort planes=       getShort();  // always 1
  ushort bitsPerPixel=getShort();  //8 or 24; allow only 24 here
```

```cpp
    ulong compression =   getLong();  // must be 0 for uncompressed
    ulong imageSize =     getLong();  // total bytes in image
    ulong xPels =         getLong();  // always 0
    ulong yPels =         getLong();  // always 0
    ulong numLUTentries =getLong();   // 256 for 8 bit, otherwise 0
    ulong impColors =     getLong();          // always 0
    if(bitsPerPixel != 24)
    { // error - must be a 24-bit uncompressed image
      cout << "not a 24-bit pixel image, or is compressed!\n";
      inf.close(); return 0;
    }
  //add bytes at end of each row so total # is a multiple of 4
  // round up 3*numCols to next mult. of 4
  nBytesInRow = ((3 * numCols + 3)/4) * 4;
  numPadBytes = nBytesInRow - 3 * numCols; // need this many
  nRows = numRows; // set class's data members
  nCols = numCols;
  pixel = new mRGB[nRows * nCols]; //make space for array
  if(!pixel) return 0; // out of memory!
  long count = 0;
  char dum;
  for(row = 0; row < nRows; row++) // read pixel values
  {
      for(col = 0; col < nCols; col++)
      {
        char r,g,b;
        inf.get(b); inf.get(g); inf.get(r); //read bytes
        pixel[count].r = r; //place them in colors
        pixel[count].g = g;
        pixel[count++].b = b;
      }
        for(k = 0; k < numPadBytes ; k++) //skip pad bytes at
row's end
        inf >> dum;
   }
  inf.close(); return 1; // success
}
```

THE SCENE AND SUPPORTING CLASSES

```cpp
// SDL.h
//definition of simple support classes:
#ifndef _SDL
#define _SDL
#include <string>
#include <iostream>
#include <fstream>
#include <strstream>
using namespace std;

#include <windows.h>
#include <assert.h>
#include <math.h>
#include <gl/Gl.h>
#include <gl/Glu.h>
```

```cpp
#include <gl/glut.h>
// include RGBpixmap if you wish to add a pix map field to
Scene:
//#include "RGBpixmap.h"
//@@@@@@@@@@@@@@@@@@ Point3 class @@@@@@@@@@@@@@@@
class Point3{
public:
 float x,y,z;
 void set(float dx, float dy, float dz){x = dx; y = dy; z = dz;}
 void set(Point3& p){x = p.x; y = p.y; z = p.z;}
 Point3(float xx,            float yy, float zz){x = xx; y = yy; z
= zz;}
 Point3(){x = y = z = 0;}
 void build4tuple(float v[])
 {// load 4-tuple with this color: v[3] = 1 for homogeneous
     v[0] = x; v[1] = y; v[2] = z; v[3] = 1.0f;
 }
};
//@@@@@@@@@@@@@@@@@@ Vector3 class @@@@@@@@@@@@@@@@
class Vector3{
public:
 float x,y,z;
 void set(float dx, float dy, float dz){ x = dx; y = dy; z =
dz;}
 void set(Vector3& v){ x = v.x; y = v.y; z = v.z;}
 void flip(){x = -x; y = -y; z = -z;} // reverse this vector
 void setDiff(Point3& a, Point3& b)//set to difference a - b
 { x = a.x - b.x; y = a.y - b.y; z = a.z - b.z;}
 void normalize();//adjust this vector to unit length
 Vector3(float xx, float yy, float zz){x = xx; y = yy; z = zz;}
 Vector3(Vector3& v){x = v.x; y = v.y; z = v.z;}
 Vector3(){x = y = z = 0;} //default constructor
 Vector3 cross(Vector3 b); //return this cross b
 float dot(Vector3 b); // return this dotted with b
};

// @@@@@@@@@@@@@@@@@@@@@ Color3 class @@@@@@@@@@@@@@@@
class Color3 { // holds a red, green, blue 3-tuple
public:
 float red, green, blue;
 Color3(){red = green = blue = 0;}
 Color3(float r, float g, float b){red = r; green = g; blue = b;}
 Color3(Color3& c){red = c.red; green = c.green; blue = c.blue;}
 void set(float r, float g, float b){red = r; green = g; blue = b;}
 void set(Color3& c)
     {red = c.red; green = c.green; blue = c.blue;}
 void add(float r, float g, float b)
     {red += r; green += g; blue += b;}
 void add(Color3& src, Color3& refl);
 void add(Color3& colr);
 void build4tuple(float v[]);
};
//@@@@@@@@@@@@@@@@@@@@@ light class @@@@@@@@@@@@@@@@@@@@@
class Light{ // for a linked list of light sources' color and position
public:
 Point3 pos;
 Color3 color;
```

```
 Light* next;
 void setPosition(Point3 p){pos.set(p);}
 void setColor(Color3 c){color.set(c);}
 Light(){next = NULL;}
};
// @@@@@@@@@@@@@@@@@@@@@@ Affine4 class @@@@@@@@@@@@@@@@@
class Affine4{// manages homogeneous affine transformations
// including inverse transformations
// and a stack to put them on
// used by Scene class to read SDL files
public:
 float m[16]; // hold a 4-by-4 matrix
 Affine4();
 void setIdentityMatrix();
 void set(Affine4 a);
 void preMult(Affine4 n);
 void postMult(Affine4 n);
}; // end of Affine4 class

//@@@@@@@@@@ AffineNode class @@@@@@@@@@
class AffineNode{
// used by Scene class to read SDL files
public:
 Affine4 * affn;
 Affine4 * invAffn;
 AffineNode * next;
 AffineNode()
 {
    next = NULL;
    affn = new Affine4; // new affine with identity in it
    invAffn = new Affine4; // and for the inverse
 }
 ~AffineNode() //destructor
 {
    delete affn;
    delete invAffn;
 }
};
//@@@@@@@@@@@@@@@@@ AffineStack class @@@@@@@@@@@@@
class AffineStack{
// used by Scene class to read SDL files
public:
 AffineNode * tos;
 AffineStack()//default constructor;puts identity on top
 {
    tos = new AffineNode; // node with identity in it
    tos->next = NULL;
 }
 void dup();
 void setIdentity();// make top item the identity matrix
 void popAndDrop();
 void releaseAffines(); // pop and drop all remaining items
 void rotate(float angle, Vector3 u);
 void scale(float sx, float sy, float sz);
 void translate(Vector3 d);
}; // end of AffineStack class
//this was Shapes.h
```

```
//Shapes class and Supporting classes
//@@@@@@@@@@@@@@@@@ Material class @@@@@@@@@@@@@@
class Material{
public:
 Color3 ambient, diffuse, specular, emissive;
 int numParams; // for textures
 float params[10]; // for textures
 int textureType;  // 0 for none, neg for solids, pos for images
 float specularExponent, reflectivity, transparency, speedOfLight;
 float specularFraction, surfaceRoughness;
 void setDefault();
 void set(Material& m);
}; // end of Material

//@@@@@@@@@@@@@@@@@@@@ GeomObj class @@@@@@@@@@@@@@@@@
class GeomObj{
public:
    //IntRect scrnExtnt;
    GeomObj * next;
    GeomObj(): next(NULL){}
    virtual void loadStuff(){}
    virtual void drawOpenGL(){}
    virtual void tellMaterialsGL(){}
};
//@@@@@@@@@@@@@@@@@@ Boolean @@@@@@@@@@@@@@@@@@@
class Boolean: public GeomObj{
public:
 GeomObj *left, *right;
 Boolean():left(NULL),right(NULL){}
 virtual void drawOpenGL()
 { // just draw its children
    if(left)left-[greater]drawOpenGL();
    if(right)right-[greater]drawOpenGL();
 }
};
//@@@@@@@@@@@@@@@@@@ UnionBool @@@@@@@@@@@@@@@@
class UnionBool : public Boolean{
public:
 UnionBool(){Boolean();} //constructor
};
//@@@@@@@@@@@@@@@@@@ IntersectionBool @@@@@@@@@@@@@@@@@
class IntersectionBool : public Boolean{
public:
 IntersectionBool(){Boolean();}
};
//@@@@@@@@@@@@@@@@@@ DifferenceBool @@@@@@@@@@@@@@@@@
class DifferenceBool : public Boolean{
public:
 DifferenceBool(){Boolean();}
};
//@@@@@@@@@@@@@@@@@ Shape @@@@@@@@@@@@@@@@@@@@@@@
class Shape: public GeomObj{
public:
 Material mtrl;
 Affine4 transf,invTransf;
 //virtual Color3 texture(HitInfo& h, int whichTexture);
 Shape(){mtrl.textureType = 0; mtrl.numParams = 0;}
```

```
 void setMaterial(Material& mt){mtrl.set(mt);}
 void tellMaterialsGL();
 virtual void drawOpenGL(){}
}; //end: Shape class

//@$@$@$@$@$@$@$@$@$@ Cube class $@$@$@$@$@$@$@$@$@$@
class Cube: public Shape{
public:
 Cube(){}
 void drawOpenGL()
 {
    tellMaterialsGL(); glPushMatrix();
    glMultMatrixf(transf.m); //load affine
    glEnable(GL_NORMALIZE);
    glutSolidCube(2.0);    // a cube with vertices -1 to +1
    glPopMatrix();
 }
};
//@$@$@$@$@$@$@$@$@$ Sphere class @$@$@$@$@$@$@$@$@$@$@
class Sphere: public Shape{
public:
 void drawOpenGL()
 {
    tellMaterialsGL();  glPushMatrix();
    glMultMatrixf(transf.m);
    glutSolidSphere(1.0,20,20);
    glPopMatrix();
 }
 Sphere() { }
};
//@$@$@$@$@$@$@$@$@$@ TaperedCylinder class @$@$@$@$@$@$@$@$@$$

class TaperedCylinder: public Shape{
public:
    float smallRadius;
    TaperedCylinder(){}
    void drawOpenGL(){ /* to be implemented */}
};
//@$@$@$@$@$@$@$@$@ Square class @$@$@$@$@$@$@$@$@$
class Square: public Shape{
public:
    Square(){}
    void drawOpenGL(){ /* to be implemented */}
};
//@$@$@$@$@$@$@$@$@ Plane class @$@$@$@$@$@$@$@$@$
class Plane: public Shape{
public:
    Plane() {}
    void drawOpenGL(){ /* to be implemented */}
};
//################## class VertexID ################
//used to define a Mesh
class VertexID{public: int vertIndex, normIndex;};
//################## class FACE #############
//used to define a Mesh
class Face{
public:
```

```
        int nVerts;
        VertexID * vert; // array of vertex and normal indices
        Face(){ nVerts = 0; vert = NULL;}
        ~Face(){delete[] vert; nVerts = 0;}
};
//@$@$@$@$@$@$@$@$@$@$@ Mesh class @$@$@$@$@$@$@$@$@$@$
class Mesh : public Shape{
private:
        int numVerts, numNorms, numFaces;
        Point3 *pt; // array of points
        Vector3 *norm; // array of normals
        Face *face; // array of faces
        int lastVertUsed;
        int lastNormUsed;
        int lastFaceUsed;
public:
        void readMesh(string fname);
        void writeMesh(char* fname);
        void printMesh();
        void drawMesh();
        void drawEdges();
        void freeMesh();
        int isEmpty();
        void makeEmpty();
        Mesh();
        virtual void drawOpenGL();
        Mesh(string fname);
        Vector3 newell4(int indx[]);
        string meshFileName; // holds file name for this Mesh
}; // end of Mesh class
//@$@$@$@$@$@$@$@$@$@$ Torus class @$@$@$@$@$@$@$@$@$$
class Torus: public Shape{
public:
        void drawOpenGL(){
            tellMaterialsGL();   glPushMatrix();
            glMultMatrixf(transf.m);
            glutSolidTorus(0.2,1.0,10,12);
            //if(doEdges) glutWireTorus(0.2,1.0,10,12);
            glPopMatrix();}
};
//@$@$@$@$@$@$@$@$@$@$ Teapot class @$@$@$@$@$@$@$@$@$$
class Teapot: public Shape{
public:
        void drawOpenGL(){ tellMaterialsGL(); glPushMatrix();
        glMultMatrixf(transf.m);
        glutSolidTeapot(1.0); glPopMatrix();}
};
//@@@@@@@@@@@@@@@@@@ DefUnit & DefUnitStack classes @@@@@@@@@@@@@@
//used in Scene to read SDL files
class DefUnit{
 // developed by Steve Morin
public:
 string    name, stuff;
 DefUnit(string n, string s) {stuff = s;name = n;}
};
class DefUnitStack {
public:
```

```
  DefUnitStack() {stack = NULL;}
  void push(string n, string s);
  void print();
  int search(string s);
  string contents(string s);
  void release();
 private:
  struct D4S {
     DefUnit *current;
     struct D4S *next;
  } d4s;
  D4S *stack;
}; // end of DefUnitStack class
//+++++++++++++ TokenType +++++++++++++
    enum mTokenType {IDENT, LIGHT, ROTATE, TRANSLATE,
    SCALE, PUSH, POP, IDENTITYAFFINE,
    GLOBALAMBIENT, BACKGROUND, MINREFLECTIVITY,
    MINTRANSPARENCY, MAXRECURSIONDEPTH, CUBE, SPHERE, TORUS, PLANE,
    SQUARE, CYLINDER, CONE, TAPEREDCYLINDER,TETRAHEDRON, OCTAHEDRON,
    DODECAHEDRON, ICOSAHEDRON,BUCKYBALL, TEAPOT,
    DIAMOND,UNION,INTERSECTION, DIFFERENCEa, MAKEPIXMAP,
    MESH, DEFAULTMATERIALS, AMBIENT, DIFFUSE,SPECULAR,
    SPECULARFRACTION, SURFACEROUGHNESS,EMISSIVE, SPECULAREXPONENT,
    SPEEDOFLIGHT, TRANSPARENCY,REFLECTIVITY, PARAMETERS, TEXTURE,
    FTCURLY, RGHTCURLY, DEF, USE, T_NULL, F_EOF, UNKNOWN };


//@@@@@@@@@@@@  Scene class @@@@@@@@@@@@@@@@@@@@@@
class Scene{
public:
 Light *light;  // attach linked list of lights here
 GeomObj * obj;  // attach the object list here
 Color3 background, ambient;
 int maxRecursionDepth;
 //must #include RGBpixmap.h to have following texture fields
 //RGBpixmap pixmap[8]; //list of attached pixmaps
 float minReflectivity, minTransparency;
 //bool isInShadow(Ray& f); // for ray tracing: implementation
left to the reader
 Scene():light(NULL),obj(NULL),tail(NULL) //default constructor
 {
    currMtrl.setDefault();
    background.set(0,0,0.6f);
    ambient.set(0.1f,0.1f,0.1f);
    minReflectivity = 0.5;
    minTransparency = 0.5;
    maxRecursionDepth = 3;
 }
 Scene(string fname){Scene(); read(fname);}
 void freeScene();
 void makeLightsOpenGL(){/* to be implemented */}
 void drawSceneOpenGL();
 bool read(string fname);
 GeomObj* getObject();
private:
 // private stuff used only for reading a scene
 int line;
 int nextline;
```

```
ifstream  *file_in;
strstream *f_in;
strstream temp_fin;
DefUnitStack *def_stack;
GeomObj * tail; // tail of object list
AffineStack affStk; // affine stack
Material currMtrl;
string nexttoken(void);
float getFloat();
bool isidentifier(string keyword);
void cleanUp();
mTokenType whichtoken(string keyword);
}; // end of Scene.h

#endif
```

//SDL.cpp
```
// support code for the classes in SDL.h
#include "SDL.h"
// Vector3 methods
Vector3 Vector3 :: cross(Vector3 b) //return this cross b
{
     Vector3 c(y*b.z - z*b.y, z*b.x - x*b.z, x*b.y - y*b.x);
     return c;
}
float Vector3 :: dot(Vector3 b) // return this dotted with b
{return x * b.x + y * b.y + z * b.z;}

void Vector3 :: normalize()//adjust this vector to unit length
{
 double sizeSq = x * x + y * y + z * z;
 if(sizeSq < 0.0000001)
 {
    cerr << "\nnormalize() sees vector (0,0,0)!";
    return; // does nothing to zero vectors;
 }
 float scaleFactor = 1.0/(float)sqrt(sizeSq);
 x *= scaleFactor; y *= scaleFactor; z *= scaleFactor;
}
// Color3 methods
void Color3 ::add(Color3& src, Color3& refl)
{ // add the product of source color and reflection coefficient
  red   += src.red   * refl.red;
  green += src.green * refl.green;
  blue  += src.blue  * refl.blue;
}
void Color3:: add(Color3* colr)
{ // add colr to this color
  red += colr.red ; green += colr.green; blue += colr.blue;}

void Color3 :: build4tuple(float v[])
{// load 4-tuple with this color: v[3] = 1 for homogeneous
  v[0] = red; v[1] = green; v[2] = blue; v[3] = 1.0f;
}
//Affine4 methods
Affine4::Affine4(){ // make identity transform
 m[0] = m[5]  = m[10] = m[15] = 1.0;
```

```
      m[1] = m[2]  = m[3]  = m[4]  = 0.0;
      m[6] = m[7]  = m[8]  = m[9]  = 0.0;
      m[11]= m[12] = m[13] = m[14] = 0.0;
   }
void Affine4 :: setIdentityMatrix(){ // make identity transform
   m[0] = m[5]  = m[10] = m[15] = 1.0;
   m[1] = m[2]  = m[3]  = m[4]  = 0.0;
   m[6] = m[7]  = m[8]  = m[9]  = 0.0;
   m[11]= m[12] = m[13] = m[14] = 0.0;
   }
void Affine4 ::set(Affine4 a)// set this matrix to a
{
  for(int i = 0; i < 16; i++)
     m[i]=a.m[i];
}
//<<<<<<<<<<<<<<< preMult >>>>>>>>>>>>
void Affine4 ::preMult(Affine4 n)
{// postmultiplies this with n
   float sum;
   Affine4 tmp;
   tmp.set(*this); // tmp copy
   // following mult's : this = tmp * n
   for(int c = 0; c < 4; c++)
      for(int r = 0; r <4 ; r++)
      {
         sum = 0;
         for(int k = 0; k < 4; k++)
            sum += n.m[4 * k + r]* tmp.m[4 * c + k];
         m[4 * c + r] = sum;
      }// end of for loops
}// end of preMult()
//<<<<<<<<<<<<<< postMult >>>>>>>>>>>>
void Affine4 ::postMult(Affine4 n){// postmultiplies this with n
 float sum;
 Affine4 tmp;
 tmp.set(*this); // tmp copy
 for(int c = 0; c < 4; c++)// form this = tmp * n
    for(int r = 0; r <4 ; r++)
    {
       sum = 0;
       for(int k = 0; k < 4; k++)
          sum += tmp.m[4 * k + r]* n.m[4 * c + k];
       m[4 * c + r] = sum;
    }// end of for loops
}
// AffineStack methods
void AffineStack :: dup()
{
 AffineNode* tmp = new AffineNode;
 tmp->affn = new Affine4(*(tos->affn));
 tmp->invAffn = new Affine4(*(tos->invAffn));
 tmp->next = tos;
 tos = tmp;
}
void AffineStack :: setIdentity() // make top item the identity
matrix
```

```
{
 assert(tos != NULL);
 tos->affn->setIdentityMatrix();
 tos->invAffn->setIdentityMatrix();
}
void AffineStack :: popAndDrop()
{
 if(tos == NULL) return; // do nothing
 AffineNode *tmp = tos;
 tos = tos-[greater]next;
 delete tmp; // should call destructor, which deletes matrices
}
void AffineStack :: releaseAffines()
{ // pop and drop all remaining items
   while(tos) popAndDrop();
}
void AffineStack :: rotate(float angle, Vector3 u)
{
 Affine4 rm; // make identity matrix
 Affine4 invRm;
 u.normalize(); // make the rotation axis unit length
 float ang = angle * 3.14159265/ 180; // deg to
 float c = cos(ang), s = sin(ang);
 float mc = 1.0 - c;
    //fill the 3x3 upper left matrix -
 rm.m[0] = c + mc * u.x * u.x;
 rm.m[1] = mc * u.x * u.y + s * u.z;
 rm.m[2] = mc * u.x * u.z - s * u.y;
 rm.m[4] = mc * u.y * u.x - s * u.z;
 rm.m[5] = c + mc * u.y * u.y;
 rm.m[6] = mc * u.y * u.z + s * u.x;
 rm.m[8] = mc * u.z * u.x + s * u.y;
 rm.m[9] = mc * u.z * u.y - s * u.x;
 rm.m[10] = c + mc * u.z * u.z;
 // same for inverse: just sign of s is changed
 invRm.m[0] = c + mc * u.x * u.x;
 invRm.m[1] = mc * u.x * u.y - s * u.z;
 invRm.m[2] = mc * u.x * u.z + s * u.y;
 invRm.m[4] = mc * u.y * u.x + s * u.z;
 invRm.m[5] = c + mc * u.y * u.y;
 invRm.m[6] = mc * u.y * u.z - s * u.x;
 invRm.m[8] = mc * u.z * u.x - s * u.y;
 invRm.m[9] = mc * u.z * u.y + s * u.x;
 invRm.m[10] = c + mc * u.z * u.z;
 tos->affn->postMult(rm);
 tos->invAffn->preMult(invRm);
}
void AffineStack :: scale(float sx, float sy, float sz)
{ // post multiply top item by scaling
#define sEps 0.00001
 Affine4 scl;// make an identity
 Affine4 invScl;
 scl.m[0]  = sx;
 scl.m[5]  = sy;
 scl.m[10] = sz;// adjust it to a scaling matrix
 if(fabs(sx) < sEps || fabs(sy) < sEps || fabs(sz) < sEps)
```

```
        {
            cerr << "degenerate scaling transformation!\n";
        }
        invScl.m[0]  = 1/sx; invScl.m[5]  = 1/sy; invScl.m[10] = 1/sz;
        tos->affn->postMult(scl); //
        tos->invAffn->preMult(invScl);
    }
    void AffineStack :: translate(Vector3 d)
    {
        Affine4 tr; // make identity matrix
        Affine4 invTr;
        tr.m[12] = d.x; tr.m[13] = d.y; tr.m[14] = d.z;
        invTr.m[12] = -d.x; invTr.m[13] = -d.y; invTr.m[14] = -d.z;
        tos->affn->postMult(tr);
        tos->invAffn->preMult(invTr);
    }
    // Material methods
    void Material :: setDefault(){
        textureType = 0; // for none
        numParams = 0;
        reflectivity = transparency = 0.0;
        speedOfLight = specularExponent = 1.0;
        specularFraction = 0.0;
        surfaceRoughness = 1.0;
        ambient.set(0.1f,0.1f,0.1f);
        diffuse.set(0.8f,0.8f,0.8f);
        specular.set(0,0,0);
        emissive.set(0,0,0);
    }
    void Material :: set(Material& m)
    {
        textureType = m.textureType;
        numParams = m.numParams;
        for(int i = 0; i < numParams; i++) params[i] = m.params[i];
        transparency = m.transparency;
         speedOfLight = m.speedOfLight;
        reflectivity = m.reflectivity;
        specularExponent = m.specularExponent;
        specularFraction = m.specularFraction;
        surfaceRoughness = m.surfaceRoughness;
        ambient.set(m.ambient);
        diffuse.set(m.diffuse);
        specular.set(m.specular);
        emissive.set(m.emissive);
    }
    // Shape methods
    void Shape :: tellMaterialsGL()
    {
        float amb[4],diff[4],spec[4], emiss[4];
        float zero[] = {0,0,0,1};
        mtrl.ambient.build4tuple(amb); // fill the array
        mtrl.diffuse.build4tuple(diff);
        mtrl.specular.build4tuple(spec);
        mtrl.emissive.build4tuple(emiss);
        glMaterialfv(GL_FRONT/*_AND_BACK*/,GL_AMBIENT,amb);
        glMaterialfv(GL_FRONT/*_AND_BACK*/,GL_DIFFUSE,diff);
```

```
        glMaterialfv(GL_FRONT/*_AND_BACK*/,GL_SPECULAR,spec);
        glMaterialfv(GL_FRONT/*_AND_BACK*/,GL_EMISSION,emiss);

glMaterialf(GL_FRONT/*_AND_BACK*/,GL_SHININESS,mtrl.specularExpo
nent);
}
//Mesh methods
Mesh :: Mesh(){
        numVerts = numFaces = numNorms = 0;
        pt = NULL; norm  =  NULL; face = NULL;
        lastVertUsed = lastNormUsed = lastFaceUsed = -1;
}
void Mesh :: freeMesh()
{ // free up memory used by this mesh.
        delete [] pt; // release whole vertex list
        delete [] norm;
        for(int f = 0; f < numFaces; f++)
            delete[] face[f].vert; // delete the vert[] array of
this face
        delete [] face;
}
int Mesh :: isEmpty()
{
 return (numVerts == 0) || (numFaces == 0) || (numNorms == 0);
}
void Mesh :: makeEmpty()
{
 numVerts = numFaces = numNorms = 0;
}

void Mesh :: drawOpenGL()
{
        tellMaterialsGL();     glPushMatrix();
        glMultMatrixf(transf.m);
        drawMesh();
        //if(doEdges) drawEdges();
        glPopMatrix();
}
Mesh :: Mesh(string fname){ // read this file to build mesh
        numVerts = numFaces = numNorms = 0;
        pt = NULL; norm  =  NULL; face = NULL;
        lastVertUsed = lastNormUsed = lastFaceUsed = -1;
        readMesh(fname);
}
Vector3 Mesh :: newell4(int indx[])
{ /* return the normalized normal to face with vertices
  pt[indx[0]],...,pt[indx[3]]. i.e. indx[] contains the four
indices
   into the vertex list to be used in the Newell calculation */
        Vector3 m;
        for(int i = 0; i < 4 ; i++)
        {
            int next = (i== 3) ? 0 : i + 1; // which index is next?
            int f = indx[i], n = indx[next]; // names for the
                                             indices in the
pair
```

```
                m.x += (pt[f].y - pt[n].y) * (pt[f].z + pt[n].z);
                m.y += (pt[f].z - pt[n].z) * (pt[f].x + pt[n].x);
                m.z += (pt[f].x - pt[n].x) * (pt[f].y + pt[n].y);
            }
        m.normalize();
        return m;
}
//<<<<<<<<<<<<<<<<<<<<<<<<<<<<< readMesh >>>>>>>>>>>>>>>>>>>>>>>>>
void Mesh:: readMesh(string fname)
{
 fstream inStream;
 inStream.open(fname.c_str(), ios ::in); //open needs a c-like
string
 if(inStream.fail() || inStream.eof())
 {
    cout << "can't open file or eof: " << fname << endl;
    makeEmpty();return;
 }
 inStream >> numVerts >> numNorms >> numFaces;
 // make arrays for vertices, normals, and faces
 pt = new Point3[numVerts];          assert(pt != NULL);
 norm = new Vector3[numNorms];       assert(norm != NULL);
 face = new Face[numFaces];          assert(face != NULL);
 for(int i = 0; i < numVerts; i++) // read in the vertices
    inStream >> pt[i].x >> pt[i].y >> pt[i].z;
 for(int ii = 0; ii < numNorms; ii++)  // read in the normals
    inStream >> norm[ii].x >> norm[ii].y >> norm[ii].z;
 for(int f = 0; f < numFaces; f++)   // read in face data
 {
    inStream >> face[f].nVerts;
    int n = face[f].nVerts;
    face[f].vert = new VertexID[n]; assert(face[f].vert !=
NULL);
    for(int k = 0; k < n; k++)        // read vertex indices for
this face
        inStream >> face[f].vert[k].vertIndex;
    for(int kk = 0; kk < n; kk++)               // read normal
indices for this face
        inStream >> face[f].vert[kk].normIndex;
 }
 inStream.close();
} // end of readMesh
//<<<<<<<<<<<<<<<<<<<<<<< drawMesh >>>>>>>>>>>>>>>>>>>>>
void Mesh :: drawMesh()
{ // draw each face of this mesh using OpenGL: draw each
polygon.
 if(isEmpty()) return; // mesh is empty
 for(int f = 0; f < numFaces; f++)
 {
    int n = face[f].nVerts;
    glBegin(GL_POLYGON);
    for(int v = 0; v < n; v++)
    {
        int in = face[f].vert[v].normIndex;
        assert(in >= 0 && in < numNorms);
        glNormal3f(norm[in].x, norm[in].y, norm[in].z);
```

```
        int iv = face[f].vert[v].vertIndex; assert(iv >= 0 && iv
< numVerts);
        glVertex3f(pt[iv].x, pt[iv].y, pt[iv].z);
     }
    glEnd();
 }
 glFlush();
}
//<<<<<<<<<<<<<<<<<<<<<<<<<<<<< write
mesh>>>>>>>>>>>>>>>>>>>>>>>>>>>>>>>>>
void Mesh:: writeMesh(char * fname)
{ // write this mesh object into a new Chapter 6 format file.
  if(numVerts == 0 || numNorms   == 0 || numFaces == 0) return;
//empty
  fstream outStream(fname, ios ::out); // open the output stream
  if(outStream.fail()) {cout << "can't make new file: " << fname
<< endl;
  return;}
  outStream << numVerts << " " << numNorms << " " << numFaces <<
"\n";
  // write the vertex and vertex normal list
  for(int i = 0; i < numVerts; i++)
     outStream << pt[i].x   << " " << pt[i].y   << " " <<
pt[i].z << "\n";
  for(int ii = 0; ii < numNorms; ii++)
     outStream  << norm[ii].x << " " << norm[ii].y << " " <<
norm[ii].z <<
 "\n";
 // write the face data
 for(int f = 0; f < numFaces; f++)
 {
    int n = face[f].nVerts;
    outStream << n << "\n";
    for(int v = 0; v < n; v++)// write vertex indices for this
face
       outStream << face[f].vert[v].vertIndex << " "; outStream
<< "\n";
    for(int k = 0; k < n; k++)    // write normal indices for
this face
       outStream << face[f].vert[k].normIndex << " "; outStream
<< "\n";
 }
 outStream.close();
}
// Scene methods
//<<<<<<<< methods >>>>>>>>>>
string Scene :: nexttoken(void) //########## nexttoken()
{
 char c;
 string token;
 int lastchar = 1;
 if (!f_in) {return(token); }
 if (f_in->eof()) {return(token);}
 while (f_in->get(c))
 {
    if (f_in->eof()) {
```

```
                                 return(token);
                             }
                         switch (c) {
                         case '\n': nextline += 1;
                         case ' ' :
                         case '\t':
                         case '\a':
                         case '\b':
                         case '\v':
                         case '\f':
                         case '\r': {
                             if ( lastchar == 0 ) {return(token);}break; }
                         case '{': {
                             token = c; return(token); break;}
                         case '}': {
                             token = c;
                             return(token);
                             break; }
                         case '!': {
                             while ( c != '\n' && f_in->get(c)) {
                             }
                             nextline++; break;}
                         default: {
                             token = token + c;
                             lastchar = 0;
                             if ((f_in->peek() == '{') ||
                                 (f_in->peek() == '}') ) {
                                 if ( lastchar == 0 ) {
                                     return(token);
                                 } else {
                                     f_in->get(c);
                                     token = c;
                                     return(token);
                                 }
                             }
                             line = nextline;
                                 }
                     }
                 }
     return(" ");
 }
//<<<<<<<<<<<<<< getFloat >>>>>>>>>>>>>>>
float Scene :: getFloat() //############## getFloat()
{
 strstream tmp;
 float number;
 string str = nexttoken();
 tmp << str;
 if(!(tmp >> number))
 {
     cerr << "Line " << line << ": error getting float" << endl;
     exit(-1);
 }
 else
 {
     char t;
```

```
      if ( (tmp >> t ) )
      {
          cerr << "Line " << line << ": bum chars in number" <<
endl;
          exit(-1);
      }
  }
  return number;
}
//<<<<<<<<<<<<<<<<< isidentifier >>>>>>>>>>>>>>>>>
bool Scene :: isidentifier(string keyword) { //#########
isidentifier
  string temp = keyword;
  if (!isalpha(temp[0])) return(false);
  for (int count = 1; count < temp.length(); count++) {
      if ((!isalnum(temp[count]))&& (temp[count]!='.'))
return(false);
  }
  return(true);
}
//<<<<<<<<<<<<<<<<< cleanUp >>>>>>>>>>>>>>>>>
void Scene :: cleanUp() //######### cleanUp
{ // release stuff after parsing file
  affStk.releaseAffines();          //delete affine stack
  def_stack->release();
  delete def_stack; // release the DefUnitStack memory
}
//<<<<<<<<<<<<<<<<< freeScene >>>>>>>>>>>>>>>
void Scene :: freeScene()
{ // release the object and light lists
  GeomObj *p = obj;
  while(p)
  {
    GeomObj* q = p;
    p = p->next;
    delete q;
  }
  Light * q = light;
  while(q)
  {
    Light* r = q;
    q = q->next;
    delete r;
  }
}
//<<<<<<<<<<<<<<<<< whichToken >>>>>>>>>>>>>>>>>
mTokenType Scene :: whichtoken(string keyword)
{
  string temp = keyword;
  if ( temp == "light" )            return LIGHT;
  if ( temp == "rotate" )           return ROTATE;
  if ( temp == "translate" )        return TRANSLATE;
  if ( temp == "scale")             return (SCALE);
  if ( temp == "push")              return (PUSH);
  if ( temp == "pop")               return (POP);
  if ( temp == "identityAffine")    return (IDENTITYAFFINE);
```

```cpp
    if ( temp == "cube")                        return (CUBE);
    if ( temp == "sphere")                      return (SPHERE);
    if ( temp == "torus")                       return (TORUS);
    if ( temp == "plane")                       return (PLANE);
    if ( temp == "square")                      return (SQUARE);
    if ( temp == "cylinder")                    return (CYLINDER);
    if ( temp == "taperedCylinder")             return (TAPEREDCYLINDER);
    if ( temp == "cone")                        return (CONE);
    if ( temp == "tetrahedron")                 return (TETRAHEDRON);
    if ( temp == "octahedron")                  return (OCTAHEDRON);
    if ( temp == "dodecahedron")                return (DODECAHEDRON);
    if ( temp == "icosahedron")                 return (ICOSAHEDRON);
    if ( temp == "buckyball")                   return (BUCKYBALL);
    if ( temp == "diamond")                     return (DIAMOND);
    if ( temp == "teapot")                      return (TEAPOT);
    if ( temp == "union")                       return (UNION);
    if ( temp == "intersection")                return (INTERSECTION);
    if ( temp == "difference")                  return (DIFFERENCEa);
    if ( temp == "mesh")                        return (MESH);
    if ( temp == "makePixmap")                  return (MAKEPIXMAP);
    if ( temp == "defaultMaterials")            return (DEFAULTMATERIALS);
    if ( temp == "ambient")                     return (AMBIENT);
    if ( temp == "diffuse")                     return (DIFFUSE);
    if ( temp == "specular")                    return (SPECULAR);
    if ( temp == "specularFraction")            return (SPECULARFRACTION);
    if ( temp == "surfaceRoughness")            return (SURFACEROUGHNESS);
    if ( temp == "emissive")                    return (EMISSIVE);
    if ( temp == "specularExponent")            return (SPECULAREXPONENT);
    if ( temp == "speedOfLight")                return (SPEEDOFLIGHT);
    if ( temp == "transparency")                return (TRANSPARENCY);
    if ( temp == "reflectivity")                return (REFLECTIVITY);
    if ( temp == "parameters")                  return (PARAMETERS);
    if ( temp == "texture")                     return (TEXTURE);
    if ( temp == "globalAmbient")               return (GLOBALAMBIENT);
    if ( temp == "minReflectivity")             return (MINREFLECTIVITY);
    if ( temp == "minTransparency")             return (MINTRANSPARENCY);
    if ( temp == "maxRecursionDepth")           return (MAXRECURSIONDEPTH);
    if ( temp == "background")                  return (BACKGROUND);
    if ( temp == "{")                           return (LFTCURLY);
    if ( temp == "}")                           return (RGHTCURLY);
    if ( temp == "def")                         return (DEF);
    if ( temp == "use")                         return (USE);
    if ( temp == " " )                          return (T_NULL);
    if ( isidentifier(temp) )                   return (IDENT);
    cout << temp << ":" << temp.length() << endl;
    return(UNKNOWN);
} // end of whichtoken
//<<<<<<<<<<   drawSceneOpenGL >>>>>>>>>>>>>>>.
void Scene :: drawSceneOpenGL()
{ //draw each object on object list
        for(GeomObj* p = obj; p ; p = p->next)
            p->drawOpenGL(); //draw it
}
//<<<<<<<<<<<<<<< Scene :: read >>>>>>>>>>>>>>
bool Scene:: read(string fname)// return true if ok; else false
{
```

```
file_in = new ifstream(fname.c_str());
if(!(*file_in))
{
   cout << "I can't find or open file: " << fname << endl;
   return false;
}
f_in = new strstream();
line = nextline = 1;
def_stack = new DefUnitStack();
char ch;
freeScene(); //delete any previous scene
// initialize all for reading:
obj = tail = NULL;
light = NULL;
affStk.tos = new AffineNode;
affStk.tos->next = NULL;
while (file_in->get(ch)) {*f_in << ch;} // read whole file
while(1) //read file, collecting objects, until EOF or an error
{
 GeomObj * shp = getObject(); // get the next shape
 if(!shp) break; // no object: either error or EOF
 shp->next = NULL; // to be safe
 if(obj == NULL){ obj = tail = shp;} // empty list so far
 else{tail->next = shp; tail = shp;} // add new object to queue
}
 file_in->close();
 cleanUp(); // delete temp lists, etc.
 return true;
} // end of read()
//<<<<<<<<<<<<<<< Scene :: getObject >>>>>>>>>>>>>>>
GeomObj* Scene :: getObject()
{ //reads tokens from stream f_in (a data member of Scene),
 // building lights, getting materials, doing transformations,
 // until it finds a new object
 // returns NULL if any error occurs, or end of file
 string s;
 GeomObj * newShape;
 mTokenType typ;
 while ((typ = (whichtoken( s = nexttoken() ))) != T_NULL)
 {
   if(typ == UNION || typ == INTERSECTION || typ == DIFFERENCEa)
   {
     switch(typ)
      {
     case UNION:          newShape = new UnionBool(); break;
     case INTERSECTION: newShape = new IntersectionBool(); break;
     case DIFFERENCEa:  newShape = new DifferenceBool();break;
       } // end of little switch
     GeomObj* p = newShape;
     p = getObject(); // get left child
     if(!p) return NULL; // Error! should always get an object
     ((Boolean*)newShape)->left  = p; // hook it up
     p = getObject();// get right child
     if(!p) return NULL;
     ((Boolean*)newShape)->right = p; // hook it up
     return newShape;
```

```
}// end of if(typ == UNION etc....
switch(typ)
{
case LIGHT: {
    Point3 p;
    Color3 c;
    p.x = getFloat(); p.y = getFloat();     p.z = getFloat();
    c.red = getFloat(); c.green = getFloat();     c.blue =
        getFloat();
    Light *l = new Light;
    l->setPosition(p);
    l->setColor(c);
    l->next = light; //put it on the list
    light = l; break;}
case ROTATE: {
    float angle;
    Vector3 u;
    angle = getFloat(); u.x = getFloat();
    u.y = getFloat(); u.z = getFloat();
    affStk.rotate(angle,u);break;}
case TRANSLATE: {
    Vector3 d;
    d.x = getFloat(); d.y = getFloat(); d.z = getFloat();
    affStk.translate(d);break;}
case SCALE: {
    float sx, sy, sz;
    sx = getFloat(); sy = getFloat(); sz = getFloat();
    affStk.scale(sx, sy, sz);break;}
case PUSH: affStk.dup(); break;
case POP:  affStk.popAndDrop(); break;
case IDENTITYAFFINE: affStk.setIdentity();break;
case AMBIENT: {
    float dr, dg, db;
    dr = getFloat(); dg = getFloat(); db = getFloat();
    currMtrl.ambient.set(dr,dg,db); break;}
case DIFFUSE: {
    float dr,dg,db;
    dr = getFloat(); dg = getFloat(); db = getFloat();
    currMtrl.diffuse.set(dr,dg,db); break;}
case SPECULAR:{
    float dr,dg,db;
    dr = getFloat(); dg = getFloat(); db = getFloat();
    currMtrl.specular.set(dr,dg,db); break;}
case EMISSIVE: {
    float dr,dg,db;
    dr = getFloat(); dg = getFloat(); db = getFloat();
    currMtrl.emissive.set(dr,dg,db); break;}
case PARAMETERS: { // get a list of numParams parameters
    currMtrl.numParams = (int)getFloat();
    for(int i = 0; i < currMtrl.numParams; i++)
        currMtrl.params[i] = getFloat();
    break;}
case SPECULARFRACTION: currMtrl.specularFraction =
getFloat(); break;
case SURFACEROUGHNESS: currMtrl.surfaceRoughness =
getFloat(); break;
```

```
    case TEXTURE: {  // get type, 0 for none
       currMtrl.textureType = getFloat();}
       break;
    case DEFAULTMATERIALS:  currMtrl.setDefault();break;
    case SPEEDOFLIGHT: currMtrl.speedOfLight = getFloat(); break;
    case SPECULAREXPONENT: currMtrl.specularExponent =
getFloat(); break;
    case TRANSPARENCY:currMtrl.transparency = getFloat(); break;
    case REFLECTIVITY: currMtrl.reflectivity = getFloat(); break;
    case GLOBALAMBIENT:
       ambient.red = getFloat(); ambient.green = getFloat();
       ambient.blue = getFloat(); break;
    case BACKGROUND:
       background.red = getFloat();
       background.green = getFloat();
       background.blue = getFloat();break;
    case MINREFLECTIVITY: minReflectivity = getFloat(); break;
    case MINTRANSPARENCY:minTransparency = getFloat(); break;
    case MAXRECURSIONDEPTH: maxRecursionDepth = getFloat();
break;
    case MAKEPIXMAP: {  // get BMP file name for a pix map
         /* to be implemented, along the lines:
         int which = getFloat();// index of this pix map in pix
map array
         if(which < 0 || which > 7){cout << "\nbad index of
RGBpixmap!\n";}
         string fname = nexttoken(); // get file name for mesh
         cout << "I got fname = " << fname << endl;
         if(!pixmap[which].readBMPFile(fname))
         {// read BMP file into this pix map
         cout << " \ncan't read that RGBpixmap file!\n";
    return NULL;  }  */
    break;}// end of case: MAKEPIXMAP
    case T_NULL: break; // The null token represents end-of-file
    case DEF: {
       string name, temp, lb, rb;
       int l = line;
       string inp;
       name = nexttoken();
       if ( whichtoken(name) != IDENT ) {
          cout << "Error:  Identifier expected." << endl;
          return NULL;
       }
       if ( def_stack->search(name) ) {
          cout << line << ": " << name;
          cout << ": attempt to redefine. " << endl;
          return NULL;
       }
       lb = nexttoken();
       if ( whichtoken(lb) != LFTCURLY ) {
          cout << "Error: { expected." << endl;
          return NULL;
       }
       while ( whichtoken( temp = nexttoken()) != RGHTCURLY ) {
          cout << temp << endl;
          inp = inp + temp + " ";
```

```
                        if (!f_in) {
                           cout << "Error: end of file detected." << endl;
                           return NULL;
                        }
                     }
                     // Push the contents of the string onto the stack.
                     def_stack->push(name, inp);
                     break;} // end of case: DEF
                     case USE: {
                        string name;
                        name = nexttoken();
                        if ( whichtoken(name) != IDENT ) {
                           cout << line << ": " << name;
                           cout << ": identifier expected.";
                           return NULL;
                        }
                     if (! def_stack->search(name) ) {
                        cout << line << ": " << name;
                        cout << ": not defined.";
                        return NULL;
                     }

                        cout << def_stack->contents(name) << endl;
                        strstream *temp_fin = new strstream;
                        *temp_fin << def_stack->contents(name) << " ";
                        *temp_fin << f_in->rdbuf();
                        delete (f_in);
                        f_in = temp_fin;
                        break; } // end of case: USE
                     default:  { // inner switch for Shapes
                        switch(typ)
                        {
                        case CUBE: newShape = new Cube;break;
                        case SPHERE:        newShape = new Sphere;break;
                        case TETRAHEDRON: newShape = new Mesh("tetra.3vn");break;
                        case TORUS:         newShape = new Torus;break;
                        case PLANE:         newShape = new Plane;break;
                        case SQUARE:        newShape = new Square;break;
                        case TAPEREDCYLINDER:  newShape = new TaperedCylinder;
                           ((TaperedCylinder*)newShape)->smallRadius =
                              getFloat(); break;
                        case CONE: newShape = new TaperedCylinder;
                           ((TaperedCylinder*)newShape)->smallRadius = 0; break;
                        case CYLINDER:      newShape = new TaperedCylinder;
                           ((TaperedCylinder*)newShape)->smallRadius = 1; break;
                        case OCTAHEDRON:  newShape = new Mesh("octa.3vn");break;
                        case DODECAHEDRON:newShape = new Mesh("dodeca.3vn");
break;
                        case ICOSAHEDRON:newShape = new Mesh("icosa.3vn"); break;
                        case BUCKYBALL:  newShape = new Mesh("bucky.3vn"); break;
                        case DIAMOND:  newShape = new Mesh("diamond.3vn"); break;
                        case TEAPOT:   newShape = new Teapot; break;
                        case MESH: {// get a filename (with extension) for this
mesh
                           string fname = nexttoken(); // get file name for mesh
                           newShape = new Mesh(fname); break;
                                   }// end of case: MESH
```

```
                default: {
                    cerr << "Line " << nextline << ": unknown keyword "
                        << s << endl;
                    return NULL;
                        }
            } // end of inner switch
            // common things to do to all Shape's
            ((Shape*)newShape)->mtrl.set(currMtrl);
            // load transform and its inverse
            ((Shape*)newShape)->transf.set(*(affStk.tos->affn));
            ((Shape*)newShape)->invTransf.set(*(affStk.tos-
>invAffn));
            return newShape;
                    }// end of default: block
        } // end of outer switch
    } // end of while
    return NULL;
} // end of getObject
// DefUnitStack methods
void DefUnitStack :: push(string n, string s) {
 D4S *temp_d4s = new D4S;
 temp_d4s->current = new DefUnit(n, s);
 temp_d4s->next = stack;
 stack = temp_d4s;
}
void DefUnitStack :: print() {
 D4S *temp = stack;
 string t;
 while (temp) {
    cout << temp->current->name << ":" ;
    cout << temp->current->stuff << endl;
    temp = temp->next;
 }
}
int DefUnitStack :: search(string s) {
 D4S *temp = stack;
 while (temp) {
    if ( temp->current->name == s ) {
        return(1);
    }
    temp = temp->next;
 }
 return(0);
}
string DefUnitStack :: contents(string s) {
 D4S *temp = stack;
 while (temp) {
    if (temp->current->name == s ) {
        return(temp->current->stuff);
    }
    temp = temp->next;
 }
 return(NULL);
}
void DefUnitStack :: release()
{
```

```
    while(stack)
    {
        D4S* tmp = stack; // grab it
        //cerr << "releasing def_stack item: "<< tmp->current-
>name<< endl;
        stack = stack->next; // advance p
        delete tmp->current; // release 2 strings
        delete tmp; // release node
    }
    stack = NULL;
}
// end of SDL.cpp
```

NOISE CLASS

```
//Noise.h
// Noise class for generating pseudorandom noise fields
//based on noise lattice a la Peachey/Perlin
#include <assert.h>

class Noise{
public:
 Noise()//construct a noise object
 {
    int i;
    index = new unsigned char[256]; assert(index);
    for(i = 0; i < 256; i++) index[i] = i;//fill array with
        indices
    for(i = 0; i < 256; i++) // shuffle it
    {
        int which = rand() % 256; // choose random place in array
        unsigned char tmp = index[which]; // swap them
        index[which] = index[i];
        index[i] = tmp;
    }
    noiseTable = new float[256]; assert(noiseTable);
    for(i = 0; i < 256; i++) noiseTable[i] = rand()/32767.99;
 } // end of constructor
 float noise(float scale, Point3& p)
 { // linearly interpolated lattice noise
    #define lerp(f, A, B) A + f * (B - A)
    float d[2][2][2];
    Point3 pp;
    pp.x = p.x * scale + 10000; //offset avoids negative values
    pp.y = p.y * scale + 10000;
    pp.z = p.z * scale + 10000;
    long ix = (long)pp.x; long iy = (long)pp.y; long iz =
        (long)pp.z;
    float tx,ty,tz, x0,x1,x2,x3, y0,y1;
    tx = pp.x - ix; ty = pp.y - iy; tz = pp.z - iz; //
        fractional parts
    float mtx = 1.0 - tx, mty = 1.0 - ty, mtz = 1.0 - tz;
    for(int k = 0; k <= 1; k++) // get noise at 8 lattice points
    for(int j = 0; j <= 1; j++)
    for(int i = 0; i <= 1; i++)
```

```
              d[k][j][i] = latticeNoise(ix + i, iy + j,iz + k);
       x0 = lerp(tx, d[0][0][0],d[0][0][1]);
       x1 = lerp(tx, d[0][1][0],d[0][1][1]);
       x2 = lerp(tx, d[1][0][0],d[1][0][1]);
       x3 = lerp(tx, d[1][1][0],d[1][1][1]);
       y0 = lerp(ty, x0, x1);
       y1 = lerp(ty, x2, x3);
       return lerp(tz, y0, y1);
    }
    float turbulence(float s, Point3& p)
    {
       float val = noise(s    , p) / 2 +
                   noise(s * 2, p) / 4 +
                   noise(s * 4, p) / 8 +
                   noise(s * 8, p) / 16;
       return val;
    }
    float marble(float strength,Point3& p)
    {
       float turbul = turbulence(10, p);
       float val = sin(6 * p.z + strength * turbul);
       return mySpline(val);
    }
float gauss()
{ // Add up 12 independent noise samples. Sum is Gaussian
  // with mean zero and variance 1.0.
  float sum = 0;
  for(int i = 0; i < 12; i++)
     sum += noise();
  return sum - 6.0;
}
private:
 float* noiseTable; // array of noise values
 unsigned char * index; //Pseudorandom indices
 float mySpline(float x) // used for marble
 {
    if(x <-0.4) return 0.15 +  2.857 * SQR(x + 0.75);
    else if(x < 0.4) return 0.95 - 2.8125 * SQR(x);
    else return 0.26 + 2.666 * SQR(x - 0.7);
 }
 float latticeNoise(int i, int j, int k)
 { // return PR noise value on an integer lattice
    #define PERM(x) index[(x) & 255]
    #define INDEX(ix, iy, iz) PERM( (ix) + PERM((iy) + PERM(iz))
)
    return noiseTable[INDEX(i,j,k)];
 }
}; // end of Noise class
```

SOME CLASSES THAT ARE USEFUL IN RAY TRACING

```
//@@@@@@@@@@@@@@@@@@@@@ PointCluster class @@@@@@@@@@@@@@@@@@@@
class PointCluster{
public: // holds array of points for the bounding hull of a
shape
```

```
      int num;
      Point3* pt;
      PointCluster() {num = 0; pt = NULL;}
      PointCluster(int n)// make a cluster of n points
      {
          pt = new Point3[n]; assert(pt);
          num = n;
      }
};
//@@@@@@@@@@@@@@@@@@@@@@@ SphereInfo @@@@@@@@@@@@@@@@@@@@
class SphereInfo{// holds the center and radius of a sphere
public:
   Point3 center;
   float radSq;
   void set(float x, float y, float z, float rsq)
   {
       center.set(x,y,z);
       radSq = rsq;
   }
};
//@@@@@@@@@@@@@@@@@@@@@@@@@ Cuboid @@@@@@@@@@@@@@@@@@@@@@@@@
class Cuboid{ // holds six border values of a cuboid
public:
   float left, top, right, bott, front, back;
   void set(float l, float t, float r, float b, float f, float bk)
   {
       left = l; top = t; right = r; bott = b; front = f; back =
bk;}
   void set(Cuboid& c)
   {
       left = c.left;top = c.top; right = c.right; bott = c.bott;
       front = c.front; back = c.back;
   }
};


//@@@@@@@@@@@@@@@@@@@@@@ Ray @@@@@@@@@@@@@@@@@@@@@@@@@@@@@
class Ray{
public:
   Point3 start;
   Vector3 dir;
   int recurseLevel;
   int row, col; // for screen extents
   int numInside; // number of objects on list
   GeomObj* inside[10]; // array of object pointers

   Ray(){start.set(0,0,0); dir.set(0,0,0); numInside = 0;}
   Ray(Point3 origin); //constructor: set start point of ray
   Ray(Point3& origin, Vector3& direction)
       { start.set(origin); dir.set(direction); numInside = 0;}
   void setStart(Point3& p){start.set(p);}
   void setDir(float x, float y, float z)
   {dir.x = x; dir.y = y; dir.z = z;}
   void setRayDirection(Light *L); //for shadow feelers
   void setRayDirection(Vector3& dir); //for spawned rays
   int isInShadow();
   void makeGenericRay(GeomObj* p, Ray& gr);
};
```

```
//@@@@@@@@@@@@@@@@@@@ HitInfo @@@@@@@@@@@@@@@@@@@@@@
class HitInfo { // data for each hit with a surface
 public:
 double hitTime;            // the hit time
 GeomObj* hitObject;  // the object hit
 int surface;                  // which surface is hit?
 int isEntering;              // is ray entering the object?
 Point3 hitPoint;          // hit point
 Vector3 hitNormal;// normal at hit point
 HitInfo()
 {
    hitObject = NULL; hitTime = -1000; surface = 0; isEntering =
0;
 }  void set(HitInfo& h)
 {
    hitTime = h.hitTime; hitObject = h.hitObject;
    surface = h.surface; isEntering = h.isEntering;
    hitPoint.set(h.hitPoint); hitNormal.set(h.hitNormal);
 }
};


//@@@@@@@@@@@@@@@@@@ Intersection @@@@@@@@@@@@@@@@@@@@@@@@
class Intersection{ // hold the hit list
 public:
 #define maxNumHits 8
 int numHits;                // the number of hits
 HitInfo hit[maxNumHits];    // list of hits;
 Intersection(){numHits = 0;}  // default constructor
 void set(Intersection& intr)
 { // copy intersection info
    numHits = intr.numHits;
    for(int i = 0; i < maxNumHits; i++)
       hit[i].set(intr.hit[i]);
 }
};
```

APPENDIX

4

An Introduction to PostScript®

POSTSCRIPT® is known as a "page description" programming language, because it is commonly used to specify how a page should be printed. A POSTSCRIPT script is a sequence of commands in the POSTSCRIPT language. Many popular word processors send a formatted document to a printer in the form of such a script. The script is sent to a printer, where an on board POSTSCRIPT interpreter processes each command in turn. The interpreter determines precisely which dots on the page to set to various colors (usually black and shades of gray) in order to fashion the desired image, and the printer then "lays down the ink" on the page according to this pattern of dots. The POSTSCRIPT interpreter is very powerful and can draw a rich variety of shapes. For instance, given the command to draw the letter 'G,' it uses mathematical formulas to determine the shape of the contour for 'G' in the current typeface and then fills in the contour with black.

An important feature of POSTSCRIPT is its device independence. This means that a given script can be sent to a variety of different display devices and the same picture will be rendered, but each one at the highest resolution available on that device.

In this appendix we introduce the POSTSCRIPT language and show how it can be used to make high quality drawings. Learning and experimenting with POSTSCRIPT can fit nicely within a graphics course[1]: The POSTSCRIPT API provides a very different approach to graphics programming than that of OpenGL, yet there are important parallels between them, particularly in the area of coordinate transformations. And the student acquires a simple programming tool for creating intricate and detailed drawings of very high quality.

The usual way to work with POSTSCRIPT is to use a text processor to fashion a POSTSCRIPT script, and then to submit the file to a POSTSCRIPT printer. The printer can be set to interpret the script and make a picture rather than simply print the script as text.

Programs such as Ghostscript provide a convenient alternative. Ghostscript is freely available and operates on a variety of PC and workstation platforms[2]. Ghostscript interprets a POSTSCRIPT script and displays the picture on the PC monitor. This can make debugging a script much easier, since you immediately see the results of a script without the need for printing.

The following example POSTSCRIPT script draws a box one inch on a side near the center of an 8 1/2-by-11-inch page (everything from '%' to the end of the line is a comment and is ignored by the interpreter):

---

[1] Various examples and projects may be found on the book's Internet site. Also, a PostScript Language Reference manual is available at *http://partners.adobe.com/asn/developer/technotes.html,* and a tutorial in PostScript is availabe at *http://www.cs.indiana.edu/docproject/programming/postsscript/postscript/html*

[2] Ghostscript is available at *http://www.cs.wisc.edu./~*ghost/. Also see the book's Internet site.

```
300 300 moveto    % move to the center of the page
372 300 lineto    % draw across to the bottom right corner
372 372 lineto    % draw upwards to the top right corner
300 372 lineto    % draw to the top left corner
closepath         % draw to the starting point
stroke            % lay "ink" on the path just described
showpage          % print the page and eject it from the printer
```

The numerical values used here might be obscure at this point, but some of the operators, such as `moveto` and `lineto`, should be familiar. Note that each command appears *after* its parameters. This is called **postfix notation** (sometimes "reverse Polish" notation, after its inventor, the Polish mathematician Ján Lukasiewicz). It's like writing `3 4 *` rather than `3 * 4`, or `5.0 sqrt` rather than `sqrt(5.0)`. The name POSTSCRIPT is partly a pun on the usage of postfix notation.

There are several advantages to using postfix notation, as we shall see. One is that parentheses are never needed to group parts of a mathematical expression. (POST-SCRIPT can therefore attach a meaning different, from the usual one to the use of parentheses.) Also, expressions generally are shorter in postfix form. In addition, Postfix encourages you to think in terms of objects arranged in a "stack." Many people become comfortable with this mental model of the process underlying mathematical operations and find it much easier to keep track of calculational details in this way.

A4.1 ABOUT THE POSTSCRIPT LANGUAGE

Scripts in POSTSCRIPT are readable by humans; that is, they contain only "printable" characters and attach no significance to others like `escape` or `control-G`. This makes scripts easy to type in and edit. It also facilitates sending POSTSCRIPT files over a network, where certain control characters could otherwise disrupt the flow.

A4.1.1 Some Preliminaries

Different characters appearing in a script take on different meanings. We start with some simple rules.

Comments. All characters from '%' to the end of the current line are comments and are ignored by the interpreter. They are treated as exactly one space.

Case. Case is significant, so `cos`, `COS`, and `Cos` are unrelated.

White space. Characters such as spaces, tabs, or newlines (i.e., the carriage return) leave spaces on the script page, and are collectively called "white space." White space is used to separate objects. One or more white-space characters together are equivalent to a single space. Thus,

```
24 16 moveto
```

is equivalent to

```
24
16          moveto
```

The character '\' immediately followed by a newline (i.e., type \ and then a carriage return) is ignored by the interpreter, so `24 16 moveto` is identical to

```
24 16 mov\
eto
```

This feature allows you to continue a long POSTSCRIPT line to the next physical line in the script.

Numbers in PostScript

Numbers are written in the usual way, either with or without a decimal point. For example, 123 and −98 are (decimal) integers, whereas −002, −3.62, and 123.65e12 are real (floating-point) numbers. (The notation e 12 denotes 10 raised to the 12th power.)

A4.1.2 PostScript Is "Stack based"

PostScript is similar to the language Forth[3] in that it maintains a stack of objects called the **operand stack**. Recall that a stack is a list of objects that you promise to alter only at one end, known as the "top" of the stack. You can only **push** a new object onto the top of the stack or **pop** the top object off the stack. The classic push-down, pop-up metaphor is a stack of trays in a cafeteria: You can put a tray onto the top of the pile, and you can remove the top tray. A stack is often called a *last-in, first-out* data structure: Whatever object was last (most recently) pushed onto the stack is always the first object that is later popped off the stack.

The PostScript interpreter maintains several data structures in its internal memory. Most commands in a script operate on the operand stack, which can contain numbers, procedures, arrays, and other types of objects. To push a number onto the operand stack, a script simply states the number. The fragment

```
34 -5.2    % push 34 then -5.2 onto the stack
12         % push 12 on top
```

first pushes 34 onto the stack, then pushes −5.2 on top of the 34, and finally pushes 12 on top of that. Figure A4.1 shows the stack like a classic stack of cafeteria trays: As each item is placed on top, it pushes the other items further down.

FIGURE A4.1 The operand stack after each number is entered.

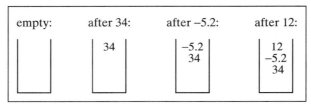

We use an easier notation to display what is on the stack after a given operation: The stack is shown "on its side" with the top item on the right. Thus, the sequence of pushes shown in Figure A4.1 is displayed as follows:

```
<empty>              (meaning the stack is empty)
34
34       -5.2
34       -5.2    12
```

A4.1.3 Some Stack Operators: `pop`, `dup`, `exch`, and `clear`

There are several PostScript operators, or "verbs," that manipulate the stack in simple ways. For instance, `pop` removes the top item (and discards it), so the sequence:

```
34 -5.2 12 pop
```

leaves the stack in the state 34   -5.2.

We will use an arrow (→) as shorthand for "leaves the stack in the state," so we can describe `pop` with the line

---

[3] See, for example, *http://www.engin.umd.umich.edu/CIS/course.des/cis400/forth/forth.html* and Brodie, Leo/Forth, INC., *Starting FORTH*, 2d ed. (Engleuood Cliffs, NJ: Prentice-Hall, 1987).

34 -5.2 12 pop → 34 -5.2

It is more concise to omit showing items that are deeper in the stack and that are un-affected by the operator in quesiton (e.g., 34 and -5.2), so we would describe pop by

12 pop → —

where the '—' doesn't mean that the stack is necessarily empty at this point, just that the item that was on top has gone.

The operator dup replicates the top element:

12 dup → 12   12

exch exchanges the top two items:

-5.2 12 exch → 12   -5.2

And clear empties out the stack:

34   -5.2   12 clear → <empty>

You might rightfully argue that dup, exch, and clear violate the spirit of a true stack, in that they do more than just push or pop. (dup, for instance, must "look at" what's at the top of the stack in order to duplicate it.) This is true, but these opera-tors are so useful that POSTSCRIPT takes some poetic license and provides them.

A4.1.4 More Advanced Stack Operators

A number of additional operators that also go beyond a simple push or pop, are often useful. They can be skipped on a first reading.

n index pops the n, counts down n items into the stack (counting the top item as the zeroth), and pushes a copy of the nth item on to the stack:

34 12 94 2 index → 34 12 94 34
6 0 index → 6   6   % same as   dup

n   copy pops the n and then pushes a copy of the top n elements of the stack:

12 6 2 copy → 12 6 12 6
12 95 23 3 copy → 12 95 23 12 95 23

num shifts roll pops shifts and num, and then does a circular shift of the top num elements shifts times (positive shifts indicates upward motion on the stack; negative shifts indicates downward motion):

-3 144 78 3 1 roll   → 78   -3   144
-3 144 78 3 -1 roll   → 144   78   -3
23 12 -3 144 78 4 -2 roll → 23   144   78   12   -3

count counts the number of items on the stack and pushes that value onto the stack.

12 35 121 count → 12   35   121   3

PRACTICE EXERCISES

A4.1 Stack frolic

The operand stack is initially 345 129 −24 366 89. Show the state of the stack after each of the following operations (applied to the initial stack):

a. dup dup pop 23 exch
b. pop pop 34 23 2 copy
c. count dup 3 index
d. 3 copy 6 copy

A4.2 The reverser

What sequence of stack operators in PostScript reverses the order of the top K items, for

a. $K = 3$
b. $K = 4$.

A4.3 copy?

If copy were not already in the PostScript language, could you create it out of other PostScript operators?   ■

A4.1.5 Some Arithmetic Operators

The top two items on the stack can be combined by using one of several arithmetic operators, such as add, sub, and mul. In each case the top two items are popped and combined according to the operator, and the result is pushed back onto the stack. If both operands are integers the result is integer. Otherwise the result is real. Examples are as follows:

```
Add:         -5.2  12 add    →   6.8
Subtract:    -5.2  12 sub    →  -17.2
Multiply:    -5.2  12 mul    →  -62.4
```

There are two operators for division, div and idiv. div performs normal division on reals and integers and produces a real. idiv operates only on integers and returns only the integer part of the result of the division:

```
-27   8  div      →  -3.375
-27   8  idiv     →  -3
```

The modulo operator mod returns the remainder formed by dividing the next-to the top integer by the top integer:

```
178 34   25 7 mod  →  178   34   4
178 18   2547  10  mod →  178  18   7
```

By means of a sequence of pushes and operators, you can use PostScript to compute the value of more complex expressions, leaving the result on the stack.

■ **EXAMPLE**

Compute $1 + 3 \cdot 5 - 6 \cdot 8 \cdot 9$, leaving the result on top of the stack.

SOLUTION:

```
1 3 5 mul add 6 8 9 mul mul sub
```

■ **EXAMPLE**

Compute $8 \cdot 24^2 - 3 \cdot 24 + 8$.

SOLUTION:

```
24 dup mul 8 mul 3 24 mul sub 8 add
```

PostScript also offers "bitwise" operators that work on the individual bits of an integer value. If n and m are integers:

```
n m and  →  (n & m) (% the bitwise and of n and m)
n m or   →  (n | m) (% the bitwise or of n and m)
n m xor  →  (n ^ m) (% the bitwise exclusive or of n and m)
n not  →(!n)        (% the bitwise complement of n
```

where we use the C language operators (&, |, ^, and !) on the right-hand side to designate the result of applying the operator to numbers. Later, will see these verbs appearing again in a different context below.

■ **EXAMPLE**

What do the following fragments place on the stack?

a. 12 5 and;
b. 34 15 or
c. 56 not
d. 12 45 xor

SOLUTION:

a. In binary, 12 is 1100 and 5 is 0101, so 12 & 5 is 0100, which is 4 in decimal.
b. In binary, 34 is 100010 and 15 is 001111, so 34 | 15 is 101111, which is 47 in decimal.
c. In binary, 56 is 111000 so !56 is 000111, which is 7 in decimal.
d. In binary, 12 is 001100 and 45 is 101101, so 12 ^ 45 is 100001, which is 33 in decimal.

POSTSCRIPT also provides a number of operators that take only a single argument. In each case the top of the stack is popped and operated on, and the result is pushed back onto the stack. The type of the result (integer or real) is the same as that of the argument. Following are the POSTSCRIPT unary operators:

```
-23.3 abs       → 23.3   % absolute value
45.6  neg       → -45.6  % negate
34.5  floor     → 34.0   % largest integer less than or equal to
-34.5 floor     → -35.0
34.6  ceiling   → 35.0   % smallest integer greater than or equal to
-34.6 ceiling   → -34.0
34.6  truncate  → 34.0   % truncate towards zero
-34.6 truncate  → -34.0
34.6  round     → 35     % round to nearest integer (round up if
                           a tie).
```

POSTSCRIPT provides familiar mathematical functions. The argument may be integer or real. The type of the result is always real. The following are some of these functions:

```
2.0   sqrt  → 1.41421356   % square root
2.0   ln  → 0.69314718     % natural logarithm
2.0   log  → 0.301029996   % logarithm to the base 10
45.0  cos  → 0.707106781   % cosine (note: the angle is in degrees)
45.0  sin  → 0.707106781   % sine (note: the angle is in degrees)
```

There is no tangent function.

Two mathematical functions pop the top two items from the stack and operate on them:

1. `exp`: The exponential function `a b exp` raises a to the power b:

$$3.0 \ 5.0 \ \text{exp} \rightarrow 243.0$$

2. `atan`: The arctangent takes two arguments, say, a and b, and returns (in degrees between 0 and 360), the angle whose tangent is a/b. Either a or b, but not both, may be zero. Following are some examples:

```
0 1 atan → 0.0
1 0 atan → 90.0
-100 0 atan → 270.0
4 4 atan → 45.0
```

Random-number Generation

The function `rand` pushes an integer in the range 0 to $2^{31}-1$ onto the stack. The number is generated by a pseudorandom-number generator. The "seed" for `rand` may be set using `seed srand`. (The internal seed is pushed onto the stack by `rrand`.) The following are examples:

```
rand            → 28394    % your results may vary.
rand            → 910293   % successive calls return different numbers
rand            → 21
56 23 srand     →     56   % set the seed to 23
rand            → 38475    % get some random value
56 23 srand     → 56       % set it again
rand            → 38475    % get the same sequence
```

A4.2 GRAPHICS OPERATORS IN POSTSCRIPT

POSTSCRIPT has operators that make it easy to draw lines, circles, Bezier curves, and many other figures. In this section, we look at methods to create pictures of any complexity using combinations of POSTSCRIPT operators (verbs). A useful model to keep in mind is that drawing operators "lay ink" down, on the page, and as each object is drawn it completely obscures any previously drawn objects in the same location.

A4.2.1 Coordinate Systems and Transformations

All drawing takes place in a coordinate system. The default coordinate system is shown in Figure A4.2(a). The origin lies at the lower left corner of the display surface (normally called the page), with x-and y-axes pointing as shown. The default unit of measure is 1/72 of an inch,[4] so the point 1 inch directly above the origin has coordinates $(0, 72)$.

FIGURE A4.2 The default POSTSCRIPT coordinate system.

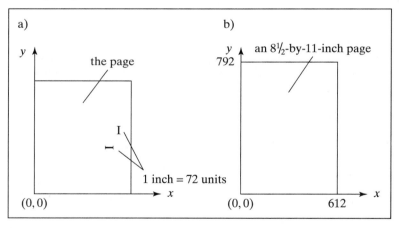

POSTSCRIPT assumes no inherent page size; the figures drawn by a script can be scaled to fit on a display of any size. Suppose, for example, that the page in question is an $8\frac{1}{2}$-by-11 inch piece of paper oriented in **portrait** orientation —that is, with the long side vertical. This orientation is shown in Figure A4.2(b). The drawing surface has its upper right corner at $(8.5 \times 72, 11 \times 72) = (612, 792)$.

Figures are drawn in POSTSCRIPT by defining a **path**, through the execution of a succession of **path construction operators**. Once the path has been formed, it can be

---

4   This is very close to the classical "printer's point", which is 1/72.27 inch.

drawn using the verb `stroke`. This is analogous to instructing a pen to produce a stroke along the path, laying down ink. Alternatively, the `fill` command can be used. This command causes the region defined by the path to be filled in with some color or shade of gray.

There are several path construction verbs, the most recognizable of which are `moveto` and `lineto`. PostScript maintains a current position (CP), which is the same as the CP discussed in Chapter 2. For instance, `lineto` pops the top two arguments to form (x, y) (that is, the first value popped is that of y, the second that of x), adds the line segment from the CP to (x, y) to the current path, and then updates the CP to (x, y).

A4.2.2 Path Construction Verbs

`moveto` pops the top two items off of the stack and set the CP accordingly:

```
x y moveto → -
```

■ **EXAMPLE**

To set the CP to (34, 56.1), use `34 56.1 moveto`.

`lineto` pops the top two items off of the stack to form (x, y), adds the line segment from CP to (x, y) to the current path, and updates the CP to (x, y):

```
x y lineto → -
```

■ **EXAMPLE**

To add the segment from CP to (1.7, −34) to the current path and set the CP to (1.7, −34), use

```
1.7  -34  lineto
```

`newpath` empties the current path.
`closepath` adds to the current path the segment from CP to the path's starting point. The value of the CP can be obtained by using `currentpoint` which pushes the (x, y) of the CP onto the stack:

```
-  currentpoint → x y
```

■ **EXAMPLE**

The following script draws the two squares shown in Figure A4.3.

```
newpath 1 1 moveto            % draw the outline of the top square
1 3 lineto 3 3 lineto
3 1 lineto closepath stroke

2 2   moveto 4 2 lineto 4 0 lineto   % fill the bottom square
2  0 lineto closepath fill
showpage
```

Two commands do **relative drawing**, as described in Chapter 3, with the arguments on the stack providing the amount to change the CP:

`rmoveto` pops the top two items off of the stack as (dx, dy) and displaces the CP by the amount (dx, dy):

```
dx dy rmoveto → -
```

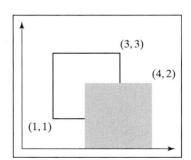

FIGURE A4.3 A figure based on two squares.

rlineto pops the top two items off of the stack as (dx, dy), adds to the current path a segment from CP to $(CP.x + dx, CP.y + dy)$, and sets the CP to the new value:

```
dx dy rlineto → −
```

■ **EXAMPLE**

The following code draws the top square shown in Figure A4.3:

```
newpath 1 1 moveto
0 2 rlineto 2 0 rlineto
0 -2 rlineto closepath stroke
showpage
```

A4.2.3 Arcs of Circles

Arcs of circles are drawn in POSTSCRIPT by using one of the two verbs arc and arcn. Both pop five items from the stack and interpret them as shown in Figure A4.4. Following is an example of each:

```
center.x center.y rad start_angle end_angle arc → −
center.x center.y rad start_angle end_angle arcn → −
```

arc and arcn add to the current path an arc of a circle having center (center.x, center.y) and radius rad, where the arc begins at angle start_angle from the positive x-axis, and extends to end_angle. arc adds a counterclockwise arc path, whereas arcn adds a clockwise arc path. (See Figure A4.4.)

FIGURE A4.4 Drawing arcs of circles.

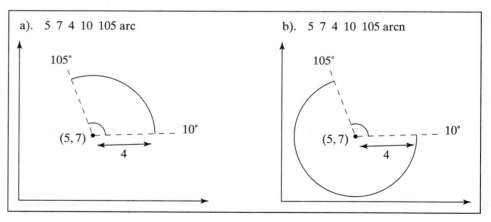

Before constructing the arc path, both operators add a straight-line path from CP to the first endpoint of the arc. If the current path is empty, no segment is added.

■ **EXAMPLE**

The following script draws the shape shown in Figure A4.5(a), consisting of two arcs and two line segments:

```
newpath 3 2 1 90 180 arc        % add first arc
3 2 2 180 90 arcn               % add line and second arc
closepath stroke                % add line and draw it
```

The first arc, of radius 1, is added to the path, and the CP is left at $(2, 2)$. Then (because the path is not empty) a line is added from the CP to the start of the second arc at $(1, 2)$. The second arc is added, and the path is closed back to $(3, 3)$. If the

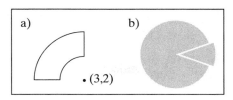

FIGURE A4.5 A figure drawn using arc-drawing tools.

final operator had been `fill` rather than `stroke`, the figure would have been filled in with the current shade of gray.

PRACTICE EXERCISE

A4.1 Pie charts

a. Write and test a POSTSCRIPT, `pieChart`, that draws a pie chart with an exploded wedge, as shown in Figure A4.5(b).
b. Extend `pieChart` so that it uses the value on the top of the stack as the fraction of the total pie the exploded wedge should be. For instance, `35 pieChart` draws a pie chart with a wedge that is 35% of the entire pie.

A4.2.4 Used for Painting Verbs

We have already seen `stroke` and `fill`. A few other verbs give fine control over a drawing:

`stroke`	"paints," a line along the current path in the current line width and color. Joints between connected line segments are drawn with the current join. (See `setlinejoin`.) Ends of open paths are painted with the current line cap. (See `setlinecap`.) Upon termination, `stroke` executes `newpath`.
`fill`	fills the area enclosed by the current path with the current color. The new color obscures any underlying drawings. `fill` executes `closepath` before it fills and `newpath` afterwards.
`setlinewidth`	pops the top item off of the stack and set the current line width to that value.
`setgray`	pops the top item, a number between 0 and 1, off the stack and sets the current gray level to that number. Here, 0 indicates black, and 1 indicates white.
`setrgbcolor`	sets the current color to (red, green, blue), each a number between 0 and 1. Its form is `red green blue setrgbcolor S —` (This verb is useful only with color displays, such as color laser printers.)
`clip`	sets the current path as the clipping path. Subsequent drawing is clipped at that boundary.
`setlinecap`	sets the shape of the "cap" at the end of open path segments. Figure A4.6 shows the effect of each of the possible parameter values. The path segment is shown as a thin inner line. Due to the line thickness the shape of the cap may bulge out in a half circle or be squared off.

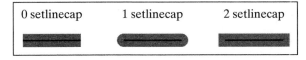

0 setlinecap	1 setlinecap	2 setlinecap

FIGURE A4.6 Ways to cap off a path.

`setlinejoin`	sets the shape of the joint between two path segments. Figure A4.7 shows the possible parameter values. For a parameter of 1, the join is an arc of diameter equal to the line thickness. ■

FIGURE A4.7 Ways to join two thick line segments.

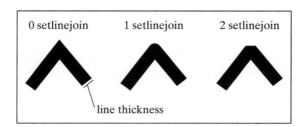

A4.2.5 Coordinate Transformations

POSTSCRIPT provides a powerful mechanism for altering drawings. The coordinate system in which drawing takes place (the **user coordinate system**) can be altered with the verbs translate, rotate, and scale. To begin with,

translate   pops the top two items off the stack as (x, y)[5] and translates the user coordinate system through the verb is amount (x, y) relative to the former coordinate system. The form of this

```
dx dy translate → −
```

Figure A4.8 shows an example, for the case of an $8\frac{1}{2}$-by-11-inch page, starting with the default coordinate system with origin at the lower left corner. The gray circle can be drawn with the following script:

```
0.5 setgray
50 50 50 0 360 arc fill
```

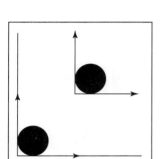

FIGURE A4.8 Translating the user coordinate system.

The black circle can be drawn by first translating the coordinate system to the center of the page:

```
306 396 translate
0 setgray
50 50 50 0 360 arc fill
```

Note that both circles are drawn by using the same code; only the coordinate system has been shifted.

If a succession of translate's is performed, each one "adds" to the others. (see Chapter 5 on composing transformations.) For instance, if 80 80 translate is now executed, the user coordinate system is shifted (80 , 80) additional units from its most recent position (at the center of the page).

rotate   pops the top item off of the stack as some angle (in degrees) and rotates the user coordinate system counterclockwise through that angle. Its form is

```
angle rotate → −
```

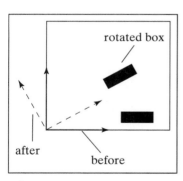

FIGURE A4.9 Rotating the user coordinate system.

Figure A4.9 shows the effect that 30 rotate has on the default coordinate system: The default axes are rotated relative to the page. If we suppose that the verb myRectangle draws the gray aligned rectangle in the figure (we see later how to define new verbs such as myRectangle in POSTSCRIPT), then the following combination draws two rectangles, one aligned with the page and one aligned with the rotated axes:

```
myRectangle % draw the rectangle aligned with the sides of the page
30 rotate   % rotate the axes
myRectangle % draw the rotated rectangle
```

---

[5] That is, the top item is taken to be y and the next down is taken to be x.

■ EXAMPLE

Drawing on a page in landscape orientation. It is more natural in some situations to draw on a page so that the picture is upright when the page is turned on its side. Figure A4.10(a) shows a row of stars that does not fit naturally on the page in portrait orientation, but is just right in landscape orientation.

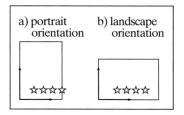

FIGURE A4.10 Changing to landscape orientation.

It is easy to prepare the user coordinate system for drawing in landscape orientation: We just shift the origin over to the right-hand corner of the page (if the page is $8\frac{1}{2}$ inches wide, this is accomplished by `612 0 translate`) and then rotate the axes through 90 degrees. (Finally, in your mind, turn the "page" 90 degrees clockwise so that you are looking at the coordinate system right side up.) The result of this operation is shown in Figure A4.10(b). The *x*-axis now points horizontally to the right along the bottom of the page, its long side. Assuming that we have a verb `drawStars` that draws the four stars in a row, the picture is drawn using the following code:

```
612 0 translate     % shift the origin to the right corner
90 rotate           % rotate the axes for landscape orientation
drawStars           % draw the picture
```

■ EXAMPLE

The verb `rotate` makes it easy to create figures with rotational symmetry. Suppose the verb `drawOval` draws the oval shown in Figure A4.11(a) relative to the origin of the given coordinate system (shown as a dot to the left of the oval). Then the sequence

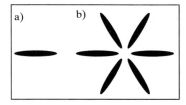

FIGURE A4.11 Drawing figures with rotational symmetry.

```
300 400 translate     % set origin near center of page
drawOval
60 rotate
drawOval
60 rotate
drawOval
60 rotate
drawOval
60 rotate
drawOval
60 rotate
drawOval
60 rotate                % restore original orientation
```

draws the pattern of Figure A4.11(b) near the center of an $8\frac{1}{2}$-by-11-inch page. Each `60 rotate` instruction adds 60 degrees more to the rotation of the coordinate system. The final `60 rotate` is not necessary, but is good practice: The original orientation of the coordinate system is left unchanged by the whole fragment of code.

As an aside, we shall see later that the preceding code can be shortened to

```
300 400 translate
6 {drawOval 60 rotate } repeat
```

The verb

```
scale
```
pops the top two items off of the stack as (sx, sy) and scales the coordinate axes by these scale factors. The form of the verb is

sx sy scale → —

For instance, if each unit is initially 1/72 of an inch, then `3 3 scale` causes each unit to be 3/72 of an inch.

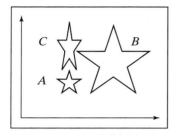

FIGURE A4.12 Scaling the coordinate system.

FIGURE A4.13 Using scale to reflect objects.

Suppose that `star` draws the star A in Figure A4.12. Then the script fragment

```
star                % draw original star
2 2 scale           % magnify by 2
star                % draw star B
0.5 0.5 scale       % back to the original system
1 2 scale           % differential scaling
star                % draw star C
```

draws stars *A*, *B*, and *C*. Star *B* is twice as large as *A* and is placed twice as far from the origin. `0.5 0.5 scale` undoes the effects of the first scaling (we will see a better way to "restore the original figure" later), and `1 2 scale` performs a **differential scaling**, wherein the two scale factors are unequal. Executing `star` now draws star *C*, which is stretched by a factor of two in the vertical direction, as well as being located twice the distance from the x-axis as star *A*. Differential scaling typically distorts figures. Reflections can be achieved by making one or both of the scale factors negative.

■ **EXAMPLE**   **Reflections**

The verb `scale` can be used to reflect an object about the *x*- or *y*- axis; just use −1 as a scale factor.

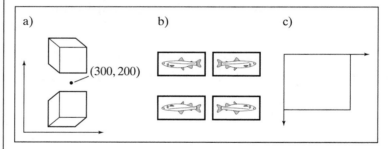

Suppose the verb `drawBox` draws the top cubelike box shown in Figure A4.13(a), after the origin has been translated to (300, 200). Then the command `1 -1 scale` will "flip" the coordinate system vertically about the point (300, 200). Drawing the box again will now draw it upside down, reflected about the *x*-axis. Thus, Figure A4.13(a) is drawn with the sequence

```
300 200 translate     % move the origin up to (300, 200)
drawBox
1 -1 scale            % reflect the y direction about the x-axis
drawBox               % draws the reflected box
```

PRACTICE EXERCISE

A4.5 Drawing four-way symmetry

Suppose the verb `drawCar` draws the upper left car shown in Figure A4.13(b). What commands will draw all four cars?   ■

PRACTICE EXERCISE

A4.6 A "screen" coordinate system

State commands that will change the default PostScript coordinate system into the one shown in Figure A4.13(c).   ■

A4.2.6 Graphics State Operators

Two POSTSCRIPT verbs, gsave and grestore, simplify many graphics tasks. Basically, gsave takes a "snapshot" of a number of current graphics parameters collectively called the **graphics state** and puts them away for safekeeping, while the program continues with further commands from the script. At a later point, grestore retrieves the snapshot and makes all the graphics parameters it contains current. To be more precise, gsave makes a copy of the "graphics state" of the interpreter and pushes it onto a separate stack, the **graphics state stack**; grestore pops the top item off this stack and stores it back into the graphics state. Thus, each grestore restores the graphics state that was current at the time of the most recent gsave.

The following items (along with some less important ones) constitute the graphics state:

- The current transformation: the composition of all of the effects of preceding calls to translate, rotate, and scale.
- the current path: the path constructed by the various path construction verbs since the most recent newpath, stroke, or fill.
- the current position, CP: the most recently addressed position on the current path
- the current font: the font most recently selected
- the gray value or color: the current gray level or color
- the line width, cap, and join: the current line width, line cap, and line join.

■ **EXAMPLE**

Recall that stroke performs an implicit newpath. To fill the house of Figure A4.14, as well as draw its outline, you could construct its path twice, using the following code:

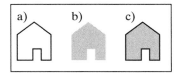

FIGURE A4.14 Filling an object and drawing its outline.

```
< lots of lines to make the path of the house>
fill                % fill the object; destroys the current path
< repeat the lines to make the path of the house>
stroke              % draw the outline
```

Here, "lots of lines" might consist of a complex sequence of instructions. But since gsave makes a copy of the current path, it is easier and more efficient to use

```
< lots of lines to make the path of the house>
gsave               % save current path in the graphics state
fill
grestore            % restore the current path
stroke
```

It is particularly convenient that gsave saves the current transformation. Suppose that in some script you have performed several transformations and are about to perform additional ones, but you know that you need to "return here" later. Then simply execute a gsave to save a record of all of the transformations to this point. Later, to return, perform a grestore. For instance, the fragment of code used to produce Figure A4.12 required "undoing" the first 2 2 scale with a 0.5 0.5 scale. A better way to write this fragment is as follows:

```
star            % draw star
gsave           % save current transformation
2 2 scale       % magnify by 2
star            % draw star B
grestore        % return to initial state
1 2 scale       % differential scaling
star            % draw star C
```

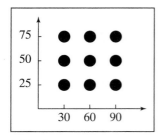

FIGURE A4.15 Using gsave and grestore.

As another example, suppose you wish to draw a regular pattern of circles, as in Figure A4.15.

Suppose the verb `circ` draws the filled circle at the origin. Start at the bottom left and draw circles across the first row, using `translate` to move the origin across the page. Then return to the leftmost circle and "move up" to the start of the next row. This "return" is easily done using `grestore`, as suggested in the following fragment of code:

```
gsave                       % save current state until the end
30 25 translate circ        % set origin for the first circle in
                                bottom row;  draw circle
gsave                       % remember where we are
30 0 translate circ
30 0 translate circ
grestore                    % back to lower left circle
0 25 translate circ         % go up to second row and draw left circle
gsave                       % push this graphics state, too; remember
                                where we are
30 0 translate circ
30 0 translate circ
grestore                    % back to left side of second row
0 25 translate circ         % up to third row, draw left circle
30 0 translate circ
30 0 translate circ
grestore                    % restore state from the beginning
```

Being able to "return" to a previous coordinate system makes it easier to organize a script and to keep track of things. We will see other examples later.

A4.3 DRAWING TEXT IN POSTSCRIPT

Although our greatest interest is graphics, most scripts in POSTSCRIPT lay out pages of carefully fashioned text—that is, long sequences of character strings. There are many POSTSCRIPT verbs to assist in this task, but the crucial ones allow you to do the following:

1. Choose the font for the string and scale the font to the desired size
2. Position the string on the page
3. Draw the string as a graphical entity

An example shows how this is done:

```
/Helvetica findfont         % request a particular font
15 scalefont                % scale it to the desired size
setfont                     % make this font the current font
100 200 moveto              % set the position of the first character
(Hi, Jess, how are you?)    % specify the string to be printed
show                        % draw the string at the CP
```

Notice the slash ('/') that precedes the name of the font. This makes `Helvertica` a "literal" and is crucial, as we discuss in the next section. Also, keep in mind that `15 scalefont` asks for a font 15 times the unit in user space. If the default unit size of 1/72 inch (a printer's point) is in effect, the command produces a 15-point font. On the other hand, if you have previously executed, say, `3 3 scale`, the resulting font is a 45-point font. Finally, strings are always enclosed in parentheses.

Some other popular choices of font are the following:

```
/Helvetica-Bold     /Helvetica-Oblique
/Times-Roman        /Times-Bold
/Times-Italic       /Times-BoldItalic
/Courier
```

A4.4 DEFINING NEW VARIABLES AND PROCEDURES

POSTSCRIPT is an extensible language, which means that you can add new commands and other objects to its repertoire. These new objects effectively become part of the language for the duration of your script. This feature makes it easier to design scripts and makes POSTSCRIPT more efficient in interpreting them.

A new object is defined by placing three things on the stack:

1. a slash ('/') followed by the new name for the object
2. the definition of the object itself
3 the keyword `def`

The two types of object we define in this section are variables and procedures.

A4.4.1 Defining Variables

A variable is easily defined, or has its value altered, using `def`. For instance, to define a variable `num` with initial value 251, place in your script. The verb `def` does very specific things: It pops the top two items from the stack and adds a new entry in the **dictionary** of words already in the language. Here the word `num` is inserted in the dictionary and associated with the value 251. Later references to `num` (without the slash), as in `34 num add`, cause POSTSCRIPT to look up the value of `num` and push it onto the stack. So if `num` is still 251 when this happens, the value 285 will be pushed onto the stack.

```
/num 251 def
```

The slash ('/') prescribes that `/num` is a **literal**, so the actual name "num" is pushed, rather than its value.

What names are valid for new items? Any sequence of characters that cannot be interpreted as a number, so Merilee, meriLee, something123, 2$abe are all valid. (But choose meaningful and readable names so that you can manage your scripts more easily.)

You can alter the value of a variable by redefining it. If `num` has been defined as having the value 251, the redefinition

```
/num 7 def
```

changes its value to 7. To add 1 to a variable, you access the current value, add 1 to it, and redefine it:

```
//num num 1 add def     % increment num
```

To add 4 to the value of `num` and then square the result, simply perform

```
/num num 4 add dup mul def     % add 4 to num and square it
```

Carefully trace the effect on the stack as each token is executed here. Notice that the addition of 4 and the squaring take place before `def` is interpreted, so the top two items on the stack when `def` is executed are /num and 121 (i.e., 11 squared).

Sometimes, in the middle of some calculation, you wish to store the value that is on top of the stack in some variable (called, say, `fred`) for later use. You can do this with

```
/fred exch def     % put the value on top of the stack into the
                          variable fred
```

For `def` to work properly, it is crucial to exchange the top two items on the stack so the the value is on top and the literal name is below it.

A4.4.2 Defining Procedures

As with all programming languages, it is very convenient to group several commands together into a procedure (also known as a subroutine or function). Usually, the procedure is given a name. Then, when the name is used later, the corresponding sequence of commands is executed. In POSTSCRIPT, the commands are placed in French ("curly") braces, as in `{dup add}`. For example, the following procedure, `smaller`, scales the current coordinate system unit by (0.8, 0.8):

```
/smaller {.8 .8 scale} def    % scale the system by 0.8
```

A new dictionary entry with the name `smaller` is created and is associated with a single "object" that is the procedure `{.8 .8 scale}`. When the procedure is used later in a script by simply stating `smaller`, the coordinate system is scaled appropriately.

■ EXAMPLE

We define the procedure `box` that draws a filled square 2 units on a side, centered at the origin, as shown in Figure A4.16(a).

FIGURE A4.16 A box primitive.

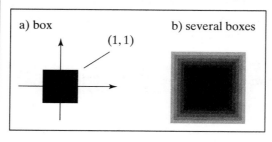

```
/box { 1   1 moveto      1 -1 lineto
      -1 -1 lineto      -1  1 lineto
      closepath         fill } def
```

We can use two procedures `box` and `smaller` together to draw the set of nested boxes of Figure A4.16(b):

```
200 200 translate 60 60 scale % set the initial coordinate system
.8 setgray box                % draw the largest box
.6 setgray smaller box
.4 setgray smaller box
.2 setgray smaller box        % draw the innermost box
```

(Why do the boxes have to be drawn in this order?)

It is often convenient to pass **parameters** to user-defined procedures. This is done by pushing the parameters onto the stack before invoking the procedure. The procedure pops the values off of the stack and uses them.

For example, we can alter the procedure `smaller` so that it takes the scale factor as a parameter. We give it the more meaningful name `scaleIt`:

```
/scaleIt {dup scale} def    % scale the system by the value on
                              the stack
```

Now we can magnify or demagnify the coordinate system with a call such as

```
.5 scaleIt   % cut the size of a unit in half
```

or

```
3 scaleIt       % triple the size of a unit
```

■ EXAMPLE Draw a "Dot"

You can draw a single dot at location (x, y) with the procedure

```
/drawDot {newpath 2 copy moveto lineto stroke} def
```

This routine expects x and y to be on the stack. A copy of each of x and y is pushed onto the stack by using `2 copy`, and both copies are removed from the stack with the use of `moveto` and `lineto`. On most POSTSCRIPT printers, moving to a point and then drawing a line to the same point draws a dot. We would express the effect `drawDot` has on the stack by

```
x y drawDot  →  −
```

and a typical usage of `drawDot` by

```
240 367 drawDot
```

■ EXAMPLE Using more parameters, to draw a box of any size

We can add more power to the routine `box` by having it both scale and position the square to be drawn. Its effect on the stack is given by

```
size x y drawBox    } −    % draw box of size units on a side
                                centered at (x, y)
```

and a suitable definition is

```
/drawBox { gsave             % avoid any global effects on system
           translate         % set the center of the box
           2 div dup scale   % adjust the size
           box               % draw the box
           grestore          % restore the previous system
         } def
```

First, the x and y values are used by `translate`. Then, since `box` draws a square that is two units on a side, we divide the `size` parameter by 2, placing `size/2` on the stack. This value is duplicated and both values are used by `scale`. Then the box is drawn. We enclose the action in a `gsave grestore` pair to prevent the transformations from altering the coordinate system.

■ EXAMPLE Writing text on the "next line"

When writing strings of text, you ultimately reach the right margin of the page and need to do a "newline"; that is you move down to the next line and start at the left margin. Suppose the following variables have been defined:

```
/LM 72 def          % left margin 1 inch from left edge of page
//RM 540 def        % right margin 1 inch from right edge of page
/lineHeight 12 def  % vertical distance between adjacent lines of
                        text
```

In addition, the variable `ypos` contains the current y position at which text is being written on the page. Then the procedure

```
/doNewline
{/ypos ypos lineHeight sub def   % decrease ypos and save it
LM ypos moveto{ def              % move to next line
```

first reduces `ypos` by the amount `lineHeight` and then moves to the left margin on the new line.

PRACTICE EXERCISES

A4.7. A variation on drawBox

Consider a formulation of `drawBox` that expects its parameters in a different order from the one previously set forth:

```
x y size drawBox → −      % draw box centered at (x, y) with size
                                 units on a side
```

With this formulation, you can't simply scale first and then translate. (why not?) Write two versions of this `drawBox` procedure using the following two approaches:

a. Define a local variable, say, `/S` in which you store the top parameter of the stack and use it later in the procedure, as in `/drawBox{/S exch def ...} def`.
b. Inside `drawBox`, manipulate the order of the parameters on the stack so that they are in the order `size x y`, and then use the original formulation of the procedure.

A4.8 Drawing big dots

Write the procedure `bigDot` with stack processing:

```
x y size bigDot → −
```

the procedure draws a circle of radius `radius` centered at `x y`.

A4.9 Draw the big dipper

Write a POSTSCRIPT script that draws the Big Dipper of Figure 2.11, using dots for the stars.

A4.10 Drawing shapes through procedures

Define procedures for drawing each of the objects shown in Figure A4.17, making suitable decisions as to the size and position of each. Execute your procedures by composing an interesting scene that uses all of the primitive shapes.   ■

FIGURE A4.17 Some primitive shapes to draw.

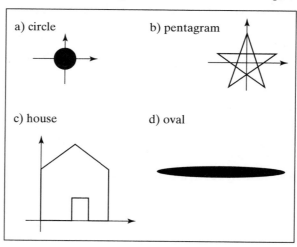

a) circle

b) pentagram

c) house

d) oval

■ **EXAMPLE   Defining the center of the page**

It is convenient to have procedures that return the location of a center of page. Assuming an $8\frac{1}{2}$-by-11-inch page in portrait orientation (and that the coordinate system is the default one), the definitions

```
/halfwayAcross 8.5 72 mul def     % define the variables
/halfwayUp       11 72 mul def
/pageCenter {halfwayAcross halfwayUp} def
```

Now the fragment `pageCenter moveto` moves the CP to the middle of the page.

Question: What's the Difference?

Note that `halfwayAcross` could have been defined as a procedure rather than a variable:

```
/halfwayAcross { 8.5 72 mul} def    % define it as a procedure
```

What's the difference? When `halfway Across` is defined as a variable, the 8.5 72 mul is performed just before `def`, and the resulting value is the value associated with `halfwayAcross`. When `halfway Across` is defined as a procedure, the `8.5 72 mul` is executed each time the interpreter sees `halfwayAcross` later in the script. Hence, both the variable version and the procedure version end up doing the same thing but in different ways: They push the value 612, onto the stack. In other cases, however, the result can be erroneous. For instance, suppose you try to write pageCenter as a variable:

```
/pageCenter halfwayAcross halfWayUp def
```

This pushes the first three items onto the stack, and then def pops the top two and tries to make sense of them, leading to an error.

Binding Procedures

The verb `bind` may be placed after a procedure definition, as in

```
/bigCirc { 2 2 scale circ .5 .5 scale} bind def
```

`bind` has no effect on the stack; rather, it forces POSTSCRIPT to compile the associated definition. In effect, `bind` "looks up" the definition of each word between the braces, such as `scale` and `circ`, and replaces it with the associated machine code. This provides two benefits:

1. When `bigCirc` is invoked later, it will execute faster, because its definition need not be reinterpreted.
2. If any of the words in the definition, such as `drawDot`, have been redefined in the meantime, this change does not "leak" to `bigCirc`; the original meaning of `circ` is bound to `bigCirc`.

A4.4.3 A Simple Form of Iteration Using `repeat`

We examine various ways to do controlled repetition of procedures in Section A4.5.3, but one verb is so handy that we introduce it here. `repeat` causes a procedure to be executed a specified number of times. It pops the top two arguments off of the stack to obtain (1) the number of iterations desired and (2) the procedure

```
num proc repeat → −
```

For example,

```
6 }5 0 translate box{ repeat      % draw 6 boxes in a row
```

executes the procedure shown six times, to draw six filled boxes in a row.

■ EXAMPLE   Draw a pentagram

The star shown in Figure A4.18 can be drawn by five repetitions of the horizontal line called "theLine" in the figure, interspersed with successive rotations of the coordinate system by 72°. That is, if procedure `drawStarEdge` draws "theLine", then the code

```
5 { drawStarEdge 72 rotate} repeat      % draw the star
```

FIGURE A4.18 Drawing a star as five rotated lines.

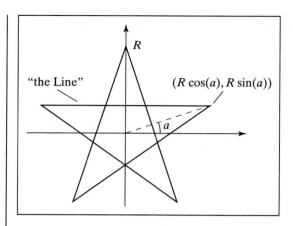

draws the entire star. The use of `repeat` makes this command easy to express. (What is the net rotation of the coordinate system when the process is complete?) Now "theLine" has endpoints $(R\cos(a), R\sin(a))$, where a is 18°. (Why?) Suppose the radius R is stored in the variable `starRad`. Within `drawStarEdge`, we build variables `tmpX` and `tmpY` to hold $R\cos(18°)$, and $R\sin(18°)$, respectively, and then draw the desired line. (Recall that `cos` and `sin` take degrees as their arguments.) Putting these ideas together, we obtain the procedure

```
/drawStarEdge {
  /tmpX starRad 18 cos mul def      % tmpX = Rcos (18°)
  /tmpY starRad 18 sin mul def      % tmpY = Rsin(18°)
  tmpX tmpY moveto                  % draw "theLine"
  tmpX neg tmpY lineto stroke
}def
```

PRACTICE EXERCISE

A4.11 An alternative star

The following procedure also draws a star, without any complicated trigonometry:

```
/drawStar{                         % stack: x y
  moveto currentpoint translate
  4{ 72 0 lineto
    currentpoint translate
    -144 rotate
  } repeat closepath fill
} def
```

Explain how this algorithm operates when it is invoked by `300 400 drawStar`. Where is the center of this star located? Where is the origin of the coordinate system after the star has been drawn? ■

A4.5 DECISIONS AND ITERATIONS

All programming languages provide ways to test values stored in memory and to execute different operations based on the results. They also provide commands to control how some action is repeated a number of times. POSTSCRIPT, of course, provides these features, too.

POSTSCRIPT defines two **Boolean** values, *true* and *false,* and has the capability of pushing and popping either of these values. Boolean values are generated by the operators in the list that follows this paragraph. Each of the verbs shown pops the top two arguments off of the stack and compares them. Each verb pushes onto the stack the Boolean value *true* if the stated condition is true; otherwise it pushes *false.* So each Affects the stack according to

```
num1 num2 operator → bool
```

where `num1` and `num2` are numbers, `operator` is one of the operators listed, and `bool` is *true* or *false.*

Suppose *a* and *b* are numerical quantities. Then, using "iff" to denote "if and only if", we have

```
a b eq    yields    true    iff a = b;
a b ne    yields    true    iff a ≠ b;
a b ge    yields    true    iff a ≥ b;
a b le    yields    true    iff a ≤ b;
a b gt    yields    true    iff a > b;
a b lt    yields    true    iff a < b;
```

(These verbs are equivalent to the C operators ==, !=, >=, <=, >, and <, respectively.)

The preceding verbs also work when *a* and *b* are character strings. For instance, a b eq yields *true* if and only if string a is the same as string b. On the other hand, a b gt is *true* if and only if a is "lexically greater" than b. The lexical ordering of strings is sometimes called "dictionary order." Suppose a and b are identical up through the *n*th character. Then a b gt is *true* if and only if the next character of a has a larger ASCII value than the next character of b (or if b has no next character, but a does). For example, each of the following expressions is *true*:

```
(rug)(rag) gt          %  'u' is "bigger" than 'a'
(lionize) (lion) gt    %  the longer string is "bigger"
(bob)(Bob)  gt         %  lowercase letters are "bigger" than
                               uppercase letters
```

A4.5.1 Verbs That Take Boolean Values for Arguments

Boolean values can also be combined to create another Boolean value. If `b1` and `b2` are Booleans (*true* or *false*), then using "iff" to mean "if and only if", we have

```
b1 b2 and     yields    true iff b1 and b2 are both true;
b1 b2 or      yields    true iff b1 or b2 (or both) are true;
b1 b2 xor     yields    true iff b1 or b2 (but not both) is true;
b1 not        yields    true iff b1 is false.
```

The values *true* and *false* can also be pushed by the verbs:

```
true      pushes true onto the stack;
false     pushes false onto the stack.
```

PRACTICE EXERCISE

A4.12 What do the following put on the stack, true or false?

a. `34 12 gt 5 7 eq or`
b. `23 2 add 5 mul 6 lt`
c. `56 67 exch ge 12 14 2 sub ge xor`

A4.5.2 Making Decisions

Boolean values are used by two verbs, `if` and `ifelse`, to control the sequence of operations performed in a script:

1. The operator if pops the top two items off of the stack as a Boolean and a procedure and executes the procedure if the Boolean is *true*:

```
bool proc if → −
```

2. The operator `elseif` pops the top three items off of the stack as bool1 proc1 proc2 and executes proc1 if bool is *true*; otherwise it executes proc2:

```
bool proc1 proc2 elseif → −
```

■ **EXAMPLE   Test for reaching the right margin**

When writing strings of text, we must test whether the right margin of the page has been reached. The procedure `atEndOfLine` tests whether the CP has gone beyond the right margin RM, and if so, it invokes the procedure `doNewline` defined earlier:

```
/atEndOfLine{
currentpoint pop       % get x position
RM g                   % beyond right margin?
{doNewLine} if         % if so, go to next line
} def
```

■ **EXAMPLE   Truchet tiles**

Figure A4.19 shows a beguiling pattern of "Truchet tiles," named for Sebastien Truchet, who experimented with these patterns in 1704. The pattern consists of an arrangement of the two "tiles" shown in Figure A4.20(a) and (b), laid side by side to cover the plane. The tiles are identical except for a 90° rotation, and the pattern is constructed by choosing the tiles randomly. The result is a collection of continuous curves [see Figure A4.20(c)], some of which form "islands" and some of which form undulating shapes across the plane.

FIGURE A4.19 Truchet tiles.

FIGURE A4.20 Building Truchet tiles.

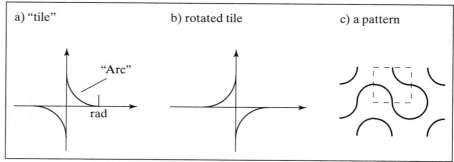

In POSTSCRIPT, the basic tile of Figure A4.20(a) is formed as a quarter circle, along with its reflection in *x* and *y*. Procedure `tile` draws these two arcs with radius `rad` at the origin:

```
/width 10 def            % width of tile
/rad width 2 div def     % radius = width/2


/Arc {newpath rad rad rad 180 270 arc stroke} def
/tile { Arc gsave -1 -1 scale Arc grestore} def
```

The number of rows and columns is stored in `num`. The pattern is drawn inside two `repeat` loops: The outer loop draws `num` rows, for each of which the inner loop draws a row of `num` tiles. After each row has been drawn, the origin of the coordinate system is brought back to the left side with a `grestore`, and then it is raised by the width of the tile in preparation for drawing the next row:

```
/num 20 def                   % number of rows and columns
72 72 translate               % set initial origin
num{ gsave
       num{ rand 2 mod 0 eq       % true or false with equal likelihood
             {tile}
                {gsave 90 rotate tile grestore}ifelse
             width 0 translate   % move to the right
       } repeat
     grestore

     0 width translate          % move up a row
}repeat
showpage
```

Each tile is chosen by "flipping a coin": `rand 2 mod` generates the value 0 or 1 randomly with equal likelihood, and `0 eq` places *true* or *false* on the stack accordingly. If true is at the top of the stack, the `ifelse` verb executes {`tile`}; otherwise it first rotates the tile by 90° and then draws it.

A4.5.3 Iterating

We have already seen the simplest form of iteration that uses `repeat`:

> `repeat` pop the top two items off of the stack as *N* and a procedure, and execute the procedure *N* times

▪ EXAMPLE

The snowflake of Figure A4.21 uses `repeat` to draw six rotated versions of a simple shape drawn by some procedure motif. The code is 6 {`motif 60 rotate`} `repeat`.

POSTSCRIPT provides two other ways to control repetition. In one,

> `loop` pops the top item off of the stack as a procedure and then repeatedly executes it

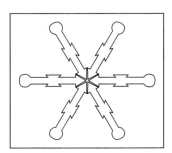

FIGURE A4.21 Using `repeat` and `rotate`.

To avoid an endless iteration, there must be a way to escape. The verb `exit` causes execution to jump out of the innermost active loop without having an effect on the stack. `loop` with `exit` is typically used when the number of iterations to be performed cannot be predicted beforehand. Iteration terminates when some condition causes `exit` to be executed.

■ EXAMPLE

Suppose we wish to draw a sequence of randomly spaced rectangles across a page, as shown in Figure A4.22. After each bar is drawn, the *x* position is incremented by a random amount. The process repeats an unknown number of times, until the *x* position reaches the right side of the page.

FIGURE A4.22 A random string of bars.

The following fragment of code draws such a row of bars, using `exit` to escape from the loop:

```
/xpos 10 def                % initial x position
/drawBar
{ 0 90 rlineto              % assumes CP is at lower left corner
  13 0 rlineto
  0 -90 rlineto
  closepath fill} def       % the main loop to draw the row of bars
} /xpos xpos 16 add         % make increment at least 16
  rand 30 mod add def       % plus a random amount: set xpos
  xpos 600 gt {exit} if     % escape if xpos > 600
  xpos 500 moveto drawBar%  draw next bar
}loop
showpage
```

A third way to control repetition is with the `for` loop. When the number of iterations is known in advance, a `for` loop provides some extra control of the iterations. The `for` verb maintains a "counting variable" that controls the iterations. This variable doesn't have an actual name; it is simply pushed onto the stack at each iteration of the loop, as we shall see. Here we call it CV for convenience. There are four parameters expected on the stack by the `for` loop:

the initial value of CV (call it `init` here)
the increment CV experiences at each iteration (call it `incr` here)
the limiting value of CV that terminates the iteration (call it `limit` here)
a procedure that is executed at each iteration (call it `proc` here)
The form of the `for` command is

```
init incr limit proc for    → −
```

The `for` verb acts slightly differently, depending on the sign of the increment.

When `incr` Is Positive

When `incr` is positive, CV is initialized to `init`. If CV has not exceeded `limit`, the value of CV is pushed onto the operand stack (for possible use within the procedure), and `proc` is executed. Then CV is incremented by `incr`. CV is again compared with `limit`, and if it does not exceed `limit`, the procedure is executed. The action is easiest to see by comparing it with how a `for` loop in the C language is executed:

```
for(CV = init; CV <= limit; CV += incr)
}
    < push CV >; /* pseudo-code: push the value of CV */
    < execute proc >;
{
```

■ EXAMPLES

Carefully trace the contents of the stack at each iteration of the following fragments of code:

a. Push the values 1 2 3 4 5 onto the stack:

```
1 1 5 { } for      % note the empty procedure
```

Since the values of CV are pushed by for but are not popped inside the procedure, they remain on the stack.

b. Put the first 10 powers of 2 (i.e., $1, 2, 4, 8, \ldots, 1{,}024$) on the stack:

```
1     0 1 10 {pop dup 2 mul} for
```

The stack is seeded with a 1 to get things started. Here the value of CV is not used, so it must be popped at each iteration.

c. Sum the numbers between 1 and 10, and leave the result on the stack:

```
0     1 1 10 {add} for
```

The leading 0 before the parameters of for is necessary to put the initial sum (0) on the stack.

d. Draw the chessboard of Figure A4.23, using gray levels .3 and .7, with the origin at the lower left corner.

FIGURE A4.23 Drawing a chessboard.

The script that follows has two imbedded for loops that iterate over the eight rows and columns of the chessboard. The calculation of which gray level to use takes the sum of the row and column counters and tests whether it is even or odd. The script would have the following equivalent code in C:

```
if( (row + col) % 2 == 0)     /* is row + col even? */
    setgray(.3);              /* yes, use dark color */
else setgray(.7);             /* no, use light color */
```

To implement this code in POSTSCRIPT, the CV for the outer loop is stored in row each time through the loop, since this value must be used eight times in the inner loop, which has its own CV, viz, is the column counter. The code row add 2 mod returns 0 when the row and column counters sum to an even number. The position of the next box to be drawn is moved along in the now familiar way of translating the coordinate system at each iteration. One implementation is as follows:

```
/W 40 def                           % width of each square
/box {0 0 moveto 0 W lineto
     W W lineto W 0 lineto closepath fill} def
72 72 translate                     % initial lower left corner
1 1 8{ /row exch def                % draw next row of squares
  gsave
  1 1 8{ row add 2 mod              % 0 if row + col is even
        0 eq
        {0.3 setgray}
        {0.7 setgray} ifelse
     box
      W 0 translate                 % move to right
     }for
     grestore                       % back to left side
     0 W translate                  % up to next row
{for
showpage
```

When `incr` Is negative

The notion of using a negative increment for `for` is to "count down" to some lower limit. The action is nearly that for positive increments, except the CV is tested against the limit differently. The following is equivalent code in C:

```
for(CV = init; CV >= limit; CV += incr)
{
     < push CV >;                /* pseudocode: push CV */
 < execute proc >;
}
```

The increment (a negative quantity) is still added to CV at the end of each iteration, but now the test is CV `>=` limit rather than CV `<=` limit. In other words, iteration continues until CV is strictly less than the `limit`.

■ EXAMPLES

a. Sum the first 10 integers, $1 + 2 + \ldots + 10$:

```
0       10 -1 1 {add} for
```

b. Push the values 3.0, 2.5, 2.0, 1.5, and 1.0 onto the stack:

```
3 -.5 1 {} for
```

c. Draw the "smeared" character string shown in Figure A4.24.

FIGURE A4.24 Smearing a message for visual effect.

The string can be drawn with a simple `for` loop that successively draws it in slightly offset positions (from right to left here), with a decreasing value for `setgray` from 0.95 towards 0, so that the string keeps getting darker in successive positions. The process is: finished up by superposing a bright white version of the string. The code is as follows.

```
/Times-Italic findfont 60 scalefont setfont
/ShowIt { 0 0 moveto (Gee Whiz) show} def     % to draw it once
320 400 translate                             % set placement
.95 -.05   0                                  % init, incr, limit
                                                 of the for loop
{setgray ShowIt -1 .5 translate} for          % draw many
                                                 versions
1 setgray ShowIt                              % the final one
showpage
```

PRACTICE EXERCISES

A4.13

Place the first 20 square numbers (i.e., 1, 4, 9, 16, 25, … , 400) on the stack.

A4.14

Place the first 20 Fibonacci numbers (1, 1, 2, 3, 5, 8, …) on the stack. Here each number is the sum of the previous two in the sequence. (Use POSTSCRIPT to compute the successive values algorithmically, of course.)

A4.15

Write scripts to draw each of the figures shown in Figure A4.25. These resemble solid spheres bathed in light.

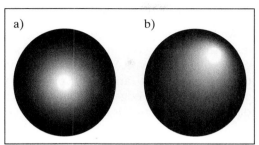

FIGURE A4.25 Spheres bathed in light.

A4.16

Write a script that draws the seven "kissing" circles shown in Figure A4.26. ■

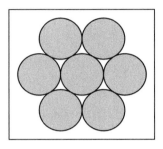

FIGURE A4.26 Seven circles meet perfectly.

A4.6 PRINTING VALUES

Sometimes you need to print out numerical values on the POSTSCRIPT page. For instance, you may wish to interrogate the values of some internal variables while debugging a script, or you may need to label the axes of a graph you wish to print. Either of these is done by converting a numerical value to a string and then printing the text string. The line

```
/str 15 string def      % create a string of 15 characters
```

sets aside memory to hold a string of 15 characters and associates the variable name `str` with that string. The verb `cvs` converts a numerical value to the desired string. It pops the top two off of the stack items, as a value and the name of a string and pushes the string representation of the value onto the stack:

```
12 6 mul str cvs → (72)      % i.e., the string holding the
                               characters '7' and '2'
```

■ **EXAMPLE**

Starting at (20, 20), print 12 random values in the range 0..35:

```
/Times-Bold findfont 16 scalefont setfont
20 20 moveto                % set the starting point
/str 30 string def          % space for a string
12{rand 36 mod str cvs show % print a random value
    ( ) show}
repeat                      % print a space (to separate values)
showpage
```

Printing the Stack (Nondestructively)

It can also help during debugging to examine the stack at certain key points during the execution of a script. The verb `pstack` prints out all the items on the operand stack, without altering the stack in any way:

```
pstack      % nondestructive stack printout
```

The stack values are not printed on the page; rather, they are sent back to the utility that passed the script to the POSTSCRIPT interpreter. With GhostScript, for instance, the stack values are sent back to the interactive GhostScript window.

FIGURE A4.27 A test PostScript image.

A4.7 DRAWING GRAY-SCALE IMAGES

PostScript can also print gray-scale images based on bit maps. (See Chapter 10.) The principal tool is the verb `image`. Here, we will not describe every nuance of this operator (see *the PostScript Language Reference Manual*), just its most common usage.

We begin with an example and then see that the example generalizes easily. The image shown in Figure A4.27 has 100 rows and 116 columns, and each pixel can have 256 possible gray levels. We wish to print it in a rectangular region 3 inches wide, having the same aspect ratio as the original image. The lower left corner should be 2 inches from the left edge of the page and 3 inches above the bottom edge. The script to produce this picture is as follows:[6]

```
/nRows 362 def            % number of rows in the image
/nCols 282 def            % number of columns in the image
/nBits 8 def              % number of bits per pixel in the image
/inch {72 mul} def        % handy conversion from units to inches
2 inch 3 inch translate   % location of lower left corner of image
                              on page
3 inch 1.28 3 mul inch scale % set up the picture size;
                                 preserve aspect ratio
/picstr hCols string def    % make space for a string of
                              characters
nCols nRows nBits         % size of image and 8 bits/pixel
[nCols 0 0 nRows 0 nRows neg]  % mapping from unit square to the
                                  image
{currentfile             % starts just after the image
                             command
picstr readhexstring pop}  % read the data as hex digits
image                    % print the image
A4A4A4A4A4A4A4A4A4A4A4A4A4A4A4A4A4A4A5A5A5A4A4A4A4A4A4A4A4A4A4A4A4A4A4A4
A4A4A4A4A4A5A5A5A4A4A4A4A4A4A4A4A4A4A4A4A4A4A4A4A4A4A4A4A4A5A5A5A4A4A4A4A6
A6A6A6A6A6A6A6A6A6A6A6A6A5ASA5A5A5
about 7960 lines of hex data in here
989C9C9C9F9F9F9F9F9FA2A2A2A4A4A4A2A2A2A2A2A2A2A2A2A2A2A1A1A19E9E9E9B
9B9B9898989494949292929292929292
```

Several new ideas are presented in this script. One simple trick is the use of the verb `inch`, which makes it easy to specify lengths in inches.

The verb `image` presupposes five items on the stack:

1. The number of columns in the image
2. The number of rows in the image
3. The gray-scale "depth" (bits per pixel) of the image (see Chapter 4).
   Values of 1, 2, 4, and 8 may be used, signifying that each pixel has 2, 4, 16, or 256 gray levels, respectively.
4. An array of six values that constitute a transformation, as we shall explain shortly.
5. A procedure for reading the pixel values, also explained shortly.

It looks like there are many choices to make, but most images are done the same way. In fact, they are usually done as in the preceding example. The image of Figure A4.27 has `nRows` rows and `nCols` columns and each pixel has `nBits` bits.

---

[6] The complete data file for the image, as well as for several others, can be found on the book's web site. (See the preface to the book.)

How is the array of six values used by POSTSCRIPT? POSTSCRIPT views an image as a rectangular array of squares (the pixels), each one unit on a side. The lower left square has opposite corners $(0, 0)$ and $(1, 1)$. The upper right square has opposite corners (nCols -1, nRows -1) and (nCols, nRows). Figure A4.28 shows an image lying in this "image space"; the image occupies a rectangular region in the space.

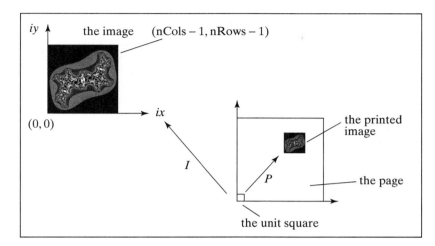

FIGURE A4.28 The transformations used by `image`.

The array of six values, as in `[nCols 0 0 nRows 0 nRows neg]`, prescribes an affine transformation, defined by a matrix such as the one in Equation (5.4). The first four values are those of the upper left two-by-two submatrix, and the final two values are m^{13} and m^{23}. The transformation is denoted I in the figure. So a point (x, y) in user space is mapped into a point (ix, iy) in image space by

$$\begin{pmatrix} ix \\ iy \\ i \end{pmatrix} = \begin{pmatrix} nCols & 0 & 0 \\ 0 & nRows & -nRows \\ 0 & 0 & 1 \end{pmatrix} \begin{pmatrix} x \\ y \\ i \end{pmatrix}$$

or simply, $ix = $ nCols x, *and* $iy - $ nRows $y - $ nRows. More general transformations are possible, but these suffice for most image work.

POSTSCRIPT reads pixel values from left to right and from bottom to top and uses the inverse of I to draw the pixels in the unit square of user space. Such a tiny image is of no use, of course, so you must first translate and scale this unit square to the desired position, size, and shape by using combinations of `translate` and `scale` (and even `rotate` if you wish). The combination of such transformations is denoted P in the figure. Hence, the overall transformation is $I^{-1}P$ from the hypothetical image-space rectangle of pixel squares to the final image. POSTSCRIPT handles this transformation automatically.

The final argument required by the word image is a procedure. The procedure used to read image data is usually

```
{currentfile picstr readhexstring pop}
```

`image` executes this procedure repeatedly until it has obtained the necessary number of pixel values. The data are expected to be in the same file as the image operator itself, directly after the verb `image` (and a carriage return) is encountered. Each call to this procedure sends to `image` a sequence of hexadecimal digits, which `image` interprets as needed.

`readhexstring` reads a sequence of the hexadecimal digits '0'..'9' and 'A'..'F' (or 'a'..'f'). It ignores nonhexadecimal characters, so it doesn't hurt to intersperse spaces, newlines, etc., in the file. The routine pushes a string containing the characters received and a Boolean value: *true* under normal conditions, *false* if end-of-file was encountered before all of the required data was received.

For example, if nBits is 8, each pair of hexadecimal digits is converted to a number between 0 and 255. For the specific data stream 73A42406..., the values are 115, 168, 36, 6,.... On the other hand, if nBits is 1, each hexadecimal digit represents four separate pixel values. For the stream 73A8..., the values are 0111 0011 1010 1000....

APPENDIX

5

An Introduction to SDL

Scene Description Language (SDL) is a very simple language for describing geometric objects and light sources in a clear, human-readable fashion. It is understood by the `read()` method of the `Scene` class. (See the definition of the class in Appendix 3.) We first look briefly at the basics of the `Scene` class and then describe SDL and discuss how it is used.

To read a scene file, say, `myScene.dat`, written in SDL, we first define a global `Scene` object, say, `scn`, and call the `read()` method for it, giving it the name of some SDL file to process:

```
Scene scn; // create a Scene object
  :
scn.read("myScene.dat"); // read the SDL file; make the scene
```

The file `myScene.dat` is read and interpreted, and a list of objects is built. A list of light sources is also built. These lists are available through the fields `scn.obj` and `scn.light`, respectively. The lists are used by the `drawOpenGL()` method described in Chapter 5 to render the scene using OpenGL's facilities or, alternatively, by `shade()` described in Chapter 14, to render the scene by using ray tracing.

The `Scene` Class

An object of the `Scene` class has several fields that describe the nature of a scene. The principal ingredient is a list of the geometric shapes that reside in the scene. The field `obj` is a pointer to the first shape in the list. To draw all of the objects on the list, we simply move through the list, telling each object to draw itself:

```
for(GeomObj* p = scn.obj; p != NULL; p = p->next)
        p->drawOpenGL();
```

Objects listed are of one type of `Shape` or another (such as `Sphere`, `Cube`, `Icosahedron`, etc.), and each type of `Shape` knows how to draw itself. Polymorphism is used here: All `Shape` types are derived from the base type `GeomObj` (short for "Geometric Object"), so any `Shape` type can reside on a list that points to `GeomObj`.

The following four fields are in the `Scene` class:

```
Light* light;          // the light-source list
GeomObj* obj;          // the object list
Color3 background;     // the background color
Color3 ambient;        // the global ambient color
```

In addition, there are three fields used for ray tracing (see Chapter 14): `maxRecursionDepth`, `minShinyness`, and `minTransparency`.

A5.1 SYNTAX OF SDL

SDL is case sensitive, but free form: Multiple white-space characters (space, tab, newline, form feed, etc.) are equivalent to a single space. Comments begin with a '!' and continue to the end of the line. Keywords in SDL are used to specify different affine transformations, geometric objects, light sources, and attributes of the scene, such as the background color.

Creating Geometric Objects

An object is created and placed in the object list simply by stating its type. For instance,

```
cube        adds a cube object to the object list, and
sphere      adds a sphere object.
```

Other geometric objects include (see `Sdl.h` for a complete list) `torus`, `plane`, `square`, `cylinder`, `cone`, `tetrahedron`, `octahedron`, `dodecahedron`, `icosahedron`, `buckyball`, `diamond`, and `teapot`. When any of these object types is specified in the file, the corresponding object is added to the (end of the) object list.

There are additional geometric object types that require a parameter, which is either a floating-point value or a file name. The parameter is placed directly after the name of the object, as in

```
taperedCylinder .312 !make a tapered cylinder with small radius .312
mesh pawn.3vn        !make a mesh
```

The first example creates a tapered cylinder object that uses the parameter to define its exact shape; the second creates a mesh object whose vertex and face lists are described in the file `pawn.3vn`. (A number of sample files in the 3vh format including those for the icosahedron, diamond, and buckyball, are available on the book's Internet site.)

Managing Affine Transformations

An affine transformation is stored with each object as it is created. (The inverse of this transformation is also stored; it is used when ray tracing.) The specific transformation that is installed with the object is the current transformation (CT) that is in effect at that moment. Various keywords in the SDL file alter the CT. For example,

```
identityAffine
```

places the identity transformation (given by a unit four-by-four matrix) in the CT, which is initially the identity transformation when `read()` begins to interpret an SDL file.

SDL uses the words `scale`, `rotate`, and `translate`, each followed by suitable parameters, to alter the CT, in a manner similar to how OpenGL uses `glScalef()`, `glRotatef()`, and `glTranslatef()` to alter the modelview or projection matrices. Specifically, each word postmultiplies the CT by the corresponding transformation and places the product back into the CT, as in

CT = CT* Trans

where Trans is the four-by-four matrix that represents the new transformation.

The three verbs are as follows:

```
scale <sx> <sy> <sz>
rotate <ang> <ux> <uy> <uz>
translate <dx> <dy> <dz>
```

`scale` takes three floating-point parameters that are the scale factors in the x-, y-, and z-directions, respectively. `rotate` takes four parameters: the angle (in degrees) of the rotation and the x-, y-, and z-components of the axis about which the rotation is to be made. (Positive values of `ang` produce CCW rotations about the u-axis, as seen looking from point u towards the origin.) `translate` takes three parameters: the x-, y-, and z-components of the vector through which the translation is to be made. For example, the commands

```
scale 2 1.3 -5.33
translate 4 -5 6
rotate 45 0 1 0
```

respectively create the matrices

$$
Sc = \begin{pmatrix} 2 & 0 & 0 & 0 \\ 0 & 1.3 & 0 & 0 \\ 0 & 0 & -5.33 & 0 \\ 0 & 0 & 0 & 1 \end{pmatrix}, Tr = \begin{pmatrix} 1 & 0 & 0 & 4 \\ 0 & 1 & 0 & -5 \\ 0 & 0 & 1 & 6 \\ 0 & 0 & 0 & 1 \end{pmatrix}, \text{ and } Rot = \begin{pmatrix} 0.707 & 0 & 0.707 & 0 \\ 0 & 1 & 0 & 0 \\ -0.707 & 0 & 0.707 & 0 \\ 0 & 0 & 0 & 1 \end{pmatrix},
$$

and each command postmultiplies the CT by its matrix and places the result back into the CT.

Stack of Affine Transformations

The CT is actually the top matrix in a stack of matrices. The words `push` and `pop` manipulate this stack:

- `push` makes a copy of the CT and pushes it onto the stack (making the top two items identical).
- `pop` pops the CT off of the stack and discards it. The matrix that was just below the top item becomes the CT. If there is no item below the top item, `pop` does nothing.

Managing Material Properties

Installed in each object as it is created is a record of material properties, called the current materials (CM). This record consists of the following fields:

- four color fields, each an (r, g, b) triple: `ambient`, `diffuse`, `specular`, and `emissive`;
- six scalar fields `specularExponent`, `specularFraction`, `surfaceRoughness`, `speedOfLight`, `transparency`, and `reflectivity`; (the last five are used in raytracing.)
- three fields to describe texture properties of the object: `textureType` designates which texture is applied to the object, `numParams` is the number of parameters defined for the object, and `params []` is an array of 10 parameter values.

Changes to the CM are managed by the following SDL words, each followed by one or more `float`'s:

```
ambient     <r> <g> <b>
diffuse     <r> <g> <b>
specular    <r> <g> <b>
emissive    <r> <g> <b>
specularExponent <value>
specularFraction <value>
surfaceRoughness <value>
speedOfLight <value>
transparency <value>
reflectivity <value>
textureType <value>
parameters <value> <value> <value> ...
```

The `parameters` keyword is followed by the number of parameters being specified and the list of parameter values. For example, to place the three values 4.5, 6, and −12 in the `params[]` array of subsequently defined objects, you would use

```
parameters 3 4.5 6 -12
```

The CM initially contains the following default values:

```
ambient =  ( 0.1, 0.1, 0.1)
diffuse =   (0.8, 0.8, 0.8)
specular =  (0, 0, 0)
emissive =  (0, 0, 0)
specularExponent 1
specularFraction 0
surfaceRoughness 1.0
speedOfLight = 1
transparency  = 0
reflectivity  = 0
textureType 0
```

The word `defaultMaterials` can be used to return the CM to these default values.

The following are keywords having to do with light sources, global attributes, Boolean objects and pixmaps:

Light Sources

```
light  <x> <y> <z> <r> <g> <b>    !place a light at (x,y,z)
                                  !having color (r,g,b)
```

Specifying Global Scene Attributes

```
globalAmbient <r> <g> <b>   !give the global ambient source the
                            !color (r,g,b)
minReflectivity <value>
minTransparency <value>
maxRecursionDepth <value>
background    <r> <g> <b>
```

The following is a sample SDL file:

```
! myScene1.dat - f.s.hill
! has several simple glowing objects

globalAmbient .4 .2 .3
light 0 10 0 1 1 1     ! white light at (0,10,0)
background 0 0 .5
ambient .2 .2 .2
diffuse .8 .7 .6
emissive .8 0 0 ! objects emit red
cube ! put a generic cube at the origin
emissive 0 1 0
! put a glowing ellpsoid at (2, 0, 0)
push translate 2 0 0 rotate 45 0 0 1 scale .5 .5 2 sphere pop
push translate -2 0 0 cone pop !and a cone at (-2, 0 0)
```

Boolean Objects

SDL also supports the specification of boolean objects, using the keywords

```
union
intersection
difference
```

Each of these verbs creates a boolean object of its specified type and places it in the object list. Each such object must be followed in the SDL file by two objects (each of which may be a geometric or a boolean object), which are placed as the left and right children of the boolean object that was originally created.

The following SDL code describes a scene that contains two boolean objects. The first is an intersection of a cube and the union of a tetrahedron and a bucky ball. The second is a difference of a tetrahedron and the intersection of a plane with the union of a torus and a dodecahedron.

```
light 1 2 3 0.2 0.3 0.4
intersection
cube     !left child of intersection
union    ! right child of intersection
diffuse .2 .5 .7 tetrahedron !left child of union
rotate 180 3 4 5 buckyball !right child of union
difference !another boolean
tetrahedron intersection
plane union
torus   dodecahedron
```

The verb

```
makePixmap <value> <fname>
```

defines a pixmap to be used for texturing. The first argument is an interger used to identify the pixmap; the second is the name of a BMP file that contains the texture image. For example, the following SDL code

```
makePixmap 5 clouds.bmp
makePixmap 2 stone.bmp
texture 5
parameters 4 0 1 1 0
push scale 3 4 2 cube pop
texture 2
parameters 3 .2 .8 2
sphere
```

creates two textures. It then associates number 5 (along with four parameters) with a scaled cube, and number 2 (along with three parameters) with a sphere. (The issue of how the texture is actually applied to an object is, of course, left up to the programmer).

A5.2 MACROS IN SDL

As a convenience, the keyword `def` allows you to combine any number of SDL commands into a macro and give them a single name. The SDL commands that form the body of the macro are enclosed is braces. For example,

```
def red {ambient 1 0 0 diffuse 1 0 0 }
```

associates the macro named `red` with the words shown. If, later in the SDL file, the command

```
use red
```

is encountered, the phrase `ambient 1 0 0 diffuse 1 0 0` is placed at that point as if you had typed it there in the file. Macros can save typing and allow definitions to be reused. For instance, an "L"-shaped stack of four cubes can be defined with the code

```
def Lstack {push cube translate 2 0 0 cube
                   translate -2 2 0 cube
                   translate 0 2 0 cube pop}
```

This macro can be used later to place several different shaped L's in a scene. Code to do this might look like

```
use Lstack
push translate 3 2 4 scale .5 .5 .5 use Lstack pop
push translate -3 -2 -4 scale .5 .5 .5 use Lstack pop
```

A5.3 EXTENDING SDL

It is straightforward to add keywords to SDL. We describe how to do this through two examples.

■ EXAMPLE 5.3.1 Adding an attribute to scenes

Suppose you wish to add to the `Scene` class a new field, `fogThickness`, that describes the thickness of fog in the scene. To control the value to be placed in this field, you add a keyword, say `fogginess`, to the SDL language. The phrase

```
fogginess 0.5
```

in an SDL file will change the value of `fogThickness` to 0.5. To accomplish this, you would make the following changes.

Changes Made in the File Sdl .h

1. Add the field `float fogThickness` to the `Scene` class.
2. Add the item `FOGTHICKNESS` anywhere in the `TokenType` enumeration list.

Changes Made in the File Sdl .cpp

1. In function `whichtoken()`, add the line

```
if (temp == "fogginess") return (FOGTHICKNESS);
```

2. In the function `getObject()`, add the line

```
case FOGTHICKNESS: fogThickness = getFloat(); break;
```

The issue of how to *use* this new field is, of course, up to the programmer. For instance, while developing a ray tracer, the programmer may add some code to the `Scene::shade()` method, such as: `if(fogThickness > 0)` *do something..*;

■ EXAMPLE 5.3.2 Defining a new type of object

Suppose you want to add a *pie slice* to the collection of possible objects appearing in scenes. This will be a portion of a thin circular disc lying in the *xy*-plane. The slice starts at angle 0 (directed along the *x*-axis) and continues CCW (as seen looking from (0,0,1) towards the origin) to angle *sweep*, measured in degrees. Thus, if *sweep* is 180, the pie slice is half a pie in the positive *y*-halfspace, and if *sweep* is 360, the pie slice is a complete pie. We extend SDL so that the keyword `pieSlice` followed by a parameter for the *sweep* angle is recognized, as in

```
pieSlice 90
```

Changes Made in the File Sdl .h

1. Define the `PieSlice` class with a field to hold the *sweep* angle; by means of the following code:

```
class PieSlice : public Shape {
 public:
    float sweep;
        etc.
};
```

2. Code the appropriate methods, such as `drawOpenGL()`, for this class.
3. Add the item `PIESLICE` anywhere in the `TokenType` enumeration list.

Changes Made in the File Sdl `.cpp`:

1. To the function `whichtoken()`, add the line

```
if (temp == "pieSlice") return (PIESLICE);
```

2. In the function `getObject()`, add the line

```
case PIESLICE:
    newShape = new PieSlice;
    ((PieSlice*)newShape) ->angle = getFloat(); break;
```

REFERENCES

Certain journals and texts are referred to so frequently they are cited in an abbreviated fashion in this bibliography.

SIGGRAPH

This refers to the journal Computer Graphics, the Conference Proceeding of the Special Interest Group on Computer Graphics of the Association of Computing Machinery in New York, published annually. A reference to SIGGRAPH92, for instance, refers to the 1992 proceedings.

GEMS

This refers to the series of five books, Graphics Gems, published by Academic Press in Boston, MA. The five books, their editors, and their dates of publication are:

Graphics Gems   - Andrew Glassner, Ed., 1990
Graphics Gems II   - James Arvo, Ed., 1991
Graphics Gems III   - David Kirk, Ed., 1992
Graphics Gems IV   - Paul Heckbert, Ed., 1994
Graphics Gems V   - Alan Paeth, Ed. 1995

Abelson, H., and A.A. di Sessa. 1981. *Turtle Geometry.* Cambridge, MA.: MIT Press.

Acton, F. S. 1970. *Numerical Methods That Work.* New York: Harper & Row.

Angel, Edward. 1970. Interactive Computer Graphics, a Top-Down Approach with OpenGL. Reading, MA: Addison-Wesley.

Apostol, T. M. 1961. *Calculus.* New York: Blaisdell.

Arvo, J., and D. Kirk. 1989. "A Survey of Ray Tracing Acceleration Techniques," in An Introduction To Ray Tracing. Andrew Glassner, ed. New York: Academic Press.

William D. Atkinson. *Method and Apparatus for Image Compression and Manipulation.* U.S. patent number 4,622,545, Nov. 11, 1986.

Ayers, F. 1967. *Projective Geometry.* New York: McGraw-Hill.

Ball, W. W. R., and H. M. S. Coxeter. 1974. *Mathematical Recreations and Essays.* Toronto: University of Toronto Press.

Ballard, D. H., and C. M. Brown. 1982. Computer Vision. Englewood Cliffs, NJ: Prentice-Hall.

Barnsley, M. F. 1993. Fractals Everywhere, 2d ed. Boston: Academic Press.

Barnsley, M. F., R. L. Devaney, B. B. Mandelbrot, H. O. Peitgen, D. Saupe, and R. F. Voss. 1999. The Science of Fractal Images. New York: Springer-Verlag.

Barr, A. 1981. "Superquadrics and Angle-preserving Transformations." *IEEE Computer Graphics* 1 (January): 11–25.

Barr, Alan. "Global and Local Deformations of Solid Primitives." *Siggraph 84*, pp. 21–30.

Bartels, R. H., J. C. Beatty, and B. A. Barsky. 1987. *An Introduction to Splines for Use in Computer Graphics and Geometric Modeling.* Los Altos, CA.: Morgan Kaufman Publishers, Inc.

Beckmann, P., and A. Spizzichino. 1963. The Scattering of Electromagnetic Waves From Rough Surfaces. New York: Pergamon Press.

Behrens, Uwe. 1994 "Fence Shading." *Graphics Gems IV.*

Bergeron. R. D., P. R., Bono, and J. D. Foley. 1978. "Graphics Programming Using the CORE System." *ACM Computing Surveys* 10: 389–443.

Berlekamp, E. R., J. H. Conway, and R. K. Guy. 1982. *Winning Ways.* New York: Academic Press.

Bigelow, C. 1985. "Font Design for Personal Workstations." *Byte* (January): 225–270.

Bier, E. A., and K. R. Sloan, Jr. 1986. "Two-part Texture Mappings." *IEEE CG&A* (September), pp. 40–53.

Billmeyer, F. W., and M. Saltzman. 1981. *Principles of Color Technology.* New York: Wiley.

Birkhoff, G., and S. MacLane. 1967. *A Survey of Modern Algebra.* New York: Macmillan.

Bishop, G., and D. M. Weimer. 1986. "Fast Phong Shading". *SIGGRAPH 86. Computer Graphics* 20 (August): 103–106.

Blinn, J. F., and M. E. Newell. 1976. "Texture and Reflection in Computer Graphics." *Comm ACM* 19(10), 542–7.

Blinn, J. F. 1977. "Models of Light Reflection for Computer Synthesized Pictures." *Computer Graphics* 11(2) (Proc. SIGGRAPH, '77).

Blinn, J. E., and M. E. Newell. 1978 "Clipping Using Homogeneous Coordinates." *Computer Graphics* 12 (August): 245–251.

Blinn, J. F. "A Scan Line Algorithm for the Computer Display of Parametrically Defined Surfaces." *SIGGRAPH 78*

Blinn, J. F. "Simulation of Wrinkled Surfaces." *SIGGRAPH '78*, 12(3), 286–92.

Blinn, J. E., L. Carpenter, J. Lane, and T. Whitted. 1980. "Scan-line Methods for Displaying Parametrically Defined Surfaces." *Communications of the ACM* 23 (January): 23–34.

Blinn, J. F. 1987 "Platonic Solids." *IEEE CG&A* (November), p. 62–66.

Blinn, J. 1996. Jim Blinn's Corner: A Trip Down the Graphics Pipeline. San Francisco: Morgan Kaufman.

Blinn, J. Jim Blinn's Corner: Dirty Pixels. 1998. San Francisco: Morgan Kaufman.

Bloomenthal, J., ed. 1997. Introduction to Implicit Surfaces. San Francisco: Morgan Kaufman.

Bouknight, W. J. 1970. "A Procedure for Generation of Three-Dimensional Half-Tone Computer Graphics Presentations." *CACM*, 13(9) (September): 527–536.

Bresenham, J. E. 1965. "Algorithm for Computer Control of Digital Plotter." *IBM Systems Journal* 4: 25–30.

Browne, M. W. 1990. "Bizarre New Class of Molecules Spawns Its Own Branch of Chemistry" *New York Times,* Dec. 25, p. 13.

Burden, Richard L., and J. Douglas Faires. 1985. Numerical Analysis. Boston: Prindle, Weber, and Schmidt.

Butland, J. 1979. "Surface Drawing Made Simple." *Computer-aided Design* 11 (January): 19–22.

Carlbom, I. and Paciorek, J. 1978. "Planar Geometric Projections and Viewing Transformations." *ACM Computing Surveys* 10 (4), pp. 465–502.

Catmull, E. 1975. "Computer Display of Curved Surfaces." *Proc. IEEE Conf. Computer Graphics Pattern Recognition Data Structures* (May), p. 11.

Clark, J. H. "A Fast Scan-line Algorithm for Rendering Parametric Surfaces." 1979. *Computer Graphics* 13 (supplement to SIGGRAPH 79).

Clason, R. G. 1990, 1991. "Tile Patterns with Logo." *Journal of Computers in Mathematics and Science Teaching.* 10 (1), Fall 1990, pp. 11–23; 10 (2), Winter 1990/91, pp. 59–69; 10 (3), Spring 1991, pp. 59–71.

Claussen, Ute. 1990. "On Reducing the Phong Shading Method." *Computers and Graphics* 14(1): 73–81.

Conrac Corporation. 1985. *Raster Graphics Handbook,* 2d ed. New York: Van Nostrand Reinhold.

Conte, S. D., and C. deBoor. 1980. *Elementary Numerical Analysis.* New York: McGraw-Hill.

Cook, R. L., and K. E. Torrance. 1981. "A Refectance Model for Computer Graphics." *Computer Graphics* 15 (August): 307–316.

Cook, R. L., T. Porter, and L. Carpenter. "Distributed Ray Tracing." *SIGGRAPH 84,* pp. 137–145.

Coons, S. A. 1967. *Surfaces for Computer-aided Design of Space Forms.* Report MAC-TR-41, Project MAC, Massachusetts Institute of Technology, Cambridge, MA.

Courant, R., and H. Robbins. 1961. What is Mathematics? New York: Oxford University Press.

Coxeter, H. M. S. *Regular Polytopes.* 1963. New York: Macmillan.

Coxeter, H. S. M. Introduction to Geometry. 1969. New York: J. Wiley and Sons.

Crow, F. C. "Shadow Algorithms for Computer Graphics." *Computer Graphics* 11(3), 242–8 (SIGGRAPH '77).

Crow, F. C. 1981. "A Comparison of Antialiasing Techniques." *IEEE Computer Graphics and Applications* 1 (January): 40–49.

Crow, F. C. 1987. "The Origins of the Teapot." *IEEE Computer Graphics and Applications* (January): 8–19.

Cyrus, M. and J. Beck. 1987. "Generalized Two- and Three-dimensional Clipping." *Computers and Graphics* 3: 23–28.

DeBoor, C. 1978. *Practical Guide to Splines.* New York: Springer-Verlag.

Demko, S., L. Hodges, and B. Naylor. 1985. "Construction of Fractal Objects with Iterated Function Systems." *SIGGRAPH 1985, Computer Graphics* 19 (July): 271–278.

A. K. Dewdney. 1988. The Armchair Universe. New York: W. H. Freeman and Co.

Ebert, D., F. K. Musgrave, D. Peachey, K. Perlin, and S. Worley. 1998. Texturing and Modeling, 2d ed. San Diego: Academic Press.

Farin, G. 1990. *Curves and Surfaces for Computer-aided Geometric Design,* 2d ed. Boston: Academic Press.

Faux, I. D., and M. J. Pratt. New York: 1979. *Computational Geometry for Design and Manufacture.* J. Wiley and Sons.

Feynman, R. 1963. "Color Vision," in *The Feynman Lectures on Physics.* Reading, MA: Addison-Wesley.

Fisher, F., and A. Woo. 1994. "R. E. versus N. H Specular Higlights." *Graphics Gems IV.*

Foley, J. D., A. Van Dam, S. K. Feiner, and J. F. Hughes 1990. *Computer Graphics, Principles and Practice.* Reading: MA: Addison-Wesley.

Foley, J. D., A. Van Dam, S. K. Feiner, J. F., Hughes, and R. L. Phillips. 1994. *Introduction to Computer Graphics.* Reading, MA: Addison-Wesley. 1994.

FRACTINT, a freeware program available in several places on the Internet.

Freeman, H. 1974. "Computer Processing of Line Drawing Images." *Computer Surveys* 6(1): 57–98

Freeman, H. *Tutorial and Selected Readings in Interactive Computer Graphics.* 1980. Silver Spring, MD: IEEE Comp. Soc. Press.

Fuchs, H., Z. M., Kedem, and B. G. Naylor. "On Visibile Surface Generation by A Priori Tree Structures" *SIGGRAPH 80,* pp. 124–133.

Fuchs, H., G. D. Abram, and E. E. Grant. "Near Real-Time Shaded Display of Rigid Objects." *SIGGRAPH83,* pp. 65–72.

Fuller, R. B., and R. Marks. *The Dymaxion World of Buckminster Fuller.* 1973. New York: Doubleday/Anchor Books.

Fuller, R. B. 1975. *Sinergetics.* New York: Macmillan.

Gardner, M. 1975. "Piet Hein's Superellipse," in *Mathematical Carnival.* New York: Knopf.

Gardner, M. 1961. *Second* Scientific American *book of Mathematical Puzzles and Diversions.* New York: Simon & Schuster.

Gardner, M. 1971. *New Mathematical Diversions from* Scientific American. New York: Simon & Schuster.

Gardner, M. 1978. "White and Brown Music, Fractal Curves and One-over-f Fluctuations. *Scientific American* (April): 16–32.

Gardner, M. *Time Travel.* 1988. New York: W. H. Freeman and Co.

Gardner, M. Penrose Tiles to Trapdoor Ciphers. 1989. New York: W. H. Freeman and Co.

Graphics Gems I–V, a series of five books:

    Andrew Glassner, ed., Graphics Gems. 1990. Boston: Academic Press.

James Arvo, ed., *Graphics Gems II*. 1991. Boston: Academic Press.

David Kirk, ed., *Graphics Gems III*. 1992. Boston: Academic Press.

Paul Heckbert, ed., *Graphics Gems IV*. 1994. Boston: AP Professional.

Alan Paeth, ed., *Graphics Gems V*. 1995. Boston: AP Professional.

Gervautz, M., and W. Purgathofer .1990. "A Simple Method for Color Quantization: Octree Quantization" *Graphics Gems I,* pp. 287–293.

Glassner, A. S., ed. 1989. An Introduction to Ray Tracing. New York: Academic Press.

Goldman, R. N. 1985. "Illicit Expressions in Vector Algebra" *ACM Transactions on Graphics* 4 (July): 223–243.

Goldman, R. "Matrices and Transformations," in GEMS, pp. 472–475.

Ronald Goldman. "More Matrices and Transformations: Shear and Pseudo-Perspective," in *GEMS II*, p. 338.

Ronald Goldman. "Decomposing Projective Transformations," in *GEMS III*, p. 98.

Ronald Goldman. "Decomposing Linear and Affine Transformations," in *GEMS III,* p. 108.

Golomb, S. 1965. *POLYOMINOES*. New York. Scribner's.

Gonzalez, R. C., and P. Wintz. 1987. *Digital Image Processing*. Reading, MA: Addison-Wesley.

Gordon, W. J., and R. F. Riesenfeld. 1974. "B-spline Curves and Surfaces" in *Computer-aided Geometric Design*, edited by R. E. Barnhill and R. F. Riesenfeld. New York: Academic Press.

Gouraud H. 1971. "Continuous Shading of Curved Surfaces." *IEEE Transactions on Computers* (June): 623–629.

Gray, Alfred. 1993. *Modern Differential Geometry of Curves and Surfaces with Mathematica*. Boston: CRC Press..

Greene, N. "Environment Mapping and Other Applications of World Projections." 1986. *IEEE CG&A* 6(11), 21–9.

Greene, N., & P. S. Heckbert. "Creating Raster Omnimax Images from Multiple Perspective Views Using the Elliptical Weighted Average Filter." 1986. *IEEE CG&A* 6(6), 21–27.

Greene, N. "Transformation Identities," in *GEMS I*, p. 485.

Griffiths, J. G. 1983. "Table-driven Algorithms for Generating Space-filling Curves." *Computer-aided Design* 17 (January): 37.

Grunbaum, B., and G. C. Shephard. *Tiling and Patterns*. 1986. New York: W. H. Freeman.

Haeberli, P., and M. Segal (*http://www.sgi.com/grafica/texmap/*). 1993. "Texture Mapping as a Fundamental Drawing Primitive." Fourth Eurographics Workshop on Rendering, M. F. Cohen, C. Peuch, and F. Sillion, eds. pp. 259–266.

Halliday, D., and R. Resnick. 1970. *Fundamentals of Physics*. New York: John Wiley.

Hawley, S. 1990. "Ordered Dithering," in *GEMS I*, 1990, p. 176.

Hayes, B. 1984. "On the Ups and Downs of Hailstone Numbers." *Scientific American* 250 (January): 10–13.

Hearn, D., and M. P. Baker. 1994. *Computer Graphics*, 2d ed. Englewood Cliffs, N.J.: Prentice Hall.

Heckbert, P. 1982. "Color Image Quantization for Frame Buffer Dispaly." *Computer Graphics* 16: 297–307.

Heckbert, P. "Survey of Texture Mapping." 1986. *IEEE CG&A* (November): 56–61.

Heckbert, P. S. "Writing a Ray Tracer," in *An Introduction to Ray Tracing* 1989. Edited by Glassner, A. S. New York: Accademic Press.

Heckbert, P., and Moreton, H. P. 1991. "Interpolation for Polygon Texture Mapping and Shading" in *State of the Art in Computer Graphics: Visualization and Modeling,* edited by David F. Rogers and Rae A. Earnshaw. New York: Springer-Verlag, pp. 101–111.

Heckbert, P. S. 1994. "Bilinear Coons Patch Image Warping," in *Graphics Gems IV*, pp. 438–446.

Hilbert, D., and S. Cohn-Vossen. 1952. *Geometry and the Imagination*. New York: Chelsea.

Hill, F. S., Jr. 1978. "Phi—Precious Jewel." *IEEE Communications Society Magazine* (September: 35–37.

Hill, F. S., Jr. 1979. "What's New in Ellipses." *IEEE Communications Magazine* (July): 23–27.

Hill, F. S. Jr. "The Pleasures of the Perp-Dot Product," in *GEMS IV,* p. 138.

Hofstadter, D. R. 1985, *Metamagical Themas*. New York: Basic Books.

Hoggar, S. G. *Mathematics for Computer Graphics*. 1992. New York: Cambridge University Press.

Huntley, H. E. 1970. *The Divine Proportion: A Study in Mathematical Beauty*. New York: Dover.

Ingalls, D. H. 1978. "The Smalltalk-76 Programming System Design and Implementation." Fifth ACM Symposium on Principles of Programming Languages (January).

H. W. Janson. 1986. History of Art, vol. 1. Englewood Cliffs, NJ: Prentice Hall.

Jarvis, J. F., C. N. Judice, and W. H. Ninke. 1976. "A Survey of Techniques for the Display of Continuous Tone Pictures on Bilevel Displays." *CGIP* 5, pp. 13–40.

Journal of Graphics Tools. Natick, M. A., A. K. Peters, Ltd., *http://www.akpeters.com*.

Jurgens H., H. O. Peitgen, and D. Saupe. 1990. "The Language of Fractals." *Scientific American* (August): pp. 60–67.

Kajiya, T. 1983. "New Techniques for Ray Tracing Procedurally Defined Objects." *ACM Transactions on Graphics 2* (July): 161–181.

Kappraff, J. "*Connections: The Geometric Bridge between Art and Science.*" 1991. New York: McGraw Hill.

Kerrod, B. 1979. *Stars and Planets*. New York: Arco Publ., Inc.

Knuth, D. E. 1973. *The Art of Computer Programming. Vol. 1: Fundamental Algorithms.* Reading, MA: Addison-Wesley.

Knuth, D. E. 1987. "Digital Halftones by Dot Diffusion." *ACM Transactions on Graphics* 6 (October): 245–273.

Knuth, D. E. 1998. *The Art of Computer Programming. Vol 2: Seminumerical Algorithms,* 3d ed. Reading, MA: Addison-Wesley.

Kochanek, D. H. U., and R. H. Bartels, "Interpolating Splines with Local Tension, Continuity, and Bias Control." *SIGGRAPH 84, Computer Graphics* 18(3), pp. 33–41.

Kopec, T. E. 1985. *Adaptive Quantization of Color Images.* Master's thesis, University of Massachusetts.

Kruse, R. L. 1984. *Data Structures and Program Design.* Englewood Cliffs, NJ: Prentice-Hall.

Lane, J. M., and L. C. Carpenter. 1979. "A Generalized Scan Line Algorithm for the Computer Display of Parametrically Defined Surfaces." *Computer Graphics Image Processing* 11, pp. 290–297.

Lane J. M., L. C. Carpenter, T. Whitted, and J. F. Blinn. 1980. "Scan Line Methods for Displaying Parametrically Defined Surfaces." *CACM* 23, pp. 23–34.

Liang, Y, and B. Barsky. 1984. "A New Concept and Method for Line Clipping." *ACM Trans. on Graphics* 3(1): 1–22.

Lindley, C. 1992. *Practical Ray Tracing in C.* New York: J. Wiley and Sons.

Lopez-Lopez, F. J. "Triangles Revisited," in *Graphics Gems III*, p. 215.

Lucky, R. W. 1989. Silicon Dreams. New York: St. Martin's Press.

Maillot, Patrick-Gilles. "Using Quarternions for Coding 3D Transformations," in GEMS I, pp. 498–515.

Mandelbrot, B. 1983. *The Fractal Geometry of Nature.* New York: Freeman.

Martin, G. 1982. Transformation Geometry. New York: Springer-Verlag.

McGregor, J., and A. Watt. 1986. *The Art Of Graphics for the IBM PC.* Reading, MA: Addison-Wesley Publishing Co.

McReynolds, Tom, and David Blythe. "Programming with OpenGL: Advanced Rendering" (course notes) *SIGGRAPH '97.*

Meyer, G., and D. Greenberg. 1980. "Perceptual Color Spaces for Computer Graphics." *Computer Graphics* 14: 254—261

Miller, Gavin, Mark Halstead, and Michael Clifton, 1980. "On-the-Fly Texture Computation for Real-Time Surface Shading." *CG&A* 18(3), pp. 44–58.

Moret, B. M. E., and H. D. Shapiro. 1991. *Algorithms from to NP, Vol. 1.* Reading MA: Benjamin Cummings.

Mortenson, M. 1985. *Geometric Modelling.* New York: Wiley.

Munsel, A. H. 1941. *A Color Notation*, 9th ed. Baltimore: Munsell Color Co.

Nelson, Mark. *The Data Compression Book,* 2d ed. 1996. New York: M&T Books.

Newell, M. E., R. G., Newell, and T. L. Sancha. "A Solution to the Hidden Surface Problem." *Proceedings of the ACM National Conference 1972*, pp. 443–450. Also in H. Freeman, *Tutorial and Selected Readings in Interactive Computer Graphics.* pp. 236–243.

Newman, W. M., and R. F. Sproull. 1979. *Principles of Interactive Computer Graphics.* New York: McGraw-Hill.

Ogilvy, S. Excursions in Geometry. 1969. New York: Oxford University Press.

Oppenheim, A. V., and A. S. Willsky. 1983. *Signals and Systems.* Englewood Cliffs, NJ: Prentice-Hall.

O'Reilly, T., V. Quercia, and L. Lamb. 1988. *The X Windows System User's Guide, Vol. 3.* Newton, MA: O'Reilly and Assoc.

Paeth, A. W. "A Fast Algorithm for General Raster Rotation," in *GEMS I*, p. 197.

Alan W. Paeth. 1991. "A Half-Angle Identity for Digital Computation: The Joys of the Half Tangent," in *Graphics Gems II,* edited by James Arvo. New York: Academic Press. p. 381.

Peachey, D. R. "Solid Texturing of Complex Surfaces." SIGGRAPH 85, pp. 279–86.

Pedoe, Dan. 1970. Geometry, a Comprehensive Course. New York: Dover Publications.

Pedoe, D. 1976. Geometry and the Visual Arts. New York: Dover Publications.

Peitgen, H. O., and P. H. Richter. 1986. *The Beauty of Fractals.* New York: Springer-Verlag.

Peitgen, H. O., and D. Saupe. 1988. The Science of Fractal Images. New York: Springer-Verlag.

Peitgen H. O., H. Jurgens, and D. Saupe. 1992. Chaos and Fractals, New Frontiers of Science. New York: Springer-Verlag.

Penna, M., and R. Patterson. 1986. *Projective Geometry and Its Applications to Computer Graphics.* Englewood Cliffs, NJ: Prentice-Hall.

Penrose, R. 1989. *The Emperor's New Mind.* New York: Oxford University Press.

Perlin K. "An Image Synthesizer." *SIGGRAPH '85*, pp. 287–296.

Phong, B-T. 1975. "Illumination for Computer Generated Images." *Communications of the ACM* 18: 311–317.

Pickover, Clifford A. 1990. *Computers, Patterns, Chaos, and Beauty.* New York: St. Martin's Press.

Pickover, C. 1992. Mazes for the Mind. New York: St. Martin's Press.

Piegl, L., and W. Tiller. "A Menagerie of Rational B-Spline Circles." *IEEE CG&A,*, Sept. 1989, pp. 48–56.

Piegl, L. "On NURBS: A Survey." 1991. *IEEE Computer Graphics and Applications* (January), pp. 55–71.

Piegl, L., and W. Tiller. 1997. *The NURBS Book* (Monographs in Visual Communications). New York: Springer-Verlag.

Pike, R. 1983. "Graphics in Overlapping Bitmap Layers." *Computer Graphics* (July): 331–356.

Pipes, L. A. 1985. *Applied Mathematics for Engineers and Physicists.* New York: McGraw-Hill.

Pitteway, M. L. V., and D. J. Watkinson. 1980. "Bresenham's Algorithm with Gray Scale." *Communications of the ACM* 23: 625–626.

Plaugher, P. J. 1992. *The Standard C Library.* Englewood Cliffs, NJ: Prentice Hall.

Preparata, F., and M. I., Shamos. Computational Geometry, an Introduction. 1985. New York: Springer-Verlag.

Prusinkiewicz, P. 1980. *Lindenmayer Systems, Fractals, and Plants Lecture Notes in Biology,* #79. New York: Springer-Verlag.

Rogers, D. E., and J. A. Adams 1990. *Mathematical Elements for Computer Graphics.* New York: McGraw-Hill.

Rogers, D. 1998. Procedural Elements for Computer Graphics. New York: McGraw-Hill.

SIGGRAPH. Conference proceedings, the Association for Computing Machinery's Special Interest Group in Computer Graphics.

Roth, Scott D. 1982. "Ray Casting for Modeling Solids." *Computer Graphics and Image Processing* 18: 109–144.

Schlick, C. 1994. "A Fast Alternative to Phong's Specular Model," *Graphics Gems IV.*

Schroeder, Manfred. 1991. Fractals, Chaos, Power Laws. New York. W. B. Freeman.

Sederberg, T. W., R. N. Goldman, and D. C. Anderson. 1985. "Implicitization, Inversion and Intersection of Rational Cubic Curves: Computer Vision," *Graphics and Image Processing* 31: 89–102.

Segal, M., C. Korobkin, R. van Widenfelt, J. Foran, and P. Haeberli. "Fast Shadows and Lighting Effects Using Texture Mapping." *SIGGRAPH92,* pp. 249–252.

Von Seggern, David H. 1990. *CRC Handbook of Mathematical Curves and Surfaces.* New York: CRC Press.

Semple, J. G., and G. T. Kneebone. 1952. *Algebraic Projective Geometry*. Oxford: Oxford Univ. Press.

Sheperd. R. *Mind Sights*. 1990. New York: W. H. Freeman and Co.

Shikin, E. V. 1995. *Handbook and Atlas of Curves.* New York: CRC Press.

Shoemake, Ken. "Polar Matrix Decomposition," in *GEMS IV,* p. 207.

Schumacher, D. 1991. "A Comparison of Digital Halftoning Techiniques," in *GEMS II.* p. 57.

Smith, A. R. "Plants, Fractals, and Formal Languages." *SIGGRAPH '84,* pp. 1–10.

Sorenson, P. 1984. "Fractals." *Byte* (September): 157.

Steinhart, Jonathan E. "Scanline Coherent Shape Algebra," *GEMS II*, pp. 31–45.

Steinhaus, H. 1969. Mathematical Snapshots. New York: Oxford University Press.

Stone, M. C., W. B. Cowan, and J. C. Beatty. 1988. "Color Gamut Mapping and the Printing of Digital Color Images." *ACM Transactions on Graphics* 7: 249–292.

Sutherland, I. E., R. F., Sproull, and Schumacker, R. 1974. "A Characterization of Ten Hidden Surface Algorithms." *ACM Computing Surveys* 6(1), pp. 1–55.

Thomas, G. B. 1953. *Calculus and Analytic Geometry.* Reading, MA: Addison-Wesley.

Thomas, S. E. "Decomposing a Matrix into Simple Transformations," in *GEMS II*, p. 320.

Tiller, W. "Rational B-Splines for Curve and Surface Representation." 1983. *IEEE Computer Graphics and Applications* 3(6), pp. 61–69.

ACM Transactions on Graphics, published quarterly.

Torrance, K. E., and E. M. Sparrow. 1967. "Theory of Off-specular Reflection from Roughened Surfaces." *Journal of Optical Society of America* 57: 1105–1114.

Touloukian, Y. S., D. P. DeWitt, eds. 1970. "Thermophysical Properties of Matter, the TPRC Data Series," *Metallic Elements and Alloys*, Vol. 7. New York: Plenum.

Trowbridge, T. S., and K. P. Reitz. 1975. "Average Irregularity of a Roughened Surface for Ray Reflection." *J. Optical Society of America* 65(5): 531–536.

Ulichney, R. 1987. *Digital Halftoning.* Cambridge, MA: MIT Press.

Wagon, S. 1991. Mathematica in Action. New York: W. H. Freeman and Co.

Walker, J. 1985. "On Kaleidoscopes." *Scientific American* (September): 134–145.

Wang, W., and Barry Joe. 1997. "Robust Computation of the Rotation Minimizing Frame for Sweep Surface Modeling." *Computer-aided Design* 29(5): 379–391.

Warnock, J. 1969. "A Hidden-surface Algorithm for Computer Generated Half-Tone Pictures." Technical Report TR 4–15, NTIS AD–753 671, Computer Science Department, University of Utah, Salt Lake City, UT (June).

Watkins, G. S. 1970. *A Real Time Visible Surface Algorithm*. Ph.d. thesis, Thech. Report UTEC–CSs–70–101, NTIS A 762 004, Computer Science Department, University of Utah, Salt Lake City, UT (June).

Watt, A. and M. Watt. 1992. *Advanced Animation and Rendering Techniques.* Reading, MA: Addison-Wesley Publ. Co.

Weiler, K., and P. Atherton. 1977. "Hidden Surface Removal Using Polygon Area Sorting." *Computer Graphics* 11(2): 214.

Wenninger, Magnus J., 1971. New York: Polyhedron Models Cambridge Univ. Press.

Whitted, T. 1980. "An Improved Illumination Method for Shaded Display." *Communications of the ACM* 23 (June): 343–349.

Wirth, N. 1976. Algorithms + data structures = programs. Englewood Cliffs, NJ: Prentice-Hall.

Woo, A., P. Poluin, and A. Fournier. 1990. "A Survey of Shadow Algorithms." *IEEE CG&A* 10(6): 13–32.

Woo, M., J. Neider, and T. Davis. 1997. "*OpenGL Programming Guide,*" 3d ed. Reading, MA: Addison-Wesley Developer's Press.

Yaglom, I. M. 1962. Geometric Transformations. Toronto. Random House.

Yates, R. C. 1946. *Curves* Dept. of Mathematics, U. S. Military Academy, West Point, NY.

INDEX

Koch snowflake, 475
  drawing, 475–76
K-reptile, 491
Kth iterate, 70

L

Lambe, Gabriel, 125
Lambert's law, 415
Landscape orientation, 60
Laser printer, 23
Laser printers, 30
Lateral inhibition, 432
Latitude, 830
`latticeNoise()`, 773-74
Left-handed coordinate systems, 146–47
`Length()`, 415
`lerp()`, 170
Liang-Barsky algorithm, 388
Library files, linking, 819
Lid, teapot, 669
Light, 672–74
  refraction of, 795–96
Light contributions, combining, 420–21
`line()`, 39
Line, perspective projection of, 375–79
Linear B-splines, 628
Linear combinations of vectors, 149–50
Linear dot product, 153
Linear interpolation, 170
Linear polynomials, 603
Linear precision, Bezier curves, 616
Line-drawing displays, 22–23
Line drawings, 51–63
  aligned rectangles, 59–60
  aspect ratio of, 60
  polylines/polygons, 53–58
  using moveto() and lineto (), 58
Line graphs, drawing, 54
`lineRel()`, developing, 105-6
Lines:
  in 2D and 3D space, 173–74
  attributes of, 11–12
  line intersections, application of, 184–85
  moving from one representa-tion to another, 176–77
  parametric representation of, 174–75
  parent line, 173, 182
  with planes, intersections of, 186–87
  point normal form for the equa-tion of, 175–76
  respresenting, 173–81
  segments, 173, 181–85
Line segments, 173
  finding the intersection of, 181–85
Line stippling, 75–76
`lineto`, 873
`lineTo ()`, 39, 248-49, 258
  drawing lines using, 58
`line(x1, y1, x2, y2)`, 39

Linux, and OpenGL, 819
Liquid crystal display (LCD), 29
Lissajous figures, 664
List-priority HSR methods, 705–13
Locator, 32
Logarithmic spiral, 127
Logical combinations of pixmaps, 552–53
Logic gates, 137–38
Logistic map:
  defined, 130
  studying, 130–31
Lookup table (LUT), 26–29
Lossy compression scheme, 501
L-Systems, 478
L-th-degree polynomial in t, 603
Luminance, 674
LUT indices, 535

M

Mach band, 432
Macintosh, and OpenGL, 819
Magnitude, complex numbers, 829
Magnitude of the determinant, 232
`makeBoxExtent()`, 803
`makeEdgeStack()`, 731
Mandelbrot, Benoit, 474, 504
Mandelbrot sets, 475, 504–13
  creating pictures of, 27
  defining, 508–9
  drawing, 511–12
  drawing orbits in, 527
  dwell of the orbit, 510–11
  and iterated function systems, 505–8
  notes on, 512–13
Mandelbrot snowflake, 481, 524–26
Mapping:
  between world window and viewport, 81, 83–85
  building, 86–87
  bump, 452–53
  chrome, 462–63
  contraction, 496
  environment, 463
  of points into new points, 214
  reflection, 461–65
  window-to-viewport, 81, 83–85, 86
`Marble()`, 773
Marble texture, adding, 777–78
Marsaglia, George, 778
Mask, 582
Masking, 765–66
Master coordinate system, 256
Matched viewports, making, 94–95
Mathematics, 820–32
Matrix:
  commuting, 822
  defined, 820
  determinant of, 824
  dot/cross product, 823
  identity, 820
  inverse of, 824–26
  linear combination of, 821
  main diagonal, 820

manipulations with, 821
m-by-n, 820
multiplying, 821–22
multiplying a vector by, 822
nonsingular, 824
one-by-four, 820
partitioning, 823
postmultiplying, 822
premultiplying, 822
quadruple, 820
scaled, 821
shape, 821
square, 820
symmetric, 821
transpose of, 821
zero, 820
Mazes, 77–79
  generating, 79
  proper, 77
  running, 79
M-by-n matrix, 820
Meander, 109
Median-cut algorithm, 692–93, 697
Medians, 169
Meridians, 327, 337
Mesh, 289
  See Polygonal meshes
Mesh approximations to smooth objects, 321–46
Microsoft Windows 95/98/NT, and OpenGL, 819
Midpoint, 48, 174
Modeling curved surfaces, 654–62
  Bezier surface patches, 656–57
  ruled surfaces based on B-splines, 654–55
  surfaces of revolution based on B-splines, 655–56
Modeling transformation, 256
Models, for Platonic solids, 303
Modelview matrix, 249, 260–61, 361, 390
Modulus, complex numbers, 829
Monochrome video displays, 26
Monohedral tilings, 486–88
Motif, 88, 138
  making patterns from, 254
Motion, capturing, 35
Mouse, 33
  controlling the Sierpinski gasket with, 65
  creating a polyline using, 65
  "freehand" drawing with a fat brush, 66
  interaction with, 63–66
  motion, 66–67
  placing dots with, 64
  specifying a rectangle with, 64
`moveRel()`, developing, 105–6
`moveto`, 873
`moveTo()`, 39, 248-49, 258
`moveTo()`, drawing lines using, 58
Mul, 870
Multiple control points, 638–39
Multiple knots, 632–33
Multiview orthographic projec-tions, 400
`myDisplay()` function, 46